INDEX TO THE
1850 CENSUS OF
DELAWARE

Compiled by

VIRGINIA L. OLMSTED

GENEALOGICAL PUBLISHING CO., INC.
BALTIMORE   1977

Library of Congress Catalogue Card Number 77-76790
International Standard Book Number 0-8063-0770-6

TABLE OF CONTENTS

INTRODUCTION

The 1850 United States Census of Delaware is a valuable genealogical tool for research in the Middle-Atlantic region. One of the original Thirteen Colonies, Delaware was, for a time, under the jurisdiction of the Dutch colony of New Netherland and became, subsequently, the "Three Lower Counties" of the Province of Pennsylvania. The earliest settlement was established by the Swedes in 1638; Finnish colonists arrived in 1656, but, broadly speaking, between 1655 and 1664 Delaware was a part of New Netherland. Consequently, colonial records are scattered and may be found in the archives of either New York or Pennsylvania.

The 1850 Census of Delaware, the first every-name census of the state, often reflects the incompetence of the enumerators. In this *Index* the reader should look for all possible spellings of surnames, for the census takers sometimes used phonetic spellings which had little resemblance to the actual name. Keep in mind, too, that the handwriting of 1850 is frequently difficult to read. Certain letters, such as "r" and "n" and capitals "J" and "I," are particularly troublesome, and ink blots and write-overs make some of the original census entries illegible. Each name is here indexed with the spelling used on the original census record.

The three counties of Delaware have been separately indexed with an alphabetical listing of each person. Each name is followed by a reference to age, birthplace, and the original census sheet number of the enumeration. A word of caution concerning the sheet numbers of New Castle County enumerations must be given. The original census records for New Castle County were microfilmed on two rolls, and there is a duplication of sheet numbers (272-383) on both rolls. The researcher may have to consult both microcopy nos. 53 and 54 in order to locate a New Castle family enumerated on the duplicated sheets.

The preparation of this *Index* has taken over two years, and I should like to thank my mother, Lella Langham, and my aunt, Minnie Laws, for their assistance. They spent many hours helping me with indexing and proof reading.

The tables on the following pages will aid the reader in effective use of the *Index*.

TABLE I

Index to County Locations
in National Archives Microfilms
State of Delaware

Microfilm for the Seventh Census of the United States: M432

Roll No.	County	Sheet Nos.
52	Kent	1-270
53	New Castle	272-401; 1-168
54	New Castle	170-384
55	Sussex	1-297

TABLE II

Birthplace Abbreviations

AA--At sea	IE--Ireland	NY--New York
AF--Africa	IL--Illinois	OH--Ohio
AG--Argentina	IN--Indiana	PA--Pennsylvania
AL--Alabama	KY--Kentucky	PO--Poland
AR--Arkansás	LA--Louisana	RI--Rhode Island
BE--Belgium	MA--Massachusetts	RS--Russia
BV--Bavaria	MD--Maryland	SA--South America
CH--China	ME--Maine	SC--South Carolina
CN--Canada	MI--Michigan	SP--Spain
CT--Connecticut	MO--Missouri	ST--Scotland
CU--Cuba	MS--Mississippi	SW--Sweden
DC--District of Columbia	MX--Mexico	SZ--Switzerland
DE--Delaware	NB--Nebraska	TN--Tennessee
FL--Florida	NC--North Carolina	TX--Texas
FR--France	NE--Netherlands	UC--Upper Canada
GA--Georgia	NF--Newfoundland	VA--Virginia
GB--Great Britain	NH--New Hampshire	VT--Vermont
GE--Germany	NJ--New Jersey	WI--Wisconsin
HL--Holstein	NK--New Brunswick	WL--Wales
HN--Hanover	NS--Nova Scotia	WN--West Indies
IA--Iowa		

TABLE III

Specific Locations

County	Locality	Roll No.	Sheet Nos.
Kent	Dover Hundred	52	153-203
	Duck Creek Hundred	52	1-54
	Little Creek Hundred	52	55-82
	Milford, Mispillion Hundred	52	83-152
	Murderkill Hundred	52	203-270
New Castle	Appoquinimink Hundred	54	212-248
	Cantwell's Bridge	54	169-174
	Christiana Hundred	53	315-373
	First Division	53	272-315
	Middletown	54	175-179
	New Castle	54	276-312
	Pencader Hundred	54	313-344
	Port Penn	54	179-183
	Red Lion Hundred	54	249-275
	St. George's Hundred	54	183-211
	Third Division	53	374-401
	Wilmington	53	1-168
Sussex	Baltimore Hundred	55	111-144
	Broad Kiln Hundred	55	1-42
	Cedar Creek Hundred	55	64-92
	Dagsborough Hundred	55	144-175
	Eleventh Subdivision	55	195-297
	George Town	55	1-8
	Indian River Hundred	55	176-194
	Lewes, Rehoboth Hundred	55	43-64
	Milton	55	31-40
	Nanticoke Hundred	55	93-111
	South Milford	55	82-86

TABLE IV

Enumeration Dates--1850

Date	County	Locality	Roll No.	Sheet Nos.
8 July	Kent	Milford, Mispillion Hundred	52	83-84
	New Castle	Wilmington	53	1-2
	New Castle	Port Penn	54	179-183
	Sussex	George Town	55	1
9 July	Kent	Milford, Mispillion Hundred	52	85-86
	New Castle	Wilmington	53	3-6
	Sussex	George Town	55	2-6
10 July	Kent	Milford, Mispillion Hundred	52	87-89
	New Castle	Wilmington	53	7-19; 11; 13
	New Castle	St. George's Hundred	54	183-185
	Sussex	George Town, Broad Kiln Hd.	55	6-9
11 July	Kent	Milford, Mispillion Hundred	52	90-92
	Sussex	Broadkiln Hundred	55	9
12 July	Kent	Milford, Mispillion Hundred	52	93-96
	New Castle	Wilmington	53	9-12; 15; 17
13 July	Kent	Milford, Mispillion Hundred	52	96-97
	New Castle	Wilmington	53	13-19
	Sussex	Broadkiln Hundred	55	10
14 July	New Castle	Wilmington	53	19-20
15 July	Kent	Milford, Mispillion Hundred	52	98-99
	New Castle	First Division	53	272-273
	New Castle	Wilmington	52	20-22
	New Castle	St. George's Hundred	54	185-186
	New Castle	Red Lion Hundred	54	249-250
	New Castle	New Castle	54	291
	Sussex	Broad Kiln Hundred	55	11-13
	Sussex	Baltimore Hundred	55	111-113
	Sussex	Eleventh Subdivision	55	195-197
16 July	Kent	Milford, Mispillion Hundred	52	99-100
	New Castle	First Division	53	274
	New Castle	Wilmington	53	23-24
	New Castle	St. George's Hundred	54	187
	New Castle	Red Lion Hundred	54	251-252
	New Castle	New Castle	54	292-293
	Sussex	Broad Kiln Hundred	55	13-16
	Sussex	Baltimore Hundred	55	113-115
	Sussex	Eleventh Subdivision	55	197-198
17 July	Kent	Milford, Mispillion Hundred	52	101-102
	Kent	Duck Creek Hundred	52	1-3
	New Castle	First Division	53	275
	New Castle	St. George's Hundred	54	188-189
	New Castle	Red Lion Hundred	54	252-253
	New Castle	New Castle	54	293-294
	Sussex	Broad Kiln Hundred	55	16-18
	Sussex	Baltimore Hundred	55	115-116
	Sussex	Eleventh Subdivision	55	199-200
18 July	Kent	Duck Creek Hundred	52	4
	Kent	Milford, Mispillion Hundred	52	103
	New Castle	First Division	53	276-277
	New Castle	Wilmington	53	25-28
	New Castle	Red Lion Hundred	54	253-254
	New Castle	New Castle	54	294
	Sussex	Baltimore Hundred	55	117-118
	Sussex	Eleventh Subdivision	55	200-201
19 July	Kent	Duck Creek Hundred	52	5
	Kent	Milford, Mispillion Hundred	52	104
	New Castle	First Division	53	277-278
	New Castle	Wilmington	53	29-32
	New Castle	New Castle	54	295-296
	Sussex	Broad Kiln Hundred	55	19
	Sussex	Baltimore Hundred	55	118-119
	Sussex	Eleventh Subdivision	55	201-202
20 July	Kent	Duck Creek Hundred	52	6-7
	Kent	Milford, Mispillion Hundred	52	104-106
	Kent	Murderkill Hundred	52	203-204
	New Castle	First Division	53	278
	New Castle	St. George's Hundred	54	189
	New Castle	Red Lion Hundred	54	254-255
	New Castle	New Castle	54	296-297
	Sussex	Baltimore Hundred	55	119-120
	Sussex	Eleventh Subdivision	55	202-204
22 July	Kent	Duck Creek Hundred	52	8

Date	County	Location	Roll No.	Sheet Nos.
22 July	Kent	Milford, Mispillion Hundred	52	107
	Kent	Murderkill Hundred	52	205-206
	New Castle	First Division	53	279-280
	New Castle	Wilmington	53	33-37
	New Castle	St. George's Hundred	54	190-191
	New Castle	Red Lion Hundred	54	244-255
	New Castle	New Castle	54	298-299
	Sussex	Broad Kiln Hundred	55	20-22
	Sussex	Baltimore Hundred	55	120-121
23 July	Kent	Duck Creek Hundred	52	9-11
	Kent	Milford, Mispillion Hundred	52	108
	Kent	Murderkill Hundred	52	207-208
	New Castle	First Division	53	281-282
	New Castle	Wilmington	53	37-40
	New Castle	St. George's Hundred	54	192-193
	New Castle	New Castle	54	299-300
	Sussex	Broad Kiln Hundred	55	22-27
	Sussex	Baltimore Hundred	55	121-122
	Sussex	Eleventh Subdivision	55	204-205
24 July	Kent	Duck Creek Hundred	52	12-16
	Kent	Milford, Mispillion Hundred	52	109-111
	New Castle	First Division	53	283
	New Castle	St. George's Hundred	54	194-195
	New Castle	Red Lion Hundred	54	256-257
	New Castle	New Castle	54	301-302
	Sussex	Baltimore Hundred	55	123-124
	Sussex	Eleventh Subdivision	55	206-207
25 July	Kent	Milford, Mispillion Hundred	52	111-114
	New Castle	First Division	53	284-285
	New Castle	Wilmington	53	41-42
	New Castle	St. George's Hundred	54	196
	New Castle	Red Lion Hundred	54	257-258
	New Castle	New Castle	54	302-303
	Sussex	Baltimore Hundred	55	124-125
	Sussex	Eleventh Subdivision	55	207-208
26 July	Kent	Duck Creek Hundred	52	17-20
	Kent	Milford, Mispillion Hundred	52	114-116
	Kent	Murderkill Hundred	52	208-211
	New Castle	First Division	53	285
	New Castle	St. George's Hundred	54	197-198
	New Castle	New Castle	54	304-305
	Sussex	Baltimore Hundred	55	125-128
	Sussex	Eleventh Subdivision	55	209-210
27 July	Kent	Duck Creek Hundred	52	21-22
	Kent	Milford, Mispillion Hundred	52	116
	Kent	Murderkill Hundred	52	211-212
	New Castle	First Division	53	285-287
	New Castle	St. George's Hundred	54	198-201
	New Castle	Red Lion Hundred	54	258
	New Castle	New Castle	54	305-306
	Sussex	Baltimore Hundred	55	128-130
29 July	Kent	Murderkill Hundred	52	212-213
	Kent	Duck Creek Hundred	52	23
	Kent	Milford, Mispillion Hundred	52	116-118
	New Castle	First Division	53	288-290
	New Castle	Wilmington	53	43-48
	New Castle	St. George's Hundred	54	202
	New Castle	Red Lion Hundred	54	259-260
	New Castle	New Castle	54	307-308
	New Castle	Mill Creek Hundred	54	345
	Sussex	Broad Kiln Hundred	55	27-30
	Sussex	Baltimore Hundred	55	131-133
	Sussex	Eleventh Subdivision	55	211-212
30 July	Kent	Duck Creek Hundred	52	24-25
	Kent	Milford, Mispillion Hundred	52	118-119
	Kent	Murderkill Hundred	52	214
	New Castle	First Division	53	291-292
	New Castle	Wilmington	53	49-52
	New Castle	St. George's Hundred	54	203-204
	New Castle	Red Lion Hundred	54	260
	New Castle	New Castle	54	309-310
	Sussex	Milton	55	31-32
	Sussex	Baltimore Hundred	55	133-135
	Sussex	Eleventh Subdivision	55	212-213
31 July	Kent	Milford, Mispillion Hundred	52	120-121
	Kent	Murderkill Hundred	52	215-216

Date	County	Location	Roll No.	Sheet Nos.
31 July	New Castle	St. George's Hundred	54	204-206
	New Castle	New Castle	54	310-311
	Sussex	Milton	55	33-40
	Sussex	Baltimore Hundred	55	136-138
	Sussex	Eleventh Subdivision	55	214-215
1 August	Kent	Milford, Mispillion Hundred	52	121-122
	New Castle	First Division	53	292-293
	New Castle	St. George's Hundred	54	207
	New Castle	Red Lion Hundred	54	261-262
	New Castle	New Castle	54	312
	New Castle	Mill Creek Hundred	54	346
	Sussex	Baltimore Hundred	55	138-140
2 August	Kent	Milford, Mispillion Hundred	52	123-124
	Kent	Murderkill Hundred	52	217-218
	New Castle	First Division	53	294-295
	New Castle	Wilmington	53	53-56
	New Castle	Red Lion Hundred	54	262
	New Castle	Mill Creek Hundred	54	348-349
	Sussex	Baltimore Hundred	55	143-144
5 August	Kent	Milford, Mispillion Hundred	52	124-125
	New Castle	First Division	53	295-296
	New Castle	Wilmington	53	59-60
	New Castle	Red Lion Hundred	54	263-264
	New Castle	New Castle	54	276-281
	New Castle	Mill Creek Hundred	54	349
6 August	Kent	Duck Creek Hundred	52	26
	Kent	Milford, Mispillion Hundred	52	126-127
	New Castle	First Division	53	297
	New Castle	Christiana	53	315-320
	New Castle	Wilmington	53	61-64
	New Castle	Cantwell's Bridge	54	169-170
	New Castle	Red Lion Hundred	54	264-265
	New Castle	New Castle	54	281-284
	New Castle	Mill Creek	54	350-351
	Sussex	Dagsborough	55	145-146
7 August	Kent	Duck Creek Hundred	52	27-32
	New Castle	First Division	53	298-300
	New Castle	Christiana Hundred	53	320-323
	New Castle	Cantwell's Bridge	54	171-174
	New Castle	New Castle	54	284-288
	Sussex	Dagsborough Hundred	55	146-148
8 August	New Castle	First Division	53	300-303
	New Castle	Christiana Hundred	53	324-325
	New Castle	Wilmington	53	65-70
	New Castle	New Castle	54	288-290
	New Castle	Mill Creek Hundred	54	351-353
	Sussex	Dagsborough Hundred	55	148-150
9 August	Kent	Duck Creek Hundred	52	33-34
	New Castle	First Division	53	303-305
	New Castle	Christiana Hundred	53	326-329
	New Castle	Wilmington	53	71-74
	New Castle	Mill Creek Hundred	54	354
	New Castle	Middletown	54	145-179
10 August	Kent	Duck Creek Hundred	52	34
	Kent	Milford, Mispillion Hundred	52	127-129
	New Castle	Wilmington	53	99-102
	New Castle	Red Lion Hundred	54	265
	New Castle	Mill Creek Hundred	54	354
12 August	Kent	Milford, Mispillion Hundred	52	129-132
	Kent	Murderkill Hundred	52	222-225
	New Castle	Wilmington	53	95-98
	New Castle	Red Lion Hundred	54	266-267
	New Castle	Mill Creek Hundred	54	355-357
	Sussex	Dagsborough Hundred	55	150-152
13 August	Kent	Duck Creek Hundred	52	35-36
	Kent	Little Creek Hundred	52	132
	Kent	Murderkill Hundred	52	225-226
	New Castle	First Division	53	306-309
	New Castle	Wilmington	53	91
	New Castle	Mill Creek Hundred	54	358
	Sussex	Dagsborough Hundred	55	152-154
14 August	Kent	Duck Creek Hundred	52	37-38
	Kent	Murderkill Hundred	52	227-229
	New Castle	First Division	53	310
	New Castle	Wilmington	53	93-94
	New Castle	Mill Creek Hundred	54	358

Date	County	Location	Roll No.	Sheet Nos.
14 August	Sussex	Dagsborough	55	154-156
	Sussex	Lewes, Rehoboth Hundred	55	43-45
15 August	Kent	Duck Creek Hundred	52	39-40
	Kent	Milford, Mispillion Hundred	52	133-134
	Kent	Murderkill Hundred	52	230-231
	New Castle	First Division	53	311-315
	New Castle	Christiana Hundred	53	330-331
	New Castle	Wilmington	53	91-92
	New Castle	Red Lion Hundred	54	267
	New Castle	Mill Creek Hundred	54	359
	Sussex	Lewes, Rehoboth Hundred	55	46-48
	Sussex	Dagsborough	55	156-158
16 August	Kent	Duck Creek Hundred	52	41-43
	Kent	Milford, Mispillion Hundred	52	135-136
	Kent	Murderkill Hundred	52	231-232
	New Castle	First Division	53	313-314
	New Castle	Wilmington	53	83; 35-90
	New Castle	Red Lion Hundred	54	268-269
	New Castle	Mill Creek Hundred	54	359-360
	Sussex	Lewes, Rehoboth Hundred	55	48-50
	Sussex	Dagsborough Hundred	55	159-160
17 August	Kent	Murderkill Hundred	52	233-234
	Kent	Milford, Mispillion Hundred	52	136
	New Castle	Wilmington	53	81-82; 83-84
	New Castle	Mill Creek Hundred	54	360-361
	Sussex	Dagsborough Hundred	55	160-161
19 August	Kent	Murderkill Hundred	52	234-235
	New Castle	Third Division	53	374-376
	New Castle	Wilmington	53	77-80
	New Castle	Mill Creek Hundred	54	361-362
	Sussex	Lewes, Rehoboth	55	51-54
	Sussex	Dagsborough Hundred	55	161-162
20 August	Kent	Milford, Mispillion Hundred	52	137
	New Castle	Christiana Hundred	53	332-333
	New Castle	Third Division	53	376
	New Castle	Red Lion Hundred	54	269-270
	Sussex	Lewes, Rehoboth Hundred	55	54-55
	Sussex	Dagsborough Hundred	55	163-164
21 August	Kent	Milford, Mispillion Hundred	52	138
	New Castle	Christiana Hundred	53	334-337
	New Castle	Third Division	53	377-379
	New Castle	Wilmington	53	75-76
	New Castle	Red Lion Hundred	54	270-271
	Sussex	Lewes, Rehoboth Hundred	55	55-56
	Sussex	Dagsborough Hundred	55	164-165
	Sussex	Eleventh Subdivision	55	215-217
22 August	Kent	Milford, Mispillion Hundred	52	139
	Kent	Murderkill Hundred	52	236-238
	New Castle	First Division	53	314-315
	New Castle	Third Division	53	379-381
	New Castle	Red Lion Hundred	54	271-272
	New Castle	Mill Creek Hundred	54	363-364
	Sussex	Lewes, Rehoboth Hundred	55	56-59
	Sussex	Dagsborough Hundred	55	166-167
	Sussex	Eleventh Subdivision	55	217-219
23 August	Kent	Little Creek Hundred	52	55-58
	Kent	Milford, Mispillion Hundred	52	140
	Kent	Murderkill Hundred	52	238-240
	New Castle	Christiana Hundred	53	338-339
	New Castle	Third Division	53	381-382
	New Castle	Mill Creek Hundred	54	364
	Sussex	Lewes, Rehoboth Hundred	55	60-62
	Sussex	Dagsborough Hundred	55	167-168
	Sussex	Eleventh Subdivision	55	219-221
24 August	Kent	Milford, Mispillion Hundred	52	141-142
	Kent	Murderkill Hundred	52	240-242
	New Castle	Third Division	53	383-384
	New Castle	Mill Creek Hundred	54	365-366
	Sussex	Lewes, Rehoboth Hundred	55	62-64
	Sussex	Dagsborough Hundred	55	169-170
	Sussex	Eleventh Subdivision	55	222-223
26 August	Kent	Duck Creek Hundred	52	43-45
	Kent	Milford, Mispillion Hundred	52	142-143
	Kent	Murderkill Hundred	52	243
	New Castle	Appoquinimink Hundred	54	212-213
	New Castle	Christiana Hundred	53	340-343

Date	County	Location	Roll No.	Sheet Nos.
26 August	New Castle	Third Division	53	384
	New Castle	Wilmington	53	103-104
	New Castle	Red Lion Hundred	54	272-274
	New Castle	Mill Creek Hundred	54	366-368
	Sussex	Dagsborough Hundred	55	170-172
	Sussex	Eleventh Subdivision	55	223-224
27 August	Kent	Duck Creek Hundred	52	45-46
	Kent	Milford, Mispillion Hundred	52	144
	Kent	Murderkill Hundred	52	244-245
	New Castle	Wilmington	53	113-114
	New Castle	Mill Creek Hundred	54	369
	Sussex	Eleventh Subdivision	55	225-226
28 August	Kent	Milford, Mispillion Hundred	52	145-146
	New Castle	Wilmington	53	107-112
	New Castle	Mill Creek Hundred	54	370
	Sussex	Cedar Creek Hundred	55	64-66
	Sussex	Eleventh Subdivision	55	227
29 August	Kent	Milford, Mispillion Hundred	52	146-147
	Kent	Murderkill Hundred	52	245-247
	New Castle	Christiana Hundred	53	344-347
	New Castle	Wilmington	53	113-114
	New Castle	Mill Creek Hundred	54	371-373
	Sussex	Dagsborough Hundred	55	173-175
	Sussex	Eleventh Subdivision	55	228-229
30 August	Kent	Duck Creek Hundred	52	47
	Kent	Milford, Mispillion Hundred	52	147-148
	Kent	Murderkill Hundred	52	248-249
	New Castle	Wilmington	53	115-118; 120
	New Castle	Mill Creek Hundred	54	375
	Sussex	Cedar Creek Hundred	55	66-67
	Sussex	Indian River Hundred	55	176-177
	Sussex	Eleventh Subdivision	55	230
31 August	Kent	Milford, Mispillion Hundred	52	148-149
	Kent	Murderkill Hundred	52	250-251
	New Castle	Wilmington	53	119-124
	New Castle	Mill Creek Hundred	54	374-375
	Sussex	Indian River Hundred	55	178-179
	Sussex	Eleventh Subdivision	55	230-232
2 September	New Castle	Wilmington	53	125-130
	New Castle	Red Lion Hundred	54	274-275
	New Castle	Pencader Hundred	54	313-314
	New Castle	Mill Creek Hundred	54	376-377
3 September	Kent	Duck Creek Hundred	52	48-49
	Kent	Milford, Mispillion Hundred	52	149-150
	Kent	Murderkill Hundred	52	251-252
	New Castle	Wilmington	53	131-134
	New Castle	Pencader Hundred	54	314-315
	Sussex	Indian River Hundred	55	179-180
4 September	Kent	Duck Creek Hundred	52	50
	Kent	Milford, Mispillion Hundred	52	150
	Kent	Murderkill Hundred	52	253-255
	New Castle	Christiana Hundred	53	348-349
	New Castle	Third Subdivision	53	385-387
	New Castle	Wilmington	53	135-140
	New Castle	Appoquinimink Hundred	54	214
	New Castle	Pencader Hundred	54	315-316
	Sussex	Cedar Creek Hundred	55	67-69
	Sussex	Indian River Hundred	55	181-182
	Sussex	Eleventh Subdivision	55	232-234
5 September	Kent	Duck Creek Hundred	52	51
	Kent	Milford, Mispillion Hundred	52	151
	Kent	Murderkill Hundred	52	255-257
	New Castle	Christiana Hundred	53	350-353
	New Castle	Wilmington	53	140-142
	New Castle	Appoquinimink Hundred	54	214-216
	New Castle	Pencader Hundred	54	317
	New Castle	Mill Creek Hundred	54	377-379
	Sussex	Cedar Creek Hundred	55	69-72
	Sussex	Indian River Hundred	55	183
	Sussex	Eleventh Subdivision	55	235-238
6 September	Kent	Duck Creek Hundred	52	52
	Kent	Milford, Mispillion Hundred	52	152
	Kent	Murderkill Hundred	52	257
	New Castle	Christiana Hundred	53	354-355
	New Castle	Third Division	53	387-389
	New Castle	Wilmington	53	143-148

Enumeration Dates--1850

Date	County	Location	Roll No.	Sheet Nos.
6 September	New Castle	Appoquinimink Hundred	54	216-218
	New Castle	Pencader Hundred	54	317-319
	New Castle	Mill Creek Hundred	54	380
	Sussex	Cedar Creek Hundred	55	73-75
	Sussex	Indian River Hundred	55	184
	Sussex	Eleventh Subdivision	55	238-240
7 September	Kent	Dover Hundred	52	153-154
	New Castle	Christiana Hundred	53	356-357
	New Castle	Wilmington	53	149-152
	New Castle	Pencader Hundred	54	319-321
9 September	Kent	Little Creek Hundred	52	59-61
	Kent	Murderkill Hundred	52	258-259
	New Castle	Third Division	53	390-393
	New Castle	Wilmington	53	153-158
	New Castle	Pencader Hundred	54	321
	New Castle	Mill Creek Hundred	54	381-382
	Sussex	Cedar Creek Hundred	55	76-77
	Sussex	Indian River Hundred	55	184-186
10 September	Kent	Little Creek Hundred	52	61
	Kent	Murderkill Hundred	52	259-260
	New Castle	Christiana Hundred	53	258-359
	New Castle	Third Division	53	393-395
	New Castle	Wilmington	53	159-160
	New Castle	Appoquinimink Hundred	54	219
	New Castle	Pencader Hundred	54	322-323
	New Castle	Mill Creek Hundred	54	382-383
	Sussex	Cedar Creek Hundred	55	78-81
	Sussex	Indian River Hundred	55	187-188
11 September	Kent	Little Creek Hundred	52	62-64
	Kent	Murderkill Hundred	52	261-262
	New Castle	Christiana Hundred	53	360-361
	New Castle	Third Division	53	396-397
	New Castle	Wilmington	53	161-162
	New Castle	Appoquinimink Hundred	54	220-221
	New Castle	Pencader Hundred	54	323-324
	Sussex	South Milford	55	82-86
	Sussex	Indian River Hundred	55	188-190
12 September	Kent	Little Creek Hundred	52	64-66
	Kent	Murderkill Hundred	52	263-264
	New Castle	Christiana Hundred	53	362-365
	New Castle	Third Division	53	398-399
	New Castle	Pencader Hundred	54	325-326
	Sussex	Indian River Hundred	55	191-193
13 September	Kent	Murderkill Hundred	52	265-267
	New Castle	Christiana Hundred	53	366-367
	New Castle	Appoquinimink Hundred	54	225-227
	New Castle	Pencader Hundred	54	327
	Sussex	Indian River Hundred	55	193
14 September	Kent	Murderkill Hundred	52	267-270
	New Castle	Christiana Hundred	53	368-371
	New Castle	Wilmington	53	163-164
	New Castle	Pencader Hundred	54	327-328
	New Castle	Mill Creek Hundred	54	383
	Sussex	Indian River Hundred	55	194
	Sussex	Eleventh Subdivision	55	241-242
15 September	New Castle	Christiana Hundred	53	372-373
	New Castle	Wilmington	53	165-166
	New Castle	Mill Creek Hundred	54	384
16 September	Kent	Little Creek Hundred	52	66-68
	Kent	Dover Hundred	52	154-155
	New Castle	Third Division	53	390-401
	New Castle	Pencader Hundred	54	328
	Sussex	Cedar Creek Hundred	55	87
17 September	Kent	Dover Hundred	52	155-157
	New Castle	Pencader Hundred	54	329-330
	Sussex	Cedar Creek Hundred	55	88-89
18 September	Kent	Little Creek Hundred	52	68-70
	Kent	Dover Hundred	52	157-160
	New Castle	Pencader Hundred	54	330-331
19 September	Kent	Dover Hundred	52	161; 163-164
	New Castle	Appoquinimink Hundred	54	227-228
	New Castle	Pencader Hundred	54	331-332
	Sussex	Cedar Creek Hundred	55	89-91
20 September	Kent	Dover Hundred	52	164
	New Castle	Appoquinimink Hundred	54	229-230
	New Castle	Pencader Hundred	54	332-333

xiv

Date	County	Location	Roll No.	Sheet Nos.
20 September	Sussex	Cedar Creek Hundred	55	91-92
21 September	Kent	Dover Hundred	52	165-166
	New Castle	Appoquinimink Hundred	54	230-231
	New Castle	Pencader Hundred	54	333
23 September	Kent	Little Creek Hundred	52	71-72
	Kent	Dover Hundred	52	166-167
	Sussex	Nanticoke Hundred	55	93-96
24 September	Kent	Little Creek Hundred	52	73-75
	New Castle	Pencader Hundred	54	335-336
	Sussex	Nanticoke Hundred	55	96-100
	Sussex	Eleventh Subdivision	55	243
25 September	Kent	Little Creek Hundred	52	75-77
	Kent	Dover Hundred	52	168-169
	New Castle	Pencader Hundred	54	336-337
	Sussex	Nanticoke Hundred	55	101
	Sussex	Eleventh Subdivision	55	243-244
26 September	Kent	Dover Hundred	52	170-171
	New Castle	Pencader Hundred	54	337-338
	Sussex	Nanticoke Hundred	55	101-103
	Sussex	Eleventh Subdivision	55	244-245
27 September	Kent	Little Creek Hundred	52	77; 78-79
	New Castle	Pencader Hundred	54	338-339
	Sussex	Nanticoke Hundred	55	103-107
	Sussex	Eleventh Subdivision	55	245-246
28 September	Kent	Duck Creek Hundred	52	54
	Kent	Little Creek Hundred	52	81-82
	Kent	Dover Hundred	52	171-172
	New Castle	Pencader Hundred	54	340-341
30 September	Kent	Dover Hundred	52	173
	New Castle	Pencader Hundred	54	341-342
	Sussex	Nanticoke Hundred	55	107-111
2 October	Kent	Dover Hundred	52	173
	New Castle	Appoquinimink Hundred	54	231-233
	New Castle	Pencader Hundred	54	343-344
	Sussex	Eleventh Subdivision	55	246-247
3 October	Kent	Dover Hundred	52	174
	New Castle	Appoquinimink Hundred	54	234-236
	Sussex	Eleventh Subdivision	55	248
4 October	Kent	Dover Hundred	52	175-176
	New Castle	Appoquinimink Hundred	54	236-242
	Sussex	Eleventh Subdivision	55	249
5 October	Kent	Dover Hundred	52	177-178
	New Castle	Appoquinimink	54	250-251
	Sussex	Eleventh Subdivision	55	249
7 October	Sussex	Eleventh Subdivision	55	250
8 October	Kent	Dover Hundred	52	179
	New Castle	Appoquinimink Hundred	54	251-252
9 October	Kent	Dover Hundred	52	180-181
	New Castle	Appoquinimink	54	243-246
	Sussex	Eleventh Subdivision	55	252-254
10 October	Kent	Dover Hundred	52	182-183
	New Castle	Appoquinimink	54	247-248
	Sussex	Eleventh Subdivision	55	254-255
11 October	Kent	Dover Hundred	52	184-185
	Sussex	Eleventh Subdivision	55	256
12 October	Kent	Dover Hundred	52	186-188
14 October	Kent	Dover Hundred	52	188-190
15 October	Kent	Dover Hundred	52	191-193
16 October	Kent	Dover Hundred	52	193-194
17 October	Kent	Dover Hundred	52	195-197
18 October	Kent	Dover Hundred	52	197-200
19 October	Kent	Dover Hundred	52	200-202
22 October	Sussex	Eleventh Subdivision	55	256-257
23 October	Sussex	Eleventh Subdivision	55	257-258
24 October	Sussex	Eleventh Subdivision	55	258-259
30 October	Sussex	Eleventh Subdivision	55	259-260
31 October	Sussex	Eleventh Subdivision	55	261-262
1 November	Sussex	Eleventh Subdivision	55	262-263
2 November	Sussex	Eleventh Subdivision	55	264-265
4 November	Sussex	Eleventh Subdivision	55	256-266
5 November	Sussex	Eleventh Subdivision	55	267-268
6 November	Sussex	Eleventh Subdivision	55	268-269
7 November	Sussex	Eleventh Subdivision	55	270-272
14 November	Sussex	Eleventh Subdivision	55	272-274
15 November	Sussex	Eleventh Subdivision	55	275
16 November	Sussex	Eleventh Subdivision	55	275

Date	County	Location	Roll No.	Sheet Nos.
19 November	Sussex	Eleventh Subdivision	55	276-277
20 November	Sussex	Eleventh Subdivision	55	278-279
21 November	Sussex	Eleventh Subdivision	55	280
22 November	Sussex	Eleventh Subdivision	55	281
23 November	Sussex	Eleventh Subdivision	55	282
25 November	Sussex	Eleventh Subdivision	55	282-284
26 November	Sussex	Eleventh Subdivision	55	284-285
27 November	Sussex	Eleventh Subdivision	55	286-287
28 November	Sussex	Eleventh Subdivision	55	288-289
29 November	Sussex	Eleventh Subdivision	55	289-290
2 December	Sussex	Eleventh Subdivision	55	291-292
3 December	Sussex	Eleventh Subdivision	55	292-293
4 December	Sussex	Eleventh Subdivision	55	294-295
5 December	Sussex	Eleventh Subdivision	55	295-296
6 December	Sussex	Eleventh Subdivision	55	297
undated	Kent	Duck Creek Hundred	52	52-54
	Kent	Little Creek Hundred	52	78-80

Name	Age	State	Page	Name	Age	State	Page	Name	Age	State	Page
Aaron, David	24	DE	39	Atkins, Alexander	22	DE	108	Allen, Elizabeth	67	DE	152
Frances Ann	27	DE	57	Ann	27	DE	146	Emeline	9	DE	192
Latitia	15	DE	39	Boaz	75	DE	90	Emma	4	NJ	88
Latitia	62	DE	39	Eliza	1	DE	86	George	14	DE	34
Lewis	30	MD	80	Eliza	34	DE	86	Harriet	11	DE	192
Mary	4	MD	80	Elizabeth	20	DE	95	Hester A	22	DE	144
Morris	26	DE	57	Elizabeth B	10	DE	91	Isaac	20	DE	149
Rachael	25	MD	80	Ellen	30	DE	91	Jacob	15	DE	201
Thomas	6	MD	80	George S	2	DE	91	James	60	MD	246
Thomas	18	DE	39	George S	43	DE	91	Jane R	55	DE	149
Abbot, George	59	DE	176	Georgianna	7	DE	91	John	6	DE	152
James	17	DE	249	Henry	11	DE	86	John	7	DE	213
Nancy	49	DE	176	John W	6	DE	86	John	18	DE	129
Abbott, James	24	DE	117	John W	17	DE	86	Jonathan	5	DE	192
Jonathan	18	DE	172	Julia A	13	DE	91	Jonathan	50	DE	192
Louisa	1	DE	240	Julia A S	43	DE	91	Joseph	40	DE	137
Lydia	63	DE	117	Rachel	2	DE	90	Joseph C	38	NJ	88
Robert	60	DE	117	Robert	23	DE	149	Louisa	25	DE	152
Stephen	56	DE	108	Sally	4	DE	86	Mahala	14	DE	60
Warner	22	DE	117	Sarah E	18	DE	91	Martha E	30	NJ	204
Abel, David	14	PA	11	Sarah J	5	DE	95	Mary	4	DE	130
Elizabeth	9	PA	11	Synthia	1	DE	95	Mary	6	DE	239
Able, George	17	PA	29	Adkinson, William	23	DE	144	Mary A	15	DE	34
Ables, Elizabeth	30	DE	134	Adkison, Ann	51	DE	130	Mary A	31	MD	11
Fransena	14	DE	133	Henry	52	DE	130	Peter S	18	MD	3
Henry	47	DE	134	John W	14	DE	130	Rhoda	7	DE	192
John H	22	DE	111	Keturah	9	DE	130	Rhoda	45	DE	192
Louisa	20	DE	126	Lurena	12	DE	130	Robert	8	DE	239
Mary A	12	DE	134	Rachel R	18	DE	130	Sarah	3	DE	192
Philemon	17	DE	115	Robert	21	DE	130	Sarah A	8	DE	152
Thomas E	15	DE	115	Agdor, John	12	DE	171	Wesley	27	DE	54
William C	11	DE	115	Airs, Ann	20	DE	248	William	22	NJ	5
Abraham, Alexander	7	DE	212	Elizabeth	24	DE	165	Wm	11	DE	185
Beckey	30	DE	212	Lewis	16	DE	165	Zadock	31	DE	153
Grace A	20	DE	211	Mary	3	DE	248	Allford, Ann	25	DE	74
John	21	DE	235	Alexander, Ann	42	DE	242	Harriet	3	DE	74
Robert	24	DE	211	George	22	DE	9	Allison, Elizabeth	71	DE	263
Zekiel	25	DE	212	Hosea	15	DE	149	Allman, Martha	65	DE	224
Adams, Alexander	3	DE	40	Isaac	4	DE	108	Allston, Angeline	24	DE	32
Ann	2	DE	40	James H	22	DE	108	John	33	DE	32
Aranor	18	DE	239	Martha	60	DE	108	Mary	9/12	DE	32
Benjamin	12	DE	223	Martha E	19	DE	108	Richard	3	DE	32
Charles	3/12	DE	143	Mary A	8	DE	103	Alston, Anna	14	DE	18
Charles	12	DE	130	Robert	22	DE	32	Araminta	43	DE	18
Edward	29	DE	143	Sarah	28	DE	108	Charles	1	DE	18
Elizabeth	28	DE	147	Thomas	6	DE	108	Daniel	16	DE	18
Elizabeth	30	DE	92	Alfred, Harriet	20	DE	257	David	42	DE	19
Harrison	8	DE	142	Philip	21	DE	73	Elias	40	DE	59
Henry	12	PA	6	Sarah	70	DE	268	Elizabeth A	12	DE	3
Hester	7	DE	146	Allabane, Louisa	27	DE	248	Henry	6	DE	19
Hester	23	DE	79	Mary	4	DE	248	Kennard	8	DE	19
Hewlet	34	DE	146	Richbell	29	DE	248	Sarah	45	DE	59
Jacob	21	DE	239	Samuel	6	DE	248	America, Charles	20	DE	170
Jane L	25	DE	136	William	2	DE	248	Elizabeth	7	DE	170
John	1/12	DE	40	Allabone, Loretta	4	DE	248	John	14	DE	171
John	32	DE	49	Martin	10	DE	248	Johnson	21	DE	162
Joseph	5	DE	223	Sarah	36	DE	248	Mary	23	DE	170
Joseph	18	DE	244	Wm	36	DE	248	Moses	16	DE	170
Joshua	32	DE	214	Allee, Abraham	16	DE	5	Moses	49	DE	171
Leura	31	DE	142	Ann	69	DE	158	Nancy	57	DE	171
Levin H	48	DE	223	Barlow	3	DE	30	Richard	10	DE	171
Maria	8	DE	239	George W	18	DE	30	Sally	8	DE	170
Mary	23	DE	239	Hannah A	10	DE	32	Sally	47	DE	171
Mary	35	DE	244	Henrietta R	11	DE	30	William	10	DE	171
Mary	55	DE	239	Jacob	23	DE	30	Aminia, Charles	37	DE	159
Mary E	4	DE	92	James	36	DE	158	Margaret	4	DE	159
Mary J	24	DE	40	James D	39	DE	30	Mary	30	DE	159
Nicholas	13	DE	148	John N	14	DE	30	Amos, Ann	5	DE	54
Peter	16	DE	146	Jonathan	36	DE	9	Ellador	4	DE	190
Peter	35	DE	214	Mary Ann	31	DE	9	George	3	DE	54
Richard	30	DE	136	Mary F	2	DE	9	James	33	DE	190
Robert H	4	DE	142	Allen, Alexander	4	DE	246	John	2	DE	190
Roger	31	DE	239	Alvin	17	DE	15	Mary	10	DE	190
Ruth E	14	MD	128	Angeline	4	DE	152	Stephen	30	DE	190
Sally	45	DE	223	Ann	24	DE	22	Amsy, Mary	3/12	DE	156
Sarah A	2	DE	92	Anna	10	NJ	204	Anders, Charles	20	DE	229
Sarah J	1	DE	142	Asa	33	NJ	204	Anderson, Aaron	50	DE	79
Sherry	61	DE	239	Benjamin B	12	MD	11	Almira	5	DE	85
Susan	6	DE	142	Christiana	28	NJ	88	Amy	4	DE	166
William	8	DE	127	Daniel	1	DE	152	Amy	12	DE	174
William	28	DE	92	Edward	25	DE	22	Andrew	62	DE	128
William F	1	DE	92	Elizabeth	45	MD	246	Andrew	63	DE	239

Name	Age	State	No.
Anderson, Angeline	20	DE	76
Ann	13	DE	237
Ann	16	DE	236
Ann	30	DE	230
Anna E	20	DE	88
Benjamin	24	DE	186
Benjamin D	37	DE	85
Benjamin F	11	DE	30
Benniah	13	DE	138
Benona	1	DE	268
Catherine	7	DE	166
Catherine	8	DE	199
Catherine	17	DE	243
Charles	39	DE	154
Charles	65	DE	43
Charlotte	60	DE	179
Clementine	10	DE	138
Cornelius	14	DE	167
Curtis	6	DE	173
Curtis	45	DE	173
Daniel	12	DE	95
Daniel G	9	DE	85
David	15	DE	138
Debora	1	DE	166
Debora	13	DE	173
Eban W	8	DE	30
Edward	12	DE	73
Edward	17	DE	179
Edwin	2	DE	199
Elias	20	DE	173
Elias	25	DE	164
Eliza	2	DE	152
Eliza	14	DE	163
Eliza	18	DE	236
Eliza	20	DE	128
Eliza	50	DE	154
Elizabeth	12	DE	154
Elizabeth	28	DE	232
Elizabeth	51	DE	124
Elizabeth	52	DE	219
Elizabeth	69	DE	230
Elizabeth M	32	DE	85
Ellen P	23	DE	92
Emeline	3/12	DE	128
Emily	13	DE	243
Emily	31	DE	166
Emily A	24	MD	152
Enolds	27	DE	128
Eunicy	45	DE	207
Ezekiel	6	DE	138
Ezekiel	12	DE	166
Ezekiel	36	DE	152
Garrison	2	DE	129
Garritt	20	DE	100
George	22	DE	240
Grace	50	DE	231
Hannah	13	DE	25
Harriet L	7	DE	138
Henrietta	47	DE	79
Henry	5	DE	232
Henry	10	DE	166
Henry	16	DE	164
Henry	32	DE	232
Isaac	4	DE	128
Isaac	6	DE	24
James	9	DE	34
James	10	DE	199
James	12	DE	207
James	25	DE	268
James	37	DE	132
James	40	DE	230
James	59	DE	243
James B	25	DE	218
James F	7	DE	85
James S	17	DE	166
Jane	42	DE	128
John	2	DE	207
John	5	DE	199
John	10	DE	223
John	13	DE	70
John	13	DE	167
John	15	DE	173
Anderson, John	24	DE	76
John	29	DE	92
John	43	DE	168
John	45	DE	207
John	70	DE	236
John C	11	DE	137
John D	41	DE	199
John N	18	DE	7
John W	10/12	DE	7
Jonathan	14	DE	158
Joseph	10	DE	243
Joseph H	23	DE	6
Josephine	3	DE	85
Junifer	53	DE	219
Keziah	42	DE	173
Kitty	45	DE	168
Latitia	45	DE	237
Levi	20	DE	55
Levick	12	DE	158
Lewis	9	DE	167
Lewis	49	DE	166
Louisa	16	DE	166
Lydia	8	DE	137
Mahala	17	DE	268
Mahala	60	DE	95
Margaret	13	DE	79
Margaret	25	DE	166
Margaret A	19	DE	129
Martha	13	DE	250
Martha	17	DE	173
Mary	6/12	DE	231
Mary	1	DE	173
Mary	3	DE	199
Mary	6	DE	137
Mary	8	DE	230
Mary	10	DE	232
Mary	17	DE	240
Mary	21	DE	6
Mary	30	DE	199
Mary A	38	DE	138
Mary E	2	DE	128
Mary E	3	DE	7
Mary E	10	DE	85
Mary R	9	DE	138
Matilda	28	DE	128
Mingo	70	DE	95
Nathaniel	41	DE	244
Nisum	75	DE	34
Oliver	11/12	DE	232
Outten	8	DE	173
Outten	33	DE	128
Pauline	2/12	DE	92
Pauline	5	DE	244
Penel	7	DE	236
Priscilla	7	DE	167
Rachel	21	DE	128
Rebecca	2	DE	137
Rebecca	32	DE	137
Reuben	61	DE	88
Rhoda	9	DE	143
Salina	2	DE	34
Sally	17	DE	166
Sally Ann	47	DE	166
Samuel	2	DE	138
Samuel	11	DE	79
Samuel	31	DE	34
Samuel	42	DE	138
Samuel G	13	DE	7
Samuel P G	5/12	DE	85
Sarah	7	DE	232
Sarah	12	DE	173
Sarah	14	DE	236
Sarah	37	DE	248
Sarah	48	DE	239
Sarah	50	DE	243
Sarah A	13	DE	137
Sarah A	20	DE	218
Sarah A	51	DE	88
Sarah Ann	26	DE	79
Sarah E	2	DE	92
Stephen H	29	DE	128
Susan	16	DE	219
Anderson, Susan	43	DE	30
Susan C	17	DE	138
Syrus	22	DE	82
Thomas	3	DE	230
Thomas	10	DE	173
Wesley	21	DE	179
William	4	DE	137
William	6	DE	230
William	12	DE	166
William	14	DE	95
William	50	DE	137
William H	1	DE	128
Wm	48	DE	166
Zippora	31	DE	34
Andrew, Ann E	10	DE	131
Clement	25	DE	145
Eliza A	36	MD	144
Elizabeth	21	MD	142
Elizabeth	52	DE	131
Hester A	8	DE	144
James	26	MD	141
James H	2	DE	146
John	8	MD	142
John	50	DE	141
John W	13	DE	132
Lavicy	22	DE	131
Margaret J	4	DE	144
Marietta	4/12	DE	146
Mary	17	DE	131
Mary	18	DE	143
Mary E	3/12	DE	142
Mary E	10	DE	141
Polly	46	MD	141
Sarah	26	DE	145
Sarah A	14	DE	131
Sarah E	2	DE	144
William H	35	MD	144
Andrews, Mary	44	DE	78
Wilson	47	MD	78
Aners, Eliza	26	DE	102
John	33	DE	102
Anthony, Benjamin	12	DE	128
Daniel	43	DE	128
Eliza	32	DE	132
Elizabeth	14	DE	128
James H	4/12	DE	128
John	39	DE	132
John D	2	DE	132
Joseph	8	DE	128
Nathan	9	DE	128
Robert	33	DE	128
Robert G	4	DE	128
Sarah	21	DE	128
Sarah	41	DE	139
Sarah	43	DE	128
Thomas "	1	DE	128
Ardes, Wm	16	PA	200
Argadine, Elizabeth	19	DE	211
Argo, David	16	DE	224
David	32	DE	157
John	22	DE	25
Joseph	30	DE	161
Mary	35	DE	161
Prudence	22	DE	31
William	7	DE	161
Argoe, Alexander	13	DE	170
Ann E	9	DE	112
Anna	6	DE	170
Betsey	46	DE	170
Charles	14	DE	170
Charles	51	DE	170
Elizabeth	11	DE	170
Fanny	21	DE	170
John	62	DE	111
Joseph	17	DE	111
Levin	18	DE	170
Mary	44	DE	111
Mary E	13	DE	111
William	1	DE	170
Aris, Mary	31	DE	153
Arlin, Andrew	30	DE	225
Sarah	24	DE	225

Name	Age	State	Page
Arm, Eliza	12	DE	188
John	17	DE	188
Lydia	4	DE	188
Martha	10	DE	188
Peter	15	DE	188
Thuzdy	19	DE	188
William	7	DE	188
Armstrong, Beckey	40	DE	213
Herbert	22	DE	221
John	35	MD	228
Mary	30	MD	228
Sarah	14	DE	46
Arnot, William H	16	DE	109
Aron, Caleb	11	DE	184
David	47	DE	182
Hannah	50	DE	189
Hetty	37	DE	184
James	10	DE	182
Martha	1	DE	188
Martha	16	DE	184
Mary	4	DE	188
Powell	23	DE	188
Rebecca	40	DE	182
Thomas	13	DE	184
Thomas	21	DE	188
Wm	40	DE	184
Art, Emma F	25	PA	2
George	6/12	DE	2
James	3	PA	2
James	28	DE	2
Mary Ann	5	PA	2
Artes, Hester	73	DE	196
James	7/12	DE	183
James	36	DE	183
Margaret	12	DE	222
Mary	1	DE	168
Mary	26	DE	183
Mathew	29	DE	168
Sarah	6	DE	183
Sarah	30	DE	168
Arthers, Arthur	9	DE	239
Arthurs, Elizabeth	64	DE	197
Joshua	8	DE	197
Mathew	6	DE	197
Susan	3	DE	197
William	11	DE	197
Wm	41	DE	197
Artis, Ann	45	DE	227
Anna	5	DE	227
Eliza	22	DE	239
Eliza	24	DE	134
Frances	60	DE	115
James	19	MD	224
John	22	DE	242
John	23	DE	220
Robert	18	DE	238
Robert	35	DE	239
William	32	DE	124
William H	3	DE	120
Asbury, Jeremiah	26	DE	222
Louisa	15	DE	201
Waitman	1	DE	222
Ash, Caleb	17	DE	158
Ellen	25	DE	143
Harriet A	4	DE	112
Isaac	19	DE	153
Levy	55	DE	202
Ashley, Harriet	23	MD	22
Mary	7	MD	22
Thomas	35	MD	22
William	7/12	DE	22
Ashton, Henry	30	DE	53
Rachel	50	DE	53
Asper, William	21	DE	56
Asprill, Joseph	32	DE	94
Mariah E	6	PA	94
Sarah E	32	MD	94
Sarah J	2	MD	94
Thomas L	8/12	MD	94
Atkins, Angelina	15	DE	166
Ann	12	DE	166
Debora	34	DE	166
Atkins, George	8	DE	166
Harriet	10	DE	167
Jacob	7	DE	166
James	31	DE	77
James A	24	DE	57
Jane	5	DE	166
John	6	DE	166
John	7	DE	77
Manlove	14	DE	166
Mary	4	DE	77
Mary	9	DE	166
Myers B	20	DE	57
Rachel	2	DE	78
Rachel	14	DE	166
Rebecca	4/12	DE	77
Rebecca	31	DE	77
Richard	9	DE	76
Sarah	6	DE	77
Timothy	4	DE	166
William	20	DE	166
William	49	DE	166
William K	27	DE	95
Attix, Edward	8	DE	41
Edward	16	DE	41
Edward	56	MD	41
Henrietta	19	DE	41
James	11	DE	41
Margaret	52	DE	41
Mary P	1	DE	41
Stephen	31	DE	41
Susan	29	DE	41
Thomas	20	DE	41
Timothy	4	DE	41
Austin, Elizabeth	17	MD	262
Ayres, William	10	DE	81
Babe, Williamina	14	DE	150
Bacon, Catharine	10	DE	16
Catharine	38	DE	16
Jane	16	DE	16
John	22	NJ	13
John	51	NJ	16
Louis	4	DE	16
Mary E	18	DE	13
William	11	DE	16
Baggs, Harriet	20	DE	223
John M	2/12	DE	4
Mathew	16	MD	204
Sarah M	19	DE	4
William	23	MD	4
Bailey, Ann R	5	DE	44
Charles P	2	DE	38
Edward	4	DE	44
James E	16	MD	38
Jane	19	DE	37
John	41	DE	38
John C	15	DE	37
John E	2	DE	44
John R W	13	DE	38
Joseph T	18	DE	38
Margaret	7	DE	44
Martha	23	DE	50
Mary E	35	DE	38
Mason	55	DE	37
Rachel	29	DE	38
Ruth Ann	21	DE	37
Sarah	48	DE	37
Sarah R	10	DE	37
Thomas E	13	DE	37
William A	9/12	DE	38
Bailiff, William	23	DE	57
Baily, Ann E	9	DE	211
Anna	14	DE	236
Catherine	6	DE	211
Catherine	18	DE	206
Charles	12	PA	228
Edmond	10	DE	236
Eliza	50	DE	236
John	53	DE	236
Lorenzo D	13	DE	211
Martena	11	DE	211
Mary	16	DE	236
Baily, Mary	32	DE	211
Mary E	1	DE	211
Matilda	12	DE	236
Nathaniel	33	DE	211
Samuel	4	DE	211
Sarah J	7	DE	211
Wilmina	13	DE	155
Bainard, Araminta	1	DE	155
Gilbert	28	DE	154
Mary	24	DE	154
Baker, Alexander	13	DE	122
Amelia	6	DE	168
Ann	14	DE	168
Ann	41	MD	122
Ann E	11	DE	122
Benjamin	5	DE	122
Charles	24	DE	269
Elizabeth	13	DE	168
Elizabeth	58	DE	269
George	10	DE	168
Harriet	18	DE	240
Isaac	1	DE	168
Isaack	38	DE	168
Jacob	15	DE	168
James	9	DE	122
James O	2	DE	208
John	1	DE	17
John	29	VA	17
John	51	DE	122
John H	6/12	DE	123
John H	17	DE	122
Mary	3	DE	168
Mary	22	DE	269
Mary A	22	DE	123
Peregrine	51	DE	269
Rachel	22	DE	17
Rebecca	20	DE	122
Samuel	4	DE	17
Sarah	28	DE	168
Shadrack	2	DE	122
Thomas	22	DE	123
Unity L	21	DE	208
William H	25	DE	208
Bancroft, Adalvia	10	PA	159
Elemuel	38	NJ	159
Stephen	6	DE	159
Susetta	11	PA	159
Susetta	33	PA	159
William	6/12	DE	159
Banks, Elizabeth	28	DE	97
John E	30	MD	97
John W	3	DE	97
Banning, Elizabeth	16	DE	115
Mary J	16	DE	148
Sarah A	36	DE	148
Bantem, Mary J	12	DE	127
Barber, Charles	10	DE	79
Debe	30	DE	162
Deborah	32	DE	58
Edward	46	DE	187
Elizabeth	9	DE	187
Flora	55	DE	165
Harriet	1	DE	187
Henry	14	DE	153
Hester	45	DE	205
Hester	74	DE	249
James	6	DE	187
James	42	DE	167
John	13	DE	187
Joseph	16	DE	187
Sally Ann	43	DE	187
Sarah	11	DE	187
Sarah	40	DE	177
Sarah	49	DE	162
Simion	55	DE	205
Barchnel, Eliza	26	DE	211
Elizabeth	54	DE	211
Joseph	69	DE	211
Thomas	20	DE	211
Barcklow, Elizabeth	55	DE	227
Barcus, Ann	52	MD	39
Ann	53	DE	246

Name	Age	State	Page
Barcus, Arian	36	DE	60
Edward	12	DE	39
Edward	54	DE	39
Elizabeth	16	DE	246
Elizabeth	29	DE	69
George	2	DE	177
Greensbury	20	DE	60
Henrietta	10	DE	60
James	5	DE	69
James	30	DE	246
James	37	DE	177
James W	9	DE	39
John	17	DE	255
John	35	DE	69
Laban	18	DE	36
Martha	32	DE	246
Mary	25	DE	177
Mary	34	DE	185
Mary E	6/12	DE	69
Moses	15	DE	177
Nathan	5	DE	177
Priscilla A	9	DE	69
Richard	6	DE	267
Rodeman	38	DE	257
Sallyann	45	DE	257
Sarah Emma	3	DE	69
Stephen	21	DE	61
Steven	27	DE	246
Warner	56	DE	246
William	27	DE	52
William H	18	DE	60
Barker, Benjamin	3	DE	139
Elizabeth	9/12	DE	139
Emily J	16	DE	120
George P	29	NJ	56
Gibaliel	9	DE	120
Jacob	90	DE	210
John	8	DE	121
John	27	DE	29
Joseph	24	DE	139
Louisa	29	DE	211
Mary	22	DE	125
Matilda	23	DE	139
McKilry	13	DE	109
Ruth	25	NJ	56
Ruther	1	DE	29
Sarah A	4	DE	139
Susanna	26	DE	29
Thomas	10	DE	121
Thomas	39	DE	211
Barnes, James	55	DE	95
Mary	2	NJ	253
Mary	25	NJ	252
Wm	35	DE	252
Barnet, Nathaniel	25	DE	57
Thomas	12	DE	32
Thomas	66	DE	32
Barney, Eliza	26	MD	29
Frances	1	MD	29
John	12	DE	66
Martha	10	DE	66
Rich	33	DE	29
Susan	41	DE	66
William R	5	MD	29
Barr, Alexander F	32	PA	202
Charles	18	DE	30
Daniel	8	DE	29
Georgina	10	DE	29
Hester	45	DE	29
Jeffry	3	DE	29
Kate	2	MO	202
Martha	7	DE	29
Mary A	8	DE	29
Nancy	6/12	DE	202
Quincy	59	DE	29
Sarah F	5	MO	202
Sarah J	23	KY	202
Barret, Abner	65	DE	235
Caleb M	14	DE	216
Elmira	7	DE	216
Henry	49	DE	216
Isaac	13	DE	201
Barret, Judy	60	DE	163
Maria	40	DE	235
Mary	37	DE	216
Miriam	82	DE	228
Patience K	5	DE	217
Philip	16	DE	211
Sarah	3	DE	216
Barrett, Andres	30	DE	220
Charles	3	DE	26
Charles	27	DE	26
Daniel	1	DE	26
Frances	30	DE	26
Frank	10	DE	199
George	12	DE	198
Hannah	16	DE	195
Hester	17	DE	198
Hetty	28	DE	220
James	6	DE	198
James	17	DE	195
James	47	DE	198
John	11	DE	195
Joseph	8	DE	172
Joseph	14	DE	195
Joseph	70	MD	172
Loker	9	DE	198
Louisa	13	DE	195
Lydia A	6	DE	220
Margaret	4	DE	195
Mary	4	DE	27
Mary	9	DE	195
Mary	43	DE	195
Mary	44	DE	198
Rachel	7	DE	195
Susan	6	DE	195
Susan	50	DE	172
William	1	DE	198
William B	8	DE	27
Wm	43	DE	195
Barrow, Francis A	1	DE	60
Barrows, Elizabeth	51	DE	55
Henrietta	7	DE	265
Jane	13	DE	201
John P	7	DE	55
Matilda	14	DE	201
Peter	16	DE	264
Bartlet, Henry	7	PA	36
Barton, Elizabeth	45	DE	157
John	17	DE	157
Sally	13	DE	157
Thomas H	18	PA	18
Barwick, Eliza	37	DE	140
Eliza J	14	DE	140
John	10	DE	140
Mary	80	DE	220
Mary E	17	DE	140
Solomon	45	DE	140
Basset, Joseph	13	DE	179
Joseph	16	DE	70
Margaret	7	DE	179
Samuel	9	DE	179
Samuel	50	NJ	179
Sarah	52	DE	179
Bast, Isaac	23	DE	165
Baston, Catherine	7	PA	268
Elizabeth	5	PA	268
Joseph	1/12	DE	268
Joseph	32	DE	268
Margaret	37	PA	268
Phillip	9	PA	268
Sarah	3	PA	268
Bateman, Anna	9	DE	231
Buky	40	MD	231
Daniel	53	DE	108
Eliza	9	DE	234
Elizabeth	13	DE	234
Elizabeth	47	DE	234
George	51	DE	234
John	17	DE	234
John H	20	MD	73
Robert	4	DE	231
Sarah J	14	DE	108
Bates, George W	27	NJ	5
Bates, Martha W	18	MA	5
Martin	1	DE	215
Martin	64	CT	163
Mary	61	DE	163
Bath, Anna	6	DE	168
Bertha	27	DE	168
Joseph	2	DE	168
Mary	4	DE	168
Owen	40	DE	168
Sarah	7	DE	168
Tamar	70	DE	168
Battell, James	29	DE	82
Thomas	25	DE	82
Battle, Ann	34	DE	167
Thomas	28	DE	167
Bayard, Caroline	32	DE	19
Joseph	32	DE	19
Bayley, James H	18	DE	138
Lydia	59	DE	138
Sarah E	15	DE	138
Baynard, Alfred	11	DE	126
Asbury	4	DE	134
Caleb	40	DE	134
Charles H	15	DE	141
Charles W	11	DE	54
Charlotte E	23	DE	141
Clarisa	43	DE	134
Emeline	2	DE	134
Ferdinand	40	DE	141
John	53	DE	54
John A	4/12	DE	141
Joseph	2	DE	54
Lawson	7	DE	134
Lewis	17	DE	132
Margaret	15	DE	54
Maria	11	DE	54
Mary A	6	DE	54
Mary C	17	DE	141
Robert H	13	DE	54
Susan	42	DE	54
Susan E	8	DE	54
Thomas H	9	DE	141
Warner	7	DE	134
William H	16	DE	54
Beacham, Ann	31	DE	177
Fanny	40	DE	188
Henry	20	DE	188
Henry	35	DE	177
John	9	DE	177
Julia	30	DE	235
Sarah	5	DE	177
Susanna	7	DE	177
Beachem, Cesar	45	DE	238
Charles	10	DE	188
Edward	5/12	DE	238
George	7	DE	238
Henrietta	4	DE	238
Isah	9	DE	238
James	20	DE	270
Joseph	12	DE	188
Julianna	25	DE	238
Lydia	16	DE	188
Margaret	14	DE	188
Mary	11	DE	238
Matilda	8	DE	219
Samuel	3	DE	188
Wesley	4	DE	188
Beachum, James	34	DE	179
Beal, James	18	DE	237
Beardley, Hannah	50	DE	43
Jeremiah	55	DE	43
Beasey, Elmira	6	DE	17
Margaret	2	DE	17
Mariah	25	DE	17
Matilda	30	DE	17
Beauchamp, Catherine	30	DE	217
Gidiah	50	KY	245
James	11	DE	245
Mary	8	DE	245
Susan	15	DE	245
Beck, Edward	21	MD	10
Jacob	22	GE	84

Name	Age	St	Pg
Beck, John E	17	MD	14
Becker, Daniel	27	PA	18
George	2	NY	18
Harriet	23	PA	18
Margaret	5/12	NY	18
Beckett, Abraham	14	DE	73
Charles	3	DE	72
George	11	DE	4
Hester	30	DE	72
John	28	DE	72
John W	5	DE	72
Beddell, George	21	DE	98
Bedwell, Amey	52	DE	188
Basha	40	DE	190
Caleb	25	DE	185
Elija	60	DE	190
Elizabeth	10	DE	190
George D	21	DE	48
Hannah	45	DE	183
Henry	32	DE	39
Hester	14	DE	183
James	35	DE	190
James	36	DE	185
Jesse	60	DE	79
Joanna	40	DE	185
Johanna	38	DE	191
Jonathan	13	DE	183
Jonathan	70	DE	188
Margaret	28	DE	39
Mary	7	DE	183
Mary	13	DE	190
Matilda	16	DE	4
Rachel	20	DE	190
Rachel	20	DE	194
Ruth	24	DE	185
Susan	6	DE	39
Thomas	11	DE	183
Trusten	28	DE	182
William	9	DE	183
William H	3	DE	39
Wm	45	DE	183
Beecham, Gabriel	60	DE	115
Henrietta	14	DE	116
Hester A	14	DE	116
John	7	DE	116
Margaret	49	DE	115
Margaret A	18	DE	115
Beer, Micha	44	DE	248
Beetle, Elizabeth	23	DE	209
John W	2	DE	209
Wm	35	DE	209
Wm H	5/12	DE	209
Beggs, Andrew	25	MD	224
Bell, Aaron	22	DE	91
Alexander	24	DE	167
Alfred	29	DE	80
Ann	32	DE	216
Ann	51	DE	91
Anna	8	DE	167
Araminta	25	DE	18
Benjamin	3	DE	209
Caleb	7	DE	209
Caleb	26	DE	235
Caleb	38	DE	209
Celia	33	DE	111
Cloe	56	DE	216
Daniel	12	DE	237
Eliza	19	DE	251
Eliza	64	DE	76
Eliza A	1/12	DE	12
Elizabeth	10	DE	209
Elizabeth	16	DE	251
Elizabeth	20	DE	235
Ellen	13	MD	159
Ellen A	14	MD	18
Hannah	6/12	DE	216
Isaac	12	DE	167
Jacob H	28	DE	12
James	14	DE	209
James H	23	DE	91
John	6/12	DE	254
John	24	DE	139
Bell, John	26	DE	254
John	54	DE	167
John A	2	DE	12
John C	7	DE	36
John H	9	DE	209
John H	18	DE	36
John S	38	DE	36
Jonathan	23	DE	235
Joseph	18	DE	167
Leonard	4	DE	167
Lydia	1	DE	155
Margaret T	25	DE	12
Martina	3	DE	111
Mary	3/12	DE	190
Mary	3/12	DE	267
Mary	14	DE	167
Mary	26	DE	235
Mary	37	DE	209
Mary	40	DE	167
Mary	65	DE	82
Mary E	6	DE	209
Mary F	4	DE	216
Nancy	22	DE	254
Nathaniel	1	DE	209
Nathaniel	3	DE	216
Nehemiah	6	DE	111
Rebecca	28	DE	139
Rees F	5	DE	36
Rees J	40	DE	18
Richia	35	DE	267
Robert	9	DE	209
Sally	1	DE	254
Sarah	10	DE	267
Sarah	35	DE	209
Sarah E	6	DE	217
Sarah E	18	DE	18
Sarah J	12	DE	209
Silfa	4	DE	209
Susan	41	DE	36
Thomas	1	DE	139
Thomas	15	DE	252
Thomas	31	DE	216
William	2	DE	254
William	12	DE	209
William	45	DE	111
William	70	MD	254
William M	22	DE	5
Wm	34	MD	267
Bellville, John	36	PA	230
Mary	36	DE	230
Benger, Jacob	15	DE	13
Bengy, Daniel	13	PA	228
Benn, Emma	2	DE	160
George	14	DE	160
John	12	DE	160
Martha	37	DE	160
Rebecca	5	DE	160
Rebecca	30	MD	160
William	9	DE	160
Bennet, Benjamin	27	NJ	161
Catherine	26	DE	161
Charles P	24	NJ	161
Ebenezer	28	DE	255
Elizabeth	3	DE	255
Frances Ann	20	DE	2
Henry	1	DE	161
Margaretta	26	MD	255
William	4	DE	255
Bennett, Ann	29	DE	102
Charles	25	NJ	34
Deborah	49	DE	99
Elizabeth	15	DE	203
James	56	DE	72
Jarusa A	30	DE	99
John	28	DE	99
John T	1	DE	99
Joshua	2	DE	102
Joshua	28	DE	102
Joshua A	5	DE	99
Margaret	10	DE	72
Mary	1	DE	255
Mary	57	DE	72
Bennett, Mary A	2	DE	102
Rebecca	25	DE	34
Ruth	29	DE	102
Sarah	18	DE	260
Sarah	21	DE	102
William G	3	DE	99
Benninghoe, Ann	51	DE	13
Ann M	4	PA	15
Emma	24	PA	15
Emma L	1	PA	15
Jacob F	24	PA	15
Mary A	17	PA	13
William	23	PA	9
Bennit, John R	21	DE	98
Mary	25	DE	89
Benson, Albert	13	DE	130
Alexander	10	DE	120
Alfred	1/12	DE	241
Andrew	43	DE	263
Ann	40	DE	263
Ann E	32	MD	78
Anna M	8	DE	78
Benjamin	59	MD	11
Bias	50	DE	121
Catherine	27	DE	209
Edmond	18	DE	54
Eliza	9/12	DE	16
Elizabeth	6	DE	264
Elizabeth	10	DE	241
Elizabeth	35	DE	120
Elizabeth	41	DE	241
Ellen	7	DE	244
Handy	6	DE	120
Henry	20	DE	263
Henry	48	DE	241
Hepburn S	35	DE	78
Hester	16	DE	244
Ida P	1	DE	78
Ivan	40	DE	120
James	1	DE	263
James	9	DE	120
John	3	DE	244
John	6	DE	120
John	8	DE	263
John	33	DE	211
John T	7	DE	209
Joseph B	20	DE	11
Joshua	19	DE	99
Leah	27	DE	121
Mahala	14	DE	241
Margaret	5	DE	244
Maria	25	DE	16
Maria	60	PA	111
Mariana	23	DE	211
Mary	38	DE	244
Mary Ann	16	DE	1
Mary E	4	DE	209
Mathew	38	DE	244
Nancy	14	DE	244
Rhoda	45	DE	121
Rhoda A	7	DE	120
Richard	17	DE	241
Robert	7	DE	241
Samuel	9	DE	244
Samuel	12	DE	260
Sarah	14	DE	263
Sarah	70	DE	209
Sarah A	2	DE	211
Sarah E	2	DE	209
Solomon	5	DE	135
Thomas	35	DE	16
Virginia A	11	MD	78
William	5	DE	241
William J	1/12	DE	209
Zenus	28	DE	209
Bentley, Mary A	14	DE	20
Rebecca	80	MD	40
Susan	12	DE	50
Berry, Adaline	19	DE	66
Alice	9	DE	250
Ann	14	DE	250
Ann	47	DE	83

Berry, Ann E 11 DE 64
Augustus 36 DE 64
Caleb 56 DE 269
Caroline 49 DE 269
Celia 50 MD 64
Charles 9 DE 269
Charlotte 2 DE 86
Cornelius P C 1 PA 16
Daniel 5 DE 269
Elizabeth G 11 PA 16
Frances Ann 9 DE 64
Francis M 1 DE 65
George W 4 DE 65
Harriet 1 DE 250
Harriet 8 DE 86
Henrietta 7 DE 250
Isaac 19 DE 64
Isaac 32 DE 64
James 11 DE 250
John 25 DE 65
John H 6 DE 64
Kitty 34 DE 250
Kitty 40 DE 265
Leah 7 DE 269
Leah 30 DE 11
Lydia 32 DE 64
Mariah 30 DE 86
Peter 23 DE 226
Peter 25 DE 224
Rebecca B 14 PA 16
Robert 11 DE 226
Sarah 4 DE 250
Susan 35 DE 16
Tansey 10 DE 269
Thomas 15 DE 250
Thomas 15 DE 269
Thomas 16 DE 253
Thomas 37 MD 250
Vincent 16 DE 251
Vincent 18 DE 269
William 7 DE 64
William 55 DE 64
William A 6 DE 64
William B 42 DE 16
William H 6 PA 16
Beswicks, Angelina 17 DE 99
Brinckley 54 DE 99
George 8 DE 99
Robert J 14 DE 99
Sarah A 11 DE 99
Sarah S 44 DE 99
William P 22 DE 99
Bethards, Ann B 52 DE 107
George 40 DE 107
George Smith 15 DE 107
James 10 DE 107
John W 11 DE 107
Samuel 5 DE 107
William H 17 DE 107
Betts, Gracy 67 DE 97
Samuel 16 MD 10
Beulah, Emma F 1 DE 10
John H 28 MD 10
Mary J 27 DE 10
Bewley, Ann C 24 MD 3
James L 32 MD 3
Bickell, John 2 DE 99
John A 28 PA 99
Mary A 27 PA 99
William H 3 PA 99
Biddle, Ann 25 DE 183
Ann M 14 DE 36
Augusta 14 DE 35
Elizabeth 1 DE 183
Elizabeth 5 DE 183
Frances A 34 MD 4
George 13 MD 4
Jerry 7 DE 110
John 8 DE 183
John 25 DE 119
Wm 2 DE 183
Wm 26 DE 183

Bidwell, Daniel 1 DE 181
Daniel 40 DE 180
Elizabeth 30 DE 180
James 9 DE 180
Mary 6 DE 180
Susan 7 DE 180
Bignore, Mary L 11 DE 111
Biles, Amanda 23 PA 177
Emma 3 PA 177
John 19 DE 177
Laura 1 DE 177
Rebecca 18 DE 177
Samuel 31 PA 177
William 1 DE 177
Billens, Eliza 4 DE 267
James 42 DE 267
Martha 9/12 DE 267
Martha 21 DE 267
Billing, Clarissa 2 DE 268
Hannah 20 DE 252
John 11 DE 268
Margaret 47 DE 268
Mary 15 DE 268
Retina 15 DE 268
Sarah 6 DE 236
Thomas 12 DE 268
Thomas 46 DE 268
William 10 DE 236
William 40 DE 236
Billings, Elizabeth 33 DE 74
Everet 21 DE 244
Binn, Benjamin F 37 PA 97
Louisa 37 DE 97
Binor, Elizabeth 13 DE 52
Bishop, Ann 26 DE 172
Harriet 1 DE 172
Harriet 45 DE 66
John 6 DE 66
William S 46 DE 66
Black, Alexander 12 DE 172
Alphonzo C 37 DE 4
Annie 4/12 DE 218
Benjamin 10 DE 242
Caroline M 10 DE 148
Eliza 14 DE 160
Eliza 34 DE 242
Elizabeth 3 DE 239
Elizabeth 15 DE 242
Emerson 8 DE 170
Eugenia 5 MD 4
Ezekiel 18 DE 192
Francis 5 DE 234
Frederick 33 DE 148
George 1 DE 95
George 55 IE 97
Hannah 22 DE 171
Henrietta 4 DE 242
James C 16 MD 4
Jane 10 DE 241
John G 47 MD 4
Jonathan 55 DE 160
Joseph S 23 DE 218
Latitia 7 DE 238
Latitia 12 DE 239
Levin 12 DE 131
Lydia A 22 DE 218
Margaret 50 DE 234
Margaret E 6/12 DE 148
Margaret W 8 MD 4
Mariam 40 DE 238
Mary 25 DE 94
Mary F 3 DE 148
Massey 8 DE 148
Nathan 16 DE 214
Rebecca 25 DE 218
Samuel 22 DE 218
Samuel 60 DE 234
Sarah 10 DE 74
Sarah 35 DE 148
Steven 18 DE 249
Susan 12 DE 234
Susan C 13 MD 4

Black, Thomas 15 DE 160
Thomas 16 DE 234
Thomas 47 MD 238
William 8 DE 242
Wm 35 DE 242
Blackishire, Sarah 17 DE 23
Blackiston, Ann E 15 DE 50
Benjamin F 20 DE 50
David 8 DE 50
Eben 43 DE 72
Elizabeth 15 DE 50
Elizabeth 18 DE 20
Ezekiel 20 DE 48
George W 39 DE 23
James 12 DE 50
James 14 DE 52
James 41 DE 42
James 76 DE 52
Jane 60 MD 53
Mary 3 DE 40
Mary F 3 DE 72
Michael 91 DE 19
Moses 7 DE 52
Richard A 50 DE 23
Sarah 41 DE 71
William T 5 DE 16
Blackshire, Michael 25 DE 82
Blackston, Ann E 2/12 DE 32
Hannah 24 DE 32
William 30 DE 32
Blackstone, Charles 5 DE 168
Charles 15 DE 161
Elizabeth 12 DE 168
Elizabeth 17 DE 164
Ellen 27 DE 163
Hannah 51 DE 167
John 3 DE 163
Martha 13 DE 167
Mary 1 DE 167
Mary 14 DE 167
Rebecca 19 DE 198
Richard 9/12 DE 198
Samuel 21 DE 198
Samuel 60 DE 198
Susan 22 DE 159
Toney 19 DE 167
Toney 54 DE 167
Wm 16 DE 167
Blades, Alexander 8 DE 132
Ann E 1 DE 152
Bowdel 28 DE 215
Elizabeth 33 MD 264
George 10 DE 103
James 13 DE 139
John 13 DE 102
John 16 DE 132
Levin 35 MD 264
Lydia 32 DE 102
Major 8 DE 102
Mary 9 DE 264
Mary W 14 DE 102
Noah 34 DE 102
Peter 19 DE 223
Phoebe A 3 DE 102
Sarah 12 DE 265
Thomas 11 DE 139
Unice 46 DE 132
Wesley 12 DE 264
William 19 DE 139
William H 30 MD 102
Blake, Eunicy 31 DE 236
Henry 13 DE 236
James 40 MD 236
Mary 2 DE 236
Samuel 1 DE 236
Sarah 11 DE 236
Wesley 10 DE 236
William 8 DE 236
Blizzard, Benjamin 28 DE 229
Elizabeth 29 DE 229
Sarah 2 DE 229
Blood, Adaline 36 MD 204

Name	Age	State	No.
Blood, Lucinda	4	DE	204
Mary E	9	DE	204
Simion	1	DE	204
Simion	39	CT	204
William H	7	DE	204
Bloomer, William H	19	PA	57
Bloxom, Mariah	35	DE	85
Mary	13	DE	90
Bosler, Esther A	25	PA	12
James M	27	PA	12
John	4	PA	12
Boardman, Abus A	15	DE	29
Boggs, Caleb	5	DE	60
Catharine	33	DE	60
Celia A	10	DE	30
David	6	DE	60
David	35	DE	81
David N	4/12	DE	30
Elizabeth	32	DE	81
James	6	DE	81
James	26	DE	68
John	8	DE	60
John	39	DE	60
John H	12	DE	30
Joseph	1	DE	60
Joseph	24	DE	68
Lydia	4	DE	30
Margaret	3/12	DE	81
Martha	3	DE	60
Mary	32	DE	30
Newell	34	DE	30
Rebecca	10	DE	81
Rebecca	23	DE	68
Ruth	8	DE	30
William	6/12	DE	68
William H	10	DE	60
Boils, Anna	1	DE	62
Celia	35	DE	63
Christopher	4	DE	38
Elizabeth	25	DE	38
Garrison	35	DE	38
George	9	DE	53
Hannah	35	DE	55
Henrietta	5	DE	38
Henry	20	MD	53
James	1	DE	38
James	15	DE	53
James	45	DE	53
James S	29	DE	62
Joseph	42	DE	53
Josephus	18	MD	53
Sarah	23	DE	62
Sophia	17	MD	53
Sophia	54	MD	53
William	11	DE	54
William	22	DE	56
Bolgar, James	34	IE	1
Bon, Margaret	1	DE	217
Bonsal, Jester J	11	DE	208
Joseph	18	DE	208
Joseph	52	DE	257
Nancy	47	DE	208
Bonville, Charles	14	DE	227
William	50	DE	227
Wm	17	DE	227
Bonwell, Elizabeth	12	DE	233
George	60	MD	236
Mary	26	DE	233
Mary	31	DE	236
Peter	31	DE	233
Boon, Ann	56	DE	60
John	21	DE	204
Louisa	15	DE	60
Louisa	22	DE	215
Lucinda	17	DE	204
Mary	40	DE	204
Sarah E	10	DE	204
Thomas	7	DE	204
Thomas	40	DE	204
William	4	DE	204
Boone, Ann	30	DE	222
Caroline	5/12	DE	222
Boone, Charles	7	DE	218
Elizabeth	20	DE	218
Henrietta	7	DE	222
James	3	DE	219
James	4	DE	222
James B	11	DE	210
James H	32	DE	219
James P	34	DE	222
Josephine	7	DE	249
John W	36	DE	222
Margaretta	4	DE	218
Margaretta	33	DE	219
Mary	59	DE	218
Mary C	16	DE	218
Mary E	2	DE	218
Nancy	35	DE	222
Sarah A	13	DE	218
Stephen C	36	MD	218
Susan	1	DE	218
Susan	6	DE	222
Susan	37	DE	218
Wm	18	DE	160
Booth, Adeline T	4	DE	149
Ann	6	DE	115
Charles T	10	DE	149
Elias T	32	DE	149
Elizabeth	9	DE	137
Elizabeth	22	DE	125
Elizabeth	22	DE	149
Henrietta	25	DE	126
Henrietta A	15	DE	116
Hester	3	DE	115
Hester J	3/12	DE	116
George W	26	DE	126
Jane	2	DE	149
John	46	DE	115
John E	12	DE	149
John T	2	DE	116
Joseph	34	DE	116
Margaret	7	DE	137
Martha	14	DE	115
Mary E	4	DE	116
Mary E	29	DE	149
Mary L	8/12	DE	150
Sarah Ann	27	DE	115
Sarah J	24	DE	116
Thomas	54	DE	116
Thomas J	1	DE	126
Boots, Ann	25	DE	21
Ann	60	DE	53
Bostic, Ann	66	DE	259
Benoni	3	DE	233
Catherine	12	DE	241
Debora	38	DE	253
Easter	61	DE	265
Eliza	30	DE	233
Elizabeth	10	DE	241
Elizabeth	44	DE	241
Emeline	9	DE	253
James	9/12	DE	253
James	37	DE	233
James	65	DE	259
John	1	DE	121
John	17	DE	250
Jonathan	29	DE	253
Joshua	3	DE	269
Lydia	4	DE	253
Margaret	7	DE	250
Margaretta	6	DE	253
Maria	36	DE	250
Mary	11	DE	250
Mary	67	DE	241
Nathaniel	45	DE	241
Rebecca	30	DE	269
Robert	1	DE	269
Ruth	42	DE	121
Sarah	6	DE	241
Warner	25	DE	269
William	2	DE	241
Bostick, Albert	2	DE	215
Andrew	17	DE	20
Catherine	45	DE	215
Bostick, Francis A	6	DE	215
Frances Ann	9	DE	2
Garret S	34	DE	122
Hester A	8	DE	215
James	16	DE	215
James D	42	DE	215
John	30	DE	53
Martha A	2	DE	52
Mary C	11	DE	216
Rebecca	72	DE	122
Ruth Ann	15	DE	2
Sarah	44	DE	2
Sarah	49	DE	10
Sarah E	17	DE	215
Susan	12	DE	10
Thomas	45	DE	2
William	5	DE	53
Boulden, Ann	12	DE	65
Dolly	60	DE	28
Elizabeth	5	DE	72
Elizabeth	16	DE	69
Henry	50	DE	28
John	15	DE	65
Joseph	86	DE	43
Louis	10/12	DE	65
Lucy	2	DE	72
Lydia	35	DE	8
Mary	25	DE	72
Perry	6	DE	65
Prince	2	DE	65
Rachel	11	DE	65
Rachel	65	DE	65
Samuel	8	DE	65
Samuel	43	DE	65
Sarah	34	DE	65
William	40	DE	8
Bowen, Daniel	19	DE	134
Elizabeth	70	DE	231
Jabez	28	DE	90
Levi	26	DE	133
Major	51	DE	133
Mary A	32	DE	133
Rebecca	55	DE	133
Rebecca A	1	DE	133
Scynthia C	4	DE	133
Bowers, Ann	7	DE	228
Jabez	28	DE	96
John	43	DE	214
Malvina	14	DE	215
Martha A	18	PA	58
Mary	2	DE	96
Matilda	25	DE	96
Sally	74	DE	214
Samuel	4	DE	96
Bowles, Mary	9	DE	232
Bowman, Catherine	11	DE	88
Charles	15	DE	21
Charles	50	DE	21
Elizabeth	39	MD	106
Emmaline O	9	DE	106
Foster R	12	DE	106
George	40	DE	106
Jane	45	DE	92
Mary H	7	DE	106
Milly	50	DE	109
Milly A	16	DE	109
Rachel C	3	DE	106
Reuben	40	DE	106
Sanders	50	DE	92
Sarah	33	DE	21
Thomas H	11/12	DE	106
Boxwell, Ann	50	DE	159
Boyce, Angelina	16	DE	134
Elizabeth	24	DE	93
Margaret	16	DE	114
Margaret	30	DE	172
Margaret	67	DE	172
Thomas	19	DE	114
Boyd, Amanda	13	DE	57
John	10	DE	61
Joshua	13	DE	61
Martha	8	DE	41

Name	Age	State	Page
Boyd, Mary Ann	24	DE	61
William	7	DE	42
William	47	MD	61
Boyer, Charlesina	9	DE	17
Eliza A	4/12	DE	22
Elizabeth	55	DE	220
Emma	4	DE	17
Eunity J	14	DE	17
George	22	DE	22
George	47	DE	59
George F	10	DE	59
James	20	DE	59
James	69	DE	35
James E	60	DE	220
James F	29	DE	35
James H	28	DE	39
James V	6	DE	35
John	8	DE	40
Margaret	52	MD	42
Mary	24	DE	35
Mary	25	DE	40
Mary	30	DE	59
Mary	70	DE	162
Mary	72	DE	162
Mary R	7	DE	17
Melvina	3	DE	35
Nancy	2	DE	40
Priscilla	11	DE	42
Priscilla	18	DE	22
Rebecca	40	DE	17
Robert McC	48	DE	17
Samuel	7	DE	40
Samuel	24	DE	62
Sarah E	11	DE	10
Sarah E	12	DE	17
Thomas R	14	DE	59
Washington	24	DE	39
William	5	DE	40
William	26	DE	40
William	55	DE	42
William E	37	DE	35
William H	18	DE	35
William M	1	DE	59
Brachears, Catherine	2	DE	157
Elizabeth	8	PA	157
John	4	PA	157
Mary	13	PA	157
Rachel	6	PA	157
Rachel	36	NJ	157
Zacheus D	47	MD	157
Braddick, Nancy	11	DE	61
Bradford, Harietta	37	PA	162
John	14	DE	48
Thomas H	34	PA	162
Bradley, Andrew	20	DE	135
Ann	30	DE	243
Ann	33	DE	239
Eliza J	4	DE	135
Ellen	7	DE	243
Garret	9	DE	125
George	4	DE	152
Harriet	3	DE	243
Henry	37	DE	100
Henry	40	DE	109
Hester	16	DE	113
Hester	23	DE	135
James	1	DE	239
James	5	DE	65
James	8	DE	55
James	35	DE	239
Jane	15	DE	217
Jane	59	DE	137
John	7/12	DE	83
John	12	DE	243
Joseph	10	DE	239
Josiah	30	DE	244
London	74	DE	135
Lucinda	3	DE	135
Major	32	DE	240
Mary	9	DE	197
Mary Ann	23	DE	83
Nancy	12	DE	65
Bradley, Nancy	83	DE	65
Nancy	85	DE	55
Nathaniel	8	DE	135
Nelly	30	DE	101
Rachel	7	DE	135
Rhoda	8	DE	239
Sarah	1	DE	55
Sarah	6	DE	239
Sarah	10	DE	243
Sarah	34	DE	55
Sarah	50	DE	65
Sarah P	6	DE	152
Solomon	25	DE	135
Sophia	66	DE	239
Susan	30	DE	86
Tamar	71	DE	135
Thomas	1	DE	65
William	2/12	DE	243
William	3	DE	239
Bradly, Emily	25	DE	235
Rhody	6	DE	242
Brainard, Jacob	55	DE	228
Sarah	30	DE	228
Braman, Eliza	46	PA	62
Matilda	16	PA	62
Randal	42	NJ	62
Theodore	6	DE	62
Bramble, Alexander	6	MD	145
Francis	42	MD	47
Hannah	15	DE	49
John	18	DE	49
Mary	2	MD	54
Nancy	19	DE	51
Rebecca	12	DE	53
Rebecca	26	MD	54
William	1	MD	54
William	25	MD	54
Branson, Eliza	5	DE	161
Joseph	37	PA	161
Josephine	1	DE	161
Mary	3	DE	161
Mary	33	DE	161
Brathell, Elizabeth	40	DE	125
Brazier, Absalom	23	OH	176
Breck, Louisa	7	DE	197
Breeding, Eliza	21	MD	146
Lewis	19	MD	146
Briam, Elizabeth	16	DE	104
Brian, Francis	18	MD	229
Briant, Joseph	11/12	DE	16
Rebecca	25	DE	16
Sarah	47	DE	60
Thomas	29	MD	16
William	14	DE	60
Brien, Rachel	76	DE	246
Bright, Edward	43	DE	136
Henrietta	14	DE	136
John H	7	DE	136
Julia A	5	DE	136
Mahala	10	DE	136
Maria J	3	DE	136
Mary	35	DE	136
Sarah E	5/12	DE	136
Brinckloe, Robert	17	DE	85
Brincklor, Alexander	1/12	DE	96
Alexander	34	DE	96
Elizabeth	33	DE	96
John	2	DE	96
Leah Ann	11	DE	84
Martha A	16	DE	96
Brinkley, Ann	28	DE	229
Cesar	15	DE	197
Elizabeth	70	DE	229
Henrietta	8	DE	229
John	14	DE	213
Lydia	21	DE	163
Malaki	15	DE	229
Mary	15	DE	229
Nathaniel	30	DE	229
Ruth	17	DE	201
Sarah	28	DE	229
Brinkley, Solomon	65	DE	256
Thomas	9	DE	211
Thomas	18	DE	229
Wm	35	DE	229
Brinkly, Abraham	4	DE	246
Abraham	31	DE	246
George	3	DE	246
James	3	DE	234
Linda	5	DE	234
Martha	7	DE	246
Mary	20	DE	247
Brinton, John B	34	PA	53
Brinson, Samuel	13	DE	41
Brister, Curtis	3	DE	46
Elizabeth B	48	DE	42
Isaac	40	DE	46
Isaac W	4/12	DE	46
James	48	DE	42
Margaret	23	DE	46
Nancy A	2	DE	46
Bristis, Bayard	34	DE	44
Curtis	75	DE	44
Nancy	69	DE	44
Broadaway, Wm	14	DE	181
Broadway, Amanda	5	DE	252
Ambrose	9/12	DE	252
Ambrose	8	DE	200
Ambrose	40	DE	252
Ann	36	PA	252
Elizabeth	9	DE	252
Emily	13	DE	252
Isabella	6	DE	252
Margaret	15	DE	252
Mary	49	DE	10
Susan	10	DE	252
William	14	DE	252
Brocksop, Amelia	44	GB	47
Elizabeth	16	PA	47
Rebecca	14	PA	47
Robert	47	GB	47
Ralph S	7	PA	47
Brookins, Caleb	8	DE	24
Elizabeth	25	DE	24
John	2	DE	24
Presley	38	DE	25
Sarah	9	DE	25
Wesley	1	DE	25
Brooks, Sarah	40	DE	82
Brown, Abraham	4	DE	200
Alice	8	DE	92
Amanda	10	DE	186
Amy	33	DE	132
Andrew	12	DE	213
Ann	2	DE	41
Ann	25	DE	20
Ann	31	DE	14
Ann	35	DE	179
Ann E	3	DE	213
Araminta	5	DE	179
Araminta	30	DE	179
Augustus	14	DE	161
Bazel	57	DE	213
Benjamin	10	DE	24
Benjamin	18	DE	76
Benjamin	25	DE	207
Caleb	9	DE	162
Charlotte	40	MD	61
Caroline	3	DE	52
Charles	3	DE	71
Charles	7	DE	179
Charles	9	DE	144
Charles	14	DE	179
Charlotta	28	DE	230
David	6/12	DE	160
David	4	DE	139
David S	27	NY	4
Edward	14	DE	214
Eliza J	7	DE	53
Elizabeth	6	DE	237
Elizabeth	15	DE	8
Elizabeth	17	DE	139
Elizabeth	22	DE	2

Name	Age	St	No.	Name	Age	St	No.	Name	Age	St	No.
Brown, Elizabeth	29	DE	249	Brown, Mary C	4	DE	17	Buck, Kate	5	PA	5
Elizabeth	30	DE	225	Mary J	9	DE	91	Mary N	28	PA	5
Elizabeth	38	DE	200	Melvina	17	DE	198	Rachel	12	DE	210
Elizabeth	46	DE	24	Minus	50	MD	230	Robert	5	DE	74
Emily	6	DE	24	Nancy	17	DE	227	Thomas N	9	PA	5
Francis	51	DE	159	Nancy	30	DE	262	William	1	DE	74
Frisby	19	MD	10	Nathan	10	DE	129	William S	36	PA	5
Garrett	14	DE	185	Nathan	17	DE	76	Buckingham, Isaac	42	DE	177
George	2	DE	24	Nathan	66	DE	1	Isaac	68	DE	177
George	8	DE	61	Nathaniel	16	DE	24	Mary	68	DE	177
George	12	DE	72	Nelly	48	DE	213	Buckmaster, Alex	27	DE	219
George	26	MD	52	Patience	21	DE	176	Ann	31	DE	221
George	35	DE	91	Pennel	21	DE	224	Ann	37	DE	76
George	42	DE	166	Peter	5	DE	61	Ann E	14	DE	221
Gorn	45	DE	91	Rachel	8	DE	262	Ann M	14	DE	77
Hannah	20	DE	24	Rachel	11	DE	19	Caleb	1	DE	109
Harriet	10	DE	213	Rachel	20	DE	207	Charles	3	DE	219
Harriet	13	DE	91	Rachel	44	DE	98	Charles	8	DE	77
Henry	22	DE	108	Rachel	45	DE	71	Edwin	6	DE	77
Hester	20	DE	160	Rachel	48	DE	71	Elizabeth	34	DE	55
Hester Ann	9	DE	52	Rachel	51	DE	21	Emily	10	DE	109
Hester R	8	DE	91	Rebecca	1	DE	2	Frederic	3/12	DE	77
Isaac	29	DE	17	Rebecca	10	DE	175	George	34	DE	55
James	6	DE	139	Rebecca	49	DE	161	George W	39	DE	109
James	17	DE	213	Robert	21	DE	219	Georgiana	1	DE	55
James	20	DE	223	Robert J	14	DE	140	James	4/12	DE	221
James H	11	DE	52	Ruth	5	DE	2	James	5	DE	219
Jane	9	DE	10	Sampson	17	DE	49	James	30	DE	219
Jane	9	DE	179	Samuel	8	DE	7	James A	45	DE	221
Jane	10	DE	53	Samuel	53	DE	161	John	3	DE	109
Jefferson	9	DE	71	Samuel	62	MD	53	Joseph	8	DE	109
John	3	DE	179	Sarah	5/12	DE	237	Lydia	7	DE	55
John	3	DE	213	Sarah	6	DE	11	Maria	39	DE	47
John	6	DE	17	Sarah	6	DE	233	Mary	7	DE	221
John	13	DE	52	Sarah	9	DE	238	Mary	67	DE	217
John	14	DE	71	Sarah	14	DE	53	Mary	73	DE	158
John	24	DE	128	Sarah	18	DE	128	Mary D	38	DE	109
John	24	DE	140	Sarah	18	DE	139	Mary E	7/12	DE	37
John	25	DE	160	Sarah	64	DE	222	Mary E	5	DE	109
John	35	DE	132	Sarah A	13	DE	35	Mary E	9	DE	55
John	35	DE	179	Sarah A	39	DE	87	Nathaniel	16	DE	221
John	58	DE	71	Sarah E	6	DE	91	Olivia	10	DE	77
John L	9/12	DE	215	Solomon	18	DE	132	Rachel	11	DE	221
John R	22	DE	24	Surrena	5	DE	230	Rhoda	28	DE	37
Jonathan	13	DE	24	Susan	7	DE	238	Rohama	69	DE	47
Jonathan	16	DE	71	Susan	10	DE	139	Sarah	24	DE	219
Jonathan	48	DE	24	Susan A	3	DE	132	Thomas	13	DE	221
Joseph	10	DE	132	Thomas	1	DE	238	Thomas	15	DE	109
Joseph	10	DE	201	Thomas	16	DE	252	Thomas D	17	DE	77
Joseph	11	DE	238	Thomas	38	DE	238	Thomas H	1	DE	219
Joshua	7/12	DE	19	Thomas	45	DE	139	Thomas S	39	DE	76
Joshua	17	DE	100	Timothy	43	DE	78	Walter	3	DE	77
Joshua	18	DE	194	Tilghman	11	DE	132	William W	24	DE	247
Joshua	49	DE	197	Tilghman	20	DE	132	Buckner, Rebecca A	12	DE	68
Julia	30	DE	237	Tilghman	53	DE	132	Buckson, Augusta	1	DE	56
Letitia	37	DE	120	Virginia	17	DE	181	Jervis B	6	DE	58
Liddy	36	DE	52	Wesley	15	DE	132	John	49	DE	58
Lucy M	4	DE	14	Wesley	24	DE	2	Lavinia	25	DE	56
Major	2	DE	132	William	11	DE	50	Louisa	5	DE	56
Margaret	18	DE	161	William	20	DE	5	Sarah L	6	DE	56
Margaret	35	MD	53	William H	29	DE	91	Tamsey	46	DE	58
Margaret	65	DE	225	William T	1	DE	14	William	30	DE	56
Margarett	17	DE	90	Wm	10	DE	178	Bullock, Ann	5	DE	239
Maria	17	DE	197	Wm	29	DE	207	Ann M	32	MD	147
Mariah	16	DE	64	Wm	30	DE	237	Charles M	2	DE	147
Mariah	30	DE	40	Brumaker, George	14	DE	197	David H	4	DE	147
Martha	7	DE	157	Bryant, John	14	NY	13	Elizabeth	17	MD	14
Martha A	4	DE	53	Buchanan, Ann	33	DE	73	Emma	8	DE	239
Mary	2	DE	230	Ann L	33	DE	217	John F	1	DE	145
Mary	6	DE	71	Mary	59	DE	87	John H	6	DE	147
Mary	9	DE	86	Buchnal, Hannah	75	DE	262	Martha	4/12	DE	147
Mary	9	DE	132	Buck, Bethena	60	DE	159	Nancy	34	DE	145
Mary	15	DE	221	David	50	DE	22	Nathaniel	33	DE	239
Mary	22	DE	197	Eliza Ann	30	DE	74	Rhoda	34	DE	239
Mary	29	DE	238	Emma	2	DE	5	Thomas B	33	DE	147
Mary	42	DE	139	Henry	9	DE	74	William	1	DE	239
Mary	44	DE	1	James	16	DE	18	William	6	DE	145
Mary	48	DE	132	James	35	DE	74	Burch, Sarah	74	DE	29
Mary	54	DE	197	James H	7	DE	5	Burdick, Royal S	32	VT	86
Mary	64	GB	28	John	8	DE	74	Burgess, Amanda	17	DE	48
Mary Ann	5	DE	14	John	13	PA	224	Charles	11	DE	49
Mary B	16	DE	87	Joseph	9	DE	201	Clayton	5	DE	49

Name	Age	St	Pg	Name	Age	St	Pg	Name	Age	St	Pg
Burgess, Eliza A	43	DE	49	Burrows, Nicholas	46	MD	1	Buxton, Prudy	22	DE	259
John	15	DE	49	Peter	6	DE	70				
Margaret G	13	DE	49	Rachel	1/12	DE	51	Cahal, Alfred H	9	DE	141
Martha A	8	DE	49	Rachel E	19	DE	94	Ann	47	DE	141
Sarah F	2	DE	49	Rebecca	8	MD	50	Benjamin	1	DE	196
William	53	DE	49	Rebecca	10	DE	230	Emily S	11	DE	141
Burk, Andrew	4	DE	44	Rebecca	15	DE	51	James	8	DE	196
Arrianna	2	DE	44	Richard	24	DE	269	James B	19	DE	124
Elizabeth	18	DE	207	Richard	57	DE	265	John	12	DE	196
Emily	1	DE	207	Ruth	10	DE	265	John A	22	DE	141
George	14	DE	207	Sally	30	DE	265	Lawrence	20	DE	124
Henrietta	2/12	DE	44	Samuel	12	DE	21	Marietta	13	DE	141
Henry	4	DE	207	Samuel	21	DE	246	Mary	32	DE	196
James	13	PA	59	Samuel	59	DE	245	Mary	41	MD	196
Julia A	26	DE	44	Sarah Ann	21	DE	51	Robert H	5	DE	141
Margaret	45	MD	44	Susan	42	DE	42	Samuel	42	MD	196
Mary	33	DE	207	Warren	22	DE	18	Sarah	4	DE	196
Mary C	7	DE	207	William	8	DE	265	Sarah A	19	DE	217
Mary E	20	DE	44	William	28	DE	94	Thomas	30	DE	217
Samuel	17	DE	29	William	29	DE	230	William	10	DE	196
Sarah	17	DE	29	William	45	DE	50	Wm	25	MD	196
William	25	DE	44	William A	8	DE	21	Wm E	17	DE	141
William	28	DE	35	William B	57	MD	42	Cahall, James	4/12	DE	242
William	45	DE	207	Wm	25	DE	164	James	33	DE	242
Wm Edward	11	DE	207	Wm	35	DE	265	Mary	3	DE	242
Burke, Peter	28	IE	258	Burton, Ann	16	DE	85	Mary	28	DE	242
Burley, Anna	8	DE	88	Ann C	37	DE	83	Rachel	6	DE	242
Elizabeth	38	DE	88	Asa	19	DE	116	Samuel	9	DE	242
James T	46	DE	88	Benjamin F	7	DE	109	William	4	DE	242
Burnal, Caleb	32	DE	233	Daniel R	15	DE	109	Cahoon, Alphonso B	9	DE	16
Elizabeth	6	DE	233	Dinah	65	DE	87	Benjamin B	4	DE	16
Joseph	4	DE	233	Erasmus	27	DE	234	Catherine E	4	DE	6
Margaret	28	DE	233	Henry P	10	DE	109	Eltse Ann	24	NY	6
Thomas	1/12	DE	233	Lydia A	18	DE	109	Louisa B	5	DE	16
Burr, Joseph A	19	PA	87	Mary Ann	21	DE	6	Louisa B	32	DE	16
Nelson	30	NJ	167	Mary M	34	DE	109	Lydia A	8	DE	16
Burrows, Ann	13	DE	50	Rhoda H	8	DE	84	Margaret	12	DE	14
Ann	19	DE	245	Robert S	25	DE	57	Maria E	15	DE	16
Ann	40	MD	233	Samuel J	23	DE	77	Mary Anna	10/12	DE	6
Ann E	1	DE	42	Sarah A	17	DE	109	Mary E	12	DE	16
Anna	7	DE	230	Thomas D	12	DE	109	Rachel J	5	DE	6
Angeline	1	DE	246	William	60	DE	84	Rebecca	1	DE	16
Benjamin	14	DE	42	Bush, Abraham	21	DE	23	Thomas L	30	DE	6
Catharine	7	DE	44	Buster, Isaac	9	DE	74	William	19	DE	17
Catherine	13	DE	245	Butcher, Alexander	42	DE	22	William	51	DE	19
Ebenezer	33	DE	50	Alice	11	DE	9	William R	6	DE	16
Edward	35	DE	50	Cornelia	7	DE	22	William R	36	DE	16
Edward	35	MD	233	Ephraim	50	DE	22	Cain, Ann	33	DE	130
Eliza	25	DE	230	Isaac D	4	DE	22	Arthur J	2/12	DE	128
Elizabeth	5	DE	265	Manlove	40	DE	81	Atwell	33	DE	93
Elizabeth	6	DE	42	Mary	4	DE	81	Caleb	12	DE	262
Elizabeth	23	DE	136	Mary C	17	DE	22	Clarissa	45	DE	249
Elizabeth	40	DE	21	Rachel	3	DE	81	Eliza	2	DE	128
Elizabeth	51	MD	56	Risdon	15	DE	39	Eliza	11	DE	133
Emeline	3	DE	265	Sarah	6	DE	81	Elizabeth	19	DE	129
Emily	8	MD	233	Sarah	23	DE	81	Elizabeth	27	DE	128
Emily A	8/12	DE	50	Sarah	25	DE	22	George	6	DE	129
Emily Ann	22	DE	50	Sarah	50	DE	68	Hasty	69	DE	126
Francis	4	DE	42	Sarah	52	DE	22	Hester	33	DE	262
George	20	DE	262	Stephen	1	DE	81	Isaac	7	DE	133
Hannah	19	DE	20	Sidney	70	DE	80	James	4	DE	262
Hannah A	41	MD	1	Thomas	23	DE	22	James	9	DE	129
Henry	20	DE	51	Thomas	75	DE	80	John	16	DE	214
Hester E	15	MD	3	Buth, Rebecca	24	DE	50	John	28	DE	128
James	20	DE	50	Butler, Ader	21	DE	208	John	40	DE	133
Jane	14	DE	51	David	18	DE	34	John of Daniel	44	DE	128
John	4	DE	233	Enolds	24	MD	142	John W	8	DE	129
John	12	DE	50	Ezekiel	16	DE	7	Levi	34	DE	129
John P	7	DE	56	Jesse	28	MD	142	Levin	4	DE	133
Joseph	19	DE	119	Joel	21	DE	88	Lodewick	32	DE	129
Julia	27	DE	267	John	7	DE	179	Lodwick	2	DE	262
Louis	45	DE	21	Mary	14	DE	68	Major	9	DE	262
Louisa	10	DE	50	Mary	26	DE	94	Major	33	DE	262
Lydia	7	DE	50	Mary	60	MD	142	Martha	18	DE	126
Margaret	22	DE	246	Sarah	18	DE	257	Mary	5	DE	128
Mary Ann	21	MD	50	Sarah	25	MD	142	Mary	10	DE	262
Mary Ann	39	DE	50	Thomas	55	DE	45	Noah	29	DE	134
Mary J	16	DE	15	William	22	MD	142	Phener	23	DE	134
Mary Jane	5	DE	50	Wm	13	DE	202	Phener	60	DE	126
Mary P	1	DE	94	Zedekiah	19	DE	160	Rachel	42	DE	109
Matilda	38	DE	50	Butt, Thomas	13	DE	74	Rebecca F	36	DE	128
Naoma	50	DE	266	Buxton, Elizabeth	16	DE	260	Rhoda	25	DE	130

Name	Age	St	Pg
Cain, Robert	8	DE	128
Robert	31	DE	144
Ruben	14	DE	262
Sarah	61	DE	130
Sarah A	29	DE	129
Sarah F	3	DE	129
Stephen	37	DE	130
William	9	DE	126
William	16	DE	216
William	26	DE	126
William	34	DE	109
William T	4	DE	109
Wm H	14	DE	207
Calahan, Alexander	22	DE	186
Alexander	27	DE	256
Brumer	18	DE	202
Edward	3	DE	194
Isaac	55	DE	195
James	5/12	DE	194
Margaret	15	DE	255
Mary	22	DE	194
Mary	27	MD	256
Samuel	14	DE	189
Wm	23	DE	194
Calaway, Ann	33	DE	134
Benjamin	35	DE	127
Catherine	22	DE	131
Curtis	18	DE	127
Curtis	57	DE	126
Eli	29	DE	130
Elizabeth	14	DE	133
Elizabeth	20	DE	127
Ellen	22	DE	127
Frances	4	DE	131
Garrit	7	DE	134
Henry	31	DE	142
Isaac	6	DE	134
James	13	DE	127
James	17	DE	131
James	38	DE	134
John	8	DE	134
John	16	DE	127
John	29	DE	134
Jonathan	27	DE	130
Joseph	15	DE	131
Joseph A	2	DE	134
Lewis	13	DE	127
Louisa	13	DE	137
Luther	10	DE	137
Lydia	1	DE	134
Lydia	32	DE	134
Margaret	8	DE	127
Margaret	19	DE	137
Margaret	39	MD	142
Margaret	43	DE	127
Mary	4	DE	127
Mary	27	DE	131
Mary	35	DE	127
Mary	59	DE	137
Mary E	1	DE	142
Mary E	10	DE	134
Mary M	27	DE	131
Mary T	17	DE	131
Minerva	4	DE	134
Nancy	56	DE	131
Peter	6	DE	134
Peter	19	DE	131
Peter	21	DE	118
Peter	56	DE	131
Phener	21	DE	127
Reynear	24	DE	127
Rhoda A	4	DE	134
Ruth	6	DE	127
Sarah	17	DE	84
Sarah A	12	DE	127
Sulah	9	DE	127
Thomas	54	DE	128
Wesley	31	DE	137
William	1	DE	127
William	24	DE	137
William	54	DE	128
William H	9	DE	134
Caldwell, Alice	60	DE	26
Charles	55	DE	249
Daniel	9/12	DE	182
Edward	28	DE	182
Elijah	19	DE	116
Elizabeth	6	DE	182
Hannah	16	DE	262
Jacob	2	DE	243
John	8	DE	47
Julia	30	DE	228
Martha	8	DE	182
Martha	10	DE	189
Mary	26	DE	182
Sarah	11	DE	182
Sina	70	DE	249
Thomas	30	DE	228
Caleb, Eliza	39	DE	7
Gideon N	3	DE	7
James	42	MD	7
James A	13	DE	7
Joseph H	2	DE	7
Mary E	5	DE	7
Susan F	9	DE	7
Vincent S	11	DE	7
William T	14	DE	7
Calihan, James	19	DE	188
Cality, Jerry	21	IE	169
Calk, John	37	DE	184
Mary	27	DE	184
Sarah	2	DE	184
Call, Deborah	8	DE	64
Elnora	2	DE	64
John	46	DE	64
Rebecca	6	DE	64
Sarah	37	DE	64
Callaway, Ann	32	DE	115
Callay, Andrew	2	DE	246
Andrew	34	DE	246
Joseph	4	DE	246
Manlove	30	DE	165
Mary	30	DE	246
Matilda	5/12	DE	246
Matilda	7	DE	165
Sarah	28	DE	165
Camamile, David	14	DE	33
Michael	70	DE	40
Cambell, James	6	DE	162
Cambridge, Ann	54	DE	174
Benjamin	30	DE	25
Charles	1/12	DE	25
Frederic	52	MD	25
George	20	DE	25
Hannah	37	DE	25
James	15	DE	25
Latitia	50	MD	25
Lydia A	4	DE	25
Mary	81	DE	249
Sally Ann	27	DE	174
Cameron, Catherine	3	DE	34
Elizabeth	12	PA	34
Evanda	14	NJ	34
John	16	NJ	34
John	44	VA	34
Margaret	11	DE	34
Margaret	43	NJ	34
Mary	9	DE	34
Richard	7/12	DE	34
Susan	5	DE	34
Thomas	7	DE	34
William	17	NJ	34
Cammam, Priscilla	67	DE	40
Cammila, Rachel	104	DE	40
Camomile, David	4/12	DE	40
David	14	DE	32
Delia	3	DE	40
Edward	2	DE	40
Ellen	11	DE	40
George	3	DE	41
George	7	DE	50
George	47	MD	41
Hannah	1	DE	50
Hester	2	DE	41
Camomile, James	4/12	DE	16
Jane	17	DE	49
Jane	32	DE	40
Jerry	36	MD	50
Julia	30	DE	50
Lydia	3	DE	50
Martha	24	DE	41
Matilda	25	DE	41
Michel	5	DE	50
Rachel	32	DE	76
Samuel	7	DE	41
Shadrick	30	DE	41
William	9	DE	40
Campbell, Adalaid	7	DE	58
Ann E	3	DE	27
Ashel	16	DE	59
Elizabeth	18	DE	27
Elizabeth	44	NJ	57
Elnora	10	DE	77
Francis	13	DE	81
Henry	4	DE	58
Jefferson	39	NJ	57
John O	7	DE	57
John W	42	DE	27
Levicy	10	DE	57
Mary	32	PA	58
Matilda S	6	DE	27
Oliver	66	NJ	58
Peter	34	NJ	57
Rachel A	11	DE	27
Rebecca	2	DE	58
Sarah	64	NJ	58
Westcott	33	NJ	57
Camper, Alevilda	1	DE	121
Angelina	16	DE	122
Clement	9	DE	121
Elizabeth	9	DE	123
James	36	DE	122
James H	4	DE	121
James W	23	DE	122
John W	8	DE	27
Joseph	6	DE	108
Latitia	29	DE	121
Mary	31	DE	122
Mary	35	DE	108
Mary E	2	DE	108
Matilda	11	DE	108
Nancy	9	DE	108
Philamon	7	DE	121
Rachel	5	DE	122
Richard S	15	DE	108
Thomas	6	DE	121
Quinton	37	DE	108
William	2	DE	122
Cane, Catherine	12	DE	224
James A	30	DE	61
Canner, Elizabeth	60	DE	42
Cannon, Aaron	19	DE	129
Amy	40	DE	92
Angelina	5	DE	96
Ann	31	DE	58
Bevus	53	DE	91
Elijah	5/12	DE	96
Elizabeth	1	DE	96
Ella	2	DE	58
Henry	5	DE	58
Jacob W	9	IN	92
James	18	DE	91
Jane	13	DE	89
Jeremiah	16	DE	88
John H	18	DE	108
John W	6	DE	96
Joseph	1	DE	96
Lewis	22	DE	92
Mahala	27	DE	96
Mary	48	DE	91
Mary E	12	IN	92
Matilda	25	DE	40
Matthew	53	DE	92
Peter	45	DE	203
Ross	32	DE	96
Sarah	33	DE	96

Name	Age	State	Page
Cannon, Shadrack	30	DE	40
Susan	19	PA	92
Wilson L	35	DE	58
Cantell, George W	4	DE	5
Margaret	31	DE	5
Mary E	6	DE	5
Sarah J	10	DE	5
William	40	DE	5
William C	8	DE	5
Winfield L	2	DE	5
Caperson, Lydia	14	DE	215
Sarah	11	DE	215
Capesome, Margaret	34	DE	232
Cara, Charles	22	DE	219
Card, James	29	DE	217
John	51	MD	217
Polly	44	DE	217
Cardeen, Sarah	50	DE	241
Carey, Elizabeth	19	DE	115
Hetty	10	DE	115
James	21	DE	65
John P	5	DE	115
Louisa	14	DE	115
Nancy	58	DE	83
Nehemiah	8/12	DE	115
Nehemiah	40	DE	115
Phillip	12	DE	115
Rachel	41	DE	115
Samuel	13	DE	77
Sarah A	17	DE	115
Carlisle, Capril	14	DE	157
Capril	20	DE	175
Capril	75	DE	175
Caroline	42	MD	161
Catherine	3	DE	178
Charlotte	28	DE	178
Cynthia	5	DE	178
Elizabeth	2	DE	175
Elizabeth	31	MD	144
Emaly P	10	DE	84
James	10	PA	160
James P	1	DE	144
James P	27	MD	144
John W	29	DE	152
Lavinia	28	DE	152
Leah	60	DE	175
Louisa	8	DE	178
Paris	15	DE	221
Paris J	48	DE	221
Pernel	44	DE	160
Peter	36	DE	178
Priscilla	9	DE	178
Rachel	55	DE	221
Roger	12	DE	178
Samuel	29	DE	146
Samuel G	40	DE	217
Sarah J	2	DE	152
William	3	DE	144
William T	3	DE	152
Carney, Eliza	8	DE	63
Gustavus	21	DE	63
James	19	DE	67
John	24	DE	67
John	25	DE	67
John	52	DE	67
John	52	DE	63
Levi	22	DE	63
Louisa	44	DE	67
Mary A	18	DE	67
Melvina	20	DE	59
Montgomery	55	MD	180
Morris	14	DE	63
Rhody	12	DE	180
Rhody	50	MD	180
Sarah	13	DE	63
Sarah	40	DE	63
Sherry	22	DE	68
Thomas	16	DE	63
Thomas	73	DE	63
William	25	DE	59
Wm	14	DE	172
Carpenter, Amanda	13	DE	221
Carpenter, Anna	11	DE	221
Caleb	85	DE	201
Charles W	21	DE	36
Elija	15	DE	202
Eliza	19	DE	179
George	6	DE	222
Hannah	15	DE	1
Henry	10	DE	221
Henry	25	DE	184
Hester	23	DE	200
Hetty	40	DE	221
Lemuel	37	DE	98
Maria	25	DE	184
Mary	6	DE	200
Mary	38	DE	176
Mary E	1	DE	221
Mary J	22	DE	151
Mathew	25	DE	179
Nancy	53	DE	201
Rebecca	3	DE	200
Robert	24	DE	151
Samuel	4	DE	221
Samuel	35	DE	176
Samuel	45	DE	221
Samuel T	40	NJ	1
Stephen	4	DE	200
William	1	DE	200
William	8	DE	221
Wm	27	DE	200
Carr, Eliza	28	GB	29
Eliza	37	CT	10
Margaret	16	DE	10
Mary Ann	14	DE	10
Peter	40	PA	10
William	34	GB	29
William H	12	DE	10
Carrol, Charles	22	DE	5
Zipporah	51	DE	5
Carroll, Charles	9	DE	227
Eliza	30	DE	227
James	16	DE	227
Sarah	5	DE	227
William	21	DE	227
William	47	DE	227
Carrow, Ann D	1	PA	5
Ann Eliza	7	DE	8
Ann Emily	1	DE	6
Caroline F	8	DE	5
Edward	51	DE	67
Eliza	26	MD	163
Eliza R	10	DE	94
Enoch	1	DE	8
Goldsmith D	26	DE	163
Harriet	32	DE	6
Harriet R	30	DE	5
James	17	DE	6
James H	12	DE	94
James P	39	DE	94
James T	8	DE	6
John	35	DE	6
John	66	DE	81
John H	12	DE	6
Joseph	4	DE	6
Joseph	32	DE	11
Laura J	9	DE	5
Lydia	42	DE	8
Lydia G	5	DE	94
Lydia S	36	DE	94
Martha	31	NJ	9
Mary	3	DE	11
Mary	64	DE	81
Mary A	6	DE	8
Mary J	5	DE	8
Perry	47	DE	36
Rachel	40	DE	36
Rebecca B	29	DE	11
Sarah	10	DE	163
Sarah	30	DE	81
Sarah L	8	DE	11
Thomas	2	PA	163
Thomas	36	DE	5
Thomas G	4	DE	5
Carrow, Timothy	4	DE	5
Timothy	38	DE	8
William	14	DE	8
William	22	DE	94
William	34	DE	12
William F	8	DE	6
William J	6	DE	5
Carry, William	19	NJ	10
Carson, Anna M	14	DE	217
Edward	11	DE	217
Elizabeth	8	DE	217
Elizabeth	37	DE	217
Elma	1	DE	217
Jane	40	DE	44
John	5/12	DE	253
John	25	DE	253
Jonathan	45	DE	217
Martha	27	DE	248
Mary A	19	MD	80
Mary F	13	DE	217
Richard	4	DE	217
Robert	4	DE	253
Sarah	22	DE	253
Thomas	19	DE	217
Carsons, William	18	DE	134
Carter, Aner	3	DE	262
Ann	27	DE	261
Ann	39	DE	190
Ann	54	MD	243
Catherine	22	DE	12
Catherine	40	DE	237
Charles	6	DE	243
Charlotte	5	DE	257
Charlotte	7	DE	253
Charlotte	35	DE	257
Daniel	18	DE	190
David	2	DE	52
David	35	DE	52
Edward	25	DE	256
Elijah	12	DE	139
Eliza	3	DE	261
Elizabeth	24	DE	256
Elizabeth	26	MD	52
Elizabeth	30	DE	262
Ellen	9/12	DE	257
Elmira	8	DE	177
Emily	3	DE	257
Eunity	23	DE	261
Harriet	14	DE	190
Herman	4/12	DE	256
Henry	5	DE	261
Henry	10	MD	52
Henry	14	DE	121
Henry	26	DE	132
Henry	38	DE	257
Henry	43	DE	237
Henry J	15	DE	45
Henry M	20	DE	117
Isaac	4	DE	190
Isaac	13	MD	52
James	3	MD	52
James	9	DE	257
James	34	DE	262
Jane	5	DE	253
Jane	11	DE	232
John	1/12	DE	190
John	5	DE	262
John	9	DE	231
John	30	DE	261
John L	15	DE	132
John W	6	MD	52
Josephine	8	DE	237
Levi	41	DE	253
Louisa	10	DE	253
Louisa	16	DE	257
Luff	50	DE	258
Lydia	16	DE	110
Lydia	19	DE	132
Margaret	10	DE	190
Margaret	18	DE	46
Martha	11	DE	243
Mary	2	DE	256

Name				Name				Name			
Carter, Mary	6	DE	262	Casson, Wm	24	DE	176	Chadawick, James	18	DE	61
Mary	7	DE	261	Caster, Albert	10	PA	227	John	14	DE	64
Mary	10	DE	237	Francis	3	PA	227	Mariam	8	DE	59
Mary	11	DE	253	George	37	PA	227	Thomas	16	DE	59
Mary	14	DE	243	Henry	26	DE	222	Chadwicks, Mary	35	DE	253
Mary	20	DE	226	Mary	12	DE	205	Chaffinch, Ann	19	DE	146
Mary	37	DE	231	Mary	14	PA	227	Ann	51	DE	146
Mary	40	DE	117	Mary	31	PA	227	Catherine	14	DE	146
Mary L	6	DE	207	Sarah	6	PA	227	John	8	DE	146
Philemon	35	DE	261	Catell, Amos	4	DE	161	Larena	12	DE	146
Rachel	1/12	DE	52	Ann	38	NJ	161	Lucy	17	DE	146
Rebecca	55	DE	258	Charles	39	NJ	161	Masey	24	DE	146
Rhoda	1	DE	132	Rebecca	4	DE	161	Priestly	22	DE	146
Rhody	7	DE	257	Rhody	1	DE	161	Priestly	61	MD	146
Robert M	34	DE	207	Cates, Lydia	9	DE	175	Chaisdon, Stephen	47	DE	41
Roxana	28	NJ	207	Catherine, Charles	9	DE	214	William	10	DE	41
Sallyann	15	DE	243	Thomas	12	DE	214	Chamberlain, Lewis	43	NJ	87
Samuel	6	DE	261	Cathiel, Martha	40	DE	99	Mary R	2	DE	87
Samuel	12	DE	190	Priscilla	37	DE	99	Mary R	38	DE	87
Samuel	46	DE	190	Catlin, Aner	69	DE	231	Spencer	5	DE	87
Sarah	6	DE	261	Robert	63	DE	231	Chambers, Ainon	55	DE	210
Sarah	14	DE	257	Catts, Amelia	24	DE	226	Ann	25	DE	233
Sarah J	4	DE	207	Amelia	55	DE	226	Benjamin D	9	DE	210
Sarah J	18	DE	143	Anna	16	DE	17	Elaphene	10	DE	240
Sun	53	DE	243	Charles W	3	DE	17	Elizabeth	18	NJ	211
Susan	3	DE	237	Elizabeth	54	DE	225	Ellen	12	DE	81
Susan	3	DE	261	Evalina	13	DE	17	Frances	2	DE	233
Susan	8	DE	190	Hannah	29	DE	23	Frances	12	DE	240
Susan R	1/12	DE	46	Harriet	18	DE	226	John	35	DE	240
Thomas	4	DE	253	Hy Clay	8	DE	17	John	68	DE	209
William	1	DE	261	James	10	DE	155	Julia	50	MD	156
William	6	DE	190	James	17	DE	90	Mark	23	DE	233
William	8	MD	52	James S	11	DE	23	Mary	8	DE	240
William	15	DE	226	John	16	DE	3	Mary	34	DE	240
William	26	DE	12	John T	16	DE	23	Samuel	64	DE	210
Wm	3	DE	220	Mary	12	DE	155	Samuel W	19	DE	210
Carty, Mary J	13	DE	21	Mary	21	DE	226	Sarah	53	DE	197
Moses	53	DE	21	Rachel	1	DE	155	Thomas	31	DE	197
Rebecca	1	DE	21	Rachel	37	DE	155	Unity	4	DE	233
Temperance	4	DE	21	Ruth A	5/12	DE	23	Chance, Alexine	2	DE	136
Case, Charles	2	DE	239	Samuel	11	DE	17	Elizabeth	30	DE	136
Charles	14	DE	243	Samuel	50	DE	17	Ellen	9	DE	82
Charles A	11	NJ	2	Sarah	43	DE	17	Fanny	8	DE	78
Elizabeth	49	DE	243	Sarah E	13	DE	23	Mary E	5	DE	136
James	34	DE	231	Sarah E	18	DE	17	Chandler, Andrew	2	DE	157
John	7	DE	239	Stephen	40	DE	155	Edwin	3	DE	157
John	33	DE	239	Thomas J	48	DE	23	Eliza	25	DE	16
Louisa	44	DE	243	Thomas M	30	DE	87	Joshua	30	PA	157
Mary	5	DE	239	Vincent	15	DE	155	Lydia	5	PA	157
Mary	23	DE	231	Causey, George	1	DE	75	Margaret	31	MD	157
Rachel	15	DE	243	Jane	16	DE	75	Chapman, Ann	18	DE	160
Sally	26	DE	239	John W	9	DE	90	Ann	60	MD	160
William	11	DE	243	Marie E	3	DE	90	David	51	DE	160
Wm	9	DE	239	Mariah	45	DE	90	Eliza A	15	DE	13
Wm	43	DE	243	Peter F	12	DE	90	James	11	DE	10
Casender, Margaret	14	DE	183	Peter F	49	DE	90	James	52	DE	10
Cashell, Thomas	18	IE	251	William F	17	DE	90	Lydia	15	DE	10
Casner, Mary	25	DE	95	Cavender, Caroline	11	DE	130	Mary	50	DE	10
Mary E	1	DE	95	Eliza	9	DE	130	Newman	9	DE	10
Robert	28	DE	95	Francis	26	MD	14	Wm	26	DE	160
Casperson, Charles	4	DE	45	John	3	DE	130	Charles, Amy	75	DE	43
David S	40	NJ	26	John	32	DE	14	Daniel W	31	DE	213
Emma	2	DE	45	Joseph	10/12	DE	14	Mary	61	DE	213
John	12	DE	26	Louisa	12	DE	130	Mary B	4/12	DE	213
Mary	8	DE	26	Mary	30	DE	130	Sarah A	22	DE	213
Mary	18	DE	45	Mary A	20	DE	132	Chase, Ann	5	DE	165
Richard	32	DE	45	Mary E	8	DE	14	Dorcas	67	DE	249
Sarah	1	DE	26	Phebe	3	DE	14	Henry	75	MD	40
Sarah	34	NJ	26	Reuben	56	DE	130	James	7	DE	165
William	14	DE	26	Theodore T	5	DE	14	John	6/12	DE	165
Cassacoon, Garrett	14	DE	72	William	2/12	DE	130	John	10	DE	179
Cassim, George W	23	DE	86	Cawdrey, Andrew	10	DE	75	Mary	25	DE	165
Cassins, Henry	12	DE	135	Ann E	8	DE	75	Philip	35	DE	165
Casson, Ann	50	DE	176	Isaac	6	DE	75	Sameul	3	DE	165
Ferdinand	10	DE	179	John	34	DE	75	Sarah	60	PA	40
Harriet	30	DE	179	Mary	1	DE	75	William	20	DE	39
Hester	11	DE	179	Mary	29	DE	75	Chatham, Benjamin F	29	PA	58
John	9	DE	179	Theodore	4	DE	75	Mary E	28	DE	58
Martha	17	NJ	178	Ceasar, Elizabeth	100	DE	76	Rohama M	2	DE	58
Myers	21	DE	178	Cedars, William W	13	MD	142	Cheesman, Clinton	30	NJ	57
Myers	38	DE	179	Chadawick, Elizabeth	52	DE	13	Chew, Aaron	22	DE	34
Sally Ann	4	DE	176	James	18	DE	61	Cato	15	DE	79

Chew, Enos	16	DE	33	Clark, Charles	3	DE	125	Clark, John W	25	DE	129
Gabriel	36	DE	33	Charles	17	DE	37	Jonathan	17	DE	247
Hannah	40	DE	33	Charles	21	DE	256	Joseph	9	DE	55
Julia	30	DE	33	Charlotte	5	DE	61	Joseph	21	DE	60
Margaret	7	DE	33	Daniel	20	DE	75	Joseph	24	DE	194
Priscilla	1	DE	33	David	66	DE	138	Joseph	39	MD	259
Rebecca	9	DE	33	David J	11	DE	39	Joshua	7	DE	256
Rebecca	40	DE	79	Ebenezer	21	DE	55	Joshua	45	DE	99
Rebecca	62	DE	33	Edith	11	DE	191	Julia Ann	10	DE	75
Chiffens, James	28	DE	15	Edward	13	DE	191	Lemuel	3	DE	190
John	24	DE	15	Edward	14	DE	248	Lemuel	30	DE	260
Maria	21	DE	15	Egnacious	3	DE	258	Lucy A	27	DE	92
Marietta	1	DE	15	Eliza	24	DE	138	Margaret	35	MD	260
Mary	50	MD	38	Elizabeth	6	DE	157	Margaret	37	DE	259
Chiffins, Benjamin	13	DE	53	Elizabeth	7	DE	260	Margaret	37	DE	268
Elizabeth	44	DE	53	Elizabeth	10	DE	248	Maria	50	MD	226
Enoch	15	DE	53	Elizabeth	12	DE	99	Martha	41	DE	61
James G	51	DE	53	Elizabeth	18	DE	61	Mary	6	DE	269
Margaret	5	DE	53	Elizabeth	21	DE	188	Mary	8	DE	260
Mary	6/12	DE	53	Elizabeth	21	DE	190	Mary	15	DE	226
Sarah E	8	DE	53	Elizabeth	26	NJ	157	Mary	19	DE	256
Susan	18	DE	30	Elizabeth	29	MD	192	Mary	23	DE	167
Chipman, Ann	28	DE	162	Elizabeth A	8	DE	217	Mary	28	DE	134
Benjamin	7	DE	162	Elizabeth P	26	DE	84	Mary	31	DE	159
Emeline	11	DE	162	Ellen	2	DE	251	Mary	49	DE	258
Ruthana	2	DE	162	Ellen	16	DE	258	Mary A	24	DE	128
Samuel	5	DE	162	Enoch	8	DE	258	Mary Ann	14	DE	55
Samuel	48	DE	162	Enoch Guy	6	DE	39	Mary E	3	DE	134
Susan	8	DE	162	Ephram W	8	DE	39	Mary E	25	DE	129
Chippey, Elizabeth	25	DE	204	Eveline	12	DE	66	Mary M	2/12	DE	129
Lavinia	4	DE	204	Ezekiel	28	DE	174	Mary M	3/12	DE	129
Sarah M	10	DE	204	Ezekiel	29	DE	259	Mordecai	31	DE	38
Wm	16	DE	157	Francena	12	DE	256	Nathan	8	DE	256
Chisden, Ann	4/12	DE	28	Francis A	1/12	DE	134	Nathaniel	45	DE	259
Benjamin	53	DE	28	Frisby	26	DE	226	Nemiah	19	DE	191
Elizabeth	4	DE	28	George	17	DE	258	Paul G	20	DE	93
Rachel	20	DE	28	George W	1	DE	218	Peter	10	DE	258
Stephen	23	DE	28	Gideon	45	DE	256	Peter	19	DE	264
Chrisdon, Augustine	11	DE	48	Grace	38	DE	218	Prudy	29	DE	259
George	16	DE	39	Harriet	10	DE	66	Rachel	16	DE	186
Gustavus	15	DE	35	Harriet A	25	DE	125	Rachel A	1	DE	92
Louisa	46	DE	39	Henry	10	DE	256	Rebecca	8/12	DE	260
Mary	16	DE	39	Henry	23	DE	226	Rebecca	10	DE	201
Nathan	17	DE	39	Henry	29	DE	237	Rebecca	15	DE	256
Samuel	4	DE	38	Henry	31	DE	134	Rebecca	43	MD	256
Stephen	5	DE	38	Henry	38	DE	191	Richard	11	DE	251
Stephen	47	DE	40	Henry H	5/12	DE	83	Robert	5	DE	256
William	10	DE	40	Hetty	2	DE	191	Robert	72	DE	126
Christein, Chris	19	GE	169	Hezekiah	5/12	DE	259	Robert H	31	DE	83
Christen, Shadric	8	DE	119	Isabella	23	DE	259	Robert S	2	DE	129
Cirl, Jacob H	24	NY	86	Jacob	43	DE	247	Sally	18	DE	217
Clamer, Solomon	1	DE	119	James	1	DE	188	Sally	40	DE	201
Clampet, Elizabeth	17	DE	234	James	1	DE	190	Sallyann	35	DE	191
Isaac	11/12	DE	234	James	1	DE	256	Samuel	2	DE	260
James	23	DE	234	James	4	DE	159	Samuel	14	DE	258
Jane	14	DE	234	James	9	DE	251	Samuel	41	DE	260
John	4	DE	234	James	12	DE	66	Sarah	6	DE	169
John	39	DE	234	James	26	DE	259	Sarah	13	DE	251
Jonathan	5	DE	234	James	30	DE	251	Sarah	13	DE	256
Louisa	2	DE	234	James	31	DE	159	Sarah	18	DE	258
Margaret	30	DE	234	James	33	DE	190	Sarah	19	DE	226
Martha	7	DE	234	James D	17	DE	39	Sarah	21	DE	39
Richard	39	DE	248	James E B	52	DE	40	Sarah	29	DE	174
Sarah	16	DE	208	James W	20	DE	55	Sarah	50	DE	99
Clark, Albert	4	DE	128	Jamima	17	DE	226	Sarah A	2	DE	129
Alice	8	DE	248	Jane	4	DE	260	Stephen	12	DE	55
Andrew	16	DE	201	Jane	6	DE	142	Susan	4	DE	252
Andrew	21	DE	129	Joel	7	DE	191	Susan	6	DE	247
Angelina	7	DE	92	John	10	DE	159	Susan	28	DE	251
Ann	23	DE	39	John	10	DE	234	Susan	40	DE	247
Ann	54	DE	217	John	10	DE	259	Tamsey	20	MD	226
Anna	21	DE	226	John	12	DE	200	Thomas	2	DE	159
Aramina	6	DE	260	John	13	DE	122	Thomas	5	DE	191
Beckey	11	DE	247	John	20	DE	180	Thomas	9	MD	192
Benjamin	14	DE	217	John	23	DE	188	Thomas	20	DE	217
Caleb	2	MD	192	John	30	MD	192	Waitman	18	DE	126
Caleb	24	DE	260	John	31	DE	260	Wesley	4	MD	192
Caroline	14	DE	195	John	55	DE	61	William	2	DE	157
Caroline	17	DE	260	John	55	DE	201	William	4	DE	256
Catherine	6	DE	134	John	56	DE	258	William	5	DE	248
Catherine	11	DE	226	John	67	DE	217	William	6	MD	192
Catherine	19	DE	158	John N	22	DE	39	William	8	DE	159

Name	Age	State	No.
Clark, William	17	DE	250
William	18	DE	140
William	26	DE	128
William	27	DE	226
William	51	DE	55
William M	31	DE	92
Winney	66	DE	138
Wm	37	DE	157
Zadock	25	DE	125
Clarke, Catherine	13	DE	228
Catherine	50	DE	228
David	53	DE	228
Ellen	7	DE	228
Steven	9	DE	228
Clarkson, Araminta	6	DE	236
Caroline	12	DE	114
Catherine	10	DE	112
Eliza J	3	DE	112
Edward W	17	DE	144
George	3	DE	112
Henry	45	DE	112
Hester	37	DE	112
Jane	55	DE	236
Mary A	23	DE	108
Perry	55	DE	236
Phoeba	50	DE	112
Susan A	5	DE	112
Wm H	11/12	DE	112
Clason, William C	39	DE	4
Clayton, Alice	5	DE	154
David	33	DE	158
Elizabeth	5	DE	66
Emily	13	DE	66
Frances	52	MD	66
Isaac	17	DE	66
Isaac	48	MD	66
James	18	DE	159
John	12	DE	39
John	25	DE	44
Louisa	4	DE	158
Martha	6	DE	158
Matilda	28	MD	66
Nancy	24	MD	12
Philip	26	MD	66
Rebecca	40	DE	66
Sally Ann	9/12	DE	158
Sarah	21	DE	66
Susan	24	DE	158
William	3	DE	66
William	12	DE	74
William	32	DE	66
Cleason, Mary	29	DE	4
Cleaver, Balinda	5	DE	26
Charles	5	DE	26
Charles	30	DE	26
Clayton	30	DE	6
Eliza	32	DE	26
Frances	7	DE	26
Henry	1	DE	26
John	3	DE	26
Julia Ann	5	DE	6
Margaret	28	DE	26
Mary E	1	DE	26
Noah	33	DE	26
Rachel	28	DE	6
Ruth M	2/12	DE	6
Sarah E	2	DE	6
Cleaves, Ann	20	DE	53
Balinda	68	DE	70
Charles	72	DE	70
Elizabeth	12	DE	70
James M	7/12	DE	53
John	4	DE	261
John	23	DE	53
Maria	1	DE	261
Nathan	50	DE	261
Rhody	35	DE	261
Richard	16	MD	261
Sarah	8	MD	261
Thomas	12	MD	261
Clegg, Charlotte	5/12	DE	11
Ellen	23	PA	11
Clegg, Samuel	30	GB	10
Samuel B	5	PA	11
Susan	28	GB	10
Thomas T	6	PA	11
William	3	DE	11
William	27	PA	11
Clement, David	3	DE	250
Emma	3/12	DE	250
Ezekiel	35	DE	250
James	10	DE	250
Laura	4	DE	250
Leonard	1	DE	250
Margaret	19	DE	169
Mary	2	DE	250
Miriam	31	DE	250
Rachel	6	DE	250
Rebecca	20	DE	192
Thomas	30	DE	192
Clements, Anna	19	DE	256
Anna C	6	DE	10
Caleb	26	DE	250
Catharine	36	DE	10
Charles R	2	DE	10
Elizabeth	68	MD	256
James R	42	MD	10
Joel	69	MD	256
John	24	DE	256
Joshua	27	DE	256
Louisa	21	DE	256
Mary	61	DE	252
Thomas	62	MD	252
Wilber F	4	DE	10
Clendaniel, Ahab	26	DE	61
Alfred	7	DE	101
Anna W	3	DE	94
Eliza Ann	19	DE	61
Elizabeth	26	DE	61
Emmaly	25	DE	94
Isabella	8	DE	215
James	22	DE	61
John	24	DE	61
Joseph	13	DE	215
Margaret	6	DE	215
Mary E	3	DE	61
Rachel	30	DE	108
Sarah	1	DE	61
Sarah A	13	DE	97
Sarah A	14	DE	97
Syntha	4	DE	94
Watson	33	DE	94
Clifton, Alfred	23	DE	243
Angeline	6	DE	99
Anna	14	DE	155
Casander	12	DE	43
Catharine	17	DE	80
Clement	69	DE	144
Daniel	35	DE	99
Daniel	49	DE	255
Delilah	66	DE	144
Elizabeth	19	DE	243
Elizabeth H	45	DE	124
George	22	DE	155
George	40	DE	155
George	63	DE	154
Henry	43	DE	107
James	3	DE	155
James	35	DE	155
James A	15	DE	80
John	55	DE	245
Margaret	17	DE	155
Margaret	17	DE	243
Maria	27	DE	255
Mary	2	DE	99
Mary	35	DE	99
Mary	45	MD	255
Mary	47	DE	243
Pemberton	44	DE	124
Rachel	20	DE	204
Ruthy	30	DE	156
Sally	20	DE	155
Sarah	55	DE	155
Sarah A	7	DE	99
Clifton, Sinderella	5	DE	204
Thomas	40	DE	204
Thomas B	11/12	DE	204
William	10	DE	155
Climer, Celia	42	DE	128
Greenbury	71	DE	121
James	8	DE	128
John	10	DE	128
Joseph	36	DE	128
Margaret	25	DE	121
Nancy	4	DE	128
Cloak, Caroline E	8	DE	29
Christiana	21	DE	15
Eben	22	DE	51
Ebenezer	58	DE	15
Emma	6	DE	29
John	60	DE	29
Louisa	41	PA	29
Sarah	43	DE	51
Clothier, Edward	20	DE	39
Cloud, Ann	77	DE	52
James	46	DE	52
William	49	DE	52
Clouds, Ann E	13	DE	26
Benjamin	42	DE	26
David	15	DE	26
Frances	20	DE	1
Frances	57	MD	1
James	22	DE	77
Mary	39	DE	26
Mary R	10	DE	26
Rhoda A	23	DE	20
Susan	8	DE	26
William	28	DE	20
Clow, Caleb	23	DE	71
Charles	3/12	DE	71
Clarissa	17	DE	201
Edney	7	DE	195
Elizabeth	20	DE	10
Emily	5	DE	195
Emily Ann	28	MD	50
George	2	DE	195
James	25	MD	195
John	34	MD	59
Joseph	5/12	DE	59
Mary Ann	19	DE	71
Sallyann	25	MD	195
Susan	25	DE	59
Clymer, Ann	18	DE	237
Isabella	20	DE	237
James	14	DE	165
James	29	DE	237
John	25	DE	237
Coal, Elizabeth	32	DE	103
James A	7/12	DE	103
John	3	DE	103
John	52	DE	249
Manlove	40	DE	103
Margarett	5	DE	103
Mary E	11	DE	103
Nehemiah	13	DE	103
Scaber	55	DE	212
William H	7	DE	103
Coalman, Sarah E	6	MD	33
Coalscott, Ann E	8/12	DE	207
Ann M	20	MD	207
Eliza A	33	DE	208
Elizabeth	63	DE	208
Henry	74	MD	208
John	19	DE	208
John H	21	DE	152
Martha E	14	DE	152
Ruth A	15	DE	208
Wm	26	DE	207
Coarse, Israel	31	DE	249
Rebecca	15	DE	55
Solomon	80	DE	55
Wm	12	DE	197
Cochran, Daniel	18	MD	255
Elizabeth	28	DE	165
Hannah	15	DE	165
James	9	DE	165

Name	Age	St	Pg	Name	Age	St	Pg	Name	Age	St	Pg
Cochran, James	45	DE	165	Collier, Agatha	45	DE	127	Collins, John C	1	DE	208
Richard	1	DE	165	George W	53	DE	127	John H	11	DE	89
Cocklin, Ella	21	IE	186	Mary E	16	DE	127	John M	13	DE	30
Garrett	35	IE	186	Collins, Abraham	8	DE	187	John R	67	DE	32
Margaret	33	IE	186	Agatha	45	MD	128	John W	1/12	DE	109
Coe, George	1	MD	141	Alexander	7	DE	151	John W	30	DE	85
George	25	MD	141	Alexander	9	DE	152	John W	58	DE	86
Henrietta	23	MD	141	Alexander	29	DE	170	Joseph	9	DE	219
Marcelles	2	DE	141	Andrew	3	DE	165	Joseph L	4	DE	14
Coffin, Cornelius	3	DE	211	Ann	15	DE	167	Josiah	42	DE	217
Cornelius W	37	DE	205	Ann	16	DE	170	Josiah	45	DE	159
John	40	DE	211	Ann	50	DE	83	Julia A	9	DE	29
Lydia	37	DE	205	Anna E	22	MD	83	Leah A	42	DE	13
Mary E	39	DE	211	Anna R	1	DE	96	Leonard	9	DE	150
Samuel	10	DE	211	Araminta	25	DE	89	Leonard	49	DE	13
Sarah E	12	DE	211	Araminty	10/12	DE	68	Levi	2	DE	68
Sarah F	12	DE	205	Araminty	65	DE	33	Lydia	25	DE	72
Coge, Mary	63	DE	224	Augusta A	2	MD	150	Margaret	5	DE	225
Cohee, Ann	2	DE	269	Benjamin	33	DE	68	Margaret	30	DE	187
Ann	34	MD	269	Benjamin	60	DE	33	Margaret A	31	DE	84
Ann	51	DE	267	Benjamin F	5	DE	15	Maria	6	DE	187
Benjamin	27	DE	270	Benjamin L	46	DE	15	Maria L	31	DE	12
Cynthia	67	DE	269	Benjamin Y	16	DE	89	Mariah	1	DE	98
Edward	4/12	DE	269	Caleb	6	DE	165	Marietta	10	DE	30
Elizabeth	3	DE	253	Catherine	10	DE	69	Martha	4	DE	187
Elizabeth	7	DE	268	Catherine	18	IE	68	Martha	16	DE	30
Elizabeth	15	DE	267	Charles	9	DE	124	Martha	45	DE	180
Elizabeth	19	DE	270	Charles	16	DE	210	Martha A	23	DE	96
Elizabeth	23	DE	270	Charles Jas	7/12	DE	32	Mary	10	DE	187
Elizabeth	28	DE	253	Charles W	3	DE	15	Mary	26	DE	150
Harriet	14	DE	12	Charlotte	25	DE	217	Mary	33	NJ	56
Henry	12	DE	269	Clark	3	DE	4	Mary	82	DE	60
Hinson	13	DE	267	David W	45	VA	83	Mary A	15	DE	14
Isaac	19	DE	267	Edward	5	DE	97	Mary A	37	DE	210
Jacob	24	DE	267	Edward	11	DE	148	Mary Ann	2	DE	97
James	10	DE	254	Edward	37	DE	84	Mary C	4	DE	12
James	17	DE	267	Eliza	3	DE	97	Mary E	10	DE	29
James	30	DE	269	Eliza	12	DE	187	Mary E	16	DE	128
Joanna	30	IE	54	Eliza	20	MD	150	Mary J	5/12	DE	84
John	7	DE	181	Eliza A	7	DE	14	Mary J	7	DE	15
John	22	DE	252	Eliza Ann	3	DE	56	Mary J	29	DE	98
John	25	IE	54	Elizabeth	12	DE	32	Michael	20	IE	251
Jonathan	9	DE	267	Elizabeth	17	DE	210	Ned	11	DE	90
Joseph	1	DE	269	Elizabeth	21	DE	80	Peter	5	DE	30
Lemuel	6	DE	267	Elizabeth	49	DE	151	Peter	40	DE	30
Lemuel	12	DE	253	Elizabeth	56	DE	77	Phebe	41	DE	67
Lydia	9	DE	269	Ellen E	11	DE	77	Rachel	15	DE	30
Mary	8	DE	253	Elma	7	DE	97	Rachel	24	DE	170
Miriana	24	DE	180	Emelina	27	DE	97	Rebecca	24	DE	56
Nehemiah	40	DE	253	Evelina D	17	DE	77	Rebecca	55	DE	170
Rachel	6	DE	269	George	32	DE	56	Robert	2	DE	187
Samuel	4	DE	269	George	35	MD	150	Robert	6	DE	88
Samuel	40	DE	269	George D	22	DE	15	Robert	14	DE	67
Sarah	15	DE	267	George P	20	DE	13	Robert	20	DE	33
Thomas	10	DE	269	George W	2	DE	150	Robert	60	DE	77
Vincent	30	DE	180	George W	11	DE	30	Robert P	14	DE	32
William	1	DE	253	George W	53	MD	126	Ruth	21	DE	33
William	11	DE	267	Gibson	27	MD	143	Ruth A	11/12	DE	143
William	27	DE	269	Gracy	45	DE	165	Samuel	50	DE	151
Coker, Daniel	9	DE	78	Hannah B	21	DE	208	Sarah	4	DE	72
Daniel	84	MD	78	Harriet D	30	DE	83	Sarah	6	DE	170
Eliza	36	DE	78	Henderson	61	DE	89	Sarah	41	DE	30
James	34	MD	78	Henderson Jr	37	DE	88	Sarah A	37	DE	88
Mary	5	DE	78	Henry	39	DE	210	Sarah A	39	DE	32
Moses	1	DE	78	Isaac	2	DE	72	Sarah B	29	DE	109
Sarah	67	MD	78	Isaac	14	DE	151	Sarah E	1	DE	88
Cole, Annanias	19	DE	21	Isaac D	17	DE	15	Sarah E	12	DE	15
Cader	1	DE	213	James	34	DE	105	Sarah E	19	DE	89
Henry	10	DE	167	James	34	DE	164	Sarah E	23	MD	143
Henry	41	DE	167	James	35	DE	224	Sarah J	12	DE	14
James	45	DE	31	James	37	DE	180	Sarah L	3	DE	32
John	5	DE	47	James A	6	DE	68	Sarah S	46	DE	15
John	23	DE	35	James B	29	DE	96	Sophia	4	DE	69
Nehemiah	24	DE	21	James N	1	DE	14	Stephen A	32	DE	97
Rachel	13	DE	33	Jesse	25	MD	250	Susan	50	DE	86
Samuel	1	DE	21	John	1	DE	113	Thomas	20	IE	202
Sarah	51	DE	31	John	18	DE	170	Thomas	28	MD	160
Sarah A	24	DE	21	John	25	DE	56	Thomas F	3	DE	208
Susan	35	DE	167	John	27	DE	72	Thomas M	7	DE	86
Wm	35	DE	202	John	37	DE	187	Wilhelmina	18	DE	15
Coleman, Sarah	30	DE	75	John A	46	DE	152	William	1	DE	72
Thomas	36	IE	75	John B	20	DE	15	William	15	DE	33

Collins, William	19 MD 142	Conner, John D	33 DE 197

Collins, William 19 MD 142
William 41 DE 32
William A 4 DE 68
William B 2 DE 30
William B 26 DE 109
William M G 22 DE 85
William T 9 DE 32
William T 18 DE 89
Wm 25 DE 152
Wm H 27 DE 208
Collison, George W 3 DE 138
Henry 12 DE 138
James A 1 DE 131
Mary L 4/12 DE 138
Sarah A 35 DE 138
Sarah E 10 DE 138
Shadrack 39 MD 138
Sophia 25 DE 131
William 27 DE 131
William H 1/12 DE 131
William W 8 DE 138
Colwell, Ann 8 DE 228
Jacob 24 DE 227
Mary 10 DE 228
Mary 18 DE 227
Mary 34 DE 228
Oliver 6 DE 228
Palm 2 DE 228
Palm 30 DE 228
Prince 35 DE 228
Rebecca 30 DE 228
Thomas 11 DE 228
William 4 DE 228
Comegys, Anna 4 DE 160
C P 70 MD 160
Cornelia 7 DE 157
Harriet 9 DE 157
Joseph 36 DE 157
Margaret A 34 DE 157
Maria 23 DE 160
Rebecca 72 DE 224
Walter 12 DE 157
Comerford, Mary Ann 30 DE 35
Thomas 24 DE 35
Conell, Sarah 35 PA 223
Conely, Catherine 55 DE 194
Eliza 5 DE 253
Elizabeth 18 DE 194
Hannah 26 DE 253
Henrietta 7 DE 253
Hetty 65 DE 183
John 22 DE 194
Tilman 30 DE 184
Connely, Catharine 52 MD 38
Connelly, John 17 DE 68
Conner, Aaron 7 DE 264
Aaron 52 DE 264
Alexander 17 DE 264
Alice 4 DE 232
Alvan 2 DE 232
Aner 16 DE 264
Ann 6/12 DE 66
Ann 32 DE 20
Barret 47 DE 232
David 9 MD 221
Denis 26 DE 264
Dennis 5 DE 251
Dennis 6 DE 197
Dennis 25 DE 66
Dennis 64 DE 251
Eliza 17 DE 209
Eliza A 45 DE 209
Elizabeth 20 DE 66
Emely 25 DE 232
George W 13 DE 20
Hannah 8 DE 209
Hester 28 MD 221
James 19 DE 259
James 26 DE 232
John 19 DE 232
John 25 IE 74
John B 52 DE 209

Conner, John D 33 DE 197
John H 20 MD 22
John H 20 DE 209
John P 3 DE 20
Kitty 56 MD 264
Lorenzo 24 DE 264
Mary 8/12 DE 232
Mary 10 DE 232
Mary 14 DE 264
Mary 21 DE 232
Mary 22 DE 209
Mary 26 DE 64
Mary 29 MD 220
Mary 45 DE 232
Magdilla 62 DE 251
Preston 45 MD 252
Rachel 64 DE 264
Samuel 2 DE 64
Samuel 24 DE 251
Samuel 31 DE 258
Samuel 40 DE 20
Sarah 2 DE 258
Sarah 40 DE 197
Sarah 86 MD 266
Susan 23 DE 258
Thomas C 4 DE 64
Thomas D 2 DE 221
W Henry 30 DE 64
William E 2 DE 20
Wm A 32 MD 221
Connor, Andrew 3 DE 51
Andrew 4 DE 121
Anne 12 DE 121
David 19 DE 121
Elijah 5/12 DE 97
Elizabeth 12 DE 51
Elizabeth 17 DE 121
Ellen 10 DE 121
Frances W 4 DE 51
Ignatious 6/12 DE 51
James 13 DE 51
James 49 DE 51
Jeremiah 16 DE 89
Joseph 14 DE 51
Lydia 37 DE 121
Mahala 27 DE 97
Mary 37 MD 51
Sarah E 10 DE 51
Solomon 7 DE 121
Solomon 48 DE 121
Traphena 15 DE 121
Vermidella 2 DE 51
William 15 DE 51
Conseder, Benjamin 2 DE 179
Edward 26 DE 179
Prudy 22 DE 179
Conway, Henry 79 DE 151
Louisa 8 DE 190
Conwell, Ann 40 DE 211
Ann E 24 DE 207
Catherine 6 DE 207
Charles 17 DE 243
Charles 35 DE 207
Henry 1 DE 222
Henry 33 DE 222
Hester 30 DE 222
John G 43 DE 211
Lydia A 3 DE 207
Margaret 9/12 DE 207
Martha 7 DE 222
Cook, Aaron 43 DE 34
Alexander 40 DE 76
Ann E 11 DE 76
Anna 7 DE 244
Armina D 13 DE 76
Catherine 17 DE 219
Catherine 50 DE 76
Charles 13 DE 75
Daniel 9 DE 76
Daniel 48 MD 76
David 11 DE 257
Debe 6 DE 213

Cook, Eliza 3 DE 76
Elizabeth 1 DE 244
Elizabeth 7 DE 55
Elizabeth 30 DE 244
Elizabeth N 44 DE 76
George 5 DE 244
George 5 DE 269
George W 30 MD 14
Hannah 55 DE 34
James 3/12 DE 76
James 14 DE 36
James 17 DE 267
James 23 DE 192
James 25 DE 219
James A 8 DE 56
James E 12 DE 14
John 8 DE 213
John 12 DE 36
John 16 DE 268
Jonathan 11 DE 244
Joseph H 4 DE 211
Josephine 16 DE 15
Louisa 4 DE 213
Lydia 5 DE 18
Lydia 47 DE 219
Margaret 15 NJ 269
Margaret A 12 DE 213
Mary 3 DE 244
Mary 9 DE 219
Mary 11 DE 247
Mary 12 DE 160
Mary 14 DE 213
Mary 18 DE 223
Mary 35 DE 160
Mary 39 MD 14
Mary 45 DE 34
Mary A 7 DE 76
Mary Ann 18 DE 251
Mary E 7 DE 210
Napoleon 22 PA 14
Nathan 14 DE 233
Rachel 2 DE 213
Rachel 9 DE 244
Rachel 37 DE 213
Risden 23 DE 235
Samuel 3/12 DE 213
Samuel 16 DE 58
Samuel 37 DE 213
Sarah 7 DE 269
Sarah C 5 DE 77
Sarah E 10 DE 213
Sarah O 12 DE 219
Thomas 34 DE 244
Thomas 72 DE 253
Thomas B 21 MD 9
William 22 DE 219
William A 8 DE 44
William H 2 DE 63
Wm 11 DE 243
Zippora 31 DE 76
Cooke, Ann 9 DE 259
Benjamin 37 DE 259
Hester 30 DE 259
Mary 7 DE 259
Susan 2 DE 259
William 5 DE 259
Coombe, Ann 35 DE 226
Catherine 30 DE 226
Charlotte 71 DE 249
Elizabeth 30 DE 226
John 47 DE 226
Latitia 28 DE 226
Margaret 25 DE 226
Coombs, Harriet 10 DE 175
Margaret 14 DE 175
Samuel 47 DE 175
Sarah 45 MD 175
Cooper, Alexander 1/12 DE 111
Andrew 23 DE 224
Angeline 9 DE 265
Ann 1 DE 253
Ann 14 DE 265

Name	Age	St	Pg	Name	Age	St	Pg	Name	Age	St	Pg
Cooper, Ann	16	DE	253	Cooper, Maria	17	DE	253	Copper, Phebe	18	DE	157
Ann	23	DE	154	Mariah	46	DE	110	Rachel	35	DE	228
Ann	33	MD	265	Mark	36	DE	117	Samuel	46	DE	228
Ann	35	DE	264	Mary	3/12	DE	74	Cordrey, Charles H	9	DE	144
Ann	35	DE	270	Mary	6	DE	253	Hester A	8	DE	151
Ann	42	DE	253	Mary	10	DE	259	Jacob	2	DE	144
Ann E	34	DE	3	Mary	20	DE	63	Jacob	36	DE	150
Anne M	49	DE	111	Mary	20	DE	183	Jeremiah	41	DE	144
Benjamin	3	DE	264	Mary	26	DE	215	Mary	2	DE	150
Benjamin	17	DE	268	Mary	27	DE	74	Michael D	4	DE	144
Benjamin	22	DE	183	Mary	46	DE	183	Nathan	43	DE	151
Benjamin	48	DE	154	Mary	52	DE	255	Noble	7	DE	144
Brumel	1	DE	215	Mary	58	DE	253	Noble	66	DE	152
Caroline	16	DE	183	Mary A	9	DE	111	Rachel	34	DE	150
Catherine	2	DE	259	Mary A	30	DE	219	Rebecca	36	DE	151
Catherine	9	DE	253	Mary E	17	DE	137	Robert	5	DE	151
Catherine	81	DE	269	Mary J	9	DE	123	Samuel	12	DE	152
Charles	10	DE	216	Minte	80	MD	212	Sarah	6	DE	150
Charles	12	DE	265	Miriam	1/12	DE	251	Sarah	77	DE	151
Charles	65	DE	268	Nehemiah	18	DE	254	Sarah A	32	DE	144
Daniel	14	DE	254	Pary	43	DE	195	Sarah C	6	DE	144
Deborah A	6	DE	123	Peter L	27	DE	137	Thomas	9	DE	150
Edith	6/12	DE	63	Rachel	2	DE	270	Williamina	11	DE	144
Elenor	37	DE	259	Rachel	12	DE	80	Cork, Catherine	35	DE	246
Elisa	36	MD	253	Rhoda	8	DE	111	Deborah	12	DE	59
Eliza	5	DE	258	Richard	14	DE	269	Deborah	13	DE	247
Elizabeth	22	DE	258	Richard	16	DE	255	Harriet	16	DE	59
Elizabeth	23	DE	117	Richard	38	DE	253	Hannah	45	DE	59
Elizabeth	30	DE	54	Richard	55	MD	255	Hester	9	DE	59
Elizabeth	53	DE	154	Robert	22	DE	183	John	19	DE	46
Elizabeth	60	DE	54	Samuel	4	DE	259	Levin	9	DE	246
Elizabeth	65	DE	241	Samuel	6	DE	270	Peregrine	50	DE	59
Elmira	10	DE	258	Samuel	10	DE	260	Robert	4	DE	246
Emily	10	DE	215	Samuel	16	DE	254	Sarah	2	DE	246
Emily	19	DE	251	Samuel	17	DE	225	William	7	DE	246
Emma	13	DE	268	Samuel	24	DE	253	Wm	40	DE	246
Ezekiel	12	DE	225	Samuel	31	DE	270	Corkain, Clementine	35	MD	219
Ezekiel	17	DE	254	Samuel	35	DE	63	Cornish, Andrew	11	DE	213
Ezekiel	19	DE	255	Samuel	36	DE	256	Ann	35	DE	70
Ezekiel	20	DE	253	Samuel	60	DE	253	Elizabeth	43	MD	122
Ezekiel S	47	DE	123	Sarah	6	DE	259	James	14	DE	213
Garrett	13	DE	37	Sarah	7	DE	74	John	41	DE	70
Georginna M	1/12	DE	123	Sarah	8	DE	264	Joseph	13	DE	122
Hannah	2	DE	54	Sarah	8	DE	268	Margaret E	6	DE	122
Hannah	22	DE	183	Sarah	9	DE	253	Mary	22	MD	264
Hannah	32	DE	54	Sarah	19	DE	259	Mary J	23	MD	122
Harriet	23	DE	137	Sarah L	2	DE	123	Samuel	11	DE	122
Henry	27	DE	241	Scyntha	5	DE	111	William	45	MD	122
Ignacious	8	DE	188	Solomon	19	DE	219	William H	20	DE	122
Isaiah	9	DE	72	Susan	2	DE	225	William J	1	DE	122
Jabez	12	DE	251	Susan	5	DE	258	Cosden, John	22	DE	13
James	2	DE	111	Susan	21	DE	270	Mary J	22	DE	13
James	4	DE	54	Susan	25	DE	260	Cose, Rachel	17	DE	21
Jefferson	17	DE	76	Susan	37	DE	256	Costen, Susan	29	DE	164
John	2/12	DE	117	Susan	52	DE	254	Mary A	17	MD	13
John	2	DE	258	Thomas	7/12	DE	260	Costin, Benjamin	42	DE	73
John	2	DE	270	Thomas	4	DE	253	David	4	DE	26
John	3	DE	260	Thomas	8	DE	253	Eliza	11	DE	26
John	4	DE	265	Thomas	25	DE	270	Frances	9	DE	26
John	5	DE	264	Thomas	27	DE	73	John	5/12	DE	26
John	6	DE	253	Thomas B	29	DE	251	Lanty	40	DE	26
John	8	DE	259	Tilly	57	DE	268	Lucy	55	DE	73
John	13	DE	137	Waitman	11	DE	111	Mary	7	DE	26
John	18	DE	255	William	5	DE	49	Mary	50	DE	74
John	31	DE	258	William	8	DE	260	Nathan	13	DE	2
John	31	DE	260	William	13	DE	75	Rachel	3	DE	26
John	44	DE	111	William	21	DE	137	Sarah	77	DE	198
John	45	MD	259	William R	8	DE	3	William	5	DE	26
John A	4	DE	123	Wm	4/12	DE	215	William	25	DE	26
John H	2	DE	74	Wm	34	DE	254	Cott, Deborah	8	DE	67
John R	5	DE	3	Wm P	19	DE	222	Elmira	2	DE	67
Jonathan	37	DE	265	Zeke	17	DE	225	John	12	DE	34
Joseph	5	DE	253	Zekiel	25	DE	215	John	46	DE	67
Joseph	9	DE	75	Coper, Outten	12	DE	162	John	76	DE	68
Louisa	2/12	DE	256	Copes, Rachel	22	DE	55	Mary	78	DE	68
Louisa	30	DE	123	Thomas	46	DE	55	Obediah	3/12	DE	62
Lucretia	8	DE	117	Thomas Jr	23	DE	55	Rebecca	6	DE	67
Luther	1	DE	251	Coppage, Edward	28	MD	56	Sarah	37	DE	67
Luther	5	DE	260	Elizabeth	26	DE	56	Cotton, Ann	49	DE	28
Lydia	3	DE	253	Martha	1	DE	56	James	16	DE	1
Margaret	2	DE	252	Sarah F	4	DE	56	Coulscott, Martha	14	DE	148
Maria	4	DE	256	Copper, Charles	5	DE	228	William R	25	MD	147

Name	Age	State	No.
Coulter, John	53	DE	43
Liveria	26	NJ	43
Mary J	9	DE	43
Sarah E	7	DE	43
Councelor, Benjamin	15	DE	178
Elisha	35	DE	178
Rebecca	22	DE	178
Thomas	3	DE	178
William	5	DE	178
Wilson	1/12	DE	178
Course, Jackson	30	DE	180
John	3	DE	180
Maria	24	DE	180
Susan	1	DE	180
Coursey, James	44	DE	31
Lydia	10	DE	31
Mary	16	DE	239
Mary E	7	DE	31
Mary J	29	DE	31
Ruth	5	DE	31
Ruthana	14	DE	239
Sarah	5	DE	239
Sarah	40	DE	239
Sarah C	2	DE	31
Thomas	44	DE	239
Thomas W	1/12	DE	31
William G	19	DE	77
Courtis, James	26	DE	63
James	30	DE	55
Margaret	25	DE	63
Margaret A	27	DE	55
Martha	2	DE	63
Martha E	4	DE	55
William	9/12	DE	63
William	1	DE	55
Coverdale, Abigail	16	DE	103
Caroline	17	DE	45
David	13	DE	103
Eliza	42	NJ	31
Elizabeth	8	DE	45
George	11	DE	103
George W	6	DE	45
Henry	3	DE	103
Hiram	13	DE	6
Jane	38	DE	45
Job	55	DE	103
John	12	DE	45
John	23	DE	104
John	54	NJ	31
Luke	55	DE	45
Margaret E	3	DE	47
Mariah	7	DE	103
Mary	1/12	DE	45
Mary	35	DE	103
Mary A	16	DE	104
Mary E	1/12	DE	47
Rebecca J	1	DE	45
Samuel	8/12	DE	104
Samuel	20	DE	103
Samuel L	31	DE	47
Sarah A	10	DE	45
Sarah A	18	DE	106
Sarah A	31	MD	47
Watson	15	DE	45
Covey, Henry	35	DE	147
Henry C	2	DE	147
Joseph	5	DE	147
Robert G	3/12	DE	147
Sarah	32	DE	147
Covington, Mary	49	DE	236
Matilda	25	DE	7
William	24	MD	7
Cowdright, Ann	40	DE	227
Elizabeth	11	DE	227
Cowgill, Albert	20	PA	158
Angelica	38	DE	268
Camilla	3	DE	73
Charles	48	DE	26
Clara	15	DE	158
Clayton	24	DE	259
Daniel	25	DE	170
Daniel	47	DE	159
Cowgill, Daniel C	30	DE	74
Edward	10	DE	268
Effa A	8	DE	26
Effie	46	NY	158
Elizabeth	12	DE	26
Ezekiel	7	DE	268
Ezekiel	58	DE	170
Hannah	38	DE	73
Henry	38	PA	268
Jacob Stout	10	DE	26
James	16	DE	170
James	48	MD	158
John	16	DE	268
John	18	DE	170
John L	25	DE	73
Joseph C	4	DE	74
Lavenia	1	DE	73
Lydia	24	DE	159
Mary	38	DE	26
Mary	44	DE	159
Mary A	2	DE	74
Palmer	15	DE	26
Sarah	52	MD	170
Sarah	86	DE	74
Susan	26	DE	74
Thomas	5	DE	74
Virginia	15	DE	170
Warner	1	PA	159
Warner W	52	DE	162
William	12	DE	26
Cowley, James	12	DE	178
Cowper, Joseph	6	DE	107
Mary	35	DE	107
Mary E	2	DE	107
Matilda	11	DE	107
Nancy	9	DE	107
Quentin	37	DE	107
Richard S	15	DE	107
Cox, Alsey	38	DE	266
Amos	3	DE	190
Ann	73	DE	249
Daniel	35	DE	190
Ellen	45	DE	180
Gore	62	DE	120
Harriet	2/12	DE	266
Hetty	24	DE	183
John	24	DE	120
Joseph	23	DE	183
Lavinia	30	DE	190
Nathan	51	DE	180
Nehemiah	7	DE	190
Sarah	13	DE	190
Sarah	63	DE	120
Thomas	7	DE	266
Wm	29	DE	266
Coxe, Mary	63	DE	223
Craig, Ann	30	DE	192
Eliza	28	DE	179
Elizabeth	22	DE	70
Emily	1	DE	70
Emily	26	DE	179
Frances	33	DE	179
Jacob	37	DE	192
John	4	DE	192
John	19	DE	179
Joseph	6	DE	192
Latitia	2	DE	192
Leonard	16	DE	140
Rachel	58	DE	179
Rebecca	21	DE	179
Samuel	30	DE	70
Sylvia	62	DE	10
Wm	20	DE	193
Crainer, Henry	9	MD	47
Rebecca	41	DE	47
Samuel	19	DE	48
Cramer, Charles	9	DE	143
Ruben	30	DE	144
Crammer, Ann	9	DE	256
Araminta	6/12	DE	256
Elizabeth	3	DE	256
Elizabeth	30	DE	256
Crammer, Eve	7	DE	256
George	3	DE	256
James	13	DE	256
Joseph	48	DE	256
Mary	15	DE	256
Ruben	1	DE	256
Shadrac	79	DE	256
Thadeus	79	DE	256
Craner, Charles	42	DE	126
Henry	14	DE	147
Crapper, Daniel D	19	DE	157
Crater, Christian	14	GE	169
Ludwig	51	GE	169
Magdaline	51	GE	169
Crather, Chris J	21	GE	48
Credie, Ann	17	DE	232
Caroline	7	DE	232
Elizabeth	42	DE	239
John	10	DE	239
Joseph	1	DE	232
Martha	5	DE	232
Peter	16	DE	239
Samuel	8	DE	239
William	3	DE	232
William	13	DE	239
Wm	25	NC	232
Wm	58	MD	239
Creed, John	23	PA	84
Cregg, Abigail	16	DE	153
Abner	24	DE	153
Emaline	14	DE	153
Louisa	19	DE	153
Mary	1	DE	153
Mary	20	DE	153
Mary	55	DE	153
Wm	1	DE	153
Wm	56	DE	153
Creig, James	30	DE	268
John	65	DE	268
Sarah	65	DE	268
Crisdon, Elizabeth	25	DE	5
Crocket, Ann	60	DE	5
Henry	23	DE	5
John	18	DE	184
Sarah	15	DE	184
Crockett, Alfred T	19	DE	27
Eliza	26	DE	27
Mariam	53	DE	39
Robert D	32	DE	27
Crookshank, George	18	MD	1
Cropper, Alexander	13	DE	106
Elenor	53	DE	86
Harriet	19	DE	112
Jabez H	22	DE	86
Jabez H	53	DE	86
Jane	80	DE	107
Phebe	35	DE	172
Crosberry, Abel T	13	DE	23
David	22	DE	23
Elizabeth	17	DE	24
Margaret	74	DE	6
Martha	7	DE	24
Mary E	9	DE	23
Matilda	50	DE	23
Rachel	22	DE	4
Risdon	5	DE	22
Sarah H	90	DE	22
Sarah Ann	3	DE	22
Susan	26	DE	22
Thomas	14	DE	24
Thomas	50	DE	23
Thomas	69	DE	6
Crosley, Eben	10	DE	50
Jacob	7	DE	50
Jacob	47	MD	50
James	1	DE	50
John	19	MD	47
Risdon	18	MD	47
Sarah	13	DE	50
Sarah	33	DE	50
Cross, Henry	51	DE	63
Martha	15	DE	63

Name	Age	State	Page
Cross, Mary	53	MD	63
Crotchet, George	28	DE	227
Crouch, Caroline	11	DE	161
Isaac	35	DE	161
Hester	16	DE	161
James	17	MD	78
Margaret	33	DE	161
Mary	13	DE	161
Crouse, Charles E	2	DE	58
Josiah H	29	NJ	58
Laura	2/12	DE	58
Mary	25	NJ	58
Rhoda L	60	NJ	58
Crow, Andrew	8	DE	4
Catherine R	12	DE	4
Eugene	5	DE	4
Franklin	3/12	DE	4
Mary A	3	DE	4
Mary A	34	DE	4
Owen	10	DE	4
Owen C	41	MD	4
William H	11	DE	4
Cubbage, Albert	7	DE	60
Andrew	21	DE	137
Aner	90	DE	264
Ann	57	DE	73
Benjamin	17	DE	255
Daniel	5/12	DE	73
Easter	50	DE	189
Elizabeth	6	DE	255
Elizabeth	24	DE	257
Elizabeth	43	DE	175
Emma S	1	DE	94
George	30	DE	180
John	27	DE	190
John	28	DE	257
John	30	DE	94
Joseph	11	DE	59
Joseph	50	DE	73
Lydia	3	DE	73
Margaret	23	DE	255
Mary	3	DE	255
Mary	5	DE	73
Mary	20	DE	190
Mary C	2	DE	94
Mary E	15	DE	255
Mary J	21	DE	94
Sallyann	18	DE	190
Sarah	9	MD	255
Sarah	28	DE	257
Susan	24	DE	73
Susan	26	DE	190
Susan A	12	DE	129
Sylvanus	13	DE	190
Thomas	28	DE	257
Thomas	41	DE	255
William	5	DE	257
William	30	DE	59
William	20	DE	255
Cuessford, David	10	DE	39
Eliza A	34	DE	39
Georgianna	2	DE	39
Isaac	7	DE	39
John	14	DE	39
John	40	MD	39
Joseph	9	DE	39
William	12	DE	39
Culbreth, Allice	8	DE	22
Emily R	1/12	DE	22
Fanny C	10	MD	22
George S	6	DE	22
Mary A	2	DE	22
Mary A	35	MD	22
Richard	41	MD	22
Wm	23	MD	164
Culihan, James	19	DE	187
Cullen, Ann	12	DE	244
Eliza	25	MD	217
Elizabeth	8	DE	167
Elizabeth	42	DE	220
Elizabeth	45	DE	1
Ellen	15	DE	244
Cullen, Emily	8	DE	244
George	45	DE	217
Hezekiah	11	DE	167
James	10	DE	167
John	11	DE	244
John	13	DE	167
John	32	DE	220
John	47	DE	244
John	49	DE	168
Louisa	20	DE	244
Margaret	4	DE	244
Mariam	8	DE	244
Mariam	49	DE	244
Mary	1	DE	167
Mary	8	DE	220
Mary	32	DE	167
Rachel	7/12	DE	220
Really	5	DE	220
Rebecca	6	DE	220
William	12	DE	220
Wm	23	DE	239
Wm J	9/12	DE	218
Culley, Elizabeth	23	DE	50
Robert	30	DE	50
Cullin, Eliza E	17	DE	100
Harriett E	2	DE	100
James P	49	DE	100
Josephine	5	DE	100
Rachel C	10	DE	100
Sarah	47	DE	100
Sarah A	17	DE	88
Sarah A	19	DE	100
William	15	DE	100
Cummins, Ann	27	DE	68
Ann	77	DE	75
Ann E	12	DE	69
Andrew H	8	DE	8
Benjamin	3	DE	69
Benjamin F	5	DE	68
Daniel	2	DE	68
Daniel	30	DE	54
David	70	DE	4
David J	26	DE	4
Eliza B	6	DE	54
Elizabeth	40	DE	8
Ellen F	34	DE	3
Evelina	41	DE	3
Florence	1	DE	3
George	4	DE	69
George	24	DE	75
George R	12	DE	3
George R	41	DE	3
George W	10	DE	8
Henry	11	DE	69
James	17	DE	68
James	37	DE	69
John	6	DE	8
John	42	DE	3
Joseph	2	DE	8
Louisa A	8	DE	3
Margaret L	4	DE	3
Martha Ann	30	DE	54
Mary	36	DE	69
Mary Ann	8	DE	68
Philip	9	DE	69
Philip	28	DE	68
Philip	72	DE	75
Rachel J	13	DE	8
Sally Ann	10	DE	3
Susan	1	DE	69
Walter	3	DE	3
William	9/12	DE	3
William	35	DE	3
William A	4	DE	8
Cunningham, Catharine	31	IE	56
Elizabeth J	2/12	DE	56
Henry	32	IE	56
Lettetia	22	IE	56
Martha	11	PA	80
Mary	9	PA	80
Mary Ann	7	DE	56
Currey, Bayard	34	DE	148
Catharine	57	DE	91
Cena	23	DE	140
Elizabeth	39	DE	131
James S	39	DE	131
John	67	DE	91
John R	1/12	DE	131
Margaret A	10	DE	131
Mary E	2	DE	140
Mary E	10	DE	92
Mitchell	30	DE	140
Sarah J	2	DE	131
Sirena	9	DE	131
Thomas B	3	DE	131
William C	5	DE	131
Currisan, Levi	4	DE	78
Curry, Daniel	38	DE	86
Francis	17	PA	17
Robert	18	DE	91
Curtis, Ann E	36	DE	110
Grace	54	DE	25
John P	9	DE	110
John R	39	DE	110
Thomas	11	DE	110
Custis, William	11	DE	44
Dacre, Charles	12	DE	230
Edward	40	DE	215
Eliza	37	DE	215
Margaret	6	DE	215
Mary	4	DE	215
Philip	4/12	DE	215
Sarah A	17	DE	215
Unity	10	DE	215
Wesley	5	DE	215
William H	8	DE	215
Dady, Adam	56	PA	11
Elizabeth	46	DE	11
Esther	6	DE	11
Jonathan	5	DE	11
Mary D	8	DE	11
Dahamal, Daniel	5	DE	190
Susan	52	DE	190
Dahorty, Alexander	28	DE	123
Amy	7	DE	123
Ann	21	DE	124
Elizabeth	8	DE	123
Ely	33	DE	123
George	4	DE	123
Henrietta M	30	DE	123
John	5/12	DE	123
John	66	DE	124
Luther	1	DE	123
Marietta	2	DE	123
Silvann	2	DE	122
Susan A	5	DE	123
Unity	26	DE	123
William B	12	DE	123
Daily, Anna	1/12	DE	75
Daniel	22	IE	76
Joanna	27	IE	75
Joseph	31	IE	75
Dairs, Celia	60	DE	109
Dakes, Rebecca	32	DE	75
Dalbor, William	40	DE	86
Daly, Edward	16	PA	4
Daniel, Ann E	12	DE	141
Caroline M	32	PA	3
James	25	DE	163
Lucy C	2	DE	3
Mary	18	DE	89
William	40	NJ	3
Daniels, Ann	30	NJ	59
Charles	2	NJ	59
Clinton W	5	NJ	59
Mary	10	NJ	59
Samuel	37	NJ	59
William	7	NJ	59
Danset, Elizabeth	11	DE	28
Darberough, David	53	DE	203
Eliza	19	DE	203
John	18	DE	203

Name	Age	State	No.	Name	Age	State	No.	Name	Age	State	No.
Darberough, Rachel	42	DE	203	David, Rachel	24	DE	155	Davis, John M	26	DE	186
Darbury, James	32	DE	27	Rees	1	DE	61	John P	10	DE	12
Julia A	29	DE	27	Rees	47	DE	61	Jonathan	13	DE	263
Darby, John	11	DE	221	Sarah	14	DE	164	Joseph	18	DE	49
Mariam	4	DE	221	Susan	35	DE	61	Julia	24	DE	186
Mariam	17	DE	221	William H	4/12	DE	61	Lewellen	13	DE	152
Mary	42	DE	221	Wm	11	DE	167	Lewis	4	MD	87
Warren	18	DE	221	Davis, Abigail	67	DE	162	Littleton	25	DE	249
Darius, Carolota	10	DE	44	Albert	4	DE	74	Lizzie B	3	DE	12
Susan	74	MD	43	Alexander	3	DE	212	Manlove	2	DE	75
Darlin, Debe A	4	DE	212	Alexander	6	DE	220	Manlove	28	DE	75
John	12	DE	270	Alexander	13	DE	54	Margaret	36	DE	63
Lutar	7	DE	214	Alexander D	32	DE	220	Margaret A	4	DE	12
Thomas	8	DE	213	Amelia	9	DE	71	Margarett	45	PA	85
Darling, Anna	6	DE	201	Angelina	14	DE	85	Margarett A	14	DE	111
Asa	10	MD	212	Ann	12	DE	248	Margarett L	20	DE	98
Elizabeth	2	DE	182	Ann	30	DE	86	Maria	26	DE	46
Henry	7	DE	265	Ann	46	DE	72	Maria	27	DE	75
Isabella	17	DE	256	Ann E	7	DE	12	Mariah	17	DE	85
James	9	DE	257	Ann M	4	DE	104	Mark J	34	DE	85
James	39	DE	265	Anna B	3	DE	85	Martha M	23	DE	214
John	9	DE	201	Annie	4	PA	157	Mary	8	DE	87
Joseph	5	DE	201	Augusta	11	PA	157	Mary	11	DE	162
Joseph	47	MD	201	Augustus	17	DE	59	Mary	14	DE	62
Mary	28	DE	265	Benjamin	1	DE	69	Mary	15	DE	74
Miriam	35	DE	265	Benjamin	10	DE	101	Mary	22	DE	185
Rachel	18	DE	201	Caleb	6	DE	134	Mary	23	DE	244
Rebecca	46	DE	201	Caroline	30	DE	74	Mary	25	DE	140
Ruth	60	DE	230	Charles	2/12	PA	157	Mary	40	DE	104
Sally	1	DE	265	Charles	1	DE	134	Mary	78	DE	213
Sally	23	DE	182	Charles	47	DE	134	Mary A	1	DE	6
Sally Ann	15	DE	163	Clementine	6	PA	157	Mary Ann	5	DE	75
Unity	11	DE	201	Daroline	23	DE	217	Mary E	11	DE	101
Unity	15	DE	265	David	23	DE	256	Mary H	17	DE	12
Vincent	4	DE	265	Deborah	63	DE	186	Mary H	29	DE	220
William	3	DE	265	Eliza J	12	DE	134	Mary J	1	DE	214
Wm	24	DE	182	Elizabeth	7	DE	263	Mary J	2	DE	140
Darnel, Ann	24	DE	210	Elizabeth	22	PA	12	Mary P	5	DE	134
Henry	24	DE	198	Elizabeth	22	DE	211	Mary T	37	DE	12
William A	5	DE	210	Elizabeth	48	NJ	23	Matilda	15	PA	157
Wm	30	DE	210	Emily	10	DE	186	Morris	3	DE	46
Daugherty, Ann	40	DE	72	Emma F	15	DE	12	Nancy	8/12	DE	74
Charles	17	DE	68	Frederick	4	DE	46	Nathan	27	DE	214
Eugenia	5	DE	2	Frederick	28	DE	46	Nathaniel	50	DE	87
Hannah	30	DE	2	George	24	DE	244	Nehemiah	10	DE	62
James	4	DE	72	George	44	DE	12	Nehemiah	44	DE	86
James	30	DE	2	George S	1	DE	101	Noah	6	DE	46
James	49	DE	72	Hannah	3	DE	263	Outten	16	DE	26
Jane	7	DE	72	Hannah	27	DE	5	Phebe	15	DE	74
Joseph	19	DE	70	Hannah	48	DE	263	Priscilla	11	DE	87
Sarah	12	DE	30	Hannah	60	DE	29	Rebecca	2	DE	185
Susan	10	DE	57	Henry	35	DE	140	Rhoda	21	DE	58
Susan	10	DE	75	Henry W	12	DE	90	Rhoda Ann	40	DE	85
Davenish, John E	3	DE	2	Hester	43	DE	87	Robert	1	DE	74
Martha	25	MD	2	Hester F	1	DE	85	Robert	9	DE	24
Mary	4	DE	2	Hetty	8	PA	157	Robert	49	DE	23
William	39	MD	2	Hetty	37	DE	134	Sarah	3	DE	75
Davenport, Mary	46	DE	106	Hezekiah	14	DE	214	Sarah	17	DE	14
Mary A	9	DE	106	Isaac	5/12	DE	263	Sarah	41	DE	101
Noah	30	DE	106	Isaac	25	DE	63	Sarah	41	DE	186
Susana	6	DE	106	Isaac	42	DE	157	Sarah	70	DE	72
William T	12	DE	106	Isaac	85	DE	3	Sarah D	24	DE	85
David, Alexander	2	DE	155	Jacob	19	DE	7	Sarah E	12	DE	59
Angeline	6	DE	72	James	8/12	DE	72	Sarah E	16	DE	87
Elizabeth	18	DE	180	James	9/12	DE	244	Sarah E	16	DE	94
Enoch	42	DE	68	James	27	MD	217	Sophia	38	PA	157
Henry	3	DE	72	James	40	DE	101	Susan	11	DE	264
Henry	5	DE	155	James A	12	DE	101	Susan	35	DE	62
Henry	20	DE	166	James B	38	DE	85	Susan	42	DE	248
Henry	45	DE	72	James H	9	DE	220	Susan E	4	DE	220
Jacob	27	DE	155	James H	30	DE	107	Theodore	18	DE	3
James	3	DE	61	James L	28	DE	12	Thomas	1	DE	217
John	12	DE	171	Jehu	14	DE	101	Thomas	18	DE	241
John F	19	DE	61	John	3	DE	75	Thomas	46	DE	263
Joseph	8	DE	167	John	4	DE	185	Trusten	60	DE	186
Josephine	4	DE	72	John	6	DE	101	Virginia	13	PA	157
Margaret A	14	DE	61	John	15	DE	197	Washington	18	PA	186
Mary	12	DE	61	John	24	DE	143	William	5	DE	74
Mary	44	DE	68	John	28	DE	185	William	8	DE	134
Mary J	18	DE	20	John	35	DE	74	William	14	DE	88
Nehemiah	10	DE	61	John H	7	DE	74	William E	9	DE	104
Rachel	1	DE	155	John L	53	DE	186	William J	10	DE	206

Davis, Wm	47	DE	248	Dechamel, John P	17	DE	74	Dempsey, Julian	1	DE	205
Zedekiah	1	DE	101	Mary	40	DE	74	Margaret J	1/12	DE	205
Davy, Benjamin	15	DE	158	Mary E	10	DE	74	Mary	30	DE	231
Daws, Absolem	53	DE	234	Susan S	12	DE	74	Robert	2	DE	231
Barney	27	DE	257	Wilhelmina	4/12	DE	74	Sarah	26	DE	205
Leah	41	DE	234	Decker, Darkey	60	DE	213	Thomas	3	DE	205
Lydia	39	DE	139	Mariah	21	DE	213	Wm	29	DE	205
William	24	DE	70	Nisse	9/12	DE	213	Dempster, Alexander	35	GB	97
Dawson, Albert	4	DE	151	Deen, Angelica	13	DE	24	Jane	40	GB	97
Ann	39	ND	141	Ann	26	DE	60	Lydia A	16	GB	97
Ann	32	DE	144	Caroline	11	DE	66	Dempsy, Catherine	13	DE	118
Anna	6	DE	219	David	15	DE	17	Curtis	47	DE	118
Asa	30	DE	219	Enoch	13	DE	66	George J	7	DE	118
Charles	25	DE	237	Hester	44	DE	66	Hester	47	DE	118
Elizabeth	6	DE	151	James	10	DE	24	John C	8	DE	118
Elizabeth	30	DE	36	Jesse	49	DE	66	Denney, Adalaide	2	DE	68
Elizabeth	46	DE	146	Lavinia	16	DE	59	Anadeltia	14	DE	9
Isabel	2	DE	151	Letitia	1	DE	66	Ann	4	DE	172
James	15	DE	151	Lewis	5	DE	60	Ann	30	DE	172
James	37	DE	144	Lydia	7	DE	66	Ann	43	DE	19
Jonathan	25	DE	151	Martha	15	DE	66	Ann	73	DE	29
Laura	3/12	DE	247	Mary	10	DE	24	Catherine R	22	DE	67
Margaretta	6/12	DE	37	Mary	18	DE	60	Charles	3	DE	172
Maria	23	DE	237	Mary E	11	DE	60	David	2	DE	32
Mary	3	DE	247	Rebecca	17	DE	66	Dorcas	46	MD	36
Mary	40	DE	151	Robert	16	DE	60	Emily	3/12	DE	70
Mary E	4/12	DE	144	Robert	21	DE	60	George	2	DE	32
Mary J	2	DE	36	Sarah	3	DE	60	Henry	35	DE	19
Matilda	10	DE	151	William	13	DE	60	Isaac	8	DE	172
Miriam	42	DE	219	William	14	DE	60	Isaac	22	DE	70
Nancy	20	DE	151	William	22	DE	60	James F	5	DE	32
Rebecca A	8	DE	151	William	47	DE	60	John	8	DE	172
Richard	82	DE	138	Wilson	19	DE	59	John	57	DE	172
Sarah	24	MD	247	Degraff, Eugene	8/12	DE	15	John F M	37	DE	172
Sarah	50	DE	226	Hiram	26	MD	15	John W	11	DE	12
Thomas G	4	DE	36	Margaret	19	PA	15	Margaret	10	DE	32
Wesley	17	DE	151	Dehadawn, John	4	DE	193	Marietta	12	DE	30
Willard	26	DE	246	Delaha, John	18	DE	108	Martha	2	DE	19
Willard S	3	DE	144	Delaney, Vincent	5	DE	256	Mary	3	DE	19
William	4	DE	219	Delany, Amy	1	DE	256	Mary	15	DE	33
William	32	DE	36	George	3	DE	256	Mary	18	DE	172
William	50	DE	151	Henry	30	DE	256	Mary	49	MD	172
William E	19	DE	151	Judah	23	DE	256	Mary W	5	DE	31
Day, Ann	12	DE	169	Demby, Ann	18	DE	51	Matilda	56	MD	172
Charles	12	DE	74	Ann M	6	DE	40	Philip	19	DE	31
Charles	23	DE	192	Araminty	37	DE	51	Rachel	16	DE	72
George	42	MD	169	Cornelia	26	DE	21	Rachel	44	DE	32
John	5	DE	169	Daniel	15	DE	22	Samuel	7	DE	31
Joseph	18	DE	192	Eliza	10	DE	51	Sarah	21	DE	70
Martha	15	DE	192	Elizabeth	41	DE	40	Sarah	40	DE	31
Martha	52	DE	192	Emily	4	DE	30	Sarah	45	DE	29
Matthias	3	DE	169	George	8	DE	51	Sarah	49	DE	167
Matthias	14	DE	192	Hester	9	DE	22	Sarah E	10	DE	30
Rebecca	1/12	DE	169	Isaac	35	DE	21	Susan	13	DE	172
Sarah	8	DE	169	James	12	DE	49	Thomas H	28	DE	67
Susan	41	DE	169	James	18	DE	45	William	4	DE	31
Dayton, Alexander	8	DE	125	John	1	DE	21	William	16	DE	30
James	11	DE	125	John	9	DE	40	William	19	DE	172
James	15	DE	121	John	13	DE	5	William	56	DE	33
Joseph A	9	DE	134	Joseph	70	DE	51	William D	11	DE	32
Dean, Anna	11	DE	162	Leah	6	DE	52	Denning, Anna E	30	PA	95
Caroline	25	MD	258	Louisa	2/12	DE	40	Caroline	2	DE	4
Charles	3	DE	258	Mahala	1	DE	52	Daniel L	7	DE	4
Edward	14	DE	162	Mary A	6	DE	22	Elizabeth	36	MD	4
Eliza	35	MD	162	Mary J	4	DE	52	Emma	7	PA	95
George	14	DE	187	Nathan	25	DE	20	Frederick W	14	DE	4
Harriet	40	DE	187	Perry	1	DE	34	Hy Clay	9	DE	4
Henry	7	DE	162	Perry	31	DE	20	James P	5	DE	95
John	20	DE	198	Rebecca	17	DE	41	John H	12	DE	4
Joshua	2	DE	162	Rebecca	27	DE	30	John H	37	DE	95
Mary	8	DE	187	Rhoda	69	DE	40	John M	42	DE	4
Martha	2	DE	187	Risdon	41	DE	22	Mary E	4	DE	4
Napoleon	8	DE	162	Samuel	26	DE	30	Mary E	11	PA	95
Rebecca	14	DE	187	Sarah	8	DE	72	Phebe A	9	PA	95
Robert	11	DE	187	Susan	6	DE	21	Susan B	3	DE	95
Salisbury	49	MD	162	Susan	35	DE	22	Dennis, Adaline	1	DE	98
Sarah	11	DE	187	Stephen	11	DE	142	Eliza J	8	DE	98
Solomon	18	DE	186	Stephen	40	DE	40	Ellen	9	DE	36
William	15	DE	187	Stephen	70	DE	40	George	13	DE	36
Wm	45	DE	187	Demise, James	25	DE	162	George	16	DE	9
York	25	MD	258	Mary	31	DE	251	George B	42	DE	98
Dechamel, Anna	6	DE	74	Dempsey, James	10	DE	208	George W	10	DE	98

Name	Age	St	Pg
Dennis, Harriet	9	DE	178
Harriet	47	DE	178
James	46	DE	178
John	20	DE	178
John	59	MD	178
Mahala	40	DE	98
Margaret	40	DE	36
Mary	13	DE	178
Mary A	3	DE	98
Sarah E	15	DE	98
Sophia M	5	DE	98
William	38	DE	36
William H	13	DE	98
Denny, Robert	21	DE	4
Deputy, Abraham	21	DE	110
Ann E	20	DE	97
Anna	12	DE	111
Betsey	50	DE	98
Elizabeth	26	DE	110
James	21	DE	110
James	22	DE	88
Jeremiah	24	DE	97
Sarah	55	DE	83
Derborough, Armwell	38	DE	56
Mary	29	DE	56
Derry, Ann	8	DE	56
Benjamin	11	DE	186
Eliza	2	DE	186
Elizabeth	19	DE	186
Harriet	5	DE	186
Mary	48	MD	186
Richard	21	DE	186
Samuel	10	DE	186
Samuel	16	DE	186
Samuel	56	IE	186
Thomas	7	DE	186
Wilson	14	DE	186
Devilon, Barney	26	PA	269
Dewase, Draper A	25	DE	160
Deweale, Julia	14	DE	85
Johanna	62	DE	85
Dewees, Anna S	3	DE	207
Cornelius	28	DE	207
Elizabeth	56	DE	215
Ellen E	3	DE	220
Mary	1	DE	220
Mary A	24	DE	215
Mary A	26	DE	220
Samuel	31	DE	215
Sarah C	22	DE	207
William C	38	DE	229
Deweese, Mary	10/12	DE	243
Sarah	23	DE	243
Wm	25	DE	243
Dhority, Harriet	23	DE	173
James	3	DE	174
John	30	DE	173
Martha	11	DE	174
Presley	7	DE	174
Rebecca	30	DE	174
Sarah	10	DE	174
Susan	2	DE	174
Wm	15	DE	174
Dickerson, Adaline	13	DE	100
Albert	6	DE	151
Asa	31	DE	114
Benjamin	41	DE	100
Caleb R	3	DE	100
Caroline C	3	DE	152
Emily	5	DE	123
Elizabeth	1/12	DE	152
Elizabeth	7	DE	100
Elizabeth	34	DE	151
James H	1	DE	114
John H	5	DE	100
John W	4	DE	152
Jonathan T	9	DE	151
Josiah	35	DE	151
Nancy	37	DE	100
Naomi A	17	DE	100
Sarah A	24	DE	114
Sarah E	2	DE	114
Dickerson, Sarah E	3	DE	87
William	4	DE	87
Wm H	11	DE	151
Dickson, Abraham	42	DE	1
Catharine	14	DE	40
Jacob	18	DE	43
James	44	DE	198
John	18	DE	49
John R	51	DE	43
Mary	50	DE	40
Nissa	44	DE	198
Phillip	55	DE	40
Phillip H	7	DE	40
Sarah	18	DE	198
Sarah	50	DE	43
Thomas	20	DE	240
William	6	DE	40
William	23	DE	36
Dier, Alexander	8	DE	135
Henrietta	24	DE	124
Hetty	26	DE	113
Jeremiah	37	DE	135
Mitchell	16	DE	135
Nancy	37	DE	135
Sarah	12	DE	149
Stephen	4	DE	135
Thomas	12	DE	144
William	26	DE	124
Dighton, Nancy	40	DE	163
Dilaha, Benjamin	4	DE	105
Curtis	9	DE	105
James W	11	DE	105
John	18	DE	105
Rachel	3	DE	105
Sarah	52	DE	27
Sarah A	50	DE	105
Sarah H	2	DE	105
Dill, Abner	1	DE	260
Abner	27	DE	263
Alexander	25	DE	224
Alexander	27	DE	257
Ambrose	13	DE	123
Ambrose	14	DE	261
Andrew	11	DE	261
Ann	1	DE	252
Benjamin	3	DE	263
Benjamin	8	DE	254
Benjamin	13	DE	262
Benjamin	47	DE	263
Benson	17	DE	261
Benson	47	DE	261
Caroline	35	MD	123
Catherine	26	DE	263
Celia	26	DE	224
Charles	1	DE	255
Charlotte	37	DE	237
Chary	66	DE	236
Cheny	45	DE	262
Debora	32	DE	263
Eli	24	MD	141
Eliza	4	DE	261
Eliza	9	DE	257
Elizabeth	1	DE	260
Elizabeth	7	DE	262
Elizabeth	10	DE	224
Elizabeth	24	MD	260
Elizabeth	36	DE	255
Elizabeth A	10	DE	123
Emeline	34	DE	261
Emily	5	DE	123
Ephraim	24	DE	255
Ezekiel	31	MD	252
George	19	DE	254
Georgiana	1	DE	141
Hester	22	DE	259
Hezekiah	12	DE	262
Hezekiah	48	DE	261
Isaac	35	DE	259
James	4/12	DE	224
James	5	DE	257
James	5	DE	259
James E	4	DE	141
Dill, James K	28	MD	141
James W	40	DE	205
John	4	DE	255
John	6	DE	263
John	13	DE	209
John	16	DE	270
John	27	DE	266
John T	8/12	DE	123
John W	1	DE	141
Julia	6	DE	261
Margaret	42	DE	79
Marietta	2	DE	257
Maritta	49	DE	262
Martha	6	DE	224
Martha	16	DE	205
Martha	39	DE	205
Martin	19	DE	129
Mary	2	DE	205
Mary	2	DE	257
Mary	6	DE	255
Mary	8	DE	123
Mary	12	DE	192
Mary	13	DE	254
Mary	17	DE	260
Mary	22	DE	257
Mary	25	DE	266
Mary	30	DE	261
Mary	41	DE	254
Mary	63	DE	260
Mary J	23	MD	141
Nancy	8	DE	261
Nancy	35	DE	217
Nancy	53	DE	258
Peter	24	DE	260
Philemon	8	DE	257
Philemon	22	DE	261
Rachel	58	DE	252
Rebecca	34	DE	252
Rhoda	21	MD	141
Richard	4	DE	263
Robert	19	DE	205
Samuel	7	DE	261
Samuel	15	DE	254
Samuel	31	DE	255
Sarah	3/12	DE	257
Sarah	9/12	DE	257
Sarah	2	DE	263
Sarah	3	DE	253
Sarah	22	DE	258
Sarah A	3	DE	123
Sarah E	6	DE	205
Surency	17	DE	55
Susan	14	DE	261
Susan	18	DE	261
Thomas	11	DE	205
Thomas	11	DE	257
William	3	DE	263
William	5	DE	254
William	7	DE	263
William	15	DE	261
William	26	DE	260
William	39	MD	123
William	43	DE	79
William H	17	DE	209
Wm	27	DE	252
Wm	50	DE	249
Dillaha, Mary F	17	DE	105
Dilleah, John	37	DE	151
Stacy	38	DE	151
Dillihunt, Rebecca	12	MD	11
Dior, William	8	DE	70
Disch, Ann C	16	DE	17
Joseph	55	GE	17
Joseph Edm	18	DE	17
Phebe Ann	46	DE	17
Rebecca	12	DE	17
Diten, Samuel	16	DE	120
Ditom, Leah	13	DE	237
Divine, Michael	30	IE	11
Dixon, Ann	14	DE	158
Caroline	20	DE	224
Elizabeth	61	DE	224

Dixon, George B	28	DE	158
Mary	31	DE	158
Samuel	61	MD	224
Sarah	60	DE	264
Sarah A	14	DE	42
Virginia	1	DE	54
William	26	DE	224
Wm	16	DE	186
Dobson, Catherine	27	DE	48
Harriet A	11	DE	48
James	28	DE	48
James H	6	DE	48
Julia A	2	DE	48
Julia A	26	DE	3
Libby	9	DE	48
Samuel	32	DE	241
Sarah E	4	DE	48
Thomas	36	DE	3
Docherty, Ann	29	DE	258
Joshua	29	DE	258
Julianne	4	DE	258
Mary	10	DE	258
Thomas	8	DE	258
William	6	DE	258
Dodd, Avery	13	DE	79
Elizabeth	22	DE	86
Harriet	5	DE	79
Jacob	45	DE	79
James	37	DE	67
Mariam	3	DE	67
Martha	42	DE	67
Priscilla	9	DE	79
Priscilla	45	DE	79
R	35	DE	87
Susan	17	MD	197
William	14	MD	197
William H H	11	DE	79
Dolan, Garret	1/12	DE	224
Mary E	1	DE	224
Sarah	23	DE	224
Wm	24	DE	224
Dolby, Edward	15	DE	227
Elizabeth	43	DE	227
Isaac	53	DE	227
Phebe	12	DE	227
Phebe	59	DE	227
Sarah	10	DE	227
Virginia	6	DE	227
Dolin, Eliza	5	DE	168
Dolley, Charles	19	DE	29
Dolly, George	10	DE	4
Hester	39	DE	46
James	6/12	DE	46
Sarah A	5	DE	43
William	48	DE	46
Donell, Anna	14	DE	223
Sarah	9	DE	223
Wm	11	DE	223
Wm	38	DE	222
Donner, John	6	DE	255
Donoho, Benjamin	33	DE	17
Edwin	10/12	DE	17
Josephine	2	DE	17
Marian	25	PA	17
William T	4	DE	17
Donovan, Ann	60	DE	132
James	25	DE	133
John	20	DE	117
Rachel	15	DE	117
Rachel	62	DE	117
Rachel A	24	DE	133
Thomas	22	DE	117
Dorman, Eliza	16	DE	248
George W	25	DE	125
Lydia	27	DE	125
Mary B	18	DE	134
Mary E	7/12	DE	125
Rachel	38	DE	248
Sarah J	13	DE	124
Solomon	15	DE	124
Thomas H	20	DE	125
Dorothy, John	64	MD	20
Dorothy, Mary	53	DE	20
Dorrall, Thomas	25	DE	91
Dorrel, Ann	22	DE	51
Daniel	41	DE	51
Elizabeth	4	DE	51
Henry	28	DE	51
James	3	DE	51
Rebecca	4	DE	51
Susan	39	DE	51
William	8/12	DE	51
Dorrell, Hester A	59	DE	92
Dorris, Hester A	50	DE	91
Dorsey, Crucinda	1	DE	90
Elizabeth B	35	DE	90
Elizabeth E	9	DE	90
Henrietta S	7	DE	90
W N W	38	MD	90
William J	3	DE	90
Douglas, John	13	DE	100
Douglass, Catherine	7	DE	101
Daniel	3	DE	101
Daniel	38	DE	101
David	28	DE	101
Eliza	15	DE	226
Martain	1	DE	103
Mary	22	DE	103
Mary A	2	DE	103
Mary E	1	DE	101
Rachel	12	DE	101
Rosanna	34	DE	101
Solomon	17	DE	109
Susan	5	DE	103
William	3	DE	103
Dowden, Wm	22	DE	188
Downham, Ann	28	DE	160
Ann	30	PA	265
Ann	41	DE	245
Ann	50	DE	232
Annis	7	DE	268
Catherine	9	OH	266
Charles	8	DE	267
Ellen	5	DE	245
Ellen	23	DE	187
Enoch	6/12	DE	245
Emilyetta	2	DE	160
Isaac	2	DE	245
James	25	DE	236
James	27	DE	245
James	56	DE	267
Jasper	43	DE	245
John	8	DE	245
John	26	DE	189
John	45	DE	266
Jonathan	37	DE	245
Joseph	20	DE	267
Joseph	49	DE	267
Joseph	57	DE	232
Kasiah	7	DE	267
Margaret	13	OH	266
Martha	20	DE	189
Mary	11	DE	267
Mary	16	DE	188
Mary	49	DE	267
Mary	60	DE	245
Miriam	11	OH	265
Rachel	7	DE	245
Ruth	20	DE	245
Sarah	11	DE	268
Sarah	60	DE	247
Susan	40	DE	267
Susannah	8	DE	268
Tamsey	51	DE	267
Thomas	14	DE	267
Thomas	32	DE	268
Thomas	43	DE	160
William	6/12	DE	187
William	2	DE	269
William	9	DE	267
Wm	80	DE	169
Downing, Eliza	17	DE	210
Downits, Ann	29	DE	258
David	1	DE	258
Downits, George	23	DE	258
Downs, Amy	19	DE	140
Ann	40	DE	140
Ann	45	DE	210
Ann E	3	DE	38
Ann M	16	DE	38
Ann M	21	DE	38
Ann R	39	DE	55
Angeline W	8	DE	55
Benjamin	43	DE	125
Daniel	22	DE	193
David	7	DE	198
David O	26	DE	38
Edwin L B	6	DE	55
Elbert	21	DE	55
Eli U	5	DE	115
Elizabeth	8	DE	115
Elizabeth	19	DE	224
Elizabeth E	27	DE	55
Ellen	8	DE	214
Enoch S	4	DE	55
Francis W	1	DE	55
George W	5	DE	55
Henrietta	52	DE	124
Henry	33	DE	55
Henry	38	DE	115
Isaac	75	DE	178
James	21	DE	127
James F	29	DE	37
James M	2	DE	55
James S	49	DE	216
Jane M	10	DE	124
John	9	DE	210
John	26	DE	196
John W	15	DE	115
Jonathan	53	DE	140
Joseph B	4	DE	216
Joseph C	32	DE	55
Joshua	45	DE	210
Joshua K	15	DE	210
Julia A	10	DE	115
Leadman E	51	DE	38
Lydia	27	DE	193
Lydia F	1	DE	38
Margaret	1	DE	193
Margaret	5	DE	196
Margaret	9	DE	233
Margaret	39	DE	214
Margaret	70	DE	38
Maria	52	DE	38
Martha E	18	DE	55
Martha E	30	MD	37
Mary	26	DE	196
Mary A	13	DE	115
Mary J	18	DE	38
Mary W	20	DE	216
Miriam	28	DE	233
Nehemiah C	16	DE	38
Rachel	47	DE	115
Rebecca	65	DE	178
Rhoda	38	DE	216
Sarah	56	DE	216
Sarah A	15	DE	140
Sarah J	16	DE	115
Thomas	2	DE	196
Thomas C	10	DE	38
William	7	DE	196
William H	17	DE	115
William L	9	DE	216
William L	11	DE	55
Draper, Ann H T	38	DE	90
Avey	17	DE	207
Avery	58	DE	250
Benjamin T	10	DE	90
Charles	4	DE	161
Charles	5	DE	161
Daniel	13	DE	260
Edward	14	NJ	80
Elias	50	DE	80
Eliza	1	DE	123
Elizabeth	18	DE	260
Elizabeth	45	DE	250

Draper, Emily	7	DE	171	Duhadawn, Eliza	6/12	DE	193	Durham, Frances Ann	19	DE	67
Green	35	DE	261	Elizabeth	31	DE	193	George	3	DE	68
Henry	18	DE	250	James	32	DE	193	Henry	37	DE	176
Hester	25	DE	161	Margaret	3	DE	193	Hester	14	DE	67
Hester	27	DE	171	Sarah	5	DE	193	Isaac	13	DE	176
James	14	DE	250	Duhamel, William	51	MD	74	Jeremiah	20	DE	23
James	21	DE	261	Dukadaway, Catharine	3	DE	2	Joel	32	DE	68
Jefferson	13	DE	260	Catharine S	35	DE	2	Jonathan	13	DE	67
John	8	DE	260	John H	9	DE	2	Mahala	28	DE	174
John	10	DE	261	Sarah E	12	DE	2	Margaret	6	DE	174
John	32	DE	161	Thomas J	1	DE	2	Margaret	34	DE	68
Lemuel J	16	DE	90	William E	1	DE	2	Mary	16	DE	67
Louis	33	DE	171	William P	38	DE	2	Nemiah	1/12	DE	174
Louis	41	MD	260	Dukes, David	16	DE	151	Priscilla	56	DE	67
Margaret	5	DE	260	George	6	DE	193	Rachel	19	DE	176
Martha	1	DE	161	Jesse	33	DE	193	Rebecca	3	DE	67
Mary	4	DE	261	Maria	32	DE	193	Rebecca	7	DE	176
Mary	5	DE	171	Mary	10	DE	193	Rebecca	38	DE	67
Mary	35	DE	123	Sarah	4/12	DE	193	Sallyann	22	DE	174
Mathew	30	DE	161	William	3	DE	193	Sarah	7	DE	174
Nehemiah	16	DE	250	Dulin, John	13	DE	9	Susanna	12	DE	176
Nehemiah	19	DE	207	Mary E	9	DE	12	Thomas	7	DE	67
Oliver	6	DE	261	Dunaphin, Eliza	20	DE	79	Wm	32	DE	174
Oliver	30	DE	123	Isaac	25	DE	79	Dyce, John	5	DE	68
Philemon	7	DE	250	Dunaven, Sarah	22	DE	168	Dyer, Bennett	9	DE	208
Priscilla	48	DE	161	Dunaway, George	8/12	DE	28	Bennett	58	DE	203
Rachel	13	DE	202	James	5	DE	28	James	20	DE	203
Rachel	42	ND	261	John	31	DE	28	John	38	DE	208
Rachel	50	DE	96	Nancy	58	DE	137	Lucretia	6	DE	208
Rhoda	10	DE	123	Sarah	36	DE	28	Mary	41	DE	203
Sally	3	DE	260	Duncan, Fanny	22	IE	162	Mary Ann	30	DE	208
Sallyann	30	MD	260	Dunigan, Hester A	40	DE	215	Ruth Ann	22	DE	7
Samuel	3	DE	171	John	50	DE	215	Sarah	20	DE	203
Samuel	49	DE	90	Duniven, Ann	22	DE	228	William	22	DE	203
Sarah	11	DE	250	George	4	DE	228	Wm	22	DE	162
Sarah E	17	DE	85	James	18	DE	228	Dyton, James	50	DE	158
Thomas H	27	DE	207	Martin	6	DE	228	Martha	12	DE	186
Wilber F	2	DE	90	Robert	45	DE	228				
Wilhelmina	12	DE	157	Sarah	40	DE	228	Eagleton, Alexander	35	IE	169
William	20	DE	260	Thomas	3	DE	228	Early, Sarah	48	DE	218
Drigers, Alfred	31	DE	210	William	8	DE	228	Easton, John	52	MD	54
Mary A	29	DE	210	Dunn, Ann	37	DE	252	Samuel C	16	DE	54
Driggars, Wm	20	MD	215	Anna M	25	MD	14	Eaton, Absolem	20	DE	270
Driggs, Daniel	1	DE	61	Daniel H	26	DE	14	Benik	30	MD	222
Frederic	34	DE	61	Edwin	15	DE	251	Benjamin	5/12	DE	16
George	10	DE	61	Frances	8	DE	252	Eliza	7	DE	53
John	6	DE	61	Este C	10/12	DE	14	Jeremiah	2	DE	222
Mary	34	DE	61	Margaret	8	DE	253	John	25	MD	16
Nancy	3	DE	61	Mary	13	DE	252	John W	14	DE	53
Samuel	4	DE	61	Robert	16	DE	250	Louisa	8	DE	53
Driver, Henry	21	DE	189	Sarah	62	DE	36	Rachel	22	DE	16
Rachel	16	DE	192	Thomas	5	DE	252	Rebecca	48	MD	53
Wm	19	DE	190	Dunning, Anna	9	DE	163	Sally	22	DE	222
Dryden, Mary	25	DE	171	Caroline	11	DE	163	William	4	DE	222
Ducre, Amy	2	DE	138	David	14	MD	174	Ebitts, John	23	DE	130
Charles	14	DE	128	Emeline	3	DE	174	Eccleston, Anna	31	MD	91
Charles	15	DE	142	Erasmus	7	DE	163	Charles	12	DE	78
Delah	51	DE	138	James	3/12	DE	163	Charles F	13	DE	91
Elizabeth	14	DE	138	James	10	DE	163	Elizabeth	33	MD	91
Hester	42	DE	142	James	38	MD	174	Elizabeth	55	DE	91
Hester A	3/12	DE	142	John	6	DE	174	John H	55	MD	91
Isaac	13	DE	142	John	12	DE	169	John W	15	DE	91
Isaac	15	DE	138	John	35	MD	174	Mary	16	DE	91
John	24	DE	138	Margaret	32	DE	163	Edge, Eunice	35	DE	239
Mashack	5	DE	138	Mary	5	DE	174	Levin	14	DE	239
Mashack	50	DE	138	Mary	9	DE	169	Mary	7	DE	239
Sarah	7	DE	138	Sarah	13	DE	174	Mary	20	DE	258
Shadrack	5	DE	142	Thomas	2	DE	163	Robert	29	DE	258
Shadrack	41	DE	142	Dunway, Cale	23	DE	240	Sallyann	2/12	DE	258
William	12	DE	138	Durburow, Rachel	13	DE	77	Edgerson, Robert	50	DE	75
Duff, Edward	48	DE	44	Durham, Amelia	2	DE	68	Edgertson, Araminty	60	DE	75
Elizabeth	22	DE	9	Angelica	4	DE	174	Edgewell, William H	30	MD	22
Isaac	17	DE	44	Benjamin	27	DE	174	Edwards, Ann	19	DE	259
Rachel	5	DE	105	Charles A	8	DE	68	Edward	18	DE	22
Sarah	50	DE	44	Clayton	9/12	DE	68	Eliza	15	DE	264
Duffy, Ann	29	DE	63	Daniel	1	DE	174	Elizabeth	7/12	DE	19
Edward	11	DE	197	Daniel	43	DE	67	Elizabeth	5	DE	162
Luraney	1	DE	63	David	17	DE	67	Eunity	44	DE	259
Lydia	5	DE	63	Elijah	5	DE	68	George	33	DE	162
Samuel	7	DE	63	Elisha	10	DE	68	James	4	DE	264
Samuel	35	DE	63	Elisha	56	DE	67	James	19	DE	199
Sylvia	11	DE	63	Eliza	5	DE	176	John	12	DE	28

Name	Age	State	Page
Edwards, John	22	DE	260
Job	12	DE	28
Margaret	30	DE	162
Martha	13	DE	10
Philemon	16	DE	264
Philemon	43	DE	259
Prudence	15	DE	264
Prudence	46	DE	264
Rachel	24	DE	19
Richard	70	DE	264
Sally	9	DE	264
Sally	18	DE	259
Susan	7	DE	264
Unity	12	DE	264
William	17	DE	259
William	20	DE	264
William	23	DE	19
Wm	7	DE	162
Wm	46	DE	264
Eisenbury, Chas L	23	PA	10
Eliot, Caleb	14	DE	119
Caroline	29	MD	5
Edward	18	DE	119
Hannah M	3	DE	5
James	29	DE	5
James H	1	DE	5
Rachel C	45	DE	119
Eliott, Caleb	73	DE	119
Elias	17	DE	144
Margaret A	9	DE	120
Maria	15	DE	144
Mary E	12	DE	119
Elisha, Elizabeth	12	MD	51
Rebecca	7	DE	51
Ellinsworth, Eliza	1	DE	97
Joseph W	33	DE	104
Nancy	40	DE	97
Orfy F	3	DE	97
Elliot, Ann	1	DE	19
Elizabeth	31	DE	19
Ellis, Mary	35	DE	236
Stephen	19	DE	91
Ellsberry, Henry	22	DE	26
Mary	13	DE	170
Mary J	12	DE	69
Elsbury, Mary	60	DE	249
Samuel	26	DE	160
Emerson, Angelina	24	DE	252
Ann	36	DE	236
Ann S	58	DE	78
Anna	4	DE	220
Benjamin D	31	DE	219
Elizabeth	17	DE	252
Emily	9	DE	237
George	14	MD	6
James	6	DE	220
John	30	DE	236
John	36	DE	237
Jonathan	9	DE	220
Mary	12	DE	237
Mary	32	DE	237
Miriam	29	DE	219
Pennell	38	DE	78
Pennell	70	DE	78
Sarah	3	DE	237
Virginia	6	DE	237
Vincent	18	DE	252
Emery, Albiner	10	DE	222
Ann	26	DE	222
Betsey	70	DE	172
Catherine	10	DE	205
Charles	13	DE	172
Charles	22	DE	175
Hannah	21	DE	175
Harriet	35	DE	171
John	35	DE	222
Lauretta	1	DE	199
Letitia	12	DE	222
Lewis	27	ME	199
Margaret	12	DE	205
Margaret	45	DE	205
Martha	29	DE	199
Emery, Samuel	2	DE	172
Samuel	39	DE	171
Sarah	5	DE	222
Sarah	6	DE	172
Solomon	40	DE	4
Thomas	8	DE	222
Thomas	45	DE	205
William	11	DE	172
Emmerson, Anna	37	DE	81
Eldridge W	2	MD	89
James N	40	MD	89
John H	29	MD	89
Julielma H	21	DE	74
Mary	50	DE	81
Sarah L	29	MD	89
William L	21	DE	74
Emory, Charles	12	DE	137
Jacob	26	DE	177
James	19	DE	15
Joseph	14	DE	15
William	9	DE	54
Endsor, John	50	GB	70
Sophia	10	DE	58
Sophia	52	DE	58
William	15	DE	70
English, Isaac	14	DE	62
James	12	DE	62
James	61	DE	62
Mary	10	DE	62
Rachel	6	DE	62
Rebecca J	15	DE	62
Sarah	43	DE	62
Sarah A	18	DE	62
Thomas	22	DE	62
Ennis, Alfred	41	DE	77
Benjamin B	36	DE	100
Elizabeth	35	DE	100
Hannah	2	DE	174
James	30	DE	173
James P	1	DE	100
Jesse	25	DE	37
John	24	DE	27
John H	2	DE	36
John W	3	DE	100
Joseph	19	DE	36
Margaret A	11	DE	68
Mary	6	DE	174
Mary	23	DE	27
Mary A	25	DE	37
Obediah	4	DE	174
Patience	30	DE	68
Richard M	5	DE	100
Sarah	22	DE	36
Susan	40	DE	77
William	36	DE	68
William F	4	DE	37
Enolds, Grandy	70	DE	145
Sarah	50	DE	145
Enos, Anna M	2	DE	10
John	28	DE	10
Rebecca	28	DE	10
Erexon, Anna	3	DE	218
Elma	7	DE	218
John	1	DE	218
John	38	DE	218
Joseph	10	DE	218
Sarah	8	DE	218
Sarah	35	DE	218
Ericson, Edward	7/12	DE	14
Jane S	28	DE	14
Jonathan	6	DE	14
Jonathan	34	DE	14
Mary	2	DE	14
William C	4	DE	14
Erry, Eliza	4	DE	265
Ellen	2	DE	265
Miranda	7	DE	265
Sarah	25	DE	265
Wm	37	DE	265
Ervin, Ann	29	DE	260
Elizabeth	9	DE	260
Emily	2	DE	260
Ervin, George	4	DE	260
John	35	MD	260
Mary	7	DE	260
Eubanks, Anna	18	DE	96
Henry	44	MD	35
Hester A	41	DE	35
John	19	DE	163
John D	51	DE	96
Joseph	9	DE	35
Lavinia	46	DE	96
Mary E	9	DE	35
Sophia	1	DE	35
Susanna	7	DE	35
William	16	DE	88
Evans, Abel	9	DE	47
Abraham	2	DE	31
Ann	3	DE	31
Ann	56	DE	25
Benjamin	26	DE	31
Catherine	5	DE	25
Catherine	35	DE	103
Charles	4/12	DE	25
David	19	DE	12
Elizabeth	3	DE	243
Elizabeth	18	DE	23
Elizabeth	21	DE	57
Elizabeth	64	DE	243
Emaline	29	DE	243
James	8	DE	103
James	18	DE	23
James	28	DE	243
James T	8	DE	152
John	6	DE	47
John	12	DE	152
John	30	DE	23
John M	1	DE	103
Joseph H	4	DE	103
Nathaniel J	14	DE	152
Peter	14	DE	35
Rachel	22	DE	31
Rachel	28	DE	25
Rebecca	21	DE	23
Richard	2	DE	25
Richard	21	DE	8
Richard	58	DE	25
Samuel	17	DE	46
Sarah	9	DE	25
Sarah	15	DE	35
Solomon	1/12	DE	25
Susan	3	DE	25
Thomas	2	DE	25
Thomas	25	DE	23
Thomas	39	DE	103
Thomas B	3	DE	103
William	1	DE	243
William	7	DE	25
William	17	DE	5
William	20	MD	20
William	34	DE	25
Evens, John	11	PA	207
Everett, Elizabeth	22	DE	187
Ellen	3	DE	63
Enoch	16	DE	197
John	7	DE	63
Rachel	23	DE	65
Samuel	1	DE	63
Sarah	22	DE	63
Vachel	23	DE	187
Valentine	32	DE	63
William	5	DE	63
Everitt, Benjamin	18	GB	251
Catherine	27	DE	61
Jane	27	GB	251
John	1	DE	251
John	34	GB	251
Lydia	5	MD	251
Mary	7	MD	251
Mary E	11/12	DE	61
Nathaniel	26	MD	61
Ewell, Rachel	23	DE	64
Farbelow, Ann	37	DE	229

Name	Age	St	No.
Farbelow, Daniel	30	DE	229
Farmer, Abraham	7	DE	67
Catherine	23	DE	23
Elizabeth	25	DE	67
Enoch	9	DE	67
Henry	28	DE	23
James H	7	DE	206
John	5	DE	67
John	24	OE	23
Joseph	27	DE	66
Mary	58	DE	23
Nancy	22	DE	23
Sarah	1	DE	67
Farrel, Emily	13	DE	8
James	10	MD	15
John	16	DE	8
Joseph	16	DE	53
Wesley	12	DE	53
Farrell, Anna M	16	DE	13
Edward	21	DE	5
Elizabeth	36	DE	64
George	11	DE	64
George	40	DE	64
Henrietta	5	DE	64
John	9	DE	64
John	14	DE	13
Mary E	7	DE	64
Rebecca	1	DE	64
Sophia	3	DE	64
Farries, Abel L	3	DE	12
Adeline P	5	DE	12
Alexander	42	DE	14
Edwin	9	DE	12
Eliza T	14	DE	14
Emeline P	28	DE	12
Isaac H	3	DE	14
Joseph	46	DE	12
Laura	1	DE	12
Mary	42	DE	14
Mary E	16	DE	14
Sarah B	12	DE	14
William A	3	DE	14
Farris, Alexander	11	DE	16
Araminty	20	DE	2
Araminty	53	DE	20
Daniel	17	DE	16
Eliza	4	DE	16
Frances A	24	DE	45
James	7	DE	15
John	33	DE	15
Joseph	16	DE	16
Mary	71	MD	15
Mary A	3	DE	3
Mary A	28	DE	15
Mary E	10	DE	14
Robert	37	DE	15
Samuel	8	DE	16
Sarah	6	DE	16
Susan	5	DE	15
Theresa	40	GE	16
Thomas	9	DE	15
William	1	DE	16
William	23	DE	45
William	47	DE	16
Farrow, Ann	38	DE	67
Ann M	37	DE	61
Anna	30	DE	174
Caroline	15	DE	59
Daniel	16	DE	67
David	3	DE	174
Frances A	1	DE	59
Harriet	5	DE	67
James	47	DE	67
James S	8/12	DE	67
John	14	DE	174
Joseph	19	DE	67
Joseph	33	DE	61
Lydia	12	DE	67
Mary	26	DE	67
Mary E	7	DE	67
Nathan	27	DE	174
Sarah	20	DE	12
Farrow, Sarah Ann	10	DE	67
Sarah Ann	20	DE	59
Susan	14	DE	67
William	30	DE	59
Farsons, Edward P	13	DE	35
James	37	DE	35
James G	7/12	DE	35
Laura	8	DE	35
Samuel	14	DE	35
Sarah	2	DE	35
Sarah	36	DE	35
Faulkner, Letty	24	DE	268
Wm	19	DE	172
Wm	23	DE	268
Fearies, Ellen	32	DE	172
Jonathan	1	DE	173
Manlove	41	DE	172
Mary	8	DE	171
Tamer	87	DE	171
William	8	DE	172
Fearns, Eliza	1	DE	142
Elizabeth	9	DE	142
Elizabeth	27	DE	142
Elizabeth	45	DE	142
Emeline	10	DE	142
James	20	DE	142
John	23	DE	142
John	54	MD	142
Jesse	16	DE	142
Mary	15	DE	142
Mary	46	MD	142
Nancy	12	DE	142
Rachel	13	DE	142
Rebecca	17	DE	142
Sarah	9	DE	142
Femming, Alexander	30	DE	243
Irene	27	DE	243
James	5/12	DE	243
John	4	DE	243
Mary	5	DE	243
Sarah	8	DE	243
Willamina	2	DE	243
Fennemore, Benjamin	14	NJ	81
Benjamin S	14	NJ	56
Elizabeth	12	NJ	56
George W	10	NJ	56
Henry G	18	NJ	56
Isaiah R	8	NJ	56
John W	20	NJ	56
Sarah C	6	DE	56
Fenwick, John	19	DE	161
Ferchis, Andrew	28	DE	306
Fergason, William	24	PA	30
Fezents, James	27	DE	189
Miriam	68	DE	189
Rebecca	28	DE	189
Fiddaman, Maria	39	DE	88
Mary	15	DE	11
Rachel	60	DE	142
Fiddleman, Sarah	59	DE	251
Fields, John	38	DE	256
Fillswater, Caroline	31	DE	95
George	2	DE	95
George F	37	DE	95
Filman, Elizabeth	10	DE	212
Finlaw, Arthalindy	1	DE	59
Elizabeth	38	NJ	59
Emily	17	NJ	59
Hiram	38	NJ	59
Mary	14	NJ	59
William	10	NJ	59
Finley, Albert W	7/12	DE	21
Ann	22	NJ	21
Archibald	33	NJ	21
Barsheba	32	DE	207
Benjamin F	1	DE	21
Eliza	36	DE	231
Elizabeth	27	DE	21
Elmira	4	DE	231
Harriet	18	DE	71
Jacob	46	DE	231
Finley, John D	5	DE	207
John G	6	DE	21
Jonathan	10	DE	231
Joseph	16	DE	231
Joseph H	6	DE	207
Joshua	31	DE	207
Mary E	4	DE	21
Richard	26	NJ	21
Susan A	8	DE	21
Thomas	8	DE	231
Finn, John	40	IE	53
Finney, Margaret	70	DE	160
Finsthwait, Ann C	46	DE	206
Anna E	14	DE	206
Thomas H	58	DE	206
Firby, Sarah Ann	40	DE	53
Fisher, Abaritta	31	DE	71
Alexander	1	DE	114
Alexander	10	DE	217
Alexander	18	DE	154
Alice A	1	DE	141
Andrew	2	DE	217
Ann	2	DE	154
Ann	9	DE	165
Ann	9	DE	198
Ann E	3	DE	116
Araminta	14	DE	249
Araminta	30	DE	154
Artemus	17	DE	164
Barrett	9	DE	250
Bayard	3	DE	123
Bayard	12	DE	128
Bayard	40	DE	123
Beckey	15	DE	164
Catherine	2	DE	107
Charles	36	DE	233
Charles	38	DE	154
Daniel	40	DE	114
David W	13	DE	148
Edward	10	DE	148
Edwin	4	DE	5
Eli	17	DE	151
Eli	26	DE	166
Elias	21	DE	146
Eliza	19	DE	165
Eliza	35	DE	35
Eliza	47	DE	164
Eliza A	8	DE	123
Eliza J	16	DE	148
Elizabeth	11	DE	260
Elizabeth	13	DE	103
Elizabeth	21	DE	154
Elizabeth	25	DE	114
Elizabeth	27	DE	164
Elizabeth	51	DE	260
Elizabeth	55	DE	223
Elizabeth	88	DE	21
Ellen	17	DE	198
Emeline	35	DE	233
Elmira	13	DE	164
Emaly J	7	DE	114
Frances A	1	DE	71
Francis A	7	DE	89
George	1/12	DE	198
George	4	DE	154
George	5	DE	123
George	6	DE	107
George	18	DE	165
George	20	DE	166
George	40	DE	165
George A	11	DE	148
Henry	13	DE	146
Henry	50	DE	260
Isaac	33	DE	141
Jabez	5	DE	148
Jabez	44	DE	148
Jacob	14	DE	148
James	1	DE	164
James	4	DE	107
James	8	DE	164
James H	18	DE	148
Jeffery	4/12	DE	71

Name	Age	State	Page
Fisher, Jeffery	29	DE	71
John	5	DE	71
John	5	DE	164
John	6	DE	198
John	28	DE	223
John	30	DE	198
John W	16	DE	148
Jonathan	14	DE	266
Margaret	30	DE	198
Mark	45	DE	148
Mary	4	DE	233
Mary	7	DE	127
Mary	13	DE	165
Mary	30	DE	181
Mary A	29	DE	217
Mary E	8	DE	148
Mary E	17	DE	73
Mary F	4	DE	141
Mary J	4	DE	71
Mary R	2	DE	89
Matilda	38	DE	165
Matthew	12	DE	146
Milky	69	DE	142
Monday	68	DE	142
Nancy	68	DE	123
Peter	42	DE	107
Phillip H	42	DE	89
Rachel	8	DE	233
Rachel	27	DE	107
Rebecca	14	DE	260
Rebecca	15	DE	76
Rhody	2	DE	165
Richard	3	DE	164
Richard	25	DE	260
Richard	49	DE	164
Robert H	10	DE	100
Robert J	10	DE	114
Samuel	12	DE	76
Samuel	24	DE	166
Samuel	68	DE	260
Samuel G	5	DE	114
Sarah	6	DE	165
Sarah	15	DE	255
Sarah	55	DE	115
Sarah A	10	DE.	71
Sarah A	20	DE	148
Sarah E	9	DE	89
Sarah J	28	DE	142
Susan	13	DE	233
Susan	16	DE	166
Thomas	19	DE	76
Timothy	17	DE	166
Tuckston	70	DE	146
Unity	6	DE	123
Wheatley	23	DE	129
William	2	DE	198
William	8	DE	71
William	15	DE	185
William J	6	DE	141
William J	11	DE	89
William J	12	DE	107
Wm	10	DE	164
Wm	16	DE	153
Fisler, George	20	DE	17
Mary C	12	DE	3
Samuel M	53	NJ	3
Susan A	41	DE	3
Fittsgareld, Amy	2	DE	102
Elijah	6	DE	102
Elijah	37	DE	102
Elizabeth	7	DE	102
Elizabeth	33	DE	101
Ezekiel	2	DE	101
Ezekiel	30	DE	101
George E	9	DE	101
John	23	DE	117
Rebecca	2/12	DE	102
Rebecca	35	DE	102
William D	5	DE	101
Fittsgerald, Lydia	19	DE	117
Fittsjarreld, Geo F	25	DE	103
Sarah A	26	DE	103
Fitzgarrald, Mary E	3	DE	103
John T	1	DE	103
Fitzgerald, Alex	12	DE	118
Charles	34	NJ	227
Eliza	39	DE	124
Elizabeth	50	DE	118
Ezekiel	6	DE	124
Ezekiel	64	DE	124
Garret	17	DE	118
George	2	DE	227
Joseph	29	DE	143
Mary	34	DE	227
Unice	27	DE	143
William B	33	DE	124
William H	9	DE	124
Fitzmorris, Mary	18	IE	156
Fitzwater, Caroline	11	DE	94
George	2	DE	94
George	37	DE	94
Flagler, William	30	NY	78
Flamer, Charlotte	39	DE	265
Clementine	3	DE	133
Elijah	31	DE	133
Eliza	10	DE	270
Ivan	13	DE	119
John	10	DE	263
John	37	DE	270
John	75	DE	133
Louisa	1/12	DE	265
Margaret	6	DE	264
Samuel	42	MD	265
Sarah	3	DE	265
Sarah	57	DE	133
William H	17	DE	139
Flanary, Elizabeth	8	PA	223
Louisa	11	PA	223
James	38	IE	223
Margaret	36	PA	223
Rachel	6	PA	223
Wilbur	9	PA	223
Flanegan, William	52	IE	9
Flanery, Cyrus	13	PA	55
Flarall, Charlotte	39	DE	264
Louisa	1/12	DE	264
Samuel	42	DE	264
Sarah	3	DE	264
Fleetwood, Charles	51	DE	96
Elizabeth	47	DE	81
Elizabeth A	50	DE	96
Fleming, Ann E	9	DE	134
Ann M	29	DE	134
Ann M	34	DE	134
Benjamin	11	DE	221
Benjamin F	3/12	DE	134
Benjamin T	38	DE	134
Charles H	17	DE	134
Easter	68	DE	150
Easter	70	DE	134
Elizabeth	4	DE	134
Elizabeth	32	DE	134
Frances A	11	DE	134
George	34	DE	134
Horatio	75	DE	134
Isaac	30	DE	134
John C	13	DE	134
Mahala A	2	DE	134
Mary	32	DE	139
Mary	49	DE	134
Mary E	6	DE	134
Mary E	15	DE	134
Mary F	8	DE	118
Matthew	32	DE	139
Nathan	54	DE	134
Sarah E	8	DE	134
Silas	12	DE	214
Thomas L	10	DE	134
Wesley	22	DE	134
William	39	DE	249
Zadock C	6	DE	134
Flemming, Alexander	35	DE	117
Ann	17	DE	91
Beniah	5	DE	117
Flemming, Catherine	2	DE	117
Charles	10	DE	117
Charles T	44	DE	91
Ezekiel	13	DE	117
Harriet	1	DE	91
Harriet	11	DE	91
Isabella	12	DE	200
James	14	DE	91
Jane	4	DE	91
Mary A	35	DE	117
Nathan	15	DE	214
Robert	21	DE	87
Samuel	16	DE	242
Samuel	28	DE	92
Sarah A	27	DE	92
Sarah E	12	DE	117
Starling	64	DE	108
Fletcher, Maria	13	DE	162
Flinn, Daniel	6	DE	169
Flowers, Henry	34	DE	227
James	6	DE	227
Mary	31	DE	227
Osburn	3	MD	227
Sarah E	16	DE	106
William H	17	DE	105
Folke, George	52	DE	270
Fon, Benjamin	30	DE	19
Elizabeth	43	DE	72
Joab	47	DE	58
John	15	DE	71
John W	22	DE	71
Jonathan	18	DE	72
Josephine	1/12	DE	58
Mary J	11	DE	72
Peter W	21	DE	72
Sarah	23	NY	19
Sarah E	16	DE	72
Sarah J	4	DE	58
Susan	10	DE	7
Susan	36	DE	58
William	8	DE	58
William	54	DE	72
Forbes, Henry	10	PA	6
Forcum, Garret	46	DE	38
Hy Clay	12	DE	38
Moses	7	DE	38
Rebecca	36	DE	38
Sarah E	9	DE	38
Ford, Anderson	14	DE	24
Aner	4/12	DE	191
Ann	16	DE	185
Ann	31	DE	191
Araminty	9	DE	57
Benjamin	4	DE	194
Brumwell	30	DE	27
Caleb	35	DE	65
Caroline	1	DE	186
Charles	2	DE	191
Christopher	38	DE	186
Daniel	30	DE	72
Daniel	36	DE	183
Daniel	50	DE	49
David	13	PA	56
Delilah	3	DE	186
Eliza	4	DE	24
Eliza	6	DE	28
Eliza	30	DE	161
Elizabeth	8	DE	191
Elizabeth	9	DE	186
Elizabeth	15	DE	65
Elizabeth	16	DE	24
Elizabeth	32	DE	64
Ellen	53	DE	24
George	40	DE	64
George	78	DE	197
Hannah	69	DE	69
Harriet	2	DE	64
Harriet	12	DE	24
Harriet	20	DE	65
Henry	5	DE	64
Henry	33	DE	64
James	45	DE	65

Name	Age	St	Pg	Name	Age	St	Pg	Name	Age	St	Pg
Ford, James T	9	DE	49	Foreacres, Mary	40	DE	176	Fosset, Miriam B	2	DE	211
Joanna	14	DE	191	Mary	40	DE	201	Samuel S	5	DE	211
John	2	DE	186	Mary E	2	DE	69	Foster, Austin	69	DE	145
John	15	DE	191	Mary E	28	DE	55	Benjamin	28	DE	145
John H	1	DE	50	Maskell	15	DE	201	Daniel	17	MD	12
Lucinda	3/12	DE	64	Melvina	21	DE	58	David	20	DE	56
Lydia	13	DE	185	Noble	26	DE	175	Elizabeth	53	DE	36
Mahala	26	DE	64	Robert	2	DE	197	Henrietta	30	DE	151
Margaret	56	DE	193	Robert	29	DE	39	Henrietta	65	DE	145
Maria	8	DE	197	Rody	64	DE	175	Julia A	10	DE	145
Maria	23	DE	186	Sally Ann	12	DE	201	Rhodes E	24	DE	56
Martha	20	DE	191	Sarah	4/12	DE	175	Samuel	10	DE	145
Martin	29	DE	194	Susan	29	DE	175	Thomas	34	DE	36
Martin	30	DE	69	Susan	36	DE	185	Fouler, Ann	6	DE	255
Martin	67	DE	193	Thomas	8	DE	175	Charles	12	DE	255
Mary	15	DE	197	Thomas	42	DE	175	Joseph	8	DE	255
Mary	16	DE	191	William	14	DE	185	Lydia	39	MD	255
Mary	27	DE	194	Wm	25	DE	176	Margaret	3	DE	255
Mary	50	DE	197	Wm	30	DE	185	Robert	13	DE	255
Mary Ann	45	MD	49	Foreman, Andrew	3/12	DE	167	Samuel	17	DE	255
Mary F	11	DE	49	Araminta	20	DE	186	William	18	DE	255
Mary J	6	DE	27	Araminta	30	MD	2	Foulks, Ellin	19	DE	86
Matthew	1/12	DE	24	Charles	30	DE	167	Jacob T	23	DE	86
Matthew	20	DE	24	Eliza	27	DE	167	Fountain, Aaron	22	DE	65
Moses	47	DE	191	Eliza J	22	DE	43	Albert	6	DE	130
Nancy	6	DE	191	Elizabeth	28	DE	166	Alexander	32	MD	245
Nehemiah	6	DE	197	Ezekiel	21	DE	155	Ann M	2	DE	98
Owen	6	DE	24	Francis	14	DE	155	Benjamin	13	DE	130
Owen	12	DE	24	George W	24	MD	43	Clementine	16	DE	130
Presley	8	DE	24	Harriet	3/12	DE	166	Daniel	55	DE	97
Presley	43	DE	24	Isaac	3	DE	166	Eliza	54	DE	223
Presley T	1	DE	24	Isaac	30	DE	166	Elizabeth	1	DE	89
Rachel	26	MD	24	James H	1	DE	43	Elizabeth	18	DE	223
Rebecca	17	DE	24	John	6	DE	167	Emily	2	DE	130
Rebecca	24	MD	24	John	9	DE	166	George H	9/12	DE	98
Rhoda	53	DE	65	Mary	5	DE	166	Georgiana	6	DE	245
Rhoda A	4	DE	64	Nancy	80	MD	41	Greenbury	45	MD	130
Sallyann	18	DE	191	Sarah	13	DE	155	Harriet	40	MD	130
Sarah	7	DE	186	Sarah	45	DE	155	James	3	DE	130
Sarah	29	DE	186	William F	26	MD	43	James	58	MD	223
Sarah A	35	DE	27	Fortner, Adaline	14	DE	259	John W	3	DE	98
Solomon	26	DE	24	Ann	6	DE	259	Julia	26	DE	239
Solomon	50	DE	65	Ann	37	DE	245	Mariah	35	DE	88
Sophia	45	DE	65	Ann	43	DE	63	Mary	42	DE	245
Stephen	21	DE	185	Ann J	34	DE	206	Massey	3	DE	245
Susan	10	DE	34	Beckey	44	MD	258	Nehemiah	32	DE	98
Susanna	3	MD	27	Caroline	13	DE	63	Rebecca	21	DE	223
Susanna	3	DE	64	Cornelia A	6	DE	206	Richard	12	DE	223
Thomas	2	DE	194	Deborah	15	DE	259	Rosanna	52	DE	98
Thomas	30	DE	6	Edward	13	DE	75	Sarah	2	DE	239
Thomas	35	DE	185	Elizabeth	5	DE	259	Sarah A	26	DE	98
Thomas S	70	DE	24	Elizabeth	19	DE	51	Stephen	29	DE	239
Vincent	29	DE	24	Elizabeth	40	DE	260	Susan	7	DE	130
William	6	DE	194	Frances Ann	15	DE	63	Thomas	17	DE	223
William H	7	DE	24	Henrietta	20	MD	258	Warner	11	DE	130
William H	7	DE	50	Henry	21	DE	201	Wm	20	DE	162
William T	7	DE	64	James	12	DE	259	Fourakers, Rachel	78	DE	41
Foreacres, Ann	29	DE	69	James	17	DE	257	Fowler, Adam S	10	DE	87
Caroline	23	DE	38	James	42	MD	259	Ann	36	DE	93
Elizabeth	30	DE	175	James F	10	DE	206	Araminta	10	DE	103
Elizabeth	31	DE	185	John	11	DE	245	Archabald	3	DE	215
Elizabeth	39	DE	3	Latitia	42	DE	201	Benjamin	20	DE	172
Elizabeth	45	DE	44	Louisa	19	DE	257	Charles	12	DE	255
Frances	12	DE	197	Margaret	8	DE	259	Edward	21	DE	220
Frances	60	DE	38	Mariam	45	DE	78	Elias	34	DE	107
Harriet	5	DE	175	Marim	49	DE	60	Eliza A	13	DE	220
Harriet A	3	DE	69	Martha	18	DE	259	Elizabeth	4	DE	103
Henry	10/12	DE	69	Melvina	6	DE	63	Elizabeth	8	DE	107
Isaac	9	DE	197	Nathan	1	DE	259	Elizabeth	19	DE	172
Isaac	14	DE	167	Richie E	14	DE	206	Elizabeth	31	DE	215
Isaac	49	DE	201	Robert	43	MD	63	Ellen	38	DE	20
Isaac T	1	DE	55	Rosanna	65	DE	55	Emeline	18	DE	57
James	44	DE	197	Samuel	13	DE	259	George	29	DE	215
John	27	DE	69	Samuel	70	DE	55	George W	8	DE	103
John W	3	DE	55	Sarah J	11	DE	63	James	34	DE	20
Joseph	11	DE	3	Thomas	5	DE	251	James	45	DE	220
Joseph	26	DE	55	Thomas	44	MD	257	James B	5	DE	107
Joseph	48	DE	185	Washington	23	DE	201	John	23	DE	71
Kitty	21	DE	185	Wm	46	MD	157	John A	4	DE	107
Margaret	18	DE	185	Fortune, Thomas	17	DE	182	Jonathan P	15	DE	87
Mary	19	DE	185	Fosset, Elizabeth	24	DE	211	Josiah	23	DE	71
Mary	35	DE	197	James	35	DE	211	Lavinia	13	DE	87

Name	Age	St	No	Name	Age	St	No	Name	Age	St	No
Fowler, Lavinia	35	DE	98	Frazier, Margaret	13	DE	74	Fulman, Emeline	5/12	DE	230
Letitia	38	DE	103	Martin	40	DE	23	Harriet	6	DE	230
Levin C	43	DE	87	Mary	1/12	DE	255	James	2	DE	230
Olivia	14	MD	84	Mary	6	DE	269	Robert	23	DE	230
Margaret E	9	DE	71	Mary	15	DE	254	Funk, Augustus	14	PA	38
Margarett	30	DE	103	Mary	18	DE	91	Furches, Caroline	9	DE	44
Mary	17	DE	220	Mary	24	DE	255	Nancy	85	DE	60
Mary	40	DE	220	Peter	19	DE	269	Furgason, Amanda	20	DE	19
Mary E	1	DE	103	Piercy M	10	DE	110	Ann	4	DE	180
Mary F	3	DE	71	Rachel	51	DE	255	Charles	15	DE	180
Nancy	38	DE	98	Rachel C	16	DE	110	Eliza	25	DE	180
Phillip F	3	DE	87	Rebecca	10	DE	254	Emanuel	1	DE	180
Rachel A	12	DE	107	Rebecca	18	DE	255	Jacob	32	DE	19
Rachel E	6	DE	103	Rebecca	43	DE	254	Henry	14	DE	186
Rebecca J	6	DE	71	Richard	9	DE	269	Henry	40	DE	186
Rebecca S	36	DE	71	Robert	5	DE	255	Rebecca	2	DE	180
Robert	5	DE	71	Robert	28	DE	255	Richard	45	DE	180
Robert	15	DE	192	Sarah	8	DE	254	William	24	DE	29
Robert J	41	DE	71	Susan A	22	DE	108				
Roxilinia	1/12	DE	216	Thomas	6	DE	254	Gailey, Wm	25	IE	222
Samuel J	14	DE	71	Thomas	22	DE	269	Gales, Benjamin	1	DE	70
Sarah	3/12	DE	172	Thomas E	49	DE	254	Charles	21	DE	76
Sarah	12	MD	84	Thomas F	12	DE	110	Cornelius	6	DE	156
Sarah	69	DE	57	William	3/12	DE	255	Daniel	3	DE	179
Sarah A	6	DE	20	William	11	DE	270	Daniel	8	DE	156
Sarah E	18	DE	91	William	17	DE	254	Eliza	40	DE	179
Sarah M	42	DE	87	William	19	DE	110	Francis	29	DE	70
Stephen J	7	DE	20	William H	6	DE	23	Jeremiah	20	DE	2
Susan	23	DE	91	Wm	24	DE	255	Joseph	31	DE	2
Susan	60	DE	91	Freeman, Ann	13	DE	203	Julia	25	DE	70
Thomas	23	DE	206	Charlotte	51	DE	268	Lydia	4	DE	70
Warren	41	DE	103	Daniel	39	DE	203	Lydia	19	DE	180
William	25	DE	57	Edward	9	DE	203	Martha	69	DE	2
William	35	DE	103	Elizabeth	58	DE	157	Priscilla	3	DE	70
William D	22	DE	91	James	13	DE	213	Pruit	19	DE	156
William G	1	DE	72	James	15	DE	203	Rachel	10	DE	156
Wm	19	DE	267	John	16	DE	209	Rachel	42	DE	156
Wm	20	DE	192	Mary	4	DE	203	Rebecca	45	DE	2
Fox, Abram	19	DE	30	Mary	45	DE	203	Sarah	1	DE	156
Amy	66	NJ	30	Rachel	36	DE	203	Gall, William	13	PA	12
Elizabeth	16	DE	158	Wesley	7	DE	160	Gambell, Wm	35	DE	164
Mariah	60	DE	27	Freestone, Eliza	11	DE	18	Garby, Elizabeth	25	DE	92
Fraley, Josephine	12	DE	257	George W	7	DE	18	Joseph C	27	DE	92
Frame, Hannah	37	DE	162	Henry M	19	DE	18	Josephine	1	DE	92
Francis, James	35	ST	193	Martha A R	14	DE	18	Margarett C	3	DE	92
Mary	34	MD	193	Mary C	9	DE	18	Garmant, James	22	DE	4
Franklin, Hannah	14	DE	197	Mary C	52	PA	18	Garner, Cena	75	DE	141
James	26	DE	197	Robert	56	PA	18	William	18	DE	141
Rachel	24	DE	197	William	23	PA	18	Garretson, Ebenezer	8	DE	28
Rebecca	6	DE	197	French, Ann	15	DE	246	Hester G	13	NJ	28
Zadoc	50	DE	197	Elias	20	DE	263	John	1	DE	28
Frashier, Thomas	22	DE	12	Eliza	33	DE	108	Juldia	10	DE	28
Frazier, Alexander	14	DE	264	Elizabeth	35	DE	105	Margaret A	17	NJ	28
Alexander	14	DE	269	Emmaline	6	DE	105	Garriger, Andrew	12	PA	82
Alexander	22	DE	269	George	44	DE	263	Garrison, Ephream	21	NJ	28
Alexander	54	DE	269	James	3	DE	246	Gammamliel	46	NJ	28
Ann	10	DE	128	John	9	DE	263	Sarah	44	NJ	28
Ann	20	DE	256	Joseph	5	DE	105	Gayfer, Eliza A	12	DE	41
Carey	1	DE	108	Joseph	48	DE	105	James H	8	DE	41
Casey	21	DE	108	Meriah	10/12	DE	105	Mary J	1	DE	41
Catherine	17	DE	269	Nathaniel	10	DE	105	Sarah	3	DE	41
Catherine	45	DE	269	Rachel	6	DE	246	Solomon	40	DE	41
Charles	4	DE	23	Rebecca	46	DE	263	Susan	35	DE	41
Eliza	18	DE	225	Sarah	8	DE	246	Gelkey, Edward	46	DE	16
Eliza	45	DE	82	William	9	DE	105	James A	11	DE	16
Elizabeth	22	DE	255	William	15	DE	246	John	17	DE	16
Ezekiel	24	DE	255	Friend, Isaac	45	DE	114	Mary	6	DE	16
Francis	2	DE	255	Lucinda	16	DE	114	Mary Ann	32	DE	16
Harriet	31	DE	23	Mary	23	DE	110	Obediah	14	DE	16
James	11	DE	74	Sophia	50	DE	114	Sarah E	9	DE	16
James	31	DE	255	Frisby, Absolem	8	DE	196	George, Ann	50	DE	204
James	61	DE	255	Daniel	21	DE	159	Ann E	14	DE	7
Job	21	DE	254	John	14	DE	196	Ann E	14	DE	28
John	48	DE	82	John	45	DE	159	Ann Jane	17	DE	204
John M C	7	DE	110	Philip	12	DE	196	Betsey	35	DE	229
Joseph	26	DE	108	Frustino, William	23	PA	56	Charles	17	DE	54
Kate A	14	DE	82	Fuller, Joanna	36	IE	214	Daniel	14	DE	191
Louis	1	DE	23	Patric	1	PA	214	Daniel	44	DE	191
Lydia	45	DE	110	Robert	8	IE	214	Elizabeth	53	DE	28
Lydia B	14	DE	110	Robert	35	IE	214	Hannah	16	DE	227
Mahala	14	DE	39	Robert	37	IE	214	Henrietta	16	DE	191
Margaret	1	DE	254	Fulman, Eliza	22	DE	230	James	12	DE	191

Name	Age	State	No.
George, James	24	DE	56
James	46	DE	204
James H	12	DE	204
Jane	11	DE	74
Jane	11	DE	229
John	4	DE	229
John	9	DE	191
John	23	DE	167
John	27	DE	28
Joseph	6	DE	191
Joseph	49	DE	7
Joseph T	10	DE	7
Joseph W	26	DE	86
Mary	19	DE	167
Mary	43	MD	191
Matilda	13	DE	226
Newel	61	DE	248
Palm	14	DE	243
Palm	36	DE	229
Palmira	12	DE	7
Patience	6	DE	229
Rachel T	20	DE	7
Robert	55	DE	28
Sarah A	37	DE	7
Sarah M	6	DE	7
Susan E	1	DE	7
Thomas	19	DE	191
Thomas R	17	DE	28
William	4	DE	191
William	8	DE	149
Wm Roe	15	DE	7
Gerg, Nancy	73	DE	249
Gerry, Eliza	27	MD	29
John	11	MD	29
Joseph	10	MD	29
Margaret J	15	MD	29
Phillip	48	MD	29
Gibb, Araminty	2	DE	65
Joseph	30	DE	65
Joshua	1	DE	65
Martin	6	DE	65
Mary	28	DE	65
Stephen	11	DE	65
Gibbs, Abel	40	DE	225
Abraham	32	DE	229
Absalom	15	DE	225
Absolem	11	DE	250
Alexander	12	DE	49
Alfred	21	MD	199
Allsey	60	DE	195
Amey	2	DE	180
Angelica	3	DE	180
Anna	4	DE	229
Antony	43	DE	201
Beckey	10	DE	225
Caleb	42	DE	187
Charles	21	DE	18
Debora	5	DE	187
Edward	60	DE	40
Elizabeth	16	DE	200
Elizabeth	29	DE	187
Elizabeth	30	DE	240
Enoch	9	DE	187
Frances	6	DE	187
Frederic	8	DE	66
Frederic	9	DE	186
George	7	DE	225
George	8	DE	200
George	25	DE	229
Hagar	25	DE	187
Henrietta	18	DE	52
Henry	11	DE	187
Henry	23	DE	198
Hewitt	7	DE	187
Isaac	13	DE	229
Isaac	20	DE	201
James	1/12	DE	38
James	8/12	DE	55
John	3	DE	55
John	6	DE	246
John	7	DE	186
John	9	DE	240
Gibbs, John	13	DE	187
Joseph	65	DE	201
Joshua	6	DE	229
Julia	45	DE	187
Levinia	23	DE	187
Levinia	33	DE	186
Louisa	15	DE	37
Louisa	26	DE	229
Lutin	7	DE	240
Mahala	46	DE	40
Margaret	24	DE	249
Martha	6/12	DE	180
Martha	2	DE	246
Martha	3	DE	187
Martha	18	DE	100
Martha	31	DE	246
Mary	1	DE	187
Mary	8	DE	226
Mary	21	DE	180
Mary	22	DE	158
Mary	55	DE	40
Mary A	7	DE	40
Matilda	3/12	DE	249
Nancy	5	DE	186
Nancy	57	DE	172
Nancy	57	DE	201
Nathan	2	DE	229
Nathan	39	DE	180
Nicholas	2	DE	187
Patience	8	DE	246
Prince	35	DE	186
Priscilla	61	MD	51
Rachel	8/12	DE	187
Rachel	7	DE	246
Rachel	17	DE	225
Rebecca	2	DE	229
Rebecca	30	DE	55
Rebecca	33	DE	36
Rebecca	34	DE	225
Richard	20	DE	187
Richard	21	DE	11
Richard	57	DE	51
Ruth	14	DE	187
Ruth	45	DE	200
Sally	12	DE	200
Samuel	4/12	DE	246
Samuel	11	DE	240
Samuel	11	DE	258
Samuel	32	DE	246
Stephen	24	DE	186
Stephen	49	DE	200
Stephen	79	DE	200
Susan	2	DE	186
Susan	8	DE	41
Tamer	21	DE	229
Thomas	60	DE	40
Timothy	6	DE	186
Warner	6	DE	240
William	5	DE	200
William	12	DE	18
William	12	DE	45
Gibson, Isabella	8	DE	178
John	4	DE	69
John	25	DE	169
John H	3	DE	78
Levin	1	DE	173
Levin	53	DE	69
Mariam	23	DE	78
Mary	16	DE	69
Phebe	15	DE	156
Rachel	12	DE	69
Rhoda	55	DE	69
Richard	15	DE	69
Samuel	30	MD	178
Sarah A	17	DE	69
Thomas	25	MD	78
Warner M	1	DE	78
William	1	DE	69
Gideon, Joseph	21	DE	20
Gilbert, Wm	45	DE	165
Gilbreath, Emmet	2	DE	161
Mary	23	DE	160
Gilbreath, Samuel	33	MD	160
Gildersleeve, Benj	35	DE	207
Daniel	18	DE	75
Elizabeth	49	DE	209
George H	5	DE	207
Mary	25	DE	225
Mary J	23	DE	207
Nehamia	1/12	DE	207
Rebecca	8	DE	225
Sarah	1	DE	225
William	4	DE	225
Wm	35	DE	224
Giley, Sarah	76	DE	212
Gilkey, Andrew	21	DE	9
James	11	DE	65
James	12	DE	13
Marthy	2	DE	13
Gillespie, William	20	NY	10
Glanden, Mary	60	MD	21
William	24	DE	21
Gleming, Benniah	9	DE	135
Godfrey, Alfred	30	NJ	50
Andrew	22	DE	57
Eliza A	28	DE	209
James	24	NJ	209
Lydia A	1/12	DE	209
Godwin, Ann E	13	DE	118
Benjamin	1/12	DE	267
Daniel	10	DE	234
Daniel C	33	DE	86
Daniel Sr	75	DE	85
Eliza	17	DE	234
Elizabeth	3	DE	267
Elizabeth	57	MD	42
Elizabeth	63	DE	85
Elizabeth	65	DE	151
Ellen	5	DE	234
Elmira J	5	DE	86
Emma R	13	DE	86
George	7	DE	118
Harriet	8	DE	234
Hester	67	DE	91
Isaac	3	DE	234
Isaac	43	DE	234
James	6	DE	234
James	29	DE	267
John	1	DE	234
John	5	DE	267
John W	18	DE	117
John W	18	DE	118
Martha	17	DE	118
Mary	1	DE	159
Mary A	38	DE	85
Mary E	10	DE	118
Peter	1	DE	267
Rebecca E	11	DE	86
Sarah	4	DE	267
Sarah	15	DE	234
Sarah A	31	DE	86
Sarah A D	18	DE	85
Sarah J	8	DE	118
Susan	31	DE	234
Susanna	2/12	DE	234
Tamsey	23	DE	267
Thomas A	4	DE	86
William	13	DE	234
William F	9	DE	86
William H	18	DE	5
William W	40	DE	118
Wm	51	PA	162
Gold, Joseph	27	DE	49
Goldsborough, Amanda	3	DE	33
Anna W	5	DE	33
Grace	50	DE	17
Jeremiah	7	DE	33
John	41	DE	33
John T	15	DE	33
Joseph C	12	DE	33
Lydia	17	DE	33
Lydia	41	DE	33
Mary	6	DE	33
Susan	37	MD	33

Goldsmith, Araminta	11	DE	226
Edward	10	DE	77
Emeline	15	DE	169
Golt, Angelica	32	DE	1
Anna	8	DE	173
Elizabeth	2	DE	173
Elizabeth	26	DE	173
Ezekiel	33	DE	1
Jane	7	DE	173
Joseph	6	DE	48
Joseph	19	DE	26
Lewis	40	DE	173
Martha	6	DE	173
Mary E	15	DE	63
Matthew	13	DE	63
Susan R	2	DE	1
Gooden, Ambrose	1	DE	251
Anna	1	DE	253
Benjamin	60	DE	266
Catherine	33	DE	253
Charles	8	DE	266
Daniel	39	DE	251
Easter	9	DE	251
Ellen	36	DE	253
Elizabeth	12	DE	253
George	9	DE	249
George	14	DE	253
Henry	8	DE	253
Hinson	15	DE	251
Isaac	28	DE	266
James	7	DE	251
John	12	DE	253
John	32	DE	251
Louisa	6	DE	253
Lydia	23	DE	251
Mary	5	DE	251
Peter	10	DE	253
Rebecca	38	DE	251
Sally	50	DE	266
Samuel	4	DE	253
Samuel	30	DE	158
Sarah	4	DE	253
Sarah	16	DE	266
Theophelus	9	DE	171
Thomas	38	DE	252
William	8	DE	253
Wm	36	DE	253
Goodin, Anna	55	DE	255
Isaac	18	DE	255
Jane	42	DE	161
John	67	DE	254
Goodman, Wm	6	DE	215
Goodnight, Anna	2	DE	178
Henry	27	DE	178
Hilary	11	DE	178
Robert	4/12	DE	178
Sally	23	DE	178
Goodson, Alexander	33	DE	158
Goodwin, Alexander	12	DE	240
Ann	13	DE	251
Sarah	32	DE	158
Gordon, Alfred	2	DE	63
Elizabeth	58	DE	39
Jonathan	37	MD	2
Hannah M	9	DE	39
Henrietta	12	DE	39
Jacob	7	DE	39
James	16	DE	39
Jonathan	68	DE	39
Mary E	32	MD	2
Melvina	18	DE	53
Gosberry, Hannah	14	DE	227
Goslin, Aner	20	DE	150
Matthew	23	DE	150
Gough, Rebecca	20	MD	253
Thomas	25	MD	253
Grace, James	17	DE	89
Margaret	2	DE	206
Maria	17	DE	237
Martin	39	NJ	206
Mary	15	DE	237
Mary A	25	DE	206
Grace, Mary F	4	DE	206
Samuel	53	MD	237
Graham, Ann	18	DE	137
Anna M	17	DE	53
Antony	55	DE	133
Benjamin	21	DE	37
Cesar	40	DE	140
Edmund	3	DE	133
Eliza	19	DE	124
Elizabeth	11	DE	38
Elizabeth	40	DE	127
Elizabeth T	18	DE	127
Emory	65	DE	127
Emory S	29	DE	78
Ezekiel H	5	DE	78
George	2	DE	140
George	7	DE	127
George	21	DE	131
Gideon	3	DE	66
Harriet	27	DE	78
Henry	24	DE	130
Isaac	4	DE	130
Isaac	14	DE	143
Jacob	7	DE	130
James	16	DE	134
Jane	51	DE	66
Jane	60	DE	133
John	17	DE	133
John	21	DE	225
Louis	25	DE	37
Mary	13	DE	232
Mary	29	MD	145
Mary	48	DE	53
Mary	52	DE	38
Mary	60	DE	124
Mary A	27	DE	130
Mary E	2	DE	130
Phillip J	6	DE	140
Pleasanton	3	DE	78
Polk	8	DE	140
Rachel	19	DE	128
Rebecca A	6	DE	130
Rebecca J	8	MD	66
Robert	16	DE	143
Robert	29	DE	38
Robert E	27	DE	133
Ruthann	23	DE	245
Samuel	32	DE	130
Samuel T	5	DE	133
Sarah	2	DE	138
Sarah	20	DE	239
Sarah E	27	DE	133
Simeon	11	DE	142
Starling	50	DE	133
Sulah	41	DE	127
Thomas	12	DE	243
Thomas G	5	DE	137
Wesley	34	DE	93
Wheatley	53	DE	124
William	18	DE	37
William	48	DE	52
William T	14	DE	55
Wm	25	DE	245
Grailer, Jacob	57	GE	75
Mary	47	GE	75
Mary C	16	GE	75
Grainger, Ann	24	DE	71
Charles	4	DE	71
William	25	DE	71
Grant, Ann	39	DE	15
Ann E	14	DE	15
Ellen M	2	DE	15
John	43	DE	15
Martha S	4	DE	15
Mary J	8	DE	15
William G	7	DE	15
Graves, Ann E	5	DE	28
Cloe	23	DE	153
Elias	39	DE	153
Hannah E	8	DE	28
James	33	DE	27
Joseph	19	DE	46
Graves, Julia A	26	DE	28
Manuel	28	DE	24
Richard	70	?	40
Sarah C	1	DE	28
Susan	50	DE	40
William G	3	DE	28
Gray, Ann C	12	DE	102
Ann M	2/12	DE	95
Benjamin	4	DE	111
Benjamin	15	DE	215
Benjamin	42	DE	110
Caleb	1	DE	111
Catherine	17	DE	110
Elizabeth	28	DE	95
Elizabeth	63	DE	97
James	15	DE	110
John G	5	DE	102
Joshua	32	DE	95
Joshua	69	DE	95
Julia A	13	DE	110
Mary	2	DE	95
Mary	5	DE	111
Mary J	9	DE	103
Peter	7	DE	95
Rachel	48	DE	102
Rachel C	9	DE	102
Rebecca	36	DE	110
Ruth	11	DE	110
Sarah	8	DE	110
Thomas	42	DE	97
William B	38	DE	102
Greaves, William	27	MD	9
Green, Alexander	13	DE	6
Andrew	67	DE	263
Aner	13	DE	199
Ann	9	DE	6
Ann	10	DE	67
Ann J	9	DE	51
Anna	3	DE	37
Anna	3	DE	199
Augustus	36	DE	21
Barrett	4	DE	29
Charles	5	DE	236
Charles W	9/12	DE	45
Cornelius	30	IE	42
Daniel	11/12	DE	8
Daniel	11	DE	67
David	7	DE	6
David	8	DE	184
Edward	26	DE	164
Elijah	30	DE	29
Eliza	30	DE	37
Elizabeth	22	DE	76
Elizabeth	28	DE	22
Elizabeth	36	DE	199
Elizabeth	57	DE	263
Elizabeth	72	DE	226
Ella	2	DE	77
Ellen	31	DE	57
Emma	2	DE	199
George W	3/12	DE	6
Hannah	65	NJ	3
Henry	8	DE	67
Horace	37	MD	236
Isaac	6	DE	45
Isaac	35	DE	45
Jacob	6	DE	6
James	3	DE	45
James	5	DE	196
James	5	DE	238
James	6	DE	199
James	15	DE	224
James	41	DE	224
James P	47	DE	67
Jesse	9	DE	67
Joanna	11	DE	248
Joanna	17	DE	184
John	3	DE	37
John	11	DE	45
John	21	DE	188
John	27	DE	37
John	43	DE	110

Name	Age	St	Pg	Name	Age	St	Pg	Name	Age	St	Pg
Green, John	45	DE	3	Greenage, Rachel	37	DE	196	Grewell, Prince	18	DE	184
Jonathan	8	DE	199	Samuel	11	DE	197	Grey, Amanda	10	DE	228
Jonathan	12	DE	184	Sarah	35	DE	69	Andrew	26	DE	211
Jonathan	42	DE	199	Sherry	36	DE	69	Catherine	69	DE	216
Joseph	18	DE	184	Washington	6	DE	196	Cato	20	DE	228
Joseph T	3	DE	57	Greene, Alexander	12	DE	219	Cato	35	DE	242
Leah	30	DE	238	Charles	20	DE	218	Caleb	9	DE	211
Levi	45	MD	51	Charles	20	DE	221	Daniel	30	DE	219
Lucinda	5	DE	185	George	29	DE	247	David	5	DE	261
Margaret	55	DE	38	Louisa	10	DE	247	Deby	7	DE	242
Margaret Ann	7	DE	57	Mary	5/12	DE	247	Eliza	6	DE	158
Margaretta	15	DE	199	Mary	17	DE	218	Eliza	8	DE	228
Marion	24	DE	184	Rachel	2	DE	247	Eliza	30	DE	242
Martha	1	DE	185	Robert J	8	DE	219	Elizabeth	3	DE	219
Mary	3	DE	76	S M	8	DE	247	Elizabeth	31	DE	211
Mary	6	DE	184	Sally	48	DE	218	Ellen	55	DE	211
Mary	8	DE	248	Sallyanne	32	DE	247	George	39	DE	261
Mary	11	DE	236	Greenell, Elizabeth	16	DE	268	Hester	18	DE	228
Mary	25	DE	37	Hannah	33	DE	267	Isabella	2	DE	242
Mary	25	DE	51	John	10	DE	267	James	12	DE	218
Mary	27	DE	29	John	53	DE	267	Jane	20	DE	261
Mary	30	DE	21	Kesiah	57	DE	267	John	16	DE	211
Mary E	3	DE	45	Letitia	7	DE	267	John	52	DE	228
Mary M H	5	DE	67	Letitia	35	DE	267	Latitia	40	DE	228
Michal	1	DE	236	Peter	18	DE	267	Lydia	12	DE	261
Miriam	24	DE	37	Susan	14	DE	267	Lydia	14	DE	218
Miriam	40	DE	224	Wm	4	DE	267	Major	64	MD	247
Nathan	22	DE	182	Greenfield, Ann	25	DE	177	Maria	3	DE	228
Patrick	21	IE	42	John	1	DE	177	Maria	35	DE	211
Philemon	13	DE	224	Truitt	35	DE	177	Maria A	16	DE	212
Philip	24	IE	42	William	5	DE	177	Mary	1	DE	242
Priscilla	37	DE	45	Greenlee, Ann	18	DE	263	Mary	1	DE	261
Rachel	2	DE	236	Arthur	27	DE	264	Mary	35	DE	261
Rachel	4	DE	6	Charles	7	DE	260	Mary A	23	DE	219
Rachel	9	DE	238	Charles	47	DE	263	Peter	4	DE	228
Rachel	10	DE	199	Elizabeth	14	DE	264	Rachel	4	DE	242
Rachel	42	DE	6	Hester	19	DE	264	Rachel	62	DE	247
Rachel S	40	DE	110	Louisa	8	DE	192	Robert	23	IE	36
Rebecca	15	DE	182	Mary	23	DE	265	Roger	71	DE	216
Rebecca A	7	DE	110	Phebe	25	DE	159	Ruth	3	DE	228
Robert H	5	DE	29	Robert	54	DE	264	Ruthy	13	DE	217
Ruben	12	DE	236	Sally	17	DE	264	Samuel	7	DE	261
Salina	40	DE	8	Sarah	52	MD	260	Sarah	5	DE	242
Samuel	3	DE	21	Sarah	53	DE	264	Sarah	6	DE	21
Samuel	9	DE	236	William	12	DE	264	Sarah	12	DE	228
Samuel	13	DE	51	William	16	DE	192	Sarah	14	DE	211
Samuel	16	DE	6	Wm	50	DE	260	Susan	50	DE	247
Sarah	7	DE	238	Greenley, Ann	6	DE	258	Thomas J	1	DE	219
Sarah	14	DE	184	John	14	DE	253	Unity	74	DE	167
Sarah	40	DE	184	Lavinia	28	DE	253	William	8	DE	242
Saulsberry	2	DE	6	Louisa	10	DE	253	Grier, George	30	GB	84
Sewel	30	DE	57	Margaret	4	DE	253	Isabella	12	DE	215
Susan	1/12	DE	238	Samuel	9	DE	253	James	7	DE	215
Susan	7	DE	183	Washington	33	DE	253	James	50	GB	215
Susanna	14	DE	248	Greenwood, Alex	36	DE	224	John E	3	DE	215
Thomas	2	DE	51	Benjamin H	21	MD	10	Mary	70	DE	245
Thomas	23	DE	76	David	20	DE	39	Mary J	20	DE	215
Thomas	28	DE	2	Eliza	40	DE	223	Michal	17	DE	173
Thomas M	17	DE	3	Eliza	51	DE	39	Robert K	10	DE	215
Washington	42	DE	6	Elizabeth	29	DE	224	Willimina	18	DE	215
William	5	DE	21	George	5	DE	171	Griffen, Delia	4	DE	49
William	9	DE	45	George	8	DE	81	Hester	15	DE	52
William	11	DE	224	Hannah	9	DE	224	Jane	60	DE	55
William	13	DE	67	James	27	DE	200	John	68	DE	55
William	17	DE	3	John	16	DE	82	John E	61	DE	52
William F	1	DE	30	Maria	16	DE	200	John R	23	DE	7
William M	5	DE	57	Mary	12	DE	39	Lydia E	18	DE	54
Wm	30	DE	238	Mary	12	DE	49	Samuel	21	DE	26
Greenage, Abigail	8	DE	197	Mary	16	DE	224	Sarah	13	DE	52
Amelia	8	DE	69	Mary	11	DE	224	Sarah	57	MD	52
Ann	2	DE	196	Sarah	1	DE	224	Sarah E	18	DE	45
Benjamin	39	DE	196	Warner C	15	DE	49	Susan	14	DE	55
James	12	DE	196	William	16	DE	49	Susan	17	DE	52
John	8	DE	196	William	40	DE	39	William	18	DE	82
John	19	DE	197	Greer, Ann T	65	VA	84	William	29	DE	52
John	43	DE	197	Anna P	13	DE	84	Griffin, Albert	8	DE	258
Josiah	13	DE	196	John	46	DE	85	Alexander	3	DE	43
Louisa	4	DE	69	Mark A	17	DE	85	Alexander	6	DE	241
Mary	10	DE	69	Mary G	40	DE	85	Alexander	12	DE	53
Melissa	18	DE	197	Mary M	8	DE	85	Alphonzo	6/12	DE	80
Miriam	4	DE	196	Sarah M	15	DE	85	Angelica	25	DE	13
Rachel	1	DE	69	Grewel, Wm	25	DE	242	Ann	14	DE	178

Name	Age	State	No.
Griffin, Barsheba B	25	DE	22
Catherine	30	DE	80
Caton	40	DE	259
Charles	4	DE	80
Charles	15	DE	178
Charles	43	DE	178
David J	2	DE	22
Eliza	34	DE	43
Elizabeth	19	DE	157
Elizabeth	35	DE	258
Elizabeth	43	DE	44
Fredis	7	DE	178
George	7	DE	22
George	16	DE	252
Georgeanna	8	DE	44
Hetty	35	DE	264
James	12	DE	258
James	65	DE	22
James F	17	DE	18
Jerry	2	DE	178
John	7	DE	178
John	8	DE	80
John	30	DE	80
John W	5/12	DE	22
Joseph	7/12	DE	43
Joseph	10	DE	178
Lydia A	13	DE	44
Margaret	3	DE	178
Margaret	36	DE	178
Mary G	6	DE	43
Mary J	30	DE	22
Melvina	18	DE	54
Noah	15	DE	200
Robert	30	DE	258
Sally Ann	5	DE	178
Samuel	5	DE	22
Samuel	10	DE	80
Samuel	53	DE	44
Susan R	5	DE	44
Tilman	13	DE	251
Thomas	10	DE	43
Thomas	10	DE	265
William	2	DE	80
Wm	52	DE	193
Griffith, Abagail	69	DE	90
Alfred P	7	DE	16
Ann	26	DE	132
Ann	45	DE	89
Ann	50	DE	244
Charles P	6	DE	87
Daniel	21	DE	89
David	9/12	DE	111
Elexena	12	DE	257
Elizabeth	26	DE	255
Elizabeth	29	DE	87
Elizabeth	71	DE	216
George	17	MD	215
Hester	28	DE	249
Hilyard	61	DE	97
James	43	DE	257
James H	2	DE	87
James H	10	DE	97
Jane	35	DE	89
John	30	DE	255
John H	9	DE	16
Jonathan	2	DE	249
Joseph C	50	DE	16
Margaret E	4	DE	132
Mariam	10	MD	252
Marjorie	69	DE	89
Martin	14	DE	257
Mary	27	DE	244
Mary	65	DE	97
Mary A	6	DE	111
Mary C	5	DE	132
Mary C	38	DE	16
Nehemiah	11	DE	87
Peter	37	DE	150
Peter	67	DE	89
Potter	67	DE	90
William	2	DE	111
William	3	DE	113
Griffith, William	9	DE	87
William D	31	DE	111
William L	35	DE	132
Zadock	30	DE	127
Gross, Ann	6	DE	219
Celea	4	DE	110
Lewis	8	DE	219
Maria	17	DE	214
Wm	2	DE	238
Groves, Solomon	34	DE	174
Susan	43	DE	174
Grumell, Eliza	18	DE	257
Isaac	14	DE	257
John	16	DE	257
Joseph	22	DE	257
Mary	49	DE	257
Guessford, Harriet	57	DE	41
James	17	DE	39
James	33	DE	41
Sarietta	11	DE	41
Guillett, Mary E	19	DE	151
Gullett, Alex W	14	DE	147
Eli C	10	DE	147
Henry C	14	DE	147
Mary A	5	DE	147
Sarah J	11	DE	147
Susan E	3	DE	147
Guy, Absolem	23	DE	248
Absolem	53	DE	248
Alfred	4	DE	44
Ann	4	DE	73
Ann	30	DE	73
Ann	37	DE	44
Ann M	11	DE	71
Bayard	11	DE	44
Eliza	51	DE	248
George	18	DE	168
Harriet	50	DE	168
Hester	15	DE	248
Isaac	2	DE	44
James	17	DE	168
James	70	DE	168
John	6	DE	73
John	20	DE	168
John	21	DE	174
Joshua	47	DE	44
Louisa	14	DE	71
Louisa	15	DE	56
Matilda A	7	DE	71
Nancy	50	MD	71
Rebecca	8	DE	73
Sarah	12	DE	168
Sarah A	13	DE	44
Sewell	7	DE	44
Susan	2	DE	73
Susan	29	DE	248
Thomas	4	DE	168
Wesley	17	DE	54
William H	17	DE	44
Haas, Christopher	4	DE	64
Hacket, Emeline	12	DE	186
John	15	DE	213
Lavinia	16	DE	203
Hackett, Charles H	18	MD	13
Hagerman, Mary	35	DE	244
Purnell	7	DE	244
Wm	23	PA	244
Hagner, Barbary	12	DE	36
Columbus	10	DE	34
Mary J	18	DE	10
Haines, Ann	18	DE	105
Harriet	50	DE	93
John	42	DE	96
John Henry	15	DE	96
Lisha	12	DE	96
Peter	1	DE	240
Rachel	35	DE	219
Retty	29	DE	96
Robert	65	DE	93
Wilber	6/12	DE	96
Hainsley, Amos	52	DE	255
Hainsley, Lydia	21	DE	255
Lydia	37	DE	255
Mary	17	DE	256
Sarah	4	DE	255
Hairgrove, Henry	18	DE	249
Joseph	19	DE	226
Sanderson	59	DE	225
Susan	45	DE	225
Haleberry, John	21	DE	250
Hall, Alexander	4	MD	183
Alexander	15	DE	87
Allice Ann	1	DE	52
Ann P	49	DE	89
Anna	13	DE	89
Caleb	56	DE	78
Caleb T	18	PA	78
Caroline	24	DE	222
Catharine	15	PA	78
Charles	9	MD	183
Charles P	5	DE	100
Charlotte	13	DE	51
Clara W	5	DE	89
Comfort	54	DE	51
David	8	DE	69
David	16	DE	101
David B	46	DE	51
Draper	43	DE	101
Edward	7	DE	52
Eliza	8	DE	89
Eliza	12	MD	183
Eliza	38	MD	183
Elizabeth	6	DE	93
Elizabeth	21	DE	49
Elizabeth	22	DE	42
Elizabeth M	35	DE	52
Emily	7	DE	78
George	16	MD	183
George	25	DE	94
George	41	DE	173
George S	1	DE	100
Hannah	8/12	DE	49
Henry	42	DE	66
Hester	4	DE	53
Hester	38	DE	100
Isaac	50	DE	93
Isabel	36	DE	78
Israel	9	DE	52
Israel P	42	DE	52
James	10	MD	183
James	20	DE	41
James	22	DE	49
James	33	DE	53
James H	11	DE	52
James M	15	DE	89
James T	12	DE	100
John	16	DE	174
John	19	DE	9
John A	15	DE	101
John D	13	DE	52
John M	33	DE	107
John W	3	DE	222
John W	15	DE	100
John W	34	DE	222
Jonathan	1	DE	41
Josephine	3	DE	78
Joshua M	53	DE	150
Laura J	2	DE	78
Levina	30	DE	93
Lydia	7	DE	51
Margaret	24	DE	173
Margarett	53	DE	101
Mary	2	DE	53
Mary	7	DE	78
Mary	42	DE	66
Mary	65	DE	173
Mary A	40	DE	96
Mary E	5	DE	52
Mary P	58	DE	96
Nancy	37	DE	96
Nathan	55	DE	51
Parker	4/12	DE	53
Peter W	28	DE	96

Name	Age	State	No.	Name	Age	State	No.	Name	Age	State	No.
Hall, Purnell	1	DE	89	Hamilton, Sarah	37	DE	50	Hanly, Parker	37	DE	71
Rebecca	26	DE	48	Sarah E	3	DE	151	Hannah, John	22	IE	52
Rebecca	26	DE	53	Sarah J	18	DE	149	Hannet, Bridget	24	DE	77
Robert	20	DE	26	Theodore	5	DE	149	Hanocks, Henry	12	DE	201
Robert	23	DE	87	Timothy	4	DE	181	Hansley, Margaret	49	DE	165
Samuel	34	DE	78	William	6	MD	50	Mary	4	DE	165
Samuel J	11	DE	96	William	6	DE	70	Phillip	2	DE	165
Samuel L	20	DE	150	William	24	DE	16	Phillip	41	DE	165
Samuel W	6	DE	213	William	34	DE	151	Hanson, John W	20	DE	219
Sarah	2	DE	222	William	42	MD	50	Julia	25	DE	30
Sarah	6	MD	183	Williamina	2	DE	151	Hardcastle, Alexina	10	MD	94
Sarah	12	DE	45	Williamina	21	DE	16	Ann	5	DE	154
Sarah	16	DE	237	Hamm, Anna	11	DE	73	Anthony	37	DE	230
Sarah	54	DE	51	Benjamin F	34	DE	73	Charles	2	DE	154
Sarah	55	NJ	78	Charles	70	DE	37	Comfort	70	DE	209
Sarah A	20	PA	78	Kate	38	DE	37	Elizabeth	28	DE	153
Sarah A	21	DE	41	Laura	15	DE	73	Louisa	40	MD	54
Sarah E	3	DE	41	Latitia	67	DE	37	Mary	30	DE	230
Sarah G	2	DE	89	Pleasanton	38	DE	78	Peter	4	DE	154
Stephen	26	DE	41	Sarah E	27	DE	78	Peter	35	DE	153
Thomas	14	MD	199	Wilhelmina	16	DE	37	Thomas	10	DE	226
Thomas	14	MD	183	Hammersley, Eliza	19	DE	90	William	8	DE	154
Thomas	24	DE	48	Eliza	50	DE	90	William D	50	MD	80
Willard	11	DE	69	James	21	DE	90	Harden, Benjamin	11	DE	23
Willard	15	DE	52	Thomas F	16	DE	90	James	36	NJ	23
William	3	DE	52	Thomas S	50	MD	90	Jane	2/12	DE	23
William	6	DE	53	Hammeton, Isaac	16	DE	110	Margaret	1	DE	23
William E	8	DE	100	Hammond, Ann H	9	DE	98	Mary	35	DE	23
Winlock	6	DE	100	Daniel	8	DE	144	Mary E	9	DE	23
Zephora	48	DE	150	Edmund	1	DE	137	Samuel J	7	DE	23
Halleday, James	24	DE	31	Eli A	13	DE	98	William T	3	DE	23
Hallman, Christopher	15	PA	20	Eli F	42	DE	98	Hardenborg, Jacob	17	DE	209
Eliza J	11	PA	20	Elias	20	DE	98	Hardesty, Alfred T	1	DE	148
Jacob	49	PA	20	Elizabeth	30	DE	98	Ann M	30	DE	147
Margaret	9	PA	20	Emmaly	3	DE	98	Elizabeth	33	DE	148
Margaret	33	PA	20	Isaac	49	DE	237	Emeline	8	DE	148
Martha	4	PA	20	Isaan	28	DE	98	Garrison	6	DE	148
Mary A	13	PA	20	Jacob	38	DE	136	George	22	DE	18
Rachel	9/12	PA	20	Jacob H	4	DE	136	James E	10	DE	148
Hamel, Lewis	23	MD	85	Jacob H	10	DE	98	Rachel	46	DE	148
Hamell, Bridget	24	DE	78	John W	18	DE	136	Sarah A	4	DE	148
Hamilton, Alexander	13	DE	181	Lovey	14	DE	136	Thomas	34	DE	148
Alexander	30	DE	159	Margaret	18	DE	136	William H	34	DE	147
Ann	30	DE	159	Martha	35	DE	137	Hardin, Hannah	9	DE	248
Ann	50	DE	97	Mary	30	DE	129	Harding, James	13	DE	89
Ann E	10	DE	102	Mary	38	DE	137	Hardisty, Hester L	25	DE	113
Ann E	13	DE	70	Mary E	3	DE	98	Levin	30	DE	112
Ann M	4	DE	151	Moses	65	DE	136	Nancy	43	DE	112
Clara	3/12	DE	151	Nicholas D	17	DE	98	Hardy, Jonathan	6	DE	72
Daniel	6	DE	9	Oliver	27	DE	136	Mary	37	DE	72
Edward	16	DE	110	Patience	63	DE	138	Parker	37	DE	72
Elizabeth	16	MD	51	Rebecca B	43	DE	98	Hargadine, Ann	35	DE	173
Elizabeth	21	DE	149	Samuel	2	DE	136	Henry	33	DE	231
Elizabeth	57	DE	149	Sarah A	3	DE	129	John	20	DE	175
Fanny	60	DE	181	Sarah J	9	DE	98	John	55	DE	175
George	3	DE	9	Susan A	28	MD	136	Mary	4	DE	231
George	3	MD	50	Susan C	6	DE	98	Robert	6	DE	231
George	10	DE	81	William	3	DE	137	Ruthana	26	DE	231
Georgianna	1	DE	16	William A	6	DE	98	William	2	DE	231
Henry	21	DE	178	Hampton, William	22	NJ	12	Hargrove, Elijah	56	MD	51
Jacob	1/12	DE	70	Handson, Henry	2	DE	34	Hester	17	DE	51
Jacob	25	MD	50	Nancy	2/12	DE	34	Leah	15	DE	51
James	8	DE	70	Peregrine	28	DE	33	Leah	50	DE	51
James	47	DE	70	Prudence	4	DE	33	Thomas	23	DE	203
James	65	DE	181	Sarah	7	DE	33	Harington, Ann	39	DE	236
James B	26	DE	149	Sarah	27	DE	33	Harkins, Anna	6	DE	190
John	8	DE	9	Handy, Eben	2	DE	73	Charlotte	15	DE	190
John	23	MD	10	Edward	1	DE	249	Daniel	23	DE	190
John C	8	DE	151	Edward	2	DE	74	Fanny	4	DE	190
Jonathan	67	DE	149	Effa	13	DE	73	Lydia	42	DE	190
Jonathan M	18	DE	149	Elizabeth	21	DE	171	Thomas	12	DE	190
Liston	1	DE	149	Elizabeth	23	DE	249	Thomas	49	MD	190
Louis	2	DE	70	Isaac	44	DE	73	Harlock, Sarah	42	DE	10
Louis	31	DE	9	Jacob	16	DE	171	Harman, Eliza	9	DE	224
Lydia	60	DE	19	John	25	DE	68	Robert	15	DE	207
Mary	11	DE	181	Mary	11	DE	73	Harmen, David	4	DE	235
Mary	32	DE	70	Mary	44	DE	73	Elizabeth	28	DE	235
Mary	40	DE	181	Rebecca	5	DE	73	Emanuel	33	DE	235
Mary J	19	DE	7	Robert	7	DE	73	George	9	DE	235
Rachel	30	DE	9	Samuel	25	DE	74	James	2	DE	235
Rebecca	25	DE	151	Hanes, Lucy	15	DE	156	James	16	DE	226
Sarah	11	DE	171	Hanly, Mary	37	DE	71	John	9	DE	226

Name	Age	St	Pg
Harmen, John	18	DE	235
Joshua	3	DE	235
Mary	10	DE	226
Milly	22	DE	235
Nathaniel	6	DE	235
Nathaniel D	36	DE	235
Nisa	36	DE	238
Sarah	4	DE	235
Thomas	6	DE	235
Harmon, Bowen	17	DE	152
Eliza J	17	DE	211
Jane	17	DE	234
John	3	DE	234
Letty	43	DE	234
Mary A	15	DE	87
Nancy	10	DE	234
Purnel	24	DE	211
Sophia	13	DE	234
William	2	DE	234
Wingate	6	DE	234
Wingate	44	DE	234
Harper, Alexander	9	DE	72
Andrew N	29	DE	68
Ann	37	DE	68
Charles	2	DE	6
Charles	37	DE	6
Edward B	7	DE	6
Elizabeth	27	DE	56
Francis	12	DE	68
Francis B	41	DE	72
Franklin A	11	DE	6
George W	3/12	DE	6
Henry R	1	DE	68
John	21	DE	201
Joseph	4	DE	72
Lucretia	55	DE	201
Lydia	42	DE	72
Martha	30	MD	6
Matilda	17	DE	72
Olivia	4	DE	6
Rachel	11	DE	72
Sophia	13	DE	72
Thomas S	26	DE	56
Warren	3	DE	56
Harrington, Agnes	14	DE	218
Alexander	9	DE	218
Alexander	12	DE	238
Alphonso	3	DE	153
Andrew	3	DE	221
Ann	7	DE	238
Ann	38	DE	164
Ann E	23	DE	116
Araminta	13	DE	164
Augustus	1/12	DE	158
Caleb	5	DE	238
Catherine	4	DE	238
Charles	3	DE	139
Cornelia	4	DE	170
Darby	67	DE	241
David	31	DE	158
Eliza A	3	DE	218
Elizabeth	3	DE	158
Elizabeth	32	DE	198
Elizabeth	37	DE	146
Elizabeth	39	DE	238
Elizabeth	52	DE	158
Elizabeth	59	DE	241
Elizabeth H	6/12	DE	116
Francis	8	DE	153
Frederic	6	DE	158
George	3	DE	244
George	19	DE	198
George	58	DE	199
George P	56	DE	121
Hannah	12	DE	194
Harriet	1	DE	170
Harriet	29	DE	153
Helen	1	DE	158
Henry	17	DE	238
Henry O	31	DE	146
Hezekiah	34	DE	153
Isaac	7	DE	218
Harrington, Isaac	25	DE	116
Isaac	35	DE	153
Jacob	9	DE	170
Jacob	22	DE	212
Jacob	42	DE	164
James	7	DE	158
James	12	DE	199
James	17	DE	238
James	28	DE	218
James	34	DE	170
James H	9	DE	138
Jane	3	DE	239
Jefferson	2/12	DE	221
Jonathan	5	DE	244
Jonathan	26	DE	150
John	7	DE	138
John	29	DE	238
John	31	DE	241
John	37	DE	194
John O	1	DE	146
Joseph	8	DE	198
Joseph	25	DE	164
Joshua	11	DE	238
Juliana	25	DE	158
Latitia	41	DE	238
Lydia	7	DE	158
Lydia	10	DE	153
Margaret	10	DE	194
Martha	11/12	DE	139
Martha	15	DE	218
Mary	7	DE	194
Mary	12	DE	153
Mary	14	DE	158
Mary	25	DE	170
Mary	33	DE	218
Mary	37	DE	158
Mary	39	DE	194
Mary	71	DE	248
Mary C	15	DE	221
Mary E	3	DE	218
Mary E	14	DE	12
Mary E	18	DE	218
Mary E	19	DE	219
Mary J	6	DE	146
Mathew	6	DE	164
Milly	37	DE	238
Miriam	54	DE	199
Nancy	32	DE	138
Nathan	3	DE	198
Nathaniel	31	DE	241
Peter	7	DE	175
Peter	9	DE	238
Philip	5/12	DE	198
Richard	3	DE	158
Richard	5	DE	194
Richard J	28	DE	138
Rhoda	2	DE	139
Ruth	6	DE	198
Ruthana	13	DE	239
Sally A	37	DE	221
Samuel	5	DE	139
Samuel	5	DE	221
Samuel	9	DE	158
Samuel	14	DE	244
Samuel	21	DE	238
Samuel	35	DE	138
Samuel	41	DE	221
Samuel	47	DE	158
Sarah	5	DE	164
Sarah	14	DE	195
Sarah	17	DE	221
Sarah	21	DE	241
Sarah	39	DE	218
Sarah	46	DE	244
Sarah	71	DE	248
Sarah A	39	DE	138
Sarah E	12	DE	218
Susan	2	DE	164
Susan A	7	DE	138
Susan B	11	DE	116
Susanna	14	DE	238
Thomas	5	DE	239
Harrington, Thomas	9	DE	175
Thomas	32	DE	198
Thomas B	16	DE	221
Vincent D	8	DE	221
Warren	17	DE	238
William	3	DE	194
William	4	DE	164
William	5	DE	153
William	16	DE	239
William	23	DE	56
Wm	1	DE	218
Wm	21	DE	252
Wm	43	DE	238
Wm	60	DE	248
Wm D	37	DE	218
Harris, Albert	13	DE	244
Alexena	5	DE	268
Andrew	6	DE	235
Ann	10	DE	222
Ann	15	DE	158
Ann	35	MD	178
Anna	11/12	DE	235
Baird	14	DE	245
Bayard	14	DE	119
Benedic	35	DE	232
Benjamin	55	DE	268
Caleb	15	DE	243
Caroline	6	DE	254
Caroline	29	DE	32
Charles	11	DE	80
Charles	18	DE	202
Clara	22	DE	230
Clementina	3	DE	268
Daniel	9	DE	245
Daniel	20	DE	77
Daniel	47	DE	245
David	18	DE	235
Deborah	20	DE	80
Elija	60	DE	195
Eliza	15	DE	222
Elizabeth	23	DE	254
Elizabeth	50	DE	222
Elizabeth	50	DE	254
Ellen	7	DE	233
Ellen	21	DE	245
Ellen	35	DE	235
Elmira	9	DE	236
Emily	3	DE	236
Enoch	14	DE	254
Frederic	8	DE	268
Hannah	10	DE	80
Harriet	10	DE	254
Henrietta	48	DE	268
Henry	43	DE	235
Henry	71	DE	244
Hester	7	DE	80
Isaac	29	DE	245
James	22	DE	254
James	35	DE	254
James	86	DE	164
John	4/12	DE	230
John	2	DE	72
John	8	DE	254
John	17	DE	257
John	50	DE	72
John	55	DE	222
John W	14	DE	52
Jonathan	10	DE	235
Jonathan	18	DE	81
Joseph	4	DE	236
Joseph	20	DE	52
Joseph H	17	DE	32
Julia	1	DE	245
Julia A	27	DE	118
Latitia	6	DE	241
Latitia	56	DE	241
Lemuel	17	DE	52
Louisa	7	DE	254
Louisa	15	DE	268
Luther	2	DE	248
Lydia	45	DE	72
Malvina	15	DE	254

Name	Age	St	Pg	Name	Age	St	Pg	Name	Age	St	Pg
Harris, Malvina	15	DE	254	Hatfield, John	40	DE	73	Hays, Christopher	4	DE	64
Martha	7	DE	245	Matilda	43	DE	217	Elizabeth	14	DE	149
Martha	45	DE	245	Nisce	15	DE	217	Elizabeth	36	DE	64
Martha E	2	DE	118	Haughey, Elizabeth	43	DE	21	Emeline	16	DE	65
Martha J	22	DE	105	Hauser, John	16	DE	161	Enoch	11/12	DE	126
Mary	19	DE	222	Hawkins, Adrianna	1	DE	200	George W	4	DE	65
Mary	30	DE	236	Ann	10	DE	251	Hannah	18	DE	150
Mary	49	MD	52	Benjamin	46	MD	269	Harriet	35	DE	148
Mary E	6	DE	32	Catherine	1/12	DE	102	Henry	17	DE	164
Mary J	24	DE	52	Clayton	25	DE	153	John	10	DE	149
Milasant	60	MD	158	David	53	DE	40	John	16	DE	184
Moses	32	DE	118	Emily	5	DE	251	John	21	DE	167
Peter	18	DE	252	Ellen	60	MD	178	John	23	DE	65
Phebe	40	DE	222	Enoch	20	DE	89	John	52	DE	126
Rachel	9	DE	72	Francis	5	DE	200	John K	46	DE	65
Rebecca	7	DE	72	George	13	DE	251	John W	6	DE	126
Robert	20	DE	251	George	29	DE	200	Joshua	13	DE	66
Robert	65	DE	254	Isaac	21	DE	178	Joshua	52	MD	64
Rody	11	DE	245	James	3	DE	251	Kemp	7	DE	64
Sally	30	DE	254	James	15	DE	248	Leah	53	DE	161
Samuel	4	DE	254	James	19	DE	127	Lydia	1	DE	65
Samuel	9	DE	105	James	23	DE	17	Manlove	33	DE	81
Sarah	7	DE	254	James	47	DE	251	Margaret	10	DE	64
Sarah	8	DE	235	John	42	DE	248	Maria	30	DE	161
Sarah	10	DE	72	Margaretta	12	DE	248	Mary Ann	10	DE	50
Sarah	15	DE	178	Mary	15	DE	178	Matilda	4	DE	65
Sarah	20	DE	244	Mary	15	DE	251	Nancy	42	DE	65
Sarah	20	DE	248	Mary	36	DE	197	Rachel V	5/12	DE	65
Sarah	20	DE	270	Mary	43	DE	251	Ruth	38	DE	126
Sarah	55	DE	195	Mary E	18	DE	99	Sarah	16	DE	65
Sarah	56	DE	47	Oregon	2	DE	248	Sarah	41	DE	201
Sarah	70	DE	245	Perry	63	MD	178	Thomas	40	DE	201
Sarah A	8	DE	52	Rachel	21	DE	102	Washington	12	DE	50
Sarah D	7	DE	32	Randy	50	DE	269	Wesley	8	DE	65
Serena	9/12	DE	268	Rebecca H	54	DE	40	Wesley	35	DE	65
Sidney	46	DE	80	Sampson	60	DE	99	William	11	DE	126
Sleighter	58	DE	52	Samuel	13	DE	168	William	24	DE	201
Solomon	4/12	DE	118	Sarah E	8	DE	226	Hazard, Alexander	26	DE	166
Steven	35	DE	236	Susan	9	DE	99	Cynthia	24	DE	166
Susanna	4/12	DE	32	Susan	38	DE	248	Hazel, Benjamin A	5	DE	50
Thomas	1	DE	245	Susannah	8	DE	251	Clarence	1	DE	57
Thomas	19	DE	234	Temperance	28	DE	200	Eliza	40	DE	72
Thomas	20	MD	178	Thomas	17	DE	251	Elizabeth	48	DE	67
Thomas	52	MD	158	Victorine	7	DE	200	Frances A	18	DE	57
Walker	12	DE	77	William	29	DE	102	Francis	37	DE	48
Walker	48	DE	80	Wm	44	DE	197	Franklin B	4	DE	58
Washington	18	DE	256	Hawzer, Angelica	76	DE	174	George	9	DE	48
William	23	DE	230	Hay, George	20	DE	183	George	18	DE	58
William	29	NJ	248	Mary	60	DE	183	George	51	DE	48
Wm	21	DE	252	Thomas	24	DE	183	George N	12	DE	50
Harrison, Celia	45	DE	58	Hayden, Ann	1	DE	195	Henrietta	11	DE	48
Jacob	20	DE	59	Ann	20	DE	195	Henry K	35	DE	72
James	43	MD	58	Charles	30	DE	180	Isaac	18	DE	20
John	7	DE	212	Daniel	12	DE	195	Isaac	48	DE	164
Lydia	7	DE	58	Daniel	63	DE	195	James	2	DE	48
Harrows, John R	17	DE	221	Elizabeth	16	DE	195	James F	9	DE	50
Hart, George	3	DE	252	Elizabeth	25	MD	195	James H	6	DE	72
Joseph	35	GB	252	Isaac	2	DE	196	James P	12	DE	62
Miriam	1	DE	252	John	6	MD	180	John	24	DE	1
Sarah	32	DE	252	Joseph	1/12	DE	180	John T	7	DE	50
Harvey, Anna	16	DE	81	Julia	3	DE	180	John W	5	DE	56
Francis	7	DE	81	Mary	25	MD	180	Lydia	40	DE	50
James	12	DE	81	Peter	1	DE	180	Manlove	20	DE	56
John	26	MD	142	Peter	25	DE	196	Margaret	9	DE	72
Sarah	49	DE	255	Sarah	10	DE	196	Martha	16	DE	48
Stephen	19	DE	255	Sarah	53	DE	195	Mary	32	DE	62
Susan	29	DE	81	William	4	DE	195	Mary E	1	DE	50
Wm	17	MD	141	Hayes, Ann	40	MD	181	Mary E	9	DE	62
Harwood, Caroline	23	DE	200	Eliza	1	DE	181	Mary J	10	DE	56
James	16	DE	200	Elizabeth	4	DE	181	Matthew	24	DE	63
John	44	DE	95	Frances	12	DE	181	Matthew	63	DE	63
Louisa	16	DE	171	Harriet	35	DE	81	Melvina	31	DE	63
Margarett	44	DE	95	John	9	DE	181	Rebecca	11	DE	72
Margarett A	7	DE	95	John	40	DE	181	Rosanna	58	DE	63
Mary E	9	DE	95	Martin	6	DE	181	Samuel	11	DE	67
Miriam	11/12	DE	200	Morris	6	DE	181	Sarah	1/12	DE	48
Thomas	21	MD	171	William	16	DE	181	Sarah	38	DE	56
William R	5	DE	95	Hays, Ann	10	DE	65	Sarah E	13	DE	56
Hasting, Jane	15	DE	100	Ann	13	DE	126	Temperance	30	DE	57
Hatfield, Charles	42	DE	217	Ann	52	MD	65	William	4	DE	72
David	20	DE	90	Ann	74	MD	81	William	5	DE	48
Emeritta	7	DE	217	Basel	34	DE	201	William	19	DE	150

Name	Age	St	Pg
Hazel, William A	42	MD	50
William D	11	DE	50
William G	27	DE	57
William H	8	DE	56
William L	41	DE	62
William M	40	DE	56
Hazill, Eliza	9	DE	159
Hazzard, David	1/12	DE	26
Ezekiel	25	DE	25
James	24	DE	20
Jonathan	11	DE	182
Lydia	2	DE	26
Margaret	20	DE	26
Mary	15	DE	97
Rachel	48	DE	234
Susan	3	DE	26
William E	4	DE	29
Wm	14	DE	251
Heath, Abaritta	1	DE	81
Ann	19	DE	81
Elizabeth	5	DE	229
Francis	12	DE	69
George	23	DE	81
Harriet	9	DE	160
Maria	24	DE	160
William	1	DE	160
Heather, Michael	28	DE	104
Thomas	19	DE	114
Heaveloe, Elisha	16	DE	100
Joshua A	13	DE	101
Margarett	7	DE	100
Mary	14	DE	100
Nancy	40	DE	100
Solomon	9	DE	100
Solomon	52	DE	100
Susan	8	DE	100
Heavelow, George	11	DE	100
Heck, James	69	DE	60
Heford, John	7	DE	175
Helembolt, Edward	1	DE	69
Edward	24	PA	69
George	4	DE	69
Louisa J	22	DE	69
Helfer, Sarah	4	DE	225
Helford, Elizabeth	26	DE	156
Hezekiah	21	DE	231
Joe	27	DE	161
Hemmons, Elizabeth A	10	DE	89
Mary J S	15	DE	89
Nancy	46	DE	89
Rhoads S	49	DE	89
Sarah A	20	DE	89
Hemsley, Ann	33	DE	1
Henderson, Benjamin	58	DE	97
Elizabeth D	4/12	DE	97
James	63	DE	245
James G	48	MD	220
Mary	31	DE	97
Mary A S	29	DE	97
Ruth	68	DE	245
Susan J	22	DE	220
Hendricks, Emily A	13	MD	4
Enoch	21	DE	49
John W	18	MD	10
Hendrickson, Eliza	22	DE	55
Emma	25	DE	21
James	30	DE	21
John	21	DE	20
Joshua	33	DE	55
Hendrix, Daniel	22	DE	50
John	20	DE	53
Mary	7	DE	63
Noah	5/12	DE	63
Rebecca	40	DE	63
Henry, Adeline	8/12	DE	117
Alexander	17	DE	141
Alfred	14	DE	212
Bill	5	MD	88
Eliza A	19	DE	117
Ellen	47	DE	163
John	4	MD	262
John	25	MD	252
Henry, Joshua	60	DE	143
Lydia	45	DE	143
Marcelas	4/12	MD	88
Mariah	39	MD	88
Martha	25	MD	262
Mary A	55	DE	117
Nicholas	10	DE	231
Peter	74	DE	249
Sarah	1	DE	262
Sarah	60	DE	78
Simon	65	DE	117
William	7	DE	78
Hensley, Elizabeth	11	DE	165
Ezekiel	12	MD	10
Ezekiel	50	MD	165
Jane	45	DE	165
Mary	8	DE	165
Herbington, Alex	30	DE	230
Enoch	1	DE	230
George	3	DE	230
Rebecca	25	DE	230
Herd, Ann	12	DE	259
Ann	22	DE	185
Ann	30	DE	264
Araminta	9	DE	184
Benjamin	3	DE	258
Charles	10	DE	187
Daniel	25	DE	198
David	6/12	DE	264
Edward	17	DE	216
Eliza	4	DE	187
Eliza	5	DE	180
Eliza	37	DE	219
Elizabeth	6	DE	252
Elizabeth	9	DE	264
Elizabeth	12	DE	258
Elizabeth	16	DE	259
Elizabeth	55	DE	259
Ellen	14	DE	259
Emma	6	DE	219
Frances	8	DE	180
George	20	DE	181
George	57	DE	187
James	2/12	DE	259
James	6	DE	258
James	10	DE	180
James	38	DE	258
Jane	11	DE	185
Jesse	7	DE	187
John	16	DE	179
John	29	DE	242
Joseph	25	DE	185
Louis	1	DE	185
Margaretta	2	DE	259
Mary	2	DE	198
Mary	12	DE	264
Mary	25	DE	242
Mary	31	DE	180
Mary	31	DE	252
Mary	44	DE	258
Miriam	24	DE	198
Noah	16	DE	182
Philip	13	DE	185
Rachel	19	DE	185
Rachel	34	DE	259
Rachel	50	DE	187
Rebecca	4	DE	252
Rebecca	8	DE	258
Rebecca	10	DE	259
Sallyann	2	DE	242
Samuel	6	DE	198
Samuel	11	DE	258
Samuel	29	DE	252
Samuel	41	DE	180
Sarah	6	DE	264
Sarah	8	DE	252
Sarah	10	DE	233
Sarah	12	DE	70
Sarah	13	DE	180
Sarah	16	DE	187
Sarah	18	DE	259
Serepha	4	DE	259
Herd, Susan	18	DE	187
Thomas	3	DE	264
Thomas	18	DE	258
Thomas	24	DE	185
Thomas	40	DE	256
Thomas	68	DE	259
William	1	DE	252
William	40	DE	259
William H	3	DE	141
Herdman, Peter	52	DE	188
Susan	42	DE	188
Herdson, Eliza	40	DE	231
Henry	10	DE	231
John	14	DE	231
Mary	12	DE	231
Nathaniel	6	DE	231
Wm	48	DE	231
Hering, James	10	DE	234
Margaretta	14	DE	234
Sarah	48	DE	234
Wm	51	DE	234
Heritage, George	52	NJ	62
Harriet M	23	NJ	62
Ruth	59	NJ	62
William W	14	MD	62
Herkey, Sally Ann	20	DE	183
Herman, Robert	13	DE	207
Herring, Abner	46	DE	236
Ann	34	DE	99
Benjamin T	10	DE	99
Catherine	38	DE	236
Elizabeth A	14	DE	99
John	72	DE	242
John W	25	DE	222
Mary	13	DE	236
Mary	16	DE	124
Mary E	7	DE	99
Samuel	16	DE	236
Samuel	51	DE	99
Sarah	10	DE	236
William	16	DE	225
Wm	20	DE	238
Herrington, Abner	17	DE	136
Adam M	24	DE	113
Albert	4	DE	125
Alexander	17	DE	126
Alexine	1	DE	132
Angelina	11	DE	125
Ann J	38	DE	129
Anna A	6	DE	94
Asa	23	DE	117
Asa	59	DE	117
Benjamin	15	DE	125
Benjamin	74	DE	125
Benjamin H	9	DE	94
Benjamin Jr	29	DE	125
Benniah	14	DE	126
Charles	15	DE	129
Charles	15	DE	136
Clement	15	DE	131
Clementine	3	DE	126
Daniel	12	DE	117
Daniel	31	DE	124
David	34	DE	125
Eli	24	DE	150
Eliza	40	DE	126
Elizabeth	4	DE	132
Elizabeth	14	DE	111
Elizabeth	21	DE	144
Elizabeth	22	DE	113
Elizabeth	26	DE	113
Elizabeth	33	DE	121
Elizabeth	75	DE	113
Ellin	7	DE	117
Emaline	15	DE	110
Emeline	2	DE	126
Emeline	11	DE	118
Emeline	14	DE	87
Gartery	3/12	DE	125
George D	6	DE	129
Harriet	18	DE	129
Henry	25	DE	117

Name	Age	St	No	Name	Age	St	No	Name	Age	St	No
Herrington, Henry W	34	DE	121	Herrington, William	9	DE	117	Hickman, John	2	DE	122
Hester A	12	DE	110	William	25	DE	120	John	25	DE	241
Hetty B	4	DE	94	William	53	DE	125	John	27	DE	95
Hezekiah	1	DE	121	William H	5	DE	121	John	40	DE	148
Isaac	1	DE	144	William T	16	DE	125	Lewis	24	DE	252
Isaac	22	DE	117	Hersey, William	16	DE	194	Luff	54	DE	120
James	9	DE	126	Hess, Amanda	31	PA	207	Lydia	49	DE	120
James	16	DE	105	Anna M	9	NJ	207	Lydia M	4	DE	120
James	30	DE	113	Catherine	10	PA	210	Margaret	11	DE	122
James	49	DE	126	Charles F	4	PA	206	Margaret J	8	DE	122
Jemima	5	DE	136	David C	1	DE	206	Mary	18	DE	29
Jeremiah	44	DE	110	David C	30	NJ	206	Mary	18	DE	119
John	15	DE	22	Eliza	13	PA	210	Mary	69	DE	232
John	17	DE	117	Emely A	27	PA	206	Mary C	3/12	DE	122
John	19	DE	110	Henrietta	2/12	DE	207	Miriam	1	DE	241
John	38	DE	94	Henry B	11	NJ	207	Sally	24	DE	241
John	39	DE	88	John	43	NJ	210	Traphina	30	DE	120
John H	8	DE	125	John H	7	NJ	206	Hicks, Elizabeth	47	DE	259
John S	4	DE	124	Joseph	18	PA	210	John	14	DE	156
John S	26	DE	90	Sarah	45	DE	210	John	20	DE	258
Jonathan	1/12	DE	132	Wesley	32	NJ	207	Lydia	15	DE	258
Jonathan	13	DE	125	Hevalow, George	4	DE	175	Myers	17	DE	176
Jonathan	55	DE	131	George	41	DE	175	Nathan	60	MD	259
Littitia	15	DE	117	Mary	37	DE	175	Peter	24	DE	176
Lydia	5	DE	126	Oney	7	DE	175	Robert	30	DE	86
Lydia	7	DE	131	Heverin, Alphonso	10	DE	166	Robert	37	DE	164
Lydia	42	DE	131	Charlotte	5	DE	166	William	17	DE	158
Major	20	DE	131	Eliza	2	DE	166	Willie	23	DE	3
Marah	33	DE	110	Elizabeth	22	DE	167	Higans, George	23	DE	30
Martha	10/12	DE	126	James	7	DE	166	Higgins, Ann	4	DE	230
Martha	20	DE	125	James	35	DE	166	Ann	26	MD	230
Martha	27	DE	124	Mary	3	DE	166	David	8	DE	230
Martin W	12	DE	136	Outen	24	DE	167	Davis	14	PA	230
Mary	6	DE	124	Pauline	1/12	DE	167	James	40	DE	225
Mary	12	DE	126	Priscilla	30	NJ	166	John	2	DE	230
Mary	32	DE	94	William	8	DE	166	Joseph	10	DE	230
Mary	60	DE	117	Hevern, Mary	8	DE	12	Lydia	23	DE	230
Mary A	20	DE	121	Hevirin, Henry	27	DE	167	Higman, Harriet	23	DE	57
Mary E	2	DE	94	Hewes, Alexander	23	DE	262	Tilghman	8	PA	57
Mary E	2	DE	113	Angelina	6	DE	258	William	50	DE	57
Mary E	6	DE	121	Ann	22	DE	262	Hignut, Celia	23	DE	131
Mary E	25	DE	125	Asa	3	DE	258	Martha A	1	DE	131
Mary S	14	DE	117	Frazier	25	PA	188	Thomas J	26	DE	131
Matilda	9	DE	125	Harriet	15	DE	245	Hignutt, Emanuel	32	MD	205
Matilda	45	DE	125	James	43	MD	258	Hannah	34	NJ	205
Matilda	50	DE	117	John	8	DE	258	Hannah C	3	DE	205
Moses	7	DE	126	Kitty	60	DE	245	Hezekiah	23	MD	212
Moses	45	DE	129	Louisa	14	DE	258	Joanna	4	DE	205
Nancy A	45	DE	136	Margaret	54	DE	187	John A	1	DE	205
Nathan	18	DE	131	Margaretta	22	PA	188	William H	6	DE	205
Necy A	12	DE	120	Mary	12	DE	258	Hilford, Ellen	35	DE	173
Nimrod	37	DE	125	Rachel	38	DE	258	Harriet	12	DE	117
Peter	8	DE	121	Richard	66	DE	245	Job	74	DE	117
Peter	24	DE	144	Robert	14	DE	188	Martha	6	DE	117
Reuben	21	DE	108	Samuel	56	PA	187	Mary J	14	DE	117
Reynear W	18	DE	125	William	17	DE	258	Morgan	13	DE	117
Rhoda	9	DE	131	William	21	DE	188	Hill, Alexander	36	NJ	56
Rhoda	11	DE	121	Hickey, Eliza	43	DE	54	Amelia	10	DE	169
Rhoda	27	DE	125	Eliza	51	MD	62	Amelia	47	DE	169
Rhoda	54	DE	120	George	6	DE	51	Ann	6/12	DE	227
Richard	57	DE	138	George	7	DE	62	Ann	3	DE	174
Robert	24	DE	121	George W	12	DE	54	Ann	24	DE	56
Ruth	17	DE	117	James	2/12	DE	59	Ann E	16	DE	114
Samuel S	27	DE	117	James	9	DE	62	Anna	1/12	DE	175
Sarah	4	DE	126	Jane	7	DE	62	Araminty	11	DE	75
Sarah	14	DE	131	John	16	DE	54	Catherine	9	DE	93
Sarah	24	DE	105	John	46	DE	54	Catherine	10	DE	15
Sarah	27	DE	125	Mary	26	DE	59	David	5	DE	174
Sarah	43	DE	136	Mary E	4	DE	54	Diana	39	DE	93
Sarah	64	DE	111	Rachel	11	DE	54	Eliza	8	DE	88
Sarah A	34	DE	94	Samuel	8	DE	54	Elizabeth	2	DE	260
Sarah A	45	DE	117	Samuel	32	DE	59	Elizabeth	20	DE	15
Sarah E	7	DE	136	Sarietta	3	DE	51	Elizabeth	40	DE	1
Sarah J	16	DE	129	Thomas	6	DE	59	Ellen A	17	DE	118
Sarah M	3	DE	121	William	7	DE	54	George	8	DE	124
Solomon	2	DE	125	William	43	DE	62	George	28	DE	90
Susan	13	MD	49	William H	10	DE	54	George	38	DE	102
Susan	62	MD	49	William H	10	DE	62	George L	10/12	DE	3
Thomas	23	DE	125	Hickman, Alexander	10	DE	120	George W	8	DE	36
Waitman	37	DE	94	Ann E	5	DE	122	Harriet A	15	DE	2
William	4	DE	117	Jacob	11	DE	122	Harriet J	20	DE	118
William	4	DE	125	Jacob	43	DE	122	Henry	7	DE	93

Name	Age	St	Pg
Hill, Henry	31	DE	227
Henry F	32	DE	7
Isaac T	19	DE	2
Jacob	11	DE	34
Jacob	12	DE	169
Jacob	12	DE	179
Jacob N	52	DE	169
James	14	DE	238
James	35	DE	179
James	53	DE	3
James C	18	DE	115
James F	11	DE	118
Jane	10	DE	81
John	24	DE	83
John	28	DE	174
John	46	DE	115
John D	12	DE	115
John H	15	DE	118
John W	3	DE	2
Joshua	6	DE	115
Joshua	28	DE	114
Joshua	30	DE	124
Layfield	12	PA	219
Lydia	4	DE	124
Lydia	43	DE	124
Lydia A	9	DE	115
Margaret	27	DE	174
Margaret	57	DE	20
Margaret Ann	5	DE	3
Margarett	43	DE	88
Marietta	1	DE	7
Mary	5	DE	169
Mary	18	DE	83
Mary	19	DE	93
Mary	40	DE	3
Mary	43	DE	15
Mary A	14	DE	114
Mary A	18	DE	15
Mary J	3	DE	56
Mary J	10	DE	36
Mary W	9	DE	88
Matilda	1	DE	124
Matilda	16	DE	91
Nicy	18	DE	108
Outten	7	DE	169
Patience	58	DE	249
Peter	47	DE	93
Peter A	6/12	DE	93
Rachel A	10	DE	93
Rebecca	24	DE	169
Rebecca	24	DE	253
Rhoda	27	DE	12
Rhoda	75	DE	83
Rhody	23	DE	227
Robert	56	DE	2
Robert J	13	DE	88
Rosett	32	DE	179
Ruth	25	DE	119
Samuel	12	DE	1
Samuel J	7	DE	7
Sarah	1/12	DE	56
Sarah	8	DE	75
Sarah	20	DE	90
Sarah	22	DE	169
Sarah	40	DE	114
Sarah A	44	DE	2
Sarah E	4	DE	7
Sarah E	14	DE	115
Sarah Eliza	15	DE	1
Stephen	22	DE	151
Susan	9	DE	173
Thomas	3	DE	175
Thomas	4	DE	88
Thomas	27	DE	87
Thomas	47	DE	1
Wesley	11	DE	68
Wesley	12	DE	104
William	5	DE	88
William	42	DE	15
William	45	DE	88
William S	4	DE	93
Wm J	18	DE	219

Name	Age	St	Pg
Hillford, Theodore	9	DE	221
Hilliard, Sarah A	23	DE	13
Hillis, John A	13	DE	73
Hillman, Ann E	2	DE	93
Elizabeth	15	DE	85
Jane	25	DE	93
Thomas J	23	DE	93
Hillyard, Albus	56	DE	21
Ann Eliza	4	DE	42
Charles	12	DE	20
Charles	24	DE	4
Christopher	60	DE	32
Eliza	50	DE	163
Frances	6	DE	21
George	35	PA	20
James	9	DE	32
James H	2	DE	42
Levicy	62	DE	32
Lydia	24	DE	42
Margaret A	5	DE	20
Maria	39	DE	20
Martin	20	DE	163
Mary A	20	DE	43
Robert C	24	DE	43
Susan	19	DE	45
Thomas	29	DE	42
Willard	19	DE	5
William	27	DE	45
William	56	DE	46
Hindsley, Mary	14	DE	164
Hineman, Lavinia	20	DE	229
Hines, Elizabeth	25	DE	51
John	27	DE	51
Mary F	2/12	DE	51
Hinesley, Amos	1	DE	192
Amos	36	DE	192
Ann	15	DE	194
Charlotte	25	DE	193
Daniel	30	DE	193
Garret	6	DE	192
Henrietta	11	DE	192
Hester	30	DE	192
James	21	DE	194
John	1/12	DE	192
John	11	DE	194
John	14	DE	192
Joseph	2	DE	189
Lydia	9/12	DE	103
Mary	3	DE	192
Mary	40	DE	192
Mathew	9	DE	192
Matilda	44	MD	194
Patience	18	DE	194
Robert	53	DE	192
Sarah	19	DE	190
Sarah	73	DE	191
Hinesly, Catherine	15	DE	201
Hinsley, Amanda	9	DE	158
Mary A	12	DE	80
Sarah	9	DE	192
Susan	5	DE	48
Susan	35	DE	158
Hinson, Alexander	11	DE	62
Andrew	26	DE	165
Ann	13	DE	156
Benjamin	27	DE	156
Benjamin	54	MD	156
Betsey	3	DE	156
Charlotte	23	DE	16
Edmund	48	DE	20
Frances Ann	12	DE	20
Francis	5	DE	16
Garritt S	20	DE	99
George	12	DE	37
Hannah	2	DE	20
Hannah	15	DE	81
Harriet	20	DE	165
Henrietta	56	MD	60
Henry	17	DE	156
James H	17	DE	60
John	19	DE	141
Lacretia	30	DE	19

Name	Age	St	Pg
Hinson, Mary	8	DE	20
Mary E	2/12	DE	19
Peter	50	DE	60
Rachel	1	DE	156
Rachel	6	DE	20
Rachel	12	DE	156
Rachel	35	DE	156
Rebecca	5	DE	20
Rebecca	23	DE	156
Rebecca	32	DE	20
Rosanna	21	DE	156
Salinda	1/12	DE	165
Samuel	16	DE	156
Sarah	2/12	DE	156
Sarah E	3	DE	16
Thomas	36	DE	19
William	9	DE	156
Hirons, Celia	64	DE	35
Elizabeth	24	DE	79
Hannah A	12	DE	214
Joseph	2	DE	79
Margaret	38	MD	214
Mariam E	18	DE	214
Mary E J	3/12	DE	215
Robert L	20	DE	214
Samuel	12	DE	79
Samuel	21	DE	60
William	10	DE	214
William	15	DE	79
William	40	DE	80
William	51	DE	214
Hitch, Specher	22	DE	108
Hitchens, Caroline	5	DE	112
Cezar	15	DE	88
Cezar	17	DE	88
Daniel	10	DE	157
David	6	DE	112
James A	10	DE	172
John A J	21	DE	113
Peter	50	DE	112
Sarah	50	DE	112
Hivilow, Charles	3	DE	101
Hobbs, Elizabeth	45	MD	140
James	12	MD	140
Lydia A	7	MD	140
Nancy	2	DE	140
Nathan	4	MD	140
Mary H	14	MD	140
Peter	9	MD	140
Peter	50	MD	140
Thomas H	17	DE	131
Hobson, Ann	41	MD	201
Deborah	10	DE	153
James	5	DE	153
James	6	DE	201
John	23	DE	166
John	43	DE	19
Joseph	1	DE	153
Lavicy	9	DE	19
Lucinda	7	DE	153
Lucinda	14	DE	19
Martha	10	DE	201
Martha	19	DE	166
Sally Ann	45	DE	153
Sarah	15	DE	153
Thomas	17	DE	167
Thomas	18	DE	67
Thomas	49	DE	153
Wm	21	DE	167
Wm	21	DE	200
Wm	59	DE	201
Hodge, Catherine	16	DE	166
Isaac	17	DE	80
John	40	DE	81
Joshua	7	DE	170
Hodgson, Sina	67	DE	281
Hoffecker, Albert T	9	DE	14
Anna	2	DE	169
Araminty	4	DE	8
Benjamin	19	DE	8
Caroline	6/12	DE	8
Castilia	9	DE	7

Name	Age	St	No.	Name	Age	St	No.	Name	Age	St	No.
Hoffecker, Castilia	59	DE	6	Holding, James R	44	MD	21	Honey, Mary J	12	DE	64
Catherine	7	DE	176	Lucy Ann	1	DE	21	Sarah A	10	DE	64
Catherine	11	DE	7	Rebecca	30	MD	21	Thomas	18	DE	64
Daniel C	35	DE	169	Samuel A	35	MD	4	Wm	17	DE	184
Edwin	6	DE	169	Sarah E	3	DE	48	Hong, Loadman	15	DE	194
Eliza	9/12	DE	176	Susanna	3	DE	48	Mary	11	DE	194
Eliza	40	DE	176	William H	39	DE	48	Hood, Manuel	52	DE	171
Elizabeth	16	DE	7	William T	9	DE	21	Mary	53	MD	171
Elizabeth	39	DE	7	Holeger, Hetty	20	DE	116	Hook, James	69	DE	61
Elmira	8	DE	169	Holiday, James	6	DE	46	Hooper, Anna	3	DE	17
Emily	4	DE	7	Jane	46	DE	46	Esther	58	DE	85
Emily H	20	DE	30	Martha	13	DE	46	Foster	40	MD	17
Francis	13	DE	169	Thomas	46	MD	46	George	16	MD	17
Henry	14	DE	176	Holingsworth, Ferdinand	35	DE	206	James	11	VA	17
Henry T	45	DE	6	Mary A	35	DE	206	John	13	MD	17
Hiram	11	DE	176	Holland, Amelia	13	DE	41	Mary	1	DE	17
James	9/12	DE	176	Ann	20	DE	106	Mary	27	PA	9
James	16	DE	30	Charlotta A	9	DE	49	Mary E	36	MD	17
James	21	DE	7	Elizabeth	13	DE	106	William	5	PA	17
James	29	DE	8	George	27	MD	129	Hopkins, Abraham	25	DE	57
Jessefely	24	DE	8	Harriet	16	DE	106	Ann	18	DE	20
John H	22	DE	30	Hemseley	47	MD	49	Benjamin	20	DE	240
John S	16	DE	14	James	40	DE	106	Bennett	2	DE	145
Joseph	11	DE	169	Lydia	51	DE	147	Charles	1	DE	154
Joseph	18	DE	30	Mark	34	DE	106	Charles	18	DE	232
Joseph	48	DE	15	Mary	19	DE	147	Charles	32	DE	154
Joseph	65	DE	30	Mary	22	DE	106	Curtis	65	DE	145
Joseph B	12	DE	14	Mary E	14	DE	49	Debora	11	DE	240
Joseph S	9	DE	35	Ruth	46	DE	49	Eliza	45	DE	20
Louis	18	DE	176	Sarah	11	DE	106	Elizabeth	7	DE	122
Mary	24	DE	14	William	11	DE	49	Ellen	4	DE	145
Philip	2	DE	176	Hollet, Eliza Jane	2	DE	51	George	3	DE	139
Philip	41	DE	176	Joseph H	17	DE	48	Henry	9	DE	132
Presley	49	DE	7	Sarah	39	DE	51	Henry	11	DE	166
Rachel	13	DE	30	Sarah E	19	DE	48	Henry	15	DE	146
Rachel H	41	DE	30	Solomon	38	DE	51	Hester A R	23	DE	128
Robert D	20	DE	47	Hollice, Charles	17	DE	164	Hooper B	35	DE	145
Sarah	18	DE	7	Holliday, Angeline	3	DE	227	James	2	DE	132
Sarah	32	DE	169	Eliza	20	DE	227	James	25	DE	240
Sarah E	21	DE	14	James	24	DE	32	James	35	DE	132
Seba	47	DE	14	Wm	25	MD	227	James	59	DE	240
Susan A	10/12	DE	7	Holliger, Eliza	22	DE	153	Jane	30	DE	145
William	23	DE	8	Hollingsworth, James	39	DE	77	John	3	DE	154
William A	24	DE	7	Lourena	22	DE	253	John	6	DE	46
Hogans, Hannah	17	DE	215	Prudence	38	DE	77	John	39	DE	122
Hoge, Margaret	11	DE	160	Hollis, Caroline	2	DE	137	John	50	DE	20
Hogins, Aner J	4	DE	215	Charles	75	DE	70	John	57	DE	144
Daniel	35	DE	215	Charles W	15	DE	104	John Jr	36	DE	147
Elizabeth	12	DE	229	Henry	40	DE	149	John W	1	DE	128
Fence	50	MD	229	James W	12	DE	136	John W	11	DE	20
Jacob	4	DE	229	John	40	DE	104	Joseph H	13	DE	20
Jacob	12	DE	216	John H	13	DE	74	Lavinia	12	DE	122
Letty	30	DE	215	John M	5	DE	104	Margeanna	5	DE	89
Mahala	2	DE	215	Lavinia	32	DE	136	Mary	17	DE	240
Manuel	1	DE	215	Margaret E	11	DE	136	Mary	25	DE	145
Mary	13	DE	215	Margaret P	10	DE	104	Mary	27	DE	154
Miriam	4	DE	229	Martha J	7	DE	137	Mary	36	DE	122
Nathaniel	7	DE	229	Mary	40	DE	148	Mary	49	DE	240
Sarah	12	DE	242	Mary E	2	DE	104	Mary A	1	DE	139
Holdan, Ann	2	DE	240	Robert H	17	DE	104	Mary E	2/12	DE	122
Edmund	10	DE	240	Sarah A	12	DE	104	Michael T	7	DE	20
Eliza	33	DE	240	Sarah W	40	DE	104	Nancy	32	DE	145
Emeline	8	DE	240	William H	9	DE	136	Peter	10	DE	105
Mary	4	DE	240	Holstein, John	49	MD	245	Robert	38	DE	27
Noah	37	DE	240	Holsten, Clement	2	DE	231	Robinson	34	DE	139
Sarah	12	DE	240	Elizabeth	20	DE	248	Ruth	73	DE	234
William	14	DE	240	John	16	DE	227	Samuel	11	DE	122
Holden, Alexander	20	DE	265	Mary	20	DE	231	Samuel	15	DE	240
Andrew	13	DE	265	Ruthann	2/12	DE	249	Samuel	40	DE	139
Charles	50	DE	265	Wm	27	DE	231	Sarah	29	DE	132
Ellen	3	DE	265	Holston, Caleb	1	DE	81	Sarah	34	DE	145
Susan	3/12	DE	265	James	47	DE	82	Sarah	62	DE	139
Wesley	10	DE	265	Matilda	25	PA	81	Sarah	68	DE	145
William	6	DE	265	Thomas	26	MD	80	Sarah A	1	DE	89
Holding, Ann C	36	DE	48	Thomas	52	DE	226	Sarah E	5	DE	20
Anna	1	DE	48	Holt, Benjamin	9	DE	2	Solomon	77	DE	140
Catherine	13	DE	159	Honey, Ann	34	DE	64	Susan A	22	DE	139
Catherine C	15	DE	48	Eliza P	6	DE	64	Thomas	9	DE	110
Ebenezer	26	DE	1	James	9	DE	64	Vermadella	8/12	DE	20
George P	11	DE	48	Joseph	6	DE	197	Waitman	4	DE	132
Henrietta	22	DE	1	Leadman	59	MD	64	Waitman	26	DE	128
Henrietta D	9	DE	48					Waitman	69	DE	139

Name	Age	St	No
Hopkins, Willard	7	DE	145
William	5	DE	139
William	7	DE	132
William	14	DE	122
William	36	DE	145
William H	25	DE	150
William N	30	DE	145
Zebulon	21	DE	144
Hopper, Shadrack	67	MD	72
Hord, George	93	MD	65
Houlston, Ann E	15	DE	83
James	41	DE	83
Sarah	39	DE	83
William N	10	DE	83
Houston, Charles C	10	DE	109
Eliza	26	DE	99
Hetty	56	DE	104
Joseph	49	DE	104
Joseph W	15	DE	109
Liston A	54	DE	109
Susan	5/12	DE	99
William	22	DE	99
Williamina	17	DE	109
Hovington, Alexander	16	DE	167
Ann	16	DE	93
George	14	DE	167
George	52	DE	109
George Sr	90	DE	109
Hannah	70	DE	109
Harriet	7	DE	245
James	19	DE	240
Major	10	DE	114
Major	44	DE	93
Nathan	72	DE	91
Philis	64	DE	91
Susan	14	DE	109
William P	5/12	DE	93
Zilla	46	DE	93
Howard, Absalom	28	DE	66
Ann	50	DE	66
Cornelia	8	DE	66
Levice	16	DE	171
Margaret	51	DE	171
Mary	11	DE	66
Sarah	3	DE	68
Stephen	60	DE	171
William	20	DE	66
Howe, Bolivar	26	MA	166
Howel, Ruben	50	DE	235
Howell, Elizabeth	27	NJ	48
Thomas H	59	DE	229
William	33	DE	48
Hoxster, Aner	40	DE	133
Benjamin	13	DE	133
Benjamin	14	DE	128
David	12	DE	133
Elijah	18	DE	128
Elijah	19	DE	133
Elizabeth	2	DE	133
Henry	14	DE	123
Ivan	21	DE	133
John	19	DE	123
John	20	DE	133
John	44	DE	133
Louisa	1/12	DE	133
Margaret E	10	DE	133
Ruth A	9	DE	133
Sab	23	DE	236
Sabe	23	DE	133
Sarah	5	DE	133
Hoxter, Emily	17	DE	237
Hubbard, Benjamin	26	MD	192
Edward	24	MD	192
Enolds	1	DE	135
Eugene	2	MD	146
James	8	DE	115
James	10	DE	135
John W	5	DE	135
John W	40	DE	135
Julia A	30	DE	135
Lydia	12	DE	135
Mary	31	MD	146
Hubbard, Mary	51	MD	192
Mary A	30	DE	115
Mary J	7	DE	135
Newton	57	MD	192
Peter	3	DE	115
Peter	45	DE	115
Sarah A	14	DE	135
Thomas	23	MD	192
Hudson, Alice	8	DE	94
Amy	26	DE	49
Ann	26	DE	94
Ann E	15	DE	85
Asa	24	DE	83
Charles H	16	DE	46
Delia	53	DE	49
Delia A	21	DE	49
Dennis	49	DE	34
Edward	35	DE	114
Elizabeth	12	DE	34
Elizabeth	60	DE	111
George	22	DE	110
George W	3	DE	14
James	10	DE	94
Henry	28	DE	49
Henry	68	DE	85
Henry J M	8	DE	83
Isaac	2	DE	49
Isaac	23	DE	49
Isaac	71	DE	49
James	21	DE	111
James	23	DE	101
James	46	DE	34
John	6	DE	14
John	43	DE	33
Joseph	6	DE	34
Joseph	12	DE	108
Joseph	46	DE	34
Martha	2	DE	34
Mary	35	MD	33
Mary J	17	DE	111
Rachel E	16	DE	101
Rebecca	10	DE	34
Rhoda	10	DE	85
Ruth	30	DE	111
Samuel	4/12	DE	34
Sarah	16	DE	34
Sarah	50	DE	85
Susan	33	MD	14
Thomas P	22	DE	85
William	8	DE	134
William	14	DE	34
William H	3/12	DE	49
Huffington, Ann	8	DE	189
George	12	DE	81
Henrietta	40	DE	37
Isaac	12	DE	212
Jacob	12	DE	246
Jesse S	33	DE	37
Malvina	14	DE	200
Maria	18	DE	78
Mariah	21	DE	76
Rebecca	25	DE	75
Samuel	12	DE	80
Thomas E	3	DE	37
William	35	DE	75
William F	6	DE	37
Hugg, Benjamin	61	DE	46
Hughes, Cornelia	27	DE	91
Ebenezer	18	DE	123
Elizabeth	15	DE	123
Elizabeth	47	DE	123
Ellen	4	DE	123
Frazier	24	PA	150
Isaiah	15	DE	31
James	20	DE	123
John	15	DE	25
Rachel	10	DE	123
Samuel	12	DE	123
Samuel	53	MD	123
Susan	15	DE	123
Hull, Eben	14	DE	8
Enoch	44	DE	17
Hull, Henry	12	DE	34
Julia	21	DE	17
Martha	7	DE	17
Rebecca	34	DE	44
Susan	4	DE	17
William	16	DE	24
Hume, Asbury	9	DE	169
Caroline	2	DE	169
Elizabeth	31	DE	228
Ezekiel	32	DE	169
Sarah	7	DE	169
Tamar	25	DE	169
Humphreys, Alexandr	25	DE	18
Elizabeth	21	DE	18
Joseph	11	DE	18
Joseph	63	DE	18
Leah	56	DE	18
Martha E	16	DE	18
Mary P	3	DE	18
Rebecca	26	DE	18
Stephen	19	DE	18
Humphries, Eliza	3	DE	152
Humphris, Joshua	6	DE	105
Hunt, Robert	50	PA	265
Hunter, Samuel	5	TX	89
Sophia	40	CN	89
Hurley, Ann	60	DE	222
George W	25	DE	84
Martha	19	DE	84
Hurlock, Alice S	4	DE	49
Ann	64	MD	49
Benjamin P	24	DE	49
Edna L	18	MD	49
Elizabeth	29	MD	49
Henrietta M	30	DE	49
Jacob	69	DE	49
John A	22	MD	49
John D	24	MD	11
John S	30	MD	49
Jonathan	8	MD	49
Mary	36	DE	49
Matilda	20	DE	11
Nicey	8	DE	42
Priscilla	34	DE	49
Samuel R	1	DE	49
Sarah	42	DE	49
Vincent	20	DE	54
Wilhelmore	20	MD	49
William A	9/12	DE	11
Hurry, William	60	?	142
Hurst, Henry	3	DE	86
Husband, Ann	35	DE	178
Elizabeth	11	DE	178
Isaach	35	DE	178
John	13	DE	178
Sarah	16	DE	178
Husbands, Adaline	16	DE	69
Ann	43	MD	69
Benjamin	15	DE	69
Benjamin	60	DE	69
Catharine	3	DE	78
John	10	DE	69
John	56	DE	69
John	82	DE	72
Mary Ann	48	DE	69
Mary Eliza	18	DE	69
Rachel	2	DE	69
William	34	DE	78
Huston, Ann	50	PA	110
Liston A	20	DE	110
Hut, Joseph	12	DE	180
Hutcheson, John	5/12	DE	93
Joseph	6	DE	93
Sarah A	17	DE	100
Sina	33	DE	93
Benjamin	9	DE	93
Hutchins, Ann	39	DE	50
Charlotte	44	DE	192
Daniel	1	DE	192
James	3	DE	192
John	12	DE	50
John	56	DE	192

Name	Age	St	Pg
Hutchins, Louisa	13	DE	192
Lydia	25	DE	251
Nathan	9	DE	192
Nathaniel	1	DE	50
Nathaniel	42	DE	50
Rebecca	10	DE	192
Samuel	15	DE	50
Sarah	5	DE	192
William	16	DE	50
William	20	DE	192
Hutchinson, Clara	5	DE	165
Edward	11	DE	165
Elenora	3/12	DE	81
Eliza	5	DE	185
Eliza	36	DE	185
Ellen	3	DE	185
Estelle	8	DE	165
Francis	5	DE	81
Hannah	35	DE	165
Henry	4/12	DE	185
John	38	DE	185
Louisa	12	DE	185
Lydia	14	DE	185
Martina	3	DE	81
Mary	9	DE	185
Matthew	33	DE	81
Rachel	26	DE	81
Peter	15	DE	212
William	2	DE	165
William T	7	DE	81
Wm	38	DE	165
Hutt, Levinia	9	DE	58
Margaret	28	DE	7
Presley	40	DE	7
Richard	7	DE	42
Richard	45	DE	42
Sarah A	5	DE	42
Hynson, George	6	DE	14
Rachel	8	DE	14
Hyrons, Levick	20	DE	180
Hyser, John W	31	DE	5
Irish, Matty	22	IE	224
Irons, Mary	52	DE	185
Sarah	70	DE	164
Thomas	11	DE	185
Timothy	45	DE	185
Irvin, Isabella	10	IE	159
Island, Ann	20	DE	40
Ann	23	DE	50
Henry	1	DE	40
John	25	DE	40
John	27	DE	50
Philip	1	DE	50
Jack, Elizabeth	10	DE	172
Frank	3	DE	172
Matilda	6	DE	172
Sarah	5	DE	172
Sarah J	4	DE	206
Sina	35	DE	172
Susan	6/12	DE	172
Tilman	35	DE	172
Timothy	8	DE	172
Jackson, Alexander	18	DE	66
Alexander	20	DE	46
Alexander	22	DE	248
Alexander	52	DE	248
Andrew	5	DE	196
Andrew	18	DE	156
Angelica	19	DE	177
Ann	30	DE	237
Ann E	10	MD	22
Ann E	14	DE	62
Antony	30	DE	213
Benjamin	7/12	DE	208
Bersheba	29	DE	199
Catherine	11	MD	229
Catherine	13	DE	48
Charles	2	DE	201
Charles	3	DE	209
Daniel	5	DE	62
Jackson, Daniel	12	DE	66
Daniel	26	DE	210
Daniel	41	DE	62
Daniel	62	DE	210
Edward	48	MD	229
Eliza	8	DE	199
Eliza	28	DE	29
Eliza	40	DE	248
Elizabeth	8	DE	196
Elizabeth	11	DE	248
Elizabeth	12	DE	54
Elizabeth	19	DE	22
Elizabeth	35	DE	84
Emeline	4	DE	222
Emily	8	DE	248
Francis	2	DE	237
Garrett	6	DE	208
George	14	DE	49
Harriet	41	MD	3
Henrietta	35	DE	62
Henry	20	DE	6
Hetty	6/12	DE	222
Indiana E	15	MD	22
Irene	1	DE	54
Jacob	40	DE	41
James	3	DE	62
James	6	DE	237
James	7	DE	66
James	7	DE	185
James	10	DE	208
James	11	DE	210
James	17	DE	248
James	23	DE	249
James	49	DE	208
James	60	DE	199
Jane	21	DE	254
Joel P	5	DE	22
John	9	DE	185
John	10	DE	62
John	14	DE	168
John	18	DE	208
John	32	DE	29
John	38	DE	237
John	53	MD	229
John	70	DE	66
John A	50	DE	54
John F	1	DE	29
John H	2	DE	209
John H	36	DE	209
John W	4	DE	145
Jonathan	4	DE	199
Jonathan	20	DE	20
Jonathan	56	DE	206
Joseph	13	DE	41
Lambert	33	MD	26
Lewis	16	DE	164
Mahala	13	DE	208
Margaret	2	DE	196
Margaret	6	DE	62
Maria	28	DE	145
Martha	10	DE	29
Martha	80	MD	206
Martha E	13	MD	22
Mary	6	DE	196
Mary	8	DE	237
Mary	10	DE	66
Mary	15	DE	41
Mary	16	DE	208
Mary	18	DE	248
Mary	24	DE	201
Mary A	31	DE	54
Mary E	37	DE	209
Mathew	5	DE	217
McElroy	5/12	DE	210
Monroe	6	MD	229
Nancy	3	DE	120
Nancy	40	DE	186
Peter	59	DE	22
Rebecca	12	DE	176
Rebecca	17	DE	188
Rebecca	18	MD	229
Rebecca	23	DE	229
Jackson, Robert	5	DE	29
Robert	26	DE	201
Samuel	20	DE	216
Samuel	24	DE	21
Samuel	60	DE	120
Sarah	2	DE	248
Sarah	9	DE	29
Sarah	19	MD	229
Sarah	35	DE	222
Sarah	37	DE	208
Sarah	48	DE	66
Sarah A	2	DE	22
Sarah A	35	MD	22
Sarah E	1/12	DE	145
Stephen	32	DE	254
Susan	16	DE	183
Temperance	5	DE	201
Thomas	1	DE	254
Thomas	12	DE	185
Thomas	18	DE	21
Thomas	21	DE	248
Thomas	40	MD	22
Thomas M	56	MD	84
Unity	5	DE	209
Unity	61	DE	210
Unity	73	DE	228
Warner	19	DE	120
William	1/12	DE	199
William	4	DE	237
William	9	DE	222
William	40	DE	222
William D	15	DE	145
Willis	40	DE	145
Wm	9	DE	154
Wm	32	MD	196
Wm H	4	DE	208
Jacobs, Aaron M	8	DE	92
Alfred	3	DE	115
Alice	54	DE	126
Ann E	9	DE	115
Aquila	2	DE	174
Benjamin	3/12	DE	63
Cato	40	DE	163
David	7	DE	174
E	15	DE	92
Eli	13	DE	62
Elijah	10/12	DE	126
Eliza	5	DE	174
Elizabeth	9	DE	62
Elizabeth	19	MD	87
Elizabeth	20	DE	126
Elizabeth	30	DE	48
Elizabeth	34	DE	174
Elizabeth	40	DE	223
Ellen	30	DE	163
Ellin	22	DE	97
Ennold S	50	DE	92
Enoch	4	DE	49
Frances	16	DE	174
George	12	DE	126
Henrietta	19	MD	142
Henry	7	DE	62
Henry	12	DE	174
Hester A	16	DE	126
Isaac	19	DE	175
Jacob	15	DE	62
James	1	DE	49
James	9	DE	174
James H	12	DE	115
Jane	17	DE	126
John	9	DE	126
John B	5	DE	115
Lot	10	DE	175
Louisa	38	DE	115
Maria	44	DE	175
Mary	19	DE	94
Mary	21	DE	63
Merton	16	DE	64
Morten	47	DE	115
Richard	35	DE	174
Sarah	40	DE	92
Sina	19	DE	90

Name	Age	State	No.	Name	Age	State	No.	Name	Age	State	No.
Jacobs, Smith	22	DE	126	Jarvis, John	27	DE	223	Jessups, Mary A	12	DE	145
Stokely M	6	DE	92	John H	8	DE	120	Serina	18	DE	145
Thomas	56	DE	126	John W	15	DE	120	Solomon	2	DE	145
William	23	DE	49	Joseph	14	DE	120	Solomon	50	DE	145
William	39	DE	63	Joseph	28	DE	261	Temperance	2	DE	145
William A	10	DE	115	Mary	57	DE	261	Temperance	49	DE	145
Jakes, John	17	DE	224	Mary	60	DE	265	Jester, Aaron	8	DE	104
Nancy	57	DE	248	Mary A	11	DE	122	Albert	3	DE	102
Thomas	47	DE	248	Mary E	1	DE	120	Alexander	35	DE	171
James, Alexander	13	DE	38	Philemon	10	DE	122	Angelina	12	DE	133
Ann	2	DE	202	Susan	35	DE	122	Ann	23	DE	102
Caroline	6	DE	41	Susanna	4/12	DE	122	Ann	31	DE	120
Elizabeth	34	DE	41	Thomas	12	DE	120	Ann	40	DE	102
Hannah	26	PA	211	William R	4/12	DE	122	Ann M	36	DE	144
Harriet	25	DE	190	Jefferies, Rachel	40	MD	21	Caleb C	19	DE	119
Jacob	4	DE	41	Jefferson, Benjamin	48	DE	19	Caroline	8	DE	102
John	6/12	DE	41	Caroline	16	DE	209	Charles	7	DE	171
Major	14	DE	71	Charles H	3	DE	47	Charles	13	DE	103
Najor	45	DE	41	Edward	3	DE	10	Charles	40	DE	101
Rachel	21	DE	202	Elihu	39	DE	60	Debby	16	DE	157
Thomas	40	NJ	211	Eliza Ann	34	DE	60	Deborah	4	DE	106
William	3	DE	41	Elmira	29	DE	10	Deborah	66	MD	144
Jarman, Elizabeth	33	DE	188	Emily R	2	DE	60	Edward	10	DE	155
Harriet	2	DE	188	Ephraim	6	DE	60	Eli	59	DE	102
John	7	DE	188	Ephraim	32	DE	47	Eliza	44	DE	54
Martha	6	DE	188	George	1	DE	19	Elizabeth	17	DE	148
Mary	12	DE	188	George	10	DE	22	Elizabeth	27	DE	102
Robert	35	MD	252	Henry	17	DE	4	Elizabeth	70	DE	161
Samuel	10	DE	188	Henry	35	DE	21	Elizabeth A	26	DE	207
Sarah	17	DE	193	James	11	DE	19	Emeline	4	DE	104
Susan	8/12	DE	188	John	1/12	DE	60	George	8/12	DE	102
Thomas	36	DE	188	John R	5/12	DE	47	Isaac	14	DE	106
Jarrell, Alexander	1	DE	52	Latetia	4	DE	60	Isaac	18	DE	144
Alexander	8	MD	53	Lavenia	40	DE	19	Isaac	37	DE	171
Debora	11	DE	269	Martha	26	DE	21	Isaac	41	DE	102
Eliza	15	DE	244	Mary A	9	DE	19	Isaac	59	DE	144
Elizabeth	5	DE	160	Rachel	12	DE	227	Isabel	20	DE	144
Elizabeth	29	DE	265	Rebecca L	56	DE	5	James	4	DE	171
Elizabeth	30	DE	244	Ruth H	32	NJ	47	James	10	DE	133
Elizabeth	35	DE	54	Samuel	12	DE	60	James	12	DE	120
Emeline	10	DE	253	Samuel	32	DE	85	James	24	MD	224
Ezekiel	20	DE	265	Susan	9	DE	60	James	29	DE	207
George	11	DE	160	Thomas	1	DE	10	James	49	DE	242
James	7	DE	244	Thomas E	31	DE	10	James H	1	DE	207
James	8	DE	253	Thomas M	5/12	DE	47	Jane	6	DE	104
James	10	DE	247	William T	6	DE	19	John	2	DE	142
Jeremiah	8	DE	265	Jenkins, Andrew	4	DE	232	John	7	DE	120
Jeremiah	34	DE	253	Ann	33	DE	226	John	45	DE	37
John	10	DE	253	Caleb	69	DE	249	John M	34	DE	22
John	16	DE	247	Charlotte	18	DE	25	John R	53	DE	218
John	44	DE	247	Elizabeth	12	DE	202	John S	24	DE	116
Jonathan	39	DE	160	Elizabeth	15	DE	227	John T	44	DE	106
Joseph	9	DE	244	Ellwood	3	DE	227	Jonathan	18	DE	101
Lorenzo	20	DE	247	Ezekiel	47	DE	227	Jonathan	19	DE	168
Mahala	49	DE	182	Jabez	18	DE	227	Jonathan	50	DE	103
Margaret	3	DE	160	Jabez	23	DE	226	Joseph	14	DE	242
Margaret	34	DE	160	Jabez	57	DE	226	Joseph	53	DE	102
Martha	15	DE	247	Jacob	30	DE	25	Joshua	5	DE	102
Martha	32	DE	3	John	15	DE	226	Latitia	8	DE	133
Mary	1	DE	265	Joseph	1	DE	25	Lydia	17	DE	30
Mary	8	DE	247	Joseph	6	DE	227	Manlove	11	DE	144
Mary	10	DE	160	Mary	20	DE	226	Mark A	6	DE	133
Mary	69	DE	234	Patience	45	DE	226	Martha	18	DE	104
Sally Ann	8	DE	160	Patience	45	DE	227	Mary	2	DE	133
Sarah	4	DE	244	Rachel	12	DE	233	Mary	7	DE	170
Sarah	11	DE	265	Ruth	66	DE	226	Mary	20	DE	102
Sarah	13	DE	247	Samuel	13	DE	227	Mary	32	DE	168
Sarah	38	DE	253	Vina	90	DE	178	Mary	34	DE	106
Sarah	42	DE	247	Wm	38	DE	231	Mary	35	DE	142
Solomon	6	DE	253	Jerman, Eli	37	DE	181	Mary	37	DE	242
Thomas	4	DE	247	Eliza	36	DE	17	Mary	41	DE	144
William	4	DE	265	John	11	DE	17	Mary	50	DE	102
William	12	DE	244	Joshua	8	DE	17	Mary	60	DE	227
William	32	DE	265	Martha	1	DE	182	Mary A	6	DE	103
Wilmina	1	DE	247	Mary	16	DE	17	Mary E	4	DE	119
Wm	44	DE	244	Noble T	46	DE	17	Mary E	10	DE	106
Jarvis, Aner	6	DE	120	Rebecca	49	DE	182	Mary E	23	DE	144
Caleb	32	DE	120	Jessups, Abigail	6	DE	145	Mary J	5	DE	107
Cornelius	7	DE	132	Abner	13	DE	128	Mary J	24	DE	116
Elizabeth	33	DE	120	Britania	9	DE	145	Mary S	47	DE	119
George	6	DE	262	Elizabeth	25	DE	145	Matilda	16	DE	242
James	27	DE	261	John	16	DE	145	Molly	9	DE	171

Name	Age	State	Page	Name	Age	State	Page	Name	Age	State	Page
Jester, Molly	45	MD	166	Johnson, Eliza	26	DE	191	Johnson, Mary	32	DE	151
Rachel	48	DE	103	Eliza	32	DE	161	Mary	67	DE	182
Rachel	70	DE	224	Eliza	70	NY	8	Mary E	21	DE	112
Rachel C	15	DE	106	Eliza A	6	DE	216	Mary J	22	DE	84
Rebecca	1	DE	106	Eliza A	24	DE	151	Mary J	22	DE	96
Robert	27	DE	227	Eliza J	12	DE	149	Mitchell	35	DE	46
Robert J	1	DE	103	Elizabeth	2/12	DE	249	Nancy	11	DE	108
Ruth A	14	DE	119	Elizabeth	8/12	DE	150	Nancy	50	DE	151
Sarah	38	DE	133	Elizabeth	1	DE	84	Nathan	52	DE	171
Sarah	44	DE	22	Elizabeth	6	DE	239	Nathaniel B	21	DE	112
Sarah	54	DE	144	Elizabeth	27	DE	182	Nicy	19	DE	151
Sarah A	12	DE	106	Elizabeth	33	DE	46	Noah	6	DE	30
Sarah E	9	DE	103	Elizabeth	40	DE	149	Permelia A	21	DE	112
Sarah F	4	DE	142	Elizabeth	78	DE	150	Perry	64	DE	205
Sina	4	DE	103	Emely	3	DE	253	Perry C	27	DE	96
Sina E	8	DE	106	Emma	2	DE	24	Philip	6	DE	19
Susan	6	DE	106	Enoch	5	DE	253	Philip	42	DE	19
Thomas	2	DE	120	Frances	1	DE	195	Prisse	35	DE	191
Thomas	39	MD	133	Francis A	17	DE	126	Purnel	16	DE	149
Thomas	46	DE	54	George	8/12	DE	149	Rachel	40	MD	19
Thomas A	3	DE	103	George	1	DE	216	Rachel	40	DE	88
Thomas H	39	DE	120	George	1	DE	233	Rebecca	1/12	DE	216
William	9	DE	120	George	19	DE	108	Rebecca	11	DE	177
William	15	DE	133	George	23	DE	182	Rebecca	37	DE	217
William	22	DE	84	George	26	DE	210	Reuben	14	DE	234
William	22	DE	102	George	32	DE	216	Rhoda A	4	DE	151
William	25	DE	104	Hannah	8	DE	21	Rhody	4	DE	177
William A	4	DE	207	Harriet	13	DE	68	Robert	1/12	DE	151
William E	21	DE	119	Henry	5	DE	230	Robert	31	DE	151
William M	47	DE	119	Henry	8	DE	19	Rosanna	50	DE	234
Jewell, John	21	?	143	Henry	8	DE	216	Ruben	60	DE	234
Margaret	33	DE	248	Henry	17	DE	247	Ruth	21	DE	21
Margaret	43	DE	220	Henry	21	DE	182	Ruth	25	DE	238
Margaret A	17	DE	146	Henry	65	DE	40	Sally	8	DE	241
Mary	16	DE	148	Henry R	2	DE	150	Samuel	3	DE	68
Johns, Enos	5	DE	195	Hester	23	DE	249	Samuel	4	DE	205
George	10	DE	195	Hester	55	DE	40	Samuel	8	DE	73
James	41	DE	195	Hester	73	DE	46	Samuel	40	DE	30
Joseph	6	DE	195	Hester A	6	DE	84	Sarah	7	DE	32
Margaret	3	DE	195	Isaac	7	DE	53	Sarah	12	DE	233
Maria	17	DE	171	Isaac	42	DE	177	Sarah A	27	DE	32
Sarah	32	DE	195	James	6	DE	191	Sarah C	1	DE	96
Thomas	11	DE	195	James	8	DE	233	Sarah E	8/12	DE	210
William	14	DE	195	James	14	MD	233	Shadrack	25	DE	252
Johnson, Adaline	11	DE	205	James	18	DE	234	Susan	2	DE	191
Albert	3	DE	151	James	40	DE	191	Susan	10	DE	228
Alexander	25	DE	178	James	54	DE	112	Susan	11	DE	6
Alexander	37	DE	150	James	90	DE	168	Temperance	45	DE	82
Alphonso	14	DE	251	James P	13	DE	151	Thomas	4	DE	191
Amy	1	DE	19	Jeremiah	16	DE	108	Thomas	6	DE	177
Amy	9	DE	32	Jerry	9	DE	99	Thomas	21	DE	19
Amy	50	DE	205	John	4	DE	40	Timothy	4	DE	19
Ananias	37	DE	217	John	5	DE	151	Timothy	32	DE	21
Aner	36	DE	233	John	6	DE	233	Victoria	3	DE	205
Angelina	14	DE	149	John	8	DE	177	Wilamina	1	DE	241
Ann	19	DE	210	John	11	DE	191	William	1/12	DE	46
Ann	25	DE	82	John	39	DE	191	William	1	DE	151
Ann M	5	DE	40	John H	24	DE	112	William	1	DE	192
Anna	4	DE	161	John T	8	DE	113	William	2	DE	32
Anna	87	DE	108	Jonathan	17	DE	34	William	2	DE	104
Arminta	10	DE	30	Joseph	24	DE	238	William	2	DE	253
Balinda	3	DE	197	Julia A	13	DE	112	William	4	DE	216
Benjamin	12	DE	161	Keziah	52	DE	112	William	4	DE	233
Benjamin	39	DE	32	Lewis	30	DE	151	William	8	DE	217
Betsey	12	DE	114	Lydia	5	DE	197	William	35	DE	83
Burton	5	DE	46	Martha	1/12	DE	19	William	50	DE	86
Caleb	25	DE	121	Margaret	6	DE	177	William	62	DE	40
Candace B	17	DE	85	Margaret	14	DE	3	William A	22	DE	7
Catherine	75	DE	176	Margaret	15	MD	10	Williamina	23	DE	150
Charles	5	DE	53	Margaret	38	DE	177	Williamson	3	DE	149
Charlott	50	DE	110	Mark A	7	DE	149	Wm	33	DE	253
Clarisa	40	DE	108	Martha	10	DE	234	Wm	35	DE	195
Clark	35	DE	57	Martha	10	DE	253	Joiner, Alexander	37	MD	189
Clement	25	DE	84	Martha	33	DE	253	Moses	3	DE	194
Cornelius	36	DE	233	Martin	14	DE	191	Jolston, Elizabeth	53	DE	227
Darling	14	DE	182	Mary	1	DE	195	Jones, Albert	36	DE	104
David	1	DE	46	Mary	20	DE	30	Alexander	3/12	DE	54
David	28	DE	98	Mary	24	DE	234	Alexander	28	DE	54
David	61	DE	110	Mary	24	DE	241	Amanda	1	DE	196
David H	3	DE	110	Mary	27	DE	210	Amelia	33	DE	107
Dianna	73	DE	114	Mary	27	DE	216	Amey	47	DE	173
Elias	24	DE	211	Mary	30	MD	195	Ann	9/12	DE	58

Name				Name				Name			
Jones, Ann	25	DE	55	Jones, James	25	DE	15	Jones, Mary	41	DE	187
Ann	40	DE	237	James	32	DE	248	Mary	46	DE	57
Ann	44	DE	22	James	50	DE	54	Mary	58	DE	25
Ann	52	DE	54	James A	3	DE	54	Mary	60	DE	72
Ann	55	DE	228	James B	2/12	DE	149	Mary A	4	DE	107
Ann	65	DE	18	James D	22	MD	4	Mary A	10	DE	47
Ann H	14	DE	148	James E	2	DE	107	Mary A	12	DE	210
Ann L	2	DE	95	James E	22	DE	4	Mary A	29	DE	18
Ann M	26	DE	148	James F	12	DE	52	Mary A	41	DE	95
Ann S	47	DE	148	James H	1	DE	33	Mary C	1	DE	15
Anna M	10	DE	52	James H	5	DE	145	Mary E	3	DE	142
Anna M	12	DE	45	Jane	7	DE	23	Mary E	5	DE	95
Benjamin	37	DE	8	Jane	22	MD	214	Mary E	5	DE	149
Caleb	21	DE	18	Jane	24	DE	25	Mary E	8	DE	3
Caleb	55	DE	45	Jeremiah	16	DE	31	Mary E	24	DE	143
Catherine	4	DE	61	Jesse	14	DE	191	Matilda	16	DE	1
Catherine	10	DE	167	Jesse	15	DE	199	Melvina	2	DE	55
Catherine	22	DE	147	Jesse	32	DE	15	Nancy	13	DE	195
Catherine	23	DE	22	Jesse	61	DE	22	Nancy	15	MD	214
Charity	5	DE	173	Jesse M	47	DE	198	Nathan	1	DE	104
Charity A	1	DE	143	John	2	DE	54	Nathan	54	DE	185
Charles	41	DE	216	John	5	DE	228	Nehemiah	14	DE	7
Charles W	19	DE	148	John	8	DE	220	Nicholas	6	DE	213
Charlotte	5	DE	145	John	13	DE	61	Peregrine	6	DE	31
Charlotte	22	DE	8	John	20	DE	228	Peregrine	69	DE	31
Clayton	13	DE	199	John	23	DE	72	Philip	55	DE	43
Clementine	9	DE	199	John	32	DE	31	Philis	18	DE	45
Daniel	8	DE	45	John	35	DE	129	Priscilla	6/12	DE	8
Daniel	21	DE	38	John	36	DE	107	Purnel	40	DE	94
Daniel	35	DE	213	John	37	DE	61	Rachel	41	DE	22
David	28	DE	231	John	65	DE	129	Rebecca	4	DE	173
David H	60	DE	95	John C	24	DE	44	Rebecca	13	DE	187
Dorcas	25	DE	31	John H	9	DE	149	Rebecca	28	DE	15
Ebenezer	30	DE	185	John H	11	DE	95	Rebecca L	49	DE	21
Edward	23	DE	22	Jonathan	17	DE	198	Richard	13	DE	47
Edward F	11	DE	54	Jonathan	58	DE	49	Richard	70	PA	228
Eliza	7	DE	198	Joseph	19	DE	52	Richard M	26	PA	202
Eliza A	17	DE	130	Joshua H	4	DE	147	Robert	20	DE	185
Eliza J	4	DE	149	Josiah	13	DE	54	Rufus	13	DE	126
Elizabeth	4	DE	167	Julia	33	DE	167	Rufus	30	DE	2
Elizabeth	24	DE	213	Latitia	5/12	DE	2	Ruth	23	DE	15
Elizabeth	27	DE	128	Latitia	27	DE	45	Salina	20	DE	268
Elizabeth	30	DE	18	Laura	7	DE	126	Sally F	3	PA	202
Elizabeth	30	DE	49	Lauretta	30	DE	58	Samuel	6/12	DE	185
Elizabeth	31	DE	44	Lavenia	9	DE	21	Samuel	5	DE	33
Elizabeth	38	DE	126	Lavinia	7	DE	149	Samuel	6	DE	61
Elizabeth	52	DE	67	Lensora	13	DE	143	Samuel	10	DE	198
Elizabeth	56	DE	31	Levin	23	DE	200	Samuel	20	DE	70
Elizabeth	60	DE	2	Levinia	21	DE	104	Samuel	49	DE	21
Ellen	15	DE	81	Loatman	59	DE	52	Samuel E	21	PA	4
Ellen	45	DE	228	Louisa	12	DE	143	Samuel L	2	DE	147
Ellen	59	DE	36	Lovey	30	DE	149	Samuel O	33	DE	149
Elvira	1	DE	198	Lucretia	60	DE	185	Sarah	2	DE	15
Emma	5	DE	31	Lydia	8	DE	8	Sarah	3	DE	58
Emma	6	DE	22	Major T	5	DE	143	Sarah	5	DE	198
Ezekiel	25	DE	148	Manlove	20	DE	31	Sarah	11	DE	200
Felica H	4	DE	142	Margaret	15	DE	68	Sarah	16	DE	3
Frances	6	DE	173	Margaret	15	DE	173	Sarah	16	DE	187
Frances	22	DE	2	Margaret	45	DE	195	Sarah	20	DE	17
Frances M	6	DE	148	Margaret	50	DE	248	Sarah	20	DE	49
George	2	DE	8	Margaret A	14	DE	135	Sarah	28	DE	143
George	7	DE	199	Maria	9	DE	187	Sarah	41	DE	198
George	11	DE	187	Maria	11	DE	173	Sarah	60	DE	127
George	20	DE	198	Maria	16	DE	173	Sarah A	11	DE	61
George	31	DE	18	Maria	26	DE	72	Sarah A	17	DE	148
George	35	DE	21	Mariah	52	DE	52	Sarah E	7	DE	143
George	44	DE	187	Martha	2	DE	61	Sarah M	1	DE	149
George R	11	DE	126	Martha	3	DE	126	Sarietta	10	DE	52
George T	6	DE	32	Martha	11	DE	15	Scipio	29	DE	33
George W	10	DE	148	Martha	23	DE	185	Seba	26	DE	2
Gertrude	1/12	DE	126	Martha	34	DE	61	Snow	58	MD	148
Hannah	18	DE	187	Martha A	5	DE	2	Sophia	66	DE	25
Hannah	53	DE	44	Martha E	17	DE	52	Stephen	6	DE	115
Hannah	60	DE	49	Martha J	2	DE	150	Susan	7	DE	69
Hannah N	24	DE	54	Mary	9	DE	58	Susan	12	DE	195
Henry	30	DE	72	Mary	9	DE	126	Theresa	1	DE	31
Henry S	28	DE	147	Mary	14	DE	187	Thomas	5	DE	7
Hester	23	DE	185	Mary	16	DE	45	Thomas	7	DE	187
Isaac	16	DE	54	Mary	19	DE	195	Thomas	34	DE	7
James	7	DE	58	Mary	23	DE	198	Thomas	34	DE	25
James	17	DE	30	Mary	25	DE	33	Thomas	45	DE	58
James	23	DE	185	Mary	30	DE	7	Thomas	63	DE	245

Name	Age	State	Page
Jones, Thomas F	1/12	DE	15
Timothy	6	DE	25
Unity A	4	DE	213
Waitman	32	DE	143
Wesley	8	DE	7
Wesley	12	DE	47
William	5	DE	187
William	6	DE	8
William	6	DE	107
William	10	DE	58
William	20	DE	54
William	24	CT	1
William	24	VT	18
William	29	DE	142
William	36	DE	6
William	36	DE	31
William B	30	DE	37
William E	10	DE	143
William H	4	DE	31
William H	8	DE	61
William H	13	DE	7
William H	14	DE	213
William H	21	DE	148
William T	4	DE	25
Wm	22	MD	220
Wm	27	DE	239
Wm	43	DE	195
Zachariah	45	DE	173
Jordan, Sarah	12	DE	25
Jourdan, Eban	11	DE	25
John	42	DE	25
Mary	5	DE	25
Sarah	13	DE	25
Susan	48	DE	25
Jump, Albert	10	DE	114
Ann	55	DE	208
Anna S	13	DE	77
Catherine	6	DE	256
Elizabeth	51	MD	256
Emily J	10	DE	137
Isaac	39	DE	163
James L	1	DE	114
John W	21	DE	114
Josiah W	3	DE	114
Louisa	12	DE	256
Margaret	13	DE	208
Mary	21	DE	256
Mary B	49	DE	77
Mary E	8	DE	77
Nancy	8	DE	114
Narcissa	15	DE	114
Robert B	38	MD	77
Robert P	6	DE	77
Samuel J	6	DE	114
Sarah	14	DE	256
Sarah A	40	DE	114
Susan	9	DE	256
William	19	DE	208
William C	15	DE	77
William L	57	DE	114
Wm	20	DE	264
Wm	45	DE	208
Kalahan, Nathan	16	DE	256
Karney, Elizabeth	5	DE	174
James	3	DE	174
James	26	DE	174
Malvina	1	DE	174
Martha	10	DE	174
Phebe	2	DE	174
Phebe	38	DE	174
Robert	7	DE	174
Robert	8	DE	174
Robert	36	DE	174
Sally	23	DE	174
Sarah	14	DE	174
Kean, Mary	54	MD	262
Patrick	26	IE	262
Ruben	54	DE	262
Keil, Patric	23	IE	213
Keith, Andrew	3	DE	46
Eliza Ann	13	DE	46
Keith, Elizabeth	57	DE	60
Fondelia	10/12	DE	59
Francis H	6	DE	46
Henrietta	8	DE	46
Henry R	31	DE	59
James	14	DE	46
Mary	34	DE	46
Susan	27	DE	59
Thomas	40	DE	46
Thomas L	8/12	DE	46
Thomas Snow	19	DE	61
William	45	DE	22
William	63	DE	60
Kelley, Ann	17	MD	55
Ann	47	MD	55
David	4	DE	204
Elizabeth	19	DE	1
Hester A	28	DE	204
John	27	MD	1
Joshua	12	MD	55
Madison	35	DE	204
Mary	9	MD	55
Mary A	4/12	DE	1
Samuel	18	MD	55
Thomas	13	MD	55
William	19	DE	45
William	60	MD	55
William C	10	DE	204
Kelly, Ann	34	DE	203
Caleb	8	DE	234
Catherine	3	DE	203
Eliza A	11	DE	203
Elizabeth	45	DE	234
Elizabeth	54	GE	161
Elizabeth	65	DE	203
George	23	DE	156
James	35	DE	203
James M	5	DE	203
John	11	DE	215
Joseph	19	DE	234
Mary E	8	DE	203
Richard	13	DE	14
Thomas	13	DE	234
Tritania	25	DE	261
William	5/12	DE	261
Wm	46	DE	261
Kelson, Emeline	14	DE	25
Kemmey, George	12	DE	81
Lydia	49	DE	81
Nathaniel	39	DE	81
Kemp, Angeline	25	DE	263
Ann	1/12	DE	210
Anna	7	DE	198
Caroline	25	GE	210
Catherine M	11	DE	140
Dorcas	65	DE	263
Elizabeth	4	DE	266
Elizabeth	5	DE	198
Elizabeth	33	DE	198
George	30	DE	266
Jacob	8	DE	266
Jacob	37	DE	266
John	9	DE	266
John	12	DE	266
Latitia	16	DE	266
Ludric	37	GE	210
Malvina	10	DE	198
Margaret	11	DE	263
Margaret	12	GE	210
Mary	8/12	DE	263
Mary	1	DE	266
Mary	8	DE	198
Mathew	27	DE	263
Mathew	68	DE	263
Mathew	10	DE	266
Miriam	34	DE	266
Peter	6	DE	266
Rachel	14	DE	263
Sally	22	DE	266
Samuel	1	DE	263
Samuel	2	DE	198
Susan	9	MD	223
Kemp, Thomas	12	DE	263
Thomas	37	DE	198
Thomas	38	DE	263
William	2	DE	266
Kenard, Lydia	13	DE	70
Kendal, John B	22	PA	17
Kenedy, Anna N	3/12	DE	88
George W	41	PA	88
John	62	DE	4
Mary E	10	KY	88
Sarah M	36	MD	88
Stiles	12	KY	88
Kenner, Phebe	14	DE	179
Kensey, Hannah	45	PA	34
Kenton, Ann	42	DE	22
Ann	49	DE	18
Catherine	23	DE	18
Eli	35	DE	197
Eliza	13	MD	197
Enock	4	DE	197
Francis L	14	DE	120
Georgiana	1	DE	266
James	7	DE	197
Julia	23	DE	266
Mary	16	MD	197
Mary	23	DE	266
Mary C	4	DE	120
Nathaniel	23	DE	266
Rachel	9	DE	197
Rebecca	3	DE	18
Sally	34	DE	197
Sarah	2	DE	197
Sarah	5	DE	266
Sarah	50	DE	120
Susan	17	DE	18
Thomas	54	DE	120
Thomas J	19	DE	120
Tilly	11	DE	197
Wilamina	3	DE	266
William	26	DE	22
William	54	DE	18
Wm	4	DE	197
Wm	27	DE	266
Kerby, Benjamin	12	DE	267
Elizabeth	16	DE	267
Elizabeth	18	DE	269
James	17	DE	267
Joanna	48	DE	267
John	21	DE	267
Parrot	48	DE	267
Susan	15	DE	267
Thomas	8	DE	267
Kersey, Aaron	14	DE	191
Ann	6	DE	194
Elizabeth	9/12	DE	184
Elizabeth	14	DE	194
Elizabeth	33	DE	194
Hannah	37	DE	184
Hetty	18	DE	194
James	12	DE	194
James	29	DE	183
John	33	DE	183
John B	30	DE	193
Jonathan	27	DE	183
Mary	23	DE	183
Moses	10	DE	194
Priscilla	11	DE	198
Sarah	5	DE	194
Susan	14	DE	193
Susan	29	DE	184
Thomas	16	DE	193
William	43	DE	194
Kese, Robert	16	DE	5
Kethcart, John	16	AA	2
Keyes, Elijah	8	MD	7
Keys, Elijah J	3	DE	18
Harriet	15	DE	158
John	3	DE	64
John T	8	DE	19
Margaret	41	DE	64
Martha	13	MO	43
Martha	23	DE	18

Name	Age	St	Pg	Name	Age	St	Pg	Name	Age	St	Pg
Keys, Mary	40	DE	19	Kinneman, Ambrose	31	DE	140	Knowles, Sarah	24	DE	218
Samuel	11	DE	23	Mary	50	DE	140	Wm L	28	DE	218
Sarah	38	DE	18	Samuel	18	DE	140	Laas, Wm	16	DE	171
Sarah A	7	DE	18	Kinson, John	17	DE	204	Labden, Polley	14	DE	220
Susan	15	DE	64	Kirben, James	37	DE	159	Lackerman, Joseph-			
Susan G	40	DE	7	James	70	DE	159	ine	11	MD	244
William	22	DE	18	Susan	55	DE	159	Lacompt, Joseph	21	DE	184
William	53	DE	64	Kirby, Martha	63	DE	46	Mary	40	DE	190
Killan, Elizabeth	44	DE	265	William	62	DE	46	Samuel	10	DE	190
James	41	DE	265	Kirk, Francis	4	MD	194	Sarah	14	DE	190
Killen, Alexander	25	DE	44	John	14	DE	195	Wm	14	DE	189
Angelica	4	DE	171	Mary	32	DE	194	Lacont, John	14	DE	253
Catherine	25	DE	73	Kirkley, Catharine	6	DE	58	Lacy, Thomas	22	DE	222
Edward	16	DE	242	James	10	DE	56	Lafferty, Alphonso	4	DE	155
Eliza	3	DE	266	Jonas	54	DE	37	Amanda	3	DE	155
Elizabeth	1	DE	258	Mary A	1	DE	58	Jackson	39	DE	155
George	18	DE	242	Mary J	3	DE	37	James	9/12	DE	155
James	28	DE	266	Sarah	4	DE	58	Rachel	27	DE	155
John	2	DE	266	Sarah	32	DE	56	Lamb, Georgiana	4	DE	53
Leah	25	DE	266	Sarah	54	DE	37	James P	20	DE	53
Louisa	13	DE	258	Sarah A	23	DE	58	Margaret R	19	DE	53
Margaret	30	DE	171	Sarah J	24	DE	37	Mary A	30	MD	53
Martha	20	DE	44	Thomas	34	DE	58	Rebecca	10	DE	53
Mary	36	DE	258	Thomas	38	DE	56	Thomas	53	DE	53
Mary	37	DE	269	William T	7	DE	58	Thomas H	1	DE	53
Nancy	36	DE	265	Kitchins, Daniel	10	DE	158	Lambden, Elizabeth	35	MD	10
Peter	15	DE	269	Kitts, Alfred	20	DE	31	James	9	DE	10
Rebecca	12	DE	266	Francis P	12	DE	110	John L	48	MD	10
Samuel	3/12	DE	44	Knight, Charles	30	PA	82	Sarah E	15	DE	10
Susan	7	DE	266	George	26	DE	212	Thomas	5	DE	10
Thomas	1	DE	266	George H W	29	MD	111	Unity W	59	DE	10
Thomas	38	DE	265	Hannah	47	DE	197	Lambertson, Daniel	45	DE	23
Timothy C	32	DE	171	Hughitt	22	DE	7	Sarah	18	DE	23
Killin, Catherine	11	DE	269	James	44	DE	66	Lamore, Ruth	49	DE	196
Daniel	1	DE	269	James S	16	DE	66	Landmen, Nancy	8	DE	219
John	4	DE	269	John	14	DE	197	Williamina	10	DE	219
John	9	DE	258	John	16	DE	14	Lane, Ann E	15	DE	136
Mary	5	DE	258	John	17	DE	70	Ann M	28	DE	127
Mary	7	DE	269	Lavicy	20	DE	82	Anthony	40	DE	136
Sarah	13	DE	269	Margaret A	20	DE	111	Elizabeth	2	DE	145
Susan	17	DE	269	Mary	22	IE	77	Elizabeth	24	DE	145
William	46	DE	258	Mary	26	DE	246	Elizabeth	26	DE	90
Wm	44	MD	269	Mary E	13	DE	66	Enos	40	IE	198
Killy, Elizabeth	16	DE	161	Morgan	19	DE	174	Francis A	11	DE	132
Kimmey, Charles	7	DE	157	Napoleon	11	DE	66	Hester A	3	DE	121
Charles	41	DE	157	Oliver	1/12	DE	66	Hester A	3	DE	122
Deborah	28	DE	156	Phebe	74	DE	257	Jacob	31	DE	127
Elizabeth	57	DE	228	Rachel	25	DE	212	James	6	DE	90
Fanny	8	DE	170	Rebecca	8	DE	66	James	8	DE	136
Hannah	5/12	DE	157	Rebecca	40	DE	66	John	24	DE	145
James	1/12	DE	157	Robert	25	DE	246	Joseph H	3	DE	90
James	10	PA	25	Sarah A	9	DE	66	Margarett Ann	9	DE	90
James	32	DE	156	Susan	18	DE	189	Mary	41	DE	136
James	71	DE	156	Susanna	1	DE	246	Mary	55	DE	267
Joseph	60	DE	228	Tilghman	22	DE	80	Mary A	1	DE	127
Julia	3	DE	156	William	6	DE	66	Nathan	6	DE	132
Margaretta	31	DE	156	Wm	67	DE	197	Richard	21	MD	261
Margretta	7	DE	156	Knock, Ann	24	DE	65	Richard J	20	MD	123
Mary	9	DE	157	Elizabeth	3	DE	65	Sarah A	24	DE	120
Mary	32	DE	170	Elizabeth	75	DE	65	Sarah M	6	DE	127
Mary	36	DE	157	John	37	DE	65	Thomas C	7	DE	136
Rebecca	37	DE	221	Joseph	23	DE	65	Timothy	32	IE	269
Samuel	47	DE	170	Susan	10	DE	49	William	16	DE	121
Sarah	20	DE	228	Thomas	26	DE	65	William A	8/12	DE	121
Sarah	30	DE	156	Thomas	75	DE	65	William S	11	DE	136
Selah	67	DE	161	Knott, David	1/12	DE	187	Laner, Nathan	24	DE	28
Susan	24	DE	228	Mary	1	DE	187	Langrell, Elizabeth	26	DE	263
Thomas	30	DE	228	Rachel	35	DE	187	John	20	DE	263
William	11	PA	257	Robert	14	DE	187	Phebe	14	DE	263
Kims, Henrietta	3	PA	171	Knotts, Benjamin	39	DE	59	Phebe	48	DE	263
John	8	PA	171	Benjamin F	8	DE	59	William	45	DE	263
Lucinda	2	PA	171	Elizabeth	34	DE	59	Lank, Ann	47	DE	218
Margaret	25	PA	171	Hester Ann	16	DE	59	David	19	DE	217
Mary	6	PA	171	John	19	DE	183	Francis A	12	DE	218
Peter	30	PA	171	Josephine	17	DE	59	Jane	20	DE	218
Sarah	5	PA	171	Margaret A	5	DE	59	John	41	DE	217
King, Abraham	22	DE	219	Mary	9	DE	198	Louisa	13	DE	217
Ann	43	DE	12	Mary E	13	DE	59	Nathaniel	10	DE	218
James	14	DE	249	Miriam	50	DE	197	Nathaniel	55	DE	218
Mary	19	DE	225	Perry	42	MD	187	Robert	15	DE	217
Richard	35	DE	211	Sarah J	3	DE	60	Sarah	38	DE	217
Robert	16	DE	245	William	10	DE	60				

Name	Age	State	No.	Name	Age	State	No.	Name	Age	State	No.
Lank, Sarah B	10	DE	218	Laws, Leah	35	DE	125	Layton, Mary	15	DE	262
Sarah E	6	DE	217	Lucinda	9	DE	235	Mary	42	DE	247
Laramore, Alexander	1	DE	122	Mahamia	2	DE	212	Mary	49	MD	29
Ann E	3	DE	122	Manuel	7	DE	67	Mary A	30	DE	86
Ann M	19	DE	121	Manuel	24	DE	61	Nathan	13	NJ	42
Eli	27	DE	121	Margaret	14	DE	168	Peter	3	DE	248
Elizabeth	29	MD	121	Martha	4/12	DE	165	Philip	7	DE	37
George T	7	DE	122	Mary	5	DE	67	Rachel	23	NJ	42
Henrietta	34	MD	121	Mary	16	DE	239	Richard	4	DE	87
Jacob	16	MD	148	Mary	64	DE	60	Richard	13	DE	247
James	10	DE	122	Mary Jane	27	DE	221	Roany	10	DE	163
Joel	18	MD	147	Mehulda	6	DE	211	Safty	19	NJ	42
John T	13	DE	121	Nero	61	DE	221	Sarah	39	DE	249
Joseph	36	DE	122	Noah	38	DE	67	Sarah A	15	DE	115
Martha J	4	DE	121	Outen	5	DE	156	Scynthia	30	DE	115
Mary	37	MD	147	Outen	29	DE	166	Thomas	17	MD	29
Mary	29	MD	121	Paris	6	DE	168	Thomas	21	NJ	42
Mary	67	MD	121	Paris	15	DE	212	Thomas	22	DE	86
Mary E	6	DE	121	Paris	17	DE	215	Thomas	43	DE	247
Mary J	6	DE	122	Phebe A	2	DE	220	Thomas	46	DE	146
Sarah A	35	DE	122	Rachel C	8	DE	211	Thomas	47	DE	29
Sarah J	1	DE	121	Rhoda	50	DE	107	Warner S	14	DE	66
Thomas	36	MD	121	Richard	3/12	DE	67	Willard	6	DE	146
Thomas	66	MD	121	Rosanna	36	DE	67	Leatman, Amy	4	DE	8
Thomas L	10/12	DE	121	Sally	23	DE	165	Ann	14	DE	8
Latchem, Harriet	34	DE	124	Sarah	1	DE	125	Elizabeth	38	DE	8
James H	4	DE	124	Sarah	11	DE	61	Lutitia	1	DE	8
Levin	38	DE	124	Sarah	17	DE	75	Mary	6	DE	8
Mary A	2	DE	124	Sarah	35	DE	211	Leatherberry, John	16	DE	10
Mary E	20	DE	124	Sarah A	11	DE	67	Lecat, Wesley	24	DE	4
Latham, William	16	DE	44	Susan	35	DE	160	Lednum, John	17	DE	89
Latimer, Dorcas	26	DE	214	Susan A	3	DE	53	Lee, Emily	17	MD	145
James H	8	DE	214	Thomas	3	DE	125	Hannah	31	PA	58
John	29	MD	214	Thomas	14	DE	100	Henry	12	PA	132
Mary E	6	DE	214	William A	5	DE	220	Jonathan	58	GB	48
Nancy W	4	DE	214	Layton, Albert	8	DE	248	Lydia	1	DE	58
Sarah E	3	DE	214	Albert	47	NJ	42	Leg, Henry	11	DE	246
Williamina	9/12	DE	214	Albert V	17	NJ	42	Mary	7	DE	255
Laton, Elizabeth	14	DE	217	Amanda	12	DE	248	Mary	52	DE	255
Lauder, Ann	27	DE	262	Amanda	24	DE	163	Solomon	13	DE	255
Ellen	4	DE	262	Ann	29	DE	146	Legar, Ann	68	DE	193
James	27	DE	262	Ann	40	DE	87	Emily	10	DE	188
Margaret	6	DE	262	Ann Jane B	6	DE	42	James	17	DE	188
Samuel	5/12	DE	262	Ann M	25	DE	96	James	44	DE	194
Lawless, Gardener	13	DE	211	Beecham	2	DE	146	John	14	DE	41
Letty C	5	DE	211	Benjamin	35	DE	85	Margaret	24	DE	188
Robert J	8	DE	211	Charles	9	DE	146	Mary	5	DE	184
Sarah	47	DE	211	Deborah	62	DE	12	Mary	35	DE	188
Thomas	18	DE	213	Elizabeth	36	DE	146	Samuel	37	DE	188
Laws, Adam	45	DE	168	Elmira	34	DE	248	Susan	8	DE	223
Alexander	8	DE	168	Frederic	8	DE	85	William	16	DE	188
Alexander	22	DE	58	George	39	DE	115	Leger, Ephraim	55	DE	104
Ann	35	DE	221	Hannah	62	DE	7	Hester	22	DE	104
Ann	36	DE	220	Henry A D	20	DE	86	John H	3	DE	104
Anna	35	DE	166	Henry L	14	DE	85	Legg, Dewitt C	21	DE	11
Basset	27	DE	61	Hiram B	25	NJ	38	Elizabeth	49	DE	22
Bassett	2	DE	67	Hughitt	70	DE	7	George W	11	DE	116
Benjamin	9	DE	67	James	2	DE	246	Henry	70	DE	60
Benjamin	17	DE	61	James	30	DE	96	James	53	DE	22
Benjamin	18	DE	76	James	63	DE	146	John	6	DE	109
Caroline	11	DE	95	James A	5	DE	85	Letitia	10	DE	105
Charles	3	DE	212	Jane	16	DE	116	Mary	70	DE	81
Charles	34	DE	212	Jane	63	DE	146	William	18	DE	11
Curtis	17	DE	107	Jehu	15	DE	108	Legris, Jacob	38	DE	78
Curtis	60	DE	107	John	5	DE	146	Martha	33	DE	78
David	9	DE	77	John	5	DE	248	Leister, James	13	DE	261
Debe	2	DE	212	John	24	DE	146	Joshua	28	MD	261
Deborah	28	DE	60	Joseph	12	DE	247	Margaret	20	DE	261
Ebenezer	11	DE	153	Levi	12	MD	29	Martha	7	DE	261
Elizabeth	23	DE	168	Levicy	62	DE	163	Martha	47	DE	261
Ellen	11	DE	212	Louisa	29	DE	115	Mary	20	DE	261
George	30	DE	220	Lowder	37	DE	248	Lekite, Benjamin M	1	DE	92
Henry	19	DE	107	Lucy	9	DE	125	Christopher S	48	DE	92
Henry	27	DE	165	Luther	17	DE	146	Daniel C	4	DE	92
Hester A	27	DE	212	Lydia A	15	NJ	42	Eliza J	19	DE	92
James H	3	DE	128	Lydia Ann	46	NJ	42	Jane	18	DE	92
John	1	DE	212	Mahala A	11	DE	115	Phoebe	29	DE	92
Joshua	1/12	DE	212	Major	17	DE	115	Roland P	21	DE	92
Julia	13	DE	6	Major	18	DE	124	William H	5	DE	92
Kate	19	DE	221	Margaret	9	DE	42	Leonard, John	6	DE	55
L G	40	DE	162	Margaret J	20	DE	38	Nancy	36	DE	55
Leah	16	DE	85	Mary	12	DE	163	Nathan	38	DE	55

Name	Age	State	No.	Name	Age	State	No.	Name	Age	State	No.
Leonard, Sarah	13	DE	55	Lewis, Elizabeth	21	DE	226	Lewis, Mary	30	DE	245
Letherbay, Amelia	49	DE	29	Elizabeth	23	DE	230	Mary	36	DE	251
Charles	15	DE	29	Elizabeth	25	DE	169	Mary	53	DE	219
David A	8	DE	29	Elizabeth	29	DE	110	Mary Ann	12	DE	230
Frances	14	DE	29	Elizabeth	50	DE	169	Mary E	3	DE	77
Hannah A	12	DE	29	Elizabeth	68	DE	144	Mary E	9	DE	212
Peregrine	58	DE	29	Elizabeth	74	MD	95	Mary E	15	DE	213
Sarah A	17	DE	29	Enoch	9	DE	251	Mary M	9	DE	147
William H	24	DE	29	Erin	27	MD	164	Mary M	11	DE	150
Letherbury, James	10	DE	163	Francis	19	DE	250	Millie	50	DE	212
Phebe	34	PA	163	Franklin	3	DE	163	Mitchel	16	DE	73
Samuel	7	DE	163	Garret	4	DE	135	Nimrod	24	DE	145
Samuel	40	DE	163	Garret	13	DE	250	Peter	47	DE	72
Sarah	15	PA	163	George	1	DE	132	Phener	35	DE	89
William	12	PA	163	George	13	DE	74	Philip	47	DE	210
Leveridge, Ann	5	MD	41	George	25	DE	30	Phillis	25	DE	30
Ann	38	DE	41	George	35	DE	235	Rachel	43	DE	129
Elizabeth	12	MD	41	Hannah	2	DE	230	Rebecca	10	DE	137
Nathaniel	18	MD	41	Hannah	25	DE	77	Rebecca	18	DE	210
Robert	9	MD	41	Harriet	17	DE	129	Reese	34	DE	43
Robert	40	MD	41	Harrison	10	DE	120	Reuben	2	DE	120
Levick, Anna	1	DE	155	Henrietta	20	DE	135	Rhoda	36	DE	137
Mary	36	DE	155	Henry	2	DE	18	Robert	6	DE	250
Richard	4	DE	155	Henry	13	DE	251	Robert	26	DE	95
Sarah	7	DE	155	Ivan	9	DE	129	Robert	31	MD	77
Stephen	5	DE	155	Jacob	22	DE	130	Robert	64	DE	230
Stephen	40	DE	155	Jacob F	43	DE	129	Ruth	20	DE	172
Susan	10	DE	155	Jacob O	13	DE	129	Ruth A	4	DE	118
Leviston, William	17	DE	247	James	4	DE	230	Sally	7	DE	230
Levy, Katy	60	DE	213	James	6	DE	212	Sarah	9/12	DE	72
Nathan	65	MD	213	James	7	DE	241	Sarah	28	DE	118
Lewis, Abigail	62	DE	125	James	8	DE	150	Sarah	33	DE	144
Abner	9	DE	46	James	10	DE	135	Sarah	33	DE	164
Abner	28	DE	118	James	25	DE	230	Sarah	43	DE	93
Abner	31	DE	147	James H	7	DE	147	Sarah	53	DE	172
Abner	35	DE	150	James H	8	DE	137	Sarah E	3	DE	150
Abner	74	DE	125	Jane	16	DE	241	Sarah E	4	DE	147
Alexander	18	DE	121	Jane	47	DE	72	Sarah E	13	DE	104
Alfred	3/12	DE	118	John	8	DE	93	Sebra	1/12	DE	197
Anderson	4	DE	120	John	11	DE	72	Sebra	29	MD	197
Andrew	18	DE	230	John	14	DE	7	Sidonham	49	DE	256
Aner	56	DE	127	John	15	DE	129	Solomon	8	DE	39
Ann	7	DE	118	John	17	DE	241	Solomon	11	DE	145
Ann	10	DE	219	John	23	DE	226	Solomon	27	DE	144
Ann	11	DE	251	John	23	MD	262	Stephen	7	DE	129
Ann	19	DE	250	John	26	DE	35	Stephen	23	DE	169
Ann	30	DE	147	John	30	DE	110	Stephen	39	DE	134
Ann	36	DE	150	John	42	DE	127	Stephen	40	DE	154
Ann	41	DE	212	John	47	MD	93	Stephen	68	DE	137
Ann	49	DE	250	John	60	DE	172	Stephen C	4	DE	137
Ann	57	MD	250	John	90	DE	135	Steven	15	DE	251
Benjamin	8	DE	212	John H	21	DE	127	Susan	12	DE	226
Benniah	2	DE	129	Jonathan	1	DE	212	Sydia	11	DE	138
Caleb	15	DE	250	Joseph	17	DE	250	Sylvester	28	DE	264
Caroline	14	DE	241	Joseph J	50	DE	219	Thomas	21	DE	135
Caroline	15	DE	256	Josephine	3	DE	197	Thomas	34	DE	197
Catharine	11	DE	72	Joshua	5	DE	93	Thomas J	23	DE	219
Catherine	17	DE	101	Julia	43	DE	210	Truston	8	DE	144
Cesar	35	DE	245	Julia A	21	DE	127	Virginia	6	MD	197
Charles	1	DE	120	Laura	1	DE	226	William	5	DE	77
Charles	6	DE	118	Lavinia	11	DE	135	William	9	DE	93
Charles	31	DE	230	Lavinia	16	DE	169	William	11	DE	125
Charles H	6/12	DE	77	Leah A	20	DE	129	William	14	DE	135
Daniel	3	DE	251	Leah Ann	18	DE	95	William	18	DE	126
Daniel	7	DE	77	Lewis	15	DE	211	William H	18	DE	70
Daniel	16	DE	250	Lucretia	11	DE	212	William S	11	DE	129
Darlin	39	DE	212	Luff	13	DE	169	William T	5	DE	43
David	7 da	DE	147	Lurena	11	DE	127	Wilson	14	PA	210
David	1	DE	212	Lydia	8	DE	110	Wm	28	DE	250
David	2	DE	110	Mahala	7/12	DE	95	Wm	49	DE	250
David	14	MD	262	Malvina	15	DE	251	Wm A	22	DE	250
David	20	DE	169	Margaret	11	DE	250	Libbey, Sarah	53	DE	61
David	49	DE	120	Margaret	30	DE	230	Lightfoot, Betsey	60	MD	178
David G	56	DE	269	Margaret A	10	DE	43	George	14	MD	178
Edward	9	DE	250	Maria	37	DE	162	Limeric, Clarissa	55	DE	6
Eisen	64	DE	251	Mark	50	DE	38	Linch, Andrew	8	DE	115
Eliza	17	DE	132	Martha	12	DE	120	Ann	1	DE	154
Eliza	34	DE	43	Martha	17	DE	47	Catherine	10	DE	137
Eliza	55	DE	135	Martha	39	DE	120	Catherine	40	DE	99
Elizabeth	1/12	DE	110	Mary	6	DE	251	Eliza Jane	11	DE	99
Elizabeth	10	DE	73	Mary	10	DE	197	Elizabeth	16	DE	115
Elizabeth	13	DE	256	Mary	22	DE	219	Ellen	34	DE	137

Name	Age	State	No.	Name	Age	State	No.	Name	Age	State	No.
Linch, George B	4	DE	115	Lister, Leah	45	DE	84	Loatman, Rachel	20	DE	9
Henry C	6	DE	115	Margaret L	20	MD	123	Rachel	24	DE	24
James T	12	DE	99	Margarett	50	DE	92	Rebecca	26	DE	24
John W	7	DE	99	Martha	47	MD	123	Rebecca	36	DE	71
John W	19	DE	115	Martha A	7	MD	123	Samuel	23	DE	33
Levina	56	DE	96	Mary	20	MD	123	Sarah	8	DE	24
Margaret	2/12	DE	99	Mary M	16	DE	96	Sarah	30	DE	181
Mariah C	14	DE	99	Thomas	14	DE	161	Sarah A	32	DE	38
Mary	36	DE	154	Trifiner	50	DE	161	Sarah E	8	DE	82
Mary E	8	DE	99	William A	19	DE	4	Sarah E	11	DE	38
Minus	2	DE	115	Little, Alexander	3	DE	56	Simon	63	DE	178
Noah	6	DE	137	Amy	33	DE	3	William	3	DE	178
Noah	35	DE	137	Ann	17	DE	15	William	4	DE	24
Richard	4	DE	154	Elbertson	26	PA	84	William	42	DE	9
Riley	14	DE	115	Emeline	5	DE	56	William	45	DE	71
Riley	42	DE	115	Nathan	35	DE	56	Wm	9	DE	178
Sarah	7	DE	154	Samuel	1	DE	56	Lober, Ann	58	DE	226
Sarah A	12	DE	115	Seba	28	DE	56	John	1	DE	217
Sarah W	2	DE	137	Littleton, Ann Eliza	6	DE	204	Margaret	16	DE	226
Stephen	5	DE	154	Hannah	18	DE	204	Mikel	66	DE	226
Stephen	40	DE	154	John	14	DE	204	Lockerman, Josephine	4	DE	243
Susan	10	DE	154	John	42	NJ	204	Lockman, Elisha	48	DE	234
Susan	39	DE	115	Margaret	38	DE	204	Isaac	4	DE	234
Thomas L	42	DE	99	Margaret J	2	DE	204	James	15	DE	234
William J	13	DE	115	Rebecca	12	DE	204	Hetty	10	DE	234
Zadock	2	DE	99	Wm J	6/12	DE	204	Martha	71	DE	234
Lindale, James	22	DE	71	Litzenbery, Wm	25	PA	18	Sarah	15	DE	234
Lindel, Catherine	4	DE	231	Livingston, John	4/12	DE	102	Sarah	45	DE	234
Catherine	55	DE	231	John	72	DE	102	Steven	16	DE	234
Edward	12	DE	225	Milly	61	MD	102	Lockwood, Armwell	48	PA	175
Eliza A	35	DE	212	Nathan	42	DE	102	Catharine H	13	DE	5
Eliza T	6/12	DE	214	Lloyd, Edward	28	PA	2	Charles P	11/12	DE	83
Elizabeth	6	DE	212	George	1	DE	2	Comfort	65	DE	5
Elizabeth	16	DE	213	Margaret	19	PA	2	David	38	DE	5
Elizabeth	17	DE	231	Loat, Alexander	12	DE	156	Eliza	32	DE	219
Elizabeth A	24	MD	214	John	14	DE	76	Elizabeth	17	DE	203
Henry	19	DE	163	Samuel	9	DE	31	Elizabeth	36	DE	248
James L	46	DE	212	Wesley	23	DE	54	Elmira	5	DE	47
James M	12	DE	212	Loate, James	11	DE	202	Francis T	13	DE	204
John	35	DE	214	Lavinia	8	DE	155	Garrett S	6	DE	204
John W	18	DE	214	Loatman, Alfred	8	DE	164	George H	14	DE	204
Joshua	62	DE	231	Amanda	4	DE	38	Henry	30	DE	187
Louisa	12	DE	231	Amy	65	DE	24	John	13	DE	184
Margaret	21	MD	229	Ann	1	DE	229	John C	6	DE	47
Margaret	21	DE	231	Ann	30	DE	24	John C	29	DE	83
Margaret	26	DE	214	Ann	45	DE	229	Maria	36	DE	203
Maria E	1	DE	214	Ann	62	DE	178	Martha	29	DE	47
Mary	50	DE	225	Caroline	5	DE	38	Martha	68	DE	184
Peter	9	DE	212	Catharine	6/12	DE	24	Mary	10	DE	184
Peter	71	DE	214	Catharine	3	DE	71	Mary Ann	25	DE	83
Peter M	26	DE	214	Catharine	10	DE	45	Matilda	80	MD	187
Thomas	39	DE	231	Charles	6	DE	71	Philene	15	DE	219
Thomas S	4	DE	212	Charles	33	DE	38	Priscilla	76	DE	225
W N	23	DE	229	David	37	DE	82	Sally Maria	4	DE	204
W N	56	DE	225	Deborah	11	DE	10	Samuel	47	DE	203
William	2	DE	231	Edward	17	DE	24	Samuel A	11	DE	204
William P	16	DE	212	Edward	48	DE	164	Susan	6	DE	219
Lindeman, Anna R	4	DE	84	Elizabeth	22	DE	229	Thomas	1	DE	47
Clara Ann	15	PA	84	George	7	DE	38	Thomas	49	DE	219
Joseph L	12	PA	84	George	8	DE	24	Thomas B	31	DE	47
Joseph L	44	GE	84	George	30	DE	71	Virginia	15	DE	5
Martha	7	DE	84	Hannah	25	DE	82	William	15	DE	47
Samuel J	5/12	DE	84	Henry	18	DE	24	William	62	DE	225
Sarah A	30	DE	84	Isabella	15	DE	164	Wm R	8	DE	204
William T	2	DE	84	Israel	31	DE	181	Lodine, Edward	2	DE	252
Lindle, Elizabeth	60	DE	87	Israel	48	DE	229	Eliza	28	DE	191
John S	3	DE	204	Jacob	16	DE	68	Eliza	37	DE	248
William	25	DE	87	James	3	DE	181	Elizabeth	10	DE	248
Lines, Ann	50	DE	150	James D	2	DE	38	George	14	DE	227
Lingo, Cyrus	27	DE	57	John	13	DE	71	Henry	30	DE	7
Henry	2	DE	57	John	16	DE	174	Isabel	22	DE	7
Henry D	32	DE	56	Jonathan	2	DE	82	James	6	DE	252
Mary	21	DE	211	Levi	15	DE	164	Jonathan	58	DE	191
Patience	28	DE	56	Lydia	47	DE	71	Josephine	6	DE	248
William C	24	DE	211	Margaret	17	DE	24	Joshua	28	DE	191
Linnen, Matthew	30	IE	53	Martha	8	DE	71	Julia	9	DE	252
Lisca, Isaac	9	DE	165	Martha	63	DE	68	Major	30	DE	252
Lister, James E	8	DE	92	Mary	1	DE	71	Mary	11	DE	221
James E	12	MD	123	Mary S	1/12	DE	71	Noah	5	DE	191
Joseph	50	DE	84	Peter	4	DE	71	Patricia	47	DE	19
Joshua	27	MD	123	Phoney	7	DE	42	Rebecca	17	DE	267
Josiah	12	DE	92	Priscilla	6	DE	164	Rebecca A	3	DE	7

Name	Age	Co	Pg
Lodine, Roseanna	7	DE	191
Samuel	6/12	DE	7
Samuel	54	DE	248
Sarah	29	DE	191
Susan	4/12	DE	191
Susan	30	DE	252
William	10	DE	254
Wm	17	DE	156
Lofland, Ann	36	MD	84
Ann D	24	DE	117
Ann	4/12	DE	184
Asa	55	DE	202
Benjamin Y	44	DE	85
Catherine	1	DE	116
Catherine	37	DE	94
Edward C	41	DE	84
Elias T	30	DE	117
Eliza	4/12	DE	117
Elizabeth	21	DE	89
Gabriel P	42	DE	94
Isaac	23	DE	202
James P	32	DE	116
James P	57	DE	90
James R	23	DE	164
Jane	15	DE	90
John	67	DE	94
John M	38	DE	116
John P	1	DE	110
Joseph A	32	DE	109
Joseph B	5	DE	116
Joshua	17	DE	233
Mariah	25	DE	116
Mark G	20	DE	90
Martha	6	DE	184
Martha	19	DE	211
Martha	37	DE	184
Mary	22	DE	104
Mary	45	DE	90
Mary A	3	DE	116
Peter L	10	DE	90
Purnel	30	DE	89
Rachel H	24	DE	110
Sarah	17	DE	202
Sarah A	4	DE	110
Sarah Ann	38	DE	94
Sarah E	13	DE	94
Selerena	8/12	DE	90
Susanna	8	DE	202
Zadock	4	DE	184
Zadock	60	DE	184
Long, Hester A	52	DE	124
Rachel	65	DE	71
Longfellow, Amy	3	DE	261
Araminta	26	DE	160
Clarissa	52	DE	160
Cynthia	79	DE	260
Easter	59	DE	258
Hester	48	DE	258
James	5	DE	160
James	5	DE	261
James	18	DE	264
James	48	DE	258
James	52	DE	264
John	12	DE	243
John	24	DE	159
John	50	DE	160
Jonathan	2	DE	247
Jonathan	35	DE	261
Jonathan	49	DE	243
Latitia	25	DE	243
Lydia	10	DE	243
Mahala	15	DE	258
Margaret	6	DE	243
Mary	30	DE	261
Peter	3	DE	160
Richie	1/12	DE	243
Susan	49	DE	264
Susanna	17	DE	264
William	25	DE	258
Longo, Ann E	18	DE	73
Candia	80	MD	224
Eben	53	DE	172
Longo, Harcklas	28	DE	203
John	22	DE	172
Louisa	24	DE	203
Margaret	13	DE	172
Rachel	47	DE	172
Sarah	13	DE	172
Sarah E	1	DE	203
Loper, Alexander	14	DE	207
Andrew	28	DE	156
Ann	15	DE	234
Ann	33	DE	216
Anthony	92	DE	208
Benjamin	29	DE	237
Caleb	17	DE	215
Caroline	17	DE	217
Charles	12	DE	210
Christina	3	DE	156
Cloe	45	DE	232
Daniel	68	DE	237
David	9	DE	245
Eliza	10	DE	237
Eliza	24	DE	156
Eliza	35	DE	233
Elizabeth	16	DE	233
Ephraim	55	DE	103
George	7	DE	237
Hester	22	DE	103
Jacob	35	DE	216
Jacob	71	DE	220
James	4	DE	216
James	6	DE	216
Jane	19	DE	155
Jane	38	DE	210
John	1	DE	216
John	2	DE	216
John	5	DE	210
John	10	DE	263
John	19	DE	155
John H	3	DE	103
Jonathan	31	DE	226
Latitia	45	DE	156
Louisa	1	DE	156
Lydia	9	DE	158
Lydia	45	DE	233
Major	18	DE	233
Margaret	2	DE	216
Martha	7	DE	235
Mary	37	DE	237
Mary E	8	DE	216
Miah	12	DE	237
Miter	92	DE	208
Peter	15	DE	209
Peter	24	DE	155
Peter	33	DE	216
Philene	4	DE	216
Rebecca	64	DE	220
Rebecca A	6	DE	220
Robert	4	DE	233
Rosanna	81	DE	237
Ruth	27	DE	235
Sally	8	DE	233
Sarah E	13	DE	103
Thomas	15	DE	155
William	1	DE	233
William	24	DE	157
Wm	35	DE	233
Lord, Alexander	10	DE	147
Andrew	18	MD	135
Ann E	3	DE	148
Ann M	40	MD	135
Anna	9	DE	225
Annie	9	DE	261
Edward	10	DE	223
Edward	42	DE	223
Elizabeth	10	DE	261
Elizabeth	35	DE	223
Frances C	1	DE	135
George	6	DE	223
George W	17	MD	135
Henry C	16	MD	135
James	6	DE	225
James	56	MD	225
Lord, James K	5	DE	147
John	5	DE	261
John B	11	DE	147
Julia	11	DE	225
Laid	13	DE	261
Lizzie	3	DE	223
Margaret A	10	DE	135
Martha	15	DE	225
Martha	46	DE	225
Martha M	1	DE	147
Mary	14	DE	223
Mary	17	DE	225
Mary E	4	DE	135
Priscilla	19	DE	225
Rebecca	33	MD	147
Robert	46	MD	135
Sarah J	16	MD	147
Shadrach W	8	DE	147
Solomon K	14	DE	135
Thomas	5	DE	223
Thomas	15	DE	261
Thomas	37	MD	147
William	6	DE	135
William	12	DE	223
William	12	DE	261
William E	14	DE	144
William E	15	DE	147
Lote, Ann	5	DE	250
Elizabeth	12	DE	154
Elizabeth	32	DE	154
George	3	DE	154
George	25	DE	217
Henry	11	DE	250
Hetty	5	DE	154
Joshua	1	DE	154
Sally	1/12	DE	154
Samuel	35	DE	154
Loteman, Araminta	32	DE	246
Eliza	31	DE	246
Elizabeth	42	DE	154
Israel	6	DE	246
James	7	DE	154
Levi	2	DE	246
Martha	4	DE	246
Nathan	6/12	DE	154
Samuel	2	DE	154
Simon	10	DE	154
Thomas	6	DE	154
Wm	47	DE	154
Lott, Rose	4	DE	246
Lovegrove, James	6/12	DE	16
James	29	DE	16
Susan	24	DE	16
Thomas	3	DE	16
Low, Thomas	90	DE	6
Lowber, Ann	42	DE	24
Elizabeth	35	DE	219
George	1	DE	24
James	48	DE	79
John	19	DE	14
Joseph	25	DE	24
Mary	35	DE	176
Mary	48	DE	79
Peter	60	DE	44
Rachel C	16	DE	219
Robert J	42	DE	219
Thomas H	14	DE	219
William	3	DE	24
Lowden, John	60	DE	223
Margaret	56	MD	223
Lowery, Eliza	25	DE	86
Justus	26	DE	86
William B	7/12	DE	86
Lowrey, Maria	60	MD	162
Mary	32	DE	59
Lucas, George	4	DE	59
Mary	32	DE	59
Luff, Anna	6	DE	83
Araminty	6	DE	7
Benjamin	12	DE	104
Caleb	18	DE	222
Caleb	19	DE	94
Catherine	2	DE	104

Name	Age	St	Pg	Name	Age	St	Pg	Name	Age	St	Pg
Luff, Elizabeth	15	DE	104	Macy, John W	8	DE	27	Manlove, Mary J	2	DE	84
Elizabeth	43	DE	104	Joseph	5	DE	33	Mary J	14	DE	206
Garrett	45	DE	224	Joseph	37	DE	33	Mary M	8/12	DE	78
George	16	DE	222	Mary E	5	DE	45	Mathew	68	DE	113
George N	19	DE	104	Peter Q	13	DE	45	Matthew T	15	DE	113
James	3	DE	73	Rebecca M	3	DE	27	Nancy	68	DE	249
James	52	DE	73	William M	5	DE	27	Sarah	37	DE	113
Jane	29	DE	156	Madden, Annie	4	DE	249	Sarah A	10	DE	113
Joshua	19	DE	91	Mary	28	DE	249	Sarah Mason	4	DE	84
Lettitia	51	DE	73	Mary	50	DE	11	Solomon	31	DE	78
Levi	42	DE	104	Thomas	36	IE	249	Susan	3	DE	113
Nancy	66	DE	55	Magee, Levi	8	DE	194	Susan C	27	DE	84
Nathaniel	58	DE	219	Maginis, Ellen	19	DE	235	Thomas	21	DE	6
Rebecca	17	DE	219	George	7	DE	235	Wm W	33	DE	201
Sarah	7	DE	224	Jeanette	9	DE	235	Mannering, John	21	MD	29
Sarah	40	DE	224	John	17	DE	235	Julia A	40	DE	35
Sarah	50	DE	101	Louisa	5	DE	235	Martha	30	DE	3
Thomas	16	DE	199	Mary	5/12	DE	235	Sarah	2	DE	199
William	23	DE	6	Mary	43	DE	235	Mansfield, Ann	15	DE	4
Wm	8	DE	234	Nathan	3	DE	235	Ann	57	DE	22
Lusby, Robert	25	MD	4	Thomas	12	DE	235	Anna M	59	DE	4
Luther, Celia	60	DE	112	William	14	DE	235	Francis	8	DE	161
Lynch, Catherine	10	DE	136	William	45	MD	235	John	35	DE	161
Ellen	34	DE	136	Magner, Cornelius	26	IE	123	Piner	58	MD	4
Kendle	30	DE	114	Mallalieu, Ann J	1	DE	48	Sarah	10	DE	161
Mahala B	32	DE	114	James M	6	PA	48	Sarah	29	DE	161
Mary E	2	DE	114	John	33	GB	48	Maree, Ann	63	DE	16
Noah	6	DE	136	Joseph	8	PA	48	Marine, Charles	45	DE	73
Noah	35	DE	136	Mary	35	GB	48	Marisne, David	26	DE	261
Sarah A	8/12	DE	114	Mary R	2	DE	48	Marker, Charlotte	62	DE	268
Sarah W	2	DE	136	Samuel	14	GB	48	Henry	26	DE	268
Lyons, Mary	22	DE	224	Thomas	35	GB	48	Isaac	64	NC	268
Patric	21	IE	269	Maloney, Ada C	7	MD	141	Rebecca	20	DE	268
				Amelia	42	MD	141	Sarah A	20	DE	107
Maclary, Charles F	5	DE	71	Andrew	21	DE	100	Markle, Ellen	29	DE	247
Eliza	39	DE	58	Elisha	43	MD	141	Isaac	10	DE	247
Ellen M	9	DE	58	Elisha T	4	MD	141	James	6	DE	247
Emily	23	DE	58	James E	10	DE	141.	Sarah	3	DE	247
Jacob	19	DE	71	John	15	DE	100	Thomas	39	DE	247
John	59	DE	71	John	46	DE	100	William	7	DE	247
John W	14	DE	71	Martha W	13	MD	141	Marsh, Elizabeth	13	DE	240
Margaret E	3/12	DE	58	Martin W	19	MD	141	Fanny	40	DE	240
Mary	38	DE	71	Mary	41	DE	100	Joseph	43	DE	240
Mary E	1	DE	71	Mary C	6	DE	61	Mariam	22	DE	199
Mary E	13	DE	57	Mary J	18	MD	141	Mary	49	DE	193
Sarah	2	DE	57	Rachel C	11	DE	100	Moses	45	DE	68
Sarah	22	DE	57	Robert	42	DE	20	William	18	DE	118
Sarah E	10	DE	71	Robert F	11/12	DE	141	Wm	52	MD	193
Thomas	53	DE	57	Sarah A	16	MD	141	Marshall, Catherine	13	DE	94
Thomas W	24	DE	57	Susan	16	DE	100	John	15	DE	94
Washington	20	DE	79	Susan	18	DE	205	John	56	DE	94
William H	23	DE	57	Thomas	23	DE	205	Margaret	26	DE	28
Maclay, Jane	24	NJ	26	William	2	DE	21	Margaret A	9/12	DE	28
William T	30	DE	26	Wm	23	DE	203	Mary	49	DE	94
Macklin, Ann	28	DE	103	Wm H	15	MD	141	Mary E	3	DE	28
Ann E	3	DE	103	Manlove, Alfred Jr	34	DE	84	Samuel	30	DE	28
Ann E	11	DE	99	Amelia	29	DE	201	William	5	DE	28
Elias Burton	3	DE	100	Angeline	6	DE	78	Martain, James A	2	DE	107
George	1	DE	99	Ann	7	DE	101	John	45	DE	107
George	38	DE	72	Benjamin S	10/12	DE	113	Mary D	35	DE	107
Henry	18	DE	90	Boaz M	4/12	DE	84	Richard A	12	DE	107
Isaac	5	DE	76	Catherine	76	DE	101	Sarah E	13	DE	107
James	4	DE	72	Daniel	57	DE	206	Martin, Ann	7	DE	213
John	2	DE	72	Elizabeth	22	DE	157	Ann	25	DE	213
John H	7	DE	99	Elizabeth	53	DE	173	Delph	2	DE	165
Mary E	6	DE	103	Ezekiel	30	DE	230	Eliza	5/12	DE	213
Obadiah	25	DE	103	George	9	DE	201	Eliza	37	DE	215
Rachel	22	DE	103	George M	62	DE	173	Elizabeth	32	DE	182
Rebecca	25	DE	72	George S	5	DE	84	Elser	18	DE	165
Sarah C	1/12	DE	103	George S	41	DE	113	Emily	9	DE	212
Sarah E	7	DE	103	Henry	28	DE	230	Hetty	40	DE	165
William	8/12	DE	72	James G	13	DE	113	John	7	DE	189
Macy, Ann	36	DE	45	Jane	30	DE	78	John	35	DE	213
Eliza	39	DE	33	John	24	DE	218	Joseph	7	DE	215
George	11	DE	9	John L	5	DE	113	Joseph	9	DE	204
Hester	40	DE	27	Juda	25	DE	101	Joseph	29	DE	215
Isaac	8	DE	45	Lavina	16	DE	101	Mary	9	DE	213
James	41	DE	27	Maria	10	DE	230	Mary	10	DE	215
James H	3/12	DE	27	Martha	3	DE	78	Samuel	9	DE	165
John	11	DE	45	Martha	21	DE	206	Sarah	3	DE	213
John	35	DE	45	Mary	2	DE	201	Susan	5	DE	213
John C	10	DE	33	Mary	61	DE	162	Theodore	14	DE	215

Name	Age	St	No.
Martin, William T	15	DE	216
Wm	13	DE	189
Wm	14	DE	167
Martingale, Eliza-beth	15	DE	224
Margaret	39	DE	224
Miriam	17	DE	224
Stephen	5	DE	224
Thomas	7	DE	224
Thomas	49	MD	224
William	3	DE	224
Marvel, Alphonsey	12	DE	198
Ambrose	11	DE	201
Ann	66	DE	252
Avery	16	DE	182
Benjamin	6	DE	201
David	2	DE	201
David	24	DE	250
David	46	DE	201
David	75	DE	252
Edward	15	DE	205
Elizabeth	10	DE	182
Ellen	10	DE	198
Harriet	5	DE	182
Henry	13	DE	182
Hester	19	DE	192
Isaac	10	DE	201
James	11	DE	156
John	20	DE	164
John	56	DE	156
Joseph	13	DE	201
Josephine	21	DE	156
Kitty	45	DE	182
Louisa	17	DE	201
Mary	46	DE	156
Philena	4	DE	199
Philip	20	DE	182
Philip	49	DE	182
Rachel	48	DE	225
Robert	16	DE	252
Ruben G	32	DE	192
Sally Ann	40	DE	198
Sally Ann	41	DE	201
Samuel	4	DE	201
Sarah	19	DE	250
Theodore	18	DE	156
Thomas	8	DE	198
Thomas J	41	DE	198
Willamina	1	DE	192
William	14	DE	198
Marvell, Emory	23	DE	108
Margaret	51	DE	113
Phillip	55	DE	113
Marvill, Adam	65	DE	113
Clarissa	34	DE	113
Daniel	25	DE	93
David	26	DE	115
Henry	43	DE	114
James	38	DE	115
James H	2	DE	93
James H	12	DE	113
Jane	49	DE	113
John A	19	DE	150
Josiah	32	DE	115
Margaret J	16	DE	113
Milly A	16	DE	113
Rebecca	18	DE	113
Sarah	22	DE	114
Sarah E	10	DE	113
Sarah J	21	DE	93
Thomas U	7/12	DE	114
William	25	DE	113
William H	4	DE	114
Mason, Alexander	4	DE	104
Alfred	3	DE	216
Ann	23	DE	159
Ann C	32	DE	108
Anna	6	DE	216
C J	38	DE	206
Caleb	2	DE	221
Caleb	30	DE	206
Catherine	3	DE	237
Mason, Catherine	15	DE	104
Catherine	45	DE	104
Charles	17	DE	104
Daniel	12	DE	176
Daniel	31	DE	96
Daniel	52	DE	176
Daniel	75	DE	91
David	10	DE	23
David H	29	DE	108
Edward	10	DE	176
Edward H	16	DE	14
Elizabeth	13	DE	104
Francis	5	DE	159
George	9	DE	257
George P	51	MD	1
Hester	1	DE	96
Hester	29	DE	96
Hetty	27	DE	216
Isaac	11	DE	104
Isaac	14	MD	53
Isaac	25	DE	159
Isaac	86	DE	164
James	9	DE	104
James R	25	MD	57
John	4	DE	176
John	14	IE	153
John	15	IE	156
John	28	DE	237
Joseph	10	DE	96
Joseph H	9	DE	23
Louis	21	DE	176
Lydia	25	DE	57
Margaret	63	MD	257
Mary	7	DE	176
Mary	72	DE	176
Mary E	6	DE	96
Mary J	6	DE	57
Miriam	58	DE	221
Nancy	19	DE	226
Rachel	20	DE	104
Robert P	3	DE	1
Ruth A	26	DE	219
Sally	41	DE	257
Samuel	4	DE	96
Sarah	10	DE	176
Sarah	25	DE	221
Sarah	44	DE	1
Sarah S	6	DE	108
Susan A	11	DE	216
Susanna	2	DE	108
Thomas	9	DE	216
Thomas	12	DE	96
Thomas	12	DE	105
Thomas	19	DE	104
Thomas	50	DE	104
Trustin	28	DE	221
William	18	PA	16
William	35	DE	216
William H	8	DE	108
Massey, Alfred	18	DE	35
Edward	14	NY	48
Elisha	7	DE	36
Elisha	32	DE	249
Elizabeth	40	DE	40
Erasmus	21	DE	84
Hannah	8	DE	232
Hester A	25	DE	206
Isaac	45	MD	40
James	4	DE	36
James	5	DE	232
James	43	DE	232
Jonathan	65	DE	249
Joseph H	9	DE	206
Julia	25	DE	249
Mary	6	DE	36
Mary	48	DE	249
Peter	40	DE	206
Rachel	71	DE	71
Rixon	4	DE	206
Sarah	37	DE	36
Sarah E	6/12	DE	36
William	1	DE	232
Massey, William	1	DE	232
Wolsey	15	DE	60
Masson, William	5/12	DE	160
Masten, Aaron	55	DE	154
Alfred	1	DE	154
Angelina	5	DE	126
Benjamin	7	DE	176
Benjamin H	13	DE	138
Catherine	52	DE	126
Clement	17	DE	105
David	11	DE	138
David	32	DE	131
David R	39	DE	111
Elizabeth	13	DE	126
Ellin G	14	DE	105
Habe	39	DE	121
Harriett	41	DE	138
Hezekiah	23	DE	171
Hughitt	47	DE	176
Isaac	9	DE	131
Isaac	10	DE	176
James P	16	DE	138
Jane	25	DE	142
John	22	DE	104
John P	6	DE	131
John P	17	DE	151
John R T	44	DE	131
John W	6	DE	126
Joseph	26	DE	131
Joseph	60	DE	126
Joseph A	10	DE	121
Latitia	54	DE	111
Mary	8	DE	138
Mary	18	DE	106
Mary	52	DE	106
Mary A	5	DE	105
Mary J	6	DE	142
Mary J	31	DE	107
Oliver	14	DE	106
Rachel	2/12	DE	106
Reuben	27	DE	105
Rhody	35	DE	176
Sarah	12	DE	138
Sarah	24	DE	105
Sarah E	3	DE	105
Sarah M	37	DE	131
Sarah T	11	DE	138
Saunders D	19	DE	106
William	20	DE	105
William	75	DE	121
William D	48	DE	106
William H	44	DE	131
William L	13	DE	121
William T	18	DE	105
Winney	29	DE	130
Winney	40	DE	154
Master, Boaz	1	DE	91
Priscilla	26	DE	90
Thomas	34	DE	91
Maston, Aaron	21	DE	102
Alexander	20	DE	216
Charles	7	DE	116
Clementine	6	DE	117
David	8	DE	237
Flora	50	DE	117
Henry	11	DE	116
Hetty	47	DE	227
James	15	DE	167
John	72	DE	116
Mary	14	DE	222
Mary	51	DE	116
Rebecca	1	DE	117
Sarah E	12	DE	117
Starling	35	DE	117
Thomas	61	DE	117
Wm	17	DE	167
Matee, Marcellas	9	DE	159
Mathews, Eliza	12	MD	256
John	14	MD	256
Joseph	9	MD	256
Lavinia	6	DE	208
Sally A	9	DE	208

Name	Age	State	No.
Mathews, Sarah	27	DE	208
William	4/12	DE	208
Wingate	27	DE	208
Matteford, Benjamin	4	DE	52
Denney	9	DE	52
James	10	DE	52
John	11	DE	52
John D	41	DE	52
Sarah E	2	DE	52
Temperance	25	DE	52
William	11	DE	52
Matthews, Henrietta	11	MD	22
Henry	27	MD	142
Maul, Thomas	9	DE	23
Mauney, Angelina	1	DE	28
Elizabeth	27	DE	28
Martha A	5	DE	28
William	28	DE	28
William H	9	DE	28
Maxim, Richard	22	DE	1
Maxson, Andrew W	7	DE	218
Elizabeth	38	DE	218
Nathan H	2	DE	218
Wm	37	DE	218
Maxwell, Emmory	23	DE	109
John	21	DE	244
May, John W	30	MD	5
Nancy	35	DE	244
Eli	23	MD	50
Mayberry, Benj F	7	DE	50
Charles T	12	DE	71
James	12	DE	50
James A	7	DE	54
John	52	DE	54
John B	9	DE	54
Martha	25	DE	50
Sarah F	11	DE	54
Temperance	35	DE	54
Thomas	33	DE	50
William	1	DE	50
McAfee, Mary Ann	19	IE	1
William	23	IE	1
McAffery, Robert	35	IE	223
McBlain, Hannah A	21	DE	30
John	24	IE	30
McBride, Amanda	21	DE	157
Amelia	13	DE	157
Amy	1	DE	193
Ann	3	DE	193
Daniel	28	DE	204
Daniel J	3	DE	204
Eliza	31	DE	193
Elizabeth	18	DE	177
Elizabeth	23	DE	163
Henry	9	DE	157
James	1	DE	231
James	7	DE	193
James	45	DE	157
Joseph	24	DE	226
Martha E	1	DE	204
Mary	37	DE	157
Mary E	24	DE	204
William	5	DE	193
William	6	DE	157
Wm	34	DE	193
McCahy, Margaret	20	IE	169
McCall, Harrison	15	DE	60
McCalley, Anna B	7	DE	83
Elizabeth B	26	DE	83
James H	30	DE	83
Matilda	13	DE	83
Theodosia	1	DE	83
McCarter, Eliza M	10	DE	207
James B	17	DE	207
Mary H	37	DE	207
Phebe	24	DE	207
Phebe L	7/12	DE	207
Roxana	5	DE	207
Samuel	2	DE	207
Samuel	40	DE	207
McCauley, John	4	DE	76
Justin	27	DE	76
McCauley, Mary	27	DE	76
McCay, Elizabeth	13	DE	59
Mary E	13	DE	10
William	10	DE	59
McClain, Sally	14	DE	230
McClasken, Wm H	11	PA	82
McClelland, Cynthia	45	DE	202
Jane	10	DE	202
Mary	7	DE	202
McClement, Alex	67	DE	18
John	4	DE	135
Joseph H	13	DE	61
McClyment, James R	20	DE	62
Mary M	50	DE	62
William T	17	DE	6
McColley, Andrew J	32	PA	86
Anna	8	DE	94
Clement S	19	DE	113
Eliza J	23	DE	113
Eliza M	3	DE	110
Elizabeth	48	DE	113
George M	26	DE	114
George R P	4	DE	86
Hester	7	DE	94
Hester J	27	DE	86
Hester O	2	DE	86
Hiram W	34	DE	94
John P	6	DE	86
Joseph O	26	DE	110
Leonard	27	DE	78
Mariah P	8	DE	86
Mary A	1	DE	115
Mary A	13	DE	113
Mary A	22	DE	110
Mary R	8/12	DE	110
Outten	64	DE	113
Rachel A	16	DE	113
Robert W	22	DE	113
Sarah	22	DE	114
Susan	35	DE	94
Trusten P	4	DE	110
McCormick, George	37	IE	169
McCoy, John	8	DE	175
McDaniel, Elizabeth	45	DE	78
Joseph	16	DE	157
Martha	4	DE	189
Nathaniel	25	PA	165
John	3	DE	189
John	24	DE	78
Sarah	15	DE	157
Susanna	21	DE	189
Wm	29	DE	189
McDavid, Arthur	5	DE	164
Francis	25	DE	164
Joseph	41	DE	164
Sarah	17	DE	164
Virginia	9	DE	164
William	4	DE	164
McDonegal, Anna	65	DE	167
Hester	22	DE	167
John	1	DE	167
Samuel	39	DE	167
Wm M	32	DE	167
McDowell, Ann	2	DE	12
Ann	49	DE	2
Elizabeth	56	DE	12
Frances	50	DE	162
James	4	DE	11
James	31	DE	11
John	53	DE	162
Lydia	22	DE	11
Mary	65	MD	9
Mary	71	MD	9
Thomas	24	MD	14
Wesley	64	DE	14
McGee, Louis H	11	PA	56
William J	25	DE	135
McGinnis, Elizabeth	70	MD	236
Rebecca	30	DE	236
Susan	17	DE	140
McGonigal, Eleazer	16	DE	114
Mary	26	DE	167
McIlvain, Emily	24	DE	208
Hester J	29	DE	208
John M	4	DE	211
Josephine	2	DE	208
Lawrence F	21	DE	211
Nancy	63	DE	208
Narcissa	2	DE	211
Samuel	5/12	DE	211
Thomas A	8	IN	208
Thomas H	33	DE	208
Wrigham	31	DE	211
Wm S	29	DE	208
McIlvaine, Eliza	15	DE	257
Elizabeth	38	DE	210
Eugenia	2	DE	257
Henry	30	DE	257
McElroy	36	DE	210
Phebe	6	DE	257
Phebe	35	DE	257
Ruthana	8	DE	210
Sarah E	7	DE	210
Thomas A	2	DE	210
William H	11	DE	210
McKee, Harriet	9	DE	248
Maria A	12	DE	27
McKendred, William	5	DE	27
McKerway, Ruth	57	PA	224
McKnatt, Elijah	49	DE	87
Harriet	49	DE	87
James H	10	DE	87
Luther	12	DE	117
Mariah	56	DE	87
McKnitt, Ann	13	DE	242
Eliza	35	DE	242
George	35	DE	242
Margaret	4	DE	242
Mary	7	DE	242
McLaferty, John	23	DE	5
McLance, Martha	5	DE	166
McLane, Allen	30	DE	166
Allice	9	DE	76
Debora	2	DE	166
Hester	10	DE	166
John	4	DE	166
Maria	4/12	DE	166
Sally	30	DE	166
Samuel	9	DE	246
McMullen, Eugene	7/12	DE	10
Lydia	23	DE	10
Walter	33	DE	10
McMullin, Charlot	4/12	DE	46
Robert	26	DE	46
Samuel H	1	DE	46
Sarah C	21	DE	46
McNatt, Burton	23	DE	137
Daniel	30	DE	118
Ebenezar	21	DE	134
Eliza	25	DE	127
Elizabeth	13	DE	130
Elizabeth	23	DE	129
Elizabeth A	10/12	DE	137
Frances	58	DE	137
George	32	DE	263
Isaac	33	DE	127
James	2	DE	127
James	24	DE	137
John	5	DE	264
John	56	DE	129
Julia	45	DE	129
Lemuel	23	DE	129
Leura	35	DE	131
Levin	56	DE	137
Luff J	20	DE	129
Major D	1	DE	117
Mary	17	DE	137
Mary	20	DE	118
Mary	35	DE	118
Mary A	9	DE	127
Mary F	5	DE	127
Nancy	40	DE	129
Nathan	9	DE	264
Sarah	2	DE	264

Name	Age	St	Pg	Name	Age	St	Pg	Name	Age	St	Pg
McNatt, Sarah	34	DE	263	Melvin, Margaret	73	DE	13	Meredith, Thomas	15	DE	252
Sarah	68	DE	129	Margaretta	29	DE	142	Thomas	23	DE	251
Sarah E	10	DE	118	Mariah E	1	DE	71	Uriah	49	DE	147
Thomas H	6	DE	118	Mary	13	DE	264	Whiteley	17	DE	269
Unity	14	DE	129	Mary	20	DE	173	William	12	DE	257
William	7	DE	264	Mary	38	DE	227	William	20	DE	21
William	22	DE	129	Mary A	20	DE	140	William	45	DE	151
William J	4	DE	118	Mary A	31	DE	140	William A	7/12	DE	87
McNeal, William	23	MD	4	Mary E	17	DE	124	William H	13	DE	126
McNease, James	11	MD	186	Matilda S	6	DE	115	Wm	17	DE	237
Wm	9	MD	186	Rachel	7/12	DE	264	Wm	42	DE	257
McNeese, Elizabeth	40	MD	192	Rachel	55	DE	152	Meridy, Amy	30	DE	166
McNelly, James M	16	PA	87	Riley	10/12	DE	143	Sally	14	DE	166
McNib, Benjamin	14	DE	240	Riley	33	DE	140	Taylor	33	DE	166
McNitt, Joseph	17	DE	212	Ruth A	8	DE	115	Merriken, Elizabeth	11	DE	145
Manlove	22	DE	164	Samuel	5	DE	70	John	10	DE	145
Manlove	27	DE	166	Sarah	4	DE	264	Mary	41	DE	144
McNutt, Robert	25	IE	74	Solomon	27	DE	264	Richard H	51	MD	144
Meadows, Philip	18	MD	11	Sydenham	33	DE	142	Richard N	24	MD	148
Meaker, Abel	5	DE	268	Thomas A	2	DE	124	Susan	7	DE	145
John	9	DE	268	Thomas A	4	DE	143	Zachariah	19	MD	148
Samuel	7	DE	268	Truit	41	DE	70	Messick, Ann	29	DE	209
Sarah	31	DE	268	Willard	8	DE	140	Anna	44	DE	84
Wm	30	DE	268	William	21	DE	81	Caroline	7	DE	209
Mears, Robert	22	DE	94	Melvine, Brumwell	69	DE	77	Charles H	12	DE	209
Mecklin, Catherine	54	DE	233	Margaret	16	DE	10	Hester	14	DE	84
Julia	19	DE	233	Matilda	60	MD	77	James B	10	DE	114
Medford, Margaret	16	DE	141	Sarah	20	DE	77	L	53	DE	114
William W	20	DE	141	Mercer, Charles	1	DE	13	William A	19	DE	114
Meeds, William C	38	MD	4	James	33	DE	13	Wingate	39	DE	209
Megar, Daniel	13	DE	45	Mary	20	DE	13	Metten, Jane	24	DE	159
Daniel	54	DE	44	Meredith, Alexander	3	DE	269	Middleton, Elenor	57	PA	3
Hester	6	DE	45	Amelia	18	DE	106	Hannah	18	DE	206
Hester	48	DE	44	Ann	46	DE	229	Miers, William H	17	PA	89
Mary E	19	DE	44	Ann R	25	DE	87	Mifflin, Ann J	34	DE	212
Sarah	17	DE	45	Benjamin	5	DE	258	Daniel	2	DE	73
Susan	11	DE	45	Caroline	8	DE	77	Daniel	41	DE	226
Thomas	15	DE	45	Catherine	1	DE	269	Daniel	75	DE	223
Mellanay, George	23	DE	13	Celea J	3	DE	106	Eliza	43	DE	73
James	56	DE	13	Charles H	16	DE	147	Emma	1	DE	212
Priscilla	55	DE	13	Daniel F	17	DE	106	Mary	27	DE	226
William W	16	DE	13	Dickerson	44	DE	106	Nathaniel	15	DE	204
Melvin, Almyra	26	DE	264	Elizabeth	16	DE	257	Nathaniel	39	DE	213
Amanda	8	DE	181	Elizabeth	17	DE	258	Pleasanton	9	DE	73
Angelina	11/12	DE	140	Ezekiel	12	DE	269	Samuel	32	DE	212
Bartholomew	45	DE	115	George	13	DE	238	Susan	50	MD	223
Clementine	19	DE	124	Henry F	3	DE	87	Thomas	54	DE	223
David	52	DE	140	Hugh	5	DE	106	Walker	36	DE	73
Deborah	63	DE	140	Jacob	14	DE	257	Milaway, James H	2/12	DE	5
Deborah A	11	DE	124	John	22	DE	106	John	28	DE	5
Edmund	16	DE	184	John	42	DE	126	Martha P	2/12	DE	5
Eliza	36	MD	264	John K	19	DE	147	Susan	29	DE	5
Elizabeth	1	DE	216	Lavicy	55	MD	147	Milburn, Edwin	3/12	DE	199
Elizabeth	17	DE	227	Levin	28	DE	87	Frances	26	MD	199
Elizabeth	34	DE	70	Lewis	21	DE	194	Mary	6	DE	199
Emily	3/12	DE	140	Lydia	6	DE	134	Samuel	29	DE	199
Emma L	10	DE	140	Lydia	11	DE	103	Sarah	5	DE	199
Greenberry	48	DE	227	M Elizabeth	8	DE	106	William	16	DE	199
Hester A	11	DE	115	Major	13	DE	125	Mileham, Ann	6	DE	263
Hester A	39	DE	115	Mary	10	DE	257	Catherine	16	DE	263
Hinson	34	DE	264	Mary	14	DE	258	Deborah	18	DE	263
Isaac J	14	DE	124	Mary	38	DE	126	Mary	20	DE	263
Jacob	2	DE	115	Mary	39	DE	257	Susan	13	DE	263
Jacob	6	DE	124	Mary	44	DE	106	Willamina	10	DE	263
James	5	DE	143	Mary E	6	DE	87	William	2	DE	263
James	10	DE	264	Nancy	60	DE	149	Wm	47	DE	263
James	23	DE	113	Nancy J	19	DE	87	Milksay, Anne	7	DE	154
James	45	DE	123	Peter	16	DE	258	Eliza	30	DE	154
James F	9	DE	70	Peter	27	DE	269	Emily	12	DE	154
James W	4	DE	124	Peter	61	DE	269	Joseph	41	DE	154
John	14	DE	178	Phener	51	MD	151	Mary	10	DE	154
John	19	DE	216	Robert J	10	DE	107	Miller, Alfred	14	DE	36
Joshua	9	DE	195	Sally Ann	37	MD	257	Alfred	15	DE	67
Joshua	19	DE	158	Samuel	10	DE	269	Alfred	18	DE	35
Joshua	19	DE	227	Samuel	25	DE	190	Alfred	21	DE	187
Joshua	60	MD	195	Sarah	29	DE	269	Amaritta	47	DE	68
Latitia	50	DE	181	Sarah	50	DE	194	Ann	17	DE	25
Lavinia	45	DE	124	Sarah	59	DE	269	Ann	31	DE	269
Lewis	2	DE	216	Sarah A	5	DE	106	Ann	46	MD	67
Lewis	44	MD	216	Sarah A	35	DE	106	Anna	3	DE	204
Louisa	8	DE	264	Sarah E	5	DE	108	Araminta	13	DE	127
Margaret	29	DE	216	Susanna	16	DE	13	Araminta	16	DE	176

Name	Age	St	Pg
Miller, Caroline	12	DE	170
Caroline	36	MD	160
Catharine	12	DE	17
Catherine	13	DE	188
Catherine	24	DE	175
Catherine	37	DE	155
Charles	15	DE	267
Charles	50	DE	155
Charles	65	DE	175
Charlotte	12	DE	268
Comfort	70	DE	174
David	9	DE	21
David	16	DE	170
David	18	DE	171
Deborix	7	DE	26
Deborix	19	DE	66
Easter	65	DE	159
Ebenezer	3	DE	17
Eliza	32	DE	25
Eliza	33	DE	38
Eliza T	12	DE	12
Elizabeth	1	DE	26
Elizabeth	18	DE	4
Elizabeth	18	DE	256
Elizabeth	64	DE	73
Ellen	3	DE	165
Emanuel	1	DE	256
Emily	13	DE	38
Enoch	29	DE	26
George	4	DE	165
George	6	DE	38
George	11	DE	76
George	14	DE	35
George	49	MD	29
George	79	DE	225
Hannah	16	DE	188
Hannah	47	DE	188
Hannah	71	DE	228
Henry	5	DE	38
Henry	8	DE	268
Henry	36	DE	160
Henry	46	DE	268
Hester	10	DE	80
Hester	11	DE	165
Hester	14	DE	68
Hezekiah	38	DE	38
Isaac	1	DE	268
Isaac	48	DE	68
Jacob	7	DE	59
James	4	DE	160
James	22	DE	256
James	59	DE	46
James	69	DE	225
Jane	11	DE	208
Jane	22	DE	25
Jeremiah	10	DE	173
John	4	DE	25
John	4	DE	268
John	13	DE	73
John	25	DE	159
John	40	DE	157
John	47	DE	66
Josiah	4	DE	66
Josiah	33	DE	25
Jude	7	DE	26
Killen	48	DE	165
Levin	6	DE	204
Louisa	20	MD	256
Margaret	7	DE	66
Margaret	10	DE	137
Margaret	12	DE	165
Margaret	69	DE	46
Mariah	10	DE	73
Martha	14	DE	17
Martha	17	DE	66
Mary	4/12	DE	175
Mary	5	DE	268
Mary	10	DE	165
Mary	10	DE	188
Mary	13	DE	66
Mary	23	DE	188
Mary	36	MD	29
Miller, Mary	40	DE	4
Morris	28	DE	175
Nancy	35	DE	256
Perry	20	DE	42
Peter	1/12	DE	188
Peter	14	DE	165
Peter	56	DE	188
Phebe	26	DE	26
Rachel	7	DE	160
Rachel	10	DE	69
Rachel	12	DE	25
Rachel	40	DE	225
Rebecca	10	DE	21
Rebecca	16	DE	28
Rebecca	36	DE	165
Rebecca	38	DE	175
Rebecca	40	DE	73
Robert	18	DE	171
Robert	41	DE	17
Sarah	2	DE	38
Sarah	7	DE	268
Sarah	24	DE	204
Sarah	39	DE	17
Sarah	62	DE	25
Sarah E	6	DE	204
Stephen	10	DE	25
Stephen	23	DE	188
Thomas	5	DE	26
Tobias	76	DE	34
Virginia	2	DE	166
William	8/12	PA	165
William	15	DE	73
Wm	10	DE	179
Wm	13	DE	170
Wm	19	PA	161
Milligan, Sarah J	16	DE	150
Scynthia	40	DE	150
Millis, Isaac P	11	DE	92
John B	3	DE	92
Mary	14	DE	228
Peter	6	DE	228
Pouty	35	DE	228
Robert C	1/12	DE	92
Samuel	4	DE	228
Samuel	40	DE	228
Sarah	5/12	DE	228
Sarah A	31	MD	92
Sarah E	8	DE	92
William	16	DE	224
William H	10	DE	92
William H	31	MD	92
Mills, David	4	DE	101
Edward	31	DE	101
George	2	DE	101
Margaret	20	DE	101
Sarah	24	DE	101
Miner, Major	51	DE	206
Margaret	2/12	DE	206
Maria	21	DE	268
Samuel	11	DE	268
Minner, Alexander	3	DE	117
Alexander	5	DE	119
Angelina	13	DE	120
Ann	15	DE	50
Ann E	2	DE	119
Ann E	10	DE	116
Ann E	11	DE	138
Anna	28	DE	137
Catherine	9	DE	121
Dennis	14	DE	120
Dennis	30	DE	137
Eliza	15	DE	117
Elizabeth	27	DE	119
Elizabeth	45	DE	110
Elizabeth	50	DE	117
Elizabeth L	34	DE	116
Hannah	28	DE	120
Henry	5	DE	120
Henry	5	DE	137
Hezekiah	19	DE	132
Hezekiah	49	DE	110
James P	4	DE	142
Minner, James P	4	DE	142
James W	8	DE	137
Jane	4	DE	138
John	12	DE	131
John	28	DE	119
John	32	DE	142
John W	1	DE	120
Jonathan	23	DE	117
Joshua	15	DE	110
Lydia	1/12	DE	138
Lydia J	3	DE	121
Margarett J	7	DE	116
Martain V	12	DE	116
Martha	7	DE	120
Mary	31	DE	138
Mary A	7	DE	110
Mary A	8	DE	138
Mary C	2	DE	116
Nathan W	40	DE	120
Nimrod	37	DE	139
Patience	20	DE	167
Samuel	6	DE	138
Sarah	53	DE	139
Sarah	60	DE	142
Sarah A	30	DE	142
Sarah E P	5	DE	116
Stephen	23	DE	170
Stephen	78	DE	129
Thomas	9	DE	120
Thomas	40	DE	138
Unice	15	DE	120
William	10	DE	138
Minnor, Jane	75	MD	162
Jesse	14	DE	240
John	16	DE	240
Joshua	16	DE	238
Leura	3	DE	240
Lydia	33	DE	240
Major	9	DE	240
Mary	12	DE	240
Mary	19	MD	162
Nathaniel	17	DE	240
Rebecca	2	DE	240
Sarah	8	DE	237
Sarah	10	DE	240
Sarah	17	DE	269
Thomas	5	DE	240
Thomas	35	DE	240
Minty, Anna M	50	GE	206
Conrad	51	GE	206
Lewis	20	DE	206
Silistane	18	DE	206
Theodore	10	DE	206
Minus, Albert	27	DE	193
Alexander	3	DE	193
Alexander	25	DE	193
Ann	3	DE	193
Ann M	11	DE	83
Anna	4	DE	255
Anor	9	DE	189
Beckey	8	DE	255
Benjamin	13	PA	6
Catherine	2	DE	193
Charles	6	DE	155
David	5	DE	155
Elizabeth	1	DE	193
Elizabeth	26	DE	189
Elizabeth	42	DE	83
Emery	28	DE	189
Eve	26	DE	193
George	1	DE	155
George P	8	DE	83
Grace	27	MD	193
Hannah	27	MD	255
Jacob	45	MD	193
James	1	DE	193
John	3	DE	189
John	5	DE	193
John	35	DE	255
Joshua S	5	DE	83
Laura	1	DE	189
Levi	14	DE	256

Name	Age	State	Page
Minus, Louisa	15	DE	255
Luther	4	DE	193
Margaret	4	DE	193
Martha	5	DE	193
Mary	1	DE	193
Mary	10	DE	255
Mary	27	DE	155
Matilda	5	DE	255
Pernel	40	DE	155
Robert John	14	DE	83
Sarah M	17	DE	83
Willy	23	DE	193
Wm	12	DE	168
Mitcham, Edward	25	DE	266
Julia	6	DE	266
Rebecca	62	DE	266
Mitchel, David	13	PA	80
Elizabeth A	3	DE	23
Elizabeth P	20	DE	23
Hannah A	10	DE	23
Hester	29	DE	23
Hester A	37	DE	47
James	25	DE	23
James	41	GB	80
John	66	DE	73
Margaret	35	GB	80
Mary	10	DE	167
Mary	15	DE	79
Nancy	60	DE	73
Robert	36	DE	23
Thomas	18	IE	2
William C	34	DE	47
William H	1	DE	23
Mitchell, Charles	2	DE	63
David	28	NY	63
Eliza	9	DE	172
Elizabeth	31	PA	1
Elizabeth	39	DE	85
Elizabeth	51	MD	154
George	2/12	DE	1
George	10	DE	178
George	43	DE	178
Henry	19	DE	47
Hester	20	DE	207
Hester A	30	MD	63
James	6/12	DE	178
James R	6	DE	85
James R	43	MD	85
John	45	DE	1
Joseph	16	DE	181
Joshua	49	MD	181
Mary	3	DE	178
Mary	36	DE	85
Mary	72	MD	154
Parris	16	DE	178
Rachel	4	DE	181
Rachel	49	DE	181
Robert	2/12	DE	210
Robert	14	DE	178
Robert	71	MD	154
Samuel	11	DE	181
Sarah	6	DE	178
Sarah	12	DE	154
Sarah	41	DE	178
Sarah V	6/12	DE	85
Scynthia E	10	DE	85
Thomas	5	DE	63
Thomas	60	ST	63
William	15	DE	181
Mitten, Alexander	65	DE	109
Ann	25	DE	109
James	15	DE	109
Mary	51	DE	110
William B	23	DE	107
Mittin, Alexander	5	DE	105
Anna	3	DE	105
Daniel	32	DE	99
James	23	DE	93
Mary	6	DE	105
Mary	31	DE	105
Matthew	37	DE	105
Rachel	1	DE	105
Mittin, Roxaline	2	DE	99
Sarah	8	DE	105
Sarah A	24	DE	99
William C	4	DE	99
Moffett, Alexander P	9	DE	37
George	12	DE	53
Mary	16	DE	53
Susan	13	DE	37
Moffitt, Franklin	24	DE	55
Hester A	5	DE	68
Molasten, Deric	4	DE	175
Derick	50	DE	169
Leah	6	DE	175
Louisa	2	DE	175
Lydia	28	DE	175
Martha	40	DE	169
Priscilla	3/12	DE	175
Roger	8	DE	175
Roger	32	DE	175
Molastin, George	8	DE	255
Molaston, Clementine	7	DE	247
Molisten, Benana	3	DE	234
Money, Mary	57	MD	15
Monk, Napoleon	4	DE	234
Peter	46	MD	249
Montague, Ann	20	DE	189
Daniel	12	DE	189
Elizabeth	14	DE	189
Elizabeth	15	DE	189
Ellen	10	DE	189
George	7	DE	189
Henry	14	DE	189
Hester	48	DE	189
Jesse	45	MD	189
John	13	DE	189
Mary	8	DE	229
Penelope	10	DE	229
Seth	10	DE	171
Wm	15	DE	188
Monty, Hannah	14	DE	159
Hetty	45	DE	159
Joseph	20	DE	159
Mary	8	DE	159
Moody, Alfred	10	DE	64
Charel	15	DE	47
John	17	DE	158
John	45	DE	64
John S	36	DE	85
Margaret	1	DE	85
Mary Ann	37	DE	85
Samuel	8	DE	64
Sarah	13	DE	158
William	12	DE	150
William T	6	DE	85
Moor, Abraham A	30	DE	11
Abraham N	42	DE	68
Amy	30	DE	11
Andrew	14	DE	67
Anna	19	DE	30
Caroline	7	DE	95
Caroline	33	DE	95
Collins	13	DE	69
David G	12	NJ	61
David R	40	NJ	61
Elizabeth	6	DE	68
George	2	DE	68
Hannah	18	DE	67
Hester	6	DE	67
Isaac	4	DE	70
Israel	65	NJ	61
Jacob	67	DE	69
James	3/12	DE	67
James S	29	DE	30
John	18	DE	67
John W	7	DE	61
Joseph K	6	DE	109
Lydia	14	DE	68
Lydia	52	DE	67
Lydia R	16	NJ	61
Mary A	1	DE	11
Mary Ann	5	DE	68
Mary C	12	DE	67
Moor, Mary J	39	NJ	61
Nehemiah	26	DE	70
Philip H	18	NJ	61
Rachel	29	DE	68
Rachel	58	DE	29
Rachel C	13	DE	109
Robert D	19	DE	73
Robert J	21	DE	29
Sarah	8/12	DE	70
Sarah	20	DE	55
Sarah	24	DE	70
Stephen	6	DE	69
Susanna	11	DE	67
Sylvia	66	DE	69
Thomas	46	DE	67
William H	16	DE	67
Moore, Abraham	6	DE	175
Abraham	30	DE	20
Abraham	67	DE	77
Alpher	38	DE	191
Amanda	2	DE	69
Andrew	6	DE	176
Ann	1/12	DE	200
Ann	13	DE	175
Betsey	40	DE	176
Catherine	49	DE	241
Clarissa A	22	DE	218
Clayton	20	DE	153
Daniel	21	DE	197
Daniel	33	DE	191
David	6	DE	197
David	7	DE	193
Ellen	4	DE	249
Ellen	6	DE	79
Ellen	36	DE	79
Elmira	1	DE	175
Elmira	6	DE	241
Emeline	5	DE	249
Emily R	16	DE	78
George	9	DE	249
George	10	DE	241
George	35	DE	249
George	36	DE	69
Griffin	33	DE	249
Henry	30	DE	177
Henry H	24	DE	78
Hester	9	DE	79
Hester	17	DE	246
Hester	18	DE	257
Hester	25	DE	249
Hetty	6	DE	191
Hetty	33	DE	191
Isaac	4	DE	191
Isaac	13	DE	79
Isaac B	39	DE	217
James	14	DE	193
James	16	DE	153
James	18	DL	183
James	20	DE	241
James	51	DE	153
James A	26	DE	217
James C	23	DE	59
John	1	DE	179
John	11	DE	200
John	22	DE	246
John	24	DE	57
John M	24	DE	162
Jonathan	20	DE	214
Jonathan	12	DE	193
Joseph	13	DE	194
Joseph	11	DE	79
Joseph S	35	DE	175
Lavinia	14	DE	78
Louisa	13	DE	200
Lydia	9	DE	200
Lydia	4	DE	158
Margaret	5	DE	193
Margaret	7	DE	200
Margaret	20	DE	217
Martha	48	DE	249
Mary	4	DE	175
Mary	7	DE	191

Name	Age	St	Pg	Name	Age	St	Pg	Name	Age	St	Pg
Moore, Mary	8	DE	175	Morgan, Hannah	15	DE	158	Morris, Henry	7	DE	82
Mary	14	DE	241	Henrietta	24	MD	177	Henry	15	PA	78
Mary	19	DE	68	Ivan	14	DE	144	Henry	23	DE	58
Mary	21	DE	189	James	12	DE	144	Hester	15	DE	33
Mary	26	DE	177	James	29	DE	177	Hester	20	DE	150
Mary	30	DE	14	Jane	28	DE	139	Hester J	14	DE	46
Mary	30	DE	146	John	10	DE	172	Hester J	15	DE	48
Mary	33	DE	175	John	34	DE	173	Irby	55	DE	84
Mary	43	DE	193	John Shores	6	DE	26	Isaac	45	DE	169
Mary E	16	DE	218	Lydia	60	DE	139	James	6/12	DE	210
Moses	32	DE	200	Margaret A	2	DE	26	James	1	DE	25
Nancy	37	DE	200	Mariah	28	DE	109	James	3	DE	240
Nancy	55	DE	77	Mary	11	DE	144	James	6	DE	266
Nancy Lydia	22	DE	78	Mary	25	DE	69	James R	19	DE	116
Nathan	1/12	DE	191	Mary	31	DE	172	John	7	DE	62
Nathan	3	DE	200	Mary	32	DE	173	John	11	DE	240
Nathan	27	DE	248	Mary E	13	DE	26	John	14	DE	163
Nathan	43	DE	176	Martha	18	DE	64	John	21	DE	127
Noah	43	DE	192	Martha	52	DE	134	John	62	MD	227
Noah	62	DE	246	Miranda	30	DE	98	John C	9	DE	134
Owen	3	DE	249	Nancy	65	DE	109	John H	8	DE	48
Rebecca	17	DE	193	Nathan	16	DE	139	Joseph	11	DE	79
Rebecca	30	DE	158	Nathan	62	DE	139	Joseph B	25	DE	57
Rebecca Ann	12	DE	69	Nelson	5	DE	144	Lemuel	23	DE	129
Richard	37	DE	200	Nelson	46	DE	143	Lydia	36	DE	212
Robert	6	DE	191	Nicy	21	DE	109	Major	15	DE	153
Robert	7	DE	158	Rebecca	5	DE	172	Major	22	DE	117
Robert	40	DE	158	Robert E	18	MD	14	Major A	1	DE	117
Sally	25	DE	241	Sally	7	DE	172	Margaret	12	PA	79
Sallyann	30	MD	200	Samuel	4/12	DE	177	Margaret	28	DE	62
Samuel	3	DE	79	Samuel	10	DE	69	Maria	5	DE	210
Samuel	11	DE	200	Samuel	30	DE	69	Mariah M	72	DE	227
Samuel	20	DE	78	Samuel H	1/12	DE	99	Mary	1	DE	263
Samuel	22	DE	153	Sarah	53	DE	134	Mary	10	DE	149
Samuel	35	DE	119	Sarah A	12	DE	77	Mary	10	DE	266
Samuel	40	DE	79	Sarah A	26	DE	109	Mary	36	DE	249
Sarah	1	DE	176	Sarah E	1	DE	122	Mary	43	DE	240
Sarah	5	DE	177	William	33	DE	98	Mary	47	DE	12
Sarah	10	DE	153	Wm	46	DE	172	Mary	55	DE	180
Sarah Ann	35	DE	69	Morrell, Elizabeth	19	DE	88	Mary	71	DE	163
Sewell G	20	DE	32	Louisa	7	DE	88	Mary E	1	DE	114
Sina	11	DE	175	Morris, Aaron	45	DE	48	Matilda	22	DE	25
Susan	4	DE	191	Aaron T	18	DE	48	Milly	60	DE	93
Susan	9	DE	69	Abritta	8	DE	9	Nathaniel	60	DE	200
Susan	15	DE	79	Alexander	35	DE	266	Parker	17	DE	93
Susan	22	DE	257	Allice	22	DE	163	Patience	30	DE	266
Susan G	14	DE	218	Ambrose	1	DE	268	Perry	50	DE	93
Susanna	3	DE	177	Aner	71	DE	249	Phebe	18	DE	4
Thomas	2	DE	191	Ann	40	PA	169	Phebe	50	DE	25
Thomas	6	DE	249	Anna	20	DE	117	Philip	60	DE	25
Thomas	8	DE	191	Anna	37	DE	163	Rachel	48	DE	48
Thomas	8	DE	241	Beacham	27	DE	200	Rachel V	13	DE	48
Thomas	15	DE	249	Bosey	4/12	DE	266	Rhoda Ann	11	DE	64
Thomas	33	DE	191	Celia	25	DE	137	Richard	48	DE	7
Thomas	47	DE	241	Charles	12	DE	64	Robert	9	DE	92
Thomas H	20	DE	218	Charles W	37	DE	114	Robert H	6	DE	139
Victorine	17	DE	57	Clement	10	DE	129	Roxena	4/12	DE	129
Vincent	31	DE	218	Cornelius	16	DE	53	Samuel	6	DE	79
William	2	DE	191	Cornelius	16	DE	64	Samuel	31	DE	117
William	9	DE	249	Cornelius	59	DE	64	Samuel	63	DE	263
William	10	DE	26	David	32	DE	32	Sarah	15	DE	184
More, Mary	1/12	DE	240	Elexena	9	DE	266	Sarah	21	DE	32
Owen	24	DE	240	Elias	4	DE	79	Sarah	29	DE	82
Sarah	20	DE	240	Elihu J	24	DE	208	Sarah E	3/12	DE	62
Moreland, George	6	DE	16	Elija	43	DE	240	Sarah E	1	DE	32
Morgan, Alsey	1	DE	172	Elijah	6	DE	134	Sarah E	9	DE	93
Angeline	10	DE	144	Elisha	9	DE	64	Sarah E	16	DE	48
Ann	45	DE	134	Eliza	18	DE	25	Scely	51	DE	200
Catherine	16	DE	176	Elizabeth	2	DE	212	Susan	8	DE	64
Chana	50	DE	143	Elizabeth	3	DE	64	Thomas	1	DE	64
Daniel	9	DE	26	Elizabeth	18	DE	127	Virginia	12	DE	54
Edmund	27	DE	122	Elizabeth	21	DE	210	William	3	DE	62
Edward	28	GB	89	Elizabeth	38	DE	64	William	6	DE	32
Eleanor A	23	DE	110	Emily	5	DE	25	William	8	DE	79
Eliza A	34	DE	122	Emily	32	DE	163	William	9	DE	240
Elizabeth	9	DE	172	George	1	DE	82	William	10	DE	27
Elizabeth	22	DE	64	George	6	DE	62	William	20	DE	104
Evan	65	DE	109	George	14	DE	24	William	34	DE	82
Ezekiel	25	DE	110	George	15	DE	25	William	35	DE	62
Frances	50	DE	64	Harriet Ann	6	DE	64	William C	3	DE	48
George	20	DE	131	Henrietta	1/12	DE	32	Wm W	66	MD	163
George	60	DE	134	Henrietta	22	DE	114	Morrison, Priscilla	70	DE	231

Name	Age	State	Page
Morrison, Roger	70	DE	231
Samuel	18	DE	231
Moseley, Alexander	13	DE	108
Amanda	2/12	DE	110
Benjamin	5	DE	173
Benjamin	28	DE	110
Comfort	2	DE	173
Eleanor	24	DE	110
Elsey	7	DE	173
Isaac	9	DE	173
John	8	DE	176
John	35	DE	173
Joseph	4	DE	108
Josephine	3	DE	173
Mary	11	DE	173
Morris	9	DE	108
Purnel	2	DE	110
Purnel	32	DE	108
Purnel	80	DE	173
Rebecca	30	DE	108
Sally	35	DE	173
Sarah	7	DE	108
Sina	5	DE	173
Zepporah	10	DE	108
Mosely, Betsey	3	DE	174
Ephraim	1	DE	174
James	7	DE	174
Nancy	25	DE	174
Purnel	5	DE	174
Wingate	10	DE	176
Wingate	30	DE	174
Mosley, Elizabeth	28	DE	206
George W	1	DE	206
James	33	DE	206
Mount, Ann	34	NJ	3
Barberry	3	NJ	3
Biryin	8	NJ	3
John C	39	NJ	3
Samuel	13	NJ	3
Mudd, William C	38	MD	3
Muldoon, James	38	IE	9
Mary	6	IE	9
Mary	39	IE	9
Mullin, Rebecca	35	DE	161
Wm	37	DE	161
Mumford, John	15	DE	206
Munce, Angeline	5	DE	68
Anjelica	2	DE	68
Hannah	7	DE	68
James	12	DE	67
Jemima	37	DE	67
John	13	DE	23
Josiah	15	DE	67
Lydia	17	DE	67
Margaret	10	DE	68
Mary E	9	DE	68
Robert	1/12	DE	68
Robert	40	DE	67
Muncy, Harriet	12	DE	81
Jonathan	3	DE	81
Margaret	6	DE	81
Mary	10	MD	10
Mary	34	DE	81
Thomas	1/12	DE	81
Thomas	40	DE	81
Muney, Margaret	4	DE	176
Martha	12	DE	176
Phebe	10	DE	176
Robert	16	DE	176
Sally	8	DE	176
Munsey, Charles H	7	DE	207
Clarissa	51	DE	207
Samuel	12	DE	207
Muonckin, Frances	7	DE	222
Lewis	5	DE	222
Lewis D	51	MD	222
Margaret	10	DE	222
Rebecca	45	MD	222
Murphey, Ann E	31	DE	48
Benjamin	6	DE	113
Caleb	35	DE	96
Charles	4	DE	163
Murphey, Charles	12	DE	223
Clement	40	DE	113
Collins	4	DE	113
David J	32	DE	48
Eliza J	31	DE	96
Elizabeth	4/12	DE	223
Elizabeth	15	DE	113
Elizabeth	31	MA	163
Florence	2	DE	163
Henry	2	DE	48
Isaac	16	DE	113
James	13	DE	140
Jenkens	9	DE	223
John	13	DE	113
Jonathan	14	DE	223
Maria	8	DE	113
Mary	14	DE	82
Nicy E	3	DE	113
Robert	5	DE	223
Samuel M	4	DE	48
Sanford	2/12	DE	163
Sarah	2/12	DE	249
Sarah	37	MD	223
Sarah	8	DE	223
Thomas	8	DE	223
Thomas	39	DE	223
Thomas G	33	DE	163
Timothy	24	IE	202
William P	1	DE	96
Zipporah	30	DE	113
Murphy, Ann E	4	DE	151
Daniel	3	DE	151
Eliza A	30	DE	151
John C	6/12	DE	151
Jonathan	4	DE	139
Jonathan	50	DE	139
Leura	7	DE	139
Maria	22	DE	249
Mary	52	DE	82
Rebecca	10	DE	139
Robert A	7	DE	151
Samuel	10	DE	82
Samuel	46	DE	82
Sarah E	1	DE	110
Solomon	30	DE	151
Susan	30	DE	139
Violet	7	DE	139
William	17	DE	123
William	24	DE	82
William H	8	DE	151
Murray, Icabod	20	NJ	161
Mary	75	DE	118
Murrey, Alexander	3	DE	242
Anna	65	DE	242
Asa	3/12	DE	242
Asa	30	DE	242
Charles	3/12	DE	229
Charles	30	DE	229
Eliza	3	DE	229
Elizabeth	35	DE	2
Emanuel	6	DE	242
Emanuel	37	MD	2
George	7	DE	242
Henrietta	30	DE	242
John	8	DE	2
Levin	68	DE	242
Sally	27	DE	242
Sarah	27	DE	229
Sarah E	7	DE	2
Sina Ann	6	DE	242
Thomas	3	DE	2
Thomas	5	DE	229
Murry, Ann	45	DE	232
Asa	8	DE	236
Catherine	2	DE	236
Catherine	25	DE	236
Charles	24	DE	203
Eugene	5	DE	159
Harriet	30	DE	159
Isaac	6	DE	232
Isaac	44	DE	232
James	5	DE	236
John	9	DE	240
Murry, Joseph	13	DE	232
Mary	10	DE	236
Mary	30	DE	116
Sarah	1	DE	236
Stanbury	6	DE	236
Stanbury	33	DE	236
Murtage, Emma	29	PA	69
Robert	33	PA	69
Mustard, Horace	9	DE	82
John	14	DE	82
John	45	DE	82
Margaret	6	DE	82
Mary	12	DE	82
Othniel	17	DE	82
Temperance	45	DE	82
Nail, Sarah	51	DE	10
Nasum, Mary	38	DE	185
Naudain, Arnold	19	DE	81
Catharine	14	DE	81
Elias	11	DE	81
James	21	DE	81
Margaret	8	DE	81
Margaret	41	DE	81
Sarah	5	DE	81
Neal, Ann	15	DE	153
Cyrus	11	DE	242
Needles, Alexander	34	DE	247
Ann	22	DE	247
Ann	48	DE	241
Benjamin	8/12	DE	99
Benjamin P	40	DE	105
David	26	DE	241
James	30	DE	241
John	7	DE	200
John	7	DE	241
John	36	DE	179
John P	25	DE	99
Joseph	1	DE	241
Mary	4	DE	241
Mary	26	DE	99
Mary	69	DE	99
Nancy	12	DE	241
Nancy	22	DE	99
Nancy	33	DE	105
Rachel	7	DE	247
Sallyann	17	DE	241
Samuel	22	DE	241
Sarah	24	DE	241
Thomas	7/12	DE	247
William	3	DE	247
Neeld, Charles J	28	PA	16
Dewitt C	6/12	DE	16
Margaret	21	PA	16
Nelson, Ann	8	DE	36
John B	14	DE	36
Mary	2	DE	36
Mary	34	DE	36
Sarah E	11	DE	36
William F	6	DE	36
William W	38	VA	36
New, James	13	DE	237
Newcomb, Ann R	14	DE	111
Reuben	27	DE	53
Sarah	23	DE	53
Newman, Cornelia V	28	MD	54
Daniel	6	DE	195
Denny	15	DE	28
Edward	4	MD	54
James	8	DE	195
James	25	DE	43
Patrick	18	IE	16
Sarah A	25	DE	43
Thomas	1	MD	54
Thomas	34	MD	54
William	12	MD	233
Newnin, Michael	55	IE	36
Newsom, Alfred	5	DE	116
Alfred	41	DE	116
John E	9	DE	116
Mary E	11	DE	116
Phillip E	3	DE	116

Name	Age	State	No.
Newsom, Ruth A	6	DE	116
Ruth A	47	DE	116
Newton, Amelia	12	NJ	68
Charles	16	NJ	68
Hannah	45	NJ	70
Rebecca	7	DE	70
Richard S	52	NJ	70
Sarah	17	NJ	56
Sarah	17	NJ	70
Nichols, Daniel	36	DE	125
Isaac W	17	DE	125
Lydia A	5	DE	125
Mary A	34	DE	125
Mary E	8	DE	125
Matthew	3	DE	125
Nehemiah	1	DE	125
William E	10	DE	125
Nicholson, Angelina	24	DE	162
John	1	DE	162
John A	22	DE	162
Nickerson, Ann	17	DE	10
Ann	34	DE	226
Charles	4/12	DE	195
Elizabeth	10	DE	226
Elizabeth	28	MD	196
Elsberry	24	DE	196
Emily	25	MD	196
Henrietta	4	DE	67
James	17	DE	201
Joseph	37	DE	226
Joshua	28	DE	195
Levi B	24	DE	196
Margaret	25	DE	67
Martha	5	DE	196
Martha	17	DE	196
Owen	5	DE	196
Owen	40	DE	196
Philemon	4	DE	226
Rosene	2/12	DE	196
Sarah	2	DE	196
Sarah	62	DE	196
Susan	28	DE	195
Thomas	1	DE	226
William	5	DE	67
William	5	DE	226
William	7	DE	195
William P	29	DE	67
Wm	60	DE	196
Nickles, Beckey	30	DE	160
Elizabeth	2	DE	160
Harriet	7	DE	160
Wesley	30	DE	160
Mickolds, Daniel	66	DE	108
Nickson, Grace	40	DE	28
Hester	11/12	DE	28
Isaac	40	DE	28
Lydia	4	DE	28
Margaret	45	DE	28
Mary	8	DE	28
Mary	18	DE	196
Samuel	14	DE	27
Sarah C	10	DE	28
Night, Daniel	9	DE	164
Daniel	47	DE	164
Mary	46	DE	164
Noble, Clement	21	DE	69
Nock, Elizabeth	25	DE	222
Mary	4	DE	222
Thomas P	26	DE	222
William	2	DE	222
Nokes, Delia	22	MD	11
Edward	2	DE	11
James	35	MD	11
Rebecca	7	MD	11
Susanna	8/12	DE	11
Nolding, William D	1	DE	48
Norris, Elijah	33	DE	203
Henry S	8	DE	203
John K	26	DE	203
Lydia	61	DE	203
North, George	28	DE	24
James	32	DE	7
Note, Harriann	14	PA	69
Notts, Debora	30	DE	196
Edward	17	DE	190
Elizabeth	1	DE	196
George	28	MD	196
Henry	30	DE	182
Wm	40	DE	175
Nowel, Clement T	33	DE	209
Elanesa	5	DE	209
Henrietta	29	DE	209
Thomas E	3	DE	209
Wm	20	DE	163
Nowell, Abraham P	28	DE	58
Clement	57	DE	79
Eliza Ann	22	DE	79
George H	3	DE	58
Grace	52	DE	79
James S	18	DE	79
John S	8	DE	125
Mary	22	DE	58
Mary	40	DE	113
Mary	78	DE	125
Mary A	10	DE	143
Mary E	23	DE	248
Mary J	16	DE	79
Peter	35	DE	125
Phener	20	DE	125
Phener	36	DE	125
Samuel	11	DE	125
Samuel	25	DE	166
Wesley	2	DE	43
Wesley	2	DE	249
Nox, Thomas	21	DE	199
Numbers, Charles	2	DE	53
Charles	7	DE	62
Charles	35	DE	53
Elizabeth	33	MD	62
Jane	27	DE	53
John	1	DE	62
John	30	DE	19
John	42	DE	62
John	70	DE	19
Martha	48	DE	19
Mary A	6	DE	53
Mary A	8	DE	62
Sarah	35	DE	19
Seba	22	DE	19
William	4	DE	62
William	8	DE	53
Nunam, Elizabeth	50	DE	26
James	52	DE	26
James H	16	DE	26
Mary	15	DE	26
Sarah	17	DE	26
Susan	11	DE	26
Nunem, Amelia	2	DE	197
Elizabeth	4/12	DE	197
James	23	MD	197
Nancy	22	DE	197
Nutter, Alfred H	7	DE	92
Clement	33	DE	92
Mary M	3	DE	92
Unice	27	DE	92
Wm	9	DE	242
Oakes, Hannah	24	PA	9
Mary E	2	PA	9
Samuel B	26	PA	9
Oakford, Lloyd	41	PA	69
Oaks, Ann	29	PA	173
Benjamin	41	PA	173
Mary Ann	5	DE	173
Taylor	2	DE	173
Obier, Hinson	9	DE	133
John	18	DE	144
Thomas E	20	DE	145
William H	14	DE	133
Ocane, James	30	IE	62
O'Connor, Cornelius	38	IE	75
Hannah	6	IE	75
Jane	3/12	NY	75
John	15	IE	75
O'Connor, Mary	27	IE	75
O'Donnel, Patrick	18	IE	17
Offley, Mary A	11	DE	18
Mary F	52	DE	18
Rebecca	16	DE	18
William P	13	DE	18
Oldfield, Charles W	12	DE	145
Eliza C	15	DE	145
James L	9	DE	145
Jane	22	DE	145
John M	27	DE	145
Mary A	24	DE	145
Miriam	50	DE	145
Rebecca	52	DE	66
Sarah E	20	DE	145
William W	18	DE	145
Oliver, John	18	DE	143
Joseph	14	DE	90
Mary	60	DE	91
Scynthia	50	DE	94
O'Neal, Henry	50	DE	235
Martha	47	DE	235
Susanna	7	DE	235
Oney, Ellen	28	DE	210
Frederic	1/12	DE	210
Hester	4	DE	210
Leah B	9	DE	210
Luther	29	DE	210
Mary A	7	DE	210
Phebe	5	DE	210
Sally	8	DE	210
Ophwell, John	22	GE	83
Oppenham, Martin	28	FR	4
Orange, Elizabeth	70	DE	19
Orel, Charles	7	DE	176
Hetty	36	DE	173
Mary	4	DE	173
Orr, Alexander	55	NJ	209
Edward	16	NJ	209
Jesse	20	NJ	209
John	12	NJ	209
Louisa	55	NJ	209
William	14	NJ	209
Orrel, David	14	DE	156
James	6	DE	76
Osborne, Wm	31	NJ	162
Oskins, David	15	DE	175
Nancy	7	DE	175
Rachel	45	DE	175
Otwell, Elizabeth	7	DE	146
Mary E	19	DE	146
Mathew	1	DE	146
Phoebe	50	DE	146
Thomas	23	DE	146
William	10	DE	146
Otwill, Edward	21	DE	148
Joshua	25	DE	148
Outen, Charles	38	DE	218
Harriet	25	MD	218
Hebron	4	DE	218
John H	6	DE	218
Sarah E	1	DE	218
Sophia	22	DE	218
Thomas	9	DE	218
Owele, David	31	DE	30
Harriet	12	DE	30
Sarah	6	DE	30
Sophia	4	DE	30
Owen, Elizabeth	18	DE	90
Owens, Ann	30	DE	165
Ann	69	MD	14
Bill	4	DE	213
Eli	1	DE	92
Elizabeth	34	DE	108
Elizabeth B	20	DE	98
George	9	DE	248
Isaac	16	DE	199
James	19	DE	199
John	8	DE	213
Joseph H	41	DE	108
Maria	22	DE	78
Mary	8	DE	250

Name	Age	St	Pg
Owens, Mary	51	DE	199
Sarah	75	DE	198
Sarah N	15	DE	98
Sina	67	DE	100
William	17	DE	108
William H	14	DE	108
Wm	20	DE	239
Owins, Aaron	83	MD	114
Alexander	25	DE	110
Eliza	22	DE	100
Elizabeth	53	DE	114
Isaiah	24	DE	98
James L	24	DE	100
Josephine P	5	DE	114
Mary	20	DE	83
Washington H	17	DE	114
William H	38	DE	98
Packard, Hester T	38	DE	93
James S	14	DE	93
Pain, Leah	35	DE	129
Paine, Elizabeth	4	DE	76
Mary A	22	IE	76
Susan	51	DE	227
Painter, Mary	16	DE	186
Paisley, Edmund	25	DE	95
Ellin	68	DE	97
Franics A	14	DE	97
Henry	26	DE	88
James H	1	DE	88
Mary A	26	DE	88
Mary E	24	DE	95
Phoebe	55	DE	95
Samuel	54	DE	97
William	65	DE	97
Palmatary, Adaline	32	DE	20
Ann E	12	DE	20
Charles	5	DE	20
Daniel P	31	DE	23
Evalina	11	DE	20
Lavinia	8	DE	20
Manlove	9	DE	58
Rachel	37	DE	32
Robert	33	DE	19
Robert	42	DE	23
Robert	63	DE	3
Ruth	45	DE	58
Sarah	6	DE	20
Sarah	64	DE	23
Sarah A	28	DE	23
Sarah A	42	DE	3
Thomas	35	DE	32
William	7	DE	58
William	26	DE	23
Palmer, Abigail	43	DE	94
Alfred	18	DE	34
Cornelia	28	PA	58
Daniel	26	DE	57
Edward	35	DE	80
Eliza	19	DE	224
Elizabeth	70	DE	165
George	9	DE	34
James	21	DE	233
James P	2	DE	94
Joseph	5	MD	80
Julia A	18	DE	89
Juliet	33	MD	80
Levick	30	DE	58
Mary	3	DE	80
Osburn	7	MD	80
Rachel	10	PA	94
Stephen H	13	DE	110
Thomas	10	DE	80
Palmeter, Anna	3	DE	90
Mary A	25	DE	90
Silas C	35	PA	90
Pamar, Catharine	32	DE	5
Emma	12	DE	5
Jacob A	6	DE	5
James T	14	DE	5
Pauline	8	DE	5
Pamatry, Bulah P	29	DE	30
Pamatry, Caroline P	10	DE	30
Cornelius P	4	DE	30
Lavenia	10/12	DE	30
Theodore	8	DE	30
Timothy C	30	DE	30
Pandee, Ann	55	DE	209
John	33	DE	209
Matilda	24	DE	209
Stephen	2	DE	209
Thomas	9/12	DE	209
Pane, John F	8	MD	129
Panel, Elizabeth	14	DE	203
Mary C	17	DE	203
Phebe	12	DE	203
Sarah	9	DE	203
Sarah Ann	36	DE	203
Sylvester	6	DE	203
Sylvester	44	DE	203
Thomas C	20	DE	203
Paradie, Caroline	30	DE	208
Edward	3	DE	208
Edward	31	DE	208
Mary Ann	5	DE	208
Sarah E	7/12	DE	209
Paris, Anna	13	DE	128
Elizabeth	21	DE	128
Louisa	6	DE	128
Mary	45	DE	128
Mary B	18	DE	128
William	17	DE	128
William	45	DE	127
Parker, Alescine	2	DE	23
Alexander	10	DE	70
Alfred	22	DE	74
Ann E	11	DE	43
Charles	10/12	DE	70
Eliza Ann	3	DE	203
Elizabeth	32	DE	203
George	41	DE	174
Isaac	3	DE	32
Isaac	45	DE	160
James	7	DE	203
James	15	NJ	31
James A	3	DE	70
John	9	DE	32
John	12	DE	70
John	37	DE	23
John	41	DE	70
John A	18	DE	203
John W	7	DE	23
Josephine	2	DE	23
Joshua	21	DE	161
Julia A	33	DE	70
Lucretia	44	DE	161
Lugene	6/12	DE	203
Margaret	17	DE	156
Martha	22	DE	161
Mary	10	DE	203
Mary	14	NJ	31
Mary	43	DE	23
Mary A	10	DE	23
Mary E	5	DE	70
Mitchell	6	DE	32
Mitchell	36	NJ	31
Nancy	16	NJ	31
Perry	7	DE	32
Phillis	59	DE	248
Richard	5	DE	203
Sally	24	DE	175
Sarah	8/12	DE	32
Sarah	32	DE	207
Sarah	36	NJ	31
Thomas	7	DE	70
William	12	NJ	31
William	13	DE	52
William F	12	DE	215
Wm	40	DE	203
Parmar, James	12	DE	13
Mary	50	DE	213
Pauline	8	DE	33
Parr, Thomas	19	DE	63
Parris, Eliza J	10	DE	58
Parris, George	41	NJ	58
Jane	36	NJ	58
John	12	DE	58
Parrott, Ann	55	DE	15
Parsons, Ann	44	DE	22
Elizabeth	61	DE	132
Joseph	14	DE	100
Mary	40	DE	13
Mary	42	DE	14
Nathaniel	26	DE	16
Nelson	27	CT	204
Rebecca	21	DE	16
Sarah	24	DE	132
Thomas	30	MD	54
Parvis, Amelia	59	DE	125
Edith	28	DE	125
Elizabeth	14	DE	193
Elizabeth	15	DE	125
Hannah	40	DE	115
Henrietta	39	DE	196
Henry	11	DE	269
James	6	DE	115
James B	6	DE	125
John	18	DE	240
John	58	DE	248
John H	2	DE	125
John T	31	DE	125
Joseph	14	DE	183
Mary	1	DE	237
Mary	24	DE	125
Mary J	17	DE	125
Matthew	10	SW	115
Miriam	40	DE	183
Moses	9	DE	250
Patience	29	DE	237
Richard	43	DE	115
Sarah	17	DE	115
Sarah A	4	DE	125
Sarah E	1	DE	125
Solomon	29	DE	237
Susan	16	DE	183
Thomas	12	DE	193
William	22	DE	125
William	55	DE	125
William W	4	DE	125
Wm	37	DE	183
Paskins, Daniel	2	DE	204
Joshua	4	DE	204
Lucy	21	DE	204
Mary	1/12	DE	204
Wm	27	DE	204
Passwater, Ann	25	DE	100
Patten, John	52	DE	267
Miriam	22	DE	253
Patterson, Alexander	32	DE	217
Ann	46	DE	1
Ann E	11	DE	8
Charles	9/12	DE	8
Francis	8	DE	217
Grace	31	DE	217
James	2	DE	8
Marie E	13	DE	217
Mary	39	DE	8
Mary	48	DE	1
Mary A	7	DE	8
Mary A	10	DE	217
Robert	82	IE	1
Samuel	5	DE	8
Samuel	33	DE	8
Thomas H	5	DE	217
William T	8	DE	8
Patton, Andrew	8	DE	154
Ann	40	DE	154
Araminta	31	DE	201
Betsey	24	DE	177
Charles	10	DE	154
Elizabeth	12	DE	154
Garrett	3	DE	201
Garrett	36	DE	177
James	7	DE	201
James	27	DE	186

Name	Age	St	No.
Patton, James	35	DE	201
Joanna	7	DE	177
John	1/12	DE	189
John	16	DE	154
Joseph	6	DE	201
Lydia	6	DE	189
Lydia	35	DE	189
Margaret	1	DE	177
Margaret	8	DE	189
Mary	1	DE	201
Mary	20	DE	186
Patience	18	DE	162
Phillip	26	DE	19
Rachel	66	DE	200
Richard	65	DE	189
Ruth	6	DE	177
Sarah	3	DE	182
Stephen	1	DE	189
Taylor	5	DE	189
Thomas	6	DE	254
Warner	13	DE	190
Wesley	23	DE	188
William	17	DE	156
William	45	DE	154
Wm	20	DE	202
Zedra	24	DE	198
Pearson, Abraham	9	DE	181
Ann	48	DE	181
Ann E	4	DE	70
Castitta	4	DE	6
Daniel G	8	DE	6
Edmond	1/12	DE	181
Eliza	17	DE	181
Isaac	2	DE	181
Isaac	29	DE	181
James	12	DE	6
James W	8	DE	70
John	10	DE	27
John	15	DE	181
Kitty	28	DE	263
Lydia	21	DE	181
Martha	13	DE	181
Mary	48	DE	6
Rachel	24	DE	181
Rebecca E	1	DE	70
Rhody	19	DE	181
Robert L	25	DE	52
Robert N	6	DE	70
Sarah	3	DE	181
Sarah E	16	DE	6
Sarah E	21	MD	52
Susan	5	DE	263
Thomas	31	DE	70
William	4	DE	34
William	4	DE	181
William	24	DE	181
Pearsons, Rachel	31	DE	70
Peeke, John	23	DE	153
Peirce, Eliza A	1	DE	208
Hannah A	10	DE	208
James	9	DE	208
James L	36	DE	208
Mary	8	DE	208
Mary A	36	MD	208
Phebe	3	DE	208
William	12	DE	208
Pembleton, Charles	1	MD	228
Edward	40	MD	228
Mary	5	MD	228
Rosetta	9	MD	228
Sarah	14	MD	228
Susan	30	MD	228
Peniwell, Isaac	30	MD	26
Mary	11	DE	78
Mary Ann	30	DE	26
Pennington, Mary F	14	MD	12
Penniwell, Caleb	18	DE	157
Elizabeth	42	DE	157
John	20	DE	157
Robert D	52	DE	157
Penniwill, Alice	5	DE	77
Ann	4	DE	77
Penniwill, Charles	2	DE	77
Harriet	1/12	DE	80
Hester	35	DE	80
Jacob	5	DE	80
Julia A	7	DE	80
Levin	37	DE	80
Mary	1	DE	77
Mary	42	DE	77
Matthew	43	DE	77
Susanna	3	DE	80
Pennywell, Ann	24	DE	168
Eben	3	DE	168
Elias	5	DE	168
Robert	9	DE	168
Robert	30	DE	168
Pepper, Frances	13	DE	12
Henrietta	12	DE	167
Rebecca J	13	DE	42
William H	15	DE	42
Peregrine, Charles	16	DE	62
Elijah	53	DE	62
Elizabeth	56	DE	62
Isaac	12	DE	62
Lydia	41	DE	21
Nathan	41	DE	21
Rebecca	15	DE	62
William	19	DE	20
Perkins, Eliza A	47	MD	4
Hester	31	DE	61
Hester A	4/12	DE	61
John	32	DE	61
John D	59	MD	4
Mary E	2	DE	61
William C	24	MD	4
Perry, Alderman	17	DE	30
Catherine	30	DE	28
Cornelia	5	DE	30
Cynthia	18	DE	266
David	32	MD	266
Eleanor	39	DE	130
Elias	44	DE	195
Eliza	13	DE	269
Eliza	15	DE	266
Eliza	47	MD	266
Elizabeth	9	DE	236
Elizabeth	40	DE	195
George	4	DE	195
Hannah	25	DE	197
Hester	3	DE	266
Jacob	13	DE	30
James	7	DE	266
John	3/12	DE	197
John	6	DE	30
John	11	DE	195
Margaret	1	DE	266
Mary	5	DE	266
Mary	65	DE	195
Mary A	19	DE	12
Phebe A	15	DE	30
Rachel	35	DE	195
Sarah	5/12	DE	236
Sarah	38	DE	236
Sarah J	9	DE	30
Solomon	6	DE	236
Spencer	7	DE	236
Spencer	20	DE	236
Spencer	53	DE	236
Susan	40	DE	30
Thomas	13	DE	195
Thomas	38	DE	197
William	2	DE	197
William	3	DE	236
William	28	DE	28
William	47	DE	30
Pervis, Lydia	57	DE	164
William	36	DE	164
Peters, James B	13	DE	146
Louisa	6	DE	146
Mary	44	DE	146
Mary W	8	DE	146
William R	17	MD	146
Peterson, Abram	35	DE	28
Peterson, Alexander	7	DE	70
Ann	7	DE	247
Ann J	27	DE	23
Deborin	22	DE	22
Elizabeth	22	DE	57
Hannah	12	DE	247
Jacob	27	DE	247
James	15	DE	172
James	25	DE	23
James H	14	DE	67
John	1	DE	22
Jonas	17	DE	15
Joseph	16	DE	176
Lettitia	40	DE	28
Lydia A	6	PA	79
Maria	1	DE	28
Martha	4	DE	70
Mary	42	DE	9
Mary A	19	DE	22
Temperance	45	DE	70
William	25	DE	6
Philip, Edward T	24	DE	59
Hester A	4	DE	59
Patience	21	DE	59
William A	8/12	DE	59
Philips, Ann	33	DE	13
Ann	62	MD	26
Delia P	59	DE	59
Edward C	58	DE	59
Elizabeth	65	DE	59
George	21	DE	184
James	20	DE	199
John	5	DE	13
Mary A	8/12	DE	13
Robert	41	DE	13
Sally	42	DE	181
William T	2	DE	13
Phillips, Ann	42	DE	247
Benjamin	57	DE	247
Cornelius	3	DE	247
Edward	21	DE	238
Eliza	1/12	DE	247
Henrietta	9	DE	247
Hetty	11	DE	247
Martha	25	DE	89
Sally	6	DE	247
Samuel	45	DE	218
Sarah	48	DE	238
Sarah A	60	DE	106
Wm	24	DE	208
Pickering, Jane	45	PA	203
Thomas	20	DE	203
Thomas	54	DE	203
Pierce, Charles	10	DE	167
Charles	12	DE	69
Elizabeth	52	DE	112
George	46	DE	112
Latitia	32	DE	167
Mary	8	DE	167
Mary	22	DE	169
Mary	60	VA	169
Nicey	15	DE	59
Rebecca	14	DE	159
Sarah	50	DE	159
Thomas	35	DE	159
Unity	17	DE	159
William	21	DE	97
Wm	40	DE	167
Pierson, Cassa	31	DE	265
John	8/12	DE	265
John	56	DE	265
Martha	3	DE	265
Mary	11	DE	265
Rebecca	6	DE	265
Wm	32	DE	265
Pincot, Wesley	26	DE	166
Pindar, Edward	48	MD	260
Elizabeth	5	DE	260
Emeline	12	DE	260
John	7	DE	260
Margaret	2	DE	260
Mary	4	DE	260

Name	Age	St	Pg
Pindar, Susan	11	DE	260
Piner, Ambrose	1	DE	40
Delia	37	I D	40
Henrietta	9	DE	40
Jacob	3	DE	40
Jacob	40	DE	40
John	5	DE	40
John	40	DE	40
Lydia	3	DE	40
Lydia A	6	DE	40
Mary	24	DE	40
Mary A	11	DE	40
William	24	FE	32
Pinfield, Elizabeth	81	I D	221
Pinket, Daniel	22	DE	8
David	4	DE	8
Elizabeth	13	DE	72
Grace	44	DE	72
Hester	8	DE	72
Jane	10	FE	72
Levin	52	FE	72
Lewis	20	DE	76
Peter	26	DE	8
William	6	DE	59
Pinor, Jane	15	DE	47
Lydia	17	DE	52
Pippin, Ann	1	DE	194
Elijah	25	MD	194
James	3	MD	194
Robert	5	MD	194
Sarah	25	MD	194
Pleasanton, Ann	12	DE	163
Anna	47	DE	169
Beckey	16	DE	169
David	36	DE	7
Eliza	9	DE	169
Elizabeth	35	DE	7
Hannah	11	DE	228
Lydia	73	DE	70
Patience	13	DE	169
Susan	1	DE	6
Susan	20	FE	226
Thomas	6	DE	170
Warner	2	DE	170
William	8	DE	170
Pleasenton, Alex	28	DE	161
Benjamin	59	FE	170
Mary	19	DE	161
Pleasonton, Amanda	1	DE	79
Daniel	6	DE	79
Edward	38	DE	79
Franklin	7/12	DE	79
Hannah	9	DE	79
Harriet	12	DE	79
Henry F	3	DE	79
John	28	DE	79
Lydia	18	DE	79
Mary J	34	DE	79
Nathaniel	8	DE	79
Nathaniel	21	DE	7
Priscilla	31	DE	6
Rebecca	16	DE	74
Samuel	15	DE	79
Sarah E	4	DE	79
Stephen	10	DE	73
Susan	7	DE	82
William	12	DE	79
Pointer, Comfort	54	DE	102
Isaac	28	DE	109
Lydia	37	DE	102
Mariah	24	FE	109
Rachel	14	DE	98
Polk, Ann E	14	DE	91
Anna M	18	DE	102
Bethany	25	DE	90
Caroline	24	DE	102
Charles J	14	DE	102
Daniel	8	DE	153
Eliza	50	DE	167
Elizabeth	20	DE	135
Ezekiel	8	DE	167
Foster	37	DE	135
Polk, George	3/12	DE	90
Henrietta	10	DE	102
Hudson	5	DE	90
James	5	DE	102
James	19	DE	90
James H	11	DE	102
James K	22	DE	234
John	10	DE	165
Joseph A	2	DE	90
Lavinia	13	DE	110
Leah	45	DE	90
Leonard	12	FE	80
Levinia	9	DE	230
Livey	3	DE	102
Marcellas	6	FE	90
Mary E	54	DE	102
Peter	32	DE	155
Rachel	23	DE	234
Richard	16	DE	90
Robert	16	DE	89
Sarah	1	DE	234
Theodore E	7	DE	102
Thomas	1	DE	154
Thomas	12	DE	202
Thomas H	10	FE	90
Trustin	24	DE	7
Unity	18	DE	226
William	12	DE	102
William	33	DE	102
William	50	DE	90
William John	13	DE	90
Pollock, Thomas	14	PA	27
Ponzo, Henry	18	DE	1
Poor, Amelia	11	DE	198
Amelia	56	DE	195
Ann	7	DE	174
Ann	15	DE	55
Benjamin	2	DE	45
Benjamin	25	DE	8
Elizabeth	20	DE	52
Elizabeth	21	DE	45
Enoch J	6	DE	45
George	10	DE	200
George	15	DE	199
Hannah	14	DE	45
Hannah	16	DE	8
Hester	7	DE	185
John	10	DE	174
John	27	DE	185
John	30	DE	174
John T	10	DE	45
Lucy	12	DE	184
Martin	20	DE	185
Mary	8	DE	195
Mary	21	DE	8
Mary	47	DE	45
Nancy	38	DE	185
Rachel	3	DE	185
Rachel	5	DE	174
Rebecca	14	DE	199
Rebecca	16	DE	45
Robert	3/12	DE	174
Robert	32	DE	174
Ruth	25	DE	177
Sarah	13	DE	185
Sarah	28	DE	174
Sarah A	9	DE	45
Thomas	51	DE	45
Poore, Edward J	78	DE	248
Mary	59	DE	248
Porter, Ann	32	DE	130
Charles	6/12	DE	182
Charles W	8	DE	130
David	14	DE	132
Edward	47	DE	132
Elizabeth	24	DE	219
Elizabeth A	9	DE	127
Emily	1	DE	127
Francis	3/12	DE	130
Henry	22	DE	130
James	14	DE	144
Henry	22	DE	130
Porter, James	14	DE	144
James	15	DE	130
James	37	DE	127
John	20	DE	130
John	45	DE	130
John F	8	DE	127
Joseph	8	DE	134
Luretta	26	DE	239
Lydia	10	DE	130
Margaret J	1	DE	132
Mary	23	MD	132
Mary	33	DE	127
Mary A	4	DE	132
Nehemiah	3	DE	130
Philip	17	DE	130
Robert	9/12	DE	229
Robert	8	DE	182
Sandel	18	DE	145
Sarah	25	DE	182
Sarah E	3	DE	132
Stephen H	6	DE	127
Susan A	29	DE	132
Washington	26	MD	219
Wm	31	DE	182
Posels, Caleb	4	DE	206
Eliza J	16	DE	206
Harriet	28	DE	211
Jacob	8	DE	216
James	7	DE	225
James	20	DE	236
Levi	8	DE	206
Miah	42	DE	211
Peter	24	DE	206
Ruth A	1	DE	211
Sally Ann	14	DE	206
Samuel	12	DE	206
Wm	4	DE	211
Postels, Abraham	6	DE	247
Anna	11	DE	247
Elizabeth	32	DE	242
Ellen	7	DE	242
James	9	DE	242
Jeremiah	2	DE	247
Job	4	DE	248
John	16	DE	247
Joseph	15	DE	247
Lake	57	DE	247
Levin	10	DE	247
Mary	47	DE	247
Rachel	5	DE	247
Sarah	24	DE	247
Stephen	38	DE	242
William	12	DE	242
Wm	32	DE	247
Postle, Henry	29	DE	229
Postles, Alex	3	DE	111
Charles	18	DE	98
Comfort	47	DE	164
Elizabeth	40	DE	98
Emeline	11	DE	157
George	15	DE	98
Hester	25	DE	111
James	15	DE	164
James	29	DE	153
James	43	DE	98
James H	25	DE	98
John	7	DE	111
John W	8	DE	98
Louisa	25	DE	164
Luke	77	DE	109
Mary	5	DE	157
Mary A	19	DE	109
Nancy	42	DE	109
Purnel	43	DE	109
Rachel E	14	DE	109
Rebecca	33	DE	157
Sarah	8	DE	157
Sarah E	12	DE	98
Sarah M	11	DE	109
Scynthia	52	DE	98
Shadrach	49	DE	98
Thomas	43	DE	157

Postles, Tindley T	17 DE 109
William	12 DE 164
Zadock	10 DE 164
Zadock	40 DE 164
Zadok	21 DE 92
Potter, Alexander	3 DE 79
Ann E	19 DE 79
Ann E	16 DE 89
Ann E	18 DE 75
Celea	54 DE 108
Cesar	52 DE 108
Elizabeth	11 DE 108
Farris	40 DE 79
George	29 DE 214
Harriet A	5 DE 131
John	31 DE 79
John A	15 DE 75
Lydia A	5 DE 79
Mary	29 DE 79
Mary A	20 MD 80
Mary E	7/12 DE 79
Morgan	25 MD 80
Samuel	2 DE 214
Sarah	5 DE 141
Sarah	25 DE 214
Sarah A	1 DE 214
Wilhelmina	2 DE 79
William T	7 DE 79
Potts, William	15 MD 16
Pouhet, Caroline	17 DE 231
Poulsen, Abraham	6 DE 3
Abraham	44 NJ 3
Andrew	4 DE 3
Catharine	40 PA 3
Charles W	10 DE 3
George	7/12 DE 3
Mary C	8 DE 3
Susanna	17 DE 3
William C	12 DE 3
Powders, William	24 MD 87
Powel, Agnes	8 DE 230
Amelia	46 DE 196
Charles	12 DE 196
Elizabeth	5/12 DE 196
Elizabeth	42 DE 230
George	23 DE 167
James	3 MD 185
James	6 DE 196
James	30 MD 185
Joseph	42 DE 230
Josephine	5 DE 231
Margaret	1 DE 185
Martha	12 DE 230
Mary	10 DE 196
Michal	16 DE 196
Rebecca	8 DE 196
Rebecca	30 DE 185
Samuel	50 DE 196
Sarah	10 DE 230
Susan	24 DE 196
Willamina	7 DE 230
William	3 DE 196
Wm	22 DE 201
Powell, Anancy	61 DE 107
Ann	30 DE 19
Araminty	55 DE 65
Arena	18 DE 194
Britannia	12 DE 194
Caroline	16 DE 65
Catherine	7 DE 170
Catherine	27 DE 135
Daniel	2 DE 120
Elisha	25 DE 194
Elizabeth	1 DE 120
Elizabeth	7 DE 136
Elizabeth	21 DE 194
Francis J	14 DE 135
George	3 DE 197
George	70 MD 135
James	8 DE 49
James	28 DE 135
James	46 DE 182

Powell, John	6 DE 120
John	13 DE 182
John H	33 DE 135
John W	28 MD 186
Jonathan	3/12 DE 197
Jonathan	27 DE 197
Louisa	8/12 DE 182
Lydia	48 DE 170
Margaret	3 DE 182
Margaret G	9 DE 135
Martha	11 DE 182
Mary	2 DE 197
Mary	7 DE 120
Mary	17 DE 182
Mary	28 DE 65
Mary	63 DE 135
Mary E	4 DE 135
Mary E	12 DE 135
Matilda M	36 DE 135
Murel	22 DE 194
Nathaniel C	36 DE 135
Prince	24 DE 66
Prince	25 DE 82
Pulasky	10 DE 135
Robert	51 DE 170
Samuel	37 DE 119
Samuel	74 DE 194
Sarah	11 DE 170
Sarah	15 DE 182
Sarah	42 DE 182
Sarah M	7 DE 135
Sirenius L	10 DE 135
Susan C	5 DE 135
Susan H	32 DE 135
Thomas	9 DE 170
William	4 DE 120
William	54 DE 170
William F	2 DE 135
William H	21 DE 65
William H	42 DE 135
Wm	9 DE 182
Zadock	20 DE 170
Pratis, Alexander	8 DE 238
Allen	7 DE 237
Ann	17 DE 220
Ann	30 DE 231
Clementine	5 DE 237
Elija	5 DE 238
Elija	35 DE 238
Eliza	3/12 DE 238
Eliza	32 DE 238
Elizabeth	3 DE 238
Harriet	10 DE 238
Henry	4 DE 231
Henry	34 DE 231
James	5 DE 231
James	13 DE 231
James	35 DE 237
Jane	6 DE 238
Jane	24 DE 233
Mary	10 DE 231
Mary	40 DE 237
Mathew	9 DE 237
Miriam	3 DE 238
Philena	2 DE 233
Robert J	26 DE 222
Ruben	12 DE 231
Ruth	70 DE 235
Susanna	8 DE 231
Thomas	1 DE 233
Thomas	27 DE 233
William	3 DE 237
Wm	69 DE 235
Pratt, Albina A	1 DE 10
Alexander	14 DE 220
Alphonzo	2 DE 251
Ann	63 DE 179
Ann E	11 DE 147
Ann M	1 DE 121
Catherine	34 MD 9
Celia Ann	20 DE 37
Daniel	7 DE 239

Pratt, Daniel	18 DE 153
Eli C	7 DE 147
Eliza	32 DE 94
Elizabeth	2/12 DE 251
Elizabeth	3 DE 138
Elizabeth	30 DE 138
Elizabeth	34 DE 150
Ellen	29 DE 251
Emily	12 DE 184
George	4 DE 179
George	39 DE 150
Green	34 DE 121
Hannah	85 DE 121
Henry	2 DE 94
Henry	9 DE 184
Henry	45 DE 184
Henry	61 DE 37
Hester	12 DE 7
Isaac	38 DE 179
James	1 DE 179
James H	36 DE 10
John	6 DE 179
John	14 DE 184
John	16 DE 153
John H	15 DE 150
John R	8 PA 9
Joseph	3 DE 9
Louisa	3 DE 184
Louisa	8 DE 150
Lydia	8 DE 251
Lydia	12 DE 256
Lydia	31 DE 51
Lydia	61 DE 37
Martha	1 DE 51
Martha	17 DE 184
Mary	35 DE 179
Mary A	13 DE 150
Mary E	1 DE 138
Mary E	6 PA 9
Mary E	23 DE 10
Mary E	27 MD 83
Nancy	11 DE 150
Nancy	18 DE 121
Nathan	8 DE 7
Nathan	16 DE 184
Nathan	49 DE 169
Nathaniel	22 DE 37
Peter	12 DE 117
Phebe B	1 DE 9
Rachel A	9 DE 138
Rus	36 PA 9
Ruth	2 DE 150
Ruth	13 DE 179
Sarah	6 DE 251
Sarah	10 DE 197
Sarah E	5 DE 150
Stephen T	33 MD 94
Thomas	28 DE 251
Unity	1 DE 184
Unity	40 DE 184
William	14 DE 153
William	27 DE 51
William	40 DE 138
William H	9 DE 147
Preston, Elizabeth	28 DE 221
Margaret J	11 DE 216
Mary	47 DE 216
Sarah	24 DE 36
Thomas	21 DE 207
Prettyman, Alfred P	19 DE 150
Burton	50 DE 150
Catherine	35 DE 227
Catherine E	9 DE 150
Cornelia	14 DE 224
Elizabeth	32 DE 97
Henrietta	11 DE 150
Henry	26 MD 224
James B	15 DE 150
James D	22 DE 89
John S	23 DE 89
John W	17 DE 150
Lavinia	35 DE 129

Name	Age	State	No.
Prettyman, Lavinia	45	DE	150
Levinia C	13	DE	130
Mary E	18	DE	130
Palestina A	3	DE	129
Pemberton	13	DE	150
Sallie	32	DE	224
Thomas	4	DE	227
William	56	DE	129
William T	9	DE	129
Williammina	7	DE	97
Price, Adam	10	DE	139
Alfred	12	DE	139
Amanda	6/12	DE	61
Amy	7	DE	139
Ann	3/12	DE	256
Catherine	17	DE	221
Clementine	7	DE	228
Elizabeth	60	DE	131
Ellen	10	DE	183
Emeline	29	DE	61
Harriet	34	DE	209
George	4/12	DE	228
George	40	DE	228
Henry	19	DE	76
James H	16	DE	120
James H	16	DE	139
John	4	DE	183
John	30	MD	256
John	31	MD	171
Louisa	17	DE	209
Louisa	26	DE	256
Lydia	41	MD	139
Mary	11	DE	228
Mary	22	DE	133
Mary	34	DE	162
Mary	35	DE	183
Mary	38	DE	221
Mary	44	DE	182
Mary A	17	MD	15
Matilda	84	MD	232
Moses	30	MD	61
Nathan	1/12	DE	183
Nicholas B	4	DE	139
Rebecca	60	DE	240
Ruthann	16	DE	182
Samuel	48	DE	139
Sarah	3	DE	228
Sarah	15	DE	182
Sarah	40	DE	228
Solomon	45	DE	182
Susan	20	DE	186
Thomas	13	DE	183
Thomas	33	DE	183
William	8	DE	183
William	14	DE	139
William	20	DE	66
Wm	53	DE	162
Primrose, Amelia	68	DE	88
Anna	5	DE	91
Elias	74	DE	88
Elizabeth	15	DE	91
Elizabeth H	26	DE	90
George	40	DE	91
George R	16	NY	100
Hester A	25	DE	100
James	8	DE	91
James	27	DE	90
John W	36	KY	100
Lydia	16	DE	91
Mary	10	DE	88
Rhoda	38	DE	91
Scynthia	13	DE	91
Thomas J	4/12	DE	90
William	8	IE	230
Prinderel, Garret	37	IE	156
Mary	44	IE	156
Redman	15	IE	156
Prior, Alexander	5	DE	41
Alexander	12	DE	49
Ann	31	DE	51
Ann E	6	DE	51
Ann N	1	DE	41
Prior, Catherine	25	DE	41
Delia	8/12	DE	51
Eben	20	DE	41
Emory	13	DE	50
George	2	DE	41
Hester	10	DE	51
James	17	DE	41
Jeremiah	34	DE	53
John	1	DE	41
John	5	DE	51
John	14	DE	51
John	24	DE	41
John W	3	DE	53
Lydia	62	DE	41
Mary E	7	DE	51
Perry	15	DE	50
Rachel	4	DE	41
Robert	6	DE	51
Samuel	6	DE	41
Samuel	24	DE	41
Susan	27	DE	53
Temperance	25	DE	41
William	2	DE	52
William	15	DE	47
William	34	DE	52
William G	8	DE	53
Pritchet, Elizabeth	14	DE	245
Hester	3	DE	245
Hester	40	DE	245
James	9	DE	245
James	40	DE	245
Jeremiah	19	DE	245
Margaret	16	DE	245
Rachel	10	DE	245
Silas	10	DE	231
Warner	5	DE	246
Prouse, William S	18	DE	223
Pruitt, Ann	30	DE	60
David	2	DE	60
William	31	MD	60
William A	4	DE	60
Purnel, Julia	23	DE	4
Sarah	19	DE	3
Purnell, Amanda	26	MD	95
Ann	50	DE	255
Benjamin	13	DE	207
Charles	8	DE	9
Edward	8	DE	27
Elias	2	DE	95
Elizabeth	52	DE	223
Emily	10	DE	27
Fanny	7	DE	9
Flora	13	DE	9
Isaac	52	DE	83
Isaac	66	DE	9
James Henry	22	DE	83
John	25	DE	83
John	29	DE	95
John H	3	DE	9
John H	9	DE	96
Jonathan	34	DE	27
Joseph	5	DE	95
Letta	53	DE	83
Levi	21	DE	83
Lydiann	23	DE	83
Margaret	6	DE	27
Mary	4	DE	27
Mary	11	DE	9
Mary	14	DE	223
Mary	35	DE	96
Mary	40	DE	89
Mary E	8	DE	83
Rachel	55	DE	9
Racher	20	DE	14
Sarah A	5/12	DE	27
Sarah A	32	DE	27
Thomas	59	DE	223
William J	25	DE	89
Wm	60	DE	255
Purse, Cassandra	32	DE	44
Catherine	32	DE	44
James	12	DE	44
Purse, John Hall	53	DE	44
Thomas	75	MD	44
Quillan, Mary	30	DE	226
Sarah	42	DE	227
Quillen, Armwell	20	DE	17
Edward	16	DE	109
Elizabeth	3	DE	104
Elizabeth	27	DE	109
Hannah	27	DE	104
Isaac	7	DE	42
Jacob	26	DE	109
James	7	DE	108
James	20	DE	41
James	57	DE	105
John	22	DE	109
John	25	DE	84
John	38	DE	108
John A	11/12	DE	84
John Arnold	1/12	DE	84
Joseph	2	DE	109
Joseph	5	DE	99
Joseph	28	DE	104
Lydia	2	DE	108
Mary	10/12	DE	109
Mary	27	DE	99
Mary E	9	DE	99
Mary M	23	DE	84
Moses	10	DE	41
Moses	51	DE	41
Parker	25	DE	30
Phebe S	15	DE	108
Robert	18	DE	99
Samuel S	7/12	DE	99
Sarah	4	DE	108
Sarah	75	DE	108
Sarah A	33	DE	108
Sarah L	7	DE	99
Susan	51	DE	41
Thomas	17	DE	41
William	31	DE	99
William B	3	DE	99
William C	12	DE	108
Quimby, Robert	29	DE	51
Quinley, Rachel	78	DE	33
Radon, Curtis	20	DE	21
Rafferty, Ellen	19	IE	2
John	27	IE	2
Rakes, John	4	DE	80
Lydia	29	DE	57
Lydia	30	DE	171
Margaret	7	DE	171
Mary	1	DE	75
William	3	DE	171
Wm	22	DE	168
Ralph, Mary	46	DE	248
Ralston, George	36	DE	85
Henry	17	DE	150
Jonathan	17	DE	150
Robert	30	DE	150
Sarah A	40	DE	150
Ranson, Albert K	13	CT	46
Sarah M	47	CT	46
Sarah S	17	CT	46
Sumner W	13	CT	46
William	20	CT	46
Ranyolds, Mary	4	DE	176
Rebecca	23	DE	176
Robert	2	DE	176
Robert	27	DE	176
Rash, Andrew	24	DE	183
Andrew	43	DE	220
Ann	5	DE	181
Ann	7	DE	23
Ann	12	DE	199
Ann	34	DE	27
Ann	36	DE	176
Ann	40	DE	175
Ann	44	DE	19
Ann	50	DE	13
Ann M	22	DE	35

Name	Age	State	Page
Rash, Charles	13	DE	201
Daniel	8	DE	180
Darling	38	DE	176
Elizabeth	17	DE	7
Ellen	22	DE	183
Eugene	2	DE	181
George	18	DE	185
Harriet	4	DE	176
Harriet	43	MD	220
Henry	8	DE	176
James	15	DE	173
James	48	DE	181
John	1/12	DE	183
John	12	DE	176
John	14	DE	35
John	16	DE	181
John	42	DE	55
John	47	DE	19
John H	54	DE	375
John W	7/12	DE	27
Joseph	18	DE	181
Joseph	20	DE	19
Laura	8	DE	27
Margaret	5	DE	180
Margaret	17	DE	35
Maria	39	DE	181
Mariah	4	DE	27
Mark	36	DE	180
Martha	55	DE	35
Martin	6	DE	176
Mary	2	DE	183
Mary	11	DE	35
Mary	14	DE	181
Mary	46	DE	181
Moses	40	DE	181
Myers	12	DE	181
Nancy	70	MD	225
Nathan	12	DE	192
Phebe	1	DE	19
Presley	22	DE	19
Rebecca	6	DE	27
Rebecca	34	DE	55
Robert	21	DE	19
Rodney	18	DE	55
Sarah	9	DE	19
Sarah	10	DE	181
Sarah	19	DE	176
Sarah	32	DE	180
Sarah	45	DE	11
Sarah	46	DE	19
Sarah E	11	DE	27
Sarah J	20	DE	35
Susan	2	DE	55
Susan	5	DE	19
Susan	9	DE	204
Thomas	14	DE	192
Thomas	39	DE	13
William	3	DE	180
William	33	DE	27
Rasin, Ann E	10	MD	21
Rasinor, Mary	1	DE	53
Peter	33	PA	53
Rachel	1/12	DE	53
Sarah A	25	DE	53
Rathel, John	53	MD	156
Margaret J	18	DE	139
Wm J	4	DE	148
Rathell, Adeline	4	DE	127
Hinson	9	DE	127
Matilda	37	DE	127
Thomas	26	DE	127
Rathwell, Rachel	5	DE	68
Ratledge, Elizabeth	11	DE	111
George	46	DE	111
James H	16	DE	111
John	28	MD	176
John G	7	DE	111
Mary	20	DE	176
Nathaniel	1	DE	176
Susan	39	DE	111
Tamsay	3	DE	111
William	1/12	DE	176
Ratlidge, John H	6	DE	80
Margaret	78	DE	176
Nathaniel	53	DE	176
Sarah	24	DE	80
William	2	DE	80
William	36	DE	80
Ratliff, Ann	30	MD	44
Catherine A	6	DE	44
Harriet L	9	DE	44
Thomas	39	DE	44
Raughley, Ann	14	DE	8
Ann E	1/12	DE	31
Ann M	10	DE	127
Argann	10	DE	172
Argann	50	DE	172
David	15	DE	172
Draper	7	DE	31
Easter	35	DE	149
Eliza J	5	DE	149
Elizabeth	23	DE	92
Emily	12	DE	127
George	14	DE	172
Hannah	38	DE	31
James	1	DE	92
James	9	DE	172
James	19	DE	8
James	24	DE	99
James	47	DE	8
James	56	DE	149
James W	5	DE	149
Joanna E	13	DE	149
John	12	DE	8
John	54	DE	172
John W	19	DE	149
Joseph R	8	DE	149
Louisa	45	DE	127
Lydia	18	DE	128
Margaret	16	DE	172
Margaret A	6	DE	149
Mary	8	DE	31
Mary E	16	DE	127
Peter	39	DE	31
Risdon B	25	DE	92
Robert	26	DE	128
Robert H	3/12	DE	149
Sarah Ann	41	MD	8
Sarah E	15	DE	149
Sarah J	4/12	DE	99
Shadrack	12	DE	172
Shadrack	42	DE	127
Sophia	25	DE	99
Thomas	17	DE	149
Unice	33	DE	149
William	10	DE	31
William	25	DE	128
Raughly, Araminta	45	DE	177
Martha	14	DE	177
Mary	26	DE	177
William	3	DE	177
Wm	47	DE	176
Rawley, Barsheba	29	DE	244
Elizabeth	22	DE	213
Henry	24	DE	17
John	39	DE	213
Lydia	22	DE	17
Rachel	17	DE	178
Robert	23	DE	178
Samuel P	22	DE	150
Sarah E	1	DE	213
Sarah E	7	DE	130
Susan	54	DE	244
Thomas	26	DE	244
William	10	DE	178
Ray, Robert	16	PA	38
Raymond, Edmund	3	DE	156
Eliza B	58	DE	23
Elizabeth	37	DE	27
Elizabeth	59	DE	1
Henry R	1	DE	27
Jacob	62	DE	23
James	5	DE	156
James	44	DE	156
Raymond, John C	37	DE	27
Martha	9	DE	156
Mary	34	DE	156
Mary	70	DE	71
Sarah	15	DE	156
Susan H	33	DE	23
Walter	1	DE	156
William G	4	DE	27
Wm	13	DE	156
Raynolds, Elizabeth	30	DE	15
Emma J	9	DE	15
George	12	DE	15
Mary	4	DE	175
Rebecca	23	DE	175
Robert	2	DE	175
Robert	27	DE	175
Samuel	35	DE	15
Rayolds, Aaron	9	DE	43
Ready, Francis	1	DE	87
James	34	DE	87
James W	7	DE	87
Mary	36	DE	87
Mary E	6	DE	87
William J	10	DE	87
Reason, Charles	7	DE	85
Wm	54	DE	181
Redden, Almira	16	DE	143
Angelina	13	DE	143
Caroline	14	DE	97
Catherine	17	DE	97
Catherine	22	DE	143
Columbia A	1	DE	143
Eliza	19	DE	97
Elizabeth	6	DE	144
Elizabeth	43	DE	97
George	29	DE	133
Hester A	30	DE	144
James D	10/12	DE	144
Jane B	23	DE	133
John	45	DE	97
John O	13	DE	144
John W	12	DE	97
John W	25	DE	144
Laura A	2	DE	133
Margaret	20	DE	144
Margaretta	5	DE	144
Mary A	20	DE	143
Mary C	6	DE	113
Mary J	11	DE	144
Sarah A	23	DE	113
Sarah E	17	DE	85
Sarah E	17	DE	143
Stephen	63	DE	144
Stephen Jr	39	DE	144
Theophilus	32	DE	113
Thomas S	11/12	DE	133
William	19	DE	143
Redman, Garret	6/12	DE	51
Milcah	33	MD	51
Thomas	27	DE	51
Reed, Alexander	7	DE	263
Ann	40	DE	214
Benjamin	3	DE	164
Benjamin	10	DE	268
Benjamin	18	DE	66
Benjamin	44	DE	270
Bilania	76	DE	123
Caleb	6	DE	171
Caroline	6	DE	254
Caroline	7	DE	122
Catherine	2	DE	57
Catherine M	39	DE	121
Charles	17	DE	246
Charles	60	DE	155
Clement	31	DE	171
Daniel	6	DE	191
Daniel	8	DE	268
Daniel S	42	DE	193
David	7	DE	191
David	12	GA	262
Dorcas	55	DE	66
Edward	22	DE	262

Name	Age	St	Pg
Reed, Edward	29	DE	121
Elias	18	DE	257
Eliza	32	DE	263
Elizabeth	11	DE	122
Elizabeth	21	DE	262
Elizabeth	34	DE	122
Elizabeth	75	DE	122
Ellen	2	DE	154
Ellen	20	DE	156
Emily	4	DE	120
Ezekiel	5	DE	119
Ezekiel	14	DE	270
Ezekiel	30	DE	120
Ezekiel W	35	MD	57
Frederick	4	DE	192
George	3	DE	122
George	10	DE	155
Hannah	10	DE	119
Hannah	50	DE	155
Hester	21	DE	250
Isaac	9	DE	120
Isabella	42	ST	263
James	10	DE	263
James	18	DE	269
James	37	DE	184
Jesse	10	DE	66
Jesse	57	DE	66
John	7	DE	184
John	7	DE	270
John	9	DE	257
John	15	DE	215
John	15	DE	257
John	18	DE	157
John	20	DE	247
John	22	DE	246
John	24	DE	62
John	25	DE	250
John	28	DE	154
John	36	DE	184
John	45	MD	257
John	45	DE	263
John B	51	DE	123
John T	24	DE	121
John W	39	DE	122
Joseph	19	DE	246
Letitia	37	DE	270
Lemuel	6	DE	164
Lemuel	13	DE	66
Lemuel	33	DE	164
Littleton	46	DE	191
Lydia	4	DE	270
Lydia	8	DE	120
Lydia	63	DE	121
Mahala	35	DE	193
Margaret	1/12	DE	184
Margaret	18	DE	74
Margaret	42	DE	268
Margaret	66	DE	193
Margaretta	11	DE	257
Martha	7	DE	119
Martha	16	DE	246
Mary	9	DE	191
Mary	31	DE	164
Mary	48	DE	257
Nancy	13	DE	122
Nancy	48	DE	122
Peter	13	DE	154
Rachel	6	DE	164
Rachel	9	DE	122
Rachel	49	DE	246
Richard	4	DE	171
Robert	2	DE	270
Robert	5	DE	184
Ruth	26	DE	171
Ruthann	12	DE	246
Samuel	14	DE	184
Sarah	1	DE	191
Sarah	27	DE	154
Sarah	35	DE	184
Sarah Ann	26	DE	57
Susan	5	DE	122
Susan	22	DE	267

Name	Age	St	Pg
Reed, Susan	25	DE	120
Susan	28	DE	191
Thomas	7	DE	257
Thomas	11	DE	171
Thomas	16	DE	184
Thomas	47	MD	214
Thomas P	68	DE	121
Vincent	6	DE	120
Warren	13	DE	123
William	7/12	DE	170
William	1	DE	120
William	1	DE	123
William	4	DE	154
William	5	DE	164
William	7	DE	262
William	20	DE	191
William	21	DE	121
Willie	3	DE	263
Wm	23	DE	267
Rees, Ann	46	DE	46
Catherine	65	MD	19
David	9	DE	47
Elizabeth	23	DE	70
Elizabeth	34	DE	47
Francis	24	DE	70
George	70	DE	19
James	2	DE	70
James	46	DE	70
John	5	DE	46
John P	4	DE	47
John P	40	DE	47
John R	50	DE	46
Mary E	17	DE	46
Mary J	9	DE	47
Priscilla	42	DE	70
Priscilla	66	DE	71
Priscilla M	11	DE	47
Sarah	8	DE	46
Sarah	29	DE	47
Sarah Ann	23	DE	70
Sarah E	1	DE	47
Susanna	6	DE	47
Thomas	10	DE	46
Thomas A	3	DE	47
William	4/12	DE	70
William R	9	DE	46
Reeve, Benjamin	30	NJ	240
Charles	13	NJ	240
Mary	56	NJ	240
Register, Charles	15	DE	155
David	47	DE	111
Eliza	49	DE	35
Elizabeth	14	DE	218
Elizabeth	55	DE	218
Ezekiel	13	DE	155
Francis	32	DE	218
Francis	54	DE	155
Isaac	10	DE	155
Isaac	40	DE	35
Mary	8	DE	155
Mary	47	DE	155
Mary	66	DE	111
Samuel	13	DE	35
Samuel	70	DE	35
Sarah	15	DE	35
Unity	18	DE	155
Reihm, Charles S	3	DE	68
Elizabeth	32	GE	68
George H	5	DE	68
John	36	GE	68
John T	8	PA	68
Ren, Mary	60	DE	27
Rese, Harriet A	19	DE	5
Resh, Elizabeth	5	DE	189
Elizabeth	45	DE	189
John	15	DE	189
Mary	9	DE	189
Peter	13	DE	189
Samuel	45	MD	189
Susan	11	DE	189
William	8	DE	189
Reston, Samuel W	18	DE	211

Name	Age	St	Pg
Revill, Louisa	35	DE	91
Reynolds, Alonso	26	MD	85
Ann	17	DE	260
Ann E	2	DE	29
Curtis	30	DE	209
David	4	DE	270
Elizabeth	11	DE	43
Elizabeth	18	DE	260
Elizabeth	35	DE	205
Fanny	17	DE	270
Francis	9	DE	262
Francis	18	DE	43
George	10	DE	260
George	45	DE	267
George	51	DE	260
Harriet R	7	DE	29
Hester	23	DE	21
James	2	DE	208
James	5	DE	32
James	21	DE	43
John	13	DE	262
John	41	DE	262
John	43	DE	43
John W	5	DE	208
John W	11	DE	32
Joseph	2	DE	43
Joseph	33	DE	28
Lattitia	34	DE	29
Lydia	13	DE	32
Margaret	8	DE	260
Margaret	38	DE	362
Margaret	44	DE	260
Martha	13	DE	43
Mary	1	DE	262
Mary E	6	DE	208
Peter	2	DE	43
Rachel	6	DE	32
Rachel	9	DE	43
Rebecca	3	DE	32
Rebecca	11	DE	262
Rebecca	43	DE	43
Robert	12	DE	270
Robert	15	DE	3
Robert	49	MD	1
Robert W	46	DE	270
Samuel	6	DE	29
Sarah	18	DE	270
Sarah	44	DE	109
Sarah	46	DE	270
Sarah A	25	DE	208
Sarah C	9/12	DE	205
Thomas	8	DE	262
Thomas	14	DE	270
Thomas	20	DE	109
Thomas	22	DE	260
Thomas	38	NJ	21
Thomas	49	DE	236
William	5	DE	205
William	6	DE	262
William	24	DE	43
William	38	DE	205
William T	1	DE	21
Wm C	1	DE	32
Rhodes, Richard	72	PA	163
Rias, Fanny	65	DE	157
Rice, Alexander	1	DE	243
Edward T	18	DE	30
Martha	34	DE	243
Richards, Ann	21	DE	90
Ann	40	DE	179
Anthony	13	DE	163
Anthony	18	DE	163
Beckey	15	DE	159
Benjamin	38	DE	104
Celia A	38	DE	224
Clementine	7	DE	74
Curtis	50	DE	159
Elizabeth	40	DE	82
Emaline	35	DE	140
Fisher	1	DE	148
Garret	59	DE	162
George H	3	DE	104

Richards, Hannah	1 DE 159	
Henrietta	25 DE 159	
Henry C	13 DE 102	
Hetty A	38 DE 104	
James	1 DE 159	
James C	1 DE 103	
Jane	7 DE 163	
Jane	22 DE 19	
Jehu	24 DE 125	
John	22 DE 77	
John	22 DE 204	
John	24 DE 19	
John	29 DE 103	
Joshua	5 DE 159	
Lovey	25 DE 103	
Lydia	8 DE 163	
Lydia	69 DE 85	
Mary	4 DE 163	
Mary	6 DE 267	
Mary	12 DE 150	
Mary	22 DE 179	
Mary	30 DE 91	
Mary	44 DE 225	
Mary E	11 DE 102	
Mary J	10 DE 104	
Peter	7 DE 163	
Peter	45 DE 179	
Rachel	28 DE 159	
Robert G	6 DE 102	
Roseann	20 DE 179	
Sally	29 DE 162	
Samuel	17 DE 163	
Sarah	11 DE 162	
Sarah A	4 DE 102	
Sarah A	30 DE 102	
Susanna	33 DE 159	
Tamar	12 DE 164	
Tamar	14 DE 163	
Tilly	19 DE 163	
William G	2/12 DE 103	
William H	36 DE 102	
William J	9 DE 102	
Richardson, Ann	35 DE 62	
Benjamin	8 DE 60	
Daniel B	54 DE 60	
Deborah	50 DE 55	
Elizabeth	17 DE 165	
Elizabeth	17 DE 155	
Elizabeth	18 DE 77	
Elizabeth	53 DE 155	
Frances A	33 MD 60	
George	6 DE 65	
Henry	13 DE 35	
Hester A	30 DE 65	
Isaac	45 DE 62	
James	4 DE 78	
James	12 DE 155	
James	28 DE 65	
James	63 DE 155	
James B	39 DE 78	
Jane	15 DE 155	
John P	4 DE 60	
John S	4/12 DE 60	
Luke	95 DE 65	
Margaret	23 DE 65	
Mary	13 DE 249	
Mary	41 DE 78	
Mary E	5 DE 60	
Mary J	7 DE 78	
Sarah	8/12 DE 62	
Sarah A	2 DE 60	
Sarah A	12 DE 60	
Sarah A	45 DE 60	
Sarah E	3/12 DE 65	
Sarah E	11 DE 78	
Sarah J	3 DE 142	
Susanna	8 DE 60	
William	4 DE 65	
William	14 DE 163	
William H	16 DE 78	
Rickards, Amanda M	8 DE 83	
Barbara	28 DE 119	
Rickards, Catherine	14 DE 149	
Charles	5 DE 149	
Charles	21 DE 170	
Charles	42 DE 149	
Christiana	6 DE 213	
David J	25 DE 225	
Emily A	11 DE 83	
Emma	9 DE 35	
Garrett	3 DE 241	
George	9 DE 248	
Hester A	34 DE 151	
Isaac	8 DE 35	
James	11 DE 205	
James	21 DE 83	
James	23 DE 179	
John	8 DE 149	
John	18 DE 213	
John T	18 DE 35	
Joseph	17 DE 35	
Lydia	19 DE 179	
Margaret	2 DE 149	
Margaret A	9 DE 119	
Mary	1 DE 179	
Mary	38 DE 205	
Mary	39 DE 149	
Mary	44 DE 83	
Mary A	12 DE 35	
Mary E	10 DE 149	
Nelson R	48 DE 83	
Parnell	6 DE 205	
Perry	16 DE 83	
Priscilla	4 DE 250	
Rachel	13 DE 90	
Rachel	74 DE 92	
Rebecca	37 DE 35	
Sarah	9/12 DE 250	
Sarah	21 DE 250	
Sarah	19 DE 225	
Sarah	50 DE 213	
Sarah	65 DE 205	
Sarah E	3 DE 35	
Sarah E	5 DE 131	
Sarah E	13 DE 83	
Solomon	25 DE 250	
William	11 DE 149	
William	13 DE 35	
Ridgely, Edward	19 DE 160	
Eugene	28 DE 179	
Henry	35 DE 170	
Mary	90 DE 162	
Ruthanna	2 DE 170	
Sally Ann	45 DE 160	
Virginia	33 DE 170	
Ridgers, Mary	27 DE 39	
Sarah	2 DE 39	
Ridgaway, Joseph	64 MD 233	
Sally	52 DE 233	
Ridgeway, Jacob	41 NJ 95	
Louisa	8 PA 84	
Mary	23 DE 95	
Rigeway, Beckey	20 DE 161	
Francis	24 DE 161	
Riggins, Thomas H	11 DE 85	
Riggs, Amelia	13 DE 235	
David	5 DE 235	
David	32 DE 224	
Eliza	34 DE 152	
Elizabeth	35 DE 235	
Ezekiel	15 DE 172	
James	10 DE 235	
James	13 DE 113	
James	41 DE 235	
John	10 DE 172	
John	62 DE 172	
Josephine	2 DE 235	
Julia A	22 DE 111	
Leah	55 DE 101	
Loudon	29 DE 78	
Louisa	16 DE 104	
Nathaniel	70 DE 152	
Mary	1/12 DE 235	
Mary	51 DE 59	
Riggs, Mary J	1 DE 78	
Nathaniel	8 DE 235	
Rebecca	12 DE 172	
Ruthy	2 DE 155	
Samuel	59 DE 59	
Sophia	27 DE 78	
Unity	55 DE 72	
Zepporah	66 DE 152	
Riley, Ann	40 DE 92	
Ann E	11 DE 86	
Daniel	14 IE 202	
Eliza J	26 DE 87	
Elizabeth	30 DE 86	
Francis A	5 DE 87	
Johanna	56 IE 214	
John	27 DE 87	
John H	4 DE 86	
Joseph H	38 DE 86	
Joseph W	8 DE 86	
Mary B	2 DE 86	
Ruth	16 NJ 56	
Spencer	1 DE 87	
Rilman, Samuel	14 DE 180	
Rines, Ann J	2 DE 44	
James	35 DE 44	
John H	5 DE 44	
Mary A	28 DE 44	
Ringold, Charlotta	14 DE 49	
William	55 DE 3	
Ringgold, Charles	9 DE 51	
Frances	18 DE 38	
Hannah	47 DE 40	
Mary	3 DE 40	
Risdon	10 DE 40	
Robert	45 DE 40	
Sophia	15 DE 41	
Wesley	7 DE 40	
William	9 DE 40	
Rins, Alexander	45 DE 160	
Alvanus	24 DE 175	
Amey	38 DE 169	
Ann	17 DE 169	
Elizabeth	8 DE 175	
Elizabeth	50 DE 175	
James	16 DE 175	
James	18 DE 175	
John	18 DE 173	
Joseph	18 DE 175	
Mary	14 DE 169	
Moses	10 DE 175	
Nero	65 DE 175	
Peter	9 DE 169	
Sally Ann	13 DE 175	
Risden, Philis	54 DE 26	
Solomon	62 DE 26	
William	16 DE 28	
Ritchie, James	23 DE 33	
Roache, John A	6 PA 14	
John A	36 MD 14	
Mary C	31 NJ 14	
Richard W	9 PA 14	
Spencer L	1 PA 14	
Roads, Joseph	20 GE 83	
Roberts, Ann	1 DE 165	
Anna S	4 DE 3	
Arianna	31 PA 3	
Charlotte	23 DE 199	
Elizabeth	5 DE 42	
Elizabeth	10 NJ 11	
Ellen	2/12 DE 199	
George	9 DE 199	
George	35 DE 165	
Hannah	7 NJ 11	
Harriet	30 DE 165	
Irene	1 DE 3	
Jacob	11 DE 199	
James	32 DE 3	
James	40 DE 38	
Lettitia	37 DE 38	
Margaret	11 DE 165	
Mary	4 DE 199	
Mary	13 DE 165	

Name	Age	St	Pg	Name	Age	St	Pg	Name	Age	St	Pg
Roberts, Melvina	18	DE	36	Robinson, Wilhel-				Ross, James	3	DE	142
Philip	17	DE	192	mina	6	DE	76	James	8	DE	207
Philip	40	DE	199	William	23	DE	51	James B	26	DE	129
Sarah	3	DE	199	Robbitson, Charlott	47	MD	158	John	11	MD	243
Stephen	13	DE	199	Henrietta	18	DE	158	Mary	15	MD	243
William	4	DE	165	Rochester, Eliza	15	DE	250	Mary	21	DE	243
William	5	NJ	11	John	60	MD	250	Mary E	17	DE	248
Robins, William	20	DE	83	Lavinia	20	DE	252	Mary P	13	DE	142
Robinson, Adeline	5	DE	98	Martha	20	DE	223	Peter	19	MD	243
Alexander	6	DE	6	Savinia	50	DE	250	Rebecca	33	DE	142
Anjelica	25	DE	34	Roderfield, Anna	37	NJ	62	Rebecca	48	MD	243
Ann	8	DE	74	Susan	6	PA	62	Rebecca J	8	DE	142
Ann	36	DE	6	William	62	PA	62	Reuben	36	DE	142
Ann	40	DE	2	Rodney, Albert	22	DE	7	Robert	57	DE	243
Ann	47	DE	74	Casar A	68	DE	60	Sarah E	10	DE	142
Anna	33	DE	33	Cezar	11	DE	88	Sarah J	16	DE	143
Catharine	7	DE	35	Ezekiel	17	DE	61	Sarah J	18	DE	207
Catharine	26	DE	51	John	10	DE	59	William	10	DE	144
Charles	3/12	DE	254	John	69	DE	59	William E	6	DE	142
Charles	1	DE	75	Joseph	20	DE	60	Williamina	32	DE	147
Charlotte	18	DE	35	Mary	51	DE	82	Wm	22	MD	243
Clayton	28	DE	200	Matilda	17	DE	59	Round, Mary	21	DE	88
Daniel	21	DE	51	Sarah	64	DE	59	Roust, Clement	69	DE	113
David	10	DE	33	Thomas	18	DE	81	Rowlett, George	36	DE	77
David	50	DE	96	Roe, Abner	32	DE	190	Rowns, Elizabeth	17	DE	239
Edward	10	DE	76	Andrew	20	MD	5	Rumbles, John T	14	PA	71
Edward	11	DE	76	Ann	23	DE	239	Rura, Louisa	26	PA	144
Elizabeth	15	DE	226	Charity	55	DE	245	Rush, Charles	11	DE	29
Elizabeth	48	DE	18	Elizabeth	4	DE	261	Frances	10/12	DE	182
Elmira	8	DE	200	Elizzbeth	17	DE	245	George	15	DE	11
George	7	DE	33	Elizabeth	55	DE	261	Harriet	5	DE	182
George	43	DE	33	Elizabeth	59	DE	52	Isaac	8	DE	182
Hannah	68	DE	79	Ellen	25	DE	239	Joseph	6	DE	182
Henry	17	DE	74	Ellen	28	DE	190	Martin	27	DE	182
Henry	41	DE	73	James	15	DE	141	Mary	40	DE	189
Hester	4/12	DE	73	James	40	DE	245	Sally	27	DE	182
Hester	1	DE	74	James W	29	DE	52	Rusin, Henrietta	16	MD	18
Hester	27	DE	171	Jane	54	DE	232	Russ, Charles	32	DE	242
Jacob	20	DE	33	John W	6	MD	141	Elizabeth	32	DE	242
James	19	DE	35	Jonathan	7	DE	245	Sarah	2	DE	242
James	36	DE	76	Martha	25	DE	52	Russel, Alexander	33	MD	140
James	52	DE	35	Mary	10	DE	261	Charles W	5/12	DE	140
James H	11	DE	98	Mary E	3	DE	141	David	38	DE	83
Jeremiah R	31	DE	34	Rachel	30	DE	239	Elizabeth	4	DE	83
John	18	DE	193	Robert	1	DE	245	Elizabeth	23	MD	140
John	22	DE	74	Samuel	16	DE	239	Elizabeth E	20	DE	146
John	40	DE	6	Sarah	4	DE	141	Francis	1	DE	146
John H	1	DE	76	Susan	1	DE	141	James	10	DE	83
Jonathan	24	DE	76	Thomas	10	DE	245	John	28	DE	146
Julia A	9	DE	73	Unity	2	DE	191	John H	4	MD	140
Luther	104	MD	153	William	15	DE	245	Joseph	30	DE	37
Margaret	6	DE	74	William	32	PA	141	Margarett	37	DE	83
Margaret	29	DE	200	William C	1	DE	52	Mary	1	DE	83
Margaret	32	DE	76	William D	19	DE	124	Robert	12	DE	83
Mary	1/12	DE	33	Wm	21	MD	261	Sarah	6	DE	83
Mary	6/12	DE	200	Wm	60	DE	239	Russell, Catherine	40	DE	5
Mary	7/12	DE	34	Rogers, Ann	6	DE	225	Eliza J	16	DE	16
Mary	12	DE	73	Arthur	70	VA	150	Elizabeth	8	PA	269
Mary	15	DE	87	Charles	27	DE	230	Hannah	33	PA	269
Mary	23	DE	76	Elizabeth	22	DE	225	John	7	PA	269
Mary	81	NJ	43	James	24	DE	225	John	19	IE	195
Mary A	12	DE	76	John	1	DE	225	Mary	3	DE	269
Matilda	12	DE	33	Nicy	62	DE	150	Morris	5	DE	269
Peter Q	11	DE	35	Rachel	47	PA	34	Robert	12	DE	136
Priscilla	50	DE	96	Sally	2	DE	156	Thornton	1	DE	269
Rachel	3	DE	33	Rolly, Joshua	2	DE	231	Thornton	35	VA	269
Rachel	50	DE	231	Sarah	28	DE	231	Rust, Eliza B	1	DE	149
Rebecca	22	DE	74	Rory, Eleanor	39	DE	129	Elizabeth	22	DE	149
Rebecca	25	DE	254	Rose, Elizabeth	35	DE	186	James	28	DE	149
Rebecca	47	DE	35	James	11	DE	186	James A	6/12	DE	149
Robert	1	DE	76	James	36	DE	186	Rusten, Charles	36	GB	195
Rosett	3	DE	73	Mary	9	DE	186	Ruth, Cloe	70	DE	224
Ruth	4	DE	76	Sylvanus	1	DE	186	James	56	DE	71
Ruth	14	DE	73	Sylvester	1	DE	186	James W	42	MD	12
Ruth	60	DE	76	Ross, Alexander	14	MD	243	John H	11	DE	12
Samuel	21	DE	254	Almira	14	DE	142	Mary	6	DE	12
Samuel	60	DE	231	Anna	9/12	DE	142	Rebecca	45	DE	12
Sarah	8	DE	76	Catherine	70	DE	106	Sarah	46	DE	12
Sarah	18	DE	33	Emily	10	DE	223	Rutledge, James	32	DE	168
Terry Ann	33	DE	73	Henry	25	DE	134	Joshua	1	DE	168
Warner	7	DE	74	Hetty	10	DE	152	Mary	4	DE	168
Warner	51	DE	74	Hooper B	5	DE	142	Mary	30	DE	168

Name	Age	State	Page
Rutledge, William	10	DE	168
Ryands, Deborah A	20	DE	170
Salesberry, Mary	7	DE	104
Mary	36	DE	234
Sarah E	15	DE	104
Salisbury, Margaret	60	MD	262
Willard	9	DE	216
Wm	39	MD	262
Wm	44	DE	234
Salmon, Elizabeth	47	DE	98
James	45	DE	98
Joseph D	10	DE	98
Milly A	2/12	DE	118
Robert H	15	DE	98
Sarah J	2	DE	98
Thomas J	19	DE	98
Salsbury, Alexander	35	DE	146
Alfred	2	DE	254
Eli	2	DE	146
Eli	31	DE	146
Ezekiel	12	DE	254
Gabe	24	DE	163
Garrison	26	DE	148
Henrietta	41	DE	146
Henry	4	DE	148
Henry	36	DE	254
James	4	DE	254
John	30	DE	148
Margaret	9/12	DE	163
Margaret	26	DE	146
Margaret	70	DE	146
Margaret A	12	DE	146
Mary	7	DE	254
Mary	60	DE	148
Mary E	4	DE	146
Rebecca	33	DE	254
Rosina	21	MD	163
Sarah	9	DE	254
Sarah E	8	DE	146
Thomas	14	DE	254
Thomas	34	DE	175
Sammon, Robert	40	DE	249
Sammons, Alfred	6	DE	144
Benjamin	12	DE	31
Benjamin	55	DE	31
David B	5	DE	103
Elizabeth	45	DE	33
Ellin	5 da	DE	86
Hester	8	DE	31
Isaac	8	DE	33
Isaac	15	DE	106
Isaac	50	DE	31
James	15	DE	33
James	20	DE	31
John	42	DE	33
Littleton	26	DE	86
Mariah	28	DE	86
Mary	13	DE	32
Mary J	9	DE	118
Milly	32	DE	118
Minus	39	DE	118
Morris	10	DE	31
Rhoda A	12	DE	118
Robert	19	DE	33
Sarah	11	DE	33
Sarah	57	DE	31
Sarah E	5	DE	118
Susan	12	DE	31
Thomas	7	DE	221
William	20	DE	149
William S	2	DE	118
Samons, Benjamin	25	DE	179
Sanard, Susan	50	DE	185
Susanna	5	DE	185
Sanders, Alexander	7	DE	43
Ann	42	DE	2
Ann	60	DE	177
Ann M	3	DE	40
Caroline	28	DE	44
Charles	6	DE	43
Daniel	3	DE	2
Sanders, Daniel	70	DE	37
Debora	22	DE	177
Eliza	5	DE	43
Eliza	7	DE	36
Emory	13	DE	36
Enoch	27	DE	44
Esther	55	DE	9
Frances	14	DE	37
George	6	DE	44
George	23	DE	177
Harriet	70	DE	37
Hester	11	DE	40
Hester	13	DE	44
Isaiah	4	DE	44
Jacob	38	DE	2
Jane E	9/12	DE	40
John	1/12	DE	177
John	5	DE	2
John	40	DE	176
Joseph	5/12	DE	177
Julia A	2	DE	44
Lydia	13	DE	43
Lydia A	2	DE	2
Margaret	25	DE	36
Margaret	25	DE	43
Mary	4	DE	36
Perry	45	DE	43
Priscilla	60	DE	39
Rachel	1	DE	44
Sarah	4	DE	36
Sarah	4	DE	43
Sarah	28	DE	40
Sewel	22	DE	44
Susan	6/12	DE	2
Susan	1	DE	36
Susan	1	DE	43
William	26	DE	43
William	29	DE	36
William	40	DE	177
Sands, John	16	MD	4
Sapp, Agnes	40	DE	116
Andrew	30	DE	119
Angelina	11	DE	119
Ann	26	DE	95
Ann E	3	DE	80
Curtis	23	DE	137
Daniel	8	DE	116
David	9	DE	119
Edward	3	DE	119
Elias	28	DE	137
Elias	36	DE	208
Elijah	16	DE	119
Elijah	75	DE	119
Elizabeth	30	DE	137
Emaline	4/12	DE	116
Emeline	53	DE	203
Emily	22	DE	236
Hester	57	DE	95
Hester A	19	DE	95
Hezekiah	7	DE	119
Isabel	14	DE	119
Jacob	17	DE	116
James	21	DE	116
John	6	DE	116
John	29	DE	268
John	42	NJ	203
John	54	DE	95
John A	1	DE	118
Lavinia	30	DE	119
Lewis	1	DE	119
Lydia	61	DE	137
Lydia	71	DE	119
Margaret E	42	DE	119
Mary	1	DE	80
Mary	8	DE	119
Mary	43	DE	21
Mary A	15	DE	119
Nicholson	27	DE	116
Noah	1/12	DE	119
Reuben	9	DE	119
Robert H	7	DE	208
Sarah	6	DE	119
Sapp, Sarah	23	DE	80
Sarah	69	DE	116
Sarah S	17	DE	118
Solomon	24	DE	118
Susan	50	DE	116
Susan A	4	DE	208
Susan A	36	DE	208
Thomas	24	DE	80
William	4	DE	116
William	10	DE	119
William	47	DE	119
William J	34	DE	116
William M	2	DE	118
William M	2	DE	121
Wm	22	DE	236
Sarde, Ann	55	DE	223
Francis	10/12	DE	225
James	2	DE	225
Mary	28	DE	225
Mary	35	DE	223
Robert	57	MD	223
Samuel	21	DE	223
Thomas	18	DE	223
William	28	DE	225
Saterfield, Ann	55	DE	238
Asberry	51	DE	249
Caroline	19	DE	238
Charles	16	DE	238
Elizabeth	56	MD	234
Harriet	17	DE	221
Joseph	12	DE	238
Margaret	22	DE	238
Nathaniel	11/12	DE	234
Samuel	7	DE	194
Sarah	60	DE	189
William	24	DE	238
Wm	57	DE	238
Satterfield, Aaron	6	DE	117
Bruffil	16	DE	117
Harriet W	20	DE	126
John	34	DE	116
Levi	8	DE	98
Margaret	23	DE	117
Mary	26	DE	116
Phillip J	3	DE	117
Sarah	57	DE	117
Washington	16	DE	126
William G	13	DE	126
William H	19	DE	117
Saudler, William	60	DE	40
Saulsberry, Susan	18	DE	2
William	22	MD	2
Savin, James T	16	DE	24
John A	20	DE	7
Richard	28	DE	77
Samuel	33	DE	77
Sarah	42	DE	30
Sarah	60	MD	77
Susan A	18	DE	30
William	31	DE	77
William	74	MD	77
Sawyer, Abraham	38	MD	49
James	50	DE	8
Perry	17	DE	47
Saxon, George W	6	DE	98
Mary E	3	DE	98
Sarah J	24	DE	98
William	40	DE	98
Saxton, Ann	52	DE	214
Anna	3/12	DE	153
Anna S	10	DE	214
Cornelius	10	DE	153
Debora	15	DE	153
Emma	14	DE	214
Harry	19	DE	153
James	6	DE	153
John	39	DE	214
Josephine	3	DE	153
Margaret	13	DE	153
Margaret	52	MD	12
Sally Ann	17	DE	153
Samuel	8	DE	153

Name	Age	State	Page
Saxton, Samuel	53	DE	153
Sarah	40	DE	153
Susan A	1/12	DE	98
Scenly, Cornelius	5	DE	251
Elmira	7	DE	251
Henry	54	DE	251
John	1	DE	182
Mary	20	PA	182
Mary	40	DE	251
Matilda	2	DE	251
Thomas	32	DE	182
Scott, Adeline	13	DE	122
Alexander	1	DE	137
Alexander	10	DE	133
Ann Mariah	2	DE	83
Anna	19	DE	83
Benjamin	5	DE	152
Caleb	8	DE	101
Catherine	23	DE	205
Celia	31	DE	133
Charles E	9	MD	123
Clement	11	DE	137
Clement	46	DE	137
Daniel	10	DE	101
Dorcas	49	DE	96
Ebenezer	7	DE	122
Elias	3	DE	133
Elicia	70	DE	267
Elijah	18	DE	137
Eliza	30	DE	267
Eliza	40	DE	101
Eliza A	13	DE	133
Eliza A	16	DE	101
Eliza A	33	DE	116
Eliza E	9	DE	152
Elizabeth	15	DE	139
Elizabeth	25	DE	21
Emeline	3	DE	129
Emma	4	DE	21
Garrison	17	DE	101
George	1	DE	133
Georgiana	6	DE	205
Harmony	40	DE	139
Harriet	40	DE	152
Harrison	8	DE	137
Hasty	5	DE	152
Hester	13	DE	129
Isaac	5	DE	137
Isabella	10	DE	133
Ivan	9	DE	140
Ivan	35	DE	138
James	4	DE	205
James	14	DE	128
Jesse	49	DE	137
John	13	DE	101
John	20	DE	90
John	35	DE	267
John R	11/12	DE	138
John W	3	DE	137
Joseph J	13	DE	140
Josiah	60	DE	241
Julietta	9	DE	152
Lauretta	2	DE	267
Levi	16	DE	133
Lorenzo	4	DE	267
Lowden	30	?	143
Luther	1	DE	140
Luther S	13	DE	152
Lydia	4	DE	96
Lydia	4	DE	149
Lydia	38	DE	152
Lydia A	3	DE	152
Margaret A	3	DE	133
Margaret A	7	DE	129
Margaretta	23	DE	241
Marrietta	1	DE	143
Mary	5	DE	133
Mary	5	DE	137
Mary	38	DE	122
Mary J	23	DE	150
Matilda	1	DE	102
Matthew	4	DE	49
Scott, Miranda	3	DE	122
Miriam	48	DE	137
Nancy	24	MD	143
Nancy	46	DE	129
Nathan	55	DE	139
Nathan W	40	DE	122
Nathaniel	11	DE	152
Nathaniel	15	DE	137
Nathaniel	16	DE	131
Nehemiah	18	DE	192
Nelson	10	DE	140
Nelson	11	DE	128
Nelson	12	DE	140
Noah	38	DE	152
Noah B	10/12	DE	152
Peter	26	DE	241
Peter	75	DE	96
Peter W	15	DE	122
Rebecca	38	DE	133
Rhoda A	8	DE	133
Robert	4	DE	101
Robert	18	DE	91
Robert	60	DE	101
Ruth A	7	DE	152
Sarah	7/12	DE	241
Sarah	7	DE	101
Sarah	30	DE	138
Sarah C	6	DE	133
Sarah E	8/12	DE	152
Sarah E	2	DE	205
Sarah E	10	DE	122
Sarah J	15	DE	152
Serepta	14	DE	137
Serepta	16	DE	96
Stephen	46	DE	129
Susan A	13	DE	85
Thomas	50	DE	152
Violet	16	DE	152
Wesley	25	DE	137
Wesley	35	DE	133
William	10	DE	96
William	11	MD	256
William	26	DE	205
William	43	DE	132
William H	7	DE	132
William H	17	DE	129
William W	2	DE	21
William W	3	DE	138
Wm	12	DE	195
Zela	20	DE	137
Scotten, Ann	4	DE	195
Caroline	13	DE	195
Charles	16	DE	194
Edith	59	DE	62
Elizabeth	51	MD	195
Hannah	6/12	DE	199
John	9	DE	199
John	14	DE	168
Jonathan	25	DE	194
Joseph	3	DE	195
Julia	41	MD	199
Kitty	9	DE	194
Levi	7	DE	199
Mahalah	64	DE	27
Martha	11	DE	194
Nancy	50	MD	194
Philomon	28	DE	194
Merrit	60	DE	194
Rebecca	27	DE	195
Sally Ann	8	DE	194
Sally Ann	30	MD	195
Sarah	3	DE	199
Spencer	22	DE	194
Susan	1	DE	195
Thomas	13	DE	194
Willard	15	DE	195
Wm	45	MD	199
Wm	47	MD	195
Scotton, Ann M	3	DE	42
Eliza	32	DE	42
Jacob	1	DE	42
James	10	DE	50
Scotton, John G	13	DE	58
Joshua	20	MD	16
Louis P	14	DE	58
Phebe	24	DE	62
Scoudoni, Sarah	23	DE	62
Scoudrick, James	28	DE	38
Mary E	24	DE	38
Sarah E	4	DE	38
Scout, Anna	32	DE	44
Anna A	4	DE	44
Augustus	32	DE	17
Eliza	15	DE	3
George	6/12	DE	44
Henrietta	5	DE	44
Henry	33	DE	44
John	2	DE	44
Mary	7	DE	44
Robert	18	DE	12
Sarah	48	DE	3
Sarah A	21	DE	3
Sidney B	3	DE	17
Temperance	22	DE	17
Walter	8/12	DE	17
Scuse, James	1	DE	200
John	3	DE	200
Martha	5	DE	200
Susan	25	DE	200
Thomas	25	DE	200
Seals, Ennel	34	DE	177
Seger, Frances A	8/12	DE	42
George	7	DE	41
Jacob	38	DE	41
Jane	32	DE	41
Josiah	9	DE	41
Martha	4	DE	41
Mary E	2	DE	42
Rachel	15	DE	38
Segris, Anna	3	DE	79
Jacob	8	DE	79
Jacob	38	GE	79
Martha	33	PA	79
Sarah	11	DE	79
Seighfreid, Edmund	21	PA	43
Selby, Scynthia	80	MD	117
Selden, Ann	64	DE	232
Marvin	47	CT	232
Sell, Elizabeth	21	DE	81
Selvy, Ann	6	DE	181
Elizabeth	27	DE	181
Virginia	2	DE	181
Washington	35	DE	181
Seney, Ann E	10	DE	64
Catherine	41	DE	64
Ellen	1/12	DE	64
James	9	DE	64
James	29	DE	65
John	1	DE	65
John	2	DE	64
Luther	2	DE	64
Martha	11	DE	64
Melvina	3	DE	65
Rebecca	22	DE	64
Rebecca J	4	DE	64
Rhoda	4	DE	65
Rhoda	75	DE	65
Samuel	28	DE	64
Sarah	23	DE	64
Thomas	10	DE	65
Washington	33	DE	64
Sergent, Hannah	27	DE	61
William	29	DE	61
Seth, Elizabeth	21	DE	249
Severson, Abraham	18	DE	33
Allen	13	DE	33
Benjamin	16	DE	33
Elizabeth	56	DE	35
Gideon	16	DE	35
Jane	50	DE	14
John	22	DE	35
John	44	DE	33
Nathaniel	54	DE	35
Sarah	44	DE	33

Severson, Sarah Ann	6	DE	33	Sharp, Mary M	35	DE	84	Sherwood, John C	28	DE	85
William	16	DE	33	Milly	44	DE	113	Layton	50	DE	106
Sevil, David R	4	DE	1	Peter	33	DE	83	Louisa	19	DE	106
Elizabeth	24	DE	1	Rachel	33	DE	108	Lydia	8	DE	47
John	8/12	DE	1	Richard	13	DE	9	Margaret	15	DE	250
John P	34	DE	1	Samuel	12	MD	88	Margaret	48	DE	250
Nathan T	23	DE	53	Sarah	59	DE	108	Martha J	10	DE	47
Rebecca	23	NJ	53	Sarah A	9	DE	108	Mary	7	DE	250
William T	9	DE	1	Sarah A	42	DE	112	Ninon	12	DE	47
Sevill, Amanda D	9	DE	12	Sarah E	6	DE	108	Rachel	44	DE	47
Elizabeth	49	DE	12	Thomas	61	DE	108	Rachel E	5	DE	47
Mary M	11	DE	12	Thomas E	4	DE	108	Robert	25	DE	250
Seward, Griffin	8	DE	184	William	10	DE	112	Sarah	20	DE	250
James	14	DE	184	William	15	DE	9	Sarah A	13	DE	106
John	26	DE	184	William	45	DE	9	Susan	12	DE	250
Martha	24	DE	184	William H	2	DE	84	Thomas	15	DE	94
Nathan	19	DE	184	William T	7	DE	108	Thomas	17	DE	12
Sewdrick, James H	12	DE	39	Sharpe, John W	32	DE	224	Thomas	18	DE	47
John W	39	MD	39	Shaw, Anna M	4	DE	126	Thomas	48	DE	47
Mary	7	DE	39	Balinda M	4	DE	1	Wm	22	DE	256
Mary	43	DE	39	Catharine	26	DE	1	Shieby, Martha	63	MD	47
Sewell, Charles	45	DE	44	Hannah	5/12	DE	210	William	67	MD	47
Elizabeth	68	PA	11	James	36	DE	232	Shockley, Amelia	16	DE	97
John	21	DE	143	James	44	NJ	210	Ann E	2	DE	119
William F	37	DE	64	James W	12	DE	126	Antony	22	DE	232
William H	17	DE	142	Lucy A	33	DE	210	Caleb	1/12	DE	155
Sexton, Catherine	9	DE	164	Mary	16	DE	232	Caroline	7	DE	136
Shahan, David	1	DE	49	Mary	48	DE	232	Edward	14	DE	216
George	3	DE	49	Mary L	10	DE	126	Elias	23	DE	155
Jacob	9	DE	49	Samuel L	7	DE	126	Eliza	45	DE	232
Jacob	14	DE	176	Sarah C	1	DE	1	Elizabeth	4	DE	229
James	24	DE	52	Susan A	1	DE	126	Elizabeth	18	DE	91
John	4	DE	49	Susan G	38	DE	126	Ellen	20	DE	232
John	16	DE	176	Wilhelmina	12	DE	34	George	2	DE	229
Jonathan	4	DE	49	William	35	DE	126	George	23	DE	155
Jonathan	35	DE	176	Shearwood, Mary	19	MD	59	George	31	DE	152
Joseph	7	DE	176	Sheet, Miles T	28	DE	63	Hester	2	DE	97
Mary	22	DE	176	Sheimer, Henry	25	PA	10	Hetty	41	DE	97
Mary	42	DE	52	Shelcott, Joshua	7	DE	121	Isaac J	6	DE	97
Maryann	34	DE	176	William P	10	DE	121	Jabez E	41	DE	85
Rachel	8	DE	49	Shelton, Angelica	15	DE	168	Jacob	10	DE	97
Thomas	1/12	DE	52	Ann	3	DE	201	Jacob	47	DE	97
William	12	DE	176	Ann	18	DE	51	James W	5	DE	152
William	13	DE	49	Elizabeth	13	DE	51	Joanna R	10/12	DE	85
William	20	DE	49	Francis	1	DE	168	John	12	DE	90
Shain, Edward	24	DE	34	George	63	DE	168	John G	12	DE	97
Emily	13	PA	17	John	4	DE	168	John W	19	DE	150
Helen M	23	PA	17	John	10	DE	51	Joshua	1	DE	155
James M	52	DE	34	John	22	DE	168	Leah	4	DE	119
Mary	40	DE	34	Joseph	1/12	DE	201	Leah	47	DE	93
Mary G	20	PA	4	Joseph	26	DE	201	Mariah	16	DE	232
Samuel	5	DE	34	Mary	26	DE	168	Mariah L	27	DE	152
Sarah	2	DE	34	Ruthann	21	DE	201	Martha A	6	DE	93
Thomas	50	DE	17	Thomas	48	DE	51	Martha J	4	DE	97
Shanahan, John	45	IE	156	Shepard, Benjamin	39	DE	209	Mary	22	DE	159
Shannon, Martha A	45	DE	23	Daniel	11	DE	209	Mary C	14	DE	97
Sharp, Abraham	9	DE	9	Daniel	15	DE	209	Milly	19	DE	232
Abraham	31	DE	76	Elenor	71	DE	209	Nancy	36	DE	136
Amanda	17	DE	9	James H	8	DE	209	Rachel	17	DE	155
Ann	5	DE	84	Jonathan N	12	DE	209	Rachel Ann	13	DE	93
Anna	9	DE	88	Mary E	2	DE	209	Rachel C	4	DE	136
Benjamin	17	DE	86	Sarah	5	DE	209	Regina D	37	DE	85
Carsa	30	DE	83	Shepherd, Daniel	50	MD	43	Regina M	3	DE	85
Catharine	12	DE	9	Henrietta	11	DE	43	Ruth E	2	DE	136
Catherine	22	DE	76	James	2	MD	43	Sally	30	DE	155
Clement L	34	DE	112	James	17	DE	129	Sarah	17	DE	232
Elizabeth	35	DE	88	Joseph	7	DE	43	Sarah A	1	DE	152
Frances Ann	1	DE	83	Margaret	4	DE	43	Sarah A	14	DE	136
Henry C	9	DE	112	Mary	14	DE	12	Tilghman	20	DE	74
Henry W	40	PA	84	Noah	7	DE	129	Whittington	35	DE	136
Isaac E	13	DE	88	Sarah	17	DE	129	William	16	DE	88
James	15	DE	88	Sherman, Robert	12	PA	38	William	16	DE	134
James	32	DE	108	Sherwood, Ann	50	DE	94	William A	2/12	DE	97
James L	1/12	DE	108	Elizabeth	5/12	DE	250	William H	25	DE	87
Jesse J	32	DE	113	Elizabeth	22	DE	256	William P	3	DE	152
John	44	DE	83	Elizabeth J	27	DE	85	Williamina	13	DE	232
John B	9	DE	84	Ezekiel	10	DE	250	Zachariah	50	DE	93
Joseph	6	DE	9	Jesse	6	DE	94	Shockly, Elizabeth	27	DE	235
Joseph	6	DE	88	Jesse	24	DE	250	Isaac	5	DE	235
Joseph G	13	DE	84	Jesse	49	DE	94	James	27	DE	228
Laura	1	DE	88	John	21	DE	250	Jimanda	7/12	DE	229
Mariah	11	DE	86	John	53	DE	250	John	19	DE	214

Name	Age	St	No.	Name	Age	St	No.	Name	Age	St	No.
Shockly, John	27	DE	235	Shorts, Emory	12	DE	180	Simpson, Ezekiel K	12	DE	29
Mary	6	DE	228	John	18	DE	180	Grace	49	DE	213
Mary	26	DE	228	Letty	20	DE	180	Isaac	37	DE	138
Peter	1	DE	235	Martha	13	DE	180	James A	11	DE	9
Peter	75	DE	235	Mary	46	DE	180	James T	7	DE	129
Sarah	18	DE	214	Sarah	15	DE	180	John	2	DE	231
Shores, George	41	DE	26	Shortter, Catharine	5	IE	29	John	13	DE	9
Mary	38	DE	26	John	1	DE	29	John	29	DE	235
Short, Amanda	5	DE	33	Margaret	36	IE	29	John H	9	DE	13
Amanda	22	DE	33	Michael	36	IE	29	John H	20	DE	214
Amanda W	20	DE	65	Thomas	4	CN	29	Joseph	61	PE	242
Angelina	2	DE	118	Shower, Rachel	80	DE	109	Joseph L	23	DE	32
Ann	4	DE	118	Shull, Daniel	7	DE	23	Julina	2	DE	133
Anna	9	DE	166	George	13	DE	23	Mary	2	DE	133
Catharine	49	DE	33	Robert	4	DE	23	Mary	9	DE	224
Charles	8	DE	105	Sarah Ann	35	DE	23	Mary	14	DE	204
Charles	35	DE	166	Shurwood, Samuel	20	DE	69	Mary	15	DE	129
Deborah	26	DE	118	Sibel, Wm	35	DE	164	Mary	19	DE	242
Elizabeth	17	DE	118	Sibley, Sarah	53	DE	60	Mary E	2	DE	13
Elizabeth H	21	DE	65	Signor, Ann	56	DE	21	Matthew	37	DE	13
Edward	10	DE	105	Derry	35	DE	21	Mitchell	6	DE	9
Edward	23	DE	118	Silvers, Eliza	21	DE	15	Norma	63	DE	242
Esther A	11	DE	63	William	4/12	DE	15	Rebecca	23	DE	13
Greensberry H	23	DE	65	William	26	DE	15	Rhoda	22	DE	242
Hannah A	12	DE	65	Silway, Benjamin	8	PA	174	Richard J	10	DE	129
Hannah A	55	DE	65	Simmons, Amey	41	DE	177	Richard L	8	DE	9
Hiram	17	DE	128	Angeline	16	DE	217	Robert	5	DE	224
Isaac	14	DE	33	Ann	40	DE	217	Samuel	4	DE	138
Isaac	59	DE	33	Araminta	20	DE	50	Samuel	16	DE	223
Isaac S	52	DE	65	Benjamin	13	DE	177	Sarah E	8	DE	133
Isaac W	2	DE	65	Catharine	24	DE	45	Susannah	47	DE	204
Isabella	34	DE	111	George	35	DE	212	Thomas	14	DE	133
James	42	DE	111	Hester	49	DE	42	Thomas	25	DE	172
James H	14	DE	105	James	19	DE	177	Thomas	38	DE	213
James M	25	DE	65	James	27	DE	45	Thomas	46	DE	223
James P	12	DE	63	James H	5	DE	212	Thomas	50	DE	204
John	2	DE	166	John	9	DE	177	Thomas H	7	DE	138
John	19	DE	203	Julian	1/12	DE	224	Thomas N	7	DE	213
John	40	DE	105	Lavinia	30	PA	224	William	19	DE	22
John H	17	DE	33	Levi	6	DE	42	William J	8	DE	138
John S	13	DE	65	Lewis	30	DE	266	William T	6	DE	133
Joshua A	15	DE	65	Margana	10	DE	217	William W	33	DE	133
Julia A	5	DE	111	Margaret	40	DE	249	Wm	30	DE	231
Kensey J	18	DE	63	Margaretta	3	DE	212	Sipple, Albert	1/12	DE	212
Lavenia	55	DE	63	Mariah	4	DE	177	Ann	6	DE	262
Leah	35	DE	166	Mary	4	DE	224	Ann E	16	DE	36
Liston A	1	DE	66	Mary	29	DE	266	Ann E	21	DE	133
Mahala E	10	DE	111	Mary	79	DE	249	Augustus	15	DE	169
Mahala H	14	DE	63	Mary A	10	DE	42	Benjamin	18	DE	237
Margeretta	14	DE	88	Mary A	27	DE	212	Betsey	70	DE	231
Mary	7	DE	166	Mary C	9	DE	212	Caleb	13	DE	89
Mary	18	DE	118	Mary E	13	DE	217	Caleb	25	DE	86
Mary	22	DE	18	Prince	19	DE	176	Caleb	50	DE	8
Mary	27	DE	33	Reese	20	DE	45	Caleb H	52	DE	157
Mary E	14	DE	110	Robert	2	DE	224	Caroline S	20	DE	212
Mary E	26	DE	105	Robert	38	DE	224	Catherine	11	DE	265
Mary J	8/12	DE	36	Ruthana	7	DE	224	Catherine	38	DE	265
Milly	7	DE	111	Samuel	59	DE	42	Charles	9	DE	172
Minus	36	DE	33	Sarah	7	DE	177	Comfort	32	DE	218
Peter	65	DE	63	Sarah E	13	DE	212	Comfort	50	DE	215
Rachel A	20	DE	66	Sarah J	8	DE	217	Deborah	45	DE	141
Rebecca	22	DE	65	Susan A	6/12	DE	212	Eliza	12	DE	203
Robert	23	DE	118	Thomas P	4	DE	217	Eliza B	36	DE	89
Robert J	3	DE	111	Wm L	42	MD	217	Elizabeth	13	DE	266
Samuel	10	DE	118	Simon, Robert P	12	DE	108	Elizabeth	18	DE	215
Samuel	13	DE	118	Simpler, Eliza	44	DE	48	Elizabeth	26	DE	265
Samuel	18	DE	105	Elizabeth	10	DE	48	Elizabeth A	19	DE	141
Samuel A	65	DE	118	Simpson, Alexander	16	DE	129	Ellen	16	DE	8
Sarah	48	DE	105	Amelia	46	DE	9	Emily	18	DE	252
Sarah E	11	DE	118	Ann	32	DE	231	Frances A	21	DE	44
Susan	22	DE	33	Ann	41	DE	129	Garret	30	DE	81
Susan	36	DE	118	Ann	46	DE	223	Hannah	35	DE	231
Susan A	4	DE	118	Ann E	4	DE	133	Henry C	6	DE	56
Susan A	11	DE	111	Ann M	5	DE	130	Hetty	45	DE	180
Susan A	13	DE	108	Anna	7	DE	224	James	2	DE	133
Thomas N	10/12	DE	65	Benjamin O	40	DE	9	James	5	DE	262
William	19	DE	33	Caroline	3/12	DE	9	James	15	DE	238
William S	27	DE	66	Clement C	41	DE	129	James B	29	DE	105
Shortas, George	21	DE	33	David	4/12	DE	133	James M	4/12	DE	91
Sarah	20	DE	33	Elizabeth	23	DE	242	John	5	DE	265
Shorts, Amelia	6	DE	180	Elizabeth J	35	DE	138	John	7	DE	89
Augustus	48	DE	180	Emily	25	DE	235	John	9	DE	232

Name	Age	State	No.
Sipple, John	27	DE	91
John	36	DE	265
Jonathan	4	DE	215
Jonathan M	43	DE	215
Lavinia	8	MD	212
Luff	26	DE	133
Mahala	37	DE	267
Margaretta	1	DE	215
Mariah	14	DE	215
Mariah	29	DE	262
Martha	1	DE	166
Martha A	24	DE	87
Mary	1/12	DE	243
Mary	42	DE	56
Mary	70	DE	27
Mary A	17	DE	141
Mary B	34	MD	212
Mary J	13	DE	38
Matilda	45	DE	204
Nathaniel	28	DE	257
Noah J	5	DE	141
Rachel A	21	DE	91
Rebecca A	17	DE	145
Rhoda	11	DE	142
Rhoda M	11	DE	38
Richard	3	DE	262
Robert	2	DE	262
Roseanna	27	DE	166
Ruth	28	DE	243
Sally Ann	46	DE	157
Samuel	12	DE	8
Samuel	50	DE	35
Samuel	50	DE	215
Sarah	1	DE	215
Sarah	1	DE	265
Sarah	7	DE	262
Sarah	80	DE	154
Sarah A	13	DE	141
Sarah Ann	21	DE	91
Sarah L	1	DE	87
Sarah M	13	DE	145
Seba	42	DE	8
Sylvia	48	DE	35
Tamar	9	DE	203
Thomas	23	DE	9
Thomas	31	DE	243
Thomas	34	MD	212
Thomas J	6	DE	242
Unity	43	DE	215
Uriah	30	DE	262
Waitman	32	DE	218
Waitman	45	DE	267
Warner	26	DE	171
William	4/12	DE	133
William	10	DE	114
William	20	DE	8
William B	3	DE	212
William H	22	DE	90
Zadock	8	DE	142
Zadock	50	DE	141
Zeich	28	DE	261
Sisco, Anna	5	DE	173
Araminta	34	DE	173
Isabella	6	DE	173
William	3	DE	173
Wm	33	DE	171
Skervin, Catherine	18	MD	16
John	11	VA	11
Thomas	17	MD	11
Skyler, Ann	7	DE	230
Beckey	40	DE	229
Slack, Judith	69	DE	14
Slaughter, Agnes	23	GB	71
Andrew	1	DE	75
Andrew	4	DE	164
Andrew	6	DE	265
Andrew	48	DE	254
Ann	14	DE	215
Ann	20	DE	31
Ann	22	DE	168
Caroline	22	DE	76
Catherine	35	DE	265

Name	Age	State	No.
Slaughter, Daniel	6/12	DE	76
Daniel	4	DE	265
Elizabeth	10	DE	265
Elizabeth	25	DE	179
Elizabeth	30	DE	198
Elizabeth	47	DE	254
Elizabeth	55	DE	179
Elsberry	15	DE	198
Emily	11	DE	179
Ephraim	2	DE	168
Ezekiel	5	DE	76
George	11	DE	75
George	50	DE	31
George A	3	DE	71
Henry	23	DE	74
Isaac	13	DE	75
James	6	DE	192
James	13	DE	265
James	23	DE	192
James	30	DE	164
James	33	DE	71
James T	5	DE	71
John	5/12	DE	165
John	13	DE	254
John	15	DE	75
John	17	DE	179
John	56	DE	75
Laura	2	DE	76
Levicy	40	DE	75
Luther	5	DE	254
Margaretta	6	DE	198
Martha	3	DE	75
Mary	7	DE	265
Mary	20	DE	179
Mary	24	DE	192
Mary E	9	DE	75
Nathan	11	DE	198
Nathan	69	DE	179
Nathaniel	3	DE	164
Pameter	60	DE	31
Rebecca	33	DE	164
Sarah	5	DE	196
Sarah	7	DE	198
Sarah	12	DE	254
Solomon	10	DE	254
Susan	12	DE	198
Susan	32	DE	266
Thomas	2	DE	265
Thomas	4	DE	168
Timothy	28	DE	168
William	5/12	DE	192
William	9	DE	198
William	16	DE	254
William	25	DE	76
William T	1	DE	71
Wm	37	DE	198
Wm	30	DE	265
Slay, George	20	DE	184
John	5	DE	184
John	11	DE	199
John	32	DE	184
Louisa	31	DE	199
Martha	7	DE	199
Mary	1	DE	184
Mary	9	MD	199
Mary	60	DE	184
Sarah	28	DE	184
Sophia	63	DE	125
Thomas	24	DE	184
William	5	DE	199
William	9	DE	184
Wm	40	DE	199
Sluby, Nancy	60	DE	42
Smallwood, Ann	10	MD	170
Anna	10	DE	158
James	14	DE	12
Mary	20	DE	161
Mary	24	MD	170
Sarah	2	DE	170
Wm	24	DE	170
Smith, Albert G	2	DE	151
Alexander	6	DE	119

Name	Age	State	No.
Smith, Alexander	10	DE	124
Alexander	10	DE	229
Alexander	13	DE	206
Alexander	17	DE	143
Alfred H	3/12	DE	143
Alfred H	2	DE	131
Alfred H	12	DE	147
Almira	9	DE	123
Angelina	6/12	DE	123
Ann	25	DE	12
Ann	26	DE	229
Ann	41	DE	36
Ann	45	DE	163
Ann	54	DE	69
Ann	55	DE	232
Ann E	4	DE	124
Ann E	8	DE	107
Ann E	9	DE	143
Ann E	21	DE	136
Ann M	8	DE	39
Ann M	33	MD	132
Ann W	45	MD	9
Araminta	34	DE	148
Araminta	59	MD	143
Artemas	25	DE	136
Asbury	1	DE	27
Benjamin	14	DE	36
Benjamin	29	DE	1
Burr	37	DE	148
Caroline	8	DE	131
Catherine	21	DE	84
Catherine	27	DE	119
Catherine	33	DE	98
Catherine	37	DE	158
Charles	1	DE	189
Charles	10	DE	143
Charles	10	DE	188
Charles A	5/12	DE	107
Charles A	8	DE	124
Charles B	34	DE	16
Charles S	29	DE	12
Charles W	2	DE	136
Charlotte	22	DE	97
Clement	34	DE	130
Dafney	79	DE	246
Daniel	40	DE	246
David	2	DE	259
David	5	DE	188
David	18	DE	150
David	20	DE	119
David	20	DE	163
David	22	DE	162
David	28	DE	188
David	41	DE	39
David M	50	DE	163
David W	18	DE	147
Deborah A	13	DE	149
Edmund B	7	DE	123
Edney Ann	22	MD	11
Edward	8	DE	230
Edward	19	DE	17
Edward H	28	DE	56
Eli	22	MD	47
Eliza	4/12	DE	131
Eliza	4	DE	188
Eliza	8	DE	260
Eliza	34	DE	148
Eliza	43	MD	188
Eliza	46	DE	118
Eliza A	11	DE	118
Eliza A	13	DE	98
Eliza J	12	DE	131
Elizabeth	2	DE	188
Elizabeth	28	DE	120
Elizabeth	35	DE	131
Elizabeth	39	DE	193
Elizabeth	41	DE	124
Elizabeth	46	DE	193
Elizabeth	55	DE	193
Elizabeth A	25	DE	130
Elizabeth B	36	DE	147
Ellen	1	DE	119

Name				Name				Name			
Smith, Ellen E	3	DE	109	Smith, Lewis	2	OH	107	Smith, Samuel	9	DE	259
Ellendor	19	DE	188	Lewis C	5	DE	27	Samuel	12	DE	143
Emily J	5	DE	132	Louisa	4	DE	145	Samuel	38	MD	11
Emma F	3	DE	147	Louisa	15	DE	188	Samuel	40	DE	260
Eugene W	2	DE	132	Lydia	10	DE	131	Samuel B	8	MD	9
Ezekiel	28	DE	86	Lydia	35	DE	148	Sarah	10	PA	159
Frances	3	DE	246	Lydia A	4	DE	148	Sarah	11	DE	90
Francis	8	DE	159	Malton W	6	DE	110	Sarah	23	DE	27
Garrison	6	DE	131	Marcellas	35	DE	149	Sarah	26	DE	188
George	19	DE	138	Margaret	17	DE	17	Sarah	42	PA	159
George	55	DE	216	Margaret	21	DE	189	Sarah E	5	DE	11
George F	4	DE	149	Margaret	26	DE	143	Sarah E	5	DE	98
George W	11	DE	124	Margaret	27	DE	119	Sarah E	11	DE	148
George W	13	DE	143	Margaret	33	DE	11	Sarah E	14	DE	216
Haden	69	DE	193	Margaret A	9	DE	109	Sarah E	25	DE	151
Hannah	16	DE	229	Margaret R	8/12	DE	143	Sarah J	6	DE	107
Hannah	60	DE	188	Maria	4	DE	188	Sarah M	12	MD	50
Harriet	4	DE	259	Maria	5	DE	256	Sarah P	8	DE	147
Harriet	24	DE	158	Maria	14	DE	190	Sophia	7	DE	188
Henry	19	DE	217	Maria	19	DE	246	Susan	7	DE	12
Henry	28	DE	259	Maria O	6	DE	147	Susan	30	DE	158
Hester	50	DE	86	Marietta	17	DE	124	Susan	43	DE	260
Hester A	14	DE	123	Martha	8	DE	188	Susan A	14	DE	143
Hester A	18	DE	148	Martin	36	DE	9	Susanna	25	DE	56
Hester A	21	DE	131	Martin	37	DE	148	Sylvester	27	DE	151
Ivan	8	DE	120	Mary	5/12	DE	36	Theophilus W	4	DE	151
James	1	DE	12	Mary	1	DE	163	Thomas	11	DE	260
James	1	DE	194	Mary	2	DE	78	Thomas	24	DE	131
James	6	DE	143	Mary	3	DE	12	Thomas	48	DE	118
James	6	DE	229	Mary	6	DE	259	Thomas J	6	DE	148
James	7	DE	235	Mary	8	DE	246	Thomas R	1	DE	149
James	9	DE	193	Mary	22	DE	189	Thomas S	1	DE	118
James	10	DE	233	Mary	25	DE	256	Tilly S	11	DE	147
James	23	DE	14	Mary	27	DE	39	Walter	1	DE	159
James	27	DE	131	Mary	32	DE	107	Wesley	8	DE	143
James	32	IE	75	Mary	36	DE	193	Willard	11	MD	11
James	32	DE	109	Mary	40	DE	123	William	9/12	DE	259
James	32	DE	163	Mary	56	DE	216	William	2	DE	87
James A	5	DE	123	Mary A	2	DE	143	William	4	DE	260
James H	1/12	DE	109	Mary A	26	DE	16	William	6	DE	211
James H	8	DE	98	Mary A	35	DE	109	William	14	PA	159
James H	10	DE	107	Mary B	28	DE	143	William	17	DE	188
James H	39	MD	123	Mary C	9	MD	132	William	56	DE	124
James M	21	DE	143	Mary E	2	DE	130	William	63	DE	69
James T	7	MD	132	Mary E	3	DE	123	William A	14	DE	124
James W	21	DE	124	Mary E	4	DE	27	William B	39	DE	98
Jane	46	MD	11	Mary E	6	DE	39	William C	29	DE	27
Jane A	15	DE	221	Mary E	9	DE	98	William F	45	DE	36
Jeanetta	25	DE	194	Mary M	7	DE	143	William G	2	DE	98
John	3/12	DE	39	Mary M	9	MD	11	William T	21	DE	36
John	3	DE	259	Mary P	19	DE	221	William T	23	DE	13
John	4	DE	221	Mathew	10	DE	247	William W	2	DE	124
John	6	DE	159	Mathew	17	DE	207	Williamina	3	DE	143
John	16	DE	57	Milly A	4	DE	143	Williamina	17	MD	148
John	19	DE	97	Minta	70	DE	228	Wm	30	DE	189
John	20	DE	188	Miriam	5	DE	124	Wm H	7	DE	149
John	25	DE	163	Nancy	40	DE	124	Smithers, Alfred	2	DE	75
John	46	DE	193	Nathan	33	DE	107	Andrew	39	DE	161
John	55	DE	131	Nathan	49	DE	124	Ann C	17	DE	217
John	59	DE	57	Nathaniel	17	DE	38	Anna	37	DE	75
John B	2	DE	147	Nicholas O	5	DE	147	Anna J	12	DE	75
John B	11	DE	107	Nicholas O	49	DE	147	Caleb	8	DE	220
John B	45	DE	159	Peter	70	DE	228	Caleb	13	DE	217
John C	64	DE	97	Phebe	50	DE	221	Caleb	51	DE	220
John L	10/12	DE	143	Prince	23	DE	229	Catherine	8	DE	211
John M	11	DE	36	Rachel	32	DE	149	David	13	DE	161
John R	45	MD	143	Rachel A	4	DE	132	Elias	6	DE	88
John W	5	DE	131	Rebecca	7	DE	36	Elias	50	DE	88
John W	32	DE	143	Rebecca	8	DE	211	Elizabeth	20	DE	221
Jonathan	7	DE	190	Rebecca	26	DE	163	Elizabeth	22	DE	110
Joseph	5	DE	12	Rebecca	41	DE	143	Elizabeth	38	DE	88
Joseph	12	DE	188	Rebecca	59	DE	193	Emeline	9/12	DE	222
Joseph	24	DE	194	Risden	15	DE	37	Emeline	25	DE	222
Joseph	45	DE	188	Risden B	32	DE	132	Emeline C	9	DE	110
Josephine	16	DE	88	Robert	8	DE	159	Emma	12	DE	88
Julia A	3	DE	119	Robert	28	DE	143	George	39	DE	217
Lavenia	52	DE	37	Robert H	11	DE	123	Hester A	3	DE	88
Leona A	1/12	DE	136	Ruth	45	DE	229	Hester Ann	15	DE	75
Levi	48	DE	229	Ruth	52	DE	57	John	3	DE	217
Levin	4	OH	107	Sally	2/12	DE	246	John	9	DE	88
Levin	26	DE	130	Samuel	7	DE	78	John	30	DE	222
Levin H	7	DE	130	Samuel	7	DE	260	Joseph	14	DE	161

Smithers, Joseph	24	DE	220
Josephine	14	DE	110
Margaret	31	DE	217
Mary	7	DE	73
Mary	9	DE	217
Mary	49	DE	110
Nathaniel B	33	DE	164
Rebecca	24	DE	110
Richard J D	13	DE	89
Sally	47	DE	220
Samuel D	15	DE	110
Sarah	4	DE	222
Sarah	11	DE	217
Sarah	18	DE	110
Theodore	4/12	DE	88
Thomas J	6	DE	75
Waitman	8	DE	222
William	11	DE	161
William H	8	DE	75
William P	41	DE	75
Snake, George	23	GE	163
Snider, Catherine	22	PA	13
Eliza	1	DE	13
Peter	36	PA	13
Snow, Amelia	27	DE	75
Andrew T	33	DE	5
Ann	33	DE	76
Daniel	5	DE	75
Daniel	35	DE	75
Deborah	3	DE	75
Eben	10	DE	78
Eliza	31	DE	75
Elizabeth	23	DE	6
George	19	DE	6
Jacob	35	DE	75
James	19	DE	6
James P	32	DE	6
John	57	DE	6
Joseph	28	DE	6
Joseph	62	DE	6
Rachel	4	DE	75
Rachel	56	DE	6
Rebecca	53	DE	76
Sarah	7	DE	75
Sarah	57	DE	6
Silas	14	DE	6
Susan	25	DE	6
Thomas	19	DE	60
Sollaway, Robert	54	DE	92
Soloway, Charles W	10	DE	92
Elizabeth	49	DE	92
Robert	23	DE	153
William	33	DE	104
Songo, Ann E	18	DE	74
Francis	10	DE	31
John	15	DE	59
Songoes, Wm	25	DE	174
Soper, Caleb	19	DE	101
Cornelia	3	DE	77
George M D	5	DE	77
Harriet	23	DE	77
William	5/12	DE	77
William	30	MD	77
Sorain, Amy	68	DE	142
Susan	19	DE	27
Sorden, Alfred	30	DE	88
Amy	3	DE	124
Amy	23	DE	135
Araminta	25	DE	93
Benniah	8	DE	136
Catherine	19	DE	102
Charles	8	DE	128
Charles	9	DE	129
Charles E	11	DE	102
Clementine	3/12	DE	127
Eliza	35	DE	127
Eliza A	2	DE	127
Elizabeth	10	DE	129
Elizabeth	12	DE	149
Elizabeth	32	DE	136
Elleanor	12	DE	135
Hannah	21	DE	135
Sorden, Hester	4	DE	127
Isaac	31	DE	127
James	6	DE	136
James	28	MD	27
James H	10	DE	149
Jesse	31	DE	125
John	9	DE	136
Louisa	9	DE	255
Mann C	6	DE	127
Margaret A	26	DE	27
Mary	14	DE	255
Mary	35	DE	255
Mary E	14	DE	102
Mary H	11	DE	149
Mathew	14	DE	168
Mathew	45	DE	135
Pere	21	DE	93
Peter	4	DE	136
Peter	60	DE	102
Rachel	55	DE	102
Rebecca	44	DE	135
Robert	45	DE	255
Sarah E	6	DE	149
Sarah J	10	DE	127
William	11	DE	136
William	14	DE	137
William	33	DE	149
Williamina	2/12	DE	149
Souard, John	6	DE	56
Nancy	36	DE	56
Nathan	38	DE	56
Sarah	13	DE	56
Sourden, Joseph	8	PA	2
Soward, Ann	26	DE	82
Anna	7	DE	79
Eliza	40	DE	79
Emerson	11	DE	79
John	8	DE	184
Joseph	40	DE	79
Mary	8/12	DE	79
Sarah	23	DE	188
Thomas	16	DE	66
Tilly	35	DE	188
Unity	8	DE	182
William P	9	DE	79
Sparkland, Caroline	14	MD	161
Mary E	1	DE	213
Salsbury	28	MD	213
Sarah	23	MD	161
Sarah	56	DE	161
Susan	21	DE	213
Sparks, Alexander	7	DE	232
Ann	29	DE	13
Bennet	4	MD	232
Georgiana	2	DE	183
Isaac	9	DE	232
Jane	21	DE	183
Joseph	7	DE	231
Merrit	32	MD	13
Sarah	49	DE	232
Solomon	28	MD	183
William S	7	DE	13
Sparr, Caroline	18	DE	4
Catherine	21	DE	4
Catherine	58	DE	4
Emily	13	DE	4
Spearman, Alexander	5	DE	161
Caleb	30	DE	161
Charlotte	60	DE	175
Elizabeth	11	DE	14
Elizabeth V	55	DE	4
Emeline	45	DE	11
Enoch	28	DE	46
Isaac	61	MD	175
Lizzie D	10	DE	4
Louisa	7	DE	3
Mary	27	DE	161
Mary E	12	DE	37
Mary V	27	DE	4
Moses	41	DE	8
Nancy	43	DE	48
Peter	15	DE	47
Spearman, Rachel J	3	DE	48
Sarah	4	DE	161
Sarah	17	DE	3
Susan A	6	DE	48
Spence, Alexander	40	DE	91
Ann	32	DE	139
David	16	DE	139
Edmund	1	DE	139
Elias	41	DE	139
Elias W	8/12	DE	140
Elizabeth A	1	DE	142
Elma	14	PA	227
Emeline	22	DE	147
Emory	14	DE	139
Harriet	15	DE	227
Henry	26	DE	147
Hester	32	DE	232
Hester	58	DE	141
Hester A	19	DE	118
Isabel	25	DE	142
James	6	DE	232
James	37	DE	140
James H	6	DE	140
Joel	10	PA	227
John	23	DE	141
John	70	MD	141
Joseph	27	DE	118
Luther E	1	DE	147
Mary	5	DE	232
Mary	8	PA	227
Mary	49	DE	145
Mary E	9	DE	140
Mary E	14	DE	144
Nancy	74	MD	132
Noah	28	DE	142
Patrick	65	MD	145
Peirson	5/12	DE	232
Pierson	42	DE	232
Rebecca	30	DE	140
Rhoda	19	DE	149
Rhody	10	DE	232
Richard	6	DE	139
Sarah	2	DE	232
Sarah E	2	DE	147
Susan	9	DE	139
Susan	21	DE	140
Susan E	4	DE	140
Thomas	27	DE	140
William	74	MD	132
William T	10	DE	140
Spencer, Anthony	56	DE	93
Charles	1	DE	80
Charles F	1	DE	29
David	23	DE	77
Eliza	49	DE	35
Elizabeth	25	DE	29
Emanuel	7	DE	106
Hannah	8	DE	80
Harriet	42	PA	227
Henry	22	DE	96
Henry	25	DE	94
Hester A	8	DE	106
Isaac	7	DE	229
James	16	DE	56
James	16	DE	79
James	19	DE	242
Jane	15	DE	225
John	11	DE	86
Joshua	18	DE	237
Julia A	25	DE	106
Landon	53	DE	204
Leah	53	DE	204
Leonard	21	DE	77
Lydia	21	DE	242
Lydia	41	DE	249
Mark A	12	DE	93
Mary	11	DE	229
Mary	13	DE	204
Mary	21	DE	77
Mary	50	DE	93
Mary E	20	DE	91
Matilda A	21	DE	96

Name	Age	State	No.
Spencer, Nutter	30	DE	29
Perry	32	DE	20
Peter	20	DE	215
Priscilla	74	DE	249
Rachel	18	DE	94
Rebecca	32	DE	229
Robert	19	DE	82
Ruthanna	7	DE	242
Samuel	18	DE	13
Sarah	30	DE	80
Sarah E	6	DE	106
Stephen	35	DE	80
Susan	7	DE	80
Susan A	9	DE	93
Thomas	8	DE	91
Wesley	29	DE	93
William	11	DE	85
William	15	DE	77
William	27	DE	242
Wm	65	DE	242
Spering, Anna	23	PA	57
Franklin	25	PA	57
Laura R	4	PA	57
Sally E '	2	DE	57
Spicer, George W	19	DC	58
Sylvester	60	DE	114
Spitall, Clement	30	DE	80
Clement	37	DE	171
Hester	11	DE	171
Margaret	25	DE	171
Margaret	30	DE	80
Spruance, Alexander	13	DE	18
Anna	50	DE	18
Enoch	34	DE	18
Enoch	62	DE	18
Henry	15	DE	18
Horace	14	DE	1
James	22	DE	21
James	69	DE	37
Lewis H	1/12	DE	21
Lydia	60	DE	15
Mary E	20	DE	18
Mary E	23	DE	18
Presley	26	DE	18
Presly	65	DE	1
Rebecca	21	DE	15
Rhoda	38	DE	15
Sarah C	12	DE	1
Sarah C	55	PA	1
William C	19	DE	1
William E	10	DE	18
Spry, Thomas	36	DE	256
Spurry, Adaline	24	DE	206
Catherine	28	DE	207
George	28	DE	206
James W	4	DE	207
Joshua	28	MD	218
Joshua	32	DE	221
Mary J	7	DE	206
Nathan	21	MD	218
Nathan	22	MD	222
Rachel	12	DE	207
Roseanna	4	DE	206
Samuel	1	DE	207
Wm H	35	DE	207
Squires, Elizabeth	35	DE	196
Mary	10	DE	196
Rebecca	2	DE	196
Richard	4	DE	196
Richard	55	DE	196
Samuel	3/12	DE	196
Thomas	9	DE	196
Srouden, Martha	59	DE	87
Thomas	66	DE	87
Stack, Edward	30	IE	36
Wesley	22	MD	21
Stadley, George	2	DE	9
George	34	DE	9
Henry L	6	DE	9
John B	3	DE	9
Roselmer	29	PA	9
Staford, James	14	DE	175
Staford, John	17	DE	70
Stant, Sally	45	DE	224
Stanton, Mariah	46	DE	214
Stapleford, Edward	69	DE	83
Mary	59	MD	83
William	32	DE	83
Staplford, James	42	DE	249
Starr, Elizabeth	77	DE	15
Elizabeth D	45	DE	93
Start, Ephraim	28	MD	11
Ephraim D	7/12	DE	11
James J	38	MD	11
John W	5	MD	11
Mahala	31	DE	11
Martha A	9/12	DE	11
Mary A	23	DE	11
Mary E	7	MD	11
Mary J	28	MD	14
Sarah A	4/12	MD	14
Sarah C	3	MD	11
Sarah J	3	DE	11
William H	31	MD	14
Staton, David	48	DE	224
Eliza	5	DE	224
Eliza	46	DE	224
Isaac	8	DE	224
James	20	DE	224
Mary	23	DE	224
Staunton, James	17	MD	233
Stayton, Ann E	45	PA	10
Charles	15	DE	19
David	12	DE	19
Elizabeth	30	DE	116
John W	37	DE	116
Joseph H	50	DE	10
Martha	7/12	DE	19
Mary	9	DE	19
Mary E	2	DE	116
Nehemiah	41	DE	19
Rhoda	20	DE	116
Sarah M	1/12	DE	116
Susanna	41	DE	19
Steadham, Jane	56	DE	15
Mary Ann	19	DE	9
Steadley, John	20	DE	219
Stedman, Elvy	9	NJ	15
Steel, David	15	DE	34
James	60	DE	100
Steele, Ann	33	DE	254
Arthur	23	DE	251
Christine	15	DE	161
Clementine	25	DE	251
Edward	7	DE	254
Elizabeth	4	DE	254
George	16	DE	190
Harriet	35	DE	200
Henry	1	DE	254
Henry	11	DE	230
James	15	DE	200
John	13	DE	254
Josiah	46	DE	254
Joseph	66	DE	190
Malan	2	DE	200
Martha	15	DE	254
Mary	23	DE	245
Mordacai	6	DE	200
Nathan	6	DE	254
Robert	21	DE	245
Sallyann	12	DE	200
Sophia	8	DE	200
Susan	10	DE	254
William	1/12	DE	200
William	1	DE	245
Wm	38	DE	200
Stephens, Emory	22	DE	42
Henry	29	DE	42
John	31	MD	53
Martha	18	DE	42
Mary	26	DE	42
Mary R	4	DE	42
Mason	15	DE	42
Peter	25	DE	35
Stephens, Rebecca	11	DE	42
Rees	8	DE	42
Sarah	6	DE	42
Sarah	48	DE	42
Sarah E	5	DE	42
Susan F	2	DE	42
Thomas	7	DE	42
William A	2	DE	45
Stephenson, Adaline	3	DE	84
Ann D	9	DE	84
Charles	10/12	DE	84
Denney	18	DE	13
Denney	56	DE	13
Henry C	34	DE	84
Mary	31	DE	84
Sarah	21	DE	13
Sarah	52	DE	13
William H	5	DE	84
Stephins, Mary W	37	NJ	45
William	27	DE	45
Stern, Morris	19	GE	4
Stevens, Alfred	21	DE	84
Ann	38	DE	162
Arah A	23	DE	92
Azel	45	MD	84
Cezar	42	DE	92
Charles	8	DE	194
Charles	18	DE	194
Charlotte	3	DE	194
Collins	55	DE	98
Daniel	13	DE	83
Daniel	70	MD	207
Elira	40	DE	162
Eliza	18	DE	247
Elizabeth	5	DE	194
Elizabeth	28	DE	240
Emory	2	DE	177
George	1	DE	240
George	22	DE	256
Harriett	13	DE	92
Harrison	16	DE	247
Henrietta	14	DE	84
Hulit	10	DE	247
James	7	DE	84
James	7	DE	194
James	32	DE	194
Jane	28	DE	91
John	6	DE	247
John	18	MD	229
John	25	DE	200
John	53	DE	247
Josephus	23	MD	84
Latitia	64	MD	194
Levin B	34	DE	116
Lucretia	42	DE	247
Mariah	19	MD	84
Mary	2	DE	200
Mary	7	DE	247
Mary	22	DE	200
Mary	33	DE	248
Mordecai	1/12	DE	200
Nancy	43	MD	84
Perry	3	DE	247
Rebecca	30	DE	194
Sarah	20	MD	224
Sarah	60	DE	98
Susan	4	DE	200
Wesley	23	DE	240
William	14	DE	248
William B	25	DE	98
Wm	12	DE	233
Stevenson, Ann	45	DE	237
Ann	46	DE	2
Anna	1	DE	186
Anna	58	DE	163
Charles	18	DE	257
Charles C	20	DE	2
Charles L	50	DE	2
Edwin	16	DE	163
Emma	6	DE	2
George	11	DE	2
George	26	DE	186

Name	Age	St	No.
Stevenson, Gertrude	3	DE	158
Gertrude	31	DE	158
James	12	DE	237
James	35	PA	237
John A	29	DE	158
Margaret	26	DE	223
Mary	13	DE	163
Melvina	22	DE	186
Mordecai	10	DE	163
Samuel	2	DE	223
Sarah	21	DE	163
Temperance	40	DE	163
Thomas	2	DE	2
Thomas	5	DE	158
Thomas	12	DE	163
Thomas	63	DE	163
Steward, Ann E	13	DE	88
Catherine	41	DE	88
Elmia	9	DE	88
Henry	17	PA	202
John	26	DE	111
John	46	PA	88
John P	5	DE	88
Josephine	11	DE	88
Lydia A	19	DE	111
Margarett E	8	DE	88
Stewart, Amos	13	DE	154
Ann	26	DE	75
Burton	8	DE	202
Duncan	86	ST	35
Elizabeth	25	DE	154
George	7	DE	9
Hannah	80	ST	35
James	10	DE	202
James	20	DE	7
James	20	DE	154
James	52	DE	154
John	66	DE	80
Joseph	26	DE	75
Kasiah	29	DE	225
Louisa	6	DE	154
Margaret	4	DE	75
Margaret	48	DE	35
Mary	1	DE	202
Mary	46	DE	35
Pompy	80	DE	36
Richard	1	DE	75
Sarah	15	DE	154
Susan	35	DE	202
Wm S	40	DE	202
Still, Alexander	13	DE	87
Ann	63	DE	87
David	10/12	DE	87
Elizabeth	34	DE	87
James	34	DE	87
James H	7	DE	87
Sarah E	15	DE	87
Stilman, Lydia	70	DE	199
Stites, Angelica	12	DE	179
Jonathan	59	NJ	179
Mary	14	DE	179
Mary	53	NJ	179
Stockley, Ayres	51	VA	4
Jared H	12	DE	4
John G	15	DE	4
Margaret	54	DE	4
Stockly, Andrew M	7	DE	205
Henry	13	DE	205
Jacob	17	DE	205
Mary J	15	DE	205
Sally A	23	DE	205
Samuel	11	DE	205
Sarah C	5	DE	205
Woodman	1	DE	205
Woodman	40	DE	205
Stokes, Elijah J	1	DE	146
Garrison	37	DE	146
Latitia	26	DE	146
Priestley	37	DE	112
Rachel	24	DE	112
William	7	PA	41
Stone, Ann	54	DE	63
Stone, Eliza P	6	DE	63
Leadman	59	DE	63
Mary J	12	DE	63
Sarah A	10	DE	63
Stout, Anna	4	DE	198
Anna	16	DE	198
Jacob	82	DE	6
Jonathan	1	DE	198
Jonathan	45	DE	198
Lavin	14	DE	198
Mary	12	DE	198
Nathan	10	DE	198
Rachel	8	DE	198
Sarah	6	DE	198
Sarah	42	DE	198
Stowey, George	11	PA	13
Henry	23	PA	13
Stradley, Elizabeth	18	DE	244
Latitia	62	DE	243
Street, Edward	35	DE	13
Jacob G	5	DE	13
Mary B	29	DE	13
Thomas H	2	DE	13
Streets, Amos	21	DE	191
James	16	DE	191
James	45	MD	191
John	18	DE	191
Mary	14	DE	191
Matilda	60	DE	15
Sallyann	42	DE	191
Sarah	8	DE	192
Stringer, James	17	DE	120
Stron, Charles	21	MD	17
Stuart, James	11	DE	81
Sarah E	9/12	DE	81
Susan	36	DE	81
William	7	DE	81
Stubbs, Drucilla	2	DE	251
Edmondson	9	DE	203
Elizabeth	13	PA	158
Elizabeth	33	DE	203
Emily	26	DE	251
George	20	GB	158
Henry	48	GB	158
James H	6	DE	203
John	16	PA	158
Mary	12	DE	158
Mary	42	GB	158
Sarah A	11	DE	203
Susan	1	DE	251
William	5	DE	251
William	6	DE	158
William	34	DE	251
Wm	36	MD	203
Wm	69	MD	204
Stuck, William	14	NJ	182
Sudler, Abraham	6	DE	39
Alphonzo	12	DE	2
Antonia	36	DE	2
Emory	33	DE	2
Frances A	3	DE	25
Isaiah	6	DE	25
Jacob	22	GE	75
Jacob	60	DE	19
James	24	MD	34
James T	1	DE	25
Jane	6	DE	57
Lydia	14	DE	3
Martha	26	DE	25
Mary	9	DE	25
Nathan	4	DE	39
Rachel	40	DE	39
Temperance	7	DE	39
Wallace	18	MD	1
William	16	DE	3
William	34	DE	25
William	60	DE	39
Sullivan, Benjamin	27	PA	11
Charles	3	DE	74
Daniel	32	IE	74
Dennis	22	IE	202
Elizabeth	7	DE	74
Sullivan, John	20	MD	16
Julia Ann	28	DE	74
Noah	20	DE	178
Patrick	18	IE	11
Susan	26	DE	74
William	4	DE	74
Summers, Amy	10	DE	7
Ann	27	DE	250
Anna	10	DE	256
Ailey	58	DE	252
Alphonzo	10	DE	254
Caleb	6	DE	254
Catherine	52	DE	254
Elizabeth	17	DE	254
Emily	18	DE	252
Harrison	11	DE	252
James	23	DE	252
Jane	8	DE	254
Jonathan	3	DE	250
Juda	85	DE	254
Rachel	54	DE	7
Ruth	15	DE	254
Susan	18	DE	7
Thomas	4	DE	250
Thomas	35	DE	250
Thomas	57	DE	252
Viletta	44	DE	245
Vincent	1/12	DE	250
Vincent	55	DE	254
William	5	DE	250
Surty, Ebenezer	11	DE	20
Ebenezer	43	DE	20
Elizabeth	41	DE	20
Enoch	5	DE	20
James	7	DE	20
John W	14	DE	20
John W	29	DE	20
Mary A	26	DE	20
Mordecai	2	DE	20
Rachel	3	DE	20
Sariella	3/12	DE	20
William H	20	DE	20
Sutherland, Emma	1	DE	222
John	1	DE	222
Joseph	37	PA	227
Margaret	21	DE	222
Mary	21	DE	227
Samuel	11	PA	227
Sophia	31	PA	227
Sutton, Albert S	34	NJ	25
Elizabeth	33	DE	48
Emma	7	NJ	48
Henry	1	DE	48
Henry F	65	MD	9
Isaac	21	DE	19
John	17	DE	4
Joseph	34	PA	48
Margaret	30	MD	25
Mary Ann	46	DE	9
Sarah	27	DE	19
Susan	5	PA	48
Thomas	24	MD	1
Sweger, Elizabeth	70	DE	231
Swift, Aner E	12	DE	248
Angelina	3	DE	262
Anthony	6/12	DE	249
Swiggett, Henry	22	DE	137
Henry	67	MD	153
John	6	DE	262
Luther	49	DE	127
Martin	42	DE	262
Mary	50	DE	262
Miriam	41	DE	262
William	8	DE	262
Swiggit, Luther	3	DE	241
Swiggit, Darkes	27	DE	241
David	8	DE	241
David	30	DE	241
John	9	DE	241
Sarah	10	DE	241
Susan	6	DE	241
Thomas	1	DE	241

Name	Age	State	Page
Swigitt, Ann	19	DE	244
Kitty	16	DE	244
Sarah	20	DE	244
Sarah	60	DE	244
Witanna	27	DE	244
Swindon, Addo	4	DE	226
Catherine	25	DE	226
Emma	6	PA	226
Samuel	31	DE	226
Swires, Elizabeth	69	DE	250
Sykes, James	22	DE	45
James H	1/12	DE	45
Lucinda	22	DE	45
Rebecca	3	DE	45
Sylvan, James H	13	DE	125
Sylvester, Benjamin	20	DE	259
Charlotte	26	DE	259
David	1/12	DE	265
David	33	MD	265
Elizabeth	18	DE	258
Eunice	57	DE	259
Henna	1	DE	196
James	3	DE	196
John	8	DE	196
Margaret	14	DE	190
Margaret	63	DE	132
Mary	11	DE	196
Rachel	27	DE	46
Rachel	34	MD	196
Robert	4	DE	196
Samuel	7	DE	196
Samuel	25	DE	258
Susan	3	DE	265
Susan	20	DE	132
Thomas	6	DE	265
Thomas	35	MD	196
William	8	DE	265
William	16	DE	259
William	17	DE	32
Wm	10	DE	196
Syres, Elizabeth	45	DE	82
Talbert, Elizabeth	15	DE	100
John	1	DE	100
Mary Ann	24	DE	100
Mary E	8	DE	100
Peter	31	DE	100
Phillip	29	DE	100
Sarah A	31	DE	100
Sarah E	4	DE	100
Silvester	2	DE	100
Stephen	35	DE	100
William	6	DE	100
William E	26	DE	100
Talbot, Priscilla	13	NJ	14
Tash, John	5	DE	56
Mary	18	DE	56
Tatman, Collins	44	DE	113
Eliza A	11	DE	113
Eliza R	13	DE	152
Henry	30	DE	243
James	9	DE	262
James	53	DE	152
James P	22	DE	152
Jane	51	DE	152
John M	16	DE	152
Mariah	37	DE	113
Mary	3	DE	262
Mary	35	DE	262
Mary E	15	DE	113
Rachel	7	DE	262
Tilman	27	DE	125
Wm	32	DE	262
Taught, Charles	55	DE	11
Tavin, John W	17	DE	3
Taylor, Abel	4	DE	13
Abigail	17	DE	177
Aerah E	14	DE	144
Alexander	30	DE	162
Ann	11	DE	177
Ann	51	DE	91
Ann	56	DE	149
Taylor, Ann E	8	DE	91
Ann Eliza	2	PA	39
Anna	20	DE	38
Catharine	1	DE	21
Catherine	14	DE	189
Catherine	43	DE	189
Charles	4	DE	252
Daniel	28	DE	137
Daniel	28	DE	177
David	7	DE	177
David	18	DE	144
David	52	DE	144
Edward	10	DE	252
Eliza Ann	12	DE	13
Elizabeth	2	DE	177
Elizabeth	17	DE	54
Elizabeth	25	DE	177
Elizabeth	43	DE	254
Elizabeth	51	DE	144
Elizabeth	59	DE	143
Emeline	23	DE	127
Emma	15	DE	55
Emma	18	DE	38
Enoch	18	DE	177
Ester	2	DE	189
George	16	DE	1
George W	14	DE	13
George W	30	DE	172
Hannah	5	DE	252
Hannah	26	NJ	68
Harriet	7/12	DE	177
Harriet	5	GB	39
Harriet	30	DE	152
Henry	2	DE	69
Henry	17	DE	177
Henry	54	MD	91
Henry	65	DE	69
Hester	44	DE	38
Ignatias	29	DE	110
Isaac	1	DE	13
James	3	GB	39
James	3	DE	154
James	35	GB	39
James	37	DE	13
Jenifer	27	DE	110
John	6	DE	177
John	9	DE	252
John	19	DE	160
John	28	DE	189
John	33	DE	252
John	34	DE	177
John	38	DE	177
John	52	DE	189
John T	1/12	DE	38
Latitia	37	DE	160
Lewis	45	DE	160
Margaret	17	DE	70
Margaret A	26	DE	39
Margaret E	2	DE	38
Martha	3/12	DE	68
Martha	2	DE	177
Martin	24	DE	177
Mary	8	DE	222
Mary	9	DE	37
Mary	12	DE	160
Mary	23	DE	154
Mary	61	DE	177
Mary A	22	DE	144
Matilda	32	DE	39
Matilda	35	DE	252
Miriam	20	DE	189
Nathaniel	26	DE	168
Noah	17	DE	55
Priscilla	7	DE	95
Reade	23	DE	177
Rebecca	53	DE	18
Reckey	5	DE	160
Richard	26	DE	38
Robert	7	DE	252
Sally	8	DE	160
Samuel	9	DE	13
Samuel	11	DE	257
Taylor, Sarah	10/12	DE	177
Sarah	2	DE	252
Sarah	10	DE	32
Sarah	20	DE	64
Sarah	31	GB	39
Sarah	44	DE	177
Sarah A	4	DE	21
Sarah A	12	DE	144
Sarah A	37	DE	13
Sarah C	7	DE	13
Sarah E	22	DE	38
Sarah E	25	DE	117
Shadrach D	24	DE	145
Stephen	1	DE	154
Stephen	28	MD	21
Stephen	29	DE	154
Susan	52	DE	70
Susan C	8/12	DE	37
Temperance	23	DE	21
Thomas	8	GB	39
Thomas	11	DE	91
Thomas	15	DE	43
Thomas	15	DE	248
Thomas K	27	DE	68
William	1	DE	39
William	17	DE	160
William	33	DE	39
William	61	DE	177
William A	38	DE	37
William H	26	DE	127
Wm	49	MD	154
Tea, Mary	35	DE	173
Michal	45	DE	173
Teas, John	35	DE	90
Mercy	34	PA	90
Temple, Charles	24	DE	227
Edwin	5	MD	12
Emery	32	MD	12
Francis	40	DE	227
Franklin	3	DE	12
Hannah	43	DE	227
James	12	DE	74
James M	18	DE	10
Josiah	5	DE	9
Margaretta	28	DE	12
Mary	14	DE	227
Priscilla	50	DE	9
Robert	55	DE	9
Sarah A	32	DE	3
Thomas	1	DE	227
Thomas	51	MD	227
William	36	MD	3
William G	10	DE	3
Temples, Harriet	27	DE	226
Harry	25	DE	226
Tener, Francis	4	IE	169
Isaac	2	IE	169
Isaac	41	IE	169
Margaret	12	IE	169
Sarah	8	IE	169
Tennant, Ann	24	DE	94
Tennent, Aaron G	5	DE	96
Caroline	10/12	DE	96
Catherine	8	DE	93
Eliza	7/12	DE	93
Emma J	30	DE	93
John	46	DE	95
Leah A	4	DE	93
Levin	40	DE	93
Mariah	44	DE	93
Martha E	11	DE	96
Mary C	14	DE	96
Tenner, Frances	40	DE	170
Terry, Ann E	1	DE	206
Elizabeth	24	DE	206
Jonathan	36	NJ	58
Martha	1	DE	58
Mary	34	DE	58
Sarah	7	DE	58
Thomas	5	DE	206
Timothy	30	NJ	206
William Q	3	DE	58

Name	Age	St	No.
Thadars, Susan A	11	DE	207
Thankston, Sarah	70	MD	107
Tharp, Almira	16	DE	91
Almira	16	DE	131
Ann	19	DE	89
Benjamin H	17	DE	87
Benjamin H	19	DE	131
Benniah	5	DE	137
Benniah	45	DE	137
George	24	DE	133
Georgianna	13	DE	137
Henrietta	28	DE	133
James B	1	DE	133
James L	14	DE	89
Jehu	10	DE	131
Jehu	34	DE	143
Jehu	35	DE	86
Joanna	14	DE	89
John W	4	DE	133
Jonathan	8	DE	89
Laura	3	DE	137
Lewellen	40	DE	131
Mariah	11	DE	87
Martina	14	DE	89
Mary	37	DE	137
Mary A	47	DE	89
Mary E	17	DE	89
Richard R	27	DE	146
Ruth	40	DE	137
Samuel	7	DE	137
Sarah P	7/12	DE	137
William	9	DE	137
William	46	DE	89
William H	3	DE	133
Williammina	11	DE	89
Thawley, Amy	9	DE	128
Catherine	13	DE	128
Elizabeth	30	DE	128
James	37	DE	128
James H	5	DE	128
John P	3	DE	128
Josephine	12	DE	12
Martin	17	MD	223
Mary	45	DE	14
Mary J	12	DE	128
William T	14	DE	128
Thistlewood, Ann E	14	DE	124
Benjamin	43	DE	124
Benjamin F	3	DE	124
Davis	9	DE	124
Henry	30	DE	244
James N	15	DE	124
Mary	25	DE	244
Mary M	11	DE	124
Napoleon	13	DE	124
Peter	3	DE	244
Phillip J	7	DE	124
Sarah J	25	DE	124
Susan	5/12	DE	244
Thomas, Albert	6	DE	268
Albert W	10	DE	220
Allan	37	DE	268
Allen	3	DE	268
Allen	20	DE	130
Allen	52	DE	130
Andrew	16	DE	106
Andrew	17	DE	107
Ann	11	DE	268
Ann	14	DE	190
Ann	50	DE	190
Ann	58	DE	231
Anna	8/12	DE	220
Anna	3	DE	162
Anna	25	DE	91
Benjamin	1	DE	24
Caleb	52	DE	25
Caroline	22	DE	139
Catherine	28	DE	103
Clarisa	48	DE	106
Edmund	32	DE	94
Edward	10	DE	113
Edwin W	3	DE	220
Thomas, Elijah	2	DE	139
Eliza	25	DE	69
Eliza	40	DE	214
Eliza A	1	DE	95
Elizabeth	1	DE	139
Elizabeth	21	DE	95
Elizabeth	22	DE	107
Elizabeth	33	DE	220
Ellen	5	DE	181
Emily	19	DE	181
George	1	DE	181
George	28	DE	103
Hannah	51	DE	124
Harriet	10	DE	181
Harriet	36	DE	229
Harriet	39	DE	181
Hester A	15	DE	150
Isaac	19	DE	190
Isaac	54	DE	190
Isaac M	11	DE	106
Jacob	30	MD	27
James	1	DE	103
James	13	DE	25
James	14	VA	91
James	40	DE	220
James A	11	DE	220
Jane	27	DE	27
John	7	DE	268
John	13	DE	220
John	14	DE	180
John	15	DE	150
John	24	DE	130
John	40	DE	151
John	59	DE	231
John H	4	DE	107
John Wm	9	DE	56
Jonathan	6	DE	181
Jonathan	43	DE	181
Joseph	23	DE	181
Leura	49	DE	144
Lucretia	30	DE	231
Mahala	25	DE	139
Margaret E	5	DE	130
Maria	32	DE	56
Mariah C	6/12	DE	95
Mariam	90	DE	32
Martha	12	DE	190
Martha	22	DE	160
Martha A	12	DE	130
Mary	4	DE	246
Mary	16	DE	163
Mary	36	DE	268
Mary	40	DE	25
Mary	42	DE	151
Mary	64	DE	193
Mary A	4	DE	139
Mary A	16	DE	25
Mary A	25	DE	94
Mary E	6	DE	220
Mary E	8	DE	144
Mary E	18	DE	130
Mary J	22	DE	87
Melissa	22	DE	24
Nancy	50	DE	180
Nancy J	14	DE	85
Nathaniel	28	DE	107
Philamen	9	DE	130
Rachel	21	DE	190
Rebecca	15	DE	130
Rebecca	25	DE	190
Rebecca	83	DE	95
Robert	18	DE	214
Robert	19	DE	231
Robert	47	DE	144
Robert H	13	DE	151
Robert J	12	DE	20
Samuel	13	DE	214
Samuel	20	DE	113
Samuel	38	DE	56
Samuel	46	DE	214
Samuel J	6	DE	56
Sarah	6	DE	180
Thomas, Sarah	7	DE	130
Sarah	8	DE	180
Sarah	15	PA	180
Sarah	15	DE	190
Sarah	38	DE	38
Sarah	72	MD	69
Sarah A	11	DE	151
Sarah J	2	DE	189
Sarah J	14	DE	113
Susan	7	DE	151
Susan	23	DE	190
Susan	29	DE	181
Thomas	6	DE	229
Thomas	26	DE	166
Thomas	57	DE	181
Thomas T	12	DE	27
Wesley	10	DE	190
William	1/12	DE	180
William	2	DE	25
William	14	DE	106
William	15	DE	107
William	21	DE	33
William	38	DE	180
William	42	DE	106
William G	1	DE	107
William H	26	DE	139
Wm	37	DE	229
Zebulon	8	DE	144
Thompson, Amelia	28	DE	93
Andrew D	4	DE	93
Andrew M	11	DE	106
Ann	20	DE	31
Ann	48	PA	229
Ann E	16	DE	107
Anna M	18	DE	46
Benjamin	6	DE	107
Betsey	52	DE	103
Caroline	15	DE	86
Catherine A	17	DE	107
Catherine E	9	DE	46
Charles	28	MD	158
Cuthbert	19	PA	229
Daniel	25	DE	154
Daniel A	10	DE	107
Elias	6/12	DE	107
Elisha W	6	DE	210
Eliza	33	DE	101
Eliza J	4	DE	210
Elizabeth	11	DE	210
Elizabeth	18	DE	185
Elizabeth	21	DE	154
George	9/12	DE	146
George	14	OH	230
George	24	DE	162
Hannah	14	DE	34
James	1/12	DE	196
James	30	DE	93
James	65	DE	107
James A	10	DE	46
James H	7	DE	93
Jesse	8	MD	239
Jesse	50	DE	229
John	13	DE	19
John	17	NJ	230
John	22	DE	84
John	34	DE	101
John	54	DE	106
John A	3	DE	107
John B	21	DE	106
John W	2	DE	210
Joseph	4	DE	185
Joshua H	5	DE	107
Leah	12	DE	103
Levin	34	DE	210
Mahala	51	DE	103
Maningforce	12	DE	230
Margaret Ann	20	DE	34
Martha	5	DE	230
Mary	32	DE	107
Mary	37	DE	210
Mary	50	DE	106
Mary	97	DE	31

Name	Age	St	Pg	Name	Age	St	Pg	Name	Age	St	Pg
Thompson, Mary E	5/12	DE	107	Tilghman, Hester	9	DE	42	Tindley, Rachel	6	DE	263
Mary E	8	DE	103	Isaac	12	DE	18	Rajiene	5	DE	263
Mary E	8	DE	107	Mary	6	DE	42	Sarah	11	DE	263
Mary E	10	DE	210	Mary	32	DE	42	Tindly, Sarah	10	DE	206
Mary L	13	DE	46	Mary A	16	DE	22	Tinley, Harriet	18	DE	70
Moses	16	DE	101	Noah	5	DE	42	Tirel, Alice	1	DE	233
Napolion	2	DE	93	Stephen	65	DE	42	Catherine	28	DE	233
Obediah	20	DE	185	Thomas	16	DE	43	Charles	5	DE	233
Obediah	44	DE	174	Till, Ann	14	DE	19	Eliza	6	DE	233
Priscilla	55	DE	34	Ann	35	DE	74	Hetty	7	DE	233
Purnell	18	DE	34	Ann	36	DE	71	Peter	31	DE	233
Rebecca	11	DE	185	George	46	DE	173	Tobin, John	21	IE	1
Rebecca	24	DE	162	Harriet	8	DE	19	Todd, Amy	31	DE	170
Rebecca	47	DE	185	Henry	8	DE	78	Anna	11	DE	162
Robert	22	DE	34	Isabell	36	DE	173	Christian	19	DE	86
Robert H	6	DE	210	James	1	DE	74	Elizabeth	9/12	DE	162
Sally	3	DE	162	James	3	DE	71	Elizabeth	35	DE	162
Samuel O	17	DE	106	James	23	DE	19	Frederic	3	DE	162
Sarah	14	DE	185	John	19	DE	68	Henry	47	DE	162
Sarah	39	DE	174	Joseph	53	DE	19	James	9	DE	162
Sarah	43	DE	107	Louis	10	DE	72	James	12	DE	170
Sarah	48	DE	46	Margaret	20	DE	19	Mary	14	DE	170
Sarah	58	DE	242	Mary	50	DE	19	Robert	6	DE	162
Sarah P	6/12	DE	180	Rachel	6	DE	171	Sarah	4	DE	170
Selby	21	DE	107	Tillman, Charles	1	DE	95	Susan A	13	DE	150
Sidney	16	DE	185	Jane	23	DE	95	William	9	MD	170
Silas	10	DE	174	John	25	DE	95	William	22	DE	33
Stephen	50	DE	103	Margarett	3	DE	95	Zebadiah	41	MD	170
Thomas	8	DE	107	Sarah A	24	DE	97	Tomilson, Eliza	41	DE	153
William	13	DE	174	Tilman, Alfred	8	DE	101	James	7	DE	153
William	51	DE	107	Ann	23	DE	233	Josephine	13	DE	153
William	58	DE	46	Benjamin	2	DE	233	Mary	15	DE	153
William A	13	DE	107	Daniel	14	DE	241	Pauline	5	DE	153
William H	16	DE	3	Daniel	45	DE	101	Robinson	3	DE	153
William J	16	DE	46	Elias	25	DE	97	Sarah	18	DE	153
Wm	9	DE	185	Elizabeth	13	DE	101	Sophia	11	DE	153
Wm	47	DE	185	Emaline	11	DE	101	William	9	DE	153
Thomson, Ayres H	2	DE	31	Emma	19	DE	179	Wm	49	DE	153
Clarissa	21	DE	28	George	1	DE	233	Tomlinson, Austin	43	DE	34
Daniel W	48	DE	28	John	4	DE	233	Barsheba	46	DE	109
Eliza M	16	DE	28	John	37	DE	178	Benjamin	11	DE	104
Elizabeth	44	DE	31	Julia A	32	DE	101	Daniel	19	DE	109
Elmira	8	DE	28	Lydia	65	DE	187	Eliza	60	DE	110
Hannah	22	DE	28	Lydia	70	DE	198	Elizabeth	34	DE	110
Hannah M	2	DE	28	Lydia A	1	DE	101	Elizabeth	41	DE	24
James	12	DE	31	Margaret	9	DE	220	James	30	DE	104
Jeffery	19	DE	31	Mariah	14	DE	87	James	44	DE	24
John	57	DE	31	Moses	35	DE	233	James D	21	DE	110
John D	21	DE	31	Prince	75	DE	179	Louis	6	DE	34
Joseph	14	DE	31	Rachel	15	DE	101	Mary	37	DE	34
Mary F	14	DE	28	Samuel	13	DE	175	Matilda	16	DE	24
Rachel	34	DE	28	Sarah	9	DE	233	Peter W	6/12	DE	104
Rachel E	10	DE	28	Sarah	16	DE	179	Prince	14	DE	24
Sarah E	5	DE	31	Sarah	50	DE	179	Rachel	35	DE	104
Sarah H	12	DE	28	Violet	3	DE	101	Samuel	7	DE	24
William A	18	DE	28	Tilton, Catherine	42	DE	125	Thomas	44	DE	109
William F	28	DE	28	Charles	35	DE	125	Thomas W	24	DE	110
Thorn, Adam	56	DE	93	Josiah	4	DE	125	Sarah	6	DE	24
Angelina A	9	DE	93	Margaret J	7	DE	125	William	21	DE	109
Catherine	12	DE	90	Mary	12	DE	125	William	29	DE	110
Daniel	5	DE	93	Ruth A	10	DE	125	William	72	DE	110
Georgianna	1	DE	93	Sarah E	9	DE	125	Winlock	20	DE	105
Hester	19	DE	12	Thomas J	1	DE	125	Toney, James	29	DE	64
James	26	DE	44	William	15	DE	125	Melissa	3	DE	64
James	7	DE	30	Timmins, Bolitha	20	DE	36	Rhoda	4	DE	64
Mary J	15	DE	93	Caroline	18	DE	44	Rhoda	70	DE	64
Milly	34	DE	93	Martha	18	DE	61	Sarah	23	DE	64
Thornton, George	30	MD	233	Samuel	12	DE	44	Tood, Clementine	19	DE	87
Isabella	20	DE	233	Tindale, James	22	DE	70	Tooth, Elizabeth	50	DE	170
John	24	DE	195	Tindle, Catherine	35	DE	135	Mary	46	DE	212
Martha	28	DE	195	George	1	DE	135	Sam	56	DE	212
Mary	1	DE	233	John	1	DE	135	Tootle, Charles	19	DE	246
Salsberry	3	DE	233	Jorday	38	DE	135	Elizabeth	13	DE	243
Thomas	28	DE	252	Tindley, Draper	8	DE	263	Harriet	1	DE	236
William	5	DE	233	Elizabeth	32	DE	263	Harriet	30	DE	236
Thuragood, Paul	18	DE	179	Jacob	14	DE	263	John	30	DE	236
Tigner, Frances Jane	10	DE	1	John	17	DE	263	Towers, Maria	13	MD	140
James W	7	DE	1	Jonathan	44	DE	263	Nathaniel	13	DE	121
John W	5	DE	1	Lydia	2	DE	263	Townsend, Absalom	81	DE	114
Sarah	28	DE	1	Mary	8	DE	263	Anna	7	DE	221
Tilghman, Andrew	18	DE	45	Mary	69	DE	120	Benjamin	8	DE	122
Daniel	3/12	DE	22	Patience	7/12	DE	263	Benjamin	12	DE	246

Townsend, Benjamin	53	DE	226	Travis, John	22	DE	123	Truett, Ruth	21	DE	170
Benetta	2	DE	226	John	26	DE	159	Truitt, Ann	18	DE	203
Betsy	60	DE	129	John D	35	DE	123	Catherine	47	DE	47
Brickers	42	DE	246	Martha A	10	DE	123	Elisha	42	DE	205
Catherine	46	MD	226	Mary A	20	DE	141	Elisha W	7	DE	205
Charles	31	DE	114	Mary J	12	DE	123	Eliza	21	DE	95
Charles	45	DE	222	Patty	33	DE	123	Elizabeth	25	DE	84
Charles B	1	DE	114	Samuel	11	DE	123	Ellen	15	DE	205
Clementine	10	DE	122	Sarah E	3	DE	123	Ferdinand	10	DE	205
Daniel	6	DE	246	Unity	8	DE	123	George	38	DE	101
Eli	22	DE	79	Wheatly	17	DE	124	Isaac	1	DE	84
Elias	4	DE	240	Wm	16	DE	262	James	21	VA	205
Elias	59	DE	240	Trenton, Ann	42	DE	23	James H	17	DE	205
Elizabeth	7	DE	240	William	26	DE	23	John	2	DE	202
Elizabeth	15	DE	222	Tribbet, Amanda	2	DE	266	John	8	DE	95
Elizabeth	32	DE	105	Ann	29	DE	266	John	64	DE	203
Elizabeth	37	DE	221	Avery	28	DE	266	John C	32	DE	84
Ester	47	DE	220	Beckey	6	DE	237	John W	13	DE	205
Hester	19	DE	239	Benona	1	DE	266	Joseph	7	DE	203
Hester A	16	DE	79	Daniel	24	DE	191	Joseph	8	DE	205
Isaac	2	DE	243	Easter	77	DE	265	Joseph S	30	DE	84
Isaac	24	DE	119	Edward	10	DE	266	Martha E	12	DE	205
Isaac	42	DE	239	Elizabeth	25	DE	266	Mary	35	DE	205
James	13	DE	195	Elizabeth	62	DE	249	Mary E	5	DE	205
James	14	DE	239	Ellen	2	DE	266	Mary E	16	DE	205
James	18	DE	239	Francis	50	DE	159	Noah	21	DE	65
James H	6	DE	114	Harriet	1	DE	182	Noah	24	DE	202
James H	16	DE	122	Hester	19	DE	237	Peter	27	DE	210
John	7	DE	105	Isaac	76	DE	266	Rachel A	2	DE	95
John	13	DE	184	James	28	DE	266	Robert H	7	DE	83
John	24	DE	239	John	26	DE	266	Samuel	21	DE	90
John B	18	DE	221	Mary	4	DE	266	Samuel	55	DE	95
John W	4	DE	122	Pompey	38	DE	265	Sarah	40	DE	94
Joseph	6	DE	105	Rosanna	74	MD	266	Sarah	44	DE	101
Major	16	DE	184	Steven	13	DE	267	Sarah	51	DE	210
Margaret	17	DE	226	Susan	23	DE	182	Sarah H	24	DE	203
Margaret A	4	DE	114	Warner	22	DE	251	Solomon	33	DE	224
Martha	5	DE	226	Warner	23	DE	182	Thomas J	19	DE	210
Martha	20	DE	193	William	5	DE	266	William	11	DE	95
Mary	10	DE	131	Wm	20	DE	201	Willie	35	DE	202
Mary	13	DE	226	Wm	24	DE	184	Wm H	6	DE	210
Mary	15	DE	221	Tribbett, Benjamin	12	DE	130	Trusty, Eliza	10	DE	25
Mary	33	DE	246	Elizabeth	20	DE	102	Eliza	25	DE	24
Mary	34	DE	243	James W	11	DE	132	Elizabeth	51	DE	25
Mary	60	DE	114	Lydia	25	DE	139	Jacob	7	DE	24
Mary E	8	DE	114	Mary	2	DE	149	Jacob	23	DE	25
Nancy	40	DE	239	Susan	1	DE	139	Judith	9	DE	24
Rachel	12	DE	105	Tribbit, Elizabeth	19	DE	266	Latetia	46	DE	24
Rachel	25	DE	226	Jacob	18	DE	266	Matilda	8	DE	43
Rachel	35	DE	114	Tribbits, Benjamin	48	DE	263	Sarah	6	DE	69
Rachel	35	DE	240	David	12	DE	263	William	17	DE	25
Robert	7	DE	105	Easter	39	DE	263	Tschuder, William	19	MD	10
Samuel	14	DE	189	Martha	8	DE	263	Tucker, Ann	45	DE	9
Sarah	10	DE	193	Tribet, Ann	7	DE	221	Ann	77	MD	50
Sarah	12	DE	226	Triblet, Nathan	64	DE	231	Ann E	5	DE	48
Sarah	17	DE	239	Mary	58	DE	231	Ann E	12	DE	20
Silas	14	DE	105	John	19	DE	232	Catherine	2	DE	48
Smartley C	2	DE	105	Philip	10	DE	76	Elizabeth	14	DE	9
Solomon	18	DE	210	Truax, Abraham	29	DE	71	Elizabeth	28	DE	50
Susan	8	DE	226	Benjamin F	1	DE	28	Elizabeth A	15	DE	111
Thomas	8	DE	246	Ebenezer	7	DE	71	Ellen	19	DE	35
Thomas	18	DE	79	Eliza J	13	DE	29	Hannah	30	DE	50
Warren	4	DE	105	George	8	DE	29	Isaac	11	DE	48
Warren	45	DE	105	Hannah	24	DE	27	James	12	DE	9
William	2	DE	246	Henry	3	DE	27	Jane	39	DE	210
William	8	DE	240	Isaac S	9	DE	28	John	2	DE	50
William	12	DE	239	James	38	DE	28	John	20	DE	9
William	24	DE	80	James T	4	DE	28	John	42	DE	20
William B	13	DE	122	John	29	DE	29	John	48	DE	219
William J	10	DE	114	John	31	DE	27	John H	10	DE	9
Wm	41	DE	221	John S	10	DE	28	Leah A	2	DE	112
Trainer, Ann	18	GB	72	Mary	30	DE	28	Mary	1	DE	48
Traverse, Wm	33	DE	249	Miriam	7	DE	27	Mary	8	DE	21
Travis, Biard	24	DE	260	Morgan	5	DE	71	Mary E	6	DE	112
Eli	8/12	DE	124	Peter	5	DE	27	Matilda	29	DE	48
Eliza	50	DE	159	Samuel	3	DE	28	Nancy	30	DE	150
George	5	DE	123	Sarah	1	DE	27	Nathaniel	21	DE	219
George	6	DE	169	Sarah	29	DE	71	Nathaniel	36	DE	226
Henrietta B	13	DE	132	Susanna	6	DE	28	Nathaniel	79	DE	226
Henry	16	DE	128	Wesley	12	DE	10	Rachel	31	DE	111
John	2	DE	124	William	1	DE	71	Samuel	27	DE	48
John	10	DE	262	William	27	DE	56	Sarah	72	DE	226

Name	Age	State	Page
Tucker, Sarah C	7	DE	9
Thomas	35	DE	50
Wilhelmina	4	DE	48
William	6	DE	21
William	47	DE	111
William E	10	DE	111
Tumbleson, Elizabeth	18	DE	221
Tumblin, Caroline	9	DE	86
Charles	15	DE	86
George	25	DE	86
Henry	6	DE	86
James	51	DE	86
John	13	DE	86
Martha J	20	DE	86
Mary	50	DE	86
Mary A	17	DE	86
Turner, Abraham	54	DE	42
Abraham	55	DE	162
Adam	1/12	DE	46
Adine	12	DE	162
Alexander	10	DE	46
Amelia	68	DE	147
Ann	3	DE	76
Ann E	6	DE	108
Ann M	10	DE	34
Ann M	21	DE	134
Ann M	30	DE	126
Antony	35	DE	121
Benjamin	3	DE	46
Benjamin	37	DE	34
Benjamin T	15	DE	109
Cassa	3	DE	112
Catherine J	5	DE	108
Charles	5	DE	126
Charles	19	DE	35
Charles	19	MD	50
Christeann	4	DE	111
Clement	13	DE	105
Cynthia	8	DE	162
Daniel	13	DE	34
Daniel	33	DE	45
Elias	28	DE	74
Eliza	35	DE	112
Eliza A	22	DE	13
Elizabeth	14	DE	21
Elizabeth	15	DE	34
Elizabeth	20	DE	43
Elizabeth	26	DE	74
Emeline	4	DE	131
Enoch	6	DE	34
George W	4	DE	126
George W	5	DE	99
Henetta	25	DE	99
Henry	8	DE	106
Henry	10	DE	162
Henry	19	DE	165
Henry L	8	DE	108
Hester A	23	DE	94
Hetty	14	DE	157
Isaac	4/12	DE	76
Isaac	6	DE	126
Isaac	13	DE	61
Isaac	30	DE	99
James	20	DE	130
Jane	8	DE	104
Jane	8	DE	150
Jane	55	DE	159
Jane	60	DE	112
Jane	75	DE	249
John	12	DE	108
John	25	DE	111
Jonathan	8/12	DE	74
Joseph	12	DE	148
Joseph	14	DE	162
Joseph	20	DE	105
Joseph	25	DE	75
Joseph	91	DE	136
Joshua	9	DE	126
Levice	35	DE	88
Lewis	25	DE	134
Louisa	21	DE	162
Luraney	3	DE	74
Turner, Lydia	2	DE	74
Major	2	DE	99
Maria	37	DE	34
Mariah	33	DE	108
Mary	18	DE	167
Mary E	1/12	DE	13
Mary E	1	DE	46
Mary E	5	DE	45
Mary E	5	DE	74
Mary J	3	DE	34
Milcah	50	DE	162
Nehemiah	7	DE	134
Nisa	14	DE	250
Priscilla	43	DE	136
Rachel	27	DE	112
Rebecca	23	DE	45
Samuel	5/12	DE	112
Samuel	6	DE	99
Samuel	12	DE	45
Samuel	40	DE	112
Samuel	60	DE	134
Samuel Sr	70	DE	111
Sarah	8	DE	34
Sarah	23	DE	75
Sarah A	7	DE	46
Sarah A	9	DE	99
Sarah P	1	DE	111
Scynthia	3	DE	108
Spencer W	24	DE	111
Stansberry J	20	DE	112
Stephen	24	DE	35
Susan	19	MD	48
Sylla	8	DE	159
Thomas	2/12	DE	125
Thomas	12	DE	45
Virginia P	5/12	DE	94
Wesley	25	DE	29
William	12	DE	34
William	12	DE	131
William	24	DE	94
William	35	DE	13
William J	3	DE	94
Turney, Elizabeth	56	DE	19
Elmira	13	DE	19
Isabel	12	DE	37
Turry, Littitia	67	DE	117
Tuttle, John	16	DE	121
Samuel	27	DE	138
Twiford, Elizabeth	14	DE	116
Twigg, Caroline	6	DE	94
Catherine	16	DE	93
James	13	DE	93
Jenetta	40	DE	93
John	8	DE	93
John	51	DE	93
Martha A	1	DE	94
William	4	DE	94
Underwood, Elizabeth	17	DE	45
Emily C	27	DE	45
Mary A	26	DE	45
Nathan T	25	DE	45
Sarah	55	MD	45
Usher, John C	23	IE	29
Margaret	1/12	DE	29
Margaret	22	IE	29
Vanbarklow, Eliza	10	DE	180
Hester	12	DE	180
Moses	18	DE	180
Ruth	35	DE	180
Vanbucklow, Wm	27	DE	222
Vancoast, Anna M	2/12	DE	206
Jacob	35	NJ	206
Jacob A	2	DE	206
Malvina	27	DE	206
Vandergrift, Wm	30	MD	12
Vane, Ann E	15	PA	13
Christianna	12	PA	13
Frances	10	PA	13
Frances	42	SZ	13
Vane, Frances A	17	NJ	31
Frances D	3/12	NJ	31
James	46	NJ	13
James H	6	NJ	31
Jesse	13	NJ	31
John W	4	NJ	31
Maria	18	PA	13
Mary A	36	NJ	31
Mary C	9/12	DE	13
Mary J	8	NJ	31
Rebecca	2	NJ	31
Sarah E	17	NJ	31
Sarah J	3	DE	13
William	11	NJ	31
William S	47	NJ	31
Vanfosten, Stephen	25	GE	13
Vangasken, Anna	10/12	DE	5
Harriet	23	NJ	5
Hy Clay	4	DE	5
John	30	DE	5
Mary	33	PA	5
Mary F	1	DE	5
Rachel	13	MI	5
Wesley	12	PA	5
VanGesel, Angelina	24	DE	43
Ann Maria	19	DE	1
Asbury	1	DE	42
Benjamin F	5/12	DE	36
Celia	31	DE	139
Ezekiel T	6	DE	36
Hope A	2	DE	36
Hope Ann	29	NJ	36
John	54	DE	42
John H	16	DE	43
John N	42	MD	36
John W	5/12	DE	36
Joseph R	6	DE	42
Mary E	8	DE	36
Priscilla	8	DE	43
Priscilla	47	DE	43
William T	12	DE	43
VanGisel, Edwin	22	DE	1
Vann, Angeline	18	DE	97
Benjamin	17	DE	86
Charles	14	DE	97
Hester	49	DE	97
Isabel	15	DE	88
Isabel	15	DE	95
John	23	DE	95
John B	16	DE	97
Leah A	4	DE	95
Littleton	45	DE	97
Mariah	21	DE	95
Mary	11	DE	97
Mary A	44	DE	95
William	12	DE	95
Vansant, Benjamin	33	MD	10
George	29	NJ	4
George W	29	PA	56
Harriet	30	MD	10
James C	8/12	DE	10
Mary E	7	MD	10
VanWinkle, Benjamin	59	DE	57
Charles	22	DE	22
James	23	DE	57
Mary E	2	DE	57
Sarah A	21	DE	57
Susan	18	DE	57
William C	1	DE	57
Vaughn, Alice	54	DE	141
Vaules, Delilah	9	DE	96
Elizabeth	26	DE	104
Elmira	10	DE	92
James D	26	DE	104
James H	2	DE	104
John	14	DE	92
John R	56	DE	92
Mary E	16	DE	93
Sarah	60	DE	113
Sarah E	3/12	DE	104
William T	23	DE	92
Vause, Ellen	18	DE	136

Name	Age	St	No.	Name	Age	St	No.	Name	Age	St	No.
Vause, Emily	9	MD	141	Virden, Thomas E	13	DE	105	Voshell, Ann E	8	DE	36
Harriet	47	MD	140	William	45	DE	105	Daniel	14	DE	25
James	30	DE	141	Virdon, Alexander	2	DE	200	Eliza N	14	DE	46
John	22	MD	143	Edwin	2/12	DE	200	George	5	DE	61
John W	49	MD	140	Eliza	51	DE	235	Harriet	11	DE	25
Josephine	25	DE	142	Ellen	12	DE	200	James	22	DE	192
Margaret	80	MD	151	James	10	DE	200	James	67	DE	46
Martha	60	DE	142	Mary	31	DE	200	James H	12	DE	36
Mary A	2	DE	136	Samuel	21	DE	235	James S	25	DE	56
Mary C	3	DE	142	Samuel	51	DE	235	Jane	25	DE	36
Sarah	50	DE	151	Sarah	16	DE	235	John	33	DE	23
Sina A	11	DE	150	Unity	8	DE	200	John	38	DE	36
Willard	4/12	DE	142	William	4	DE	200	John M	3/12	DE	23
William H	28	DE	136	Wm	43	DE	200	Lydia	12	MD	15
Vickers, Edward	22	DE	238	Virgin, Rachel	14	DE	62	Lydia A	28	DE	46
Henry	38	DE	232	Vocine, Charles	28	MD	155	Margaret	26	DE	61
Vickery, Elizabeth	41	DE	216	Vore, Charles	28	MD	155	Martha	8	DE	23
James H	9	DE	139	Voshel, Alexander	25	DE	182	Mary	57	MD	46
Margaret	13	DE	35	Ann	23	DE	262	Mary A	32	DE	23
Sarah A	2	DE	139	Anna	28	DE	182	Mary E	15	DE	31
Thomas	46	DE	216	Betsey	60	MD	189	Mary E	20	DE	46
William	33	DE	139	Clementine	12	DE	190	Melvina	3	DE	25
William A	1	DE	139	Daniel	6	DE	182	Obadiah	3	DE	23
Williamina	4	DE	139	Daniel	20	DE	227	Obediah	47	DE	192
Vickory, Margaret	13	DE	28	Draper	4	DE	170	Obediah	60	DE	25
William	17	DE	35	Draper	30	DE	170	Ruth	18	DE	25
View, Elizabeth	14	DE	43	Elisha	2	DE	170	Ruth	56	DE	192
George	46	DE	43	Elizabeth	21	DE	182	Sarah	46	DE	25
Zilpha	49	DE	43	Emily	3	DE	190	Susan	21	DE	192
Vincent, Hannah	9	DE	232	Fenor	30	DE	189	William	8	DE	25
James	11	DE	232	Francis	7	DE	190				
James	29	DE	61	Garrett	28	DE	262	Wadkins, Amelia A	10	DE	101
James	41	DE	232	George	2	DE	182	Ann	1	DE	153
John	5	DE	232	George	2	DE	189	Celea A	14	DE	101
John	50	DE	35	Hannah	3	DE	182	Charles P	12	DE	101
John	56	DE	115	Hannah	12	DE	189	Eli R	38	DE	101
Levi	13	DE	232	Hannah	48	DE	190	Ellen	6	DE	153
Margaret	49	DE	61	Harriet	33	MD	190	Henry	30	DE	141
Mary	40	DE	232	James	14	MD	189	Hester E	5	DE	101
Mariah	48	DE	115	Johanna	12	DE	190	John R	8	DE	101
Miriam	2	DE	232	John	26	DE	203	Joseph	36	MD	153
Nicolas	17	DE	232	John	30	DE	184	Lavicy	6	DE	101
Richard	13	PA	90	John	33	DE	190	Mary	23	DE	153
Thomas	14	DE	230	John W	12	DE	80	Mary E	13	DE	101
Thomas	15	DE	232	Joseph	22	DE	248	Nancy	38	DE	101
Thomas	20	DE	246	Laretta	15	DE	203	Theodore E	4	DE	101
William	7	DE	232	Levinia	20	DE	248	William G	1	DE	101
Vineyard, Ann	27	DE	104	Levi	13	DE	169	Wainwright, Thomas	70	MD	223
Vining, Daniel	24	DE	18	Lorenzo	18	DE	203	Waitman, Benjamin	45	NJ	172
Elijah	20	DE	25	Louisa	2	DE	262	Charles	13	DE	172
Elizabeth	45	DE	24	Margaret	1	DE	190	Elizabeth	1	DE	172
Henry	30	DE	24	Margaret	27	MD	184	Hannah	3	DE	172
Henry	53	DE	24	Margareta	7/12	DE	262	Jonathan	6	DE	172
Jacob	55	DE	163	Mariam	4	DE	182	Samuel	8	DE	172
James	1	DE	18	Martha	7	DE	182	Sarah	11	DE	172
John	1	DE	8	Mary	2	DE	182	Sophia	36	NJ	172
John D	25	DE	9	Mary	2	DE	184	Walcot, Emma	13	DE	15
Mariah	39	DE	8	Mary	6	DE	190	John	23	DE	257
Mary	4	DE	25	Mary	8	DE	182	Mary	70	DE	249
Mary	23	PA	9	Mary	28	MD	190	Thomas	22	DE	159
Melvina	50	DE	19	Mary	34	DE	18	William	25	DE	164
Prince	53	DE	8	Mary	37	DE	170	Wales, Hetty	18	DE	232
Rachel	56	DE	24	Mary	37	DE	189	John	23	DE	232
Rachel E	4	DE	8	Mary	56	DE	203	Nesa	49	DE	232
Sarah	10	DE	25	Obediah	7	DE	189	Rhody	18	DE	232
Sarah	21	DE	18	Peter	33	DE	189	Samuel	62	DE	232
Seba	1	DE	25	Rebecca	4	DE	190	Walker, Ann	6	DE	157
Seba	12	DE	25	Rebecca	63	MD	190	Ann	55	DE	136
Seba	50	DE	25	Robert	1/12	DE	184	Benjamin	1	DE	199
Susan	51	DE	24	Ruth	6	DE	80	Benjamin	44	DE	200
Vinyard, Anna	3	DE	104	Samuel	5	DE	189	Catherine	16	DE	101
Curtis	1	DE	104	Samuel	10	DE	80	Charles	25	DE	125
Curtis	25	DE	100	Samuel	50	DE	189	Charles W	22	DE	67
Curtis	60	DE	114	Sarah	6	DE	170	Eliza	23	DE	157
Henry	23	DE	114	Sarah	75	DE	189	Elizabeth	24	DE	105
James	29	DE	104	Susan	35	DE	189	Elizabeth	26	DE	135
Phillip J	7	DE	104	Titus	10	DE	189	Ezekiel	27	DE	134
Sarah	56	DE	114	William	3/12	DE	182	George	50	DE	207
Sarah E	5	DE	104	William	24	DE	203	George D	4	DE	134
William E	19	DE	114	Wm	34	DE	182	Harriet B	15	DE	136
Virden, Mary E	16	DE	105	Wm	40	DE	190	Hester	56	DE	135
Rachel	43	DE	105	Voshell, Ann E	2	DE	61	James	12	DE	200

Name	Age	State	No.
Walker, James C	9	DE	136
James H	18	DE	107
James J	45	DE	136
Julia A	17	DE	136
Leah	24	DE	99
Lettitia	68	DE	109
Margaretta	14	DE	200
Maria	1	DE	199
Maria	39	DE	200
Martha L	28	DE	5
Mary	59	DE	5
Mary Ann	32	DE	5
Mary E	3	DE	134
Mary P	24	DE	135
Nehemiah	49	DE	211
Peter	90	DE	125
Robert	27	DE	158
Rhoda	47	DE	211
Sarah	11	DE	200
Sarah Ann	18	DE	67
Sarah E	10/12	DE	135
Susan	16	DE	200
Susan	23	DE	207
William	20	DE	100
Wm	32	DE	157
Wall, Daniel	33	DE	65
Wallace, Angeline	29	DE	89
Ann	10	DE	165
Benjamin	27	DE	58
Benjamin	48	DE	225
Catharine	23	DE	58
Eliza	12	DE	188
Elizabeth	43	DE	165
Ellen	80	DE	189
James	3	DE	89
James	4	DE	183
James	24	DE	82
James C	47	DE	165
John	5	DE	89
John	11	DE	249
John	15	DE	194
John	64	DE	249
Joseph	10	DE	183
Joseph	26	DE	39
Joseph	48	DE	183
Louisa	19	DE	39
Margarett	7	DE	89
Martha A	25	DE	208
Mary	5/12	DE	208
Mary	6	DE	183
Mary	8	DE	165
Mary	8	DE	249
Mary	37	DE	88
Mary	44	DE	183
Mary E	1	DE	58
Miriam	15	DE	249
Rebecca	16	DE	180
Rebecca	48	DE	183
Rebecca	60	DE	61
Richard	31	DE	208
Samuel	15	DE	183
Sarah	19	DE	249
Sarah	56	MD	249
Sarah A	2	DE	208
Susan	44	MD	225
Susanna	9	MD	225
Synthia	73	DE	88
Thomas	1	DE	89
Thomas	14	DE	183
Thomas	22	DE	61
Thomas	33	DE	183
Thomas	34	DE	89
Thomas	49	DE	183
William	15	MD	225
William	23	DE	249
William	25	DE	85
Wm	53	DE	250
Waller, Charles	1	PA	225
Frank	4/12	DE	225
Henrietta	27	NY	225
John	23	DE	225
Tracy	35	DE	225
Waller, William	3	PA	225
Wallis, Charles H	11	DE	147
Emeline	28	DE	147
Mary P	3	DE	147
Robert	8/12	DE	147
Walls, Ann	22	DE	63
Campbell C	43	DE	15
Caroline	4/12	DE	15
Catherine	24	PA	141
Charles	6	DE	225
Daniel	2	DE	180
David	46	DE	98
Eliza A	11	DE	125
Elizabeth	47	DE	185
Emmaline	9	DE	98
George	6	DE	65
George W	3	DE	98
Hensely R	39	DE	225
James	5	DE	63
James	40	DE	185
James	59	MD	63
James B	10	DE	15
James H	20	DE	127
Jane	10	DE	225
Jane	38	PA	225
John	9	DE	225
John	11	DE	63
John H	3	DE	114
Julia A	1	DE	114
Louisa	27	DE	156
Margerett	36	DE	114
Martha	8	DE	156
Martha	13	DE	225
Mary	3/12	DE	180
Mary	4	DE	156
Mary	6	DE	185
Mary	32	DE	180
Mary	36	DE	15
Mary	46	DE	98
Mary J	7	DE	15
Mathew	31	DE	180
Nancy	5	DE	180
Nathaniel	48	DE	39
Parnel	20	DE	98
Rachel	3	DE	225
Samuel	6	DE	156
Samuel	20	DE	65
Sarah	44	DE	63
Sarah A	14	DE	15
Sophia	8	DE	180
Thomas	4/12	DE	141
Thomas	4	DE	156
William	2	DE	225
William	16	DE	185
William D	4	DE	15
Walsworth, Mary	40	DE	268
Walter, James	10	DE	30
Rosa	59	DE	87
Samuel	10	DE	30
Slator	17	DE	30
Walters, Jacob	18	DE	100
Walton, Absolem	44	DE	83
David	23	DE	84
David	62	DE	84
Elizabeth	17	DE	84
Elizabeth	68	DE	220
John	16	DE	77
Lydia	14	DE	84
Nancy	55	DE	98
Peter	50	DE	98
Sally	45	DE	90
Sarah E	30	DE	98
Sarah P	8	DE	113
Susan	25	DE	84
Thomas	6	DE	84
Thomas	22	DE	75
William	26	DE	84
Waltons, Ezekiel	14	DE	158
Wamsley, Celia	23	DE	140
Charles	12	DE	128
David	25	DE	186
David A	6	DE	140
Wamsley, Garrison	2	DE	140
Thomas	40	DE	140
Waples, Ann	4	DE	168
Charles	4	DE	164
Harriet	15	DE	168
James G	42	DE	168
Mary	12	DE	168
Sally	42	DE	168
Waravin, Elizabeth	8	DE	173
Hannah	5	DE	173
Hannah	40	DE	173
John	11	DE	173
Joseph	16	DE	173
Joseph	47	DE	173
William	14	DE	173
Ward, Andrew J	17	DE	143
Ann E	21	DE	205
Clementine	9/12	DE	130
Deborah	19	DE	205
Edward	30	DE	18
Eliza A	27	DE	143
Elizabeth	47	DE	205
Elizabeth T	8	DE	143
George	31	DE	50
George W	9	DE	148
Grace	70	DE	74
Hannah	53	MD	5
James	55	DE	205
James	66	DE	74
James H	25	DE	130
Jane	48	DE	148
Jesse	22	DE	143
John	17	DE	205
John D A	13	DE	143
John W	12	DE	148
Joseph	20	DE	143
Joseph	55	DE	143
Julia Ann	32	MD	50
Mary	23	DE	130
Mary C	15	DE	143
Mary E	2	MD	32
Murphy	49	DE	128
Ruthanna	46	DE	179
Samuel	24	DE	127
Samuel S	7	DE	148
Sarah	6	DE	205
Sarah	49	DE	143
Susan	15	DE	258
Susan	73	DE	146
Willard	21	DE	16
William	8	DE	205
William	11	DE	5
William	54	DE	148
Ware, Emily	5	DE	181
James	8	DE	182
Jane	38	DE	182
John	1/12	DE	182
John	17	DE	181
John	43	DE	181
Layton	6	DE	182
Margaret	10	DE	182
Margaret	12	DE	181
Mary	3	DE	182
Mary	40	DE	181
Rebecca	15	DE	181
Samuel	2	DE	181
Sarah	9	DE	181
Susan	15	DE	181
William	13	DE	182
Wm	39	DE	182
Warner, Abigail	22	DE	162
Charles	35	DE	68
Elizabeth	28	DE	29
James	60	DE	119
John	45	DE	29
Warren, Amelia	13	DE	173
Angelica	7	DE	118
Anna	4	DE	214
Anna E	9	DE	206
Charles	6	DE	216
Charles	7	DE	206
Charles	32	DE	118

Name	Age	State	Page
Warren, Charles	33	DE	238
Clarena	3	DE	119
David	60	DE	237
David	65	DE	237
Eliza	25	DE	215
Elizabeth	57	DE	237
Elizabeth	62	DE	237
Emeline	35	DE	120
Emily	16	DE	237
Florence	1	DE	119
George	5	DE	212
George R	36	DE	212
Hannah	30	DE	73
Harriet	16	DE	179
Harriet	35	DE	111
Henry	35	DE	216
Henry Hill	2	DE	111
Hester A	5/12	DE	216
Isabella	13	DE	206
Jesse	10/12	DE	206
John	20	DE	237
John	29	DE	237
John	40	DE	213
John	53	DE	217
John E	1/12	DE	214
John W	9	DE	118
Kitty M	39	MD	212
Lydia	3/12	DE	73
Malvina	19	DE	179
Margaret	34	DE	206
Margaret	44	DE	214
Margaret	70	DE	121
Margaret A	32	DE	213
Margaretta	14	MD	212
Mariah L	14	DE	214
Mariam	75	DE	221
Mariam E	12	MD	212
Mary	4/12	DE	238
Mary	9	MD	212
Mary	29	DE	193
Mary	32	DE	238
Mary	40	DE	216
Mary J	4	DE	214
Mary J	5	DE	216
Mary J	30	DE	212
Mary S	3	DE	206
Miriam	4	DE	238
Nathaniel	39	DE	73
Nathaniel L	1	DE	214
Nathaniel L	43	DE	214
Nelly	60	DE	211
Phebe A	25	DE	221
Rachel C	13	MD	212
Richard	22	DE	257
Richard	29	DE	221
Samuel	2	DE	238
Samuel	3	DE	216
Samuel	4	MD	212
Samuel	44	DE	215
Sarah	49	DE	213
Sarah A	10/12	DE	111
Sarah A	30	DE	118
Sarah E	5	DE	119
Sarah J	15	DE	206
Solomon T	40	DE	212
Sophia T	7	MD	212
Susan A	12	DE	216
Susan E	6	DE	214
Susanna	56	DE	214
Thomas	2	DE	212
Walter	5	DE	206
Walter	40	DE	206
Warner	1	DE	215
William	1	DE	216
William	12	DE	47
William	29	DE	111
William A	4	DE	111
William H	2	DE	215
Warrington, Louisa	18	DE	192
Nathaniel	28	DE	57
Washington, Abraham	19	DE	171
Ann	15	DE	205
Washington, Catherine	7	DE	205
Charles	45	MD	171
Dorothy	25	DE	38
George	9	DE	205
George	12	DE	176
Henry	20	DE	101
Lydia	17	DE	171
Patience	45	DE	171
Susanna	3	DE	205
Waston, George	47	DE	244
Rachel	16	DE	245
Sarah	40	DE	244
Susan	14	DE	245
Waters, Andrew	20	DE	138
Cezar	28	DE	76
Charlotte	68	DE	127
Dana	5	DE	126
Gilbert	14	DE	125
Hannah	50	DE	76
Henry	21	DE	77
Hester A	6	DE	106
Jacob	46	DE	126
Jacob B	10	DE	126
James	23	DE	43
Joseph	12	DE	82
Joseph	19	DE	268
Lydia	18	DE	70
Mahala	2	DE	106
Mahala	48	DE	126
Mary	24	DE	127
Mary A	6	DE	127
Milly	35	DE	106
Nathan	8	DE	212
Peter	15	DE	268
Phoebe	18	DE	126
Phoebe A	4	DE	121
Rachel	3	DE	106
Rachel	22	DE	43
Rachel C	8	DE	126
Robt	1	DE	126
Samuel	21	DE	200
Sarah E	14	DE	126
Sarah E	21	DE	127
William	40	DE	106
Wm	16	DE	236
Watkins, Betsey	80	DE	213
Franklin	18	DE	170
Hester	3	DE	158
Mary	9	DE	248
Nehemiah	13	DE	248
Priscilla	15	PA	158
Watson, Ann E	8	DE	105
Bethewel	33	DE	86
Charles	12	DE	90
Clinton	25	DE	41
David H	4	DE	114
David K	34	DE	105
Edward J	18	DE	114
Eli	28	DE	85
Elias Shockley	12	DE	114
Elizabeth	3	DE	41
Emily	1	DE	41
Isabella	14	DE	97
James	5	DE	41
James M	3	DE	105
James M	8	DE	114
Jesse	45	DE	114
Jinetta	30	DE	93
John	30	DE	93
Joseph	10	DE	173
Lydia	14	DE	114
Lydia	43	DE	114
Manlove	24	DE	105
Mann	40	DE	84
Margaret	2	DE	159
Mary A	21	DE	88
Mary Ann	17	DE	6
Mary B	16	DE	114
Mary E	3	DE	86
Mary J	4/12	DE	105
Priscilla	19	DE	88
Watson, Priscilla	22	DE	41
Rebecca	10	DE	93
Robert	2	DE	93
Robert	29	DE	93
Ruth	21	DE	86
Samuel	24	DE	159
Sarah	32	DE	105
Serena	21	DE	159
Thomas A	5	DE	105
William	4	DE	159
William	7	DE	39
William G	11/12	DE	87
Wm	35	MD	234
Webb, Charles A	3	DE	107
Elias	33	DE	91
Eliza	11	DE	155
Ellen	60	DE	86
George	27	DE	13
Hannah P	18	DE	73
Harriet	1/12	DE	170
Henry	19	DE	170
Hester	3	DE	155
James	8	DE	155
James H	15	DE	106
John	13	DE	61
John	13	DE	201
John C	40	DE	106
John M	7	DE	107
John W	6	DE	105
Joseph	39	MD	155
Margaret	12	DE	169
Margarett	2	DE	105
Margerett A	12	DE	106
Mary	29	DE	105
Mary	43	DE	170
Mary J	5	DE	91
Mitchell	37	DE	116
Rachel	32	DE	116
Rachel C	5	DE	106
Rebecca	35	DE	91
Sarah	9	DE	170
Sarah	17	DE	209
Sarah	26	DE	170
Sarah	33	DE	106
Sarah	35	DE	155
Sarah A	2	DE	116
Sarah A	9	DE	105
Sarah E	10	DE	106
Silvester	1/12	DE	107
Silvester	34	DE	105
Susan	16	DE	155
Susan S	19	DE	73
William	15	DE	73
William H	9	DE	116
Wm	30	DE	170
Webster, Albert	46	CT	223
Benjamin	13	DE	223
Catherine	38	DE	223
Eliza	8	DE	223
Ira	8	DE	223
Joseph	4	DE	54
Lavinia	4	DE	223
Weeks, Jane	2	DE	59
Julia	24	DE	264
Margaret	66	DE	26
Mary	7	DE	264
Sarah	24	DE	59
William	27	DE	264
Welch, Elizabeth	45	DE	140
Elizabeth	50	DE	152
Jacob	16	DE	116
Jacob	17	DE	140
Jacob	50	DE	140
Sarah	10	DE	140
Sarah A	22	DE	95
Sarah E	3	DE	95
Shadrach	20	DE	91
Susan	13	DE	140
Susan	14	DE	116
Thomas H	15	DE	140
William	26	DE	95
William	85	DE	152

Name	Age	St	Pg
Welkinson, Catherine	23	DE	190
Wells, Albert	4	DE	208
Clorinda	1	DE	208
Elizabeth	49	DE	73
John	54	MD	208
Joseph	10	DE	208
Rebecca	40	DE	208
Smith	7	DE	208
Sophia	55	MD	14
Susan	13	DE	208
William	34	DE	113
Welsh, Elizabeth	22	DE	242
Robert	22	IE	166
Wendel, Ann	63	DE	34
Benjamin	29	DE	34
Elizabeth	18	DE	34
Joseph	25	DE	34
William	68	DE	34
West, Ann	21	DE	100
Ann E	30	DE	220
Anna	8	DE	219
Catherin	70	DE	83
Edward	27	DE	169
Eli F	4	DE	12
George	25	DE	228
George W	9	DE	47
Harriet	5	DE	218
J Burton	14	DE	47
James	45	MD	47
John	1	DE	220
John	5	DE	169
John	38	DE	218
John C	6/12	DE	218
John W	7	DE	47
Louisa	9	DE	12
Luke	32	DE	12
Mary	6	DE	169
Mary	35	DE	12
Mary A	8	DE	47
Milcah	73	MD	162
Rachel	12	DE	218
Rachel	26	DE	169
Rachel A	5/12	DE	47
Richard	90	DE	83
Sarah	33	DE	162
Sarah E	14	DE	218
Thomas	3	DE	47
William	15	DE	71
William F	1	DE	12
William H	17	DE	47
Wetherby, Clayton	38	NJ	161
Pitman	8	DE	161
Prudence	39	DE	161
Whaley, Eliza A	23	DE	151
John	58	DE	151
John R	22	DE	143
Thedora	1	DE	151
Whartinberry, Laura	9/12	DE	4
Wharton, Alexine	6	DE	156
Ann	23	DE	155
Anna	1/12	DE	156
Bolitha	27	DE	155
Charles	1/12	DE	155
Charles	1	DE	213
Charles M	37	DE	156
Clement B	25	DE	151
Eliza	25	DE	207
Ella	4	DE	155
Ernest	2	DE	156
Harriet	60	DE	213
Henry	8	DE	171
John B	1	DE	211
John C	4	DE	151
Joshua B	24	DE	211
Manlove	9	DE	267
Martha	5	DE	267
Mary	9	DE	156
Mary	20	DE	211
Mary	31	DE	32
Mary A	18	DE	35
Mary E	10	DE	151
Matilda	29	DE	156

Name	Age	St	Pg
Wharton, Rhoda	36	DE	151
Samuel	28	DE	156
Unity	27	DE	156
William	11	DE	156
Whartonberry, Ann	25	DE	22
George	1	DE	22
Susan	5/12	DE	22
Thomas	30	DE	22
Whatly, Ann	37	DE	236
Caroline	4	DE	236
Elizabeth	2	DE	236
John	27	DE	236
Noah	27	DE	236
Wheatley, Elizabeth	11	DE	157
Henry	31	DE	104
James	14	DE	185
John	38	DE	116
John	41	DE	111
Margarett	20	DE	104
Mary	50	DE	111
Mary	60	DE	104
Tina	23	DE	104
Wheatly, Brainard	15	DE	178
Brainard	49	DE	178
George	20	DE	178
Martha	11	DE	178
Mary	49	DE	178
Sally Ann	16	DE	178
Sidney	8	DE	178
Wheeler, Jacob	20	DE	261
John	11	DE	261
Margaret A	22	DE	213
Mary	18	MD	171
Miriam	1	MD	171
Robert	34	DE	213
Sally	46	DE	261
Samuel	2	DE	213
William	17	DE	137
William	18	DE	132
Wm	29	DE	171
Wheetley, William	21	DE	78
Whelen, Thomas	16	DE	260
Whiacre, Elizabeth	25	DE	217
Joseph	4	DE	217
Joseph H	27	DE	217
Penelope	11	DE	251
Whitaker, Eliza	23	DE	219
Jacob	21	DE	120
Miriam	20	DE	120
Whitby, Analy	30	DE	223
David R	13	DE	113
Elizabeth	34	DE	223
Elizabeth	47	DE	113
John R	46	DE	113
Joseph	35	DE	191
Martha	13	DE	191
Mary	6	DE	191
Mary	34	DE	191
Nancy	28	DE	227
Nathan	10	DE	191
Ruth A	9	DE	113
Sarah	2	DE	191
William	7	DE	223
White, Andrew	18	DE	156
Ann	3/12	DE	14
Ann	6	DE	162
Ann	10	DE	234
Ann	15	DE	101
Ann	24	DE	220
Ann	30	DE	168
Ann	41	DE	92
Ann	83	DE	248
Ann E	3	DE	57
Anna	21	DE	209
Ansley	2	DE	96
Ansley	44	DE	96
Ansley	75	DE	192
Anthony	60	DE	101
Araminta	18	DE	90
Arry	35	DE	244
Benjamin	4/12	DE	7
Benjamin	7	DE	262

Name	Age	St	Pg
White, Benjamin	28	DE	171
Benjamin	35	DE	168
Benjamin	76	DE	171
Betsey	40	DE	162
Britannia	9	DE	262
Caleb	22	DE	58
Caleb	23	DE	249
Charles	3	DE	188
Charles	72	MD	37
Clement	34	DE	108
Edward	12	DE	231
Eliza	30	DE	188
Eliza A	30	DE	111
Elizabeth	2	DE	220
Elizabeth	3	DE	241
Elizabeth	7	DE	244
Elizabeth	8	DE	96
Elizabeth	11	DE	111
Elizabeth	28	DE	241
Elizabeth	46	DE	57
Elmira G	1/12	DE	209
George	3	DE	96
George W	14	DE	123
Hannah	35	DE	73
Hannah A	40	DE	90
Harriet	44	DE	96
Henry	11	DE	96
Isaac	5	DE	244
Isaac	14	DE	147
Isaac A	6	DE	92
Jacob	12	DE	156
James	9	DE	244
James	11	DE	75
James	24	DE	171
James E	4	DE	108
James H	46	DE	192
James T	45	DE	37
John	9	DE	220
John	11	DE	37
John	19	DE	150
John	19	DE	215
John	24	DE	57
John	57	MD	1
John M	4	DE	92
John M	48	DE	95
John W	27	MD	209
Joseph	4/12	DE	244
Joseph	4	DE	14
Joseph	17	DE	59
Joseph G	2	DE	111
Josiah	3	DE	108
Julia	10	DE	165
Laura	5	DE	168
Levin	33	DE	241
Lavinia	2/12	DE	171
Litty C	1	DE	108
Louisa	22	DE	218
Lydia	15	DE	96
Major	30	DE	114
Margaret	8	DE	37
Mariah	46	DE	37
Mary	4	DE	111
Mary	8	DE	168
Mary	25	DE	108
Mary	48	DE	95
Mary E	1	DE	212
Mary E	19	DE	92
Mary E	26	DE	119
Mary J	20	DE	160
Mary J	21	DE	57
Marybel	12	DE	76
Nathaniel	37	DE	188
Nehemiah	28	DE	96
Nelitha	50	DE	101
Peter	4	DE	96
Philemon	17	DE	242
Priestley	10	DE	96
Rachel	27	DE	171
Richard	32	DE	220
Robert	40	DE	111
Sarah	3	DE	244
Sarah	35	DE	14

White, Sarah	35	DE	244	Wilds, Susan	11	DE	168	Williams, Eliza A	6	DE	213
Sarah A	3	DE	109	William	33	DE	1	Elizabeth	6	DE	60
Sarah Ann	13	DE	92	William D	2	DE	37	Elizabeth	39	DE	213
Sarah E	19	DE	96	Wiley, John	73	DE	175	Elizabeth	45	DE	42
Savilla	17	DE	14	Wilkinson, Harriet	9	DE	189	Elizabeth	47	DE	205
Silas	4/12	DE	241	James	47	DE	189	Elizabeth	49	MD	147
Solomon	11	DE	244	Joshua	14	DE	63	Elizabeth B	4	DE	216
Susan	39	DE	96	Mary	16	DE	189	Ellwood	17	PA	16
Thomas	9	DE	55	Mary	18	DE	63	Emeline	4	DE	213
Viletta	1	DE	168	Mary	40	DE	189	Emeline	40	DE	74
William	2/12	DE	188	Wm	21	DE	190	Emma	3	DE	164
William	5	DE	172	Wilkerson, Hannah	12	DE	63	Emma	11	DE	201
William H	9	DE	92	Risdon	16	DE	63	Enos R	2	DE	216
Wm	14	DE	186	Risden	53	DE	63	George	14	DE	6
Whiteacre, Catherine	6	DE	221	Sarah	54	MD	63	George	35	PA	82
Catherine	60	DE	156	Wilkinson, Eliza	27	DE	180	George W	17	MD	141
Elizabeth	8	DE	221	Lydia	53	DE	160	Gracy	38	DE	102
George	17	DE	240	Susan	6/12	DE	180	Hannah	50	GB	27
George	58	DE	240	Wm	64	DE	160	Hanson	20	DE	24
Henry	1	DE	221	Will, Ann	1	DE	264	Harriet	18	DE	230
Henry	35	DE	221	Willaby, Eliza	34	DE	260	Henry	18	DE	205
James	6	DE	167	John	59	MD	260	Henry	47	MD	42
John	8	DE	167	Mary	5	DE	260	Henry	54	DE	213
John	15	DE	233	Mary	53	DE	255	Hester	6	DE	74
Letitia	58	DE	240	Willey, Caleb	2	DE	245	Hester	60	DE	219
Margaret	12	DE	240	Eliza	7	DE	245	Hester J	12	DE	32
Martha	8	DE	252	George	8	DE	245	Hiram	21	DE	92
Mary	42	DE	252	Gideon M	21	DE	103	Isaac	52	DE	32
Peter	4	DE	221	Joseph	30	DE	245	Jacob	7	DE	62
Ruth	70	DE	241	Joshua	18	DE	103	Jacob	41	DE	27
Susan	30	DE	221	Louisa E	8/12	DE	136	James	5	DE	112
William T	11	DE	221	Mahaley	15	DE	103	James	8	DE	11
Wm	38	DE	221	Mary	4	DE	245	James	9	DE	147
Whitehead, Mary	44	DE	101	Mary	32	DE	245	James	20	DE	205
Sarah	30	DE	101	Mary A	6	DE	103	James	21	DE	183
Whiteley, Albert	33	MD	220	Pinkey	9	DE	103	James	24	PA	61
Amsley	75	DE	191	Scynthia	3	DE	103	James	31	DE	94
Benjamin	6	DE	220	Sylvester	7/12	DE	245	James	38	DE	186
Elizabeth	8	DE	220	Sylvester	32	MD	245	James J	51	DE	205
Emeline	11	MD	220	William	49	DE	103	Job	22	PA	57
Madeline	3	DE	220	Zippora	35	DE	103	John	11/12	DE	11
Whitely, Ann	10	DE	229	William, Albert	25	DE	68	John	4	DE	195
Elizabeth	27	DE	220	George	11	DE	60	John	15	DE	62
Rebecca	25	DE	190	James	7	DE	185	John	18	DE	222
Whiteman, Elizabeth	15	DE	188	James	10	DE	186	John	20	DE	26
Ellen	17	DE	166	John	2	DE	185	John	22	DE	147
Wible, George	26	DE	83	Jonathan	2	DE	186	John	23	DE	243
Wicks, Elizabeth	35	DE	132	Mary	5/12	DE	199	John	38	DE	116
Elizabeth	4	DE	132	Mary	30	DE	199	John	38	DE	201
James	7	DE	132	Phillip	11	DE	214	John	40	DE	7
Joseph	27	MD	160	Robert	4	DE	185	John H	3/12	DE	213
Mary	10	DE	132	Thomason	10	MD	230	John H	11	DE	27
Robert H	39	DE	132	Wm	30	DE	199	John T	6	DE	116
Susan A	14	DE	132	Williams, Allen	8	DE	60	John T	7	DE	122
William H	15	DE	132	Allen	15	DE	27	Jonathan	35	DE	186
Wilds, Anne E	14	DE	37	Amanda	6	DE	205	Joseph	14	DE	114
Catherine	10	DE	168	Andrew	9/12	DE	60	Joseph	22	DE	213
David S	18	DE	37	Ann	3	DE	11	Joseph E	13	DE	27
Elizabeth	33	DE	168	Ann	4	DE	201	Josephine	4	DE	89
Elizabeth	59	DE	54	Ann	34	DE	207	Joshua	37	DE	35
Elizabeth A	33	VA	1	Ann	36	DE	60	Julia	24	DE	11
Emma	5	DE	168	Ann	36	DE	203	Lanta	14	DE	86
Francis	35	DE	10	Ann	36	DE	257	Lavinia E	18	DE	146
James	7	DE	168	Ann A	29	DE	10	Levin C	2/12	DE	216
James B	46	DE	37	Ann E	1	DE	65	Louisa	10	DE	121
James P	4	DE	37	Ann M	31	DE	89	Luke	27	DE	216
James P	46	DE	157	Benjamin	30	DE	147	Lurena	64	DE	131
John M	9	DE	37	Caleb	4	DE	74	Lydia A	28	DE	62
Lydia A	12	DE	37	Caleb	8	DE	213	Margaret	11	DE	146
Lydia E	38	DE	37	Caleb	37	DE	102	Margaret J	7	DE	147
Lydia S	5	DE	15	Caroline	38	PA	82	Mary	6	DE	164
Margaret R	8	DE	10	Catherine	3	DE	146	Mary	9	DE	96
Mary	13	DE	168	Charles	2	DE	213	Mary	12	DE	164
Mary	35	DE	10	Charles	9	DE	60	Mary	16	DE	157
Mary J	33	DE	15	Charles F	15	DE	146	Mary	17	DE	152
Mary R	7	DE	37	Charles W	6	DE	27	Mary	22	DE	205
Nathaniel	7	IL	1	Curtis	50	DE	74	Mary	30	MD	243
Nathaniel B	37	DE	168	Denney	10	DE	62	Mary	33	DE	216
Nathaniel F	6	DE	10	Ebby Jane	21	DE	85	Mary	42	DE	7
Robert	4	DE	1	Elijah	40	DE	203	Mary A	5	DE	121
Samuel	10/12	DE	1	Eliza	35	DE	96	Mary A	8	DE	23
Sarah A	4	DE	10					Mary E	5	DE	116

Name	Age	St	Pg
Williams, Mary H	30	DE	85
Melvina	3/12	DE	63
Miriam	9	DE	201
Nancy	14	DE	7
Nathan E	6	DE	89
Nathan G	12	DE	116
Nicy	28	DE	116
Priscilla	6	DE	32
Rachel	9	DE	32
Rachel	13	DE	87
Rachel	14	DE	96
Rebecca	45	MD	141
Reynear	9	DE	85
Richard	12	DE	74
Risden	35	DE	216
Robert H	3	DE	116
Robert H	6	DE	85
Robert K	8	DE	205
Samuel	12	DE	43
Samuel	39	DE	62
Samuel J	8	DE	89
Sarah	1/12	DE	186
Sarah	26	DE	27
Sarah	30	DE	94
Sarah	30	DE	186
Sarah	51	DE	32
Sarah	67	DE	257
Sarah A	9	DE	116
Sarah A	14	DE	32
Sarah A	19	DE	97
Sarah J	10	DE	27
Sarah J	31	DE	147
Susan	16	DE	43
Susan A	17	DE	147
Tamsey	45	DE	146
Thomas	3/12	DE	204
Thomas	8	DE	186
Thomas	11	DE	213
Thomas	15	DE	27
Thomas	21	DE	182
Thomas	26	DE	97
Thomas	50	DE	146
Thomas B	8	DE	146
Virginia	8/12	DE	201
Wassmand	7	DE	203
William	4	DE	60
William	5	DE	186
William	15	DE	44
William	19	DE	27
William	22	DE	146
William	25	DE	11
William	37	DE	60
William	40	DE	147
William	63	GB	17
William B	11/12	DE	97
William D	14	DE	89
William T	19	MD	141
Williamson, Adeline	13	DE	148
Anna M	1	DE	102
Charles	45	MD	148
Charles W	9	DE	148
Clinton L	11/12	DE	148
Columbus F	4	DE	148
Elijah	24	MD	102
Elizabeth	20	DE	102
John	17	MD	145
Martha J	15	DE	148
Sarah	19	DE	5
Sarah A	11	DE	148
Sarah A	44	DE	148
William T	24	DE	148
Willis, Caleb	15	DE	239
Catherine	36	DE	113
Elizabeth	48	MD	194
James H	19	DE	136
John L	17	DE	136
Joseph	10	DE	136
Joseph W	42	MD	136
Lavinia A	28	DE	149
Lewis	29	DE	113
Louisa	5	DE	136
Mary	18	DE	194
Willis, Mary E	7	DE	136
Mary K	2	DE	149
Nancy	44	DE	136
Nathan	35	DE	149
Sarah A	1	DE	149
Sarah E	12	DE	136
Sarah E	19	DE	92
Serrah	47	MD	194
Susan A	14	DE	136
William	21	MD	92
William	23	MD	194
William A	21	DE	136
Willoughby, Eliza A	1	DE	130
Eliza A	28	DE	132
Job	30	DE	130
Margaret	29	DE	130
Mary	7	DE	130
Rachel	67	DE	132
Richard	27	DE	132
William	4	DE	130
Willowby, John	21	DE	261
Wills, Daniel	14	DE	45
Wilmer, Fanny	89	DE	167
Wilson, Adam	9	DE	42
Alexander	4	DE	5
Alexander	30	DE	5
Amanda	14	NJ	181
Andrew J	21	DE	57
Ann	7	MD	186
Ann	42	DE	42
Ann	57	DE	57
Ann M	27	PA	5
Anna	1	DE	77
Catharine	17	DE	57
Catharine	54	DE	17
Catharine M	17	DE	17
Charles	7	DE	184
Cowgill William	42	DE	73
Debora	3	DE	153
Edward	15	DE	146
Edward W	34	DE	76
Elisha	11	DE	153
Eliza A	20	DE	214
Elizabeth	26	DE	8
Elizabeth	36	DE	204
Elizabeth	65	DE	83
Ellenora	9	DE	5
Emeline	20	DE	181
Francis	12	PA	3
Gustavus	70	DE	57
Hannah	55	DE	214
Harriet	19	DE	37
Henry	1	DE	11
Henry	10	DE	214
Henry W	13	DE	57
Hester	3	DE	42
Hester	50	DE	73
James	1	DE	181
James	42	DE	37
James A	8	DE	8
James H	11/12	DE	38
Jane	7	NJ	181
Jane	40	PA	181
Jervis	10	DE	38
John	1	DE	8
John	8	DE	242
John	11	DE	242
John	37	DE	204
John	44	NJ	181
John C	26	DE	211
John C	32	DE	8
Jonathan	58	DE	146
Joseph	20	NJ	181
Lewis	6	DE	204
Lydia	4	DE	242
Margaret	1	DE	42
Margaret	56	DE	240
Margaret A	12	DE	214
Mark	10	DE	85
Martha	4	DE	186
Mary	1	DE	186
Mary	10	DE	242
Wilson, Mary	16	MD	153
Mary	31	MD	186
Mary	63	MD	146
Mary A	16	DE	11
Mary E	1	DE	5
Mary E	9	DE	204
Moses	60	DE	73
Peter	41	MD	153
Phebe	20	DE	212
Priestly	36	DE	146
Priscilla	11	DE	42
Rachel	12	DE	242
Rachel	60	DE	242
Rachel H	8	DE	5
Rebecca	28	DE	211
Rebecca	30	DE	146
Robert	21	DE	17
Robert	34	DE	186
Robert	70	DE	42
Robert B	5/12	DE	211
Robert K	19	DE	57
Ruth	28	DE	73
Ruth	60	DE	193
Sarah	4	DE	76
Sarah	5	DE	42
Sarah	6	DE	242
Sarah	10	DE	153
Sarah	63	DE	182
Sarah A	28	PA	76
Sarah E	18	DE	17
Sarah J	2	DE	205
Sarah J	16	DE	150
Sophia	29	DE	77
Susan	6/12	DE	242
Theodore	10	DE	210
Thomas	60	DE	214
Thomas W	31	MD	77
Warner	27	DE	229
William	3	DE	8
William	7	DE	153
William	13	DE	204
William	20	DE	214
William	23	DE	193
William	63	DE	17
William	66	DE	193
Wm	8	DE	203
Wm	34	DE	242
Wingate	21	DE	77
Windal, Mary	33	DE	24
Mary E	2	DE	24
William	33	DE	24
Windsmere, Alexander	3	DE	219
Alexander	47	DE	219
Caroline	8	DE	219
Eliza	5	DE	219
Margaret A	42	DE	219
Winford, Angeline	8	DE	244
Elizabeth	40	DE	232
John	32	DE	222
Latitia	14	DE	244
Lemuel	36	DE	244
Mary	22	DE	222
Sela	35	DE	244
Wing, Mary	45	DE	143
Mary	75	DE	150
Robert	77	DE	150
Wise, Ann	22	DE	231
James	21	DE	231
With, Araminta	28	MD	259
Mary	62	MD	259
William	21	DE	259
Wobb, Sarah	7	DE	210
Wodard, Charles	5/12	DE	230
Hester	43	DE	230
Robert	45	DE	230
Sally	3	DE	230
Wodars, Elija	7	DE	208
Levin	37	DE	207
Wolcott, Elizabeth	39	DE	125
James L	10	DE	125
John R	16	DE	21
Joseph	11	DE	214

Name	Age	State	No.
Wolcott, Joseph	24	DE	125
Josiah	57	DE	125
Levin	26	DE	4
Rachel A	13	DE	125
Wolford, Mary	55	DE	230
Wolmar, Mariah	19	DE	164
Wonsley, John	23	DE	243
Wood, Anna	38	MD	71
Catherine A	28	DE	113
Elizabeth	22	DE	105
George	14	DE	113
James J	44	DE	113
James P	1/12	DE	113
Jane	8	DE	16
John	11	DE	71
Martha G	14	DE	39
Mary M	10	DE	113
Nancy	60	DE	105
Samuel	12	DE	39
Stephen	25	DE	105
William J	12	DE	113
Woodal, Ann M	32	DE	76
Daniel	9	DE	76
Edward	13	DE	76
Emma J	10	DE	8
George	12	DE	8
Henry	30	DE	76
John	9	DE	8
John	40	DE	76
Mary	4	DE	76
Matilda	11	DE	76
Woodall, Cornelia	21	DE	169
Eliza	45	DE	168
Francis A	17	DE	18
Franklin	18	DE	169
Thomas	47	MD	18
Woodel, Julia	3	DE	233
Louisa	14	DE	233
Margaret	37	DE	233
Terry	40	DE	233
Thomas	18	DE	168
Woodells, Francis	4	DE	159
Wooders, William H	13	MD	132
Woodhall, Anna	8	DE	230
Ezekiel	38	DE	230
Joshua	11	DE	230
Woodley, Betsey A	10/12	DE	81
Charles	7	DE	81
Harriet E	29	DE	81
Jonathan	45	DE	81
Woods, Thomas	3	DE	215
Woodward, Thomas	20	DE	69
Woolford, George	6	DE	222
Mariah	24	DE	222
Rachel	2	DE	222
Wooters, Abner	23	DE	242
Abner	24	DE	239
Abner	60	DE	241
Alexander	13	DE	241
Ann	36	DE	267
Cynthia	41	DE	220
Daniel	32	DE	59
Elija	16	DE	241
Eliza	13	DE	260
Francis L	12	MD	132
James	7	DE	267
James	8	DE	260
James	38	MD	260
James	40	MD	220
John	10	MD	261
John	52	DE	239
Julia A	36	DE	117
Lemuel	15	MD	1
Maria	10	DE	260
Mary	7	DE	261
Mary	10	DE	267
Mary	18	DE	239
Mary E	12	DE	117
Miriam	34	DE	241
Phillip	47	DE	267
Presley	14	DE	7
Rachel	20	DE	261
Wooters, Rachel	45	DE	239
Reuben	1	DE	117
Reuben	42	DE	117
Robert	5	DE	267
Robert J	17	DE	117
Ruth	1	DE	267
Ruthana	1	DE	220
S____	32	DE	241
Sarah	15	DE	239
Sarah	46	DE	267
Sarah A	22	DE	220
Sarah E	14	DE	220
Tansey	9	DE	267
Thomas	36	DE	261
Thomas J	7	DE	117
William	7/12	DE	261
William	12	DE	239
William	16	DE	258
William	18	DE	241
William	46	MD	220
Wootten, James	3/12	DE	219
John	58	DE	219
Mary	35	DE	219
Wooters, John	8	DE	81
Woters, Sarah	14	DE	161
Wrench, Henry	41	DE	32
Margaret	4	DE	32
Margaret	31	DE	32
Mary	12	DE	32
Rachel	1	DE	32
Sarah	9	DE	32
Susanna	6	DE	32
Washington P	8	DE	32
Wright, Adam	4/12	DE	1
Ader	14	DE	230
Andrew	26	DE	262
Ann	56	DE	109
Cassa	35	DE	158
Charles	2	DE	187
Ebenezer	12	DE	1
Elisha	17	DE	187
Eliza T	27	DE	12
Elizabeth	27	DE	1
Elizabeth R	42	DE	112
Frederic	40	DE	206
Hannah	6	DE	206
James	24	DE	246
James D	3	DE	47
John	3	DE	187
John	8	DE	47
John	16	DE	246
John	41	DE	47
John D	3	DE	12
Julia	27	DE	187
Lavicy	21	DE	70
Lavicy	19	MD	143
Louisa	31	DE	40
Lovy	10	DE	206
Margaret A	23	NJ	11
Maria	12	DE	206
Martha	3	DE	206
Mary	16	DE	246
Mary	23	DE	255
Mary A	14	DE	47
Mary E	5	DE	1
Naomi	71	DE	45
Peregrine	8	DE	1
Peregrine	40	DE	1
Rachel J	3	DE	47
Robert	5	DE	187
Robert	34	MD	187
Ruth	23	DE	262
Salina	25	DE	206
Samuel	1	DE	13
Samuel P	31	DE	12
Sarah	6	DE	187
Sarah A	32	DE	187
Sarah C	2	DE	1
Sarah E	12	DE	47
Sina	15	DE	116
Susan C	5	DE	47
Wesley	32	DE	40
Wright, William	1	DE	187
William	10	DE	1
William	17	NJ	11
William P	15	DE	47
Wroten, Ann	31	DE	145
Ann M	15	DE	145
Caroline	29	DE	145
Charles	53	DE	145
Charles W	5	DE	145
Eli	23	DE	145
Eli	57	DE	145
Jacob R	8	DE	145
James	27	DE	147
James H	20	DE	145
Margaret	25	DE	145
Mary A	19	DE	147
Mary E	20	DE	145
Nancy	50	DE	145
Noah L	17	DE	145
Sarah A	17	DE	145
Sarah E	8/12	DE	147
Wyatt, Aaron	45	DE	264
Andrew	13	DE	120
Ann	21	DE	158
Ann	45	DE	100
Ann E	33	DE	119
Celia	7	DE	128
Charity A	7	DE	131
Charles P	13	DE	83
Charlotte	9/12	DE	181
Daniel	1	DE	240
Daniel	35	DE	240
Daniel	45	DE	131
David	17	DE	224
George Edward	2/12	DE	100
Edwin	7/12	DE	158
Eliza	3/12	DE	256
Eliza	19	DE	140
Eliza A	6	DE	119
Elizabeth	2	DE	122
Elizabeth	33	MD	253
Elizabeth	37	DE	264
Elizabeth A	24	DE	118
George	4	DE	120
Georgiana	3	DE	131
Hannah	44	DE	138
Harriet	50	DE	120
Hasty	35	DE	119
Henry	52	DE	118
Isaac	14	DE	138
Jacob	9	DE	119
James	7/12	DE	119
James	13	DE	118
James	45	DE	100
James B	20	DE	131
John	11	DE	265
John	12	DE	182
John	16	DE	120
John	23	DE	240
John	29	DE	158
John	30	DE	120
John	34	MD	253
John R	16	DE	131
John W	16	DE	138
Joseph	9	DE	100
Latitia	60	DE	141
Lodewick	33	DE	119
Lydia	6/12	DE	119
Major	6	DE	132
Major	23	DE	140
Major	53	DE	138
Major	77	DE	141
Maria	38	DE	224
Margaret	1	DE	240
Margaret	9	DE	119
Margarett	49	DE	118
Mary	8	DE	224
Mary	14	DE	131
Mary	15	DE	83
Mary	32	DE	119
Mary	44	DE	131
Mary	65	DE	252

Wyatt, Mary A	24	DE	122	Wyatt, William	21	MD	256	Young, James	2	DE	80
Priscilla	3	DE	158	William A	3	DE	100	Jane	46	DE	238
Rebecca	15	DE	264	William W	12	DE	139	John	25	DE	235
Reuben	16	DE	119					John	30	DE	36
Richard C	5	DE	131	York, Comfort	65	DE	81	John	50	DE	80
Robert	9	DE	119	Eliza D	30	DE	80	John W	2	DE	36
Robert	27	DE	122	Elizabeth	24	DE	81	Jonathan	53	DE	238
Ruthy	2	DE	265	Elmira	6	DE	80	Joseph	60	DE	238
Samuel	6	DE	119	Helen	7	DE	60	Martha	5	DE	238
Samuel	11	DE	119	Laura	2	DE	81	Martha A	5	DE	36
Samuel	17	DE	118	Mary	34	DE	60	Mary	18	DE	237
Samuel	23	DE	104	Mary E	1	DE	80	Mary	22	DE	235
Sarah	2	DE	119	Samuel C	33	DE	80	Mary Ann	38	DE	97
Sarah	6	DE	119	Thomas	72	DE	81	Mary E	25	DE	36
Sarah	16	DE	85	Virginia	5	DE	60	Mary J	3/12	DE	36
Sarah	16	DE	119	William T	4	DE	80	Nathaniel	7	DE	194
Sarah	20	DE	240	Young, Alexander	16	DE	238	Nathaniel	44	DE	237
Sarah	56	DE	222	Ann	9	DE	220	Rachel	4	DE	238
Sarah E	9/12	DE	122	Ann	37	DE	235	Rhody	9	DE	238
Sina	3	DE	119	Ann	46	DE	80	Robert	21	DE	219
Sina	25	DE	119	Ann	55	DE	238	Samuel	6	DE	119
Sina	63	DE	139	Catherine	7	DE	235	Sarah	2	DE	237
Susan	13	DE	264	David	39	DE	97	Sarah	3	DE	236
Susan	18	DE	240	Eliza	17	DE	235	Sarah	16	DE	238
Susan A	14	DE	100	Eliza	50	DE	235	Sarah	37	DE	237
Thomas	3	DE	119	Elizabeth A	3	DE	214	Thomas	5	DE	236
Thomas H	20	DE	119	Ester	15	DE	237	William	19	DE	238
Unity	11	DE	138	Harriet	7	DE	235	William T	6	DE	36
Wesley	1/12	DE	119	Isaac	35	DE	235	Zachariah	60	DE	236
William	9	DE	138								

Name	Age	St	No.
Abbet, Alfred V	14	DE	111
Ann	44	NJ	111
Cyrus	51	PA	111
Mary D	16	DE	111
Sarah	11	DE	111
Abbot, David	23	DE	362
John	27	GB	123
Mary	33	DE	55
Rebecca	20	DE	123
Abbott, Alfred V D	11	DE	301
Benjamin	50	NJ	220
Catherine A	23	DE	362
Jane	30	PA	311
John	10	PA	311
Mary	33	?	167
Mary	54	DE	220
Mary	57	NJ	278
Samuel	34	NJ	311
Abels, Andrew	36	PA	71
Catherine	9	PA	71
Coturo	7	PA	71
Eliza	15	PA	71
Eliza	16	DE	308
Hester	10	PA	71
Sarah	35	DE	71
William	14	PA	71
Abert, Samuel	4	MD	203
Able, Biddy	18	IE	132
Achison, Thomas	30	IE	79
Achley, Martha A	25	NJ	398
Acley, Caroline	22	MD	335
John L	1	MD	335
John	35	NJ	335
Adair, Ann	40	DE	328
Ann J	9	DE	328
Hannah	74	DE	314
Jacob	12	DE	314
Louis	14	DE	314
Margaret	32	DE	343
Robert G	7	DE	328
Adams, Adolphus	7	DE	387
Ann	16	DE	188
Ann	74	DE	387
Ann E	46	PA	112
Catherine	17	NY	296
Catherine W	9	DE	113
Charles	6	DE	153
Charles	18	PA	210
Christiana	7	DE	215
David	35	DE	378
Dorcas	56	DE	153
Edward	24	DE	257
Elizabeth	5	NJ	79
Fanny	17	PA	308
Foster	34	DE	255
George R	6	DE	378
Gideon	14	NJ	79
Harrison	40	DE	257
Harriet B	12	OH	71
Harriet F	35	MD	153
Henry	11	DE	303
Hester A	3	DE	188
Howard J	14	OH	71
Isabella	48	ST	71
Jacob	19	DE	183
Jacob	21	DE	211
James	1	DE	391
James	30	DE	387
James	40	MD	389
Jenifer	54	DE	71
Jennet	18	OH	71
Jeremiah	3/12	DE	378
John	16	DE	255
John	24	DE	215
John H	29	DE	98
John Q	9	DE	378
Joseph A	20	PA	100
Judith	34	NJ	79
Levi	60	DE	153
Malan	39	NJ	79
Margaret	4	DE	98
Margaret	50	DE	113
Adams, Martha	15	DE	215
Mary	25	DE	392
Mary A	26	DE	98
Mulford	11	DE	79
Nathaniel	23	DE	185
Rebecca	16	NJ	79
Samuel L	4/12	DE	79
Samuel S	19	DE	244
Sarah	30	DE	188
Sarah	31	DE	378
Susan	62	DE	112
William	55	DE	215
William L	13	DE	215
Addams, George	19	DE	341
Hester J	25	DE	331
Addy, George	6	DE	106
George	56	GB	106
Susan	42	PA	106
Theodore	9	DE	106
Adkinson, Anne	47	NJ	283
Elizabeth	9	DE	303
Jacob	47	GB	283
Joseph	21	DE	283
Theodore	9	DE	303
Age, Alfred P	1	DE	83
Anna G	10	PA	83
Joshua P	45	PA	83
Samuel H	5	DE	83
Sarah	35	PA	83
Thomas J	12	PA	83
Agnew, Lewis W	18	PA	43
Agnis, Charles	26	DE	12
Vilet	70	DE	12
Aiken, Elizabeth	32	IE	351
Elizabeth S	35	DE	3
James	8	DE	351
James	33	IE	337
James	39	IE	351
James C	43	IE	3
John	6	DE	351
Lydia	4	DE	351
Mary A	28	PA	337
Robert	18	DE	117
Samuel	1	DE	351
Sarah J	14	DE	3
William	9	DE	351
Aikin, Alexander	2	DE	121
Amanda	19	DE	125
Anna	4/12	DE	125
Elizabeth	45	DE	125
Ezekle T	22	DE	132
James C	1	DE	137
Jane	64	IE	132
John	3	DE	137
John	38	IE	137
Martha	5	DE	137
Mary	21	DE	121
Mary	31	NJ	137
Samuel	67	DE	132
Samuel M	26	DE	132
Samuel T	9	DE	137
William	8	DE	137
William	26	DE	121
Aikins, Catherine	23	NJ	189
Joseph	40	NJ	189
Rebecca S	6	DE	189
Sarah B	4	DE	189
Selicia	60	IE	314
Ainscow, Alfred	11	DE	143
Evan	18	DE	143
George	3/12	DE	143
Mary	40	MD	142
William	40	GB	142
Aisa, Caleb	7	NJ	97
Michael H	2	NJ	97
Rachel W	4	NJ	97
Sarah A	5	NJ	97
Susan	29	NJ	97
Alben, W H	13	PA	163
Alcalde, Catherine	33	FR	343
David	3	DE	343
Alcorn, Anne E	8	DE	382
Alcorn, Elizabeth	46	DE	382
George	16	de	382
George P	51	MD	381
Hannah	12	DE	374
James	6	DE	382
Lemuel	3	DE	382
Margaret	36	DE	382
Martha J	15	DE	382
Susanna	22	DE	373
William	23	DE	382
Alderdice, A	56	DE	1
Eliza	47	MD	1
Joseph	19	DE	1
Mary	16	DE	1
Ruth	40	DE	30
W Hill	22	DE	1
Aldriches, Charles	17	DE	328
John	20	DE	328
Mary A	7	DE	328
Mary A	45	DE	328
Rebecca	9	DE	328
Samuel	12	DE	328
Sarah	14	DE	328
Peter	4	DE	329
Aldricks, Caroline	10	MD	330
George S	10	DE	189
James B	25	DE	189
John	7	DE	189
John	32	DE	189
Mary S	5	DE	189
Rachel B	24	DE	189
Sarah L	2	DE	189
Alee, Ellen F	7	DE	182
Alerdice, Isabella	24	DE	81
John A	26	VA	81
Alexander, Adaline	47	DE	24
Andres	30	DE	394
Charles	2	DE	271
Charles	6	DE	16
Charles	24	PA	30
Charles	30	MD	16
Edward	3	DE	30
Elizabeth	12	DE	341
Elleander L	1	DE	315
Emma	13	PA	271
Frances M	4	DE	237
George	12	PA	306
George	44	DE	306
George W	3	DE	341
George W	9	MD	315
H T	4	DE	305
Humphry	7/12	DE	305
James	6	PA	306
James	65	MD	287
James C	5	DE	237
James W	38	MD	315
Jane	40	DE	123
Jesse	39	DE	271
Jesse H	38	PA	305
John	4	PA	306
Joseph	14	PA	306
Julia A	11	MD	315
Louisa	31	PA	271
Louisa J	36	GB	315
Margaret A	2	DE	237
Mary	28	DE	30
Mary	28	MD	287
Mary	39	PA	306
Mary A	17	MD	315
Mary J	25	DE	16
Phebe	30	PA	305
Rachel	2	DE	16
Rebecca	24	PA	337
Rebecca J	2	DE	305
Richard	5	DE	271
Robert	26	MD	123
Robert	30	MD	341
Robert	35	MD	237
Robert W	10/12	DE	341
Sarah	16	PA	306
Sarah	28	PA	32
Sarah	28	PA	138

Name	Age	St	Pg	Name	Age	St	Pg	Name	Age	St	Pg
Alexander, Sarah	30	PA	341	Allen, Joshua	33	NJ	180	Allston, Harriet	39	DE	170
Sarah A	28	PA	237	Josiah	25	NJ	172	Joab	30	DE	256
Sarah J	15	MD	315	Julia	6	DE	383	John	4/12	DE	256
Smith	10	PA	306	Laura	5	DE	383	John	14	DE	219
Susan W	7	DE	341	Louis	5	DE	297	John E	10	DE	171
Thomas B	9	DE	237	Louisa	1	PA	102	Josephine	4	DE	171
William	3	DE	201	Lydia	28	DE	221	Lydia	8	DE	219
William	8	PA	306	Lydia	60	DE	108	Lydia	18	DE	257
William	33	PA	138	Lynias	15	DE	314	Mary E	8	DE	171
Wm	11	PA	271	Margaret	3	DE	192	Rachel	6	DE	219
Algoe, John	23	IE	353	Margaret	17	DE	258	Raymond	1	DE	219
Allanson, Mary	22	DE	308	Margaret	36	DE	383	Sarah	40	DE	235
Allbright, Charles	23	GE	5	Margaret A	5	PA	102	Sarah A	12	DE	219
Allen, Abigail	22	DE	158	Margaret J	9	DE	368	Temperance	49	DE	257
Adeline	10	DE	296	Martha J	48	DE	331	Thomas	45	DE	171
Alfred	1	DE	192	Mary	20	DE	48	Thomas H	11	DE	171
Alice	28	DE	346	Mary	34	DE	102	William	11	DE	219
Amanda	10	DE	377	Mary C	8/12	DE	369	William C	42	DE	219
Amanda	13	DE	383	Mary J	6	DE	3	Almond, Elizabeth	13	DE	306
Amanda	34	DE	297	Matilda	37	DE	108	Elizabeth	22	DE	130
Andrew	30	GB	102	Peggy	13	DE	116	George	27	DE	130
Ann	50	DE	377	Perry	2	DE	369	John	15	DE	307
Ann J	23	IE	319	Perry	26	DE	318	John	21	DE	297
Anna	20	DE	3	Perry	30	DE	3	John	62	DE	297
Anna L	6	DE	108	Perry	33	DE	368	Julia E	10	DE	306
Anna M	13	DE	377	Perry	70	DE	226	Mary	55	DE	297
Anna N	43	PA	158	Phoebe	33	DE	369	Mary A	22	DE	297
Aron M	17	NJ	238	Phoebe Jane	5	DE	366	Mary H	9/12	DE	130
Benedict	13	DE	207	Purcy	30	DE	346	Phebe	53	DE	306
Benjamin L	13	DE	180	Rachel	30	DE	297	William	56	DE	306
Byard	14	DE	360	Rachel	32	DE	367	Alrich, Amelia	16	DE	138
Byard	35	DE	367	Rebecca	40	DE	377	Anna	40	DE	51
Caroline	9	DE	383	Rhoda	32	NJ	180	Elizabeth	12	DE	56
Caroline	20	DE	112	Samuel	2	MD	383	Elizabeth	80	DE	51
Charles	4	DE	297	Samuel	24	PA	158	Harriet	19	DE	138
Charles	7	PA	297	Samuel	24	DE	231	Henry	46	DE	56
Charles	9	DE	221	Samuel	46	PA	383	Jacob	74	DE	56
Charlotte	1	DE	238	Samuel G	3	DE	108	John	40	DE	382
Charlotte	2	DE	239	Sarah	22	MD	239	Lydia	9	DE	56
Charlotte A	10	DE	180	Sarah	30	DE	192	Margaret	35	DE	266
Cora	3	DE	180	Sarah	49	DE	276	Martha M	14	DE	382
Elias	9/12	DE	267	Sarah	62	DE	141	Mary E	8/12	DE	382
Eliza	11	DE	318	Sarah E	8	DE	221	Mary J	20	GB	144
Elizabeth	7	DE	180	Sarah E	12	DE	368	Peter	10	DE	382
Elizabeth	8	DE	108	Sarah G	6	DE	354	Robert H	12	DE	382
Elizabeth	37	PA	297	Sarah J	10	MD	238	Samuel	8	DE	382
Ellen	50	DE	225	Sarah R	11	DE	238	Sarah	6	DE	57
Emeline	3	DE	369	Scatergood	17	DE	383	Sarah	30	DE	56
Emeline	25	PA	354	Stephen	32	DE	346	Sarah	44	PA	57
Emily	13	DE	258	Susanah	10	DE	354	Sarah A	39	DE	382
Enoch	3	DE	238	Susannah	7	DE	368	Sarah M	3	DE	382
Frances A	34	MD	238	Theodore	7	DE	158	Sidney	35	DE	56
Francis	8/12	DE	383	Thomas	22	DE	48	Thomas C	65	DE	138
Frederick	11	DE	383	Thomas	49	NJ	158	William	11	DE	57
Gemima	23	DE	81	Thomas A	5	DE	369	William	14	DE	138
George	26	DE	318	William	5	DE	221	William T	24	DE	288
George	32	DE	297	William	7	DE	367	Alrichs, Martha P	61	DE	307
George	33	DE	296	William	8	DE	354	Peter S	64	DE	307
George W	8/12	DE	239	William	60	GB	354	Alsop, Rachel	5	PA	165
Hannah	21	DE	225	Wilmina	2	DE	192	Rachel G	32	NJ	165
Hannah	23	DE	318	Winfield Scott	1	DE	180	Samuel	9	PA	165
Hester	2	DE	354	Aller, Emily	12	MD	230	Samuel	37	PA	165
Hester A	11	DE	368	Allfry, Ann	25	DE	244	Alston, Ann S	63	MD	295
Hetty	10	DE	299	John C	9	DE	244	John	50	MD	205
Hutson	22	DE	316	William	50	DE	244	Amer, Edward	19	PA	164
Isaac	1	DE	221	William A	1	DE	244	John	33	ST	272
Isaac	35	DE	221	Allis, Caroline	16	DE	384	Amoy, Wm	21	PA	261
Jacob	18	DE	231	Allison, Andrew	28	IE	2	Amphery, Edward	25	DE	398
Jacob	18	DE	244	Joseph	36	IE	185	Anderson, Abanus	13	DE	122
James	35	DE	346	Mary	30	IE	185	Abraham	40	DE	153
Jammah	23	DE	318	Allman, Lewis	42	DE	218	Abraham	40	DE	309
Jane	40	PA	354	Allmon, Sarah	13	MD	382	Albert	3	DE	118
Jane	48	DE	289	Almond, Jane	48	DE	293	Alexander M	22	DE	310
Jane	74	DE	298	John G	19	DE	293	Alfred	7	DE	122
Jeremiah	25	DE	239	Allrichs, John	4	DE	328	Alfred J	12	DE	146
Jeremiah	64	NJ	238	Allston, Abner	2	DE	256	Alice	49	DE	125
Jerry	30	DE	192	Abner M	59	MD	256	Allen	13	DE	11
John	6/12	DE	158	Anthony	5	DE	170	Amanda	9	DE	325
John	3	DE	221	Arthur	56	DE	234	Andrew	23	DE	262
John	3.	DE	367	Eliza	4	DE	218	Andrew	45	DE	4
John	48	DE	377	Eliza	32	DE	218	Ann	9	DE	42
Joshua	26	DE	346	Francis A	15	DE	170	Ann	17	PA	371

Name	Age	State	Page
Anderson, Ann	36	DE	11
Ann	73	DE	167
Anna	52	DE	267
Araminta	5	DE	125
Betty	2	DE	242
Caroline	3	DE	325
Caroline	33	DE	263
Caroline	48	DE	90
Catherine	10/12	DE	152
Catherine	18	DE	230
Catherine	26	DE	152
Charles	8	DE	252
Charles	28	NJ	25
Charles E	25	DE	175
Charlott	35	MD	316
Christopher	19	DE	230
Clara	1	DE	11
Clementine	8	DE	213
D B	41	DE	153
Daniel B	16	DE	153
David	11	DE	263
David	45	DE	262
Deby A	22	DE	157
Dennis	19	DE	182
Edward	6	DE	152
Edward	12	DE	230
Edward H	36	DE	152
Elias	20	PA	323
Eliza	12	PA	112
Eliza	16	DE	100
Eliza J	8	DE	157
Elizabeth	23	DE	285
Elizabeth	27	MD	336
Elizabeth	30	DE	118
Elizabeth	36	MD	366
Elizabeth	64	DE	57
Elizabeth J	43	DE	310
Elmira	24	PA	33
Emma	11	DE	157
Emma	19	DE	309
Eve	60	DE	41
Ezekiel	30	DE	222
Frank	7	DE	252
George	1	DE	267
George	5	DE	118
George	20	DE	290
George	23	DE	326
George	30	DE	324
George	40	DE	155
Hannah	20	DE	114
Hannah	23	DE	255
Hannah	24	DE	33
Harriet	15	DE	263
Harriet	32	DE	252
Harriet J	12	DE	153
Hester	16	DE	65
Hester A	24	PA	153
Hester E	22	DE	170
Hester J	9	DE	287
Isabella	60	DE	339
Jacob	9	DE	11
Jacob	10	DE	255
Jacob	38	DE	11
James	1	DE	65
James	6	DE	84
James	9	DE	231
James	19	DE	309
James	21	IE	375
James	23	VA	29
James	46	DE	122
James	49	DE	322
James	50	MD	65
James L	9	DE	153
James M	3	DE	366
James R	27	PA	170
Jane	3	DE	153
Jane	13	DE	29
Jane	22	VA	19
Jane	35	MD	153
Jane	47	PA	287
Jane	50	DE	309
Jane	74	MD	278
Anderson, Jesse	24	DE	285
Jessie D	65	DE	289
John	8	DE	125
John	14	PA	163
John	23	DE	33
John	25	PA	267
John	35	MD	307
John	40	DE	47
John	42	DE	263
John	50	DE	90
John D	9/12	DE	4
John D	22	DE	183
Joseph	8	DE	42
Joseph	11	DE	11
Joseph	12	DE	319
Josephine	7	DE	153
Josiah	16	DE	125
Josiah	35	DE	118
Josiah	45	DE	377
Layman	50	MD	125
Levi	30	DE	42
Lucy	12	DE	69
Lydia E	8	PA	295
Margaret	3/12	DE	196
Margaret	14	DE	325
Margaret	30	DE	196
Margaret	31	MD	327
Margaret	35	DE	121
Margaret	45	NJ	156
Maria	40	DE	392
Martha	7/12	DE	153
Martha	6	MD	327
Martha	25	DE	4
Mary	7/12	DE	153
Mary	5	DE	263
Mary	14	DE	325
Mary	25	DE	242
Mary	25	GB	267
Mary	28	DE	42
Mary	45	DE	41
Mary	50	DE	175
Mary	50	DE	255
Mary E	4	DE	222
Mary R	11	DE	156
Matilda	16	DE	255
Matilda	16	DE	260
Matilda	18	DE	69
Matilda A	19	PA	295
Morris	6	DE	118
Nancy M	17	PA	295
Nelson	20	DE	211
Perry	50	MD	321
Phillis	56	DE	387
Priscilla	55	DE	47
Rachel	3	DE	252
Rachel	13	DE	326
Rachel	25	DE	244
Rachel	29	DE	325
Rachel	60	MD	157
Rachel	68	DE	167
Rebecca	16	DE	263
Rebecca	39	DE	65
Reuben	28	DE	267
Richard	22	DE	208
Robert	45	DE	156
Sally	58	DE	289
Sam	17	DE	251
Saml	3	DE	255
Saml	9	DE	252
Saml	10	DE	252
Saml	45	DE	255
Samuel	20	DE	309
Samuel	22	DE	277
Sarah	1	DE	252
Sarah	10	DE	65
Sarah	13	DE	263
Sarah	15	DE	252
Sarah	25	DE	377
Sarah	44	DE	262
Sarah	45	MD	157
Sarah	49	DE	122
Sewell	30	DE	244
Anderson, Susan	5	DE	325
Susannah	1	DE	222
Susannah	25	DE	222
Theodore	10	DE	122
Thomas	5	IE	84
Thomas	40	DE	252
Thomas	45	DE	366
Unity	18	DE	359
Watson	12	PA	163
Wesley	8	MD	327
William	4/12	DE	242
William	2	DE	325
William	18	DE	65
William	23	DE	331
William	26	MD	185
William	76	DE	118
William A	3	DE	4
William S	18	DE	153
William T	6	DE	222
Wm	6	DE	255
Wm H	8/12	DE	285
Andrews, Alexander	24	DE	210
Bina	35	DE	127
Ella	4	DE	311
Hannah A	3	DE	210
Harriet	22	DE	210
Harriet	50	DE	211
James	25	DE	313
John	6	DE	41
John N	12	DE	311
John W	36	DE	311
Mary	28	DE	210
Mary	35	PA	311
Mary E	14	DE	211
Mary N	14	DE	311
Richard	1	DE	211
Robert	16	DE	311
Wesley	1	DE	210
William A	11	DE	210
Andrie, Marianna	16	PA	81
Angle, Margaret	25	IE	396
Ankins, Albina	57	PA	149
Susan	17	DE	149
Ansen, Sarah	3	DE	149
Ansley, E A	45	CN	163
Anson, David	34	GB	149
George	10	GB	149
James	1	DE	149
Mary	8	DE	149
Sabra	33	GB	149
William	6	DE	149
Anthony, Catherine	20	DE	224
Catharine	58	MD	380
Eliza	75	NY	282
Ellen A	19	MD	380
Frances	1	DE	224
Joseph	24	MD	380
Samuel	42	MD	380
Applebee, Franklin	35	NJ	261
Isabella	25	DE	261
Sarah	7	DE	261
Appleby, David	7	DE	302
David	27	GB	197
George W	15	DE	64
James	5	DE	64
Jane	3	DE	63
Jesse	3	DE	302
John	9	DE	64
John	40	GB	64
John T	3	DE	197
Martha	7	DE	63
Martha	35	DE	64
Oliver H	9	DE	302
Rachel A	32	DE	302
Rebecca	21	DE	197
Richard T	10	DE	302
Sarah	26	PA	63
Sarah J	4/12	DE	64
Sarah J	1	DE	197
Thomas	3	DE	64
Thomas	5	DE	302
Thomas	20	DE	122

Name	Age	St	Pg
Appleby, Thomas	36	GB	302
William	1	DE	303
Applegate, Fran	1/12	DE	313
Jane	30	ST	313
Jemima	3	DE	313
John	30	DE	313
William	25	PA	313
Appleton, Ann E	7	DE	196
Anna E	2	DE	182
Anna E	27	DE	210
Edward	10	DE	210
Eliza C	40	NJ	196
Eugene	4	DE	182
John	17	DE	196
John M	46	DE	210
John M	15	DE	210
John W	15	DE	182
Lavinia	26	DE	182
Lucy L	11	DE	182
Nicholas B	42	DE	196
Rachel	48	DE	210
Thomas D	38	DE	182
Whilmina	13	DE	196
William	15	DE	196
Araboy, Eliza	30	DE	256
Arbuckle, Henry	20	DE	199
Sarah	27	PA	302
Archary, Joseph	13	DE	315
Joseph	50	DE	315
Maria	44	DE	315
Arche, Ann E	19	DE	322
Grace	60	MD	322
William H	19	DE	322
Archer, Aaron	5	DE	215
Charlotte	60	PA	251
Emily	7	DE	215
Isaac	35	DE	215
Joseph	3	DE	249
Joseph	83	PA	251
Judy	45	DE	249
Margaret	7	DE	249
Rachel	25	DE	215
Archy, Elias	30	DE	257
Maria	7	DE	215
Philip	10	DE	215
Ardis, Amanda	22	PA	285
Mary	3	PA	285
Robert	28	DE	285
Sarah E	7/12	PA	285
Argrove, Patrick	20	IE	195
Arment, Newlin	53	PA	272
Phebe A	16	PA	272
Sidney A	23	PA	272
Armey, Jesse	38	PA	310
Armor, Ann	68	DE	365
Catherine	17	DE	365
Caroline	7	DE	365
Ellen C	5	DE	373
George S	8	DE	373
James	38	DE	365
Mariam	31	DE	372
Smith	25	DE	322
Sophia	6	DE	365
Thomas	33	DE	372
William	4	DE	365
Armstrong, Adaline	11	DE	387
Alexander N	11	DE	191
Amanda E	17	DE	364
Andrew	52	IE	301
Andrew	80	DE	369
Ann	25	DE	364
Ann	34	DE	364
Ann	44	DE	357
Ann	80	PA	389
Ann E	9	DE	358
Ann Mary	5	DE	357
Anna C	4	PA	114
Anna J	6	DE	387
Anna L	2	DE	389
Anna M	9	DE	363
Archibald	29	DE	380
Benjamin	24	DE	191
Armstrong, Benjamin	45	DE	174
Benjamin	46	DE	357
Benjamin E	2	DE	363
Benjamin V	69	DE	191
Bridget	33	IE	156
Catherine	13	NJ	302
Catherine	15	DE	244
Caroline	22	DE	301
Caroline	22	DE	383
Dorcas	25	DE	8
Edgar P	2	DE	152
Edmund	4	DE	351
Edward	63	DE	333
Eleanor J	2	DE	333
Eliza	25	DE	33
Eliza	38	PA	56
Elizabeth	6	IE	136
Elizabeth	21	DE	353
Elizabeth	23	DE	393
Elizabeth	50	PA	364
Elizabeth E	4	DE	363
Ella E	5	DE	359
Ellen	5	DE	8
Ellen	8	DE	214
Emily	6	DE	8
Ester A	25	DE	3
Frances	15	DE	214
Frances	45	DE	214
George	35	DE	102
George D	28	DE	33
Hannah L	22	DE	345
Harriet A	6	DE	174
Henry	28	PA	118
Henry C	2	DE	357
Hester	12	DE	301
Hester	40	DE	351
Hiram	6	DE	389
Isabella	3	DE	33
James	9/12	DE	118
James	18	IE	316
James	28	DE	362
James	35	IE	136
James	39	DE	389
James	55	IE	316
James E	11	IE	136
Jane	13	IE	33
Jane	41	PA	56
Jane	52	DE	66
Jane	70	DE	358
John	9/12	DE	33
John	18	DE	345
John	40	DE	358
John	64	DE	345
John C	19	DE	214
John G	5	DE	191
John M	8	DE	389
John P	42	DE	363
John S	2	PA	114
Joseph	21	DE	196
Joseph M	1	DE	191
Joseph M	34	DE	191
K A	15	MD	165
Lewis P	28	PA	152
Luran D	20	DE	345
Lydia	55	DE	110
Malon	11	DE	357
Margaret	18	DE	353
Margaret	50	IE	316
Margaret	70	DE	364
Margaret J	17	DE	191
Maria	20	DE	301
Maria J	10	DE	389
Martha	15	DE	357
Mary	11	ME	165
Mary	22	DE	69
Mary	28	DE	152
Mary	30	DE	387
Mary	34	DE	368
Mary	40	IE	33
Mary	45	DE	353
Mary	64	DE	192
Mary A	27	DE	301
Armstrong, Mary D	28	DE	345
Mary E	3	DE	191
Mary E	8	DE	174
Mary E	12	MD	389
Mary E	23	DE	364
Mary F	14	DE	333
Mary J	33	DE	191
Mary P	14	DE	387
Mary W	39	DE	333
Matilda	15	DE	301
Matilda	33	DE	314
Nancy	5	DE	392
Naomi K	8/12	DE	387
Nathaniel	15	DE	345
Patric	21	IE	136
Phebe A	35	PA	118
Priscilla	40	DE	174
Rachel	19	DE	364
Rachel	32	DE	364
Rachel Ann	17	DE	348
Rachel G	40	DE	358
Rebecca	14	DE	345
Rebecca	49	DE	301
Rebecca A	4/12	DE	152
Richard	25	DE	193
Robert	18	DE	387
Robert	43	DE	387
Robert A	4	IE	136
Robert J	17	DE	293
Robert F	15	DE	364
Saml	40	DE	358
Samuel	40	DE	351
Samuel	51	DE	214
Samuel F	22	DE	8
Sarah	12	NJ	207
Sarah	19	DE	353
Sarah	50	DE	158
Sarah	50	PA	389
Sarah	52	DE	293
Sarah A	7	DE	333
Sarah A	37	MD	389
Sarah D	23	DE	193
Sarah R	20	DE	191
Sarah S	32	DE	380
Spencer P	16	DE	387
Susan	22	IE	316
Susan	25	PA	114
Susan	35	IE	318
Susan C	35	DE	363
Susan D	20	DE	345
T Anne	10	DE	304
Thomas	20	IE	316
Thomas	26	IE	33
Thomas A	10	DE	174
Thomas L	9	DE	345
Washington M	6	DE	191
William	4	DE	118
William	15	IE	295
William	16	IE	316
William	19	DE	377
William	20	DE	357
William	30	DE	364
William	31	DE	358
William	49	NJ	303
William H	12	IE	136
William W	5	DE	152
William W	22	DE	244
Arnal, James	25	MA	171
Arno, John	30	PA	135
Arnold, Abagale	2	FR	107
Alie	6/12	DE	107
Elizabeth	21	NH	165
Mr	23	FR	106
Pauline	22	FR	107
Arnstead, Delia	10	VA	161
George	50	VA	161
Mary	48	VA	161
Aserig, Sophia	56	DE	287
Ash, Amanda	18	DE	263
Charles	10	DE	263
Cornelia	12	DE	263
Ellen	24	DE	283

Name	Age	ST	No.
Ash, Emma	3	DE	263
George	14	DE	263
Helen	25	DE	276
Jesse	23	PA	263
John	24	IE	93
Laura	6	DE	263
Mary	3	DE	276
Matilda	30	MD	263
Phebe	32	IE	93
Susan	7/12	DE	276
Susan	35	DE	263
William	60	IE	93
Ashbowhan, Elizabeth	68	IE	143
Ashbridge, Catherine	4	DE	329
John	1	DE	329
Mary A	25	PA	329
Thomas	30	PA	329
Ashcraft, Wells	22	MD	90
William	25	NJ	239
Ashley, Christopher	44	GB	312
John	7	NJ	312
Martin	9	PA	312
Mary	44	PA	312
Ashton, Adelina S	33	NJ	297
Albert D	1	DE	297
Charles K	8	MD	297
Cynthia	63	NJ	375
Lewis	63	NJ	375
Lewis Jr	38	NJ	297
Lewis W	3	DE	297
Sarah	83	MD	371
Asia, Thomas	30	NJ	96
Askew, Ann	5	DE	151
Edward	23	MD	55
Elizabeth R	13	DE	106
Fannie E	17	DE	106
H F (Dr)	45	DE	106
Hannah	22	GB	151
Joseph	90	PA	64
Joseph W	21	MD	4
Mary H	42	DE	106
Mary L	7	DE	106
Thomas	32	GB	151
Aspril, Ann	50	DE	202
Ann Eliza	17	DE	202
Charles B	10	DE	202
Hestalina	17	DE	202
Isaac	16	DE	200
James	24	DE	200
John	62	DE	202
John A	19	DE	202
Lawrence	26	DE	200
Maria	52	DE	200
Asprill, David	2	DE	171
Leonard	30	DE	171
Leonard V	5/12	DE	171
Mary	30	DE	171
Atherton, Charles	14	PA	17
Elizabeth	45	PA	17
Henry	15	PA	17
Thomas	49	PA	17
Attison, James	26	DE	324
Atwell, John	30	IE	194
Augusta, Rachel	35	DE	244
Augustus, Amelia	56	MD	74
David	27	MD	74
Hannah	85	DE	335
John	51	DE	335
Perry	80	MD	74
Ault, Martha M	10	PA	358
Austin, Anna E	7	DE	391
Anna S	8	PA	372
Catherine A	28	MD	391
Eliza	25	IE	328
Elizabeth	18	PA	372
Elizabeth	48	PA	372
Harriet	18	NY	266
Hiram	39	MD	391
Mary A	14	PA	372
Rachel M	21	PA	372
Sarah	11	PA	372
Susan	2	DE	391
Austin, Susan A	16	PA	372
William D	5	DE	391
Aydelott, George H	35	DE	186
John B W	12	DE	186
Julia A	32	DE	186
Roselle	5/12	DE	186
Sarah S	10	DE	186
Zadoc	5	DE	186
Ayden, Amanda	7	DE	87
Caroline	13	DE	87
Jonathan	38	GB	87
Margaret	35	DE	87
Tamer	9	DE	87
Thomas	14	DE	87
Thomas	72	GB	87
Ayers, Edward	42	DE	126
Eliza	3	DE	387
Emily	35	NJ	126
Hannah	26	PA	398
John W	18	PA	363
Margaret A	11	PA	400
Sarah E	5	DE	126
William	16	PA	362
Ayres, Ann	29	IE	373
Anna M	5	NJ	284
Catherine	8	DE	373
Charles	14	PA	271
Eliza	1	DE	271
Eliza	47	NJ	271
Elizabeth	2	DE	373
James B	50	PA	271
Jeptha	29	NJ	284
John	35	IE	373
Joseph	10	DE	271
Margaret	35	IE	264
Mary	11	DE	373
Sarah N	28	NJ	284
Sophia	6	DE	373
Babcock, Lucy	25	CT	130
Babet, Margaret	53	DE	10
Bacchus, Alfred	13	DE	387
Ann	23	DE	231
David	51	DE	231
Elizabeth	13	DE	391
George	15	DE	377
Hester	5	DE	231
Isaac	36	DE	394
Israel	40	DE	387
John	1	DE	231
Margaret	54	DE	394
Richard	17	DE	377
Sewall	8	DE	231
Susan	38	DE	387
William	12	DE	182
Bachelor, Bruno	44	NH	365
Charles G	5	PA	365
Harriet C	10	SC	365
Sarah	42	VT	365
Susannah	9/12	PA	365
Bachus, Anna	11	DE	251
Asa	1	DE	251
Benjamin	5	DE	251
David	3	PA	77
David	11	DE	81
Elizabeth	30	DE	81
Henry	12	PA	77
Isaac	--	DE	291
Isaac	30	DE	81
Isaac	35	DE	298
James	8	DE	251
James	40	PA	77
Liston	40	DE	251
Margaret	30	DE	251
Nancy	68	DE	360
Nat	1	DE	251
Nero	5	PA	77
Priscilla	50	DE	137
Rachel	35	PA	77
Backhouse, Agnes P	3	DE	382
Ann E	10	MD	308
Clara	33	MD	308
Backhouse, Elizabeth	14	DE	295
Ellen J	1	DE	308
Henry	9	DE	382
Isabella	12	DE	295
Jacob	38	DE	295
Jeremiah	5	MD	308
John	8	MD	308
John	34	DE	308
Margaret	40	MD	295
Martha A	11	MD	308
Martha M	5	DE	382
Percy C	3	MD	308
Sarah J	6	DE	295
William	11	DE	295
Backson, John	30	DE	222
Rodney A	2	DE	222
Sarah A	19	DE	222
Isaac	35	MD	299
Bacon, Anne	23	PA	177
Joseph	25	PA	177
Mary	11	DE	363
Wm	9	DE	321
Baer, Patrick	20	IE	336
Baety, Catherine	27	PA	388
Bagger, Ann	20	PA	340
Charles L	25	DE	340
Eliza J	8	MD	340
Baggs, James	19	DE	158
William	24	DE	340
Baghouse, Eli	38	GB	379
Hannah	35	GB	379
Bagley, Margaret	27	IE	53
Bagner, Mich	35	IE	274
Bags, Alfred	5	DE	71
Eli	29	PA	71
Sarah	23	PA	71
Theodore	1	DE	71
Bailey, Abner	8	DE	107
Abner	33	DE	107
Edward	2	DE	91
Eli	17	DE	197
Elizabeth	8	DE	373
Elizabeth	18	DE	78
Emma	4	DE	107
Emmanuel	10	DE	383
George	5/12	DE	107
George	7	DE	47
George	35	DE	47
Grace	98	DE	47
Henry	10	DE	107
Jacob	17	DE	358
James	43	DE	358
James B	13	DE	160
John	4	DE	47
Joseph J	52	DE	160
Levinia	35	DE	107
Louis	20	DE	383
Margaret	3/12	DE	47
Margaret	29	DE	91
Margaret	38	PA	358
Maria	29	DE	47
Martha A	8	DE	214
Martha M	14	DE	358
Mary	27	DE	170
Priscilla H	18	PA	160
Samuel A	10	DE	358
Sarah	8	DE	47
Sarah	21	DE	214
Sidney	22	DE	160
Thomas	42	DE	369
William	22	DE	346
Baily, Alfred	30	DE	377
Anna A	8/12	DE	377
Anna L	22	DE	373
Charlotta	45	DE	153
Daniel	50	DE	153
Eliza	21	PA	371
Elizabeth	27	GB	365
Elizabeth	29	NY	372
George	6	DE	153
George	15	DE	377
Hannah	30	IE	374

Name	Age	St	Pg
Baily, Hannah J	55	NY	372
Hannah M	17	DE	373
Isaac	9/12	DE	371
Jane	5	DE	374
Jane	13	DE	153
Jamimah	18	DE	246
John	40	DE	365
John W	5	DE	377
Joseph	3	DE	377
Malinda	37	DE	377
Margaret	3	DE	377
Margaret	50	DE	370
Martha E	20	DE	373
Mary	3	DE	374
Mary A	12	DE	377
Mary J	27	DE	373
Matilda	1	DE	375
Philena	14	DE	368
Rachel A	8	DE	377
Rebecca C	24	DE	373
Robert	8	DE	153
Samuel	40	IE	374
Samuel	56	DE	372
Sarah A	25	DE	373
Sarah E	4	DE	365
Sharlott	50	DE	355
Stephen C	57	PA	373
Thomas	25	GB	371
Thomas T E	15	DE	373
Baines, Elizabeth	46	PA	337
Ellen	18	PA	337
Jess	61	PA	337
Baites, Daniel M	29	DE	100
George H	5	DE	100
Margaret H	25	MD	100
Sarah H	1	DE	100
Baker, Aaron	33	PA	399
Ann C	6	DE	160
Curtis	32	DE	198
Elias	30	DE	171
Eliza E	1	DE	169
Elizabeth	25	DE	292
Elizabeth	32	DE	160
G R (Dr)	37	PA	160
George	2	DE	171
George W	5	DE	285
Georgianna	7	DE	169
Henrietta	3	DE	285
Henry	28	MA	274
Henry R	35	DE	170
Isabella	24	PA	260
John	4/12	DE	120
John	17	PA	219
John	20	IE	323
John	65	NJ	285
John D	45	PA	264
Joseph	31	PA	260
Joshua	35	DE	85
Levi	7	DE	285
Lydia A	5	DE	292
Margaret	38	NJ	264
Mary	6/12	DE	260
Mary	30	MD	121
Mary	32	DE	169
Mary A	4	DE	171
Millard	2	PA	260
Reba G	4	DE	161
Samuel	10	DE	120
Samuel	13	DE	380
Sarah	8	DE	120
Sarah	28	MD	231
Sarah	30	PA	399
Sarah	40	NJ	285
Sarah J	9	DE	169
Susan	24	DE	171
Thomas C	2	PA	399
William	7	DE	120
William	35	MD	120
William G	5	DE	169
Wm	5	PA	260
Wm	27	GB	266
Balcher, Araminty	14	DE	319
Balcher, John	19	DE	319
Baldwin, Ann	45	DE	372
Ann	50	PA	374
Benjamin	43	DE	332
Caroline	44	IE	297
Clark M	2	DE	278
Eli	9	DE	331
Elizabeth	3/12	DE	44
Eugenie	3	DE	44
George	6	DE	44
George	14	DE	356
Harlen	38	DE	44
Joseph M	12	DE	374
Laura	28	DE	374
Lewis H	14	DE	374
Lydia	61	DE	348
Lydia Ann	37	DE	348
Margaret	35	DE	44
Mary	19	DE	58
Mary	20	DE	372
Mary E	4	DE	278
Mary E	9	DE	374
Mary Jane	32	DE	348
Reece	27	PA	278
Robert	29	PA	278
Samuel S	21	PA	397
Sarah	22	MD	389
Sarah	24	DE	278
Sarah A	16	DE	374
Susannah	43	NJ	332
Thomas	28	DE	347
Thomas	70	DE	348
Victorine	28	DE	382
William	8	PA	44
William	18	DE	374
William	26	DE	130
William	63	DE	374
Balinger, Mary	74	NJ	95
Ball, Ales A	26	PA	322
Anabell	4	DE	375
Andrew	31	DE	141
Anna	38	DE	381
Benjamin	30	DE	385
David	45	DE	381
David L	3/12	DE	385
Eliza	28	DE	141
Emmy	58	DE	382
George	28	DE	350
George W	5	DE	385
Hannah	30	DE	104
Isabella	9/12	DE	370
James	31	DE	104
James	35	DE	381
Jesse B	31	DE	370
John	10/12	DE	322
John	22	DE	382
John	35	DE	322
John	60	DE	382
Joseph	55	DE	375
Josiah	23	DE	381
Margaret	18	DE	382
Margaret	60	DE	322
Mary	30	DE	370
Mary	34	PA	385
Montgomery	1	DE	350
Rachel	8	DE	381
Rachel	32	DE	137
Rebecca J	39	DE	341
Reuben	25	DE	382
Samuel	2	DE	104
Sarah	20	DE	350
Sarah	80	IE	49
Sarah E	2	DE	322
Susanna	35	DE	375
Victoria	7	DE	385
William H	6	DE	385
Ballar, Emma	3	DE	134
Lydia	36	PA	134
Robert	31	DE	134
Balm, Alice	25	GB	122
John T	13	DE	122
William	26	GB	122
Banard, Sarah	13	DE	78
Bancroft, Joseph	47	GB	332
Samuel	10	DE	332
Sarah P	46	DE	332
Wm P	15	DE	332
Bandy, Dinah	30	DE	331
John	2	DE	400
John	26	DE	331
Victorine E	52	FR	342
Bange, William H	15	NJ	292
Baning, Caroline	21	MD	368
Josephine	2	DE	368
Robert	34	DE	368
Banks, Ann	1	DE	22
Charles	14	DE	38
Charlotte	12	VA	365
Elizabeth	2	DE	366
Elizabeth	12	DE	38
Emeline	20	PA	100
George W	23	PA	100
Henrietta	25	DE	22
Henry	4/12	DE	38
Henry	45	DE	38
Jane	22	GB	366
Joseph W	23	DE	22
Margaret	16	DE	269
Martha	39	MD	38
Mary J	28	IE	308
Saber	25	GB	366
William	18	DE	210
William	32	GB	308
Bannard, Charles	21	DE	77
Eliza	56	DE	77
Eliza J	7	DE	77
Ester	38	DE	77
Mary C	17	DE	77
William	4	DE	77
William	30	DE	77
William	54	DE	77
Banner, Eliza	40	DE	131
Elizabeth	4	DE	76
George	2	DE	76
George	5	DE	68
George	38	DE	76
Henry	28	DE	78
James	34	DE	68
John	8	DE	131
John	36	DE	131
Lewis	6	DE	131
Margaret	25	DE	76
Martha E	4	PA	78
Martha H	11	DE	131
Mary	31	DE	68
Robert	2	DE	68
Sally A	12	DE	131
Sarah	26	NJ	78
William	11	DE	68
William H	2	DE	78
Banning, Alice P	24	DE	359
Elizabeth	57	DE	359
Emely	24	AG	98
Henry G	34	MD	98
James	2	DE	98
John	30	DE	359
John A	60	DE	359
Margaret	14	DE	86
Mary	7	DE	359
Sarah A	20	DE	359
Sarah G	72	DE	98
William S	9	DE	359
Bannister, Ann	70	GB	72
Thomas	80	DE	189
Barabas, Emma	20	GB	380
George	1/12	DE	380
James	27	GB	380
Barands, Elizabeth	31	DE	283
Ellen	9	PA	283
John E	6	PA	283
William	7	PA	283
William	34	PA	283
Barber, Amanda	14	PA	151
Amanda K	15	NJ	131

Name	Age	State	Page
Barber, Anna M	7	DE	301
Elizabeth	4	DE	137
Elizabeth	53	DE	90
Hannah	4/12	DE	137
Hester	9	DE	207
J L	38	PA	137
James	21	MD	327
John	73	DE	90
Lewis	9	MD	327
Mary	37	DE	137
Mary	51	DE	315
Mary E	12	DE	301
Peter	41	DE	301
Rachel	39	DE	301
Rebecca J	19	PA	151
Samuel	12	DE	137
Sarah	13	DE	151
Sarah	15	DE	53
Sarah	48	NJ	151
Thomas	40	DE	315
William	24	MD	327
William H	'9	DE	301
Bardsly, Daniel	35	GE	127
John T	5/12	DE	127
Martha	32	GB	127
Sarah	12	GB	127
Barge, Anna	14	DE	109
Barkely, James	32	PA	381
Barker, Ann	40	DE	58
Elizabeth	12	PA	360
Hannah	8	DE	360
Henry	28	NJ	89
James	25	DE	57
John	42	MD	308
Joseph	10	PA	360
Joshua	5	DE	360
Joshua B	39	DE	360
Martha	15	DE	89
Martha	37	PA	360
Patrick	20	IE	361
Phenix	35	MD	31
Priscilla	18	DE	89
Rebecca	3	DE	360
Sarah	15	PA	360
Sarah	36	DE	308
Williamina	4	DE	57
Barkley, Ann E	5	PA	355
George	28	PA	355
Jane	14	GB	159
Margaret	4	PA	355
Margaret	40	MD	355
Mary E	3	PA	355
Mary J	21	DE	56
Rebecca Jane	11	PA	355
Samuel	32	IE	36
Barlow, Ann E	14	PA	353
Ashton	52	GB	353
Caroline	5	DE	276
Curtis	57	PA	276
David O	24	DE	281
Deborah	15	DE	276
Elizabeth	17	DE	276
Elizabeth	18	DE	281
Ellen	22	PA	353
Felix	23	DE	243
George	12	DE	381
Gideon E	35	DE	240
Harriet	22	PA	282
Mary A	48	NJ	276
Mary A	48	DE	353
Milton S	29	DE	276
Rachel	25	MD	276
Susan	11	DE	240
Susan	44	DE	240
Barm, Francis	24	DE	230
Henry	25	GE	273
Barman, Henry	18	DE	310
Barnaby, Andrew	23	DE	258
Ella	4	DE	295
Joseph	39	DE	295
Joseph W	2	DE	295
Josephine	3	DE	295
Barnaby, Rosanna	27	MD	295
Barnard, Charlotte	22	DE	82
Coleman	9/12	DE	82
John	23	DE	82
Barnatt, Jane	19	PA	265
Barnell, Almira	6	DE	390
John	25	DE	390
Sarah	24	DE	390
William	2	DE	390
Barnes, Frances	24	DE	229
Samuel	14	DE	199
Barnet, Amelia	15	DE	360
John	17	DE	364
Barnett, Alfred	40	GB	333
Andrew	40	GB	333
Caroline	21	DE	364
Elizabeth	24	DE	218
Elizabeth	48	DE	366
Elizabeth	55	DE	218
Elizabeth E	2	DE	218
Emma	1	PA	333
George	60	DE	366
Jacob	5	DE	232
John	16	NJ	232
John	18	DE	366
John	26	DE	218
John	52	NJ	232
Joseph	18	DE	366
Margaret	6/12	DE	218
Mary	30	GB	333
Matilda	50	NJ	232
Samuel	14	DE	232
William A	12	DE	217
Barney, Edward	30	DE	79
Elizabeth	29	DE	79
Elizabeth H	3	DE	304
Elmer	3	DE	79
Emma	7/12	DE	79
James	40	DE	104
Malen	5	DE	79
Solomon	30	DE	7
Barnhill, Eliza	12	PA	305
Elizabeth	24	DE	305
George	1	DE	305
Michael	27	PA	305
Barns, Alexander	30	IE	345
Elizabeth	28	DE	93
Grady	40	DE	93
Henry	9	DE	93
James	15	DE	93
James	42	DE	93
John	1	DE	345
Rebecca	50	IE	345
Sarah	6	DE	345
Sidney	28	DE	345
William	4	DE	345
Barr, Adam H P	10	DE	132
Alexander	28	DE	213
Ann	35	IE	328
Ann E	17	DE	296
Anna H	8	DE	296
Caroline D	14	DE	287
Caroline T	48	DE	287
Catherine A	33	DE	132
Catherine F	29	PA	395
Christiana	11	DE	369
Clara A	15	PA	395
Edmond	3/12	DE	132
Elizabeth A	13	DE	132
Elizabeth P	50	DE	279
Emily	10	DE	281
Emma	12	DE	80
Enos	14	DE	132
George	3	DE	272
George P	18	PA	279
Henrietta	1	DE	383
Henry	10	DE	380
Isaac B	5	DE	43
Isabella	42	DE	80
James	2	DE	281
James	7	DE	369
James	55	IE	356
Barr, Jane	17	DE	369
John	15	DE	369
John	33	DE	272
John	59	ST	296
John H	21	DE	80
John H	49	PA	80
John T	19	DE	111
Joseph	3	DE	132
Joseph	40	DE	132
Joseph	51	DE	314
Joseph	58	DE	395
Joseph M	26	DE	160
Margaret	19	DE	80
Margaret	41	DE	16
Margaretta	2	DE	16
Margaretta	47	DE	296
Mary	20	DE	383
Mary	55	DE	314
Mary A	8	DE	16
Mary R	25	DE	279
Paul	33	DE	281
Rachel	22	DE	281
Robert H	25	DE	296
Robert H	61	PA	279
Robert H Jr	23	PA	279
Robert M	4	DE	16
Ruth	30	CT	272
Samuel	11	DE	286
Samuel	43	DE	16
Sarah	7	DE	272
Sarah	40	DE	367
Sarah	47	MD	369
Sarah	56	DE	395
Sarah F	1	DE	281
Susan	20	DE	367
Wesley	5	DE	281
William H	9	DE	16
William H	40	IE	328
Wm	13	IE	328
Wm H	23	IE	337
Barrel, Catherine	1	IE	337
Christian	3	DE	337
Sarah	6	PA	127
Barrett, Anne	3	DE	127
Charles	4	DE	127
Elizabeth	2	DE	368
George	26	DE	368
George	3	DE	188
John	2	DE	127
Kate	26	DE	188
Latitia	26	DE	163
Margaret	6/12	DE	368
Marian	35	VT	143
Mary A	28	PA	127
Mrs	10	PA	373
Romuel	21	DE	368
Sarah	16	DE	368
Susan	25	DE	368
Thomas	20	IE	349
William	30	PA	127
William	36	DE	188
Barry, Alexander	24	DE	119
Anna	18	DE	2
Samuel	21	DE	18
Thomas	18	IE	250
Thomas	28	DE	32
Barstow, J G (Dr)	29	DE	132
Rebecca	14	DE	34
Bartells, Frances D	6	GB	87
Hannah	37	GB	87
Jane E	4	GB	87
William	1	GB	87
William	35	GE	87
Barten, Edward	4	DE	117
Henrietta	24	DE	117
James	27	DE	117
James E	3/12	DE	117
Margaret	20	IE	7
Margaret J	--	DE	377
Patric	30	IE	7
Barthel, Hannah	31	DE	369
Thomas	36	MD	369

Bartlet, Elizabeth	49	MD	284	Basset, Emma	12	NJ	32	Batting, Sarah	8	PA	26
Sarah	40	MD	337	Franklin	4	DE	32	Batton, Alfred	10	DE	154
Bartlett, Alexander	5	DE	309	Granville	14	NJ	32	Andrew	25	DE	400
David	30	DE	219	Irene	10	NJ	32	Caroline	5	DE	154
Jacob	22	PA	263	Josiah	54	NJ	75	Elizabeth	2	DE	276
James M	14	DE	308	Mark S	44	NJ	32	George	8	DE	154
John T	15	DE	308	Martha	41	NJ	32	Joseph	2	DE	154
Joseph	10	DE	308	Mary	8	NJ	32	Margaret	12	DE	154
Joseph	38	MD	308	Nathan	6	NJ	32	Maria	40	DE	154
Juniper	3	DE	308	Rachel	40	DE	76	Mary	29	PA	276
Lucretia	40	MD	308	Rebecca	15	NJ	75	Matilda	20	DE	154
Maria	33	DE	219	Ruth	55	NJ	76	Rebecca	14	DE	154
Mary	35	DE	219	Susan M	47	DE	75	Ruben	19	DE	154
Mary A	7	DE	308	William	16	NJ	32	Thomas	32	DE	276
Susan	25	DE	219	Bassett, Elizabeth	93	IE	290	William	8	DE	351
William	1	DE	308	Jonathan	4	DE	240	William	54	DE	154
Bartley, Hasland	12	PA	359	Mary M	23	NJ	240	Batty, Sarah	26	IE	6
Honor	58	DE	332	Wesley	31	NJ	240	Bauchler, James A B	24	MD	182
James	58	DE	332	William F	5/12	DE	240	Baugh, Eliza	26	DE	99
Joseph	56	DE	281	Bassia, Margaret	37	SZ	153	Elizabeth	9	DE	99
Joseph H	14	DE	281	Frederic	42	SZ	153	George	6	DE	99
Josiah	47	DE	330	Bast, Joseph	11	?	313	George	36	DE	99
Lewis H	27	DE	332	Mary	15	?	313	William	5	DE	99
Lydia A	2-	DE	332	Baston, Ann	9	DE	74	Baxter, Alexander	19	IE	145
Margaret	16	DE	281	David	8/12	DE	74	Alexander	54	IE	333
Mary	47	DE	281	Ellen	36	DE	74	Andrew	45	IE	278
Bartly, Alfred	4	DE	237	Josiah	4	DE	74	Catherine	40	IE	326
John W	12	DE	241	Robert	39	DE	74	Catherine A	11/12	DE	278
Mary A	24	DE	237	Bateman, Edward	2	DE	271	E Isabella	7	DE	326
Nancy	50	DE	241	Elias	49	MD	271	Edward	16	IE	313
Samuel	8/12	DE	241	John	11	DE	271	James	27	IE	340
Samuel	30	DE	237	Margaret	14	DE	271	Jane	12	IE	326
Samuel	63	DE	241	Matilda	10	DE	271	Jane	22	IE	333
Sarah	47	DE	329	Rachel	3	DE	271	Jane	60	IE	333
William T	5	DE	237	Rachel	38	DE	271	John	22	GB	322
William T	7	DE	241	Richard	5	DE	271	Mary	18	IE	326
Bartman, Benj	36	PA	353	Bates, Amanda	6	NJ	40	Mary	26	IE	278
Benj F	3	DE	353	Ann E	7	NJ	114	Mary J	10/12	DE	278
Elizabeth	37	DE	353	Anna	8	PA	282	Michael	4	DE	326
Elwood	10	DE	353	Catherine	36	NJ	40	Peter	19	IE	102
Barton, Ann L	1	DE	83	Cornelius	22	PA	39	William	21	DE	385
John B	31	DE	83	David	8	DE	341	Bayan, John R	20	DE	330
Lydia	20	DE	363	Eliza J	14	DE	142	Bayard, Absolem H	3	DE	74
Margaret	20	DE	382	Elizabeth	2	DE	282	Adam	25	DE	74
Miller	18	DE	383	Elizabeth	23	VT	393	Albert B	8	DE	190
Sarah	29	PA	83	Elizabeth	33	NJ	114	Alexander	3	DE	188
William	16	DE	363	Elizabeth	54	DE	287	Alfred	10	DE	17
William	27	IE	163	Ellis	8	NJ	40	Andrew	30	DE	84
Bartram, Anne E	14	DE	69	Elwood	3	DE	114	Andrew J	16	MD	84
Charles H	12	DE	69	Eustace	13	NJ	40	Ann	47	MD	340
Hannah M	39	DE	69	Gideon	43	NJ	40	Ann F	46	PA	160
Henry W	42	PA	69	Hugh B	1/12	DE	341	Anna E	11/12	DE	84
Bartrum, Sarah A	17	DE	206	James	46	MD	341	Benjamin	5/12	DE	318
Barwick, Alexander	24	MD	341	James L	14	DE	341	Catherine	9	DE	84
Anna	20	MD	341	Jas A	35	PA	282	Caroline	12	DE	13
Joshua	1	DE	341	Lewis	14	NJ	40	Charles	4	DE	188
Rebecca	24	DE	341	Margaret	5	NJ	40	Charles M	8	MD	16
William J	17	MD	246	Margaret	6	PA	282	Charlotte	8	DE	74
Bashton, Martha	--	DE	290	Mary A	30	PA	282	Charlotte	21	DE	74
Baskut, Ann	14	DE	177	Robert	19	DE	292	David	42	DE	112
Baslove, John	16	IE	210	Samuel	17	IE	280	Edward	60	DE	190
Bass, Adda	10/12	DE	17	Sarah	10	NJ	40	Eliza	6	DE	84
Anna	52	DE	56	Sarah	40	DE	341	Eliza	14	DE	13
Eli	15	DE	298	William	10	NJ	114	Eliza	41	DE	112
Elizabeth	40	DE	54	William	36	DE	114	Eliza J	2	DE	319
Erwin	23	PA	362	Batman, Elias	18	MD	265	Eliza J	15	PA	75
Franklin	2	DE	17	Emily	2	MD	265	Elizabeth	3	DE	297
Henry T	1	DE	362	John	16	MD	265	Elizabeth	5	MD	16
Isaac B	5	DE	44	Mary	4	DE	265	Elizabeth	14	DE	84
Jacob	4	DE	17	Matilda	37	DE	265	Elizabeth	30	MD	16
Jacob	40	DE	17	Perry	6	MD	265	Elizabeth J	10	DE	190
James	21	DE	39	Rebecca	10	MD	265	Emma	16	DE	262
Jane	45	DE	54	Batten, Mary	14	PA	85	Eveline	40	DE	197
Jonathan	12	DE	17	Batterill, Anna	51	GB	399	Florence	8	DE	160
Lydia	35	DE	44	Joseph	49	GB	399	Frances	5	DE	74
Mary	28	PA	362	Battic, Anne	22	IE	148	Frances	24	DE	84
Mary	50	DE	56	John J	2	DE	148	Gemima	3/12	DE	84
Matilda	25	DE	17	Mary A	1	DE	148	George	8	DE	188
Marias	8	DE	17	William	28	IE	148	George	26	DE	331
Rebecca	38	DE	17	Battimere, Charles	23	GE	125	George	29	DE	267
Basset, Anne	59	NJ	76	Batting, Charles	21	GB	26	George W	2	DE	190
Elizabeth	60	NJ	76	Louisa	20	DE	26	Hannah	16	DE	208

Name	Age	St	Pg
Bayard, Harriet	29	MD	322
Harry	36	DE	319
Henard	25	DE	84
Henrietta	16	PA	187
Henrietta	32	DE	350
Henrietta	60	MD	187
Henry	6/12	DE	297
Henry	5	DE	188
Henry	38	DE	65
Hetty	35	DE	84
Isaiah	24	DE	65
Jacob	55	GE	295
Jacob	19	DE	340
James	7	DE	13
James	35	MD	13
James	53	MD	301
James A	60	DE	160
James H	2	DE	318
Jeremiah	59	DE	340
John	19	DE	267
Joseph	7/12	DE	322
Joseph	1	DE	13
Joseph	1	DE	188
Joseph	18	DE	252
Joseph	27	DE	187
Joseph	57	DE	322
Latitia	3	DE	13
Mable	11	DE	160
Margaret	33	MD	13
Margaret A	10	DE	112
Martha	13	DE	144
Martha	19	MD	33
Mary	16	MD	98
Mary	19	DE	64
Mary	20	DE	75
Matilda	5	DE	13
Millicent	33	DE	190
Millison	8	DE	322
Minte	4	DE	64
Minte	40	DE	64
Minte	56	DE	340
Oliver	25	DE	16
Rachel	22	DE	297
Rachel	31	DE	319
Rachel	35	MD	16
Richard	24	DE	297
Saba	2	DE	297
Sally A	16	DE	326
Sally A	24	MD	318
Saml	15	DE	309
Samuel	3	DE	322
Samuel	7	DE	188
Samuel	30	DE	188
Sarah	4/12	DE	64
Sarah	3	DE	84
Sarah	26	MD	58
Sophia	10	DE	64
Stephen	30	MD	84
Susan	25	DE	188
Thomas	9/12	DE	208
Thomas	6	DE	188
Thomas	44	MD	263
Thomas	71	MD	187
Thomas L	21	DE	160
William	6	DE	122
William	28	MD	318
William	33	MD	16
William F	2	DE	84
Bayer, Joseph	18	PA	135
Bayha, Eliza	12	DE	314
Bayles, Martha	35	DE	26
William	40	DE	26
Bayless, Anna	3	DE	86
John	7	DE	86
John R	39	DE	86
Mary	5	DE	86
Mary	27	PA	86
Samuel	1	DE	86
William	8	DE	86
Bayley, Catharine	15	DE	235
Edward	40	NJ	136
Emeline	32	MD	155
Bayley, Emerilla	10	DE	155
Florence	14	MD	165
Frances L	1	DE	155
Hannah	20	IE	137
John	33	MD	155
Margaret	13	DE	235
Margaret	22	IE	25
Mary	51	DE	235
Mary A	7	DE	155
Mary S	17	DE	235
Nathaniel	22	IE	25
Robert	19	DE	235
Sarah A	21	DE	235
Sarah E	2	DE	155
Wilson	17	IE	25
Bayliss, Charles	18	DE	291
John	63	MD	291
Hannah	22	DE	291
Margaret	63	NJ	291
Baynard, Eliza	50	MD	330
Elizabeth C	16	DE	133
Ellen C	35	MD	133
Frances	41	MD	31
George	30	MD	330
Henrietta	32	DE	351
Henry	32	DE	350
Margaret	29	MD	31
Margaret E	18	DE	133
Mary	21	MD	32
Mary	36	DE	146
Robert	51	DE	31
Sarah C	9	DE	133
Susan	8	MD	32
Susan A	12	DE	133
T H	45	DE	133
Williamina W	5	DE	133
Bayne, Ann	47	PA	392
Daniel	9	De	392
James	1	DE	390
James	24	PA	390
Mary S	25	DE	390
Nathaniel	4	DE	392
Robert	50	PA	392
Samuel	14	PA	392
William D	4	DE	392
Baynes, Azirah	15	DE	311
Eliza	32	DE	311
Emma E	2	DE	311
George	45	PA	311
George W	5	DE	311
Gilbert	13	DE	311
Bazin, Louis	20	DE	384
Bea, Benjamin	28	DE	367
Beach, James	36	DE	156
Beachman, Emma	3	PA	38
Hannah	26	DE	38
Margaret	4	PA	38
Thomas	1	PA	38
William	36	PA	38
Bealer, Catharine	32	GE	294
Jacob	25	GE	294
Beam, Isaac R	20	PA	304
Bean, Catherine	15	MD	164
Beard, Charles	14	DE	70
George	44	DE	70
Isaac	19	DE	70
Mary	41	DE	99
Mary A	44	DE	70
William	21	DE	70
Beare, Mary	21	GE	142
Beasly, Mary	52	DE	96
Thomas	39	GB	96
Beason, Amanda	6	PA	349
Amanda	41	PA	349
Elizabeth	11	PA	349
Elizabeth	66	PA	349
Filena	16	PA	349
George W	4	PA	349
John	2	PA	349
John	14	PA	349
John	41	DE	349
Sarah Ann	9	PA	349
Beason, Susan	20	PA	349
William	22	PA	349
Beastan, Ephraim	36	DE	210
Irene	2	DE	210
Leila A	3/12	DE	210
Wilmina	25	DE	210
Beaston, Sarah E	35	MD	343
Beatts, Ephraim	19	GB	380
Beatty, Alexander	2	DE	326
Eliza Jane	1	DE	326
Faithy	24	IE	326
John	18	PA	324
Lydia B	50	PA	323
Robert	26	IE	326
Beaty, Benjamin	42	DE	353
Edith S	13	DE	353
Elizabeth	66	DE	353
Ellen	11	DE	353
George A	13	DE	353
Harriet M	25	DE	353
Joseph H	17	DE	353
Lydia S	6	DE	353
Margaret	19	IE	13
Martha	47	PA	353
Mary A	30	DE	353
Sarah	17	PA	166
Beaumont, Mary H	14	PA	348
Beck, Amanda	16	DE	150
Ann V	4/12	DE	150
Elizabeth	8	DE	150
Frances	14	DE	150
Isaac	22	GB	291
Isabella	35	DE	231
James	18	DE	150
John	2	DE	231
John	7	DE	134
Joseph	35	DE	231
Joseph A	3	DE	134
Joseph W	30	MD	134
Milana	43	MD	150
Margaret A	5	DE	231
Mary	40	DE	134
Samuel	21	DE	224
Sarah E	10	DE	134
Walter	16	GB	251
William	7	DE	150
William	50	MD	150
Wm	23	GB	251
Becket, Alexander	5	DE	310
Ann	9/12	DE	318
Belinda	13	DE	190
Cecilia	25	DE	310
Charles	32	DE	310
Deborah	30	DE	244
Greensbury	37	DE	244
Henry	69	DE	351
John	2	DE	245
John	4	DE	318
Joseph H	1	DE	310
Joshua	3	DE	190
Louisa	7	DE	251
Lydia	10	DE	318
Maria	40	DE	318
Maria	42	MD	190
Mary	8	DE	244
Perry	5	DE	245
Peter	69	DE	351
Rachel	25	DE	92
Rebecca	2	DE	92
Rebecca	3	DE	310
Susan	12	DE	318
William	35	DE	190
William	35	DE	318
Zachariah	7	DE	244
Beckhart, Rachel	25	DE	143
Beckley, Catherine	10	DE	103
Rebecca	21	GB	103
Robinson	34	DE	103
Beckly, Albert J	8	PA	145
Amanda L	8	PA	283
Andrew J	9	PA	145
Anna M	28	PA	145

Name	Age	St	Pg	Name	Age	St	Pg	Name	Age	St	Pg
Beckly, George W	8	DE	104	Bell, Emily	2/12	DE	251	Bennet, William	34	DE	379
Harlen J	35	DE	145	Hannah E	5	DE	133	Wm	1	PA	272
Margaret A	6	DE	104	Henry	9	PA	294	Bennett, Amanda	4	DE	121
Mary	21	DE	149	Henry	25	DE	106	Alfred	20	DE	119
Sarah	55	DE	87	Isaac	13	DE	318	Catherine M	12	DE	228
William H	18	DE	87	Isaac	58	DE	45	Charles H	29	DE	110
William R	2	DE	104	John	2/12	MD	251	Elizabeth	9	DE	186
Becraft, Francis	24	PA	390	John M	35	NJ	133	Elizabeth	30	PA	305
Francis M	1	DE	390	Josiah	35	DE	355	Ezekle	6	DE	110
Catherine	60	PA	390	Lavinia	14	DE	185	George	4/12	DE	186
Bedford, Hannah	50	DE	155	Louisa	12	PA	164	George T	2	DE	369
Harriet	22	DE	33	Louisa	23	MD	251	James	15	DE	5
Henrietta J	50	DE	112	Margaret	32	DE	294	James	36	NJ	305
Sippell	57	DE	155	Maria	43	PA	330	John	13	DE	186
W H H	11	TN	163	Mary	60	PA	396	John	18	DE	5
Bedwell, Elizabeth	27	DE	229	Mary E	7	DE	133	Joseph	24	DE	119
James	3	DE	229	Robert	10	PA	294	Joseph L	38	DE	228
John	6/12	DE	229	Ruth	35	DE	45	Laurence	23	IE	122
John	31	DE	229	Samuel	74	PA	396	Lydia J	9/12	DE	369
Leonora	2/12	?	270	Samuel T C	21	DE	396	Mary	2	DE	186
Lewis	21	DE	105	Susannah	8	DE	45	Mary	28	NJ	121
Nancy	28	?	270	Tempy	65	DE	204	Mary	35	GE	186
Rebecca	45	DE	105	Thomas	19	PA	390	Mary	38	DE	228
Sarah	12	DE	105	William	36	DE	193	Mary A	15	DE	5
William	7	MD	105	William L	3	PA	396	Mary A	20	IE	122
William	7	MD	105	Wm L	33	DE	251	Mary A	26	DE	110
Beers, Elizabeth H	53	NY	113	Y James	17	DE	55	Mary A	60	DE	119
Joshua	56	NY	113	Bellah, Edward T	33	DE	306	Mary E	18	DE	228
Beeson, Anna	4/12	DE	305	Bellville, Anne	24	PA	256	Mary F	1	DE	110
Anna M	8	DE	292	Catherine	6	DE	256	Purnell	16	DE	228
Beulah A	25	DE	293	Edward	7	DE	258	Rachel	10	DE	186
Charles	13	DE	276	Eliza	2	DE	278	Sally	66	NJ	73
Charlotte	10	DE	276	Elizabeth	23	PA	256	Sarah	6	DE	186
David H	28	DE	293	Elizabeth	34	DE	278	Sarah	12	DE	239
Edward	34	DE	305	J P	9	DE	258	Sarah	23	DE	369
Edward	73	DE	292	John P	30	DE	256	Solomon	51	MA	27
Eliza	18	DE	292	Joseph	6	DE	278	Susannah	42	DE	5
Elizabeth A	8/12	DE	293	Joseph A	32	DE	278	Thomas	15	DE	231
Emily	10	DE	276	Lucy	3	DE	258	William	5	DE	186
Jane	4	DE	305	Mary	60	PA	256	William	30	NJ	121
John	35	DE	305	Mary J	10	DE	278	William	49	DE	186
John	76	DE	292	Mary P	30	PA	256	William W	50	DE	5
John A	29	DE	293	Robt	2	DE	256	Benning, Asbury	24	DE	91
Leah	28	DE	305	Sarah	1	DE	258	Benoit, Francois	25	FR	192
Lydia A	11	DE	292	Sarah	66	DE	261	Benser, Margaret	15	DE	143
Margaret	16	DE	276	Thomas	9/12	DE	256	Benson, Adeline	35	DE	170
Mary	50	DE	292	Thomas W	37	DE	258	Andrew	16	DE	163
Mary E	7	DE	305	Belt, Anna E	32	DE	108	Ann	6	DE	155
Mary J	16	DE	292	Emma	5	DE	108	Ann	8	IE	301
Rebecca	7	DE	276	John H	11	DE	108	Anna	22	MD	50
Rebecca	49	DE	276	Mary L	6	DE	108	Benjamin R	36	DE	95
Robinson	52	DE	276	Osborne	37	MD	108	Caleb	34	DE	285
Wesley G	19	DE	276	Beltz, Elias G	66	PA	397	Charles B	3	DE	170
Beggarly, Elizabeth	14	PA	286	Ellen	16	PA	397	Cornelia	40	DE	95
Martha	38	DE	286	Esther	63	PA	397	Edith A	12	MD	316
William	11	MA	286	Samuel	22	MD	398	Elizabeth	23	IE	336
Beihl, Jane	15	DE	189	Bemont, Ann	25	GB	339	Emily	13	MD	50
John	20	DE	189	Bender, Hester	9	DE	206	Fanny	40	MD	50
Joseph	12	DE	189	Beneson, Eliza	29	DE	390	Frances	18	MD	50
Joseph	55	PA	189	Benner, Margaret	28	DE	368	Frances A	16	DE	170
Sarah	7	DE	189	Benneson, Jane	70	DE	392	Francis	18	MD	369
Susan Sarah	48	DE	189	Margaret	42	DE	392	George	15	DE	170
William	23	DE	189	Maria	40	DE	392	Henrietta	6	DE	170
Beleton, John	23	PA	334	Tabitha	38	DE	392	Henrietta	16	MD	50
Belford, Bridget	48	IE	47	William L	13	DE	392	Henry	4	DE	285
Edward	8	DE	47	Bennet, Ann	50	DE	379	James A	23	MD	316
James	14	IE	47	Elizabeth	45	DE	370	James H	5	DE	155
Michel	4	DE	47	George	28	DE	369	James M	1	DE	170
Michel	50	IE	47	George M D	5	DE	370	Jane	17	MD	50
Beline, Henry	7	NY	343	Hannah L	15	DE	370	John	16	IE	301
Henry	46	PA	343	Jacob	5	DE	232	John	22	IE	353
Isabella	35	PA	343	James	11	DE	370	John H	5	DE	92
Louisa	13	PA	343	John	11	DE	370	Jube	40	DE	92
Mary	11	PA	343	John	41	DE	370	Kate	12	DE	95
Mary	72	PA	343	Kate	8	PA	272	Joshua	9	DE	155
Bell, Adeline C	8	DE	116	Margaret	21	DE	216	Joshua	40	DE	155
Alexander	25	DE	176	Martha J	1	DE	216	Luisa	24	DE	10
Amos	63	DE	204	Mary	32	PA	272	Margaret	24	DE	152
Ann	26	DE	133	Mary J	2	DE	216	Martha	8	MD	50
Caroline	24	DE	396	Norton	24	NJ	216	Mary	18	IE	301
Cornelia R	9	DE	133	Rachel	16	DE	379	Mary	19	MD	51
Earnest	16	PA	165	William	14	DE	370	Mary A	2	DE	285

Name	Age	St	No	Name	Age	St	No	Name	Age	St	No
Benson, Mary A	36	DE	155	Berry, Robert	5	DE	348	Bidale, Rose	7	DE	25
Mary A	40	IE	301	Sarah	25	PA	257	Sarah	15	DE	25
Mary E	12	DE	155	Sophia	50	MD	316	Biddeman, James A	60	FR	353
Mary S	22	MD	316	Susan T	14	DE	119	Biddle, Alex	51	DE	252
Melvina	25	DE	285	Bervell, Sarah	74	DE	66	Alexander	26	DE	188
N R	30	DE	152	Beson, Augustin H	30	DE	323	Andrew	47	DE	319
Rachel	7	DE	95	Thomas	49	DE	323	Andrew	60	DE	189
Rebecca	6	DE	170	Best, Mary	15	GB	299	Andrew Jr	22	DE	189
Rebecca S	5	DE	152	Betson, Ann	30	MD	146	Ann E	21	DE	199
Richard	19	IE	353	Josephine	10/12	DE	146	Ann J	8	MD	294
Sarah	20	IE	301	John	27	MD	146	Anne E	42	DE	199
Sarah E	3	DE	92	Martha	2	DE	146	Araminty	12	DE	336
Sarah H	8/12	DE	152	Betts, Albert	19	DE	68	Augustus	4	DE	189
Sebila	25	DE	92	Alfred	2/12	DE	83	Benjamin	8	DE	196
Susan	3	DE	152	Alfred	14	DE	162	Caroline	24	MD	266
Susan	9	MD	50	Ann	3	DE	9	Catherine	3	MD	396
Thomas	10	DE	95	Benjamin	30	DE	15	Catherine	5	NJ	89
William	6	IE	301	Charles	22	DE	68	Charles	2	DE	336
William	19	DE	212	Charles	53	PA	68	David	23	MD	294
William	45	DE	170	Edward	25	DE	162	David S	15	DE	189
William	52	IE	301	Eliza	15	DE	68	Deborah	35	MD	336
Benston, Andrew	3	DE	192	Elizabeth	53	DE	68	Dorcas	35	DE	227
Andrew	36	DE	192	Emanuel	25	DE	396	Dorcas	68	DE	196
Ann E	6	DE	172	George	1	DE	10	Eli	56	MD	199
Charles	35	MD	172	George	1	DE	396	Elijah	24	DE	327
Charles Jr	8	DE	172	Hannah	23	DE	30	Eliza	1	DE	327
John T	7	DE	192	Hannah	28	DE	15	Eliza J	36	MD	281
Joseph	9	DE	192	Hannah	84	PA	113	Elizabeth	27	NJ	86
Margaret P	4	DE	172	Harry	1	DE	83	Elizabeth M	33	PA	294
Olivia R M	29	DE	172	James	8	VA	68	Emily	35	DE	251
Rachel A	3/12	DE	192	Jesse	7	DE	9	Ezekle	28	NJ	86
Sarah A	31	DE	192	Jesse	86	PA	113	Frances	33	MD	261
Bentley, Anna	27	IE	391	John	5	DE	9	George	4	MD	294
Arthur	71	IE	330	Laura	4	DE	83	Hannah	23	DE	327
Harland	12	PA	358	Malon	55	PA	162	Harriet	60	DE	190
John	6	DE	239	Mary	3	DE	15	Harriet A	2	DE	176
John	35	DE	207	Mary	8	DE	83	Henry	18	DE	207
Mary	65	PA	330	Mary	24	DE	83	Horace C	8	DE	281
Benton, Alonzo	25	NY	192	Mary	28	DE	68	Isaac	2	DE	294
Hannah	36	DE	90	Mary	55	PA	162	Jacob	3	DE	261
Harriet	9	DE	90	Mary W	12	DE	162	James	8	DE	336
Jacob	65	MD	90	Rachel	21	DE	396	James	9	MD	80
Jonathan	7	DE	90	Rachel	62	PA	113	James	9	DE	319
John M	40	DE	90	Samuel	29	DE	83	James	25	DE	277
Margaret	11	DE	90	Samuel	30	DE	9	Jane	2	NJ	89
Sally	1	DE	90	Sarah	14	DE	68	John	8	NJ	89
William	4	DE	90	Sarah	28	DE	9	John	6	NJ	86
Benzinger, Augusta	12	MD	164	Virginia	11	VA	68	John	10	DE	336
Cecilia	15	MD	164	William	1	DE	15	John	37	DE	178
Bergen, Elizabeth	40	DE	376	Bevridge, Silvester	26	DE	382	John	55	DE	190
Berguerce, Amanuel	14	CU	163	Beyer, Deborah	28	DE	173	John R	4	MD	176
Joacam	12	CU	163	Perry	32	DE	204	Josephine	20	DE	252
Peter	19	CU	163	Biard, Amanda	16	DE	346	Lucy E	5	DE	281
Phillip	17	CU	163	Lea	60	DE	377	Lydia	40	DE	319
Bering, Maria	22	MD	366	Marcey	19	DE	377	Margaret	4	DE	86
Bernal, John	35	DE	318	Perry	40	DE	377	Margaret	5	MD	395
Joseph	16	DE	385	Sibbillia	14	DE	371	Margaret	25	MD	176
Bernard, Westley	21	MD	368	Bias, Charles	35	DE	334	Martha	2/12	DE	336
Bernel, Lewis	11	DE	353	Charlotte	15	DE	396	Mary	21	DE	86
Berry, Catherine	23	DE	325	Charlotte	18	DE	396	Mary	42	DE	252
Charlotte	50	DE	250	Chloe A	56	DE	396	Mary	62	DE	178
Elizabeth	16	DE	197	Moses	56	MD	396	Mary A	34	DE	178
Ellen	13	DE	250	Samuel	5	DE	396	Mary E	7	NJ	89
Frank	20	DE	309	Thomas	14	DE	391	Mary J	9	DE	190
George	33	PA	325	Bicking, Catherine L	6	PA	123	Mathew	40	DE	325
George	35	DE	59	Elizabeth	33	PA	123	Mrs	32	NJ	89
Hannah	11	DE	348	Isaac	15	PA	28	Priscilla	4/12	DE	294
Henry	12	DE	250	John S	34	PA	123	Saml	33	DE	261
Jacob	12	DE	348	Margaret	55	PA	123	Samuel	7	DE	319
Jacob	48	DE	280	Melissa	1	PA	123	Samuel	41	DE	281
James	18	DE	250	Rebecca	21	MD	123	Samuel C	1	DE	281
James	19	DE	255	Richard	25	PA	123	Sarah	2	DE	196
James	35	DE	257	Samuel	19	PA	123	Sarah	18	DE	260
John	15	DE	348	Susan	34	PA	123	Sarah A	24	DE	277
John	37	DE	348	Bicta, Henry	8	DE	38	Sarah A	40	DE	189
Joseph	14	PA	237	Joseph	24	GE	38	Sarah E	2	DE	86
Lorenzo	15	DE	250	Mary	1	DE	38	Sarah E	9	DE	189
Maria	9	DE	348	Mary	27	DE	38	Sarah S	16	DE	313
Martha	8/12	DE	348	Bidale, Benjamin	9	DE	25	Sophia	9	DE	261
Mary	30	DE	59	David	11	DE	25	Stephen L	45	MD	336
Mary A	2	DE	325	Mary	35	DE	25	Susan	6	MD	294
Rachel	35	DE	348	Moses	35	DE	25	Teeny	40	MD	201

Biddle, Thomas 5 DE 336
  Thomas T 78 MD 319
  Wesley 3 DE 327
  William 30 DE 176
  William M 1/12 DE 176
Biddlehaus, John 35 PA 355
Bidheman, Emma 3 DE 37
  Hannah 26 DE 37
  Margaret 4 PA 37
  Thomas 1 DE 37
  William 36 PA 37
Bidelle, Ann J 8 MD 322
  Susan P 6 MD 322
Bids, Moses 21 DE 332
Bien, Daniel 24 IE 303
Bigger, Ann 4 DE 271
  Charles 16 DE 271
  Charles 42 NJ 271
  Emma 2 DE 271
  Joseph 13 DE 271
  Mary 6 DE 271
  Matthew 10 DE 271
  Ruth 22 NJ 271
  Saml 18 DE 271
Biggs, Alexander 19 DE 296
  Anna 5 DE 148
  Araminta B 24 DE 210
  Benjamin T 28 DE 318
  Catherine 15 DE 296
  Dianna 50 DE 318
  Elizabeth 3 DE 148
  Isaac 32 DE 301
  J 35 DE 148
  James 31 DE 148
  James 46 DE 296
  Jane E 22 DE 318
  Jewell C 26 DE 318
  John 61 MD 318
  Joseph 1 DE 148
  Joseph 16 DE 318
  Martha L 53 DE 296
  Mary A 8 DE 318
  William H 8 DE 148
  William P 11 DE 318
Bill, Benjamin 10 DE 238
  Elizabeth 26 DE 238
  George 9/12 DE 238
  Mary A 13 DE 238
  Philemon 42 DE 238
  Rebecca 6 DE 238
Billarry, Ann 56 GB 113
  Mary E 15 DE 113
  Sally A 13 DE 113
  William H 18 DE 113
Billman, Wm 22 GE 252
Billop, Catharine 2 DE 304
  Catharine 40 MD 304
  Charles 4 MD 304
  Christopher 14 MD 304
  Frank 8 MD 304
  John 6 MD 304
  Mary 6/12 DE 304
  Robert 10 MD 304
  Thomas 12 MD 304
  Thomas F -- NY 304
  William 16 MD 304
Binan, Thomas 20 IE 304
Bingey, Fanny 5 DE 255
Bingham, Andrew 32 DE 70
Bingle, James 20 PA 347
Bird, Amanda M 2 DE 287
  Amos 49 DE 314
  Andrew 1 PA 315
  Charles 12 DE 318
  Charles M 18 DE 287
  Eliza 17 DE 314
  Elizabeth 22 DE 278
  Elizabeth 50 DE 315
  Elizabeth V L 15 DE 287
  Hannah 50 DE 314
  Hannah A 14 DE 315
  Henry 1 DE 278

Bird, Henry B 17 DE 318
  Hiram 6 PA 315
  James C 22 DE 318
  James T 53 DE 318
  Jno D 54 DE 287
  John 60 DE 314
  John 65 DE 285
  Joseph 59 DE 277
  Julia A 38 DE 287
  Levi 8 DE 318
  Lewis 31 DE 277
  Lewis W 3 DE 287
  Lydia C 13 DE 287
  Margaret 15 DE 277
  Margaret T 5 DE 288
  Mary 13 DE 318
  Mary 19 DE 277
  Mary 56 DE 288
  Mary 82 PA 288
  Mary E 17 DE 287
  Matilda 9 DE 315
  Neonie 69 DE 314
  Rachel 36 DE 288
  Rebecca 7 DE 314
  Rebecca S 49 DE 287
  Sarah 22 DE 277
  Susan 46 DE 318
  Susan E 15 DE 318
  Thomas 27 DE 253
  Thomas G 15 DE 287
  Thomas P 22 DE 285
  Unis 25 DE 277
  William 10 DE 318
  William 28 DE 294
  William 49 DE 287
  William 71 DE 314
  William H T 9 DE 287
Birly, Eliza A 40 DE 316
  Nathaniel 48 MD 316
Birmingham, Ellen 60 IE 39
Birnham, Caroline 7 DE 207
Bisbee, Bolivar 24 NY 400
Bishop, Elizabeth 19 DE 157
  Hannah M 3/12 DE 384
  Henry 24 DE 384
  Jesse 54 DE 345
  John 23 DE 101
  John 25 DE 157
  Joseph 23 DE 254
  Levi 12 DE 345
  Martial 24 DE 345
  Mary A 2 DE 384
  Rachel 49 DE 345
  Sarah J 22 DE 384
  Susan 18 DE 101
  Susan 18 DE 345
Black, Abby 48 DE 38
  Absolem 31 DE 65
  Aletha 30 DE 191
  Alex 14 DE 255
  Alfred 17 DE 322
  Amanda 1 DE 319
  Ann 24 DE 45
  Ann 42 DE 160
  Ann J 35 DE 282
  Caroline 13 DE 254
  Charles 6 DE 376
  Charles 22 MD 10
  Chas A 6 DE 282
  Chas H 41 DE 282
  Daniel 20 DE 132
  David H 32 DE 391
  Diane 30 DE 363
  Dora A 8 DE 282
  Dorcas 60 DE 17
  Dorcas A 60 DE 391
  Elisha 2/12 DE 92
  Eliza 23 DE 51
  Elizabeth 15 DE 23
  Frank M 6/12 DE 282
  George 7 DE 393
  George 21 IE 331

Black, Hannah 21 DE 324
  Harriet 45 DE 69
  Harriet L 4 DE 282
  Harriet M 4 DE 340
  Helen 15 DE 268
  Hester 30 DE 114
  Isaac 12 DE 343
  Isaac 70 DE 343
  James 12 DE 113
  James 16 DE 28
  James 35 DE 363
  James L 3 DE 340
  Jane 1/12 DE 376
  Jane 40 DE 160
  John 14 DE 282
  John 17 DE 208
  John 17 PA 250
  John 22 DE 151
  John 30 DE 13
  John J 12 DE 282
  Joshua 30 PA 375
  Levi 25 DE 206
  Loisa 40 DE 319
  Lucretia 50 DE 343
  Lucy 14 DE 264
  Malinda 29 MD 65
  Margaret 16 DE 114
  Margaret 20 DE 338
  Margaret J 10 DE 282
  Maria 65 MD 9
  Marina 3 DE 65
  Martha 4 DE 92
  Martha 20 DE 53
  Martha 30 DE 192
  Mary 4 DE 65
  Mary 12 DE 363
  Mary 20 DE 97
  Mary 25 DE 161
  Mary A 40 MD 89
  Mary J 20 DE 391
  Mary J 25 DE 340
  Matilda 16 DE 76
  Matilda 19 DE 144
  Minty 30 DE 376
  Murtana 10 DE 363
  Robert M 4/12 DE 340
  Robert M 37 DE 340
  Samuel H 32 DE 340
  Sarah 23 DE 14
  Sarah 28 DE 92
  Sarah 50 DE 10
  Sidney 40 DE 31
  Susan 10 DE 272
  Susan 18 IE 30
  Susan 22 DE 76
  Thomas 2 DE 92
  Thomas 30 DE 92
  William 23 MD 322
  William 50 DE 38
  William 84 PA 396
  William J 2 DE 282
Blackborn, Benjamin 10 DE 159
  Charles W 3 DE 159
  Edward 12 DE 159
  Elener 39 DE 159
  James 16 DE 159
  James 19 DE 116
  James 42 DE 159
  Jane 27 NJ 138
  John 9 DE 159
  William H 14 DE 159
Blackburn, Benj F 2 DE 323
  Euretta N 44 DE 323
  Hannah F 5 DE 323
  Hannah T 7 DE 323
  Joseph 48 DE 323
  Joseph P 13 DE 323
  Mary E 15 DE 323
  Samuel J 17 DE 323
  Sarah J 11 DE 323
  Theodore T 7 DE 323
  Wm J 9 DE 323

Name	Age	State	No.
Blackhorn, William	22	PA	135
Blackiston, George W	17	DE	400
Sarah	8	DE	390
Blackman, Joseph	13	DE	365
Blackmore, George	55	GB	32
Blackshire, John	25	MD	318
Blackson, Charles	28	DE	16
Elizabeth	27	DE	16
Blackston, Aaron	3	DE	116
Ann	40	NJ	209
Ann M	2	DE	209
Benjamin	52	MD	73
Elener	28	DE	167
Eliza	19	DE	209
Elizabeth	3	DE	216
Elizabeth	14	DE	73
Ezekiel	35	DE	203
George	1	DE	202
George	6	DE	73
Henry	9	DE	202
Jacob	25	DE	202
James	54	DE	341
Jonathan	4/12	DE	209
Julia A	25	MD	116
Levi	1	PA	337
Lorenzo	40	PA	337
Luisa	3	DE	73
Major	6	DE	209
Malvina	28	MD	170
Mary A	48	GE	73
Peter	32	MD	170
Phillis	30	DE	202
Rebecca	3	DE	202
Rebecca	16	DE	73
Richard	10/12	DE	116
Richard	28	MD	116
Samuel	10	DE	116
Sarah A	4	DE	209
Sarah J	7	DE	202
Susan	37	PA	337
Susan	40	DE	244
Susan	45	DE	216
Thomas	4	PA	337
William	18	DE	73
William	18	MD	149
William H	11	DE	116
William H	12	DE	235
Blackstone, Hannah	70	DE	377
Levi	1	DE	378
Lorenzo	32	DE	378
Mary	50	DE	155
Mary E	10	DE	377
Sarah	5	DE	377
Sarah	35	MD	377
Susanna B	26	PA	378
Thomas	35	DE	377
Thomas L	5	PA	378
Thomas M	7	DE	377
Blackwell, Ann M	1	DE	141
Harrison	2	DE	141
Henry D	28	NJ	141
Sarah	25	GB	141
Stephen C	32	NJ	293
Blackwood, Mary W	21	PA	111
Rebecca	18	PA	111
Rebecca J	46	DE	110
Blag, Alace	6/12	DE	66
Anna	31	GB	66
Frank	3	GB	66
Sarah A	6	GB	66
Richard	40	GB	66
Blair, Aaron	47	PA	360
Ann	17	DE	360
Catharine	19	DE	360
Egbert	23	DE	360
Emily	2	DE	360
Frederick	21	DE	360
Hannah	43	DE	360
Henrietta	11	DE	144
John	17	DE	152
Jonas	8	DE	360
Sally	40	DE	55
Blair, Phebe	13	DE	360
Blake, Alcey A	1	DE	283
Ann	32	DE	389
Anne	2	DE	389
Annette	26	DE	252
Elijah	35	NJ	84
Eliza	9	DE	186
Eliza	18	DE	289
Elizabeth	47	DE	84
Ellen	30	DE	84
Frances	2	DE	283
George H	25	DE	283
John	26	NJ	9
John	56	MD	65
John H	25	DE	84
Joseph	3	DE	252
Joseph	35	DE	316
Julia	13	DE	318
Julia A	31	DE	155
Leah	20	MD	29
Lucinda	22	DE	288
Margaret	18	DE	316
Mary	15	DE	284
Mary	51	MD	65
Peter J	11	DE	84
Rachel	6	DE	288
Robert	40	DE	84
Samuel	6/12	DE	84
Thomas	34	DE	173
William	29	VA	155
Blandy, Francis P	S48	MD	395
Graham	10	DE	395
James H	12	DE	395
John F	17	DE	395
Thomas R	21	DE	395
Blanes, Henreitta	25	DE	220
James	3	DE	220
Jerry	2	DE	220
Jerry	30	DE	220
William H	7	DE	220
Blaney, Elizabeth	50	DE	290
Fanny	20	DE	290
Blanken, Thomas	25	PA	136
Blayer, Elizabeth	70	GE	128
George	3	DE	107
John B	44	GE	107
John H	17	DE	107
Magalena	41	PA	107
Magdelina	6	DE	107
Margaret	9	DE	107
William	14	DE	107
Blear, John	--	DE	290
Blerer, Eliza	28	DE	381
Marey E	8	DE	381
Margaret A	2	DE	381
William	5	DE	381
William	30	DE	381
Blessington, Ann	28	IE	74
James	43	IE	348
Margaret	3	DE	348
Margaret	30	IE	348
Mary A	10	IE	348
Michel	36	IE	74
Rosanna	5	DE	348
Blest, Adaline	8	PA	133
Brian W	49	DE	374
Emeline	45	PA	133
George W	12	GE	374
George W	13	DE	108
James	35	PA	107
James T	15	DE	374
John F	4	DE	107
Laura A	9	DE	107
Mary	33	DE	107
Mary A	7	DE	107
Mary Jane	19	DE	374
Phoebe Ann	21	DE	374
Rebecca M	17	DE	374
Thomas T	55	PA	133
William	23	DE	374
Blibran, Sarah	65	DE	371
Bliskey, Elizabeth	30	DE	85
Blister, Mary	12	DE	260
Blizard, Charlota	24	DE	119
George	26	DE	119
Matilda	26	DE	119
William	7	DE	119
William	30	DE	119
Z (Capt)	35	DE	119
Blizzard, Benj	11	PA	311
Emily	30	DE	230
James	47	MD	311
Lydia	13	PA	311
Maria	15	PA	311
Mary	48	PA	311
Sarah	8	PA	311
Thomas	11	PA	311
Bloumer, Sarah	8	PA	178
Blount, Ann	40	DE	286
James	44	DE	286
John Y	3	DE	286
Lydia	37	DE	286
Sarah A	5/12	DE	286
Blucher, John	16	DE	253
Blue, Charlotta	21	DE	28
Jane	17	DE	32
Mary	27	DE	29
Mary E	9	DE	128
Sarah	27	DE	55
Blyer, Charles	24	GE	6
Elizabeth	43	GE	5
George	5	DE	6
Henry	40	GE	5
Levinia	27	DE	6
William	31	DE	6
Blythe, Jacob	15	DE	111
Boardly, Lewis	30	MD	4
Nathaniel	40	DE	284
Bobbits, Mary	5/12	DE	277
Bock, Frances	21	PA	28
Samuel	30	PA	360
Susan	23	DE	360
Bockman, Edith	44	DE	167
Bockshale, Solomon	40	PA	17
Boddy, Anna	3	DE	36
Anna L	2	DE	36
Benjamin	31	GB	36
Byran	5	DE	36
Charles	4	DE	36
Francina	18	VA	395
John	28	GB	36
Hannah M	30	DE	144
Henrietta	24	MD	36
Henry	26	DE	395
Hester	26	DE	36
Latitia	8/12	DE	36
Loyed L	2	DE	144
Mary	2	DE	36
William	32	GB	144
Bodle, Amelia K	11	DE	109
Catherine	28	DE	109
Edward	30	DE	109
Bodley, Adam	28	DE	156
Dolly	30	DE	156
Frank	14	DE	143
John	32	DE	143
Margaretta	20	DE	143
Margaretta	52	PA	143
Sally A	27	DE	156
Stephen	66	DE	143
Bogan, Ann	37	DE	337
Catherine	32	IE	29
Charles	40	IE	311
Fanny	63	IE	350
Mary Jane	4	DE	337
Paul	16	DE	337
Paul	37	IE	337
Thomas	2	DE	337
Bogia, Alphonso	7	DE	277
Anna	2	DE	277
Benjamin	11	DE	277
Catharine	17	NJ	277
Charles G	13	DE	277
Ferdinand	9	DE	277

Name	Age	St	Pg
Bogia, Godwine	41	DE	277
John A	18	NJ	277
John F	41	PA	277
Josephine	15	DE	277
Mary	10/12	DE	277
William	4	DE	277
Boggs, Alexander	7	DE	208
Elizabeth T	4	DE	208
Esther	9	DE	256
Henry	4	DE	256
James H	51	DE	208
John	28	PA	274
Mary	35	PA	208
Saml	42	DE	256
Sarah	35	DE	256
Bogues, Henry L	6	DE	236
John W	3	DE	236
Louisa	35	DE	236
Sarah E	11	DE	236
Susan	3	DE	236
William	40	DE	236
William D	11/12	DE	236
Bohl, Henry	25	GE	401
Boils, Adela L	5/12	DE	396
Alexander	24	MD	335
Ann M	50	MD	335
Anthony	3	DE	335
Catherine	22	DE	335
Eliza J	22	DE	396
Henry	22	MD	335
James A	7/12	DE	335
Sala	4	DE	335
William	25	MD	396
Bois, Irenah S	19	MD	323
James T	17	MD	323
Joseph S	54	NB	323
Mary T	48	MD	323
Sarah H	15	MD	323
Bolden, Elizabeth	76	MD	374
Jerry	40	MD	195
Robert	14	DE	385
Susan	48	DE	358
William	21	DE	121
William F	11	DE	388
Bolinson, Catherine	29	DE	377
Bolly, Jane	10	NJ	379
Bolton, Benjamin	32	GB	281
Francinia	67	DE	294
George	35	DE	294
James	72	DE	294
James Jr	14	MD	314
James L	31	DE	314
Jane	1	DE	294
Martha	21	DE	281
Mary	48	DE	193
Mary E	14	DE	193
Virginia	15	DE	294
William	4	DE	294
William	16	DE	193
Bond, Ann	45	NJ	336
Caroline	7	DE	336
J Oliver	14	MD	194
James S	38	MD	194
John	45	IE	336
Julius A	16	MD	195
Laura H	7	MD	195
Mary A	38	MD	194
Virginia	3	MD	195
William G	12	MD	195
Boner, Catherine	19	IE	161
Edward	25	IE	62
Ellen	4/12	MA	62
Ellen	24	IE	62
Margaret	17	IE	161
Boneur, Robert	29	DE	355
Bonjour, Sarah	44	DE	327
Bonnell, Elmira	6	DE	391
John	25	GB	391
Michael	21	DE	337
Sarah	24	DE	391
William	2	DE	391
Bonner, Catherine	19	IE	112
Bonner, Rosanna	30	IE	55
Bonney, Elizabeth	14	DE	358
William	12	DE	358
Bonor, Catharine	19	IE	307
Bonsel, Bennet P	16	DE	355
Charles B	19	PA	355
Hannah	56	DE	112
Hannah E	12	DE	355
Israel R	55	PA	355
Joseph P	21	PA	355
Mary H	55	DE	112
Samuel	24	PA	355
Stephen	58	DE	112
Bonsell, Chaulkly	38	DE	78
Booke, Edmond	24	MD	341
Mary	63	MD	341
Rachel	22	MD	341
Booker, _____	35	IE	339
Margaret	9	IE	339
Mary	24	IE	339
William	7	IE	339
Boon, Alexander	32	PA	36
Elizabeth F	47	DE	372
Emily	37	DE	111
Layton	1	DE	36
Lois	35	MD	105
Rebecca	16	MD	105
Sidney	29	PA	36
Boose, William	16	DE	149
Booth, Amelia	27	MD	280
Anna	2/12	DE	299
Bartholomew	36	MD	145
Benjamin M	8	DE	310
Benjamin S	40	DE	310
Catharine	59	DE	299
Charity	43	DE	279
Charles	19	GB	90
David	14	DE	186
David	26	FR	137
David	66	DE	185
Elizabeth	5	DE	332
Elizabeth	18	DE	332
Elizabeth	27	DE	282
Elizabeth	40	DE	282
Elizabeth J	17	DE	304
Elmira	4	DE	299
Emily A	7/12	DE	145
Enoch	18	DE	279
George	34	GB	332
Hannah	40	DE	310
Hannah W	50	DE	282
Henry C	11	DE	310
Isaac	21	DE	279
J G	28	DE	137
James	1	DE	280
James	8	AA	332
James	21	DE	304
James R	22	DE	282
Jas (Hon)	60	DE	282
Jane	1	DE	332
Jane	30	GB	332
Jemima	9	DE	279
John	6	DE	279
John	29	DE	299
Julia M	16	DE	282
Julia M	17	DE	332
Maria R	23	DE	304
Martha	39	NJ	145
Mary	13	DE	310
Mary	41	DE	304
Mary A	20	GB	90
Mary E	7	DE	299
Mary E	24	DE	282
Nathaniel	11	DE	279
Nathaniel	50	PA	279
Paris	40	MD	280
Rebecca	45	DE	185
Sally A	30	DE	299
Sarah	4	NJ	145
Sarah	16	DE	279
Squire	11	GB	332
Susan H	28	DE	282
Booth, Thomas	69	DE	298
Thomas H	20	DE	282
William	7	DE	332
William	50	DE	304
Boots, Barbara	12	GE	132
David	14	GE	151
Elizabeth	24	GE	132
Emily	1	DE	234
George	15	GE	62
George	16	GE	151
Jacob	17	GE	151
Jacob	45	GE	151
James	30	GE	158
James L	4	DE	224
John	7	GE	151
John	36	DE	234
John W	10	DE	224
Madaline	8	GE	151
Martha	34	MD	234
Martha A	7	DE	234
Mary E	9	DE	234
Mary L	6	DE	224
Mr	50	GE	158
Rebecca	32	DE	224
Robert	40	DE	224
Sarah E	5	DE	234
Sarah J	2	DE	224
William A	7	DE	224
Borderieux, Adolph	7	PA	104
Adolph	45	FR	104
Agatha	41	FR	104
Caroline	9	PA	104
Elizabeth	2	PA	104
Francis	4	PA	104
Joseph	13	FR	104
Bordley, William	19	DE	156
Bordly, Mary	15	DE	152
Susan	50	DE	59
Boren, Wm	9	DE	320
Borlan, Abram	75	IE	329
Martha	27	MD	329
Mary	63	MD	329
Boroughs, Joseph	13	DE	308
Borrel, Alexis	25	DE	336
Catherine	23	IE	336
Christian	1	DE	336
Sarah	3	DE	336
Borrough, William	30	MD	319
Boskit, John	1	DE	224
Margaret A	24	DE	224
Richard	34	DE	224
Sarah A	3	DE	224
Bostic, Ann	15	DE	279
Betsey	28	DE	259
Cynthia	7	DE	252
Elizabeth	17	DE	301
George	4	DE	252
Hannah	1	DE	259
Hannah	3	DE	74
Isaac	15	DE	382
James	6	MD	73
James	22	DE	377
John	40	MD	73
Martha	30	DE	252
Mary	5/12	DE	252
Mary S	2	DE	74
Perry	10	DE	255
Perry	37	DE	259
Rachel	19	DE	377
Rachel	22	DE	70
Sally	4	MD	73
Sarah	39	MD	73
Sarah A	4	DE	74
Sarah J	23	DE	117
Susannah	24	DE	74
Temperance	11	DE	259
Thomas	10	DE	252
Thomas	40	DE	252
William H	30	MD	74
Bostick, Isaac	11	DE	384
Isaac	39	MD	384
Joseph	1	DE	384

Name	Age	St	No	Name	Age	St	No	Name	Age	St	No
Bostick, Martha E	6	DE	384	Boulden, Samuel T	13	DE	362	Bowman, Alonzo	10	DE	273
Mary	40	MD	384	Sarah	21	DE	167	Alpheus	10	DE	184
Mary E	13	DE	384	Sarah	60	DE	54	Alphonso	16	DE	200
Sarah	5	DE	384	Sarah A	25	DE	362	Ann	43	DE	200
Spencer	9	DE	384	Sarah E	4	DE	78	Anna	30	DE	287
Susanna	3	DE	384	Sarah L	15	DE	326	Anna R	14	DE	184
Thomas	20	DE	185	Susan	22	DE	54	Benjamin	30	DE	259
Boston, John	19	DE	191	Susan	39	DE	105	Catherine	14	DE	18
Boul, George	33	DE	341	Thomas	48	DE	362	Catherine	33	DE	273
Hannah C	1	DE	341	Thomas E	51	DE	326	Charles	40	DE	200
Joshua	12	DE	341	Virginia	13	DE	105	Cornelia	3	DE	305
Mary A	7	DE	341	William	9	DE	105	Curtis F	5	DE	184
Rachel	39	DE	341	William	11	DE	316	Elizabeth	44	DE	151
Rachel	55	DE	323	William	12	DE	333	Elma	8	DE	200
Samuel	1/12	DE	341	William	15	DE	341	Emma	11	DE	200
Virginia	4	DE	341	William H	5/12	DE	155	Flora	40	DE	18
Bouldel, Elizabeth	39	DE	68	William H	16	DE	400	George K	8	MD	184
Susannah	74	DE	68	Boulder, Charles	55	NJ	33	Hannah	17	DE	26
Boulden, Albert	35	DE	333	Jacob	32	DE	19	Hannah	70	DE	366
Alexander	8	DE	362	Mary	8	DE	39	Henry	3	DE	20
Amelia	4	DE	326	Boulton, Emma	24	NY	389	Henry A	39	DE	184
Ann	19	DE	341	Bouser, George	8	DE	23	Jacob	22	GE	5
Anna L	9	DE	326	Elizabeth	16	DE	251	Jacob	55	DE	26
Calvin	4	DE	323	James	14	DE	251	James	6	DE	273
Catherine S	6	DE	362	James	32	MD	23	James	36	DE	273
Caroline	38	DE	333	Joseph	12	DE	23	James	45	DE	287
Charles	41	DE	323	Paul	9	DE	251	James C	53	DE	200
Clarissa	26	MD	323	Rebecca	10	DE	23	Jeremiah	43	DE	287
David	11	DE	326	Sarah	28	MD	23	Jesse	19	DE	26
Edward	13	DE	326	Boutcher, Hannah	21	PA	373	John	9	DE	20
Eliza	19	DE	333	Joseph	19	DE	373	John	18	DE	381
Ellen	15	DE	324	Mary	48	PA	373	John	21	DE	26
Emeline	14	DE	323	William	40	PA	373	John	25	DE	366
Frances	12	DE	341	Bouyour, Sarah	44	MD	328	John	70	DE	366
Frisby	8	DE	326	Bowen, Ann	50	NJ	269	Joseph	22	DE	385
Frisby	46	DE	322	Edward	25	IE	61	Joseph	42	PA	20
George	7/12	DE	326	Eliza	16	DE	269	Louisa	18	DE	145
George	39	DE	326	Ezekiel	15	DE	265	Lydia	13	DE	305
George T	3/12	DE	322	George	5	DE	265	Lydia	39	DE	20
George W	14	DE	362	James	9	DE	265	Margaret	7	DE	273
Hannah	7	DE	326	James	40	DE	265	Margaret	30	DE	316
Hannah	77	PA	321	John	11	DE	265	Margaret	65	DE	316
Hannah J	6	DE	324	John	21	DE	269	Martha	16	DE	184
Harriet A	1	DE	362	John	50	DE	269	Martha D	31	DE	184
Isaac	40	DE	324	Lydia	9	DE	269	Mary	2	DE	273
Jacob	80	DE	324	Mary	7	DE	265	Mary	9	DE	305
James	8	DE	333	Mary	12	DE	269	Mary	12	DE	20
James	28	DE	324	Mary	25	IE	10	Mary	40	DE	305
James	30	DE	78	Prudence	32	DE	265	Mary A	5	DE	309
Jesse Jr	22	DE	324	Rebecca	14	DE	265	Mary J	32	PA	309
Jesse Sr	76	DE	324	Wm	3	DE	265	Orphy	14	DE	26
John	6/12	DE	333	Wm	28	DE	269	Peter	53	DE	305
Joseph	2	DE	322	Zekiel	16	DE	190	Rebecca	3	NJ	184
Levi L	16	MD	400	Bowers, Ann E	23	PA	311	Robert	6	DE	184
Lewis	28	DE	155	Emma	3	DE	158	Sarah	2	DE	184
Lewis H	4	DE	362	George	38	GE	86	Sarah	70	DE	200
Louisa	37	MD	326	Henry P	1	DE	158	Sarah Ann	37	DE	184
Margaret	40	DE	322	John	22	DE	158	Sarah E	6	DE	151
Margaret A	16	DE	323	Leonard	16	DE	158	Susan	6	DE	20
Marion	7/12	DE	323	Martha	24	PA	49	Susan	77	DE	287
Martha	2	DE	326	Mary	50	DE	158	Thomas	26	IE	311
Mary	7	DE	78	Mary A	5	DE	158	Virginia	10	DE	305
Mary	22	DE	292	Sarah	21	NY	86	William	13	PA	366
Mary	42	DE	324	Sarah	55	DE	251	William	34	DE	200
Mary	45	MD	341	Sarah A	28	DE	158	William	53	DE	200
Mary A	3	DE	155	Thomas W	29	DE	158	William Jr	19	DE	200
Mary A	15	DE	326	Bowing, Eli	8	DE	371	William R	9	PA	342
Mary A	20	DE	287	Eliza	49	DE	371	Bowner, John	26	MA	103
Mary A	25	MD	155	Ephragm	22	DE	371	Bowonun, Joseph	25	DE	360
Mary E	2	DE	323	George	17	DE	371	Mary E	22	DE	360
Mary H	38	MD	323	Phoebe	13	DE	371	Bowser, Joseph	35	DE	316
Mary J	11	DE	362	Stacey	62	NJ	371	Bowsinger, Ann	45	SZ	364
Nathan L	20	DE	324	Bowl, George	34	DE	293	Martin	63	SZ	364
Olivia	6	DE	326	Rachel	35	DE	322	Bowyer, Elizabeth	12	DE	294
Priscilla	49	DE	326	Bowlen, Anna	17	DE	280	George	20	DE	294
Rebecca	2	DE	324	Charles	47	PA	280	Perry	64	DE	168
Richard	13	DE	332	Charles W	15	DE	280	Boyce, Abraham	49	DE	342
Richard	14	DE	333	John	21	DE	284	Ann E	12	DE	342
Richard	54	DE	341	Mary J	22	PA	280	Ann J	50	DE	210
Rosby	19	DE	326	Sarah	1	DE	280	Charles P	14	DE	342
Ruby J	19	DE	320	Sarah	47	DE	280	Ellen	30	DE	316
Samuel	30	MD	157	Bowman, Aaron	45	DE	151	Henry	26	GB	297

Name	Age	St	Pg
Boyce, Jacob	25	DE	317
James	8	DE	343
John	16	PA	297
Mahala	42	DE	342
Mary	26	GB	296
Mary A	36	PA	58
Mary J	21	DE	342
William	3	DE	342
Boyd, Charles S	11	DE	200
Elizabeth	14	DE	200
Elizabeth S	40	DE	200
James	25	IE	335
John L	6	PA	278
John M	12	DE	200
John R	49	DE	200
June	16	DE	200
Mary A	18	DE	200
Mary S	73	DE	200
Micha	40	IE	330
Romia R	10/12	DE	200
William S	3	DE	200
Boyden, Jeremiah	19	DE	330
Boyed, Ann E	24	DE	96
George M	18	DE	70
Harriet M	22	DE	70
James	56	MD	82
John	27	IE	82
Margaret	70	IE	51
Mary A	1	DE	96
Mary A	50	DE	70
Mary J	24	DE	70
Mr	36	DE	96
Thomas J	12	DE	70
William	10	NY	165
William	25	PA	97
William S	15	DE	70
Boyer, Charlotte	6/12	DE	259
Darius	14	DE	249
Darius	14	DE	259
Elizabeth	21	DE	175
Emeline	16	DE	271
Harriet	28	DE	259
Henry	12	PA	357
Henry	25	DE	256
Hezekiah	45	MD	195
Isaac	35	MD	262
Isaiah	4	DE	269
James	25	DE	252
Joseph	8	DE	259
Joseph	31	DE	259
Louisa	4	DE	259
Louisa	18	PA	357
Manual	8	DE	259
Maria A	27	DE	259
Martha	3	DE	269
Martha	36	MD	269
Mary	57	PA	357
Mary A	32	DE	259
Michel	25	DE	84
Reese	20	PA	357
Reese	60	PA	257
Samuel	37	MD	269
Samuel	41	DE	259
Shadrack	10	DE	259
Shadrack	37	DE	259
Shadrack	70	MD	259
William	25	DE	244
Boyle, Charles	7/12	DE	151
Ellen	30	IE	318
Francis	2	DE	151
Hugh	38	IE	151
James	6	DE	151
Margaret	61	IE	167
Mary	5	DE	150
Sarah	27	DE	150
William	22	PA	143
Boyles, Rozy	35	IE	282
Boys, Abraham	11	DE	27
Abraham	50	DE	17
Catherine	15	DE	27
Edward	13	DE	27
Elizabeth	77	DE	172
Boys, Hannah G	31	DE	372
Harriet	48	DE	118
Henry	52	DE	27
Isabella	15	DE	118
Isaiah	20	MD	335
John	22	ST	362
John	55	DE	118
Joseph	8	DE	27
Lucinda	15	NJ	140
Mary	10	IE	37
Mary	38	IE	37
Mary	52	DE	27
Mary E	19	DE	118
Neal	30	IE	37
Susanna	21	DE	27
Thomas	18	DE	27
William	20	DE	27
Bozins, Wesley	22	PA	397
Bozwell, Wm (Rev)	22	PA	336
Braceland, Ellen	20	IE	45
Sarah	17	IE	45
Thomas	28	IE	45
Brachen, Hannah	74	DE	269
Matthias	36	GB	353
Brachin, Ann	22	PA	36
Benjamin	26	DE	141
Benjamin W	60	DE	36
Catherine	25	IE	6
Elizabeth	1	DE	141
Elizabeth F	3/12	DE	382
Ellen	30	IE	162
Hellen	30	DE	384
Henry	65	DE	365
James M	38	DE	384
Jane	32	DE	382
John	32	DE	382
Mary	4	DE	382
Mary	50	IE	162
Mrs	24	DE	141
Rachel	58	DE	36
Sarah	13	DE	365
Sarah	20	DE	36
Sarah A	2	DE	382
Thomas	55	DE	364
Brachine, Thomas	16	DE	398
Brachinson, Lewis	17	DE	354
Mary	75	DE	354
William	84	DE	354
Bracken, Mary E	20	DE	314
Rebecca	8	DE	364
Richard R	8/12	DE	353
Sarah Jane	2	DE	353
William	24	DE	364
William	61	DE	353
Brackin, Charlotta	14	MD	355
Susan	49	DE	364
Thomas	7	DE	384
Watson	6	DE	382
William	11	DE	384
Bradey, Michael	16	IE	277
Bradford, Ann	62	PA	289
Ann Eliza	11	NJ	294
Anna M	7	DE	294
Catherine	26	PA	148
Charity C	10/12	DE	289
Charles	9	DE	295
Cornelia	3	DE	55
David J	4	DE	148
Edward	20	MD	383
Edward	23	DE	289
Edward G	2	DE	55
Edward G	31	MD	55
Elizabeth	22	DE	211
Enos	30	NJ	239
Eugenia	7	MD	109
George	3	DE	148
George	23	DE	383
George W	4	DE	294
James	15	DE	131
James	21	PA	75
James	27	DE	148
James	40	DE	131
Bradford, James H	6	DE	55
Jane	39	DE	131
John	16	DE	131
John	18	PA	294
John	35	DE	289
John	40	PA	294
John	58	DE	282
Joseph	21	DE	289
Julian	21	DE	109
Margaretta	54	DE	281
Martha Linda	4	DE	240
Mary J	27	PA	289
Morgan R	5/12	DE	294
Moses	61	MA	109
Phillip	26	DE	210
Rebecca	38	PA	294
Rebecca C	13	NJ	294
Richard	7	DE	239
Robert	3	DE	294
Sarah	28	NJ	239
Sarah	37	DE	109
Sarah A	28	MD	210
Susan	2	DE	239
William	7/12	DE	240
William	1	DE	148
William	29	DE	289
William	62	DE	289
William H	3	DE	289
William M	15	PA	294
Bradfort, Agness	43	GB	375
James B	22	RI	375
Stephen	46	GB	375
Bradley, Adaline	16	DE	390
Agnes	14	DE	390
Amos T	12	DE	330
Andrew	19	DE	331
Ann	20	GB	379
Ann	21	DE	46
Ann	59	IE	46
Ann J	18	IE	350
Anna A	10	DE	390
Anna O	8	DE	331
David	30	PA	46
Edmond	13	GB	379
Edmond B	40	GB	379
Edwin	13	IE	373
Ellen S	3	DE	330
Francis	29	PA	391
George W	4	DE	391
George W	7	DE	330
Hannah	36	PA	330
Hannah M	1	DE	330
Henry H	9	DE	330
Jane	32	DE	391
John	8	PA	379
John	25	IE	336
John	67	IE	46
Joseph	10	GB	379
Lewis	32	DE	295
Maria M	4	DE	330
Martha	6	PA	379
Martha	41	GB	379
Martha J	13	DE	391
Mary	40	DE	331
Mary	52	DE	390
Mary	57	DE	285
Mary E	11	DE	331
Narcissa	9	DE	391
Nathaniel	40	MD	285
Patterson	6	DE	331
Sarah	1	DE	331
Sarah	23	PA	46
Sarah	78	DE	331
Susan	1/12	DE	379
Susan	2/12	DE	391
Thomas	41	PA	330
Thomas A	23	DE	331
Thomas C	45	DE	331
Thomas M	24	DE	390
William H	2	DE	379
William S	15	DE	331
Z Taylor	4	DE	331

Name	Age		Pg
Bradly, Emeline	28	DE	143
Bradshaw, Hannah	70	MD	153
Bradshire, Anna	75	MD	123
Brady, Alice R	2	DE	178
Ann	2	DE	6
Ann	19	IE	279
Ann	30	IE	52
Augustus	6	DE	178
Caleb	83	DE	373
Catherine	20	PA	164
Edward	7	PA	178
Edward	30	PA	178
Eliza	35	MD	178
Elizabeth J	19	DE	203
Ellen	18	IE	52
Ellen	30	DE	6
Eugene	3	DE	6
Fanny	33	IE	276
Frances	5	PA	178
George L	25	PA	210
Hannah	11	MD	373
Harry	20	DE	210
James	26	IE	295
James	55	IE	310
Jane	43	DE	373
John	12	DE	282
John	30	IE	103
John	38	IE	276
John	50	IE	310
John F	4	MD	276
John F	24	DE	203
John J	32	DE	6
Margaret	26	IE	210
Margaret	60	IE	210
Mary	13	IE	276
Mary	85	IE	347
Mary E	2/12	DE	178
Matilda	20	MD	316
Rose	31	IE	8
Samuel	31	IE	210
Sarah	21	IE	210
William	26	DE	316
William	28	PA	210
Braidy, Bernard F	46	IE	379
Bridget W	46	IE	379
James	6	DE	379
Mary A	8	DE	379
William	4	DE	379
Braman, Catherine	73	IE	362
John	80	IE	362
John Jr	39	DE	362
William	9	PA	128
Bramble, Eliza P	37	DE	373
George M	33	MD	373
John R	11	PA	374
William R	7	PA	374
Branch, John L	14	PA	319
Brand, Anna	52	MD	23
Charles	31	PA	32
Ella	9/12	DE	32
Mary	3	DE	32
Mary	23	PA	32
Brann, Francis	68	IE	48
Brannan, Barnard	47	IE	115
Elizabeth	6	PA	115
Francis	10	PA	115
James	11	IE	115
Mary	3	PA	115
Rosanah	43	IE	115
Samuel	18	PA	164
Brannon, Elizabeth	19	DE	137
John W	11	DE	137
Priscilla	47	DE	137
William	44	DE	137
William R	7	DE	137
Brannin, Abigal	25	PA	310
Charles H	7	MA	287
Elizabeth	15	IE	287
Ellen M	4	MA	287
G W	5	DE	310
James	32	DE	310
James N	1	DE	310
Brannin, John	9	MA	287
Mary	40	IE	287
Samuel	48	IE	287
Sarah A	11	MA	287
Brannon, Margaret	88	DE	327
Michael	16	NJ	234
Brant, Isaac T	11	DE	96
Sarah E	27	DE	96
William	45	NJ	96
William A	3	DE	96
Branton, Adalade	4	DE	16
Alace	5	DE	75
Alace	20	DE	75
Eve	50	DE	75
Jacob	26	DE	16
Mary J	23	DE	16
Bratten, Alexander	38	DE	115
Ann	38	PA	376
Anna L	1	DE	376
Cather G	3	DE	115
Elizabeth T	12	DE	115
George W	5	DE	115
James H	7	DE	115
Mary A	35	GB	115
Mary E	8/12	DE	115
Mary E	7	DE	376
Bratton, Abraham	51	DE	215
Abraham Jr	16	DE	215
Ann	30	DE	288
Ann	49	DE	215
Ann E	20	DE	171
Caleb	39	DE	288
Catharine	11	DE	246
Charles M	10	DE	169
Elizabeth	14	DE	216
Elizabeth	17	DE	302
Elizabeth	56	NJ	171
Ellen	22	DE	301
Emily	11	DE	215
Emma J	11	DE	345
Frank	3	DE	245
George	66	DE	301
Henry	28	DE	169
James	36	DE	345
James A	9	DE	302
John	1	DE	288
John C	8	DE	169
Jonas	3	DE	288
Lugene N	2	DE	169
Margaretta	3	DE	345
Mary	33	DE	169
Mary	64	DE	301
Mary A	28	DE	302
Sarah	7	DE	288
Sarah	34	PA	345
Sarah E	12	DE	302
Susan	7	DE	215
Susana	6	DE	288
Susannah	17	DE	171
Thomas	21	DE	215
Thomas	54	DE	215
Thomas Jr	4	DE	215
William	4	DE	288
William	9	DE	345
William	20	DE	215
William	32	DE	376
William	41	DE	302
Braw, Anna	2	DE	73
Catherine	7	DE	73
James	25	MD	73
Josiah	8	DE	73
Julia	25	DE	73
Percy	4	DE	73
Sarah	2/12	DE	73
Bready, Phillip	37	IE	346
Brean, Mark	13	DE	317
Brease, Deborah	11	PA	109
John	13	PA	109
Mr	40	PA	109
Mrs	38	PA	109
Bredman, Catharine	22	GE	263
Henry	30	GE	263
Breen, Bridget	56	IE	302
Lewis	15	DE	302
Lewis	70	IE	167
Mary E	19	DE	302
Breene, Maria	22	MD	328
Bren, Henry	24	IE	80
Brene, James	35	IE	85
Brennan, Catharine	72	IE	300
Mary	5/12	DE	300
Mary	29	DE	300
Peter N	33	GB	300
Breslow, Margaret	50	IE	263
Brettenhouse, Ed-ward	40	MA	378
Brewer, John	50	GB	255
Joseph	35	?	270
Brewster, Eben	14	DE	220
Wilson	13	DE	220
Brian, Delancey	12	PA	293
Elizabeth	16	PA	293
Elizabeth	46	GB	293
Ellen	16	PA	293
George	60	MD	155
John	46	PA	293
Mary	39	DE	155
Thomas	75	DE	155
Brice, Cornelius	16	DE	198
Elizabeth	3	DE	197
George	35	MD	197
John	8	DE	187
Sarah J	6/12	DE	197
Bricen, Eliz J	11	DE	128
Elizabeth J	28	DE	128
James	2	DE	128
James H	39	DE	128
John	10/12	DE	128
Mary	4	DE	128
Rosanah	13	DE	128
Bride, Elizabeth	15	DE	332
Bridge, Ann	11	GB	333
Anne	33	GB	333
David	1	DE	333
David	36	GB	333
John R	5	DE	333
Sarah E	8	DE	333
Bridgeman, Margaret	20	IE	350
Brien, Catharine	25	IE	16
Frances	38	IE	167
Isabella	25	GB	34
James J	8	DE	8
Joseph	2	DE	8
Joseph	17	DE	302
Joseph	34	NH	7
Margaret	9	DE	7
Martha J	32	PA	7
Matilda	4	DE	8
Brier, Abel	9	DE	117
Abigal	23	PA	78
Ann	25	GB	78
Elizabeth	2	DE	117
Ellen	40	PA	117
Hiram	11	DE	117
John	6	DE	117
Joseph	43	GB	117
Mark	13	DE	117
Mark	64	GB	78
Sally	20	DE	78
Sarah	62	GB	78
Brigeman, Terrence	31	IE	300
Briggs, Catherine	18	DE	367
David	5	DE	367
Joseph	7	DE	367
Margaret	21	IE	318
Robert	32	DE	367
William H	8	DE	367
Bright, Abraham	25	DE	59
Adalaide	3	PA	67
Anna	10/12	DE	9
Ellen	3	DE	272
George	40	GB	67
Hannah	13	DE	76
Jacob	15	NJ	67

Name	Age	State	No.
Bright, John	9	DE	9
John	22	DE	211
Laura	3	DE	9
Lydia	29	DE	272
Lydia	42	DE	67
Lorenzo	1	MD	59
Maria	6	NJ	67
Mary	13	NY	67
Sarah	29	DE	76
Sarah J	10	DE	9
Victorene	5	DE	9
William	36	DE	76
Wilmer	30	DE	237
Wm	25	NJ	272
Brigner, Lawrence	18	IE	323
Brigs, Betty	55	MD	310
Catherine	12	DE	365
David	5	DE	373
Joseph	6	DE	373
Mary	34	DE	373
Mary	39	DE	368
Robert	35	DE	373
William	12	DE	373
Brindley, James J	67	DE	324
Sallie	22	DE	324
Rebecca B	23	DE	324
Richard	19	DE	324
Brindy, Philip	37	IE	347
Brine, Stephen	43	DE	78
Bringhurst, Anna	34	DE	31
Hannah H	26	DE	154
Henry	24	DE	31
James	53	PA	154
John	5	DE	31
Joseph	42	DE	31
Margaret	3	DE	31
Mary	22	DE	154
Sarah	24	DE	154
William	17	DE	31
Bringhurt, Margaret	15	DE	142
William	17	DE	142
Bringhust, Edward	14	DE	55
Edward	41	DE	55
Ferris	12	DE	55
Sarah	38	DE	55
Brinkle, Anna	27	DE	373
Elizabeth	22	DE	373
George	35	MD	140
Jacob	57	DE	22
John R	56	DE	373
Julia	52	DE	373
Mary	30	MD	140
Samuel C	54	DE	373
Samuel C Jr	14	PA	373
Susan R	19	PA	373
Temperance	20	DE	144
Brinkley, Anderson	34	DE	283
Anderson	35	DE	365
Eliza	23	DE	211
Eliza P	3	DE	211
Elizabeth	25	DE	324
Ellenor	85	DE	318
Hannah	52	PA	324
Jacob	53	MD	316
John R	56	DE	322
Joshua	33	DE	211
Joshua R	3/12	DE	211
Mary F	18	DE	277
Nathan	20	DE	303
Nathan	21	DE	283
Robert	64	MD	283
Samuel R	54	DE	322
Thomas B	5	DE	211
Brinklow, Amia	13	DE	75
Bathina	50	DE	75
Eliza	15	DE	75
John	10	DE	75
Perce	50	DE	75
Brinkly, Comfort	20	DE	203
Nathan	21	DE	283
Wilmina	4/12	DE	203
Brinton, Amos E	30	PA	82
Brinton, Caleb	32	DE	260
David	60	DE	253
Elwood	17	PA	43
Evans	17	PA	82
Hannah	1	DE	82
Hannah E	22	DE	82
Jacob	19	DE	293
Margaret	45	MD	253
Mary A	18	DE	279
Sabena	18	DE	354
Sarah	32	PA	82
Susan	13	IE	307
Thomas	21	IE	328
William	8	IE	307
William	12	PA	358
Brisco, Emma	8/12	DE	253
James	55	DE	253
Jane	50	DE	253
John	6	DE	253
Mary	11	DE	253
Rachel	10	DE	253
Saml	4	DE	253
Wm	8	DE	253
Briscoe, Anne	10	PA	174
Edward L	21	DE	333
Eli	22	DE	194
Elizabeth	31	PA	174
George	14	DE	75
Henry	10	DE	247
Isaac	21	MD	246
Isaac	28	DE	214
James	25	DE	242
Jane	3	DE	254
John	3	DE	228
John	14	DE	218
John	21	DE	32
John	25	DE	244
Mary	4/12	DE	156
Mary	8	PA	174
Mary M	25	DE	244
Philip	2	DE	382
W	35	PA	174
Briscow, Abraham	30	DE	382
Edward L	23	DE	334
Margaretta	23	DE	381
Mary	5	DE	381
Susan	3	DE	381
Brise, Thomas	74	DE	167
Brison, Ann M	18	MD	232
Anna	4	DE	158
John	2	DE	158
John C	38	DE	158
Margaret	27	DE	158
Rosanah	12	DE	158
Thomas E	10	DE	158
Brissey, Sarah	18	MD	164
Bristen, Charlotta	40	MD	74
Dinah	50	DE	74
Edward L	21	DE	101
Emeline J	4	DE	102
George W	10	DE	101
Georgianna	19	DE	101
Jacob W	13	DE	101
James	36	DE	74
James L	8	DE	101
Maria	46	DE	101
Mary A	22	DE	101
Robert	62	MD	101
Robert W	17	DE	101
Samuel	55	DE	74
Virginia B	15	DE	101
Brister, Alexander	23	DE	238
Alexander	24	DE	236
Ann	38	DE	238
Ann	52	DE	147
Betsey	35	DE	225
Charlota	23	DE	241
Charlott	36	DE	226
Curtis	20	DE	229
Frisby	22	DE	230
George W	7	DE	317
Hannah	46	DE	239
Brister, Hannah	11	DE	239
Henry	30	DE	196
Hezakiah	10	DE	226
Isabel	2	DE	239
Jacob	3	DE	238
Jacob	30	DE	226
Jacob	50	DE	237
James	25	DE	238
Jenny	33	DE	196
Jerry	30	DE	225
John	9	DE	238
John	25	DE	194
John	30	DE	237
John	65	DE	238
Joseph	30	DE	217
Leah	40	MD	92
Lorenzo	4	DE	239
Maria J	6	DE	241
Mary	20	DE	238
Mary A	9/12	DE	238
Mary E	9	DE	241
Matilda	25	DE	237
Rachel	8	DE	241
Rebecca	8	DE	238
Richard	15	DE	238
Rosanna	50	DE	237
Sarah	6	DE	238
Sarah A	6	DE	237
Sarah E	4/12	DE	239
Stephen	19	DE	230
Stephen	46	DE	239
Susan	7	DE	238
Sydney	12	DE	239
William	2	DE	241
William	11	DE	238
William	33	DE	238
William	40	DE	241
Bristes, Eliza	30	DE	367
Gabriel	28	DE	367
Bristow, Jacob	13	DE	365
Briten, John	24	DE	93
Brittington, Jane	35	MD	401
Britton, Benjamin F	29	MD	181
Mary A	19	DE	181
Broadbeth, Edward	65	GB	310
George	22	GB	310
Henry	12	PA	310
James	14	PA	310
John	30	GB	310
John E	16	PA	310
Joseph	8	PA	310
Martha	6	PA	310
Martha	42	GB	310
Mary E	10	PA	310
Sarah	3	PA	310
Thomas	20	PA	310
William	19	PA	310
Broadway, Martha	13	DE	266
Robert	30	DE	202
Brobson, Elizabeth	53	PA	81
Francis B	14	DE	81
James	20	DE	81
Joseph L	17	DE	81
Brockman, Major	22	GE	262
Brockson, Alice	1	DE	223
Elizabeth	25	DE	223
Elizabeth	35	DE	228
Hannah A	2	DE	228
James	30	DE	219
John	1	DE	219
Margaret A	20	DE	219
Martha L	2/12	DE	219
Richard C	3	DE	219
Brodbert, Abigal	77	CT	135
Catherine	34	CT	135
George	1	CT	135
Robert C	3	CT	135
Samuel	39	CT	135
Samuel W	8	CT	135
Brodbery, Perry	57	DE	168
Brody, Michael	16	DE	276
Brogan, Dennis	40	IE	286

Name	Age	State	Page	Name	Age	State	Page	Name	Age	State	Page
Broker, Saml	19	MD	267	Browing, Stacey	11	DE	372	Brown, Elizabeth	19	DE	82
Bron, Augustus	28	GE	312	Brown, _____	33	DE	232	Elizabeth	20	DE	141
Brook, Charles J	10	DE	336	Abraham	33	DE	232	Elizabeth	22	DE	303
Gaberella	2	DE	336	Agness	10	DE	320	Elizabeth	23	PA	299
Gaberella	37	DE	336	Alace	2	DE	41	Elizabeth	32	DE	42
George S	13	DE	336	Albert	8	DE	232	Elizabeth	46	GB	363
Georgianna	21	MD	310	Albina	19	PA	383	Elizabeth	60	PA	306
William	37	PA	336	Alexander	15	DE	363	Ellen	9	DE	317
Brooke, Charles	30	MD	161	Alfred	9/12	DE	264	Emeline	18	PA	312
James B	36	PA	75	Alfred	6	DE	309	Emeline	20	DE	71
Mary H	42	PA	75	Alfred C	1	DE	298	Emery	40	DE	308
Brookfield, Alfred	27	MD	303	Allace	40	DE	41	Emma	18	DE	368
Alice	4	DE	281	Amanda	7	DE	322	Emma	25	DE	74
Ann	22	PA	303	Amelia	3	DE	346	Emory	23	DE	366
James	10	DE	281	Amelia	21	DE	101	Ferdinand	17	DE	297
Julia	1	DE	281	Ann	20	MD	54	Frances	7	DE	38
Margaret	16	DE	281	Ann	21	PA	349	Frances	15	DE	206
Thomas	14	DE	281	Ann	22	DE	317	Francis	73	GB	312
Thomas	45	GB	281	Ann	28	IE	265	George	3/12	DE	252
Brooks, Amanda	3	DE	222	Ann	29	PA	317	George	4/12	DE	186
Ann	41	MD	371	Ann	36	MD	155	George	2	DE	232
Anna M	16	DE	381	Ann	50	DE	268	George	12	DE	306
Anna V	8	DE	182	Ann E	1	DE	196	George	25	PA	299
Benjamin	25	DE	222	Ann E	6	DE	365	George	35	PA	264
Christopher	71	DE	387	Ann E	13	DE	205	George	35	DE	339
David	1	DE	327	Ann M	1	DE	375	George	38	DE	186
David	70	DE	168	Ann M	56	DE	362	George	45	DE	206
Eliza	9	DE	327	Anna	19	DE	57	George C	3/12	DE	198
Elizabeth	25	DE	222	Anna	25	DE	91	George H	2	DE	317
Elizabeth	30	DE	379	Anna	28	DE	101	George W	11	DE	91
Esther D	18	DE	387	Anna	36	DE	102	Georgianna	3	DE	264
George	2	PA	371	Anna A	10	DE	355	Hannah	20	GB	102
George	45	?	346	Anna M	12	DE	140	Hannah	25	IE	30
George T	4	DE	379	Arnold	22	DE	252	Hannah T	28	PA	126
Henry L	3	DE	298	Arthur	36	MD	199	Harriet	2	DE	140
James	6	DE	381	Asbury	18	DE	185	Harriet	2	DE	186
James T	7	MD	298	Augustus C	14	MA	317	Harriet	20	DE	198
John	7	PA	371	Benj	39	PA	305	Henna	24	DE	132
John	12	DE	381	Benj T	5	PA	305	Henry	4	DE	232
John	66	PA	34	Benjamin	14	DE	362	Henry	5	DE	38
Joseph	36	GB	372	Benjamin	40	DE	41	Henry	16	DE	196
Joseph W	16	DE	298	Betsey	35	DE	138	Henry	23	PA	350
Josephine	2	DE	379	Caroline	33	DE	309	Henry	30	DE	251
Josiah	44	DE	381	Catharine	3	DE	315	Henry	37	DE	375
Margaret	55	PA	34	Catharine	6	DE	310	Henry	65	MD	326
Maria	40	PA	381	Catharine	22	IE	342	Hester	22	DE	60
Martha	30	MD	327	Catharine	24	DE	306	Hester	30	MD	264
Martha A	10	DE	182	Catharine	30	DE	35	Hester	41	DE	4
Mary	30	GB	371	Charles	1	DE	309	Isaac	9	DE	196
Mary J	5	DE	222	Charles	5	DE	74	Isaac	14	DE	317
Mary M	12	DE	182	Charles	36	MD	91	Isaac	24	GB	317
Mary S	37	DE	298	Charlotta	46	DE	61	Isabella	22	GB	322
Mary W	61	DE	387	Charlotta	47	DE	60	Isabella	35	DE	346
Nathan	18	PA	272	Charlotta	60	DE	156	J Holland	3	NY	271
Rachel	11	DE	381	Charlotte	12	DE	186	Jacob	23	DE	306
Rachel J	9	DE	298	Chloe	17	MD	277	Jacob	59	PA	306
Robert	35	MD	327	Clement	45	DE	363	Jacob	60	DE	60
Samuel	15	PA	371	Danial	2/12	DE	101	James	3	DE	196
Sarah	12	PA	371	Danial	14	DE	81	James	3	DE	327
Sarah A	7	DE	379	David	6	PA	40	James	9	DE	186
Sarah E	6	DE	182	David	14	DE	263	James	12	DE	362
Sarah M	4	DE	381	David	21	DE	203	James	15	PA	60
Sarah M	42	DE	182	David	25	GB	322	James	15	DE	81
Thomas	33	DE	379	David	56	DE	98	James	16	CN	53
William	50	DE	298	Diana	16	DE	391	James	21	DE	98
William C	46	MD	182	Dianah	7	DE	74	James	30	IE	274
William L	14	DE	298	Dinah	40	DE	40	James	30	IE	309
Broom, Ann	39	DE	90	Dinah	50	DE	263	James	30	GB	317
Margaret	6	DE	90	Ebenezer	30	DE	322	James	55	IE	148
William	45	DE	90	Edward	4	DE	101	James	61	DE	203
Broomall, Anna E	3	PA	284	Edward	48	RI	60	James	68	IE	53
Adaline	26	PA	399	Elias	18	DE	232	James F	3	DE	126
Brother, Patrick	14	IE	210	Elisha	29	PA	383	James J	1	DE	317
Broughton, William	36	PA	298	Eliza	4	DE	74	James J	20	DE	203
Broun, George	25	GE	340	Eliza	12	DE	375	James H	8	DE	309
Brounton, Elizabeth	32	PA	102	Eliza	16	PA	60	James H	16	DE	232
Joseph	39	PA	102	Eliza	16	DE	268	James M	35	NJ	250
Broval, Mary J	18	DE	273	Eliza	23	DE	205	James T	3	DE	204
Brow, Elenor	65	DE	44	Eliza A	1	DE	327	Jane	6	DE	346
Browing, Ann	20	DE	372	Elizabeth	4	DE	346	Jane	22	DE	112
Beula	15	DE	372	Elizabeth	6	DE	265	Jane A	12	DE	56
David	5	DE	372	Elizabeth	19	DE	38	Janet	26	DE	322

Name	Age	State	No.
Brown, Jeremiah	7	DE	196
Jesse C	18	DE	382
John	7/12	DE	322
John	4	DE	317
John	11	DE	305
John	20	DE	255
John	21	DE	268
John	23	DE	248
John	26	DE	101
John	35	MD	221
John	45	DE	257
John	50	DE	268
John	69	IE	143
John A	40	MA	317
John C	7	DE	206
John M	47	NJ	203
John R	1	DE	204
John T	28	GB	365
John W	1	DE	251
John W	12	DE	304
Joseph	5	DE	57
Joseph	20	DE	306
Joseph	20	DE	371
Joseph	25	DE	57
Joseph	26	DE	101
Joseph A	35	DE	126
Joseph F	1	DE	126
Josephine	3	PA	383
Julia A	7	DE	363
Julia A	31	DE	251
Juliet	45	NJ	49
Kate	2	DE	271
Lark	11	DE	353
Letty	40	DE	186
Louisa	18	DE	112
Lewis	8	DE	295
Lucinda	8	PA	347
Lucy	45	DE	43
Luisa	16	DE	98
Lydia	7	MD	309
Lydia	9	DE	268
Lydia	27	DE	22
Lydia E	26	DE	203
Lydia J	17	DE	81
Lydia M	29	DE	365
Lyman W	5	NY	317
Margaret	4/12	DE	140
Margaret	9	DE	79
Margaret	16	PA	362
Margaret	24	NY	271
Margaret	36	PA	162
Margaret A	5	DE	362
Margaret A	15	DE	310
Margaretta	25	DE	315
Maria	2	DE	264
Maria	34	DE	271
Maria	50	MD	57
Maria K	2	DE	362
Martha	3/12	PA	383
Martha	3	DE	37
Martha	15	DE	74
Martha	35	MD	37
Martha J	14	DE	203
Martha M	26	MD	294
Mary	1/12	DE	250
Mary	5/12	DE	155
Mary	1	DE	315
Mary	6	MD	221
Mary	9	DE	74
Mary	9	DE	186
Mary	10	DE	34
Mary	12	DE	268
Mary	16	DE	261
Mary	17	DE	99
Mary	20	IE	302
Mary	24	MD	140
Mary	25	DE	9
Mary	33	MD	221
Mary	35	DE	47
Mary	37	DE	206
Mary	38	DE	188
Mary	38	DE	375
Brown, Mary	39	NJ	257
Mary	50	PA	70
Mary	50	PA	351
Mary	53	DE	60
Mary	60	DE	232
Mary A	6	DE	232
Mary A	11	NY	164
Mary D	36	DE	204
Mary E	4	DE	191
Mary E	5	DE	140
Mary E	14	PA	380
Mary E	22	PA	333
Mary J	25	DE	250
Mary W	35	PA	361
Melvina	12	DE	257
Meriam	9	DE	101
Miriam	60	DE	101
Mitty	3	DE	186
Mrs	32	PA	40
Mrs	60	DE	53
Nancy	37	MA	317
Nancy	40	DE	235
Nathan	45	PA	353
Nathaniel	5	DE	4
Nathaniel	28	IE	327
Nathaniel	70	MD	4
Nelson	3	DE	309
Nicey A	5	DE	363
Perry	12	DE	188
Perry	31	MD	140
Perry	50	DE	263
Peter	1	DE	205
Peter	38	DE	101
Peter	62	DE	101
Phebe J	19	NY	155
Phillip	74	IE	371
Pursey P	6/12	DE	362
Rachel	10	DE	81
Rachel	20	MD	22
Rachel	40	DE	81
Rachel A	3	DE	155
Rebecca	2	PA	40
Rebecca	4	DE	140
Rebecca	5	DE	186
Rebecca	7	DE	375
Rebecca	20	DE	296
Rebecca	33	DE	232
Rebecca	35	DE	363
Rebecca	36	DE	355
Rebecca	40	DE	125
Rebecca	55	MD	184
Richard	22	DE	293
Ridgway	1	DE	74
Robert	1	PA	37
Robert	20	DE	9
Robert	24	IE	356
Robt	23	IE	336
Sally	25	DE	160
Samuel	7	DE	101
Samuel	8	DE	346
Samuel	10	MD	59
Samuel	14	DE	306
Samuel	14	IE	327
Samuel	26	DE	30
Samuel	45	DE	125
Samuel	70	MD	269
Sarah	4	MD	221
Sarah	8	PA	40
Sarah	8	DE	159
Sarah	9	DE	266
Sarah	15	PA	356
Sarah	17	DE	38
Sarah	20	DE	132
Sarah	22	IE	327
Sarah	23	DE	199
Sarah	30	DE	101
Sarah	50	DE	235
Sarah	54	PA	99
Sarah	67	MD	324
Sarah	66	DE	143
Sarah E	6/12	DE	322
Sarah E	15	DE	186
Brown, Sarah J	1	DE	4
Sarah J	5	DE	205
Sarah J	8	DE	204
Sarah J	9	DE	140
Sarah J	12	RI	317
Sarah J	16	DE	305
Susan	7	DE	370
Susan	16	MD	171
Susan	30	DE	138
Susan	39	DE	305
Susan	45	PA	70
Susan	52	MD	171
Thomas	2	DE	317
Thomas	9	DE	81
Thomas	11	DE	364
Thomas	12	DE	40
Thomas	12	DE	350
Thomas	16	DE	306
Thomas	21	MD	184
Thomas	24	IE	347
Thomas	41	NY	81
Thomas H	28	DE	315
Thomas W	25	MD	22
Till	10	DE	302
Viney	35	DE	232
Washington	8	PA	362
Wesley	4	DE	207
Wesley	35	DE	205
Westley	21	DE	252
William	2	DE	74
William	4	NY	98
William	7	DE	81
William	8	DE	375
William	14	DE	343
William	15	DE	309
William	16	NY	49
William	16	DE	57
William	30	DE	198
William	33	PA	135
William	34	PA	361
William	52	MD	156
William	66	DE	43
William	67	IE	353
William	77	DE	49
William E	10/12	DE	206
William H	8	DE	200
Wilson	17	DE	253
Wm	6	NJ	257
Wm	28	DE	268
Wm Jr	24	PA	365
Zilpha	3	DE	322
Browning, George	22	MD	213
Brox, William	23	PA	94
Brozine, Rachel	60	DE	90
Bruin, Joseph	29	DE	331
Brun, James	68	IE	302
Bruster, Catharine	27	DE	96
Cornelia	1	DE	96
Franklin	30	DE	96
Jane	3	DE	96
Jane	63	PA	96
Bryan, Celia	37	DE	281
Charles	26	MD	177
Donophan	41	DE	380
Harriet	11	DE	380
J Henson	27	DE	249
James	4	MD	281
James	44	DE	281
James W	5	DE	281
John R	20	DE	330
Margaret A	4	DE	380
Martha	48	DE	273
Mary A	29	NJ	356
Richard H	24	DE	184
Robert	9	DE	380
Sarah	65	DE	15
Sarah E	2	PA	356
Susan	7	DE	380
Susan	40	DE	380
William	26	PA	356
William A	32	MD	209
Bryant, George	27	GB	357

Name	Age	State	Page
Bryant, James B	2	PA	13
Joel B	29	NH	13
Lucretia	28	NH	13
Sarah J	5/12	DE	13
Thomas	19	GB	357
Bryne, Ann	37	NJ	136
Cyrus	34	PA	30
Georgana	12	NJ	136
Mary	9	DE	30
Rebecca	35	DE	30
Thomas J	9	DE	136
Thomas J	49	NJ	136
Bryson, Frances	36	DE	389
Madison	23	DE	389
Martha	8	DE	389
Mary	51	DE	389
Bubon, Alfred	16	LA	164
Buchanan, Angelina	3	DE	219
Anne D	11	DE	219
Bathsheba	4	DE	219
Catherine	1	DE	219
George	13	DE	219
George W	37	DE	219
Mary A	30	DE	219
Mary E	16	DE	219
Bucher, John	9	DE	254
Whilemina	9	DE	252
Buck, Annie	50	DE	337
Anthony	21	DE	320
Charles	16	DE	207
Eliza	13	DE	169
Eliza	18	PA	132
Elizabeth	23	DE	204
George	20	DE	373
Henrietta	20	DE	321
Jacob	60	DE	373
John	12	DE	321
John	23	DE	319
Maria	8	DE	337
Mary	58	DE	373
Serena	9	PA	132
Thomas	23	MD	255
Buckenhorst, Henry	29	GE	274
Mary	29	GE	274
Buckert, Hannah	3	PA	176
James	5	PA	176
John D	26	DE	176
Mary E	24	DE	176
Matthew C	1	NJ	176
Buckingham, Albin	39	DE	362
Alvin	7	DE	362
Catherine	28	DE	391
David	10	DE	362
Elizabeth	5	DE	362
Globyour	75	DE	362
Isaac G	7	DE	391
James	53	DE	351
John	2	DE	362
John	32	DE	391
Margaret	26	DE	351
Martha	60	PA	351
Mary	24	DE	350
Mary	24	DE	357
Mary	46	PA	362
Mary	50	IE	347
Richard	9	DE	362
William	23	DE	331
Buckley, Eliza	23	DE	149
Elizabeth	43	PA	149
Emma	1	DE	271
Nathaniel P	44	GB	149
Otterbine	17	PA	149
Peter	48	GB	271
Ralph	19	GB	324
Rosetta	14	PA	149
Sarah	40	DE	271
Washington	15	PA	149
Buckly, Alfred	4	DE	299
Benj	7	DE	299
Casner	2	DE	299
Ellen	2	GB	128
John	40	GB	295
Buckly, Joseph	30	GB	128
Lydia J	19	MD	328
Mary A	30	GB	128
Rachel	30	DE	299
Robert	22	MD	208
Susan	40	PA	295
Thomas	34	GB	299
Buckman, Wm T	12	DE	294
Buckmaster, Ann E	23	DE	235
George L	1	DE	235
Louis	34	DE	235
Lydia A	4	DE	235
Sarah E	6	DE	235
Buckminster, Nathan	17	DE	400
Buckson, James	22	DE	376
Reed	45	DE	376
Buckworth, Amelia J	5	DE	373
Benjamin T	9	MD	373
Charles	18	MD	373
Eliza	44	MD	373
Eliza	48	MD	367
Ellen R	13	MD	367
Joshua	16	MD	367
Joshua E	15	MD	373
Saml	45	MD	367
Samuel	43	MD	373
Budd, Catharine	20	DE	236
Elias	12	DE	291
James	25	DE	235
James N	1	DE	236
John	30	DE	332
John	66	DE	236
Sarah A	15	DE	295
Thomas	9	DE	236
William	25	DE	236
Bucy, Henry	74	SZ	107
Bugler, Catherine	39	IE	277
James	39	IE	277
Mary	1	IE	277
Patrick	4	IE	277
Phillip	6	IE	277
Bugles, James	50	PA	323
Buling, Price	22	DE	399
Bull, Rachel	9	DE	381
Bullen, Charles	5	DE	263
Emma	17	DE	263
George	11	DE	262
John	20	DE	263
Mary	39	NJ	263
Wm	7	DE	252
Bullock, Anna	13	DE	273
Charles	20	PA	273
Charles K	13	PA	400
Curtis	25	PA	291
Elizabeth	25	DE	337
Emeline	21	DE	306
Hannah	3	DE	273
James S	7	DE	273
John	10	PA	204
John M	37	PA	273
Laura	11/12	DE	306
Lewis	31	PA	306
Livingston	5	PA	273
Margaret	14	DE	273
Mary	29	PA	109
Mary E	3	DE	306
Moses S	12	PA	273
Ravanna S	1	DE	273
Samuel M	36	PA	109
Samuel R	2	DE	109
Sarah	63	PA	129
Sarah J	9	DE	273
Sarah M	2	DE	337
Thomas	18	DE	162
Vilott	37	DE	273
W B	15	PA	165
William	26	DE	337
William W	5	DE	273
Bunden, John	12	DE	44
Bundy, John	26	DE	332
Bungey, Margaret J	13	DE	307
Bungy, Amanda	6/12	DE	308
Bungy, Elma	2	DE	308
Jacob	5	DE	308
Lewis	9	DE	301
Rebecca	34	DE	308
William	8	DE	308
William	40	DE	308
Bunker, Henry	35	DE	205
Joshua	9	DE	205
Margaret	30	DE	205
Bunkin, Elizabeth	49	DE	70
Ellen	23	PA	70
James M	24	PA	70
Bunnell, Hannah J	21	DE	175
Henry	28	NJ	175
Mary E	6/12	DE	175
Bunting, Anna M	35	DE	348
Hannah	21	DE	348
John	18	DE	348
Lurena	27	DE	348
Lydia	23	DE	348
Mathew	67	IE	348
Thomas	10	DE	348
Bunyan, Josiah	9	DE	294
Jesse	53	MD	294
Burchard, David	1	DE	231
Elizabeth A	2	DE	231
Peter	25	DE	231
Sarah E	25	DE	231
Burchet, Ann	17	IE	348
Burges, Martha	46	DE	185
William	28	GB	23
Burgess, Elizabeth	23	DE	241
Ellen	21	IE	291
Emma	3	DE	187
George	1	DE	187
George	9	DE	315
George O	40	DE	187
Isabella	2	DE	315
James	25	DE	314
Jno	23	DE	291
John	57	DE	315
Joseph	6	DE	187
Margaret J	4	DE	315
Martha	2	DE	187
Martha	65	DE	313
Mary	6	DE	315
Mary	40	DE	315
Mary A	29	DE	241
Peter	26	FR	203
Rachel	35	DE	187
Sarah	14	DE	203
Sarah E	15	DE	315
Spencer	10	DE	315
Tairson	8	DE	315
Thomas	11	DE	315
Burgy, Catherine	24	DE	14
Catherine	51	GE	14
Fran	40	SZ	52
Hannah	16	DE	14
Henry	22	DE	14
John	14	DE	14
John	52	SZ	14
Joseph	10	DE	14
Mary	12	DE	14
Rosanna	19	DE	14
Sebastian	35	SZ	52
Burk, Anna	2	DE	378
Catharine	6	DE	378
Edmond	7/12	DE	378
James	4	DE	378
James	20	DE	384
John	24	PA	384
John N	10	DE	378
Lyttleton	50	DE	199
Margaret	20	DE	182
Margaret	35	DE	378
Mary	21	IE	311
Mary J	9	DE	378
Piretta	17	DE	384
Rachel	3	DE	378
Rachel R	3	DE	378
Rebecca J	30	MD	378

Burk, Sena	58	DE	384	Burns, Martha	23	NJ	289	Burton, Matilda	74	MD	366
Washington	44	MD	378	Mary	8	IE	234	Rachel	28	DE	303
William	8	DE	378	Mary	18	DE	327	Rebecca L	16	DE	304
William	26	DE	378	Mary	50	IE	320	Richard	11	DE	304
Burke, Ellen	62	IE	42	Mary J	8	IE	334	Richard	24	DE	322
Frances	44	SZ	6	Michael	12	IE	234	Richard	27	DE	366
John	8	DE	6	Michael	22	DE	327	Richard	40	PA	304
Luisa	17	DE	6	Michael	22	IE	347	Robert	35	DE	7
Peter	40	IE	6	Mrs	28	GB	102	Ruth	36	DE	304
Thomas	66	IE	42	Mrs	65	DE	52	Ruthana	3	DE	304
Ulrick P	42	IE	80	Nicholas	25	DE	327	Sarah	10	DE	303
Burkely, Andrew	37	IE	35	Patrick	2	IE	234	Sarah M	2	DE	304
Eliza	4	DE	35	Patrick	8	IE	327	William	16	DE	364
James	13	IE	35	Patrick	22	IE	347	Bush, Ann	17	DE	86
Jane	11	IE	35	Patrick	40	IE	234	Anne E	33	DE	86
Margaret	32	IE	35	Robert	25	DE	150	Catherine	2	DE	87
Samuel	6	IE	35	Sarah	7	DE	158	Catherine	37	GE	87
Burle, William	32	DE	345	Sarah	20	IE	366	Charles	45	PA	162
Burleigh, Margaret	59	DE	52	Smith H	18	DE	208	Charles C	12	PA	162
Burley, Samuel	16	DE	317	Susan	4/12	DE	334	David	75	DE	86
Burner, Henry	19	DE	379	Thomas	30	IE	334	David P	16	PA	162
Burnam, Eliza J	15	DE	290	Burnsides, Eliza	21	IE	11	Elizabeth K	20	PA	162
Elizabeth	56	DE	290	John	6/12	IE	11	Ellen	44	PA	162
Jno	20	DE	290	John	30	IE	11	Eugene E	1	DE	127
Samuel	61	DE	290	William	18	IE	11	Frederic	6	DE	67
Burnet, John	45	PA	354	Burr, Franklin	21	MD	175	George	12	DE	67
Burnett, Aner	4	DE	48	James	15	DE	202	George	20	DE	372
Anna E	11	PA	48	Jane	22	MD	175	George	53	DE	86
Catherine M	12	DE	229	Martin	56	PA	175	George W	24	DE	86
Charles W	14	MD	67	Samuel	30	DE	97	Hannah C	30	DE	138
David	50	MD	67	William H	25	DE	176	Henry	4	DE	87
David	17	MD	67	Burra, Daniel	13	DE	40	Henry S	7	DE	86
Edith	5/12	DE	48	Burrell, Sarah	14	CT	10	John F	5	DE	87
Emma	6	DE	48	Frances	10	CT	10	John T	37	GE	87
Fanny	25	PA	65	Frederic	18	DE	10	L P (Dr)	38	DE	126
George	5/12	DE	65	McCoy	12	CT	10	Leonard	24	GE	87
John	2	DE	65	Percy	26	MD	205	Lewis P	6	DE	126
John	9	DE	48	Sarah M	48	DE	10	Luisa V	10	DE	86
John	26	MD	65	Thomas T	43	NY	10	Martha	61	NJ	86
John	48	PA	48	Burren, Elizabeth D	19	PA	173	Martha P	9	DE	126
Joshua L	38	DE	229	Burrows, Mary J	28	DE	210	Maria	38	DE	126
Margaret	32	PA	49	Nemiah	33	DE	210	Mary H	10	DE	126
Mary	13	DE	49	Susan	1	DE	210	Mary R	3	DE	138
Mary	38	DE	229	Burshal, Abert J	1	DE	83	Samuel	19	PA	162
Mary E	18	DE	229	Marshal H	30	MD	83	William	39	DE	138
Purnell	16	DE	229	Mary A	23	MD	83	William C	3	PA	162
Rachel	63	PA	279	Burt, George W	6	DE	117	Bushwell, Charles	18	DE	373
Sarah	46	MD	67	John	21	PA	327	Busick, Henry	50	DE	297
Sarah E	19	MD	67	Lydia	24	DE	117	Mary	55	DE	297
William N	22	MD	67	Mary A	23	PA	327	Busmen, John	25	IE	290
Burnham, Elizabeth	39	DE	207	Mary B	3	DE	117	Bussey, Sarah	18	MD	165
Elizabeth J	14	DE	207	Thomas	25	DE	117	Butcher, Amelia	28	DE	323
Emma	9	DE	207	Burtain, Alfred L	9	DE	304	Bassett	20	DE	238
James H	52	DE	207	Anna M	7	DE	304	Eli	37	DE	342
Jno	20	DE	291	Hannah	53	DE	304	Eliza	4	DE	323
Mary A	13	DE	207	Jane	27	DE	304	Eliza	30	DE	233
Samuel	61	DE	291	John W	34	DE	304	Hannah	6	DE	323
Thomas	10	DE	207	Orlando	2	DE	304	Henry	72	DE	59
William	1	DE	207	Burten, Sarah	54	DE	88	James	11	DE	182
Burns, Andrew	16	DE	23	William	52	DE	88	James J	10	DE	233
Ann	28	IE	163	Burton, Albert	38	MD	373	Jerry	40	MD	197
Anna	9	IE	334	Alhaney	15	DE	139	John	8/12	DE	233
Bridget	6	IE	234	Anna	10	DE	373	John	2	DE	323
Bridget	30	IE	334	Burres	2	DE	7	Margaret E	13	DE	233
Danial	75	DE	52	Catherine	10	DE	7	Robert	8	DE	233
David	30	IE	327	Daniel W	7	DE	304	Robert	50	DE	233
Elizabeth	3	IE	334	Edward C	9	DE	304	Susan	65	DE	59
Ellen	20	IE	52	Elizabeth	18/12	DE	366	Thomas	28	DE	323
George W	40	GB	319	Elizabeth W	5	DE	304	William J	12	DE	233
James	6/12	IE	234	Emily	31	NJ	7	Butler, Abraham	50	DE	92
James	2	DE	327	Hannah M	2	DE	304	Ann	40	DE	92
James	25	IE	289	Henrietta	23	DE	366	Ann E	17	VA	165
John	4	IE	234	Henry	35	DE	366	Anne	11	IE	103
John	21	DE	23	Henry	50	DE	12	Anne	20	PA	101
John	30	IE	102	Isabella	6	DE	373	Anne M	12	PA	157
Joseph	27	CN	289	Jacob	35	DE	303	Barnard	50	IE	103
Lydia	22	DE	150	Jane	24	PA	322	Catherine	15	IE	103
Margaret	5	IE	334	John A	15	DE	304	Eleazer	48	NJ	133
Margaret	23	IE	366	Louisa	4	DE	373	Elender	49	IE	103
Margaret	26	IE	59	Margaret	18	DE	140	Elener	44	PA	33
Margaret	30	IE	327	Margaret J	5	DE	303	Eliza	4	DE	92
Martha	22	IE	289	Matilda	5	DE	366	Elizabeth	3	PA	157

Name			
Butler, Elizabeth	6	DE	374
Elizabeth	16	DE	92
Elizabeth	17	NJ	133
Ellen	10	IE	103
George	13	DE	224
Hannah J	30	DE	388
Hester	29	PA	38
Hester	90	DE	167
Ira	42	PA	33
Isaac	50	NJ	374
James	8	DE	236
James	15	PA	33
James	35	MD	38
James	70	MD	65
Jane	12	DE	92
Jefferson M	8	PA	157
John	16	IE	103
John	18	DE	296
John	40	DE	102
John O	9/12	DE	374
Josephine	6/12	PA	157
Lemuel	22	PA	374
Margaret	9	DE	374
Margaret	44	NJ	374
Maria	40	WN	41
Martha A	11	DE	329
Mary	14	DE	57
Mary	25	DE	121
Mary	30	PA	157
Mary A	11	DE	374
Mary A	19	NJ	133
Mary J	13	PA	157
Rebecca	21	DE	49
Samuel	15	NJ	133
Sarah	54	NJ	133
Susan	16	DE	143
Susanah	18	PA	33
Thomas	25	MD	335
Thomas B	22	DE	386
Washington J	14	PA	157
William B	18	DE	92
Butte, Sarah	18	DE	236
Butterworth, Charles	12	DE	358
Buyard, Hestalice	2/12	DE	174
James	2/12	DE	174
Buyers, Mary	1	DE	107
Samuel	23	DE	107
Sarah	23	DE	107
Buzby, David L	22	DE	99
Eliza A	41	NJ	165
Ella	14	DE	99
Florence	6/12	DE	99
Frank	8	DE	99
Henry	18	DE	99
Maria	44	NJ	9
Mary	20	MD	99
Samuel	55	NJ	99
Buzine, Amanda	19	DE	80
Ella	3	DE	108
George	30	MD	108
Henry	15	DE	80
Msria	54	MD	80
Martha	23	DE	80
Martin	10	DE	80
Rebecca	28	PA	108
Robert	6	DE	108
Samuel	63	DE	80
Susannah	8	DE	108
Byam, Charles	40	DE	310
Byard, Alexander	13	DE	381
Ann	25	MD	300
Charles	30	DE	297
Emson	18	MD	318
George	25	DE	391
Henry	13	DE	280
Henry	30	DE	383
Henry	69	MD	383
John	13	DE	84
Josephine	11	DE	398
Julia A	25	DE	297
Laura	4	DE	391
Laura	7	MD	300
Byard, Leah	19	DE	303
Lucy A	11/12	DE	297
Lucy Ann	34	DE	401
Mary	60	DE	383
Perry	22	DE	380
Rachel	14	DE	380
Ruth	55	DE	84
Thomas	8	DE	135
Byards, Anna R	22	DE	287
James	5	DE	325
Jerry	29	DE	325
John J	5	DE	287
Lavenia	27	DE	325
William A	33	DE	287
William H	5	DE	287
Byas, Jereldean	5	DE	83
Mary	29	DE	83
Bye, Benjamin T	28	PA	1
Bill	32	PA	1
P P	25	PA	1
Pusey P	4	PA	1
Ruth A	6	PA	1
Byers, George	28	DE	333
Byes, Sarah	20	DE	394
Byrne, James	28	IE	130
John W	4/12	DE	130
Mary A	23	NF	130
Timothy F	4	NJ	130
Byrns, Margaret	26	DE	10
Mary	20	DE	10
Cade, Anna A	4/12	DE	89
Elizabeth	13	DE	274
John	4	DE	89
John	55	NJ	88
Martha	7	DE	89
Martha	36	PA	89
Mary	9	DE	89
Rebecca	11	NJ	89
Caffant, Benjamin	19	DE	66
James	22	DE	66
Mary	13	DE	66
Mary	39	DE	66
Thomas	52	DE	66
Cahill, Elizabeth	11	DE	301
Elizabeth	23	IE	301
Mary	7	DE	301
Sarah	9	DE	301
Thomas	45	IE	301
Cain, Alli	6	DE	342
Almira A	8	DE	356
Ann	11	PA	278
Ann L	14	DE	319
Anna	49	DE	356
Bennet J	17	DE	356
Catherine	10	PA	278
Charles	17	DE	319
Elizabeth	6	DE	278
Flecher	11	DE	319
James	14	PA	278
Jane E	9	DE	319
Jesse H	55	PA	356
John	30	IE	356
John	38	PA	278
John	40	DE	319
Louisa	3	DE	278
Margaret A	9	DE	342
Margaret A	32	DE	342
Mary F	12	DE	342
Nancy	40	MD	319
Robert	40	DE	342
Robert F	3	DE	342
Sarah	8	DE	278
Theodore	5	DE	319
William	16	DE	278
Cairy, Andrew	11	DE	380
Calahan, Amelia J	14	DE	349
Ann M	18	DE	349
Charles J	2	DE	349
Daniel	10	DE	349
Elizabeth	7	DE	349
Frances P	4	DE	349
Calahan, James	23	DE	341
Joseph H	11	DE	349
Mary	37	FR	349
Michael	39	IE	349
Calder, Charlotte	57	MD	170
J Cookman	2	DE	261
John	28	MD	261
Joseph	16	PA	139
Martha	6	DE	261
Mary	4	DE	261
Mary	33	DE	261
Caldwell, Alex	70	DE	102
Alfred	14	DE	85
Anna	7	DE	307
Anna W	12	PA	284
Anne	26	DE	87
Charles	9	DE	67
Charles	17	DE	232
Charles	40	DE	87
Caroline	6	DE	67
Catherine	18	DE	286
Catherine	19	DE	303
Catherine	36	MD	67
Daniel	4	DE	307
David	44	DE	284
David F	15	PA	284
Elizabeth	40	DE	101
Ezekiel	2	DE	307
Ezekle	35	DE	102
Fran R	12	DE	307
Henry W	9	DE	284
Hesekiah	14	DE	102
Isabella	12	DE	67
James	15	DE	67
James	16	DE	307
James	36	MD	307
Jane	2	DE	92
John A	28	DE	281
Jonathan T	30	DE	102
Joseph	58	DE	281
Julia	42	NJ	284
Laura	5	DE	307
Lucinda	15	DE	101
Luisa	6	DE	87
Lydia	6	DE	307
Margaret	3/12	DE	307
Mary	4	DE	92
Mary	31	MD	101
Mary	35	MD	307
Mary	50	PA	127
Mary A	10	DE	101
Mary E	2	DE	87
Mele	1	DE	87
Melie	25	DE	92
Menassa	25	DE	67
Rachel	40	PA	281
Rebecca	9	DE	324
Richard	19	DE	300
Rosana	12	DE	101
Sarah	14	DE	307
Sarah	50	DE	287
Sarah	75	DE	187
Sidney	30	DE	32
Susan	21	DE	101
Timothy	26	DE	92
Valety	10	DE	300
Wesley	32	DE	140
William	18	DE	102
William	18	DE	288
William	18	DE	307
William	19	PA	216
Cale, Dual	40	DE	277
Mary	52	DE	277
Calesbury, Charles	17	MD	373
Martha H	12	MD	373
Caley, Joseph	16	DE	224
Calhoun, Ann	6	DE	313
Ann	30	DE	254
Caroline	15	DE	267
Harriett	30	DE	313
James	3	DE	313
John	17	DE	370

Name	Age	State	No.
Calhoun, John W	29	DE	254
Lynias	15	DE	313
Martha	18	DE	267
Mary E	2	DE	254
Sarah	54	DE	267
Thomas	30	IE	320
William	31	DE	313
Wm	3	DE	254
Call, Albin A	45	DE	362
Andrew	50	IE	4
Eli	36	DE	362
Margaret	55	IE	4
Callahan, Ann	35	DE	301
Catherine	19	IE	312
Catherine	29	PA	68
Daniel	10	DE	301
Dennis	4	DE	301
Dennis	45	DE	301
Frances	3	DE	301
Hannah Ann	14	DE	346
Jeremiah	29	IE	301
John	23	DE	283
Lucretia	16	DE	346
Luisa	6	DE	68
Patric	33	IE	68
Patrick R	77	IE	301
Sarah	1	DE	301
Secilia	6	DE	301
Susan	11	MD	178
William	12	DE	301
Callaway, Anna M	9	PA	123
Catherine	7	PA	123
Elener	16	PA	123
Elizabeth	18	PA	123
Emma	4	DE	123
James	10/12	DE	123
James	43	PA	123
Mary A	38	PA	123
Mary J	19	PA	123
William	12	PA	123
Cally, Hannah	16	DE	224
Joseph	16	MD	225
William	29	DE	188
Caln, Mary	20	IE	374
Calvert, Albert L	21	MD	99
Ann	26	DE	41
Anna	2	DE	41
Bethena	42	DE	38
Caroline	46	MD	99
Charles W F	14	MD	99
George	11/12	PA	272
Hannah M	19	DE	99
Harriet B	19	MD	99
Henry	3	PA	272
Josephine	33	PA	271
Joshua	5	DE	41
Mary	9	DE	41
Walter	60	PA	38
William	23	PA	41
William H	16	MD	99
William H	46	MD	99
Wm	27	PA	271
Calvery, Joseph	35	GE	278
Persyla	34	GE	278
Cambirs, Harriet	13	DE	381
Jacob	50	DE	381
Jemima	30	DE	381
Camblin, James	9	MD	341
Cambridge, Harriet	2	DE	368
Hetty	28	DE	368
Jacob	3/12	DE	368
John	22	DE	368
Cameron, Charles C	3	DE	206
Daniel	40	IE	334
Ephraim	25	DE	194
Frances E	14	DE	206
Frank W	1	DE	206
Isabella	11/12	DE	295
Jane	30	MD	295
John	55	DE	206
Josephine	11	DE	194
Levi	9/12	DE	194
Cameron, Mary	41	DE	206
Rachel	17	DE	194
Rebecca	23	DE	194
Sarah E	10	DE	206
Susan	12	IE	206
Thomas H B	6	DE	206
Virginia	8	DE	206
Camey, Susan	12	IE	84
Cammel, Charles	9	DE	300
Hannah	8	DE	300
James	8	PA	365
John	35	IE	302
Owen	23	IE	302
Cammile, Ann	35	DE	281
Cammill, Catherine	45	IE	289
Peter	17	IE	301
Sarah	46	DE	286
Cammomile, (male)	30	DE	248
Margaret	19	DE	231
Samuel	12	DE	227
Cammon, John J	16	DE	401
Susan E	2	DE	375
Camp, Charles H	6	DE	151
Joseph	38	NJ	151
Joseph C	4	DE	151
Laura	8/12	DE	151
Tabitha	27	DE	151
Campbell, Acenith	35	DE	361
Agnes	40	IE	338
Alfred	9/12	NJ	14
Amos	4	DE	361
Ann J	28	NH	5
Ascenith	33	DE	356
Betsey	70	DE	42
Catherine	28	DE	29
Charles	21	NJ	14
David	34	DE	361
Edward D	3	DE	8
Eli	28	NJ	355
Elizabeth	39	DE	361
Ellen	3	DE	5
Ellen	9	PA	27
Ellen	30	IE	358
Emeline	30	PA	303
Felix	32	IE	5
Franklin	1	DE	317
George	10	DE	8
George W	28	PA	314
Hugh T	3/12	DE	5
James	2	DE	26
James	28	DE	303
James	52	DE	353
James M	6	MD	303
Jane	28	DE	26
Jane	40	DE	351
Jesse	2	DE	361
John	12	PA	294
John	27	IE	197
John	35	DE	32
John L	5	DE	5
Joseph S	1	MD	303
Lazero	20	DE	354
Margaret B	23	DE	310
Mary	8	DE	24
Mary	33	MD	8
Mary	56	IE	353
Mary A	20	DE	310
Mary J H	8/12	DE	8
Neal	26	IE	392
Neal	30	IE	45
Parmenos	7	DE	361
Patric	35	IE	29
Rachel	18	NJ	14
Rebecca	26	DE	361
Rebecca	77	DE	361
Samuel	7/12	DE	361
Sarah	78	DE	361
Sarah E	7	MD	8
Thomas @	5	DE	8
William	16	DE	249
William	39	DE	26
William H	35	DE	8
Campbell, Wm L	7	DE	303
Campell, Anna G	27	DE	111
Catherine	2	IE	108
Catherine	4	DE	63
Catherine	55	IE	167
Charles H	2	DE	111
Charles S	25	NJ	111
Charlotta	11	DE	63
Elizabeth	22	DE	167
Ellen	26	MD	68
George	25	IE	108
George W	1	DE	63
Hannah	86	DE	168
James	4	IE	108
John	19	DE	58
John	25	MD	68
John	26	IE	79
Joseph	40	DE	68
Mary	6/12	DE	167
Mary	11	DE	63
Mary	73	IE	68
Michel	80	IE	107
Rebecca	52	DE	58
Samuel	22	VA	55
Sarah	20	DE	58
Sarah A	40	NJ	63
Sarah E	2	DE	68
Susan	26	IE	108
Tempe	11	DE	138
William	3	DE	68
William	45	PA	79
Campwell, William	16	IE	250
Canada, Ann	52	IE	286
James	52	IE	286
Margaret	78	DE	336
Martin	80	IE	286
Canady, Ira	15	DE	359
Canale, Alexander	17	MD	56
Canary, Henry	26	PA	284
Jane	26	DE	284
John W	1	PA	284
Canby, Amelia	2	DE	338
Anna	17	PA	162
Anna B	26	DE	65
Catherine R	11	DE	10
Charles	52	PA	32
Edmond	2	DE	137
Edward F	3/12	DE	65
Eliza	50	DE	162
Elizabeth	12	DE	338
Elizabeth	22	DE	137
Elizabeth	68	PA	10
Ellen	5	DE	137
Fanny	8	DE	137
Frances	5	DE	338
Francis	45	DE	338
Isabella	2	DE	338
James	17	DE	137
James	23	IE	350
James	69	DE	10
Jane	6	DE	338
Joshua	50	DE	261
Lydia	27	DE	31
Margaret	10	DE	137
Mary	19	DE	137
Mary A	8	DE	337
Mary T	42	DE	137
Martha	15	DE	162
Merrell	52	DE	162
Robert M	27	DE	10
S	23	DE	355
Samuel	13	DE	137
Susan	14	DE	338
William	19	PA	162
William	28	DE	65
Candress, Margaret	19	MD	360
Cane, Bridget	18	IE	318
Henry	11	IE	322
Joseph	30	DE	16
Sarah	20	IE	317
Cann, Adela	2	DE	317
Amelia	16	DE	327

Name	Age	St	Pg
Cann, Amelia	32	NH	317
Amelia A	6	NH	317
Amos B	13	NH	317
Ann	19	DE	341
Ann H	31	PA	342
Clara L	4	DE	317
Daniel	59	DE	327
Daniel S	33	DE	342
Eliza	35	DE	273
Elizabeth	71	DE	377
George T	30	DE	208
James	36	NH	317
James	45	DE	377
James A	8	NH	317
Janeth E	31	DE	317
Laura	8/12	DE	208
Lydia A	20	DE	327
Mary A	10	NH	317
Mary E	8	DE	342
Rebecca	29	DE	208
Richard	1	NH	317
Richard F	34	DE	317
Robert	4	NH	317
Robert H	2	DE	342
Samuel W	5	DE	342
Sarah	50	DE	327
Theodore H	4	DE	208
Thomas H	8	DE	317
William H	11	NJ	317
Cannon, Abraham	44	DE	375
Alexander	1/12	DE	305
Ann	35	DE	38
Ann	45	IE	287
Anna	9	DE	263
Anthony	6/12	DE	12
Biddy	38	IE	358
Cecilia	25	IE	305
Charles H	7	DE	375
Clarissa	15	DE	185
Cornelia	17	DE	375
Daniel	36	IE	331
Dennis	4	IE	305
Dennis	30	IE	305
Doming	4	IE	305
Edith	28	DE	354
Elizabeth	18	DE	183
Ellen	11	DE	263
Emily	4	DE	212
Hannah	11	DE	212
Hannah	45	DE	212
Henry	15	DE	206
Hugh	48	IE	287
Isaac	5	DE	277
Isaac	26	DE	206
James	3	DE	12
James	11	IE	305
John	2	DE	305
John	15	IE	287
John	36	PA	287
Joseph	8	DE	354
Joseph A	3	DE	287
Joseph T	9	DE	287
Levi	55	DE	212
Levi Jr	14	DE	212
Lydia	23	DE	19
Margaret	9	IE	305
Mariana	12	DE	375
Mary	23	DE	206
Mary	38	DE	375
Mary J	31	DE	287
Michael	35	IE	358
Noah	40	DE	38
Patrick	12	IE	287
Patrick	17	IE	355
Rebecca S	9	DE	375
Ruth A	17	DE	185
Samuel	40	DE	354
Sarah	38	MD	305
Theodore	6	DE	206
William	1	DE	354
William	26	DE	212
William H	5	DE	287
Cannon, William W	5	DE	375
Canon, Joseph	15	DE	354
Cantwell, William	25	IE	284
William	26	IE	294
Canun, Mary	20	DE	354
Capelle, Eliza W	24	DE	252
Joseph E	25	DE	252
Marcus	1	DE	252
Cappell, Alexander	11	DE	116
Catherine	46	DE	116
Catherine J	9	DE	116
George	14	DE	116
Maria	23	DE	116
Mary	17	DE	116
Cara, Elizabeth	33	DE	246
James	10	DE	246
James	32	MD	220
Maria	3	DE	220
Martha A	4	DE	220
Mary C	8	DE	220
Mary E J	8	DE	246
Sarah A	13	DE	246
Susan	31	DE	220
Thomas	6	DE	246
Thomas	35	DE	246
William G B	2	DE	246
William L	6	DE	220
Carden, Patric	30	IE	89
Cargingly, Ellen	24	GB	51
Carl, Caroline	12	DE	263
Catherine	7	DE	263
Emeline	50	DE	302
Elizabeth	6	DE	263
Elizabeth	34	GE	263
Joseph	2/12	DE	263
Magdalena	9	DE	263
Michael	36	GE	263
Samuel	50	DE	302
Thomas	2	DE	263
Carlaw, Louisa	20	DE	140
Noah	17	DE	140
Carle, Ann	27	IE	18
Joseph	9	PA	163
Carley, Catherine	41	IE	12
James	40	IE	12
Sophia	29	IE	12
Carlin, Cecilia	8	DE	22
Elizabeth	40	DE	22
John	6/12	DE	22
Mary	6	DE	22
Michael	38	DE	224
Michel	50	IE	22
William	5	DE	22
Carlise, Francis	5	DE	77
James	3	DE	77
Nelson	31	DE	77
Traphena	30	MD	77
William	3/12	DE	77
Carlisle, Abigail	36	PA	349
Abigail	50	PA	31
David	6	DE	349
Jane B	25	DE	77
Paris S	15	DE	400
Robert	3	DE	349
William	32	DE	77
William	36	DE	349
William N	5/12	DE	349
Carly, Eliza	13	DE	176
Levi	14	MD	176
Carmel, Caroline	18	IN	166
Caressa D	20	DE	351
Carmell, Elizabeth	67	PA	283
Isaac	38	PA	283
Carmikle, James	18	MD	85
Carnahan, James A	12	OH	360
Carnan, Ann	27	IE	142
Carney, Amanda	6	DE	154
Christina	1	DE	154
James	30	DE	199
James	45	DE	255
Levi	24	MD	318
Madalena	4	DE	154
Carney, Mary	24	DE	154
Carnilon, Elizabeth	53	DE	33
Carnnon, William	21	DE	365
Carny, Anne L	4	PA	150
Ellen V	3	DE	296
Elmira J	2	PA	150
Emma	31	PA	296
Ester	21	MD	150
George W	5/12	PA	150
James	25	MD	150
Jane	24	IE	59
Margaret	28	IE	43
Mary	50	IE	59
Wm J	1	DE	296
Wm R	35	IE	296
Caroll, Anna	13	IE	377
Anna	35	IE	377
Catherine	2	DE	377
Francis	8	DE	377
Mary	5	DE	377
Patrick	15	IE	377
Carpenter, Alfred	12	DE	354
Ann	38	MD	35
Ann E	4	DE	354
Benjamin	35	DE	354
Charles	45	DE	149
Eliza A	54	DE	280
Elizabeth	3	DE	354
Elizabeth	22	DE	49
Elizabeth	25	DE	31
Elizabeth	54	PA	348
Emma	26	PA	60
Erastus S	5	DE	354
George	2	DE	35
George	14	DE	309
George	15	DE	355
Isabella	8	DE	35
Jacob	75	PA	282
James	4	DE	31
James	25	DE	159
James	49	DE	188
James S	33	PA	354
Jane	6	DE	35
Jane	35	PA	282
John	11	DE	309
John	21	DE	145
John	28	DE	354
John B	3	DE	354
John L	42	DE	278
John S	2	DE	354
Jonah	23	DE	28
Jonathan	50	DE	150
Joseph	37	GB	60
Joseph	39	DE	282
Joseph S	9	DE	354
Josephine	6	DE	354
Josephine	8	PA	164
Julia A	25	DE	159
July A	40	DE	282
Lewis	1	DE	4
Lewis	20	DE	3
Lydia	30	DE	354
Margaret	20	DE	4
Margaret	28	DE	354
Margaret A	8	DE	354
Maria L	10	PA	164
Mark	40	PA	284
Martha	20	DE	159
Martha	50	DE	35
Martha J	8	DE	282
Mary	3	DE	31
Mary	4	DE	35
Mary	5	DE	149
Mary	15	NY	142
Mary	20	PA	304
Mary	48	DE	35
Mary A	35	DE	149
Phebe A	18	DE	149
Robert	12	DE	149
Samuel	55	DE	188
Samuel	67	PA	280
Sarah	2	DE	149

Name	Age	St	No
Carpenter, Susan	33	DE	278
Thomas	26	DE	31
Thomas E	10	DE	35
William	13/12	DE	354
William	54	MD	314
William	56	DE	327
Carr, Abraham	16	DE	368
Alice H	13	PA	330
Ann E	19	PA	330
Augustus	17	DE	180
Barbara	44	GB	293
Barnard	35	IE	12
Catherine	14	IE	344
Charles	12	IE	344
Charles S	9	PA	354
Cornelius	42	IE	344
David	56	PA	354
Elizabeth	10	DE	108
Elizabeth	28	PA	354
Elizabeth	39	DE	108
Elizabeth C	2	DE	293
Ellwood T	3	PA	309
Frances	40	IE	344
George S	4	DE	293
George T	6	PA	309
Henry	3	DE	149
Henry	12	DE	240
Hiram	14	PA	330
Hiram	52	PA	330
Hiram	60	PA	323
Isabel	17	PA	330
James	5	IE	344
Jane	10	IE	344
Jane	62	PA	354
John	5	DE	240
John	39	PA	309
John	40	MD	110
John W	8	PA	309
Joseph	21	DE	293
Joseph	57	GB	293
Joseph L	10	PA	309
Lucy G	5	DE	294
M A	15	DE	165
Margaret	15	DE	293
Margaret	33	PA	309
Margaret	50	MD	110
Margaret	74	PA	293
Margaret E	12	PA	309
Margery	50	PA	331
Mary	18	DE	293
Mary	30	IE	149
Mary	49	PA	240
Mary	60	IE	148
Mary A	18	DE	178
Mary J	1	DE	309
Mary S	24	DE	293
Michael	21	DE	258
Michael	70	DE	313
Michel	40	IE	149
R	8	DE	165
Ravenna	9	DE	293
Rebecca	38	DE	12
Rebecca J	6	DE	108
Sarah	12	DE	108
Sarah A	15	PA	309
Susannah	20	DE	108
Thomas R	1	DE	108
V E	11	DE	165
Virginia	12	DE	293
Washington	23	PA	354
William	4	DE	109
William	16	IE	344
William	28	DE	293
William P	46	DE	108
Wm	22	DE	255
Carrell, Mathew	25	IE	163
Carrigan, Bridget	6	IE	326
Bridget	38	IE	326
James	3	IE	326
James	36	IE	326
Jane	7	IE	326
Mary	13	IE	326
Carroll, Albert	14	MD	163
Allice	50	IE	310
Ann	18	DE	311
Charles	25	MD	86
Hugh	25	IE	311
John	16	DE	311
John	50	IE	395
John	62	IE	310
Margaret	1	DE	395
Mary	4	DE	395
Mary	20	DE	311
Mary	35	IE	395
Carry, Andrew	12	DE	100
Anna	8/12	DE	100
Cornelius	37	DE	100
Elizabeth	36	DE	100
Elizabeth	68	DE	56
Mary	10	DE	100
Carsner, Ann	20	DE	294
Carson, Adam	25	MD	193
Amos	30	NJ	258
Catherine S	30	PA	386
Edward	7	MD	301
Edward	30	MD	301
Eliza	12	DE	291
Elizabeth	34	DE	271
Elizabeth	40	MD	301
Frank	3/12	DE	273
Harry	6	DE	273
Henry	9	MD	301
James	4	DE	258
John	9	DE	273
John	22	MD	296
John	47	ST	273
Kesiah	28	NJ	258
Rachel	39	MD	266
Rebecca	14	MD	301
Ruth	47	DE	296
Thomas	12	MD	301
Tobias	47	MD	296
Victorine	14	DE	273
Wm	3	DE	273
Wm	43	NJ	266
Carsons, Joseph	2	DE	296
Leah	23	MD	296
Carswell, Ada V	1	DE	116
Clara	3	DE	154
Edward T	7	DE	116
Eliza	21	DE	154
Eliza	66	DE	154
Frances W	6/12	DE	124
Henry	1	DE	154
Howard M	2	DE	124
Jane	35	DE	124
Laura E	4	DE	124
Mary G	9	DE	116
Rachel A	29	DE	116
Robert	38	DE	116
Susan	35	DE	154
Susanah E	25	PA	124
Wilson	29	DE	154
Carter, Alexoma	34	DE	272
Amous	26	DE	320
Ann	7/12	DE	272
Ann	12	DE	266
Anne M	2/12	DE	298
Christopher	6	MD	272
David	23	PA	310
Eliza	13	KY	23
Elizabeth	3	DE	298
Elizabeth	30	MD	298
Emma	20	DE	109
Fernanda	19	VA	23
Frederic	21	KY	23
George	34	GB	334
George W	5	DE	334
Hannah	24	PA	31
Harriet	19	PA	311
Henry	4	DE	266
James	8	DE	266
Jane	25	DE	23
Jonathan	6	DE	298
Carter, Joseph	33	PA	298
Josephine	16	VA	23
Kerdelia	8	PA	334
Mary	9	MD	298
Mary	20	DE	320
Mary	35	DE	266
Mary	45	DE	23
Mary A	30	DE	334
Mary E	19	DE	349
Mary V	5/12	DE	334
Nathan	36	MD	266
Phebe	2	DE	320
R W	24	PA	349
Rebecca	8	MD	298
Richard E	3	DE	334
Samuel	23	PA	117
Samuel	25	PA	31
Sarah	10	DE	266
Spencer	34	MD	32
Theodore	37	MD	272
Walraven	23	PA	23
William	20	DE	292
Zeporah	62	NJ	311
Cartner, George M	22	DE	380
Cartwell, Elizabeth	37	GB	291
George	39	DE	291
Hannah	1	DE	291
John	44	DE	291
John B	9	DE	291
Margaret E	4	DE	291
Mary	52	DE	291
Rebecca	34	DE	291
Sarah A	42	DE	291
Thomas	50	DE	291
William	12	DE	291
Cartwright, Henri-etta	31	MD	33
Mary	28	DE	213
Sarah	7	DE	33
Spencer	45	DE	33
Carty, Cahrles	6	GB	384
Elizabeth	12	GB	384
George	14	GB	384
Hannah	38	GB	384
Joseph	10	GB	384
Lewis	16	DE	295
Richard	8/12	DE	384
Richard	43	GB	384
Sarah	8	GB	384
Susan	23	DE	251
Susan	51	DE	375
Cary, Mary A	25	IE	317
Casady, John	14	PA	54
Casalow, Ann	37	DE	341
John T	4	DE	341
Sarah E	11	DE	341
William G	51	DE	341
William H	13	DE	341
Case, Howard	28	PA	340
Lewis	17	DE	130
Casell, James	15	NY	353
Casere, Margaret	14	MD	165
Casey, Andrew	26	IE	274
Anna	25	IE	274
Michael	22	IE	347
Wm	1	DE	274
Cash, Eliza	40	DE	6
Eliza Ann	7	DE	6
Joseph	17	PA	6
Joseph	17	DE	53
William	13	PA	6
Cashaw, Ann	49	GB	66
Edward	12	GB	66
John	18	GB	66
Joseph	16	GB	66
Joseph	50	GB	66
William	20	GB	66
Casho, Anna	4	DE	395
Eliza	34	DE	395
George A	31	MD	395
James	7	DE	395
William W	17	MD	395

Name	Age		
Caslow, William	16	DE	328
Casperson, John	12	NJ	254
Margaret	6	DE	254
Mary	2	DE	254
Sarah	38	NJ	254
Wm	38	DE	254
Cass, Bridget	20	IE	67
Joseph	17	DE	54
Lewis	2/12	DE	229
Cassady, Anne	5	ME	124
Catherine	37	IE	124
Edward	17	ME	124
Ellen	20	IE	290
Francis	23	ME	124
John	10	ME	124
John	47	IE	124
Julia	8	ME	124
Maria	19	PA	124
Mary	23	CN	81
Mary	30	PA	282
Mary	49	IE	310
Mary	50	IE	301
Matilda	13	ME	124
Peter	40	IE	282
Rebecca	50	DE	282
Robert L	3	DE	124
Cassan, Mary	22	DE	32
Casseday, Edward	34	IE	347
Cassell, Joseph E	24	DE	251
Eliza W	24	DE	251
Marcus	1	DE	251
Cassey, ____	2/12	DE	280
Elizabeth	9	DE	280
Joseph	4	DE	280
Margaret	13	DE	280
Mary E	30	DE	280
Robert	11	DE	280
Robert	48	NY	280
Thomas C	2	DE	280
William	29	NY	284
Caster, Hannah	14	PA	166
Castle, Theodore	20	NY	380
Castlow, Anabella	13	DE	181
Elizabeth	8	DE	181
Jeremiah	43	DE	180
John	35	DE	356
John F	10	DE	180
Margaret	35	DE	356
Rachel	4	DE	356
Sarah	6	DE	356
Susan	1	DE	356
Susan	42	DE	180
Thomas C	5	DE	181
William	7	DE	356
William	15	DE	180
William	16	DE	211
Cathcart, Hannah	50	IE	283
William	15	PA	400
Cather, Martha	65	DE	113
Cathers, Anna	44	IE	327
James	17	IE	327
John	10	IE	327
John	64	IE	327
Mary A	14	IE	327
Robert	12	IE	327
Catlin, Ann C	7	DE	178
Heber C	4	DE	178
Jonathan	54	DE	178
Justice	2	DE	178
Mary E	9	DE	178
Mary J	54	DE	178
Robert	11/12	DE	178
Cauders, Anna	16	MD	351
Caulk, ____	35	DE	177
Abraham	26	DE	301
Absolem	32	DE	74
Alfred	2	DE	221
Alfred	22	DE	255
Alice	6	DE	226
Andrew	7	DE	221
Angelina	8	DE	237
Ann	30	DE	210
Caulk, Benjamin	51	DE	376
Boulden	64	DE	220
Caroline	16	DE	221
Columbus	12	MD	294
Cornelius	32	MD	294
David A	23	DE	317
Deborah	1	DE	221
Deborah	40	DE	220
Dennis	2	DE	276
Eliza	45	DE	226
Elizabeth	6	DE	109
Elizabeth	16	DE	166
Elizabeth	16	DE	255
Elizabeth	30	DE	72
Emeline	16	DE	221
Emeline	19	DE	192
Frances O	10	DE	377
George	6	DE	237
George	75	MD	226
Harriet	47	DE	237
Hester	40	MD	276
Isaac	14	DE	241
Isaac	50	DE	241
Israel	55	DE	1
Jacob	32	DE	236
James	35	DE	72
James	60	DE	308
Jane	25	DE	189
Jane C	6	DE	294
Jane W	35	MD	376
Jesse	26	DE	305
John	8	DE	72
John	9	DE	221
John	35	DE	294
John	40	DE	47
Judith	6	DE	294
Levi	2	DE	237
Levi	49	DE	276
Louisa V	6	DE	276
Lydia	14	DE	108
Lydia M	18	DE	221
Margaret	32	DE	74
Margaret	50	DE	316
Mary	2	DE	108
Mary	25	DE	53
Mary	27	PA	108
Mary	57	DE	255
Mary A	5	DE	236
Mary J	5/12	DE	276
Mary M	9	DE	294
Minty A	25	DE	236
Nancy	47	MD	1
Nicholas	6/12	DE	236
Perry	--	DE	290
Perry	14	DE	30
Perry	65	DE	316
Phoebe	10	DE	237
Priscilla	1	DE	72
Priscilla	10	DE	175
Rachel	8	DE	316
Rachel	11	DE	241
Rachel	23	DE	1
Rachel	24	DE	237
Rebecca	1	DE	189
Rebecca	20	DE	241
Sally A	11	DE	72
Sally A	21	DE	4
Sarah Ann	13	DE	216
Sarah C	3	DE	294
Siney	50	DE	102
Susan E	21	DE	317
Thomas	5	DE	210
Thomas	50	DE	108
William	20	DE	217
William	24	DE	317
William	25	DE	197
William	50	DE	237
William F	3	DE	236
William G	30	DE	288
William H	15	DE	238
Wilmina	4	DE	221
Caun, William	16	PA	279
Caurner, James	20	IE	343
Causey, Alexander	35	DE	170
Charles W	10	DE	170
Conrad	31	GE	134
Edward	3	DE	134
Hannah	32	DE	170
Hannah A	6	DE	170
Maria	40	DE	208
Mary	9/12	GE	134
Mary	29	GE	134
Millicent	23	DE	170
Phillip	60	MD	208
Thomas	28	DE	170
Thomas G	13	DE	173
William A	3	DE	170
William F	16	DE	401
Cavalere, Fanny	60	MD	140
Cavanaugh, John	22	IE	347
Cavender, Alexander	36	DE	300
Ann	2	DE	207
Ann J	4	DE	300
Bryan	25	IE	322
Ebenezer	1	DE	260
Elenora	6/12	DE	328
Elizabeth	40	DE	207
Emeline	30	DE	260
George W	3	DE	324
Harry	6	PA	282
Hector	23	DE	205
Henry	30	DE	324
Herdelia	8	DE	327
Hester	10	DE	327
Hester A	11	MD	280
James	7	DE	300
James	40	DE	327
Jane	4	DE	260
John	10	DE	260
John	11	DE	300
John	36	DE	260
John W	4	DE	194
Lydia	30	DE	194
Lydia E	1	DE	194
Martha	27	PA	324
Martin	12	DE	260
Martin	40	IE	334
Mary Eliza	4	DE	194
Mary J	9	DE	300
Rachel	5	DE	327
Rebecca	38	DE	300
Sarah	15	DE	327
Sarah E	11/12	DE	207
Susan	30	DE	327
Thomas	35	DE	194
William	35	DE	207
Wilson F	6	DE	194
Caves, George	27	IE	356
Sarah	30	IE	356
Cavinder, James	29	DE	363
Mary Ann	4	DE	364
Mary Ann	30	DE	363
Sarah Jane	7	DE	363
Thomas A	2	DE	364
Cawley, Elizabeth	37	PA	360
Cawsden, Elizabeth	54	DE	338
Elizabeth M	2	DE	360
Evelina	18	DE	338
Samuel	39	DE	360
Wilamina	18	IE	338
Celles, Bryan	35	IE	302
Cennard, Catharine	32	MD	345
David	39	MD	345
Cernegy, Alexander	8	ST	281
Isabella	1	PA	281
Isabella	27	DE	281
Mary J	5	ST	281
Peter	32	IE	281
Chadwic, Wm	21	GB	331
Chadwick, Anne	20	GB	85
Caroline	18	DE	85
Charles	19	PA	282
Isabella	22	GB	85
Mary	11	DE	85

Chadwick, Mary	50	GB	85	Chambers, George	4	DE	192	Chandler, Benj	68	DE	351
Mary	65	GB	284	George	19	DE	227	Benjamin	76	DE	160
Radcliffe	56	GB	85	George R	3	DE	316	Caroline	11	DE	228
Thomas	21	GB	85	Hellen	7	DE	363	Caroline	20	DE	156
Watts	22	GB	85	Henry	9	DE	249	Courtland	33	MD	350
William	13	DE	85	Henry	9	DE	316	David	27	DE	160
Chaffant, William	17	PA	135	Isaac	26	DE	204	David W	7	DE	350
Chaffin, Benjamin	11	DE	335	Isabella	25	IE	340	Dewett W	4	DE	345
Jesse	39	DE	335	James	2	DE	249	Dr	65	DE	27
Mary	13	DE	335	James	2	DE	319	Eliza H	23	DE	350
Mary	35	DE	335	James	15	DE	220	Elizabeth	3	DE	355
Chairs, Alexander	29	DE	93	James	26	DE	249	Elizabeth	6	DE	351
Benjamin	19	DE	93	James	27	DE	244	Elizabeth	15	PA	22
Elizabeth	26	IE	145	James	30	DE	231	Elizabeth	16	DE	228
Ferdenand	4	DE	93	James	41	DE	319	Elizabeth	30	DE	355
Margaret	5	DE	145	Jesse W	18	DE	355	Elizabeth	35	DE	227
Martha	3	DE	145	John	2	DE	340	Elizabeth	44	DE	274
Mary	29	MD	93	John	11	DE	249	Elizabeth	54	PA	22
Samuel	30	IE	145	John	25	IE	340	Elizabeth	67	DE	351
Chalfant, Benjamin	11	DE	273	John	45	DE	192	Ella R	5	DE	355
Chalk, Mary A	5	DE	237	John	50	DE	355	Ellen	13	DE	33
Challenger, David	17	DE	283	John	69	DE	306	Emery	6	DE	228
David	17	DE	287	John B	23	DE	355	Enoch	5	PA	358
Edward	15	DE	283	John H	9/12	DE	363	Filmore G	1	DE	345
John G	25	DE	288	John M	3	DE	316	Frances J	7	DE	351
Rebecca	18	DE	283	Joseph	36	DE	316	Grace	6/12	DE	228
Sarah	50	DE	283	Joseph	39	DE	259	Greeg	38	DE	111
Thos	61	GB	283	Joseph Henry	9	DE	363	Hannah	26	DE	345
Chamberlain, Clara	10	DE	42	Lydia	57	DE	355	Hannah	29	PA	109
Christiana	46	PA	393	Lydia A	1	DE	191	Hannah	43	DE	363
Elizabeth B	17	PA	393	Margaret A	18	DE	231	Hannah	55	DE	350
George T	10	PA	393	Martha A	25	DE	247	Hannah H	2	DE	277
Grace	50	DE	42	Mary	5	DE	69	Hannah H	14	DE	277
Hannah	26	DE	42	Mary	30	DE	231	Hayes	28	DE	273
Isaac	30	PA	32	Mary	42	MD	319	Henry H	5/12	DE	345
James H	13	PA	393	Mary	45	DE	231	Isaac	50	DE	156
Margaretta	16	DE	42	Mary A	43	DE	69	Jacob	8	DE	361
Martha	14	DE	42	Mr	21	DE	32	Jacob	33	DE	345
Martha A	14	PA	393	Myra G	1	DE	70	James	29	DE	358
Mary A	8	PA	393	Perry	45	MD	125	James A	4	DE	228
Mary E	17	DE	42	Rachel B	20	DE	26	Jane	30	PA	358
P (Dr)	58	DE	42	Rebecca	11	MD	192	Jane	67	PA	358
Patience	12	DE	296	Rebecca	38	MD	259	Jesse	5	DE	350
Pearce	46	DE	393	Richard	21	DE	396	Jesse	8	DE	348
Chamberlin, Anna	21	DE	393	Richard	74	DE	396	Johan	13	PA	361
Benj	41	PA	305	Robt	21	IE	344	John	3	DE	361
Eliza	41	PA	305	Samuel	4	DE	363	John	6	DE	228
Eliza A	5	PA	306	Samuel	13	MD	192	John	25	DE	325
Elizabeth	28	DE	393	Samuel	15	DE	231	John	40	DE	228
Elizabeth	56	MD	393	Sarah	35	DE	29	John	42	DE	277
Hannah	17	PA	306	Sarah Ann	30	DE	363	John	46	DE	274
Jacob	8	PA	305	Sarah J	8	DE	319	John	53	PA	22
Joseph	12	PA	305	Sewall	20	DE	206	John C	6	PA	358
Joseph P	19	DE	393	Simon	1/12	DE	319	John T	36	DE	351
Josephine	13	DE	393	Susan	1	NY	125	Joseph	18	DE	325
Rosetta	2	DE	306	Susan	8	MD	192	Joseph	20	DE	352
Samuel E	16	DE	393	Susan	45	DE	192	Joseph H	11	DE	355
Thomas	17	PA	305	Susanna	63	DE	396	Joseph P	1	DE	351
Chambers, Alex	5/12	DE	340	Thomas	5	DE	259	Joseph P (MD)	40	DE	355
Andrew	57	DE	191	Thomas	6	DE	192	Joseph W	9	DE	350
Ann	26	DE	172	William H	17	DE	231	Joshua	19	DE	106
Anna Jane	11	DE	363	X C (Rev)	49	IE	69	Keziah H	28	DE	358
Benjamin	40	DE	363	Champ, Sally	7	DE	300	Lydia	10	DE	228
Caroline	12	DE	260	Champion, Benjamin	39	MD	330	Margaret E	18/12	DE	355
Caroline	30	NY	125	Catherine	22	DE	330	Maria S	36	DE	111
Carry	4	DE	70	Hester	25	DE	330	Mary	36	DE	351
Catherine A	22	DE	355	Levi	78	DE	330	Mary	74	DE	390
Charlotte	7	DE	259	Champre, Gabriel	45	PA	357	Mary A	4	DE	351
David	16	DE	232	Champson, James	6	DE	38	Mary A	45	DE	351
David	63	DE	359	Chance, Sarah	35	MD	230	Mary E	11	DE	228
David	85	MD	342	Chandler, Abigal	35	PA	277	Mary E	17	DE	274
Elizabeth	5	DE	249	Adaline	35	DE	351	Mary G	11	DE	363
Elizabeth	19	DE	231	Alexander	27	DE	25	Mary Jane	18	DE	361
Elizabeth	24	DE	396	Alexander	45	DE	227	Michael B	35	DE	348
Elizabeth	26	DE	249	Alice	76	DE	348	Nathan	18	MD	354
Elizabeth	28	DE	316	Ann	18	PA	22	Pathena	51	DE	33
Elizabeth	38	MD	192	Ann	18	DE	363	Peter A	8	DE	355
Elizabeth	50	DE	359	Ann	75	DE	353	Philomonia	22	DE	361
Emily	1	DE	249	Anna	20	DE	274	Phillip	2	DE	350
Empson	3	NY	125	Anna	64	DE	273	Rachel	25	DE	228
Enoch P	7	DE	231	Anna Mary	3	DE	345	Rachel E	14	DE	274
Ezekiel	16	DE	191	Benj	9	DE	351	Rachel G	31	PA	348

Chandler, Rachel W	34 DE 350	Chesney, Mary E	21 DE 93	Christy, William	2 DE 85
Rebecca	17 DE 350	William	28 MD 93	William H	24 DE 93
Rebecca	58 DE 160	William F	1 DE 93	Chumley, Henry	24 DE 187
Ruth A	12 DE 353	Chester, Elizabeth	60 NJ 130	John	18 DE 187
Ruthana	34 DE 350	Thomas	20 NJ 130	Rebecca	16 DE 187
Samuel	47 DE 363	Chew, Isabella	14 DE 361	Richard	40 DE 186
Sarah	26 PA 22	James	24 DE 363	Church, Elizabeth	23 MD 334
Sarah	43 DE 361	Julia	30 DE 363	Churchman, Alex R	6 DE 303
Sarah	50 DE 156	Margaret	64 DE 348	Ann E	36 PA 283
Sarah	52 PA 273	Sarah E	4 DE 348	Augustine	11/12 DE 303
Sarah A	9 DE 361	Chewns, Ann	22 DE 167	Caleb	11 DE 283
Sarah A	9 DE 361	Childs, Anna	12 TN 318	Charles	1 DE 283
Sarah A	26 MD 393	Ellen	10 TN 318	Frederic	9 DE 283
Sarah E	3 DE 277	Chippa, James	12 DE 390	George	5 DE 283
Spencer	26 DE 350	Chippe, Anna	25 DE 74	George W	39 DE 283
Swithen	20 DE 350	Edward	10 DE 74	Henry L	29 PA 303
Thomas	7 PA 22	Edward	25 DE 73	Maria	3 DE 283
Thomas	16 DE 361	George	6 DE 59	Martha	4 DE 303
Thomas	20 DE 363	Hester	23 DE 73	Micajah	58 PA 300
Thomas C	40 DE 350	Margaret	32 DE 69	Samuel	2 DE 303
Thome	11 MD 345	Mary	3 DE 59	Sarah	28 PA 303
Thome	49 DE 361	Mary	7 DE 74	Sarah M	56 PA 300
Thos A	15 DE 350	Mary H	9/12 DE 59	William H	7 DE 283
W P	29 DE 109	Moses	35 DE 59	Churnsides, Agness	70 GB 122
Wesley	1 DE 228	Peter	39 DE 75	Elizabeth	38 PA 122
Wilberforce M	13 DE 111	Rosa	32 DE 59	George	40 GB 122
William	26 DE 39	Sarah	5 DE 74	Chusnut, Dorcas	15 DE 129
William	34 DE 156	Chivers, Frank	1 DE 223	Hannah M	38 DE 129
William	72 DE 33	Sarah	23 DE 224	Sarah	27 DE 129
William S	12 DE 350	Chivins, Benjamin	45 DE 224	William D	38 DE 129
William T	10 DE 274	Eli	18 DE 235	Cistern, Christian	20 GE 51
Chanlove, James	26 IE 305	Elizabeth	30 MD 224	Clancy, William	45 IE 313
Chaplain, Caroline A	28 MA 366	James	30 DE 224	Clane, Joseph	35 PA 351
Daniel	30 MA 366	Mary	6 DE 224	Mary E	8 DE 351
Ellen	1 MA 366	Rebecca	3 DE 224	Sabina M	50 DE 307
James	2/12 GB 366	Sarah	2 DE 224	Sarah A	5 PA 351
Chapman, Ann	63 GB 61	Chouerton, Eliza-		Sarah J	35 PA 351
Frances	60 GB 61	beth	35 GB 322	Susan	13 PA 351
Charde, Elizabeth	36 DE 33	Ellen	4 DE 322	Claranar, William	24 DE 168
Reuben	55 NJ 33	George	6 DE 322	Clare, Lewis	6 DE 288
Charles, Amanda	1 DE 367	George	40 GB 322	Emma W	12 DE 288
Ann L	2 DE 367	Sarah	10 PA 322	Hannah J	13 DE 288
Bella	50 GB 363	Thomas	13 PA 322	Jesse	34 PA 288
Clara	12 DE 366	Christe, Elizabeth	27 DE 109	Samuel C	1 DE 288
Ellen L	6 DE 366	Harry	4 DE 109	Sarah E	30 PA 288
Francis	40 GB 363	James	16 IE 2	William	8 DE 288
George	35 DE 366	James	19 DE 164	Clark, A Mark	35 PA 393
Hannah	26 DE 366	James	30 DE 109	Adaline	15 DE 58
James R	21 DE 363	Margaret	12 IE 2	Adaline	20 DE 53
Louisa T	16 DE 363	Margaret	45 IE 2	Abigail A	8 PA 378
Mary A	13 DE 366	Mary E	20 DE 94	Abisha	38 PA 273
Sarah E	5 DE 367	Mary F	2 DE 110	Albina	14 DE 261
Chase, Ann	14 MD 133	Patric	47 IE 2	Alexander	12 DE 316
Charles	7 DE 393	Christian, Cather-		Alexander	15 DE 111
Eugene	12 DE 285	ine	37 DE 223	Alexander	15 IE 151
Grace	26 DE 391	John	37 VA 223	Alexander	45 DE 111
Henry	10 DE 393	Lucinda	11 DE 223	Alice M	3 DE 150
Isabella	14 DE 360	Rachel A	5 DE 223	Alonzo	10 DE 273
Juliann	38 PA 285	Christmas, Adam	28 MD 165	Amia	2 DE 20
Laura	1 DE 393	Aunty	80 DE 264	Andrew J	8 DE 150
Lucian M	43 MA 285	George	30 DE 264	Andrew S	35 IE 150
Lucian R	13 DE 285	Mary A	10 DE 198	Ann	23 DE 393
Melvina	9 DE 285	Rachel A	22 DE 197	Ann	38 IE 140
Owen	24 DE 393	Saby	55 DE 264	Ann	43 DE 258
Priscilla	64 MD 84	Samuel	30 DE 197	Ann	50 DE 364
Samborn	30 DE 359	Christmus, Delia	19 PA 331	Ann	72 DE 34
Sewall	15 DE 393	Levi	11/12 DE 331	Anna	5 DE 365
Chatter, Elizabeth	1 DE 368	Solomon	35 DE 331	Anna	10 DE 58
Elmer	7 DE 368	Christy, Alonzo T	1 DE 86	Anna E	15 DE 212
John	35 MD 368	Ann	57 DE 93	Anne	7 DE 257
Phebe	35 DE 368	Anna M	4 DE 140	Annie	9 DE 338
Sarah	5 DE 368	Anna M	27 DE 86	Benjamin	17 DE 249
Chawburg, Eliza E	50 DE 350	Anthony	27 DE 85	Benjamin F	33 DE 53
Chaylor, Anna E	10 MD 113	Anthony	89 GE 93	Bridget	6 DE 150
Amanda D	4 DE 113	James	32 IE 140	C Elliott	5 DE 249
Araminia	34 PA 113	James T	3 DE 140	Cantwell	43 DE 338
George W	6 DE 113	John V	30 DE 86	Caroline	2 DE 257
Osborne	2 DE 113	Lydia	22 PA 85	Catharine	10 DE 342
Sarah	76 MD 113	Mary A	3 DE 86	Catharine	11 DE 338
Sarah A	8 DE 113	Mary A	30 MD 140	Charles	19 DE 257
W (Dr)	35 MD 113	Sarah A	18 DE 93	Charles A	21 IE 152
Cheeman, Martha D	6 NY 166	Victorine	21 DE 93	Charles E	6 MD 243

Name	Age	State	Page
Clark, Clara	35	DE	393
Clement	22	DE	23
Clinton	12	DE	273
Cornelia	6	DE	316
Daniel	18	PA	251
Dean	14	DE	355
Dorcas	70	MD	101
Edmond	40	IE	140
Edward	6	DE	273
Edward P	13	NJ	378
Edwin	3/12	DE	261
Eliza	7	DE	253
Eliza	22	DE	113
Eliza	38	NY	266
Eliza	40	MD	58
Elizabeth	22	DE	257
Elizabeth	30	NJ	378
Elizabeth	34	DE	109
Elizabeth	35	MD	342
Elizabeth	45	DE	252
Elizabeth	52	DE	34
Elizabeth	55	DE	371
Elizabeth A	5	PA	273
Elizabeth B	35	DE	338
Elizabeth C	23	DE	110
Ellenor	28	PA	273
Emily E	16	DE	208
Emma	5	DE	249
Emma	13	DE	58
Emma W	12	PA	289
Emory	27	MD	209
Estella Amelia	3	DE	365
Esther	3/12	DE	249
Esther	30	PA	365
Eve	45	ND	155
Fanny	50	MD	273
Frances A	10	DE	150
Frank M	1	DE	161
George	16	DE	273
George	20	DE	144
George	20	DE	252
George	36	DE	316
George B	44	DE	266
George D	53	NY	296
George H	5	DE	110
George H	7	DE	249
Hannah	8	DE	111
Hannah	50	GB	142
Hannah G	3	DE	289
Harriet	15	DE	257
Harry	3	DE	261
Harry	8	DE	252
Henrietta	8	PA	273
Henry	12	MO	266
Henry	16	VA	113
Henry	17	DE	333
Henry	37	PA	281
Henry	50	NJ	212
Henry	52	DE	364
Henry	55	IE	113
Henry Clay	6	DE	281
Henry F	1	MD	243
Henry H	2	DE	53
Hetty	14	DE	253
Ingeber H	56	DE	310
Ingebur	40	DE	268
Isaac	25	DE	192
Isaac	46	PA	58
Isaac	52	MD	253
Isaac V	34	DE	261
Isabella	20	IE	152
Isabella	72	DE	281
James	3	DE	342
James	4	DE	253
James	5	DE	252
James	5	DE	356
James	12	DE	111
James	12	DE	254
James	22	DE	337
James	23	PA	364
James M	69	IE	7

Name	Age	State	Page
Clark, James T	4	DE	378
Jane	2	DE	111
Jane	25	IE	56
Jane	29	DE	281
Jane	44	DE	111
Jane	74	DE	288
Jefferson	12	DE	249
Jerome	13	DE	317
Jesse	34	PA	289
John	3	DE	316
John	7	DE	338
John	10	MD	224
John	11	DE	58
John	16	MD	243
John	16	DE	252
John	24	IE	339
John	26	GB	249
John	45	MD	243
John	50	DE	371
John	71	DE	314
John	78	DE	34
John C	51	DE	252
John M	59	DE	342
John T	28	VA	113
John W	8	DE	342
Jonathan	34	NJ	20
Joseph	17	DE	319
Joseph	21	DE	58
Joseph W	5	VA	113
Joshua	8/12	DE	300
Julia	14	DE	273
Keziah	24	GB	249
Laura	2	DE	338
Leanora	5	DE	338
Lenore	5	DE	173
Levi	33	DE	161
Levi H	35	DE	249
Lydia	5	DE	261
Lydia	32	DE	109
Margaret	7	DE	261
Margaret	14	DE	254
Margaret	16	DE	257
Margaret	17	DE	393
Margaret	30	DE	253
Margaret	55	DE	305
Margaret	58	IE	7
Margaret E	3	MD	243
Margaret J	8	DE	281
Margaret R	12	PA	274
Maria	1	DE	338
Martha A	8	MD	243
Mary	3	DE	343
Mary	9	VA	113
Mary	12	DE	212
Mary	13	DE	257
Mary	22	DE	20
Mary	24	DE	316
Mary	25	IE	150
Mary	26	DE	113
Mary	43	DE	268
Mary A	5	DE	140
Mary D	21	NY	296
Mary E	10	DE	364
Mary E	13	DE	343
Mary F	27	DE	249
Mary J	3	DE	110
Mary M	45	DE	113
Matilda	2/12	DE	257
Matilda	14	DE	316
Matilda	14	DE	321
Miles	4	DE	257
Milly	34	DE	316
Obadiah	6	DE	254
Obadiah	48	DE	254
Paul	17	DE	359
Pauline	49	NY	296
Permelia	12	DE	58
Phillip	18	DE	252
Philip	21	DE	257
Priscilla	28	DE	318

Name	Age	State	Page
Clark, Rachel	8	DE	254
Rachel	59	MD	334
Rebecca	10	DE	212
Rebecca	12	VA	113
Rebecca	18	DE	273
Rebecca	28	DE	224
Rebecca	40	MD	243
Rebecca	45	DE	268
Rebecca	55	NJ	23
Samuel	3	DE	212
Sarah	11	DE	257
Sarah	22	PA	21
Sarah	35	DE	261
Sarah	45	NJ	212
Sarah	54	DE	58
Sarah	60	DE	314
Sarah	75	DE	109
Sarah A	19	IE	142
Sarah E	19	DE	58
Sarah E	20	MD	241
Sarah M	40	DE	79
Stephen	15	DE	321
Stephen	16	DE	316
Stewart	27	DE	110
Susan	7	DE	212
Susan	8	DE	316
Susan	18	DE	254
Susan	18	DE	257
Susan J	7	DE	161
Susan M	29	DE	249
Susan W B	27	DE	161
T J	50	DE	273
Theodore	12	DE	252
Thomas	1	DE	150
Thomas	7	DE	140
Thomas	9	DE	257
Thomas	9	DE	262
Thomas	24	DE	23
Thomas	38	DE	113
Thomas	44	DE	257
Thomas J	74	DE	314
Thomas T	43	NJ	378
Warner	3/12	DE	53
William	9	PA	307
William	14	DE	58
William	25	DE	190
William	25	DE	300
William	27	DE	365
William	75	DE	113
William B	37	DE	249
William E	14	VA	113
William G	10	MD	243
William Hadly	3	DE	249
William Hurlock	3	DE	249
William R	9/12	GB	249
William T	8/12	DE	212
Wm	10	DE	252
Wm	16	DE	254
Clarkson, David	56	DE	300
George	15	DE	300
John	18	DE	382
Joseph	27	DE	382
Sarah	46	DE	300
Clasner, Mary	9	DE	70
Clatts, Ann E	15	DE	7
Elizabeth	41	NJ	7
Joseph	44	GE	7
Lewis	11	OH	7
Clavey, Christian	28	PA	68
June	24	PA	68
William	3	PA	68
Clawford, Wm	16	DE	251
Clay, Ann	23	GB	262
Anna	4	DE	236
Catherine	9	DE	236
Florence	1	DE	236
Henry	10	DE	236
Jacob	27	GB	262
Joseph	2	DE	262
Rachel	7	DE	236
Rebecca	3	DE	264

Clay, Rebecca	36	GB	264
Sulivan	5/12	DE	262
Wm	6	DE	264
Wm	37	GB	264
Wm	72	DE	252
Claypole, Abraham	37	NJ	271
Ann E	8	PA	134
Ann E	33	PA	134
Emma	6	PA	134
George	34	PA	134
Harrison	1	PA	271
John	12	PA	134
Mary A	4	DE	134
Rachel	12	MD	271
Sarah	36	NJ	271
Ward	3	PA	271
Washington	10	PA	134
Wm	14	PA	271
Clayton, Ann	49	PA	314
Anna F	8	PA	208
Anna M	47	DE	208
Anna W	45	DE	192
Caroline	13	ND	248
Charles	11	DE	191
David	12	DE	219
Elias B	25	PA	172
Eliza	11	DE	219
Elizabeth	47	DE	105
Emeline	35	MD	248
Enoch	25	DE	109
Enoch S	2	DE	224
George	18	MD	17
Hannah	63	MD	141
Henry	11	DE	192
Henry	21	DE	96
Henry	55	MD	67
Isaac T	10	DE	222
James	2	DE	233
James	42	MD	248
James F	26	DE	295
James W	15	MD	400
John	50	DE	314
John D	8	DE	233
John D	17	DE	224
Joshua	6	DE	191
Joshua (Col)	48	DE	191
Joshua (Esq)	55	DE	192
Levi	28	PA	115
Louisa	6	DE	314
Louisa	8	DE	219
Lydia	4	DE	222
Lydia	36	PA	115
Lydia	70	PA	115
Manlove	8	DE	222
Margaret	14	DE	219
Margaret	15	PA	314
Maria	3/12	DE	222
Martha	37	DE	219
Martha A	3	DE	219
Martha E	24	DE	192
Mary	5	DE	219
Mary	28	DE	224
Mary A	5	DE	224
Mary E	4	DE	233
Melvina	10	DE	314
Rachel	35	DE	222
Rebecca B	22	DE	172
Rebecca J	3	DE	224
Reece	12	DE	314
Richard	8	DE	192
Richard H	10	DE	208
Richard T P	38	DE	208
Sarah A	25	DE	233
Sarah E	7	DE	224
Susan	40	PA	115
Thomas	16	DE	400
Thos (Hon)	73	DE	281
Timothy	36	DE	224
William	32	DE	233
William	34	DE	222
William	40	DE	219
William H	2	PA	172

Cleaden, Eliza	34	MA	301
James	31	MA	301
John	11	PA	301
William	12	PA	301
William	33	MA	301
Clealand, Derain	22	DE	201
Clean, Abby M	38	ME	58
Cleare, Christiana	4	DE	378
Elisha	5	DE	378
James	40	DE	378
Margaret R	10	DE	378
Sarah	28	MD	378
Sarah E	1/12	DE	378
Cleaver, Amanda	24	DE	180
Angeline	13	DE	180
Catherine	40	DE	180
Charles H B	14	DE	180
Cora	3	DE	185
David	12	DE	185
Durrach	12	DE	180
Edmond D	16	DE	180
Eliza W	8	DE	180
Elizabeth	17	DE	180
Elizabeth	20	DE	185
George	30	DE	321
George G	27	DE	185
Henry	2	DE	180
Isaac	56	DE	185
Isaac Jr	13	DE	185
Isaac L	20	DE	180
Jane	52	DE	185
John	54	DE	189
John A	2	DE	185
John A B	6	DE	180
Joseph	51	DE	180
Joseph C	16	DE	180
Julia T	5	DE	180
Julius	1	DE	185
Martha	18	DE	185
Mary Ann	47	DE	180
Peter	19	DE	185
Priscilla	43	NJ	180
Rachel	11	DE	185
Rachel	40	NJ	189
Samuel B	20	DE	180
Sarah	33	PA	180
Sarah B	10	DE	180
Thomas	39	DE	180
William	21	DE	186
William	24	DE	189
William	79	NJ	180
William III	20	DE	180
William E	7	DE	180
William Jr	44	DE	180
Cleaves, Angeline	14	DE	394
Ann	10	?	270
E D	17	?	270
Elizabeth	8	?	270
Ellen	30	DE	382
Emma	1	?	270
Emma	3	DE	382
G G	49	?	270
James M	32	DE	292
Jane	33	?	270
John H	6	DE	382
Martha	5	?	270
Mary	3	?	270
Sarah	6	?	270
Cleavland, Margaret	50	MD	366
Cleland, Ann C	41	DE	136
Elizabeth	64	IE	301
Elizabeth A	24	DE	320
Ellen	54	IE	320
Ellen M	26	DE	320
Emily M	8	DE	136
Hannah A	14	DE	136
George	17	DE	320
James	21	IE	28
James	33	IE	311
John	63	IE	320
Margaret	14	DE	320
Mary	16	IE	28

Cleland, Mary A	19	DE	320
Mary E	10	DE	136
Nelson	40	DE	136
Robert	30	DE	17
Sarah	50	IE	320
Sarah A	27	DE	318
Sarah E	8	DE	320
Clelland, Alfred N	8	DE	318
Arvilla	4	DE	318
George	3	DE	318
George	33	DE	318
Clemens, Angeline	12	DE	250
Clement, Charles	16	DE	322
Elizabeth F	17	DE	365
Francis	57	DE	355
Franklin W	40	NJ	365
Harriet F	30	DE	365
Margaret	54	DE	322
Mary	15	DE	365
Richard	52	NJ	355
Sylvester	21	DE	322
Clements, Samuel	20	DE	213
Clemson, Catherine	23	DE	367
Elizabeth L	12	DE	367
Henry	25	DE	367
James	60	PA	367
Jemima	16	DE	367
John	14	DE	367
Mary	53	DE	367
Clendaniel, John	20	DE	230
Clendenin, Lewis	10	DE	336
Elizabeth	12	DE	336
Samuel	45	PA	336
Clendening, Joseph	22	PA	78
Clendennan, Margt	49	PA	330
Clens, Jane	31	DE	71
Clenther, Joseph	16	MO	163
Cleson, Albert	4/12	DE	255
Cleven, Sarah	35	DE	289
Click, John W	17	DE	332
Clifton, Andrew	6	DE	221
Caesar	17	DE	221
Caroline	36	DE	217
Catherine	9	DE	171
Eliza	27	DE	329
Hudson	64	DE	194
Jacob	21	DE	197
Jacob	50	DE	221
James	1	DE	329
Julia A	40	DE	171
Juliet	5	DE	171
Mary	16	DE	221
Mary	54	DE	194
Matilda	45	MD	221
Richard	40	DE	329
Clinch, James	5	DE	24
Julia	25	IE	24
Margaret	25	IE	24
Michael	27	IE	24
Cling, Alonzo A	5/12	DE	387
Catherine E	23	DE	387
James L	33	DE	144
Mary	30	MD	316
Robert	41	DE	387
Sarah	60	PA	278
Thomas	29	DE	316
Clinger, Charles	19	DE	152
Clingey, Catharine	38	IE	336
Ellen	18	NS	336
John	13	NS	336
Mary E	3	MD	336
Wm	45	IE	336
Clinton, Ann	16	IE	332
Araminta	15	DE	87
Catherine	40	IE	332
James	12	IE	332
James	40	IE	332
James H	10	DE	87
Josephine	3	DE	87
Joshua	5	DE	87
Lewis	39	DE	87
Malichi	9	DE	87

Clinton, Mary	20	IE	332
Mick	14	IE	332
Phebe A	13	DE	87
Rebecca	1	DE	87
Susanah	37	MD	87
Cloak, Jane	4	DE	96
John	10	DE	96
John	40	DE	96
Mary	6	DE	96
Mrs	29	DE	96
Clothier, Freling-			
hausen	5	DE	179
John	28	MD	179
Sophia	28	MD	179
Cloud, Abner	50	DE	120
Alzira	28	PA	280
Amos A	20	PA	107
Andrew	31	PA	49
Ann	14	DE	352
Ann	28	DE	280
Ann E	10	PA	330
Ann M	8	DE	282
Anna	2	DE	356
Charity	6	DE	282
Charity	50	DE	284
Clarkson	21	PA	18
David M	12	DE	106
Elena	22	DE	329
Elizabeth	8	DE	280
Elizabeth	44	DE	120
Ellen E	22	DE	106
Elmira	13	DE	283
Emma	10	DE	353
Emma E	9	DE	106
George	4	DE	356
George S	10	DE	282
Glencam	20	DE	352
Harlan	43	PA	356
Harmony B	5	DE	330
Henry H	8	PA	330
Hiram H	16	DE	330
Isaac	32	DE	280
Jackson	7/12	DE	356
James H	1	DE	106
Jane	43	PA	106
Jane A	3	DE	330
Jane E	35	DE	330
Jesse	10	DE	280
Joel	11	DE	282
John	6	DE	352
John	55	PA	352
Lew C	7	PA	330
Lott	38	DE	282
Margaretta	23	DE	49
Maria	40	DE	282
Maria E	2	DE	282
Martena V	5	DE	106
Mary	85	PA	77
Mary H	54	PA	356
Mary J	18	PA	106
Mary J	18	DE	329
Morris C E	8/12	DE	330
Rachel	40	DE	346
Rebecca	38	DE	282
Samuel	17	DE	352
Sarah	16	DE	352
Sarah	17	DE	18
Sarah	28	IE	152
Sarah	34	PA	356
Sarah	44	DE	352
Sarah	67	PA	77
Serena	12	DE	352
Stephen	32	DE	330
Stephen W	13	DE	330
Thomas	1	DE	152
Thomas	73	DE	346
Thomas P	20	PA	69
Volney	19	DE	352
Walter	28	PA	152
Washington	34	PA	18
William	4	DE	282
William B	14	PA	330
Cloud, William F	1	DE	50
William M	19	DE	282
Clough, Ann	5	DE	378
James	31	GB	315
John	11/12	DE	378
Mary E	2	DE	378
Sarah	31	GB	378
Thomas	30	GB	378
Clow, Nathaniel	21	DE	222
Clugston, Asher	10	DE	254
Asher	49	NJ	254
Catherine	38	NJ	254
David	18	NJ	254
Ezeniah	13	DE	254
Gertrude	12	DE	254
Levinia	7	DE	254
Mary	14	DE	254
Ruth	6	DE	254
Clunside, George	7	DE	353
John	30	GB	353
Mary E	5	DE	353
Philena	28	DE	353
Sarah E	3	DE	353
Williamena	7/12	DE	353
Clute, Amelia	38	MD	208
Clyde, Anna	2	DE	284
George W	5	DE	284
Margaret S	8	DE	284
Rebecca	33	PA	284
Thomas	37	PA	284
William	10	DE	284
Coag, James	21	MD	317
Coal, Jesse	13	DE	382
Coalmary, Caroline	11	DE	384
Elena P	3	DE	384
Mary A	14	DE	384
Mary J	37	DE	384
Washington	38	MD	384
William S	9	DE	384
Coat, Joseph	15	PA	351
Coates, Acquilla J	7	PA	135
Ann E	19	PA	135
Isaac	16	PA	135
Joseph	14	PA	135
Lydia	43	PA	135
Coats, John	28	MD	353
Ruth	7	DE	399
Coborn, Joseph	24	DE	110
Cochern, Elizabeth	30	IE	28
S	15	MD	165
Cochran, Alice L	3	DE	196
Alice R	13	DE	207
Ann	21	IE	288
Ann	36	DE	367
Ann	45	PA	249
Aquilla	52	DE	205
C F	27	PA	196
Charles	4	DE	127
Charles P	11	DE	194
Cicily	6	MD	367
Dan M	5/12	DE	207
David	11	PA	249
David R	4	PA	249
Edwin R	12	DE	227
Eliza	7	DE	194
Eliza	38	DE	194
Elizabeth	13	PA	249
Frances	2	DE	296
Frances E	3	DE	227
Harry	3	DE	196
Isaac	45	PA	249
James F	6	DE	227
John	9	DE	194
John P	41	DE	194
John W	8	MD	367
Joseph	2	DE	367
Julian	1	DE	194
Margaret R	6	DE	196
Mary L	28	MD	227
Mary T	11	DE	207
Oliver	4	DE	367
R W	27	DE	196
Cochran, R Eugene	1	DE	196
Rebecca	13	DE	194
Richard	10	DE	207
Robert A	1	DE	227
Robert A	14	DE	207
Robert A	47	DE	227
Robert T	35	DE	207
Roland	8	PA	249
Sarah	4/12	DE	196
Sarah	28	PA	196
Sarah J	16	PA	249
Sarah M	49	DE	205
Sophia	33	DE	107
Thomas	6	DE	207
Violetta	15	PA	249
William	32	MD	367
William	49	DE	205
William A	30	DE	196
William H	8	DE	227
William R	16	DE	194
Cochrane, Eliz M	19	DE	127
James M	20	DE	127
John	50	PA	127
Susan	28	MD	127
Code, Elizabeth	13	NJ	274
Coffield, Alven	13	MD	163
Eugene	17	MD	163
William	10	MD	163
Coge, Anna	5	DE	257
Elizabeth	25	DE	257
Frances	9	DE	257
James	30	MD	257
John	8	DE	257
Wesley	30	PA	287
Cogrief, Peter	21	IE	194
Coil, David	19	IE	324
Ellen	13	DE	324
John	54	IE	324
Margaret	22	IE	324
Mary	50	IE	324
Mary A	15	DE	324
Sarah T	11	DE	324
Wm	14	DE	324
Colam, James	54	FR	354
Mary S	45	FR	353
Colaman, John	25	GE	84
Mary	21	GE	84
Colbert, George	70	DE	245
Sarah	41	DE	245
Colby, Lydia	60	DE	161
Robert	25	GB	311
Susan	14	DE	161
William	29	DE	187
Colcord, Virgil P	15	PA	401
Coldwell, Wesley	32	DE	141
Cole, Abraham	72	DE	178
Ann	28	IE	167
Ann	43	MD	332
Benjamin H	10	DE	332
Christopher	17	DE	123
Delia	40	DE	278
Elias	8	DE	332
Elias	41	DE	332
Elizabeth	70	DE	317
Emma	4	NJ	253
George	6	DE	308
George	37	DE	308
Hannah	50	PA	308
Harry	52	DE	278
Henry	15	PA	308
Henry	22	DE	89
James	2	DE	146
Jefferson	51	DE	317
Jesse	12	PA	308
John E	18	MD	178
Mary A	14	DE	152
Mary A	15	DE	146
Rebecca	5	DE	146
Sarah	38	DE	146
Sarah E	12	DE	146
Theodore	7	DE	233
Wesley	14	PA	330

Name	Age	St	No.
Cole, William	10	DE	233
William	10	PA	308
William H	12	DE	332
Coleman, Ann E	17	PA	313
Araminta	38	MD	213
John	3	MD	213
Mary	69	IE	301
Mary A	19	PA	126
Philander	32	MD	126
Samuel	20	DE	213
William	18	DE	226
Colgate, Alexander	3	DE	241
Hannah	63	DE	241
James	63	DE	241
Sarah	10	DE	241
Thomas	11	DE	241
Colligan, W L	13	NJ	164
Collin, James	22	IE	262
Collings, Blair	22	DE	399
Collins, Andrew J	24	DE	217
Angelina	28	DE	397
Angeline	17	DE	215
Ann	29	IE	275
Ann C	3	DE	215
Augustus	8	PA	275
Bayman	24	DE	232
Benjamin	11/12	DE	246
Bridget	20	IE	314
Clayton Clay	1	DE	397
Edward	27	DE	190
Edward	53	DE	341
Edward	70	IE	314
Edward B	33	DE	398
Eliza	2	DE	190
Elizabeth	16	DE	341
Elizabeth	27	DE	246
Elizabeth	54	MD	341
Ellen	19	IE	302
Emma A	3	DE	397
Franklin	18	DE	215
George	5	DE	246
George	5	DE	360
George	65	DE	215
George D	25	DE	215
George W	27	PA	350
Harriet	50	MD	98
Henrietta	20	DE	215
Henrietta	60	DE	215
Isaac	32	DE	3
James A	1	DE	350
James R	33	DE	217
Jane	24	DE	155
Jane E	28	PA	350
John	1	DE	275
John	3	DE	246
John	15	DE	251
John	21	DE	215
John	28	IE	188
John	35	DE	246
John	43	PA	360
Lawrence	10	IL	275
Lewis E	8	DE	397
Margaret	15	DE	215
Margaret	22	IE	314
Margaret	31	DE	128
Maria	34	DE	3
Mary	4	DE	190
Mary	24	DE	190
Mary	24	IE	314
Mary	45	PA	360
Mary A	6	DE	246
Mary E	8	DE	3
Mary J	5	DE	397
Mary J	26	DE	217
Morris	35	DE	217
Neosha J	6/12	DE	217
Peter	28	IE	302
Rebecca	18	MD	176
Rebecca	54	NJ	227
Richard	7	DE	3
Robert C	35	DE	246
Rosa	17	IE	314
Collins, Ruth	20	DE	258
Samuel	38	PA	128
Sarah	11	DE	203
Sarah	30	IE	314
Sarah	35	PA	357
Sarah Louisa	1/12	DE	190
Sarah S	58	DE	111
Thomas	5	PA	275
Thomas	31	GB	137
Timothy	4	PA	275
Timothy	45	IE	275
Violetta	42	DE	205
William H	13	DE	217
William H	18	PA	190
Collons, Elias	6	DE	313
Elias	44	DE	313
Elizabeth	5	DE	313
Mary	9	DE	313
Mary	25	DE	313
Richard	1	DE	313
Sarah	11	DE	313
Susan	2	DE	313
Collum, Catharine	23	DE	307
Eliza S	9	NJ	159
Howard	7	NJ	159
J G	40	PA	159
Mary E	11	CT	159
Mary E	38	PA	159
Rebecca B	5	NJ	159
Samuel S	2	NJ	159
Colluett, Gouldy	28	NJ	137
Collwood, Elizabeth	25	DE	10
Colly, Ann	18	IE	187
Colman, Francisa	3	DE	25
George	6/12	DE	25
John	22	DE	20
John	63	DE	20
John H	5	DE	111
Mary	16	DE	21
Maximiliam	28	GB	25
Mercy	35	PA	25
Sarah	58	DE	20
William	24	DE	20
Colnolo, Catherine	15	IE	48
Colp, John	24	PA	293
Colt, Anne J	1	DE	236
Joseph	44	DE	236
Rachel	27	DE	236
Colten, Raymond C	13	PA	400
Simon H	9	PA	400
Colter, Burton	2	DE	226
Colvin, Elizabeth	27	PA	264
Esther	30	?	270
James	29	?	270
James	58	ST	264
Jane	60	ST	264
Margaret	5	?	270
Wm	15	DE	264
Colwell, David	32	DE	346
Edward	2	DE	371
Hester	76	IE	338
Jane	45	IE	328
John	9	DE	338
Jonathan	24	DE	357
Rosanna	12	DE	350
Sarah M	8	DE	371
Colwin, Eliza	50	PA	147
Joseph	52	PA	147
Lydia B	18	PA	147
Margaret H	12	PA	147
Sarah J	15	PA	147
Comberford, Margar-ette	9	DE	329
Mary	33	MD	329
Sarah E	6	DE	329
Combs, Henry	16	DE	332
Comegees, Ann	16	MD	92
Charles	8	MD	92
John	22	MD	92
Mary A	70	MD	92
Nathaniel	60	MD	92
Phillis A	25	MD	92
Comegees, Rachel	55	MD	92
William	20	MD	92
Comegy, Harriet	30	DE	340
James	1	DE	340
James	40	MD	340
Mary E	6	DE	221
Rebecca J	3	DE	221
Susan	9	DE	221
Comegys, __(male)	22	DE	248
Abner	35	MD	261
Benjamin	2	DE	261
Elizabeth	6	DE	261
Elizabeth	29	DE	261
Emma	17	DE	252
James	11	DE	261
John	13	DE	261
John	22	DE	143
Mary	7	DE	260
Mary	47	DE	260
Rebecca	16	DE	260
Rebecca	31	DE	167
Richard	16	DE	248
Sally	17	MD	166
Saml	20	DE	260
Sarah	3	DE	261
Sarah	20	DE	248
Susan	4	DE	391
Thomas	12	DE	260
William	15	DE	162
Comerford, Arthur	10	DE	360
Comfort, Asa	17	DE	50
Asia	50	PA	50
Eliza	10	DE	50
Mary	44	PA	50
Matilda	6	DE	50
Rosetta	4	DE	50
Sarah	18	DE	50
Comming, Unice M	17	DE	390
Commings, Caroline	22	DE	393
David	25	DE	388
Commons, Albert	21	PA	359
Ann	53	PA	359
Caroline E	19	PA	359
John	54	PA	359
William	16	PA	359
Conahan, James	28	IE	37
Margaret	25	IE	37
Mary	2	DE	37
Peter	5/12	DE	37
Conaway, Peter	27	IE	346
William	28	DE	186
William	50	PA	359
Concaid, Mary	8	DE	366
Concannon, Ellen	18	IE	399
John	25	IE	399
Condon, Ellen	60	IE	239
Elizabeth	59	DE	250
Condrage, Margaret	40	IE	352
Coneley, Patrick	34	MD	284
Conell, John	67	PA	318
Rebecca S	60	DE	318
Congo, Cornelius	3	DE	199
Edmond	1	DE	181
Hester	30	DE	181
Isaac	10	DE	199
James	6	DE	181
Jane	6	DE	199
John	30	MD	340
Mariah H	50	MD	340
Mary	25	MD	340
Noah	23	MD	340
Priscilla E	6/12	DE	199
R A	12	DE	199
Rachel	12	DE	256
Rachel	25	DE	199
Sarah	2	DE	181
Stephen	22	DE	330
Stepheney	21	MD	340
Thomas	8	DE	199
Timothy	5	DE	199
Timothy	30	DE	199
William	35	DE	181

Name	Age	St	No
Congo, William Jr	4	DE	181
Conklin, Edith	27	DE	160
George W	6	DE	160
Conley, Ann	35	PA	397
Catharine	18	IE	337
Diana	80	DE	397
George	7	DE	397
Hannah	60	MD	325
Hannah	64	MD	325
James	10	DE	397
James	40	IE	337
Jefferson	50	MD	325
Jeffro	60	DE	325
John	7	DE	337
Jonathan	36	DE	397
Neal	5	DE	337
Patrick L	24	IE	393
Priscilla	4	DE	397
Rebecca	3	DE	397
Sarah	18	MD	325
Spencer	15	MD	325
Susan	90	IE	337
Conlin, Edward	17	DE	282
Sarah	40	DE	62
Sarah E	21	DE	225
William	23	DE	225
Conlyn, David	20	DE	366
Jane	39	DE	318
John	17	PA	356
Margaret	35	IE	365
William	44	DE	318
Connally, Chas J	9	DE	289
Ellen	5	PA	289
Frances	32	IE	289
Jane	65	IE	289
Jas S	4	DE	289
Michael	33	IE	289
Connel, Catherine	26	IE	96
Margaret	50	IE	57
Michel	40	IE	96
Patric	11	IE	96
William A	16	PA	281
Connell, David	2	DE	2
Elizabeth	8	DE	2
John	14	DE	161
John	21	IE	256
Latitia	17	DE	133
Mary A	41	IE	133
Sarah	30	DE	2
Thomas	19	IE	258
William	31	IE	2
William H	5	DE	2
Connelly, Hannah	22	IE	88
Spencer	17	DE	192
Conner, Alace	75	IE	25
Ann	30	IE	22
Anna	65	DE	57
Caroline	29	DE	367
Catherine	21	IE	21
David	29	PA	291
Ellen	31	IE	163
Emily	8/12	DE	61
Emily	26	PA	61
Hugh	4	DE	22
Isaac	28	DE	209
James	20	MD	251
John	26	MD	61
John	30	IE	39
Louisa	16	DE	222
Margaret	22	IE	253
Margaret	24	DE	57
Margaret A	2/12	DE	349
Margarett	19	IE	300
Rachel	50	MD	154
Rebecca	20	PA	349
Sarah	34	DE	167
William	26	DE	349
Connerton, Bridget	4	IE	312
Ellen	29	IE	312
James	9	IE	312
John	11	IE	312
John	40	IE	312
Connerton, Michael	14	IE	312
Patrick R	6	IE	312
William	9/12	DE	312
Connolly, Catherine	14	IE	195
Connor, Eliza A	41	DE	222
Emma	1	DE	222
Isaac	28	DE	368
John	25	DE	222
Mary	19	IE	251
Rebecca	21	DE	222
Sarah W	10	DE	222
William	13	DE	235
Connway, Ann	67	DE	28
Conoly, Unie	18	IE	165
Conoway, James	18	IE	362
Conrad, Rachel	71	PA	30
Conroy, Margaret	61	PA	43
Conway, Alexander	11	DE	218
Ann	55	IE	336
Barney	17	IE	339
Catharine	30	IE	320
Lydia	28	DE	28
Margaret J	22	DE	208
Peter	56	IE	339
Rose	9	IE	339
Conwell, Edw	21	IE	274
Cooch, Francis L	79	DE	288
Hellen	8	DE	338
Joseph W	10	DE	338
Levi G	47	DE	338
Sarah G	36	MD	338
William	5	DE	338
Zebulon H	1	DE	338
Cook, Aaron	5	DE	281
Ada B	6	MA	96
Albert O	12	ME	96
Alby H	10	DE	368
Alfred	5	DE	368
Allen	10/12	DE	2
Ann	16	DE	297
Anna	1	DE	252
Anna	40	GE	65
Catherine	36	NS	95
Charles	18	CT	135
Eliza	45	DE	259
Elizabeth	20	DE	300
Elizabeth	34	DE	2
Flora	16	DE	281
Fortine	45	GE	65
Frances A	17	MA	95
George	8	DE	65
George	10	DE	300
George W	9	DE	281
Harna	35	DE	359
Hiram	3	MA	95
Hiram	28	NJ	379
Hiram Sr	57	NJ	379
Horacio N	10	ME	96
Jacob	50	DE	383
James	21	IE	303
Jane	18	IE	106
Jesse	23	DE	387
Job	46	DE	259
John	6	DE	65
John	11	DE	2
Joseph	35	MD	390
Lydia	4	DE	65
Margaret	24	NJ	379
Margaret	25	IE	31
Maria	13	DE	281
Maria L	13	MA	95
Mariah	40	MD	359
Mariah	44	DE	358
Martha	3	DE	383
Martha	22	DE	167
Martha	22	DE	363
Martha A	16	NJ	379
Mary	31	NJ	379
Mary	53	NJ	379
Mathew H	15	MA	95
Mrs	50	DE	51
Robert	3	NJ	379
Cook, Sally Ann	35	DE	383
Sarah	12	DE	383
Sarah	25	DE	281
Stephen	55	IE	349
Stoney P	7	ME	95
Walter	1	MA	95
Warner	74	DE	358
William	15	IE	330
William	36	DE	2
Cookemback, Geo	3/12	DE	81
Jacob	6	DE	81
Joshua	4	DE	81
Joshua	25	PA	81
Mary	20	IE	81
Cool, John M	30	DE	222
Cooling, Joseph	19	DE	149
Samuel	27	DE	149
Cooly, Ann	40	IE	400
Catherine	11	PA	400
James	40	IE	400
Mary	9	PA	400
Coombe, Corah W	16	DE	121
Edwin W	5	PA	121
Henrietta W	11	PA	121
Pennel	13	MD	121
Coombs, Penel	9	DE	224
Cooper, Adeline	20	DE	275
Alexander	12	DE	216
Alfred	12	AL	171
Alfred	14	DE	257
Alice A	10	PA	358
Amanda	8	DE	216
Ann	25	DE	114
Ann S	39	PA	325
Anne	4	DE	257
Aremitha	4	DE	353
Barbara	45	NJ	275
Benjamin	10	DE	190
Benjamin	50	NJ	275
Caleb S	16	PA	325
Catherine	6	DE	257
Charles	15	DE	275
Charles	19	DE	194
Charles	25	DE	220
Charles A	6	DE	325
Chas	20	DE	179
Daniel	20	DE	179
David W	1	MD	202
Eliza	5	DE	172
Elizabeth	20	DE	248
Elizabeth	28	DE	353
Elizabeth	68	PA	14
Emily	28	DE	262
Fanny	15	GB	391
Francis A	9	DE	353
Francis A	14	DE	313
Frank	9	PA	164
Frisby	25	DE	93
George	50	NJ	198
Harriet	16	DE	248
Helen V	14	PA	189
Henrietta	35	NJ	189
Henrietta	46	MD	146
Henry	--	DE	290
Henry	4	DE	257
Henry	5	DE	198
Henry	16	DE	216
Henry M E	11	DE	325
Isaac	12	DE	275
Isabella J	17	DE	198
James	35	MD	150
Jane	30	DE	257
Jane	34	DE	74
Jefferson	2	DE	257
John	--	PA	325
John	44	NJ	216
John	47	PA	308
John H	15	DE	198
John H	20	GB	183
John J	9	MD	194
John Jr	23	DE	216
Jonathan	8	DE	353

Name	Age	State	No.
Cooper, Joseph	9	DE	232
Joseph G	10	DE	325
Julia	55	DE	93
Leurana	40	DE	114
Margaret	38	DE	198
Margaret P	29	MD	150
Maria	9	DE	275
Maria	46	PA	308
Martha	8	DE	198
Martha Ann	8/12	DE	354
Mary	3	DE	198
Mary	4	DE	275
Mary	8	DE	257
Mary	20	IE	113
Mary	22	DE	216
Mary E	6	DE	303
Mary J	14	PA	325
Mary J	20	MD	202
Mary M	6	DE	150
Michael	40	GE	232
Molly	6	DE	190
Mr	26	MA	32
Pennel (Rev)	39	DE	122
Peter	19	DE	93
Rachel	39	DE	171
Rebecca	7	DE	353
Rebecca J	17	DE	216
Richard	12	DE	93
Robert	23	DE	93
Rosanna	17	DE	275
Samuel T	10	DE	198
Sarah A	18	DE	374
Spilo	50	DE	257
Stephen	41	DE	74
Susan	50	NJ	216
Thomas F	35	DE	189
W ORev)	46	MD	114
William	14	DE	203
William	19	ST	17
William	28	DE	93
Wm	23	DE	273
Coors, Philip	19	GE	87
Copper, Josephine	2	PA	272
Mary Ann	32	PA	272
Stephen	35	MD	272
Susan	7	PA	272
Thomas	5	PA	272
Corbert, Ann	50	MD	83
Corbit, Biddy	30	IE	395
Charles	11	GB	310
Daniel	53	PA	173
Daniel W	7	DE	173
Louisa	12	DE	173
Mary C	2	DE	173
Mary W	38	DE	173
Patrick	27	IE	395
Roger	29	IE	395
Thomas	1	DE	395
William R	10	DE	174
Corbus, Jane	30	IE	89
Corch, Edward	2	DE	240
Frederick	40	GE	240
Cordeza, Isabella	27	PA	283
John D M	4	PA	283
John T M	30	PA	283
Corey, David	25	NH	255
John W	28	NH	255
L Maria	23	NH	255
Lydia	22	NH	255
Mary V	27	NH	255
Corizan, John	20	IE	284
Corkrin, Caroline	14	PA	275
Helen	20	PA	275
Isabella	12	DE	275
John	50	PA	275
Margaret	45	PA	275
Mary	18	PA	275
Corliss, David	6	PA	283
Edward	14	PA	283
Johille	1	DE	283
Johille	37	NJ	283
Mary	8	PA	283

Name	Age	State	No.
Corliss, Mary	32	PA	283
Susan	4	PA	283
Corman, Michael	35	IE	345
Cornall, John	3	DE	245
Lewis	35	DE	245
Sarah	25	DE	245
Cornaway, Elias	30	DE	120
John	3	DE	120
Mary	26	DE	120
William	6	DE	120
Cornbrook, Caroline	13	PA	85
Cornelius, Jeremiah	29	NJ	121
Roda J	19	PA	121
Cornish, David	4	DE	74
Hannah	7	DE	352
Jane	17	DE	351
Mary	60	DE	361
Rhoda	12	DE	347
Saml	16	DE	252
Cornley, Ann	22	DE	330
Ellen	1	DE	330
Robert	3	DE	330
Samuel	33	PA	330
Corridon, Joseph C	12	DE	184
Laura J	13	DE	184
Laura L	50	DE	184
Corrie, Christopher	40	DE	231
Corsdale, Jane	19	PA	372
Martha	41	PA	372
Sarah	16	PA	372
Stephenson	58	PA	372
William	6	DE	372
Willis	15	PA	372
Corson, Abijah	6	NJ	306
Abijah	40	NJ	306
Laura	3	DE	306
Lewis H	8	NJ	306
Louisa	12	NJ	306
Lucinda	7	NJ	306
Mary M	1	DE	306
Nicholas J	32	NJ	306
Rhoda	35	NJ	306
Sarah B	27	NJ	306
Cosgrift, Alice	41	IE	173
Ann	3	IE	173
John	7	IE	173
Margaret	9	IE	173
Thomas	47	IE	173
Cossroad, Eliza A	19	PA	13
William E	29	PA	13
Coston, Ann	23	DE	191
Benjamin	11/12	DE	191
Charles	6	DE	191
Charlotte A	2	DE	191
Elizabeth	4	DE	191
Nathan	22	DE	191
Sally A	5	DE	191
Coswell, Caroline	13	DE	258
Cott, Evert	16	DE	245
Cottingham, Esther	20	IE	261
Mary	46	IE	193
Matilda	24	IE	183
William	21	IE	192
Cotton, Patric	52	IE	147
Couch, Mary M	28	DE	284
Tamer	60	DE	330
William	54	DE	330
Couden, Elizabeth	59	DE	251
Coulter, Alexander	50	DE	335
Ann M	37	DE	335
Benjamin	4	DE	336
Ellen	11	DE	336
Henry A	7	DE	336
Joseph	4	DE	336
Councillor, David	17	DE	245
Couper, Absalom	37	VA	303
Alfred	14	DE	69
Ann	29	DE	303
Catherine	28	DE	146
Charley	7	DE	324
Eliza R	27	DE	289
Elizabeth	54	PA	63

Name	Age	State	No.
Couper, George	14	DE	203
George	27	DE	146
Hannah	47	DE	289
James	1	DE	146
James	47	DE	290
Mary	6	DE	316
Mary B	39	DE	290
Saml M	45	DE	289
William	43	DE	289
Couply, James	10	DE	276
John T	1/12	DE	276
Mary	7	DE	276
Mary	37	MD	276
Sarah	2	DE	276
William	37	GB	276
William Jr	17	MD	276
Courain, Mary	19	DE	250
Courey, Edward	8	DE	174
Edward	40	DE	174
Frances	5	DE	174
John	20	DE	172
Maria	25	DE	172
Mary	19	DE	174
Mary	21	DE	174
Latitia	17	DE	174
Lydia	2	DE	174
Rachel	22	DE	174
Course, Leonkin	8	DE	48
Rebecca	68	DE	48
Sarah	40	DE	48
Susan	28	DE	48
William	26	DE	48
Court, Rachel	30	PA	18
Sarah	25	PA	18
Courtis, Anna L	16	PA	142
Anna M	40	DE	115
Charles E	5	DE	115
Edward L	21	DE	141
George W M	8	DE	141
Hannah	19	DE	133
James	24	DE	133
James H	24	DE	141
John	6/12	DE	133
John	46	DE	141
Joseph L	6	DE	141
Louisa M	3	DE	115
Margaretta S	16	PA	141
Mary E	12	DE	115
Peter	40	DE	115
Sarah A	19	DE	115
Sarah A	46	DE	141
Sarah S	2	DE	141
William	18	PA	141
William	48	DE	167
William H	10	DE	115
Cousins, Charlotta	25	GE	152
Frederic W	5	DE	152
George	30	?	152
George	2	DE	152
Coventin, Lydia	21	DE	359
Coventon, Charles	15	DE	379
George	25	DE	374
Coverdale, Charlot	8	DE	338
John D	10	DE	338
Lydia E	6	DE	338
Ninos E	11/12	DE	338
Ninos H	35	MD	338
Sarah	30	DE	338
Sarah J	4	DE	338
Covington, Benj	21	DE	376
Elizabeth	25	MD	1
Elwood	4	DE	376
George	30	DE	376
Hannah	35	MD	1
James	28	DE	376
Jane	54	DE	376
Joseph D	22	DE	190
Lydia Ann	25	DE	376
Nathaniel	64	DE	260
Rebecca	28	DE	260
Willey	2	DE	376
Cowan, Catherine	9	DE	344

Cowan, Chris	38	IE	344	Coyle, Albert R	13	PA	304	Craig, Lydia	5	DE	350
Christopher	7	DE	344	Catherine	27	PA	102	Lydia	50	DE	350
Jane	40	IE	344	George	4	DE	102	Martha	5	DE	37
Jemima	12	DE	344	James	21	IE	398	Mary	11	DE	130
Mary Ann	14	DE	344	John	6	DE	102	Mary	25	DE	67
Robert	36	IE	378	John	28	IE	102	Mary A	23	PA	354
Rosa	70	IE	338	Margaret	9	MD	157	Mary Ann	18	DE	192
Rose	19	IE	344	Margaret A	10	PA	304	Mary E	11	DE	368
Cowder, Christian	20	DE	57	Martha	20	DE	398	Mr	22	IE	130
Cowen, Catherine	50	IE	12	Martha A	40	PA	304	Mr	24	IE	130
Eliza	19	IE	359	Neil	24	IE	45	Mrs	22	IE	130
Ellen	26	IE	378	Patrick	50	IE	335	Nelson	16	PA	90
James	28	DE	82	Samuel	17	DE	70	Noah	19	DE	194
John	5/12	DE	82	Unity	50	IE	335	Noah	59	DE	299
John	21	IE	362	William	2	DE	102	Ramona	8	DE	67
John	35	IE	12	William S	25	IE	304	Ruth	40	DE	187
Margaret	22	IE	163	Cozens, Susan	45	NJ	263	Sally C	40	DE	115
Mary	55	IE	12	Cozier, Adeline	19	DE	322	Sarah	64	DE	300
Sarah	24	DE	82	Catherine A	21	DE	322	Sarah A	14	DE	240
Sarah E	8	DE	362	Elizabeth	38	MD	320	Sarah A	20	DE	90
Steward	25	IE	362	Henry	50	DE	322	Sylby	50	DE	242
William	19	DE	58	Jacob B	16	DE	322	Thomas	1	DE	67
Cowley, Hugh	22	IE	350	Jacob B	16	DE	400	Thomas	20	DE	115
Cox, Albert	23	DE	121	John	29	DE	320	Thomas	21	DE	212
Ann	17	DE	137	Robert W	20	DE	320	Walter	40	PA	350
Ann	25	DE	293	Sarah J	24	DE	320	Washington	34	PA	37
Anna	3	DE	179	Sarah J	51	NY	322	William	1	DE	347
Anna	29	PA	62	Crabb, Eliza	45	PA	53	William	16	DE	149
Anne	18	DE	157	Crabbe, John McKee	20	PA	373	William	27	PA	55
Benjamin	34	NJ	18	Craft, Matthew	26	PA	347	William	35	PA	90
Caspar	8/12	DE	200	Crage, Priscilla	6	DE	285	Crain, Sarah	30	IE	242
Catherine	30	IE	130	Susan	38	DE	285	Cramby, John	26	IE	304
Catherine	60	IE	335	Wesley	35	DE	285	Crampton, William	23	DE	399
Chany	31	PA	62	Craian, Catherine	7	DE	118	Cramsey, Edward	14	IE	308
Charles	4	DE	121	Charles	11	DE	118	William	16	IE	308
Edward L	11/12	DE	127	Hugh	30	IE	118	Cranbrook, Adelade	10	PA	13
Elizabeth	15	PA	332	James	2	DE	118	Amelia	8	PA	13
Elizabeth	20	MD	178	Mary A	28	IE	118	Caroline	13	PA	13
Elizabeth	30	DE	200	Craig, Abraham	8	DE	90	Jane	44	NY	13
Elizabeth	33	DE	358	Ann	25	DE	243	William	16	PA	13
Elizabeth	47	NJ	178	Ann	74	DE	354	William	45	GB	13
Garret Jr	10	DE	178	Caroline	9	DE	37	Crankleton, Abraham	4	DE	206
George	48	DE	200	Catherine	1	DE	130	Benjamin	37	DE	206
George	50	PA	179	Cedney	18	DE	354	Jenny	37	DE	206
Hannah	80	PA	42	Celinda	7	DE	315	Cranson, Adaline	15	DE	370
Harriet P	10	DE	136	Clara	11	DE	130	Anna	9	DE	370
Isaac	18	DE	14	Daniel	18	DE	299	Anna	68	PA	368
Ismand	46	NJ	60	David	35	DE	130	Benjamin	36	DE	368
James	1	PA	358	Duress	4	DE	347	Edward	13	DE	370
James	25	MD	329	Elwood	14	DE	350	Edwin	2	DE	368
James	32	MD	358	Estalina	16	DE	187	Elizabeth	17	DE	370
Jane A	35	NJ	136	Frederic	11	DE	130	Ellen T	40	DE	368
John	2	DE	293	George	2	DE	37	Elne	37	DE	368
Joshua	28	NJ	127	George	10	DE	130	Emma	1	DE	370
Lewis	27	DE	122	George	51	DE	115	Francis	5	DE	368
Lewis M	23	DE	178	Hannah	40	DE	176	Hannah	30	PA	368
Louisa	6	DE	179	Hannah J	12	DE	350	Hannah	40	PA	376
Margaret J	7	DE	293	Harlan	8	DE	350	James	42	DE	368
Martha	10	DE	218	Harry	7	DE	130	John	7	DE	368
Mary	24	NJ	121	Henrietta	6	DE	90	Joseph	51	DE	370
Mary E	3	DE	136	Henry	5	DE	67	Louisa	4	DE	370
Matilda	3	PA	358	Henry	25	DE	67	Mary	11	DE	370
Moses	60	PA	367	Henry	65	DE	37	Mary E	13	DE	368
Osmond	46	NJ	59	Hester	6	DE	67	Samuel	4	DE	368
Priscilla	50	DE	252	Hester	32	DE	347	Sarah	19	DE	370
Rebecca	28	DE	121	Hester	33	DE	37	Simon	84	PA	368
Samuel	20	DE	136	Hetty	60	MD	37	William	2	DE	368
Samuel	40	DE	136	Isabella	30	DE	130	Crasgrove, Albert B	9	DE	355
Samuel B	16	PA	136	Jacob	29	PA	347	Hannah	21	PA	355
Sarah	18	DE	127	Jacob T	32	PA	354	Hugh	2	DE	355
Sarah J	6	DE	137	Jane	66	MD	269	John L	4	DE	355
William	50	?	293	James	2	DE	243	Joseph W	7	DE	355
William H	5	DE	293	James	15	DE	212	Crasgrow, Chas	47	PA	352
Coxe, Edward	38	DE	123	James M	11/12	DE	90	Elizabeth J	17	PA	352
Elizabeth	13	DE	123	John	4	DE	90	James B	19	PA	352
Ellen	17	DE	123	John	10	DE	350	Joshua	2	DE	352
Emeline	14	PA	129	John	17	DE	116	Mary	11	PA	352
Esau	68	DE	122	Lamborn	5	DE	347	Oliver	5	DE	352
John	14	DE	230	Lamborn	5	DE	353	Rebecca	14	PA	352
Mary	77	DE	181	Laura	11	DE	37	Sarah	8	DE	352
Samuel	50	DE	218	Lewis	2	DE	347	Theressa	48	WL	352
Sarah	35	NJ	123	Lucy	4	DE	130	Crassen, Charlotte	30	DE	93

Name	Age	State	No.
Crassen, Israel	25	DE	93
Crausly, James	38	DE	110
Craven, David S	48	DE	201
John V	10	PA	201
Mary J	18	DE	201
R J	38	DE	201
Thomas J	13	DE	201
Crawford, A	3/12	DE	98
Abraham	13	DE	216
Alexander	27	DE	388
Alexander	30	DE	371
Alexander	67	DE	388
Ann R	4	DE	230
Anna	1	DE	24
Catherine	17	DE	179
Catherine	58	DE	179
E G	19	MD	401
Ebenezer	28	PA	24
Eldridge G	19	DE	210
Eliza Jane	23	DE	352
Elizabeth	7	NY	343
Elizabeth	55	DE	352
Elizabeth	75	DE	351
Emperor	18	MD	179
Henry V B	16	DE	400
James	77	DE	352
James T	32	DE	230
James V	23	DE	230
Jane	38	ST	343
John	4/12	DE	380
John	20	ST	388
Joseph M	23	DE	388
Lydia	56	MD	371
Maber	25	PA	24
Mary	3	DE	24
Mary	13	DE	3
Mary	16	ST	343
Mary E	2	DE	230
Mary M	27	DE	230
Rebecca	25	DE	388
Rebecca	35	DE	388
Robt	38	ST	343
Samuel	23	PA	24
Samuel L	27	DE	210
William	25	DE	210
William H	57	MD	179
William T	4	DE	343
Crawson, Sarah	20	MD	32
Craynor, Eli	19	DE	234
Creig, Abner	50	NJ	254
Anna	2	DE	274
Elizabeth	31	NJ	274
Elizabeth	38	DE	266
Elmira	16	DE	266
Emma	1	DE	274
Esther	45	DE	253
George	18	DE	266
James	8	DE	266
James	49	DE	266
John	6	DE	266
John	26	PA	266
John	32	PA	274
Noah	7	DE	253
Rachel	48	NJ	254
Sarah	3	DE	266
Sarah	7	DE	253
Wm	11	DE	254
Wm	14	DE	266
Wm	14	DE	273
Cregg, Joseph	78	GB	167
Cresley, Margaret J	11	DE	351
Crethers, John	25	MD	7
Crinand, Frances	20	IE	344
Cripen, Chas H	1	DE	288
Edward G	3	DE	288
James	28	DE	298
Sarah A	28	DE	298
Crips, John	38	DE	306
Criste, Miss	43	ST	58
Crocker, James	17	DE	301
John	22	IE	383
Rachel	40	DE	301
Crockett, Henry	26	DE	239
Samuel	19	DE	214
Croes, George S	33	IE	396
James	2	DE	396
James	45	IE	396
Jane	42	IE	396
John	17	PA	396
Joseph	8	PA	396
Nancy	12	PA	396
William	15	PA	396
Croff, David	2	DE	368
Hannah A	8	OH	368
John	10	OH	368
Joseph	12	OH	368
Louisa	6	OH	368
Mariah	44	PA	368
William	3	PA	368
William	45	PA	368
Crofford, Amelia J	8	DE	339
Andrew J	9/12	DE	340
Charles F	2	DE	340
George W	7	DE	339
George W	32	DE	341
John E	12	DE	339
Joseph	40	DE	339
Joseph D	9	DE	339
Lydia A	5	DE	339
Susanna	35	DE	339
William A	14	DE	339
Croft, Alice	55	DE	169
Edward M	22	NY	169
James	24	DE	350
Josiah L	17	DE	169
Mary J	30	NY	169
William B	20	NY	169
Crogin, Henrietta	22	DE	28
Crompton, Ann C	26	DE	336
Ann E	6	DE	336
John G	27	DE	336
Stephen J	3	DE	337
Cronen, Alexander	5	ST	372
Archivald	18	ST	372
Archibald	42	ST	372
Elizabeth	16	ST	372
James	14	ST	372
Jane	20	ST	372
John	12	ST	372
William	22	ST	372
Croney, Elizabeth	3	DE	261
Hannah	1	DE	261
Hannah	23	PA	261
Mary	30	DE	80
Philemon	31	MD	261
Cronin, Calvin	4	DE	351
Eli	31	DE	358
Elizabeth	30	DE	358
James	5	DE	358
John R	35	DE	351
Margaret	29	DE	351
Mary Francis	3	DE	358
Maurice	2	DE	351
William L	1	DE	358
Cronister, Charles	18	DE	335
Rebecca	48	DE	335
William	6	DE	335
Crooks, John	13	IE	330
Cropley, Charles	15	DE	360
Joseph	39	DE	352
Margaret	34	MD	352
Mary	45	DE	354
Susan A	18	DE	352
Cropper, Margaret	38	MD	11
Crosman, James	19	IE	294
Patrick	25	IE	335
Crooks, Robt	52	IE	329
Saml	50	IE	329
Crosby, Ann M	8	DE	326
Elizabeth	50	IE	39
Emanuel	22	DE	63
Fanny	12	PA	39
George H	4	DE	326
Henry	41	DE	301
Crosby, J C	50	IE	39
James	6	DE	326
Lydia	45	DE	63
Margarett	10	DE	326
Mary	95	DE	63
Michel	13	PA	39
Owen	20	IE	188
Phillis	25	MD	63
Rachel	40	DE	158
Samuel	45	GB	373
Sarah	30	NJ	326
Susannah	18	DE	63
Taylor	35	DE	326
Crosgrove, Albert B	9	DE	354
Hannah	21	PA	354
Hugh	2	DE	354
John S	4	DE	354
Joseph W	7	DE	354
Cross, Amanda	1	DE	236
Amy A	5	DE	187
Ann	10	DE	236
Charles	11/12	PA	144
Clarissa	40	PA	62
Eliza	28	DE	355
Hannah	19	PA	62
James	15	PA	62
John	22	DE	218
John R	35	DE	350
John T	8	DE	187
Jonathan	11	DE	62
Lydia	14	DE	62
Margaret	29	DE	350
Margaret J	27	MD	186
Mary	17	PA	62
Mary	32	DE	236
Mary	36	HN	144
Matthew	26	DE	236
Maverick	2	DE	350
Peter	31	GE	144
Thomas	45	PA	62
William	9/12	DE	186
William	25	NJ	197
Crossby, Harvey	13	DE	348
Crossin, Abigail	67	PA	358
Anna S	23	DE	358
Calvin	4	DE	357
Eli	31	DE	357
Elizabeth	33	DE	357
George F	2	DE	383
Hannah	47	DE	364
Hannah E	19	DE	364
Isaac L	33	DE	358
James	17	DE	364
James	29	DE	358
Jane	35	DE	383
John	7/12	DE	364
John	36	DE	383
John L	6	DE	383
Julian	12	DE	364
Louis H	3/12	DE	364
Margaret A	7	DE	348
Sabilla	14	DE	364
Crossly, Emanuel	22	DE	64
Hannah	45	DE	304
Phillis	25	MD	64
Susanah	18	DE	64
Crosson, Elizabeth	28	DE	383
Charlotte	20	DE	92
Clement	5/12	DE	357
Israel	25	DE	92
Louis H	28	DE	383
Lydia A	4	DE	357
Lydia A	30	DE	357
Milton	5/12	DE	357
Reuben	2	DE	383
Samuel	6	DE	357
Theodore	5	DE	357
Washington	27	DE	357
Crossgrace, Charles	4	DE	348
Joseph	26	DE	348
Rachel	25	PA	388
Crouch, Alexander	1	DE	223

Name	Age	State	Page
Crouch, Amanda A	1	MD	5
Ann	34	NJ	240
Anna K	2	PA	388
Cordelia	3	MD	5
Catherine	3	DE	223
Christopher	39	MD	388
Daniel	27	DE	183
Elisha	26	DE	215
Frances H	4	DE	240
Georgiann	13	DE	174
Hannah P	25	PA	388
James	9	DE	213
John	3	DE	174
John	5	DE	336
John	28	MD	5
John Z	37	DE	174
Josephine	18	DE	174
Margaret	28	MD	5
Martha	10	DE	174
Martha	13	MD	174
Martha	13	DE	224
Mary	13	DE	174
Mary	23	DE	309
Mary A	34	DE	174
Mary J	29	DE	215
Morgan L	4/12	DE	215
Rachel	40	DE	223
Rachel H L	4	PA	388
Sarah	6	DE	174
Sarah	16	DE	224
Sarah	35	DE	223
Susan A	6	DE	240
William	4	DE	223
William	12	DE	240
William L	31	DE	240
Crouse, Charles	16	MD	99
Crow, Andrew	30	DE	27
Ann E	19	MD	278
Ann M	18	MD	282
Ella W	22	DE	27
Ellen	53	VA	321
George	30	IE	356
George W	63	DE	321
Geroge W Jr	2	DE	321
Jemima	14	MD	280
John	22	DE	180
Margaret	18	IE	356
Mary J	16	MD	278
Susan	52	MD	278
William W	12	DE	278
Crowder, Anny	10	DE	233
Elisa	19	DE	233
Jacob	11	DE	239
Jacob V	2/12	DE	220
Marietta	13	DE	234
Martha A	22	DE	220
Nehemiah W	27	DE	220
Rebecca	14	DE	239
Rebecca L	2	DE	220
Crowley, John	45	PA	348
Crown, James	22	IE	349
Crousdale, Howard	28	PA	302
Crozier, Anna M	6	MD	83
Benj A	40	DE	315
Caroline	3	MD	83
Catharine M	4	DE	320
Charity	14	DE	320
Eli	36	MD	83
Eli	42	DE	315
Eliza J	45	DE	315
Elizabeth	16	DE	320
Elizabeth	35	PA	83
Francis	12	DE	320
Henne	24	MD	35
Henrietta	24	DE	30
James	1	DE	35
James	16	DE	30
James	35	DE	35
John H	6	DE	320
Laura	4	MD	83
Lydia	3	DE	36
Mary	2/12	DE	83
Crozier, Mary R	12	DE	315
Martha L	10	DE	320
Thomas	38	DE	30
Crumlish, Andrew	21	IE	80
Andrew	36	IE	80
Hugh H	2	DE	30
Jane	24	IE	80
John	39	IE	80
Susan	59	IE	80
Crumpton, Elizabeth	26	DE	210
Lorenzo	25	NJ	188
William	23	DE	398
Crutch, George	36	NJ	84
Mary	50	PA	84
Cruthers, Ann	3	DE	45
Ellen	2	DE	45
Rachel	1	DE	45
Samuel	39	IE	44
Sarah	38	IE	44
Crutson, Susannah	73	DE	237
Cubby, Mary A	17	NJ	302
Culbert, Catherine	25	IE	167
James	20	DE	54
James	50	IE	54
Martha	42	IE	54
Samuel	12	DE	54
Thomas	17	DE	54
Culin, Adam V	30	PA	266
Adriana	7	MD	266
George	2	DE	266
Mathew	3	DE	266
Rebecca	26	MD	266
Cullen, Ann	8	DE	272
Charles	28	IE	347
David	17	DE	237
Elizabeth	28	NJ	272
Isaac	70	MD	237
Jesse	70	MD	237
Powell	24	?	270
Wm	51	DE	272
Cullin, Milton	1	DE	252
Wm	2	DE	252
Culling, Isabella	30	PA	377
James	39	PA	377
James W	2	DE	377
John	4	DE	377
Joseph	4	DE	377
Cullins, William	30	DE	365
Cummerford, Catherin	33	GB	274
Edward	35	IE	274
Elizabeth	21	DE	174
James	16	DE	174
John	12	GB	274
John	27	DE	184
Joseph	1	DE	275
Mary	3	PA	274
Patrick	2	PA	274
Rebecca	57	DE	174
Thomas	66	DE	174
William	17	DE	174
Cummings, Susan	22	IE	338
Cummins, Alexander	28	PA	30
Ann	23	IE	300
Dorcas	35	DE	159
Emma J	6/12	DE	84
Eve	60	MD	16
Henry	50	DE	159
Joseph	46	MD	295
Joseph	70	DE	389
Luisa	13	DE	30
Mary	10/12	DE	30
Rachel	47	DE	295
Rebecca	27	DE	30
Sarah	6	DE	30
Sarah A	18	DE	83
Susan	21	DE	392
William	3	DE	30
William	25	DE	83
Cummons, Alexander	59	DE	84
Benjamin	14	DE	84
John	8	DE	134
John	22	DE	84
Cummons, Rebecca	20	DE	84
Sarah	52	DE	84
Sarah J	17	DE	84
Cunningham, Amelia	18	IE	183
Cinthia	26	DE	315
Eliza J	5	DE	315
John	30	IE	367
Mary	21	IE	194
Sarah A	30	PA	81
Sophia	2	DE	315
Stephen	28	DE	315
Susan	76	NJ	266
William	23	DE	329
William	25	DE	315
Curby, Isaac	7	PA	301
Isaac	45	NJ	301
Jane	10	DE	296
Jane	17	NJ	301
Margaret	43	NJ	301
Margaret A	21	DE	296
Richard	15	DE	301
Rhoda	40	NJ	296
Curl, Rachel	50	DE	58
Curlet, David	6	DE	139
David P	28	DE	107
Eliza	14	DE	139
Elizabeth	6	DE	107
James	11	DE	139
Jane	25	DE	107
John	8	DE	139
Lewis	3	DE	107
Lewis	18	PA	139
Lewis	44	DE	139
Margaret	35	NY	139
Matilda	13	DE	139
Samuel S	5	DE	107
Thomas	4	DE	139
Curlett, Elizabeth	47	DE	329
William	50	DE	329
Curns, James	3	DE	97
John	27	IE	97
Rosana	25	IE	97
Current, John	35	DE	39
Currinder, Catherine	14	DE	379
Catherine	49	DE	383
Charles M	2	DE	330
Eliza	43	DE	379
Frederick	51	DE	383
Jacob	15	DE	330
Jacob	45	DE	329
John	49	DE	379
Margaret	32	DE	330
Margaret L	2	DE	379
Martha L	13	DE	379
Mary	53	DE	383
Robert O	9	DE	379
Washington	5	DE	330
William B	6/12	DE	330
Curry, Ann E	19	MD	178
Eliza	35	IE	338
John	9/12	DE	178
John	25	DE	361
John	27	PA	360
John	30	DE	345
Ninos	19	PA	397
Peirce	36	PA	178
Samuel	26	IE	338
Thos E	22	IE	353
William J	11	DE	226
Curshawe, David	15	DE	353
Cursuel, Anne	40	DE	313
Caroline	12	DE	313
Curtis, Adeline H	28	MA	363
Alfred A	1	MA	392
Ann	45	PA	128
Anna	14	PA	56
Anna M	4	MA	392
Annie	4	MA	392
Benjamin	6	DE	318
Easter	3/12	DE	256
Edwin W	5	MA	368

Name	Age		Num
Curtis, Ephraim	40	MD	263
Esther	20	DE	256
Fred A	36	MA	392
Harriet M	31	MA	392
John	50	MD	191
John T	9	DE	169
Margaret	70	MD	128
Saml	40	MD	256
Sarah	3	DE	256
Sarah	32	DE	169
Sarah E	1	DE	209
Sarah H	1/12	DE	363
Solomon M	32	MA	363
William	12	PA	169
Curts, Alfred	5	DE	397
Eliza	31	PA	397
Elizabeth	7	PA	397
Jacob	3	DE	397
Jacob	35	PA	397
Sarah	18	DE	397
Cusic, James	28	IE	13
Cusick, Mary	20	IE	24
Custelow, Jacob	50	DE	374
Lydia	52	DE	374
Custis, Betsey	55	DE	183
Cornelius	1	DE	183
George	19	DE	289
John W	16	VA	400
. Neal	50	DE	183
Custos, Elizabeth	22	DE	183
Custus, George	7	PA	329
Cuthers, Benjamin	24	MD	368
Margaret E	1	PA	368
Martha	28	PA	368
Sarah J	2/12	DE	368
Cutis, Mary	29	DE	209
James L	33	DE	209
Cutter, Elizabeth	2	PA	25
Levi	31	PA	25
Rachel	25	PA	25
Dackery, Ann	35	DE	362
Granville	3	DE	362
Mathew	42	DE	362
Nathaniel	8	DE	362
Richard	5	DE	362
William H	10	DE	362
Dade, George M	13	DE	200
Daham, Catherine	35	FR	341
John	6	FR	341
Nicholas	34	FR	341
Dailey, Alfred	35	NY	284
Bridget	38	IE	345
Charles	30	IE	345
Edmond H	38	NY	284
Elenora	30	NY	284
James	11	IE	295
John C	42	MA	284
John Sr	73	GB	284
Julia A	31	NJ	284
Margaret	30	IE	39
Mary	11	DE	39
Michel	28	IE	39
Susan	40	IE	345
William	10	DE	39
Daily, Frederic	8	IE	295
Thomas	12	PA	380
Dalbo, John	7	DE	36
King	40	PA	36
Margaret	37	DE	36
Mary A	15	DE	36
William H	10	DE	36
Dalby, Jane	15	IE	4
Dale, Ann	50	MD	380
Eliza	11	DE	182
Elizabeth	29	DE	206
Ellen	4	DE	182
Ellen	33	PA	182
George W	12	DE	380
Henrietta	10	DE	206
James	9	DE	182
John	35	DE	182
Dale, John Jr	2	DE	182
Latitia	10	DE	182
Malachi	5	DE	206
Margaret	17	DE	206
Margaret	66	PA	182
Martha	2	DE	321
Peggy	22	DE	158
Rachel	70	DE	321
Rhody	15	DE	206
Richard	6	DE	182
Richard	53	DE	206
Richard Jr	14	DE	206
Sally Ann	4	PE	321
Samuel	2	DE	321
Samuel	12	DE	206
Samuel	48	DE	321
Samuel	53	MD	380
Samuel	19	DE	380
Samuel T	15	DE	321
Tempy	7	DE	206
William	7	DE	321
William	18	DE	321
Daley, Eliza	25	DE	110
Laura	3	PE	110
Tolbert	7/12	DE	110
Dallas, Jacob	6	DE	236
Dalles, Augustus	25	DE	113
Benjamin	2	DE	113
Catherine	3	DE	113
Elizabeth	25	DE	113
Matilda	1	DE	113
Dalton, A F	42	RS	401
Eliza A	30	DE	351
Elizabeth	59	DE	79
James	24	DE	204
Jane	76	IE	341
Joel	33	DE	354
John	61	DE	78
Lydia E	4	DE	354
Margaret	25	DE	341
Maria	7	DE	354
Rebecca G	28	DE	357
Sarah	60	DE	354
Sarah E	9	DE	354
Thomas	36	DE	354
Danarger, Harry	8	DE	394
Danby, Anna	2	DE	313
Caleb	70	DE	277
Elizabeth	10	DE	71
Frances	28	DE	277
Frank	4	DE	313
Hannah	44	DE	71
Hannah	59	GB	71
Henry	32	GB	313
John	62	GB	71
John Jr	25	DE	63
Maria	7/12	DE	63
Maria	35	GB	313
Mary A	2	DE	63
Morris	36	GB	71
Sarah J	23	PA	63
Danderine, Lan A	12	PA	163
Danger, Jacob	19	GE	352
Danials, George	8	DE	140
Jane	27	DE	140
Daniel, Abigal	5	DE	220
Blendict A	7	DE	220
George W	16	DE	220
Jacob	41	DE	220
Jacob A	4/12	DE	220
Joanna	19	IE	332
John	3/12	DE	234
Joseph A	3	DE	220
Mary E	12	DE	220
Mary M E	14	DE	335
Purnell S	6	DE	220
Rachel	36	DE	220
William J	15	DE	220
Daniels, Andrew F	2	DE	229
Comfort	63	DE	229
David J	27	DE	229
Eugenia	4	DE	140
Hannah	41	DE	229
Daniels, Henry	8	DE	229
Johana	11	DE	140
Louisa	4	PE	229
Martha J	11	PE	378
Mary E	6	DE	230
Noah	5/12	DE	378
Perry	40	MD	378
Rachel	22	PA	378
Sarah	55	?	270
Stokley	9	DE	229
William	31	DE	229
William H	6	DE	378
William S	10/12	DE	229
Dannell, James H	10	VA	351
Dansel, Aramantha	8	MD	242
James	35	MD	242
Latitia	29	MD	242
Mary A	10	MD	242
Sarah E	13	MD	242
Susan L	4/12	DE	242
Darby, Susan	60	DE	130
Dare, George	35	NJ	199
Dario, Elizabeth	34	DE	339
Georgianna	10	MD	336
Hannah	59	NJ	336
Peter	35	DE	339
Darle, Catherine	28	PE	157
Thomas	27	DE	157
Darling, Elizabeth	8	DE	282
Elizabeth	41	GB	282
James	4	DE	282
Lucinda S	8	MA	370
Robert	20	DE	151
Robert	23	GB	309
Darlington, Charlotte	20	NJ	272
Edward	35	PA	3
Leonidas	3	DE	393
Mary A	5	DE	393
Mary L	30	DE	393
Samuel	4/12	DE	393
Samuel	35	PA	393
Sarah L	7	DE	393
Thomas	27	PA	27
William	18	PA	70
William B	19	PA	68
Darper, Thomas	13	IE	298
Darr, Mary A	20	IE	227
Darrach, Margaret	66	DE	181
Darrah, Ann H	58	DE	287
Susan	14	DE	239
David, Anna	59	DE	261
Benjamin	45	DE	214
Benjamin F	16	DE	214
Elizabeth G	21	DE	144
James E	4/12	DE	144
James J	25	MD	144
James L	20	DE	214
Louisa J	10	DE	214
Mary	25	IE	159
Mary A	6	DE	339
Mary A	18	DE	214
Mary E	2	DE	144
Mary J	36	DE	214
William	10	DE	218
William	20	DE	343
William J	7	DE	214
Davidson, Alexander	3	DE	269
Alexander	26	MD	270
Amos	4	DE	269
Amos	24	DE	269
Ann M	4	DE	320
Clement	1	DE	269
Elizabeth	29	DE	269
George	2	DE	269
George	22	DE	270
Hannah	36	DE	269
Harvey	7	DE	320
Jane	48	MD	270
John	8	DE	270
John	10	DE	320
John	30	DE	269

Name	Age	State	No.
Davidson, John	31	GB	320
Mary	10	DE	393
Mary A	30	PA	320
Prudence H	13	PA	320
Thomas	31	DE	392
Thomas	31	DE	392
William	32	DE	269
David, Abigal	19	DE	247
Alexander	5	DE	228
Alexander	9	DE	313
Allace	60	MD	157
Alonzo	1	DE	113
Amanda	11	DE	210
Amos	5	MD	357
Amos	30	DE	360
Amos	44	DE	358
Andrew	37	DE	369
Ann	4/12	DE	229
Ann	20	MD	381
Ann	33	DE	247
Ann	38	PA	360
Ann	85	DE	241
Ann E	17	DE	357
Ann E	23	DE	236
Ann J	7	DE	307
Anna	9	DE	157
Anna	27	DE	330
Anthony C	3	DE	301
Benjamin	6	DE	157
Benjamin F	6	DE	157
Caleb	30	DE	214
Caleb	36	DE	371
Caroline W	36	DE	371
Catherine	11	DE	211
Catherine	16	DE	242
Catherine	18	DE	336
Catherine	25	DE	242
Catherine	33	DE	371
Catherine	38	DE	248
Catherine	75	DE	219
Catherine E	15	DE	248
Catherine M	12	PA	107
Charles	2	DE	301
Charles	37	DE	366
Cornelius	9	DE	247
Critendon	44	DE	371
Daniel	3	DE	247
David T	8	DE	211
Deborah A	17	DE	291
Diana	11	PA	18
Edward	1	DE	371
Edward	12	PA	358
Edward W	8	DE	357
Edwin A	8/12	DE	307
Eli	7	DE	364
Eli	44	PA	364
Elijah	7	DE	236
Eliza	28	MD	314
Eliza	29	DE	369
Eliza	30	DE	80
Eliza	48	NJ	211
Eliza A	26	DE	123
Eliza J	4	DE	299
Eliza J	8	PA	360
Eliza J	21	DE	201
Elizabeth	2	DE	123
Elizabeth	8	DE	93
Elizabeth	12	PA	106
Elizabeth	14	DE	333
Elizabeth	15	DE	358
Elizabeth	16	PA	16
Elizabeth	17	DE	216
Elizabeth	33	PA	157
Elizabeth	34	DE	338
Elizabeth	44	GB	357
Elizabeth	50	DE	242
Elizabeth	50	GB	333
Elizabeth A	15	PA	358
Elizabeth C	2	DE	247
Elizabeth K	17	DE	166
Ellen	48	DE	149
Elvan	30	DE	64
Davis, Elvan	30	DE	64
Emma	15	DE	166
Emma	20	NY	64
Emma	23	DE	74
Emma L	5	DE	202
Eran	18	DE	333
Evalina	1	DE	314
Evan	6	DE	314
Evan	8	DE	301
Frances	2	DE	80
Francis	8/12	DE	202
Frederick	29	DE	202
Frederick	5	DE	370
George	9	DE	364
George	49	PA	16
George	54	DE	198
George D	3	DE	306
George E	3	DE	280
George W	19	DE	247
Georgianna	10	DE	335
Gilpin	14	DE	365
Hannah	14	DE	399
Hannah	43	DE	236
Hannah	63	DE	91
Hannah	68	DE	331
Hannah A	35	DE	365
Harman	41	PA	358
Harriett	7	NJ	336
Harriett B	2	DE	318
Henrietta	45	MD	166
Henry	5	DE	214
Henry	8	DE	79
Henry	40	MD	91
Henry	48	DE	247
Herman L	14	GA	318
Hester	20	DE	242
Hester A	9	DE	365
Hetty	8/12	DE	157
Honor	11	DE	394
Isaac	11	DE	365
Isaac	17	DE	318
Isaac	18	DE	360
Isaac M	6	DE	247
Isabela	5	DE	300
J Ann	60	DE	192
Jacob	14	DE	290
Jacob	42	DE	204
James	10	DE	235
James	14	DE	247
James	15	DE	210
James	16	DE	332
James	21	MD	297
James	22	MD	380
James	29	NJ	336
James	32	DE	93
James	36	MD	306
James H	4	DE	123
James H J	7	DE	105
James M	27	DE	200
James W	11/12	DE	214
Jane	4	DE	206
Jane	19	DE	395
Jane	45	PA	15
Jane	50	DE	91
Jane E	35	VA	106
Jane S	38	PA	105
Jesse	5	PA	358
John	3	DE	204
John	7	DE	242
John	7	DE	299
John	14	PA	358
John	18	DE	218
John	19	DE	192
John	21	DE	198
John	24	DE	247
John	25	DE	74
John	26	MD	198
John	26	PA	257
John	27	DE	370
John	28	GB	314
John	34	DE	322
John	35	DE	94
Davis, John	35	MD	184
John	40	IE	300
John	72	DE	168
John F	6	DE	228
John H	11	DE	229
John W	3	DE	236
John W	4	DE	202
Joseph	6/12	DE	93
Joseph	23	MD	157
Joseph	49	PA	105
Joseph M	10	DE	356
Joseph S	14	PA	105
Joseph T	11	GA	319
Joshua	22	MD	369
Jube	9	DE	123
Judy	50	DE	244
Julia	30	MD	100
Julia A	3	DE	214
Kanhapuck (?)	85	DE	297
Kent D	9	DE	318
Kerboni E	7	DE	318
Laly	14	DE	235
Laura	7/12	DE	200
Lemuel	3/12	DE	198
Leonard	26	MD	203
Letitia B	4	DE	105
Lewis	9	DE	299
Lewis	28	DE	309
Lewis	32	DE	299
Lewis	35	DE	285
Littleton	40	DE	371
Louisa	31	DE	370
Luisa	30	DE	370
Lydia	33	DE	300
Lydia A	4/12	DE	123
Lydia A	39	MD	99
Manlove	22	DE	242
Manlove	40	DE	247
Margaret	9	DE	105
Margaret	19	MD	380
Margaret	35	DE	370
Margaret	45	DE	364
Margaret Ann	14	DE	364
Margaret D	24	DE	280
Maria	11	MD	357
Maria J	7	DE	365
Mark	55	DE	242
Mark H	14	DE	242
Martha	12	DE	242
Martha	35	DE	91
Martha J	15	DE	356
Martha J	20	DE	110
Martha W	2	DE	105
Mary	3/12	DE	113
Mary	16	DE	147
Mary	16	DE	253
Mary	23	DE	198
Mary	26	DE	214
Mary	27	NJ	336
Mary	32	DE	228
Mary	38	DE	247
Mary	40	DE	235
Mary	51	DE	336
Mary	58	DE	253
Mary	80	DE	70
Mary A	6	DE	370
Mary A	12	DE	247
Mary A	15	DE	243
Mary A	16	DE	236
Mary A	24	DE	242
Mary A	24	DE	285
Mary A	26	DE	202
Mary Ann	19	DE	387
Mary J	4	DE	128
Mary J	19	PA	105
Mary J	38	DE	204
Mathew	2	DE	370
Matilda	7	MD	357
Matilda	36	DE	366
Matilda	56	DE	369
Matilda E	13	DE	356
Michael	65	DE	253

Name	Age	State	Page
Davis, Morris	6	DE	356
Nemiah	10	DE	242
Nemiah	34	DE	228
Oscar	35	DE	156
Peter	35	DE	156
Peter	35	DE	338
Prince	60	DE	253
Rachel	6	DE	236
Rachel	39	MD	16
Rachel	42	PA	358
Rebecca	7	DE	74
Rebecca	26	DE	202
Rebecca	35	PA	306
Rebecca	42	DE	198
Richard T	1	DE	329
Risdon	8	DE	204
Risdon	8	DE	231
Robert	21	DE	194
Robert	22	DE	247
Robert	35	DE	189
Robert	35	DE	309
Robert H	9	DE	228
Robert J	17	DE	364
Robert L	2/12	DE	202
Robinson	45	DE	394
Samuel	13	DE	318
Samuel	30	NJ	43
Samuel B (Col)	83	DE	318
Sarah	11/12	DE	299
Sarah	1	DE	370
Sarah	2	DE	247
Sarah	3	NJ	336
Sarah	14	DE	253
Sarah	22	DE	157
Sarah	25	DE	318
Sarah A	5	DE	360
Sarah A	39	PA	128
Sarah A	41	MD	357
Sarah D	44	MD	70
Sarah E	6	DE	79
Sarah E	11	DE	306
Sarah E	17	DE	203
Sarah E	20	DE	236
Sarah J	7	DE	202
Sarah J	10	DE	247
Sarah J	14	DE	357
Sarah J	28	DE	299
Sarah Jane	19	DE	364
Sarah M	8	DE	247
Serena	21	DE	193
Sina	5	DE	365
Siney	51	DE	102
Susan	17	DE	358
Susan	21	NJ	113
Susan	30	DE	93
Susan D	11	DE	318
Synthia	4	DE	94
Thomas	1	DE	128
Thomas	8	DE	236
Thomas	14	DE	247
Thomas	35	DE	247
Thomas E	31	NJ	128
Victorine	3	DE	370
Walter W	9/12	PA	360
Walter W	43	PA	360
William	8/12	DE	74
William	1	DE	236
William	2	MD	357
William	8	DE	329
William	23	DE	202
William	24	DE	248
William	25	MD	194
William	28	GB	50
William	28	DE	329
William	30	PA	53
William	32	PA	113
William	44	DE	210
William	54	DE	102
William	56	MD	136
William	58	WL	99
William B	33	DE	123
William	12	DE	364
Davis, William	58	WL	99
William B	33	DE	123
William F	12	DE	364
William S	1	PA	358
William S	3	DE	113
William W	2/12	DE	380
Wm T	10	DE	332
Davy, Serra	16	VA	81
Shockley	35	NJ	212
Dawn, George	12	DE	363
Dawson, Catherine	35	DE	28
James	24	MD	207
James W	38	MD	70
Lydia	46	MD	70
Margaret	36	DE	132
Mary A	40	MD	70
Day, Albert	1	DE	293
Anna M	11	DE	274
Benjamin	70	DE	284
Charles	2	DE	103
Charlotte B	15	MD	332
Edwin A	16	MD	400
Edwin W S	7	DE	274
Eliza	5	DE	285
Ellen E	9	DE	274
Ellen R	24	DE	274
Emeline	37	PA	274
George	31	NJ	103
Hannah B	24	PA	274
Hellen	58	GB	274
Hester	21	DE	293
James	35	MD	187
James M	25	DE	56
John	36	DE	285
John B	1	DE	286
John W	29	DE	274
Joseph P	12	DE	274
Lydia E	2	DE	274
Mary	2	PA	88
Mary	20	MD	187
Mary	27	IE	103
Mary	33	IE	88
Mary E	15	DE	303
Matilda	23	DE	56
Matilda	27	DE	285
Priscilla	2	DE	285
Priscilla	69	DE	285
Thomas R	21	DE	274
Willemina	3	DE	274
William	28	DE	293
William A	2/12	DE	103
William A	10/12	DE	274
William M	36	DE	274
Dayley, Sarah	2	DE	146
William	15	IE	352
Dayly, Ann	30	IE	146
Barnard	5	DE	352
James	7	DE	146
James	40	IE	146
Mary A	8	DE	146
Days, Sarah	10	DE	305
Deacon, Andrew	20	DE	140
Benjamin	10	DE	201
Eliza	30	DE	140
Hannah	9	DE	63
John	13	PA	63
Mary	7	DE	63
Mary	44	NJ	63
Robert	11	DE	63
Sarah	5	DE	63
Stacy	43	NJ	63
William	40	DE	140
Deacyne, Edith	10	DE	140
Elizabeth	13	DE	140
Jacob	9/12	DE	140
James	6	DE	140
Martha A	3	DE	140
Nelson	5	DE	140
William	18	DE	140
Deakyne, Albert G	24	DE	216
Barnadoh	18	DE	231
Bashaba	13	DE	231
Deakyne, Catherine	28	DE	215
George	7	DE	225
George	61	DE	215
George A	28	MD	215
George C	22	DE	215
George F	11	DE	215
Hannah	56	DE	215
Jacob	29	DE	215
James H	7	DE	215
John	5	DE	215
John	12	DE	225
Joseph B	14	DE	215
Lydia A	28	DE	231
Martha	14	DE	226
Mary	8	DE	215
Mary	26	DE	215
Mary A	14	DE	231
Mary A E	28	PA	215
Napoleon B	22	DE	215
Peter S	28	DE	215
Rachel	40	DE	226
Sarah	50	DE	215
Sarah J	10	DE	226
Sarah J	19	DE	215
Thomas	29	DE	231
Veronica	50	DE	213
Virginia	1	DE	231
Wilhelmina	15	DE	213
William	4/12	DE	215
William	22	DE	213
William C	6	DE	215
William W	37	DE	226
Deal, Susan	25	DE	128
Dean, Angelica	22	DE	245
Ann	2/12	DE	245
Bethia	8	DE	264
Charles	1	IE	64
Charles	40	IE	64
Eleanor	29	PA	175
Elizabeth	22	MD	398
Gilbert	11	MI	139
Jacob	29	MD	298
James	7	IE	64
James	25	DE	245
James	72	GB	390
Jane	40	IE	64
Janett	14	MD	323
John	21	MD	105
Joseph	9	PA	390
Joseph	66	GB	390
Margaret	9	IE	64
Margaret	31	GB	390
Mary	3	DE	245
Mary E	5	IE	64
Oliver	11	DE	310
Rebecca	47	DE	264
Robert	8	IE	64
Robert M	70	IE	64
Solomon	44	DE	264
Susanna	7	PA	390
Thomas J	5	PA	390
William	18	MD	395
William	30	GB	390
William E	1	DE	390
William P	1	MD	398
DeAngeli, Martha	15	PA	164
Dearey, James	29	IE	310
James	40	IE	310
John	30	IE	310
Mary	8	IE	310
Mary	18	IE	302
Mary	22	IE	310
Mary	28	IE	326
Michael	12	DE	302
Michael	13	IE	310
Patrick	1	DE	310
Rose	10	IE	310
Sarah	28	IE	337
Unity	37	IE	310
Dearson, Emeline	23	DE	147
Deaton, Catherine	40	DE	91
Harriet	22	DE	305

Name	Age	St	Pg	Name	Age	St	Pg	Name	Age	St	Pg
Deaton, Mary A	4/12	DE	305	Delsaver, Sarah	10	PA	223	Dennis, Francis	30	ST	340
Deblin, Robert	27	DE	313	Susannah	9	PA	223	Henry M P	7	DE	386
Debluth, Amos P	11	PA	348	Deltny, Isaac	33	DE	373	John	40	DE	155
Ann	60	PA	348	Mariah	27	DE	373	Joshua	15	MD	327
Anna	7	DE	348	DeMagri, Martha	15	PA	164	Hester	28	MD	386
Henrietta	8	PA	348	DeManlativo, L	18	CU	164	Lucy	2	DE	386
John	50	PA	348	Dembo, Susanna	25	DE	340	Margaret A	37	MD	144
Rebecca	18	PA	348	Demby, Ann	24	DE	202	Mary	20	MD	328
Decinson, William	13	DE	336	Betty	50	PA	178	Nathan	7	DE	155
Decker, Benjamin	3	DE	316	Caleb	30	DE	189	Sarah J	5	DE	155
Hannah	28	DE	45	Charles	1	DE	199	Siney	14	MD	327
Rebecca	30	DE	316	Eliza A	58	MD	327	Susan B	40	NJ	165
Dedham, Mary	11	DE	320	Elizabeth	11	DE	242	William	38	NY	165
Rachel	37	DE	320	Fanny	15	DE	202	Zachariah G	6	DE	144
Rebecca	9	DE	320	Henry	8	DE	242	Zachariah G	38	MD	144
William	2	DE	320	Hester A	35	DE	242	Dennison, Elizabeth	23	IE	66
William	40	DE	320	James	23	DE	231	Elizabeth Ann	25	PA	362
Deharty, Elizabeth	16	MD	370	John	20	DE	232	James	28	DE	66
George H	8	MD	370	John	22	DE	203	John W	2	DE	362
Harriet	2	DE	370	Rachel	8/12	DE	242	Lydia	69	DE	362
James	15	MD	370	Rachel	55	DE	231	Lydia A	1	DE	66
Jerome	12	MD	370	Richard	61	MD	327	Robert	5	DE	49
John	13	MD	370	Sarah E	11	DE	242	Samuel	38	DE	362
John	54	IE	370	Stephen	38	DE	242	Sarah	50	DE	49
Margaret	43	PA	370	Demming, James	25	IE	176	Denny, Abigail	42	NJ	378
Margaret J	10	MD	370	Demmody, Thomas E	21	PA	142	Aimey	50	DE	381
DeHaven, Andrew	19	PA	392	Dempsey, Adeline	9	DE	313	Alfred	31	DE	46
Anna	14	PA	393	Archibald	5	DE	341	Anne	22	MD	29
David	17	PA	392	Areneth	29	DE	341	Asbury	11	DE	322
Harriet	49	PA	392	Elizabeth	17	NJ	30	Benjamin	4	DE	232
Jacob	50	PA	392	Elizabeth	56	MD	342	Benjamin	29	DE	244
Louisa	16	DE	392	James	20	DE	317	Benjamin F	3	DE	138
Margaret	12	DE	393	James H	4	DE	313	Catherine	17	DE	178
Dehuly, David	6	DE	185	Jane	6/12	DE	313	Elijah	60	DE	378
Elizabeth	10/12	DE	185	John	38	DE	341	Eliza	9	DE	320
Emeline	35	DE	185	John T	7/12	DE	341	Eliza	10	DE	62
James	10	DE	185	Martha A	6	DE	313	Elizabeth	28	DE	381
John	50	DE	185	Mary	12	DE	317	Elizabeth	32	PA	45
Mary	8	DE	185	Mary	25	DE	313	Emma	13	DE	40
Rachel	13	DE	185	Mary	55	DE	326	Emma	13	DE	138
Deihl, Adam	57	PA	197	Michael	30	DE	314	Gallena	5	DE	46
Anna	10/12	DE	200	Milton	8	DE	341	Gideon	5	DE	138
Elizabeth	49	DE	197	Denagan, Elizabeth	2	DE	13	Henry	9	MD	178
Emma	23	DE	197	Mary	4	DE	13	Henry	17	DE	384
Eugene	12	DE	197	Mary	29	IE	13	Isaac	38	DE	367
George	18	DE	197	Patric	30	IE	13	Jacob	2	DE	45
Jane	23	PA	296	Denby, Cassey	35	DE	74	Jacob	34	PA	45
Martha A	10	DE	197	Edward A	10	DE	187	James	15	DE	62
Mary	24	DE	200	Maria	35	PA	314	James	25	DE	381
Theodore	8	DE	197	Marion	32	DE	187	James	45	NY	62
Virginia	20	DE	197	Mary	3	DE	74	James	75	DE	381
William	24	DE	209	Mary A	3	DE	187	Jane	23	DE	381
Deknight, James	6	PA	283	Rebecca	@*	DE	187	Jane	45	DE	282
Rachel	33	DE	283	Sarah E	8	DE	187	Jane	40	DE	62
Delanhin, Clemen-				Dengra, Dergella	16	PA	163	John	5	DE	244
tine	20	DE	312	Denham, Rachel	50	DE	35	John	60	DE	138
Delany, Amy	6	IE	328	Denier, Catherine	3	DE	158	John R	9	DE	138
Bridget	8	IE	328	Danial	40	GE	158	Josephine	11	DE	138
Catherine	12	IE	328	Jane	30	DE	158	Leander	7	DE	46
Ellen	32	IE	328	John	2	DE	158	Lolo	8/12	DE	46
Jane	22	IE	309	Mary A	4/12	DE	158	Lydia	18	MD	138
John	18/12	IE	328	Denison, Dennis	25	IE	42	Maria	27	DE	267
Mary	14	IE	328	Jane	21	IE	42	Martha	8	DE	51
Rebecca	40	DE	54	Joseph	11/12	DE	42	Martha	49	PA	178
Susan	35	DE	54	Mary A	35	DE	326	Mary	25	DE	47
Thomas	6	IE	328	Rachel A	12	DE	10	Mary A	47	DE	138
Delaplain, Eliz	26	DE	355	Denning, Anna	4	IE	254	Mary E	2	DE	244
Francis E	10	DE	355	Catherine	12	DE	336	Mary F	16	DE	138
Hester A	29	DE	355	Eliza	32	IE	254	Mary L	2	DE	232
James	55	DE	355	Elizabeth	8	IE	254	Peter	49	PA	178
James S	20	DE	355	Elizabeth	40	IE	336	Robert B	20	MD	138
Mary	49	DE	355	Jane	11	IE	254	Sarah	1	DE	244
Mary J	23	DE	355	Jane	8	DE	336	Sarah	17	DE	62
Peter	32	DE	355	John	6	IE	254	Sarah	22	DE	163
Delarah, Mary	30	IE	151	Michael	34	IE	254	Sarah	25	DE	244
Delass, Allace	18	IE	13	Susan	1	DE	254	Sarah	45	DE	51
Bridget	20	IE	13	Dennis, Anna	35	MD	204	Solomon	18	DE	162
Delman, Charles	70	FR	342	Anna	19	MD	327	Sophia	30	PA	46
Delplane, Nehemiah	51	DE	347	Anna M	13	DE	155	Susam	40	DE	162
Suena	20	DE	347	Charles W	11/12	DE	165	Temperance	24	DE	232
Delsaver, Maria	50	PA	223	Deborah	54	IE	340	Theodore	9	DE	46
Naham	41	NJ	223	Eliza	40	MD	327	Thomas	14	DE	51

Name	Age	State	Page
Denny, Thomas	51	DE	51
Thompson	12	DE	62
William	21	DE	47
William	27	PA	18
William	28	DE	232
William J	9/12	DE	232
Zachary Taylor	19	DE	138
Denton, Hannah	40	GB	103
John	25	GB	8
Mary	21	GB	8
Sarah A	4/12	DE	8
Depity, Charles	26	DE	253
Elias	23	DE	254
Deputy, Ann E	17	MD	324
Anthony	18	DE	254
Catherine	22	MD	209
Catherine	26	NJ	294
David	6	DE	184
Elizabeth	6/12	DE	184
Elizabeth	8	DE	254
Emeline	35	DE	184
Isabella	22	DE	253
James	5	DE	254
James	10	DE	184
John	22	DE	294
John	38	DE	184
John L	52	DE	254
Mary	8	DE	184
Mary	14	DE	254
Mary	45	DE	254
Rachel	13	DE	184
Rachel	16	MD	327
Saml	10	DE	254
Silvester	35	MD	209
Solomon	19	DE	254
Susan	12	DE	254
DeReals, Aris F	9	SC	165
Derickson, Anna	23	DE	368
Cornelius	33	DE	368
Eliza	18	GB	162
Henry A	7	PA	115
Joseph	19	GB	162
Margaret	2	PA	115
Maria	15	DE	273
Mary J	4	PA	115
Maurine	12	PA	288
Dericson, Eliza	28	DE	334
James C	66	DE	313
Dering, Maria	22	DE	365
Derlenby, Isaac	24	DE	348
Derrell, Asaniah	2	DE	101
Mary	24	PA	101
William H	25	MD	101
Derrick, Charles A	7	DE	296
Ellen	21	DE	295
John A E	23	DE	110
Derrickson, Alfred	15	DE	278
Allen	67	DE	291
Ann	29	MD	214
Anna B	4	DE	210
Anna B	33	DE	210
Aquilla	9	DE	383
Aquilla	41	DE	383
Biard	5	DE	383
Calvin	6	DE	383
Catherine J	21	PA	380
Charles	9	DE	210
Chas	21	PA	329
David P	21	DE	278
Eliza A	37	PA	278
Ellen S	6	DE	365
George	7	DE	210
George	45	DE	210
Hannah	4	DE	365
Hester M	35	DE	207
Jacob	12	PA	329
James M	46	DE	232
Jane	66	DE	368
John	11	PA	329
John P	26	DE	380
Joseph	15	DE	373
Joseph	17	DE	383
Derrickson, Joseph J	1	DE	380
Joseph S	45	DE	278
Letitia	48	MD	329
Lewis	5	DE	373
Lydia	65	DE	204
Margaret	40	DE	383
Margaret	41	DE	373
Maria L	13	DE	210
Martha	40	DE	232
Mary	75	DE	207
Mary A	3	DE	215
Newton J	14	PA	329
Phineas	40	DE	308
Rebecca	40	DE	308
Rebecca S	13	DE	279
Robert	21	DE	205
Robert	79	DE	214
Robt	40	DE	214
Samuel	9	DE	214
Sarah	9	DE	373
Sarah A	73	PE	214
Sarah A	18	DE	278
Sarah H	22	DE	365
Sarah E	11	DE	214
Sarah F	1	DE	383
Sugar	16	PA	329
Susan	66	DE	291
Thomas	34	DE	275
Thomas	70	DE	368
William	17	DE	373
William C	34	DE	365
William R	17	DE	278
Zachariah	40	DE	373
Derry, Daniel	14	IE	301
Ellen	50	IE	301
Patrick	17	IE	301
Thomas	50	IE	301
Desage, David	21	MD	258
Deshane, Mary	11	DE	321
Rachel	39	DE	321
Rebecca	9	DE	321
William	2	DE	321
William	40	DE	321
Deslaw, Elisabeth	37	DE	34
Desney, William	50	PA	106
Deterline, Hiram	60	PA	62
John	4	DE	62
DeTores, Joseph M	15	CU	164
Develan, Henry	17	DE	355
Deven, Biddy	10	IE	59
James	32	IE	43
John	8	DE	43
Mary E	10	DE	43
Rebecca	32	IE	43
Dever, Andrew	31	IE	148
Barney	27	IE	89
Elizabeth	22	IE	89
James	3	DE	148
Jane	35	IE	148
John	6	DE	148
Lusianna	1	DE	89
Mary	12	IE	113
Mary E	19	IE	148
Devilyn, Biddy	19	IE	249
Devine, Mary	15	IE	227
Devis, Matilda	15	DE	29
Devlen, Edward	24	IE	300
Sarah	22	IE	300
William	26	DE	337
Devlin, David	43	DE	347
Hannah	64	DE	347
Devon, Clementina	3/12	DE	53
Elizabeth	24	MD	53
Hugh	30	IE	347
Isaac	17	DE	53
James	29	DE	53
James	57	DE	53
Joseph	7/12	DE	347
Maning	27	DE	53
Margaret	23	IE	347
Mary	2	DE	53
Ruth	55	DE	53
Devough, Ann	28	DE	288
Dewes, Charles	23	PA	17
Mary	64	DE	131
Dexter, George	26	DE	225
Dicerson, Samuel	21	NJ	301
Diches, John	25	DE	167
Dick, Ann	20	DE	329
Archibald	28	DE	315
Archibald	40	DE	329
Phebe Ann	22	DE	388
Dickanson, Wright	20	GB	357
Dickenson, Ann	13	PA	336
Cornelius	51	PA	336
Daniel S	4	PA	336
James	6	PA	336
James	45	GB	336
Jane	10	PA	336
Joshua B	22	DE	386
Mary	8	PA	336
Mary	50	DE	386
Mary A	38	PA	336
Mary E	17	DE	386
Miles	17	DE	386
Miles	50	DE	386
Warren	28	DE	374
William	12	DE	386
Dickerson, Alissa	13	DE	207
Amanda	6	DE	332
Caroline	5	DE	374
Charles	13	DE	332
Charlotte M	9	DE	374
Eliza J	7	DE	374
Elizabeth H	5	PA	115
Ellen	6	DE	209
George	10	PA	115
George	35	PA	115
George M D	3	DE	374
James	35	DE	209
James L	2	DE	209
John N	9	DE	209
John W	4	DE	333
Levi	15	DE	208
Mary	4	PA	115
Mary	29	DE	374
Mary A	10	DE	333
Mary J	30	DE	332
Mary L	10	DE	209
Rebecca D	8	PA	115
Sarah	32	DE	209
Sarah E	10	DE	374
Sarah J	8	DE	333
Susan	28	DE	115
Walter	13	DE	332
William	45	DE	332
William	45	DE	332
William H	18	MD	200
Dickey, Ann	21	PA	287
Benjamin	28	PA	16
Charles H	16	PA	287
Emma	2	DE	16
John L	5	DE	16
Martha J	24	PA	16
Dickinson, David	34	DE	280
David A	2	DE	280
George	10	PA	280
James	12	DE	206
John	34	DE	14
Joseph H	16	PA	48
Josiben	38	DE	14
Mary	6	DE	206
Mary A V	12	DE	280
Miles	18	DE	380
Morris	40	PA	48
Mrs	38	PA	48
Rebecca	49	DE	206
Sarah	10	DE	14
Sarah	8	DE	206
Susan	5	DE	280
Susan	34	DE	280
Susanah	4	PA	14
Vincent	7	PA	14
William	10	DE	206

136 NEW CASTLE COUNTY

Name	Age	St	No.
Dickinson, William	47	DE	206
Dickson, Alexander	17	DE	223
Ann E	1	DE	209
Benjamin	26	DE	223
Catherine	29	DE	216
Catherine A	3/12	DE	234
Eli	29	DE	216
Eli	30	DE	223
Elizabeth	22	DE	234
George	8	PA	319
George	13	DE	197
Hannah	69	PA	234
James	35	IE	34
John	17	DE	319
John W	15	PA	319
Maria	4/12	DE	209
Milly	28	DE	209
Sarah	60	DE	223
Stephen	21	DE	222
Stephen	23	DE	223
Thomas	15	DE	236
Vincent	29	DE	234
William	68	DE	222
William H	14	PA	295
Diehl, Albert	15	DE	273
Amanda	1	DE	293
Daniel	26	DE	296
Elizabeth	33	NJ	293
Elizabeth	57	?	293
Elizabeth	57	NJ	296
Francis	3	DE	293
George T	29	DE	271
John	35	DE	293
Martha	6	DE	293
Mary Ann	12	DE	293
Susan	4	DE	293
Thomas	9	DE	293
Dilaha, Edith	24	DE	65
Eli	5	DE	65
Eli	28	DE	16
John	1	DE	65
Mary	20	DE	16
Sarah	4	DE	16
Rachel	2	DE	16
Dill, Ebenezer	32	DE	171
George	34	NJ	142
John A	4	DE	171
Louisa	31	MD	171
Dillaha, Eli	28	DE	52
Jacob	19	DE	65
James	4	DE	65
James	30	DE	65
Margaret	60	DE	65
Sally A	22	DE	65
William	5	DE	65
William H	4	DE	65
Dillen, William	26	DE	336
Dillman, Samuel	19	PA	358
Dillon, Anne	50	DE	246
Christiana	16	DE	246
George	54	NJ	246
Martha	15	DE	204
Dilts, James	40	NJ	374
Dilworth, Charles C	14	DE	188
Clara G	10	DE	188
Eliza H	4	DE	188
Eliza S	40	PA	188
James B	8	DE	188
John D	50	DE	188
John R	12	DE	188
John D	54	DE	281
Louis C	1	DE	188
Rebecca H	24	DE	188
Sarah P	6	DE	188
Thomas T	10	DE	188
William H	17	DE	188
Dinges, Amanda	14	DE	61
David	42	DE	61
Elizabeth	20	DE	61
Mary	16	DE	61
Mary	40	DE	61
Mary	40	DE	61
Disher, Edward	6	DE	81
Ella	1	DE	81
Isabella	27	MD	81
Divine, Ann	30	IE	9
Catherine	15/12	DE	325
James	7	DE	125
James	19	IE	136
Jane	22	IE	341
John	25	IE	235
Martha	50	DE	160
Mary	12	IE	106
Sarah	24	IE	325
Thos	23	IE	341
Dixen, Isaac	64	DE	142
Lucretia R	29	PA	142
Margaret E	20	DE	142
Mary	29	DE	374
Mary	33	PA	142
Mary	58	DE	142
Samuel	14	DE	374
Dixon, Abraham	21	DE	324
Alexander H	46	DE	359
Ann	11	DE	21
Anna	19	DE	346
Benjamin	11	DE	198
Benjamin	25	DE	239
Bines	15	DE	346
Charity M	9	DE	346
Charles H	1	DE	320
Davis W	2	DE	362
Deborah	40	DE	370
Eben	7	DE	383
Elizabeth	20	DE	343
Elizabeth	24	DE	384
Elizabeth	30	DE	320
Elizabeth	50	MD	237
Elizabeth B	26	DE	113
Elizabeth T	20	DE	346
Elmyra	11	DE	379
Emeline	20	DE	379
Emeline	21	DE	237
Fisher H	49	DE	346
Frances A	6/12	DE	239
George	5	DE	113
George	13	DE	198
George	45	DE	370
Hannah	22	DE	384
Hannah	27	DE	381
Hannah	36	DE	346
Hannah A	5	DE	198
Harriet	24	DE	151
Henry	16	DE	74
Henry D	9	DE	346
Herbert	4	DE	158
Isaac	10	DE	383
Isaac	23	DE	346
Jacob	17	DE	346
James	32	DE	158
James	45	DE	346
James H	16	DE	238
John	4	DE	151
John	10	DE	303
John	17	DE	144
John	22	DE	158
John	30	DE	73
John T	11	DE	362
Joseph	10	DE	74
Joseph H	2	DE	346
Joseph M	55	DE	240
Josephine	5	DE	187
Jourdan	35	DE	361
Laura	3	DE	346
Letitia M	35	DE	361
Lewis	53	DE	288
Lucinda	7	DE	151
Lydia A	21	DE	384
M A	21	MD	166
Margaret	16	DE	355
Margaretta T	11	DE	346
Maria	5	MD	320
Martha	10	DE	383
Mary	20	NJ	103
Dixon, Mary	26	DE	73
Mary	37	DE	35
Mary	43	IE	74
Mary	46	DE	384
Mary	86	DE	384
Mary A	3	DE	113
Mary E	12	DE	346
Mary J	14	DE	346
Mary F	4	DE	384
Mary T	43	PA	346
Maxwell	6	DE	158
Morris	18	DE	384
Newlan	8	DE	113
Rebecca	6	DE	346
Rebecca	29	DE	158
Rebecca J	5	DE	381
Rhody	18	DE	239
Robert	6	DE	151
Samuel	10/12	DE	151
Samuel	6	DE	35
Samuel	13	DE	384
Samuel	55	DE	36
Samuel P	49	DE	384
Sarah	1	DE	113
Sarah	13	DE	99
Sarah A	9	DE	362
Sarah A	15	DE	384
Sarah C	4	DE	237
Sarah E	7	DE	381
Sebrina	48	DE	359
Simon	34	DE	151
Susan	26	DE	384
Thomas	2	DE	73
Thomas	7	DE	198
Thomas	30	DE	381
Thomas H	3	MD	320
Thomas S	35	DE	113
William	11	DE	384
William	14	DE	74
William	36	DE	237
William	40	MD	320
William	41	IE	74
William H	1	DE	198
Wiston	13	DE	362
Doan, Eliza	35	PA	362
Doane, Horace	39	DE	290
Dobbs, Anna	7	DE	279
Henry F	9	DE	279
Rachel	24	PA	279
Sarah	4	DE	279
William H	2	DE	279
William H	34	GB	279
Docerty, Ann	20	IE	142
Catherine	22	IE	114
Robert	14	PA	18
Docherty, Andrew	2	DE	61
Ann	8	PA	45
Ann	16	IE	99
Ann	22	IE	115
Ann	56	DE	79
Ann	60	IE	115
Anna	26	ST	34
Barney	16	IE	117
Barney	44	IE	45
Biddy	40	IE	162
Bridget	9	DE	116
Catherine	13	PA	45
Catherine	17	IE	72
Catherine	44	IE	45
Danial	2	DE	116
Dennis	5	DE	34
Edward	6	DE	61
Edward	23	PA	163
Eliza	46	IE	64
Elizabeth	25	DE	73
Elizabeth	30	IE	61
Elizabeth	33	IE	65
Elizabeth	40	IE	39
Elizabeth	60	IE	91
Fanny	25	IE	161
Franklin	12	PA	45
Grace	22	IE	111

Name	Age	State	Page
Docherty, Isaac	30	PA	125
James	1	DE	65
James	3	DE	34
James	3	DE	45
James	7	DE	116
James	30	IE	85
James	35	IE	115
Jane	17	PA	45
Jane	21	IE	65
Jannett	1	DE	34
John	6	PA	45
John	7	PA	50
John	15	DE	116
John	18	IE	64
John	21	IE	133
John	25	IE	65
John	35	IE	65
John	60	DE	79
Joseph	5	DE	45
Margaret	5	DE	116
Margaret	34	IE	116
Mary	3	PA	50
Mary	35	PA	50
Mary A	4/12	DE	61
Mary A	14	DE	116
Mary A	20	IE	100
Mary J	18	DE	125
Matson	6	PA	50
Michel	30	IE	61
Neal	17	MA	31
Neal	36	IE	34
Patric	12	DE	116
Patric	35	IE	116
Phillip	3/12	DE	115
Robert	16	PA	45
Sarah	16	DE	115
Sarah	19	IE	20
Sarah	23	IE	18
Sarah A	35	DE	99
William	15	IE	64
William	19	DE	45
Dockery, Ann	5	DE	25
Henry	32	GB	25
Margaret	28	DE	25
Mary	2	DE	25
Rebecca	2/12	DE	25
Sarah	6	DE	25
Dockhard, Anna May	13	DE	363
Dockins, James H	13	MD	69
Dodd, Ann	81	DE	341
Caroline	33	DE	374
Hester	16	PA	358
John S	9	DE	374
Joseph	8	DE	374
Silas	4	DE	374
Silas	38	DE	374
William R	2	DE	374
Dodson, Rebecca	22	MD	219
Dodsworth, Elizabeth	60	GB	352
Jeremiah	65	GB	352
Dodglden, Margaret	14	DE	166
Doherty, Ann	12	IE	343
Ann	25	IE	338
Ann E	34	IE	343
Barney	19	DE	323
Bridget	7	DE	362
Bridget	26	IE	348
Bridget	75	IE	360
Catherine	16	IE	348
Catherine	73	IE	362
Daniel	1	DE	340
Daniel	25	IE	361
Daniel	26	IE	340
Edward	16	DE	360
Edward	50	IE	360
Eliza	25	IE	340
Eliza A	23	MD	333
Elizabeth	1	DE	333
Francis	5	DE	362
George	21	IE	339
Hannah J	7	PA	333
Henry	25	IE	338
Doherty, Isabella	7	IE	343
James	3	DE	362
James	5	DE	339
James	14	IE	339
James	20	IE	347
Jane	18	IE	340
Jane	23	IE	336
John	25	IE	336
John	25	IE	348
John	37	IE	333
Joseph	12	DE	360
Julia	18	IE	339
Margaret	50	IE	339
Margaret E	10	IE	343
Mary	6	PA	356
Mary	20	IE	352
Mary	50	IE	360
Mary A	11	IE	339
Mary A	25	DE	338
Mary J	2	DE	342
Patrick	22	IE	352
Patrick	45	IE	362
Patrick	60	IE	342
Patrick W	5	DE	333
Philip	28	IE	336
Rebecca	23	IE	339
Rosanna	23	PA	360
Rosetta	5	IE	343
Sarah	35	IE	362
Sarah J	4/12	DE	362
Thomas	3	DE	340
William	9	IE	343
William	40	IE	343
Dolan, Thos	22	IE	347
Dolbo, Andrew	5	NJ	26
Daniel	2	NJ	26
Daniel	45	NJ	25
Elizabeth	7	NJ	26
Mary	10	NJ	26
Reuben	9	NJ	26
Sarah	4	NJ	26
Sarah	30	NJ	26
Dolen, John	22	IE	274
Cathrine	50	IE	326
Dolin, Martin	30	IE	326
Dolinson, Henry	17	DE	354
Dolly, Bridget	25	IE	58
Catherine	23	IE	58
Edward	16	DE	232
Joseph	60	DE	198
Mary	59	DE	198
Dolphen, Eliza	55	GB	53
James	17	DE	53
Dolton, Ann	62	PA	274
Edith	33	PA	274
Elihu	22	DE	274
Elizabeth	24	DE	274
Harriett	18	DE	274
James	6	PA	274
John	30	DE	274
Joshua	61	DE	274
Mary J	9	NY	303
Sarah	28	DE	275
Doman, Francis	5	FR	341
Francis	35	FR	341
Jane	16/12	DE	341
Joseph	12	FR	341
Josephine	31	FR	341
Margaret	10	FR	341
Peter	8	FR	341
Donagan, Elizabeth	1	DE	77
Mary A	3	DE	77
Mary A	27	IE	77
Patric	26	IE	77
Donaho, Ann	10	IE	7
Barnard	3/12	DE	7
Elizabeth	35	IE	7
Hugh	1	DE	7
Owen	35	IE	7
Donahoe, John	27	IE	250
Margaret	18	IE	9
Susan	34	IE	310
Donahoe, James	43	IE	310
Donahu, Sarah	17	IE	334
Donal, Jane O	2	DE	336
Donalas, William	23	DE	24
Donald, Andrew	8	DE	121
Ann	50	IE	43
Antonia	40	IE	326
Barra	5	DE	326
Catherine	20	IE	121
Ellen	40	IE	43
Francis	6	DE	121
Hugh	9	IE	326
Hugh	40	IE	326
Jane	10	DE	121
Jane	28	IE	108
John	16	CN	121
Kate	25	IE	127
Margaret	14	DE	121
Margaretta	7	IE	326
Mary	45	IE	121
Mary A	22	IE	121
Mary E	1	DE	326
Patric	45	IE	121
Thomas	18	CN	121
William	55	IE	43
Donaldson, Mary	18	PA	153
Donaly, Barney	2	DE	301
Barney	25	IE	301
Julia	27	IE	301
Mary A	1	DE	301
Patrick	34	IE	301
Donan, John	18	DE	253
Donell, Charlotte A	25	MD	174
Erasmus	35	NJ	174
Joseph	7	DE	174
Isaac	6	DE	174
Donelly, Catherine	12	DE	323
Daniel	20	IE	1
John	11	DE	323
Margaret	17	DE	144
Mary E	15	GB	323
Rosanna	40	IE	323
Thomas	18	DE	57
Donelson, Ann	61	IE	167
John	80	ST	145
Mary	20	IE	15
Mary	24	DE	137
Doner, Elena	45	IE	320
Michael	40	IE	320
Dones, Harriet	10	DE	319
Doniphan, Anna M	4	DE	91
Catherine	37	IE	91
Ella	2	DE	91
John	9	DE	91
John	38	IE	91
Donley, Bridget	36	IE	33
Caroline	6	DE	33
Catherine	8	DE	33
Christopher	24	DE	167
Frank	12	DE	33
James	17	DE	33
John	16	DE	33
Luke	10	DE	33
Patric	49	IE	33
Donly, Brigit	17	IE	307
Donnal, Daniel	36	IE	336
Mary A	4	DE	336
Patrick	13	IE	336
Rebecca	36	IE	336
Sarah	9	DE	336
Donnel, Elizabeth	18	DE	374
Elizabeth	53	DE	374
James	16	DE	374
James	50	OH	374
Donnell, David	17	DE	155
Henrietta	50	MD	155
Jacob	18	DE	155
Jane	22	DE	155
Thomas	50	MD	155
Wesley	10	DE	155
Donnelly, Wm	12	PA	254
Donner, Isaac	38	MD	376

Name	Age	St	Pg
Donner, Martha J	28	DE	376
Donohau, Ellen	40	IE	352
Henry	36	IE	352
Joseph	1	IE	352
Mary	6	IE	352
Donohoe, Andrew	30	DE	245
Catharine	4	DE	245
Catharine	24	IE	132
Elizabeth	7	DE	246
Elizabeth	36	DE	238
Emma	6/12	DE	245
James	6/12	DE	245
Jane	2	DE	245
John H	7	DE	238
Joseph	34	DE	238
Joseph F	5	DE	238
Mary A	5	DE	245
Matthew	2	DE	245
Rachel	27	DE	245
Rebecca	6	DE	245
Sarah	54	MD	238
William R	2	DE	238
Doolan, Ann J	9	DE	206
Catherine	8	DE	206
Charles H	20	DE	206
Elwood	3	DE	206
Henrietta	14	DE	106
James	6	DE	206
John	10	DE	206
Risden	9/12	DE	206
Sally	38	NJ	206
William	16	DE	206
Dooly, Ann	28	MD	144
Ann	32	IE	312
Charles	6	DE	144
Edward	38	IE	66
Elizabeth	32	IE	66
Elizabeth	40	IE	31
Elizabeth A	31	IE	66
Mary H	4	DE	144
Patric	30	IE	30
Thomas	35	NY	144
William	2	DE	144
Doorhety, Edward	48	IE	322
Mary	48	IE	322
Doral, Sarah	7	DE	240
Doran, Agnes	3	DE	334
Anna	22	PA	109
Catherine	80	IE	334
Francis	18	IE	334
Frank	18	IE	149
George	10/12	PA	109
Henry	46	IE	334
John	14	DE	334
John	18	DE	252
John	18	DE	252
Margaret	6	IE	339
Margaret	44	IE	334
Mary	6	DE	334
Mary	11	IE	339
Mary	32	IE	339
R (Dr)	29	PA	109
Rosanna	19	IE	334
Sarah	9	IE	339
Thomas	33	IE	339
Dorat, John	54	PA	354
Martha	48	PA	354
William	21	DE	354
Dorman, Annie	17	PA	164
Charles	50	DE	301
Elizabeth	3	DE	304
Elizabeth	30	DE	159
Grace	4	DE	301
John	4	DE	304
John	30	MD	304
John	35	DE	159
Laura	5/12	DE	304
Richard H	2	DE	159
Samuel	8	MD	295
Sarah	24	PA	304
Dorothy, Ann	22	IE	329
Dorough, Anna	28	DE	289
Doroughty, Allice	19	IE	293
Betty	22	IE	307
Michel	44	IE	307
Neil	35	IE	277
Dorris, Phillip R	12	DE	395
Dorset, Benjamin	30	DE	203
Edward	4	DE	203
Georgianna	1	DE	203
Henrietta	6	DE	203
Homer	3	DE	203
Joseph	12	DE	203
Rachel	29	DE	203
Sarah J	7	DE	203
Dorsett, Abigail	61	PA	355
Caleb	25	DE	355
Eliza A	29	DE	355
Washington	23	DE	355
Dorsey, Elizabeth	2	DE	33
Elizabeth	9	DE	309
Hannah	48	GB	309
Tamer	14	DE	309
Thomas	31	DE	368
Washington	50	MD	309
Dorson, Martha	52	PA	374
Richard	30	GB	305
Dorton, Eli	57	NJ	313
Margaret	53	PA	313
D'Orville, Amelia	7	WN	15
Amy	6/12	DE	15
Auguste	49	VA	15
Augustin	16	WN	15
Clara	14	WN	15
Edward	17	WN	15
Eliza	33	WN	15
Emma	19	DE	15
Doucherty, Mary	30	IE	28
Douden, Amy	51	NJ	300
Doudy, John	23	MD	42
Dougherty, Alen E	15	PA	400
Ann	10	IE	314
Bridget	20	DE	342
Bridget	38	IE	314
Catherine	12	DE	278
Catherine	14	DE	313
Catherine	16	IE	314
Charles	6/12	DE	312
Charles	35	IE	313
Daniel	6	DE	314
Ebenezer	13	DE	192
Edward	12	IE	313
Elizabeth	5	DE	314
Ellen	14	IE	314
Frances	16	DE	253
Francis	5	PA	283
George	4	DE	191
George	18	DE	278
George	50	IE	278
Hester	37	DE	191
James	20	IE	196
James	20	IE	375
Jane	12	DE	260
Jane	20	DE	278
John	3	PA	283
John	7	DE	313
John	15	DE	278
John	17	DE	310
John	30	PA	332
Margaret	25	IE	312
Margaret H	42	IE	313
Mary	1	DE	283
Mary	1	DE	313
Mary	18	IE	314
Mary	21	DE	283
Mary	49	IE	278
Mary W	12	DE	192
Michael	2	IE	312
Michael	2	DE	314
Michael	25	IE	312
Michael	36	PA	191
Nell	16	MD	314
Niel	44	IE	313
Patrick	4	IE	312
Dougherty, Patrick	22	IE	345
Patrick	25	IE	315
Patrick	28	IE	283
Sarah	6	DE	191
Sarah A	8	DE	313
Sarah M	22	IE	196
Susan	31	IE	313
Susannah	2	DE	191
Thomas	13	DE	314
William	23	DE	311
Doughten, Ann E	14	DE	171
Mary J	12	DE	171
Rebecca	42	MD	171
William	45	NJ	171
Doughton, Elizabeth	25	DE	246
James	26	DE	246
John B	19	DE	288
Laura	1	DE	246
Martha	13	DE	246
Mary	5/12	DE	246
Douglass, Allace	13	DE	107
Martha	60	DE	33
Dover, Ann	24	DE	241
John	4	DE	241
John	34	DE	241
Samuel	1/12	DE	241
Dowdle, John	23	PA	345
Dowen, John	35	DE	156
Margaret	32	DE	156
Dowlan, Catharine	17	IE	349
Dowling, Ellen	51	DE	381
Robert	24	DE	381
William	31	MD	381
Dowly, Catharine	19	IE	336
Down, Ann E	6	DE	146
Anna	31	DE	146
James	8	DE	146
William H	33	DE	145
Downer, Ann	28	DE	204
James	1	DE	204
William	21	DE	169
Downey, Benjamin	3	DE	279
Edward	30	IE	279
Edward	31	IE	358
Hannah M	7	DE	279
James	17	DE	171
James	28	MD	171
John	8	PA	279
Levi	21	DE	208
Mary	23	IE	32
Melvina	28	DE	279
Downing, Anna M	2	DE	82
Edward J	8	DE	129
Elizabeth	25	DE	119
Elizabeth G	21	DE	278
George	53	PA	2
Henry W	17	DE	82
James	39	DE	129
James M	11	DE	129
John	41	DE	82
John B	10	DE	82
Josephine	2	DE	278
Margaret	14	DE	278
Martha	40	DE	82
Mary A	22	PA	2
Samuel	42	IE	278
Samuel S	26	PA	2
Sarah	41	DE	278
Sarah B	53	PA	2
Sidney	39	DE	129
William A	14	DE	82
William S	3	DE	129
Downs, Alexander	3	DE	284
Amanda	12	DE	284
Ann	47	DE	169
Ann G	10	DE	169
Guner T	53	DE	169
James	17	DE	172
James	28	MD	172
John	17	DE	169
John	35	PA	284
Maria	37	DE	86

Name	Age	St	Pg
Downs, Mary	26	DE	169
Mary E	39	DE	284
Sarah J	15	DE	169
Downy, Edward	6	DE	279
Doxey, Margaret	55	IE	145
Draddy, Sipriana	10	MX	143
Drake, Augustus	33	GE	250
Elizabeth	60	DE	321
George	3	DE	379
John	25	DE	32
Letitia	37	DE	354
Martha	7/12	DE	354
Mary	16	NY	379
Maxwell	31	DE	354
Samuel	8	DE	379
Susan	47	NY	379
Theresa	24	GE	250
Uriah	14	NY	379
Uriah	54	NY	379
William	12	NY	379
Dranan, Mary	42	DE	104
Draper, Alex	19	DE	274
Alexander	8	DE	386
Anne	1	DE	255
Betsey	65	DE	255
Cecilia	50	DE	297
Daniel	7	DE	377
Elizabeth	28	GB	72
Frank	10	DE	255
Hannah	30	DE	387
Harry W	22	DE	400
Henry	30	DE	230
Henry	34	DE	387
James	16	DE	377
John	5	DE	230
John	36	DE	49
Jonathan	25	DE	255
Jonathan	48	MD	260
Lydia Ann	10	DE	377
Margaret	23	DE	230
Mary	2	DE	230
Mary	3	DE	49
Mary	21	NJ	255
Mary	30	DE	49
Mary J	12	DE	386
Melvina	22	MD	136
Noah	50	MD	386
Peter	22	DE	249
Rachel A	15	DE	217
Rebecca	16	DE	295
Saml	76	MD	255
Sarah A	26	PA	321
Sarah A	38	DE	135
Susan	4	DE	377
Susan	40	DE	377
Thomas	13	DE	377
William	17	DE	156
William W	14	DE	379
Drennan, Ann	44	DE	391
Eliza	11	DE	391
Jonathan	3	DE	391
Jonathan	42	MD	391
Rachel	14	DE	391
Thomas	16	DE	391
Drenning, Elizabeth	67	MD	391
Maria	43	MD	391
Robert	35	MD	391
Dresden, Elizabeth	24	DE	198
Drethell, Stephen	13	MD	163
Drew, Edith	57	MA	130
Lydia B	45	MA	130
Driggers, Bayman	22	DE	245
Charlotte	45	DE	245
Daniel	12	DE	245
David	18	DE	245
Eli	17	DE	245
Hester	9	DE	245
Mary	2	DE	245
William	5	DE	245
William	47	DE	245
Driner, Christian	30	GE	38
Driver, Alace P	7	DE	69
Driver, Alfred T	6	PA	339
Ann	28	GB	339
Anna	1/12	DE	339
Anna M	9	DE	69
Edith M	2	DE	69
Henry	19	DE	69
Hester S	17	DE	69
James	32	GB	339
Joshua E	13	DE	69
Joshua E	44	MD	69
Louisa R	2	DE	339
Mary E	4	PA	339
Martha	24	DE	69
Mary E	19	DE	69
Mary G	39	DE	69
Nallie G	4	DE	69
Reynolds	11	DE	69
Drummond, John	30	DE	205
John W	27	DE	374
Mary	51	DE	167
Mary	61	DE	374
Rachel	35	DE	205
Sarah	1	DE	205
Drumond, James R	38	DE	371
Richard	5	DE	371
Sarah	37	DE	371
Duboise, Martha	32	NJ	10
Duboys, Amos	6/12	NJ	141
Amos	38	NJ	140
Ann	37	NJ	141
Hannah	11	NJ	141
Jane	8	NJ	141
Robert	19	NJ	141
Dubree, John	33	PA	150
Phebe	32	IE	150
Thomas	1	DE	150
Duckley, Unice	60	MD	69
Duckrey, Ann	2	DE	264
Anna	40	DE	366
Eliza	25	DE	264
Eliza	50	DE	258
Emma	4/12	DE	264
George	27	DE	343
George A	14	PA	307
Henrietta	22	DE	325
Henry	3	DE	264
John	12	DE	312
John H	4	DE	343
Joseph H	2/12	DE	343
Mary	26	DE	343
Mary E	13	PA	307
Richard	33	MD	325
Thomas	50	DE	366
William	7	DE	300
William	35	MD	308
Ducrey, Wesley	10	DE	274
James A	33	MD	321
Margaret A	2	DE	321
Maria	34	DE	321
Martha A	10	DE	338
Patience	9	DE	321
Violet	70	MD	156
Wm	40	MD	258
Dudly, Mary	31	MD	258
Duey, Margaret	16	PA	158
Duff, Algernon S	18	IE	165
Anna	2	DE	60
Asbury	55	DE	233
Benton	8	DE	159
Elizabeth	7	PA	60
Emmett	15	ST	372
George H	4	DE	60
Henry	3	DE	159
Hugh	26	DE	159
Isaac	42	ST	60
James	50	DE	233
Lucinda	23	DE	323
Margaret	5	DE	372
Mary	11	DE	372
Nancy	43	ST	372
Phebe	30	DE	92
	45	DE	159
Duff, Sarah	21	ST	372
Sidney	34	DE	60
Susan	23	DE	159
Thomas	9	DE	372
Thomas	44	ST	372
William	4	DE	92
William	13	ST	372
Duffer, Catherine	28	IE	325
Duffey, Bridget	19	DE	83
Catherine	1	DE	316
Hugh	9	DE	316
John	38	IE	274
Neal	25	IE	316
Susan	25	IE	316
Duffy, Catherine	2/12	DE	198
George	23	DE	198
Mary	18	IE	55
Mary C	20	DE	198
Francis	--	GB	290
Dugall, Martha	24	IE	114
Dugan, John	26	IE	347
Margaret	24	DE	335
Rosanna	26	DE	335
Duglass, Joseph	26	PA	371
Duke, Daniel	11	DE	338
Sarah	40	DE	338
Duland, Daniel	6	DE	140
Hetty	30	DE	140
John	35	MD	140
Dulany, Henry	17	DE	354
Dulin, Alifair	19	DE	182
Duling, Mary	4	DE	312
Dunbar, Margaret	37	IE	30
Robert	35	IE	30
Duncan, Ann	9	IE	11
Anna	30	IE	11
Benjamin	10	DE	200
Benjamin F	10	DE	368
Benjamin W	48	DE	368
Cass	3	DE	11
Charles	10	DE	106
Christiana	34	IE	12
Eliza M	40	MD	106
Elizabeth	76	PA	106
Emma	20	PA	280
Frank	1	DE	280
George	1	DE	97
Hannah	35	MD	106
Hannah	53	DE	288
Hugh	35	TE	12
James	12	DE	12
James	29	IE	97
James	69	DE	280
James Jr	24	DE	280
Jane	4	DE	97
John	34	IE	11
John	73	MD	106
John A	44	DE	101
Kit	1	DE	12
Margaret	63	PA	280
Martha	47	MD	368
Mary	12	IE	11
Sarah	60	DE	52
Susan	26	IE	97
Dunegan, Ann	50	MD	295
Dunel, Susan A	8	PA	299
Dunham, Jane	19	DE	35
Dunlap, Anne	5	OH	258
Benjamin	7	NY	258
Benjamin	44	PA	258
Bernard	30	IE	309
Charles	16	DE	263
Charles	19	DE	163
Ellen	26	IE	309
F D	43	DE	263
Frances	4	OH	258
Frank	16	DE	263
Frank	17	DE	164
Harriet	9	NJ	393
Joseph	7/12	DE	258
Margaret	1	DE	309
Margaret	50	DE	149

Name			
Dunlap, Mary	30	IE	258
Mary	70	PA	158
Sarah	74	DE	386
Theodore	9	NY	259
William	74	DE	386
Dunman, Lewis	28	DE	122
Dunn, Benj	50	DE	364
Bridget	20	IE	1
Catharine	6	DE	346
Hugh	15	IE	346
John	13	IE	346
James	2	DE	346
Jane	4	DE	346
John	7	IE	63
Margaret	31	IE	346
Margaret	35	IE	62
Mary Ann	9	DE	342
Owin	36	IE	346
Dunnigan, George	17	DE	184
Dunning, Samuel W	21	MD	56
DuPont, Alexis J	7	DE	345
Alexis J	34	DE	345
Alfred	52	FR	342
Alfred V	17	DE	342
Amelia	8	DE	300
Amelia	54	DE	336
Ann R	35	DE	300
C J	53	SC	300
C J Jr	19	DE	300
E Ironew	20	DE	342
Eleuthera P	2	DE	345
Ellen	8	DE	342
Eugene	10	DE	345
Evelina	10	DE	342
Frances E	12	DE	345
Henry	1	DE	300
Henry	12	DE	343
Henry	38	DE	343
Irene	5	DE	345
Joanna	34	PA	345
Louisa	6	DE	342
Louisa	32	PA	343
Margaret E	43	MD	342
Mary V	24	DE	300
Pauline E	23	DE	342
Reidmond	12	DE	342
Sarah	4	DE	342
Saumnett	19	DE	342
Sophia	38	DE	300
Sophia F	15	DE	342
Victor	22	DE	69
Victorine	2	DE	342
Y T	47	NJ	300
Duquette, Paul	30	DE	192
Duragan, Margaret	15	IE	294
Dural, Wm	26	IE	339
Durand, Hannah	37	PA	68
Henry	3	PA	68
Martha	6	PA	68
Mary	11/12	PA	280
Durgan, Martha	19	DE	12
Martha	21	PA	2
Samuel	17	PA	2
Susan	24	PA	165
Thomas	16	DE	12
Durham, Alfred	9	DE	232
Amanda	1	DE	215
Ann	29	DE	232
Benjamin	9	DE	232
Bayard	8	DE	245
Charles H	12	DE	232
Clayton	15	DE	232
George	21	DE	232
Hester	4	DE	215
John	35	DE	186
John J	22	DE	245
Joseph	15	DE	374
Josiah	28	DE	215
Louis	5	DE	374
Margaret	19	DE	232
Margaret	41	DE	374
Mary	3	DE	232
Durham, Mary	44	DE	232
Mary E	2	DE	219
Mary J	26	DE	219
Mathew	50	DE	245
Matthew	29	DE	219
Rebecca	25	DE	215
Ruth A	6	DE	232
Sarah	9	DE	374
Susan	2	DE	245
Susan	46	DE	245
William	17	DE	374
William	44	DE	232
Zachariah	40	DE	274
Durmin, Charles	40	IE	342
Mary	32	IE	342
Durnett, Emily	33	NY	273
Mary	12	NY	273
Wm	10	NY	273
Wm H	33	CT	273
Durney, Adaline M	7	DE	136
Ellen	14	ME	136
Elizabeth	6	DE	136
Joseph	16	ME	136
Martha	49	IE	136
Mary	9	DE	136
Mary	42	IE	136
Samuel	11	DE	136
Sarah	13	DE	136
Durram, Jane	23	DE	33
Peter	25	DE	33
Susannah	6/12	DE	33
Dutt, Leah	22	PA	121
Dutton, Alonzo	4	DE	119
Charles	10	DE	254
Elizabeth	52	DE	306
Enoch	6	DE	133
Ethan	38	DE	133
Jacob	18	DE	133
Jacob	18	DE	143
John	5	DE	210
John	13	DE	317
Joseph	9	DE	133
Martha	5/12	DE	133
Martha	39	DE	133
Mary E	22	DE	119
Mary E M	3	DE	119
Mary G	56	DE	119
Rachel A	23	DE	119
Sarah	14	DE	133
Duval, James	16	DE	30
Dyer, William	21	NJ	227
Eliza	36	DE	315
John	13	DE	315
Margaret A	8	DE	315
Nathan	16	DE	315
William T	10	DE	315
Dyke, Ellen	5	DE	120
Harriet	8/12	DE	120
Joanna	29	DE	120
Mary A	3	DE	120
Richard	40	PA	120
William	8	DE	120
Dykes, Eliza	12	MD	319
Martha	40	MD	319
Dyott, James	6	DE	222
James	25	DE	196
Martha	1	DE	197
Martha A	26	DE	234
Mary	16	DE	197
Mary A	8	DE	222
Dyson, Jackson	22	PA	355
Dyton, James	12	DE	281
Eachus, Jane	33	PA	361
John	18	DE	361
Joseph	4	DE	361
Hannah	6/12	DE	361
Obed	54	PA	361
Orpha	15	DE	361
Eagle, Jane	12	DE	265
John	35	DE	265
Eagle, Lewis	6	DE	266
Mary	10	DE	265
Westley	8	DE	265
Earl, Edith	14	NJ	165
Early, James	38	IE	288
Earner, Patric	33	IE	163
Thomas	17	IE	163
Earnshaw, Mary	57	PA	279
William	56	GB	279
Earren, Mary	20	IE	7
Earst, Catherine	1	PA	14
James	27	DE	14
Mary	28	DE	14
Eastborn, Alinda	3/12	DE	356
Ann Eliza	18	DE	363
Ann F	3	DE	379
David	35	DE	356
Elizabeth	7	DE	355
Elizabeth	60	PA	356
Franklin	13	DE	355
Isaiah	40	DE	379
Jane	39	GB	356
John B	6	DE	379
Joseph	2	DE	355
Joseph	47	PA	355
Margaret	25	DE	356
Marion	9	DE	379
Mary	5	DE	356
Mary J	32	DE	379
Mary R	9	DE	356
Newton	32	DE	356
Oliver	4	DE	356
Oliver	26	DE	363
Samuel	16	DE	361
Samuel	28	DE	356
Sarah	65	DE	356
Sarah E	11	DE	379
Sarah J	9	DE	356
Susan	34	PA	355
Washington	12	DE	355
William	18	DE	356
Eastburn, Amos	41	DE	348
Anna A	4/12	DE	349
George T	5	DE	349
Levi B	4	DE	349
Mary J	36	DE	348
Mary R	9	DE	349
Oliver	15	DE	359
Rachel E	10	DE	348
Ruthanna	7	DE	349
Sarah M	2	DE	349
William	12	DE	348
Easter, Eliza	22	DE	142
Eastwood, Eli	30	GB	2
Melissa	2	DE	106
Thomas E	2	DE	106
William	12	DE	396
Eaton, Abigail	66	PA	181
Ann	14	DE	252
Anna J	8	DE	145
Benjamin	55	NJ	189
Casper	21	DE	181
Charles	35	DE	182
Debrah	57	NJ	181
Deborah A	9	DE	182
Elizabeth	32	DE	145
Ellen F M	7	DE	181
Elwood	18	DE	252
Emily F	1	DE	182
Eugenia	3	DE	182
Gideon	40	NJ	239
James	23	DE	238
James H	4	DE	145
James J	31	OH	182
John	5	DE	182
Joseph	58	NJ	181
Joseph D	16	DE	181
Katelin	16	DE	181
Martha	33	NJ	182
Mary	42	DE	252
Mary A	--	DE	181
Mary E	2	DE	145

Name			
Elliott, James	10	DE	287
John	4	DE	287
John	39	PE	294
John C	27	DE	303
John Lea	8	DE	294
Joseph	16	DE	287
Josephine	2	DE	295
Laura	2	DE	308
Margaret	12	DE	287
Mary	11	DE	378
Mary	20	DE	167
Rachel	7	DE	368
Robert	19	IE	288
Sarah	35	VA	321
Susana	33	VA	294
Thomas	14	DE	287
Thomas	43	DE	287
William	4	DE	368
Ellis, Eliza	13	NJ	70
Elizabeth	9	DE	225
John	6	DE	248
John	10	DE	225
Mrs	30	NJ	70
Samuel	39	DE	78
Samuel	40	DE	160
Sarah	5	DE	225
Susan	3	DE	225
Susan	32	DE	225
William	7	DE	225
William	23	DE	112
William	32	PA	225
Ellison, Cecilia S	9	DE	320
Charles	8	DE	319
Clara	12	DE	323
Curtis B	40	NJ	323
Harry C	10	DE	319
James J	28	DE	318
James M	24	NJ	204
James S	2	DE	320
James T	2	DE	319
Jennett	6	DE	320
Jonathan	35	NJ	319
Lewis	63	NJ	317
Lewis F	9	DE	319
Lewis F	39	NJ	320
Lorranna	6/12	DE	323
Lydia	2	DE	323
Lydia A	24	DE	317
Margaret B	32	DE	323
Mary	64	NJ	117
Mary B	6	DE	319
Mary E	10	DE	323
Sally	1/12	DE	319
Sarah	22	MD	204
Sarah	30	NJ	217
Sarah E	7	DE	323
Susan	34	DE	319
Susan B	4	DE	319
Susan L	11	DE	320
Susan M	28	PA	320
Thomas B	15	DE	323
Ujane L	5	DE	323
William C	5/12	DE	317
William J	13	NH	317
Ellit, Ann	12	DE	213
Ellsburg, Ann	12	DE	351
Elsbury, Emily	14	DE	159
Elvis, Andrew	44	GB	360
Elizabeth	43	GB	360
George	13	GB	360
John	21	GB	360
Mary E	12	GB	360
William	19	GB	360
Elwee, Mary A	32	PA	128
Uriah	44	NJ	128
Elwell, Joseph	60	NJ	190
Maria	17	PA	25
Ely, George W	19	PA	324
Louisa J	16	PA	324
Mary E	8	DE	324
Oliver P	45	PA	324
Susannah F	42	PA	324
Emanuel, Charles	10	DE	334
Louisa A	32	MD	334
Wm	32	MD	334
Emerite, Charles	24	PA	127
Mary J	24	MD	127
Emery, Ann	55	DE	268
Anthony	2	DE	237
Cynthia	10	DE	229
Eliza J	4	DE	229
Harriet	36	DE	75
Henry	12	DE	9
Henry	20	DE	66
Isaac	28	DE	187
Isaiah	13	DE	237
Jabes	7	DE	219
James	8	DE	229
James	45	DE	237
Jessie	45	DE	229
John	2	DE	229
John	12	DE	257
Lavinia	12	DE	237
Louis	7	DE	237
Margaret A	35	DE	237
Margaret L	6	DE	237
Mary	6	DE	229
Mary	18	DE	75
Mary	29	DE	147
Rhody	19	DE	237
Samuel	21	DE	228
Stephen	49	MD	258
Teeny	20	DE	228
Thomas H	10	DE	237
William	23	DE	147
Wm	10	DE	258
Wm	46	MD	258
Emmeline, Joseph	50	FR	302
Emmet, Elizabeth A	22	DE	378
Richard	25	IE	371
Robert	46	GB	378
Thomas	28	GB	378
Emmons, Charles	30	ME	139
Francis	1	DE	118
Mary	55	MA	139
Rebecca	28	NJ	117
Richard	21	NJ	117
William	28	MA	117
Emory, Charles	16	DE	241
Elizabeth	1	DE	391
Elzie	27	DE	203
George	53	MD	185
Henry	29	DE	283
Izaiah	12	DE	235
James	10	DE	232
James	15	DE	236
John	18	MD	323
Mary	25	DE	283
Moses	4	DE	283
William H	12	DE	283
Empson, Andrew	14	DE	193
Ann	27	DE	293
Benjamin H	6	DE	204
Emeline	34	MD	204
Hannah	5	DE	206
Hannah	17	DE	177
Isaac	49	DE	204
John	5	DE	204
Mary	1	DE	193
Mary A	3	DE	204
Mary Ann	37	DE	204
Mary E	10	DE	204
Sarah A	8	DE	204
Theodore	8	DE	204
Thomas	39	DE	204
William	17	DE	193
William J	4	DE	204
Emry, De Ann	5	DE	297
Edward	3	DE	297
Joseph	15	DE	285
Lurana	35	MD	297
William	7	DE	297
Emsley, John	29	GB	390
Hannah	12	GB	390
Emsley, Joseph B	4	GB	390
Lewis	1	DE	390
Martha W	7	GB	390
Mary	29	GB	390
William	10	GB	390
Endis, Ann	22	MA	321
Ellen	51	IE	321
John	26	IE	321
Margaret	3/12	DE	321
Margaret	45	IE	321
Engeline, Jane	25	IE	317
England, Anna	6	DE	52
Bathia	38	DE	112
Elias	42	NJ	138
Elizabeth	60	DE	112
Martha S	37	NJ	138
Mary	29	DE	112
Susan	36	DE	112
Thomas	4	DE	52
William	1	DE	52
William	19	DE	392
William	30	DE	52
Engle, Abigal	41	PA	33
Caroline E	16	MD	382
Frederick F	10	DE	185
Hezekiah B	15	DE	185
Isaac	17	PA	33
James	5	DE	33
James O	13	DE	185
John	56	PA	33
John	66	GE	185
Joseph H	13	PA	273
Sarah	48	MD	185
Engles, Amelia	20	GE	114
English, Charles	32	DE	258
Edward	28	IE	394
Ellen	70	MD	98
Ephraim	9	GB	334
Glen	70	MD	99
James	29	GB	3
James S	28	DE	373
Matilda K	17	PA	166
Sarah	24	GB	334
Sarah	54	DE	258
Ennes, Bridget	2	DE	44
Eliza	8	IE	44
Elizabeth	42	IE	44
Patric	17	IE	44
William	50	PA	2
Ennis, Frances	20	DE	284
Frances	56	DE	284
Lewis	19	DE	284
Margaretta	23	DE	284
Enos, Abraham	11	DE	28
Alexander P	14	DE	28
Ann H	29	DE	171
Annianna	30	DE	213
Archibald	59	DE	292
Clarance	6	DE	28
Elizabeth	35	DE	28
George W	20	DE	214
Henry A	2	DE	169
Hiram	5	MD	305
Jane	57	DE	292
John	12	DE	214
Joseph	85	DE	171
Julian	5/12	DE	28
Kezia	33	DE	274
Laura	4	DE	293
Mary C	1	DE	314
Mary D	3	DE	305
Newton	1	DE	305
Robert E	36	DE	305
Ruth	28	DE	169
Samuel	28	DE	169
Sarah	30	PA	305
Sarah E	6	DE	171
Serafinah	21	DE	292
Serafinah	57	DE	292
Spencer D	45	DE	28
Thomas T	32	DE	171
Veronica	18	DE	213

Name	Age	State	No.
Enos, William J	21	PA	124
Enters, Benjamin	55	NJ	190
Entriken, Caleb	27	DE	346
Hester P	22	PA	346
Phebe E	6/12	PA	346
Enturisel, Mary	65	GB	384
Ernest, Ann	40	DE	178
Jasper	8	DE	178
Joseph	56	DE	178
Richard	1	DE	178
Errington, Ephraim	20	DE	379
Ert, Augustus	23	PA	39
Ervan, Hannah	15	IE	307
Hannah	15	MD	307
Erwin, Elizabeth	7	IE	96
Elizabeth	35	IE	96
James	21	DE	190
Joseph	32	IE	96
Margaret	3	DE	96
Maria	6/12	DE	96
Nancy	10	DE	96
Eschenuca, George A	30	GE	137
Esling, Theodore	6	DE	311
Esom, Ann	18	DE	180
Esteven, G A	16	CU	164
Estlin, George	10	PA	282
Mirah	17	GB	282
Eton, Joanna	13	NJ	378
Eubanks, Anna M	15	DE	13
Maria	54	DE	13
Richard	18	DE	13
Euling, Marchus L	13	PA	400
Eurich, Frank	14	PA	164
Evans, Abram	19	DE	204
Adaline	29	MD	395
Agnes G	3	DE	332
Amelia	27	DE	296
Ann	22	PA	131
Ann	38	MD	395
Ann	62	DE	393
Ann	65	DE	363
Anna B	11	DE	332
Anna C	5	DE	8
Anna M	16	DE	400
Belinda	2	DE	195
C P	27	PA	56
Catherine	6	DE	195
Catherine E	20	DE	197
Chandler	22	DE	374
Charles	15	PA	383
Charles	20	NJ	62
Charles	22	DE	131
Charles	55	DE	374
Charles L	1	DE	131
Christopher	17	DE	235
Curtis	12	PA	315
Edward	6	DE	23
Edward	45	IE	23
Edward G	77	PA	366
Edwin B	8	DE	379
Eli	80	PA	363
Eliza	30	PA	315
Eliza A	24	DE	8
Elizabeth	4	DE	23
Elizabeth	16	PA	79
Elizabeth	28	IE	326
Elizabeth	35	NJ	62
Elizabeth	48	DE	296
Elizabeth	60	NJ	63
Elizabeth A	25	DE	54
Emeline	30	DE	379
Emma M	5	DE	332
Enos	4	MD	377
Eugene	1	DE	332
George	6	PA	306
George B	38	DE	296
George G	34	DE	393
Hannah	38	DE	393
Hannah C	15	DE	332
Henry	21	DE	396
Henry	45	MD	400
Irene R	40	DE	181
Evans, Jacob	11	DE	210
James	7	DE	306
James	25	DE	296
James	38	GB	306
James S	9	DE	198
Jane	19	MD	394
Jane C	8	DE	181
Jenetta	11/12	DE	23
John	4	DE	326
John	10	DE	306
John	19	MD	319
John	29	DE	363
John	35	NJ	187
John L	13	DE	332
John W	39	MD	332
Joseph	2	PA	315
Joseph W	27	DE	8
Josephine	14	PA	165
Joshua H	39	DE	181
Levi	35	DE	400
Levi	42	PA	315
Lucy	5	DE	394
Margaret	3	DE	23
Margaret A	33	DE	306
Margaret A	38	DE	332
Martha	25	NJ	62
Mary	8	DE	23
Mary	40	DE	235
Mary	74	DE	296
Mary A	25	MD	195
Mary E	2	DE	196
Mary E	18	DE	330
Michael L	29	DE	197
Nathan	86	NJ	62
Perry	16	DE	325
Perry	16	DE	393
Perry	17	PA	320
Rachel	59	DE	374
Rachel	75	DE	394
Rebecca	7	DE	195
Richard	38	WL	13
Rosana	40	IE	23
Sarah A	6/12	DE	198
Susan W	7	DE	332
Thomas	2	DE	306
William	12	DE	396
William	19	DE	391
William	23	DE	289
William	26	DE	192
William	32	GB	379
William	75	DE	394
William C	3	DE	8
Wm	16	DE	330
Everith, Elizabeth	18	PA	373
Everson, Alexander	12	DE	310
Elias	33	DE	310
John	35	DE	310
Matilda	2	DE	310
Evert, John	29	DE	224
Everton, Amelia	10	PA	114
Eves, Elizabeth	80	DE	155
Harriet	50	DE	254
Margaret J	45	DE	155
Ewe, Ruth	10	DE	312
Ewing, Agnes	25	ST	287
Ann	5	DE	340
Charles	37	ST	340
John	35	ST	286
Hannah	25	NJ	181
Harriet	30	ST	340
Hugh	1	DE	286
Mary	9	DE	340
Mary	16	NJ	86
Parnell	29	DE	181
Sarah A	1	DE	181
Exton, Hugh	21	DE	249
John	13	DE	249
John	62	GB	249
Julia M	50	MD	249
Mary	16	DE	249
William L	19	DE	249
Eyere, Ellen	4	PA	30
Eyere, Francis	2	PA	30
Mary	6	PA	30
Fabier, Christian	5	OH	137
Christian	32	PA	137
Sarah F	25	DE	137
Facery, Ann	35	VA	90
Fagan, Peter	19	IE	164
Fahey, Samuel	63	PA	158
Failin, Catharine	72	IE	336
Failing, Daniel	10	DE	285
Elizabeth	9	DE	285
Elizabeth	52	IE	285
Ellen	13	PA	285
Fairbank, Charles	24	MD	192
Edwin	2	DE	173
Emelia	34	DE	173
Jonathan	22	MA	317
Joseph	6	DE	173
Joseph	36	DE	173
Thomas	11	DE	173
William	9	DE	173
Fairbanks, Caroline	16	DE	169
Sarah	40	DE	169
Wilmina	14	DE	169
Fairland, Jonas	65	PA	42
Falkner, Andrew J	21	DE	222
Andrew J	22	DE	224
Emeline	17	DE	222
Emeline	17	DE	224
Fanagan, James	23	DE	135
Faragan, Sarah	25	MD	328
Farel, James	14	DE	236
Farell, Ann	21	IE	301
Bridget	15	IE	33
Mary	30	IE	301
Ellen	19	PA	301
Faris, Alfred	19	DE	376
Ann E	1	DE	376
Catharine	37	DE	342
Chas	25	PA	354
David B	17	DE	314
Jacob	76	DE	313
Margaret	20	DE	376
Samuel	22	DE	376
Sarah E	9	DE	342
Susan A	26	DE	314
William	45	DE	342
Farlan, William M	16	GB	215
Farlin, James	24	IE	300
Farmer, Ann	6	DE	231
Benjamin	18	DE	245
Elizabeth	44	IE	275
Ellen	14	PA	274
Gilbert	50	DE	231
Jane	70	PA	302
Mary	20	DE	245
Mary	40	DE	231
Patrick	37	IE	275
Farnesbury, Mary	20	NJ	30
Farny, Ann	15	DE	331
Catherine	17	DE	331
John	8	DE	331
Lydia	43	DE	331
Margaret	13	DE	331
Mary	21	DE	331
Thomas	11	DE	331
Farra, D W	26	DE	100
Mary	28	DE	100
William G	1	DE	100
Farrady, Eliza	26	DE	332
Miles	29	GB	332
Philomin	3	DE	332
William	3	DE	332
Farrah, George	1	DE	355
Hannah	33	DE	355
Thomas	87	DE	355
Farrar, Charis	35	IE	17
Franklin	2	DE	17
John	6	DE	17
Margaret	26	PA	17
Mary	6/12	DE	17

Name	Age	St	Pg
Farrar, Thomas	4	DE	17
Farrell, Catherine	7	DE	87
Catherine	12	DE	172
Elizabeth	2	DE	87
John	16	DE	218
John	35	IE	87
Margaret	5	DE	87
Mary	9	DE	87
Rosanah	34	IE	87
Farris, John	49	DE	31
Sarah	70	DE	31
Farrity, Patric	30	IE	2
Farry, Francis A	25	DE	348
Joseph	35	DE	348
Margaret A	6	DE	348
Mary E	7	DE	348
William	19	IE	337
Farsons, George	8	DE	386
John	12	DE	20
John	54	DE	20
Mary	10	DE	20
Samuel	17	DE	33
Susanna	42	DE	20
Faser, John	6/12	DE	265
John	26	GE	265
Louisa	25	GE	265
Father, William	21	DE	41
Faucen, Ann	28	NJ	89
Charles	30	NJ	89
Martha	5	DE	89
Samuel	2	DE	89
Faulk, Alexine	8	DE	178
Alfred	4/12	DE	178
Catherine C	28	PA	69
Elizabeth	23	DE	178
Elizabeth	24	DE	78
Elizabeth A	49	PA	69
Elizabeth C	15	PA	69
George T	3	DE	178
Jacob	26	DE	68
Joseph	16	DE	78
Mrs	30	DE	68
Nathaniel C	20	PA	69
Nimrod	35	DE	178
Priscilla	52	DE	78
Stephen	51	DE	78
Susan E	5	DE	178
Thomas J	20	DE	78
William	1	DE	68
Faust, Henry	27	DE	63
Henry A	2	DE	63
Margaret	26	DE	63
Favier, Charles	4	DE	80
Jane C	28	DE	80
Joseph	10/12	DE	80
Virginia	2	DE	80
Zepheniah C	38	SZ	80
Fay, Anna	4	DE	5
Anna	28	DE	5
Frances	40	IE	5
Joseph	9	CU	163
Patric	30	IE	17
Simon	11	CU	163
Thomas	1	DE	5
Fearel, Henry	25	PA	32
Fears, Thomas	74	DE	310
Featherson, John	24	IE	303
William	25	IE	303
Fee, Elizabeth	38	IE	40
Feeny, James	18	DE	296
Felker, Elizabeth	37	MD	336
George	38	GE	336
Fell, Ann	47	PA	349
Courtland J	7	DE	161
Edith	60	PA	66
Eliza	34	PA	349
Ezra	21	PA	349
Jane Ann	10	DE	349
John	17	PA	59
Jonathan H	8	DE	349
Jonathan (MD)	34	PA	365
Joseph	19	PA	349
Fell, Lewis	50	PA	349
Mary	25	PA	349
Mary S	42	PA	161
Simeon	14	PA	349
Thomas	17	PA	349
W	16	PA	349
Watson	22	PA	349
Felmet, Frederic	43	GE	160
Fennerman, Abraham	21	NJ	227
Caroline	22	NJ	227
Edward	19	NJ	227
Joshua B	47	NJ	227
Joshua Jr	14	NJ	227
Margaret	11	NJ	227
Rebecca O	18	NJ	227
Samuel	8	NJ	227
Sarah	16	NJ	227
Sarah	49	NJ	227
Fenney, Bridget	5	DE	12
Bridget	33	IE	12
Elizabeth	2	IE	12
James	4	DE	12
Mary	11	DE	12
William	7	DE	12
William	42	IE	12
Fennimore, Ann	28	DE	245
Ann	44	DE	245
Francis	12	DE	245
Hannah	80	DE	271
Jesse J	22	DE	245
John	24	DE	245
Louis	13	DE	245
Mary E	7	DE	245
Sarah	26	DE	245
Thomas	15	DE	246
William H	4	DE	246
Ferginson, Allice A	4	DE	369
Elizabeth	24	DE	371
George	14	PA	374
Jenny	18	DE	369
Laura	8	DE	369
Mary	35	DE	369
Mary	83	PA	380
Robert	65	DE	369
Ferguson, Charles	55	IE	353
Elizabeth	3/12	DE	335
John	38	DE	335
Josephine	11	DE	335
Lewis	4	DE	335
Matilda	8	PA	358
Robert	6	DE	335
Sarah A	33	DE	335
Fergusson, Bassett	48	MD	224
Feris, Susan	56	DE	314
Fernon, Benjamin F	6	DE	368
Francis	1	DE	368
John	4	DE	368
John	35	IE	368
Margaret	28	MD	368
Mary	7	MD	368
Ferra, Rosanna	30	DE	17
Ferrell, Eliza	25	IE	165
Elizabeth	31	DE	246
Margaret A	10/12	DE	246
Martha	6	DE	246
Michel	60	IE	12
Susan	4	DE	246
William	25	MD	246
Ferren, Hester C	3	DE	209
Joshua	8	DE	209
Mary A	4/12	DE	209
Rebecca	30	DE	209
Sarah E	5	DE	209
William	35	MD	209
Ferris, Anna	34	DE	34
Benjamin	70	DE	34
Deborah	36	DE	34
Eliza	53	MD	31
Hannah	57	PA	34
Martha	29	DE	34
William W	31	DE	270
Ziba	21	DE	31
Ferris, William W	31	DE	270
Ziba	21	DE	31
Ziba	64	DE	31
Fetters, Isaac	21	PA	78
Martha	29	DE	160
Field, Daniel M	6	PA	273
Elizabeth	28	NJ	273
James H	35	PA	273
John	31	DE	210
Margaret R	4	PA	273
Samuel A	8	PA	273
Tabitha	45	DE	348
Fields, Aaron	47	DE	277
Ann	16	DE	272
Anna	24	DE	47
Bassel	29	DE	277
Caroline	6	DE	198
Caroline	17	DE	256
Charles	13	DE	198
Charles	31	DE	198
Clement	18	DE	255
David	39	NY	394
Elis	2	DE	277
Eliza	23	DE	280
Elizabeth	1	DE	277
Elizabeth	13	DE	249
Elizabeth	25	MD	280
Elizabeth	27	MD	277
Emma	2	DE	309
Emma	8	DE	135
Fidelia	4	DE	277
Frances	27	MD	281
Frances	31	MD	309
George	6	DE	198
George	26	DE	309
George	28	DE	281
Harriet	15	DE	255
Henry	9	DE	272
Isabella	4	DE	198
Isabella	60	DE	368
James	13	DE	198
James	13	DE	331
Jane	30	DE	134
John	9	DE	198
John	31	DE	209
Lindy	5	DE	198
Maria	2	DE	198
Maria	32	DE	198
Maria	35	DE	383
Mary	1	DE	198
Mary	11	DE	272
Samuel	60	MD	368
Sarah	24	NY	394
Sarah	40	DE	272
Sarah	46	DE	277
Sarah A	24	DE	198
Sidney	54	NJ	277
William	25	DE	198
Wilson	7	DE	277
Filan, Hannah	16	IE	266
Michael	30	IE	266
Filding, Ann R	8	DE	112
John	35	GB	112
Mary A	32	GB	112
File, Eliza	32	DE	103
Elizabeth	12	DE	187
Elmira	12	DE	103
James	32	DE	103
Joseph	40	DE	77
Levi	25	DE	233
Lorenzo	11	DE	103
Lydia	21	DE	29
Read	35	PA	29
Filer, Anna	8	DE	2
Elizabeth M	11	DE	2
Henry H	2	DE	2
John D	6	DE	2
Sarah A	34	NJ	2
Filler, Anna	8	DE	379
Henry	1	DE	379
John	6	DE	379
Sally	35	NJ	379

Name	Age	State	No.	Name	Age	State	No.	Name	Age	State	No.
Filman, John	55	DE	273	Finny, William	12	IE	50	Fitchgarald, Robt B	8	DE	323
Martha	45	DE	273	Firth, John	21	NJ	298	Sarah A	34	DE	323
Filmore, Elizabeth	25	DE	323	Fisher, Amelia J	4	MD	308	Thomas	42	DE	323
Martha J	1/12	DE	323	Andrew	1	DE	330	William	11	DE	323
Richard	28	DE	323	Andrew H	42	DE	330	Fitsimmons, Robert	40	DE	376
William H	5	DE	323	Ann M	39	PA	330	Susanna	29	PA	376
Fincher, Amos	18	DE	298	Anna M	1	DE	394	Thomas	16	DE	376
Catharine	25	DE	298	Benjamin	20	DE	299	Thomas	32	DE	376
Elizabeth	8	DE	298	Bernard	17	DE	361	Fitzgerald, Alace	27	IE	76
George	8/12	DE	298	Byard	12	PA	348	Elizabeth	3	IE	264
George	40	PA	298	Caroline	10	DE	157	James	30	IE	264
Phebe	6	DE	298	Debrah	16	DE	120	John	4	DE	76
Thomas	25	GE	329	Debrah C H	26	DE	160	Joseph	7	MD	76
Find, Rosanna	40	DE	281	Dinah	34	MD	146	Mary	29	IE	264
Fine, Peter	25	GE	328	Edward	16	DE	349	Thomas	2	PA	264
Philip R	25	GE	331	Eliza	2	DE	277	Zaceriah	1	DE	76
Fink, Augustus	6	GE	295	Elizabeth	17	DE	377	Fitzheny, Bridget	21	IE	100
Frederick	8	GE	295	Elizabeth	52	DE	297	Fitzpatrick, Bernard	33	DE	40
Frederick	40	GE	295	Elizabeth A	8	DE	330	Catherine	29	NJ	40
Jane	36	GE	295	Ellis	9	DE	277	Catherine	38	IE	7
Matilda	15	OH	165	George	11	DE	120	Franklin	3/12	DE	40
Finlaw, Margaret	30	NJ	24	George	25	IE	346	Margaret	80	IE	40
Mary	6	PA	24	George	32	DE	146	Mary	5	DE	7
Phebe	44	NJ	24	Harriet	3	DE	330	Patrick	25	IE	212
Finley, Adaline	24	PA	14	Henrietta	28	MD	308	Peter	38	IE	7
Ann	4	NJ	265	Isaac H	7	MD	308	Thos	67	IE	334
Christopher	7	NY	265	Israel	18	PA	277	William	3/12	DE	40
David	9/12	DE	15	Jacob	2	DE	308	William	19	DE	20
David	23	MD	18	James	8/12	DE	145	Fitzsimmons, Eliz	50	DE	371
David	32	PA	98	James	16	DE	341	John	5	DE	371
Delia	4	DE	14	James J	5	DE	394	Joseph	20	DE	371
Edgar A	6	DE	392	John	9	IE	341	Mary	23	DE	371
Elizabeth	26	IE	188	John	25	DE	157	Rachel	2	DE	371
Ellen	16	PA	103	John	30	DE	297	Rebecca	16	DE	371
Georgianna	22	DE	364	John	47	MD	308	Sarah	36	DE	371
James	6/12	DE	265	John E	11	DE	330	Flanagan, Alexander	1	DE	320
John	29	IE	265	John H L	24	DE	180	Biddy O	30	IE	19
John W	9	?	273	John W	6	DE	157	Hannah	20	IE	359
Lawrence	8	NY	265	John W	24	MD	303	Margaret	23	IE	353
Lewis	24	PA	14	Joseph	3	DE	394	John	3	DE	320
Mary	25	IE	265	Joseph	14	DE	339	Joseph	34	IE	320
Mary E	15	DE	392	Joseph	51	PA	277	Margaret A	27	IE	320
Naomi	11	DE	392	Laura T	6/12	DE	308	Flanaway, Clayton C	4	DE	384
Priscilla	17	DE	392	Levi	34	DE	394	Daniel	30	DE	385
Rachel M	9	DE	392	Levin	45	DE	146	Susan	31	DE	384
Rebecca	21	PA	18	Lovey	47	DE	120	Flanigan, Alfred	1	DE	315
Samuel C	38	DE	392	Margaret	13	IE	341	Ellen	25	IE	315
Sarah S A	1	DE	392	Martha	1	DE	157	Wesley	29	MD	315
William	28	IE	188	Martha	4	DE	282	Flanory, Henry	15	PA	163
Finly, Jacob	23	DE	364	Martha	18	IE	341	Jacob	12	PA	163
Finnegan, Celestine	17	DE	301	Martha	45	IE	341	Fleeson, James	19	PA	264
Elizabeth	15	DE	301	Martha E	20	MD	99	Sarah	13	PA	264
Ellen	12	DE	301	Martha J	1	DE	303	Sarah	14	PA	272
Henry	19	DE	301	Martha J	34	DE	394	Flemens, William	20	PA	158
Henry	52	IE	301	Mary	6	DE	330	Fleming, Ann J	21	DE	5
Jane	26	DE	301	Mary	17	MD	105	Archibald	38	DE	26
Jane	50	IE	301	Mary	19	DE	299	Bridget	4/12	?	167
Thomas	21	DE	301	Mary	30	IE	145	Caroline	25	DE	116
Finney, Alexander	3	DE	279	Mary	49	PA	277	Catherine	20	IE	29
Caroline	25	DE	277	Mary E	6	DE	157	Delia	7/12	DE	146
Eliza	36	DE	277	Mary E	12	DE	307	Elener	14	DE	6
Harriet	45	DE	288	Mary E	14	DE	375	Elener	48	IE	5
Henry L	14	DE	305	Rachel J	20	DE	180	Elizabeth	22	DE	146
Jacob	34	DE	277	Samuel	11	IE	341	Fanny	22	IE	100
James	26	DE	279	Samuel	19	DE	352	Hugh	44	IE	180
Levi	14	DE	309	Samuel	24	IE	145	James	8	DE	26
Lucy	65	MD	277	Samuel	44	IE	341	James	40	MD	146
Margaret	34	IE	280	Samuel	50	DE	120	James	42	IE	42
Minty	24	DE	279	Samuel N	7	DE	394	John	15	IE	42
Finninrow, Hannah	80	GE	272	Sarah	6	DE	277	John D	5/12	DE	116
Finny, Barnard	39	IE	50	Sarah E	13	MD	308	Keisah	9	DE	111
Barny	8	IE	50	Sebastian	14	DE	361	Luff	27	DE	116
Caroline	24	DE	160	Sena B	15	MD	308	Marceles	22	PA	111
Catherine	13	IE	50	Susan A	28	DE	157	Martha	22	DE	111
Elizabeth	4	IE	50	Susan A	28	DE	303	Mary	10	NJ	42
Elizabeth	39	IE	50	Unity	37	DE	146	Mary	24	IE	259
George	15	IE	50	William	21	DE	180	Mary	25	IE	5
Harriet	49	DE	16	Fishpatt, Angeline	43	NY	142	Mary A	25	IE	159
John	1	DE	50	Clara	11	NY	142	Peter	4	DE	146
Levy	60	DE	16	Lewis	38	GE	142	Rachel A	4	DE	146
Mary	10	IE	50	Fitchgarald, Eliz	15	DE	323	Samuel	14	DE	26
Sally	5/12	DE	50	Richard	6	DE	323	Sarah	6	DE	26

Name	Age	St	No.
Fleming, Sarah	8	NJ	43
Sarah	34	PA	180
Sarah	40	DE	26
Susan	35	IE	42
Susannah	35	DE	167
Thomas	25	IE	66
William	18	DE	5
William R	5	DE	180
Flemming, Catherine	19	DE	216
Enoch J	25	DE	216
Henry	18	DE	175
Joseph	1	DE	216
Joseph	65	DE	216
Mary	5	PA	216
Nelle	6/12	DE	216
Fletcher, Alfretta	10/12	DE	117
Ellen	18	DE	145
Eugene	2	DE	117
Hannah	71	PA	47
Helena L	3	DE	117
James	50	DE	168
John D	20	DE	99
Mary	12	DE	117
Mary	30	MD	117
Thomas	39	DE	117
William	5	DE	117
Flick, Anna G	3	DE	283
Ravenna	25	NJ	283
William	28	PA	283
Flindagon, Jane	22	ST	322
John	2	IE	322
Flinn, Alexander	50	DE	145
Allice A	4	DE	368
Anna B	9	DE	370
Anna M	1	DE	367
Anthony	20	DE	19
Bridget	22	IE	85
Catherine	6	IE	339
Catherine	37	IE	339
Daniel H	27	DE	143
David	20	DE	349
Elbridge G	6	DE	369
Elizabeth	10	WI	19
Elizabeth	15	DE	373
Elizabeth	30	DE	369
Elizabeth	53	DE	19
Ellen B	27	DE	368
Emily R	2	DE	368
Evan	28	DE	366
Franklin	28	DE	368
George B	16	DE	368
Howard	16	DE	381
Hugh	46	IE	339
Isaac M	5	DE	369
Isabella	15	IE	339
James	9	IE	339
James	22	IE	339
Joanna	27	DE	367
John	12	IE	338
John	27	IE	45
John	53	DE	19
Laura E	3	DE	369
Lewis C	31	DE	367
Margaret	24	PA	81
Margaret	25	DE	143
Maria	12	DE	19
Mary	3	IE	339
Mary	17	DE	350
Mary E	1	DE	369
Mary E	38	DE	120
Michael	22	IE	286
Robert	23	DE	367
Samuel	29	DE	19
Flinn, Thomas	19	IE	286
Vincent G	5	DE	368
Westley	22	DE	350
William	33	DE	369
Flint, Moses	39	VT	182
Flinton, Owen	35	IE	380
Fletcher, James	19	GB	2
John	17	GB	2
John	45	GB	2
Flitcher, Margaret	42	GB	2
Stephen	15	GB	2
Flitcraft, Abigail	53	PA	310
Ashbel	63	NJ	310
William H	13	PA	310
Flowers, Melvina	14	MD	18
Floyed, Ann E	14	PA	140
Bird	12	PA	140
George F	13	PA	140
George W	4/12	DE	140
George W	40	PA	140
Helen	2	DE	140
Samuel	33	DE	120
Samuel	70	DE	120
Sarah A	40	PA	140
Sarah W	3	PA	140
William	10	PA	140
Floyd, Ann	47	DE	175
David H	14	DE	175
George	49	DE	175
Hester A	20	DE	175
James H	4	DE	175
John	1/12	DE	175
Mary A	2	DE	175
Rachel	40	NJ	175
Samuel	11	DE	175
Flute, Henry	5	PA	109
Flynn, Ann	25	IE	343
Foarce, Charles	14	DE	201
Eli	16	DE	201
George	9	DE	201
Richard	6	DE	201
Robert	7	DE	201
Thomas	44	MD	201
Foard, Ann	20	DE	234
Anna E B	17	MD	332
Benjamin	31	DE	233
Charles	14	DE	233
David	6	DE	343
David	49	MD	343
Eliza J	13	DE	343
Emily	22	DE	233
Hannah	9	DE	343
Hannah	43	DE	343
James	3	DE	343
John F	23	DE	233
Mary	1	DE	233
Mary	22	DE	233
Parmelia	60	DE	234
Rachel A	14	DE	343
Robert	19	DE	233
Susan	7	DE	343
William	25	DE	233
William B	15	DE	343
Fogatry, Alice	23	IE	310
Folk, Edith	48	DE	365
Jacob	58	DE	365
Lewis	19	DE	365
Sarah Ann	5	DE	365
Stephen	10	DE	365
Fooks, Harvy P	14	DE	400
Foot, Ann	50	CN	391
Anna	12	DE	363
Benjamin	20	DE	380
Caroline A	22	MA	159
Elizabeth	1	DE	351
Elizabeth	32	DE	382
George	11	DE	358
George	50	CN	391
George	81	DE	382
Hannah	15	DE	358
Harriet	20	PA	391
Herther M	11	DE	358
James	34	DE	382
Lydia	36	DE	363
Martha J	1	DE	363
Mary E	10	DE	363
Sarah	17	DE	363
Sarah	19	PA	391
Sarah	71	DE	382
Sarah C	8/12	DE	358
Susan D	17	DE	358
Foot, Susan N	42	DE	358
Thomas	44	DE	363
William	44	DE	363
William	48	DE	358
Footh, Eliza	21	DE	373
John	60	DE	373
Margaret	49	DE	373
William	46	DE	373
Foran, Margaret	30	IE	286
Forbes, Charles	30	NJ	272
Rachael	32	DE	272
Sophrona	3/12	DE	272
Forcial, Charetta	27	DE	62
Daniel D	29	PA	62
Emerson	3	DE	62
John	1	DE	62
Ford, Aaron S	13	DE	299
Abraham	30	DE	322
Ann	11	MD	268
Ann	35	?	270
Ann	43	DE	299
Ann	50	DE	152
Ann	50	PA	279
Ann	54	DE	224
Ann	55	DE	322
Ann H	56	PA	279
Bartley	20	IE	12
Benjamin	35	DE	160
Bethia	75	DE	312
Clara	30	DE	125
Edward	14	DE	224
Edward J	22	DE	305
Elisha	11	DE	224
Elizabeth	16	PA	70
Elizabeth	18	DE	366
Elizabeth	59	MD	123
Ellen	11	IE	337
Emma	4	?	270
Ezekiel	12	DE	279
George	11	?	270
Hannah	15	DE	20
Hannah	17	PA	279
Hannah	21	IE	12
Hannah	24	DE	56
Henry	50	MD	152
Isaac	61	DE	322
James	2	PA	280
James	7	DE	224
James	20	DE	188
James	22	MA	125
James	29	DE	224
Jeremiah	12	DE	366
Jesse	55	DE	279
John	15	DE	223
John	16	IE	337
Josephine	6	MD	267
Julia	2	DE	20
Louis	7	DE	224
Louisa	4	MD	267
Lydia	2	DE	125
Mary	7	DE	20
Mary	22	IE	337
Mary	28	DE	267
Mary	36	DE	17
Mary A	17	DE	322
Michael	18	IE	337
Milison	15	DE	299
Oliver	10	DE	330
Richard	8	MD	267
Rebecca	19	PA	279
Robert	14	DE	20
Rosanna	30	DE	18
Samuel	39	?	270
Sarah	13	DE	224
Sarah	19	PA	274
Stephen	30	MA	125
Susan	44	GB	20
Susan	57	DE	366
Thomas	15	IE	337
Thomas	27	IE	12
Thomas	27	DE	224
Thos	35	IE	337

Name	Age	St	Pg
Ford, William	1	DE	125
William	5	DE	20
William	14	DE	279
William	32	DE	224
William	48	GB	20
William	56	DE	224
Foreaker, Anna Mary	1	DE	362
George	3	DE	362
John	6	DE	362
Joseph	33	DE	362
Mary Jane	4	DE	362
Rebecca	33	DE	362
Sarah Ann	5	DE	362
William	12	DE	376
Foreman, Albert	28	PA	122
Amanda	13	PA	131
Anna J	11	PA	131
Elizabeth	19	PA	131
Isaac	9	PA	132
Isaac	48	PA	131
Jane	24	PA	122
John	5/12	DE	91
John	30	MD	293
John B	7	DE	41
John G	32	PA	91
John R	22	PA	131
Margaret	29	PA	41
Margaret J	3	DE	91
Mary	27	DE	91
Mary A	17	PA	131
Mary A	44	PA	131
Moses	6	PA	131
P B	32	DE	41
Samuel	5	DE	41
Thomas	1	DE	122
Forest, Margaret	25	ST	329
Forkum, Ann Emeline	9	DE	190
Henry	3	DE	190
John R	7	DE	190
Mary C	28	DE	190
Rachel	11/12	DE	190
Silas	36	DE	190
Forman, Ann	55	DE	318
Elinor B	21	DE	318
Isaac W	10	DE	318
Joseph S	28	DE	318
Martha B	61	DE	376
William	15	DE	185
Forrest, Barbell	13	DE	116
Daniel A	2	DE	116
John	6	DE	116
Margaret	4	DE	116
Margaret	35	IE	116
Mrs	80	IE	145
Samuel	11	DE	116
Samuel	32	IE	26
Sarah J	12	DE	117
William	36	IE	116
William	75	IE	147
William J	9	DE	116
Forta, John	33	IE	338
Fortener, Sarah M	65	DE	38
Forthergale, Ann	50	DE	20
Forwood, Amos	18	DE	290
Ann	56	DE	297
Cyrus	14	DE	282
David	30	DE	297
Eliza A	50	DE	282
Elizabeth	10	DE	278
Emily	15	DE	282
George	24	DE	297
George	55	DE	297
Gideon	17	DE	297
Hannah	23	DE	294
Hannah	44	DE	278
Harriet	61	DE	290
James	3	DE	290
Jane	20	DE	290
Jehu	37	DE	290
Jehu	86	DE	290
John	26	DE	297
Joseph	1	DE	290
Forwood, Lydia	35	PA	290
Martha	12	DE	278
Mary	2	DE	290
Mary	51	DE	294
Mary J	16	DE	278
Miller	5	DE	290
Rebecca	17	DE	278
Ribert	27	DE	297
Ruthan	21	DE	297
Samuel	50	DE	282
Susan	7	DE	290
Thomas	19	DE	297
Valentine	45	DE	278
William	14	DE	297
Foster, Ann	18	IE	313
Caroline M	6	DE	175
Charles	51	NJ	175
Charles H	12	DE	175
Deborah	20	DE	291
Edward	25	DE	266
Eli	49	NJ	291
Eliza	23	DE	291
Elizabeth	16	DE	74
Elizabeth	30	MD	281
Francis	14	DE	292
George	18	DE	292
Hannah	48	DE	292
Harriett	38	DE	291
Hugh	21	DE	313
Jacob M	8	DE	175
James	28	MD	124
Jno J	8	DE	292
John	1	DE	281
John	9	DE	291
John	51	GB	144
Joshua	14	DE	291
Lucy A	16	DE	292
Mahlon	40	DE	292
Maria	3	DE	292
Mary	4/12	DE	266
Mary	49	GB	144
Mary E	10	DE	175
Michael	20	DE	337
Milford	3	DE	124
Rachel	23	DE	266
Rebecca	20	MD	315
Rhody C	13	DE	175
Robert H	27	DE	209
Ruth L	18	DE	291
Sarah	6	DE	282
Sarah	27	DE	209
Sarah	49	DE	175
Sarah E	10	DE	292
Sarah J	9	DE	144
Sarah J	11	DE	291
Sarah L	15	DE	175
Susan A	22	DE	124
William	4	DE	281
William	40	DE	281
William M	22	IE	30
Fothergill, Ann	20	GB	165
Foulk, Anna M E	11	DE	279
Candia	28	DE	363
Candis	71	DE	363
Elethera C Y	13	DE	279
James H	5	DE	279
John	9	DE	279
John	27	DE	363
John	33	DE	279
John	70	DE	363
Susan	30	DE	279
Susan H	7	DE	279
Thomas H	3	DE	279
William	30	DE	363
Fountain, __(female)	40	DE	248
Elizabeth	10	DE	88
Isabella	29	DE	88
Jacob ·	18	DE	184
Jacob	40	MD	251
James	30	DE	88
Rachel	24	MD	330
Sarah A	7	DE	88
Fountain, Victor- ine	11/12	DE	88
William H	4	DE	88
Founty, Mary	56	FR	76
Fourd, Harcot	27	PA	24
Fowler, Henry	40	DE	135
Henry	40	DE	135
Jonah	21	GB	348
Jonathan	32	GB	348
Lewis	6/12	DE	135
Mary E	11	DE	135
Matilda	33	DE	135
Rebecca	8	DE	135
Synthia	5	DE	135
William	8	DE	348
Fox, Ann J	18	IE	103
Anna	16	PA	55
Charles	20	PA	55
Daniel	7	PA	55
Elizabeth	13	PA	55
Francis	16	PA	55
George	12	IE	103
Hugh	29	DE	130
James	54	IE	55
John	15	IE	103
John	62	IE	130
Margaret	20	IE	103
Mary	40	IE	103
Rachel	11	PA	55
Robert	15	DE	243
Shalot	30	?	167
Sophia	50	PA	55
Thomas	26	DE	130
William	31	IE	103
Foxwell, Angeline	29	DE	213
Carey	22	DE	213
Charles E	14	DE	213
Elizabeth	9	DE	213
Garret	7	DE	213
John	5	DE	213
Lydia A	2	DE	213
Mary J	16	DE	213
Tilghman	49	MD	213
Foy, Joseph	9	CU	164
Simon	11	CU	164
Frailey, Frances	6	DE	265
John	32	GE	265
Magdalene	30	GE	265
Mary	3	DE	265
Fraim, Benj	24	DE	277
John	49	DE	277
John W	1	DE	277
Martha	51	GB	277
Mary	22	DE	277
Robert	20	DE	277
Frain, Eliza J	1	DE	298
George W	35	DE	298
Hester	38	PA	298
Lewis	5	DE	298
Mary	7	DE	298
Fraizer, George	28	DE	32
Mary	23	DE	32
Pearce	2/12	DE	32
Frame, Alfred	1	DE	356
Allen	9	DE	356
Anna	28	PA	365
Christina	26	GE	81
Edward	9	DE	47
Eliza Jane	32	PA	365
Elizabeth	16	DE	333
George	3	DE	356
George	4	PA	365
Grace	46	DE	47
Hardy	48	DE	47
Henry	65	PA	365
John M	4	DE	356
Margaret	28	DE	356
Martha A	6	DE	356
Mary	36	DE	356
Mary	64	PA	365
Mary Ann	30	PA	365
Mary E	23	MD	194

Name	Age	State	No.
Frame, Nathan	22	DE	192
Nathan	26	PA	365
Phillip	24	GE	81
Robert	10	DE	144
Ruth Ann	20	PA	365
Sarah	3	DE	356
Sidney	1	DE	356
Susanna	5	PA	365
Taylor	1	DE	356
Thomas	12	DE	114
Thomas	26	PA	356
William	28	PA	356
France, Elizabeth	14	PA	344
Elizabeth	16	DE	332
George	22	PA	344
John	2	DE	73
John	16	PA	344
Joseph	12	PA	344
Joseph	60	GB	344
Julia	4	DE	73
Rachel	19	GB	43
Rachel	20	PA	344
Sarah	45	PA	344
Frances, Abigal	25	NJ	228
Ann	37	NJ	352
Auto	12	DE	163
Charles A	14	DE	164
Eliza	7	PA	352
Emeline	9	PA	352
Henry	40	NY	352
James H	1	DE	228
John	4	PA	352
Jonathan	23	DE	21
Lewis	2	PA	352
Lydia	35	DE	228
William	28	DE	228
Francis, Arthur	12	DE	306
Charles	13	DE	306
Cora M	10	DE	306
Daniel	73	IE	338
Hannah	18	IE	338
James	17	DE	87
Jonathan	21	DE	375
Julia	27	PA	306
Martha E	21	DE	375
Mary E	19	DE	375
Rose Theresa	19	IE	287
Sarah E	2	DE	377
Walter	1	DE	377
William M	26	DE	375
Frank, Charles	10	DE	282
Deborah A	30	PA	282
Edwin	4	DE	282
George C	7	DE	282
George C	92	NE	287
Henrietta	8	DE	282
Henry	29	DE	282
J Lewis	6	DE	282
Mary E	9/12	DE	282
Franklin, Anna R	10	PA	332
Catherine H	34	MD	332
Emily F	8	DE	332
Mary L	12	DE	332
Sarah H	4	DE	332
Walter D	12	PA	332
Walter E	35	PA	332
Frantze, Caroline	24	DE	54
Elizabeth	28	DE	54
Emma	28	DE	54
Eugenia	8	MD	54
Eugenia	26	MD	54
Jacob	40	GE	50
John	40	MA	54
Laurence	30	GE	50
Frazer, Hannah	22	?	168
Frazier, Alexander	5	DE	328
Benjamin	6	DE	333
Catharine	12	DE	340
David M	7	DE	328
Edmund	16	DE	340
Eliza	14	DE	328
Eliza	34	PA	333
Frazier, Emaline	1	DE	328
Emily	6	DE	340
Emma	42	DE	328
Emmaline	31	NJ	326
Harriet	31	NJ	326
Henry	1	DE	326
Ingeber	39	DE	340
Ingeber	39	DE	340
Isaac	8/12	DE	340
James	21	DE	328
James	35	NS	33
James	42	DE	333
James H	8	DE	333
Jane	19	DE	328
John	8	DE	340
John	10	DE	333
John	44	DE	340
Josephine	8	DE	326
Levinia	43	DE	333
Louisa	12	DE	328
Margaret	5	DE	326
Mary	2	DE	333
Mary	15	DE	340
Richard	7	DE	333
Robert	4	DE	333
Samuel	10	DE	340
Samuel	12	DE	333
Samuel	50	DE	328
Samuel B	10	DE	328
Sarah	13	DE	340
Sarah	16	DE	328
Thomas	3	DE	326
Thomas	41	DE	326
Wellington	9	DE	333
William	50	DE	333
William H	3	DE	328
Fred, Benjamin	60	DE	115
Emma	18	DE	115
Mary	55	DE	115
Mary	60	PA	24
Fredd, Caleb	24	PA	361
Charles	17	DE	361
Charles	30	IE	361
Elias	4	DE	361
Elizabeth J	23	PA	360
Isaac	52	PA	361
John P	5	DE	360
Mariah H	76	PA	360
Mary M	23	PA	361
Olive P	2	DE	360
Freeman, Catherine	23	MD	69
Dianna	20	DE	340
Edward	25	MD	340
Elias	13	DE	291
George	28	DE	71
Henrietta	58	MD	293
James	6/12	DE	340
Jesse	68	DE	293
John	16	DE	317
Mary A	16	DE	239
Mary J	4	DE	319
William	21	DE	196
Freize, Ann H	16	PA	166
Christian	90	PA	44
Mary	17	DE	44
Mary	42	PA	44
Rosana	35	PA	44
Sarah	30	DE	44
Zenes	68	PA	44
Freman, Alonzo	2	DE	156
Cass	1	DE	92
Cass	22	DE	92
Edward	4	DE	156
Eliza	30	DE	156
Isaac	17	DE	92
John	35	DE	93
John	40	NJ	156
Mary	33	DE	93
Mary J	4	DE	319
Mele	40	DE	92
Rebecca	18	MD	103
Rebecca	20	DE	92
Freman, Sarah	28	DE	92
Sarah J	6	DE	157
French, Alexina	8	DE	179
Alfred	4/12	DE	179
Amos S	39	OH	187
Elizabeth	33	DE	179
George L	3	DE	179
Henry	8	DE	187
Joseph	5	DE	187
Lydia W	30	NJ	187
Mary J	3	DE	187
Nimrod	35	DE	179
Sarah	55	DE	230
Sarah E	5	DE	179
French family:		FR	270
female	2	FR	270
female	4	FR	270
male	6	FR	270
female	50	FR	270
male	50	FR	270
Freston, Henry	21	MD	103
Frick, Hester	21	MD	24
Jediah	23	DE	24
Mary	52	DE	24
Friel, Ann	11	DE	276
Avoline	4	DE	276
Charlotte	15	DE	276
Chas	25	PA	355
John	42	PA	276
John T	9	DE	276
Letitia	1	DE	276
Mary	64	PA	276
Mary F	17	DE	276
Rebecca	7	DE	276
Rebecca	42	DE	276
William E	13	DE	276
Fries, Henry C	37	PA	179
Maria E	5	DE	179
Matilda A	33	DE	179
Frieze, Alfred	15	DE	76
Lydia	27	DE	76
Mary A	45	DE	76
Thomas	17	DE	76
Thomas	54	PA	76
Frisby, Andrew	28	DE	194
Benjamin	25	DE	204
Charlotte	9	DE	184
Elijah	35	DE	72
Eliza	30	DE	194
George	4	DE	194
Martha	14	DE	175
Mary E	9	DE	194
Phillis A	48	DE	73
Richard A	1	DE	194
Frisk, Catherine	27	DE	49
Henry	27	DE	49
Horace	2	DE	49
William	4	DE	49
Fritz, Henry	21	GE	258
David	30	PA	311
Fromberger, John H	37	PA	251
Fron, Rosanna	19	IE	282
Frontege, Caroline	24	DE	55
Elizabeth	28	DE	55
Emma	26	DE	55
Eugenia	8	MD	55
Eugenia	26	MD	55
John	40	MA	55
Frute, Ann	52	DE	289
Fruye, George	18	MD	65
Jerry	45	MD	65
John	10	DE	65
Mary	15	DE	65
Minte	43	MD	65
Fry, Elizabeth	35	PA	284
Isabella	19	PA	284
Mary	22	PA	284
Sarah	25	PA	284
Fuhr, Elizabeth	36	MD	317
George	40	PA	317
James H	16	MD	317
John S	2	DE	317

Name	Age	St	No
Fuhr, Margaret	5	DE	317
Mary A	18	MD	317
Sarah	9	DE	317
Wm F	4	DE	317
Fuller, Alfred	7	DE	350
Catharine	31	IE	367
Elizabeth	2	PA	350
James N	10	DE	350
John	40	PA	350
John M	12	?	274
Margaret	40	PA	350
Michael	4	PA	366
Patrick	35	IE	367
Rachel A	5	DE	350
Sarah	18/12	PA	367
Fullerton, Esther A	25	PA	314
Jane	5	DE	314
Jesse	32	PA	314
Mary	6	DE	314
Oliver	21	DE	314
Sarah	16	PA	251
Fulman, Abigail	9	DE	191
Ann E	10	DE	190
Anthony	8	DE	35
Augustus	11	GE	35
Barnard	56	GE	35
Elizabeth	43	GE	35
Francis	16	GE	35
George	35	DE	191
George C	30	GE	190
Henry	5	DE	35
Joseph	21	GE	35
Leah	26	DE	190
Margaret	8	DE	191
Rebecca A	6	DE	191
Fulmer, Andrew	28	GE	90
Anna	47	SZ	145
Eliza A	26	MD	90
Ferdinand	12	DE	145
Henry	9	DE	145
John	23	DE	145
John	47	GE	145
Joseph	19	DE	145
Louisa	16	DE	145
Mary	20	DE	145
Melissa	5	VA	90
Fulton, Anai	11	DE	332
Edward	14	DE	332
Elizabeth	10	DE	361
Esther A	14	DE	361
Henry C	6	DE	361
James	40	NY	332
John S	12	DE	361
Mary	40	MD	332
Mary A	4	DE	361
Samuel	51	DE	218
Sarah	6	DE	332
Sarah	35	PA	361
Sarah R	2	DE	361
Thomas	41	PA	361
Fultz, Claonia	10	DE	287
Ezekiel	27	DE	280
Israel H	30	DE	287
Julianna	3	DE	287
Julianna	30	DE	287
Martha A	18	DE	296
Furchase, James	6	DE	295
John	7/12	DE	295
Mary	24	DE	295
Sarah	3	DE	295
William	7	DE	295
William	37	DE	295
Furgason, David	20	IE	343
Furgenson, Charles	30	IE	61
Charles O	5	PA	61
Elizabeth	27	ST	61
George	3	DE	61
John G	8	PA	61
Furginson, Alice A	9	DE	368
Furgerson, Anna	22	DE	384
George	12	MD	392
Hannah A	17	MD	392
Furgerson, Hannah A	17	MD	392
Henry	5	MD	392
James D	11	MD	392
John	8	MD	392
John B	43	MD	392
Josephine	1	DE	393
Mary	18	PA	166
Mary	42	MD	392
Robert	22	DE	385
Sarah J	14	MD	393
Thomas	16	PA	280
William	7/12	DE	72
Furgeson, Elizbeth	53	MD	384
Robert	43	ST	384
Furgesson, Collins	14	DE	225
Janetta	20	DE	384
Martha A	16	DE	225
Mary E	7	DE	225
Richard	19	DE	225
Susan	11	DE	225
Susan	39	DE	225
Temperance	5	DE	225
Furgison, Elizabeth	10	DE	364
Mary	17	DE	364
Furguson, Charles	24	DE	386
Susanna	12	DE	364
Furgusson, Eliza	9	DE	375
Elizabeth	49	DE	375
Furr, Arminta M	34	DE	192
Furrows, Elijah	11	DE	364
Emroy	1	DE	364
George	75	MD	364
James	35	PA	364
Mary	33	DE	364
Rebecca	71	MD	364
Fuzards, John	30	GB	156
Mary	28	GB	156
Gabby, George B	19	GB	380
Gabinella, Evalina	56	FR	353
Gaddare, Ann	20	DE	376
Gaddes, Alice	16	DE	222
Edward	1	DE	222
James	8	DE	222
Mary	45	DE	222
Stephen	3	DE	222
William	6	DE	222
William	45	DE	222
Gage, Mary	16	DE	315
Gail, Charles M	36	IE	334
Gains, Emeline	26	DE	35
Rebecca	21	DE	361
Gairy, Abraham	50	IE	376
Catherine	48	DE	376
James H	18	DE	376
Isabella	11	DE	376
Mary A	15	DE	376
Robert	13	DE	376
Samuel T	18	DE	376
Galager, John B	2	DE	60
Sarah A	26	PA	60
William	25	DE	60
Galagher, Ellen	2	MA	350
Ellen	22	SA	350
John	36	IE	346
Thomas	22	IE	326
Thomas	22	IE	342
Galaher, Hannah	22	IE	43
Marcellus	19	VA	163
Galan, Enigeo	13	MX	304
Galatz, Rebecca	62	DE	274
Galaway, Thomas	47	DE	78
Galbreath, William	23	DE	127
Galbreth, Catherine	16	DE	16
Gemima	50	DE	16
Robert	50	DE	16
Robert C	6	DE	16
Wallace W	20	DE	16
Gale, Anna	35	DE	292
Elizabeth	19	DE	292
George	6	DE	215
Isaac	12	DE	215
Gale, Jeremiah	47	DE	215
Joseph	15	DE	215
Judy	51	DE	215
Rebecca	30	DE	288
Stephen	49	DE	292
Galena, Ann Rose	11	DE	306
Deborah Jane	9	DE	306
John	51	FR	306
Mary A	49	MD	306
Mary E	16	DE	306
Galinne, Sarah	21	DE	81
Gallagar, Bainley	16	IE	312
John	14	IE	312
John	50	IE	312
Mary	48	IE	312
Patrick	18	IE	312
William	30	IE	313
Gallager, Anna	2	DE	42
Anna	36	PA	42
Bridget	1	DE	43
Catherine	40	IE	29
Danial	10	PA	42
Daniel	30	IE	43
Ellen	12	PA	42
James	4/12	DE	43
John	36	DE	42
Lewis	8	PA	42
Lewis	18	DE	149
Martha	7/12	DE	42
Mary	25	IE	43
Gallagher, Bridget	30	IE	314
Isabel	4	MA	350
John	24	IE	274
Mary	22	IE	311
Michael	35	IE	314
Sarah	70	GE	285
Gallaher, John W	43	DE	210
Maria	43	DE	210
Gallaspy, Mrs	50	IE	5
Gallaway, Elizabeth	2	DE	117
George	2	MD	341
George W	9	DE	78
John	34	MD	117
Margaretta	6	DE	78
Martha J	18	DE	78
Mary	34	MD	117
Mary A	39	DE	78
Sarah J	25	MD	341
Susanna	16	DE	78
Thomas C	14	DE	78
Galliger, Anna	4	DE	40
Catherine	1	DE	40
Farrell	29	IE	40
Hannah	27	IE	40
Marten	20	IE	366
Gallop, Ann	18	MD	339
George	20	DE	339
George	39	MD	339
Hannah	20	MD	338
Rebecca	60	MD	339
William	30	MD	339
Gallow, Bernard	24	IE	274
Galloway, Arabella	13	DE	280
Elizabeth	18	DE	280
Emily	16	DE	280
James	23	DE	280
James	50	MD	280
John	25	DE	280
Robert	11	DE	280
Sarah	40	PA	280
Susan	17	DE	319
Galt, Eliza A	20	MD	195
Galvin, Mary	1	DE	25
Mary	22	ST	25
Peter	45	IE	25
William	3/12	DE	25
Gambel, Ann	10	NC	134
Claude	5	NC	134
John	40	NC	134
Joseph	1	DE	134
Rebecca	38	NC	134
Sarah	6	NC	134

Name	Age	ST	Page
Gambel, Susan	8	NC	134
Gamble, Amelia	26	DE	370
Ann	10	MD	138
Ann	52	DE	372
Anna	2	PA	282
Charles	5	DE	373
David	30	ST	369
Eliza	31	IE	282
James	28	DE	373
John	30	IE	282
Margaret	14	PA	282
Margaret E	1	DE	373
Nathaniel	6	PA	283
Neinhan	2	DE	373
Samuel	7	DE	373
Samuel	26	DE	370
Sarah	25	DE	373
William J	9	PA	282
Gamer, John	21	DE	317
Gansy, Mary	4	DE	318
Garby, Amanda	8	DE	359
Catherine	45	DE	359
Elizabeth	20	DE	283
Richard	39	PA	283
Garden, Charles H	4	NJ	110
David	38	NJ	35
Edward	6	DE	7
Elizabeth	40	DE	142
Emma Y	2	DE	110
George W	38	NJ	110
Henry	13	NJ	35
James	11	DE	7
Jane	30	PA	35
John	4	DE	7
John	40	IE	7
John A	40	DE	353
Margaretta	12	NJ	110
Mary	32	NJ	110
Mary	38	IE	7
Mary B	9	NJ	110
Sarah	12	PA	361
Gardener, John M	9	DE	245
Gardens, Annie W	26	PA	298
Francis R	30	ST	298
Isabela	58	ST	298
Mary C A	20	MD	298
Gardins, C W	23	WN	163
Gardner, Amanda	19	DE	245
Benjamin W	60	PA	22
Catherine	3	DE	60
Delight	31	VA	245
Edward	19	PA	136
Elizabeth	17	NJ	136
Elizabeth	44	DE	136
Ellen	5	DE	60
Ellen	22	DE	10
George	16	DE	60
George W	12	DE	143
Hannah	5	PA	21
Isaac S	2	DE	290
James	7	DE	108
James	21	DE	60
Jenetta	10	ST	108
John	16	ST	108
John	17	DE	337
John	30	DE	143
John T	8	DE	136
Josephine	9	DE	60
Lamintine	2	DE	108
Martha	10	DE	143
Martha	12	DE	60
Mary	3	PA	22
Mary	35	DE	290
Mary	42	DE	60
Mary A	12	PA	136
Mary S	3/12	DE	108
Nathan	7	PA	22
Rachel M	19	PA	22
Rebecca	27	DE	143
Robert W	42	DE	60
Rosannah	4	DE	73
Samuel	17	PA	22
Gardner, Sarah	14	PA	22
Sarah	41	PA	22
Virginia	1	DE	246
William	3	DE	290
William	21	DE	87
William H	3	DE	136
William M	32	DE	290
Garesche, Cora M	53	WN	306
John A	21	DE	306
Jno Peter	69	WN	306
Mary E	17	DE	306
Garetson, Elizabeth	24	DE	141
Peter	19	DE	23
William	26	DE	141
Gargen, Elizabeth	35	NJ	93
Garish, Elizabeth	18	DE	98
Garman, Benjamin	42	DE	223
James	12	MD	320
John	18	DE	223
Randall	12	DE	223
Sarah J	15	DE	223
Solomon	10	DE	223
Garner, Henry	45	PA	259
John	22	PA	79
Margaretta	21	PA	79
Garovin, Sarah	11	IE	283
Garret, Caroline	25	MD	394
Eliza	2	DE	339
Isaac	40	DE	356
James	24	DE	339
Maria	23	MD	394
Mary A	45	MD	394
Samuel	14	MD	394
Sarah E	20	MD	394
Garretson, Ann C	31	DE	242
Benjamin	8	DE	372
Elizabeth	14	DE	166
Elizabeth	45	DE	372
George W	3	DE	291
Hannah	24	WL	291
Hannah	39	PA	70
Hannah A	5	MD	291
Henrietta	2	DE	372
Henry G	18	DE	70
Isabella	16	DE	70
Israel	50	DE	372
James	34	MD	291
James E	21	DE	143
John W	33	DE	242
Margaret A	6	DE	372
Mary E	10	DE	70
Mary E	11	DE	372
Melvina	7	MD	291
Susannah	44	DE	70
William	32	MD	115
Garrett, Aaron	23	DE	314
Anna	30	DE	30
Benjamin	59	PA	369
C Alfred	10	DE	51
Catharine	18	NY	336
Catherine	25	DE	29
Catherine	34	DE	51
Charles C	1	DE	29
David H	7	DE	368
Eli	20	DE	29
Eliza	20	DE	339
Elizabeth	4	DE	51
Elizabeth	4	PA	357
Elwood	36	PA	51
Emily	5/12	DE	51
Gemima	40	PA	357
Harriett	75	DE	329
Harry	27	DE	29
Howard	8	DE	51
John G	7	DE	357
Kamma	6/12	DE	339
Lucilla	2	DE	357
Lydia	11	PA	54
Lydia	11	PA	357
Margaret	8	PA	357
Maria	6	DE	51
Mary	4	DE	29
Garrett, Mary A	16	PA	357
Mary H	47	PA	368
Rachel	57	DE	29
Sarah	13	PA	357
Silas	40	DE	357
Thomas	4	DE	368
Thomas	63	PA	29
Warren	2	DE	51
Garriguer, Charles	15	PA	377
Edward	50	PA	377
Louisa	13	PA	377
Louisa	48	NY	377
Garriot, Mary	15	DE	30
Garrish, Ann M	12	DE	61
Elizabeth	18	DE	97
Mary	50	PA	61
Garrison, Anna M	1	DE	183
Charles	30	NJ	183
Edward L	30	NJ	183
Ella L	5	DE	183
Fanny W	8	NJ	183
Hetty	26	NJ	183
Sarah A	26	PA	183
Garry, Abraham	21	IE	378
James A	18	MA	165
Mary J	16	IE	378
Rachel	50	IE	378
Robert	12	IE	378
Robert	49	IE	378
Samuel	19	IE	378
Garthy, Joanna	44	GE	49
John C	51	GB	49
Garven, Brook	2	PA	75
Evans	4/12	PA	75
James	30	PA	75
Sarah	25	PA	75
Garvin, James	8	PA	339
John	11	PA	339
Priscilla	22	PA	339
Reuben	49	PA	339
Susanne A	47	PA	339
Warner	13	PA	339
William	20	PA	339
William	21	PA	339
Garwood, William	26	PA	224
Gary, Erma	1	DE	324
Joseph	40	DE	210
Levi	33	PA	324
Rebecca	36	DE	324
Gasden, John	45	FR	353
Gasford, George	34	GB	297
Mary	52	NJ	297
Gaskill, Caroline	14	GB	332
Elizabeth	1	DE	332
Thomas	6	DE	332
Thos	45	GB	332
Gates, Josiah	20	DE	172
Priscilla	16	MD	117
Gault, Margaret	4	DE	44
Margaret	28	DE	44
Gaunt, Emma	25	DE	119
Harriet	60	GB	119
John B	2	DE	119
Joseph	20	DE	119
Gause, Arabella	3	DE	72
Ella	2	DE	70
Harriet	32	PA	48
Horace	5/12	DE	19
Martha	22	DE	19
Martha	23	NJ	70
Obediah	25	DE	70
Rebecca	23	PA	72
Taylor	25	PA	19
Washington	22	PA	72
Gay, Howard	15	DE	358
Joseph	14	PA	352
Gayley, Elizabeth J	16	DE	319
Margaret C	14	DE	319
Margaret J	46	PA	319
Martha M	6	DE	319
Samuel M	4	DE	319
Samuel M	48	IE	319

Name	Age	State	Page
Gayley, Samuel R	21	IE	319
Thomas C	18	PA	319
William J	10	DE	319
Gear, Ann	63	MD	4
Emily	23	MD	144
John	18	IE	360
W H	27	DE	143
Gears, Anna	10	DE	89
Dorcas	27	DE	89
John	3	DE	89
John	30	DE	89
Lucy	10/12	DE	89
William	6	DE	89
Gebbelins, Chas	26	IE	341
Cornelius	3	IE	341
Mary A	6	IE	341
Wm	15/12	IE	341
Gebelins, Charles	27	IE	341
Frances	19	IE	341
Geddes, Sophia	62	DE	98
Geleny, William	13	DE	303
Gemmell, Jane	9	ST	157
Margaret	4	ST	157
Margaret	28	ST	157
Mathew	30	ST	157
Gemmill, Anna G	5	DE	282
Anna M	32	MD	281
Chas H	9/12	PA	294
David W	15	PA	294
David W	41	DE	294
Elizabeth	33	PA	294
Elizabeth W	3	DE	282
James	6	PA	294
Jane M	13	PA	294
Margaret	8	MD	260
Martha	11	PA	294
Thomas	12	MD	260
Virginia	2	PA	294
Z	32	DE	281
Z W	6	DE	282
Genderelle, George	15	NY	164
Gennis, Ann E	19	DE	131
David	50	MD	131
Jane	40	MD	131
Mary J	21	DE	131
Samuel	24	DE	131
Gent, Sophia	40	GB	166
George, Charles	50	DE	262
Charles	50	DE	263
Edith	11	DE	260
Eliza	30	DE	262
Eliza	30	DE	263
Elizabeth	16	DE	262
Elizabeth	16	DE	263
John	22	NJ	250
Jonathan	25	DE	303
Mary	8	DE	260
Mary	16	DE	314
Olive	4	DE	260
Gerby, Robert	55	DE	367
Gereld, Elizabeth	15	DE	26
George	40	NJ	26
Jonathan	8	DE	26
Margaretta	36	GE	26
Mary	5	DE	26
William	10	DE	26
Gess, Palmer	17	PA	361
Gest, Elizabeth	92	DE	361
Evalina	22	PA	361
Joseph	60	PA	361
Peter	15/12	DE	361
Gets, Samuel	45	PA	79
Getts, William	30	GE	125
Getty, Benjamin	12	PA	324
David	8	PA	324
John	9	PA	324
John	35	PA	324
Michael	3	PA	324
Rebecca	30	PA	324
Wm	2	PA	324
Geyer, Abraham	37	DE	181
Amos	10	DE	181
Geyer, Edward	12	DE	181
Harriet	7	DE	181
John	4	DE	181
Lorenzo	2	DE	181
Mary	6/12	DE	181
Samuel	5	DE	181
Sarah	30	DE	181
Ghorham, Eleazor	20	DE	388
Gibb, Robert	35	DE	204
Gibbelins, Sarah	26	IE	341
Wm	22	IE	341
Gibbens, Caroline	19	DE	11
Elizabeth	26	DE	11
Frank	22	DE	11
Lewis	30	DE	11
Margaret	28	DE	11
Rebecca	65	DE	11
Rodman	24	DE	11
Sarah	34	DE	11
Gibbins, Ann	56	IE	331
Cathrine	17	IE	331
Chas	60	IE	331
James	12	IE	331
Sarah	19	IE	331
Gibbons, Andrew	27	IE	345
Anna	3	DE	342
Anna	44	DE	95
Archilles	28	PA	67
Bernard	23	IE	345
Bridget	27	IE	345
Catharine	26	IE	342
Charles	14/12	DE	342
Charles	22	IE	342
Cornelius	10	IE	340
Elizabeth	36	IE	284
Ellen	14	IE	340
Hannah	18/12	DE	345
Isaac C	45	DE	244
Jacob	9	DE	244
James	16	IE	340
Jane J	36	NJ	89
John	3	DE	67
John	12	IE	340
John	13	DE	244
John	29	IE	342
Joseph	51	DE	95
Margaret	30	DE	244
Mary	1	DE	67
Mary	26	DE	67
Mary	55	PA	34
Mary J	1	DE	95
Samuel B	14	NJ	89
Sarah	26	DE	95
Sarah	50	IE	340
Washington	13	DE	95
William	55	IE	340
William S	36	NJ	89
Gibbs, Ann	2	DE	230
Ann	28	DE	19
Ann	77	MD	230
Benjamin	37	DE	230
Charles	21	DE	232
Daniel	30	MD	269
Edward	18	DE	233
Elizabeth	10	MD	68
Elizabeth	45	DE	230
Garrett	3	DE	19
George	6	DE	19
George	25	DE	245
Hanah	16	DE	238
Hannah	30	DE	230
Hannah C	47	DE	230
Henry	39	DE	19
Hester	11	DE	269
Isaac	35	DE	230
James	6	DE	233
Janett	35	MD	270
Joseph S	5	DE	230
Louisa	43	DE	230
Margaret F	41	DE	230
Minty	9	DE	216
Richard	9	MD	246
Gibbs, Philip	25	DE	227
Sarah	8	DE	19
Solomon	7	DE	257
William	4	DE	19
William C	40	MD	269
Gibenson, Ann	10	DE	309
Hannah	34	DE	309
Nelson	38	IE	309
Phebe	66	PA	309
Giberson, Gideon	38	DE	110
Gibson, Ann	19	IE	341
Ann	34	MD	398
Anna	45	NJ	60
Anna M	14	DE	198
Benjamin	8	NJ	60
Bridget	40	IE	341
Charles	18	NJ	60
Della	1	VA	103
Edward	3	PA	103
Elizabeth	10	NJ	60
Elizabeth	15	PA	45
Elizabeth	16	DE	88
Elizabeth	32	DE	198
George T	5	DE	398
Hannah	25	PA	103
Helen	20	NJ	60
Isabella	24	DE	82
James	16	IE	341
James	24	DE	5
James	26	DE	316
James	28	PA	103
James	45	DE	168
James G	23	DE	82
John	10	PA	398
John	32	DE	82
John	53	IE	341
Joseph	12	PA	398
Joseph	16	NJ	60
Joseph	47	IE	45
Joseph	50	NJ	60
Louisa	25	DE	233
Lydiann T	7	PA	398
Margaret	3	DE	398
Margaret	26	DE	82
Margaret	50	IE	45
Martha	18	MD	35
Mary	21	IE	167
Mary	28	DE	82
Mary	45	IE	167
Philip	59	MD	316
Priscilla	22	DE	52
Priscilla	26	DE	316
Priscilla Jr	3	DE	316
Rachel	19	PA	302
Rebecca	28	DE	290
Sally	13	NJ	60
Sarah	20	NY	5
Sarah	42	MD	316
Sarah	45	NJ	32
Sarah G	26	DE	290
Sarah Jr	3	MD	316
Thomas D	34	MD	398
William	30	MD	302
William	43	DE	198
Giers, Darcus	30	PA	286
Giffin, Adeline	5	DE	358
Amanda	10	DE	358
Andrew	35	DE	371
Anna	17	DE	358
James	20	DE	358
James	65	DE	358
Mary	6	DE	380
Mary	48	DE	358
Mary	60	DE	375
Mary Edith	12	DE	358
Thomas	30	DE	375
William	18	DE	375
Gifford, Ann	36	DE	233
Anna	61	NJ	179
Charles	17	NJ	179
James	25	DE	189
John	1	DE	233

Name	Age	St	No
Gifford, John	55	NJ	179
Mary C	1	DE	189
Mary E	7	DE	233
Norman	30	NJ	189
Thomas	24	DE	233
Giggle, Catherine	20	DE	78
Helen	51	GB	78
Sarah	18	DE	78
Gigley, Charles	7	PA	327
Elizabeth	21	NY	327
Ellen	14	PA	327
Ellen	45	IE	327
Hannah	7	PA	327
John	12	PA	327
Margaret	20	PA	327
Michael	18	PA	327
Michael	40	IE	327
Patrick	16	PA	327
Gilbert, Harriet J	24	NY	159
Jesse H	9	DE	174
Joseph L	48	DE	374
Joseph S	4	DE	374
Lydia A	2	DE	374
Mary A	27	DE	72
Morgan	45	PA	7
Sarah	7	DE	374
Gilbreth, Mary A	28	DE	73
Gilden, Joseph	24	MD	40
Mary	24	MD	40
Giles, John	1	DE	210
Margaret	20	DE	210
Thomas	20	DE	210
Gilky, John	26	DE	172
Gill, Anna	3	DE	139
Anna	35	MD	142
Anne	7	NJ	195
Asher	19	NJ	195
Benjamin	45	NJ	195
Catherine M	22	PA	109
Daniel	20	IE	273
Debrah A	10	DE	139
Edward	60	IE	302
Edward J	7	DE	142
Elijah	5/12	DE	195
Elizabeth	14	NJ	195
Ellen	2	DE	345
Ellen	17	IE	302
Emma S	6	DE	142
George	11	DE	195
James	34	PA	139
John	21	NJ	195
John	36	IE	345
John J	29	PA	109
Lewis	5	DE	195
Mary	5	DE	195
Mary	58	IE	302
Mary A	34	PA	139
Mary E	10	DE	142
Michael	22	IE	302
Rachel	35	DE	7
Rebecca	22	IE	345
Rebecca	65	DE	353
Snow	9	DE	195
Thomas	10/12	DE	109
William	9	PA	109
Gilland, Edward	8	DE	324
Gillen, Charles	11	DE	5
John	24	DE	210
Gilliard, Alexander	32	PA	55
Gillin, Ann	20	ST	341
Gillingham, Alice A	24	PA	343
John W	30	PA	343
Jonathan	3	PA	343
Gillion, Isaac	6	DE	194
Jacob	10	DE	194
Peter	8	DE	194
Peter	40	FR	194
Susan	12	DE	194
Gillis, Edward T	6	DE	308
Elizabeth T	39	DE	308
John P	44	DE	308
John P Jr	4	DE	308
Gillis, Martha	60	IE	49
Mary T	2	DE	308
Gillous, Rosa A	20	ST	315
Gilman, Catherine	12	IE	212
John	19	IE	212
Gilmer, Elizabeth	21	IE	205
Emily G	39	DE	360
Isabella	7	IE	205
James	5	IE	205
James	22	IE	205
Martha	45	IE	205
Thomas	3	IE	205
William	18	IE	174
Gilpin, Annie	16	DE	306
Edward W	45	DE	57
Elenora A	36	PA	57
Elnora L	5	PA	10
Elizabeth	33	PA	306
Elizabeth F	36	DE	58
Ellicot	9/12	DE	54
Hannah	38	PA	54
Hellen R	8	PA	10
Jane E	10	PA	10
Joseph	60	VA	34
Laura	15	DE	165
Lydia W	60	DE	34
Meta D	7	DE	58
Pauline E	7/12	DE	58
Richard	45	DE	54
Sarah A	31	NY	10
Vincent C	40	DE	10
Gilprey, Sarah E	18	DE	174
Gilson, Charlotte	10	MD	364
Rebecca	40	MD	364
Samuel	45	MD	364
Ginder, Bernard	25	DE	39
Catherine	3	DE	120
Charles	2	DE	39
Christopher	32	DE	120
Elizabeth	4	DE	120
Elizabeth	25	IE	39
Hannah	28	DE	120
Henry	1	DE	120
John	10/12	DE	39
Josephine	65	GE	134
Peter	60	GE	134
Ginley, Biddy	30	IE	42
Ginn, Benjamin	10	DE	230
Elizabeth	60	DE	337
Euina	12	DE	286
George	14	DE	230
James	24	DE	230
Jane E	25	DE	333
John	21	DE	230
John	50	MD	286
John G	26	DE	333
Julia	17	DE	286
Margaret A	22	MD	286
Martin F	8	DE	230
Mary E	3	DE	333
Mary E	3	DE	337
Mary E	16	DE	230
Rebecca	45	MD	286
Rebecca	50	DE	230
Robert	8	DE	286
Sarah A	1	DE	334
Sarah J	15	DE	286
William	19	DE	286
William	47	DE	230
Ginnet, Ellen	15	DE	17
Gist, Byard	18	DE	19
Givies, Anna	7	NJ	283
Daniel J	32	NJ	283
Elizabeth	34	NJ	283
Elmira	5	NJ	283
John C	1	DE	283
Lydia	12	NJ	283
Martha	11	NJ	283
Glade, Jane M	53	DE	370
Mary	49	DE	370
Sharlot	36	DE	378
Glander, Eben	11	MD	246
Glasby, Albert	2	DE	307
Charles	8	MD	307
Edwin	6	DE	307
Elizabeth	37	MD	307
Jonathan	37	MD	307
Margaret	10	MD	307
Marion	4	DE	307
Glasco, Abel	31	DE	120
Anna M	16	DE	397
Edward	9	DE	126
Elizabeth	14	DE	397
Ellis	40	DE	397
Emily	10	DE	125
Filmore	2	DE	125
Hanna T	10	DE	397
Henry	11	DE	126
John	7	DE	126
Jonathan	18	DE	397
Lydia M	7	DE	397
Mahlon H	1	DE	397
Rachel	4	DE	126
Rebecca	42	DE	397
Sidney	25	DE	168
Susan	3/12	DE	126
Susan	32	DE	126
Thomas	35	DC	126
William T	3	DE	397
Glascow, Henrietta	20	DE	322
Mary	70	MD	259
Thomas	75	DE	331
Glasgo, Ellen	45	DE	400
George	10	DE	400
James E	5	DE	397
John	11/12	DE	400
Lydia A	20	DE	400
Margaret	5	DE	400
Richard	32	DE	289
Glasgow, Abagail	26	MD	333
Amelia	16	DE	331
Celley	23	DE	307
Ephraim	24	DE	320
Israel	5	DE	320
James	24	PA	307
Joseph	7/12	DE	307
Louisa	25	DE	333
Lydia	14	DE	333
Mark	40	DE	320
Mary	30	DE	320
Mary	46	DE	333
Rachel	26	MD	320
Richard	30	DE	280
Samuel	12	DE	331
Susan R	5	DE	334
Thomas	25	DE	333
William	11/12	DE	320
William H	6	DE	334
Glason, Jacob	23	DE	322
Glass, Henry	15	DE	367
John	17	DE	303
Glath, Joseph	16	IE	366
Glazier, Julia A	40	DE	160
Z B	44	VT	160
Gleaves, Anne	10	DE	248
Mary	58	DE	248
Glen, Ellen	24	PA	393
William	34	DE	393
Glendening, Christian	2	CN	322
Christian	33	IE	322
David R	8	CN	322
Janetta G	6	CN	322
John	38	SC	322
John P	4	CN	322
Mary G	12	CN	322
Robert	7/12	DE	322
Glenn, Francis	23	PA	34
Kate	9/12	PA	34
Maria	21	PA	34
Thomas	28	DE	86
Gleves, George W	45	DE	216
Julia A	8	DE	216
Martha	1	DE	216
Mary	35	DE	216

Name	Age	State	Page
Gleves, Mary E	4	DE	216
Glitty, John	17	PA	365
Glover, Christopher	35	GB	283
Edward	2	DE	283
Emma	7	DE	283
John	34	GB	283
John S	10	PA	283
Joseph B	12	CN	283
Mary	31	GB	283
Rosamond	55	GB	283
Rosanna	7	DE	284
William	62	GB	283
William H	5	DE	284
Goden, Annie M	1	DE	125
Rebecca	28	MD	125
William	29	MA	125
Godford, James	28	IE	79
Godfrey, Aaron	27	NJ	307
Heather	25	NJ	307
Robert A	17	NJ	311
William	12	DE	307
Goding, James	33	DE	256
Golby, John L	23	PA	159
Mary A S	17	PA	159
Gold, Ann E	18	DE	324
Goldburgh, William	74	DE	219
Golden, Catherine	25	IE	56
Hannah	4	DE	339
Hannah	5	DE	349
Hannah	26	MD	339
Hannah	28	DE	340
James	10	DE	340
James	15	DE	192
James	32	MD	339
James	46	DE	340
John	29	DE	318
Mary	4	DE	340
Mary	7	DE	339
Nancy	13	DE	340
Rachel	9	MD	339
Vilet	8	DE	339
William	14	DE	340
Goldsberry, Alfred	10	DE	242
Cain	35	DE	242
Elizabeth	11	DE	242
John	14	DE	242
Goldsborough, Wm	45	DE	341
Goldsbury, Samuel	13	DE	241
Golly, John	2	DE	25
John	32	IE	25
Margaret	23	IE	25
Patric	30	IE	25
Phillip	3/12	DE	25
Golrick, Catherine	30	IE	326
Golt, Eliza	19	MD	238
Eliza J	17	DE	225
Elizabeth	7	DE	225
George	25	DE	213
George W	4	DE	225
Henry	20	DE	225
James	36	DE	233
John	16	DE	236
John	39	DE	225
John W	9	DE	225
Joseph	14	DE	225
Joseph	27	DE	233
Julia A	18	DE	225
Rachel J	3	DE	233
Rebecca	5	DE	225
Sarah	39	DE	233
Sarah A	28	PA	225
Susan A	6/12	DE	225
William H	11/12	DE	233
William L	2	DE	225
Goodell, Sarah	17	PA	130
Gooden, Alexander	19	DE	348
Alfred	2	DE	348
Anthony	32	DE	350
David	38	NJ	34
Elizabeth	27	MD	348
George	10	DE	348
Henry	9/12	DE	348
Gooden, Henry	13	NJ	34
Henry	40	DE	348
Isaac	8	DE	348
Isaac	37	DE	360
James	9	DE	348
Jane	30	PA	34
Louisa	9	DE	361
Margaret	4	DE	351
Margaret	34	DE	361
Mary E	3	DE	361
Sarah A	6	DE	361
Sarah Jane	5	DE	348
Goodin, Betsey	45	DE	203
James	51	DE	203
Seely Ann	9	DE	203
Gooding, Abraham	55	MD	339
Benjamin	25	DE	219
Catherine	25	DE	219
Charlotte	25	MD	197
Chas	30	MD	293
Jabes	45	DE	219
Jesse	19	MD	313
John	19	DE	339
John	21	MD	313
Mary	15	DE	339
Patience	50	DE	219
Sally	50	MD	339
Susan	17	DE	339
Susan	25	MD	313
Tom	15	MD	274
Goodley, Catherine	22	PA	283
Elizabeth	15	DE	288
Elizabeth	66	DE	283
Jacob	3	DE	288
James	34	DE	283
Jonah	32	PA	283
Lydia A	6	DE	288
Margarett	2	DE	283
Mary	26	IE	283
Priscilla	34	PA	288
Susan	13	DE	288
Thomas	7/12	DE	283
Thomas	41	DE	288
Goodman, Alexander	16	DE	337
Ann	10	DE	337
Charles	14	DE	337
Charlotte	38	DE	41
James	44	IE	337
James	8	DE	337
Jane	4	DE	337
Margaret	39	PA	337
Sarah	6	DE	337
Susan	17	DE	337
William	40	DE	41
Goodwin, Evan	28	GB	322
Patience	13	DE	183
Goold, Lucy	13	CN	294
Goores, Jane	14	DE	343
Gooseberry, Alexan-der	11	DE	213
Ann	20	DE	169
Eliza	18	DE	196
James	40	DE	174
Martha	38	DE	174
Peter	30	DE	196
Peter Jr	2	DE	196
Sally Ann	8	DE	174
Goram, Eleazer	60	DE	246
Harrison	7	DE	246
Jane	45	DE	246
Martha Jane	10	DE	246
Gorby, Richard	55	DE	276
Gorden, Aaron	50	DE	47
Ann E	65	DE	162
Charles	2	DE	7
Charles	21	DE	80
Charles	29	DE	161
George	23	DE	80
George C	25	DE	161
George W	38	DE	109
Helen	26	DE	161
James	11	DE	47
Gorden, James	26	IE	96
Louisa	32	DE	161
Margaret A	1	DE	96
Mary A	22	IE	96
Renard	6	DE	47
Sarah H	30	DE	161
Susan	5	DE	47
Susan	47	DE	47
Gordon, Ann E	12	DE	176
Ann E	16	DE	282
Anthony	32	DE	351
Catherine	42	DE	176
Charles	12	PA	384
Charles T	60	DE	233
Eliza	19	DE	311
Eliza E	15	PA	288
Eliza J	16	DE	301
Elizabeth	10	PA	384
Fanny	40	DE	256
George W	7	PA	384
George W	82	DE	233
Harriet	15	DE	386
Henry	16	DE	374
Henry	50	DE	386
Jacob	40	MD	253
James	3	MD	253
James C	28	DE	176
John	40	DE	282
Joseph	14	DE	293
Margaret	30	MD	253
Margaret A	9	DE	386
Mary	17	DE	176
Mary A	39	DE	282
Mary E	4	DE	282
Oliver	40	DE	256
Robert C	6	DE	282
Sarah	14	PA	384
Susan	40	DE	386
Thomas	40	DE	176
William	14	DE	282
Gore, George	12	DE	169
Mr	21	MA	32
Gorgas, Edward W	12	PA	400
John	45	PA	113
Joseph	14	PA	401
Susan	5	DE	113
Gorman, Catharine	26	IE	344
James	2	DE	344
Mary Ann	4	DE	344
William	32	IE	344
Gormand, William	46	IE	81
Gormey, John	35	IE	43
Gormely, Catherine	25	IE	352
John	25	IE	352
Margaret A	6/12	DE	352
Patrick	30	IE	345
Gorrie, John H	7	DE	286
John Jr	41	ST	286
John Sr	72	ST	286
Sarah B	32	MD	286
Sarah J	7/12	DE	286
Thomas S	9	DE	286
Gosewich, Amanda M	33	PA	114
Anna C	7	DE	114
Carl E	4	DE	114
Edgar W	6	DE	114
Ernestine L	2	DE	114
Frederic Z	8	DE	114
J Charles (MD)	42	GE	114
Theodore O	4/12	DE	114
Gosnall, John C	17	DE	368
Gosnell, Charles W	15	DE	371
Eliza	48	DE	371
Elizabeth	63	IE	352
John	48	DE	371
Theodore	6	DE	371
Gosset, James	31	DE	375
Rachel	63	DE	375
Smith	26	DE	375
Gothrop, Lydia A	17	PA	348
Gottschimner, Eliza-beth	28	GE	95

Name	Age	St	Pg
Gottschimner, Fred-			
erick	10	DE	95
Henry	1	DE	95
Henry	40	GE	95
Joseph	7	DE	95
Mary	4	DE	95
Gouert, Charles	1	DE	142
Charlotta	26	HN	142
George	34	GE	142
Gould, Adaline	4	DE	39
Elizabeth	23	DE	351
Elizabeth	55	DE	351
Elmira	3	DE	42
George	26	DE	351
Heckland	63	DE	351
Hester	23	DE	42
James H	20	DE	351
Joseph	10	DE	39
Joseph	37	DE	39
Joshua	11/12	DE	39
L	12	DE	165
Lucy	13	UC	293
Margaret	17	DE	351
Mary	30	DE	351
Mary	32	DE	39
Pearce	7	DE	39
Saml	50	DE	351
Samuel	32	DE	351
Goulden, Pricilla	60	MD	58
Grace, Eli	13	DE	305
Nathan	14	DE	318
Grady, Michael	30	IE	345
Graham, Anthony	30	DE	170
Eliza J	10/12	DE	235
Elizabeth	60	IE	356
Francis	25	IE	338
Henrietta	28	DE	170
Jane	38	DE	235
John	20	DE	234
John	24	?	270
John	33	DE	39
Lighton	8	DE	290
Margaret	27	DE	290
Margaret	50	DE	214
Margaret J	2	DE	170
Maria	16	PA	397
Mary	2	DE	290
Mary A	19	IE	300
Mary E	4	DE	170
Mary J	9	DE	235
Rebecca	5	DE	290
Robert	7	DE	290
Robert	28	IE	290
Samuel	35	DE	235
Sarah E	5	DE	235
Thomas	75	IE	356
Graker, Elizabeth	21	IE	350
Gramm, Hugh M	51	IE	135
Grammar, George	55	GE	197
Mary	18	GE	197
Granger, Arthur	4	RI	271
Emily	12	CT	271
Jacob	18	MD	323
Josephine	8	CT	271
Sarah	36	PA	271
Wm	10	CT	271
Grant, Andrew	37	DE	354
Caroline	18	MD	113
Charles	14	PA	314
Charles E	2	DE	138
Indiana J	19	MD	144
James	4	PA	314
James R	25	ME	138
John	26	MD	372
John	28	DE	372
Lewis	40	PA	314
Margaret	21	PA	372
Margaret	25	PA	372
Margaret	35	IE	302
Martha	25	MA	138
Rachel	39	PA	314
William	8	PA	314
Grantham, Ann	40	MD	293
James	40	NJ	293
Grantlin, Amy J	6	DE	283
Elizabeth	27	MD	277
John	27	NJ	277
John A	6/12	DE	277
Priscilla	37	NJ	283
Sarah E	1	DE	283
Susana	14	DE	283
William	44	NJ	283
William H	4	DE	283
Grather, Wm	16	NJ	253
Graves, Albert	8	DE	156
Ann	56	DE	361
Ann	65	PA	354
Ann E	3	DE	98
Caroline C	1	DE	361
Clinton	14	DE	297
David	42	PA	365
Edward	8	DE	110
Elener	27	DE	98
Eliza J	10	IN	130
Elizabeth	13	PA	365
Henry A	2	DE	357
James	36	DE	110
James	50	DE	156
James	65	MD	255
Jane	34	DE	357
John B	7/12	IN	130
Joseph	8	DE	354
Lemuel	26	DE	353
Lewis	6	DE	354
Lewis	32	DE	361
Louisa	18	DE	156
Lucy	2	IN	130
Lydia	8	DE	37
Margaret	67	DE	357
Margaret E	11	PA	365
Margaret E	12	IN	130
Margaret J	29	DE	110
Mary	18	VA	24
Mary	30	DE	37
Mary	30	MD	156
Mary	42	PA	365
Mary A	22	DE	354
Mary A	40	DE	381
Mary A	48	DE	381
Mary Amanda	6	PA	365
Morris	8	DE	361
Nathan	22	DE	353
Patience	12	DE	156
Rachel	51	PA	353
Rebecca A	31	PA	130
Rehard	3	DE	330
Richard	18	DE	381
Robert	10	DE	156
Robert	32	MD	99
Robert	44	DE	168
Robert	45	PA	167
Robert C	80	VA	381
Robert D	6	DE	357
Samuel	41	DE	357
Samuel	45	DE	358
Sarah E	5	DE	330
Sarah Jane	9	PA	366
Sebelilla	32	DE	361
Taylor	7	DE	361
Thomas	12	DE	357
Thomas	20	DE	354
Thomas J	9	IN	130
William	4	DE	366
William	8	DE	358
William	24	DE	353
William	34	DE	130
William H	4	IN	130
Graw, Ann	40	DE	351
Elizabeth	7	DE	351
Jesse	46	DE	351
Lewis	13	DE	351
Mary A	19	DE	351
Gray, Alice	19	DE	51
Amos	33	DE	193
Gray, Alice	19	DE	51
Amos	33	DE	193
Andrew	4	DE	289
Andrew C	45	DE	289
Angeline	22	DE	176
Ann	41	GB	372
Ann Eliza	6	NJ	372
Ann V	1/12	DE	190
Anna E	6	DE	141
Anne	15	DE	294
Anne	36	DE	322
Annie	8	DE	289
Betsey	40	DE	120
Catherine	1	DE	194
E M	40	CT	289
Elizabeth	1	DE	296
Elizabeth	50	GB	294
Ellen	17	IE	7
Emily	5	DE	289
Ezray	15	DE	284
Francis	17	DE	294
George	3/12	DE	323
George	1	DE	321
George	10	DE	289
George	23	DE	60
George	29	PA	296
George W	1	DE	197
Hannah T	20	DE	60
Harald B	8/12	DE	60
Hemphill	33	DE	71
Henrietta	24	DE	197
Henrietta	33	DE	71
Henry	3/12	DE	176
Henry	12	DE	294
Henry	32	DE	322
Henry T	12	DE	284
Isaac	2	DE	322
James	25	DE	197
James	57	GB	294
James H	8	DE	322
James N	26	DE	176
John	5	DE	194
John	24	PA	51
John	29	DE	141
John	50	IE	353
John L	40	DE	194
Joseph	28	DE	194
Josephine	2/12	DE	372
Lowenstone	15	GB	372
Lucinda	7	DE	194
Lyga P	6	DE	322
Margaret	24	PA	321
Margaret	26	DE	39
Margaret	31	DE	194
Maria	14	DE	289
Maria	16	DE	195
Maria	20	NY	296
Martha A	19	DE	190
Mary	50	DE	39
Mary A H	51	PA	284
Mary Ann	17	GB	372
Mary E	4	DE	322
Montgomery	5	DE	294
Pamlia A	15	CT	165
Peter	26	MD	321
Rebecca	69	MD	120
Rebecca	70	DE	146
Richard	14	DE	294
Robert	42	GB	372
Sarah E	5	DE	372
Susanah	31	PA	141
Thomas	23	DE	195
William	26	DE	293
William	29	DE	311
William	34	DE	301
William	57	DE	284
William R	2	DE	176
Grear, Benjamin	2	DE	338
Benjamin	28	DE	338
David	23	IE	343
Rachel	25	PA	338
Greeg, Evan B	24	PA	72

Name	Age	State	Page
Greeg, Henrietta	19	DE	110
John	16	PA	28
John	20	DE	86
Lilly O	20	IE	27
Nelson	17	DE	98
Rachel	4	DE	72
Samuel	4	DE	72
Greeman, Catharine	2	DE	144
Emma	7/12	DE	144
George	3	DE	144
Joel V	33	NJ	144
Joseph H	27	NJ	144
Rachel C	25	PA	144
Green, Adeline	5	DE	256
Adeline	8	DE	237
Alexander	--	DE	186
Amanda	7	DE	297
Amelia	44	DE	324
Ann	6	DE	19
Ann	10	DE	297
Ann	30	IE	99
Ann	33	IE	367
Ann	50	DE	166
Ann J	9	DE	233
Anne	20	IE	53
Benjamin	2	DE	337
Benjamin	14	MA	26
Benjamin	28	DE	337
Benjamin	36	DE	342
Benjamin	40	DE	324
Betsey	58	MD	259
Caroline	18	DE	269
Catherine	17	DE	42
Catherine	30	DE	31
Charles	1	DE	295
Charles	24	DE	352
Charles	30	IE	335
Charles	45	DE	237
Charles H	12	DE	383
Charlotte	24	IE	335
Charlotte	28	DE	193
David	9	DE	335
David T	9	DE	337
Drucilla	20	DE	393
Eli W	15	PA	273
Elijah	10	DE	91
Elijah	17	DE	24
Eliza	30	DE	86
Eliza	50	DE	315
Eliza	56	DE	24
Eliza J	13	DE	337
Eliza J	18	DE	333
Elizabeth	1	DE	393
Elizabeth	8	MD	255
Elizabeth	15	GB	1
Elizabeth	16	DE	358
Elizabeth	39	ST	26
Elizabeth	48	GB	1
Ellen	55	IE	335
Elwood	7	DE	358
Emeline	40	DE	120
Emma	13	GB	1
Enoch	36	DE	79
Esther	44	PA	358
Evan	14	DE	358
Frances	26	DE	288
Gemima	6	DE	91
Hannah	3	DE	335
Hannah	27	DE	91
Hannah A	10	PA	273
Harriet	20	DE	185
Harriet	46	DE	171
Henrietta	11	DE	189
Henry	10	MD	196
Henry	11	PA	321
Hester	25	DE	200
Isaac	9	DE	78
Jack	--	DE	290
Jacob	7	DE	291
Jacob	6	DE	186
Jacob	27	PA	383
James	3/12	DE	91
Green, James	2	DE	19
James	3	DE	277
James	7	DE	79
James	20	DE	352
James	22	DE	256
James	22	DE	274
James	28	DE	91
James	28	IE	295
James	30	DE	171
James	65	IE	44
Jamima	17	DE	180
Jane	3/12	DE	79
Jane	14	DE	335
Jane	18	DE	40
Jane	19	MA	26
Jane	23	DE	11
Jemima	4	DE	297
Jemima	27	DE	297
Jeremy	9	PA	346
Jessie	1	DE	171
Joanna	10	DE	337
John	2	DE	288
John	8	DE	19
John	11	DE	324
John	12	DE	288
John	16	DE	43
John	20	IE	335
John	24	DE	257
John	24	DE	269
John	30	DE	200
John	44	GB	1
John	55	IE	335
John F	2/12	DE	233
John H	48	DE	172
John P	8	PA	286
John W	18	IE	340
Joseph	4	DE	325
Joseph	52	DE	244
Joseph A	3	DE	91
Joshua	35	DE	199
Leah	41	DE	324
Leah E	8	DE	200
Levi	45	MD	233
Levi	47	DE	337
Lewis	12	DE	297
Lewis	13	PA	273
Lewis	30	DE	187
Louis	8	DE	187
Louisa	5/12	DE	187
Louisa	22	DE	27
Margaret	--	DE	186
Margaret	15	DE	352
Margaret	33	PA	295
Margaret	35	DE	4
Margaret	65	DE	272
Margaret A	5	DE	91
Margarett	5	DE	278
Maria	3	DE	353
Maria	5	MD	255
Maria	17	DE	352
Maria	26	MD	255
Maria	43	PA	286
Maria	55	DE	352
Maria A	12	DE	337
Marjery	15	IE	335
Martha	20	DE	276
Martha	20	DE	282
Martha	22	DE	340
Martha F	1	DE	324
Martha R	12	DE	186
Mary	4	DE	79
Mary	8	DE	64
Mary	16	MA	26
Mary	23	IE	132
Mary	24	DE	187
Mary	25	DE	11
Mary	26	DE	233
Mary	32	DE	383
Mary	32	DE	383
Mary	40	DE	237
Mary A	14	DE	237
Mary A	48	MD	335
Green, Mary E	2	DE	337
Mary E	4	DE	200
Mary E	5	DE	383
Mary J	1	DE	278
Mary N	3	DE	89
Matilda	60	DE	91
Matthew	2	DE	315
Michael	40	DE	324
Moses	4	DE	277
Neal	26	IE	335
Owen	25	DE	203
Palmer	36	PA	383
Parker	43	PA	273
Perry	18	DE	244
Perry	19	DE	210
Philis	40	DE	381
Priscilla	35	DE	388
Rachel	25	DE	337
Rachel	60	DE	277
Rachel A	18	PA	152
Rebecca	6	DE	282
Rebecca	30	DE	48
Rebecca	37	DE	273
Richard	2	DE	297
Richard	30	DE	297
Robert	21	DE	244
Robert	22	DE	269
Robert	35	GB	187
Sally	11	DE	55
Sally A	30	DE	200
Saml	53	DE	358
Samuel	11	DE	335
Samuel	12	DE	55
Samuel	30	DE	357
Samuel	51	DE	335
Samuel A	15	DE	338
Sarah	5	DE	282
Sarah	14	DE	104
Sarah	18	IE	367
Sarah	36	DE	337
Sarah	50	IE	44
Sarah A	2	DE	200
Sarah C	12	DE	324
Sarah E	19	DE	171
Sarah J	2	DE	388
Scarlet	25	DE	168
Scharlot	25	DE	168
Schroder	16	GB	208
Solomon	36	DE	324
Sophia	3	DE	324
Stephen	4	DE	19
Susan	25	DE	352
Susan D	7	DE	200
Thomas	3	DE	233
Thomas	5	DE	381
Thomas	10	IE	44
Thomas	12	PA	26
Thomas	15	PA	286
Thomas	19	GB	1
Thomas	65	PA	286
Uriah	7	DE	315
Westley	31	MD	255
William	5	DE	186
William	10	PA	19
William	10	DE	237
William	14	DE	352
William	24	DE	143
William	35	MD	196
William	46	GB	26
William F	12	PA	286
William J	4/12	DE	335
Zebidee	12	DE	314
Zebulon	11	DE	316
Greenalak, Elizabeth	44	GB	332
George	14	GB	332
John P	2	DE	332
Margaret S	11	GB	332
Mary	18	GB	332
William J	8	DE	332
Wm	43	GB	332
Greenback, John	21	MD	166

Name	Age	St	Pg
Greenberry, William	14	DE	206
Greenby, Absolem	10	DE	1
Georgana	6	DE	1
Peter	36	MD	1
Sally A	5	DE	1
Sally A	32	MD	1
William	3	DE	1
Greenfield, Amos	30	PA	294
Benj	3	NJ	299
Elizabeth	31	DE	294
Elizabeth	32	GB	299
George H	5	NJ	299
Richard	8	PA	299
Samuel	49	GB	299
Sarah	9	PA	299
Stephen	6	NJ	299
Susan	11	DE	294
Greenwall, John	53	PA	379
John L	3	DE	379
Joseph	55	DE	380
Margaret	36	DE	379
Mary	56	DE	380
Robert	26	DE	380
William W	10	DE	379
Greenwich, James	11	DE	262
James	54	DE	262
Greenwood, Alfred A	3	DE	119
Alfred W	6	DE	154
Amanda M	6	DE	119
Ann	37	DE	154
Charles E	7	DE	154
Ella M	3	DE	154
Hannah A	10	PA	285
Harriet	7/12	DE	96
Henry T	2	NJ	96
Isaac	30	DE	96
John	45	GB	285
John J	11	DE	119
John T	30	DE	119
Margaret C	20	NY	96
Mary E	10	DE	98
Priscilla C	32	DE	119
Ralph	41	GB	154
Ralph H	4	DE	154
Sarah A	23	MD	169
Spencer	30	DE	365
Tacy	56	PA	285
Wilhelmina	14	DE	257
William	29	GB	371
William H	12	DE	119
Greer, John	24	IE	302
Mary	16	IE	302
Gregery, Levinia	15	MD	166
Gregg, Amanda	25	PA	308
Ann Eliza	7	DE	364
Benjamin	15	DE	364
Benson	26	DE	364
Caroline	20	PA	28
Edward	7	DE	28
Elizabeth	35	DE	364
George	41	PA	28
George W	2	PA	366
Hannah	49	DE	347
Henrietta	19	MI	366
Isaac	22	PA	308
James E	11	DE	364
Jehew W	9	DE	364
Jesse	60	DE	347
John	1	DE	308
John	20	PA	136
John	35	DE	347
John	40	DE	364
Levinia	4	DE	347
Maria	43	DE	28
Martha J	3	PA	308
Mary	30	DE	347
Mary	59	DE	364
Mary	63	MI	366
Rufus	28	PA	366
Sarah	26	PA	366
Sarah	29	DE	364
Sarah Ann	38	PA	364
Gregg, Thomas	6	DE	347
William	13	DE	366
William	27	PA	308
Greggs, Lydia E	5	DE	349
Mary A	29	PA	349
Peter W	31	DE	349
Samuel	8	DE	349
Gregor, Ann	36	GB	378
Charles	40	GB	378
Gregory, Philip	14	DE	382
Grenage, Georgeana	10	DE	313
James	8	DE	313
James	31	DE	313
Sally A	28	DE	313
William	6	DE	313
Grennage, Sarah	17	DE	323
Grenn, Ann C	4	DE	364
Ellen	31	DE	364
John J	52	DE	364
Thomas M	2	DE	364
Grenville, William	3/12	DE	61
Grey, Alexander	24	MD	363
Anna L	9/12	DE	363
James	10	DE	230
Joseph W	2	DE	363
Margaret	22	DE	363
Grible, Josephine	10	DE	274
Louisa	12	PA	274
Susan	40	PA	274
Grice, John	20	GB	24
Grieg, Robert	20	DE	343
Samuel	18	DE	343
Grier, Charles	16	NJ	165
David	24	IE	156
Esther	49	DE	359
Jane	20	IE	161
Mary	1	IE	256
Mary	14	IE	143
Sarah	24	IE	256
Griffe, Sarah	18	DE	10
Griffen, Mary	20	IE	342
Peter	20	DE	330
Griffenberg, Chris-			
tina	24	DE	176
Lydia M	18	DE	176
William T	1	DE	176
Griffeth, Edmond	30	DE	109
Hugh	56	WL	45
Margaret	23	DE	109
Mary	20	DE	109
Richard	25	PA	59
William D	3	DE	109
Griffett, Ann S	37	PA	60
Emma	8	PA	60
John W	33	PA	60
Mary	5	PA	60
William	10	PA	60
Griffin, Amelia	37	MD	371
Anna	8	DE	154
Anne	6/12	DE	116
Auther	19	DE	63
Asa	25	DE	384
Edward	2	DE	154
Eliza	9	DE	384
Elizabeth	6	DE	63
Emma	16	DE	30
George	34	DE	299
George W	15	DE	34
Harriet	5	DE	63
Henrietta	24	MD	116
Henry B	6	DE	154
Hiller J	3	DE	116
Isaac	1	DE	384
Jacob	11	DE	154
Jacob	12	DE	319
Jane	24	IE	299
Jane	43	DE	384
John	9	MD	153
John	21	DE	84
John	28	DE	116
Joseph	7	DE	384
Lofley	17	DE	384
Griffett, Lofley	68	DE	384
Maria	16	DE	63
Mary	5	PA	61
Priscilla	75	DE	33
Rebecca	30	DE	63
Samuel	80	DE	33
Sarah	50	NJ	30
Sarah A	32	DE	154
Sarah E	4	DE	154
Thomas	61	DE	30
W H	35	DE	154
William	5	DE	384
William	2	PA	299
Griffinby, Edwin C	4	DE	114
Ella	1	DE	114
Hannah S	28	DE	114
William F	27	PA	114
Griffith, Agnes	56	PA	333
Anna A	10	DE	358
David	1	DE	308
David	24	DE	262
Elizabeth	20	DE	333
Irvin G	17	DE	333
James	8	DE	308
James	43	DE	330
Jane J	27	PA	346
John	24	DE	348
Joseph	13	DE	333
Joseph	57	DE	333
Mr	65	DE	15
Mrs	62	DE	15
Richard	24	DE	309
Robert S	22	DE	333
Ruth	70	DE	330
William	73	DE	351
Griffiths, Charles	12	DE	194
Eliza A	14	DE	194
Griffitt, Debro	53	DE	58
Rebecca	22	PA	58
Grig, John	20	DE	318
Grimes, Amelia	28	DE	379
Benjamin	10	DE	229
Catherine	16	GE	49
Frederic	39	GE	49
George	3	DE	314
George	10	DE	291
George	14	DE	229
Isaiah	13	DE	298
James	4/12	DE	314
James	24	DE	229
John	2	DE	353
John	21	DE	229
John	25	DE	353
Joseph	23	DE	311
Joseph	25	DE	303
Joseph	60	DE	254
Joseph T	5	DE	379
Lewis	6	DE	353
Lucy	21	DE	303
Martha F	8	DE	229
Mary A	20	DE	312
Mary Ann	4	DE	353
Mary E	16	DE	229
Mary J	19	DE	21
Mary L	1	DE	379
Nancy	55	DE	254
Rebecca	29	DE	314
Robert	27	DE	314
Thomas	1	DE	312
Thomas	24	DE	312
Samuel	35	DE	379
Sarah	12	DE	380
Sarah	20	DE	303
Sarah Ann	29	DE	353
Susan	12	DE	298
Susanah	26	GE	49
Thomas	55	DE	252
William	24	MD	302
William	44	DE	353
William	49	DE	229
Grimshaw, Auther H	27	PA	69
Charlotta	36	PA	159

Name	Age	St	No.	Name	Age	St	No.	Name	Age	St	No.
Grimshaw, Eliza	20	PA	159	Groves, Henrietta A	3	DE	379	Grubb, James	16	DE	281
Elizabeth	23	DE	69	James	30	NJ	270	James	35	DE	79
Isabella	25	PA	159	James	36	DE	384	James	45	DE	288
Margaret A	3/12	DE	124	James H	9/12	DE	331	James	65	DE	27
Mary	2	DE	124	James H	13	DE	322	James Sr	37	DE	145
Grinage, Sarah	17	DE	324	Jane	14	DE	344	James T	4	DE	145
Grindage, Amelia	22	MD	328	John A	16	DE	322	James W	13	DE	288
Charlotte A	40	MD	328	John T	7	DE	379	John	24	DE	292
James H	2	DE	328	Jonathan	14	DE	292	John B	19	DE	288
John	50	MD	328	Jonathan	30	DE	95	John E	33	DE	272
Sarah C	4	DE	328	Jonathan	39	DE	379	John S	9	DE	115
William	35	MD	328	Joseph	5	DE	378	John S	9	DE	145
Grindle, Amelia	20	DE	98	Lucretia	26	NJ	270	John W	6	DE	281
Anna E	23	DE	98	Margaret J	9	DE	379	Joseph	53	DE	289
Maria	19	DE	98	Mary	11	DE	322	Joseph L	22	DE	289
Mathew	50	DE	98	Mary J	22	DE	95	Julia A	53	DE	281
Griner, John	32	GE	142	Mitchell	26	DE	253	Kesiah	70	DE	289
Grise, John	11	DE	189	Richard	3	DE	331	Kesiah B	23	DE	278
Grobe, Abby	26	PA	114	Richard	4	DE	322	Larkin	4	DE	281
Charles	35	GE	114	Richard	30	DE	23	Letha W	1	DE	278
Groff, Beulah	24	DE	28	Richard	45	DE	322	Lewis	18	DE	27
Grogan, John	15	IE	164	Robert	1	DE	322	Lewis T	23	PA	278
William	25	IE	164	Samuel	5	DE	270	Louisa	5	DE	132
Grogen, Michel	22	IE	153	Sarah	5	DE	331	Martha J	1	DE	79
Groom, Charles	15	DE	24	Sarah	27	DE	330	Martin	22	PA	260
Charles	50	MD	24	Sarah	32	DE	378	Mary	10	DE	288
Margaret	20	DE	24	Sarah E	16	DE	378	Mary E	5	DE	79
Sarah	18	DE	24	Taylor	7	DE	362	Mary E	10	DE	289
Groome, Caroline	20	DE	74	Thomas	21	DE	256	Mary J	33	DE	363
Samuel	21	DE	74	Virginia	6	DE	385	Matilda	50	DE	281
Grose, Adaline	9	DE	183	William	2	DE	270	Moses	21	DE	27
Amanda	14	DE	185	William F	10/12	DE	379	Priscilla	19	DE	281
Charles W	6	DE	200	William F	7	DE	378	Prudence	16	DE	281
Charlotte	30	Md	200	Grubb, Adam	30	DE	305	Rachel	2	DE	281
Eliza Jane	9	DE	185	Adam	63	DE	281	Rachel H	29	DE	305
Elizabeth	49	DE	185	Alfred	16	PA	310	Rebecca	20	DE	289
Jacob	54	DE	185	Ann	40	PA	27	Rebecca	45	NJ	285
James H	2	DE	200	Ann	43	DE	288	Samuel	37	DE	281
James M	13	DE	185	Ann E	3	DE	281	Sarah	34	DE	272
John W	8	DE	200	Anna A	43	PA	281	Sarah Bella	4/12	DE	272
Leona	17	DE	185	Anna M	4	DE	272	Sarah S	15	DE	288
Phillip J	23	DE	185	Anna N	21	DE	281	Susan	50	DE	20
Rachel B	11	DE	185	Anna Maria	50	DE	281	Thomas J	4	DE	79
Robert	35	DE	200	Anne	32	DE	79	Wellington	38	DE	132
Sarah C	4	DE	200	Anne E	41	DE	132	William	6	DE	281
Susan	40	DE	183	Bayard	46	DE	281	William	9	DE	27
Wilson	4	DE	183	Beulah A	5	DE	288	William A	2	DE	288
Wilson	40	MD	183	Beulah C	8	DE	290	William A	17	DE	289
Gross, Catharine	50	GE	46	Buleah	35	DE	132	Grubby, William	21	GB	301
Elizabeth	9	OH	132	Catherine	11	DE	335	Gruby, Ephraim	18	GB	310
Lewis G	6	DE	132	Charles	15	PA	357	Hannah	6/12	DE	310
Maria L	3	DE	132	Charles C	11/12	DE	281	Hannah	40	GB	310
Mary	5	DE	258	Charles E	12	DE	281	Phebe	16	GB	310
Mary	18	OH	132	Clementine B	17	PA	166	Thomas	45	GB	310
Sally C	14	OH	132	Curtis	56	PA	285	Walter	8	GB	310
Susan	40	DE	132	Edmond W	7	DE	305	William	21	GB	310
Grove, Byard	15	DE	318	Edward	6	DE	363	Grye, John	21	DE	11
Donelson	3	DE	23	Edward	7	DE	288	Guest, Alfred W	12	DE	290
Eli	13	DE	318	Elener	30	DE	145	Bayard	20	DE	290
Hanson	7	DE	318	Eliza	20	IE	27	Henrietta	17	DE	290
James	6/12	DE	23	Eliza C L	12	DE	132	James H	15	DE	290
Mary	53	DE	318	Eliza J	2	DE	288	Joseph	45	DE	290
Nathan	65	MD	318	Elizabeth	22	DE	27	Maria	44	DE	290
Grover, Catherine	28	IE	305	Elizabeth	55	DE	281	Martha	8	DE	290
George	30	IE	305	Ellen	2	DE	79	Gui, Eliza	14	DE	320
Martha	1	DE	305	Ellen B	17	DE	288	Enoch	16	DE	320
Groves, Abraham	18	DE	376	Evan	6	DE	27	Guile, Elenora	83	PA	341
Andrew	30	DE	330	Francis H	18	DE	281	Guin, William	34	MD	323
Andrew J	12	DE	379	George	1	DE	27	Guiney, John	31	PA	344
Ann	25	DE	249	George	30	DE	363	Guinn, Charles	25	DE	97
Ann B	34	MD	322	George	40	DE	27	David	6	DE	287
Benjamin	14	DE	322	George W	24	DE	289	Samuel	15	DE	230
Benjamin	25	DE	292	Hannah	35	DE	289	Guire, Amanda	19	DE	114
Benjamin	33	DE	378	Hannah	50	DE	289	Edwin B	24	DE	114
Charles H	5	DE	380	Hannah	61	PA	279	Guirey, John M	30	PA	368
Elizabeth	28	DE	23	Hannah E	15	DE	289	Mary Y	29	MA	368
Elizabeth	36	DE	379	Harriet	21	PA	56	William P	1	DE	368
Elizabeth R	3	DE	378	Hetty R	5	DE	363	Guirick, Thos	60	IE	284
Emeline	36	DE	384	Ignacious	9	DE	132	Guise, Elizabeth	60	DE	338
Emma F	7	DE	322	Isaac	30	DE	289	Gully, Joseph	37	FR	153
George	7/12	DE	270	Isaac H	26	DE	281	Gumnire, Caroline	14	PA	165
George W	14	DE	379	Jacob	9	DE	281	Gun, Darius	30	IE	285

Name	Age	Code	No.
Gun, David	18	IE	108
John	55	IE	108
Mary	21	IE	108
Mary E	15	IE	108
Ruth	49	IE	108
Ruth A	13	IE	108
Sarah	81	IE	108
Thomas	11	IE	108
William	21	IE	108
Gunison, Mary	30	NJ	180
Gunn, John	58	IE	188
Gusters, Albert	40	DE	204
Johnston	2	DE	204
Latitia	35	DE	204
Guthre, James	24	PA	100
William J	2	DE	100
Guthrie, Alexander	33	DE	386
Alexander	55	DE	363
Alexander	62	DE	379
Ann	6	DE	369
Ann	51	DE	379
Ann E	9	DE	379
Benjamin	9	DE	369
Benjamin	32	MD	369
Biddy	15	IE	343
Catharine	18	IE	343
Catherine	12	DE	97
Elizabeth	25	DE	363
Elizabeth	29	DE	287
Elizabeth	50	DE	363
Emely Ann	9	DE	363
Hannah	2	DE	386
Hannah	20	PA	100
John	2	DE	343
John	4	DE	386
John	11	DE	369
John	15	DE	363
John	28	DE	22
Joseph	19	DE	369
Joseph	25	DE	323
Margaret	72	DE	379
Maria	59	PA	287
Mary	15	IE	97
Mary	23	DE	22
Mary	39	IE	97
Mary	35	IE	343
Mary Ann	5	DE	386
Mary Anna	14	DE	287
Michael	12	IE	343
Michel	35	IE	97
Nancy	10	IE	343
Patrick	40	IE	343
Samuel	31	DE	387
Samuel J	18	DE	386
Sarah	42	DE	369
Simon	30	DE	363
Sophia	5	DE	369
Susan	21	DE	386
Susan	27	DE	287
William	12	DE	363
William	60	DE	287
Guy, Abby	35	DE	257
Abraham	7	DE	242
Amanda	6	DE	257
David	3	DE	257
Elizabeth	16	DE	257
Enoch	48	DE	257
Hannah	8	DE	257
Hannah	55	DE	231
Isaiah	1	DE	257
Joseph	16	DE	231
Mary	11	DE	257
Mary A	30	IE	205
Mary E	8	DE	242
Warner	35	IE	205
Habon, Anna M	33	PA	376
Hack, John	12	DE	326
Hacket, Alexander	22	MD	102
Benjamin	23	DE	264
Charles	2	DE	326
Charles	5	DE	54
Hacket, Frederic	27	IE	24
Hannah	39	NJ	54
Harriett	18	MD	326
Henny	35	MD	326
Hester	10	MD	326
Hester	35	DE	24
Jessean	12	DE	54
Maria	15	DE	102
Mary	15	PA	54
Mary	19	MD	102
Mary	50	DE	102
Michael	30	IE	326
Robert	2/12	DE	326
Sally A	16	MD	102
Samuel	8	MD	326
Samuel	40	MD	326
William	9	DE	54
William	43	PA	54
Hackett, Betsey	17	DE	212
Eletha	63	PA	250
Ella	6	DE	212
Henry	9	DE	216
Hester	25	DE	172
John	25	DE	172
Samuel	14	DE	213
Sarah	18	DE	215
Hackman, William D	9	PA	279
Hackson, Sarah E	4	DE	222
Hadden, Cornelia	11	DE	29
Elizabeth	40	GB	373
Emma	7	DE	29
Isabella	4	DE	29
J L	39	DE	29
James	22	DE	369
John W	20	DE	191
Sally	30	DE	29
Haddoc, Ellen S	11	MD	137
Hannah	59	PA	139
Henry	24	PA	32
James A	2	DE	118
Louisa	26	MD	118
Mary A	17	PA	139
Robert	18	MD	118
Samuel	30	MD	118
Haden, Ann	50	IE	366
Edward	50	IE	366
Haffeny, Mary	52	IE	16
Sarah	28	DE	204
Hagan, Andrew	7	DE	38
Bridget	13	IE	319
David	40	DE	38
Hannah	32	DE	38
John	13	PA	164
John	23	IE	347
Michael	17	IE	384
Hage, Eliza M	45	MD	152
Margaret E	17	MD	152
Sarah A	19	MD	152
Hagerman, Christopher	15	PA	297
Hiram	11	PA	297
Jane	44	PA	296
Jane A	18	PA	296
Jehu	21	PA	296
John	47	PA	296
Lewis	4	PA	297
Margaret	9	PA	297
Robert	7	PA	297
Hagerty, Alexander	25	IE	330
Chas	23	IE	274
James	18	IE	335
John	16	IE	323
Sarah E	18	GB	330
Haggan, John	23	PA	338
Margaret	18	IE	347
Michael	17	DE	383
Haggard, Caroline	18	DE	297
Haggerty, George	50	IE	341
John	20	IE	341
Mary	24	IE	341
Mary Sal	29	IE	341
Haggery, Anne	11	DE	31
Haggery, Ellen	4/12	DE	31
Eliza L	6	DE	31
George	36	DE	31
Margaret	25	IE	28
Mary A	28	DE	19
Robert	10	DE	31
Sarah	35	DE	31
Sarah	8	DE	31
William	28	DE	19
Hague, Hannah	54	GB	332
John	57	GB	332
Matilda	21	GB	332
Sarah	33	GB	332
Susan	15	GB	332
Haigens, Eliza	15	MD	166
Julia	17	MD	166
Haines, Ann	8	DE	365
Ann	57	NJ	189
Arthur G	1	DE	302
Caroline	1	DE	288
Elizabeth	5	DE	176
Eri M	26	MD	389
John	35	DE	176
Joseph	7	DE	176
Joshua	27	NJ	302
Mary	29	DE	176
Mary E	4	DE	288
Rebecca	29	DE	288
Sarah	21	NJ	302
Sarah E	27	NY	389
Thomas	2	DE	176
William	30	DE	288
Hains, Mary	50	DE	323
Hainsworth, Henry J	27	MD	145
Sarah A	26	MD	145
William H	2	DE	145
Hair, Aaron	47	?	359
Ann	17	?	359
Bridget	30	IE	63
Catherine	1	DE	63
Catherine	19	?	359
Edward	5	PA	63
Egbert	23	?	359
Emily	2	?	359
Frederick	21	?	359
Hannah	43	?	359
John	1	DE	63
John	3	DE	165
John	32	IE	63
Jones	8	?	359
Mary	3	DE	63
Mary	27	IE	19
Mary	31	DE	81
Phebe	13	?	359
Haire, Abigal	35	DE	106
Anna	2	DE	106
William	35	PA	106
William B	7	DE	106
Haistings, Abby	32	DE	48
Elizabeth	21	DE	48
Jesse	69	MD	48
Mary	19	DE	48
Washington	12	DE	48
Hale, Alfred	40	DE	345
John	1	DE	192
Lydia	7	DE	379
Richard	35	DE	188
Wesley	23	DE	207
Haley, Richard	19	MD	267
Hall, Abner A	7	DE	230
Albert	6	DE	19
Amanda	35	DE	19
Angelina	7	DE	301
Ann	13	DE	301
Ann	69	DE	300
Ann Louisa	4	DE	230
Caroline	10	DE	174
Caroline	24	FR	209
Charles	17	DE	265
Charles	60	GB	310
Cornelia	2	DE	155
David	18	DE	233

Name	Age	St	Pg
Hall, David	28	GB	22
Dorcas	15	DE	155
Edward	2	DE	137
Edward	35	DE	277
Eliza	25	DE	198
Eliza	44	DE	378
Eliza J	12	DE	209
Eliza L	17	DE	166
Elizabeth	45	DE	243
Elizabeth	54	PA	149
Ellen	15	DE	301
Emily H	24	MD	209
Emma	2	DE	19
Ephina	15	DE	354
George	22	NJ	265
George	35	DE	198
George P	24	DE	378
George W	35	DE	243
Hannah A	32	MD	277
Harriet H	51	DE	160
Henrietta	15	PA	160
Henry	22	MD	341
Hester	2	DE	209
James	12	DE	353
James	15	DE	359
James B	34	DE	230
James H	5	DE	209
Jane	14	DE	359
Jane	25	IE	34
Jane	3	IE	265
John	5	DE	301
John	14	DE	200
John	26	DE	19
John	29	DE	381
John	36	IE	301
John	50	DE	160
John	51	DE	392
John T	2	DE	381
John T	48	NJ	265
Joseph	4	DE	19
Joseph A	50	PA	64
Joseph L	35	MD	19
Julia A	33	PA	230
Julia V	2/12	DE	230
Letitia C	9	DE	19
Margaret	20	DE	265
Margaret	45	NJ	265
Margaret	51	DE	376
Maria	5/12	DE	22
Martha	22	DE	155
Martha	50	DE	220
Martha J	19	DE	380
Mary	60	MD	380
Mary A	19	DE	378
Mary C	7	DE	301
Mary D	10	MD	277
Mary E	10/12	DE	381
Mary E	1	DE	278
Matilda	18	DE	155
Narcissa	12	PA	160
Orpha	45	PA	160
Perry	16	DE	202
Perry	30	DE	209
Perry	60	PA	359
Rebecca	24	DE	381
Rebecca	28	DE	19
Rebecca	32	DE	137
Robert	2	DE	301
Robert C	3	DE	277
Rufus	15	DE	293
Rufus W	7	DE	378
Sabina	40	DE	155
Sally	10	DE	268
Samuel	12	DE	359
Samuel	59	MD	149
Samuel J	22	DE	149
Sarah	10	DE	301
Sarah	14	DE	233
Sarah	15	DE	19
Sarah	38	DE	301
Sarah	50	DE	359
Sarah E	2	DE	230
Hall, Sevin W	35	DE	244
Susan	10	DE	359
Susanah	22	PA	22
Thomas	18	DE	349
Thomas F	28	PA	160
Uriah	7	DE	265
Willard	69	MA	160
William	5	DE	380
William	12	DE	198
William	20	PA	160
William	23	DE	381
Hallam, Isaac H	22	DE	317
Mary	49	DE	317
Sarah A	24	PA	24
Thomas	52	DE	317
Robert	23	GB	309
Halldeson, John W	20	DE	190
Hallet, Mary	7	DE	383
Halley, Ann	6	PA	335
Edward	5·	PA	335
Ellen	22	IE	335
James	4	DE	335
James	29	IE	335
John	2	DE	335
William	5/12	DE	335
Hallman, Ann B	23	PA	320
Anthony	30	DE	320
Eliza	5	DE	320
Ellen J	4	DE	320
John C	1	DE	320
Hallowell, Jane	51	PA	324
Jesse	53	PA	324
Joseph	8	DE	324
Rebecca	11	PA	324
Hallum, Isaac	22	NY	44
Hamar, Laurence	17	PA	2
Hamby, Thomas	36	IE	347
Hamel, George	11	DE	331
Hannah	65	DE	331
Hannah A	13	DE	331
Joseph	12	DE	331
Mary J	12	DE	331
Rebecca J	4	DE	331
S D	42	DE	331
William	2	DE	331
Hamen, Rebecca	53	DE	380
Hamilton, Alexander	24	DE	13
Ann	32	DE	4
Ann E	10	DE	361
Anne P	34	DE	182
Asbury	38	DE	237
Biddy	25	IE	185
Caroline	3	DE	318
Caroline N	1	DE	174
Catherine	36	DE	234
Courtland C	6	DE	372
David	4	DE	219
David	25	DE	172
Edward	4	DE	4
Edward	11	MD	357
Eli	35	MD	357
Elias	4	DE	237
Eliza	16	MD	357
Eliza B	34	DE	237
Eliza C	4	PA	174
Eliza Jane	1	PA	185
Elizabeth	77	MD	318
Elizabeth	7	DE	182
Emma	9	DE	298
George H	15	PA	164
George W	11	DE	372
Hannah E	5	DE	318
Isaac	10	DE	318
Jacob	16	DE	215
James	1	DE	234
James	2	DE	219
James	15	DE	301
James	16	PA	101
James	26	DE	234
James	28	DE	296
James N	2	DE	183
James N	41	PA	280
Hamilton, Jane	3/12	DE	107
Jane	3	DE	234
Jane	77	IE	352
John	11	DE	219
John	11	DE	298
John L	8	DE	234
John M	12	DE	312
John M	30	PA	182
Joseph	27	DE	318
Joseph	38	PA	372
Josephine	4	DE	312
June	12	DE	4
Leah	5/12	DE	219
Leah	39	DE	219
Louisa A	1	DE	312
Margaret	15	PA	166
Maria	18	DE	4
Maria	21	NJ	295
Martha	20	IE	336
Martha	21	PA	101
Martha A	5	DE	182
Mary	16	DE	367
Mary	18	PA	101
Mary	21	DE	107
Mary	37	DE	56
Mary	38	MD	313
Mary	49	PA	101
Mary A	9	DE	312
Mary E	5	DE	237
Mary J	19	DE	241
Mary U	30	DE	174
Matilda	7	DE	318
Michel	16	DE	4
Nancy	14	PA	101
Perry	1	DE	318
Perry	39	DE	219
Perry Jr	8	DE	219
Perry H	6	DE	314
Rachel	7/12	DE	296
Rachel	12	PA	101
Robert	15	DE	247
Robert	24	DE	107
Rosanna	36	MD	312
Samuel	2	DE	4
Sarah	6	DE	219
Sarah	10	DE	218
Sarah	14	DE	4
Sarah	14	DE	132
Sarah	16	NJ	296
Sarah	32	DE	318
Sarah A	34	DE	372
Sarah J	13	PA	166
Sarah M	4	DE	183
Susan	40	DE	314
Susan	59	DE	301
Thomas	28	DE	125
Thos	24	IE	329
William	9	MD	357
William	10	PA	101
William	21	DE	295
William	34	DE	234
William	41	MD	312
William	46	DE	313
William	50	IE	101
William Jr	5	DE	234
William N	34	PA	174
Zenus	12	DE	129
Hamm, Charles	16	DE	206
Elias	20	DE	336
Margaret	62	DE	37
Hamman, Jacob	20	DE	349
Hammer, Emma	20	PA	356
Hammett, Charles	17	NJ	14
Edmond	25	NJ	14
Emaline	22	NJ	14
Rebecca	15	NJ	14
Rebecca	49	NJ	14
Thadeus	20	NJ	14
Thomas	18	NJ	14
Thomas	56	NJ	14
Hammon, Anna J	5	DE	97
Charles H	11	DE	97

Name	Age	St	Pg
Hammon, Eliza	25	PA	97
Emily	3	DE	98
George	39	PA	97
James	1	DE	97
John P	13	DE	97
Mary	25	DE	97
Mary A	16	DE	97
William	19	DE	97
Hammond, Cheny	21	PA	43
Elizabeth	26	NJ	199
Samuel W	24	DE	320
Sarah	49	DE	205
Hammonds, Craig	34	PA	340
James	30	GB	295
Hammons, Elizabeth	1	DE	298
Ellen	25	IE	340
John	44	GB	298
Martha	39	GB	298
Hamner, John	30	IE	93
Margaret	5	IE	93
Margaret	25	IE	93
William	3	DE	93
Hamon, Akin	9	DE	329
Edmond	10	DE	329
Emily	5	DE	329
James	14	DE	329
John	2	DE	329
Mary A	34	DE	329
Hampton, David	25	PA	14
Edward	1	DE	14
Elizabeth	6	DE	216
Hannah	20	PA	14
Isaac	35	DE	216
Sarah A	23	DE	216
Walter S	3	PA	282
Han, Hetty	46	DE	97
Hanager, James	21	IE	356
Hanaway, Patrick	45	IE	250
Hanby, Adam F	17	DE	280
Ann	36	PA	280
Ann	40	DE	281
Anna E	2	DE	280
Catherine L	24	DE	272
Charity	68	DE	279
Charlotte	8	DE	280
Curtis C	1	DE	279
Elias	1	DE	272
Eliza	30	PA	280
Eliza A	7	DE	281
George	7	DE	279
Harrott J	17	DE	280
Jacob H	10	DE	280
James B	19	DE	281
James G	40	DE	280
James W	2	DE	272
John	22	DE	280
John A	11	DE	281
John L	9	DE	280
John W	13	DE	281
John W	34	DE	279
Joseph	30	DE	272
Louisa J	4/12	DE	281
Malenda	5	DE	279
Margaret	14	DE	281
Mary E	2	DE	280
Mary E	9	DE	281
Mary J	14	DE	279
Priscilla	4	DE	281
Priscilla	45	DE	280
Rachel A	10	DE	280
Richard	48	DE	281
Robert A	16	DE	281
Samuel	2	DE	281
Samuel	32	DE	280
Samuel W	5/12	DE	280
Sarah A	34	DE	279
Sarah E	12	DE	279
Susan A	7	DE	282
Vilette	3	DE	279
William	44	DE	279
William	45	DE	280
William E	7	DE	280
Hanby, William H	14	DE	280
Hance, Amanda	7	DE	303
Charles	8	DE	64
Charles	14	DE	324
Charles	60	MD	189
Edward B	27	DE	381
Eliza	23	DE	381
Eliza	32	DE	64
Hester A	13	DE	276
Isabella	17	DE	276
Jeremiah	15	DE	256
Jeremiah	15	DE	276
John	35	DE	64
John L	2/12	DE	381
Mary	9	DE	189
Millicent B	3	DE	381
Minte	35	DE	189
Perry	16	DE	276
Hancock, George	3	DE	278
Mary	26	PA	278
Hand, Alexander	3	DE	277
Alexander	14	DE	277
Alexander	53	IE	277
Elizabeth	15	DE	100
Emily J	4/12	DE	277
Isaac	4	DE	277
Isaac	27	DE	277
James A	6	DE	277
John	25	DE	277
Mary	1	DE	277
Patrick	29	DE	277
Rachel	29	DE	277
Rebecca	5	DE	279
Rebecca	52	DE	277
Willamina	6	DE	277
Handling, Thomas	19	IE	358
Handocerty, Edward	4	IE	37
Joseph	20	IE	37
Mary	65	IE	37
Thomas	19	IE	37
Handy, Adeline	1	DE	290
Anna	7	DE	140
Benjamin R	29	DE	388
Charles H	2	PA	150
Cornelia	22	DE	140
Dorcas	50	DE	101
Edwin W	6	DE	387
Eliza	40	DE	167
Elizabeth	5	DE	290
Gertrude E	5	MD	181
Henry	27	DE	368
Isaac W H	34	DC	181
Jane	35	MD	388
John	6	DE	383
John	24	IE	150
John	25	DE	140
John	30	DE	55
John	30	DE	160
John	32	DE	374
John	33	MD	155
Joseph	8	DE	92
Josephine	12	DE	290
Kettie	60	MD	290
Kitty	30	DE	368
Margaret	23	MD	155
Maria	30	DE	387
Maria C	22	IE	150
Maria V P	9	MD	181
Martha R	27	MD	181
Mary	26	DE	59
Moses P	4	MO	181
Rachel	15	DE	290
Rachel	16	DE	101
Rachel	40	MD	290
Sallie M	31	MD	181
Sarah	20	DE	92
Sarah A	65	MD	388
Sarah E	1	DE	268
Tabitha	45	DE	54
Thomas	4/12	DE	59
Thomas	25	DE	59
Thomas	73	MD	388
Handy, William	7	DE	290
William	8	DE	383
William	10	DE	92
William	22	DE	290
Zederic N Y	8	MD	181
Hanes, Mary	38	FR	50
Hanghan, Ann	22	IE	366
Hanie, Edward B	27	NJ	382
Eliza	23	NJ	382
John L	2/12	DE	382
Millicent B	3	DE	382
Hankens, Frances	6	DE	222
Martha L	2	DE	222
Mary	25	DE	222
Hanking, Columbus	23	NJ	385
Hankins, Henry	18	DE	297
Henry	27	DE	188
Martha	16	NJ	239
Priscilla	20	NJ	239
Richard	12	DE	246
Hann, E A	30	DE	196
Elizabeth	4	DE	196
John	31	DE	196
Jonathan	1	DE	196
Mary	33	PA	196
Hanna, Ann	45	DE	374
Benjamin	48	DE	374
Elizabeth	5	DE	177
Emma	20	DE	374
John	35	DE	177
Joseph	7	DE	177
Mary	29	DE	177
Thomas B	2	DE	177
Hannah, Alfred	12	DE	355
Eliza	38	DE	359
Frederick	35	GE	262
Georgianna	5	DE	359
James	22	DE	367
James	20	DE	37
Jane	41	IE	37
John	9	DE	359
John	22	DE	355
John	73	DE	356
Joseph	17	DE	355
Lea	50	DE	355
Lewis	23	DE	359
Lydia R	16	DE	323
Margaret E	8	DE	359
Martha L	26	PA	356
Mary	30	GE	262
Mary E	6	DE	356
Mary J	1	DE	359
Mary L	4	DE	356
Robert	21	DE	86
Robert	40	DE	359
Samuel	36	DE	356
Thomas	20	DE	355
Thomas	54	DE	355
William	15	DE	37
William F	11	DE	359
Hannan, Patrick	28	IE	347
Hannett, Mary	20	DE	333
Hannon, Ann	30	IE	300
John	20	DE	371
Hannum, Elizabeth	20	DE	272
Kezia	39	DE	272
Thomas	13	DE	272
Hans, Alexander	18	DE	314
Hansan, Abraham	26	GB	14
Hansen, Elizabeth	50	DE	190
Elizabeth T	45	DE	286
James T	33	DE	105
Mary A	22	DC	309
Hansley, Amos	35	DE	275
Ann	70	DE	275
Hanson, Abigal	8	DE	92
Alice	20	DE	286
Ann	30	DE	192
Ann E	36	MD	191
Ann J	4	MD	195
Augustus	30	GE	6
Benjamin	7	DE	93

Name	Age	St	Pg	Name	Age	St	Pg	Name	Age	St	Pg
Hanson, Benjamin	25	DE	248	Harden, Matilda	30	MD	145	Harman, David	10	DE	395
Benjamin P	3	MD	195	Mr	30	IE	163	David	48	DE	387
Benjamin S	31	MD	195	Rachel	30	DE	160	Edward	3	DE	388
Charles	17	DE	248	Rachel	50	DE	101	Edward	12	DE	393
Edmund	10	DE	328	Ralph	77	DE	65	Edward	14	DE	380
Eleanor	46	MD	175	Thomas	60	MD	101	Elizabeth	14	DE	104
Ellen	35	DE	197	Wesley	16	DE	160	George W	7	DE	5
Emily	18	DE	286	Harding, Ailsie	45	DE	377	Hannah	2	DE	314
Enoch	2	DE	156	Mary	60	DE	221	Hannah M	11	DE	382
George	1	DE	279	James	55	DE	354	Hanson	21	DE	104
George	25	DE	310	Julia	18	DE	282	Harriet	18	DE	293
Ingeber	26	DE	310	Temperance	54	DE	354	Isaac	18	DE	303
James	10	DE	279	Wilkin	13	DE	377	Israel A	15	DE	328
James	14	DE	328	Hardy, George	17	DE	364	Jacob	2	DE	314
James	33	MD	173	Harriet	25	DE	346	Jacob	26	DE	314
James	47	DE	279	James	28	DE	346	Jacob	40	DE	104
James H	9	DE	173	John	19	DE	117	James	4	DE	5
John	4	DE	279	Joseph	25	GB	311	James	23	DE	380
John	30	DE	192	Maria	17	DE	305	Jane	12	DE	104
John	30	DE	205	Hare, Mary	24	IE	309	Jane	39	DE	104
Jonathan	11	DE	173	Hargrove, John H	14	VA	400	Jemima	24	MD	5
Joseph	5	DE	207	William W	16	VA	400	Jeremiah	40	DE	382
Joseph	29	PA	207	Harken, Grace	18	IE	298	John	4	DE	383
Joseph	40	DE	197	Harker, Alena	10	DE	126	John	8	DE	388
Joseph H	19	DE	227	Barney	14	DE	348	John	21	DE	382
Letitia A	4	DE	97	Charles	5	DE	126	Jonathan	26	DE	293
Margaret	30	NJ	250	Ellen J	40	DE	126	Joseph	19	DE	104
Mary	9	DE	250	John N	44	DE	126	Joshua	7/12	DE	314
Mary	20	PA	98	Laura	9	DE	126	Lemuel	10	DE	5
Mary	25	PA	195	Mary	49	NJ	32	Levi	3	DE	5
Mary	30	DE	185	Samuel	7	DE	126	Levi	30	DE	5
Mary	60	DE	310	Harkings, James	30	IE	308	Liza	3	DE	293
Mary A	13	DE	279	Margaret	30	IE	308	Margaret A	9	DE	5
Mary A	34	DE	328	Harkins, Anthony	7/12	DE	51	Maria	49	DE	382
Mary B	32	DE	207	Catherine	26	IE	51	Martha H	30	DE	328
Peter	12	DE	175	Fanny	50	IE	51	Mary A	35	PA	355
Phoebe A	16	DE	201	James	2	DE	51	Mary E	17	DE	328
Richard F	32	DE	228	John	35	IE	51	Mary R	16	DE	332
Sarah	29	PA	279	Mary	30	IE	316	Matilda A	32	MD	387
Sarah	33	DE	173	Mary J	1	DE	316	Sally	7	DE	340
Sarah E	11	DE	279	Patric	35	IE	316	Sarah	11	DE	328
Susan	50	DE	178	Harkness, Ann	40	DE	352	Solomon	30	DE	17
Thomas P	25	DE	195	Catherine	3	DE	352	Thomas	17	DE	104
Thomas R	6	MD	195	Catherine	16	DE	363	William	11	DE	331
William	9	DE	279	Catherine	80	GE	352	William	26	DE	283
William	25	MD	195	Elizabeth	34	DE	352	Harmen, Harriet	6	DE	382
Wm	36	DE	250	James	13	DE	352	Mary	28	DE	382
Hapenny, Nicolas	24	IE	43	Mary A	11	DE	352	Rebecca	3	DE	382
Patric	18	IE	43	Rachel	4	DE	363	Samuel	4	DE	382
Harberson, Letitia	45	PA	104	Rachel	43	PA	363	William T	28	DE	382
Harbert, George	45	PA	319	Robert	10	DE	363	Harmon, Alfred	15	DE	309
George W	5	DE	319	Samuel	48	PA	363	Bradford	17	DE	309
Margaretta B	16	DE	319	Samuel	87	IE	352	Benjamin	7	DE	324
Martha A	3	DE	319	Sarah	8	DE	352	Benjamin	27	DE	319
Sarah	37	DE	319	Susan A	8	DE	363	Eliza	44	DE	183
Timothy C	16	DE	319	William	5	DE	352	George	16	DE	252
William H	10	DE	319	William	50	DE	352	George W	64	MD	183
Harbertson, Mary	18	NJ	31	Harlan, Rachel	40	DE	349	Isaac	20	DE	59
Harbus, Hannah	11	DE	90	Harland, Benjamin	19	DE	359	James	20	MD	325
Hardcastle, Adaline	15	NY	164	Harlen, Ann J	35	DE	142	Jemima	3	DE	313
Edgar	2	DE	148	C (Dr)	37	DE	32	John	4	DE	314
John	17	DE	202	Edith	31	DE	142	John	22	DE	59
John T	10	MD	148	Elgarda	7	DE	32	John	25	PA	313
Levina	20	NY	164	Eliza	40	DE	32	Mary	15	DE	59
Mary E	6	MD	148	Elizabeth	5	DE	32	Mary	23	DE	313
Peter	35	DE	148	John	79	DE	373	Mary Elizabeth	8	DE	182
Sarah E	8	MD	148	Joshua	67	DE	373	Matilda	11	DE	309
Thomas H	23	MD	362	Leah	60	PA	115	Minty	28	DE	317
Harde, Lydia	81	NJ	105	Mary A	29	DE	142	Rachel	32	DE	314
Harden, Andrew P	1	DE	102	Samuel	41	NY	42	Rebecca	1	DE	313
Ann	40	DE	102	Sarah	17	DE	42	Harmony, Patrick	45	DE	249
Anna	3	DE	65	Susan	39	PA	42	Harmsley, Henry	7/12	DE	88
Caroline	35	MD	11	Harman, Amanda	15	DE	389	Henry	35	DE	88
Elizabeth	35	DE	65	Amelia	5	DE	293	Sarah	22	DE	88
George	2	DE	65	Andrew	--	DE	290	Harner, Emeline	22	NJ	89
George	25	DE	322	Andrew	7	DE	388	Emma	9	DE	89
Jack	30	PA	92	Andrew	40	DE	328	Samuel	23	PA	89
James	21	DE	101	Ann E	13	DE	329	Harney, Ellen	39	IE	116
James	30	DE	11	Belinda	13	MD	6	Harno, Bidde	29	IE	155
Justinia	1	DE	65	Benjamin	7	DE	325	Catherine	6/12	DE	155
Mary	7	DE	65	Daniel	3	DE	6	George O	30	IE	155
Mary A	29	DE	92	David	5	DE	394	Hugh	8	IE	155

Name	Age	St	Pg
Harno, Mary	3	DE	155
Harns, Margaret	14	DE	70
Harod, Joseph	16	DE	385
Harp, Elizabeth	32	DE	134
Ellen	4	DE	134
Hannah	9	DE	134
John	36	DE	134
Sally A	13	DE	134
William	9	DE	134
Harpe, Catherine	9	DE	280
Eliza B	4	DE	280
Henry J	11/12	DE	280
Mary	38	DE	280
Mary A	8	DE	280
Robert	35	DE	280
Harper, Ann	29	DE	303
Barbary	3	DE	303
Charles	9/12	DE	303
Dennis B	3	DE	98
Edward	56	MD	98
Edward J	5	DE	98
Enoch	30	PA	356
Harriet A	24	DE	98
Isaac	32	NJ	303
Jasper	34	PA	275
John	6	DE	356
John	7	DE	375
Lemuel	18	PA	354
Mary A	12	DE	303
Moses C	10	DE	98
Samuel	2	DE	303
Sarah	31	DE	356
Sarah	57	DE	140
Sarah J	11	DE	303
Sarah J	20	DE	140
Simeon	18	PA	355
Susan A	47	DE	98
William	17	DE	98
Harrick, Jane	25	DE	123
John	22	GB	123
Harriett, Ann	55	DE	302
George	30	PA	302
Harriety, Edward	3	DE	150
Edward	40	IE	150
Ellen	30	IE	150
Margery A	10/12	DE	150
Harrigan, Catherine	30	IE	130
John	23	PA	171
Harriman, Edward	13	GB	163
Sarah E	37	MA	134
Harris, Abraham	9	DE	255
Adam	13	DE	193
Adam	35	DE	227
Albert	30	DE	189
Albert T	5	DE	99
Alexander	5/12	DE	46
Amore	16	NJ	129
Ann	20	DE	222
Ann	30	NY	82
Ann Jane	2	DE	209
Araminta	32	DE	145
Asbury	30	MD	191
Barry	50	DE	5
Benjamin	5	DE	208
Benjamin	11	DE	46
Benjamin	16	DE	222
Benjamin	22	GB	18
Caroline	22	NJ	129
Catherine	31	DE	99
Charles	47	DE	134
Charles E	8	PA	322
Charles W	13	MD	341
Cooper	14	DE	222
David	25	NY	181
Edgar V	10	DE	99
Eliza	13	DE	353
Eliza	25	DE	293
Eliza	30	DE	29
Elizabeth	6	DE	201
Elizabeth	12	DE	249
Elizabeth	13	DE	46
Elizabeth	70	DE	29
Harris, Felicia A	3	PA	82
Francis	8	DE	99
George	3	DE	222
George	17	DE	297
George	22	DE	189
George	29	MD	249
George	40	DE	364
George W	8	DE	233
Hannah J	19	DE	181
Harriet	22	DE	319
Harriet A	9	NJ	82
Helen A	4	DE	155
Hester	44	DE	157
Isaac	45	DE	46
Jacob	13	DE	157
Jacob	14	DE	255
Jacob	15	DE	258
Jacob	29	DE	235
Jacob	60	DE	240
Jacob	66	DE	322
James	4	DE	255
James	9	DE	364
James	23	DE	247
James	37	DE	222
James	43	DE	372
Jane	10	DE	183
John	4	DE	202
John	14	DE	318
John	21	DE	206
John	23	DE	5
John	25	DE	222
John	30	DE	99
John	70	DE	29
John W	18	DE	299
Joseph	11	DE	255
Kenard	7	DE	46
Kesiah	22	DE	29
Lavina	5	DE	372
Lavina	51	MD	372
Lavinia	55	MD	232
Lester A	1	DE	99
Letitia	13	DE	5
Levic	19	DE	364
Louisa	7	DE	372
Lydia A	1	DE	181
Margaret	23	DE	211
Margaret A	8	DE	201
Maria	35	DE	299
Maria	40	DE	255
Martha	9	DE	46
Martha	22	DE	222
Martin M B	13	DE	129
Mary	6	DE	341
Mary	12	DE	130
Mary	16	DE	253
Mary	24	DE	235
Mary	25	DE	201
Mary	28	DE	29
Mary	30	DE	322
Mary	35	DE	155
Mary	49	DE	5
Mary C	2	DE	235
Mary W	2/12	DE	222
Milly	9	DE	249
Perry	38	DE	201
Phebe	47	NJ	129
Rachel	50	DE	240
Rachel A	10	DE	157
Rebecca	21	DE	65
Rebecca	46	DE	134
Rebecca	60	DE	65
Robert	46	NJ	129
Samuel	9	DE	204
Samuel	17	DE	5
Samuel	48	DE	341
Samuel	50	DE	196
Sarah	7	DE	240
Sarah	16	DE	255
Sarah	26	DE	189
Sarah	28	MD	340
Sarah	38	DE	372
Sarah	43	DE	364
Harris, Sarah A	30	DE	249
Sarah A	38	NJ	372
Sarah B	18	DE	332
Sarah E	1	DE	157
Sarah L	1/12	DE	235
Stansbury	30	DE	299
Susan R	3/12	PA	82
Susanna	11	DE	364
Temperance	19	DE	222
Theodore	20	DE	189
Thomas	10	DE	201
Thomas	19	DE	5
Thomas	25	DE	256
Thomas	47	NY	82
Wesley A	7	NJ	82
Wilhelmina	12	DE	318
William	3	DE	46
William	5	NJ	82
William	20	MD	191
William	36	DE	372
William	44	DE	157
William H	9	DE	157
Wm	1	DE	255
Zachary	2	DE	341
Harrison, Benjamin	12	NY	104
Benjamin	50	GB	104
Charles H	19	MD	238
Eliza A	5	MD	239
Emeline	29	DE	327
George	12	DE	366
Harriet	21	GB	366
Henrietta	40	DE	327
James	45	MD	238
John	23	GB	104
Joseph	3	MD	238
Levi	22	MD	238
Lucy	25	GB	104
Martha	22	DE	327
Mary A	24	MD	238
Mathew	22	IE	373
Mathew	36	IE	346
Robert	16	MD	238
Robert	30	DE	327
Sarah	16	NY	104
Sarah A	22	MD	238
Sarah J	4	MD	238
William	34	GB	366
Harriss, Abraham	60	DE	368
Sarah	19	DE	368
Sarah	55	DE	368
Harrity, James T	1	DE	120
Jane A	25	IE	120
Michel	36	IE	120
Harrold, ___	47	DE	174
Margaret F	47	DE	174
Harry, Mary	12	DE	368
Hart, Alexander	13	IE	28
Alexander	13	IE	156
Ann	2	DE	11
Benjamin G	2	DE	5
Charles	39	MD	5
Charles	56	DE	298
Charles A	10	PA	5
Edward	28	IE	11
Eli	16	DE	233
Elizabeth	25	MD	177
Elizabeth	69	DE	241
Elizabeth	70	DE	222
Ellen	23	IE	84
Emily L	9	IE	156
George	25	DE	123
George	56	PA	299
Henry	1	DE	299
Isabella	58	PA	151
Jacob	19	DE	151
James	11	IE	156
James	33	DE	284
James	35	IE	35
James	60	IE	156
Jane	20	IE	329
John	4/12	DB	123
John	50	NJ	111

Name	Age	State	Pg
Hart, John	50	DE	151
Joseph	6	IE	156
Julia	40	DE	298
Lydia	25	DE	282
Lydia	29	MD	284
Martha	48	IE	138
Martha	70	DE	26
Martha A	7	PA	5
Mary	22	IE	35
Mary A	33	MD	5
Matilda	35	IE	156
Rachel	20	DE	123
Rachel A	27	IE	11
Rosannah	12	IE	156
Sarah	7	DE	329
Sarah	38	DE	355
Wm	30	PA	329
Hartis, Ellen	18	IE	367
George	18/12	DE	367
George	30	GB	367
Margaret	24	GB	367
Richard	32	GB	367
Susannah	4	DE	367
Hartley, Abigail	55	NJ	179
Amanda	15	DE	360
Benjamin	53	PA	360
Benjamin Jr	4	DE	360
David	65	NJ	179
Eliza	42	PA	360
Hartly, David	44	PA	70
John	45	DE	360
Ruth A	45	PA	70
Hartman, Ann	45	PA	363
Ellen	8	PA	148
Frederick	50	PA	363
George	34	PA	148
Henry	12	PA	359
Isaac	5	DE	364
John	18	PA	363
Margaret	1	DE	148
Martin	32	DE	364
Orpha	28	MD	148
Robinson	6	PA	148
Tabitha	32	DE	364
Hartrip, Henrietta	48	DE	245
Thomas M	22	DE	245
Hartshorn, George	38	DE	276
Mary	3	DE	276
Mary	44	DE	276
Harty, Cyrus	21	PA	39
Hartye, Caroline	28	DE	306
George W	31	DE	306
Harvey, Anna H	43	PA	308
E A	29	PA	88
Elizabeth	4/12	DE	88
Huxley	6	DE	88
Lewis B	31	PA	285
Margaretta	5/12	DE	261
Marietta	25	DE	261
Martha	37	DE	308
Mary E	29	PA	285
Rachel E	6	PA	285
Rebecca	26	DE	68
Sarah	13	DE	308
Sarah D	28	DE	88
Thomas	25	DE	70
Thomas	26	PA	68
William	3	DE	68
William	3	DE	88
Harvy, Amos	8	PA	40
Ann	38	DE	57
Elizabeth	45	DE	43
Henry	12	PA	40
Jeremiah B	2	DE	285
Julia	47	PA	40
Mary	35	DE	45
Harwood, Thomas B	10	DE	187
Hasell, Thomas	50	VA	106
Hasen, Barry	21	IE	17
Haskill, Caroline	17	PA	166
Haskin, Charles	6	DE	346
Chas	32	IE	346
Haskin, Daviel	30	IE	346
Edward	9	DE	346
James	8	DE	346
John	2	DE	346
Mary	12	DE	346
Mary	31	IE	346
Haslett, Alexander	30	DE	304
Ann	30	MD	304
Bennett	19	DE	304
Emeline	8	DE	304
Emma	8	DE	304
George	5	DE	304
Mary	16	DE	304
Newel	62	PA	304
Samuel	7	DE	304
Sarah	54	DE	304
Sarah J	10	DE	304
Thomas	23	DE	304
William	2	DE	304
Hassan, Bridget	7	IE	357
Catherine	13	IE	357
George	--	DE	290
James	50	IE	357
Mary	15	IE	357
Michael	17	IE	357
Sarah	9	IE	357
Sarah	50	IE	357
Thomas	--	DE	290
Hassel, John	27	DE	304
Hasselton, Eliza	63	MD	201
Hassen, Elizabeth	1	DE	102
Ella	1	DE	61
George	25	PA	61
Hasset, John	53	IE	336
Hassin, Catherine	58	PA	378
Emma	24	PA	378
Hellen	60	DE	359
Kitty	20	DE	359
Peter	55	DE	359
Sarah	21	PA	378
William	38	PA	378
Hassinger, Anna	22	DE	398
Charlotte	13	DE	398
Charlotte	50	DE	398
Jane	11	DE	398
Joseph	50	DE	398
Joseph Jr	18	DE	398
Luisa	19	DE	398
Hasson, John	--	DE	398
Mary	40	IE	330
Mary J	10	PA	330
Matilda	4	DE	330
Susannah C	16	IE	330
Taney	15	PA	330
Thomas	43	IE	330
Hastings, Abraham B	3	DE	281
Anna M	39	PA	281
Annie	22	IE	360
George	35	DE	282
George W	9	DE	281
John	1	DE	281
John	24	IE	350
Martha	20	IE	360
Rebecca N	5	DE	281
Hatch, Elizabeth	26	DE	189
George	8/12	DE	189
Hatcher, George	7	DE	10
John	12	DE	10
Lewis	29	DE	10
Margaret	27	DE	10
William	13	DE	10
Hathaway, Martha	23	MD	23
Sarah	2	DE	23
William	26	DE	23
Hathorn, George	14	DE	296
Hatten, George	27	PA	16
Hatton, Andrew E	6	DE	195
Ann E	20	DE	195
Charles	25	DE	195
J Randolph	10	DE	195
Mary	18	NJ	273
Mary A	41	DE	195
Hatton, Mary T	8	DE	195
Sarah	6	DE	195
Sarah J	16	DE	195
Sewall G	14	DE	195
Spencer	46	DE	195
William M	2	DE	195
Hauck, Adam	32	PA	320
Caroline	1	DE	320
Caroline A	24	PA	320
Griffith B	2	DE	320
Henry B	9	PA	320
Isaac P	14	PA	320
Mary L	10	PA	320
Haugh, Samuel	20	DE	317
Haughey, Barney	17	IE	337
Bernard	24	IE	274
Bridget	26	IE	312
James	11	DE	326
James	36	IE	326
John	17	DE	2
John Hugh C	17	IE	324
Margaret A	9	DE	324
Owen	45	IE	324
Peter	22	IE	356
Peter J	14	IE	324
Rose	45	IE	324
Sarah	48	IE	327
Haughton, William	15	PA	164
William	80	NC	101
Haus, Alexander	19	DE	315
Hawes, John	16	DE	243
Maria	15	DE	378
Hawk, Edmond	6	DE	352
Henry M	2	DE	352
Jane	19	GB	351
John	20	GB	351
Mary	11	GB	352
Mary	40	GB	352
Mary E	22	PA	352
William	14	GB	352
William	43	GB	352
Hawkins, Ann	28	DE	170
Anna	7	DE	78
Anna E	7	DE	84
Barney	16	IE	341
Barney	25	IE	365
Catherine	30	IE	337
Elizabeth	8	MD	144
Frances	18	IE	341
Henry H	13	DE	84
Hugh	30	IE	341
James L	11	DE	84
Jane	13	IE	341
Jane	30	IE	341
Jane L	46	DE	84
John	14	IE	337
Mary	22	DE	32
Mary	40	DE	40
Mary	45	DE	305
Mary	55	PA	32
Peter	20	IE	341
Rebecca	30	NJ	78
Robert	36	DE	61
Samuel	9	DE	84
Thomas	4	DE	84
Thomas	40	DE	84
Timothy	30	IE	337
Wesley	35	DE	78
Wesly	3	DE	78
Haws, Danial	24	GE	104
Hawsey, Emeline P	11	DE	348
Maria	37	PA	348
William B	35	PA	348
Hawthorn, Ann M	16	PA	340
Charles	12	DE	273
Elizabeth	35	DE	385
Harriet	13	DE	385
John	49	DE	382
Lena	16	DE	385
Louisa	11	DE	340
Martha	2	DE	340
Martha	37	NJ	340

Name	Age	State	Page
Hawthorn, Nathan	13	PA	340
Robert	4	DE	385
Robert	38	DE	382
Sarah	60	DE	382
Sarah A	7	DE	385
Sarah Ann	22	DE	382
Susan	6	DE	340
Thomas	9	DE	385
William	2	DE	385
William	9	DE	340
William	17	DE	382
William	42	DE	385
William S	37	PA	340
Hay, Adelaide	2	DE	277
Adeline	26	MA	277
Eudora	3	MA	277
Frederick	26	SC	278
James	20	GB	133
James	24	PA	164
John	22	DE	177
Phoebe	70	PA	348
Samuel	7	MD	146
William	30	DE	348
Hayden, Abraham	35	DE	217
Abraham Jr	6	DE	217
Catherine	8	DE	217
Emily	10	DE	217
George	1	DE	217
Susan	34	DE	217
Hayes, Abigal	17	DE	299
Alexander	16	DE	187
Alexander	21	DE	313
Catherine	17	?	274
Catherine	58	DE	309
Ceazar	65	DE	328
Eliza	3/12	DE	172
George	--	DE	290
Jacob W	27	DE	242
James	56	DE	304
James	16	DE	201
John	30	IE	347
John	35	IE	364
John	46	DE	310
John W	4	DE	242
Louis	32	DE	310
Martha A	24	DE	172
Minty	60	DE	298
Peter	29	DE	172
Richard	29	DE	242
Sarah E	1/12	DE	242
Stephen	49	DE	309
William	6	MD	212
William	19	DE	284
William H	34	DE	310
William T	12	MD	142
Hayne, Ann	70	IE	12
Elizabeth	6	DE	12
Elizabeth	36	IE	12
James	4	DE	12
Mary	8	DE	12
Thomas	2	DE	12
Thomas	36	IE	12
Hays, Abigal	25	DE	29
Adeline M	14	DE	204
Adolphus	46	GE	51
Alonzo	9	DE	100
Amanda	5	DE	356
Ambrose	15	MD	175
Anderson J	21	DE	204
Andrew	29	MD	4
Anna	9	DE	138
Byard	14	DE	356
Caroline	14	DE	109
Caroline	25	DE	365
Charles	2	DE	200
Charlotta A	19	MD	4
Christian	9	PA	356
Cuthbert	12	DE	196
David	22	PA	43
Edgar	4/12	MD	196
Edward	70	DE	59
Edwin	4/12	MD	196
Hays, Elizabeth	27	DE	84
Elizabeth	35	DE	196
Elizabeth	50	PA	45
Ella	15/12	DE	29
Emeline	14	DE	204
Emeline	35	DE	38
Frances A	37	DE	200
George	7	DE	358
George	40	DE	358
George	49	DE	200
George C	16	MD	84
Hannah	75	DE	27
Henry	67	DE	27
Jacob	56	DE	356
James	4	DE	200
James P	26	DE	29
James W	4	DE	4
Jane	42	DE	358
Joanna	6	DE	4
John	70	DE	204
John S	6	DE	197
Joseph	5	DE	3
Joseph	11	DE	358
Joseph	28	DE	27
Joseph	76	DE	100
Joseph Jr	39	DE	100
Josephine	4	DE	100
Josephine	10	DE	3
Joshua	18	DE	109
Letitia	50	MD	109
Margaret	38	PA	100
Martha	46	DE	100
Martha A	2	DE	4
Mary	4/12	DE	99
Mary	4	DE	51
Mary	7	DE	365
Mary	27	GE	51
Mary A	7	DE	356
Mary E	9	DE	4
Mary Jane	5	DE	358
Matilda	16	DE	109
Matilda	18	DE	95
Mines	7	DE	3
Mines	50	DE	3
Nathaniel	21	DE	109
Nathaniel	50	DE	109
Owen	9	DE	196
Peter	15	DE	38
Phebe	15	DE	3
Phoebe	34	DE	365
Rachel	12	DE	38
Rachel	21	DE	99
Rachel	50	NJ	141
Rachel	60	DE	59
Richard	10	DE	109
Richard	45	DE	138
Richard G	24	DE	204
Robert	5	DE	196
Robert	30	DE	196
Ruben	35	DE	27
Sally	50	VA	356
Sarah	1	DE	51
Sarah	27	DE	3
Sarah	28	DE	109
Sarah	38	DE	138
Sarah	50	DE	204
Sarah	55	MD	4
Sarah A	28	MD	196
Sarah Ann	14	DE	358
Sarah E	11	DE	197
Sarah E	18	DE	3
Susan	7	DE	285
Theodore	7/12	DE	196
Thomas R	36	DE	196
Washington	40	DE	27
William	7	DE	200
William	12	DE	3
William	24	PA	46
Haywood, Decima C	52	SC	55
James T	22	SC	55
Hazlett, Ann	33	IE	17
John	63	WL	17
Hazzard, Ann	27	DE	308
John	32	PA	346
Mary	70	DE	228
Heach, Josiah	34	PA	353
Head, Mary A	50	IE	57
Heal, Jacob	15	MD	58
Samuel	11	MD	58
Heald, Alfred	4	DE	55
Caleb	51	PA	345
Charles	17	DE	119
Edward	20	DE	119
Eliza A	45	DE	99
Hannah	27	PA	55
Hannah	71	PA	345
Jacob	48	PA	345
Joseph	19	PA	345
Joshua T	29	DE	55
Martha M	43	PA	346
Mary A	22	PA	28
Mary J	3	DE	346
Mary P	2	DE	56
Philena	19	DE	346
Purcy	11	DE	346
William	6	DE	346
Healy, Ann	32	IE	22
James	10	GB	22
John	38	IE	22
Richard	4	GB	22
Sarah	7	GB	22
Heardman, James	2	DE	393
Jefferson	7	DE	393
John	47	DE	393
Hearn, Patrick	26	IE	348
Sarah C	14	DE	166
Heart, Emma	22	DE	381
William	12	DE	381
Heartish, Richard	--	GB	317
Heath, Elizabeth	14	PA	326
Isabella	4	PA	350
Mary	19	IE	334
Samuel H	7	PA	350
Sarah	37	PA	326
William H	7	PA	350
Hebron, Hyland D	10	DE	224
Heckey, Rachel	20	DE	274
Heckman, Elizabeth	29	DE	259
Hector, William	11	DE	342
Hedges, Adaline	43	DE	17
Adaline E	18	DE	7
Charles A E	15	DE	7
Elizabeth	73	DE	17
John	75	DE	17
John F	4	DE	7
Joseph S	42	DE	7
Margaret	30	DE	17
Mary J	33	PA	7
Sarah	41	DE	17
Urban	39	DE	17
Hedrick, Alfred	14	DE	89
Elizabeth	28	DE	89
Hannah	30	DE	89
Isabella	7	DE	89
Isabella	73	DE	89
Lewis	12	DE	89
Heigh, Dorothy	74	GE	145
Heinsworth, Walter	17	GB	298
Heisler, Bracilla	37	PA	105
Henry E	3/12	DE	105
Mary	28	MD	105
Mary A	9	DE	105
Rebecca S	30	MD	105
Reual	32	PA	105
Sarah E	1	DE	105
Heiss, Christopher	30	GE	352
Hannah	25	GE	352
John	8	GE	352
Sarah	2	GE	352
Heizman, Ramond	16	PA	163
Helfore, Thomas	30	IE	335
Helinger, Martin	25	GE	36
Hellings, Harriet	16	GB	375
Hellum, Anna	23	DE	248

Hellum, Charles	32	DE	148
John W	4	DE	148
Mary	3	DE	148
Thomas D	14	DE	148
William	2	DE	148
Helms, Elizabeth	14	PA	259
Israel	12	MD	259
Lydia	41	PA	259
Mary	18	PA	259
Helmsley, Edward	30	DE	195
Hemeric, William	20	PA	159
Hemmett, Thomas	18	NJ	80
Hemphill, Ann	29	DE	307
Edward C	7	DE	307
Elizabeth	1	DE	307
Esther A	3	DE	307
John	62	DE	59
Lesley C	9	DE	307
Mary J	5	DE	307
William	50	DE	307
Hemsley, James	8	DE	292
Henderson, Adaline	43	DE	395
Adaline C	6	DE	349
Amy	32	DE	329
Anna	38	PA	48
Asbury	15	DE	292
Ashbury	14	DE	394
Catharine	7	PA	335
Charles	13	PA	239
David	34	DE	102
David	52	DE	394
Eliza	49	PA	48
Ellen	31	NJ	25
Grace	8	DE	394
Hall	4/12	DE	102
Hannah G	10	DE	349
Isaac	7	DE	102
Isaac	21	DE	398
James	8	DE	395
James	39	ST	335
Jane J	40	PA	48
John	--	DE	290
John G	3	PA	335
Joseph	47	DE	301
Joseph G	4	DE	349
Joseph G	45	DE	349
Laura	15	DE	60
Levi	12	DE	180
Lydia	44	PA	48
Malcolm	3	PA	335
Maria	4	DE	395
Marshall	12	PA	219
Mary	6	DE	25
Mary	34	DE	102
Mary	55	DE	296
Mary A	3	DE	102
Mary A	10	DE	335
Mary A	19	PA	329
Mary E	7	DE	329
Nathaniel	3	DE	25
Nathaniel	32	NJ	25
Rachel	2/12	DE	25
Rebecca	25	MD	322
Rebecca	27	DE	57
Rebecca	59	DE	57
Rebecca A	12	DE	349
Richard	5	DE	102
Robert	11	DE	335
Rosanna	29	DE	335
Samuel	6	DE	395
Samuel	50	DE	296
Sarah	76	DE	301
William W	7	DE	335
Wm	34	DE	329
Hendrick, Alfred	12	MD	205
James	10	MD	238
Mordecai	24	DE	225
Hendricks, Amanda	34	DE	358
Jane E	16	DE	358
Rebecca E	14	DE	358
Samuel	12	DE	358
Hendricksen, Anna	6	DE	60
Hendricksen, George	10	PA	60
James	32	PA	60
John	8	DE	60
Joseph	3	DE	60
Mary	29	PA	60
Richard	5	DE	60
Samuel	5/12	DE	60
Hendrickson, Andrew	15	DE	359
Anna	18	DE	53
Anna	21	DE	57
Charles	27	DE	359
Debby	18	DE	3
Debby	48	DE	3
Eliza	50	DE	15
Ellwood	38	PA	314
Emma C	6	PA	314
Hannah	20	DE	359
Isaac	14	PA	81
Isaac	40	DE	359
John H	20	DE	377
Joseph	19	DE	57
Joseph	75	DE	359
Joseph T	10	PA	314
Levic	8	DE	377
Malinda	10	DE	57
Margaret	46	DE	57
Margaret V	47	DE	230
Maria	15	DE	161
Mary	21	DE	3
Mary	35	PA	314
Mary	49	DE	377
Mary	52	DE	359
Nathan	18	DE	377
Peregrine	67	MD	230
Robert	5	DE	238
Samuel	14	DE	377
Sarah	15	DE	3
Sarah	15	DE	57
Sarah	18	DE	359
Sarah	30	DE	15
Sarah	70	NJ	15
Thornton R	8	PA	314
William	16	DE	377
William	18	DE	377
Henebry, Andrew	40	IE	310
Mary	38	IE	310
Michel	42	IE	310
Patrick	36	IE	310
Heneman, Anna M	5	DE	312
John	12	DE	312
Margaret	15	DE	312
Mary J	8	DE	312
Henley, Thomas	7	DE	363
Hennelly, Michael O	--	IE	291
Hennesay, Elizabeth	54	IE	273
Hennet, Ann	54	DE	363
Elizabeth	23	DE	380
John	52	DE	363
Lucinda	5	DE	355
Lydia A	1	DE	355
Malinda	7	DE	355
Martha	36	DE	363
Mary Jane	17	DE	363
Peter	20	DE	364
William	23	DE	355
Henry, Alexander	1	DE	375
Andrew L	5/12	DE	226
Ann	3	PA	43
Ann	28	IE	361
Ann	45	MD	176
Anna	2	DE	263
Bayard	25	DE	190
Catherine	1	DE	43
Charles	1	DE	296
Charles	1	DE	319
Charles	5	DE	318
Columbus	7	DE	296
Daniel	52	DE	168
Eliza J	8	DE	226
Elizabeth	20	IE	58
Elizabeth	24	DE	261
Ellen	3	DE	48
Henry, George	3/12	DE	106
Hannah	8	DE	48
Hannah	66	IE	21
Harry	27	IE	161
Isaac R	33	PA	43
James	12	DE	383
James	67	DE	296
James A	10	DE	226
James B	30	DE	263
John	11/12	DE	204
John	1	DE	361
John	2	DE	176
John	34	IE	48
John J	28	DE	262
Joseph	7	DE	226
Joseph	12	DE	231
Joseph	35	DE	226
Joshua	22	DE	127
Margaret	6	DE	48
Margaret	20	IE	375
Mary	7	DE	355
Mary	13	DE	175
Mary	28	IE	316
Mary	32	PA	43
Mary	37	IE	48
Mary F	44	MD	388
Matilda	45	DE	296
Patric	54	DE	168
Perry	5	DE	226
Rhody	30	DE	204
Richard	4	DE	237
Robert	4	DE	176
Samuel	23	IE	375
Sarah	6	PA	43
Sarah	27	DE	262
Sarah A	2	DE	226
Susan	28	DE	226
Virginia	5	DE	191
William	5	DE	176
William	55	DE	176
Henshaw, Thomas	17	PA	390
Hensley, Charles	15	DE	102
Hannah	32	DE	102
Harriet	12	DE	102
Jacob	3	DE	102
Joseph	35	PA	102
Louisa	7	PA	102
Martha	8	DE	371
Mary	9/12	DE	371
Mary	29	DE	371
Rebecca A	5	DE	371
Susan	17	PA	102
Susanna	8	DE	102
Thomas	45	DE	370
William H	5	DE	102
Henson, Hannah	20	DE	61
Wesley	11	DE	197
William	25	DE	61
Hepple, Jacob	21	PA	351
Herbaugh, David	56	PA	309
Elizabeth	51	MD	309
John G	8	DE	308
Peter	34	PA	308
Samuel L	14	DE	308
Herbert, Catharine	18	PA	283
Eliza	53	NJ	283
Emaline	24	MD	316
Margaret	14	PA	283
Mary E	4	DE	316
Samuel	8	DE	316
Samuel	27	MD	316
Sophia	5	DE	316
William	21	PA	283
Herbinson, Ellen	22	IE	305
Herd, Rachel	35	DE	269
Herdman, Benjamin	28	DE	389
Caroline	22	DE	389
Charles	3	DE	389
Eliza	32	DE	393
Jacob	1	DE	389
Jacob F	43	DE	55
Martha	27	DE	389

Name	Age	State	No.
Herdman, Samuel B	2	DE	389
William	40	DE	389
William G	1/12	DE	389
Heritage, Charles-			
anna	16	PA	166
Herman, Araminta	21	DE	304
Herred, Charles	13	DE	335
Charles	51	MD	335
David	3	DE	335
John	11	DE	335
Mary	34	DE	335
Hersey, Alfred	27	DE	250
Julia	22	MD	250
Mary	45	DE	249
Herst, John	25	MD	310
Herting, Margaret	14	DE	328
Hertzel, Susan	17	PA	166
Hervey, Andrew J	21	DE	400
Hesmere, Israel	2	DE	112
Maria	24	PA	112
Hess, Ann	36	DE	168
Elizabeth	43	DE	313
George	54	PA	313
George W	12	PA	313
Sarah A	11	DE	313
Hessey, James	40	DE	185
Hessleman, Mary	18	IE	282
Hessy, David S	14	DE	185
James W	12	DE	185
Sarah J	17	DE	185
Hester, Charlotte	1	DE	14
Elizabeth	24	PA	14
Kessey M	32	PA	14
Sarah	5	PA	14
Susan	3	PA	14
Hesten, Joseph A	19	PA	55
Heston, Ahab	26	PA	325
Cortian Sr	66	DE	350
Elizabeth	2	DE	350
Hetcherson, Mary J	16	DE	132
Heughs, Eliza	35	PA	325
George E	12	DE	325
Rebecca A	11	DE	325
Sarah A	8	DE	325
Wm J	34	PA	325
Heusted, Jane	25	NY	38
Hevelow, John R	22	DE	317
Heveret, Jane	58	MD	224
William	35	DE	224
Hewes, Margaret A	27	DE	280
Mary	34	IE	326
William E	28	DE	280
Hewitt, Elizabeth K	58	NJ	173
Jacob	56	NJ	173
Hewlet, Anna M	4	DE	358
Josiah G	11	DE	358
Hews, Aaron	60	DE	57
Abert	4	DE	96
Alexander	2	DE	96
Elmira	26	NJ	88
Emma	20	GB	82
George	11	NJ	96
Hannah	60	PA	82
Hannah	62	DE	57
James	16	IE	82
Jane	46	GB	82
John	25	DE	81
John M	12	GB	82
Joseph	26	GB	82
Joseph	38	PA	96
Mary	28	PA	96
Mary A	22	DE	96
Mary B	3	DE	96
Richard M	14	GB	82
Swayne B	6	NJ	96
Swayne B	31	NJ	96
Hewsworth, Martha J	20	GB	339
William	25	GB	339
Hickel, Albert	13	DE	292
Hicken, Abigail	30	PA	264
Alex	8	DE	264
Anna	4	DE	272
Hicken, Charles	11	DE	272
Eliza	40	DE	272
Emma	13	DE	272
George	6	DE	264
George	35	DE	264
Henry	4	DE	264
Henry	39	DE	272
James	3	DE	272
Jesse	37	DE	264
Joseph	10	DE	264
Martha	29	DE	264
Saml	5	DE	264
Thomas	23	DE	264
Thomas	11	DE	264
Washington	7	DE	264
Wm	2/12	DE	272
Wm	4	DE	265
Hickens, Benjamin	3	MD	302
Benjamin	29	MD	302
Joseph	5	MD	302
Julia	1	MD	302
Mary E	6	MD	302
Neamiah	26	MD	302
Rachel	28	MD	302
Sarah E	8	MD	302
Hickey, James	19	DE	250
James	20	DE	255
John	16	PA	164
Patric	18	PA	164
Peter	9	PA	164
Rachel	20	DE	273
Hickman, Anna	11	PA	384
Araminta	12	DE	42
Charles C	15	DE	400
Charlotta	27	PA	62
David F	5	DE	211
Eliza M	47	DE	211
Elizabeth	29	DE	258
Elizabeth C	5	DE	211
Emeline	21	DE	123
George	7	DE	384
Jacob	56	DE	244
James	10/12	DE	384
James	31	DE	384
Joanna	30	PA	62
John F	9	DE	211
Lydia J	8	DE	217
Margaret L	16	DE	211
Margaretta	7/12	DE	123
Martha	60	DE	127
Mary	35	DE	206
Mary C	16	DE	204
Phebe E	4	DE	384
Phillip	70	DE	168
Rebecca	24	PA	62
Robert	21	DE	99
Wesley	26	DE	123
William	8	PA	384
William	49	DE	211
Hicks, Ann	70	MD	31
Ann M	12	DE	231
Anne	2	DE	31
Frances	28	MD	31
Henrietta	28	MD	31
Henry	50	MD	42
Mary	13	DE	42
Mary	45	DE	42
Robert D	41	MD	31
Hide, Margaret	70	GB	19
Thomas	70	GB	19
Higby, Edward	12	MD	289
Higgan, Peter	23	IE	337
Higgans, Luke	20	WI	148
Higgins, Anna	28	DE	368
Anthony	10	DE	251
Anthony	40	DE	251
Catherine	28	IE	17
Catherine A	9/12	DE	6
Catherine M	42	IE	6
Charles	5	DE	6
David	16	DE	201
Edward	8	DE	1
Higgins, Edward	8	DE	1
Edward	14	IE	12
Edward	14	IE	80
Eliza	8	DE	201
George	20	PA	163
Gracy	22	DE	373
Harriet	44	DE	201
James	8	DE	99
James	10	DE	6
James	19	DE	373
James	40	GB	301
James	45	IE	6
Jesse	19	DE	201
John	19	IE	12
John	21	IE	41
John C	12	DE	251
Joseph	39	DE	368
Joseph	82	NJ	373
Luke	40	IE	1
Margaret	4	DE	1
Margaret	43	IE	1
Maria	45	DE	182
Martha	16	DE	251
Mary	3	DE	251
Mary	12	DE	201
Mary	13	DE	6
Mary	19	IE	12
Mary	30	MD	132
Mary A	6	DE	1
Matthew	7	DE	12
Patrick	11	DE	12
Pernal	6	DE	251
Rodney	13	DE	161
Samuel	5	DE	201
Samuel	46	DE	201
Sarah C	39	DE	251
Susan	10	DE	201
Thomas	8	DE	251
Thomas	29	DE	374
Thomas J	50	DE	255
Higham, Edward	27	DE	61
Lucinda	4/12	DE	61
Sarah	3	DE	61
Susanah	24	DE	61
Highby, Elizabeth	22	DE	382
Highet, George W	34	PA	19
John	8	DE	19
Mary	2	DE	19
Mary	32	MD	19
Rachel	11	DE	19
Sidney	8	DE	19
Highfield, Benjamin	3	DE	357
Calvin	35	PA	357
Hellen	6	DE	357
Louisa	29	PA	357
Mary Jane	2	DE	357
Highland, Anna	11	DE	37
Christian	50	PA	37
Elizabeth	15	DE	37
George	12	DE	90
George	27	PA	37
Joseph	70	DE	90
Margaret	20	DE	37
Mary	4	DE	90
Mary	17	DE	37
Mary	40	PA	90
Sarah	8	DE	37
Sarah	49	PA	37
William	22	DE	37
Hilcot, Anthony	30	ST	157
Hilderburn, Fredrick	28	HN	259
Hilegan, George H	2	DE	245
Martha A	28	DE	245
Hilfen, Bridget	26	IE	332
Hilk, Sarah	50	DE	374
Hill, Adam	36	PA	80
Alexander	16	MD	291
Amie	35	PA	66
Amos	40	DE	317
Anna	20	NY	57
Avis Ann	33	DE	238
Benj H	29	DE	320

Name	Age	St	Pg	Name	Age	St	Pg	Name	Age	St	Pg
Hill, Benjamin E	44	DE	333	Hillman, Catherine	65	PA	88	Hinson, Millison	6	DE	325
Bennett	40	MD	155	Hilson, Francis A	2	DE	379	Morris	11	DE	365
Caroline	24	DE	308	Henry	30	DE	379	Rebecca	17	DE	191
Catharine A	36	DE	333	John W	4	DE	379	Rebecca J	7/12	DE	191
Cornelia	7	DE	117	Sarah	29	DE	379	Robert	30	MD	328
Deborah	36	GB	312	Sarah E	1	DE	379	Sally	18	DE	331
Deborah	38	GB	314	William H	9	DE	379	Sarah	8	DE	24
Elenora	25	FR	308	Hilyard, Enoch	30	DE	277	Sarah	8	DE	191
Elizabeth	76	DE	155	Mary A	2	DE	277	Thomas	32	MD	202
Hamer	11	MD	164	Mary J	25	DE	277	William	11	DE	24
Hannah	8	DE	367	William	5/12	DE	277	William	30	DE	24
Hannah	28	DE	117	Himes, John	25	PA	311	William F	11	DE	191
Hannah A	17	DE	132	Himmell, Albert	20	PA	302	Hinsworth, Charles	5	PA	302
Harriet	40	DE	374	Frederick	68	PA	302	Edward	11	GB	302
Hester A	18	PA	169	John	22	PA	302	Francis	50	GB	302
Howard	73	DE	385	Maria	53	DE	302	Frank	9	GB	302
Jacob	26	PA	132	Sarah	18	PA	302	George	13	GB	302
Jacob	30	DE	218	Hinchcliffe, Chas	7	PA	333	Hannah	45	GB	302
Jacob F	7	PA	80	Elizabeth	12	GB	333	Henry	7	GB	302
James	21	GB	353	Hugh	34	GB	333	Richard	18	GB	302
James	36	GB	311	Joseph	14	GB	333	Thomas	15	GB	302
James	38	GB	314	Sarah	33	GB	333	Hipple, Charles	3	DE	172
James H	6	PA	66	Hindman, John	12	DE	114	Elizabeth	18	DE	172
James R	4	DE	333	Hinds, Alfred	3/12	DE	20	Hiram, Mary	17	MD	20
Jane	33	NJ	218	Isabella	8	DE	20	Hirbs, John	32	GE	38
John	25	PA	360	John	4	DE	20	Hisbee, Frances	16	MD	164
John	27	GB	303	Samuel	32	GB	20	Hiser, Jacob P	44	DE	352
John	34	PA	66	Sarah	32	GB	20	Hister, George	27	GE	5
John	49	PA	80	William	30	IE	20	Hitchens, Emma	7	DE	339
John H	6	DE	331	Hines, Mary	21	IE	274	Hitchkis, A R	21	NY	180
John R	35	MD	333	Saml	23	PA	266	Hites, Arabella G	19	NJ	306
Joseph	25	PA	177	Hinley, James	34	NY	29	Hitzel, Martha	10	DE	347
Joseph	48	DE	132	Joseph	1	DE	29	Hizler, Elizabeth	58	GE	274
Joseph L	23	PA	319	Sarah	37	DE	29	Hoaltan, Emma J	11	DE	346
Louisa	38	DE	155	Hinson, Alace	6	MD	73	James	39	DE	346
Margaret	34	PA	80	Ann	28	DE	24	Margaretta	3	DE	346
Mary	22	GB	303	Ann	41	IE	375	Sarah	34	PA	346
Mary A	49	DE	132	Ann E	3	DE	202	William	9	DE	346
Mary E	1	DE	319	Anna M	3	DE	125	Hoar, Sarah	17	NJ	272
Mary E	26	PA	320	Benjamin	14	DE	203	Hobson, Charles	8	PA	152
Marvina L	1/12	DE	319	Benjamin	15	DE	190	Francis	48	GB	306
Neamiah D	24	DE	304	Charles	5	DE	191	George T	8	GB	306
Phebe	73	MD	333	Charles	16	DE	333	Harriet	36	PA	152
Phebe P	21	PA	319	Charles	25	NJ	73	James E	17	PA	152
Rachel	11/12	PA	66	Clarissa	1	DE	202	James R	8	DE	236
Samuel	29	DE	169	Eben	16	MD	221	Jane S	12	PA	153
Sarah	50	DE	373	Eliza	6	DE	24	John	25	DE	228
Sarah	61	DE	238	Eliza J	8	DE	217	John S	40	PA	152
Sarah J	2	DE	320	Elizabeth	35	DE	217	Kezia	22	GB	292
Sarah J	10	DE	333	Ellen	7	DE	217	Mary	47	GB	306
Thomas F	64	GB	308	Ellen	9	PA	250	Mary A	1	PA	152
Thomas H	1	DE	303	Ellen	17	DE	213	Sarah E	12	DE	236
Vincent A	25	DE	238	Emeline	29	MD	328	Sarah E	16	DE	228
William	30	DE	117	Emery	15	DE	125	Sarah J	11	GB	306
Hillard, Elisha	39	MD	171	Emery	33	DE	67	Thomas	86	PA	18
John	6	DE	171	Erich	--	DE	290	William	25	GB	292
Joseph	1	DE	171	George	7	DE	336	Hodgkins, John	26	DC	178
Sophia	39	PA	171	Hannah	3	DE	313	Hodgson, Catharine	66	MD	332
William	10	DE	171	Hannah A	24	DE	202	Deborah	22	DE	335
Hillary, Bridget	30	IE	354	Hannah M	2	DE	202	Deborah	38	GB	335
Daniel	35	IE	354	Harriett	42	MD	336	George	20	DE	273
Hiller, Alma	2	DE	3	Henrietta	40	MD	328	Jonathan	28	DE	273
Augustus	36	GE	80	Henry	10	DE	125	Mary	50	DE	322
Charles	25	PA	215	Henry	18	DE	228	Thos	55	GB	335
Elenor	36	GE	80	Henry	55	DE	382	Hodson, Clement	5	DE	11
Ferdinand	41	DE	80	Ida	17	DE	125	Elizabeth	2	GA	11
Frederic	47	MD	3	James	4	DE	336	Elizabeth W	39	DE	11
Jesse	1/12	DE	3	James	16	DE	220	Jacob	28	GB	120
John F	7	DE	80	James	40	DE	125	John	5	PA	120
Sarah J	21	PA	3	Jane	24	MD	63	Mary	1	GA	11
Hillis, Eli	67	PA	98	John	43	MD	191	Mary	26	GB	120
Elizabeth B	35	DE	98	John	56	DE	336	Hoffecker, Ann	35	DE	226
Israel	12	PA	350	John N	4	DE	191	Eliza	15	DE	216
John J	20	DE	98	Jonathan	11	DE	218	Henry D	42	DE	193
Margaret H	64	NJ	98	Levi	6/12	DE	73	Hetterlina	11	DE	281
Phebe	19	PA	348	Levi	28	DE	93	James R	13	DE	193
Samuel	62	PA	98	Louisa	21	DE	73	Mary E	15	DE	193
Sarah L	30	PA	58	Mancy	35	DE	125	Mary H	37	DE	193
Susan M	7/12	DE	58	Margaret	42	DE	191	William	51	DE	226
William	25	DE	58	Maria	39	DE	67	Hoffly, Sarah	28	DE	205
Hillman, Benjamin	63	NJ	88	Mary A	9	DE	217	Hoffman, Neno	24	GE	21

Name	Age	St	No.
Hofman, John	11	PA	164
Hogan, Amanda	16	DE	194
Ann	15	IE	357
Hannah	18	DE	194
Hannah	48	MD	194
Henry	60	MD	194
James	20	IE	366
John	16	IE	13
Rebecca	4	DE	194
Sarah	13	DE	289
William	21	IE	278
Hogans, David	24	DE	59
Margaret	26	DE	59
Mary	56	DE	136
Ruth	8	DE	59
Samuel	4	DE	59
Thomas	24	DE	136
Hogy, Andrew K	10	DE	87
Ann	30	DE	99
Elizabeth	70	DE	99
Ellen	26	DE	99
Hannah	36	DE	87
James	17	DE	87
James	41	MD	99
Jane	38	DE	34
Margaret J	12	DE	87
Mary	28	DE	99
Mary E	15	DE	87
Robinson	37	DE	87
Holahain, Amanda	18	PA	364
Holcomb, Bankson T	10	PA	309
Chancey P	46	CT	309
Rebecca	32	PA	309
Thomas	7	DE	309
Holden, Bartholomew	6	IE	326
Biddy	12	IE	326
Bridget	40	IE	326
Caroline	25	DE	38
Eliza	55	DE	38
James	10	IE	326
James	45	IE	326
John	20	IE	326
John	23	MD	389
Michael	17	IE	338
Patrick	8	IE	327
William	10/12	DE	327
Willis	19	DE	38
Holdgate, William	40	GB	388
Holding, Charles	11	PA	197
Holehan, Amos	11	PA	401
Holgate, Maria	21	PA	383
Holiday, Charles	14	PA	327
Holingsworth, Abner	28	DE	381
Hollagan, Mary	32	IE	125
Hollan, Jane	29	DE	361
Margaret	34	DE	361
Sarah	27	DE	361
Holland, Anna J	20	DE	317
Catharine	30	IE	285
Daniel	6	DE	294
Darcus	4	DE	342
Edward	3	DE	47
Elizabeth	13	DE	332
Elizabeth	13	DE	338
Elizabeth	29	DE	79
Evalina	15	DE	338
Frisby	4	DE	47
George W	6	DE	1
Hannah	12	DE	313
Hannah	12	DE	342
Henry	35	PA	301
Hugh	11	DE	338
Isaac	37	DE	285
James	1	DE	148
James H	6	DE	342
Jane	10	DE	342
Jane	59	DE	391
John	24	IE	148
John	29	DE	302
John	60	GB	354
Joseph	19	PA	249
Julia	29	PA	1
Holland, Margaret	3	DE	285
Margaret	6	DE	338
Margaret	30	IE	338
Margaret	56	DE	395
Martha	33	IE	301
Mary	9	DE	108
Mary	9	DE	338
Mary	22	IE	148
Mary	44	DE	342
Mary A	8	PA	1
Mary A	35	DE	302
Mary A	50	FR	338
Mary E	14	DE	342
Nicholas	16	DE	338
Patric	23	IE	29
Patrick	19	DE	338
Patrick	25	IE	262
Perry	8	DE	342
Perry	50	MD	342
Reuben	30	GB	5
Ruth	41	DE	294
Samuel	53	DE	294
Sarah	26	DE	5
Sarah	60	IE	302
Sarah A	20	DE	255
Sarah J	13	DE	312
Thomas	1/12	DE	5
Thomas	8	DE	338
Thomas	14	DE	53
Thomas	14	DE	148
Thomas	19	DE	257
Thomas	31	GB	1
Thomas	56	DE	395
Thomas	91	IE	395
William	4	DE	302
William	28	DE	312
William	45	IE	363
William	48	DE	395
William A	2	DE	5
Wilson	7	DE	294
York	15	DE	328
York	16	DE	342
Holleren, Ellen	26	IE	163
Hollet, Benjamin	8	DE	234
Eli	13	DE	234
Harriet	38	MD	234
Rebecca C	6	DE	234
Samuel	10	DE	234
Hollin, Allice	18	IE	326
Hollinbeck, Eliza-beth	19	NY	324
Hollingsworth, Al-len R	18	DE	133
Ann	62	DE	1
Anna	35	DE	1
Archillis	43	DE	98
Dinah	65	DE	196
Edward B	39	DE	133
Eli	65	DE	71
Elijah	45	DE	1
Elizabeth	19	DE	381
George	30	DE	71
George W	14	PA	133
James L	5	PA	133
John	26	DE	360
Joseph A	8	PA	133
Julia	1/12	DE	1
Julia	25	DE	196
Luisa	20	PA	71
Lydia C	63	DE	71
Margaret	50	MD	355
Mary	54	DE	355
Mary E	26	DE	71
Phebe A	17	DE	1
Rachel	24	DE	111
Ruth A	39	DE	133
Sally A	11	DE	98
Samuel H	11	PA	133
Sarah F	6	DE	1
Sarah M	31	DE	71
Susan	41	DE	98
William	21	DE	71
Hollingsworth, Wm	24	DE	360
Wm H	17	DE	133
Hollis, Ann	3	DE	37
Henry	23	DE	37
Mary	23	DE	37
Nancy	1	DE	37
Nancy	33	PA	333
Rebecca O	22	DE	333
Hollow, Robert	23	DE	308
Hollowell, Elizabeth	30	DE	115
Mr	28	OH	143
Mrs	25	NY	143
Hollyson, George	22	DE	171
Margaret	20	DE	171
Holman, David S	23	ME	143
Holmes, Abigal	51	NJ	68
Abraham	23	DE	318
Almira	23	NJ	12
Amelia	23	NJ	68
Ann	19/12	DE	373
Catherine	11	DE	55
Eliza	20	NJ	12
Eliza Jane	2	PA	345
Elizabeth	53	NJ	68
George	1	FL	254
Jackson	36	DE	345
John	3	DE	373
Jonathan	17	NJ	31
Jonathan	17	MD	68
Margaret	8	PA	345
Martha	5	PA	345
Martha	34	PA	345
Mary	3	DE	12
Mary A	24	DE	373
Phillis	25	FL	255
Poinsett	4	FL	255
Prince	50	AF	255
Rachel	55	NJ	373
Sarah	30	DE	254
Susan	7	PA	345
Thomas	25	DE	373
Thomas	31	SC	254
Holmstead, Wm H	14	PA	224
Holson, Anna	37	MD	357
Benjamin	47	PA	357
Frances E	15	PA	357
John	4	DE	357
John	42	DE	194
Josephine	17	PA	357
Lora M	1	DE	357
Mary J	5	DE	357
Phoebe A	10	PA	357
Priscilla	18	PA	357
Rachel D	35	DE	194
Sarah E	7	DE	357
Holsten, Ann	33	NJ	111
Hanna A	13	NJ	111
Joel	43	NJ	111
John M	7	NJ	111
Martha	5	NJ	111
Sarah J	12	NJ	111
Theodore A	2	NJ	111
William H	10	NJ	111
Holstine, William A	14	DE	295
Holston, Andrew	40	NJ	299
Anna M	7	DE	299
David	11	DE	299
Eliza A	39	NJ	299
Mary E	14	DE	288
Holt, Benjamin	14	DE	248
Charles	8	DE	248
Martha A	11	DE	240
Primrose	50	MD	240
Rachel	45	DE	240
Rachel J	9	DE	240
Holton, Stephen J	23	DE	228
Holtspecker, Mary	7	DE	310
Holtzhecker, Eliza	9	OH	393
Eliza	40	PA	393
George	34	DE	393
Homans, John	50	?	271
Kate	9	?	271

Name	Age	St	No	Name	Age	St	No	Name	Age	St	No
Homans, Maria	34	?	271	Hopper, Eliza	9	DE	33	Housten, William H	17	DE	190
Honomann, Erma	8/12	DE	322	Emeline	8/12	DE	33	Houston, Bayard	15	DE	210
Galiel	31	GE	322	Keziah	56	NJ	267	Franklin	17	DE	210
Louisa	21	GE	322	Martha	5	DE	33	George	14	DE	260
Hony, Margaret	22	DE	76	Mary	15	DE	33	George	24	DE	312
Hood, Amanda	19	PA	350	Mary	35	IE	32	Harriet	14	DE	210
Charles	5	DE	350	Samuel	35	IE	32	James	51	DE	260
Eli	45	DE	350	Sarah	30	DE	160	Joseph M	17	DE	400
Lewis	22	PA	361	Seth	15	NJ	267	Mary	9	DE	260
Sarah A	7	DE	351	Susannah	13	DE	33	Mary	40	DE	67
Simon	9	DE	350	Thomas	19	NJ	273	Mary	65	DE	202
Susan	22	DE	351	William	11	DE	33	Rebecca	42	MD	260
Hook, Catherine	35	GB	180	Horkenshire, Andrew	46	PA	356	Robert N	23	DE	177
Edward	33	GB	180	Louisa	16/12	DE	356	Saml	20	DE	260
Edward Jr	13	GB	180	Phoebe	5	DE	356	Sarah	60	DE	374
Elizabeth	53	PA	41	Rachel	45	DE	356	Thomas	21	DE	210
George	12	GB	180	Rebecca	6	DE	356	Washington	19	DE	210
Harriet J	5	GB	180	Horn, Adam	53	GE	35	William	22	DE	203
Mary	3	GB	180	Ann E	5/12	DE	104	William	70	IE	67
Minerva	28	PA	41	Carrissa	9	DE	109	How, Henry M	18	DE	400
Percifer	55	PA	41	Edmond	12	DE	109	Patrick	30	IE	262
Sarah E	1	GB	180	Edward	6	PA	282	Howagan, James	60	IE	147
Waldmen	30	PA	41	Emma	16	DE	35	John W	26	IE	147
William	10	GB	180	George	6	DE	171	Mary H	70	IE	147
Hooper, A	32	PA	316	George	29	PA	282	Michael	30	IE	147
John	19	DE	293	Gilbert	14	DE	109	Onie	20	IE	147
Mary E	16	DE	316	John	18	DE	109	Patric	28	IE	147
Samuel	9	DE	316	John R	8	DE	104	Howard, Albert	2	DE	368
Sarah	39	MD	316	Joseph	23	PA	282	Andrew C	12	DE	378
Susan J	11	DE	316	Joshua B	17	DE	109	Ann	65	MD	332
William	7	DE	316	Letitia	30	DE	104	Charles	8	DE	349
William W	21	DE	348	Martha	1	DE	282	Edward	15	DE	186
Hoopes, Barton	25	PA	36	Mary A	25	DE	109	Eliza	32	DE	46
Clara E	8	DE	111	Mary L	9	DE	104	Ella	8	DE	46
Clement	4/12	DE	36	Richard	23	DE	211	Emeline	25	MD	46
Edward W	15	PA	142	Sarah	34	PA	282	Franklin	1/12	DE	368
Elener	33	DE	111	Sarah	46	DE	109	George	16	DE	253
Henry	40	PA	111	Susan	4	DE	104	Harry	3	DE	370
Laura E	5	DE	111	William	3	PA	282	Henry	37	DE	370
Ruth A	24	PA	36	William	5	DE	109	Isaac	11	DE	370
Sarah J	10	DE	111	William N	45	PA	104	Jane	9	DE	370
William H	2	DE	111	Hornby, Margaret	35	GB	284	Jemima	21	DE	303
Hoops, Enos	9	DE	353	Horner, Ann	21	PA	237	John	11	DE	334
Hannah J	20	DE	354	Ann K	50	PA	237	John	40	DE	377
Jonathan	28	PA	354	Edward J	37	DE	70	John	60	MD	332
Martha	20	DE	354	Ellen F	14	PA	70	John H	10	DE	378
Mary Ann	28	DE	353	Hannah	--	NJ	186	Kate	9	DE	270
Susan	19	PA	338	Harriet	39	PA	70	Letitia	1	DE	378
Thomas	18	DE	364	William C	30	PA	237	Letitia	38	DE	377
Thomas	39	PA	353	Hortage, Elizabeth	50	NJ	372	Margaret	29	LE	370
William	8/12	DE	354	Lawrence	45	NJ	372	Margaret	67	MD	46
William	31	PA	349	Hosac, Mathew	76	IE	99	Margaret A	4	DE	378
William M	3	DE	353	Hosseker, Anna E	5	DE	364	Maria	34	DE	270
Hootton, Isaac	47	DE	304	Emma C	7	DE	364	Mary	58	DE	332
Rebecca	45	DE	304	James	29	DE	364	Mary E	6	DE	370
Hoover, Mary	77	PA	312	James H Jr	5/12	DE	364	Mary E	15	DE	378
Hope, Eliza A	4	DE	386	Sarah	27	DE	364	Rachel	18	DE	377
Elizabeth	60	NJ	79	Hotsten, Rachel	40	DE	122	Richard	18	DE	333
Emanuel P	6	DE	386	Rachel M	18	DE	122	Robert	29	MD	368
George T	14	DE	386	Hougarth, Mary	15	DE	345	Samuel	1	DE	370
Henrietta	1	DE	386	House, Margaret	3	DE	153	Samuel F	7	DE	378
Henrietta	33	DE	386	Householder, Albert	4	PA	267	Sarah	5	DE	370
Martina K	8	DE	386	James	2	PA	267	Sarah	26	DE	368
William	34	DE	386	John	16	PA	267	Sarah	68	DE	370
William R	10	DE	386	Louisa	1/12	DE	267	Sarah J	17	DE	377
Hopham, Ashton	7/12	DE	139	Sarah	23	PA	267	Terry	64	DE	324
Caleb	34	PA	139	Wm	29	PA	267	Thomas	37	MD	46
Charles A	8	VA	139	Houseman, Amy	68	NJ	283	William	10	DE	46
George S	4	DE	139	Housten, Benjamin A	9	DE	111	William H	1	DE	303
Mary	27	VA	139	Dennis	27	IE	43	Howe, Anna E A	16	DE	184
Hopkins, Catherine	17	DE	113	Drucilla	36	GB	111	Esther C	8	DE	184
Dinah	55	DE	199	Francis H	5	DE	111	James C	52	NJ	184
Ellen	19	DE	128	Henrietta	36	DE	190	Jane M	11	DE	184
Harriet	5	DE	128	Jerry	30	DE	74	John B	21	NY	184
Harriet	40	PA	128	John	42	DE	190	Letitia H	14	DE	184
James	5	DE	128	John	46	DE	136	Letitia H	47	PA	184
James	50	MD	128	Mark B	1	DE	111	Mary J	17	DE	184
John	4	IE	165	Mary	28	DE	74	Rebecca	50	DE	238
Joseph	22	PA	276	Rachel	74	PA	101	Sarah	51	DE	238
Lydia	22	PA	357	Sarah	12	DE	111	Howel, Alice	3	MD	320
Hopper, Charlotte	45	DE	272	Sarah	23	IE	43	Alexander	23	NJ	293
Edward	27	DE	382	William	40	DE	111	Augustus	5	MD	319

Name	Age	St	No	Name	Age	St	No	Name	Age	St	No
Howel, Jacob	50	MD	319	Hudson, Sarah J	18	DE	173	Hughs, Mary	3	DE	22
Mary	30	DE	47	Susan	7	DE	199	Mary	11	NJ	34
Sarah	6	MD	319	Thomas	48	DE	92	Patrick	28	GB	22
Sarah	48	MD	319	Thomas C	4	DE	82	Richard	15	NJ	34
Sarah E	1	DE	319	William	6	DE	11	Sarah	3	DE	34
Howell, Ann	27	MD	238	William	6	DE	82	Susannah	8	DE	34
E D	40	DE	316	William F	1	DE	239	Huhim, Adam	13	PA	128
Eliza A	14	DE	316	Hues, George	18	DE	3	Agniss	2	PA	128
Eliza J	35	DE	316	Margaret	24	IE	318	Ann	4	PA	128
Elizabeth	9	DE	238	Margaret	55	MD	26	Ann	33	PA	128
Henry D	30	NJ	179	Huff Edgar	4/12	MD	196	Danial	39	PA	128
John	5	MD	238	Edwin	4/12	MD	196	Elizabeth	9	PA	128
John	30	DE	238	Robert	30	DE	196	Mary J	11	PA	128
Lenora B	3	DE	316	Sarah A	28	MD	196	Sarah	6	PA	128
Martha A	14	DE	394	Huffington, Joshua	43	DE	373	Hukel, Edward M	10	DE	171
Perry	1	MD	238	Sarah J	24	PA	90	George B	1	DE	171
Rachel	53	MD	318	William	50	DE	160	Gideon	41	DE	171
Samuel	17	MD	179	Huffnall, Amanda	3	DE	314	Gideon B	5	DE	171
William	7	MD	238	Emeline	6	PA	314	Hannah E	16	DE	171
Howland, Elizabeth	36	DE	359	Joseph	36	PA	314	John L	9	DE	171
Joseph	9	DE	359	Mary A	31	PA	314	Mary C	18	DE	171
Price	4	DE	359	Hugen, Emily	19	GE	275	Sarah V	7	DE	171
Samuel	7	DE	359	Huges, Oswald	28	GB	333	Susanna	38	DE	171
Samuel	37	DE	359	Hugg, Andrew	27	DE	295	William A	14	DE	171
Howshall, Henry	14	PA	319	Benjamin	6	DE	380	Hulden, Elilila	22	IE	323
Hucharty, John	28	DE	236	Enoch	34	DE	294	Hull, Ann	60	DE	129
Huchenson, Maria	35	DE	331	Hannah A	2	DE	380	Edward	6	DE	200
William	15	DE	314	John C	9/12	DE	380	Eliza	30	PA	131
Huckel, Emily	7	DE	291	Maria	50	PA	294	Elizabeth	60	PA	131
Jeremiah	46	DE	290	Sarah	23	PA	294	Ervin	9	DE	200
John	14	DE	291	Sarah A	30	DE	380	Fess	25	DE	303
Leah	46	DE	290	Susan	65	MD	172	Hannah	30	DE	28
Sally Ann	10	DE	291	William E	3	DE	380	Henrietta	2	DE	200
William	11	DE	291	William H	32	DE	380	James	38	DE	200
Huckle, Mary	15	DE	315	Huggins, Harriet	45	DE	382	Joseph	12	DE	128
Spencer	50	DE	315	John	12	DE	382	Leah	28	DE	128
William	12	DE	316	Levi	49	DE	382	Louisa	4/12	DE	200
Hudson, Abraham	12	DE	225	Levi Jr	19	DE	382	Margaret	40	DE	128
Alfred	20	DE	198	Mary	6	DE	200	Mary	40	DE	200
Amanda	25	DE	4	Mary	16	DE	382	Mary J	22	DE	128
Ann E	7	MD	239	Robert	14	DE	200	Neamiah	23	PA	131
Catherine J	11	DE	196	Robert	41	DE	200	Rachel	60	PA	284
Edith	2	DE	225	Samuel	17	DE	200	Sabila A	19	DE	128
Elizabeth	3	DE	82	Sarah A	32	DE	200	Sarah	10	DE	128
Elizabeth	15	DE	199	Sarah M	12	DE	200	Sarah	10	DE	200
Elizabeth	25	DE	225	William	19	DE	200	Thomas	23	PA	354
Elizabeth	31	DE	82	Huggit, Samuel	10	DE	313	Hullcross, Ann	7/12	DE	209
Ellen	23	DE	230	Hughes, Albert	27	NY	2	Anna	29	PA	209
Esther	23	DE	255	Esther	48	NJ	267	Frank F	37	PA	209
Frances E	4	PA	8	James	21	NJ	267	Jacob	5	DE	209
Francis	25	IE	8	James	21	PA	379	James	3	DE	209
George W	1	DE	4	Jesse	11	NJ	267	Hullet, John	6	DE	365
Gustavus	10/12	DE	230	Jesse	52	NJ	267	Martha	45	DE	365
Isaac	34	DE	342	Joseph	8	NJ	267	Mary	7	DE	384
Isaac	40	DE	255	Lucetta	20	NJ	267	Sarah	12	DE	365
Henry	36	DE	239	Margaret	17	NJ	267	Hully, Catherine	7	DE	43
Hester	24	DE	342	Sarah	58	NY	2	Daniel	45	GB	43
James	21	DE	196	Hughey, Ann	7	DE	334	James	10	DE	43
James A	12	DE	230	Ann	38	IE	334	Mary	15	GB	43
Jno	--	DE	290	Catherine	3	DE	334	Sarah	5	DE	43
John	1	DE	199	Edward	9	DE	334	Sarah	40	GB	43
John	17	DE	204	Hugh	17	DE	334	Humline, Anna H	15	DE	120
John	25	DE	230	James	3	DE	334	Breta	35	DE	120
John H	9	MD	239	John	20	IE	334	James H	13	DE	120
John P	45	DE	198	Margaret	13	DE	334	John	1	DE	120
Joseph	16	DE	225	Mary	24	DE	263	John	52	NJ	120
Leah	35	DE	199	Mary J	15	DE	334	Lucinda	5	DE	120
Lydia A	21	MD	239	Patrick	11	DE	334	Margaretta	11	DE	120
Martha	18	DE	199	Patrick	48	IE	334	Sarah	3	DE	120
Mary	12	DE	263	Peter	1	DE	334	Humphrey, Charles	5	MD	277
Mary	22	IE	8	Thomas	24	MD	263	George	7	MD	277
Mary E	4	DE	230	Wm	35	MD	263	James	55	GB	277
Matilda	45	DE	92	Wolman	2/12	DE	263	Lydia	42	GB	277
Outen D	8	DE	196	Hughs, Catherine	1	DE	22	Humphries, Ambrose	25	GE	250
Purnell	40	DE	196	Charles	11/12	DE	34	Elizabeth	20	DE	376
Richard	19	DE	197	James P	38	NJ	34	Israel	23	DE	280
Robert	8	DE	225	John	23	IE	350	James	1	DE	280
Robert	40	MD	199	John	52	IE	84	Peter	2	DE	376
Robert H	26	RI	8	Lydia	36	NJ	34	Richard	32	DE	376
Sarah	10	DE	199	Margaret	27	GB	22	Sarah	25	MD	380
Sarah	14	DE	225	Margaretta	6	DE	34	Hunt, John M	22	PA	175
Sarah A	15	DE	196	Martha	10	DE	34	Hunter, Abba A	14	DE	21

Name	Age	Place	No.
Hunter, Abigal	7	IE	35
Andrew	10	DE	270
Anna	6	DE	270
Catherine	1	DE	3
Eliza	23	GB	183
Elizabeth	13	DE	56
Elizabeth	50	DE	21
Hannah	25	ST	165
Hellen	5	DE	306
Isaac	25	IE	35
Isaac	46	MD	270
Isabella S	18	DE	183
James	60	DE	145
Jane	26	IE	35
John	30	DE	3
John M	5	DE	3
Joseph	19	DE	22
Joseph	33	PA	306
Joseph A	8/12	DE	183
Joseph A	44	DE	56
Laura E	1	DE	306
Lucy	26	IE	84
Marcia C	3	DE	306
Margaret	35	DE	270
Martha	8	DE	56
Martha	38	DE	56
Mary	16	DE	270
Mary E	2	MD	183
Mary E	5	DE	3
Mrs	35	PA	113
Sarah	23	DE	3
Sarah	32	PA	306
Thomas	12	PA	270
William	28	FL	183
Huntington, Benj	30	ME	59
Huntsman, Hannah	38	PA	274
Hannah E	1	DE	274
Sarah A	3	DE	274
William	41	GB	274
Hupel, John	24	GE	185
Hurigan, Danial	34	IE	161
Hurlburt, Ebenezer	16	PA	197
Hurley, Catharine	16	IE	302
Hurlock, Caroline	42	DE	255
Wm J	60	DE	255
Hurst, Alexander	3	DE	346
Asbury	17	DE	199
Edward	42	IE	346
Evalina	1	DE	346
Isabella	9	DE	346
James	27	DE	305
Rebecca	22	IE	346
Rebecca	40	IE	346
Stephinius	6	DE	346
Hurt, Henry	9	DE	255
Susan	70	DE	327
Hurth, Joseph	27	FR	317
Husbands, Abraham	48	DE	313
Adolphus	24	DE	296
Andrew J	11	DE	313
Anna M	14	DE	313
Daniel	22	DE	296
Eliza A	16	DE	313
Elizabeth	29	DE	302
Ella J	7	DE	313
Ester J	14	DE	348
Hannah P	23	DE	296
Howell	26	DE	243
James	10	DE	296
Jane	44	DE	348
Jane	51	DE	296
John	33	DE	296
John A	12	DE	313
Louisa J	16	DE	313
Lydia J	9	DE	313
Margaret	27	DE	296
Rachel	26	DE	348
Rachel	34	DE	296
Rachel	44	DE	313
Rebecca	52	DE	348
Rebecca J	18	DE	348
Robt	51	DE	348

Name	Age	Place	No.
Husbands, T C	5	DE	302
Thomas	33	DE	302
Thos W	18	DE	348
Victorine	8	DE	277
Wesley J	7	DE	313
William	26	DE	348
William F	44	DE	313
William S	9/12	DE	313
Wm	64	DE	296
Wm A	6	DE	296
Wm E	3	DE	302
Wm H	6	DE	296
Hust, William	34	IE	300
Hustead, George	32	CN	14
John	22	CN	14
Husten, Ellen	14	DE	331
Emma	11	DE	331
Mary	17	PA	331
Robt T	8	DE	331
Stewart	62	IE	331
Susan	43	DE	331
Hustick, Benjamin	25	DE	336
Hustis, Elizabeth	5	DE	352
Elizabeth A	35	NY	352
Joseph	1	DE	352
Joseph	34	NY	352
Minerva	7	DE	352
Sarah	3	DE	352
William	9	DE	352
Hutchins, Priscilla	50	DE	198
William	48	DE	198
Hutchinson, Andrew	8	DE	319
Ann	70	IE	359
Augustus	40	DE	257
Benedict	60	DE	225
Catherine	22	DE	231
Charles	25	GB	20
Daniel	6/12	DE	319
Daniel	40	MD	319
Dillon	41	DE	330
Eliza J	28	MD	319
Elizabeth	46	IE	287
John	1	DE	231
John	6	DE	257
John	30	DE	225
Joseph	22	DE	231
Margaret	30	DE	257
Margaret	70	IE	359
Martha A	7	DE	319
Mary	2	DE	257
Mary	24	DE	225
Mary E	16	DE	225
Perry H	3	DE	319
Robt	6/12	DE	257
Sarah	4	DE	257
Sarah J	5	DE	319
William	1/12	DE	225
William	16	DE	349
William	39	IE	287
Hutman, Anna	10	GE	21
Anna	36	GE	21
William	9	GE	21
William	45	GE	21
Hutt, Ann	35	DE	244
Edward	11	DE	244
Harriet A	5	DE	229
Henrietta	3	DE	229
Henry	2	DE	323
Jane	25	DE	323
John	1	DE	245
Joseph	40	DE	228
Lorenzo	7	DE	229
Lydia	3	DE	244
Lydia M	16	DE	228
Priscilla	6	DE	244
Rebecca	2	DE	244
Sarah	10	DE	244
Thomas	10	DE	229
William	35	DE	244
William H	7	DE	244
Hutten, Elizabeth	28	DE	54
Mary B	45	DE	54

Name	Age	Place	No.
Hutton, Aaron	20	DE	49
Aaron	21	PA	18
Amelia	4	DE	93
Ann	40	PA	18
Ann	55	PA	41
Anna	45	NJ	93
Elizabeth	27	DE	162
Elwood	17	PA	18
Eunice	44	DE	375
Franklin	8/12	DE	280
Hannah	9	PA	18
Hannah	22	DE	41
Hannah	30	DE	280
Hult	22	DE	41
James	9	DE	347
James	25	IE	347
John	11	DE	347
John	49	DE	375
Joshua	17	DE	41
Joshua	58	PA	41
Maria	12	DE	336
Mary	13	PA	18
Mary	24	DE	93
Mathew B	1	DE	93
Patrick	28	IE	347
Sarah	16	DE	41
William	25	NJ	93
Huttone, Jesse	11	PA	285
Huxler, Catherine	17	DE	161
Elisha	56	DE	161
Hannah	40	DE	161
John	12	DE	162
Hyatt, Agnes	45	DE	244
Albert A	2/12	DE	171
Amanda	7	DE	324
Anna	2	DE	287
Catharine	42	DE	259
Charles C	3	NJ	244
Christiana E	80	PA	244
David	35	DE	287
Edward	9	PA	169
Edwin	8	PA	244
Edwin	9	MD	194
Eliza J	31	DE	324
Elizabeth	12	DE	287
Ellen	36	PA	66
Frances A	26	DE	171
Frank	19	DE	149
Frederic	15	DE	66
George	4	DE	287
George	11	DE	264
George	50	DE	259
Hannah	23	DE	287
Henry	2	NJ	244
Henry	18	DE	259
Jacob	12	DE	66
Jacob B	17	DE	96
Johanna	8	DE	259
John	5	DE	66
John T	42	PA	66
Levinia	22	DE	171
Mary	8	DE	66
Mary	45	DE	133
Mary A	10	DE	289
Mary J	1	DE	324
Noah	12	DE	249
Rachel	10	DE	66
Rebecca J	10	PA	244
Sarah	12	DE	324
Sarah E	15	PA	207
Susan	11	MD	194
Tercia	2	DE	287
Theodore	22	NY	56
Thomas	71	MD	278
Tilman	41	DE	324
Wilhelmina	9	DE	324
William	6	PA	244
William	25	DE	96
William E	43	DE	244
Wyane	3	DE	324
Hybeald, Eli	33	PA	345
Elizabeth	1	PA	345

Hybeald, Ingram	31	PA	345	Irons, Mary J	36	MD	206	Jackson, Elizabeth	13	DE 220
Jane	57	PA	345	Matilda	40	DE	299	Elizabeth	16	DE 25
Joseph	23	PA	345	Rebecca	7	DE	119	Elizabeth	21	DE 173
Martha T	5	PA	345	Rebecca	27	DE	380	Elizabeth	22	IE 58
Morris	19	PA	345	Robert	25	DE	396	Elizabeth	22	IE 150
Ruthanna	15	PA	345	Sally	4	MD	325	Elizabeth	24	DE 12
Susan	21	PA	345	Sarah	15	DE	292	Elizabeth	30	IE 88
Hyde, Albert	26	DE	139	Solomon	15	MD	339	Elizabeth	32	PA 350
George	8	DE	139	Solomon	16	MD	340	Elizabeth	35	DE 220
Joseph	21	PA	136	Susanna	5	DE	299	Elizabeth	48	DE 260
Mary	40	DE	139	Susanna	8	DE	380	Elizabeth	50	DE 19
Mary J	11	DE	139	Tempy	53	DE	292	Elizabeth B	9	PA 356
Mary J	18	DE	136	Wesley	41	MD	206	Emeline	35	DE 73
Hyland, Elizabeth	35	DE	120	Wesley R	3	DE	206	Emeline	36	MD 43
Elmira	33	DE	372	William	17	MD	339	Florida	42	DE 281
Frederick	63	NJ	372	William	18	DE	340	Frances	9	DE 220
John P	25	DE	372	William	20	DE	296	Francis	1	DE 306
Mary	55	NJ	372	William	23	DE	292	Franklin	15	DE 25
Mary E	5/12	DE	371	William	47	MD	339	George	14	DE 302
Sarah J	19	DE	371	Irvin, George	14	ST	319	George	22	PA 25
Thomas	30	IE	338	Irvine, Catherine	26	DE	311	George	26	DE 173
William H	29	DE	371	Irwin, George W	1	DE	86	George W	2	DE 73
				Isabella	29	GB	86	George W	7	DE 143
Idel, Mary A	19	PA	105	John	30	IE	194	George W	11	PA 325
Imary, Amy	7	DE	391	Margaret	8	DE	86	Georgiana	12	DE 216
David	5	DE	391	William	35	DE	86	Grandel Du Pont	4/12	DE 315
Eliza	27	DE	390	Island, Dinah	70	MD	127	Hannah C	13	DE 300
Ingersoll, Louisa	15	NY	164	Israel, Susannah	51	PA	112	Hannah N	5	DE 306
Inghram, Benjamin	25	PA	398	Ivan, Catharine	27	DE	332	Hayne	53	DE 351
Eliza	23	PA	398	James A	1	DE	332	Henrietta	15	PA 73
James	2	PA	398	Thomas	37	NJ	332	Henry	25	IE 150
Joseph	1	DE	398					Henry	32	DE 73
Kennedy	23	PA	398	Jack, Andrew	49	DE	55	Henry C	6	DE 143
Insliff, Joshua	29	GB	334	Anna	12	DE	55	Hinily	40	MD 255
Ireland, Anna	3	DE	110	Edward	40	DE	41	Howard	1/12	DE 368
David	38	NJ	79	Eleanor	39	PA	267	Isabella	30	DE 313
Elizabeth	36	PA	110	Emily	7	DE	55	James	20	DE 260
Elizabeth	49	DE	181	Emma	4	DE	267	James	30	PA 153
Frederic	3/12	DE	110	Georgana	11	DE	41	James	33	DE 346
Hannah	35	NJ	79	George	5	DE	55	James	34	DE 73
Jonathan	56	NJ	181	Hannah	6	DE	267	James	42	DE 216
Rachel	28	VA	175	Hannah	43	DE	55	James	48	MD 260
William	10	DE	110	Ingebur	1	DE	267	James A	19	PA 325
Irish, John	21	IE	255	James	50	DE	267	Jane	49	PA 302
Mary	22	IE	263	Jane	6	DE	267	Jane	60	IE 150
Irons, Ann	18	DE	158	Jane	45	DE	41	Jane	65	PA 346
Ann F	55	DE	158	John	2	DE	126	Job H	18	PA 103
Catherine	19	DE	292	Lydia	9	DE	267	John	2	DE 301
Catherine	27	DE	308	Margaret	9	DE	55	John	5	DE 220
Charles	5	DE	292	Margaret	16	DE	41	John	6	DE 59
Charles	18	MD	339	Mary	14	DE	55	John	7	DE 25
Charles	19	DE	314	Mary	16	DE	267	John	10	IE 103
Comfort	4	DE	155	Mary	28	DE	126	John	10	DE 143
Edith	7	DE	380	Rachel	28	IE	55	John	15	PA 301
Eli	12	MD	325	Sarah	14	DE	267	John	19	PA 359
Eli	70	DE	299	William	3	DE	126	John	28	DE 242
Elizabeth	3	DE	380	William	14	DE	41	John	50	DE 143
Elizabeth	11	DE	320	William	30	DE	126	John C	31	DE 350
Elizabeth	50	DE	119	Wm	11	DE	267	John M	36	PA 306
Ellen	1	DE	380	Jackson, A S	24	DE	12	John W	3/12	DE 73
Jacob	15	MD	339	Amelia	28	PA	346	John W	9	DE 313
Jacob	17	DE	192	Andrew	6	DE	368	Joseph	9	DE 25
James	6/12	DE	308	Ann	25	DE	368	Joseph	20	DE 337
James	6	DE	380	Ann	32	IE	103	Joseph	53	DE 304
James	10	DE	293	Anna M	12	PA	356	John	80	IE 290
James	17	DE	320	Benjamin	35	DE	220	Julia	3	DE 153
James	33	MD	380	Bennett	5	DE	155	Julia	34	MD 155
John	12	MD	339	Bryan	53	GE	302	Jupiter	73	DE 384
John	18	MD	325	Catherine	35	DE	375	James	5	DE 73
John	65	DE	158	Charles	12	PA	288	Kesiah	47	DE 115
Julia	3	DE	308	Charles	25	PA	381	Larega	1	DE 12
Levi	10	DE	320	Charlotte	9	DE	348	Laura	4	DE 59
Levi	10	MD	325	Clara	4	DE	300	Levi	19	DE 387
Levi	60	DE	119	Darius	22	DE	73	Lucy	8	DE 300
Lewis	8	DE	300	David	37	DE	155	Lydia	42	DE 25
Lewis	30	MD	325	David	45	DE	379	Malinda	40	DE 48
Lewis	40	DE	320	David A	11	DE	155	Margaret	9/12	DE 73
Lewis	40	MD	325	Edward F	1/12	DE	346	Margaret	10	DE 73
Lydia	25	MD	325	Elder J	10	DE	320	Margaret	13	DE 25
Lydia	30	DE	320	Eli	16	DE	391	Margaret	23	DE 201
Margaret A	10	DE	206	Eliza	15	DE	368	Margaret	27	DE 306
Marian	35	MD	325	Eliza	38	DE	380	Margaret	63	VA 284

Name	Age	State	Pg	Name	Age	State	Pg	Name	Age	State	Pg
Jackson, Maria	15	PA	350	Jacobs, John	13	DE	352	Janvier, Edwin P	22	DE	381
Maria	24	DE	320	Levi	52	MD	339	Eliza	56	DE	201
Maria	33	DE	73	Margaret Hellen	11	DE	352	Eliza C	41	DE	280
Mariettie	1	DE	381	Mary	28	MD	339	Elizabeth	18	DE	381
Martha	42	DE	216	Mary J	16	DE	352	Ellen	12	DE	314
Mary	12	DE	385	Rachel	5	DE	352	Emily	24	DE	201
Mary	29	DE	368	Sarah	5	DE	352	Emma	6	DE	314
Mary	24	DE	381	Sarah	38	DE	352	Ferdinand	28	DE	296
Mary	28	PA	153	Sylvester	17	MD	339	George	46	PA	387
Mary	45	DE	304	William	9	MD	339	Isaac	18	DE	127
Mary	59	DE	384	Jagger, Caroline	18	NJ	379	Isaac	65	DE	127
Mary A	12	DE	143	Elizabeth	25	NJ	379	James	17	DE	201
Mary A	36	DE	300	George	41	DE	352	Jane	14	DE	54
Mary A	39	PA	325	Harriet F	14	NJ	379	John	41	DE	280
Mary E	7/12	DE	173	James	27	NJ	379	John	64	DE	201
Mary E	1	DE	325	Joseph P	14	NJ	379	Joseph	20	DE	127
Mary E	2	DE	306	Matilda	50	NJ	379	Julian D	11	DE	280
Mary E	9	DE	300	Rachel	11	DE	379	Louisa	17	DE	387
Mary E	42	RI	315	Robert	16	NJ	379	Louisa	23	DE	282
Mary J	2/12	DE	216	Thomas	8	DE	337	Margaret	35	DE	54
Mary J	8	DE	73	James, Abijah	8	DE	337	Margaret W	6	DE	280
Mary L	3	DE	346	Ann	27	DE	337	Mary	10	DE	314
Matilda	45	DE	143	Ann E	14	MD	246	Mary	11	DE	54
Matilda J	3	DE	143	Anne	19	DE	9	Mary	16	DE	387
Milton	39	PA	325	Daniel	23	DE	18	Matilda	16	DE	127
Peter	40	DE	320	David	1	PA	337	Matilda	20	DE	314
Rebecca	5	DE	375	David	10	DE	337	Matilda	58	GB	127
Rebecca A	28	DE	103	E J	25	MD	1	Mercer	72	NJ	288
Richard	11	IE	103	George	12	DE	337	Rebecca	21	DE	201
Richard	44	GB	300	Grace	50	NJ	288	Reuben P	18	DE	296
Risdon	74	MD	376	Henry	8/12	DE	246	Thomas	3	DE	54
Robert	75	DE	284	Jane	5	DE	337	Thomas	4	DE	387
Ruth	45	DE	350	Jane	50	MD	337	Thomas	77	DE	288
Samuel	10	DE	384	John	10	MD	246	Thomas M D	26	DE	172
Samuel	42	PA	356	John E	10	DE	337	William	5/12	DE	54
Samuel	45	DE	368	Joseph	45	DE	337	William	22	DE	127
Samuel A	14	DE	300	Julia	35	GB	307	William	30	DE	282
Sarah	10/12	DE	153	Margaret	17	DE	337	William E	20	DE	132
Sarah A	55	DE	116	Margaret M	46	MD	333	Jaquet, James	37	DE	375
Sarah E	7	DE	368	Martha	2	DE	337	John	20	DE	32
Sharlotta	10	DE	354	Mary E	7	DE	337	Margaret	24	DE	375
Susan	8	MD	400	Mary J	13	MD	246	Mary J	7	DE	375
Susey W	7	PA	356	Richard	2	MD	246	Robt	36	NJ	264
Sylvester	9	DE	321	Samuel	4/12	DE	337	Jaquett, Amanda L	2	DE	327
Temperance	60	DE	330	Samuel	1	MD	238	Andrew N	8	DE	383
Thomas	5	DE	350	Samuel	4	DE	221	Catharine	18	DE	266
Thomas	9	DE	216	William	10	DE	317	Esther	50	PA	390
Thomas	15	DE	220	William	16	MD	246	John	39	DE	383
Thomas	16	PA	143	Zebulon	3	PA	337	John	41	NJ	146
Thomas	16	DE	302	Zebulon	60	MD	337	Levi	56	DE	323
Thomas	23	GB	32	Jameson, James	14	MD	333	Matthew J	12	DE	383
Thomas	73	DE	346	Jamison, Agnes	4	DE	202	Nathaniel	60	DE	327
Thomas H	13	DE	370	Albert	10	DE	202	Robert	15	DE	332
Travilla	26	DE	260	Anna	6	DE	202	Sarah	55	DE	146
Victoria	6	PA	325	Elizabeth	10	DE	268	Virginia	20	VA	327
Virginia	4/12	DE	381	Emma	2	DE	202	William	28	DE	390
Wayne	53	DE	350	George H	21	DE	365	William T	13	DE	383
William	4/12	DE	150	James	11	DE	266	Jarald, James	55	DE	245
William	10	DE	305	Lewis	36	DE	267	Susan	15	DE	245
William	18	PA	317	Mary	8	DE	202	Wesley	13	DE	245
William	34	MD	195	Mary	32	DE	266	Jarold, James	24	DE	215
William	36	DE	330	Mary	38	DE	267	John	36	DE	215
William	40	DE	220	Mary A	32	DE	202	Rachel	42	PA	215
William A	44	MD	313	Rebecca	63	DE	365	William H	17	DE	215
William B	7	DE	350	Sarah	6	DE	266	Jason, John	28	MD	22
William H	12	DE	220	Scynthia	18	DE	365	Jastison, George C	7	DE	293
Woodward T	5	PA	356	Thomas	17	PA	163	Elizabeth	16	DE	293
Jacob, Silvester	19	DE	313	Thomas	42	DE	202	Jean, Margaret	20	DE	11
Jacobs, Adam	21	DE	313	Wm	8	DE	266	Jeandell, Andrew	1	DE	274
Adam	22	MD	339	Wm	16	DE	252	Charles	4	DE	115
Albert	8	MD	339	Janvier, Alfred	18	DE	314	Francis	1	DE	115
Albert	19	DE	375	Ann	33	DE	172	Francis	29	DE	274
Aquilla	12	MD	339	Ann	41	DE	314	Francis	66	FR	274
Belinda	46	MD	339	Ann J	62	DE	172	George S	1	DE	115
Christiana C	15	DE	352	B A	42	DE	54	Jane	38	DE	308
David	1	MD	339	Benjamin	5	DE	54	Mary	61	DE	274
George	9	DE	352	Catharine T	58	DE	387	Rachel	28	PA	116
George Sr	83	GE	352	Charles	8	DE	314	Sarah	19	DE	274
Henery	6	DE	352	Clara	14	DE	314	W T	32	DE	115
Henry	70	GE	358	Edward	30	DE	201	William	6	DE	115
Hester A	7	DE	352	Edward B	51	DE	314	Jeans, Joseph	21	DE	398
Hyram	3	DE	352	Edwin P	22	DE	381	Priscilla	25	DE	398

Name	Age	St	Pg
Jeans, Priscilla	43	DE	398
Jester, Elizabeth	37	FR	50
Jefferies, Margaret	20	PA	339
Susan	18	PA	339
Jefferis, Allice	32	DE	309
Eugene	7	PA	298
James V	23	DE	299
James W	5	PA	298
Jervis	6/12	DE	298
Joseph	32	PA	298
Phebe	21	DE	299
Rebecca	28	PA	298
Thomas W	2	DE	298
William	13	DE	362
Jeffers, Allen	4	DE	49
Amelia	12	PA	40
Ann	45	DE	40
Ann	47	PA	81
Anna	18	DE	40
Carlton	7	DE	49
Caroline	6/12	DE	152
Caroline	16	DE	40
Charles	8	PA	40
Charles	22	PA	129
Chaulky	21	DE	64
Danial	9	PA	142
Edmond	7/12	DE	72
Edwin	9	DE	48
Elias	5	DE	72
Elias	5	DE	78
Eliza	36	PA	152
Elizabeth	23	DE	72
Ella	14	DE	40
Emmon	45	PA	40
Ester	8	DE	152
Eugene	10	PA	40
Franklin	30	PA	33
Galena	10/12	DE	142
Gemimia	39	MD	73
George	3	DE	98
Hannah	18	DE	33
Hannah	25	DE	72
Henry C	15	IN	81
Howard	2	PA	33
Isaac	21	MD	73
Jacob	37	PA	48
James	27	PA	356
Jervis	35	PA	142
Jethro	37	PA	152
John	40	DE	90
John C	25	PA	160
Joseph R	22	PA	56
Louisa	32	MD	356
Lydia A	14	PA	152
Margaret	11	IN	81
Margaret	30	DE	116
Martha	38	PA	48
Mary	6/12	DE	49
Mary	25	PA	56
Mary	30	DE	98
Mary	59	DE	72
Mary A	29	PA	33
Mary H	11	PA	152
Mary J	19	PA	81
Park	28	DE	72
Phebe A	34	DE	90
Rachel	20	MD	73
Rebecca	50	DE	64
Richard	48	DE	81
Sarah	60	NJ	69
Sarah A	26	PA	143
Susan	4	DE	40
Tabitha	18	DE	64
William	1	DE	98
William	23	MD	73
William	40	DE	110
Jefferson, Amanda	20	DE	211
Ann	38	DE	288
Ann	53	DE	211
Arzilla	15	DE	272
Caroline	12	DE	115
Charles	12	DE	272
Jefferson, Chas R	14	DE	288
Colbert	18	DE	201
David J	20	DE	201
Elbert H	2	DE	202
Elda A	14	DE	222
Elias	32	DE	173
Elihu	24	DE	213
Elihu	48	DE	288
Eliza	34	DE	321
Eliza J	12	DE	321
Eliza J	15	DE	213
Elizabeth	11	DE	202
Enoch	8	DE	321
Enoch	34	DE	321
Enos H	37	DE	115
Eugene H	5	DE	202
Eunice	13	DE	202
Frank W	7	DE	202
Frederick	2	DE	321
Henry	17	DE	129
Hester	28	DE	322
James	20	NC	268
James	30	DE	322
John	46	DE	202
John	50	DE	241
Josephine	16	DE	288
Joshua	29	DE	202
Julia	8	DE	288
Juliaelma	14	DE	272
Lydia	18	DE	202
Lydia A	16	DE	211
Margaret	47	DE	202
Mary A	24	DE	202
Mary A	30	DE	213
Penney	30	DE	248
Purnel	58	DE	202
Purnell	16	DE	202
Purnell L	29	DE	211
Rachel A	10	DE	222
Richard	10	DE	222
Richard	31	DE	208
Samuel	11	DE	321
Samuel	53	DE	211
Sarah	4	DE	321
Sarah H	36	NJ	202
Sarah J	13	DE	222
Sewall	26	DE	248
Susan	28	DE	207
Susanah	32	DE	115
Thomas	20	DE	251
Wesley	35	DE	213
William H	4	DE	288
Jeffries, Alice	32	DE	308
Bennett	65	PA	354
Mary	70	PA	354
Tamora	74	DE	362
Jefries, Martha	13	DE	323
Michael	50	IE	323
Jemison, Alexander	33	DE	149
Edward	14	DE	213
Elizabeth	60	DE	149
James	12	DE	213
Margaret	28	DE	149
Robert	32	MD	16
Jenkins, Abraham	6/12	DE	64
Abraham	30	DE	228
Abraham	35	DE	229
Caleb	12	DE	12
Catherine	7	DE	156
Cesar	37	DE	309
Cesar	70	DE	235
Daniel	17	DE	11
Daniel	17	DE	305
David	24	DE	307
David	25	DE	11
Edward	16	MA	163
Elizabeth	1	DE	235
George	3	DE	11
Henry	26	DE	64
Hester	70	DE	337
Jabes	40	DE	11
James W	17	MA	153
Jenkins, John	10	DE	11
John	10	DE	73
John	11	ST	178
John	17	DE	229
Lydia	24	DE	11
Lydia	24	DE	159
Margaret	5	DE	156
Margaret	20	DE	235
Maria	39	DE	11
Mary	1	DE	156
Mary	25	DE	64
Mary	54	DE	257
Mary	60	DE	317
Millicent	16	DE	225
Minte A	29	DE	156
Nancy	45	DE	229
Rachael	18	DE	235
Rachel	67	DE	235
Richard	67	MD	354
Samuel	2	DE	11
Sarah A	7	DE	11
Sarah E	8	DE	156
Thomas	9	DE	235
Tiny	58	DE	354
William	15	MA	163
William	15	PA	305
William	34	DE	156
William D	14	DE	11
Jennett, Rebecca	63	DE	167
Jenney, Emma L	2	PA	91
Luisa	28	CN	91
Mary C	5	PA	91
Jennings, P	30	IE	64
Jenny, Thomas	34	PA	91
Jessup, Augustus E	52	MA	314
Edward A	17	MA	314
Lydia M	50	MA	314
Jester, Amanda	8	DE	36
Ann	10	DE	243
Anna	38	DE	232
Caroline	40	DE	36
Charlotte	40	DE	316
Cornelia	6	DE	36
Edward	4	DE	36
Eliza	16	DE	30
Emily	17	PA	36
Franklin	10	PA	36
George	36	DE	324
George D	6	DE	148
Isaac B	44	DE	148
James	15	DE	36
James A	11	DE	148
James B	13	DE	243
Jane	14	DE	148
Jane	17	DE	316
John	2	DE	324
Jonathan	50	DE	232
Joshua	10	DE	324
Louisa	19	PA	36
Manlove	6	DE	316
Manlove	8	DE	324
Manlove	52	DE	316
Mary	30	DE	324
Mary	40	DE	261
Mary A	10	DE	233
O D	50	DE	36
Peter	45	DE	243
Purnel C	7	DE	243
Rebecca	37	DE	149
Rebecca	40	MD	243
Samuel T	2	DE	149
Sarah	12	PA	36
Sarah A	8	DE	149
Sarah F	11	DE	316
Thomas	2	DE	36
William	12	DE	324
Jestis, Anna M	10	DE	123
Edith	42	DE	123
Elizabeth	5	DE	123
George	7	DE	123
James	1	DE	123
Joseph	42	DE	123

Name	Age	State	No.
Jestis, Sarah J	12	DE	123
Jewell, John	26	MD	217
Jewil, Elizabeth	23	DE	285
Isaac	24	MD	285
Wilhelmina	1	DE	285
Jiffers, Oliver	21	PA	39
Joeane, Deborah	9	DE	307
John, Phebe	70	PA	33
Johns, Alexander	30	DE	197
Ann	62	DE	289
Hester	60	MD	197
James	22	DE	303
James	25	DE	212
Jane	55	DE	289
John	15	DE	289
Julia	6	NJ	140
Julia	20	DE	289
Kensey (Hon)	58	DE	289
M	56	DE	289
Mary	25	DE	289
Sarah	35	MD	197
Sarah M	25	DE	289
William	4	DE	289
William	60	MD	91
Johnson, Aaron	50	MD	153
Abel	4	DE	72
Adaline	4	DE	12
Alex	40	DE	267
Alex	--	DE	290
Alexander	9	DE	12
Alexander	24	DE	286
Alfina	24	MD	56
Alfred	18	MD	307
Amanda	15	OH	289
Amelia	32	PA	108
Amelia A	5	DE	208
Amy	19	DE	279
Amy	19	DE	304
Andrew	25	DE	376
Andrew C	1	DE	276
Ann	18	DE	29
Ann	26	DE	375
Ann	37	DE	376
Ann	50	NJ	309
Ann J	56	DE	309
Ann M	3	DE	134
Anna	1	DE	304
Anna	2	DE	12
Anna	18	DE	4
Anna	58	MD	316
Anna	82	PA	48
Anna C	14	DE	381
Anna F	2	DE	369
Anna J	2	DE	309
Anna M	25	DE	12
Anna M	28	PA	310
Anthony	61	MD	286
Benjamin	4	DE	147
Benjamin	35	PA	325
Benjamin	45	PA	56
Benjamin T	3	DE	325
Brandbling	50	DE	93
C	47	DE	304
Caleb	8	DE	317
Caleb P	28	MD	106
Caroline	15	DE	355
Catherine	13	DE	122
Catherine	15	GB	51
Catherine	19	PA	42
Catherine	22	DE	23
Causden	35	MD	325
Charles	4	DE	93
Charles	9	MD	369
Charles	16	DE	307
Charles	28	DE	92
Charles	70	MD	338
Daniel	70	DE	317
David	21	DE	126
David	27	DE	23
Dianah	45	MD	72
Donia	25	MD	37
Dr	40	DE	162

Name	Age	State	No.
Johnson, Edward	12	DE	387
Edward C	25	DE	309
Elias	22	DE	23
Elias	48	DE	78
Elijah	32	DE	90
Elisha	28	DE	134
Eliza	20	DE	309
Eliza	36	PA	363
Eliza	38	DE	141
Eliza	40	DE	276
Eliza	40	DE	281
Eliza P	33	DE	378
Elizabeth	5	DE	297
Elizabeth	13	DE	219
Elizabeth	15	DE	12
Elizabeth	29	DE	235
Elizabeth	38	DE	270
Elizabeth	40	MD	160
Elizabeth D	11	DE	276
Ellen	25	MD	145
Ellen	35	IE	149
Ellen B	44	DE	53
Emanuel	4	DE	370
Emeline	2	DE	270
Emeline	12	PA	337
Emily	9	DE	74
Emily	27	DE	134
Emily M	12	PA	108
Emma	10/12	DE	42
Eunice A	7	PA	337
Ferdinand	12	KY	309
Frances	18	DE	225
Frank	12	DE	244
Frederick	3	DE	378
George	15	DE	122
George	22	MD	85
George	26	DE	309
George	45	DE	378
George	60	IE	137
George H	1	DE	309
George W	9/12	DE	325
Gilbert	2	DE	93
Grace	28	DE	120
Hannah	26	DE	78
Hannah	47	DE	78
Harriet	35	DE	161
Henrietta	23	MD	160
Henry	12	DE	161
Henry	19	DE	337
Henry	23	SA	290
Henry	35	DE	192
Henry	36	DE	369
Hester	30	MD	369
Hiram J	20	DE	376
Isaac	8	DE	84
Isaac	17	DE	74
Isabella	4/12	DE	337
Jacob	25	DE	147
James	2	DE	13
James	4	DE	336
James	16	DE	28
James	17	VA	401
James	30	DE	83
James	40	DE	34
James	75	DE	363
James C	35	DE	108
James E	39	NJ	392
Jane	1	DE	314
Jane	16	DE	316
Jane	19	DE	97
Jane	22	DE	15
Jane	32	DE	324
Jane	36	IE	336
Jane	43	PA	33
Jane	50	DE	376
Jesse A	10/12	DE	309
Joel	13	PA	282
John	1	DE	149
John	12	DE	383
John	14	DE	161
John	17	DE	308
John	25	DE	9

Name	Age	State	No.
Johnson, John	40	DC	297
John	45	DE	12
John	75	DE	93
John C	15	DE	376
John E	26	DN	42
John H	6	DE	325
John M	16	PA	337
John W	23	MD	149
Jonathan	27	DE	233
Joseph	10	DE	161
Joseph	12	DE	312
Joseph	14	PA	351
Joseph	40	DE	141
Joseph	64	MD	342
Julia	6	DE	84
Julia A	20	DE	152
Kitty	44	DE	12
Lady Ann	58	DE	363
Laura	6	PA	68
Lauran	16	DE	385
Lawson	45	DE	270
Leah	41	PA	337
Lewis	44	PA	33
Lewis H	7/12	DE	152
Lewis H	60	PA	154
Louisa	4/12	DE	134
Louisa	1	DE	316
Louisa	19	PA	337
Louisa	28	MD	153
Louisa	39	DE	307
Louisa	50	DE	276
Lucy	18	DE	309
Luisa	40	DE	74
Lydia	35	DE	61
Margaret	5	DE	13
Margaret	16	PA	88
Margaret	20	DE	23
Margaret	22	GB	149
Margaret	40	DE	381
Margaret	60	GB	145
Margaret	66	DE	61
Margaret E	12	DE	391
Margaretta	35	DE	161
Martha	14	DE	281
Martha	22	PA	309
Martha	40	DE	64
Mary	13	GB	51
Mary	18	DE	93
Mary	20	DE	142
Mary	24	DE	147
Mary	30	DE	285
Mary	30	DE	297
Mary	35	GB	51
Mary	35	DE	314
Mary	60	DE	23
Mary A	8	DE	325
Mary A	34	PA	114
Mary Ann	21	DE	181
Mary C	18	DE	381
Mary D	36	DE	276
Mary E	5	DE	276
Mary F	12	DE	316
Mary Jane	18	DE	376
Mary L	2	DE	153
Mary S	5	DE	337
Matilda	8	DE	141
Milton	45	PA	337
Morgan	8	DE	141
Moses	43	DE	122
P S	39	DE	55
Peter	57	IE	29
Peter L	55	SW	88
Precilla	26	DE	92
Priscilla	55	DE	244
Rachel	11	DE	13
Rachel	17	DE	244
Rachel	21	NJ	88
Rebecca	43	DE	122
Rebecca	60	MD	338
Rebecca D	8	DE	376
Richard	36	GB	51
Robert	22	DE	54

Johnson, Robert	30	NY	110	Johnston, Henry	35	DE	192	Jones, Biddy	24	DE	185

Name	Age	St	Pg	Name	Age	St	Pg	Name	Age	St	Pg
Johnson, Robert	30	NY	110	Johnston, Henry	35	DE	192	Jones, Biddy	24	DE	185
Robert	39	PA	276	Hetty	63	NJ	183	C W	22	DE	164
Robert S	9	DE	276	Isaac	6/12	DE	214	Caleb	37	DE	242
Robert T	41	NC	310	Isaac E	3	DE	182	Caroline	1	DE	178
Rose	6	DE	314	James	12	DE	231	Caroline	7	DE	297
Sally A	22	DE	78	James	17	DE	218	Caroline	8	NJ	19
Sally E	9	DE	324	James	35	DE	186	Catharine	1	DE	370
Samuel	22	DE	244	James	49	DE	207	Catharine	5	DE	279
Samuel B	51	DE	244	James H	4	DE	244	Catharine	17	DE	314
Samuel M	8	DE	381	Jane	3/12	DE	182	Catherine	17	DE	27
Samuel P	8	PA	337	Jane	3	DE	205	Catherine	18	IE	307
Samuel P	55	DE	381	John	3	DE	231	Catherine	21	DE	309
Sarah	8	DE	267	John	6	DE	207	Catherine	28	DE	270
Sarah	12	DE	161	Josiah	40	DE	205	Catherine	18	MD	194
Sarah	27	PA	325	Judy	15	DE	190	Catherine	25	DE	31
Sarah	28	DE	83	Julia	4	DE	214	Catherine	62	IE	302
Sarah	35	DE	373	Julia	26	DE	214	Charles	4	DE	230
Sarah	36	DE	267	Kate	10/12	DE	233	Charles	6	DE	28
Sarah	44	PA	88	Linda M	24	NJ	184	Charles	13	DE	235
Sarah E	7	DE	325	Lindy	30	DE	183	Charles	18	DE	236
Sarah E	12	DE	381	Lydia	25	DE	200	Charles	35	NJ	270
Sarah J	19	DE	378	Margaret	2	DE	214	Charles	36	PA	17
Sarah J	29	DE	392	Margaret	28	DE	204	Charles	48	DE	235
Susan	16	DE	384	Martha	13	PA	189	Charles	50	DE	86
Susan	25	DE	110	Martha	26	DE	205	Charles E	1	DE	184
Susan	25	DE	219	Martha	35	DE	182	Charles H	6	DE	235
Susan E	17	DE	378	Martha A	3/12	DE	207	Charles W	9	DE	177
Susannah	17	PA	337	Mary A	16	DE	183	Charlotte	14	DE	177
Thomas	5	DE	134	Minty	80	DE	220	Charlotte	17	NJ	232
Thomas	15	DE	49	Moses	13	DE	172	Christian S	25	PA	131
Thomas	16	DE	392	Nathan	41	NJ	184	Daniel	15	DE	237
Thomas	22	DE	304	Nicholas	50	DE	241	David	2	DE	299
Thomas	24	DE	244	Rebecca	18	DE	172	David	3	DE	217
Thomas	36	GB	336	Richard	4	DE	205	David	60	MD	268
Thomas	58	DE	23	Sally A	15	DE	198	Debby	23	NJ	262
Thomas	60	IE	167	Samuel	10	DE	205	Deby A	5	DE	46
Thomas H	11	MD	369	Samuel	20	DE	241	Edith	12	DE	330
Wesley C	8	DE	108	Sarah	74	DE	244	Edward	2	DE	177
Willamina	12	DE	297	Sarah A	28	DE	192	Edward	16	DE	338
William	8/12	DE	304	Silas S	42	DE	182	Edward	32	DE	261
William	7	DE	369	Susan	35	DE	207	Edward	34	MD	139
William	14	PA	288	Susan	100	DE	214	Eliza	4	DE	54
William	15	DE	282	Tempy A	4	DE	207	Eliza	22	DE	286
William	16	DE	161	Thomas	4	DE	233	Eliza	24	DE	217
William	17	IE	28	William	4	DE	231	Eliza	31	DE	6
William	17	DE	126	William	6	DE	214	Eliza	33	NJ	19
William	17	MD	315	William	25	DE	200	Eliza A	6	DE	310
William	26	PA	152	William	33	DE	214	Eliza A	9	MD	373
William	30	DE	194	William	35	DE	231	Eliza A	29	MD	333
William	36	DE	12	William D	1	DE	184	Eliza J	12	DE	110
William	51	DE	376	William G	46	PA	183	Elizabeth	7	DE	299
William A	2	DE	134	William H	6	DE	205	Elizabeth	12	DE	217
William A	15	DE	378	Joice, Rebecca	21	PA	292	Elizabeth	16	DE	235
William B	25	DE	376	Thomas	17	PA	292	Elizabeth	18	MD	30
William D	9	DE	392	Jones, Absolem	30	DE	72	Elizabeth	20	DE	27
William H	11	DE	324	Absolem	33	DE	16	Elizabeth	26	DE	242
William M	25	DE	235	Adalaide	12	DE	235	Elizabeth	28	DE	332
William W	13	DE	276	Albert L	9	DE	331	Elizabeth	38	DE	299
Wm	4	DE	325	Alexander	7	DE	188	Ella	3	NJ	20
Wm F	3	DE	309	Alexander	20	MD	194	Emaline	8	DE	207
Wm H	25	DE	258	Alice	20	DE	187	Emeline	28	PA	370
Johnston, Alexander	11	DE	182	Ann	4/12	DE	190	Emma	8	DE	28
Andrew W	20	NJ	183	Ann	10	PA	274	Emma	10	DE	100
Ann	16	DE	248	Ann	25	DE	242	Emma	27	PA	39
Ann E	3	DE	207	Ann	26	IE	302	Emma F	3	DE	233
Ann Eliza	3	DE	214	Ann	35	MD	177	Enoch	1	DE	217
Annie	8	DE	192	Ann	41	PA	32	Enoch	3	DE	235
Ari	51	DE	242	Ann	54	MD	29	Enoch	33	DE	226
Benjamin	10	DE	231	Ann	64	DE	75	Ephraim	25	DE	242
Benjamin	27	DE	244	Ann	70	MD	193	Euphemia	41	MD	268
Caroline	14	DE	241	Ann E	1	DE	332	Evan	14	DE	110
Catherine	8	DE	182	Anna	1	DE	162	Ezekiel	10	DE	235
Charles H	6/12	DE	205	Anna	4	DE	28	Fanny	6	DE	32
Elisa	23	DE	231	Anna	23	DE	178	Frances	22	ST	274
Elizabeth	50	DE	225	Anna	52	DE	54	Frances	60	MD	268
Elizabeth C	13	DE	182	Anna M	35	DE	69	Francis	23	MD	303
Emeline	8	DE	192	Anna M	63	DE	131	Francis R	2	DE	279
Emily	30	DE	244	Annie	5	DE	217	Frisbey	20	DE	303
Emma	20	PA	214	Araminty	13	DE	299	Gemima	17	DE	37
George	12	DE	212	Benjamin	1	PA	16	George	2	MD	373
George	35	DE	227	Benjamin	2	DE	72	George	11	DE	365
George W	5	DE	182	Benjamin	14	DE	274	George	12	DE	230

Name	Age	State	Pg	Name	Age	State	Pg	Name	Age	State	Pg
Jones, George	17	DE	59	Jones, Julia	45	DE	1	Jones, Rebecca A	27	DE	369
George	28	DE	370	Julia A	10	DE	213	Regina	1	DE	235
George	66	DE	131	Julia A	47	DE	235	Richard	6	DE	240
George C	32	DE	339	Letitia A	65	NY	278	Richard	10	DE	242
George P	2	DE	13	Louisa	28	DE	327	Richard	54	MD	297
George R	2	DE	310	Lucretia C	6	DE	338	Richard K	43	DE	13
Grace	70	DE	219	Lucy	14	DE	190	Robert	9	DE	237
Hannah	2	DE	54	Lydia	14	DE	393	Robert	16	DE	27
Hannah	27	PA	141	Lydia	40	DE	317	Robert B	45	DE	236
Hannah E	17	DE	378	Lydia	45	DE	192	Robt H	11	DE	338
Hannah M	4	DE	349	Lydia A	7	DE	378	Ruth	40	DE	37
Hanson	4	MD	207	Lydia Anne	14	DE	192	Sallie	8	DE	331
Harriet	18	DE	184	Margaret	16	DE	311	Samuel	15	DE	378
Harriet	18	PA	338	Margaret	17	DE	378	Samuel	18	DE	122
Harriet	19	DE	175	Margaret	22	DE	261	Samuel	24	DE	187
Harriet	52	GB	338	Margaret	24	DE	233	Samuel	40	DE	19
Henrietta	42	PA	64	Margaret	30	DE	28	Samuel M	30	DE	233
Henrietta O	23	DE	131	Margaret	32	DE	236	Sarah	9/12	DE	185
Henry	19	DE	230	Margaret	37	DE	378	Sarah	2	PA	39
Henry	20	DE	212	Margaret	46	MD	3	Sarah	5	DE	237
Henry	22	DE	207	Margaret A	17	DE	299	Sarah	7	DE	217
Henry	48	DE	299	Maria	4	DE	305	Sarah	11	PA	298
Henry C	13	DE	338	Maria	29	NJ	279	Sarah	16	DE	255
Henry H	10	DE	162	Martha	1	DE	270	Sarah	18	DE	20
Hester	2	DE	46	Martha	1	DE	299	Sarah	20	DE	317
Hester	32	DE	376	Martha	24	DE	189	Sarah	27	DE	162
Hetty	35	DE	308	Martha	26	DE	2	Sarah	27	DE	251
Hetty M	9	DE	235	Martha A	13	DE	210	Sarah	30	DE	27
Irenna	44	DE	86	Martha C	10	DE	110	Sarah	30	DE	54
Isaac	4	DE	177	Mary	8/12	DE	299	Sarah	36	DE	297
Isaac	8	PA	274	Mary	1	DE	274	Sarah	38	MD	240
Isaac	44	PA	274	Mary	6	DE	54	Sarah	39	DE	184
Israel	35	DE	177	Mary	8	DE	197	Sarah	54	PA	376
J B	37	DE	162	Mary	12	DE	192	Sarah A	1	DE	378
Jacob	13	DE	328	Mary	12	DE	237	Sarah A	32	PA	378
James	1	DE	261	Mary	28	MD	139	Sarah J	5	DE	310
James	10	DE	255	Mary	29	DE	73	Sarah J	8	MD	373
James	12	DE	274	Mary	30	DE	46	Sarah J	13	PA	13
James	14	DE	37	Mary	35	DE	58	Sarah J	16	DE	235
James	28	DE	309	Mary	40	DE	349	Sewall	7	DE	177
James	29	DE	250	Mary	40	DE	262	Silas	9	DE	226
James	40	DE	35	Mary	51	DE	162	Spencer	5	DE	188
James	63	DE	330	Mary A	8	DE	297	Susan	4	DE	240
James H	6	DE	213	Mary A	19	DE	196	Susan	25	MD	373
James J	16	DE	389	Mary A	21	DE	226	Susan	30	DE	310
James M	9	DE	13	Mary E	2/12	DE	162	Susan R	11	DE	331
James T	15	DE	331	Mary E	5	DE	278	Susanna	3	DE	332
Jane	3	DE	37	Mary E	8	DE	230	Susannah	37	DE	213
Jane	6	PA	274	Mary E	14	DE	86	Theodore	9	DE	251
Jane	34	ST	274	Mary H	11	DE	69	Theopolis	70	DE	27
Jane	61	GB	399	Mary J	16	DE	299	Thomas	16	DE	400
Janette	58	DE	318	Mary J	20	DE	162	Thomas	22	PA	251
Jerry	49	MD	240	Mary P	22	DE	131	Thomas	29	DE	369
Jesse	4	DE	378	Mary S	3	DE	370	Thomas	37	DE	310
John	7	DE	197	Mary W	43	NJ	13	Thomas	48	DE	230
John	8	DE	268	Matilda	30	DE	289	Thomas	49	MD	184
John	8	DE	322	Miller	3	DE	270	Thomas	77	MD	373
John	11	PA	13	Morgan	42	DE	331	Thomas A	1	DE	213
John	11	DE	226	Moses	4	DE	297	Thomas Jefferson	16	DE	192
John	12	DE	378	Nathaniel W	3	DE	213	Thomas Jr	28	MD	373
John	17	DE	236	Octavius	25	MD	194	Thomas P	30	DE	178
John	18	DE	323	Oliver	6	DE	270	Thomas W	17	DE	13
John	21	DE	300	Owen	30	WL	295	Thos	29	DE	217
John	29	GB	32	Patrick	26	IE	302	Virginia	9	MD	45
John	32	DE	37	Perry	28	DE	69	Washington	30	MD	270
John	33	DE	349	Peter	16	DE	193	Washington	32	DE	28
John	60	DE	192	Phillip	26	DE	54	Willmina	15	DE	177
John	60	GB	399	Phillip H	58	DE	162	William	4/12	DE	28
John A	30	MD	332	Phillis	51	PA	187	William	1	DE	233
John A	56	NJ	75	Rachel	3	DE	242	William	3	PA	274
John Adams	10	DE	192	Rachel	13	DE	235	William	4	DE	72
Jonathan	57	DE	328	Rachel	18	DE	298	William	7	DE	187
Joseph	4	DE	251	Rachel	46	DE	230	William	7	DE	278
Joseph	6	DE	197	Rachel	66	PA	2	William	9	DE	378
Joseph	15	DE	330	Rachel A	15	DE	387	William	11	DE	177
Joseph	17	DE	264	Reader	25	MD	194	William	19	MD	221
Joseph	19	PA	32	Rebecca	4	DE	299	William	19	DE	236
Joseph	20	PA	338	Rebecca	15	DE	179	William	19	DE	245
Joseph	35	GB	279	Rebecca	16	MD	19	William	20	MD	150
Joseph	55	GB	338	Rebecca	35	DE	2	William	22	DE	230
Joseph	67	PA	355	Rebecca	48	DE	328	William	30	DE	2
Josephine	5	DE	139	Rebecca	66	PA	355	William	30	DE	185

Jones, William	30 DE 376	Justison, Daniel	17 DE 292	Karsner, Jane	10 PA 256

Name	Col1	Name	Col2	Name	Col3
Jones, William	30 DE 376	Justison, Daniel	17 DE 292	Karsner, Jane	10 PA 256
William	40 DE 378	George	15 DE 292	Jane	40 DE 256
William	44 MD 213	George	30 DE 298	John	3 DE 256
William	46 DE 387	John	17 DE 292	John	46 DE 256
William	66 DE 2	John	41 DE 292	Margaret	14 PA 256
William H	39 DE 69	Margaret	14 DE 292	Kate, Charles H	5 DE 199
William T	7 DE 213	Margaret	38 PA 292	Hester A	7 DE 199
William W	3 PA 16	Martin	3 DE 292	James W	3 DE 199
Wm	25 DE 252	Rebecca	20 PA 292	Rebecca	9 DE 199
Wm	30 DE 251	Richard	52 DE 292	Kay, Lewis	17 DE 392
Wm	50 MD 268	Sarah A	11 DE 292	Keale, Ann	11 DE 228
Zachariah	3 DE 178	Justus, Albert	18/12 DE 365	Betty	70 MD 228
Zachariah	45 MD 193	Elizabeth	6 DE 365	Matilda	35 DE 228
Zipher	30 DE 72	John B	34 DE 365	Keally, Ann	23 IE 336
Zophia	32 DE 16	Lavinia	28 DE 365	Mary	40 IE 336
Jordan, Agnes	63 DE 294	Sarah Ellen	4 DE 365	Michel	3/12 DE 336
Ann	13 PA 287			Michel	21 IE 336
Catherine	13 DE 226	Kaighan, Edward	8 DE 134	Thomas	23 IE 184
Charles F	12 DE 226	Jesse	60 DE 134	Thomas	23 IE 336
Charles R	45 PA 226	Patience	45 PA 134	Kean, Alexander	16 DE 18
Elizabeth	11 DE 287	Kain, Bridget	7 DE 346	Biddy	22 IE 132
Elizabeth	35 DE 226	Catherine	10 DE 287	Elizabeth	68 DE 18
Elizabeth	64 PA 314	John	7/12 DE 346	Mary	20 IE 75
Hester	35 MD 318	Henry	36 IE 346	Mary	66 DE 18
Isabella	38 DE 272	Mary	30 IE 346	Mathew	63 DE 18
James	79 DE 294	Mary	50 IE 310	Keane, Biddie	20 IE 97
John	67 DE 381	Simon	30 IE 346	Catherine	2 DE 133
John A	40 DE 272	Kalie, Ann E	9 DE 328	James	18 IE 133
Maria T	53 PA 285	Henry	5 DE 328	Mary	25 IE 133
Mary	9 DE 287	Jacob	2 DE 328	Patric	4 DE 133
Mary	33 DE 287	Jacob	40 FR 328	Patric	32 IE 97
Mary E	6 DE 226	James	5 DE 328	Keannan, James	26 IE 306
Ruth	54 DE 381	Susan	42 MD 328	Kearns, Cassander	23 DE 41
Ruth A	18 DE 381	Susan A	11 DE 328	James	20 DE 41
Sarah	7 DE 287	Kane, Alice	16 IE 333	James	49 DE 41
Sarah	33 DE 294	Allice	6 DE 345	Margaret	55 PA 41
Spencer	22 DE 381	Amos	16/12 DE 327	Virginia	17 DE 41
Susan	1 DE 226	Ann E	8 DE 327	Keasler, Henry	28 SZ 125
William	46 DE 318	Catherine	10 DE 327	Keates, Catherine	41 DE 34
William N	5 DE 226	Catherine	29 DE 337	Hannah	11 PA 35
William W	3 PA 287	Catherine	30 IE 380	Jacob	42 NJ 34
Jorden, Asia	50 MD 84	Charles	7 DE 337	John	7 PA 35
Margaret A	10 DE 381	Charles	39 IE 337	Joseph	10 PA 35
Mary	14 GB 185	Dennis	12 DE 327	Maria	15 PA 34
Sarah	35 GB 185	Dennis	2 DE 337	Maria	17 DE 144
Jordon, Henry P	26 DE 301	Ellen	14 IE 333	Mary	14 PA 34
Jorney, Henry	14/12 DE 365	James	10 DE 337	Keath, Elizabeth	45 DE 160
John	14 DE 365	James	40 IE 327	Keatly, James J	2 DE 380
Margaret	36 DE 365	Jane	16/12 DE 327	John T	22 MD 380
Moses	5 DE 365	John	36 GE 186	Mary	35 MD 380
Moses	37 DE 365	Lawrence	12 IE 333	Mary E	9 MD 380
Sarah A	9 DE 365	Margaret	12 IE 345	Richard	38 MD 380
William	17 DE 365	Mary	14 DE 327	William F	7 MD 380
Joseph, Bridget	30 IE 17	Mary	34 IE 345	Keats, George J4	30 DE 1
Josline, Francine	38 MD 151	Mary	62 IE 333	George Sr	67 NJ 1
Mary	16 NJ 151	Mary	62 ? 167	George W	5 DE 1
Thomas	19 NJ 151	Michael	34 IE 345	Henry H	3 DE 1
William	38 NJ 151	Patrick	20 IE 349	Jane	28 DE 1
Jourdan, Howard H	2 DE 381	Rachel	40 PA 327	John	1/12 DE 1
John	36 DE 381	Sarah J	4 DE 337	William	9 DE 1
Martial S	6 DE 381	Thomas	10 IE 345	Kedene, Eliza	20 IE 56
Sarah	34 DE 381	Thomas	24 IE 347	Keech, Emily A	19 PA 306
Joyce, Bertha	21 IE 9	Victoria	6 DE 327	Malinda	45 PA 306
Bridget	32 IE 341	Kanelys, Benjamin	12 DE 227	Matilda E	11 PA 306
John	3 DE 341	Eliza	45 -- 227	Samuel	47 PA 306
Michael	30 IE 341	Elizabeth	10 DE 227	Samuel J	3 PA 306
Thomas	2 DE 341	Emma	14 DE 227	Sidney E	14 PA 306
Jule, Catherine	12 DE 231	James	8 DE 227	Thomas B	9 PA 306
Sarah	15 DE 290	James	52 DE 227	Keel, Ann	46 PA 348
Thomas	13 DE 231	Mary O	6 DE 227	Anna E	21 PA 348
William	17 DE 231	William	3 DE 227	John B	12 PA 348
Jump, Ellen	25 DE 317	Karch, Jacob	15 DE 94	Lydia	14 PA 348
Jefferson	51 MD 325	Jacob	45 GE 94	Margaret J	19 PA 348
Sarah A	18 DE 198	Margaret	11 DE 94	Mary	22 PA 348
Justice, Ann M	18 DE 367	Mary	17 DE 94	Rebecca	17 PA 348
Catherine	61 DE 367	Salome	44 GE 94	Keeler, Jacob	34 NJ 261
Ellener	33 DE 318	Karnahan, Anthony	12 DE 381	Levica	34 PA 261
Rebecca	60 DE 318	Karney, Martin	24 NY 237	Wm	3 DE 261
Robert	25 DE 367	Karnian, Ellen	19 IE 306	Keene, Catherine	3 MD 31
Susan	23 DE 367	Karr, David P	24 DE 362	Elizabeth	1 DE 31
Justis, Sarah C	15 DE 332	Rebecca J	23 DE 362	James	40 PA 363
Justison, Anna L	28 DE 292	Karsner, Ebenezer	6 DE 256	Mary	32 DE 31

Name	Age	St	Pg
Keene, Saml	10	DE	253
Kees, Thomas	18	IE	43
Keever, Mary M	73	DE	167
Kegan, Ellen	1	DE	36
Keith, Daniel	28	IE	249
Keizer, Nicholas	21	GE	162
Keller, Anna	9	NJ	312
Anna	42	GE	312
Frederic	11	NJ	312
George	3	DE	312
George	42	GE	312
Rosana	14	GE	312
Simpson	66	PA	312
Thomas	15	NJ	164
Kelleson, James	24	IE	346
Kello, Charles	28	DE	139
Joseph	2	DE	139
Rachel	23	DE	139
Kellog, Mr	20	OH	137
Mary	25	IE	336
Mary	74	IE	360
Kellum, Artemis	10	DE	296
Caroline	4	DE	297
Eliza	6	DE	297
John	2	DE	297
Joseph	36	DE	297
Julia A	51	DE	296
Lewis	13	DE	296
Mary	7	DE	297
Mary E	8	DE	296
Sarah	25	DE	297
Thomas	2	DE	297
William	47	DE	296
Kelly, Abram	20	DE	366
Albania	9/12	MA	103
Alexander	5	DE	66
Alexander	35	NJ	66
Andrew	13/12	DE	327
Andrew	42	IE	327
Ann	42	IE	327
Anne	16	IE	147
Benjamin	4	DE	68
Bridget	22	IE	4
Bridget	35	IE	120
Caroline	12	PA	390
Catherine	9	IE	4
Catherine	24	IE	279
Catherine	29	IE	358
Catherine	36	IE	147
Catherine	50	DE	380
Danial	40	IE	138
Danial B	3	IE	147
Daniel	2/12	DE	42
Daniel	11	DE	216
Dennis	17	PA	163
Duncan	3	MA	103
Edward	3	OH	45
Edward	9	DE	138
Eliza	25	IE	391
Elizabeth	18	PA	390
Elizabeth	19	IE	298
Elizabeth	22	DE	380
Elizabeth	25	PA	103
Elizabeth	36	IE	120
Ellen	9/12	PA	4
Ellen	2	DE	138
Ellen	28	IE	2
Emma	12	DE	66
Ezekle	32	PA	118
Ezekle	36	MD	68
Frances	22	IE	341
Frances	23	IE	348
Frances	34	IE	2
Francis	6	IE	2
Francis	29	IE	4
George	7	IE	2
George T	42	PA	120
Hannah	13	DE	380
Hannah	22	IE	42
James	2	DE	42
James	4	DE	120
James	4	DE	312
Kelly, James	5	DE	30
James	8	DE	138
James	16	PA	327
James	18	IE	137
James	27	IE	42
James	49	IE	147
James J	40	PA	351
Jane	35	IE	312
Jane	63	IE	29
John	2	DE	120
John	7	DE	66
John	7	IE	147
John	11	DE	138
John	15	PA	312
John	17	DE	380
John	23	IE	125
John	28	IE	345
John	40	IE	312
Jonathan J	33	OH	103
Joseph	5	DE	29
Joshua	11	DE	30
Louisa	4	PA	351
Margaret	18	IE	4
Margaret	20	IE	332
Margaret	35	DE	66
Maria	30	DE	351
Martin	32	IE	29
Mary	3	DE	29
Mary	5	DE	138
Mary	7	DE	312
Mary	9	DE	66
Mary	12	IE	147
Mary	19	DE	381
Mary	40	IE	34
Mary	40	DE	54
Mary J	66	MD	30
Mary R	8	DE	68
Michel	41	IE	120
Patric	8	IE	4
Patric	35	IE	120
Patrick	23	IE	300
Rachel	7	DE	30
Rebecca	29	DE	30
Richard	--	GB	290
Robert	11	PA	312
Samuel	25	DE	381
Samuel	51	DE	188
Sarah	9	DE	45
Sarah	36	IE	138
Sarah	38	PA	120
Thomas	2	DE	312
Thomas	8	PA	327
Thomas	14	IE	147
Walter	15	PA	163
William	2	DE	30
William	2	PA	118
William	3	DE	66
William	6	DE	312
William	6	PA	351
William	14	PA	327
William	35	MD	30
William	65	DE	380
Kelroy, Catharine	5	IE	285
Mary	34	IE	285
Michael	30	IE	285
Thomas	7	IE	235
Kelton, Ellen	45	DE	138
Kelty, Clark	25	NJ	269
Rebecca	52	NJ	269
Kemble, Ann	55	NJ	243
Aron S	48	NJ	243
Caroline	16	NJ	243
Charles	55	NJ	243
Charles S	12	PA	243
Isaac J	7	PA	243
James	20	?	327
Matilda S	35	PA	243
Sarah	4/12	DE	243
Kemether, Catharine	52	GE	339
Ellentine	20	GF	339
Valentine	16	GE	339
Valentine	59	GE	339
Kemp, Charles E	7	PE	180
Edward	5	DE	385
Elizabeth D	20	NJ	180
Ellinor	1	DE	180
Joseph	5	DE	180
William H	30	MD	180
Kemple, Ann	1	DE	349
Mary A	26	IE	349
Kempt, Alice	32	DE	292
Margaret	12	DE	292
Martha J	9	DE	292
Peregrine	36	MD	292
Sarah E	11	DE	292
Kenam, Barry	2	IE	298
Mary	22	IE	298
Richard	40	IE	298
Kendle, Caspar	13	PA	351
Eliza	39	PA	351
Elizabeth	48	DE	291
Emma	4	DE	351
Gibbins	48	PA	351
Jarvis	30	DE	119
Jesse	57	DE	291
John B	22	PA	127
Margaret E	24	PA	127
Martha	60	DE	127
Mary E	11	DE	291
Philena	18	PA	351
Sarah	29	PA	119
Kendric	20	PA	154
Kenedy, Edward	30	DE	311
Ella A	4	DE	308
George W	30	DE	308
James	22	DE	311
John W	1	DE	311
Lydia	29	DE	308
Sarah A	10/12	DE	308
Kenith, James	20	DE	328
Kenkade, Amelia	10/12	IE	111
George	29	MD	111
Lydia	28	DE	111
Kennady, Elizabeth	6	PA	328
Elvora	4	PA	328
James	27	IE	328
Joseph	21	IE	284
Prudence	28	IE	328
Rebecca	17	DE	306
Robert	20	PA	328
Kennally, Michael	79	IE	290
Robert	67	IE	306
Kennan, Elenor	20	IE	33
Kennard, Anna	17	DE	18
David	40	DE	221
Eli	25	DE	37
Hannah	18	PA	126
Harriet	7	DE	355
James	16	MD	18
Joseph	14	MD	18
Laura M	10/12	DE	126
Mary	20	DE	227
Phebe	20	DE	37
Rachel	48	DE	18
Susan	35	DE	221
William	50	MD	18
William C	24	DE	126
Kenneday, Elizabeth	54	DE	275
Kennedy, Alida R	17	DE	188
Ann	21	DE	311
Anne	22	IE	58
David C	20	PA	182
Fanny	65	MD	170
George	21	DE	173
Helen	50	IE	130
John	23	IE	250
John	40	IE	188
John	55	PA	392
John L	9	DE	392
Mary	84	PA	61
Mary A	55	PA	188
Sarah	45	DE	392
Thomas	25	IE	188
William	56	DE	188

Name	Age	State	No.
Kennell, Catherine	10	IE	24
Kenney, Catherine	6	DE	80
Catherine	38	IE	79
Daniel	3	DE	80
Elizabeth	11	DE	80
John W	3	DE	305
Margaret	9	DE	80
Mary A	14	NY	79
Michel	36	IE	79
Kenny, Eliza	13	DE	365
John H	19	DE	139
Martha A	16	DE	139
Mary L	38	DE	138
Pernell	39	DE	138
Kensey, Joseph	26	MD	315
Kensley, Charles	15	DE	103
Hannah	12	DE	103
Hannah	32	DE	103
Jacob	3	DE	103
Joseph	35	PA	103
Luisa	7	PA	103
Martha	10	DE	103
Rebecca	6/12	DE	103
Susan	17	PA	103
Susannah	8	DE	103
William H	5	DE	103
Kent, Bridget	15	DE	35
Eliza	18	CN	331
Elizabeth	17	DE	35
Elizabeth	52	PA	351
Elizabeth	55	IE	35
Ellen	24	DE	355
Ellen	25	PA	351
Ellen	50	IE	331
George	20	GB	278
Henry	13	DE	351
Hinsey	12	DE	278
Jane	22	IE	331
John	16	DE	351
John W	16	DE	278
Luisa	13	DE	35
Mary	19	DE	35
Mary	20	CN	331
Penelope A	48	GB	278
Phoebe	18	DE	355
Phoebe J	20	PA	351
Sarah E	10	DE	351
Thomas	22	PA	351
Thomas	57	IE	351
William	50	IE	331
Kepland, Charles	30	PA	101
Kerby, Anna	7	NJ	88
Eliza	12	DE	118
John	21	GE	88
Joseph	39	NJ	88
Mark	11/12	DE	88
Martha	5	NJ	88
Mary	34	NJ	88
William	23	NJ	88
Kern, James D	22	PA	310
Sarah	21	DE	310
Kerns, Elizabeth	29	DE	167
Thomas	53	DE	372
Kernshaw, Margaret	54	DE	181
Kerr, Andrew	56	DE	398
George G	15	DE	398
Hannah	48	DE	398
James B	8	DE	398
John	12	DE	391
Mary E	17	DE	398
Sarah	36	IE	383
William	22	IE	379
Kerry, Ann	12	DE	15
Bersheba	48	DE	15
Ebenezer	48	DE	15
John	15	DE	15
Martha	11	DE	15
Kersey, Charity	49	PA	351
Gerard	35	DE	95
Joseph	2/12	DE	95
Margaret	20	DE	95
Kessen, A L	45	DN	401
Kessy, George	5	MD	265
Kettlewood, James	17	DE	296
John	21	DE	304
Lawrence	6	DE	296
Maria	48	GB	296
Mary J	14	PA	296
Mathew	12	DE	296
Mathew	56	GB	296
Sarah	19	DE	304
William	19	DE	130
Key, Elizabeth	30	GB	377
Robert	35	GB	377
Keyes, Andrew	10	DE	256
Henry	3	DE	256
Keyla, Catharine	34	IE	336
John	12	MD	336
Mary E	4	MD	336
Michel	8	MD	336
Michel	41	IE	336
Keys, Charles	72	IE	325
Christopher	26	IE	353
Francis A	14	IE	325
Henry	35	IE	256
Isabella	6	DE	256
John	24	IE	346
Margaret	1	DE	256
Margaret	35	IE	256
Keyser, G Eyre	17	PA	400
Peter	15	PA	400
Kibby, Julius	28	CT	253
Kienle, Henry	38	GE	6
Jacob	37	GE	6
Mary	1	DE	6
Mrs	31	GE	6
Kile, Catherine	14	IE	371
Margaret	17	IE	371
Rosanna	47	IE	371
Kilgore, Amy H	13	DE	397
Andrew J	17	PA	397
Drucilla	74	DE	370
Eliza	43	DE	397
Eliza J	1	DE	397
James	46	DE	397
James S	18	PA	369
John	15	PA	397
John K R	9	PA	369
Joseph	5	DE	397
Joseph	37	DE	370
Joseph	50	DE	369
Margaret	41	PA	369
Margaret B	4	DE	370
Mary D	14	PA	369
Samuel	10	DE	397
Sarah A	42	DE	370
Kilingsworth, John	4	DE	51
John	30	DE	51
Rachel	12	DE	51
Killinger, Ann	10	DE	206
Henrietta J	32	DE	206
William P	10	DE	182
Killingsten, Jerem	28	IE	23
Kilpatrick, Catherin	7	DE	209
Eliza J	9	DE	209
Elizabeth	13	DE	209
Elizabeth	37	DE	209
Emily	2	DE	209
James	13	PA	350
John	5	DE	209
John	41	MD	209
Joseph A	18	DE	209
Mary A	14	DE	209
Rachel	11	DE	209
Susan	4	DE	209
Virginia	1	DE	209
Kincaid, Alice	2	DE	369
Anna M	7	DE	369
Anna M	34	DE	369
Mary	8	DE	369
Samuel	62	MD	369
Thomas	5	DE	369
Kinch, Elizabeth	64	DE	370
Ruth A	28	DE	370
Kindle, Author	3	GB	388
Charles	35	GB	388
Elizabeth	36	GB	390
Emma L	4/12	GB	390
Hannah	7	GB	388
James	35	GB	390
Pauline	16	GB	388
Rebecca	50	DE	49
Sarah	36	GB	388
Sarah J	10	GB	388
William	50	DE	43
William H	12	GB	388
King, _____	2/12	DE	296
Abraham	20	DE	232
Adam	12	PA	265
Adeline	23	DE	261
Albert	2	DE	295
Andrew	44	DE	94
Angeline	21	NJ	79
Ann	15	DE	285
Ann	50	NJ	371
Ann	53	DE	94
Ann	55	DE	234
Ann J	15	IE	341
Barbary	44	GE	285
Benjamin	24	PA	341
Bridget	52	IE	85
Catharine	20	DE	341
Catharine	21	IE	295
Catharine	22	DE	279
Catharine	33	PA	265
Catherine S	11	DE	279
Charles	1	DE	261
Charles	63	GE	85
Charles F	8	DE	279
Clementine	14	PA	279
Cornelia E	11/12	DE	279
David	9	DE	285
David	24	DE	234
Deborah T	41	NJ	279
Elijah	9	GB	250
Eliza A	4	DE	279
Elizabeth	12	DE	285
Elizabeth	25	DE	336
Elizabeth F	11	DE	341
Emmet	6	DE	371
Harriet	46	DE	307
Henry	45	GE	252
Jacob	14	DE	371
James	24	DE	336
James	25	IE	2
James A	40	GB	250
Jane	5	DE	341
Jane	9	DE	371
Jane	70	IE	14
Joel	56	PA	48
John	9	DE	191
John	20	DE	279
John	22	DE	285
John	24	DE	307
John	26	NJ	295
John	41	IE	371
John	43	PA	265
John	52	DE	279
John L	8	DE	279
Joseph	15	DE	85
Joseph	18	DE	285
Kesiah	45	DE	94
Letitia	13	DE	371
Levi	1	DE	307
Levinia	40	PA	48
Margaret	30	DE	307
Margaret	50	DE	239
Margaret A	25	DE	170
Mariana	8	DE	48
Martha	16	DE	336
Martha B	6	DE	279
Martha E	3	DE	371
Mary	13	DE	341
Mary	20	MD	112
Mary	24	DE	307
Mary	29	IE	371

Name	Age	State	Page
King, Mary	40	GB	250
Mary	43	DE	279
Mary W	13	DE	279
Mathew	18	GB	250
Michael	20	DE	285
Michael	46	DE	285
Naomi	52	?	167
Noah	30	DE	307
Penal	23	DE	261
Rachel	6	DE	336
Rachel	10	DE	279
Rachel	27	DE	156
Rebecca	50	DE	32
Rebecca	57	DE	98
Reuben	12	GB	250
Richard	16	DE	371
Richard D	40	DE	371
Robert	1/12	DE	170
Robert	13	GB	189
Robert	14	DE	371
Robert	56	DE	336
Samuel	16	DE	137
Sarah	7	GB	250
Sarah	18	DE	279
Sarah	51	DE	336
Smyley W	7	DE	341
Thomas	2	DE	285
Thomas	3	DE	279
Thomas	54	GB	279
Thomas C	24	PA	170
Vincent	17	DE	94
Walter	15	GB	255
Washington	12	DE	336
William	14	DE	336
William	15	DE	239
William J	9	DE	341
William M	12	PA	400
Wm	25	GB	250
Kingly, Henry	40	GE	145
Kinkade, George	29	MD	112
Lydia	29	DE	112
Kinler, Ellen	28	IE	35
John	2/12	DE	35
John	40	IE	35
Kinley, Sarah	13	IE	282
Kinsler, Adam	19	PA	148
Adam	57	PA	148
Emeline	2	DE	148
Harriet	41	PA	148
Henry	14	PA	148
Joseph	25	PA	148
Martha	20	DE	148
Mary	16	PA	148
Kinslow, Abraham	20	DE	258
Abraham	50	DE	213
Bridget	80	IE	34
Casanda	2/12	DE	22
Charles	1	DE	313
Elenor	16	DE	34
Elizabeth	45	IE	34
Hannah	22	DE	22
John	20	DE	52
Michel	28	DE	22
Rachel	20	DE	258
Rachel A	22	DE	313
Robert	25	DE	343
Sarah	53	DE	258
Victoria	2	DE	22
William	28	DE	295
Kirby, Arnold	31	NJ	380
Caroline	2	DE	273
Georgianna	7	DE	273
Harriet H	24	NJ	380
Hope	25	DE	269
John	4	DE	273
John W	23	DE	289
Mark	38	NJ	273
Mary	1	DE	269
Mary	12	NJ	273
Mary	34	NJ	273
Richard	15	NJ	266
Samuel	32	NJ	269
Kirby, Sarah	7	PA	269
Kirk, Ann J	25	DE	126
Betsey	82	DE	71
Catherine	1	DE	302
Chaukley	24	DE	317
Clara J	5	DE	126
Clarissa	7	DE	368
David	19	DE	333
Elizabeth	24	PA	317
George	25	DE	262
J C	28	DE	126
John	12	DE	262
Julia A	18	PA	352
Lewis L	36	DE	297
Maria	22	DE	71
Maria	30	DE	302
Marshall	25	PA	355
Mary E	3	DE	297
Michael	22	PA	352
Phebe A	6	PA	317
Rachael	52	DE	333
Rebecca	22	DE	333
Rebecca	27	DE	297
Robert M	29	IE	302
Sarah	10	DE	262
Sarah	25	DE	262
Sarah J	8/12	DE	297
Sarah J	2	DE	302
William	28	DE	71
Kirkman, John	17	DE	141
John	36	GB	141
Mahulda	22	DE	179
Mary A	22	DE	141
Mary H	35	DE	141
Rebecca	15	DE	141
William	41	GB	141
Kirkpatric, Harrison	55	DE	131
James	19	IE	82
Margaret	44	IE	288
Margaretta	40	DE	114
Martha	45	DE	114
Mary	49	DE	114
Mary E	5	PA	82
Mary R	57	PA	131
Hannah	50	PA	379
Hugh	54	DE	379
Robert	17	PA	367
Kirkwood, Elizabeth	3	DE	342
Hannah	26	IE	342
James	2	DE	334
Mary A	4	IE	334
Robert	2	DE	342
Robt	10	IE	334
Robt	32	IE	342
Rose	40	IE	334
Sarah	35	IE	334
Wm	45	IE	334
Kiser, Lewis	27	GE	125
Kitchen, John	60	PA	68
Mary	50	DE	68
Kitson, Thomas	72	GB	310
Kizar, John	16	IE	14
Kizer, Margaret	13	DE	354
Thomas	16	DE	158
William	17	DE	354
Klein, Frederick	79	PA	382
George	40	PA	382
Henry	8	DE	382
Margaret A	65	PA	382
Samuel	15	DE	382
Sarah	34	DE	382
Klund, Caroline	7	DE	149
Frances	46	GE	149
Frederic	5	DE	125
Frederic	36	GE	125
Henry	44	GE	149
John H	8	DE	125
Mary A	28	PA	125
Mary L	2	DE	125
Knight, David	10/12	DE	277
Dubre	50	PA	165
Edmonde	19	DE	304
Knight, Ellen	23	DE	277
Ezek	63	RI	304
James	27	DE	277
Joseph	28	IE	285
Joseph D	10	PA	352
Margaret	23	IE	285
Margaret	55	DE	304
Martha B	56	NJ	165
Mary	9	PA	352
Rebecca	15	DE	219
Sarah	18	DE	311
Knoblet, Anne	20	DE	296
Isaac	26	DE	296
Sally A	4/12	DE	296
Knotts, Charles E	2	DE	342
George	8	DE	342
Margaret A	29	DE	342
Mary E	6	DE	342
Rebecca A	7	DE	342
Sarah A	5	DE	342
William	34	DE	342
Knowen, Sarah Beth	28	NY	389
William Ash	29	NY	389
Knowles, Eliza	21	DE	208
Ephraim	55	VA	208
Mary	27	DE	208
Rachel	56	DE	208
Knox, Joseph	12	DE	337
Mary A	15	DE	337
Sarah	52	MD	337
Thomas	22	DE	398
Thomas	23	DE	337
Thomas	52	VA	337
William H	21	DE	337
Kollick, Matilda	31	DE	184
Sarah	7	DE	184
Kollock, Anna	16	DE	20
Robert	39	DE	20
Sarah	5	DE	20
Sarah	44	DE	20
Koontz, Harriet S	19	NY	393
Mary E	16	NY	393
Matilda H	48	MD	393
Matilda J	22	NY	393
Kortley, John	45	GB	361
Krauch, Alexander	10	DE	143
Ann	2	DE	143
Ann	45	GE	143
Christian	45	GE	143
Julius	15	DE	143
Williamina	13	DE	143
Kresley, Margaret	11	DE	352
Krey, Richard	13	DE	311
Krider, William	35	?	365
Kuhns, Benjamin	25	PA	263
Kuster, Catharine	64	DE	393
George E A	28	DE	393
Mary F	30	DE	393
Sylvia	35	DE	393
Kyle, Frances	27	DE	342
Mary C	4	DE	342
Robert	4/12	DE	342
Robert	35	MD	342
Labrana, Peter	14	LA	319
Lachary, Conrad	35	GE	181
George J	2	DE	181
James H	5	DE	181
John R	10	PA	181
Martha L	29	MD	181
Lack, Stephen	43	?	370
Lackey, David	48	IE	350
David	60	IE	168
Derby	65	IE	284
Dinsmore	1	DE	49
Edward	6	DE	49
Emma	12	DE	313
George	8	DE	49
John	26	IE	344
John H	14	DE	350
Mary	41	MD	278
Milton	38	PA	49

Name	Age	St	No.
Lackey, Rebecca	31	PA	49
Sarah	49	PA	350
William	10	DE	313
Lacy, Burton	16	MD	266
Hester A	19	DE	196
Saml	18	DE	272
Laddin, Edwin	17	DE	383
Lafetry, Adlia	4	DE	323
Ann E	15	DE	323
Charles	8	DE	323
Daniel	13	DE	323
Daniel	48	DE	323
Ellenor J	19	DE	323
Hannah	10	DE	323
Hannah	45	DE	323
James S	17	DE	323
John M	11	DE	323
Lafferty, Alace	60	IE	39
Ambrose	44	DE	283
Biddy	8	IE	350
Caroline	16	DE	283
Daniel	24	IE	314
Hugh	53	IE	11
James	10	IE	350
John	32	IE	350
Latitia	16	DE	11
Letitia	17	IE	368
Luisa	12	DE	11
Margaret	9	IE	350
Margaret	39	IE	358
Martha	4	DE	11
Mary	6	IE	350
Mary	14	DE	11
Mary	32	IE	350
Mary	38	IE	55
Mary	42	DE	283
Mary A	13	PA	283
Matilda	30	IE	11
Sarah	2	DE	11
Sarah	4	IE	350
Sarah	19	DE	283
Lafra, Savior	21	FR	317
Laher, Joseph	40	GE	44
Margaret	28	GE	44
Lair, Catherine	14	PA	127
Elizabeth	11	PA	127
John W	35	PA	127
Margaret J	2	DE	127
Mary C	38	IE	127
Patric	12	PA	127
Laird, Alexander	18	PA	144
Lake, Anna	43	MD	177
Augustus	9	DE	232
Catherine	21	DE	112
James	12	DE	177
James	80	PA	177
Jesse	43	DE	177
Virginia	10	DE	177
La John, John	26	GB	328
Margaret	24	GB	328
Lalor, Latitia	58	DE	210
Minty	30	DE	210
Lamar, Saml	22	PA	354
Lamb, Anna	2	DE	81
Charles	30	GB	26
Mary	10	GB	26
Mary	30	IE	26
Mary	60	DE	248
Samuel	60	DE	248
Susannah	11	DE	248
Susannah	76	GB	230
William	11	GB	26
Lambdin, Samuel	14	DE	296
Lambers, William	20	DE	366
Lambert, Annah M	10	DE	82
Araminta	12	DE	240
Bayard	7	DE	240
Caroline	1	DE	240
Caroline	40	DE	240
Charles	21	DE	83
Charles	50	MD	83
Elizabeth	33	DE	10
Lambert, Ellen	65	DE	10
Emory	14	DE	240
Hannah	5	DE	82
James	19	DE	82
John	6	DE	10
Joseph	35	DE	228
Maria	45	DE	82
Martha	1	DE	10
Martha J	10	DE	240
Mary	22	DE	82
Mary A	9	DE	195
Mary R	3	MD	10
Michael	3	DE	240
Susan	3	DE	82
Susan	70	DE	225
William	51	DE	340
Wilson F	8	DE	240
Wm W	38	DE	10
Lamberton, George	12	DE	70
Henry	10	DE	70
Lambion, Chandler	33	DE	352
Edith	28	DE	352
John C	3	DE	352
Lamborn, Aquilla	70	PA	348
David	40	PA	348
Eliza Ann	35	PA	348
Elizabeth	16	?	375
Margaret	65	PA	348
Phebe	21	PA	396
Phebe	68	PA	353
Phebe Ann	23	DE	353
Sarah	30	DE	48
Lambson, Catherine	54	NJ	307
Chas H	23	DE	288
Eliza J	11	DE	307
Giles	17	DE	307
Giles	56	NJ	307
John R	15	DE	307
Moses	32	DE	309
Rebecca J	21	DE	307
William	12	DE	307
Lambton, Anne	2	DE	174
Thomas J	28	DE	174
Wilmina	24	PA	174
Lamden, Henry	21	DE	3
Lamm, Simeon	33	?	319
Lamon, Ann	40	NJ	244
Hannah A	4	PA	244
James	40	IE	244
Lydia	10	PA	244
William	5/12	DE	244
Lamp, Constant	22	DE	195
Lampal, Catherine	45	IE	327
Barna	47	IE	327
Margaret	16	IE	327
Lampier, Mary A	30	DE	195
Lampleigh, Isaac	15	NJ	369
Mary E	3	PA	369
Thomas	37	PA	369
Thomas Jr	9	DE	369
Quinby	6	DE	369
Lancaster, Ann E	2	DE	330
Ann J	25	PA	330
Ellen	4	PA	330
Wm R	31	NJ	330
Land, Ann E	16	NC	165
Anna L	7	NJ	105
David	70	NJ	105
Emma E	6	NJ	105
James	33	NJ	105
Mary A	33	NJ	105
Landware, George	20	FR	249
Lane, Ann	2/12	DE	47
Ann	40	GB	300
Ann	43	DE	94
Anna	14	DE	126
Anthony C	44	MD	94
Augustine S	6	DE	47
Caroline	7	DE	126
Catherine	23	MD	281
Gilpin	2	DE	47
Hannah	59	NJ	371
Lane, James	22	MD	281
James	65	DE	126
James R	11	DE	126
Jane A	36	PA	47
Jesse	48	NY	47
Joseph H	16	DE	126
Martin	4	DE	47
Mary	6	PA	353
Mary	28	DE	126
Mary H	48	NJ	126
Nathan J	34	PA	371
Rebecca	23	DE	126
William	20	DE	94
William	21	PA	18
Laner, Bridget	25	IE	33
Lang, Alfred F	21	DE	102
Amelia	1	DE	103
Eliza J	4	DE	103
Elizabeth	24	DE	102
Elizabeth	42	WL	102
Ellen	19	DE	102
James	11	DE	103
John	23	GB	102
John	45	GB	102
Mary E	16	DE	102
Phebe A	7	DE	103
William H	9	DE	103
Langan, Catherine	22	IE	354
Peter	35	IE	301
Langham, John M	22	DE	362
Langland, Ellen	20	IE	373
Langley, Mary E	10	DE	50
Rachel	74	PA	317
Rebecca	35	DE	351
Sarah	64	PA	351
William	64	DE	351
Langly, Jeremiah	4	DE	295
Joseph	35	DE	295
Mary	34	GB	295
Sarah E	7	DE	295
Lankey, John G	33	DE	374
John G Jr	9	MD	374
Lanney, John	22	IE	398
Lansdale, Emily	35	?	135
Mr	40	?	135
La Orville, Alice	8	WN	58
Augusta	13	WN	58
Augustine	35	WN	58
Lape, Henry	2	DE	167
Susanah	32	DE	167
William	30	DE	167
Lapham, Elizabeth	6	DE	72
Emeline	32	DE	72
George L W	1	DE	125
Ida	1	DE	104
James	4	DE	125
James	27	MD	72
James H	4	DE	72
John	16	DE	104
John	30	DE	125
Joseph	9	DE	104
Lucinda	11	DE	104
Mary A	30	PA	125
Rachel	3	DE	72
Rebecca	6	DE	104
Rebecca A	7	DE	125
Richard	4	DE	104
Richard	49	GB	104
Sarah J	41	DE	104
Laprel, James	16	IE	167
Largill, Ann	17	IE	363
Larigan, Peter	35	IE	302
Larkin, Marga	17	IE	316
Larry, Catherine	32	PA	64
Edward	6	DE	64
Henry	3	DE	64
Matthew	7	DE	64
Matthew	30	DE	64
Pricilla	13	DE	64
Robert	10	DE	64
Lary, Ephraim	26	PA	311
Mary R	27	DE	310

Name	Age	State	Page
Lasey, Elizabeth	16/12	DE	328
Latamis, Johanna S	18	DE	246
John S	8/12	DE	246
Levi W	38	DE	246
Louisa	30	DE	246
Latimer, Angelina	20	DE	212
Benjamin	17	DE	212
Elizabeth	50	PA	317
James	17	DE	212
James	18	DE	215
John	19	IE	198
John R	56	DE	317
Margaret	18	DE	212
Margaret	49	DE	212
Martha	15	DE	212
M R	14	DE	165
Robert	45	DE	212
Latmere, Sally	40	DE	57
Latte, Elizabeth	14	IE	326
Samuel	16	IE	326
Thomas	20	IE	326
Lattimer, Ann R	22	DE	369
Eliza	50	IE	29
Elizabeth J	24	DE	369
Henry	57	DE	369
Mary R	15	DE	369
Sarah A	49	DE	369
Thos H	3	DE	329
Lattimore, James W	8	PA	329
John	33	IE	329
Saml S	6	PA	329
Wm W	5	PA	329
Lattimus, Alexander	15	DE	245
Ann	50	DE	245
Rachel A	20	DE	245
Robert	17	DE	245
Laub, George	13	DE	217
Laudry, John	21	DE	178
Laughlin, Louisa M	17	PA	288
Laurence, Ann	40	NJ	124
Charles	3/12	DE	124
David	22	DE	79
Elizabeth	9	DE	60
Ellen	21	PA	144
George	24	NJ	124
Hannah	12	PA	60
Henry	54	PA	60
John A	2	DE	60
Joseph T	16	PA	60
Josiah	17	NJ	124
Mary	19	NJ	124
Mary	40	PA	60
Mary A	14	PA	60
Rachel	40	DE	81
Rebecca	22	DE	124
William H	4	PA	60
Laven, Alfred	14	MD	383
Lavender, Hannah	73	GB	104
Laverty, Hiram	42	PA	291
Mary A	31	PA	291
Mary J	6	PA	291
Rachel E	9	PA	291
Rebecca J	11	PA	291
William J	2	DE	291
Lavery, Anna	8	DE	89
Daniel	38	NJ	170
Elizabeth	19	DE	170
Jonathan	14	DE	172
Mary	11	IE	111
William	10	DE	89
Law, Catharine	48	DE	304
Lawder, Francis	23	DE	368
Maria V	19	DE	368
Lawley, Sarah	45	IE	323
Lawrence, Ellen	16	NJ	272
Sarah	20	NY	258
Laws, Alex	17	DE	254
Amanda	16	DE	292
Amanda	17	DE	251
Ann	60	DE	200
Ann E	16	DE	336
Benjamin F	10	DE	336
Laws, Caroline	4	DE	292
Daniel	55	DE	378
Dorcas	30	MD	336
Eliza	46	PA	292
Elizabeth	28	DE	202
Ellen	16	DE	271
Ellen R	5	DE	377
George W	3	DE	336
Harriet	12	DE	292
John	10	DE	292
John C	5	DE	336
Joseph	2	DE	377
Joshua	28	DE	377
Margaret	15	DE	291
Margaret	55	DE	83
Martha	57	MD	378
Martha J	8	DE	377
Mary	10	DE	254
Mary	18	DE	292
Mary	18	DE	296
Mary	35	DE	254
Mary E	26	DE	377
Mingo	24	DE	313
Rachel	12	DE	254
Rebecca	19	DE	254
Sarah	15	DE	292
Stephen	55	DE	292
Susanna	6	DE	254
Thomas	8	DE	254
Thomas	40	DE	254
William	12	DE	336
William	19	DE	292
William	40	DE	336
Woodward P	8	DE	336
Lawson, Ann	40	?	243
David	31	?	270
David	50	IE	356
Esther	26	?	270
Hannah A	4	?	243
Hellen	4	DE	306
Isabella	10	DE	306
James	12	PA	356
James	34	?	270
James	40	?	243
John	1	DE	306
Margaret	5	?	270
Margaret	16	PA	356
Margaret	41	PA	306
Margaret M	3	PA	357
Mary	17	PA	285
Mary	59	GB	285
Rachel	65	PA	77
Sarah	8	PA	356
Sarah	12	DE	306
Sarah	46	IE	357
Thomas	15	PA	306
Thomas	45	PA	306
Thomas C	9	PA	357
William	5/12	DE	243
William	69	GB	285
Lawton, Abraham	49	GB	381
Elizabeth	13	NY	381
Esther B	11	NY	381
George	60	DE	37
John	10	DE	381
Naomi	7	DE	381
Sarah	41	GB	381
Layer, Patrick	28	IE	298
Layman, Henry Clay	5	DE	376
John C	35	PA	376
Laura L	2	DE	376
Maria L	32	MD	376
Thomas	31	PA	376
Thomas	66	PA	376
Laymen, Edmond K	27	PA	376
Edmond O	11/12	DE	376
Margaret A	24	DE	376
Layton, Augustus	34	DE	29
Edward	32	DE	29
Enoch	29	DE	126
Josephine	2	DE	127
Layton, Martha	38	DE	29
Mary	29	PA	126
Rachel	23	NJ	195
Thomas	38	MD	32
Lazalier, Ann E	26	DE	312
Benjamin F	34	NJ	312
Caroline	5	DE	312
Rebecca A	8	DE	312
Lea, Agnes	1	DE	310
Amanda	13	MD	164
Emeline	6	DE	299
Esther	12	DE	310
George	25	DE	377
Henry	10	DE	310
James	40	GB	123
Jane	32	PA	310
John	9	PA	200
Joseph W	1	NJ	124
Margaret A	25	PA	124
Mary	4	DE	310
Mary E	3	NJ	124
Preston	8	DE	310
Rebecca	11	DE	218
William	6	DE	310
William	45	DE	310
Leach, Alice	2	DE	360
Ann	10	DE	360
Dorothy	26	PA	384
Emeline	36	DE	377
George H	10	DE	146
Hillis	30	PA	384
James	38	GB	360
James T	12	DE	146
John	45	DE	377
John B	2/12	DE	360
John T	14	NJ	146
Joseph	3	DE	360
Joseph	31	GB	360
Joseph	64	GB	384
Margaret	70	GB	384
Margaret	80	DE	377
Margaret A	8	DE	360
Margaret J	4	DE	377
Martha	33	GB	360
Mary	30	DE	360
Mary A	35	DE	146
Mary E	1	DE	360
Susan E	2	DE	146
Theodore W	4	DE	146
William	40	DE	146
William A	17	PA	146
Leahy, Catherine	4/12	DE	367
Elizabeth	7	DE	367
Margaret	27	IE	367
Mary	5	DE	367
Thomas	33	IE	367
Leal, Joseph	44	DE	45
Sarah T	42	DE	45
Leaner, Catharine	16	IE	306
Leatham, Anna	3	DE	190
Ellen	6	DE	190
James	10	DE	190
John	8	DE	190
John	35	DE	190
Martha J	12	DE	190
Martha J	48	DE	190
Mary C	15	DE	199
Leatherman, Enoch	28	DE	212
Esther	20	DE	212
Robt H	3	DE	212
Samuel	1	DE	212
Lebington, Isabel	11	DE	376
Mary	12	DE	376
Le Carpentier, Al-fred	3/12	DE	347
Charles	45	FR	347
Edward	34	FR	347
Mary S	27	DE	347
Sarah J	2	DE	347
Lecat, Catherine	70	GE	6
Lecates, Caroline	2	DE	255
Hannah	32	PA	255

Name	Age	State	No.
Lecates, James	6	DE	255
Margaret	12	DE	255
Stephen	30	DE	255
Wm	8	DE	255
Leckler, Ferdinand	37	PA	288
Margaret	27	DE	285
Lecompt, Birely	5	MD	294
Charles	35	MD	294
David	23	DE	211
Hannah	12	DE	294
James	2	DE	294
James	15	DE	173
James	39	MD	203
James A	3	DE	203
Mary	6	DE	294
Mary J	34	DE	294
Priscilla	4/12	DE	294
Rebecca	6	DE	203
Sarah	8	DE	188
Sarah	9	DE	294
Sarah A	11/12	DE	203
Sarah A	34	DE	203
Susan	8	DE	203
Lecount, Ann C	10	DE	90
Eliza A	39	DE	90
George	3	DE	90
Joseph	6	DE	90
Ledhill, John	27	GB	80
Lee, Abraham	30	DE	218
Adaline	1	DE	307
Alexander	65	DE	218
Alfred	7	DE	44
Alfred (Rev)	42	MA	10
Ann	32	GB	378
Anna	37	GB	378
Benjamin	16	CT	10
Benjamin	40	PA	181
Benjamin R	3/12	DE	376
Caesar	23	DE	203
Charles	4	MD	302
Charles	24	DE	307
Clementine J	4	DE	10
David	30	DE	217
Edith	29	NJ	379
Edward	6/12	DE	44
Edward	54	MD	302
Eliza	10	DE	64
Eliza	28	DE	64
Elizabeth	1	DE	10
Elizabeth	75	DE	218
Elizabeth D	15	PA	181
Frances	64	MD	302
Hannah	64	NJ	379
Hannah E	4	DE	379
Isaac	19	DE	16
James A	39	NJ	379
Jane	18	PA	144
Jane	50	IE	76
John	12	DE	44
John	35	GB	44
John W	3	DE	379
Julia	1	DE	10
Julia A	17	DE	76
Julia W	38	MA	10
Leighton	12	CT	10
Lemuel	13	DE	229
Lucy Ann	37	NJ	181
Luisa B	24	PA	7
Martha	21	PA	389
Margaret	7	DE	102
Margaret	30	DE	217
Mary	16	DE	44
Mary	40	DE	34
Mary A	10	DE	34
Perry	35	DE	64
Rachel	25	PA	56
Rebecca	45	DE	229
Sally A	18	MD	302
Sarah	19	DE	34
Sarah	20	DE	389
Sarah	26	GB	378
Sarah	31	DE	307

Name	Age	State	No.
Lee, Sarah	68	GB	378
Sarah A	16	PA	181
Susan	30	DE	44
William	6	DE	44
William	58	NJ	76
Leeds, Anna E	16	DE	159
Elizabeth	44	NY	45
Emely T	4	DE	159
Hannah	14	NY	45
Joseph	20	NY	45
Joseph C	47	DE	159
Joseph M	15	DE	159
Mariana	37	DE	159
Margaret	17	NY	45
Mary W	8/12	DE	159
Rachel A	23	DE	222
William C	45	DE	45
William H	22	DE	159
Lees, Albert	2	GB	276
Anna E	2	DE	276
Benjamin	5	DE	131
Elizabeth	30	GB	276
Harriet	25	NJ	131
James	31	GB	276
Ralph	27	GB	276
Samuel	5/12	DE	131
Samuel	30	OH	131
Sophia	26	GB	276
Thos	30	GB	276
Leesing, Alfred	8	DE	288
Le Fevre, Ann	4	DE	307
Ingeber	1	DE	307
John	3	DE	307
John B	32	PA	307
Mary	23	DE	307
Lefferets, Charles	30	PA	283
Legay, John	25	DE	185
Legg, Augustus S	7	DE	94
Elmira	16	DE	94
George	5	DE	94
Hannah	21	DE	94
James W	22	DE	94
John M	11	DE	94
Joseph	17	DE	94
Lewis P	2	DE	94
Sarah	43	NJ	94
W (Capt)	52	DE	94
William	20	DE	94
Legrix, Hellen	26	DE	358
John	60	DE	358
Sarah Jane	22	DE	358
Susan	58	DE	358
Leigh, Ann	52	GB	122
James	48	GB	122
Mary	16	PA	122
Lemon, David	24	IE	29
Joseph	48	IE	67
William	27	IE	54
Lendeman, Caleb	40	DE	275
Catharine	5	DE	307
Christopher	73	DE	275
Elizabeth	6	DE	307
Herman	38	DE	275
Isaac G	25	DE	275
Jacob	4	DE	307
Sarah	59	DE	275
Lender, Carie	66	MD	298
John	25	DE	298
John	73	DE	298
Josiah	30	DE	298
Robert H	11	PA	400
Lenderman, Benj	33	DE	303
Christopher	15	DE	286
Isaac	46	DE	292
Isaac B	7	DE	292
Jacob	6	DE	292
Jacob	30	DE	303
John	7	DE	303
Lewis	30	DE	297
Lewis W	2	DE	292
Margaret	9	DE	273
Margaret	11	DE	292

Name	Age	State	No.
Lenderman, Mary	30	PA	292
Mary A	21	DE	286
Sarah	10	DE	292
Sarah	31	IE	303
Thomas A	4	DE	292
Valentine	1	DE	303
William H	3/12	DE	292
Lendmen, Barbary A	39	PA	307
Lenerus, Georgianna	6	DE	224
John L	4	DE	224
Lambert	42	MD	224
Parinela	30	DE	224
Lenex, Eliza	30	DE	273
Lenix, Charles A	5	IE	370
Eli	54	DE	158
Eliza J	5	DE	370
Elizabeth J	44	DE	370
Isaac	47	DE	370
Lennard, Henry	23	IE	374
Lenox, Charles	33	PA	122
Francis	8	MD	122
Margaret	3	DE	122
Margaret	30	DE	122
Mary A	11	PA	122
Nathaniel L	5	DE	122
Leonard, Catherine	3	DE	306
Catherine	42	IE	306
Conrad	24	GE	124
Daniel	34	IE	356
Ellen	19	DE	69
Frederic	78	MD	1
James	19	IE	89
Jane	19	DE	311
John	6	DE	306
John	44	IE	306
Margaret	15/12	PA	356
Margaret	25	GE	124
Mary	23	IE	356
Rebecca	60	DE	1
Susannah	5/12	DE	125
Thomas	6	PA	308
Lesle, Maria	18	DE	116
Lesler, John	20	DE	90
Leslie, Ellen V	33	PA	290
Alpheus H	4	DE	278
Anna L	3	DE	185
Elizabeth	29	GB	278
Ellen F S	22	DE	185
Henry N	25	PA	185
Jane	10/12	DE	185
Mrs	28	NY	290
William W	10	DE	278
William W	22	PA	185
Lester, Ann J	10	DE	242
James B	13	DE	242
Pennell C	7	DE	242
Peter	45	DE	242
Rebecca	40	DE	242
Leuchsinning, Herman	22	FR	165
Leuduain, John	29	GE	216
Leuty, Moses	20	DE	314
Levett, Harriet J	34	PA	310
Levey, Thomas	20	IE	3
Levic, Ann	25	DE	302
Levin, Thomas	30	IE	25
Levingston, James	45	PA	337
Levy, Ann	29	DE	333
Hannah M	1	DE	333
William H	28	MD	333
Lewis, Aaron	9	MD	63
Albert E	49	DE	390
Alfred	13	DE	320
Almira	18	OH	166
Ann	2/12	DE	250
Anna M	12	DE	81
Anne	6	PA	121
Asher B	35	PA	157
Caroline	30	MD	321
Catherine	3	PA	121
Charles	5	DE	134
Charles	7	MD	63
Charles E	2	DE	169

Name	Age	State	Page
Lewis, Daniel	17	DE	307
David L	32	DE	282
Dauphin	35	DE	324
Delia	20	DE	113
Delia	50	MD	32
Edward	12	DE	390
Edward	21	?	151
Elija	45	DE	27
Eliza A	4	DE	221
Eliza J	46	DE	81
Elizabeth	2	DE	113
Elizabeth	21	DE	93
Elizabeth	24	PA	43
Elizabeth	25	DE	140
Elizabeth	28	DE	329
Elizabeth	33	DE	169
Elizabeth W	62	DE	309
Ella	1	DE	113
Emma	7	DE	81
Esther J	10	DE	390
Fanny Sr	23	IE	344
Frances	40	MD	30
Frances L	2	DE	171
George	1	DE	116
George	19	DE	341
George	32	PA	116
George	45	DE	338
George L	13	PA	122
Hannah M	4	DE	329
Harriet	6/12	DE	43
Harriet	17	DE	285
Harriet	34	MD	248
Henrietta	16	DE	390
Henry	10	DE	321
Jacob	5	PA	116
Jacob	9	DE	324
Jacob	40	PA	121
Jacob H	7	PA	121
James	9	PA	121
James	15	DE	323
James	24	DE	160
James	26	DE	301
James	38	DE	169
Jemima	35	DE	324
Jeremiah	22	DE	316
John	16	DE	232
John	23	DE	230
John B	51	DE	82
Joseph	2	DE	134
Levi	44	MD	321
Louisa	3	DE	113
Louisa	31	DE	171
Maria	30	DE	324
Marshal	16	NJ	4
Martha	31	GB	250
Mary	16	DE	374
Mary	18	MD	181
Mary	25	DE	134
Mary	40	DE	160
Mary	40	DE	161
Mary A	55	GB	259
Mary J	7	DE	390
Mary J	32	PA	121
Mary W	2	DE	250
Rebecca	22	NJ	157
Rebecca B	9	DE	81
Richard	2	DE	329
Richard	59	GB	259
Robert	5	DE	63
Robert	30	PA	43
Ruth	50	DE	282
Saml	34	GB	250
Samuel	7	PA	116
Samuel	23	PA	30
Samuel	24	DE	203
Sarah	26	PA	116
Sarah	43	MD	338
Solomon	7	DE	329
Synthia	21	MD	338
Tammy	23	IE	345
Thomas	6/12	DE	121
Thomas	21	DE	321
Lewis, Thomas	45	DE	134
William	3	DE	63
William	3	PA	116
William	10	DE	171
William	17	PA	75
William	38	DE	171
William	40	DE	329
Wm W	5	DE	250
Lewkins, George	22	DE	353
Joannah	20	DE	353
Licking, Elizabeth	28	DE	126
John	33	DE	126
Melissa	1	DE	126
Lidale, Eliza	17	IE	71
Liddell, Amelia	4	PA	372
Amelia	40	ST	372
John	2	DE	372
Margaret	12	PA	372
Mary	9	PA	372
Robert	7	PA	372
Robert	51	ST	372
Lidsen, Andrew	12	DE	178
Catherine	9	DE	178
Catherine	38	DE	178
Joshua	38	DE	178
Joshua M	10	DE	178
Robert H	2	DE	178
Lifin, William	7	DE	380
Lightly, Ellen	23	IE	234
Likens, Bridget	29	PA	289
Caleb	36	DE	289
Caroline	5	DE	289
Charles	10/12	DE	289
Likins, Eliza	26	DE	55
Elizabeth	3	DE	55
Francis C	7	DE	55
Leuisa	17	DE	55
Stephen	28	PA	53
Lil, Ephraim	23	GB	274
Lilley, Julia	11	MD	299
Lilly, Eliza	14	DE	84
Emma	9	NJ	295
Emeline	30	DE	84
Henry	5	DE	288
Henry	12	DE	84
Henry	35	DE	84
Joseph	6	DE	84
Mary	1	DE	84
Thomas	8	DE	84
Limmon, Allen J	30	PA	32
Linch, James	60	IE	306
John	17	DE	307
Margaret	16	DE	306
Mary	14	DE	306
Mary	48	IE	306
Nicholas	28	GE	282
William	30	DE	370
Linda, Martha	4	DE	239
Susan	2	DE	239
William	9/12	DE	239
Lincoln, Benj T	18	MA	59
Linde, Elizabeth	53	GE	226
Henry	58	GE	226
Henry Jr	23	GE	226
Rebecca	16	GE	226
Lindell, George	19	DE	328
Joseph	68	DE	328
Rachel	32	DE	328
Thomas	25	DE	328
Lindeman, Barbary A	39	DE	306
Catherine	5	DE	306
Elizabeth	26	DE	306
Jacob	4	DE	306
Linden, Cave	66	DE	297
John	25	DE	297
John	73	DE	297
Joseph	30	DE	297
Lindley, Hyland	21	DE	210
Linderman, Benj	73	DE	274
Elizabeth	63	PA	274
Margaret	9	DE	274
Lindsey, Anna	5	DE	15
Lindsey, Eliza	37	DE	347
Hannah	34	DE	347
Hannah	47	DE	15
Harry	9/12	DE	29
Henry	45	IE	29
Isaac	18	DE	190
John	12	DE	167
Joseph	29	DE	354
Joseph	57	DE	354
Luisa	20	DE	15
Maria J	22	PA	1
Mary	19	DE	52
Mary A	25	DE	354
Samuel	5	DE	29
Samuel C	23	DE	354
Sarah	2	DE	29
Sarah	21	DE	354
Sarah	23	DE	15
Sarah	33	PA	29
Sarah	48	DE	104
Sarah	54	DE	354
Walter	7	DE	5
Line, Alfred	19	DE	19
Ling, Cyrus	2	DE	259
Eliza	30	DE	227
Eliza J	8	DE	227
Elizabeth W	7	NJ	259
Jeremiah	35	DE	227
Jerry	6	DE	227
John F	4	NJ	259
Joseph	10	NJ	259
Joseph	38	GE	259
Judith	39	NJ	259
Mark W	16	PA	259
Mary	10	DE	227
Link, Abraham	42	GE	21
Anna B	7	DE	277
Caroline	3	DE	21
Christian	14	PA	21
Clara	6	DE	46
Elizabeth	4	DE	21
Elizabeth	42	GE	21
Henrietta	5	DE	21
Henry	7	DE	21
John	53	PA	277
Julian C	11	DE	277
Mary	11	DE	21
Mary	35	PA	277
Mary M	4	DE	277
Roseanna	1	DE	21
Sally	2	DE	46
Sophia	28	DE	46
William	26	DE	46
Linsey, Agnes C	10	DE	331
Elizabeth	20	DE	10
Francina B	50	DE	331
James	59	DE	331
James L	14	DE	331
Jane	21	DE	331
John W	12	DE	331
Lippincott, Benjamin F	9	NJ	176
Edward	19	NJ	176
Eli	17	NJ	176
Eliza	16	NJ	176
Ira	42	NJ	176
John C	14	NJ	176
Mary	42	NJ	176
Lisle, Maria	18	DE	115
List, Elizabeth	26	DE	119
Levina B	2	DE	119
Lewis	35	PA	119
Mary	6/12	?	167
Lister, Ann	70	DE	111
James	20	MD	280
John	20	DE	89
Liston, David	3/12	DE	285
Empson	11	DE	303
Empson	56	DE	286
Hester	36	DE	285
Lites, Charles	23	GE	260
Simon	23	DE	189

Little, Andrew	25	IE	71
Archy	21	PA	188
Eliza J	18	DE	347
Elizabeth	1	DE	345
Elizabeth	62	DE	349
Isabella	39	DE	374
James	34	DE	374
John	68	DE	349
Levi	21	DE	399
Margaret	30	DE	121
Mary E	16	DE	347
Mary E	20	DE	346
Mary Elizabeth	1	DE	346
Samuel	65	DE	346
Sarah	59	DE	374
Sarah Jane	29	DE	345
Thomas	19	DE	399
Thomas	62	DE	346
W S	65	PA	38
Washington	19	DE	374
William	24	DE	36
William	28	DE	374
William	29	DE	345
William	59	DE	374
Littleby, Jonathan	21	DE	177
Litzenberg, Catharine	18	PA	39
Sarah	19	PA	39
Litzenburg, Davis	1	DE	51
Henry	7	DE	51
John	3	DE	51
Joshua	5	DE	51
Maria	30	PA	51
Mary	8	PA	51
Richard	31	PA	51
Lively, Jacob	26	PA	391
Livingston, Albert	17	DE	336
Augustus	22	PA	336
Eliza	25	PA	336
Francis	29	PA	336
Isabel	11	DE	375
James	56	PA	336
Mary	12	DE	375
Sarah	50	PA	336
Susanna	20	PA	336
Livy, Mary	88	MD	58
Lloyd, Aaron	14	NJ	284
Amy	28	NJ	284
Barclay	11	DE	350
Beulah	35	PA	289
Beulah S	50	NY	322
Eastham	14	DE	350
Elizabeth	17	DE	350
Elizabeth	30	PA	307
Emily E	5	PA	307
Esther	2	DE	284
Franklin	32	PA	307
George H	30	NY	285
George L	9	DE	289
Isaac U	12	PA	322
John	33	DE	289
Joseph	41	PA	289
Joseph	53	PA	322
Joseph Jr	15	PA	322
Margaret P	15	DE	289
Marian B	10	DE	322
Mary	15	DE	350
Mary B	6	DE	289
Mary E	8	PA	307
Rebecca	43	DE	350
Rebecca A	46	DE	333
Samuel	47	PA	350
Samuel B	20	PA	322
Sarah E	4	DE	284
Sarah E	18	PA	322
Sophia	19	DE	333
Susan	64	DE	289
Wellington G	11	DE	289
William H	8	DE	289
Loanes, Ann	32	DE	323
James	45	DE	323
Margaret	13	DE	323
Perry	73	MD	323
Loanes, Perry	73	MD	323
Rachel	16	DE	323
Sarah	15	DE	323
William	11	DE	323
Loans, Fanny	27	DE	343
Hannah	2/12	DE	343
Henry	30	DE	343
Margaret	4	DE	343
Rachel	6	DE	343
Loates, Henry	11	DE	296
Rebecca	28	DE	313
Loatts, Aden	8	DE	323
Eliza	18	DE	322
John	57	DE	322
Nancy	49	MD	322
Rachel	12	DE	323
Lobb, Benjamin	23	DE	360
Catherine	37	NJ	309
Elizabeth	42	PA	162
Elmer	40	DE	357
George	21	DE	345
Isaac	24	DE	103
Isaac R	45	NY	309
James R	2	DE	345
John	18	DE	345
John K	14	NJ	309
Johnnah	14	DE	345
Joseph	45	DE	357
Joshua	30	DE	357
Julia M	9	DE	309
Lavinia	37	DE	345
Lydia	21	PA	103
Martha	16	DE	357
Mary	8	DE	345
Mary	10	DE	357
Mary	52	PA	14
Mary	59	DE	345
Mary	81	DE	354
Mary Ann	1	DE	345
Sarah	73	DE	357
Sarah Ellen	7	DE	359
William	20	PA	360
William H	11	PA	309
Lobdell, Addy	32	MA	130
Elizabeth B	3	DE	130
George	32	NY	130
George G	4/12	DE	130
Maria D	7	DE	130
William	6	DE	130
Lober, George	20	DE	367
Henry	14	DE	112
John	19	DE	201
Peter	14	DE	201
Rachel	16	DE	112
Rachel	60	DE	112
Lochard, Ann	33	MD	349
Ann Mary	10	MD	349
Anna Margery	2	DE	349
Hannah	26	DE	349
John	54	DE	349
John P	38	DE	349
John Thomas	7	DE	349
Mary	91	DE	349
Mary Ann	43	DE	349
Mary Elizabeth	5	PA	349
Mathew	60	DE	349
Lock, Joseph	25	DE	140
Maria	22	DE	140
Lockam, John	18	PA	163
Lockaman, Peter	49	MD	321
Rachel	48	DE	321
Lockard, George	25	PA	83
Lockerman, Ann	11	MD	227
Cantwell	43	DE	268
Catherine	13	DE	268
Elias	35	DE	244
Elizabeth	26	DE	244
Elizabeth	62	DE	219
Elizabeth J	25	DE	208
Ephraim L	40	DE	181
George E	2	DE	244
George L	29	DE	208
Lockerman, Harrison	8	DE	202
Henrietta	22	PA	251
Henry	2	PA	251
Jane	30	DE	181
John	6	DE	202
John	45	DE	202
John M	4	DE	181
Martha J	3/12	DE	208
Mary	10	DE	268
Perry	11	DE	203
Prudence	30	DE	53
Rebecca	14	DE	202
Sarah	37	DE	268
Sarah	45	DE	202
Sarah E	3	DE	244
Susan	6	DE	268
William	3	DE	208
William	8	DE	244
William D	6	DE	181
Lockhard, William	24	DE	396
Lockheard, Jacob	40	DE	296
Lockman, Alexander	1	DE	199
Benjamin	28	DE	199
Eliza J	10	DE	199
Elizabeth	24	DE	198
Henry	15	DE	309
Rachel	28	DE	199
Vincent	12	DE	262
William	30	DE	198
Wm	30	MD	255
Lockwood, Absalom	72	DE	258
Charles	23	MD	160
Clara	19	DE	128
George	23	MD	58
John J	14	MD	177
Letitia L	16	MD	177
Margaret R	9	DE	177
Mary	50	DE	177
Mary J	12	DE	363
Richard K	62	DE	177
Richard T	12	MD	177
Sarah	45	DE	258
Sarah A	22	DE	10
Sarah E	1	PA	10
Sarah T	19	DE	177
William R	21	MD	177
Lodain, Alexander	3	DE	318
Ann E	6/12	DE	318
Harriet	27	DE	318
Wesley	5	DE	318
Zekial	30	MD	318
Lodge, Adeline	5	DE	268
Adeline	31	DE	268
Alfred	21	DE	289
Anna M	17	DE	289
Clark W	14	DE	290
Elizabeth W	10	DE	290
Ellen	11/12	DE	268
George	54	DE	284
George W	31	DE	352
Hiram H	40	DE	290
Isaac	16	DE	268
Isaac	19	PA	259
Isaac W	15	DE	290
Isaac W	35	DE	290
James	10	DE	268
John	63	DE	288
John W	29	DE	288
Jonathan	55	GB	375
Joseph	40	DE	268
Louisa	18	DE	290
Malachi	11	DE	268
Margaret	40	DE	290
Martin	17	DE	288
Mary	7	DE	268
Mary	54	NJ	288
Mary	55	GB	375
Mary	62	DE	290
Prudence	66	DE	289
Saml	15	PA	278
Saml	15	DE	268
Samuel	66	DE	289

Name	Age	State	Page
Lodge, Tabitha	62	NJ	290
William C	24	DE	284
William P	22	DE	290
Lodine, Emily	24	DE	210
Ezekiel	26	DE	210
Joshua	22	DE	257
Patty	50	DE	188
Sarah A	16	DE	171
Lofland, Alfred	2	DE	258
Alfred	27	DE	258
Elias	29	DE	258
Elizabeth	1	DE	261
Elizabeth	8	DE	258
Emeline	25	DE	258
George	22	DE	252
George	28	DE	261
Henry	4	DE	258
John	20	DE	342
Matilda	25	DE	261
Mary	25	DE	261
Sarah J	1/12	DE	342
Lofthouse, Cecelia	14	WN	166
Loftland, George	2	DE	193
Jacob	23	DE	172
Jesse	6	DE	193
Samuel	23	DE	193
Sarah	27	DE	193
Solomon	27	DE	193
William	55	DE	193
Logan, Ann	21	DE	42
Anna E	2	DE	157
Eli H	23	PA	69
Frances	75	MD	3
Frances Jr	14	DE	3
Hannah	65	DE	3
Henry	27	DE	253
Hugh ·	30	IE	384
John	50	IE	350
Joseph	13	DE	133
Mary	10	DE	157
Mary	19	DE	44
Robert H	29	DE	42
Samuel	19	DE	42
Sarah	19	DE	60
Logue, Charles	25	IE	89
John	17	IE	35
Mary	23	IE	350
Robert	29	IE	350
Loire, Adalaide	9	DE	203
Alfred	31	NJ	239
Ann	28	NJ	172
Anna D	30	DE	203
Charles	19	DE	172
Dallas D	1	DE	203
Edmund S	30	NJ	239
Elizabeth J	--	AL	239
Ellen	4	DE	203
Emma	17	DE	172
Experience	56	NJ	239
Martha	6	DE	199
Priscilla	49	NJ	172
Sarah J	28	GA	239
Stephen	40	DE	199
William	30	NJ	203
Loken, Agnes	43	GE	5
Catherine R	18	DE	5
Christian	52	GE	5
Elizabeth	10	DE	5
Frances	16	DE	5
James	20	DE	5
Mary A	13	DE	5
Lolly, Ann J	7	DE	382
Daniel	40	DE	382
Eliza	5	DE	382
Emeline	35	DE	382
Mary	6	DE	382
Matilda	10/12	DE	382
William	4	DE	382
Loman, George	29	IE	368
Hannah	27	IE	368
John	29	IE	290
Margaret	22	IE	290
Loman, Mary	21	PA	396
Mary	30	IE	290
Rebecca J	1	DE	368
Rosa	20	IE	290
Sarah E	4	PA	368
William	2	PA	396
Lomax, Lewis	1	DE	27
Sarah	28	MD	27
William	30	MD	27
Londry, Elizabeth H	23	IE	367
Owen	25	IE	367
Patrick	1	IE	367
Long, Alpheus	5	MD	266
Amelia	39	DE	16
Andrew	19	IE	343
Biard	40	DE	369
Caroline	8/12	DE	201
David	34	PA	275
Elizabeth	7	DE	370
Francis	29	DE	381
George	13	PA	369
George	22	PA	263
George W	6	MD	193
Henry	41	DE	16
Hester A	27	MD	193
Isaac	11	PA	369
Isaac	18	GB	353
Isabella	55	DE	260
John	3	MD	266
John	5	NJ	353
John	52	IE	167
John D	32	MD	266
John T	47	PA	381
Joshua	3	DE	353
Joshua	38	NJ	353
Julius	2/12	DE	266
Lorenzo	3	DE	201
Lucy	52	MD	280
Margaret	6	PA	369
Mark	3	PA	370
Mary	7/12	DE	353
Mary	30	DE	201
Mary C	10	DE	201
Patrick	22	IE	347
Richard	7	DE	201
Richard	35	MD	201
Rosanna	24	NJ	252
Sarah	31	DE	266
Sarah	49	DE	386
Susan	38	PA	370
Theodore	6	DE	201
William	9	DE	201
William	20	PA	70
William C	32	MD	193
Longacre, Angelina	24	PA	158
Jacob	21	PA	158
Joseph	55	PA	158
Rosannah	58	PA	158
Longan, Mary	20	MD	31
Longbotham, Ella	4	DE	51
Henry	28	GB	51
Martha	62	GB	51
Mary	1	PA	51
Matilda	25	IE	51
Longfellow, Lavinia	24	MD	257
Margaret	55	DE	257
Thomas	30	MD	257
Longo, Mary	6	DE	232
Mary	50	DE	232
Mezzy	14	DE	232
Rebecca	60	DE	337
Samuel	67	DE	337
Look, Jane	73	DE	370
Looper, Sarah	8	DE	246
Loper, Adaline	3	DE	189
Albert	8	DE	189
Ann	22	DE	188
Benjamin F	11	DE	202
Hester	25	DE	368
Hugh	30	DE	383
Isabella	10	DE	189
John	46	DE	189
Loper, John	68	DE	247
Julia A	18	DE	189
Mary E	14	DE	189
Nicholas	7	DE	189
Rebecca	40	DE	189
Sarah	11	DE	391
Sarah C	6	DE	189
Smith	5/12	DE	189
William	35	DE	209
Loran, Mr	25	GE	39
Mrs	22	GE	39
Lord, Alonzo	6	DE	182
Charles	1	DE	122
Charles	21	DE	255
Charles	27	NJ	122
Charles	38	DE	182
Graberella	7	DE	122
Hannah S	5	DE	122
Harriet N	12	DE	182
Jane H	6/12	DE	182
John	19	PA	163
John R	40	DE	182
Mary	7	DE	129
Mary	18	PA	164
Mary E	10	DE	182
Sarah	26	NJ	122
Lorren, Bridget	25	IE	32
Losemia, Mary E	45	DE	58
Loshard, Jacob	40	FR	297
Loteman, Alexander	19	DE	246
Edward	50	DE	218
Henrietta	50	DE	218
Isabella	25	DE	202
Israel	4	DE	218
Jacob	1	DE	202
Richard	30	DE	202
William	8	DE	218
William	21	DE	211
Lotes, William	10	PA	293
Lothmond, George	30	MD	291
Lott, Margaret	72	DE	265
Lotts, Eliza	18	DE	257
Lotz, Catharine	24	DE	285
Elizabeth	26	DE	285
Mary	33	DE	285
Susan	59	IE	285
Louden, Sarah	49	PA	333
Louis, Wesley	9	PA	387
Louper, Amelia	4/12	DE	331
Amelia	40	DE	331
Anthony	47	MD	331
Joseph	10	DE	331
Lavenia	8	DE	331
Martha	12	DE	333
Thomas	3	DE	332
Love, Adelaide	3	DE	172
Alfred	30	DE	364
Alphonse	3	DE	172
Amelia	8	DE	172
Ann E	31	DE	172
Clara	5	DE	172
Harriet	26	DE	364
Henrietta	2	DE	364
Joseph A	39	DE	172
Sarah	65	PA	358
Theodore	1	DE	172
Thomas	54	PA	358
Virginia	12	DE	172
Lovekins, Anthony	51	DE	300
Caroline	9	DE	300
Louisa	11	DE	300
Rachel	15	DE	300
Sarah	21	DE	300
Lovel, Ann	24	DE	305
Richard	11	DE	293
Sarah	4	DE	299
Lovell, Annah E	9	DE	321
Elizabeth	2	DE	321
Mary J	7	DE	321
Richard S	10	DE	321
Sarah E	4	DE	321
Susannah	30	DE	321

Name	Age	State	Page	Name	Age	State	Page	Name	Age	State	Page
Lovell, William	5/12	DE	321	Loyd, Anna	53	MD	316	Lum, Clara	3	DE	343
Low, Henry	13	DE	307	Anna S	18	PA	332	Debrah	30	DE	89
John	24	DE	307	Catharine	18	DE	375	Isaac A	40	DE	343
Lowber, Adaline E	5	DE	394	Charles	45	DE	240	John	32	SW	89
Adeline	35	DE	394	Cornelia	2	DE	316	Mary B	41	MD	343
Alexander	9	DE	394	David	6	DE	341	Lumber, Augustus	15	DE	368
Alexander	43	DE	394	Eliza	23	DE	316	William	19	DE	368
Catharine M	11	DE	394	Eliza	25	MD	316	Lumbers, Edward	20	DE	339
Lowden, John	24	DE	93	Ella	4	DE	341	Mary A	18	DE	57
Mary	1	DE	93	Frisby	21	DE	303	Lumford, Mary A	30	DE	194
Mary	22	DE	93	Frisby	68	MD	316	Lumm, Elizabeth	55	MD	337
Charlotte P	17	DE	365	George	21	DE	375	Emory	20	MD	337
Eliza P	23	DE	365	Harriet	15	DE	240	John	32	MD	337
James	50	GB	365	Henry	30	DE	341	Mary	37	MD	337
James R	20	DE	365	Jane	45	DE	240	Mary J	8	DE	337
Jane	47	GB	365	Martha	45	DE	375	Samson	63	DE	320
Richard G	11	DE	365	Mary	16	PA	332	Thomas	21	MD	338
Lowe, Elizabeth L	32	DE	80	Mary A	22	NJ	303	Thomas	26	DE	293
Frederic	10	NJ	3	Mary A	25	NJ	304	Lumpkins, Edward	20	DE	338
Harriet	2	DE	3	Minty	18	DE	261	Emma	24	DE	338
James	20	IE	78	Samuel	12	DE	318	Lunny, Elizabeth	47	DE	385
Jane	25	DE	31	Samuel	16	DE	316	George	4	DE	385
Jessie	23	IE	103	Samuel	30	DE	338	James	13	DE	385
John	16	IE	78	Sarah E	14	DE	375	James	50	DE	385
John	11	NJ	3	Wesley	22	DE	316	John	8	DE	385
Mary	34	NJ	3	Wilamena	29	DE	341	Lush, Benjamin	3	DE	241
Mary E	7	DE	80	William	13	DE	375	Elias	5	DE	241
Richard	40	NJ	3	William F	48	DE	375	Isaiah	7	DE	241
Sarah	60	DE	31	Loyed, Abigal	50	PA	75	Jacob	12	DE	241
Sarah E	9	DE	80	Andrew	28	DE	27	Jacob	47	DE	241
William	14	NJ	3	Ann	13	DE	27	John	5/12	DE	241
William G	10	DE	80	Benjamin	16	DE	75	Mary A	17	DE	241
William G	40	DE	80	Benjamin	45	PA	75	Sarah	37	DE	241
Lowery, Elizabeth	25	PA	99	Edward	7	DE	75	William	10	DE	241
Jane	8	AA	349	George	21	DE	27	Luzby, George	5	DE	269
Lowman, Charles	32	DE	36	Hetty	19	DE	112	Henrietta	3	DE	267
Eliza	32	DE	36	Isaac	4	DE	75	John	25	DE	267
Franklin	7	DE	36	Jacob	29	DE	27	Margaret	30	NY	267
Henry	2/12	DE	36	Jane	20	NJ	85	Mary	26	DE	269
John	3	DE	36	Mary	25	DE	34	Susanna	35	DE	267
Mary	3	PA	396	Mary	50	MD	82	Susanna	65	MD	267
Samuel	5	DE	36	Spencer	9	DE	75	Thomas	1	DE	252
Lowry, Elenor	42	DE	22	William	18	DE	75	Wm	32	DE	267
Ellen	5	DE	22	Lucas, Ann	3	DE	217	Lyans, Emma T	5	MD	117
Hannah	11	DE	22	Charles	8	DE	386	Florence P	2	PA	117
James	13	DE	22	James	25	DE	217	Rebecca H	29	MD	117
Jemimah	7	DE	22	Louisa	34	MD	146	Lybrand, Ester	35	DE	71
Lydia	1	DE	22	Louisa	39	MD	295	James	4	PA	72
Mary	9	DE	22	Mansfield	17	DE	375	John	8	PA	72
Michel	8	DE	22	Sarah	20	DE	217	Mary	3	DE	72
Michel	45	IE	22	William	15	DE	178	Walter	13	PA	71
Rebecca	3	DE	22	Ludow, Catharine	36	CT	392	William	4/12	DE	72
Lowther, Angeline	33	PA	287	Luff, Ann	38	DE	39	William	37	PA	71
Ann	21	DE	295	Cecilia	5	DE	349	Lydia, Thomas	20	IE	135
Ann	46	IE	359	Danial	3	DE	101	Lyle, Ellen	85	PA	283
Anna	16	DE	359	Dianna	35	DE	349	Mary	18	PA	20
Christian	11	DE	359	George	18	DE	95	Lynam, Albert G	35	DE	366
Christy A	44	DE	295	George A	10	DE	349	Anna M	5	DE	367
David	7	DE	359	Hannah	11	MD	294	Anna M	7	DE	369
David D	45	DE	287	Hannah M	12	PA	349	C J	10	DE	304
Eliza P	3	DE	287	Harriet	8	DE	95	Catharine A	21	DE	218
Ella C	9	DE	295	James	38	DE	349	David S	15	DE	218
Emma M	8/12	DE	295	Jane	34	MD	34	Debro Mary	28	DE	115
Jane	12	DE	295	John	12	DE	95	Ellanor	50	DE	366
Jane	23	DE	359	John	39	DE	34	Eliza	37	DE	369
John	14	DE	295	John W	9	PA	349	Elizabeth	13	DE	365
John	19	DE	295	Judy	31	DE	95	Elizabeth	17	DE	5
Joseph	15	DE	295	Lydia	6	DE	95	Elizabeth P	17	DE	379
Major L	5	DE	359	Purnel	40	DE	95	Ellen B	11	DE	370
Margaret	9	DE	359	Sally A	16	DE	95	Emma S	11	DE	367
Margaret A	6	DE	287	Sarah J	9	DE	101	Evelina	39	DE	360
Mary	73	DE	295	Susan	15	DE	105	George T	3	DE	360
Mary J	7	DE	287	William	21	DE	95	Jacob	36	DE	373
Moses	17	DE	295	William G	14/12	DE	349	Jacob A	4	DE	218
Moses	19	DE	384	Luft, Jane	14	DE	156	James H	25	DE	366
Moses	52	DE	359	Luit, Caroline	4	DE	246	Jeremiah R	2	DE	367
Sarah	11	DE	295	John	28	GE	246	Joanna	65	DE	370
William	20	DE	295	Rebecca A	25	NJ	246	Joanna A	6	DE	360
William	21	DE	359	William H	2	DE	246	Joanna S	20	DE	367
William	47	DE	295	Luke, John	25	LA	152	Joanna J	19	DE	218
Wm H	9	PA	287	Lukins, Mary	42	NJ	69	John	42	DE	369
Lowyen, John	14	DE	331	Lum, Charles A	15	DE	343	John	50	DE	218

Name	Age	St	Pg
Luzby, John R Jr	4	DE	369
John W	14	DE	367
Joseph	80	DE	370
Joseph C	18	DE	367
Joseph G	13	DE	218
Joseph R	9	DE	360
Joseph S	40	DE	367
Josephine R	5	DE	379
Lewis C	1	DE	380
Margarett	50	PA	304
Marion C E	7	DE	367
Martha	34	DE	218
Martin W	7	DE	36
Mary	34	DE	373
Mary	42	DE	379
Mary	50	DE	115
Mary A	13	DE	379
Mary J	18	DE	218
Mary J	30	DE	366
Mary R	1	DE	369
Masina	1	DE	367
Raburn W	9	DE	369
Rebecca A	15	DE	367
Rebecca A	39	DE	367
Remus A	8	DE	367
Robert F	17	DE	369
Sarah	20	DE	115
Sarah	13	DE	369
Sarah A	5	DE	36
Sarah C	15	DE	379
Susanna S	12	DE	360
Thomas	45	DE	360
Thomas	65	DE	366
Thomas B	19	DE	369
Thomas J	19	DE	379
Virginia L	11	DE	379
William A	17	DE	360
William H	7	DE	379
William R	41	DE	379
William W	9	DE	218
Lynch, Amos W	31	MD	195
Ann E	7	DE	121
Barnard	3	DE	286
Bridget	13	DE	286
Bridget	19	IE	314
Catherine	3	DE	298
Catherine	11	DE	286
Catherine	28	PA	129
Catherine	29	DE	298
Catherine	45	IE	302
Catherine	60	DE	327
Clinton	30	MD	178
Edward	9	DE	298
Elijah	30	MD	201
Elizabeth	28	DE	121
Ellen	3	DE	326
Ellen	8	IE	302
Ellen	30	IE	286
Emma M	3	DE	178
Eugene	3/12	DE	121
Frances D	9	DE	195
George B	2	DE	201
Harriet	3	DE	195
Henrietta	7	DE	201
Hugh	5	DE	298
Hugh	15	DE	286
Hugh	16	IE	302
Hugh	36	IE	345
Hugh	55	DE	327
James W	30	PA	121
John	7	DE	286
John	18	IE	302
John	20	MD	196
John	33	IE	298
John	50	IE	302
John H	3	DE	121
Joseph	16	DE	195
Julia	20	DE	195
Julia	29	IE	326
Maria O	9/12	DE	178
Mary	7	DE	298
Mary	9	DE	286
Lynch, Mary	22	DE	195
Mary A	5	DE	129
Mary A	13	IE	302
Mary E	20	MD	178
Mary S	1	DE	203
Patrick	20	IE	302
Pernell J	27	DE	203
Rebecca	7	DE	195
Richard	14	MD	195
Rose	30	PA	159
Sally N	30	DE	201
Sarah	5	IE	302
Sarah A	26	DE	203
Sarah E	4	DE	203
Susan	3	DE	129
Thomas	9/12	DE	298
Thomas	5	DE	287
Thomas	7	DE	129
Thomas	23	DE	203
William	1	DE	286
William	34	DE	129
Wm	28	DE	327
Lynet, Elizabeth	75	IE	69
Margaret	40	IE	69
Lyniun, Ann C	14	DE	366
David	39	DE	366
David R	6	DE	366
Elenor	34	DE	366
Evan T	3	DE	366
George	5	DE	366
Lavinia	9	DE	366
Margaret	19	DE	382
Robert	28	DE	381
Lyons, Cornelius	10	MD	301
Eliza	9	PA	360
Elizabeth	38	IE	301
Joel	7	DE	360
Mary	28	DE	246
Nicholas	16	PA	163
Thomas	19	PA	164
Thomas	31	DE	246
Lyser, Ann	28	IE	372
Catherine	8	DE	372
Elizabeth	2	DE	372
John	35	IE	372
Mary	11	DE	372
Sophia	6	DE	372
Macafferty, Ellen	2	DE	30
Ellen	35	IE	30
Ellen	40	IE	30
Jane	76	IE	30
John	13	PA	30
Mary	15	DE	30
Rosean	12	PA	30
Thomas	3	DE	30
Macaw, David	17	DE	172
Macehill, Ann	18	IE	287
John	5/12	DE	287
Michael	21	IE	287
Macey, Andrew	13	ST	344
Ann	9	ST	344
Martha	25	ST	344
Mary	11	ST	344
Sarah	16	ST	344
Wm	34	ST	344
MacFarland, Ann	50	DE	172
Macintore, Owen	18	IE	306
MacIntyre, Ann	47	DE	178
Thomas	46	DE	178
Mackay, Jane	22	IE	193
Mackey, Sarah	15	DE	369
Maclean, George P	13	DE	392
Lydia	7	DE	392
Mathew	17	DE	392
Mathew	57	PA	392
Rebecca	46	DE	392
Macolerogue, Unis	22	IE	116
Macpherson, Mary J	48	PA	282
Macrosson, Jane	20	IE	303
Rose	30	IE	303
Macurdy, Robt	75	PA	24
Macurdy, Robt	75	PA	369
Madden, Catharine	40	IE	250
Elizabeth	12	IE	316
Hugh	17	IE	250
John	15	IE	250
John	40	IE	250
Mary	3	DE	318
Sarah	35	IE	271
Wm	30	IE	250
Mader, Sylvester	9	DE	320
Madison, Henrietta	4	DE	98
James	32	DE	98
James M	33	DE	295
Matilda	6	DE	98
Sally	29	DE	300
Williamina	28	MD	98
Maffer, John	40	GE	335
Magage, Mary	20	IE	78
Magarity, Edward	39	IE	105
Ellen	4/12	DE	106
George	8	IE	106
James	3	DE	106
Mary	31	IE	105
Patric	6	IE	106
Patric	22	IE	22
Patric	28	IE	106
Sarah	22	IE	106
Thomas	45	IE	22
Magear, Edward	19	GB	304
Magee, Ann	29	IE	82
Anna J	3	DE	34
Bryan	4	IE	365
Catherine	2	IE	5
Catherine	35	IE	147
Catherine	40	MD	177
Charles	20	MD	177
Daniel	30	IE	82
David A	2/12	DE	82
Edward	5	DE	147
Eliza Jane	30	IE	84
Elizabeth	23	IE	365
Elleanor	13	MD	177
Ellen	1	DE	147
George	18	MD	196
George	48	PA	108
James	14	MD	177
Jane	4	DE	147
Jane	14	DE	393
Jane	25	IE	330
Jane E	30	DE	108
Letitia	48	DE	108
Margaret	3	DE	147
Mary E	2	DE	84
Mike	14	DE	147
Nathaniel	2	DE	82
Patrick	24	IE	365
Sarah J	9	MD	177
Susan	12	DE	147
William	33	IE	84
Magener, Caroline	18	PA	125
Magill, James P	16	MD	400
Magines, Lydia	24	IE	52
Maginis, Hannah	12	IN	302
William	10	IN	302
Maginnis, Biddy	40	IE	20
Maginte, Patric	17	IE	44
Magolis, Patric	72	IE	11
Magouin, Patric	17	IE	150
Magowin, Biddy	50	IE	47
Matilda	5	IE	47
Patric	50	IE	47
Magruder, John	7	DE	151
Magugan, Ann	35	IE	138
Maguire, Ann	9	IE	97
Ann	20	IE	56
Ann	21	IE	122
Ann	30	DE	32
Anna	11	DE	35
Anna	20	DE	128
Balinda	50	PA	128
Barny	10	IE	127
Bridget	24	IE	304

Name	Age	Place	Page
Maguire, Catherine	11/12	IE	122
Catherine	16	DE	152
Catherine	38	IE	151
Charles	12	IE	151
Charles	26	DE	44
Charles	39	IE	151
Conner	55	IE	127
Cornelius	15	IE	290
Dennis	19	IE	14
Dennis	19	IE	127
Dennis	30	IE	151
Elizabeth	3	DE	151
Ellen	48	DE	94
Ellen	48	IE	127
Emeline	26	DE	60
Frances	6	DE	151
Frances	10	IE	151
Frances T	1	DE	307
Frank	9	PA	164
George	4/12	DE	97
George	7	IE	151
George	52	PA	128
Harriet	19	DE	128
Hugh	5	IE	151
Hugh	39	IE	44
Isaac	15	DE	94
James	1	DE	151
James	6	IE	97
James	38	PA	14
Jane	5	DE	44
Jerry	15	IE	81
John	11/12	DE	151
John	1	DE	
John	4	IE	97
John	6	IE	151
John	11	PA	164
Lewis	6	DE	94
Lewis	24	DE	60
Lewis	50	DE	94
Margaret	13	IE	304
Margaret	27	IE	151
Martha	22	DE	128
Mary	5	DE	152
Mary	11	DE	39
Mary	11	IE	97
Mary	35	IE	304
Mary A	16	PA	307
Mary A	17	DE	94
Mary A	18	DE	151
Mary E	13	PA	128
Michel	30	IE	122
Owen	84	IE	122
Patt	30	IE	304
Rebecca	28	IE	44
Rosa	4	IE	127
Sally	9	DE	94
Samuel	15	PA	128
Sarah	30	IE	97
Susan	8	IE	151
Sylvester	40	DE	302
Magulerie, Ellen	25	IE	11
George	27	IE	11
Mahaffy, Elizabeth H	20	DE	9
Henry C	5	DE	9
Jane R	34	DE	9
Margaret	63	IE	9
Margaret H	26	DE	9
Mary	26	DE	9
Mary	30	DE	9
Mary E	10	DE	9
Thomas	32	DE	9
Thomas	62	IE	9
Mahan, Ellen	30	IE	163
Maharly, James	20	PA	79
Mahary, John	45	IE	80
Maherd, Arthur	19	DE	304
Mahews, Henne	73	DE	168
Mahony, Catherine	19	NY	296
Edward	12	NJ	296
Maria	44	CT	296
Mary A	17	PA	296
Richard	9	CT	296
Mahony, Timothy	60	IE	296
Main, Augustia	30	GE	24
Mainey, Johanna	1	IE	252
Margaret	19	IE	252
Michael	30	IE	252
Wm	1	IE	252
Major, Sarah	40	DE	19
Thomas	51	GB	19
Makins, Caroline	18	MD	209
Maklin, Anna M	15	DE	376
Eliza	25	DE	376
Isaac	21	DE	376
John	12	DE	376
Mary	55	DE	376
Rebecca J	77	DE	376
William	53	DE	376
Malan, Mrs	28	MD	137
Malcolm, George W	7	NJ	286
John	1	DE	286
John	42	IE	286
Margaret J	3	DE	286
Martha	26	PA	286
Sarah A	5	PA	286
Maley, Marshall	14	IE	379
Malley, Augustine	16	DE	112
Augustine	46	FR	112
Charles E	18	FR	112
Eugene C	5	DE	112
Margaret E	76	FR	112
Mary C	1	DE	112
Samuel T	14	DE	112
Sarah H	40	GB	112
Malloy, Catherine	50	IE	265
John	24	IE	265
Lawrence	28	IE	265
Sarah	18	IE	348
Mallram, Betty	47	GB	378
Mary	23	GB	378
Thomas	51	GB	378
Malochlin, Anna	15	IE	18
Malon, Patrick	31	IE	250
Malone, Biddy	22	IE	196
Jacob	18	PA	34
Margaret	34	PA	335
Mary	5	PA	335
Mary Ann	7/12	PA	346
Mary Ann	22	IE	346
Sarah	3	DE	151
Susan A	25	IE	363
Maloney, Bridget	28	IE	298
Catherine	30	IE	65
Charles	3/12	IE	65
Daniel	4	IE	298
Eliza	20	IE	144
James	2	DE	65
John	7	DE	65
John	22	IE	86
John	30	NY	65
Martha	9	DE	167
Richard	7	IE	298
Sarah	29	?	167
Thomas	8	DE	65
Thomas	8	IE	298
Thomas	24	NY	70
William	5	DE	65
Malony, Arthur	10	DE	367
Isaac B	22	PA	330
Jane	15	PA	330
Margaret	16	IE	10
Mary A	51	PA	330
Michael	54	IE	330
Sarah	13	PA	330
Wm	12	PA	330
Malten, Cathrine	21	PA	317
Maly, Mary	10	DE	244
Mancill, Jane	71	PA	274
John	71	PA	274
Lydia	28	PA	274
Mander, Sarah	34	DE	156
Manderfield, August	16	Pa	163
Maney, Charles	17	IE	25
James	25	IE	285
Maney, John	1	DE	285
Susan	23	DE	285
Mange, Emanuel	6	PA	292
John	14	GB	292
Martha	42	GB	292
Mary	2	PA	292
Priscilla	9	GB	292
Samuel	4	PA	292
Theophilus	43	GB	292
Thomas	11	GB	292
William	16	GB	292
Manges, Corah	20	DE	161
Mrs	40	DE	161
Manley, Elizabeth	25	DE	298
Hester	38	DE	298
Louisa	40	DE	298
Manlove, Amelia	12	DE	277
Hudson	6	DE	194
James O	26	DE	304
Manuel	35	DE	277
Maria	40	PA	93
Mary	30	DE	277
Noah	15	DE	230
Sarah	25	DE	106
Manly, Ann	30	DE	156
Debro	22	DE	95
Fereby	54	DE	156
Hetty	19	?	284
John	23	DE	95
Josephine	8	DE	246
Mathew	30	DE	156
Peter	7	DE	74
Peter	67	DE	156
William H	11/12	DE	95
Mann, Jno	16	IE	292
Levic	19	DE	383
Mannan, Alfred	7	DE	244
Elizabeth	6/12	DE	244
Elizabeth	37	DE	244
George	12	DE	244
James	61	DE	244
John	17	DE	244
Lydia	16	DE	244
Mannering, Alphonso	5	DE	173
Elizabeth	7	DE	173
Harrison	10	DE	173
James	7	DE	173
James	20	DE	226
Margaret	41	DE	173
William	14	DE	173
William	41	DE	173
Manning, Benjamin	26	DE	242
Marietta	21	DE	242
Sewall	25	DE	226
Mannon, Alfred	9	DE	243
Elizabeth	6/12	DE	243
Elizabeth	37	DE	243
George	12	DE	243
James	25	DE	231
James	61	DE	243
James M	9/12	DE	231
John	17	DE	243
Lydia	16	DE	243
Mary A	22	DE	231
Mansfield, Jane	68	PA	282
Jas C	52	MD	282
Mary R	52	MD	282
Michel	17	PA	164
Thomas	15	PA	164
Zebediah	40	CT	114
Manship, Andrew	38	MD	94
Levi J	11/12	DE	94
Rebecca	25	MD	94
Mansley, Alice	22	GB	301
Anna	15	GB	301
Elizabeth	20	GB	315
John	24	GB	315
Sarah N	19	GB	301
Vesperna	17	GB	301
Manuel, Charles	5	DE	378
Charles	45	MD	378
Henrietta	42	MD	378

Name	Age	St	No.	Name	Age	St	No.	Name	Age	St	No.
Manuel, James	14	DE	378	Marshall, Frances	1	DE	363	Martin, Lewis	8	PA	391
Rebecca	9	DE	378	Hannah	33	PA	363	Lydia	45	PA	250
William	23	MD	378	John	38	DE	320	Lydia P	20	DE	362
Maran, Charles	34	DE	125	John B	35	PA	363	Martha	7	DE	260
Hester	35	DE	125	John E	4	PA	363	Martha E	6	PA	391
John W	7	DE	125	Joseph	22	GB	23	Mary	44	GE	242
Mary J	9	DE	125	Joseph	35	DE	247	Mary A	16	DE	278
Sarah E	2	DE	125	Josephine	27	PA	320	Mary J	6	DE	367
March, Peter	13	DE	368	Margaret E	8	PA	363	Mathew	17	DE	158
Marchant, Arzilla	3	DE	272	Mary	30	GB	377	Phillip	14	MD	107
Catharine	30	FR	272	Mary A	6	PA	363	Rebecca	42	MD	20
Charles	11	VA	272	Mary E	6/12	DE	225	Robt	25	IE	340
Charles	39	FR	272	Mary S	2	PA	320	Sarah	2	DE	260
Emma	1	DE	272	Moses	25	DE	225	Sarah	8	DE	278
Frances	7	DE	272	William	30	GB	377	Sarah	10	MD	20
Josephine	9	VA	272	Martan, Jane	50	DE	88	Sarah	12	PA	249
Marel, Martha	14	DE	244	Marten, Eliza J	33	DE	291	Sarah A	32	DE	367
Marine, Charles	17	DE	223	Margaret	3	DE	291	Susan	5	DE	367
Cornelius C	18	DE	223	Sterling	1	DE	291	Susan	27	IE	144
Elizabeth	50	DE	223	Martial, Alfred	1	DE	367	Theodore P	4	DE	391
John	24	DE	223	Anna	3	DE	367	Thomas M	16	PA	391
Maria	10	DE	223	Caleb	11	DE	367	Thos	28	IE	341
Mary E	14	DE	223	Caleb	43	PA	367	Veronica	8	GE	242
Richard S	22	DE	223	Calvin P	16	DE	367	William	9	DE	367
Thomas	55	DE	223	Elizabeth	5	DE	367	William A	9	DE	362
Marion, Peter	20	IE	274	Jane	31	PA	367	Wm	17	PA	340
Markel, John	20	GE	43	John	41	PA	367	Marton, Phebe	57	PA	384
Markey, Sarah	15	ST	370	Lydia S	14	DE	367	Marvell, Alace	22	PA	79
Markle, Mary A	18	DE	61	Mary	41	PA	367	Alexander	30	DE	26
William	22	GB	61	Mary H	17	PA	367	Isabella	6	DE	26
Markman, Chandler	15	DE	355	William	3	DE	367	Mary	40	DE	26
James	49	DE	355	Martimer, Charles H	15	PA	319	Phillip	25	NJ	79
Juliet A	34	DE	355	Martin, Adam	50	GE	242	Marvin, Ebenezer	41	NY	400
Mary E	9	DE	355	Ann	48	PA	249	Jane	6/12	DE	400
Marley, Anna L	5	DE	383	Anthony	45	GB	168	Mary	25	GB	400
Elizabeth	20	DE	383	Benjamin F	8	DE	362	Marywether, John	7	DE	152
John	27	DE	383	Catherine	15	PA	249	Susan	9	DE	291
Louisa M W	2	DE	383	Charlotte	11	PA	391	Thomas	7	DE	281
Rebecca	30	DE	390	Charlotte	40	PA	391	Mason, Adaline	12	VA	124
Richard Mc M	31	DE	390	David	3	PA	249	Albert	12	DE	176
Marlin, Catherine	29	DE	112	David	51	PA	250	Alexander	19	DE	213
Hannah E	7	DE	112	Eliza	3	DE	279	Alexander	50	MD	236
Isaac	40	PA	112	Eliza	3	DE	367	Ann	56	MD	221
Susannah	50	PA	112	Eliza	7	DE	340	Anna	9	DE	176
Thomas J	4	DE	112	Eliza	18	IE	340	Anna	15	DE	67
William S	3	DE	112	Eliza	36	DE	277	Caroline	13	NY	103
Marlow, Owen	25	IE	344	Elizabeth	23	IE	144	Caroline	21	MA	103
Marny, Rebecca	23	DE	366	Elizabeth	35	DE	362	Catherine	25	NF	69
Sarah A	17	DE	366	Elizabeth A	5/12	DE	362	Charlotta	33	DE	118
Marquet, Ann	34	GE	335	Emma	12	DE	278	Clifford	3	DE	67
Frederick	38	GE	335	Enoch	19	PA	277	David	17	DE	171
Marr, Elizabeth	4	DE	6	Evalina	9	PA	249	Eliza	22	IE	366
Elizabeth	40	DE	6	Fanny	76	IE	362	Elizabeth	12	DE	317
Catherine	2	DE	25	Frances	24	PA	249	Elizabeth	14	VA	124
Catherine	36	IE	25	Frances	26	DE	362	Elizabeth	26	DE	118
George W	2	DE	6	Francinia	12	DE	362	Ellen	2	DE	69
James	13	DE	6	George H	2	DE	250	Ellen	7	DE	176
John	10	DE	6	George H	24	DE	250	Emma	5/12	DE	69
John	39	IE	25	Hamilton	40	DE	218	Enos	6	DE	328
Michel	40	IE	35	Hamilton	48	DE	174	Francis J	28	NY	103
Patric	21	IE	37	Hiram	44	DE	99	George	4	DE	49
Rebecca J	6	DE	6	Hugh	19	IE	250	George	7	DE	118
William	38	GB	6	Jacob	42	DE	278	Hamilton	6	MA	103
William H	14	DE	6	James	34	DE	367	Hester	30	DE	67
Marriott, Martha	15	DE	204	James	35	DE	362	Isaac	4	DE	236
Mary	16	DE	204	James	40	DE	285	Isaac	41	DE	67
Sarah	40	DE	204	James S	15	PA	391	James	2	DE	124
Thomas J	56	DE	204	James S	47	SC	391	James	19	DE	213
Marrow, Jane	27	PA	305	Jane	93	DE	398	James	46	PA	124
Marsh, Amelia	31	NY	144	Jeremy	3	DE	362	James Jr	12	DE	176
Augusta	8	NY	144	John	6	DE	278	John	8	DE	328
John	35	NY	144	John	22	IE	340	John	35	DE	103
John M	54	DE	296	John	28	DE	253	John	47	DE	221
Sarah	37	NY	144	John	42	DE	122	John	55	DE	328
Viola	6	NY	144	John S	12	PA	107	Joseph	28	NY	25
Marshal, Mary	22	DE	21	Joseph	20	PA	249	Josiah	16	MD	221
Nathan	18	PA	135	Joseph	47	DE	250	Lemuel	30	MA	103
Peter	22	GB	305	Joseph E	5	DE	362	Lewis	5	DE	118
Stephen	35	PA	21	Josephine	8	PA	250	Lewis	35	DE	118
Marshall, Charles	3	GB	377	Kate	10	MS	181	Lucinda	10/12	DE	118
Comfort A	18	DE	225	Kenard W	30	MD	15	Lydia	3	DE	118
Edward W	4	PA	320	Lewis	8	PA	391	Maliki	32	DE	69

Name	Age	Birthplace	Page
Mason, Margaret	68	DE	67
Margaret A	14	DE	118
Mary	6	DE	49
Mary	11	DE	328
Mary	30	DE	49
Mary	30	DE	328
Mary	40	PA	115
Mary A	22	DE	286
Mary J	2	DE	236
Matthew F	70	PA	176
Olivia	40	VA	124
Oscar	5	DE	67
Park	8	DE	67
Park	70	DE	67
Rachel	17	DE	331
Rachel	40	MD	236
Sarah	6	DE	67
Sophia	26	DE	208
Sophia	29	DE	103
Susan	9	MD	221
Susan	32	PA	67
Tabitha	68	PA	115
Taylor	2	DE	49
Thomas	16	DE	236
Washington	28	DE	49
William	3	DE	103
William	11	DE	197
William H	11	RI	103
Massey, Ann	45	MD	200
Anne M	3	DE	274
Bernard	7	PA	274
Charlotta	14	MD	153
Elizabeth	1	DE	193
Elizabeth	17	DE	200
Gemima	18	GB	105
Harriet	60	PA	49
Henry	30	DE	258
Hensley	2	DE	47
Hensley	25	DE	47
Isabella	16	DE	230
Israel	56	PA	49
James B	36	DE	90
Jemima	18	GB	104
Jesse	36	DE	90
John	30	GB	302
Joshua	4	DE	47
Luisa J	2	DE	87
Lydia A	29	DE	274
Mary	45	MD	153
Mary A	23	DE	49
Rachel	7	DE	87
Rachel J	6	DE	200
Rebecca	34	DE	87
Rebecca J	11/12	DE	274
Sarah	30	DE	47
Sarah	68	MD	159
Sarah	73	MD	193
Sarah E	5	DE	274
Susan	19	DE	258
Thomas	5/12	DE	47
Vicey	60	DE	318
William	4	DE	87
William	9	DE	219
William	45	MD	200
William	45	DE	211
William B	28	DE	87
William T	29	DE	274
Massin, Angus	45	GB	364
Harriet	24	GB	364
Massy, Jemima	34	IE	328
Masten, Anne	6	DE	125
James	30	DE	125
John	3	DE	125
Sarah	32	MD	125
Master, Lewis W	4	PA	329
Mary	23	PA	329
Masters, Ann	25	GB	262
Ellen	2/12	DE	262
John	30	GB	262
Mary	10	GB	262
Morris	8	GB	262
Stephen	30	GB	262
Masters, Wm	28	GB	262
Matchit, Elizabeth	7	IE	305
Margaret	4	IE	305
Martha	1	DE	305
Martha	30	IE	305
Samuel	36	IE	305
William	5	IE	305
Mathels, Bridget	20	IE	30
Mathers, Ann	58	GB	36
Mary Susan	27	DE	36
Thomas	53	GB	36
Mathews, Ann E	6	DE	212
Bridget	5/12	DE	365
Charles	11	DE	242
Charles A	2	DE	343
David	20	DE	367
Elizabeth	19	PA	364
Emily	22	PA	364
Francis	15	DE	242
Francis	18	PA	341
Hannah	14	DE	242
Henry	5	DE	343
Isaac	4	DE	212
James	45	IE	319
James C	18	DE	242
James N	60	DE	242
Jamson	23	GB	336
Jemima	52	DE	242
John	30	PA	340
John	40	DE	212
Lucinda	3/12	DE	212
Margaret	33	PA	341
Maria	18	PA	341
Mary	21	IE	365
Mary	29	MD	212
Mary J	13	DE	341
Michael	22	IE	365
Peter	40	FR	341
Richard A	80	MD	302
Stewart	9	DE	212
Thomas	11	DE	212
William	13	DE	212
William	23	DE	302
Mathewson, Elizabeth	23	IE	346
George	25	DE	334
Gilbert	62	IE	345
Gilbert Jr	28	DE	345
Jane	2	DE	346
Joseph	12	DE	345
Mary	40	DE	345
Mary Ann	15	DE	345
Rebecca	25	IE	334
Mathias, Mary	41	MD	330
Mathiast, Frederic	24	SZ	5
Matias, John	33	DE	128
Matloc, Elizabeth	33	DE	129
John G	33	DE	129
William B	7	DE	129
Matlock, Bennett	8	DE	94
Charles	2/12	DE	94
Charles P	39	DE	94
Henry	12	DE	94
Mary	10	DE	94
Phebena	24	DE	94
Mattee, Marcellas	40	MD	303
Rebecca	35	DE	303
Matthew, Alfred	6	DE	310
Ann M	25	PA	364
Charles	36	DE	310
David	20	IE	368
Elizabeth	19	PA	365
Elizabeth	26	DE	310
Emily	22	PA	365
George	7	DE	11
Isabella	58	PA	364
John	12	DE	11
John E	62	PA	364
Lewis	29	DE	11
Margaret	27	DE	11
Mary L	8	DE	310
Sarah	26	DE	310
William	13	DE	11
Matthews, Charles E	4	MD	335
Edward	6	PA	273
Edward	30	PA	273
Eliza A	2	MD	335
Eliza J	20	MD	335
Elizabeth	14	IE	330
Esther	26	PA	273
Mary A	8	MD	335
William M	62	MD	181
Wm	8	PA	273
Mattis, Henry	24	GE	213
Lawrence	12	GE	213
Mary	10	GE	213
Perry	16	GE	213
Phillip	22	GE	213
Valentine	50	GE	212
Mattoc, Bennett	35	DE	119
Mary	39	NJ	119
Rebecca	40	NJ	119
Mattson, Abner	10	NJ	262
Charles	36	NJ	262
Delia	30	NJ	262
Edward	4	PA	262
Mary	12	NJ	262
Sarah	2	DE	262
Maughn, Patrick	25	IE	349
Maule, Annie	14	PA	164
Maunagh, Patrick	35	IE	310
Mavis, John	25	MD	169
Mawhirter, James	2	DE	372
Jane	15	IE	372
Margery	34	IE	372
Mary	10	IE	372
Sarah	13	IE	372
Thomas	8	IE	372
Maxwell, Alexander D	8	DE	357
Amelia	41	MD	398
Ann	70	DE	337
Ann M	13	DE	363
Anthony	14	DE	289
Arthur	23	DE	23
Benjamin D	4	DE	366
Capt	60	DE	271
Catherine	2	DE	175
Catherine	40	MD	175
Catherine S	26	MD	320
Chamberlain	10	DE	398
Charles	8	DE	327
Charles A	6	PA	320
Charles W	2	DE	363
Chas	6	IE	327
Curtis	10	DE	276
David	45	VA	175
David H	5	DE	175
Elijah T	4	DE	363
Eliza	1	DE	23
Elizabeth	14	IE	327
Elizabeth	30	PA	54
Elizabeth	30	PA	329
Elizabeth	35	MD	363
Ellen	5/12	DE	327
Ellen	40	IE	327
Franklin C	12	DE	357
George G	14	DE	357
Georgianna	15	DE	398
Hamilton	10	IE	327
Hamilton	30	IE	329
Jacob C	19	PA	357
James	51	MD	363
James R	15	PA	329
John	17	IE	327
John	27	PA	365
John M	12	PA	175
John T	10	DE	363
Joseph P	16	DE	357
Lewis	10	DE	295
Lewis	18	DE	398
Margaret	12	IE	328
Margaret	45	GB	271
Marian	50	DE	312
Marshall P	6	DE	357
Martha E	8	DE	363

Name	Age		No.	Name	Age		No.	Name	Age		No.
Maxwell, Mary	6	DE	295	McBride, Patric	11/12	DE	13	McCaley, Janet	32	IE	337
Mary	21	GB	23	Patric	30	IE	13	Nancy	7	VA	337
Mary	44	DE	161	Rebecca	2	DE	297	Susan	9	PA	337
Mary	73	DE	295	Rebecca	25	DE	296	McCall, Adaline	24	PA	62
Mary E	6	MD	320	Richard E	25	NJ	297	Andrew	14	DE	108
Mary J	4	DE	398	Sarah	2	DE	13	Ann	11	DE	108
Mary Jane	12	DE	363	Sarah A	21	NJ	297	Anna F	12	PA	62
Mary V	8	MD	175	Susan	20	NJ	29	Betsey	55	PA	48
Rachel	14	PA	175	Thomas	52	DE	296	Bradly	2	DE	53
Rachel A	6	DE	398	Thomas C	19	DE	296	Caroline	2	DE	53
Rachel C	30	PA	357	Washington	3	DE	296	Catherine	9	DE	62
Rebecca	9	DE	295	William	27	DE	314	Catherine	37	PA	62
Robert	22	DE	175	McCa, Robert	35	IE	307	Charles	3/12	DE	62
Samuel	20	IE	327	McCabe, Ann	2	DE	344	Charles	34	SC	62
Samuel A	8	DE	398	Ann	15	PA	163	David	43	DE	108
Samuel N	5	MD	320	Ann	46	IE	81	Eliza	46	DE	154
Sarah	42	PA	366	Bridget A	10/12	IE	161	Elizabeth	26	MD	53
Sarah E	2	DE	329	Catharine	14	DE	342	Elizabeth	26	PA	53
Sarah E	4	MD	320	Catharine	16	IE	330	Elizabeth	31	NJ	107
Sarah P	2	DE	366	Charles	5	PA	163	Emma	7	DE	122
Stacia	42	DE	295	Charles	9	PA	330	Emma	8	PA	62
William	4	DE	327	Edward	17	PA	163	Franklin	3	DE	53
William	18	DE	346	Elizabeth	17	DE	349	George	5	DE	107
William	18	PA	357	Francis	21	DE	349	George	23	PA	53
William	30	MD	320	Helen	13	DE	349	John	6	DE	108
William	42	PA	357	James	1	DE	81	John	29	PA	53
William	56	MD	398	James	13	PA	163	John	49	DE	154
William T	20	MD	332	James	26	DE	81	Lewis	36	PA	107
Mayberry, Rachel	19	DE	380	Jane	27	PA	349	Margaret	33	PA	62
Maybin, Elanier W	55	PA	396	John	4	DE	344	Margaretta	2	DE	62
John E	27	PA	396	John	14	DE	81	Mary	36	PA	108
Joseph A	23	PA	396	John	24	DE	349	Mary A	23	DE	116
William A	25	PA	396	John A	3	DE	330	Mary E	5	DE	122
Maye, Dinah	50	DE	192	Larkey	20	IE	161	Oscar	1	DE	116
George	6	DE	192	Larkey	25	IE	161	Ralph	28	PA	116
Jack	13	DE	192	Margaret	6	DE	344	Richard	2	DE	122
Mayfield, Morris	79	DE	293	Mary	36	IE	330	Robert	4/12	DE	53
Mayhew, Jane	26	DE	399	Mary	50	IE	345	Samuel J	17	DE	154
John W	1/12	DE	399	Mary A	3	PA	161	Sarah	24	DE	122
Joseph	26	DE	399	Mary J	23	DE	81	Sidney	60	PA	62
Rachel A	7	DE	399	Michel	30	IE	161	Theodore	2	DE	107
Stephen	3	DE	399	Patrick	17	IE	330	William	4	DE	53
Maynard, John	20	IE	347	Peter	36	IE	342	William	30	DE	122
Mayson, Jonathan	28	DE	358	Robert	49	IE	349	McCalley, John	65	DE	113
Mary	30	DE	358	Rosanna	8	DE	342	McCallister, Chris	22	PA	307
Susannah	61	PA	358	Sarah A	3	DE	81	Collin	40	PA	312
Mazzani, Theresa C	14	PA	332	Susan	29	IE	342	David	61	PA	314
McAllen, John	2	IE	345	Susan	40	IE	163	Jane	17	PA	314
Mary	28	IE	345	Wm	37	IE	330	John	4	DE	381
Mary Ann	3	DE	345	McCade, Hugh	15	IE	330	John	13	DE	314
Patrick	30	IE	345	McCafferty, Abigail	16	DE	331	John	18	DE	290
McAlter, Charles	24	IE	368	Alexander	35	IE	344	Lewis	12	DE	324
McAnessy, James	23	IE	353	Ann	6	IE	312	Lewis H	2	DE	381
McAnna, David	14	PA	379	Ann	45	PA	331	Louisa	22	PA	290
McArvy, Peter	23	IE	264	Chas	61	IE	331	Margaret	55	NJ	314
McAvoy, Margaret	65	PA	286	Edward	23	IE	291	Maria	30	DE	381
Mary A	22	DE	287	Elizabeth	15	DE	331	Mary	40	PA	312
Peter	23	IE	263	George	8/12	DE	312	Peter	30	DE	381
McBeth, William H O	42	DE	393	Grace	22	IE	345	Phillip	1	DE	312
McBride, Ann	35	IE	85	Grace	25	IE	159	Rebecca	21	DE	312
Anne	8	DE	85	James	2	DE	344	Sarah J	32	PA	312
Barnard	40	IE	85	James	10	IE	312	Thomas R	34	OH	312
Barney	24	IE	383	James	30	IE	344	William H	3	DE	312
Catherine	20	DE	27	James	34	IE	312	Wm	50	PA	324
Daniel	21	DE	296	James	40	IE	345	McCally, Cath	45	IE	328
Francis	20	IE	291	Jane	5	DE	344	Catherine	10	PA	328
Hannah	20	NJ	297	John	1	DE	344	Dennis	55	IE	328
Henry	38	IE	335	John	2	IE	312	Margaret	14	DE	328
James	23	IE	334	John	5	DE	344	Mary	21	MA	328
Jane A	46	DE	296	Lydia	14	DE	331	Patrick	18	PA	328
John	11	DE	296	Margaret	24	PA	314	McCalment, Arthur	56	DE	279
John	22	IE	350	Martha	15	DE	331	McCambridge, Arch	24	IE	345
Joseph	6	DE	296	Mary	16	DE	27	McCan, John	33	IE	334
Julia	8	DE	296	Mary	29	IE	312	McCanales, Ann	28	IE	79
Lewis	11/12	DE	297	Sarah	4	IE	312	David	30	IE	79
Margaret	30	IE	13	Sarah	25	IE	344	McCanelas	16	IE	212
Mary	13	DE	296	Susan	18	DE	331	McCanandy, Patrick	15	IE	349
Mary	21	IE	332	Susan	26	IE	344	McCann, Bernard	65	IE	51
Mary	5	DE	85	Thomas	3	DE	344	Bridget	1	IE	361
Patric	11/12	DE	13	McCalester, Rachel	35	DE	6	Catherine	21	DE	284
Patric	30	IE	13	McCaley, Alexander	43	IE	337	Clara	2	DE	71
William	5	DE	85	Janet	32	IE	337	Elizabeth	36	NE	71

Name	Age	Code	Pg
McCann, Ellen	64	IE	51
Francis	1	DE	71
Hannah E	6	DE	327
James	12	DE	327
Jerome	3	DE	71
John	10	DE	327
John	40	GB	71
John	69	IE	284
Margaret	16	DE	327
Mary	6	IE	361
Mary	18	AA	327
Mary	30	IE	361
Mary	51	IE	327
Mary	65	IE	284
Patrick	30	IE	361
William	4	DE	327
Wm M	40	IE	327
McCanna, Charles	38	IE	311
James	17	IE	311
John	8	IE	311
Sally	42	IE	311
McCannan, Alena	5	DE	141
Joel	30	DE	141
Lydia	25	DE	141
McCannen, Anna Jane	2	PA	372
Lawrence	33	DE	372
Margaret J	25	PA	372
McCannon, Isabella	57	DE	109
James	1	DE	396
John	62	PA	352
Joseph	11	PA	352
Mary	9	PA	352
Mary	28	DE	352
Thomas	71	DE	109
Trudy	69	PA	353
McCarley, Alexander	43	IE	336
Jannett	32	IE	336
Nancy	7	PA	336
Susan	9	PA	336
McCarly, Catherine	35	IE	283
McCarron, Ann	13	IE	157
Catharine	40	IE	343
Charles	14	IE	157
John	4	DE	158
Patric	10	DE	157
Phillip	7	DE	157
Rosa	38	IE	157
William	2	DE	158
William	40	IE	157
McCarter, Chas	30	IE	284
Robert	40	IE	375
McCartin, John	20	NY	164
McCartner, George	22	GB	381
McCartney, Ann	16	IE	330
Benjamin	10	PA	332
Bridget	40	IE	332
Catherine	32	IE	340
David	18	IE	330
David	19	DE	364
Elizabeth	52	PA	126
James	8	DE	340
James	12	IE	332
James	23	IE	330
James	40	IE	332
John	10	DE	340
John	46	IE	328
Joseph	14	DE	330
Mary	1	DE	340
Mary	16	IE	332
Mary	21	IE	328
Mary	22	IE	314
Nicholas	4	DE	340
Nicholas	16	IE	330
Nicholas	17	IE	328
Nicholas	35	IE	340
Robert	6	DE	340
Robert	22	GE	145
Robt	20	IE	330
Robt	50	IE	330
Sarah Jane	45	IE	330
Thomas	18	IE	332
Timothy	28	IE	163
McCartney, William	13	PA	340
William	32	IE	330
McCarton, John	45	DE	319
McCarty, David	40	IE	349
Elizabeth	27	IE	274
Elizabeth	55	?	349
Ellen	5	DE	335
Hannah	37	ST	285
James	1	DE	274
John	3	PA	274
John	35	IE	285
John	35	IE	335
Margaret	29	IE	335
Margaret E	4	DE	335
Martha	1	DE	274
Mary A	7	DE	335
Nicholas	18	IE	36
Patt	35	IE	274
Robert	21	IE	36
Sarah Jane	2	DE	335
McCasson, Elizabeth	45	NJ	285
Joseph	12	NJ	285
McCauley, Minty	26	DE	253
McCaulley, Catherine	10	DE	121
Elizabeth W	22	DE	81
Hugh	11	PA	164
John	51	MD	121
John A	4	DE	121
Samuel	49	DE	121
Samuel W	24	DE	81
Samuel W	13	DE	121
Sarah L	48	PA	81
Sarah P	16	DE	121
Tamer	46	DE	121
William	53	MD	81
William S	17	DE	317
McCaully, Anna	17	DE	317
Mary	25	IE	32
McChaffant, Ellen	25	PA	340
Jacob	28	PA	340
Vicorew E	4	DE	340
William	2	DE	340
McChathan, Collin	13	DE	143
Martha M	40	MD	143
Samuel J	37	PA	143
McChugh, Jno	7	DE	284
Margaret	6	DE	284
Martin	30	IE	284
Mary	27	IE	284
Mary E	8/12	DE	284
McCibbin, Mary J	11	DE	384
McCilben, Andrew	5	DE	351
George	3	DE	351
James	29	IE	351
Susan	27	CN	351
McCilvin, Dennis	30	IE	147
Dennis	50	IE	147
James	9	IE	355
Jerry	27	IE	147
John	24	IE	147
Mary	2	DE	147
Mary	24	IE	147
Mary	49	IE	147
Patric	20	IE	147
Roger	29	IE	147
McClafferty, Bernard	21	IE	347
John	22	IE	383
McClain, Edward	30	IE	368
Isabella	3	DE	368
Mary	53	DE	395
Mary J	7	DE	381
Margaret	6	DE	368
Margaret	26	IE	368
Minty	55	DE	355
Sarah	25	DE	381
Sarah E	4	DE	381
William	30	DE	381
McClancy, Biddy	19	IE	351
McClane, Abagail	29	DE	330
Alexander	22	IE	347
Allen	4	DE	37
Catherine	30	IE	37
McClane, Catherine	30	IE	37
Hugh	40	IE	188
Jane	43	IE	188
Jason	2	DE	37
John	14	DE	37
Joseph	30	DE	330
Josephine	5	DE	330
Mary E	5/12	DE	330
Rebecca	90	PA	129
Rebecca A	9	DE	330
Sabina	50	DE	306
Samuel	6	DE	37
Samuel	38	IE	37
McClary, Caroline	23	DE	20
Emily	17	DE	15
Margaret	25	DE	57
Samuel	25	DE	20
Samuel	62	DE	15
Sarah	21	DE	15
Susan	23	DE	15
Susan	61	DE	15
Thomas	30	DE	57
William	1	DE	20
McClawer, Robt	70	IE	328
William	30	IE	328
McClay, Ann	13	DE	14
Caroline	9	DE	14
Eliza	45	DE	35
Elizabeth	20	DE	14
Elizabeth	25	DE	56
Henry	22	DE	14
Joseph	17	DE	13
Joseph	31	MD	13
Marshal	2	DE	13
Mr	52	DE	35
Phebe	50	MD	13
Sarah	14	DE	35
Sylvester	11	DE	14
McClean, Anna B	20	DE	88
Elizabeth B	7	DE	88
Henry C	12	DE	88
John	50	IE	88
John P	18	DE	88
Samuel B	15	DE	88
McClear, John	28	IE	356
Mary	50	IE	345
McCleary, Eliza A	45	DE	28
John	56	DE	28
John B	2	DE	28
Margaret	34	DE	28
Rebecca	60	DE	28
McCleaver, Anna	2	DE	364
George	9	DE	364
Jane	30	DE	364
Sarah E	6	DE	364
Thomas	4	DE	364
William	38	DE	364
McClees, Anna	21	DE	159
Charles	19	DE	159
Edward	3	DE	100
Edward	28	DE	159
Elizabeth	30	DE	159
Everest	60	PA	159
George	24	DE	159
Helen	2	DE	100
Jane	21	DE	102
Mary	3/12	DE	100
Sarah A	26	DE	100
William K	27	DE	100
McCleland, Bridget	21	IE	334
Catharine	17	IE	334
Catharine	50	IE	334
Margaret	19	IE	334
Mary	15	IE	334
Mary	52	IE	334
McClellan, James	45	PA	354
Margaret A	12	DE	354
Jacob	16	DE	354
Rebecca	54	DE	354
McClelland, Adaline	13	DE	398
Anna	8	DE	398
Catharine	46	PA	398

Name	Age	St	No.
McClelland, Jackson	23	DE	398
Jane	55	DE	398
John	16	DE	398
John	37	DE	398
Lavinia	25	DE	398
Margaret	23	DE	398
Mary J	21	DE	398
Rachel	13	PA	398
Samuel	4/12	DE	398
Sarah	16	PA	398
William	48	DE	398
William Jr	23	DE	398
McClen, Edward	32	IE	373
Isabella	2	DE	373
Margaret	5	IE	373
Margaret	24	IE	373
McClenagan, John B	2	PA	13
Letitia	3	PA	13
Mary	26	PA	13
Robert	28	PA	13
McClenan, William H	16	PA	396
McClenegan, Dennis M	52	IE	64
Ellen	53	IE	64
McCleninan, Catherine	23	DE	265
Elizabeth L	12	DE	265
Henry	25	DE	265
James	61	DE	265
Jemima	16	DE	265
John	14	DE	265
Mary	7	DE	265
Mary	53	DE	265
McCleuse, Mary	20	IE	98
McClintock, Alexander	19	DE	120
Danial	24	NY	120
Elizabeth	15	DE	120
Frances	30	PA	279
George	7	DE	291
Happy	81	DE	48
James	9	DE	291
Jane	19	IE	262
Jane	44	IE	120
John	1	DE	279
John	38	IE	291
Lavinia	24	IE	120
Lewis C	3	DE	279
Margaret	5	DE	291
Martha	6	PA	279
Martha	39	IE	291
Robert	4	DE	291
Sarah K	8	PA	279
William	13	DE	121
William	36	DE	279
William A	10/12	DE	291
McCloud, Madora	1	DE	36
Sarah	27	DE	36
McCluen, Ann	26	PA	85
Elizabeth	11/12	DE	85
Emily	4	PA	85
John	28	PA	85
McClung, Eliza N	45	DE	27
John	3	DE	57
John	56	DE	27
John B	2	DE	27
Margaret	34	DE	27
Mary	1	DE	57
Mary	56	PA	57
Rebecca	13	PA	57
Rebecca	60	DE	27
William	9	PA	57
William	51	DE	57
McClure, David	50	IE	284
Eliza	19	PA	329
James	43	PA	329
John	7	PA	329
Margaret	12	PA	329
Mary A	20/12	PA	329
Prudy	44	IE	329
Robt	14	PA	329
Samuel	5	DE	329
Sarah J	28	PA	329
William	16	PA	329
McCluskey, Barney	36	IE	12
McCluskey, Fanny	36	DE	12
Jane	5/12	DE	38
James	5	DE	38
James	7	DE	12
James	28	IE	44
Joanna	26	IE	147
John	3	DE	12
John	40	IE	38
Margaret	3	DE	38
Maria	4/12	DE	147
Mary	25	DE	44
Michel	27	IE	147
Patric	14	DE	38
Rose	39	IE	38
Sarah	4/12	DE	147
Sarah	5/12	DE	38
Thomas	4	DE	12
William	12	DE	38
McClusky, Ann	30	IE	61
Catherine	28	NJ	125
Catherine	47	IE	63
David	10	DE	63
Frank	17	PA	163
James	21	PA	19
James	30	IE	61
John	1	DE	61
John	6	DE	362
Joseph	8	PA	125
Joseph	11	IE	63
Margaret	4	DE	44
Maria	4/12	DE	148
Mary	1	DE	44
Mary	3	DE	61
Mary	9/12	DE	125
Michel	9/12	DE	125
Patric	30	MD	125
Peter	13	IE	63
Sarah	3	DE	125
McColister, Ann E	9	DE	299
John M	5	DE	299
Norris	14	DE	299
Sevilah	10/12	DE	299
Susannah	35	DE	299
Thomas	3	DE	299
William	12	DE	299
William	38	DE	299
McColleran, Anna	23	IE	57
McCollogue, Nancy	26	IE	71
McCollough, Andrew	45	DE	325
Elizabeth	4	DE	124
Eunice	43	DE	325
George	5	DE	124
Joseph	12	DE	325
Laura	11/12	DE	45
Lewis	30	PA	124
Olle	3	DE	124
Rebecca	50	MD	124
Robert	8	DE	124
Sarah	30	IE	39
McCollum, John	55	IE	326
McConagan, Mary	20	IE	137
McConaway, Patrick	27	DE	183
McCone, Margaret	34	IE	383
McConer, John	12	DE	329
Philena	40	DE	329
Susan J	10	DE	329
Wm P	8	DE	329
McConikle, Mary	27	PA	374
McConlogue, Bridget	66	IE	104
Danial	70	IE	104
McConnaway, Patrick	15	IE	350
McConnel, Catherine	10	IE	90
James	10	DE	73
John	12	DE	73
Mary	14	DE	54
Rachel	40	DE	73
McConnell, Bernard	21	IE	347
David	8	DE	73
Eliza M	17	DE	116
Elizabeth	20	DE	150
Elmira	1	DE	77
Emma A	15	DE	116
Hannah	43	DE	150
McConnell, Harry	5	PA	77
Isaac	45	DE	116
James	65	IE	319
Margaret	29	PA	77
Rachel	15	DE	150
Rebecca M	41	DE	116
William	28	IE	17
William	34	PA	77
Wuester	7	PA	77
McConnery, Alia	35	IE	362
Charles	48	IE	362
James	7	IE	362
Patrick	15	IE	362
Sarah	2	DE	362
McConnors, James	1	DE	397
McConoha, Ann	20/12	DE	340
Ann	40	IE	340
Catharine	15	IE	340
John	13	IE	340
John	45	IE	340
Mary	18	IE	340
Rosa	11	IE	340
McConologue, Thos	22	IE	283
McConoughey, Ann	52	PA	334
David	26	PA	334
Ephraim B	16	PA	334
Jonathan B	21	PA	334
Rebecca	22	PA	334
Sarah E	11	DE	334
Susan	30	PA	334
Thomas B	14	DE	334
William	18	PA	334
McConoughy, Alex	30	DE	271
Rebecca	20	MD	271
McCoogman, John	59	DE	293
McCool, Elizabeth	24	DE	221
James	13	DE	221
John	6	DE	221
Samuel	15	DE	221
William	30	DE	221
McCombs, Henry	24	DE	19
Jane	14	DE	19
James	21	DE	19
Martha	25	PA	19
Martha	50	IE	19
William	17	DE	19
McCorckle, Letitia	12	DE	79
Thomas	45	DE	79
McCord, Elizabeth	25	MD	222
John	6	MD	222
Jonas	13	MD	222
Samuel	15	MD	222
William	30	MD	222
McCorkin, Andrew	23	IE	379
McCorkle, Anna	8	PA	78
Charles P	13	DE	1
David C	6	DE	78
George	18	DE	1
George	50	DE	1
Henry L	10	DE	1
John J	5	DE	1
Lindsey J	39	DE	1
Maria J	8	DE	1
Mary	46	DE	1
Mary	74	DE	1
Rebecca	34	DE	78
Sabila A S	3	DE	1
Thomas	3	DE	78
Thomas	16	DE	1
McCormack, Catherine	10	IE	89
Jane	20	IE	51
McCormic, Ann	22	DE	317
Catherine	6	DE	317
Jane	1/12	DE	317
John A	21	PA	43
Mary	4	DE	317
William	26	IE	317
McCormick, Anne	49	DE	349
Barney	30	IE	273
Eliza	9	DE	349
Eliza	11	PA	358
Hannah J	38	DE	347

Name	Age	St	Pg	Name	Age	St	Pg	Name	Age	St	Pg
McCormick, James	25	NJ	314	McCracken, John M	30	DE	316	McCullough, Joseph W	13	DE	352
John	36	DE	347	Joseph E	10	DE	316	Joshua H	22	DE	350
John	41	IE	358	Thomas	19	DE	316	Letitia	22	MD	107
John F	1	DE	347	McCrackin, Mary E	17	DE	379	Mary	20	DE	45
Levi	23	DE	350	McCrae, Eliza	44	PA	334	Mary	20	NJ	107
Lewis	76	DE	349	John S	42	PA	334	Mary	24	DE	72
Lewis H	10	DE	347	Martin	14	PA	334	Mary	48	DE	284
Mary	20	IE	196	Sarah	11	PA	334	Peter	26	IE	45
Mary M	5	DE	347	Thomas	16	PA	334	Rebecca A	6	DE	72
Michael	22	IE	274	William T	10	PA	334	Robert	53	DE	350
Nathan	23	DE	349	McCrakky, Ann	25	IE	375	Unice W	11/12	DE	72
Nathaniel G	8	DE	347	Colwell	30	IE	375	William	37	DE	72
Patrick E	25	PA	371	Henry	9/12	DE	375	McCune, Timothy	27	IE	250
Rachel E	12	DE	349	James	2	PA	375	McCurdy, Joseph	28	IE	305
McCovey, Jehu	25	PA	16	McCrary, Hannah	52	IE	375	Saml	23	IE	274
McCouch, Mary	28	IE	285	John	15	IE	375	McDade, George	13	DE	199
McCowan, John	28	IE	326	William	55	IE	375	Rachel	13	DE	183
Mary	32	IE	326	McCray, Ellen	16	DE	311	Rachel	13	PA	299
Mary E	3	DE	326	Henry	24	DE	311	McDaniel, Albert	6	DE	49
Sarah J	18/12	DE	326	Julia	18	DE	311	Alfred	31	DE	50
McCowen, Sarah	33	MD	143	Lena	13	DE	311	Ann	29	MD	49
McCoy, Alexander	33	IE	8	Mary E	11	DE	322	Ann	40	DE	185
Ann	10	DE	8	Rebecca	40	DE	311	Ann E	7	DE	100
Bridget	21	IE	51	Thomas	23	DE	311	Delaplane	32	DE	100
Catherine A	18	DE	124	Wm	13	DE	322	Eliza	12	DE	338
David	9	DE	361	McCrome, John Jr	29	DE	227	Eliza	25	DE	372
Douglas	13	DE	361	Mary E	23	DE	227	Elizabeth	9	DE	371
Eliza	3	DE	382	Sarah	38	DE	300	Elizabeth	18	DE	371
Eliza	25	DE	124	McCrone, Abigal D	29	NJ	304	Elizabeth	25	DE	372
Elizabeth	35	DE	361	Benjamin	4/12	DE	304	Emma	2/12	DE	49
Emily	3	DE	8	Elizabeth	8/12	DE	295	Emma	1	DE	372
George	3	DE	124	Elizabeth	55	DE	302	Emma	5	DE	371
George	14	DE	311	George	40	DE	304	Emma	24	PA	355
George	33	DE	21	George F	6	DE	304	Emma	55	DE	355
Hannah A	25	DE	231	Henry C	2	DE	304	George	40	MD	338
James	9	DE	8	James S	31	DE	302	George A	1	DE	338
James	17	VA	322	Jesse	42	DE	299	Georgianna L	16	PA	355
James	32	PA	361	John	61	IE	302	Hilbank	18	DE	371
James	44	DE	361	John H	4	DE	304	Isabella	27	PA	50
James	70	IE	122	Margaret	18	DE	302	James	34	PA	370
Jane A	38	DE	382	Rebecca	32	DE	295	Jeremiah	29	DE	49
John	4	DE	124	William B	8	DE	304	John	4	DE	372
John	11	DE	361	William B	40	IE	295	John	18	MD	334
John	36	DE	231	McCrown, Ellen	14	IE	336	John	58	DE	356
John	52	DE	295	James	10	DE	336	John A	12	DE	371
John	58	DE	322	Mary	40	IE	336	John M	18	DE	333
John W	2	DE	231	McCue, Allis	7	DE	321	John W	6	DE	146
Lewis	9/12	DE	124	Ann	27	IE	267	Joseph	40	DE	185
Louisa	12	DE	295	Bernard	10	DE	321	Joseph B	3	DE	100
Louisa	45	VA	322	Bridget	40	IE	321	Lydia A	4	DE	370
Louisa E	23	VA	322	Ellen	25	IE	283	Martha	13	DE	371
Margaret	1	DE	382	John	9	DE	283	Mary	2	DE	371
Margaret	13	DE	63	John	28	IE	267	Mary	14	DE	334
Margaret	35	DE	8	Margaret	25	IE	287	Mary	15	DE	338
Margaret	44	DE	301	Martin	46	IE	283	Mary	28	PA	355
Margaret	50	DE	295	Mary	45	IE	283	Mary	30	DE	370
Martha M	12	PA	8	Patrick	30	IE	267	Mary	35	MD	338
Mary	7	DE	8	Thomas	4	DE	321	Mary	47	PA	371
Mary	10	PA	104	McCuen, Ellen	1	DE	395	Mary E	6	DE	100
Mary	25	VA	322	Ellen	58	IE	395	Melvina	54	PA	308
Mary	27	DE	183	James	64	DE	395	Rebecca	5	DE	338
Mary J	10	DE	382	Mary	38	IE	395	Robert	13	MD	381
Nathaniel	15	DE	361	Robert	36	IE	395	Sally	35	DE	137
Robert	56	DE	382	Sophia	26	MD	395	Samuel	2	DE	50
Samuel	12	DE	382	Thomas	30	IE	381	Samuel D	1	DE	100
Samuel	14	DE	215	William	3	DE	395	Sarah	12	DE	137
Sarah	14	VA	322	McCullough, Andrew	44	DE	352	Sarah A	31	DE	100
Sarah	20	PA	361	Ann	25	DE	354	Springer	52	DE	371
Sarah	43	DE	124	David A	8	PA	107	Susan	18	IE	33
Sarah A	7	DE	382	Eliza	27	IE	49	Thomas	22	PA	371
Thomas	1	DE	361	Eliza A	51	DE	355	William	18	MD	338
Thomas	19	VA	322	Elizabeth	45	DE	351	William	23	MD	146
Thomas	27	PA	124	Elizabeth	49	DE	355	Wilson	2	DE	370
William	5	DE	8	Eunice P	37	DE	352	McDavit, Ann	14	IE	343
William	15	DE	295	Hannah	50	PA	350	Charles	17	IE	343
McCracken, Amanda	17	DE	316	James	20	DE	330	Ellen	16	IE	343
Amelia C	16	DE	386	Jane	6	DE	72	Peter	22	IE	343
Anna	7	DE	316	Jane	42	PA	107	McDaw, Rachel	13	DE	182
Catharine	15	DE	316	John	14	DE	330	McDermot, Ann	26	IE	341
Catharine	35	DE	316	John	41	DE	355	Barney	14	IE	341
Elizabeth	12	DE	316	John Jr	26	DE	354	Bridget	18	IE	341
John	4	DE	316	John 3rd	2	DE	354	Bridget	50	IE	341

Name	Age	BP	Pg
McDermot, Catharine	16	IE	341
Jane	22	IE	341
Mary	20	IE	341
Patrick	27	IE	351
Rose	26	IE	351
McDewitt, Susan	18	IE	165
McDivet, Letitia	16	IE	136
Robert	20	IE	136
McDocherty, Elizabeth	22	IE	380
Hugh	2	DE	380
Margaret J	1/12	DE	380
Robert L M	22	IE	380
McDonal, Ellen	15	IE	328
McDonald, Ann	24	IE	283
Catherine	15	DE	70
Catherine	22	IE	10
Elizabeth	25	IE	101
Ellen	20	IE	34
Grace	25	IE	66
Jane	24	DE	162
John	2	PA	283
John	24	DE	70
Joseph	28	DE	70
Leah	26	DE	70
Margaret	22	DE	70
Maria	20	DE	70
Mary	24	IE	124
Mary	27	IE	161
Mary	50	IE	162
Mary A	24	IE	10
Nancy	30	IE	10
Patrick	22	IE	283
Sally	23	IE	70
Thos M	--	DE	290
McDonnell, Aaron	18	PA	295
Anna	5	DE	53
Clara	2	DE	53
Emma	14	DE	53
Martha	8	DE	53
R B	45	GB	53
Rebecca	36	PA	53
McDonough, Bridget	30	IE	364
McDoudy, Billy	19	IE	274
McDowel, Barbara	38	DE	361
George W	8	DE	395
Hannah	45	DE	395
James	49	PA	361
Louisa	10	DE	394
Margaret J	15	DE	361
Margaret S	14	DE	394
Martha	18	DE	394
Martha E	2	DE	361
Mary	18	DE	361
Mary E	12	DE	394
Rachel A	11	DE	361
Sarah	5	DE	394
Susan	24	DE	394
William	45	DE	394
McDowell, Andrew	25	DE	316
Ellen	19	IE	69
Isabella	20	DE	252
James H	7/12	DE	316
Jane	76	DE	108
Margaret G	24	DE	69
Mary	64	DE	69
Mary C	34	DE	69
Mary E	23	MD	316
Olivia	12	DE	296
Olivia	16	DE	69
Samuel	18	PA	27
Susanah	36	PA	115
Thomas	72	DE	69
McDowl, Ann J	12	DE	319
Catherine	29	DE	321
Edward	6	DE	321
Elizabeth	33	DE	319
Hester G	17	DE	321
James	8	DE	319
James	47	DE	319
Jane	1	DE	321
John	21	DE	319
John A	21	DE	321
McDowl, Morress	14	DE	321
Phillip	13	DE	321
Phillip	45	DE	321
Phillip E	5	DE	319
William	1	DE	319
William	3	DE	321
Wilson	8	DE	321
McDuff, Edward	26	IE	346
McEleney, James	24	IE	302
McEllis, Anna	21	DE	158
Charles	19	DE	158
Edward	28	DE	158
Elizabeth	30	DE	158
Everitt	60	DE	158
George	24	DE	158
McElmer, Samuel	13	DE	220
McElver, Biddy	20	IE	365
McElvie, William	23	IE	319
McElwee, Catherine	6	NJ	383
Edward	40	DE	383
James	3	DE	383
Jane	8	NJ	383
John	9	NJ	383
Mary	1	DE	383
Mary	30	IE	383
Rosanna	5	DE	383
William	4	DE	383
McElwell, Hannah	21	IE	362
John	19	IE	13
Mary	18	IE	362
Neal	23	IE	362
Roger	30	IE	362
Roseane	27	IE	362
Samuel	13	IE	219
Sarah	5/12	DE	362
Sarah	20	IE	362
William	70	IE	362
William Jr	25	IE	362
McEntire, George	12	IE	328
Margaret	12	IE	328
Matilda	10	IE	328
Matilda	45	IE	328
Rachel	16	IE	328
Samuel	18/12	DE	328
Susan	20	IE	328
Thomas	18	IE	328
William	7	IE	328
Wm	40	IE	328
McEntyre, Ann	35	IE	343
McEvey, Bernard	5	DE	344
Bernard	19	IE	344
Daniel	7/12	DE	344
Daniel	37	IE	344
John	2	DE	344
Mary Ann	13	DE	344
Sarah	32	IE	344
McFadden, Ann	45	IE	106
Edward	17	PA	331
Ellen	43	IE	330
James	7	PA	330
John	22	IE	330
Mary	10	PA	331
Mary	43	IE	44
Neel	50	IE	330
William	12	PA	330
McFarland, Ann	50	DE	171
Anna	28	DE	41
Edward	24	DE	380
Edward	28	DE	380
Elizabeth	12	PA	64
Ellen	22	IE	308
Harry	2	DE	41
Jane	25	DE	380
John H	36	DE	311
John M	20	IE	315
Joseph	20	PA	64
Manlis	17	DE	380
Mary	25	DE	40
Richard	22	MD	388
Robert	29	DE	41
Robert	67	IE	380
Samuel	16	PA	64
McFarland, Samuel	60	IE	64
Sarah	10/12	DE	380
Sarah	60	DE	380
Sophia	47	DE	64
Sophia	8	PA	64
William	28	DE	40
McFarlin, Andrew	30	ST	371
John T	5/12	DE	346
Luran	21	PA	346
Thomas	24	PA	346
McGady, Frances	54	IE	326
Hannah	24	IE	326
Hugh	56	DE	326
Mary	23	IE	326
William	15	DE	326
McGarity, Mary	20	IE	31
McGarry, Jane	52	IE	302
Matthew	17	DE	302
Rebecca	15	DE	302
McGarty, Catharine	22	CN	338
Ellen	6/12	IE	353
James	4	DE	353
Jane	51	IE	338
John	12	IE	353
Margaret	7	DE	353
Mary	9	DE	353
Mary	31	IE	353
Michael	40	IE	353
William	5	DE	353
McGarvy, Ann	27	IE	321
Catherine	2	DE	321
John	14	IE	249
Wm	32	IE	321
McGaw, Charles	6	DE	114
Elizabeth	11	DE	114
James H	8	DE	114
Jarred	38	DE	114
Lydia A	37	DE	114
Robt	67	IE	351
McGeckin, Ellen	23	IE	332
Richard	24	IE	332
McGee, ____	50	PA	335
Alexander	9	DE	335
Anna	9	DE	373
Catharine	7	DE	373
Catherine	40	IE	340
George	7	DE	335
James	5	DE	373
James	22	PA	335
James	45	IE	340
James	45	PA	373
Jane	18	DE	143
John	16	DE	373
John	24	IE	346
John	25	PA	335
Lorra	1	DE	373
M Neal	12	PA	335
Margaret	14	DE	373
Mary	14	DE	122
Mary	30	DE	167
Mary A	36	PA	373
Sarah	26	IE	340
Susan	16	PA	335
William	21	DE	117
McGehan, James	24	IE	85
McGennes, James	25	IE	7
McGill, Henry	12	IE	253
Susan	40	IE	253
William	26	ST	171
Wm	17	IE	253
McGilligan, Anna	6	DE	349
Hannah	41	DE	349
James	4	DE	349
James	43	DE	349
Jane H	8	DE	349
Mary E	11	DE	349
Wm B	9	DE	349
McGillis, ____	50	PA	335
McGinley, Hugh	28	IE	347
James	35	IE	2
John	4/12	DE	347
Margaret	28	IE	347

Name	Age	St	Pg	Name	Age	St	Pg	Name	Age	St	Pg
McGinley, Margt	2	DE	347	McGrager, Mary	28	IE	338	McIntire, Ann	59	DE	52
Mary A	3	DE	336	McGrau, James	60	IE	167	Edward	32	DE	52
McGinn, James	7	DE	373	McGregor, Martha	74	IE	351	Florence F	3	DE	69
Patrick	19	IE	337	McGraw, Luisa	25	DE	29	Henry	6	DE	52
McGinnis, James	25	IE	6	McGrugen, John	20	DE	135	Jane	28	PA	15
McGladen, Catherine	2	DE	325	McGuiles, Catherine	20	IE	321	John	25	DE	150
Dennis	30	IE	325	John	25	IE	321	Malcolm B	4	DE	69
Ellen	3/12	DE	325	McGuin, Michel	18	IE	35	Margaret	23	DE	307
Mary	22	IE	325	McGuire, Andrew	22	DE	380	Mary	4/12	DE	15
McGlamstra, Elizabeth	22	GB	11	Andrew	47	DE	380	Mary	18	IE	151
Susan	6/12	DE	11	Ann	32	IE	272	Mary	29	DE	52
William	22	GB	11	Charles	8	DE	272	Samuel	1	DE	150
McGlancey, Ann	50	IE	360	Frances	10	DE	250	William	25	DE	15
Sarah M	17	IE	360	Lavinia	17	DE	380	McIntosh, Charles	18	DE	52
McGlaughlin, Patrick	20	IE	300	Margaret	10	IE	272	Daniel	27	DE	52
McGlinche, Thomas	13	DE	111	Mary	24	IE	304	Emeline	56	PA	52
McGlochann, Ann	35	IE	20	Mary E	6/12	DE	272	George	2	DE	52
Robert	40	IE	20	Michael	6	DE	272	George	14	DE	52
McGlockby, Fanny	25	IE	66	Michael	38	IE	272	James	21	DE	52
Nancy	4	DE	66	Roseanna	14	IE	272	Margaret	23	DE	52
William	28	IE	66	Sarah Jane	3	DE	272	Thomas	61	DE	52
McGlochlan, George	16	DE	105	McGurgan, James	22	IE	386	McIntyre, Andrew	6	MD	340
Joseph	14	DE	105	McGurley, Bridgett	14	IE	325	Charles	26	DE	271
Joseph	47	PA	105	David	7	DE	325	Edward	18	DE	271
Mary	47	DE	105	David	45	IE	325	Florence	2	DE	340
Lydia	5	DE	105	Ellen	27	IE	325	Frances	13	DE	271
McGlocklan, Andrew	5/12	DE	76	John	11	IE	325	Harden	15	DE	271
John	36	IE	76	Hugh	25	IE	325	James	30	MD	340
Mary	34	DE	76	Margaret	45	IE	325	John	53	DE	271
Sally A	2	DE	76	Mary A	4	DE	325	Joseph	10	DE	271
McGlocklin, Ann	18	DE	1	Owen	17	IE	325	Martha	28	DE	69
Bridget	16	IE	19	McHannon, Catherin	5/12	DE	372	Mary	3	DE	271
Grace	23	IE	4	McHinsley, Edward	24	IE	335	Mary	23	DE	340
James	19	IE	45	James	24	IE	360	Matilda	30	DE	340
Mary	17	PA	157	Mary	60	IE	335	Matilda	45	DE	271
Mary	21	IE	129	Patrick	22	IE	335	Rebecca	9	DE	271
William	22	PA	157	Patrick	65	IE	335	Samuel	3/12	DE	340
William	40	PA	112	McHester, Cortland	66	DE	349	Samuel	30	MD	340
McGloran, Patrick	22	IE	300	Elizabeth	2	DE	349	Sophia	4	MD	340
McGlugen, Elizabeth	22	IE	394	McHoney, Catharine	20	IE	375	McKane, Mary J	14	IE	301
McGochlin, Mary	20	IE	32	McHuey, Barnard	25	IE	335	McKay, Benjamin	27	MD	221
Michel	25	IE	1	McHurd, Benjamin	44	MD	193	Benjamin	33	DE	224
Rosanna	20	IE	1	Jemima	5	DE	193	Elizabeth	23	DE	224
McGoin, Patrick	50	IE	365	Sarah	38	DE	193	Elizabeth	31	MD	221
McGolan, Mary	12	IE	112	McIlben, James	9	DE	356	Emma	3	DE	201
McGonigal, Robert	23	IE	375	McIlheny, Amelia	20	IE	6	George	8	DE	204
McGonigle, Bridget	28	IE	342	Ann J	9	DE	107	Henrietta	4	DE	209
Elna Jane	4	DE	375	Barry	45	IE	6	Henry	74	DE	209
James	4	DE	342	Daniel	7	DE	6	James	28	MD	127
James	25	PA	51	Daniel	11	DE	107	James	30	DE	203
Jane	34	NY	375	Frank	4	DE	108	John	60	DE	224
John	30	IE	342	Henry	11	DE	6	Josephine	1	DE	203
Mary A	6	PA	375	Hugh	6	DE	107	Joshua	25	DE	221
Mary Ann	2	DE	342	John	2	DE	6	Mary	6	DE	224
Sarah	22	MD	51	Joseph	2	DE	108	Mary	24	DE	209
William J	1	DE	375	Mary	12	DE	108	Mary	36	DE	120
McGorine, Catherine	22	IE	112	Nancy	28	IE	108	Mary	30	DE	203
McGorlich, John	29	IE	347	Patric	30	IE	108	Sarah	30	DE	203
McGorman, Sarah	30	IE	357	Thomas	7	DE	108	Sarah A	23	PA	127
McGovern, Ann	23	IE	105	William	4	DE	6	Sarah W	1	MD	221
Catherine	11	DE	17	McIlherin, Eliza	4	IE	103	McKee, Alexander	16	MD	164
Daniel	30	IE	350	Eliza	45	IE	103	Alexander	22	IE	198
David	51	IE	350	Jane	16	IE	103	Alfred	18	DE	299
Edward	21	DE	17	Margaret	19	IE	103	Althethia	40	DE	172
Eliza	20	IE	350	William	9	IE	103	Andrew	35	DE	57
George	6	DE	17	McIlvain, Benjamin	27	GB	253	Andrew	38	DE	370
Hugh	14	DE	17	McIlwane, Ann	45	DE	113	Andrew	70	DE	299
Hugh	52	IE	17	Archibald	35	DE	113	Ann	15	DE	299
James M	26	IE	357	McInaffy, Ann	25	IE	359	Catherine	2	DE	57
John	3	DE	17	Ann	26	IE	359	David	9	DE	172
John	25	IE	43	Bridget	7/12	IE	359	David	38	DE	172
Julia	22	DE	17	John	26	IE	359	David B	41	DE	204
Margaret	52	IE	320	McInairy, Catharine	3	PA	264	Elizabeth	28	DE	10
Mary	9	DE	17	Catherine	30	IE	264	Ellen	37	PA	277
Mary	23	IE	357	Eliza	4	NJ	264	Elwood	5	DE	370
Mary	28	IE	113	Geneva	2	NJ	264	Frances	51	DE	299
Mary Ann	1	DE	350	James	30	IE	264	Henry	11	NY	57
Patric	15	IE	17	John	6/12	NJ	264	James	9	NY	57
Patric	17	IE	151	John	34	IE	264	John	3	DE	172
Patric	21	IE	383	Mary	8	IE	265	John	14	DE	370
McGowey, John	14	IE	250	Mary	8	NJ	265	Julia	30	NY	57
McGrager, John	30	IE	338	McIntire, Adaline	3	DE	15	Julye H	2	DE	277
								Lydia A	5	DE	277

Name	Age	State	No.
McKee, Lydia M	47	PA	299
Margaret	35	PA	370
Margaret	36	IE	198
Mr	28	IE	163
Mary	29	PA	299
Mary E	7	DE	277
Rachel	75	DE	172
Richard	16	DE	204
Robert	15	DE	172
Sarah	12	DE	172
Sarah D	65	DE	274
Sarah F	17	DE	370
Sarah P	12	DE	277
Tabitha	38	DE	204
William T	42	DE	277
McKeecrake, John	20	PA	374
McKeever, Hannah	17	DE	62
Mary	19	IE	34
Mary A	14	DE	272
Susan	12	DE	272
Susan	48	?	272
Thomas T	20	DE	272
McKegney, Biddy	17	IE	44
Lawrance	26	IE	44
Mary	18	IE	44
Mary	60	IE	44
McKend, Susan	14	IE	289
McKenney, Daniel	5/12	DE	371
Frances	6	DE	371
James	8	VT	371
John	12	VT	371
Margaret	10	VT	371
Margaret	30	IE	371
Mary	14	VT	371
Rosanna	3	DE	371
Thomas	35	IE	371
McKenner, Catharine	12	IE	288
McKenny, Allice	8	IE	312
Anna	5	IE	310
Catharine M	7	IE	310
Edward	40	IE	312
Elizabeth	15	IE	312
Ellen	26	IE	310
James	2	IE	310
James	25	IE	338
John	7	IE	312
Margaret	30	IE	312
Mary	13	IE	312
Mary	23	DE	337
Michael	5	IE	312
Owen	11	IE	312
Patrick	31	IE	310
McKenrick, James	26	IE	331
Margaret	20	IE	331
McKeon, James	29	IE	274
McKille, Adaline	22	DE	368
James	50	DE	368
John	6	DE	368
Josephine	10	DE	368
Martha	46	DE	368
Mary E	8	DE	368
Mary J	2	DE	368
Samuel	14	DE	368
McKimmey, Ann J	25	DE	81
Edward	7	DE	81
William	1	DE	81
McKimmy, Elizabeth	55	IE	67
Robert	51	IE	67
McKinland, Roger	29	IE	334
McKinley, Dennis	21	IE	347
Robert	24	IE	346
William	21	IE	194
McKinney, Alexander	22	IE	343
Andrew	47	IE	103
Emma	7	DE	102
Harry M	22	IE	111
James	26	IE	343
Jane	13	DE	101
Julia	21	IE	13
McKinnon, Ann	55	DE	372
Emaline	25	MD	378
Hector	65	ST	172
McKinnon, Isaac	31	DE	378
Joseph	18	DE	372
Mary	22	DE	372
Rebecca A	1	DE	378
William Henry	3	DE	378
McKinny, Eliza	5	DE	102
John	44	IE	102
Margaret	18	DE	102
Mary	14	NY	150
Mary	15	DE	102
Mary	42	IE	102
Sarah	17	DE	102
McKinsey, John	28	MD	338
John E	5	MD	338
Mary	20	MD	338
Mary E	5	Md	338
Sarah E	8/12	DE	338
McKivlin, Patrick	22	IE	347
McKnight, Charles	7	IE	8
Hannah	36	NJ	70
James	4	IE	8
Mary A	10	IE	8
Samuel	2	GB	8
Samuel	50	ST	8
Sarah	50	IE	8
Wm	25	IE	338
McKnit, Chas	13	DE	291
Elizabeth	12	DE	291
Ellen	6	DE	291
Rebecca	9	DE	291
Robert	55	DE	291
Sarah	17	DE	315
Sarah	48	DE	291
Thomas	4	DE	291
William A	29	NY	390
McKnowen, Sarah B	28	NY	390
McLackey, James	22	IE	351
McLain, Patric	50	IE	364
McLane, Alen	15	IE	37
Alexander	10	PA	37
Andrew	23	DE	36
Anne	2/12	DE	214
Arabella	18	DE	36
Archibald	31	DE	214
Archy	70	DE	214
Eliza	17	DE	214
Eliza	52	DE	214
Elizabeth	38	IE	37
John	3	DE	37
John	21	DE	215
John	40	IE	37
Louis	12	DE	214
Mary	6	DE	37
Mary	19	DE	214
Mary	22	DE	214
Mary B	2	DE	214
Sarah	10	DE	214
Thomas	27	DE	214
William	22	DE	214
McLaughlin, Ann	10	DE	285
Barney	22	IE	363
Bridget	20	DE	314
Catherine	16	DE	285
Ellen	33	IE	342
George	8	PA	293
James	15	DE	285
James	35	IE	342
James	38	IE	285
Joel	36	PA	308
John	7	DE	285
John	65	DE	398
Lydia	21	IE	373
Margaret	13	DE	285
Margaret	30	IE	361
Mary	56	IE	342
Mary	68	PA	308
Peter	36	IE	361
Samuel	10	PA	285
Sarah	23	IE	344
Sarah	66	GB	398
William	21	IE	366
McLeare, ____	68	DE	382
McLeare, Barton	30	DE	382
Eliza A	21	DE	382
George	30	DE	380
Louis	26	DE	382
Margaret J	23	DE	382
Mary	33	DE	382
Susanna	19	DE	382
McLeod, Alexander	29	DE	38
Jane	54	DE	38
McLerry, James	24	IE	303
McLevane, Joseph	40	IE	375
Mary	38	IE	375
McLewer, Ann	2	DE	365
George	9	DE	365
Jane	36	DE	365
Sarah E	6	DE	365
Thomas	4	DE	365
William	38	DE	365
McLohey, James	22	IE	350
McLoughlin, Caleb J	2	DE	355
Constantine	32	PA	362
Franklin	6/12	DE	362
Hannah	34	PA	355
Henry	7	DE	355
Henry	45	IE	378
James	3	DE	378
Jane	16	IE	378
John	12	PA	355
John H	12	DE	356
Joshua	4	DE	355
Mary	26	PA	378
Mary	35	PA	362
Michael	34	PA	355
Robert	2	DE	362
Robert	12	IE	378
Sarah	50	IE	378
Thomas	1	DE	378
Walter	28	GB	378
William	9	DE	355
McMacan, Bridget	26	IE	301
John	34	IE	301
Mary J	2	DE	301
Susan	1	DE	301
McMahan, Edward	30	IE	346
McMaken, Barney	22	IE	302
Elizabeth	12	IE	302
Elizabeth	19	DE	300
John	4/12	DE	300
Mary	15	IE	302
Mary	55	IE	302
Michael	27	IE	300
Patrick	25	IE	302
McMakin, John	19	PA	42
McMallary, Mary	12	IE	19
McMane, Joseph	35	PA	284
Josephine	5	DE	284
McManis, Catharine	19	IE	299
McMann, Catherine	3	DE	183
Elizabeth	29	DE	183
Frelinghuyser	5	DE	183
Harry	2/12	DE	183
Henry	33	PA	183
McMannis, Barnard	38	IE	334
Bridget	44	IE	334
Catherine	9	DE	334
Edward	20	IE	334
Edward J	20	IE	10
Elizabeth	12	DE	334
James	15	DE	334
John	3	DE	334
Mary	17	IE	334
Michael	6	DE	334
Michel	21	IE	194
Patrick	49	IE	334
Sarah	38	IE	334
Thomas	20	IE	72
McManus, Catherine	19	DE	298
James	7	DE	17
Jane	40	CN	25
Joseph	9	DE	17
Lerrisse	4	DE	17
Mary	36	IE	17

Name	Age	State	No.
McManus, Michel	11	DE	17
Michel	53	IE	25
Philomena	12	MD	164
McMaster, Eliza	20	DE	197
Francis	17	DE	197
John	6	DE	197
John	58	DE	197
Margaret	40	DE	197
William A	10	DE	197
McMenemew, Patrick	22	IE	274
McMikle, Ann	46	DE	369
Mary A	17	DE	369
Rebecca	78	DE	6
Susanna	46	DE	380
McMillen, Ann	75	DE	264
McMinim, Catherine	30	IE	157
Mary	1	DE	157
William	32	IE	157
McMiniman, Elizabeth	70	IE	351
McMonagan, Grace	10	IE	80
Margaret	1	IE	80
Mary	36	IE	80
William	40	IE	80
McMorgan, Alice	40	IE	348
Charles	4	DE	348
Francis	15	IE	348
James	8	DE	348
John	3	DE	348
Patrick	6	DE	348
Patrick	50	IE	348
William	2	DE	348
McMuckin, George	25	IE	346
John	19	IE	346
McMullen, Ann	75	DE	263
Catherine	6	DE	39
Edwin	29	PA	350
George	10/12	DE	266
George	80	IE	334
Hannah	51	MD	266
Harriet	27	DE	295
Henry	17	DE	295
Isabella	10	IE	321
Jacob	14	PA	350
James	4	DE	266
James	23	DE	318
James	53	DE	266
John	7	DE	295
Lydia	6	PA	334
Mary	20	IE	60
Mary	34	DE	266
Mary	50	DE	295
Rachel	17	GB	181
Samuel	21	DE	292
Sarah	21	DE	295
Warner	5	DE	232
Wm	31	DE	266
McMullin, Ann Jane	9	DE	183
Eliza	12	DE	183
James	15	DE	183
Josephine	7	DE	183
Margaret	37	DE	183
William	4	DE	183
William	43	DE	183
McMunar, Mary	40	IE	166
McMurphey, Agnes	4/12	DE	152
Andrew	36	DE	152
Anna	2	DE	219
Emma	9	DE	152
Frances J	12	DE	152
Henry	6	DE	152
John G	43	FR	218
Mary	8	DE	152
Priscilla	32	DE	218
Richard E	5	DE	152
Sarah J	30	DE	152
William A	2	DE	152
McMurrey, George	17	IE	259
McNamee, Alice	66	DE	301
Caroline	11	DE	392
Charles	15	DE	329
Chas	3	DE	291
Chas	27	DE	291
McNamee, Eliza	9	DE	329
Eliza	37	NJ	329
Elizabeth	24	DE	335
Emmaline	2	DE	329
John	17	DE	329
Margaret	11	DE	329
Martha	28	DE	390
Martha	56	DE	335
Mary	7	DE	329
Rachel	23	DE	291
Rebecca J	5	DE	291
Rebecca J	13	DE	329
Susan	20	DE	335
William	5	DE	329
William	41	DE	329
McNasty, Ana	60	IE	86
McNatt, Clara	4/12	DE	89
Edith	55	DE	246
James	21	DE	246
John	24	DE	89
Margaret A	20	DE	246
Sarah	17	DE	89
McNeal, Anna	25	DE	68
Hannah A	20	PA	117
Harriet	27	DE	68
Henry	14	PA	372
Henry	40	PA	372
John	4	DE	315
Letitia	36	IE	315
Malina	2	DE	315
Margaret	30	DE	68
Margaret J	2	PA	372
Joseph	13	PA	372
Mary A	30	DE	68
Mary Ann	35	PA	372
Robert Anna	4	PA	372
Thomas A	2/12	DE	372
William	11	PA	372
McNear, Edward	22	IE	331
McNeil, Catherine	20	IE	267
Horatio	28	PA	354
James	6	PA	315
John	30	IE	267
Joseph W	5/12	PA	354
Rachel	23	PA	354
McNit, Isabella	23	?	270
McNite, John	62	DE	381
McNitt, Edward	8/12	DE	92
James	40	DE	92
Jane	24	DE	92
Thomas	38	DE	92
McNulty, Anna	1	DE	133
Catherine	30	GB	133
Danial	4	DE	133
Danial	32	IE	133
John	7	DE	133
Mary	6	DE	133
McNutt, Hannah	16	IE	399
Hannah	48	IE	399
Jane	12	IE	399
Martha	10	IE	357
Mary	18	IE	399
Samuel	26	IE	371
McPherson, Jane	--	DE	326
John	2	DE	326
John	33	IE	326
Mary A	6	IE	326
Rebecca	5	IE	326
McPike, Alice	9	DE	283
Ann	40	IE	283
Edward	11/12	DE	94
Henry	8	DE	94
Henry	16	DE	283
Henry	17	DE	283
John	13	DE	94
John	14	DE	283
Mary	3	DE	94
Mary	33	ST	94
Mary F	6	DE	283
Michel	33	IE	94
McQuade, Miss	27	DE	71
Owen	56	IE	8
McQuay, Mrs	50	DE	132
Hares R	63	ST	146
James	65	ST	146
Margaret	22	DE	132
McQuilland, Eliza	15	DE	42
McQuillen, James	13	IE	332
Mary	17	IE	332
Mary	20	IE	31
Sarah	45	IE	42
McQuin, Richard	33	DE	167
McRandal, Elizabeth	25	IE	227
McRay, James E	17	IE	67
McRerson, Ann H	46	DE	289
Edward	22	DE	289
Elizabeth	17	DE	289
McShane, Benjamin	50	PA	106
James	28	IE	346
McSordley, Francis	43	IE	290
James	39	IE	290
Joseph	43	IE	290
Maria	54	IE	290
Sarah	37	IE	290
William	45	IE	290
McTagert, Peter	26	IE	339
McTague, Hugh	35	IE	334
McVail, Alexander	43	DE	205
Martha	10	DE	205
Mary	10	DE	205
Mary	36	DE	205
McVay, Benj	34	MD	313
Emma	11	DE	313
Henrietta	4	DE	210
Henry	8	DE	184
Henry	27	DE	210
James	1	DE	313
John	10	DE	184
John	32	DE	184
Leonard	25	DE	211
Louisa	34	PA	313
Mary	24	DE	210
Mary F	2	DE	184
Mary L	8	DE	313
Rebecca	32	DE	184
Rebecca	36	MD	190
Rebecca S	4	DE	313
Samuel	27	DE	190
Sarah J	5	DE	184
McVey, Andrew	5	IE	332
Ann	1	IE	332
Bridget	3	IE	332
Daniel	15	IE	332
Ellen	9	IE	332
Frederick	54	DE	272
Hugh	13	IE	332
James	11	IE	332
John	17	IE	332
Margaret	20	DE	332
Martha	15	NJ	272
Martha	47	IE	332
Martin	47	IE	332
Mary	25	MD	399
Mary	40	NJ	272
Patrick	7	IE	332
Sarah	45	IE	332
Susan	12	DE	269
Susan	52	DE	269
McVince, Margaret	18	IE	132
McVinn, Bridget	20	IE	339
McVoy, Catherine	2	IE	47
James	10	IE	47
James	30	IE	47
Jane	8	IE	47
Jane	25	IE	47
Sarah	7	IE	47
McWhorter, A J	26	DE	198
Charles H	11	DE	198
Elizabeth	17	DE	273
Ella	3/12	DE	198
John T	7	DE	198
L N	3	DE	198
L N	40	DE	198
Margaret	33	DE	273

Name	Age	St	Pg
McWhorter, Mary	15	DE	273
Mary	35	DE	198
Mary	50	DE	198
Thomas	32	DE	198
Thomas	73	DE	198
McWhortle, Mary G	14	IE	347
McWilliam, Eliza	16	DE	124
McWray, Margaret	22	DE	131
Mrs	50	DE	131
Meachim, Madora	5	NY	296
Meally, Elizabeth	2	DE	346
John	40	IE	346
Margt	32	IE	346
Maria	4	DE	346
Thomas	8/12	DE	346
William	35	DE	346
Means, Mary	25	DE	54
Meany, Sarah	23	IE	282
Mearthy, Cornelius	28	IE	360
Patrick	30	IE	360
Mecomb, Benjamin	4	DE	337
Hannah	1	DE	337
James	3	DE	337
James	30	DE	337
Rachel	32	DE	337
Mecum, Eliza	26	DC	25
Francis	1	DE	25
Galand	43	MA	25
John	14	NY	25
Rebecca	12	NY	25
Samuel	5	DE	25
William	7	DC	25
Mecurdy, Alexander	18	IE	306
Maria	19	IE	306
Ruth	75	PA	25
Medcraft, Jane	51	DE	159
Mahala	13	DE	295
Medell, Isabella	21	DE	135
Medford, Allen	3	DE	155
Ben	56	DE	55
Benjamin	34	DE	230
Benjamin	69	DE	155
Clarissa	19	DE	25
Comfort	50	DE	155
Hester	57	DE	25
Isabella	17	DE	25
Isabella	17	MD	25
James	30	DE	16
James H	4	DE	16
Joseph A	1	DE	16
Levi	39	DE	73
Levi	60	DE	25
Margaret	13	DE	172
Mary	28	WN	73
Mary	29	DE	16
Naurena	6	DE	155
Sarah	9	DE	155
Medicraft, Jane	51	IE	160
John	10	DE	167
Medill, Ann	49	DE	385
David	55	DE	385
Eliza	13	DE	385
George	10	DE	385
Mary Jane	16	DE	385
William	15	DE	385
Meekins, Sarah A	22	DE	314
Meenen, Allice C	12	DE	273
Catharine	8	DE	273
Daniel	6	DE	273
David	40	IE	273
John	5	DE	273
Mary	10	DE	273
Mary	45	IE	273
Meeteer, Ann	52	DE	394
Edward B	16	DE	394
Henrietta	18	PA	394
Joseph P	27	DE	394
Margaret	20	DE	394
Martha M	1/12	DE	394
Samuel	29	DE	394
Megahe, Araminty	75	DE	307
Megaligar, Ann	70	IE	312
Megatrick, Ellen	15	DE	135
Megatrick, Jane	32	IE	135
Megaw, David	42	DE	322
Eliza Ann	10	DE	322
Joseph W	13	DE	322
Phebe S	32	PA	322
Philena	17	DE	322
Sarah W	39	MD	322
Megear, Alter	2	PA	31
George M D	6	DE	114
Meglenshe, Bridget	35	IE	305
Charles	11	PA	305
James	6	DE	305
John	9	DE	305
Mary	2	DE	305
Michael	14	PA	305
Peter	35	IE	305
Thomas	13	PA	305
Megratten, James	26	PA	46
Martha	23	DE	46
Sarah	56	PA	46
Megregor, Martha	74	DE	352
Megubgin, John	26	IE	301
Mehamy, James	42	PA	57
Jane	13	DE	57
Sarah	32	PA	57
Mehann, Patrick	16	IE	244
Mehann, Elizabeth	50	DE	394
John	50	PA	394
Meherd, Ann	59	MD	280
Eliza	20	DE	327
Elizabeth	15	DE	280
Lige	62	MD	280
Phillis	58	DE	290
Mehinner, Caroline	25	DE	377
Isaac	31	DE	377
Rebecca A	1	DE	377
William Henry	3	DE	377
Mekeever, John	50	DE	272
Meklen, Andrew	12	DE	345
Eliza	47	DE	375
Jane	10	DE	376
Mary A	14	DE	375
Michael	49	DE	375
Sarah R	2	DE	375
Mellen, Arthur	31	IE	64
Bridget	40	IE	64
Catherine	32	IE	64
James	35	IE	27
John	2	DE	64
Elizabeth	17	PA	166
Mellin, Henry	14	DE	14
James	10	DE	14
John	2	DE	11
John	17	DE	14
Mahala	35	IE	11
Margaret	5	IE	11
Margaret	6	DE	14
Martin	12	DE	14
Mary	34	IE	14
Susan	35	IE	11
Mellon, Ann	35	IE	51
James	45	IE	51
Jane J	18	IE	309
John	48	PA	296
Kernhapkuck (?)	48	DE	308
Margaret	45	PA	296
Margaret J	20	IE	289
Mary	23	DE	85
Michael	46	PA	296
Sarah	20	DE	290
Meloy, James	30	PA	360
Lidea	84	DE	358
Simon	73	DE	358
Melton, Nathaniel	13	DE	274
Melvin, Ann	87	DE	335
Anne	24	DE	233
Elizabeth	72	MD	222
Hannah	48	DE	221
James	18	DE	382
James	35	DE	234
L S	48	DE	221
Robert	41	DE	335
Mendenhall, Ann	22	PA	30
Melvin, L S	48	DE	221
Robert	41	DE	335
Mendenhall, Ann	22	PA	30
Edward	16	DE	50
Edward	16	DE	383
Edwin	18	DE	353
Eli	19	DE	299
Eli	65	PA	141
Eliza	49	PA	359
Elizabeth	6	DE	359
Elizabeth	16	DE	351
Elizabeth	18	DE	50
Elizabeth	22	DE	359
Elizabeth	43	DE	351
Elizabeth	71	NJ	360
Elizabeth	72	DE	221
Ellwood H	11	DE	71
Hannah	21	DE	351
Hannah	22	DE	353
Hannah	28	DE	359
Harrison	48	DE	360
Henry	13	DE	50
Isaac	25	DE	359
James	19	DE	351
James	29	DE	359
James	35	DE	233
James	46	DE	351
Jesse	52	DE	50
John	14	DE	351
John	21	DE	141
Joseph	60	DE	299
Margaretta	31	DE	71
Mary	3	DE	359
Mary	9	DE	50
Mary	54	DE	299
Mary	63	PA	141
Mary	82	PA	112
Mary M	6	DE	71
Sarah	44	DE	50
Sarah	45	PA	353
Susannah	3	DE	71
William	5	DE	51
William	35	DE	71
William	49	DE	353
Menough, Clara	12	DE	161
Elizabeth C	39	DE	161
Hellen	39	IE	361
John	41	PA	161
Menoy, Michael	25	IE	310
Menton, Dennis	7	IE	316
James	33	IE	313
John	30	IE	316
Margaret	3	IE	316
Mary	5	IE	316
Mary	30	IE	316
Mercer, Caroline	1	DE	320
Catharine	45	IE	300
Charles	24	DE	320
George N	8	PA	272
Margaret	18	MD	11
Maria	20	DE	320
Samuel	14	IE	300
William	26	IE	300
Merck, Harriet	13	DE	285
Meredith, Anna M	13	PA	281
Benjamin	7	MD	221
Charlotte	55	DE	264
George Anna	6	MD	276
Hester	15	DE	24
Hugh	57	DE	221
James	19	DE	317
Mary	15	DE	24
Mary A	30	DE	247
Mary Jane	20	DE	270
Samuel	32	DE	247
Sarah	47	DE	226
Sarah A	47	DE	221
William	5/12	DE	167
William	15	MD	281
William	48	MD	299
William L	44	DE	309
Merion, John	28	PA	285
Merkins, Joshua	25	DE	256

Mermen, Martha Ann	20	DE	347
William	26	PA	347
Merran, Elizabeth	20	DE	158
Mary	18	DE	158
Merrell, Sarah M	15	DE	358
Merrick, Anna	2	DE	90
Clara	4	DE	90
E	15	MD	165
John	13	DE	89
Sarah	33	DE	90
Merrihew, Ann	20	DE	144
Ella	5	DE	144
George	7	DE	144
James	12	DE	144
James P	50	PA	144
John	17	DE	144
Sarah	48	DE	144
Stephen	22	DE	144
Merril, Ann	24	PA	121
Merrit, Linder	6/12	DE	147
Mary E	8	DE	147
Rachel	28	DE	147
Merritt, Ann E	14	DE	375
Charity	45	PA	375
Elizabeth	28	DE	69
Hannah	64	DE	313
James	12	DE	375
James	39	DE	375
John	6	DE	387
John L	34	DE	179
Joseph	15	DE	375
Martha	26	PA	387
Mary	30	DE	358
Mary E	2	DE	147
Peter	60	DE	179
Rachel	8	DE	375
Sarah	35	DE	179
Susan	2	DE	387
Thomas B	10	DE	375
Merriwether, Ann	46	DE	357
Francis	21	DE	357
Mersit, Eliza	29	DE	317
W G	29	DE	317
Messic, Catherine	28	GE	97
Laurence	37	GE	97
Rocius	25	GE	97
Messick, James B	25	DE	336
Rebecca	25	DE	336
Messig, Anthony	66	GE	271
Charles W	1/12	DE	238
Frances	7	DE	238
Francisco	26	GE	271
Inglebert	28	GE	271
John	4	DE	264
Joseph	2	DE	271
Mary	2/12	DE	264
Mary A	33	DE	238
Pauline	29	GE	264
Peter	7	DE	264
Peter	32	GE	264
Samuel	70	DE	238
Thomas	5	DE	238
Messik, Charles	1/12	DE	323
Emmaline	23	DE	323
Louden M	28	DE	323
Mary A	2	DE	323
Messinger, Foster	42	MA	50
Maria	38	PA	50
Susannah	3	DE	50
Mesum, Ann	18	GB	299
Metcalf, Jacob	14	DE	295
John W	11/12	DE	274
Mary	57	DE	295
Mary A	3	DE	274
Mary J	23	DE	274
Rebecca A	4	DE	274
Thomas	27	DE	274
Thomas	71	GB	295
Metz, Fanny V	2/12	DE	176
George	20	PA	273
George	50	PA	172
John S	24	DE	176
Metz, Mary	19	DE	176
Mary C	7	DE	172
Rebecca H	30	DE	172
Meullin, Ann	50	PA	362
Meyer, Richard	25	MD	201
Mibbley, Eliza	15	GB	394
Micherds, Jane	15	DE	276
Josiah	60	MD	276
Lige	10	DE	276
Phillis	54	DE	276
Midan, Rebecca	30	DE	193
Middleton, Benj F	8	DE	238
Eliza	1	DE	252
Elizabeth	15	DE	61
Elizabeth	30	DE	238
Emily	10	DE	238
Isabella	29	IE	253
John	2	DE	253
Mary	20	DE	393
Robert	30	IE	252
Sarah	9	DE	238
Thomas	1	DE	238
Thomas	22	DE	231
Thomas	39	PA	239
Meigs, Anna	2	DE	400
George G	5	OH	400
Mary G	3	DE	400
Mary G	29	OH	400
Matthew (Rev)	38	NY	400
William A G	7	MI	400
Miken, Elizabeth S	35	DE	2
James C	43	IE	2
Sarah	10	DE	366
Sarah J	14	DE	2
Milaken, John	25	IE	334
Nicholas	27	IE	334
Milby, Eliza	43	DE	172
Frances	21	DE	172
John	45	DE	172
Miles, Anna M	21	DE	149
Calvin	5	PA	366
Elim	3	PA	366
Elwood	2	DE	137
Harriet	42	DE	393
J W	29	DE	149
James S	45	DE	393
John	71	DE	360
Margaret W	28	DE	149
Mary	61	DE	360
Mary A	27	DE	137
Mary Ann	25	PA	366
Rosetta	14	DE	149
Ruth A	19	PA	137
Samuel G	27	PA	137
William	1/12	DE	366
William C	29	NJ	366
Milford, Artamesia	5	NJ	260
Hannah	26	NJ	260
Lorenzo	28	NJ	260
Martha	6	NJ	260
Millagan, Thomas	24	IE	43
Miller, Abram	5	DE	67
Adriana	20	DE	27
Albert	1	DE	313
Albert H	12	DE	309
Ann	1	DE	38
Ann	13	PA	369
Ann	23	DE	319
Ann	28	IE	38
Ann	43	DE	290
Ann	60	IE	280
Ann	61	DE	298
Ann E	5	DE	319
Ann E	19	MD	175
Ann E	24	MD	329
Ann M	18	DE	338
Anna	5	PA	23
Anna	10	DE	391
Anna	16	DE	280
Anna	17	DE	47
Anna	39	DE	294
Anna M	2	DE	294
Miller, Araminta	56	MD	329
Augustus	17	GB	32
Benjamin	20	DE	207
Beulah	9	DE	294
Caleb	35	DE	369
Caroline	24	PA	131
Caroline	34	MD	317
Catherine	7	IE	6
Catherine	12	DE	338
Charles	6	DE	294
Charles	23	IE	18
Charles	23	GE	33
Charles	23	DE	290
Charlotte	27	DE	382
Charlotte	25	PA	23
Christian B	8	DE	370
Clara	30	NJ	110
Danial	26	NJ	3
Danial J	7	DE	286
David	30	DE	22
David	62	MD	293
Dorcas	28	GE	32
Earnest	3/12	DE	65
Edward	10	DE	39
Edward	10	DE	320
Edward	12	DE	321
Edward	40	DE	317
Elijah	3	DE	268
Eliza	19	PA	380
Eliza	31	PA	270
Eliza J	4	DE	303
Eliza J	15	DE	290
Eliza J	16	DE	294
Eliza J	37	DE	209
Elizabeth	17	DE	370
Elizabeth	21	DE	47
Elizabeth	24	GB	39
Elizabeth	49	DE	332
Elizabeth	55	DE	311
Ellen	20	DE	311
Ellen	50	DE	289
Ellen	65	DE	226
Ellena	8	OH	370
Emma	5	PA	270
Essex	45	DE	186
Evans	22	DE	311
Fanny	21	GB	39
Ferdinand	11	DE	49
Frances	48	GB	39
Frances A	11	DE	391
Francis	19	NJ	49
Franklin T	5	DE	370
Gadlike	26	GE	152
George	8	DE	391
George	13	DE	338
George	18	DE	248
George	39	DE	314
George	80	IE	294
George G	3	DE	294
George H	3	DE	324
George M C	18	NJ	309
Grace	5	DE	317
Grace	62	DE	67
Hannah	16	DE	238
Hannah	35	PA	313
Hannah A	18	DE	370
Harriet	2	DE	303
Harriet	40	DE	58
Harriett	18	DE	293
Harriett	25	DE	294
Harriett C	40	NJ	309
Henry	5	DE	67
Henry	7	DE	38
Henry	7	DE	317
Henry	40	IE	38
Henry	60	MD	47
Henry W	8	DE	338
Hester A	8	DE	342
Isaac	5	DE	186
Isaac	20	MD	329
Isaac	51	DE	370
Isaac	60	DE	342

Name	Age	State	Page
Miller, Isabella	1	OH	370
Isabella	21	DE	311
Isaiah	10	DE	342
Jacob	2	DE	131
Jacob	28	DE	47
James	3	PA	338
James	9	DE	317
James	10	DE	203
James	21	DE	391
James	30	DE	313
James	33	MD	154
James	35	DE	303
James	44	DE	392
James	70	IE	311
James	80	DE	226
James	87	IE	67
James W	3	DE	369
Jane	24	DE	317
Jane	30	DE	355
Jane	42	PA	338
Jane	35	IE	314
Jane E	42	MD	387
Jno	45	DE	290
John	1/12	DE	268
John	5	IE	6
John	12	DE	22
John	13	DE	290
John	16	DE	382
John	18	DE	258
John	18	DE	301
John	18	DE	320
John	20	GE	185
John	30	DE	268
John	40	DE	391
John	58	IE	329
John	84	PA	359
John S	20	DE	338
John W	11	DE	387
John W	16	DE	370
Jones W	46	DE	338
Joseph	6	DE	22
Joseph	17	NJ	49
Joseph	29	DE	122
Joseph	30	MD	319
Joseph	32	NJ	131
Joseph	37	MA	370
Joseph	44	DE	294
Joseph	48	NJ	49
Joseph H	3	DE	319
Joseph J	2	DE	309
Josephine	7	PA	269
Josephine	7	DE	294
Josiah	14	DE	320
Judy A	28	GB	369
Julia	19	DE	319
July A	30	DE	371
Laura	2	DE	128
Letitia	15	DE	314
Levi	7	MD	208
Levina	25	DE	149
Lewis	20	DE	391
Lewis	22	NY	74
Lewis	40	GE	33
Lewis M	10/12	DE	294
Louisa	52	MD	175
Lydia	6	DE	325
Mara	50	PA	48
Margaret	13	NY	35
Margaret	13	MD	387
Margaret A	13	MD	387
Margaret T	16	NJ	309
Maria	10	DE	294
Maria	5	DE	243
Maria	7	DE	324
Maria	20	DE	332
Maria	21	DE	268
Maria	28	DE	303
Maria	40	DE	186
Martha	20	DE	58
Martha	50	IE	68
Martin	47	DE	294
Mary	7/12	DE	6
Miller, Mary	3	DE	22
Mary	4	DE	314
Mary	8	DE	324
Mary	11	NY	39
Mary	13	DE	186
Mary	20	DE	317
Mary	23	DE	47
Mary	23	DE	280
Mary	24	NJ	310
Mary	25	DE	342
Mary	28	DE	22
Mary	35	MD	392
Mary	36	DE	370
Mary	37	DE	320
Mary	40	IE	6
Mary	47	NJ	49
Mary	50	DE	47
Mary A	5	DE	30
Mary A	13	DE	392
Mary A	16	MD	175
Mary A	17	DE	210
Mary A	20	IE	74
Mary A	41	DE	371
Mary A	44	DE	243
Mary B	17	DE	136
Mary E	2	DE	319
Mary E	4	DE	313
Mary E	15	DE	294
Mary J	13	DE	152
Matilda	2	DE	269
Matilda	10	DE	317
Matilda	11	DE	383
Meria	7	DE	324
Michel	3	DE	38
Mitchel	3	PA	23
Mrs	50	DE	76
Natalie	18	MD	175
Neal	14	DE	319
Nevin C	39	DE	370
Patric	16	IE	80
Patric	22	DE	370
Perry	9	DE	186
Perry	20	DE	312
Perry	66	DE	208
Peter	7	PA	131
Rebecca	26	PA	23
Rebecca	60	DE	2
Rebecca	66	MD	208
Rebecca	73	DE	365
Rhody	30	DE	198
Richard	20	DE	230
Robert	5/12	DE	122
Robert	26	DE	243
Robert	29	MD	319
Robert	50	DE	387
Robert	70	IE	280
Robert J	9	DE	309
Robinson	9/12	DE	370
Sally	18	DE	341
Sally	30	MD	325
Samuel	50	PA	27
Sarah	6/12	DE	243
Sarah	2	DE	314
Sarah	9	DE	27
Sarah	18	DE	39
Sarah	30	DE	311
Sarah	38	DE	27
Sarah	63	DE	243
Sarah	74	DE	294
Sarah	78	IE	111
Sarah A	17	DE	294
Sarah D	6	DE	170
Sarah E	10	DE	87
Sarah J	2	DE	149
Sarah J	2	DE	186
Sarah J	20	DE	338
Sarah J	21	OH	370
Simeon	40	NJ	309
Susan	12	DE	201
Susannah	13	DE	370
Tempy J	1	DE	109
Thomas	4	IE	6
Miller, Tempey J	1	DE	209
Thomas	4	IE	6
Thomas	4	DE	208
Thomas	4	DE	317
Thomas	5	DE	38
Thomas	14	DE	227
Thomas	28	DE	149
Thomas	40	IE	6
Thomas S	18	MD	329
Virginia	4	PA	131
Warner	28	MD	324
Werster	21	PA	396
Wesley	15	DE	235
William	6	DE	303
William	7	DE	27
William	8	DE	314
William	9	PA	269
William	10	DE	22
William	10	DE	290
William	12	DE	311
William	15	DE	189
William	15	DE	370
William	18	DE	156
William	19	PA	324
William	22	IE	291
William	23	DE	23
William	24	DE	303
William	49	DE	332
William	57	PA	280
William	61	DE	289
William	73	DE	293
William H	35	PA	269
Zilphur	60	DE	209
Milligan, Catherine	22	DE	58
Catherine	91	MD	58
John	30	IE	43
John J	54	MD	58
Margaret	45	DE	399
Martha	13	DE	58
Martha L	51	PA	58
Mary L	25	DE	58
Robert	27	DE	58
Sarah	4	IE	12
Smith	16	PA	399
Susan	14	DE	377
Susan	18	DE	395
William	45	DE	399
Millis, Benjamin	15	DE	156
Hannah	4	DE	156
Jacob	13	DE	156
Jacob	14	DE	121
Julia A	3	DE	156
Mary A	11	DE	156
Miss	50	DE	2
Rachel	7	DE	156
Rachel	42	DE	156
Richard	20	DE	156
Sarah	9	DE	156
Millman, Caroline	6	DE	372
Isaac	4	DE	372
Joseph	29	GE	158
Maria	30	MD	372
Rachel	7	DE	372
William	5	DE	372
William	35	MD	372
Mills, Alice	18	GB	276
Charles R	19	NY	319
David	28	DE	190
Elizabeth	7	PA	276
Erwin	20	GB	298
George T	1	DE	190
Hannah C	4	DE	276
Henrietta	23	DE	218
Hiram	6	DE	339
James	14	PA	276
James	15	MD	299
John	16	PA	276
John	44	GB	276
Joseph	20	GB	276
Mary	9	PA	276
Matty	45	GB	276
Rachel	24	DE	190

Name	Age	St	No.
Mills, Robert	11	PA	276
Wilhelmina	8	DE	389
William	15	DE	188
Millven, Caleb	35	DE	74
Eliza	25	MD	74
Millwood, Edward	60	WL	110
John	18	DE	110
Margaret	19	DE	110
Martha F	46	DE	110
Mary	27	IE	266
Thomas	20	DE	110
Milner, Thomas	35	GB	119
Thomas	56	DE	114
Minaugh, Clara	12	DE	160
Elizabeth C	39	DE	160
John	41	DE	160
Minckins, Ann	19	IE	205
Jesse	22	MD	205
Miner, Albert	28	CT	23
Martha	25	PA	252
Mines, Ann	55	DE	55
Mingo, Andrew	15	DE	94
Caroline	8	DE	94
Daniel	70	DE	94
Dorcas	70	DE	94
Mele	24	DE	94
Sarah	25	DE	94
Minick, Emma	20	PA	38
James	5/12	DE	162
Mary J	24	PA	162
Phillip	28	PA	161
Phillip A	3	DE	162
Mink, Catherine	40	GE	141
John	18	PA	141
George W	1	NJ	14
Mary A	19	NJ	14
Samuel	22	NJ	14
Minner, John	19	IE	337
Minton, Dennis	7	IE	26
John	32	IE	26
Margaret	3	IE	26
Mary	5	IE	26
Mary	30	IE	26
Mires, Ambrose	14	MD	163
Baptist	22	GE	67
Charles	19	GE	67
Eliza	10	DE	65
Emmet	2	DE	75
Ezekle	30	DE	75
George W	2	DE	119
Harriet	32	DE	75
Henry	27	PA	119
Mary	20	DE	168
Mary	40	DE	46
Sarah	27	DE	119
Sarah C	1	DE	119
William	8	DE	46
William	40	PA	53
Mitchel, Alexander	60	IE	298
Amor	21	PA	42
Amos	21	DE	282
Bridget	22	IE	162
Edith	17	PA	153
Elizabeth	6	IE	302
Elizabeth	56	DE	42
Hannah	2	DE	167
Hannah M	6	DE	348
Harlan	15	DE	348
Henry	29	PA	63
Israel	10	DE	348
James	12	DE	299
James	18	PA	153
Joel	16	PA	42
Joseph	4	DE	348
Joseph	20	DE	348
Joseph	32	IE	302
Joseph	66	PA	348
Lydia	46	MD	42
Martha	8	IE	302
Martha	25	DE	142
Martha	60	DE	348
Martha J	1	DE	348
Mitchel, Mary	11	IE	302
Mary	31	IE	302
Oliver	22	DE	348
Passmore	19	PA	42
Phebe	40	PA	153
Robert	21	PA	43
Robert	35	IE	302
Sally	47	DE	298
Sarah	18	DE	348
Sarah E	2	IE	302
Sarah J	8	DE	348
Stephen	26	DE	348
Susan	27	IE	302
Susan	70	IE	302
Susana	13	IE	302
Susana	28	DE	167
Thomas	31	PA	57
Thomas	34	DE	348
William	25	DE	42
William P	19	PA	353
Mitchell, Adeline	5	DE	237
Alice	1	DE	237
Amanda M	16	DE	376
Annie Luisa	1	DE	371
Charles	8	DE	374
Charles	64	DE	297
David	62	IE	302
Edmond	25	GB	371
Edward	10	DE	374
Edward	19	DE	374
Eliza Jane	22	VA	371
Elizabeth	2	DE	360
Emaline	9	DE	237
Emely	45	NY	376
Emma F	7	DE	376
Harriet M	14	DE	376
Harry R	11	DE	376
James	53	GB	369
James H	46	PA	374
James S	18	PA	400
John	30	DE	360
John G	18	DE	376
Jonathan	12	DE	374
Julia A	28	DE	237
Mary E	21	DE	376
Margaret	6	DE	375
Margaret	49	GB	369
Mariah	41	PA	374
Martha E	23	DE	376
Mary A	11	DE	236
Mary E	4	DE	374
Rachel A	14	DE	374
Sarah	29	DE	360
Sarah A	15	DE	369
Sarah J	3	DE	237
Sarah M	2	DE	374
Sarah S	9	DE	376
Sarah W	44	PA	374
Thomas	1	DE	360
Thomas	50	NY	376
Walter	24	GB	369
William	38	MD	237
William H	16	DE	375
Mitchener, Julia A	25	PA	144
Mixin, Rebecca	50	PA	102
Thomas	56	MD	102
Moat, Anna Mary	18	DE	352
Christiana	44	DE	352
George L	20	DE	352
Hannah E	21	DE	352
Isaac	55	DE	352
Isaac J	11	DE	352
Jacob H	15	DE	352
Martha	14	MD	122
Mary	5	DE	122
Mary J	13	DE	352
Rebecca	45	MD	122
William	50	MD	122
Moffet, Edward W	1	PA	283
Joseph	2	PA	283
Joseph	36	DE	283
Martha	34	PA	12
Moat, Richard	38	PA	12
Susana	27	PA	283
William	8	PA	283
Moffett, Amanda	14	DE	208
Elizabeth	21	MD	196
Enoch	18	MD	224
George	20	MD	224
Hannah M	9	DE	224
John W	10	DE	224
Joseph	2	DE	224
Joseph	30	MD	224
Mary J	27	DE	224
Rachel J	4	DE	224
William H	7	DE	224
Mofford, William	28	PA	79
Moflam, Alice	1	DE	207
Catherine	12	DE	207
Frank	4	DE	207
James	16	DE	207
James	39	DE	207
John	10	DE	207
Mary A	44	MD	207
William	5	DE	207
Moleston, William	28	PA	393
Molinex, Margaret	30	IE	280
Momson, George	23	DE	329
Kirk	12	MD	353
Monahan, Ellen	3	DE	44
James	25	IE	44
Mary	25	IE	44
Monde, Hannah	16	DE	43
Mary	18	DE	43
Money, Benjamin	33	DE	229
Bridget	30	IE	335
Darius	35	DE	325
David	3	DE	326
Fergus	42	IE	335
George	12	DE	341
George	27	MD	263
Henrietta	5	DE	325
Isaac	11	DE	325
James	4	DE	325
James	25	DE	284
James	48	DE	325
Jerry	11	DE	326
John	7	IE	335
Levi	18	DE	326
Lewis	9	DE	326
Lewis	35	DE	325
Melvina	1	DE	325
Margaret	17	DE	171
Margaret	80	DE	325
Martin	11	IE	335
Mary	2	DE	325
Mary	4	IE	335
Michel	12	IE	335
Patrick	40	IE	335
Sarah B	21	DE	229
Susan	6/12	IE	335
Susan	23	DE	284
Savilla	35	DE	326
William H	9	DE	229
Monk, William	84	DE	168
Monkhouse, Ada E	5	DE	277
Howard	9	DE	277
John H	2	DE	277
Richard	38	GB	277
Sarah	11	DE	277
Susannah	31	DE	277
Monks, Edward B	30	GB	122
Monkton, Alonzo C	8/12	DE	88
Anna	19	DE	4
Evan C	16	DE	4
George	27	MD	49
John	1	DE	49
Margaret	19	DE	88
Phebe F	48	GB	4
Rufus	7	DE	49
Susanah	24	DE	49
William H	22	NY	88
Monlatro, L De	18	CU	163
Monro, Susan E	40	DE	112

Name	Age	St	Pg	Name	Age	St	Pg	Name	Age	St	Pg
Monroe, Abram	18	DE	186	Moody, Sarah J	14	DE	298	Moore, Elizabeth J	17	DE	311
Henry	16	DE	266	Sibila	50	MD	146	Ella S	2	DE	95
Monson, Frank	5	MD	74	Sophia H	40	DE	287	Ellen	22	MA	16
Isaac	40	MD	74	William	40	DE	146	Ellen M	25	MA	96
Jane	35	MD	74	William L	2	DE	99	Emeline	21	PA	95
Monson, Betsey	44	DE	93	Moon, Elizabeth	27	DE	192	Enoch	8	DE	95
Elizabeth	10	DE	359	Frances Ann	2	DE	192	Enoch	13	DE	117
Frisby	45	DE	93	Ira	19	DE	172	Enoch	25	DE	114
Isaac	42	DE	93	Mooney, Barnard	3	DE	342	Enoch	47	DE	95
Rachel	6	DE	93	Charles	17	IE	24	Frances Ann	2	DE	193
Sarah J	4	DE	93	Joseph	9/12	DE	342	Frances M	3	DE	361
Montgomery, Adah	9	DE	365	Mary	18	IE	369	Franklin	34	DE	336
Adaly J	7	PA	366	Mary	22	IE	342	George	1	DE	122
Alexander	36	PA	101	Niel M	33	IE	342	George	10	DE	201
Ann	17	DE	150	Thomas	20	IE	334	George	19	DE	256
Betsey	72	DE	161	Moore, Abraham	29	DE	243	George W	6	DE	8
Eliza Jane	7	IE	335	Abraham S	32	DE	314	Gideon	18	NJ	147
Elizabeth	19	DE	150	Adelaide	1/12	DE	397	Hannah	12	DE	373
Elizabeth	26	IE	335	Adelaide	4	DE	241	Hannah	28	PA	27
Elizabeth	59	PA	150	Alexander	24	IE	33	Hannah	30	DE	114
Elizabeth	47	DE	374	Alexander	64	GB	320	Hannah	30	GB	309
Emily	19	PA	45	Alfred M	13	DE	241	Hannah	41	NJ	139
Ester	18	DE	83	Amanda	22	DE	27	Hannah	43	PA	95
George	54	DE	357	Amanda	25	DE	46	Hannah	72	SC	291
George Q	2	DE	398	Ann	19	DE	309	Hannah C	3	DE	336
Hannah Jane	13	DE	358	Ann	24	MD	16	Harriet	2	DE	362
James	5	IE	335	Ann	41	PA	310	Harriet	10	DE	336
James	33	DE	83	Ann	44	DE	334	Harrison	19	NJ	97
Jane	70	DE	380	Ann	55	GB	320	Hellen	47	NJ	349
Jerry	60	DE	256	Ann C	23	DE	388	Henry	3	DE	149
John	8	DE	101	Ann D	10	DE	117	Henry	15	PA	95
John	10	DE	357	Ann E	35	DE	206	Henry	31	GB	240
John	21	DE	371	Ann Eliza	42	MD	201	Hester A	2	DE	357
John	63	DE	150	Anna M	18	DE	297	Hiram	14	DE	388
John	65	DE	377	Anna M	24	DE	336	Isaac	4	DE	8
Lewis	2/12	DE	101	Anne	13	DE	82	Isaac	64	PA	396
Louisa	3/12	DE	398	Aubenbundy H	29	DE	96	Isabella	30	DE	8
Margaret	26	DE	106	Augustine	4	DE	212	Jacob	2	DE	212
Maria	21	MD	101	Benjamin	15	DE	51	Jacob	16	DE	362
Martha B	16	DE	106	Benjamin L	50	PA	349	Jacob	57	DE	227
Mary	47	PA	357	Dorcas	74	DE	157	Jacob	86	DE	157
Mary E	18	DE	368	Catharine	32	IE	344	James	30	DE	27
Michael	16	IE	377	Catherine A	3	DE	336	James	35	IE	344
Moses	81	DE	350	Charles	2	DE	243	James	50	NJ	97
Robert	22	DE	368	Charles	8	DE	82	James	50	DE	212
Robert	27	PA	398	Charles	20	PA	397	James A	20	DE	241
Robert H	4	DE	106	Charles	21	DE	114	James B	35	MD	206
Saml	27	IE	335	Charles	28	PA	122	James B	40	PA	8
Samuel	33	DE	380	Charles	33	PA	361	James J	2	DE	8
Sarah	11	DE	357	Charles	45	DE	117	James L	6	DE	206
Sarah	50	DE	83	Charles D	2	DE	361	James V	43	DE	241
Sarah A	24	PA	398	Charles H	9	NJ	97	Jane	18	DE	320
Sarah J	22	PA	150	Charles W	29	DE	336	Jane	30	IE	149
Thomas	13	DE	382	Clara	7/12	DE	96	Jesse	58	DE	386
William	18/12	DE	335	Clark	40	NJ	147	John	5	DE	206
William	14	DE	377	Corby	60	DE	313	John	17	PA	349
William	18	PA	162	Corillea	6/12	DE	243	John	18	DE	376
Moody, Annabella	5	MD	309	David	2	IE	372	John	24	IE	345
Ann	30	DE	254	David	19	DE	349	John	25	DE	293
Ann	39	MD	309	Duan Gilbert	11	NJ	140	John	45	DE	197
David S	40	DE	99	Edward	40	DE	132	John	50	IE	149
Ellen R	8	DE	307	Eliza	18	DE	311	John	55	DE	388
Georgianna	13	MD	309	Eliza	50	DE	32	John	56	DE	51
Henry	40	DE	254	Eliza	52	DE	386	John W	4	NJ	139
Hester	3	DE	185	Eliza J	13	DE	227	John W	11	PA	400
Isaac	25	DE	301	Elizabeth	6	DE	82	John H	14	DE	132
James	58	DE	380	Elizabeth	9	DE	95	John L	8	DE	336
John	7	MD	321	Elizabeth	10	DE	140	John M	18	DE	388
John	84	DE	287	Elizabeth	14	DE	357	J P	25	DE	149
John R	33	DE	190	Elizabeth	20	MD	313	Jos P	25	PA	401
Louisa	36	DE	185	Elizabeth	22	IE	274	Joseph	7	DE	388
Maris	62	DE	190	Elizabeth	23	DE	114	Joseph	16	DE	210
Mary A	17	DE	99	Elizabeth	25	DE	293	Joseph	17	DE	173
Rachel E	5	DE	99	Elizabeth	27	DE	193	Joseph	18	DE	261
Raison G	18	MD	309	Elizabeth	39	NJ	97	Joseph	61	DE	292
Robert J	13	DE	99	Elizabeth	40	DE	357	Joseph C	17	PA	401
Saml	35	DE	254	Elizabeth	62	DE	19	Julia	21	DE	20
Sarah	15	DE	341	Elizabeth	63	DE	120	Kesiah	13	DE	95
Sarah	36	DE	51	Elizabeth	65	DE	114	Levic	4	DE	357
Sarah	38	PA	99	Elizabeth A	6	DE	345	Levina	16	DE	320
Sarah J	4	DE	298	Elizabeth H	22	DE	149	Lewis B	47	DE	357

Moore, Louisa	14	DE	362
Louisa	14	DE	386
Ludom B	32	PA	397
Lydia	36	DE	362
Lydia H	7	DE	362
Mansell	8	DE	357
Marcus C	13	PA	400
Margaret	26	DE	114
Margaret	47	DE	82
Margaret	50	MD	16
Margaret	58	DE	292
Margaret B	10/12	DE	361
Margaret E	27	DE	307
Margaret J	9/12	DE	8
Margaret J	39	DE	8
Margaretta	12	PA	95
Maria P	37	DE	361
Marian	27	GB	122
Martha	5	PA	349
Martha	7	DE	95
Martha B	12	NJ	97
Martha W	25	PA	397
Mary	17	PA	1
Mary	20	GB	311
Mary	28	NJ	147
Mary	35	DE	57
Mary	45	DE	197
Mary	45	DE	374
Mary	48	MD	95
Mary	53	DE	227
Mary	64	PA	1
Mary A	12	DE	132
Mary A	15	DE	374
Mary A	17	NJ	97
Mary A	29	PA	397
Mary Ann	11	DE	344
Mary Ann	26	PA	344
Mary E	7	DE	241
Mary E	10	DE	362
Mary E	17	DE	117
Mary J	17	PA	95
Mary J	35	DE	336
Mary Jane	8	PA	349
Mary M	52	DE	388
Mary R	1	DE	336
Mary S	13	DE	288
Mary S	19	DE	359
Mathias M	62	NJ	139
Matilda A	17	DE	357
Mulford D	3	NJ	139
Nathaniel	5	DE	96
Nathaniel	50	DE	95
Olivia	16	DE	386
Perry	60	DE	82
Peter	11	DE	82
Rachel	5	DE	362
Rachel	20	DE	386
Rachel	41	DE	241
Rachel	61	PA	397
Rachel E	11	DE	357
Rachel L	9	DE	397
Rebecca	6	DE	336
Rebecca	17	DE	348
Rebecca	19	DE	114
Rebecca	20	DE	292
Rebecca H	21	PA	349
Rheese	1	DE	97
Richard	19	IE	347
Richard	43	DE	201
Robert	2	DE	8
Robert	26	DE	320
Robert	27	IE	372
Robert	28	GB	309
Robert	35	MD	8
Rosanna	32	MD	83
Sally	4	DE	83
Sally	28	DE	46
Samuel	2	DE	213
Samuel	6	DE	147
Samuel	22	DE	46
Samuel	30	PA	83
Samuel	50	DE	212

Moore, Samuel	50	DE	323
Samuel	70	DE	313
Sarah	10	DE	388
Sarah	11	DE	227
Sarah	11	DE	266
Sarah	11	DE	362
Sarah	23	IE	372
Sarah	30	MD	318
Sarah	45	DE	212
Sarah	50	DE	372
Sarah	53	IE	312
Sarah A	12	DE	320
Sarah A	24	DE	243
Sarah A	36	DE	117
Sarah E	40	MD	132
Sarah J	6	DE	397
Sarah J	15	DE	357
Sarah Jane	17/12	DE	344
Souby	60	DE	323
Susan	55	DE	51
Susan M	10	DE	357
Susanna	4/12	DE	362
Susanna	18	PA	312
Thomas	22	IE	291
Thomas	70	DE	114
Thomas H	7/12	DE	359
Thomas J	40	DE	362
Thomas L	18	PA	401
Thomas M	14	DE	241
Tuzant	48	DE	290
Vincent	2	DE	206
William	3/12	DE	16
William	8	DE	95
William	9	DE	206
William	11	PA	349
William	28	IE	347
William	35	DE	96
William	36	IE	344
William A	25	DE	359
William B	14	NJ	97
William E	6/12	DE	336
William H	27	MD	400
William H	17	PA	8
William S	6	DE	96
William T	12	DE	357
Zachariah	44	DE	374
Moot, Martha	14	MD	123
Mary	5	DE	123
Rebecca	45	MD	123
William	50	MD	123
Moran, Catharine	22	IE	334
More, David	50	DE	347
Hester	55	DE	347
Jane	85	IE	347
Joseph	16	DE	272
Mary	18	DE	272
Morely, Francis	14	DE	171
George	24	GB	297
Morgan, Adelia C	20	PA	85
Alexander	14	DE	382
Anderson	13	DE	315
Ann E	22	DE	299
Asa	43	MD	243
Charles	1	DE	85
Daniel	27	DE	188
David	27	DE	299
David	49	DE	169
David W	16	DE	169
Eliza J	24	DE	186
Elizabeth	44	MD	243
Emily	18	MD	265
George	10	DE	232
George	18	PA	85
Georgiana	11	DE	169
Henrietta	24	DE	151
Hester	6	DE	186
James	26	MD	85
James	33	DE	374
James H	30	MD	99
John	21	PA	135
John	24	DE	270
Joseph	50	DE	245

Morgan, John	24	DE	270
Joseph	50	DE	245
Margaret	52	DE	315
Martha	14	DE	169
Mary	1	DE	270
Mary	23	MD	270
Mary	73	PA	361
Mary A	12	NY	166
Mary E	9	DE	243
Mary J	20	DE	315
Ophilla	15	NY	166
Samuel	32	MD	33
Sarah A	13	DE	243
Sarah A	21	DE	119
Sarah E	7	DE	189
Thomas	31	PA	79
William	8	DE	212
Morocco, Arthur	40	MD	328
Julia Ann	40	DE	328
Morpheth, Levi	20	DE	255
Morran, John	21	IE	48
Morrell, John	76	ME	373
Martha	14	DE	245
Mary J	29	NJ	373
Mary J	35	DE	383
Stephen	29	DE	383
William	27	DE	373
Morris, Alace	30	DE	140
Amanda	3/12	DE	78
Amanda	26	NJ	78
Amelia T	13	PA	165
Andrew	3	DE	300
Andrew	53	NJ	300
Ann	14	DE	257
Ann	44	IE	296
Ann	46	DE	76
Ann J	13	DE	124
Ann J	15	DE	121
Anna	28	MD	54
Anna	28	DE	360
Benjamin	19	DE	381
Benjamin	27	NJ	78
Benjamin	56	DE	262
Brinkley	9	DE	374
Catherine R	1	DE	121
Comfort	68	DE	294
David	10	DE	299
Debby A	6	DE	138
Edward	8	DE	230
Eliza	16	IE	296
Eliza J	10	DE	138
Elizabeth	3/12	DE	54
Elizabeth	14	DE	199
Elizabeth	19	NJ	127
Elizabeth	23	DE	298
Elizabeth	26	DE	385
Elizabeth	45	DE	294
Elizabeth	63	DE	48
Elwood W	18	DE	294
Emeline	12	DE	262
George	3	DE	128
George	5	DE	123
George	5	DE	307
George	6	DE	258
George	34	DE	309
George L	16	DE	121
Isaac	12	DE	220
Henry	8/12	DE	66
Henry	24	DE	309
Hyland	5	DE	230
Jacob	46	DE	294
Jacob	60	DE	217
James	2	DE	257
James	11	DE	300
James	29	IE	274
James	40	DE	138
James	61	IE	296
James H	11	DE	138
Jane	18	IE	296
Jane	32	DE	262
Jane	50	DE	29
John	11	DE	123

Name	Age	St	Pg	Name	Age	St	Pg	Name	Age	St	Pg
Morris, John	22	IE	274	Morrison, Anna M	17	DE	358	Morrow, Goerge	38	DE	309
John	30	DE	262	Benjamin	35	IE	374	George H	19	DE	305
John	60	DE	134	Catherine	1	DE	3	Henry	15	DE	55
John	68	PA	292	Catherine	28	IE	374	Henry B	1	DE	71
John	70	DE	281	Charlotte	21	DE	276	Henry H	5	DE	111
John J	25	DE	384	David	32	NJ	312	Hugh S	6	DE	309
Joseph T	4/12	DE	138	David	40	DE	383	Humphrey	45	PA	329
Josephine	7	DE	298	Douglas	15	DE	383	James	2	DE	291
Joshua	14	DE	294	Eliza	45	DE	304	James	15	DE	77
Levi	32	DE	140	Elizabeth	19	DE	366	James S	21	MD	103
Lewis	15	DE	123	Elizabeth	48	DE	385	Jane	3	DE	77
Lewis	23	PA	251	Elizabeth	55	IE	2	Jane	27	DE	291
Louisa	33	DE	121	Elizabeth	57	ST	358	Jane	31	IE	28
Louisa J	12	DE	294	Ellen	3	DE	3	Jane	34	DE	360
Lydia	32	DE	96	Ellen	20	DE	3	John	1	DE	150
Lydia A	5	DE	294	Emaline	12	DE	276	John	25	IE	150
Lydia E	9	DE	96	Ephraim	52	DE	168	John	28	DE	360
Mahala	50	DE	310	George W	21	DE	298	John	49	DE	305
Margaret	3/12	DE	127	Hannah	9	DE	304	John	50	IE	55
Margaret	5	DE	121	Isaac	15	PA	351	John L	11	DE	305
Margaretta	2	DE	128	Isaac	30	DE	360	Joseph	24	IE	105
Maria	11	DE	257	James	6	DE	367	Joseph	28	IE	145
Maria	37	MD	123	James	11	DE	383	Juel	14	MD	105
Maria	55	DE	134	James	16	DE	385	Mary	1	DE	28
Mary	1	DE	298	James	40	DE	367	Mary	40	DE	77
Mary	17	DE	154	James	53	DE	385	Mary A	2	DE	150
Mary	25	GB	66	James	66	DE	360	Mary S	12	DE	309
Mary	27	DE	95	James	67	IE	298	Michael	56	DE	310
Mary	35	NJ	128	Jane	19	DE	385	Robert	21	DE	305
Mary A	18	DE	123	Jane	57	IE	385	Robert	28	IE	380
Mary A	20	IE	296	John	13	DE	346	Robert	30	DE	360
Mary B	15	PA	165	John	30	DE	14	Sarah	49	DE	305
Mary E	8	DE	294	John	45	NY	304	Sarah A	23	DE	305
Mary E	8	DE	300	John	66	DE	351	Sarah A	35	DE	111
Mary E	10	DE	121	John C	24	DE	298	Susan	1	DE	291
Mary E	10	DE	319	John J	26	DE	385	William	3	DE	28
Nathaniel	50	DE	54	Kesiah	75	PA	30	William	19	PA	55
Nelson	38	DE	378	Lewis	21	DE	383	William	43	IE	111
Noah	10	DE	294	Lydia J	5	DE	276	William	45	DE	77
Noah	35	DE	121	Margarett	14	DE	276	William	72	DE	360
Perry	35	DE	230	Margarett	26	PA	14	William A	18	MD	105
Phebe	15	DE	257	Maria	57	PA	293	William R	14	DE	309
Philip	5	DE	257	Martha A	1	DE	374	Morse, Andrew	11	DE	382
Phoebe	50	DE	217	Mary	3/12	DE	360	Elizabeth	7	DE	382
Priscilla	35	DE	230	Mary	6	DE	14	Elizabeth	60	DE	382
Rachel	4	DE	54	Mary A E	6	DE	374	Georgeanna	2	DE	382
Rachel	13	DE	121	Nancy	64	IE	385	Hannah J	8/12	DE	382
Rachel	15	DE	308	Morrison, Rachel	39	PA	30	John	36	DE	382
Rachel	23	DE	360	Rachel E	20	DE	385	Margaret	33	DE	382
Rebecca	9	DE	96	Rebecca	23	DE	312	Mary	5	DE	382
Rebecca	38	DE	138	Rebecca	25	DE	245	Robert	42	DE	382
Richard	20	DE	138	Robert	7	DE	276	William	9	DE	382
Robert	7	DE	294	Robert	13	PA	367	Mortimer, Charles	8	DE	129
Rosena	34	IE	300	Robert	17	DE	298	Eliza	26	GB	129
Sally	5	DE	360	Robert	25	PA	358	George	10	DE	117
Samuel	54	MD	299	Robert	26	NY	304	George	30	GB	129
Samuel H	21	DE	385	Robert	57	PA	276	George W	36	VA	117
Sarah	7	DE	257	Morrison, Samuel	55	DE	385	Hannah	30	NJ	117
Sarah A	40	DE	251	Sarah	11	DE	304	John	6	DE	129
Susan	6	DE	230	Sarah	23	DE	83	Virginia	4	DE	117
Susan	51	PA	394	Sarah D	58	PA	351	Mortin, William	11	?	294
Tamar	50	DE	244	Sarah E	23	DE	358	Morton, Caroline	4	DE	120
Tamar	50	MD	299	Thomas	26	DE	3	Eliza	18	DE	338
Thomas	14	IE	296	William	15	PA	367	Elizabeth	55	GB	380
Thomas	17	DE	123	William	21	DE	358	George	2	DE	120
Virginia	2	DE	95	William	22	DE	15	George	45	DE	380
Wesley	31	DE	385	William	25	GB	304	Hannah	50	NJ	153
William	3	DE	298	William	35	DE	245	Jane G	25	MD	121
William	7	DE	299	William	45	DE	385	John	30	PA	318
William	9	DE	307	William A	17	DE	385	John	45	DE	338
William	12	DE	218	William H	26	DE	208	Mary E	6	MD	121
William	40	DE	298	Morrow, Agness	2	DE	309	Samuel	22	DE	121
William E	8	DE	138	Ann	32	DE	360	Mosely, Ann	50	DE	351
William H	3	DE	385	Ann	52	PA	55	Frances	14	DE	170
William H	16	DE	294	Bethia	23	PA	28	Moseley, Benjamin	40	DE	186
William H	27	DE	95	Catherine	25	IE	150	George	17	PA	351
Morrison, Abigail	35	PA	367	Charles	26	IE	291	Titus	60	DE	351
Agnes	10	DE	276	Edward	13	DE	77	William S	10	DE	351
Agnes	50	DE	276	Eliza J	34	MD	309	Moses, Ann	9	DE	175
Agnes J	15	DE	358	Elizabeth	22	DE	305	Ellen	7	DE	175
Andrew	8	DE	374	Elizabeth A	9	DE	111	James Jr	12	DE	175
Andrew	12	DE	358	George	19	DE	309	Moss, Ellen	22	IE	330

Name	Age	St	Pg	Name	Age	St	Pg	Name	Age	St	Pg
Moss, John	9/12	DE	330	Muldoon, Stephen	32	DE	345	Murguiondo, Dolores	37	WN	57
John	25	GB	330	Mulford, Charles	4	DE	207	Julia	12	AG	57
Mote, Abraham S	6	DE	363	James	6	DE	207	Lolo	16	AG	57
Ann	50	PA	392	Jemima	35	NJ	207	Murphey, Ann	12	DE	285
Eli C	9	DE	363	Margaret	13	DE	173	Burnett	10	DE	285
Eliza	25	MD	333	R W	33	NJ	208	Catherine	16	DE	285
Elizabeth	48	PA	392	Mullen, Ann	22	IE	8	Chaster	40	IE	347
Ely	44	DE	363	Bridget	3/12	DE	320	Elizabeth	18	DE	285
Harris	2	DE	363	Bridget	21	IE	7	Elizabeth	48	IE	285
Isaac T	13	DE	363	Catharine	6	DE	327	Hugh	17	IE	399
Isabell	1	DE	334	Charles	16	IE	343	Peter	22	IE	343
Isabell	52	PA	363	Charles	51	IE	8	Robert	24	DE	338
Jacob	14	DE	363	Eliza	6	DE	8	William	29	ST	285
Jacob	60	PA	396	Elizabeth	35	MD	33	Murphield, James	26	GB	312
James T	6	DE	363	James	19	IE	343	Murphy, Alfred D	28	DE	303
Jesse H	14	DE	363	James M	23	IE	317	Ana	17	DE	100
Joseph J	19	DE	363	Jane	12	IE	343	Ann	11	IE	296
John	18	DE	392	Jane	20	PA	20	Anna	3	DE	40
John S	6	DE	363	Jane	40	IE	8	Anna	12	DE	284
Rachel	41	PA	363	John	26	IE	2	Bridget	22	IE	45
Sarah C	40	DE	363	Martha	13	DE	8	Burnet	10	DE	284
Sarah J	11	DE	363	Mary	30	IE	320	Catharine	2	DE	296
Smith	53	PA	363	Mary	48	IE	343	Catharine	15	DE	284
Walter D	3	MD	333	Michael	21	IE	320	Charles	27	DE	45
William	64	PA	363	Neal	30	IE	7	Clara	24	PA	303
William H	16	DE	363	Owen	28	IE	300	Druet	29	IE	335
William S	30	DE	333	Susan	36	IE	336	Edward	1	DE	303
Mother, Jane	28	IE	147	Sydney	22	IE	40	Elizabeth	18	DE	284
John	5	DE	147	Thomas	24	IE	80	Elizabeth	48	DE	284
Mannis	30	IE	147	William	20	NJ	271	Elizabeth A	13	MD	193
Michel	4/12	DE	147	Muller, Michael	24	IE	334	Emeline W	2	DE	100
Motherall, Eliza	35	DE	309	Mullgrift, Wilson	22	DE	173	G W	43	DE	303
Henry	1	DE	309	Mullian, Ann R	15	NJ	314	Henry	20	DE	307
Mary	6	DE	309	Mullin, Allen	6	DE	346	Henry	22	IE	335
William	3	DE	309	Ann	19	DE	342	Isaac J	32	MD	110
William	44	DE	309	James	9	DE	346	Isabella S	25	NJ	110
Motley, Ann	4	GB	258	James	50	IE	346	James	3	DE	303
John	7	GB	258	Jane	16	DE	342	James	6	IE	149
John	35	GB	258	Margaret	10	DE	346	James	32	MD	100
Mary	35	GB	258	Mary	47	IE	346	James	38	IE	296
Moulton, Mary	28	IE	347	Mulville, Robert	5	DE	382	Jane	27	DE	40
Mount, Albert	22	DE	303	Munks, Agnes	25	DE	329	Joanna	50	IE	6
Albert	49	DE	341	Catharine	23	DE	329	John	7	DE	40
Eliza J	14	MD	341	Eliza A	18	DE	329	John	28	DE	40
Elizabeth	5	DE	329	Margaret	20	DE	329	John	30	IE	293
Lettitia	40	MD	341	Margaret	56	IE	329	John	58	DE	202
Margaret A	16	MD	341	Mary	32	IE	329	John B	34	MD	311
Mountain, Ann	15	DE	303	Munroe, Abraham	45	DE	197	John R	72	MD	311
Flora	27	DE	303	Ann	45	DE	197	Leander	23	DE	34
Harry	13	DE	303	Cecilia	23	DE	197	Leurana	23	NY	100
Mounts, James	30	MD	277	Charles	10	DE	197	Lydia A	40	DE	303
Mousley, Anna M	13	DE	351	Charles	14	DE	235	Lydia L	11	MD	193
Catharine	84	DE	285	Emma	9	PA	235	Margaret	25	IE	335
Charity	3	DE	280	Enoch	2	DE	235	Margaret	27	IE	149
Curtis	25	DE	285	Hester	2	DE	197	Margaret	41	MD	303
Curtis	62	DE	275	James	17	DE	235	Maria J	21	DE	311
George	34	DE	280	Joseph	5	DE	235	Mary	2	DE	45
George A	21	DE	351	Mary	4	DE	197	Mary	19	PA	274
George W	9/12	DE	280	Rebecca	4	DE	197	Mary	30	IE	85
Isaac D	2-	DE	292	Sarah	40	DE	235	Mary	45	DE	202
Joseph M	28	DE	275	Murch, Martha	87	IE	180	Mary	63	IE	335
Lewis H	3	DE	285	Murchard, Samuel	16	DE	295	Mary A	10	MD	193
Lewis H	15	DE	351	Murdock, Elmer	3/12	DE	51	Mary E	5	DE	110
Louisa	1	DE	285	George	50	DE	100	Mary E	9	DE	303
Martha E	1	DE	351	James	37	DE	143	Michel	3	IE	149
Mary	25	DE	285	James	56	DE	143	Michel	50	IE	6
Mary	59	GB	275	John	25	DE	51	Patric	29	IE	149
Mary E	7	DE	275	Martha	8	DE	143	Paul	7/12	DE	149
Mary J	19	MA	314	Mary A	17	PA	143	Rebecca	13	DE	303
Rachel	27	DE	280	Prudence	23	PA	51	Rejina	11	DE	303
Sarah A	4	DE	280	Sarah	40	PA	143	Sander	21	DE	110
Sarah M	19	DE	351	Susan G	48	DE	376	Sarah	1	DE	45
Thomas J	6	DE	280	Thomas	20	DE	100	Sarah	20	IE	335
Mulby, Eliza	43	DE	173	Thomas	48	DE	143	Sarah	23	PA	70
Frances	21	DE	173	Murfield, Caroline	25	GB	312	Sarah	59	DE	21
John	47	DE	171	Murgertroyd, Ann	22	GB	45	Susan	39	PA	193
Muldain, Andrew	57	IE	157	Ann	52	GB	45	Thomas	43	MD	193
Catherine	50	DE	177	Benjamin	19	GB	45	Thomas C	2	MD	193
Muldoon, Alice	28	DE	345	Christopher	53	GB	45	William	22	DE	70
James	35	DE	345	Sarah	26	GB	45	William	29	DE	284
Joshua	26	DE	345	Murguiondo, Charles	15	AG	57	William	71	DE	303
Pusey	30	DE	345	Credensa	37	WN	57	William A	4	DE	303

Name	Age	State	Page
Murray, Anna	20	DE	338
David	21	DE	187
Deborah	30	DE	206
Edward	35	IE	345
Elizabeth	30	DE	203
Henry Clay	3	DE	203
James	35	DE	203
Joseph L	10/12	DE	203
Margaret	15	PA	343
Margaret	15	DE	374
Margaret R	5	DE	203
Mary	37	DE	203
Mary E	8	IE	203
Mary J	2	DE	203
Sarah E	6	DE	203
Thos	22	PA	338
William	37	DE	203
William L	8	DE	203
Murrey, Elizabeth	35	DE	370
Emanuel	--	DE	290
George	39	DE	370
John	16	DE	399
Murry, Aaron	17	DE	289
Abraham	34	MD	316
Albert	10	DE	256
Alexzina	6	DE	154
Ann	8	DE	256
Anna	30	KY	256
Bridget	20	IE	347
Catharine	35	DE	388
Charles	18	DE	257
Charles A	1	DE	316
Clement	35	DE	206
Edward	5/12	DE	289
Elby	23	DE	154
Elihu	12	DE	256
Elizabeth A	3	NJ	289
Emily	11	PA	326
George	20	DE	308
George	55	DE	256
George H	7	DE	316
Hannah	36	DE	316
Hannah A	1	DE	206
Harriet	4	DE	256
Henrietta	15	DE	320
Isaac	13	DE	308
Isaac	14	DE	289
Isaac	24	DE	154
Isaac	87	NJ	289
James	6	DE	206
James	25	GB	80
James E	3	DE	316
John	4	DE	327
Jonas	32	NJ	289
Josiah	50	NJ	289
Levi	8	PA	326
Louisa E	5	NJ	289
Manuel	25	DE	303
Margaret	15	DE	373
Margaret	17	PA	326
Margaret	24	MD	72
Margaret	52	DE	113
Martha	27	PA	46
Mary	3	DE	388
Mary	6	DE	256
Mary	6	DE	289
Mary	33	NJ	289
Mary	37	DE	202
Rebecca	53	MD	308
Richard	4	DE	206
Richard	6	DE	308
Samuel	21	DE	326
Sarah	32	MA	326
Sarah	38	DE	289
Sarah E	5	DE	316
Sarah E	6	DE	202
Susan J	5/12	NJ	289
Thomas	18	IE	79
Thomas	35	MD	308
Thomas	35	DE	388
Whilemina	2	DE	256
William	9/12	DE	326
Murry, William	16	DE	356
William	25	MD	72
William	37	DE	202
William T	9	DE	202
Muser, Sophia	26	IE	207
Musgrove, Elizabeth	42	DE	394
James A	7	DE	394
Lydia L	15	DE	394
Martha	10	DE	394
Thomas H	20	DE	394
William	75	DE	387
William A	12	DE	394
William A	45	DE	394
Mussey, Anna	45	MD	199
Elizabeth	7	DE	199
John	4	DE	263
Margaret	15	DE	342
Mary	2/12	DE	263
Pauline	29	DE	263
Peter	7	DE	263
Peter	32	DE	263
Rachel J	6	DE	199
William	45	MD	199
Mustard, David L	14	DE	400
Mutter, Elizabeth	10	ST	303
John	8	ST	303
Peter	52	ST	303
Mary	5	DE	303
Mary	36	ST	303
Myers, Eliza J	21	DE	311
Ingeber L F	31	DE	279
Isaac	6	DE	250
Jacob	40	PA	320
James	14	PA	288
James L T	15	PA	279
John	10	DE	307
Josephine	13	PA	279
Lucy	4	DE	168
Mary E	15	DE	222
Naff, H H J	40	DE	51
Mrs	35	DE	51
W H	50	DE	53
Nagle, Delia	8/12	PA	75
Elizabeth	2	PA	75
Elizabeth	5	PA	49
Ellen	3	PA	49
John	14	PA	75
Joseph	10	PA	49
Margaret	28	PA	75
Mary	5/12	DE	49
Michel	34	PA	75
Mr	50	GE	131
Rebecca	32	PA	49
William	35	VA	49
Nakle, Eliza P	35	DE	211
Margaret A	15	DE	211
Samuel A	14	DE	211
Sarah E	11	DE	211
William	45	DE	211
Nally, Mary	17	MD	166
Nameless, George	28	PA	17
Nance, Henry	13	DE	174
James	40	DE	174
Naral, Conrad	50	GE	298
Nash, Bridget	29	IE	310
Elizabeth	2	GB	388
George	8	GB	388
John	4	GB	388
Martha	32	IE	350
Theodosia	34	GB	388
William	32	GB	388
Nathan, Carty Philip	4	DE	259
David	16	DE	274
Isaac	68	DE	259
John H	1	DE	185
Margaret	16	DE	259
Mary	28	IE	312
Ruth	40	DE	259
Sarah	24	MD	185
William	23	DE	185
Nats, Cumerah	12	?	333
Naudain, Ann	61	DE	385
Ann E	4	DE	226
Ann E	9	DE	239
Ann M	35	DE	385
Anna M	9	DE	239
Eliza	2	IE	190
Eliza	24	DE	319
Eliza	40	DE	226
Eliza A	7	DE	226
Elizabeth	18	DE	190
Elvis A	57	DE	190
Fountain	40	DE	247
Emeline	28	DE	228
Henry Clay	5	DE	239
Jacob V	43	DE	239
James S	13	DE	190
Jemima	61	MD	175
John	36	DE	226
John M	15	DE	226
John M	31	DE	248
John O	15	DE	190
Lawrence M	25	DE	247
Lydia E	9	DE	175
Lydia W	50	PA	190
Martha	37	DE	180
Mary C	7	DE	239
Mary E	34	DE	385
Mary R	26	DE	248
Matthew M	29	DE	385
Nicholas	29	DE	169
Posey	46	DE	190
Rebecca	21	DE	169
Sarah R	11	DE	239
Susan	28	DE	385
Theodore	5	DE	190
Thomas	53	DE	190
Naudane, Angie	8	DE	383
Arnold	5/12	DE	383
Mary	4	DE	383
Susie	6	DE	383
Naudine, Arnold	36	DE	383
Ellen	9	DE	383
Esther	38	DE	383
Naw, Ann	30	NJ	217
David	13	PA	217
Henry	45	DE	217
Joel	5	DE	217
Mary	5	DE	217
Nawdain, Alexzena S	9	DE	367
Arnold S	11	DE	367
Christopher B	15	DE	367
Elias S	40	DE	367
Estill	5	DE	367
Joseph C	3	DE	367
Sarah A	39	DE	367
Sarah S		DE	367
Naylor, Alexander	3	DE	198
Hannah	35	DE	59
Henry	7	DE	198
Hester	7	DE	226
Isaac	45	DE	198
James	4	DE	229
John	1	DE	229
John	26	DE	229
Levi	40	DE	59
Mary A	14	DE	99
Mary E	5	DE	233
Mary R	8	DE	198
Noble	47	NJ	226
Perry	17	DE	197
Rebecca	15	DE	198
Rebecca	25	DE	229
Robert	15	DE	226
Sarah	30	DE	233
William	25	DE	233
William W	9/12	DE	233
Nead, William	10	DE	46
Neal, Andrew	16	DE	322
Ann	45	DE	54
Barbary Jane	5	IE	362
Betty Ann	2	IE	362
Daniel	13	DE	239

Name	Age	Place	Page
Neal, Daniel	30	MD	212
Edith	25	MD	212
Eliza	11	DE	322
Eliza	54	MD	322
Elizabeth	32	IE	362
Elizabeth	57	MD	353
Emery	16	DE	322
Francis	9	IE	362
Isaac	34	IE	362
James	7	IE	362
Joshua T	46	DE	162
June	9	DE	172
Lydia	20	DE	178
Mary	1	DE	252
Mary	8	DE	265
Mary	38	MD	266
Perry	20	MD	203
Rachel	75	PA	162
Saml	11	DE	252
Samuel	13	DE	189
Thomas	43	DE	353
Wm	45	MD	265
Neals, Elizabeth	16	DE	50
Elizabeth	26	DE	25
Enor	12	DE	360
James	26	DE	25
John	32	DE	50
Mary	2	DE	25
Mary	44	MD	360
Milton	41	DE	360
Pearce	11	DE	50
Rebecca	54	DE	50
Sarah	40	DE	360
Nebicer, Acquilla	7	DE	141
George	14	DE	141
Mary	40	DE	141
Samuel A	10	DE	141
Neels, Stephen	20	DE	13
Neff, Emeline	26	GE	271
John	8/12	DE	271
Margaret	2	DE	271
Wm	4	DE	271
Wm	35	GE	271
Neilour, John	25	PA	359
Neis, Hester	62	PA	357
Joseph	69	PA	357
Neleker, Anna J	5	DE	373
Elizabeth	6	DE	373
Elizabeth	70	DE	373
Jane	1	DE	373
John	30	DE	373
Mary A	25	PA	373
Nelson, Albert	13	DE	373
Ann	16	IE	300
Charles	33	GB	305
Dorain	54	IE	301
Elizabeth	12	VA	312
George	12	DE	395
Henrietta F	16	DE	360
Jane	38	IE	300
Joseph	35	MD	74
Louisa	17	DE	260
Margaret	23	NJ	103
Mary A	8	DE	318
Mary J	14	DE	300
Rachel	18	PA	396
Robert	36	PA	103
Rosana H	34	DE	74
Thomas	15	GB	90
William	5	DE	103
Nanlove, John P	9	DE	305
Nennet, Henry	5	DE	272
Nesbit, S E	15	MD	165
Neuss, Catherine	13	DE	36
Mary	40	PA	36
Peter	60	GE	36
Nevil, Mary	50	DE	341
Jane E	18	DE	181
Jonathan J	25	DE	181
New, Benjamin	28	DE	368
Elizabeth	7	DE	199
Potter	26	DE	173
Newbound, Ann	16	GB	266
Esther	43	GB	266
Joseph	50	GB	266
Moses	7	GB	266
Sarah	14	GB	266
Newel, Christina	53	PA	129
Lydia	1	DE	118
Margaretta	13	DE	129
Maria	23	DE	118
Mary	21	GB	104
Robert	17	DE	129
Samuel	24	DE	118
Stephen	57	MA	129
Newell, Clara	10	DE	43
Edward	9/12	DE	43
Edward	37	DE	43
Emma	8	DE	43
Margaret	28	DE	43
Newkirk, James	6	DE	272
James	52	NJ	275
Julia	16	DE	266
William	12	DE	259
Newlan, Margaret	25	DE	149
Newlands, Mary M	16	FL	283
Newlen, Alonso	3	DE	57
Arabella	5	DE	57
Charles	8	DE	57
Hannah	40	DE	57
Harriet	6	DE	57
James	10	DE	57
Mary	60	PA	88
Samuel	43	DE	57
Samuel	63	DE	88
Newlin, Edward	45	PA	359
Hannah J	7/12	DE	384
Henry	25	IE	300
Isaac	16	MD	359
James	20	PA	340
John	13	PA	359
Louisa	17	PA	364
Margaret A	10	MD	359
Maria E	2	DE	384
Martha	45	MD	359
Mary J	18	PA	359
Robert	21	PA	359
Thomas	21	PA	274
Thomas	23	IE	360
Newlove, Alfred	5	DE	151
Catherine	13	DE	151
Henry M	13	DE	311
John W	45	GB	311
Julia	50	GB	311
Sarah	3	DE	152
Solomon	11	DE	311
William	13	PA	151
William	16	DE	311
Newman, Anna N	65	NJ	114
Delilah	40	DE	219
Delilah	40	DE	242
Eliza	12	DE	173
Elizabeth	30	DE	173
Hannah	3	DE	324
J B	75	GB	114
Jane	36	DE	267
Joel G	39	MD	173
John	6	DE	173
John W	11	DE	235
Joseph	5	DE	324
Rachel	40	DE	324
Sally	12	DE	324
William	2	DE	324
William	17	DE	219
William	19	DE	242
Newsom, Elizabeth	12	DE	105
Emely	41	MD	96
Emily	1	DE	96
Joseph	43	DE	96
Rebecca	9	DE	96
Newton, Albert O	28	DE	256
Elizabeth	34	PA	384
Julia A	30	DE	256
William	25	PA	384
Newton, Wm H	10	DE	256
Nice, Theodore	25	PA	135
Nicholas, Christina	2	PA	66
Christina	28	GE	66
Ennes	1	DE	38
Hannah Jane	22	DE	350
James	17	DE	359
Jane	29	PA	38
John A	25	NY	66
Margaret	5	NY	66
Margaret	55	DE	29
Mary	7/12	DE	66
Seth H	29	PA	38
Susan	21	DE	350
Washington	7/12	DE	66
William	4	PA	38
Nichols, Amanda J	10	DE	359
Amos	4	DE	354
Cato	40	MD	350
Clarissa D	17	DE	359
Daniel	85	DE	354
Eli	42	DE	354
Ellis	50	DE	359
Ellis M	21	DE	359
Hannah	14	DE	362
Hannah J	22	DE	359
Joseph P	6	DE	354
Lydia	45	PA	359
Margaret	40	MD	350
Martha	6	DE	350
Mary	38	DE	354
Mary A	23	DE	359
Nelson	40	PA	319
Prudence A	18	PA	319
Ruth A	40	PA	319
Sarah A	36	PA	354
William W	5	DE	350
Nicholson, Anna M	9	DE	317
Eliza	5	IE	296
Elizabeth J	8/12	DE	118
Hannah	13	PA	350
Harriett	7	DE	313
Isaac J	26	PA	118
James	6	DE	317
James	35	DE	317
Jane	6	IE	296
John	1	DE	296
John	28	IE	296
Julius S	50	MD	118
Lambert	4	DE	317
Margaret	22	DE	118
Mary	26	DE	88
Michel	24	IE	44
Millason J	11	DE	317
Paulina	4	DE	328
Rachel C	1	DE	321
Rebecca	30	IE	296
Sarah	19	?	167
Sarah	40	DE	317
Sarah	48	DE	118
William	64	DE	328
William P	7	DE	328
Nickerson, Gabriel	40	DE	218
John	6	DE	218
Sarah	35	DE	218
Sarah E	3	DE	218
Nickle, Alfred	20	NJ	264
Ann	23	NJ	264
Catherine	9	DE	264
John	11	DE	264
John	52	NJ	264
Lewis	18	DE	264
Lydia	11	DE	264
Lydia	50	NJ	264
Martha	15	DE	264
Sarah	25	NJ	264
Nickles, Hetty	25	MD	326
Nickols, Amous B	18	PA	325
Cathrine	44	PA	325
David P S	16	PA	325
Elizabeth A	22	PA	325
Mary J	21	PA	325

Name	Age	State	Page
Nickols, Milton H	14	PA	325
Milton P	48	PA	325
Prudence A	7	PA	325
Rachel A	2	DE	325
Ruth A	11	PA	325
Nicols, Mary	10	DE	303
Nield, Nice	15	PA	166
Night, Abiga	31	PA	384
Abraham	70	PA	49
Lydia A	35	PA	384
Susannah	75	PA	49
William W	14	DE	396
Nile, William	30	GB	360
Niles, Mary	35	MD	31
Niven, Hannah	40	DE	144
Rebecca	22	DE	144
William	50	DE	144
Nivin, Amanda D	21	DE	303
David G	45	DE	303
Edward F	5	DE	303
Edwin M	37	DE	303
James M	8	DE	303
Julia	3	DE	303
Louisa	6	DE	303
Margaret	10	DE	296
Maria S	44	DE	303
Mary G	9	DE	393
Noble, Capt	24	PA	83
Lucy	6	DE	83
Luisa	3	DE	83
Mary	1	DE	83
Noblet, Alfred T	1	DE	160
Boyed	30	DE	168
Charles	15	DE	57
Dell	73	PA	55
Eliza	54	DE	55
James	8	DE	57
John	32	DE	160
John H	6	DE	160
Joseph C	15	DE	55
Mary	11	DE	57
Mary P	41	DE	57
Sarah	17	DE	57
Sarah H	31	DE	160
Tersa	70	DE	57
Noel, Sarah	50	DE	380
Sarah E	17	DE	380
Nokes, Mary A	17	DE	299
Susan	11	DE	288
Nolan, James	41	DE	219
Mary	41	DE	219
Mary R	7	DE	219
Samuel T	8/12	DE	219
Sarah	20	DE	232
Susan	13	PA	164
William	29	DE	232
William J	14	DE	219
Noland, Susana	48	NJ	48
Susanah	14	PA	48
Nolin, Andrew	37	IE	274
Nones, Albert	10	DE	71
Anna H	42	PA	71
H B (Capt)	46	PA	71
Henry B	19	PA	71
Jefferson H	25	PA	71
John	16	NY	71
Mary A	8	ME	71
Samuel	13	NY	71
Washington H	22	PA	71
Nonon, John	18	IE	283
Noon, Faddy	24	IE	326
John	3	AA	327
Martin	30	IE	326
Mary	25	IE	326
Mary	28	IE	326
Michael	1	DE	326
Thomas	1	DE	326
Noot, John	64	GB	97
Mary	70	GB	97
Norbert, James	21	IE	377
Norman, Nathaniel	4	DE	232
Norrett, Charles	4	PA	86
Norrett, Charles	4	PA	86
Eliza A	3/12	DE	86
Fredericka	41	GE	86
Harlen	47	DE	86
Mary	30	DE	34
Norris, Catharine	7	DE	339
Catharine	45	DE	338
George	20	DE	338
George	21	DE	339
Hetty	7	PA	225
James	2	DE	338
Maria	4	DE	338
Moses	18	DE	193
Samuel	11	DE	338
Sarah B	32	DE	284
William	22	DE	338
Norry, Moses	18	DE	194
North, James	46	MD	118
Lydia E	18	DE	118
Malvina	5	DE	118
Margaret M	7	DE	118
Mary	45	DE	118
Mary M	16	DE	118
Rachel A	11	DE	118
Norton, Elizabeth	40	NY	401
Isabella	3	VA	18
Jaban	35	MA	18
Lucinda	31	VA	18
Wm A	45	NY	401
Norvall, Susannah	41	DE	110
Nott, Eliza J	4/12	DE	105
James	6	PA	105
James	30	GB	105
John	6	PA	105
Mary A	4	PA	105
Mary J	30	MD	105
Nowlands, Mary M	16	DE	282
Nowman, Charles	39	DE	185
Noxon, Benjamin	40	DE	72
Elizabeth	10	MD	72
Francis	12	MD	72
Henry	15	MD	72
Sarah	38	MD	72
Nuce, Henry	24	GE	263
Mary	1	DE	263
Mary	23	DE	263
Nugent, Amanda	10	PA	1
Ann	30	PA	1
Charles E	5	PA	1
George W	3	PA	1
Henry	25	PA	324
Josephine	8	PA	1
Rachel	30	PA	40
William	30	PA	1
Numbrell, Margaret	22	MA	193
Nunn, Manual	2/12	DE	295
Margaret	10	DE	295
Nunsun, Susan	9	DE	342
Nunun, Jane	8	DE	321
Noah	17	DE	321
Nunvilla, Mary	65	DE	136
Nut, Elizabeth	39	PA	69
Levi	7	IL	69
Mary J	5	IL	69
Nutt, William	23	DE	28
Nutter, Elizabeth	10	ST	302
John	8	ST	302
Mary	5	DE	302
Mary	36	ST	302
Peter	52	ST	302
Nuttle, Anna	5	DE	372
Elizabeth	12	DE	372
Elizabeth	42	GB	372
Ellen	7	DE	372
Joseph	3	DE	372
Margaret J	10	DE	372
Mary Ann	17	PA	372
Susanna	10	DE	372
Thomas	44	GB	372
Oakes, Albin	30	DE	355
Joseph	36	PA	351
Oakes, Margaret	1	DE	355
Palmer	16	DE	354
Rebecca	26	MA	355
Winfield S	3	DE	355
Oakford, Henry	6	PA	17
Rachel	1	DE	29
Oakly, Gemima	25	GB	23
Robert	23	GB	23
Sarah	2	GB	23
Oats, Ann	35	IE	36
James	8	IE	36
Peter	40	IE	36
Ober, John	17	CT	188
Obkiel, John	25	MA	264
O'Brian, Alexander	17	PA	105
Ann	21	NY	24
Catherine	15	IE	7
Ellen O	23	IE	100
James	24	PA	105
Jane	10	IE	7
John	9	IE	7
Julia	12	IE	7
Michel	19	DE	143
Patric	40	IE	7
O'Brien, Catharine	13	PA	331
Catherine	25	IE	268
John	30	IE	268
Martha J	15	PA	331
Mary	39	IE	331
Terressa	12	PA	331
Obrine, Abbis	2	DE	317
O'Brine, Allace	17	IE	159
Catherine	18	DE	133
Catherine	20	IE	109
Catherine	38	IE	157
Ellen	16	IE	29
Ellen	16	IE	109
George	5	DE	157
Hugh	10/12	DE	157
Hugh	44	IE	157
Isabel	26	IE	317
James	31	IE	317
Margaret	8	DE	157
Mary	30	IE	109
Michel	14	DE	157
Rosanah	11	DE	157
Susan	8	DE	157
Susannah	4	PA	317
William	26	GB	110
Obryan, Bridgett	28	IE	325
Catherine	4	DE	325
Charles	4	DE	325
James	8	DE	325
Mary	6	DE	325
Mary	6	DE	325
Mary	28	IE	325
Ocheltree, Eliza	53	DE	149
Elizabeth	28	DE	355
Elizabeth	56	DE	347
John	56	DE	347
Joseph	2	DE	355
Margaret A	8/12	DE	355
Mary	51	DE	150
Mary	60	DE	355
Mary J	18	DE	347
Maxwell B	47	DE	355
Thomas M	35	DE	386
William	23	DE	347
Wm D	34	DE	281
Ochiltree, Caroline	13	DE	252
Eugene	10	DE	252
Fanny	15	DE	393
Frances	15	DE	252
James	8	DE	252
John	20	DE	251
Rebecca	45	DE	251
Robt	60	DE	251
Robt E	12	DE	252
Sarah	6	DE	252
O'Connel, Catharine	3	PA	277
Charles	10	PA	277
Daniel	9/12	PA	277

Name	Age	St	No	Name	Age	St	No	Name	Age	St	No
O'Connel, Jeremiah	46	IE	277	Ogle, Anna	5	DE	268	O'Maria, Mary	30	IE	162
Joanna	39	IE	277	Benjamin	5	DE	84	O'Melia, Joseph	24	IE	44
Margaret A	7	PA	277	Benjamin	40	DE	268	O'Meria, Archibald	11	NJ	49
Mary	13	IE	277	Benjamin G	31	DE	274	Eliza	45	NY	49
O'Connell, Anne	29	IE	301	Charlotte	58	DE	266	James	15	NY	49
James	25	IE	308	Charlotte P	13	DE	376	Onatta, Justo	14	CU	164
O'Conner, Catherine	6	DE	338	Clara	30	DE	268	O'Neal, Barney	21	IE	350
Edward	16	IE	338	Eliza	30	DE	269	Dennis	39	IE	379
James	14	IE	338	Eliza J	6	DE	269	Francis	40	IE	345
John	10	DE	338	Elizabeth	68	DE	379	Hilly	50	IE	109
Mary J	8	DE	338	Ella	7	DE	266	John	10	IE	15
Rosana A	35	IE	338	Ella W	9	DE	376	John	40	IE	347
O'Connor, Bridget	17	IE	342	Ellen A	21	DE	374	Mary	13	PA	379
O'Danial, Benjamin	40	DE	84	Hannah	90	DE	266	Nancy	33	IE	379
Elizabeth	2	DE	99	Howard	4	DE	376	O'Neil, Daniel	16	PA	339
Elizabeth	30	DE	99	Howard	60	DE	266	Edward	36	IE	267
Emma	4	DE	99	John N	32	DE	269	Eliza J	15	DE	323
Francis	11	DE	99	Joseph	12	DE	278	Elizabeth	12	PA	339
Isabella	16	DE	99	Joseph	47	DE	84	Elizabeth	42	IE	339
John	18	DE	99	Josephine	7	DE	268	Ellen	60	IE	267
Julia	4/12	DE	99	Julia E	3	DE	376	Felix	40	IE	267
Martha	38	PA	84	Laura G	10	DE	269	Frances	38	IE	267
Peter	22	IE	86	Lucinda	1	DE	268	Francis	28	IE	186
William	13	DE	99	Mary E	9/12	DE	374	Francis	50	IE	339
William F	42	DE	99	Mary F	10	DE	269	Isaac	18	DE	200
Odare, John	43	DE	399	Sarah	45	PA	84	John	25	IE	263
O'Donal, Mary	20	IE	220	Tabitha N	33	DE	376	John	30	IE	186
O'Donald, Anna	28	IE	5	Thomas M	39	DE	376	John	30	IE	267
Barny	25	IE	23	Ogram, Alice	42	GB	301	Margaret	30	IE	186
Catherine	17	IE	51	James	48	GB	301	Mary	25	IE	342
Catherine	30	IE	46	Joseph	5	DE	301	Mary	32	IE	267
Charles	15	PA	164	Mary	2	DE	301	Mary	47	DE	273
Charles	40	IE	51	Thomas	7	DE	301	Thomas	21	IE	198
Dominic	40	IE	46	O'Hair, John	23	IE	394	Thomas	30	DE	254
Ellen	39	IE	51	O'Hanlon, Catherine	11	IE	3	Ophir, Catherine	25	MD	177
Hannah	39	DE	100	Hannah	20	IE	3	Orange, Benjamin	45	MD	211
James	10/12	DE	46	Malichi	73	IE	3	Oren, Andrew J	22	DE	356
Jane	20	IE	99	O'Hannan, Catherine	25	IE	116	Jane	64	DE	356
Jane	25	IE	131	O'Kean, Michel	35	IE	80	Joseph A	25	DE	356
John	4	DE	46	O'Kieve, Mary	35	IE	43	Orick, Ellen	12	PA	328
John	12	IE	51	Richard	45	IE	43	John	10	PA	328
John	30	IE	122	O'Larry, Farian	17	MA	163	Julia	6	DE	328
John	45	IE	46	O'Laughlin, Bridget	22	IE	285	Margaret	16	CN	328
Julia	30	IE	42	Oldham, Charles	16	IE	314	Mary	8	PA	328
Mary	20	IE	131	Charles H	35	DE	375	Mary	40	IE	328
Mary	22	IE	53	Daniel J	53	NJ	326	Timothy	4	DE	328
Thomas	6	IE	51	Eliza	12	DE	324	Timothy	50	IE	328
William	6	DE	46	Isaac	40	MD	324	William	14	CN	328
O'Donall, Mary	50	IE	7	Joseph	21	DE	323	Oriel, Eliza J	15	DE	324
O'Donland, Charles C	15	IE	343	Laura C	20	DE	375	O'Riley, Daniel	22	IE	346
Hugh	19	IE	343	Mary A	57	DE	375	Patrick	20	IE	346
Jane	9	IE	343	Sally	30	DE	324	Oring, Perry	90	DE	168
Margaret	12	IE	343	Walter	13	IE	314	Oroak, Alace	45	IE	19
O'Donnal, Daniel	36	IE	335	William	22	DE	323	O'Roick, Patrick	25	IE	334
Mary A	4	DE	335	O'Leary, Mary	25	IE	318	O'Roke, James	25	IE	360
Patrick	13	IE	335	Oliver, Aaron P	50	PA	394	Joseph	18	IE	360
Rebecca	36	IE	335	Andrew J	23	GA	394	Oroson, Lydia A	4	DE	356
Sarah	9	DE	335	Anna J	20	SC	394	Lydia A	30	DE	356
O'Donnel, Hugh	20	IE	344	Balinda C	2	DE	394	Samuel	6	DE	356
James	27	IE	360	Hellen	18	IE	353	Theodore	5	DE	356
John	19	IE	346	James	7	PA	380	Washington	27	DE	356
O'Donnell, Charles	26	IE	291	Joseph	10	PA	380	Wilson	2	DE	356
James	8	DE	280	Joseph	15	PA	164	Orpwood, Ann E	22	PA	89
James	25	DE	309	Mary E	13	PA	394	Sarah	24	GB	89
John	5	DE	280	Thomas	42	DE	380	Thomas	30	GB	89
Patrick	36	IE	280	Verlinda W	46	VA	394	William H	9/12	DE	89
Susan	24	IE	280	Wilhelmina	50	PA	394	Orr, Amos J	31	PA	321
Thomas	2	DE	280	Olliver, Elizabeth	19	DE	65	Benjamin	4	PA	321
O'Donold, Patric	35	IE	5	O'Lorick, Patrick	25	IE	335	Caroline	28	GB	321
O'Flanagan, Biddy	30	IE	20	O'Mally, Anna	27	IE	340	Caroline E	13	DE	337
Ogden, Clara	3/12	DE	52	George	10	GB	340	Eliza	25	PA	331
Clarkson	24	NJ	160	Joseph A	25	IE	339	Elizabeth	19	DE	291
Debrah	18	NJ	123	Mary A	14	GB	339	Jane	24	DE	291
Edward	30	NJ	52	Mary A	45	IE	339	John	5	PA	321
Elizabeth	26	DE	52	Patric	52	IE	339	Joseph	65	IE	291
Elizabeth	60	NJ	123	Sarah E	52	GB	339	Margaret	22	DE	291
Ellen	14	PA	30	Wm A	6	DE	339	Robert	26	DE	291
Ellen	21	NJ	123	O'Maria	30	IE	162	Robt	37	IE	256
Martha	18	NJ	123	O'Melia, Joseph	24	Ie	44	Samuel	28	DE	291
Rebecca	35	NJ	123	O'Meria, Archibald	11	NJ	49	Sarah	50	PA	331
Robert	2	DE	52	Eliza	45	NY	49	Sarah E	7	MD	321
Ogdon, Henry	22	NJ	312	James	15	NY	49	Thomas	1	PA	321

Name	Age	St	Pg
Orr, William	20	DE	291
Orskins, Catherine	7	DE	354
Mary E	4	DE	354
Rachel	43	DE	354
Robert	30	DE	354
Robert P	5	DE	354
Sarah Jane	12	DE	354
Thomas	17	DE	354
Orsprang, Andrew	28	FR	24
Martha	28	DE	24
Ortason, Augustus	24	DE	236
Osborn, Albert	4	DE	184
Ama	20	IE	72
Andrew	12	IE	263
Ann	38	IE	361
Anna	8	DE	277
Eliza	10	IE	361
James	4	IE	361
James	5	?	270
James	45	IE	361
Jemima	5	DE	277
John	7	IE	361
John	22	IE	72
John W	30	MD	184
Margaret	2	DE	184
Margaret	15	?	270
Margaret	25	DE	184
Margaret	49	?	270
O'Thomas	47	?	270
Rebecca A	1	DE	361
Sarah	23	?	270
William	36	MD	277
Osborne, Aaron	53	NJ	129
Aaron P	18	PA	129
Anna M	4	PA	129
Caleb	10	PA	129
James	9	PA	129
Jonathan A	20	PA	129
Marian	16	PA	164
Mary	12	PA	129
Mary A	34	DE	277
Sarah	47	PA	129
Sarah E	15	PA	129
Theodore	2	DE	80
Thomas	25	IE	212
William	22	PA	129
William S	35	MD	80
Osgood, John	50	NJ	85
Mary	76	NJ	85
Rebecca	45	NJ	85
Oskins, John	35	DE	41
Osmund, Richard	22	GB	85
Osten, Catherine E	8	MD	141
Mary	33	MD	141
Mary C	5	MD	141
William	33	MD	141
Otdo, John	13	DE	131
John	39	GE	131
Mary	37	GE	131
Otheson, Catharine	45	DE	248
Elias	14	DE	248
Ellis	9	DE	248
Garret	53	MD	248
Samuel	25	MD	248
Otto, Eliza	47	DE	39
James	8	DE	87
James	28	DE	87
John	18	DE	381
Rose	25	DE	87
William H	13	DE	167
Ottwell, James	18	DE	213
William	21	DE	213
Overton, Charles	43	GB	333
Elizabeth	13	DE	333
George	8	DE	333
Isabella	16	PA	333
John	10	DE	333
Margaret	36	PA	333
Margaret E	3	DE	333
Mary A	4/12	DE	333
Owen, David	45	PA	346
Elizabeth	35	PA	346
Owen, Henry	13	PA	346
Salida	14	PA	346
Owens, Edward	6	DE	22
Edward	45	DE	22
Elizabeth	4	DE	22
Elizabeth	55	DE	122
Hannah	58	DE	285
Jonathan	11/12	DE	22
Margaret	3	DE	22
Mary	8	DE	22
Mary	11	DE	54
Rosanna	40	DE	22
William M	17	DE	123
Packard, Abraham	46	DE	234
Henry S	19	DE	234
Hugh	16	DE	234
Isabella J	1	DE	234
Margaret	13	DE	234
Mary E	28	DE	234
William	10	DE	234
Page, John H	8	DE	290
Mary E	35	DE	290
Mary	6	MS	290
Paice, John	13	DE	309
Pailin, Michael	20	IE	358
Painter, Alfred	26	PA	117
Charlotte	55	DE	276
Eliza	28	PA	30
Elizabeth	28	PA	93
George	17	GB	313
Hannah L	1	DE	117
James	15	DE	276
James G	25	GB	292
John	75	DE	93
Lewis	25	PA	93
Margaret	21	PA	30
Mary	5	DE	284
Mary	44	DE	289
Mary J	24	PA	117
Phebe	62	MD	30
Rebecca	65	DE	93
Thomas	20	GB	360
William	65	PA	30
Paldure, George	14	DE	355
Pall, Samuel	27	DE	295
Susan	25	DE	295
Paller, Wm	12	PA	319
Palmer, Abram	12	DE	356
Allison	26	DE	289
Anna	26	DE	298
Anna M	7/12	DE	298
Bartram J	8	DE	305
Catherine	7	PA	75
Charles	48	NY	32
David H	20	DE	294
Edward E	5	PA	75
Eliza A	15	DE	299
Elizabeth	47	PA	398
Elizabeth C	14	DE	305
Esther J	16	DE	305
George	23	DE	299
James P	10	DE	305
John	26	DE	305
John	27	DE	294
Lewis	20	DE	293
Linwood	2	PA	75
Lydia A	11/12	DE	294
Martha J	9	DE	294
Mary	50	DE	305
Mary G	1	DE	305
Mary W	22	PA	75
Moses	18	DE	305
Moses	63	DE	305
Rebecca	4	DE	294
Sarah A	13	DE	398
Sarah M	12	DE	305
Sarah P	25	PA	305
Susan	27	DE	294
William	18	DE	297
William W	53	PA	298
Pancost, Franklin	28	NJ	54
Paradise, Catherine	30	NY	38
Hannah	15	NJ	48
John	2	DE	38
Mariam	4	DE	38
Rachel	56	NJ	48
William	35	NJ	38
Parker, Andrew	16	IE	344
Ann	14	DE	133
Ann	51	NJ	338
Anna	18	IE	344
Anna	39	DE	74
Catharine	12	DE	337
Caleb	17	DE	400
Chloe	55	DE	299
Cornelia	2	DE	377
Daniel	45	DE	337
David	37	DE	74
Debby	37	PA	145
Eliza	23	DE	91
Eliza	38	DE	337
Eliza A	8	MD	304
Eliza J	4	DE	337
Elizabeth	13	DE	377
Elizabeth	70	PA	361
Ellen	70	DE	291
Eugene	6/12	DE	145
Frances	7	DE	377
George S	7/12	DE	299
Hanah	4	DE	377
Hannah	32	PA	361
Hannah	41	MD	377
Isaac	1	DE	145
Isaac	30	DE	299
Isaac	35	DE	145
Isabella	7	DE	145
Jacob	2	DE	337
James	9/12	DE	377
James	12	NJ	324
James	19	GB	2
James	25	DE	91
James	54	DE	376
James	72	NJ	291
Jane	3	DE	337
Jane	33	DE	324
Jane	42	IE	344
John	3	DE	91
John	38	PA	361
John H	68	CT	324
Joseph D	35	DE	246
Mary	15	DE	377
Mary	33	DE	246
Mary	57	DE	376
Mary A	7	DE	91
Mary A	14	DE	337
Mary A	24	PA	308
Mary E	2	DE	299
Mary L	1	DE	92
Matilda	4	AA	344
Michael	46	DE	377
Nancy	22	DE	367
Rachel A	5	DE	367
Rachel C	19	DE	193
Rosana	5	DE	91
Sally A	10	DE	337
Samuel	18	DE	299
Sarah	11	DE	377
Sarah	23	DE	299
Sarah	40	DE	98
Sarah E	6	DE	361
Sarah F	6	DE	246
Sarah Jane	14	IE	344
William	12	IE	344
William	26	GB	365
William	55	IE	344
William C	26	DE	193
Parkinson, Charlotte	4	GB	298
Ellen	30	DE	390
J Donlin	35	GB	298
Mary Ann	32	NS	298
Maude	2	PA	298
Richard	30	GB	390
Parks, Andrew	16	MD	72

Name	Age	State	Page	Name	Age	State	Page	Name	Age	State	Page
Parl, Bartholomew	3	PA	354	Patten, Charles	5	NJ	79	Peach, Phebe A	33	DE	302
Eliza	26	IE	353	David	44	DE	74	William	41	DE	302
Henry	4	IE	353	Edwin	2	DE	85	William Jr	12	AR	302
John A	--	DE	354	James	10	DE	85	Peaco, Deborah	24	DE	378
William	30	IE	353	John	13	DE	316	Grace J	6/12	DE	378
Parmer, Anna M	19	DE	278	Joseph	7	DE	85	James	32	DE	378
Charles	18	DE	278	Joseph	48	DE	30	Margaret A	3	DE	378
Charles	45	DE	278	Letitia	35	PA	85	Mary A	8	DE	378
Clement	8	DE	278	Levinia	12	DE	108	William	6	DE	378
Edward	4/12	DE	42	Mary	16	MD	74	Peakey, Amelia A	34	PA	121
Edward	35	PA	42	Mary	16	DE	85	Pearce, Ami	1	DE	39
Eliza A	47	DE	278	Peter	19	DE	367	Ann	20	DE	105
John	11	DE	278	Rosanah	40	DE	74	Anna	20	DE	52
Margaret	20	DE	216	Patterson, Amelia	20	DE	80	Anna M	10/12	DE	125
Margaret	30	IE	166	Deliverance	39	NJ	265	Anna R	6/12	DE	346
Mary	32	IE	42	Eliza	52	DE	158	Clara	4	DE	125
Robert	13	DE	278	Elizabeth	13	DE	309	David	5	DE	35
Simon	23	DE	216	Elizabeth	33	IE	379	David	13	CT	125
Thomas	2	DE	42	Elizabeth M	50	PA	80	David	60	DE	52
William	15	DE	278	Ellen	12	NJ	265	Edward	5	DE	346
Wilson	19	PA	144	Ellen	16	DE	80	Edward	17	DE	43
Parr, Jacob	12	DE	364	Ellen	60	DE	373	Elener	55	?	167
Joseph	21	DE	364	Fanny	39	DE	286	Elias	40	DE	133
Orpha	25	DE	364	George	1	DE	265	Eliza	21	DE	31
Parrish, Edward	4/12	DE	58	Henry	27	DE	80	Elizabeth	30	DE	52
James R	32	DE	58	Hester	49	IE	309	Elizabeth	33	PA	134
Mary A	21	DE	58	Hugh	19	DE	32	Ella	8/12	DE	35
Parry, Charles	8	GB	29	Hugh M	19	PA	309	Emeline	16	DE	377
Edwin	13	PA	350	John	3	IE	379	Empson	14	DE	377
Fanny	17	GB	29	John	5	DE	265	Empson	48	DE	377
Priscilla	37	GB	29	John	7	DE	276	Gemima	38	PA	16
Robert	10	GB	29	John	21	PA	309	George	34	DE	346
Robert	40	GB	29	John	22	MD	251	Hannah	60	DE	109
William	4	GB	29	John	22	DE	269	Hannah E	15	DE	109
Parsons, Ann E	39	PA	115	John	33	IE	379	Jacob E	1	DE	118
Charles	18	NJ	143	John	43	IE	309	James	12	DE	39
Edward Y	11	PA	115	John W	36	NY	265	Job	50	DE	117
John	62	GB	331	Joseph	11	PA	276	John	26	PA	39
Lewis	28	PA	115	Joseph	22	MD	342	John	35	DE	52
Mary	57	DE	331	Lewis	41	DE	286	John H	30	MD	327
Mary A	13	PA	115	Margaret	15	PA	265	June S	36	PA	133
Paryes, George W	4	DE	210	Mary	5	DE	265	Justinian	46	NY	125
Mary	40	DE	210	Mary	13	DE	309	Lydia Ann	17	PA	346
Pasant, William J	25	DE	316	Mary	35	IE	276	Margaret	24	DE	95
Paschall, Charles	7	PA	294	Mary J	9	DE	276	Margaret	51	PA	117
Henry H	33	PA	294	Matilda	10	DE	309	Margaret E	12	DE	118
Mary A	36	PA	294	R N (Rev)	55	PA	158	Martina	10	DE	39
Mary S	2	PA	294	Samuel	28	DE	80	Mary	28	PA	117
Samuel	8	PA	294	Sarah	8	IE	379	Mary	32	DE	52
Pass, Ervin	23	DE	361	Sarah	10	DE	265	Mary E	1	DE	377
Henry T	1	DE	361	Thomas	19	DE	80	Mary E	7	DE	346
Mary	28	DE	361	William	15	PA	189	Melissa	19	PA	16
Passmore, Mary	12	PA	39	William	17	PA	309	Ramond	35	DE	39
Sarah	50	DE	28	William	45	IE	32	Rayonon	4	DE	377
Passons, Absolem	4/12	DE	244	Patton, Absalom	50	DE	390	Rebecca	10	DE	377
Bashann	3	DE	244	Alfred	10	DE	154	Rebecca	20	DE	52
Jesse	45	DE	244	Catharine	15	DE	369	Rebecca	30	PA	346
Jesse E	5	DE	244	Jane	9	DE	238	Rebecca	48	DE	377
Susan	25	DE	244	John	10	DE	188	Robert	71	DE	109
Passwater, Caroline	3	DE	126	John	40	DE	182	Samuel	8	DE	125
Ebenezer	60	DE	171	Joshua	42	DE	211	Sarah	12	DE	160
Emilia	30	DE	205	Peter	67	DE	230	Sarah	27	PA	35
Isaac	35	DE	205	Samuel	35	DE	235	Sarah	35	DE	39
Margaret	22	DE	197	Sarah	55	DE	230	Stephen S	40	MD	16
Mary J	8	DE	205	Wm	24	DE	262	Susan	60	DE	31
Matilda	23	DE	126	Paul, Ann	50	DE	315	Thomas	20	DE	52
William	27	DE	126	Samuel	25	DE	315	Urana	39	CT	125
Patcher, John	58	PA	44	Susan	25	DE	315	William	11	CT	125
Mary	30	PA	44	Thomas	68	DE	197	William	29	NJ	35
Pate, Elizabeth	16	GE	114	Thomas	70	DE	252	William H	3	DE	117
Paten, Samuel M	11	DE	314	Pauline, Jacob	22	NJ	273	William H	28	DE	117
Thomas G	14	DE	314	Pauls, William	21	IE	2	Pearel, Mary A	23	DE	123
Patent, Mary J	23	DE	331	Paxen, Mary A	20	DE	48	Edward	29	DE	123
Paterson, C S	30	DC	160	Paxon, J Z G	12	PA	165	William S	5/12	DE	123
Edward	55	DE	323	Paydon, William	22	IE	347	Pearson, Alfred M	2	DE	71
Hellen L	25	NJ	142	Payson, James	15	DE	282	Anna Mary	53	DE	346
Jacob	21	DE	323	John	21	GB	306	Clara	2	NJ	85
John C	34	DE	142	Peach, Anna M	27	DE	302	Daniel	21	DE	147
William	40	DE	13	Jane	31	DE	302	Ethan	8	DE	346
Patten, Alexander	14	DE	85	John	78	GB	302	Frederick	29	DE	346
Alexander	40	PA	85	Mary	14	AR	307	George	6	DE	71
Anne	31	NJ	79	Mary	75	DE	302	George B	15	DE	347

Name	Age	St	Pg
Pearson, George W	23	DE	346
Henrietta	41	PA	85
Henry C	12	DE	118
Hyram	25	DE	346
Jacob	12	DE	346
Jacob	47	DE	118
John	16	DE	346
John	40	DE	76
John L	16	DE	71
Joseph	18	DE	71
Joseph	43	DE	71
Julia	9	DE	118
Leban	48	DE	347
Lidy	6	DE	347
Margaret	18	NJ	32
Margaret	40	NJ	32
Mariah J	17	DE	347
Martha	16	DE	347
Martha	42	DE	147
Mary	47	DE	115
Mary Ann	44	DE	347
Mary E	5	DE	347
Mary M	3	DE	346
Matilda	10	DE	347
Nelson G	13	DE	347
Newlan	5	DE	71
Olivia	38	NJ	71
Philip	6/12	DE	347
Raus	15	DE	347
Rebecca	18	DE	118
Rebecca	19	DE	115
Robert A	15	DE	118
Sarah	20	NJ	32
Sarah E	5	DE	347
Sarah E	20	DE	118
Sarah F	4/12	DE	147
Sarah J	21	DE	346
Susan	31	PA	76
Susanah	46	DE	118
Thomas	24	DE	147
Thomas	49	DE	347
William	8	PA	85
William	51	DE	115
William	56	DE	346
William H	12	DE	71
William J	40	NJ	85
William L	11	DE	346
Wilson	9	DE	115
Pechering, Alfred	4	DE	365
Enos	8	DE	365
George	15	DE	365
Harlen	7	DE	365
James	45	IE	365
Sarah	7	DE	365
Sarah	38	PA	365
Silas	17	DE	365
William H	2	DE	365
Peckard, Edwin	12	DE	273
Henry L	43	DE	273
Mary	35	DE	273
Susanna	8	DE	273
Pedric, Emma	8	DE	31
Hannah	6	DE	31
Hannah	41	NJ	31
Jane	4	DE	31
Joseph L	11	DE	31
Margaret	2	DE	31
Mark	42	NJ	31
Naomi	13	DE	31
Pedrick, Elizabeth	29	NJ	288
Isaac	9	PA	288
James	10/12	DE	288
Joel	37	NJ	288
William	3	DE	288
Peeke, Lewis	27	PA	291
Margaretta	4	DE	291
Sarah	26	DE	291
Peeney, Charles	8	DE	316
Elizabeth	22	DE	316
Joseph	29	DE	316
Joseph S	11/12	DE	316
William H	4	DE	316

Name	Age	St	Pg
Peery, Stacey	30	DE	201
Peirce, Rachel	17	DE	183
Pence, Jane	64	MD	322
Rufus	13	DE	205
Pendergrass, Ann	8	DE	42
Hannah	80	MD	41
James	28	NJ	42
John	10	DE	42
Rachel	27	PA	42
Penington, Charles	1	DE	213
Eliza M	60	DE	142
George W	16	DE	142
H B	73	MD	142
Hannah C	7/12	DE	143
Lariana	16	DE	213
Mary A	13	DE	212
Mary J	23	DE	142
Philis	35	DE	213
Thomas C	6	DE	142
W R	28	MD	142
William H	3	DE	142
Penix, Jacob	3	DE	368
John A	5	DE	368
Joseph	1	DE	368
Linch F	25	DE	368
Marian G	24	DE	368
Penn, Jane	64	DE	321
Penneck, Anna	28	PA	367
Mary E	3	PA	367
Purcy	26	PA	367
William A	1	PA	367
Pennell, Able	52	PA	299
Absalom	5	DE	303
Anna M	4/12	DE	282
Emma	4	DE	282
Harriet	36	DE	303
Jane	27	PA	282
John H	2	PA	282
John L	32	PA	282
Laban	46	MD	303
Levi	6	DE	303
Martha	13	DE	303
Nathan	8	DE	282
Nelia	1	DE	303
Richard	4	DE	303
William H	6	DE	282
Pennepacker, Anna M	5	DE	126
Ellen	28	PA	126
John	30	PA	126
Pennewell, Ann R	43	DE	94
Elihu J	15	DE	94
Harriet A	19	DE	94
John	45	DE	94
Mary J	16	DE	90
Penning, Sarah A	24	DE	135
Pennington, Abraham	6	DE	322
Abraham	40	MD	322
Agnes J	1	DE	178
Albert	31	OH	178
Alrich R	4	DE	298
Ann	39	DE	392
Ann	56	DE	355
Ann E	23	DE	299
Anna	8	DE	257
Anna R	8	DE	322
Asbury	59	MD	253
Asbury J	4	DE	179
Benjamin	21	DE	253
Cato	70	MD	193
Cato	17	DE	293
Charles	1	DE	212
Charles	5	DE	258
Charlotta	50	DE	40
Christina	18	PA	208
Clara	10	DE	253
Clarence	7	DE	177
Cora	5	DE	177
Edmond B	13	DE	381
Edward	42	DE	392
Elah	2	DE	257
Elijah	20	DE	207
Elijah	20	DE	257

Name	Age	St	Pg
Pennington, Elijah	20	DE	257
Eliza J	20	DE	89
Elizabeth	8	DE	173
Elizabeth	28	PA	178
Elizabeth	28	DE	257
Elizabeth	37	DE	322
Ella	8	DE	177
Ellen	42	PA	369
Fidus	57	DE	381
Frances A	2	DE	299
Frances E	5	DE	381
Franklin	2	DE	177
Franklin	4	DE	301
Fredy R A	2	DE	196
Henrietta	43	DE	301
Henry	18	IE	330
Hester	65	DE	226
Isaac	22	PA	280
Jacob A	39	DE	182
James	11	DE	258
James	15	DE	301
James	15	GB	360
James	40	DE	89
James F	56	MD	257
Jane	7	DE	253
Jane	16	DE	381
Jane	50	MD	193
Jane	59	DE	253
Jane A	23	DE	301
Jeffers	6	PA	369
John	1	DE	193
John	8	DE	392
John	13	PA	369
John	27	IE	330
Joseph	--	DE	272
Joseph	42	MD	338
Joseph R	7	DE	182
Kellte	17	DE	338
Lavinia	16	DE	212
Leonard A	31	DE	299
Louden M	27	DE	182
Louis	33	DE	196
Margaret	30	DE	257
Margaret	62	MD	342
Margaret J	11	DE	322
Maria	23	IE	330
Marion C	1	DE	299
Martha	3	DE	389
Martha	17	DE	257
Mary	7	DE	301
Mary	27	DE	177
Mary	27	DE	257
Mary A	29	DE	182
Mary E	6	DE	392
Mary E	9	PA	369
Mary H	12	DE	382
Mary L	4	DE	389
Nicholas	44	PA	369
Phillis	35	DE	212
Peter	3	DE	193
Richard	50	DE	354
Ruth E	27	DE	182
Sally	35	DE	173
Samuel	33	DE	177
Sarah	14	DE	258
Sarah	18	DE	381
Sarah	50	MD	258
Sarah E	10	DE	278
Susan	36	DE	389
Thomas	9	DE	338
Thomas	12	DE	332
Thomas	15	DE	244
Thomas	15	PA	369
Thomas	24	IE	330
Thomas M	46	DE	301
Vilet	39	MD	338
William	2/12	DE	280
William	30	DE	389
William D	11	DE	381
Pennock, Danna	28	PA	365
Hannah	22	PA	365
Jehu	30	PA	365

Name	Age	State	No.
Pennock, Pusey	26	PA	365
Penny, Ann	63	DE	315
Clara	6	NY	52
John	28	NY	52
Matilda	4	NY	52
Matilda	24	NY	52
Penock, William	73	PA	351
Peoples, Catherine	40	PA	40
Elizabeth	17	DE	40
Emma	5	DE	88
James	3	DE	345
James	13	DE	88
James	32	IE	345
Jane	10	DE	40
Jane	25	DE	347
John	12	DE	360
John	30	IE	347
Joseph	14	DE	360
Margery	18/12	DE	345
Martha	8	DE	88
Martha	27	IE	345
Mary	8	DE	360
Mary A	35	PA	88
Mary E	9	DE	88
Mary Elizabeth	7/12	DE	347
Robert M	5	DE	345
Samuel	3	DE	40
Sarah	30	IE	342
Thomas	10	DE	360
William	7	DE	40
William	35	IE	88
William	50	IE	40
Wm Henry	3	DE	347
Pepper, Edward	30	DE	262
Enoch	13	DE	216
Percell, William J	28	PA	55
Percival, David	47	PA	178
Elizabeth	46	PA	178
Peregrine, Anthony	53	MD	146
James	4	DE	92
James	28	MD	147
John	32	DE	92
Joseph	45	DE	35
Maria	30	DE	92
Mary	4/12	DE	92
Mary	10	MD	35
Mary	30	MD	35
Phebe	50	MD	146
Phebe A	3	MD	146
Perkins, Adaline	7	DE	130
Amor	5	DE	26
Armor	42	DE	290
Asbury	11	DE	26
Beckey	25	DE	92
Benj F	18	DE	290
Caleb	60	DE	140
Caleb	79	DE	289
Caroline	6	PA	331
Catherine A	12	DE	290
Christine	47	DE	89
Daniel B	32	DE	290
Edmond S	2	DE	290
Eliza J	3	DE	290
Emeline	13	DE	140
Emely	12	DE	140
Emma	3	DE	27
Esau S	16	DE	290
Franklin	17	DE	19
G W	29	DE	130
George B	6	DE	290
George W	13	DE	331
Georgianna	8/12	DE	140
Hannah	8	DE	130
Hannah	50	DE	92
Henrietta J	19	DE	290
Henry W	8	DE	140
Hester	42	PA	331
Isabella	3	DE	86
James B	20	DE	290
James M	8	DE	89
Job	9	PA	331
John	15	DE	26
Perkins, John	15	DE	26
John	45	PA	331
John	48	NJ	289
John	50	DE	26
John A	2	DE	331
John B	21	DE	289
Jonathan	3	DE	289
Joseph	13	DE	26
Joseph	69	DE	290
Julia A	7	DE	89
Julia A	38	DE	89
Kunhappeck	38	DE	289
Lena E	14	DE	289
Lucy A	4	DE	130
Lucy A	28	NJ	131
Lydia A	11	DE	289
Margaret	12	DE	89
Margaret M	27	DE	290
Maria	32	DE	92
Martha	10	DE	140
Martha	25	DE	86
Mary	1	DE	130
Mary	9	DE	27
Mary	26	PA	140
Mary	34	DE	140
Mary A	2	DE	140
Mary E	15	DE	276
Mary J	18	PA	331
Mary M	10	DE	290
Mele	3	DE	92
Merrit	5	DE	140
Rachel	33	DE	295
Rebecca	20	DE	57
Rebecca	40	PA	289
Rebecca	45	DE	290
Rebecca M	14	DE	290
Reece	37	PA	295
Robert	36	ME	86
Sarah	1	DE	27
Sarah A	19	DE	291
Sarah J	10	DE	289
Sarah S	11	DE	331
Sidney	41	PA	26
Simon	65	DE	92
Suel	30	DE	92
Thomas	47	DE	140
Pernal, Charles	14	PA	165
Samuel	12	DE	375
Sarah	35	DE	317
Perrett, Jane	37	NJ	132
Perry, Alice A	17	PA	128
Allice A	21	PA	315
Amanda E	16	DC	166
Ann	33	*E	347
Anthony	7	DE	315
Benjamin	15	DE	359
Bently	2	DE	315
Catharine	3	DE	347
Chas	6/12	DE	347
Christopher J	16	DE	213
Davis	5	DE	315
Enos	11/12	DE	152
Francis	37	DE	347
Francis T	12	DE	213
George B	11/12	DE	152
Harris	45	DE	97
Henry C	27	DE	152
Isaac A	13	MD	323
Isabella	30	PA	315
James	10	PA	182
James	13	IE	348
James C	33	PA	182
Janah V	14	MD	323
Jane	30	IE	142
John	50	NJ	323
John R	6	DE	323
Joseph E	34	PA	315
Malinda	27	PA	152
Margaret H	61	DE	297
Martha	18	VA	288
Mary	5/12	DE	162
Mary	50	DE	213
Perry, Mary E	7	DE	347
Mary E	14	DE	213
Mary H	50	IE	152
Rachel A	35	DE	323
Samuel	12	DE	299
Stacey	30	DE	200
Thomas	16	PA	358
William	24	DE	128
Pervis, Mary	19	IE	8
Robert	18	IE	89
Peter, Abraham	13	PA	278
Christiana	15	GE	278
Francis	10	NJ	278
Joseph H	3	DE	278
Lenna	38	GE	278
Margaret	6	DE	278
Martin	40	GE	278
Mary	8	NJ	278
Peters, Amelia	55	DE	384
Ann B	48	MD	386
Benjamin	20	PA	386
Benjamin	48	PA	386
Charles	32	DE	376
Charles H	7	DE	376
Henry W	22	PA	386
James	22	DE	384
John	16	PA	279
John F T W	13	DE	386
Rebecca	19	DE	348
Susan	28	DE	376
Peterson, Alexander	28	IE	28
Amelia B	29	NY	56
Ann	18	DE	99
Anna	1/12	NJ	250
Anthony	4	NJ	250
Betsey	40	DE	93
Betsey	51	DE	97
Catherine	34	DE	24
Catherine	35	DE	94
Clarissa	21	DE	15
Edward	8	DE	29
Elizabeth	18	DE	23
Elizabeth	40	DE	24
Emily	6	DE	18
Frances	18	DE	229
George	40	DE	94
George S	32	DE	56
Jane	4	DE	18
Jane	50	DE	211
Jarius	21	DE	97
John	3	DE	286
John	17	DE	97
John	26	DE	286
John	38	NJ	246
John	49	NJ	105
Joseph	44	?	283
Leah J	16	DE	94
Margaret	28	DE	24
Martha	9/12	DE	367
Martha	44	NJ	283
Mary	7	PA	283
Mary	25	DE	24
Mary E	1	DE	56
Mary J	22	NJ	250
Miles	1	DE	12
Phebe	14	DE	105
Phebe	52	PA	105
Rachel A	28	DE	94
Rebecca	30	DE	18
Samuel	40	DE	211
Sarah	5	NJ	250
Sarah	6	DE	286
Sarah	20	DE	367
Sarah E	11	DE	161
Silby	23	NJ	250
Susanah	16	DE	105
Teresa	30	DE	286
William	19	DE	23
Petit, Joseph	24	PA	275
William	48	NJ	294
Petitdemange, Ella	10	DE	311
Francis	14	DE	311

Name	Age	State	No.
Petitdemange, Francis	51	FR	311
John	22	DE	311
Julia	16	DE	311
Julia	51	GE	311
Louisa	12	DE	311
Mary	24	DE	311
Secilia	18	DE	311
Peugh, Richard	10	DE	170
Phalen, Elizabeth	29	MD	134
Patric	37	IE	134
Richard	--	DE	203
Phile, Andrew J	16	PA	288
Benj	14	PA	288
Elenor	9	PA	288
Jacob	48	PA	288
John	11	PA	288
Maria	49	NY	288
Mary	7	PA	288
Philips, Alexander	13	DE	341
Ann	35	GB	341
Benjamin	38	DE	215
Benjamin F	5	DE	215
Calvin	37	DE	366
Charles	38	GB	341
David	23	PA	307
Francis	31	AA	334
Jane V	30	PA	336
John	9	DE	215
John	40	DE	231
John H	42	DE	352
Joseph	13	DE	352
Lewis A	9	DE	352
Louisa	6/12	DE	215
Lucretia M	8	DE	366
Margaret	1	DE	334
Mary	5	DE	341
Mary	60	GB	334
Mary	66	DE	352
Mary A	29	DE	215
Mary L	8	DE	334
Rebecca	44	DE	352
Robert	7	DE	215
Samuel J	6	DE	366
Thomas M	10	DE	352
Winna	29	DE	334
Phillinger, William	10	DE	181
Phillipa, Albanas	25	NJ	289
Albina	63	PA	358
Albina G	25	DE	358
Amanda	8	DE	151
Ann	18	DE	76
Anna B	29	PA	358
Anna M	2	DE	275
Anna M	4	DE	160
Benj F	6	DE	275
Catherine	51	GB	145
Charles	34	PA	128
Edith G	16	DE	358
Edward	18	DE	134
Edward	19	DE	151
Eliza	24	DE	358
Elizabeth	1	DE	275
Elizabeth	2	DE	160
Elizabeth	25	NJ	289
Elizabeth	26	DE	160
Elizabeth R	19	DE	288
Ellen	2	DE	294
Evan	65	DE	358
Ewen W	9/12	DE	358
Frances	1	DE	297
George	4	DE	275
George	6	NJ	289
George W	34	DE	160
Hannah J	24	PA	366
Hannah W	49	DE	291
Harvey	40	DE	358
Henry	11	DE	151
Isaac D	33	DE	358
Isabella	31	DE	297
Isabella	60	PA	295
Jane	10	DE	275
John	8	DE	275
Phillips, John	14	DE	362
John	30	DE	275
John	50	DE	147
John	67	DE	358
John W	6	PA	128
Jonas	27	NJ	289
Jonas	52	DE	291
Josephine	6	DE	160
Lavinia	30	PA	280
Lewis	31	DE	294
Lucenia	16	PA	144
Lucretia	3/12	DE	362
Lydia J	4	DE	280
Margaret	8/12	DE	151
Margaret	2	DE	280
Margaret	32	DE	294
Margaret	48	NJ	289
Marshall	50	DE	54
Mary	13	DE	362
Mary	16	PA	310
Mary	31	DE	275
Mary	48	PA	54
Mary	48	DE	147
Mary A	27	PA	128
Peter	26	DE	297
Phebe	3	DE	358
Pussy	34	DE	356
Rebecca	17	DE	151
Richard	3	IE	207
Robert	11	DE	362
Samuel	4	DE	151
Samuel	23	DE	288
Sarah	7	DE	362
Sarah	30	IE	207
Sarah	36	PA	362
Sarah A	38	DE	151
Sarah J	21	DE	109
Susan	14	DE	288
Susan	16	DE	284
Susan	31	NJ	289
Thomas	30	DE	280
Thomas	35	DE	291
William	20	IE	72
William	33	NJ	289
William	45	DE	362
William D	80	DE	353
William G	30	DE	366
William H	8	DE	358
William S	2	PA	128
Pickels, Ann	19	GB	103
Elizabeth	6	GB	103
Henry	20	GB	103
James	35	GB	103
Mary E	8	GB	103
Sarah	17	GB	103
Sarah	36	GB	103
William	10	GB	103
Zachariah	14	GB	103
Pickering, Armenies	27	MD	127
Sarah	27	DE	127
Pickle, Christopher	14	GB	302
Pierce, Aaron	44	PA	287
Adaline	30	DE	240
Adam	56	DE	279
Alban M	3	DE	310
Albain	27	DE	279
Alexus du Pont	10	DE	279
Alfred	20	DE	291
Amos	18	PA	277
Ann	78	PA	295
Ann Eliza	33	DE	311
Benjamin	4	DE	276
Benjamin	12	DE	248
Benjamin	15	DE	247
Beulah J	6	DE	310
Brandling	26	PA	279
Catherine	8	DE	277
Catherine	59	DE	325
Catherine A	15	DE	275
Charles R	24	DE	281
Christiana	18	DE	325
Christiana	54	DE	310
Pierce, Clark	12	DE	279
Clementine	14	DE	277
Curtis H	12	DE	310
David	55	DE	349
Edgar C	18	DE	306
Edward C	4	DE	279
Elias	43	DE	275
Eliza	30	PA	276
Elizabeth	10	DE	352
Elizabeth	16	DE	277
Elizabeth	16	DE	311
Elizabeth	28	DE	286
Elizabeth	49	PA	287
Elizabeth	76	PA	352
Elizabeth H	34	PA	349
Ellen	32	MD	276
Elmira	20	DE	279
Emeline	4	DE	277
Emeline	11	PA	349
Emeline	28	DE	248
Enos W	9	DE	275
Erwin	14	DE	287
Ezra	7	DE	275
Frederic	14	DE	310
Frederic	48	DE	310
George	3	DE	276
George A	11	DE	275
Hannah	7	DE	352
Hannah A	21	DE	293
Harvey	17	DE	371
Henry	2	DE	203
Henry	15	DE	347
Henry	72	DE	275
Irwin	53	PA	310
Isaac	9	DE	276
Isaac	12	DE	352
Isaac	26	PA	349
Isaac	34	DE	276
Isaac C	3/12	DE	310
Isabella	1	DE	286
Isabella	37	DE	286
Jacob	40	DE	358
James	1	DE	276
James	5	DE	276
Jesse	48	DE	303
Jemima	7	DE	276
Joel	26	DE	196
John	12	PA	276
John T	8	DE	306
Joseph	40	PA	351
Joseph	53	DE	291
Joseph	61	DE	277
Joseph	66	DE	277
Joseph J	5	DE	286
Joseph M	14	DE	291
Joseph W	26	DE	276
Joshua H	30	MD	203
Julian	42	DE	371
Lena	23	DE	276
Lena	63	DE	276
Lennat	6	DE	279
Lethia	8	DE	279
Lewis V	10	DE	310
Lindsy	47	PA	306
Lindsy L	11	DE	306
Lydia	11	DE	276
Lydia	19	DE	276
Lydia E	3	DE	281
Maranda	1	PA	276
Margaret	9	DE	276
Margaret B	4	DE	352
Marietta	28	MD	203
Marshal B	14	DE	352
Martha M	8	DE	310
Mary	6	DE	277
Mary	18	DE	306
Mary	38	MD	277
Mary	46	DE	306
Mary	60	DE	240
Mary	60	DE	276
Mary	62	DE	286
Mary A	24	DE	295

Name	Age	State	Page
Pierce, Mary E	4	DE	286
Mary E	7	DE	276
Mary E	9	DE	248
Mary J	4	DE	275
Matilda	5	DE	279
Nero	65	DE	240
Noah	19	DE	248
Noah	20	DE	248
Orpha	25	DE	365
Peter	19	DE	273
Phillip	35	DE	286
Priscilla	35	PA	352
Quizah	13	DE	275
Quizah	52	DE	279
Rachel	6	DE	276
Rachel	10	DE	248
Rachel	67	DE	277
Ralph M	17	DE	276
Rebecca	14	PA	349
Robert	2	DE	277
Sarah	17	DE	287
Sarah	25	DE	196
Sarah	41	DE	291
Sarah	45	DE	295
Sarah A	26	DE	279
Sarah A	41	DE	275
Sarah J	16	DE	295
Sarah M	1	DE	275
Stephen	18	DE	279
Susan	19	DE	315
Thomas	5	PA	349
Thomas	45	DE	371
Thomas E	22	DE	276
Tiriza C	1	DE	281
Uriel	42	DE	279
Uriel T	1	DE	279
Walter	8/12	DE	196
Walter	32	DE	282
William	8	PA	349
William	15	DE	371
William	20	DE	277
William	41	PA	349
William H	8	DE	248
William H	11	DE	291
William T	25	DE	315
Pierson, Ann	19	MD	195
Edmond	31	DE	310
Emmet	42	PA	354
Isabella	2	DE	310
James	5	DE	310
Louisa	8	DE	310
Mary A	1	DE	310
Mary A	28	DE	310
Richard	7	DE	310
Richard	30	DE	256
Susan H	32	PA	354
Pigget, John	24	PA	39
Pile, Mary E	18	PA	154
Pilling, Ann	16	GB	390
Elizabeth A	6	DE	390
John	20	GB	390
Richard	40	GB	390
Susan	40	GB	390
Thomas	14	GB	390
Pine, Abraham J	2/12	PA	342
Alace	5	NJ	62
Ann	33	NJ	62
Luisa	15	NJ	62
Mary	3	NJ	62
Samuel	25	PA	135
W S	38	NJ	62
William	7	NJ	62
William	23	DE	342
Piner, Ambrose	19	DE	176
Ambrose	21	DE	179
Anne	58	MD	176
Catherine	17	DE	176
William	50	DE	176
Pinkerton, David	42	PA	158
Emma	9	DE	158
Franklin	1	DE	158
John	7	DE	158

Name	Age	State	Page
Pinkerton, John	20	MD	338
Mary A	27	NJ	338
Mary E	6/12	NJ	338
Mathew	28	DE	338
Phebe	36	NJ	158
Rebecca	14	PA	158
Sarah A	4	NJ	338
William	11	DE	158
Pinket, Elias	1	DE	243
Harriet	27	DE	243
Moses	35	MD	1
Pinkson, Benjamin F	1	DE	191
Hannah	28	DE	183
James	32	DE	183
Lucinda	4	DE	183
M L R	30	DE	191
Margaret	30	DE	191
Rhoda	6/12	DE	183
Pinkston, John	30	DE	322
Pinnock, Alpheus	1	DE	380
Filena	3	DE	380
Lewis	45	PA	380
Sarah	32	DE	380
Pinny, Alfred	11	DE	70
Piolin, Gerard	14	DE	312
Piper, Anna J	11	PA	55
G (Dr)	37	PA	55
Hannah	52	DE	289
Sarah	22	DE	4
William	25	NJ	4
William	57	NJ	289
Pipes, Frederic	36	DE	45
Mary	15	DE	130
Pipin, Matilda	16	DE	56
Pitman, J R	14	MD	164
Pitnal, Pauling	12	?	165
Pitner, Debro	60	PA	21
Debro L	21	DE	21
Eliza	48	PA	21
Pitt, Elizabeth	65	GB	6
Elizabeth J	60	GB	102
Emma	23	DE	99
Thomas	17	GB	24
Pittman, Helen E	3	DE	174
Jane	30	DE	174
John D	30	NJ	174
Plank, Charles A	12	DE	286
George E	4	DE	286
James B	2	DE	286
Margaret A	7	DE	286
Maria	45	DE	286
Mary E	15	DE	286
Sebastin	42	GE	286
William H	9	DE	286
Plant, Eli	16	DE	296
John	23	DE	296
William	16	DE	374
Plater, Richard	50	MD	204
Platt, Alexander F	23	DE	287
Alfred	5	DE	321
Ann H	49	DE	287
Catharine	1	DE	307
Catharine	31	DE	307
Catharine G	17	DE	287
Charles	5	DE	321
Charles	10	DE	107
Clayton	33	DE	307
Elisha	32	NJ	107
Elizabeth	16	DE	321
Elizabeth F	21	PA	287
Emma	4	DE	307
Franklin	13	DE	321
George	63	DE	287
Hannah	38	NJ	107
Hugh E	25	DE	287
James	4	DE	107
Jane	60	IE	64
Jane	70	DE	361
John	9	DE	307
John	9	DE	321
John	48	DE	321
John F	21	DE	287

Name	Age	State	Page
Platt, Joseph	44	GB	149
Joshua	16	DE	30
Levina	18	DE	321
Mahala	27	MD	149
Mary	6	DE	307
Mary	48	GB	321
Mary	70	NJ	112
Mary E	2	DE	107
Mary E	15	DE	287
Samuel	2	DE	107
Samuel	11	DE	307
Samuel	27	DE	287
Susan	15	DE	321
William	58	IE	64
Plumbly, Elizabeth	10	DE	52
George	7	DE	52
Ruth A	8	DE	52
Sarah	31	DE	52
Thomas	3/12	DE	52
Thomas	37	DE	52
Plummer, Amos	18	DE	256
Thomas F	13	MD	132
Plunket, Anne	6	DE	40
Ellen	9	DE	2
Frances	3	DE	40
George	14	DE	40
George	27	IE	17
Hugh F	5	DE	2
James	7	DE	2
James	13	DE	40
James	25	VA	163
James	38	IE	40
John	4/12	DE	40
Joseph	46	IE	167
Lydia	34	PA	2
Margaret R	1	DE	2
Mary	4	DE	2
Mary	11	DE	40
Phillip	6	DE	2
Phillip	34	IE	2
Susan	38	IE	40
William	7	DE	40
Pogue, Alfred	9/12	DE	199
Ann	60	DE	358
David	24	DE	7
Ellen	25	DE	199
Francis	2	DE	199
George	65	DE	358
James	6	DE	147
James	7	DE	199
James	30	DE	199
Mary	8	DE	147
Patrick	24	IE	347
Poinset, Asa	50	NJ	117
Catherine D	26	DE	117
Charles W	7	DE	117
Eliza	48	DE	117
Rachel M	18	DE	117
Stephen	55	DE	117
Poinsett, Asia	32	DE	109
Elizabeth	32	DE	109
John	23	DE	304
William Mc	3	DE	109
Point, Anna M	32	DE	281
Benjamin	44	PA	279
Edward W	11	DE	281
Francis	2	DE	281
Hannah	41	PA	279
John	34	PA	281
John T	7	DE	281
Virginia	4	DE	281
William	9	DE	281
Pointer, Comfort	45	DE	295
Pole, Morris	6	DE	357
Poles, Emma	14	DE	347
Polk, Abraham	26	DE	288
Abraham	27	DE	74
Amelia	--	DE	194
Anna	17	DE	266
Anne	23	DE	74
Caroline	15	DE	89
Charles	15	DE	173

Name	Age	State	Page
Polk, Charles	65	DE	56
Cyrus	40	DE	173
David	10	DE	89
Dinah	70	DE	173
Elizabeth	2	DE	266
Henry	6	DE	266
Isabella	44	DE	376
James H	5	KY	286
John	4	DE	266
Joseph	12	DE	89
Juliet	--	DE	174
Margaret	--	DE	174
Margaret	31	DE	266
Martha	70	MD	69
Mary J	36	DE	173
Matilda	17	DE	89
Matilda	45	DE	185
Robert	8	DE	89
Robert	25	DE	361
Robt	12	DE	266
Robt	51	DE	266
Sarah A	38	IE	89
William	--	DE	174
William	16	DE	173
William	19	DE	218
William	25	DE	244
William	64	IE	89
William F	14	DE	400
Polkerson, Mary	30	DE	245
Pollock, Robert	21	IE	343
Polock, Absolem	37	DE	64
Marina	3	DE	64
Mary	4	DE	64
Melinda	29	DE	64
Polson, John	10	DE	155
Leah	19	DE	61
Sarah	36	DE	155
Ponger, Benjamin	2/12	DE	298
Charlotte	5	DE	298
Elizabeth	24	DE	298
John	25	DE	212
Margaret	9	DE	298
William	26	DE	298
Ponso, Cynthia	6	DE	173
Eben	35	DE	219
Eliza	5	DE	173
Ellen	75	DE	219
Hannah	14	DE	219
Jerry	26	DE	219
John	28	DE	173
Mary	10	DE	219
Mary	28	DE	173
Pont, James	48	GB	200
James T	14	DE	200
Rachel S	15	DE	200
Sarah A	18	DE	200
Susan	66	NJ	200
Ponzer, Elizabeth	8	DE	243
Elizabeth	35	DE	242
Hannah	9	DE	243
Isaac	35	DE	242
Mary	14	DE	243
Polly	12	DE	243
Sally	7	DE	243
Ponzo, Ebenezer	30	DE	221
Edward	4	DE	221
Ellen	70	DE	223
Jane	65	DE	221
Jerry	25	DE	232
Mary	7	DE	232
Richard	65	DE	221
Pool, Adeline	18	DE	337
Alfred	30	DE	365
Elizabeth	23	DE	345
Elizabeth	64	PA	282
Emily	22	PA	282
Hammet	24	DE	365
Henrietta	2	DE	365
Joseph	26	PA	345
Lewis	25	PA	282
Mary Ann	47	DE	345
Milliard F	1	PA	279
Pool, Phebe A	8	PA	279
Rachel	20	DE	345
Richard	35	PA	279
Robert	50	PA	345
Sarah	36	PA	279
Thomas	18	DE	345
William	13	PA	345
William H	5	PA	279
Poole, Alfred D	2	DE	4
Ann	22	PA	4
Elizabeth	6	DE	46
J Marton	36	DE	4
Jane T	5	PA	137
John S	9	DE	4
Julia	13	PA	56
Mary	10	DE	112
Mira	43	NJ	138
Samuel S	53	DE	138
Sarah	7	DE	112
Sarah	53	DE	110
Thomas	7	DE	4
William	19	DE	110
Popper, Elizabeth	15	DE	237
Porter, Abel J	36	DE	247
Alexander	52	DE	191
Alexander	65	DE	30
Alfred	22	DE	282
Amelia	45	DE	59
Anna	9	DE	53
Anna	14	DE	300
Anna	33	MD	303
Catherine	25	IE	78
Charles	42	MD	303
Charlotte	48	PA	2
David	4	DE	136
Elias	1	DE	318
Eliza	2	DE	136
Eliza	35	DE	136
Eliza	46	MD	382
Elizabeth	14	MD	2
Elizabeth	14	MD	303
Elizabeth D	33	DE	138
Elizabeth J	11	DE	367
Ellen	7	DE	53
Emely	50	MD	30
Emma M	3	DE	247
George	8	MD	397
George	17	DE	193
George W	7	MD	191
Hannah	25	DE	31
Hannah	45	DE	191
Harriet C	8	DE	112
Henry	34	DE	300
Henry G	3	DE	53
Isaac	16	DE	208
Isabella	4	DE	300
James	6	DE	136
James	22	DE	367
James T	5	MD	191
Jane	79	DE	375
Jane B	5	DE	112
Jehew	20	PA	367
Jenny	4	DE	191
Jesse	14	DE	204
Jesse	40	DE	318
Joel	9	DE	2
Joel	44	DE	2
John	3	DE	367
John	8	DE	136
John	12	OH	2
John	44	MD	367
John B	13	DE	53
John B	42	DE	53
John T	4/12	DE	247
John W	9/12	DE	303
Joshua	17	DE	191
Junia	2	DE	112
Lewis	5	DE	318
Lewis	19	DE	293
Lewis	23	DE	381
Lorenzo	8	DE	318
Lucinda H	9	DE	112
Porter, Lucinda H	40	DE	112
Lydia	4	DE	367
Lydia A	9	DE	247
Margaret	1	DE	300
Margaret	57	PA	287
Mary	25	DE	324
Mary	34	IE	300
Mary A	15	PA	367
Mary J	7	DE	3
Mary R	15	DE	53
Nathan G	13	DE	191
Peter B	5	DE	138
Priscilla	46	DE	318
R R (Dr)	38	DE	112
Robert	11	DE	53
Robert	28	IE	78
Robert	35	DE	38
Samuel	3	DE	303
Samuel	9	DE	300
Samuel	14	DE	317
Samuel	17	DE	378
Samuel M	11	DE	315
Sarah	26	DE	247
Sarah A	40	PA	367
Sarah E	7	DE	300
Sidney S	10	DE	300
Solomon	16	DE	373
Sophia	15	DE	191
Susannah	37	DE	53
Thomas	7	DE	138
Thomas	35	DE	136
Thomas	38	PA	250
Thomas G	14	DE	315
Thomas K	5	DE	53
William	9	MD	294
William	35	IE	300
William G	19	DE	369
William T	21	SC	4
Posit, James	48	DE	199
James T	14	DE	199
Rachel S	15	DE	199
Sarah A	11	DE	199
Susan	55	DE	199
Post, Emma	16	DE	377
Levi	60	DE	377
Mary	55	DE	377
Zadoc A	16	DE	181
Postle, Richard	50	NJ	266
Postles, Amy	44	DE	276
Isaac	45	DE	276
Paul	25	DE	295
Potter, Benjamin	18	VA	401
Charles	13	DE	383
Edward	2	DE	105
Eliza	33	DE	46
Eliza	40	DE	105
Ellis	7	DE	387
James	28	DE	46
James	40	DE	387
John	15	DE	387
Mary	40	DE	387
Mary E	10	DE	387
Ruth A	5	DE	131
Stephen	35	CT	175
Susan	10	DE	307
Thomas	13	DE	307
William	11	DE	304
Potts, Mary E	23	PA	289
Nathaniel	61	NJ	289
Sophia	55	PA	289
Stephen	20	PA	84
Susan	21	PA	289
Poulson, Abraham	46	DE	373
Mary	40	DE	366
Pound, Joseph	21	DE	365
Powel, Alfred	18	DE	69
Alfred	19	DE	59
Ann J	38	DE	142
George	40	DE	142
Rosanna	16	DE	59
Rosanna	50	DE	59
Thomas	22	DE	59

Name	Age	St	No.
Powell, James	16	DE	219
James	16	GB	334
John	47	DE	218
Joseph	78	PA	210
Joseph W	21	GB	334
Margaret	42	DE	218
Mary	51	GB	334
Mary E	14	DE	218
Michael	60	IE	252
Robert	16	DE	218
Samuel	14	GB	334
Sarah H	20	GB	334
Thomas	16	DE	218
William G	51	GB	334
Power, Ann T	3	DE	360
James	42	DE	234
James Jr	6	DE	234
John	3	IE	234
John	30	IE	360
Margaret B	5	DE	360
Martin	18/12	DE	360
Sophia	29	DE	360
Powers, Catherine	14	PA	265
Edward	7	DE	265
Edward	40	IE	265
John	12	IE	265
John	45	GB	224
Mary	36	IE	265
Richard	9	DE	265
Robert	22	IE	250
Pratt, Darwin	21	PA	27
Eliza	37	DE	219
Henry	28	NJ	368
Henry	39	DE	218
Henry	54	DE	336
Henry Jr	16	DE	218
Hester	56	DE	336
John	12	DE	218
Maria	8	DE	336
Sarah	25	DE	368
Susan	13	DE	218
Thomas	9	DE	218
Press, Anna M	13	DE	76
Hugh	55	IE	76
Jane	52	IE	76
Sarah J	20	DE	76
Preston, Isaac	22	DE	119
Elizabeth A	15	VA	165
Prettyman, Alphonso W	8	DE	208
Charlotta S	30	DE	166
Frances W H	3	DE	208
George P	5	DE	208
George W	29	DE	208
L (Rev)	51	DE	165
Maria C	1	DE	208
Maria H	20	DE	208
Mary S	34	PA	165
Sally E	18	DE	166
William B	6	DE	208
Pretzschiner, Henry	29	GE	43
Margaret	27	NJ	43
Price, Aaron	41	DE	377
Abraham	50	MD	197
Adaline	2	DE	182
Adaline	2	DE	364
Adaline	6	DE	93
Adam	24	DE	211
Agness C	15	DE	76
Alfred S	3	DE	220
Alice	8	DE	364
Ameliz J	8	DE	220
Andrew	9	DE	220
Andrew	37	DE	341
Ann E	15	DE	220
Ann M	29	DE	236
Anna M	6	DE	325
Anne G	16	DE	9
Benjamin	23	PA	82
Betsey	39	DE	185
Caleb N	10	DE	320
Camelia	2	DE	9
Catharine	17	DE	327
Price, Catherine	40	GB	283
Catherine G	6	DE	9
Catherine G	40	DE	9
Chandler P	4	MD	362
Chas	13	DE	291
Clara M	16	DE	220
Cornelia	7	DE	9
Cornelia C	14	DE	320
Danial	25	NJ	143
Daniel	26	NJ	24
David	4	DE	364
David	25	PA	337
David	39	DE	363
Dorcus	60	DE	319
Edgar	13	DE	182
Edward	37	DE	220
Edward H	30	GB	324
Edward T	8	DE	10
Eliza	30	IE	41
Eliza	30	DE	220
Eliza	30	DE	284
Eliza A	10	DE	327
Eliza J	11	DE	325
Elizabeth	4	DE	265
Elizabeth	15	DE	327
Elizabeth	17	DE	341
Elizabeth	28	MD	220
Elizabeth	31	DE	136
Elizabeth M	38	DE	228
Elmer	20	NJ	250
Emily	9	DE	265
Emily	14	DE	363
Emma	15	DE	291
Emma	21	PA	299
Emma A	13	DE	211
Esther	49	DE	360
Fanny	60	MD	325
Frances	11	DE	265
Frances	45	DE	265
Frances A	10	DE	220
George	14	DE	185
Hannah	4	MD	325
Hannah A	14	DE	325
Hannah F	4	PA	337
Harriet	20	MD	319
Harriston	7	DE	291
Harriet	33	DE	191
Harry	17	DE	185
Henry	13	DE	10
Henry C	5	NJ	62
Henry R	19	DE	182
Hester	31	DE	31
Hester	31	DE	192
Housten	6	DE	220
Hyland	24	MD	362
Hyland	28	MD	399
Isaac	28	PA	43
Isaac	33	DE	24
Isaac	36	MD	236
James	10/12	DE	136
James	1	DE	24
James	12	DE	363
James	17	DE	9
James	26	DE	299
James	43	DE	211
James E	41	DE	9
James H	15	MD	362
James H	44	MD	362
James W	2/12	DE	291
Jane	40	PA	363
Jane	43	DE	342
Jane V	36	DE	265
Jeremiah	33	MD	319
Jerry	30	DE	93
Jno W	52	DE	291
John	2	DE	265
John	4	MD	325
John	8	DE	31
John	16	DE	343
John	32	DE	136
John	46	DE	342
John B	42	MD	319
Price, John C	40	DE	31
John H	18	IE	9
John H	46	DE	76
John L	1	DE	192
John L	23	DE	117
John S	12	DE	320
John S	66	DE	182
John T	8	DE	182
Joseph	8	DE	325
Joseph	15	IE	9
Joseph	18	DE	269
Joseph	20	DE	191
Joseph	80	MD	327
Joseph H	12	DE	220
Joseph T	45	DE	9
Julia	5	DE	291
Kennard	35	DE	220
Kent	17	MD	362
Lawrence	64	MD	319
Leah A	27	MD	362
Levina	2	DE	324
Lucinda	6	DE	31
Lucinda W	39	DE	211
Luke C	42	NJ	62
Lydia H	23	PA	43
Marcellus	37	MD	325
Margaret	9/12	DE	324
Margaret	5	DE	327
Margaret	8	DE	284
Margaret	14	DE	9
Margaret	17	DE	265
Margaret	19	DE	9
Margaret	27	DE	377
Margaret	50	DE	197
Margaretta	43	PA	76
Martha	20	DE	24
Martha	31	DE	341
Martha J	36	DE	182
Mary	3/12	DE	82
Mary	6	DE	364
Mary	10	DE	9
Mary	10	DE	316
Mary	25	PA	312
Mary	56	DE	86
Mary A	3	DE	291
Mary A	5	DE	377
Mary A	11	DE	320
Mary A	22	DE	82
Mary A	30	PA	324
Mary A	31	DE	319
Mary A	36	PA	325
Mary E	5	DE	220
Mary E	7	DE	220
Mary E	20	DE	272
Mary F	1	MD	325
Mary J	18	DE	86
Mary J	25	DE	220
Mary J	30	DE	313
Mary R	9/12	DE	362
Matilda	11	DE	9
Matilda	40	PA	9
Millicent	10	DE	188
Nicholas	13	DE	265
Noah	12	DE	31
Perry	18	DE	220
Priscilla	80	DE	220
Rachel	17	DE	182
Rebecca	10	NJ	62
Rebecca	13	DE	220
Rebecca	19	DE	318
Robert	4	DE	327
Robert	56	DE	327
Samuel C	34	PA	324
Samuel S	34	DE	191
Sarah	2	DE	291
Sarah	6	DE	328
Sarah	28	DE	93
Sarah	41	DE	291
Sarah	50	DE	19
Sarah A	24	PA	81
Sarah A	10	DE	363
Sarah A	42	DE	228

Name	Age	State	Page
Price, Sarah H	3	DE	43
Sidney	6/12	DE	9
Sophia	21	DE	9
Suella H	12	MD	362
Susan	26	NJ	324
Susan	55	DE	182
Susanah	35	NJ	62
Susanna	20	DE	343
Theodore	16	DE	164
Theodore D	17	DE	211
Thomas	30	DE	313
Thomas C	41	DE	182
Thomas L	8	DE	320
Thomas T	35	DE	312
Virginia	9	DE	9
Washington R	3	DE	377
Wesley	28	DE	323
William	35	DE	380
William A	10	DE	182
William F	3	dE	192
William G	12	DE	9
Wm H	6	DE	324
Wm W	1	DE	324
Prichard, George	25	DE	379
John	50	DE	369
Joseph	93	DE	379
Mary	57	DE	379
Pricket, Abraham	30	NJ	246
Primrose, Caroline	45	MD	238
John	19	DE	229
Robert	14	DE	222
Prince, Adam	53	DE	282
Charlotte	38	DE	282
Eliza	45	PA	284
John M C	15	DE	282
Sarah	5	DE	282
Pring, Adolph	40	DE	81
Pringle, Alexander	60	DE	133
Elizabeth	54	PA	319
Emma	9	DE	319
Margaret	14	DE	133
Mary A	30	DE	133
Prior, Ann	30	DE	224
Anna	7	DE	285
James	5	DE	230
James	14	DE	229
James	28	DE	224
John	30	DE	224
Martha A	1	DE	224
Sarah E	3	DE	285
Pritchard, Abigail	13	DE	391
Acquila	35	MD	62
Allen	1	DE	395
Elizabeth	16	MD	83
Elizabeth	45	MD	83
Harriet	38	DE	62
Israel	30	DE	395
Jane	29	DE	395
Jane	42	PA	391
John F	5/12	DE	168
Joseph	9	DE	395
Joseph	41	DE	391
Joseph P	4	DE	391
Maria	25	IE	167
Margaret	2	DE	391
Margaret	22	MD	62
Mary E	14	DE	391
Rachel	18	MD	62
Sarah	4	DE	395
Susan A	5	DE	395
Thomas C	35	MD	83
Pritchet, Elizabeth A	1	DE	334
John	28	DE	334
Mary	27	IE	334
Sarah A	32	DE	334
Proctor, Alonzo	1	DE	92
Ann	24	DE	92
James	25	DE	92
Provost, Ann	48	DE	306
Benj	23	DE	306
Edmond	15	DE	306
Lewis H	12	DE	306
Provost, Sarah	14	DE	306
William	53	DE	306
Pryer, Eliza	39	DE	89
Eubus	38	MD	89
Mary J	14	MD	89
Rachel E	11	DE	89
Puff, Catherine	12	PA	77
Jacob	5	PA	77
John	19	PA	77
Joseph	10	PA	77
Joseph	43	PA	77
Margaret	9	PA	77
Mary	33	PA	77
Mary J	10/12	PA	77
Sarah	7	PA	77
Washington	15	PA	77
Puge, Wm	28	DE	325
Pugh, Alexander	40	DE	306
Andrew	35	MD	339
Ann	28	IE	377
Ann E	12	DE	66
Eliza	34	PA	18
Elizabeth	9	DE	18
Elizabeth	34	GD	339
Elizabeth	36	DE	306
Elizabeth J	33	DE	23
Francis	7	MD	377
George	5	DE	23
James	34	DE	306
James E	27	DE	377
James P	10	DE	306
Joanna	12	DE	18
John	34	DE	297
John T	9	DE	306
Joseph	33	MD	18
Lewis H	14	DE	308
Sarah	13	PA	354
Susan	6	DE	23
Susan	33	DE	297
Taylor	3	DE	18
Thomas	21	DE	55
William	2	DE	339
Pullen, Elizabeth	24	GB	45
Victor	23	PA	45
William	2	PA	45
Purchase, Rebecca	23	DE	295
William	4/12	DE	295
Purey, Elizabeth	28	DE	348
Howard	9/12	DE	346
Jacob	3	DE	346
Joseph	28	DE	346
Purnall, Cornelia	28	MD	148
Mary C	7	MD	148
Sarah	12	DE	150
Sylvester	32	DE	148
Purnel, Ann	5	DE	140
Harriet	45	DE	140
Mary	14	DE	49
Parker	50	DE	140
Ruth A	14	DE	367
Purnell, Angelina	19	DE	156
Benjamin	4	DE	153
Benjamin	30	DE	156
Charles H	3	DE	153
Clementine	19	DE	153
Daniel	15	DE	153
Harriet	25	DE	142
John	7	DE	153
John	36	DE	140
Mary	31	MD	140
Mary	45	DE	153
Nancy	90	DE	199
Plesent	63	MD	46
Sana	67	MD	46
Theodore E	17	DE	153
Purse, Henry	9	DE	220
John	21	?	270
Mary	45	DE	248
Sarah A	2	DE	248
Purvess, Alexander	28	IE	12
James	26	IE	12
James	60	IE	12
Purvess, James H	1	DE	12
Louisa	27	PA	12
William	30	IE	12
Pusey, Ann H	26	PA	357
Charles	7	DE	40
Edward	18	DE	42
Elizabeth	8	DE	45
Elizabeth	28	DE	345
Ellen	6	IE	45
Ellen	38	IE	7
Hannah	2	DE	357
Henry	4	DE	40
Howard	9/12	DE	345
Israel	39	PA	45
Jacob	3	DE	345
Jacob	57	PA	42
Jonas	20	DE	55
Jonas	59	PA	55
Joshua	8	DE	42
Joshua	32	PA	40
Joseph	28	DE	345
Lea	30	DE	357
Mary	38	PA	45
Patric	40	IE	7
Phebe	22	DE	42
Samuel N	36	DE	29
Sarah	31	PA	40
Sarah W	20	DE	42
William	4	DE	40
Pusler, Larrance	26	GE	125
Putnam, James	54	IE	395
Pyle, Allen	3	DE	86
Ann	44	WL	358
Anna	22	PA	52
Anna E	2	PA	279
Bowen	22	PA	357
Charles W	3	DE	52
Charles W	18	DE	100
Cyrus	43	PA	40
E J	13	DE	360
Edward	12	DE	396
Elizabeth	22	DE	48
Elizabeth V	7	DE	122
Ellen	3	DE	136
Emma P	10/12	DE	48
Esther A	25	PA	279
Ezekiel	7	DE	358
George	4	PA	358
George	6	PA	260
Hannah	40	DE	396
Harlen	35	DE	304
Henry M	2	DE	52
Humphry	30	PA	136
Humphry	34	DE	86
Isaac	25	DE	52
Isaac	74	DE	358
Isaac J	5	DE	122
Isabella	35	PA	358
Jane	43	DE	304
John	45	DE	304
John B	8	PA	358
Joseph	24	PA	48
Joseph	34	PA	279
Joseph	58	PA	357
Joseph P	39	DE	122
Joshua	60	DE	279
Lamborn	37	PA	396
Letitia	20	DE	136
Lucy	27	DE	86
Lydia C	1	DE	279
Mary	6	DE	40
Mary	26	PA	279
Mary	28	PA	260
Mary	27	DE	122
Mary A	5/12	DE	122
Mary C	4	DE	343
Mary J	13	PA	362
Mary Jane	10	PA	358
Moses	26	NJ	260
Phebe A	10	DE	396
Priscilla	82	PA	279
Rebecca	3	DE	343

Name	Age	St	Pg
Pyle, Rebecca	4	PA	260
Rebecca	23	PA	279
Rebecca	77	PA	304
Reese	30	PA	358
Robert	10	PA	279
Robert	17	PA	55
Ruth Elizabeth	15	PA	357
Sarah	6	PA	358
Sarah	59	PA	357
Susan	61	DE	279
Theodore	1	PA	358
Thomas W	19	PA	279
William	25	PA	55
William	27	DE	86
William	27	PA	136
William	30	PA	40
Quick, Anna	8/12	DE	346
Catharine	30	IE	346
John	5	DE	346
Margaret	7	DE	346
Michael	35	IE	346
Thomas	3	DE	346
Quigley, Anna P	4	DE	129
Bridget	26	IE	50
Elizabeth	26	DE	129
Elizabeth V	5	DE	129
James	35	IE	89
John	15	DE	347
John	30	IE	89
John F	2	DE	129
Mary	17	DE	347
Mary Ann	48	PA	347
Michel	18	PA	145
Peter	23	DE	347
Peter	50	IE	347
Phillip	32	NJ	129
Quin, Anne	18	PA	122
Barney	22	IE	227
Bridget	25	IE	162
Catherine	30	DE	11
Eliza	27	DE	15
Elizabeth	8	IE	7
Ellen J	4/12	DE	7
Hugh	35	IE	305
Joseph	1	DE	162
Martha	23	DE	133
Mary	2	DE	7
Mary	76	DE	165
Mary A	16	PA	284
Mary E	30	IE	7
Michel	4	DE	7
Michel	40	IE	162
Patric	40	IE	7
Robert	20	IE	227
Thomas	6	IE	7
William	21	DE	294
Quinby, Ab	52	DE	25
Albert M	1	DE	25
Ella	9	DE	25
John	2	DE	372
John	25	IE	337
Mary	31	DE	25
Phebe	7	DE	25
Quinagh, Patrick M	35	IE	311
Radcliff, Sarah	13	PA	165
Radclift, Jane	2/12	GB	379
Rebecca	3	GB	379
Radman, Anne	7	DE	75
Elizabeth	38	GE	75
Rag, James	22	DE	218
Ragin, Catherine L	2	DE	138
Isabella	7	DE	138
Martha	28	MD	138
Mary A	9	DE	138
William	30	DE	138
Raign, Rebecca J	17	NJ	289
Raiman, Henry	18	GE	311
Raimond, James	40	FR	340
Rain, Elizabeth	15	NJ	370
Rainbo, Samuel	51	PA	335
Rainey, Henry	25	IE	284
Joseph	1/12	DE	284
Margaret	28	DE	284
Rains, Julia	34	MD	82
Susan A	15	MD	82
Raisen, Eliza J	38	DE	34
Margaret	87	PA	34
Raison, George	28	DE	301
Jonas	6	DE	314
Raisons, Julia	16	DE	149
Rakes, Alfred	10/12	DE	250
Alfred	30	DE	250
Anna E	9	DE	250
Daniel	30	MD	270
Esther	3	DE	250
Esther	27	DE	250
Jackson	14	PA	364
Mary E	4	DE	250
Wm T	5	DE	250
Ralston, Samuel	14	IE	19
Thomas	18	IE	348
Rambo, Andrew	34	PA	387
Charlotte	17	DE	281
Elizabeth	12	DE	387
Elizabeth E	23	MD	311
Enos	19	DE	335
Ezekle Y	17	PA	142
George	27	DE	395
Jacob	24	PA	387
John	21	DE	311
Louisa	19	DE	281
Margaret	30	PA	395
Margaret	51	DE	335
Mary	9	DE	387
Mary	32	DE	387
Rachel	52	DE	281
Rathnell W	7	DE	387
Samuel	1	DE	395
Samuel	26	DE	311
Susan	21	DE	281
Thomas	52	DE	281
William	11	DE	335
William	26	PA	387
Rambow, Mary	47	DE	346
Ramo, Agatha E	22	DE	323
Christiana	44	DE	324
George W	14	DE	324
Jerome	16	DE	324
John F	12	DE	274
Peter	40	DE	323
Ramsay, John	40	IE	324
Ramsey, Andrew	12	IE	251
Catherine	1	IE	251
Charlotta	24	PA	85
John	35	IE	251
Mary	4	PA	85
Mary	10	IE	251
Rebecca	34	IE	251
Robt	6	IE	251
Thomas	50	PA	85
Wm	8	IE	251
Randall, John	18	DE	178
Margaret J	19	DE	178
Randolph, Mary	26	DE	321
Ranely, Benjamin	12	DE	228
Eliza	45	DE	228
Elizabeth	10	DE	228
Emmy	14	DE	228
James	8	DE	228
James	52	DE	228
Mary O	6	DE	228
William	3	DE	228
Raney, George	19	DE	177
Hamilton	17	DE	177
Rankin, Ann J	7	DE	351
Anna	36	PA	82
Anna M	18	DE	351
Davis	19	DE	351
Hannah	53	DE	351
Hannah M	22	DE	351
Henry	37	PA	82
James H	16	DE	351
Rankin, John	18	IE	358
Joseph	63	DE	351
Joseph C	24	DE	351
Leah	63	DE	68
Louisa	13	DE	351
Margaret	57	DE	351
Mary E	6	PA	82
Mary E	14	DE	351
Montgomery	21	DE	351
Rebecca	30	DE	351
Robert T	28	DE	351
Sarah	46	DE	351
Sarah M	26	DE	351
Thomas	53	DE	351
Thomas C	3	DE	351
William	9	DE	351
William	41	PA	333
William H	11	PA	82
Wm	60	DE	253
Ransom, Mary	18	IE	285
Raphun, Hannah A	10	PA	289
Jno	38	PA	289
Joseph E	7	PA	289
Mary J	15	PA	289
Sarah A	33	NJ	289
William H	1	DE	289
Rapple, Andrew	48	IE	356
Andrew E	16	DE	356
James G	19	PA	356
John B	9	DE	356
Mary A	47	IE	356
Mary J	12	DE	356
Samuel	2	DE	356
Sarah A	27	PA	356
Thomas	24	PA	356
William W	5	DE	356
Rash, Andrew	59	DE	339
Ann M	3	DE	339
Ashby	1	DE	236
Franklin	10	DE	236
George	8	DE	339
James	33	MD	339
John	48	DE	221
Joseph	41	DE	236
Mary	35	DE	236
Mary	40	MD	339
Mason	30	DE	216
Mathew	13	DE	235
Rosetta	11	DE	236
Sarah E	22	DE	339
Sarah J	4	DE	339
William	16	DE	221
Rassell, Eliza J	17	DE	159
James	10	DE	159
Joseph	50	DE	159
Mary A	15	DE	159
Mary A	45	MD	159
Rebecca	19	DE	159
Virginia	7	DE	159
Ratliffe, Isaac C	36	DE	242
Sarah C	1/12	DE	242
Ratlige, Martha A	3	DE	225
Mary A	23	DE	225
Nathaniel M	2/12	DE	225
Robert	25	DE	225
Susan	46	DE	225
William H	9	DE	225
Raudolph, Mary	26	DE	322
Rawley, John	34	DE	180
John T	4	DE	180
Maria A	25	DE	180
Nathan B	3	DE	180
Samuel	10/12	DE	180
Rawlins, Boice	13	MD	349
Granville	16	MD	349
Rebecca	7	MD	349
Sarah	10	MD	349
Sarah	39	MD	349
Stephen	40	MD	349
William	11	MD	349
Ray, Absalom	6	DE	225
Alexander	50	IE	318

Name	Age	St	Pg	Name	Age	St	Pg	Name	Age	St	Pg
Ray, Ann	43	IE	373	Read, Eliza	32	DE	67	Reason, Ann	46	DE	288
Ann H	29	DE	34	Elizabeth	23	IE	122	Charles	43	VA	335
Catherine A	22	NJ	394	Elizabeth	30	DE	340	Freeman	2	DE	335
Clara	15	DE	240	Elizabeth D	25	PA	93	Hester A	32	MD	335
Clara	55	DE	240	Frances B	30	PA	93	Robert	4	DE	335
David	7	DE	240	Franklin	7/12	DE	372	Susan	5	DE	288
David	60	DE	240	George	25	DE	372	Violet	65	DE	10
Edward	11	DE	330	Hannah	20	DE	120	Rebman, Carrie	5	DE	52
Elizabeth	4	PA	355	Hannah	70	PA	372	Jacob	2	DE	52
Elizabeth	15	DE	225	Harriet A	3	DE	10	Jacob	45	SZ	52
Elizabeth	29	PA	355	Henry	1	PA	667	John	15	DE	52
Elizabeth P M	27	PA	396	Henry	30	DE	97	Joseph	10	DE	52
Emeline	1	PA	355	Isaac	14	DE	364	Mary	13	DE	52
Forbes	28	DE	394	James	14	ST	377	Rosannah	46	SZ	52
Hannah	5	PA	355	James	24	IE	162	Redclift, Rebecca	3	IE	378
Horace	30	DE	34	James P	2	DE	90	Reddan, William	16	DE	164
Jacob	12	DE	217	Jane	54	IE	328	Redden, Abram	27	DE	186
Jacob	13	DE	225	Jeremy	65	DE	364	Elizabeth	30	IE	51
Jacob	30	DE	225	John	3	DE	340	John	21	IE	39
James	22	DE	217	John	11	ST	377	John G	3/12	DE	308
James H	26	DE	396	John	26	IE	122	Joseph W	15	DE	400
Jane	3	PA	355	John	27	IE	43	Laurance	26	DE	308
Jane	16	IE	375	John	33	PA	90	Mary	12	IE	165
John	9	DE	225	John	54	IE	328	Mary A	21	DE	308
Mary	25	PA	71	Joseph	35	DE	66	Mary T	6	DE	308
Mary A	28	DE	318	Margaret	16	PA	154	Nelly	45	IE	39
Oliver	26	DE	318	Margaret	31	IE	66	Richard A	4	DE	308
Phoebe	55	DE	241	Martha	15	ST	378	Sarah	11	DE	308
Rebecca	33	DE	239	Mary	4/12	DE	335	Susan	2	DE	308
Samuel	29	PA	355	Mary	25	IE	302	Susan	27	DE	186
Susan	30	DE	226	Mary	29	NJ	66	William H	17	DE	400
Susannah	3	DE	225	Mary	37	ST	377	Wilson T	9	DE	308
William	27	PA	71	Mary E	5	DE	372	Reddin, Absolem	50	DE	244
Rayborn, Anna L	2	DE	278	Mary G	45	DE	286	Adeline	3	DE	225
Eliza	21	DE	278	Mary J	9/12	DE	302	Betsey	50	DE	244
Joseph	58	DE	277	Mary J	15	DE	335	David	32	DE	225
Sarah	57	DE	277	Mary J	28	IE	328	Eliza	25	DE	225
William H	4	DE	278	Minty	63	DE	364	Emma	7	DE	225
Rayman, Alvina	1	DE	291	Rachel A	5	DE	340	George	3	DE	225
Ann	36	DE	291	Robert	2/12	DE	66	Henry C	18	DE	247
Hannah M	9	DE	291	Robert	1	DE	377	Isaac	25	DE	247
Hiram	4	DE	291	Robert	30	IE	66	Jerry	65	DE	228
John	5	DE	291	Robert	37	ST	377	Phillip	14	DE	228
Lucillia	11	DE	291	Samuel	10	NJ	66	Rachel	20	DE	218
Nicholas	7	DE	291	Sarah	25	DE	372	Susan	30	DE	211
Sebastian	37	GE	291	Sarah F	50	DE	286	William	18	DE	184
Raymond, Alexander	12	DE	39	William	9	DE	336	Redding, Catherine	18	DE	202
Ann	2/12	DE	39	William	28	IE	302	David	40	DE	393
Caroline	30	DE	39	William	40	DE	374	Hannah	35	DE	213
George H	16	DE	401	William A	1	DE	66	Isabella	24	DE	261
Presley	16	DE	199	William F	5/12	DE	90	Jerry	8	DE	213
William	30	DE	39	William L	57	DE	286	John	55	DE	213
Raynor, James	27	MD	400	Reade, Jacob	12	DE	365	Joseph	9	DE	213
Razell, Lydia	5	DE	305	Reader, Ania	12	DE	60	Philip	28	DE	261
Mary J	1	DE	305	Charles	5	DE	60	Pink	12	DE	213
Sarah	24	DE	305	Frances	4	DE	60	Richard	20	DE	252
William	25	DE	305	James	2	DE	39	Richard	22	DE	261
Reace, George	10	DE	131	John	32	DE	63	Solomon	2	DE	214
James	38	DE	104	John	51	DE	59	Stephen	3	DE	214
Margaret	42	DE	132	John J	2	DE	63	Reddon, William	16	IE	165
Margaret	60	DE	104	Joseph	16	DE	59	Reddun, George	13	DE	226
Margaret J	8	DE	131	Maria	45	MD	63	Redgate, John	50	NJ	389
Mary E	4	DE	131	Mary	14	DE	60	Redgraves, Thomas	18	DE	231
Mary J	24	DE	104	Mary A	25	MD	63	Redish, Eliza H	1	DE	281
William	45	DE	131	Mary A	31	MD	63	Frances	30	GB	281
Reach, Margaret	20	IE	109	Mary E	6	DE	63	James	29	GB	281
Read, Abigal	8	NJ	66	Minte	45	DE	59	Redman, Ann	11	NJ	357
Abigal	31	NJ	90	Rachel	73	DE	63	Ann	42	GB	357
Alexander	10	DE	359	Ruth	22	PA	39	Cornelia	27	DE	309
Alexander	20	IE	66	Stephen	11	DE	69	David	50	DE	387
Alexander	54	TN	318	William	30	MD	63	Elizabeth	8	NJ	357
Amelia	64	NJ	126	William	37	DE	39	Henrietta	28	IE	304
Andrew	35	DE	99	Reading, A P	54	DE	195	John	25	DE	303
Ann	4	DE	97	Anna	8	DE	383	Joseph	4	NJ	357
Ann	6	IE	66	Henry P	23	DE	195	Joseph	41	GB	357
Ann E	21	DE	97	James	23	DE	195	Mary M	6/12	DE	302
Anna	5	NJ	66	Lydia	50	MD	195	Mary T	1	DE	302
Benjamin	7	DE	341	Mary E	16	DE	195	Rebecca	21	GB	302
Benjamin	27	DE	340	Mary E	16	DE	332	Samuel	8	DE	77
Charles	16	DE	347	Reals, Avis F	9	DE	164	Sarah	50	DE	387
Edward A	1	DE	97	Rease, James	35	PA	112	Simon	28	GE	302
Eliza	32	DE	51	Reason, Ann	46	DE	288	Redon, Noah	22	DE	283

Name	Age			Name	Age			Name	Age		
Reece, Benjamin R	19	DE	401	Reiley, Eliza	23	IE	217	Reyla, Michael	41	DE	335
Clara	15	DE	338	Reilley, Ann	62	IE	163	Reyley, John	36	MD	160
Esther	75	DE	374	John	13	PA	164	Reynolds, Aaron	23	DE	216
Phoebe	15	DE	282	Michael	36	IE	163	Amelia	65	DE	195
Thomas	75	DE	374	Patric (Rev)	42	IE	163	Andrew	38	DE	56
Thomas H	40	DE	374	Reilly, Elizabeth	4	MO	49	Andrew C	18	DE	236
Reed, Ann	30	DE	272	Marion	2	DE	49	Andy	2/12	DE	218
Ann	35	DE	262	Michel	20	IE	49	Ann	45	IE	380
Anna	18	DE	253	Sarah	24	PA	49	Ann	48	NJ	258
Austen	11	DE	216	Reise, Alfred	10	GE	21	Ann	70	MD	53
Catharine	35	DE	216	Benitta	12	GE	21	Ann	80	DE	11
David	50	DE	262	George	8	GE	21	Anna	12	DE	308
Elizabeth	20	IE	165	Henrietta	1	GE	21	Araminta	60	MD	16
Elizabeth	43	DE	272	Josanna	14	GE	21	Asbury	2	DE	41
George	8	DE	262	Joanna	39	GE	21	Asbury	30	MD	41
Hannah	30	DE	302	Otto	6	GE	21	Benjamin	1	DE	195
Hugh	35	IE	346	Rudolph	3	GE	21	Bridget	26	IE	380
Isaac	10	DE	263	William	17	GE	21	Bridget	50	IE	380
Jacob	7	DE	302	William	48	GE	21	Catharine	35	DE	334
James H	20	DE	401	Remington, Catherine	34	PA	3	Charles	42	DE	305
James W	35	DE	216	George	5	DE	39	Charlotte	18	MD	41
Jane	31	IE	346	George	35	DE	39	Clara J	5	DE	308
John	18/12	DE	346	George W	10	DE	3	Edward	20	GB	262
John	14	DE	262	Hannah	4/12	DE	39	Elener	67	IE	115
John	17	MD	224	Jane	7	DE	39	Eliza J	9	DE	259
John	19	MD	184	John L	3	DE	3	Elizabeth	32	DE	223
John	38	DE	312	Letitia	30	DE	39	Elizabeth	49	PA	301
Margaret	5	IE	360	William	35	MD	3	Elizabeth	64	DE	334
Margaret	23	IE	329	Remson, Abraham	21	NY	131	Ella	47	DE	259
Margaret	28	IE	295	Garrett	48	NY	130	Ellen	30	MD	78
Martin	30	DE	312	Hannah	9	NY	131	Emma	1	DE	216
Mary	6	DE	346	Letitia	47	NY	●30	Emma J	6	DE	223
Mary	28	DE	209	Martha	17	NY	131	Frances	13	DE	259
Mary	28	DE	272	Sarah	19	NY	57	Frances H	2	DE	78
Mary E	10	DE	228	William	13	NY	131	Francis	23	DE	378
Melvina	16	DE	272	Rench, J Nathan	40	MD	394	Francis	28	DE	54
R	15	MD	165	Mary	40	MD	394	George	10	DE	308
Sarah	42	DE	272	Rengoll, Samuel	18	DE	247	George	45	DE	53
Sarah	62	DE	272	Renly, Joseph	22	DE	315	George	45	DE	195
William	4	DE	302	Renshaw, Samuel	20	GB	396	George V	7	DE	195
William	30	PA	302	Resley, John	50	DE	27	Georgianna	12	MD	41
Wm	12	DE	262	Ress, M Louisa	15	DE	166	Grantham	28	DE	250
Reedman, Anna M	1	DE	76	Resson, George	20	DE	185	Henry F	40	DE	308
Eliza	6	DE	76	Reth, Jane	16	IE	280	Hester	42	DE	308
Hannah	5	DE	76	Revson, Michael	65	GB	187	Isabela	10	DE	305
Jane	30	DE	76	Rosemander	63	GB	187	Isabela	33	DE	305
Lewis	23	GE	158	Reybold, Barney	34	DE	253	James	6	DE	308
Philip	32	DE	76	Beulah	32	NY	188	James	9	DE	223
Samuel	8	DE	76	Caroline	34	SC	252	James	10	DE	41
Reenan, Richard	45	IE	304	Catherine	6	DE	252	James	32	DE	236
Rees, Elizabeth	5	DE	172	Catherine	22	PA	263	Jane	7	GB	262
Minte	60	DE	172	Clayton	3	DE	274	Jane J	24	PA	250
Reese, Ann	29	DE	174	Edwin	3	DE	188	Jeremiah	15	DE	195
Harman	22	DE	350	Elizabeth	6	DE	273	Joe	18	DE	274
Jane	62	DE	389	Elizabeth	12	DE	188	John	11	DE	377
John	40	DE	174	Elizabeth	67	PA	249	John	11	IE	380
Joseph	19	DE	213	Frederick	13	DE	252	John	30	GB	258
Mary	63	SZ	364	George	5/12	DE	188	John A	36	DE	377
Saml	30	DE	253	George	8	DE	273	Joseph	25	DE	260
Sarah	15	DE	380	Henry	9	DE	188	Joseph	26	GB	262
Sarah	32	DE	395	John	4	DE	252	Joseph	50	IE	301
Sarah J	10/12	DE	395	John	5	DE	273	Lewis	43	DE	308
Reeve, James	40	PA	362	John	40	DE	273	Lydia	7	DE	53
Reeves, Clement	30	NJ	259	Josephine	12	DE	252	Lydia	35	DE	53
Regan, John	27	IE	36	Mary	5	DE	188	Lydia	7	DE	78
Rosannah	25	IE	36	Mary	34	PA	273	Margaret	23	DE	381
Reggan, Bridget	28	IE	338	Matilda	32	DE	249	Martha A	3	DE	236
Register, Elijah	28	DE	13	Maxwell	7/12	DE	274	Mary	11	DE	379
Eliza P	51	DE	288	Phillip	37	DE	252	Mary	15	PA	301
Isaac H	38	DE	288	Phillip	67	PA	249	Mary	26	DE	334
Isaac L	8	DE	288	Sophrona	30	CT	253	Mary	35	IE	303
Henry C	6	DE	288	William	35	IE	188	Mary	42	DE	377
John B	4	DE	288	Wm	1	DE	252	Mary A	17	DE	305
Mary A	31	DE	288	Reybolds, Ann	32	NJ	249	Mary A	23	DE	236
Sarah	2	DE	13	Anthony	30	DE	249	Mary E	2	DE	236
Sarah A	24	MD	13	Philip	2	DE	249	Mary E	16	DE	308
William	6	DE	13	Reyla, Catherine	34	DE	335	Matilda	2	DE	41
Reheybold, Clayton	28	DE	263	John	12	DE	335	Matthew	3/12	DE	250
Rehm, George	20	GE	186	Mary E	4	DE	335	Matthew	17	GB	262
Reid, John	19	DE	184	Michael	8	DE	335	Michael	66	IE	380
William	4	DE	347	Michael	41	DE	335	Minor A	11	DE	218
Reiley, John	29	IE	217	Reyley, John	36	MD	160	Patrick	27	IE	380

Name	No	St	Pg
Reynolds, Perry	5	DE	259
Perry	49	DE	259
Peter	19	GB	262
Rachel	6	DE	218
Rachel	9	DE	41
Rebecca	14	DE	308
Rebecca J	28	PA	216
Richard	31	IE	78
Robert	8/12	DE	303
Robt	29	DE	274
Samuel M	8	DE	377
Sarah	13	GB	262
Sarah	13	DE	379
Sarah	23	DE	334
Sarah	25	MD	41
Sarah	30	DE	54
Sarah	50	GB	262
Sarah	54	DE	236
Sarah	67	DE	308
Sarah A	9	DE	218
Sarah A	35	MD	195
Sarah C	1/12	DE	236
Sarah E	11	DE	236
Sarah E	17	DE	308
Sarah J	11	DE	305
Suley	2/12	DE	219
Susan	33	DE	334
Thomas	2	DE	303
Thomas	11	GB	262
Thomas	24	DE	250
Thomas	30	IE	380
Thomas	40	GB	303
Walter	1	DE	223
Washington E	10	DE	377
Wilhelmina	12	DE	259
William	3	DE	218
William	4	DE	78
William	13	DE	377
William	50	DE	378
William F	5	DE	236
William H	8	DE	308
William H	29	DE	308
William P	16	DE	237
Willmina	10	DE	267
Zadock	2	DE	308
Rhees, Anna J	8	PA	28
Grace	43	PA	28
John	17	NJ	28
Morgan J (Rev)	47	PA	28
Mary	11	NJ	28
R Rust	18	NJ	28
Rhodes, Catharine	9	DE	228
Elizabeth	64	DE	291
Emma	16	DE	249
Enoch	56	DE	24
George	1	DE	249
Hannah	47	NJ	24
Harriet	25	MD	228
Jno	10	DE	292
Joseph	1	DE	228
Joseph	12	DE	292
Joseph	19	PA	24
Margaret	1	DE	183
Margaret	37	MD	292
Mary E	11	DE	292
Perry	10	DE	195
Perry	30	MD	228
Rebecca	15	DE	292
Rebecca	56	DE	292
Robert	59	DE	291
Sallie	18	DE	183
Samuel	19	DE	310
Sarah	13	DE	301
William	17	DE	292
William	51	DE	292
Rhodey, Charles	25	IE	231
John	22	IE	231
Riace, Catherine	60	DE	30
Riason, Abraham	60	MD	67
Mary A	35	DE	67
Rice, Ann	14	DE	41
Ann	30	GB	42
Rice, Ann M	29	DE	374
Anna	26	DE	375
Anne E	2	DE	132
Betsey	17	VA	113
Chandler P	4	DE	361
Edward H	2	DE	41
Edward L	39	DE	41
Eliza	37	DE	83
Elizabeth	25	DE	137
Elizabeth	35	PA	212
Elizabeth	81	DE	137
George	1	DE	374
George W	26	DE	374
Henry	39	PA	321
Henry	85	DE	137
Henry T	17	DE	361
Hiland	4	DE	132
Hyland	27	DE	361
Jacob	7	DE	83
Jacob	40	DE	70
James	19	DE	70
James	59	DE	70
James H	15	DE	361
James H	44	DE	361
James L	11/12	DE	375
James L	3	DE	374
John	11	DE	376
John	16	DE	70
John	52	DE	160
John A	36	DE	376
Joseph	13	DE	368
Joshua H T	43	DE	83
Kate	10	DE	41
Leah A	27	DE	361
Margaret J	11	DE	83
Margaret T	25	DE	387
Margaretta	24	DE	70
Maria	20	DE	137
Martha	6	PA	321
Martha E	30	DE	132
Mary	39	DE	41
Mary	42	DE	376
Mary A	45	DE	70
Mary B	7/12	DE	361
Mary E	12	DE	71
Mary J	2	DE	83
Mary J	2	DE	321
Mary J	7	DE	41
Mary J	22	DE	70
Mary J	28	PA	321
Matilda	21	DE	70
Samuel M	8	DE	293
Sarah	16	DE	293
Sarah	35	DE	70
Sarah	50	DE	365
Sarah A	57	DE	121
Sarah E	32	MD	313
Secilia H	12	DE	361
Thomas B	33	DE	132
Washington	6	DE	381
Washington E	10	DE	376
William	24	DE	375
William	13	DE	376
William	26	DE	137
William	54	DE	76
William H	13	DE	83
William H	42	DE	381
Rich, Jacob	35	NJ	267
John	30	PA	176
Martha	16	DE	179
Mary	29	NJ	176
Mary B	5	PA	176
Richard, Noble	13	DE	341
Richards, Amelia	6/12	DE	203
Ann	43	DE	234
Ann	50	GB	60
Anna C	19	DE	215
Caroline	5	DE	120
Curtis C	7	PA	297
David	1	DE	213
Dutton	4	DE	375
Edward	14	DE	375
Richards, Edward	14	DE	375
Elizabeth	32	PA	297
Elizabeth	36	DE	213
Elizabeth	50	PA	43
Emma E	4/12	DE	297
George	46	DE	215
Hannah B	23	DE	203
Harriet	74	DE	203
Hester	6	DE	215
Hester	46	DE	215
Hetty	70	DE	120
Isaac	7	DE	120
James	17	DE	234
James	50	DE	234
Jane	35	DE	375
Jane W	6	DE	375
John	15	DE	382
John	53	DE	368
John R	5	PA	297
Jonfaver	6	DE	234
Joseph	21	PA	102
Levi	40	DE	120
Lewis	12	DE	120
Lewis	26	DE	203
Margaret	16	DE	234
Mary	1	DE	215
Mary	3	DE	234
Mary	65	DE	10
Mary A	1	DE	120
Mary A	16	DE	10
Miles M	37	DE	213
Mitchel	16	DE	120
Morton	30	DE	213
Nathaniel	52	DE	375
Priscilla	35	DE	120
Rachel	11	DE	234
Sophia	13	DE	215
Susanna	2	DE	375
Thomas	15	DE	375
Thomas	19	DE	234
Thomas J	34	MD	297
Thomas W	3	PA	297
Wesley	17	DE	209
Richardson, Albert	11	PA	62
Alden B	24	MA	58
Ann	7	MI	366
Ann	17	DE	123
Ann	18	DE	312
Ann	27	DE	261
Ann	38	DE	307
Ashton	74	DE	369
Ashton Jr	20	DE	369
Benj	9	DE	307
Catherine	50	MD	34
Charles	18	?	270
Daniel	6	DE	307
Edward	18	DE	182
Eldridge	2	DE	61
Eliza A	50	DE	58
Elizabeth	5	MI	366
Elizabeth	30	DE	366
Elizabeth	60	DE	261
Ellen	8	MD	62
Elsey	28	DE	261
George	4	NY	259
George	6	DE	219
George	10	DE	366
George	34	DE	142
George S	50	PA	123
Georgiana	10	DE	123
Hannah	31	DE	369
Harman	18	DE	74
Hannah R	11	DE	376
Henry	12	DE	251
Henry	44	DE	156
Henry B	4	DE	142
Irda	3	DE	46
Jackson	16	DE	219
Jacob	26	DE	46
Jacob	40	DE	307
James	20	DE	234
James	39	PA	62

Richardson, James 39 DE 198
James 65 DE 16
James Jr 14 DE 198
Jane 2 MI 366
John 3 DE 307
John 13 PA 62
John 67 DE 366
John Jr 26 DE 366
John L 8 DE 123
Joseph 1 DE 142
Joseph 7 DE 366
Joseph 9 MD 62
Joseph 26 DE 61
Joseph 58 PA 58
Joseph P 23 DE 366
Joshua 19 PA 308
Lewis 9 DE 366
Loro 6 DE 61
Lucy 20 MA 58
Lucy 25 DE 369
Margaret 24 DE 61
Martha 6 DE 197
Mary 4 MI 366
Mary 26 PA 46
Mary 30 ST 259
Mary 35 DE 369
Mary 36 DE 62
Mary 44 DE 123
Mary 65 PA 369
Mary A 7/12 DE 307
Mary E 1 DE 366
Minte 25 DE 168
Oliver 75 DE 326
Priscilla 30 PA 366
Rebecca 13 DE 16
Rebecca 30 DE 301
Robert 18 DE 198
Ruth A 9 DE 277
Sally M 17 MD 166
Saml 44 MI 366
Samuel 40 MD 309
Sarah 12 DE 54
Sarah 15 DE 219
Sarah 39 DE 198
Sarah T 35 DE 366
Sarah W 28 DE 142
Sidney 6/12 DE 46
Sidney 16 DE 123
Susan 16 DE 39
Susan 34 MI 366
Susan W 2 DE 142
Thomas 3 DE 366
Thomas 46 DE 161
William 5 DE 366
William 14 DE 345
William 45 DE 366
William 46 DE 34
William P 30 DE 366
Riche, Catherine 40 DE 86
James 8 DE 86
James 50 DE 86
John 12 DE 86
Maria 50 DE 5
Robert 52 DE 5
Sarah A 18 DE 86
Thomas 25 DE 5
William 25 DE 86
Richinson, John S 30 PA 380
Kesiah 21 PA 350
Margaret 3 PA 380
Rebecca 28 PA 380
Stephen D 2 PA 380
Richmond, Earnestine 17 MD 37
Susan 40 GE 37
William 14 MD 37
William 50 GE 37
Richter, Hetty 20 DE 279
Hetty 59 DE 279
Rickard, Carthgina 8/12 DE 207
Elizabeth 24 DE 207
Ezekiel 27 DE 207
Daniel 1 DE 214

Rickard, David 38 DE 272
Eliza A 23 DE 217
Elizabeth 31 MD 214
George 3 DE 207
George 6 DE 272
George 20 DE 268
James 12 DE 268
James 37 DE 217
James 45 DE 268
John 2 DE 272
Jonathan 5 DE 217
Marian 17 DE 272
Martin 11 DE 239
Mary 14 DE 268
Mary 36 DE 272
Mary 48 DE 268
Molton 30 DE 214
Rickarts, Mr 30 DE 114
Ricker, Eliza 5 DE 3
Hannah E 10 DE 3
Henrietta 25 DE 3
John B 1 DE 3
William 3 DE 3
William 29 DE 3
Rickert, Miles M 37 DE 214
Ricket, Ann 35 DE 359
Lewis 7 DE 359
Thomas 29 DE 359
Ricketts, Josephine 6 DE 280
Riddle, Eliza 19 DE 161
G R 30 DE 161
Hannah 34 MD 328
Harriet 46 MD 176
Hosea T 44 MD 399
James 46 IE 328
Jane 4 DE 328
Jas 60 DE 284
Leander F 8 PA 328
Margaret 29 VA 161
Margaret 54 IE 284
Mary 60 IE 279
Mary A 30 DE 76
Penelope 57 PA 399
Penelope L 18 DE 399
Rachel 10 DE 248
Saml 24 IE 329
Sarah 22 DE 284
William 14 DE 284
Rider, Araminty 31 MD 321
Emily 33 IE 43
Emla 36 IE 323
James 12 DE 258
James 35 DE 321
Rachel 10 DE 277
Rachel 10 DE 321
Saba 5 DE 321
Sarah A 18 DE 311
Wilson 13 DE 321
Ridgely, E 22 DE 164
Ridgeway, Anna R 7 PA 86
Emma 31 DE 86
Emma L 4 DE 86
John K 6 NJ 350
Samuel 38 NJ 86
Susan 18 NJ 350
Ridgly, Henry 32 PA 283
Mary 30 MD 283
Mary E 1 DE 283
Ridgway, David 11 DE 169
David B 11 NJ 306
Harriett L 20 NJ 306
Isaac P 14 NJ 306
James W 8 NJ 306
John 48 NJ 305
Josiah 41 NJ 169
Kesiah 9/12 DE 306
Martha A 13 DE 169
Martha J 15 NJ 306
Matilda 49 DE 169
Roselinda 5 DE 169
Samuel 18 NJ 306
Sarah 43 NJ 306

Ridings, Anna 47 GB 278
Clara 9 DE 278
Elizabeth 6 DE 278
Frederick 15 PA 278
Frederick 46 GB 278
John 20 PA 278
Sarah J 12 PA 278
Thomas 17 PA 278
Riely, Ann 18 IE 282
Hannah M 30 DE 298
John 50 IE 28
Peter 42 IE 298
Rieman, Susan 26 IE 2
Rigby, Elizabeth 31 DE 288
Francis E 10 MD 289
Isabela 5 DE 305
Joseph J 11 DE 305
Samuel 41 DE 305
Samuel T 8 DE 305
Sarah L 37 DE 305
Rigdon, Sarah 12 PA 361
Riggs, Abel 1 DE 15
Abel 2 DE 235
Abraham 36 DE 15
Buleah 4 DE 15
Buleah 33 PA 15
Emeline 9/12 DE 235
Lavinia 9 DE 235
Mary R 7 DE 235
Sarah 5 DE 235
Sarah A 32 DE 235
William E 33 DE 235
Righ, John 34 DE 301
Righby, Rachel A 13 DE 305
Right, Catherine 9 PA 372
John 12 NJ 372
John 54 ST 371
Margaret 40 ST 371
Margaret J 12 NJ 372
Mary Ann Jane 17 PA 372
Robert 14 ST 372
Sela 12 DE 104
Thomas 10 PA 372
Thomas 41 DE 155
Righter, Anderson 25 DE 72
Anna 10/12 DE 72
Anna 13 DE 275
Anna 27 DE 72
Anna 34 DE 275
Benjamin B 15 DE 76
Christopher 3 PA 307
Elizabeth 16 DE 76
Ella M V 1 DE 275
George 17 DE 76
Isaac 67 DE 275
Jacob B 13 DE 76
James 35 DE 275
John 10 DE 275
John 29 DE 307
John 47 DE 76
John V 7 DE 275
Margaret 1 PA 307
Margaret 29 PA 307
Mary 2 DE 73
Mary E 18 DE 76
Rebecca 19 PA 307
Sarah 46 DE 76
Rigs, Andrew 25 DE 369
Catherine 14 DE 369
Catherine 40 MD 369
Daniel 59 MD 369
Eliza A 30 DE 93
George 19 DE 312
Joseph 1 DE 369
Levi 12 DE 93
Mary 51 PA 98
Mary A 22 DE 369
Mary E 7 DE 93
Rebecca 5 DE 369
Robert 16 DE 98
Robert 17 DE 369
Sarah 12 DE 369

Name	Age	St	Pg	Name	Age	St	Pg	Name	Age	St	Pg
Rigs, William	12	DE	98	Risburry, Robert	15	PA	364	Robenson, Joel	42	DE	282
William	49	IE	98	Risdin, Lydia N	25	DE	316	John	10	DE	76
Riley, Alice	18	DE	177	Risdon, Sally	8	DE	297	Kezia	50	DE	282
Alice	46	GB	177	Riser, Mary	60	PA	348	Robert, Ringold	33	DE	354
Benjamin	50	MD	207	Ritche, A A	11	DE	280	Roberts, Adaline	14	DE	223
Benjamin T	4	DE	207	Ellen H	9	CH	280	Albin	46	PA	299
Betsey	30	MD	207	Hetty	3	NY	280	Alexander	8	MD	384
Catherine	1	DE	207	Hetty	20	PA	280	Alexander	21	DE	194
Catherine	14	DE	177	Hetty	59	PA	280	Alfred	14	DE	223
Charles	19	DE	18	Hugh H	5	CH	280	Alfred	23	DE	10
Charles A	8	DE	118	Martha H	13	DE	280	Alice A	30	DE	136
Dennis	6	IE	259	Martha H	39	PA	280	Amy	31	MD	384
Eliza	23	DE	218	William	7	CH	280	Ann	3	DE	343
Elizabeth	32	DE	18	Ritchwell, Ann	18	DE	178	Ann	35	PA	366
Ellen	23	IE	306	Riter, Elizabeth	35	DE	106	Ann E	1	DE	326
Emma	12	DE	118	Enoch L	2	DE	221	Ann J	44	NJ	95
George W	14	DE	118	Evan	30	DE	106	Anna M	12	DE	227
Henry	10	DE	177	Harriet M	2	DE	106	Anna M	55	DE	227
John	1	NJ	259	Isaac	6	DE	106	Bernard	3	DE	229
John	26	IE	306	John	7	DE	106	Bodacia	30	PA	369
John	29	DE	218	Mary A	5	DE	221	Catharine	24	DE	235
John	30	IE	259	Mary A	28	DE	221	Catharine	59	MD	388
John L	21	PA	118	Rebecca	20	NJ	79	Charles	3	DE	140
Joseph	10	DE	118	Rebecca	26	NJ	106	Charles	10	ST	343
Joseph	43	PA	118	Rebecca J	4	DE	221	Charles H	7	DE	136
Joshua	3	DE	307	Sarah E	6	DE	221	Christiana	26	ST	343
Judith	42	IE	330	Timothy	32	MD	221	Curtis	35	PA	135
Lucy	5	DE	118	Wesley	24	DE	78	Dorcus	50	MD	84
Lydia A	8	DE	207	William	25	DE	79	E M	62	PA	10
Margaret	39	DE	18	William	27	DE	106	Edward	4	DE	384
Maria	16	DE	178	Rittenhouse, Abram	12	DE	367	Edwina	2	DE	222
Martha	9	DE	188	Catharine E	4	DE	367	Eliza	31	DE	140
Mary	1	DE	306	Edward	40	DE	377	Eliza	36	PA	135
Mary	9	DE	208	Sarah A	27	DE	367	Eliza A	24	NJ	311
Mary	17	DE	188	Sarah A J	7	DE	367	Elizabeth	13	ST	343
Mary	26	IE	259	William H	3	DE	367	Elizabeth	31	DE	227
Mary	60	DE	18	William H	30	IE	367	Elizabeth	54	DE	10
Mary A	17	PA	118	Riz, John	42	DE	298	Ellen	27	MD	326
Mary A	42	DE	118	Roach, Ann C	66	NJ	312	Elwood	4	DE	136
Mary E	3	DE	218	Edwin W	16	MD	376	Enoch	44	DE	43
Philip	12	DE	177	Ellen B	36	NJ	376	Ewen	15	DE	229
Philip	50	NJ	177	Emma	21	DE	135	G M	25	NJ	164
Priscilla	20	DE	177	John	13	DE	359	George	12	ST	343
Rachel	24	DE	226	Niona	32	IE	336	George	46	GB	329
Rose	2/12	DE	306	Patrick	35	IE	336	George	50	GB	315
Samuel	21	DE	188	Percy L	16	PA	163	George	60	MD	84
Samuel	24	DE	18	Sarah	18	PA	109	George W	42	PA	143
Samuel	51	DE	188	Spencer	22	PA	109	Gideon	60	MD	327
Sarah E	4	DE	218	Thomas	46	MD	376	Hannah	7	DE	221
Spencer	10	DE	207	Thomas M	13	MD	376	Hannah	30	IE	98
Susan	16	DE	188	Wm	34	IE	376	Harriet	68	MD	98
Thomas	22	DE	226	Roache, Anna	11	DE	28	Henry	9	DE	219
William	20	MD	380	Edward M	35	DE	28	Henry	19	DE	223
William H	19	PA	118	Emma	9	DE	28	Henry	33	DE	140
Riller, Maria	10	DE	4	Fanny	5	DE	28	Hugh	29	PA	136
Rily, Sarah W	19	DE	247	Hannah	32	DE	28	Isabel	15	ST	343
Rince, Christian	58	PA	176	Helen	2	DE	29	James	4/12	DE	343
Rine, Michael	35	IE	304	James L	42	DE	129	James	7	DE	231
Ring, Eliza	30	DE	228	James M	4	DE	98	James	12	DE	192
Eliza J	8	DE	228	James M	60	DE	129	James	12	ST	343
Jeremiah	35	DE	228	Mary A	30	NY	129	James	31	DE	10
Jerry	6	DE	228	William	7	DE	28	James	60	DE	227
Mary	10	DE	228	William H	2	DE	129	James H	10	DE	369
Ringale, James	20	DE	104	William S	4	DE	129	James H	29	DE	221
Ringgold, Camel	37	DE	306	Roads, George	19	DE	332	James M	41	PA	134
John	7	DE	288	Samuel	16	DE	385	Jane	3	DE	343
Ringle, Araminty	5	MD	338	Roan, Ann	62	DE	104	Jane	4	ST	343
James	20	DE	346	Robb, Charles S	14	NJ	313	Jane	22	ST	343
Ringold, Elizabeth	22	MD	341	Edmond T	17	NJ	313	Janet	16	ST	343
John	6	DE	320	George	16	PA	313	John	2	DE	284
Kinsey	18	DE	258	Louisa	22	PA	313	John	6	DE	222
Mary	14	DE	320	Mary	42	PA	24	John	6	ST	343
Mary	35	DE	300	Mary E	2	DE	313	John	23	DE	369
Perry	13	MD	278	Sophia	38	PA	313	John	38	ST	343
Rachel	16	DE	289	William	42	PA	313	John M	1	DE	296
Sarah	77	DE	300	William J	7	NJ	313	Joseph	9	DE	95
William	11	DE	257	Robenson, Amos	36	DE	282	Joseph	21	DE	227
Ringolds, Robert	22	DE	227	Charity	75	DE	282	Joseph	27	WL	292
Ripley, Elizabeth	3	DE	14	Hannah	3	DE	76	Joseph	27	DE	326
Mary	1	DE	14	Hester A	34	DE	76	Joseph	64	DE	10
Sarah	24	MD	14	James	36	DE	76	Julia	60	MD	322
Thomas	34	PA	14	James H	6	DE	76	Julia A	45	PA	134

Roberts, Lambert	14	DE	221	Robinson, Ann	15	DE	399	Robinson, James	1	DE	100
Louisa	24	DE	296	Ann	40	DE	27	James	12	DE	57
Lydia	37	DE	222	Ann	60	ST	148	James	28	ST	263
Margaret	16	DE	132	Ann E	11	DE	114	James	30	GB	26
Margaret	20	DE	10	Ann E	13	DE	288	James	41	DE	298
Mariah R	5	DE	369	Anne	11	DE	131	James	59	DE	241
Martha	29	DE	227	Anne	18	DE	103	James	60	ST	148
Martha	31	GB	311	Aron	63	DE	354	James	73	DE	388
Martha A	36	NJ	229	Atwood A	5	DE	114	James A	8	DE	288
Martha A C	13	DE	229	Caroline	10	DE	56	James J	25	DE	370
Mary	2	DE	343	Caroline B	7	DE	353	James W	3	DE	170
Mary	3	DE	136	Catherine	2	DE	88	Jane	6	DE	88
Mary	42	DE	329	Catherine	2	DE	396	Jane	25	IE	331
Mary	50	DE	315	Catherine	29	DE	378	Jane	80	MD	68
Mary	39	ST	343	Catherine M	15	IN	322	Jane E	19	DE	141
Mary L	5	DE	231	Celinda	1	DE	375	Janet	59	NY	325
Matilda	25	DE	204	Charles	4	DE	65	Jemima	20	IE	331
Melissa	22	DE	78	Charles	8	DE	267	Jerusha B	44	DE	141
Norma St. Clair	9	DE	229	Charles	14	DE	375	Job	32	DE	88
Rachel	4	ST	343	Christiana A	22	DE	317	John	2	DE	44
Rachel	59	MD	327	Cornelia	7	DE	95	John	9	DE	399
Rachel A	11	DE	226	Davis	3	DE	375	John	25	MD	307
Robert	10	DE	315	Edith	17	DE	64	John	25	DE	377
Robert H	12	DE	329	Edward	7	DE	103	John	28	DE	279
Samuel	5	DE	384	Edward	41	DE	103	John	31	DE	170
Samuel	24	DE	234	Eleanor	52	DE	270	John	34	DE	101
Samuel	36	MD	384	Elijah H	39	NJ	376	John	35	DE	44
Samuel J	4	DE	326	Eliza	22	DE	27	John	38	DE	31
Samuel P	44	PA	369	Eliza	38	IE	115	John	68	GB	324
Samuel W	32	DE	95	Eliza	40	NJ	65	John	85	DE	76
Sarah	2/12	DE	384	Eliza	50	PA	360	John A	5	DE	375
Southwell	2	DE	369	Eliza A	19	IE	331	John B	26	DE	317
Stephen	65	MD	98	Eliza J	4	DE	170	John F	30	DE	186
Sudler P	1	DE	229	Elizabeth	3	DE	263	John L	30	DE	379
Theodore	4	DE	135	Elizabeth	10	DE	370	John T	46	DE	56
Thos	36	ST	343	Elizabeth	14	DE	370	John T	16	DE	370
Thomas B	39	DE	10	Elizabeth	15	DE	284	Joseph	20	DE	234
William H	72	DE	222	Elizabeth	20	PA	360	Joseph	36	DE	370
William T	36	DE	222	Elizabeth	23	PA	375	Joseph E	7	DE	114
William P	24	DE	296	Elizabeth	32	NJ	29	Joseph F	6	DE	349
William Z	1/12	DE	296	Elizabeth	44	DE	155	Joshua K	7	GB	396
Zachariah M	45	DE	229	Elizabeth	72	DE	106	Julia	4	DE	88
Zachariah M Jr	6	DE	229	Elizabeth H	73	DE	388	Kate	13	DE	53
Robertson, Alfred S	2	DE	30	Elizabeth J	26	PA	324	Kitty	45	DE	53
Eliza A	24	DE	30	Elizabeth M	69	DE	310	Lewis H	12	DE	103
Martha	21	DE	30	Elizabeth W	36	DE	87	Lydia	27	DE	186
Robinett, A McLane	19	PA	4	Ella	2	DE	271	Lydia	52	DE	317
A McLane	50	DE	4	Emit M	40	DE	322	Margaret	3	DE	379
Anna A	45	DE	78	Emma E	8	DE	88	Margaret	6	PA	381
Catherine	31	DE	141	Frances	8	GB	396	Margaret	10	MD	207
David	26	DE	141	Frances	9	GB	300	Margaret	10	DE	370
David	52	DE	116	George	1	DE	263	Margaret	11	DE	241
Evan H	12	PA	116	George	8	DE	44	Margaret	18	DE	130
George H	8	DE	116	George	13	DE	375	Margaret	24	PA	324
Hannah L	7	VA	4	George	14	DE	262	Margaret	39	DE	57
Hannah S	31	DE	3	George	14	DE	301	Margaret	50	DE	372
Henry C	9	VA	4	George	32	DE	29	Margaret	58	DE	87
Jane	21	DE	4	George H	34	DE	100	Margaret	60	PA	44
Joseph R	22	PA	4	Gertrude	45	NJ	376	Margaret A	13	DE	95
Joseph R	50	DE	2	Gilbert	7/12	DE	271	Margaret J	2	DE	370
Kesiah	46	DE	116	Hannah	3	DE	29	Marina	5	DE	29
Lewis	5	DE	141	Hannah	4	DE	396	Martha	14	DE	27
Mary S	16	PA	4	Hannah	51	GB	399	Mary	4	DE	44
Sarah	15	PA	4	Hannah	62	DE	303	Mary	7	DE	65
Sarah	47	DE	3	Hannah E	2/12	DE	170	Mary	19	DE	167
Sarah J	50	DE	78	Hannah J	12	MD	322	Mary	20	DE	370
Susan	46	PA	4	Hannah R	4	DE	95	Mary	22	DE	87
Theodore	12	PA	4	Harriet	10	DE	95	Mary	22	DE	263
William	3	DE	141	Harriet	13	DE	241	Mary	25	DE	130
Robins, Gerard	14	MD	313	Harriet A	7	DE	170	Mary	29	DE	263
Hannah	53	NJ	89	Harris	1	DE	263	Mary	30	DE	100
Thomas	40	NJ	89	Henrietta	17	DE	286	Mary	32	DE	131
Robinson, Abraham	45	DE	64	Henrietta	38	DE	64	Mary	32	GB	300
Acquilla G	31	DE	56	Henry N	2	DE	322	Mary	35	IE	331
Adaline H	6	DE	370	Hester	5	DE	370	Mary	36	NJ	114
Agnes	15	DE	64	Hester	65	DE	286	Mary	60	IE	331
Alban	16	DE	295	Hester A	18	DE	106	Mary	63	ME	43
Albert	20	DE	263	Isaac	37	PA	375	Mary	76	DE	148
Alfred	21	BE	400	J L (Capt)	42	DE	131	Mary A	28	DE	88
Alice	25	DE	170	Jacob	29	DE	54	Mary A	10	DE	170
Amanda	1	DE	186	Jacob	52	DE	270	Mary A	15	DE	370
Amelieth	25	DE	271	James	2/12	DE	26	Mary A	17	MD	322

Robinson, Mary A	28	DE	353	Robinson, William B	27	DE	271	Roe, Elizabeth	57	DE	370
Mary A	37	NJ	298	William E	10/12	DE	88	Joseph	18	DE	274
Mary A	37	DE	388	William H	2	DE	353	Mary	18	NJ	174
Mary Ann	28	IE	338	William H	5	DE	100	Roestow, Bridget	34	IE	345
Mary C	36	DE	56	William H	8	DE	322	Catherine	5	DE	345
Mary E	17	DE	288	William H	31	GB	396	Elizabeth	3	DE	345
Mary E	18	DE	56	William Jr	25	DE	287	John	12	DE	345
Mary J	3	DE	186	William P	30	DE	359	Madeline	11	DE	345
Mary J	17	DE	343	William T B	7	DE	376	Mary Ann	8	DE	345
Mary L	2	DE	353	Wm	31	DE	267	Mary Jane	1	DE	345
Mary R	9	DE	317	Wm C	30	ST	263	Peter	27	SZ	345
Mary R	10	DE	88	Robson, William	20	GB	311	Rosanna	15	DE	345
Mary W	1	DE	298	Rochester, John H	18	DE	305	Rogers, Alace	52	IE	35
Matilda	30	PA	363	Rock, John	22	IE	351	Alice	18	GB	390
Michael	23	DE	186	Mary	13	DE	295	Ann	16	IE	343
Mysinger	29	MD	349	Sarah	28	DE	288	Ann	48	DE	118
Naomi	6	DE	54	William	12	DE	76	Ann	102	IE	350
Nathaniel	50	DE	154	Rockhill, Alice	26	PA	367	Anna	38	MD	330
Phillis	55	DE	91	Ann	6	PA	367	Anna B	12	DE	312
Phoebe	14	DE	64	Daniel	5	DE	367	Bridget	6	IE	343
Phoebe A	34	DE	349	Edward	34	NJ	367	Bridget	40	IE	343
Rachel H	25	DE	359	Margaret	1	PA	367	Catherine	8	IE	35
Rebecca	7	GB	26	Roscoe	3	DE	367	Charles	17	DE	379
Rebecca	24	DE	65	Rockwell, Caroline	22	DE	122	Charles	22	DE	32
Rebecca	28	DE	379	Francis W	6	NY	100	Dinah	60	DE	41
Rebecca	40	DE	241	Frederic F	3	DE	100	Elijah	17	PA	310
Richard	10	DE	241	Hamilton P	3/12	DE	100	Eliza	18	DE	387
Richard	14	DE	53	J E (Rev)	34	VT	100	Eliza	22	IE	401
Richard	18	PA	360	Mary A	5	NY	100	Eliza L	1	DE	330
Richard	23	GB	399	Mary E	32	NY	100	Elizabeth	75	MD	120
Richard	40	NJ	114	Rodan, Elizabeth	48	IE	59	Emmaline	9	DE	330
Richard	40	DE	388	John	48	IE	59	Eugene	30	DE	304
Richard	60	GB	360	Rodden, Ellen	19	IE	88	George	25	PA	187
Richard H	14	DE	114	Mary	18	IE	88	Hugh	10	IE	343
Robert D	55	DE	317	Rodes, Lydia	9	DE	374	Hugh	40	IE	343
Robert L	13	DE	317	Rodgers, Francis	4	DE	342	Hugh	50	IE	350
Samuel	27	GB	360	Francis	29	IE	342	Isabella	20	DE	28
Samuel A	2	DE	170	Jefferson	25	DE	337	James	70	DE	304
Samuel W	9	DE	100	John	31	IE	342	James B	37	DE	312
Sarah	17	MD	221	Mary	20	IE	401	Jesse	50	DE	118
Sarah	19	DE	64	Mary Ann	2	DE	342	John	15/12	DE	341
Sarah	26	MD	370	Mary R	3	DE	337	John	20	IE	35
Sarah	28	DE	44	Thos J	2	DE	337	John	20	IE	343
Sarah	34	NJ	95	Victorine	29	DE	342	Joseph G	40	GB	390
Sarah	38	DE	301	Rodic, James	3/12	DE	336	Joseph H	29	DE	304
Sarah A	16	DE	241	Mary	24	IE	336	Julian	27	DE	304
Sarah A	28	DE	88	Timothy	27	IE	336	Louisa	11	PA	164
Sarah A	35	DE	369	Rodney, Alverde	1	DE	300	Margaret	18	IE	137
Sarah C	11	DE	376	Angelina C	19	PA	282	Margaret	18	IE	343
Sarah C	42	PA	322	Caesar A	8	DE	251	Maria	14	DE	332
Sarah E	10	DE	349	Celeste	1	DE	251	Maria	60	DE	304
Sarah M	20	DE	317	Cesar	10	DE	155	Maria B	14	DE	312
Spencer	31	DE	65	Cesar	60	DE	155	Mary	53	DE	316
Stephen D	2	DE	379	Daniel	17	PA	282	Mary A	12	DE	330
Susan	22	DE	59	Eliza C	2	PA	175	Mary C	35	MD	9
Susan	26	DE	279	Emily	9	DE	282	Matthew	14	IE	148
Susan	35	DE	53	Francis	44	DE	300	Melton C	11	DE	312
Susanah	69	PA	54	George	4	DE	300	Patric	50	IE	35
Thomas	5	DE	288	George W	30	PA	175	Robert	42	DE	330
Thomas	10	DE	375	Geo B	45	DE	282	Robert	60	IE	350
Thomas H	38	DE	95	Geo B Jr	7	DE	282	Robert C	26	DE	305
Thomas M	40	DE	288	Hannah	28	PA	175	Sarah	30	DE	145
Thomas S	4	DE	298	Henry	6	DE	251	Sarah A	32	PA	312
Vincent	16	PA	6	James	2	DE	300	Sarah E	22	DE	337
Volumnia	30	GB	26	James L	13	DE	282	Susan	19	IE	126
Washington	11	DE	270	John	7/12	DE	175	Thomas	30	MD	321
Westlegh	28	NJ	353	John C	3	DE	251	Thomas W	5	DE	312
William	10	DE	44	John Henry	11	DE	282	Thos	21	IE	341
William	11	DE	288	Margaret	16	DE	282	Thos W	68	DE	282
William	17	DE	103	Margaret B	16	DE	332	W H	39	DE	9
William	22	DE	28	Mary	5	DE	300	William	20	PA	387
William	22	IE	346	Mary	25	DE	300	Rogerson, Anna J	38	DE	145
William	23	DE	383	Rachel	66	DE	155	Edward	6	DE	145
William	25	DE	286	Susan M	34	DE	251	Evans	29	GB	96
William	38	DE	26	Thomas M	45	DE	251	Mary	26	GB	96
William	40	DE	370	Rodolph, Charlotta	43	DE	32	Thomas	40	ST	145
William	45	PA	349	Franklin	19	DE	32	William T	4	DE	145
William	46	GB	399	Horace	2	DE	32	Rogman, Esther	26	DE	272
William	56	DE	353	John	53	PA	32	George	3	DE	272
William	58	DE	298	Martha	24	DE	32	George	40	GB	272
William	67	DE	286	William	26	DE	32	Mary	2	DE	272
William B	18	DE	399	Roe, Elizabeth	57	DE	370	Rohan, Charles G	3	DE	173

Name	Age	State	Page
Rohan, Daniel	1	DE	173
Joseph R	5	DE	173
Lavinia A	20	DE	173
Robert	26	DE	173
Roland, Adaline	3	DE	154
J M	32	DE	379
Joanna	40	DE	154
Joseph	50	DE	154
Lydia A	6	DE	379
Manluf D	1	DE	379
Mary E	7	DE	154
Ruth A	45	DE	154
Sarah E	31	MD	379
William H	3	DE	379
Roley, James	3	DE	156
Rolla, Eliza	60	DE	86
Rollick, Hetty A	40	DE	162
Rollins, Alexander	11	DE	153
Harriet A	15	DE	153
June	22	DE	152
Nancy	49	MD	153
Robert	24	ME	152
Samuel	20	DE	153
William	23	GB	302
Rolly, Mary E	16	DE	166
Ronalds, Sarah F	35	DE	307
Roney, Barclay	27	PA	175
Ellen	2	DE	175
James	4/12	DE	147
John	23	DE	147
Rachel	26	DE	175
Susanah	21	PA	147
Ronich, Bartholomew	32	IE	399
Roop, Almira	13	DE	314
Francis A	37	PA	314
James	63	PA	314
Joseph	10	DE	314
Joseph F	11	MS	314
Kesiah J	38	DE	314
Lydia M	24	DE	314
Margaret	7	MS	314
Maria D	18	DE	314
Maria J	50	DE	314
Robert	4	DE	314
Sarah T	20	DE	314
Roope, Constantine	39	GE	107
George	8	PA	107
John	6	DE	107
Susanah	42	GE	107
Ropers, James	9	DE	371
David	44	DE	371
Ellen	17	DE	371
Mary Jane	6	DE	371
John	12	DE	371
Margaret	15	DE	371
Robert	10	DE	371
Samuel	4	DE	371
Rork, Catharine	11/12	DE	388
Charlotte	1	DE	388
James	32	IE	388
Mary M	27	IE	388
Timothy	3	IE	388
Rorrick, Thomas	30	IE	398
Rose, Angeline	4	DE	170
Ann	11	DE	307
Ann E	5	DE	170
Anna	8	DE	170
Anna E	4/12	DE	169
David C	27	DE	169
Eliza A	24	MD	171
Greensberry	29	NJ	169
Henry L	39	DE	170
Henry T	1	DE	170
Lurene J	2	PA	169
Margaret	22	PA	169
Martha	8/12	DE	169
Mary	24	DE	169
Mary A	35	DE	170
Mary L	14	IN	170
Ruth A	27	DE	169
Sarah E	2	DE	169
Sarah L	3	DE	170
Rose, Thomas	26	PA	366
Trueman	3/12	DE	169
Turpin	24	DE	119
William E	11	DE	170
William W	40	DE	170
Rosell, Mary	65	NJ	136
Rosen, Mary	35	MD	246
William	30	PA	246
William	25	IE	246
Roslain, Mary	16	DE	159
Ross, Alexander	40	IE	375
Amelia	20	DE	299
Amelia	55	MD	299
Ann	19	DE	343
Ann	22	DE	260
Ann	74	DE	155
Ann E	26	MD	291
Anna M	3	DE	381
Anne	27	IE	30
Caleb	23	DE	299
Caleb	65	DE	299
Charles G	22	DE	343
David	50	MD	96
Edward	28	MD	291
Eliza	30	PA	60
Elizabeth	24	DE	343
Emeline	22	DE	299
Emeline	24	DE	48
Hannah J	14	PA	104
Henry	53	DE	343
James	3	MD	60
James	3	DE	299
James	6	DE	291
James	30	DE	168
James	40	IE	60
James S	17	DE	343
John	14	DE	298
Joseph	30	DE	380
Margaret	1	DE	60
Martha	35	DE	166
Martha	77	DE	392
Mary	4	DE	291
Mary	14	DE	299
Mary	23	IE	96
Matilda	8	MD	60
Matilda	22	DE	380
Sarah	51	DE	343
Sarah E	15	DE	343
Sina	18	DE	299
Susanah	5	MD	60
Thomas J	9/12	DE	381
William	20	DE	206
William H	8/12	DE	96
William H	21	DE	343
Rosser, Andrew W	4	DE	376
Caroline	20	DE	260
Charles W	2	DE	376
Henrietta	65	DE	260
John	5	DE	260
John	25	DE	260
Lemuel	40	MD	376
Mary E	6	DE	376
Mary J	32	DE	376
Roth, Edward	28	IE	163
Rothwell, Abraham	8	DE	240
Abraham	30	DE	114
Abraham	50	DE	240
Alexander	19	DE	240
Alfred	12	DE	276
Amelia J	3	DE	240
Angeline	15	DE	247
Ann	2	DE	233
Ann	5	DE	208
Ann	18	DE	179
Ann	40	MD	208
Anne	18	DE	276
Benjamin	34	DE	368
Caroline	20	DE	276
Catharine	13	DE	220
Catharine	14	DE	208
Catherine	25	DE	233
Deborah	56	DE	368
Rothwell, Debra	4	DE	114
Ebenezer	64	DE	208
Eliza	37	DE	276
Eliza J	1	DE	197
Ellen	13	DE	276
Emaline	7	DE	197
George	2	DE	247
George	5	DE	233
Gideon E	33	DE	233
Grace	16	MD	354
Hannah	48	DE	240
Hannah E	14	DE	240
Henrietta	3	DE	233
Henry	20	DE	197
Isaac	5	DE	276
Isaac	39	DE	276
Isaac D	9	DE	240
Jacob	1	DE	114
Jacob	70	DE	368
James P	12	DE	228
Joellen	10	DE	247
John M	16	DE	228
Joseph	8/12	DE	277
Lydia	1	DE	228
Lydia	45	DE	247
Lydia A	9	DE	247
Lydia R	40	DE	228
Margaret	16	DE	276
Maria E	6/12	DE	247
Martha	10	DE	228
Mary	6	DE	114
Mary A	12	DE	240
Mary E	8	DE	364
Perry	1	DE	247
Perry	45	DE	247
Priscilla	45	DE	240
Rachel	11	DE	240
Rebecca	3	DE	277
Rebecca	16	DE	247
Richard T	6/12	DE	240
Robert R R	20	DE	228
Ruth Ann	12	DE	208
Samuel	6	DE	276
Samuel H	52	DE	208
Samuel L	2	DE	208
Sarah	29	DE	114
Sarah A	15	DE	359
Sarah E	6/12	DE	240
Thomas H	8	DE	228
Washington	4	DE	228
Wilhelmina	9	DE	208
William	15	DE	240
William	24	DE	197
William	44	DE	240
William	67	DE	228
William A	2	DE	212
Wilmina	4	DE	248
Wilmina	7	DE	240
Roulson, Jane	18	DE	37
Roup, Elizabeth	18	VA	264
Rowand, Anna T	36	NJ	284
Ellen F	18	NJ	284
Wilmina	19	NJ	284
Rowe, Dennis	4	DE	343
Dennis	48	IE	343
Eliza	6	DE	343
Elizabeth	35	ST	343
Ellen	16	ST	343
Jane	10	ST	343
Mary A	12	ST	343
Richard	14	ST	343
Thomas	2	DE	343
William	23	ST	343
Rowen, Henry	45	DE	382
John	14	DE	382
Mary	44	DE	382
Mary C	18	DE	382
Thomas	24	MD	183
William P	9	DE	382
Rowland, Beulah	58	NJ	284
Emma	2	DE	293
George	19	PA	293

Name	Age	St	Pg
Rowland, Hannah	10	DE	293
Jeuba S	15	PA	293
Lydia	5	DE	293
Mary	43	PA	293
Mary A	17	PA	293
Priscilla	7	DE	293
Richard	61	IE	293
Sarah R	12	PA	293
William	63	NJ	293
Rowley, John	30	VA	4
Roy, Alexander	50	DE	319
Hiland	24	DE	316
Jane	46	MD	324
John	11	DE	324
Maria	23	DE	316
Martha A	4	DE	324
Mary A	28	DE	319
Mary J	12	DE	324
Oliver	25	DE	324
Oliver	26	DE	319
Reuben	6	DE	324
Reuben	47	DE	324
Sophia	7	DE	324
Whilamena	16	MD	324
William	16	DE	316
Royal, Catherine J	23	MD	119
Dolly	51	NJ	89
Ephraim	24	NJ	119
Mary	18	NJ	119
William	7/12	DE	119
Royce, Ellen	7	DE	20
Eva	30	PA	20
Frederic	28	DE	52
Henry	5	DE	20
Herbert	2	DE	20
William	9	PA	20
William P	33	MA	20
Rozell, John P	28	DE	313
Mary H	29	VA	313
Sarah	1/12	DE	313
Rozene, Anna M	33	MD	314
Charles C	6/12	DE	315
Frederick	17	MD	314
Frederick	48	FR	314
George N	5	DE	314
John E	3	DE	314
John G	45	FR	314
Mary F	8	DE	314
Susan	45	FR	314
Susan A	10	DE	314
Ruake, Charles	30	IE	17
Rubincome, Charles H	5	DE	372
Jacob	37	DE	372
John	30	DE	372
Margaret H	8/12	DE	372
Mary	24	DE	372
Mary E	2	DE	372
Rebecca	40	DE	372
Rebecca Ann	9	DE	372
Rudd, Elizabeth	4	DE	222
Susannah	1	DE	222
William	31	DE	222
Ruderic, Catherine	38	IE	150
George	48	GB	150
Rudman, Anna M	1	DE	77
Eliza	6	DE	77
Hannah	5	DE	77
Jane	30	DE	77
Phillip	32	DE	77
Rudoff, Elizabeth	10	DE	372
Rudolf, John	12	PA	398
John	--	DE	290
Rudrow, Jane	8	NJ	379
Rue, Ann J	18	DE	130
Edward	4	DE	130
Evan	18	DE	130
James L	45	PA	380
Lucy	7	DE	130
Lutitia	48	PA	380
Mary	46	DE	130
Mary E	41	DE	130
Rebecca	53	DE	130
Rue, Washington	10	DE	130
William	13	DE	130
William W	45	DE	130
Ruely, John	19	DE	316
Samuel	16	DE	318
Rumburger, Jacob	21	GE	174
Rumer, Ann J	6	DE	295
Eliza J	38	DE	382
Elizabeth	24	DE	295
Elizabeth	36	GB	295
Ellen	55	DE	295
George	40	DE	383
Georgianna	7	DE	384
Hannah	13	DE	384
Henrietta	6	DE	384
Henry	68	PA	374
John	8	DE	295
John	29	DE	295
Mariah	9	DE	384
Mariah	40	DE	383
Martha	17	DE	383
Martha	17.	DE	384
Mary	4	DE	295
Mary	15	DE	384
Mary	65	PA	374
Matilda	3	DE	384
William	38	DE	295
Rumford, Alfred	6	DE	145
Charles	9	DE	115
Edward	9	DE	145
Elizabeth G	11	PA	58
Francis	12	DE	56
Helen	11	DE	145
Henry	4	DE	145
Isaac	16	DE	43
Isaac	16	DE	56
Jonathan	50	DE	145
Margaret	16	DE	115
Margaret	30	DE	115
Margaret	68	DE	115
Maria	40	DE	145
Mary	21	DE	56
Rebecca	14	DE	56
Sarah	53	NJ	56
Sidney J	37	DE	145
William	19	DE	56
William	50	DE	115
William H	18	DE	115
Rummer, Amanda	8/12	DE	384
Rummis, David	28	DE	333
Sarah A	25	DE	333
Rush, Margaret	13	DE	172
Rusk, James	3	DE	174
Mary J	12	DE	174
Mary J	37	DE	174
Matilda	6	DE	174
Phoebe A	9	DE	174
Ruben	40	DE	174
Sarah E	16	DE	174
Russ, William	20	DE	205
Russel, Amelia	45	DE	183
Ann	5	DE	345
Ann	25	IE	326
Ann	35	IE	345
Ann	41	DE	372
Ann Elizabeth	2	DE	348
Anna	13	DE	373
Benjamin R	34	PA	144
Caroline	10	DE	45
Catharine	9/12	DE	345
Chamberlin	12	DE	351
Eliza	9	DE	345
Eliza	18	IE	360
Elizabeth	4	DE	373
Elizabeth	18	DE	45
Elizabeth	50	IE	45
George W	3	DE	348
George W	9	DE	351
George W	16	DE	372
Gilbert	19	DE	397
Hebe	75	DE	347
Irwin	18	DE	8
Russel, Isaac P	17	DE	372
Jackson	9	DE	8
Jacob	50	GB	8
James	3	DE	345
James	10	DE	373
James	36	IE	345
James	40	GB	373
James R	5	DE	351
Jane	24	DE	78
Jane	32	DE	347
Jennie	15	IE	8
John	3	DE	326
John	15	IE	8
John	20	DE	45
John	22	IE	326
John	25	IE	326
John	51	PA	356
John L	17	DE	351
Joseph	20	IE	345
Joshua	26	DE	78
Ken	78	IE	348
Latitia A	14	DE	351
Lydia S	42	DE	351
Margarella	73	IE	58
Margaret	12	DE	345
Margaret	38	DE	372
Mariana	17	DE	375
Mary	6	DE	373
Mary	35	DE	8
Mary	45	DE	331
Mary E	12	DE	372
Mary T	44	DE	375
Morris	16	DE	159
Rachel	45	DE	331
Rachel	60	PA	68
Rebecca J	12	DE	347
Robert	2	DE	78
Robert	40	PA	372
Rosanna	11	DE	347
Samuel	51	PA	351
Samuel T	7	DE	351
Sarah	39	GB	373
Sarah J	8	DE	373
Simeon	19	GB	353
Thomas	7	DE	45
Thomas	14	DE	365
Virginia	14	DE	8
Washington	51	DE	375
William	8	DE	347
William	16	DE	159
William	38	DE	348
Russell, Absalom	12	DE	185
Absalom	13	MD	259
Alfred	18	GE	117
Amy J	25	DE	276
Ann M	50	MD	391
Annabella	16	RI	315
Anthony J	4/12	DE	276
Arthur W	27	DE	389
Daniel	5	DE	259
Daniel	38	MD	259
Eliza	16	PA	148
Elizabeth	19	DE	393
Elizabeth	25	IE	311
Elizabeth	34	DE	286
Ellen	22	DE	58
Jacob	30	DE	276
James H K	31	DE	307
John	20	DE	31
Joseph	13	PA	348
Levi	38	DE	286
Lewis	16	GE	117
M T C	7	DE	307
Maria	40	MD	260
Mary	24	IE	342
Mary	55	PA	393
Mary	60	DE	283
Mary L	21	DE	391
Mathew	8	DE	145
Moses	65	DE	283
Phillip	21	GE	117
Rebecca	4	DE	258

Russell, Rosanna	10	DE	258
Sampson	40	DE	261
Samuel	6	DE	145
Sarah	7	MD	259
Sarah	24	DE	261
Sarah S	12	DE	286
Sarah T	18	DE	161
William	14	DE	286
William	18	DE	117
William	20	DE	393
Russle, David	18	IE	356
Sophia	62	CN	295
William	35	IE	356
William	37	DE	346
Rust, Levi	22	GE	142
Rusten, Edward	17	PA	80
Rebecca	4	PA	80
Thomas	38	PA	80
Rusum, Benjamin	18	DE	291
Eliza	40	MD	282
Ruth, Allen	10	DE	385
Amos	19	DE	385
Hannah	50	DE	357
Harriet A	13	DE	357
John	12	DE	385
John	47	DE	357
John P	18	DE	357
Levi	8	DE	385
Levi	30	DE	386
Levi C	9	DE	358
Margaret	16	DE	358
Margaret J	1	DE	386
Mary E	3	DE	386
Mary J	20	DE	357
Mary J	20	DE	377
Phebe	38	DE	385
Rebecca	27	DE	386
Saml	35	DE	254
Theodore	2	DE	385
Thomas	7	DE	254
Thomas	19	DE	193
Virginia	10	DE	177
William	15	DE	385
William	41	DE	385
William H	9	DE	176
Wm	9	DE	254
Ruther, Blythe	40	PA	274
Elizabeth J	15	DE	274
Esther A	17	DE	274
Francena	22	DE	383
Isabella	68	DE	272
James B	4	DE	274
Ketinah	9	DE	274
Lydia	38	PA	274
Sarah V M	1	DE	274
Wilhemina	7	DE	274
Rutherford, Elizabeth	6	PA	109
Elizabeth	42	MD	109
Hugh	4/12	PA	109
Jane	10	PA	108
Mary	16	PA	108
Rachel S	3	PA	108
Samuel	12	PA	108
Samuel	43	IE	108
Sarah	8	PA	108
Thomas H	14	PA	108
Ruthvin, Anna J	17	PA	350
Catherine	21	PA	350
Emily F	8	PA	350
Emora	3	PA	350
John	44	PA	350
John H	6	PA	350
Phoebe A	14	PA	350
Rebecca	11	PA	350
Rebecca	47	NJ	350
Samuel A	18	PA	350
Rutter, Isabella	68	DE	273
Jane	20	DE	76
Jemima R	10/12	DE	76
John E	23	DE	76
Joshua	10	PA	76
Ruzere, Charles	32	GE	33
Ryan, Ann	12	DE	148
Catherine	36	IE	148
Elizabeth	40	DE	176
Hannah	26	IE	130
John	19	IE	349
John	22	IE	3
Julia	18	IE	148
Levi	51	DE	176
Martin	9	IE	148
Mary	2	DE	148
Mary	3	DE	3
Mary	35	IE	3
Mathew	9	IE	136
Michel	5	IE	136
Patric	38	IE	136
Patric	40	IE	148
Patric	3	FR	3
Samuel	10/12	DE	3
William	23	DE	176
Ryans, Edward	25	IE	157
Elizabeth	32	IE	341
Fargas	25	IE	341
Percy	19	IE	157
Ryder, Charles	78	DE	377
James	26	DE	377
Jane	5/12	DE	381
Joseph	32	MD	381
Margaret A	13	DE	375
Mary A	21	DE	378
Rachel	50	MD	375
Rachel	54	MD	381
Sarah E	20	DE	375
Susan J	21	MD	381
Ryen, Agusta	1	FR	343
Catharine	25	FR	343
Frances	33	FR	343
Lewis	5	FR	343
Mitchel	3	FR	343
Ryland, Hannah A	2/12	DE	235
Jacob	25	DE	235
Mary	21	DE	235
Ryley, Susan	18	PA	137
Ryman, Frances	45	WL	352
Sacks, Stephen	43	GE	371
Sadler, Frances	5	DE	92
Mary A	6/12	DE	92
Phoebe	60	DE	47
Saddler, David J	1	DE	208
Elizabeth R	1	DE	191
Isaac C	6/12	DE	208
James	30	MD	191
James W	6	DE	191
John A	24	MD	208
Louisa	8	MD	191
Margaret	20	DE	208
Mary	28	MD	191
William T	3	DE	208
Salmon, Robert	16	DE	194
Salon, Jane	65	DE	331
Salsbury, Hannah	55	DE	168
Samborn, Elizabeth	16	DE	376
Mary	1	DE	37
Rebecca	20	DE	37
Sarah	30	DE	49
Thomas	26	DE	37
Sammond, David H	10	DE	321
Sammons, Daniel	29	DE	329
George H B	32	DE	329
Hassari	62	DE	329
James	19	DE	329
Jane	30	DE	331
John	23	DE	329
Joseph	15	DE	329
Mary	30	MD	329
Rachel A	20	DE	329
William H	26	DE	329
Sampel, John	1	DE	311
John	40	DE	311
Margaret	25	DE	311
Mary	60	DE	311
William	25	DE	311
Sampel, Mary	60	DE	311
William	25	DE	311
Sample, Elizabeth	60	DE	397
Sampler, Susan	25	DE	47
Sampson, Ann E	14	GB	296
Elizabeth	38	GB	296
Ester	3	NJ	33
Israel	33	MA	33
John	5	RI	33
Sarah	10	DE	34
Sinthy	33	NY	33
Sophia	48	MD	183
Thomas	35	DE	114
Thomas	41	GB	296
Viola	1	DE	33
Samsal, Julia	11	IE	329
Mary E	17	MD	339
Patrick	14	IE	329
William	6	IE	329
Sanborn, David (Dr)	45	NH	46
Hester	35	NY	46
Hyland	56	NH	43
Jennett	17	DE	46
Julia	43	PA	43
Mahala	16	NH	43
Martha	15	DE	46
Sanburn, Albert	25	NH	317
Sanders, Abermella	8	DE	192
Alice	5	DE	191
Alice	10	DE	318
Amos	2	DE	380
Amos Jr	33	DE	380
Amy E	3	DE	187
Ann	79	PA	380
Anna	29	MD	285
Anne	52	DE	15
Catharine	32	DE	281
Charlotte	9	DE	318
Clarissa	7	DE	187
Daniel	3	MD	38
Daniel	19	DE	37
David	40	DE	209
Edward	4	DE	101
Elias	11	DE	202
Eliza	32	DE	187
Ellis	55	DE	15
Franklin	7	DE	318
George	58	DE	329
Hannah	52	DE	331
Harriet	15	DE	101
Harriet	35	MD	38
Harwood	60	DE	209
Henry	27	DE	230
Hetty	10	DE	101
Hetty	44	DE	101
Houston	8	DE	101
Hyland	60	DE	210
Isaac	17	DE	318
Isaac	18	DE	191
Isaac	35	DE	285
Isaac	45	DE	288
Israel	6/12	DE	191
Jacob	17	DE	37
Jacob	70	DE	397
James	1	DE	68
James	5	DE	380
James	11	DE	191
James	13	DE	318
Jefferson	20	DE	331
John	2	DE	285
John	6	MD	38
John	20	DE	54
John	21	DE	37
John	30	MD	38
John	36	DE	191
John B	20	DE	191
John J	24	DE	68
Joseph	1	DE	191
Joshua	21	PA	101
Julia A	5	DE	192
Levi	30	DE	281
Levi	40	DE	187

Name	Age	St	Pg
Sanders, Louisa	15	DE	318
Louisa	16	DE	191
Lydia	50	DE	37
Margaret	20	MD	68
Mary	40	DE	230
Mary E	16	DE	329
Mary J	27	DE	380
Nathan	28	DE	380
Peter	17	DE	101
Phebe A	7	DE	380
Rachel	35	DE	191
Rachel	51	DE	318
Rachel	56	DE	329
Rachel	60	DE	397
Robert	20	DE	54
Ruth A	27	DE	230
Solomon	60	DE	331
Thomas	8	DE	191
Thomas	12	DE	318
William	4/12	DE	101
William	13	DE	173
William	16	DE	318
William	50	DE	101
William H	13	DE	191
Sandhusen, Frederic	30	GE	250
Sandor, Benjamin	13	MD	163
Sands, Margaret	28	DE	10
Sandy, William	13	DE	172
Sanjuan, Leander	17	CU	154
Sankey, John G	35	DE	375
John G Jr	9	MD	375
Sanner, Anna	65	IE	15
Mary	16	IE	15
Santage, Anne	7	DE	139
Catherine	5	DE	139
Charles	2	DE	139
Henry	7/12	DE	139
Henry A	36	GE	139
Maria	10	PA	139
Williamina	35	GE	139
Sapp, Ann	19	MD	31
Sargent, Benjamin	26	MD	32
Saring, Edward	2	PA	75
Elizabeth	80	PA	75
Samuel	40	PA	75
Sasender, Hannah	73	GB	105
Sash, Francis A	11	DE	229
Jacob	3	DE	229
James	56	DE	229
James A	5	DE	229
Louisa	8	DE	229
Maria	38	DE	229
William A	6	DE	229
Sathel, Henry	35	DE	226
Martha	2	DE	226
Mary	25	DE	226
Samuel	6	DE	226
Sarah	4	DE	226
William	8	DE	226
Sauden, Emeline	20	DE	311
Emma	2	DE	311
Thomas	27	DE	311
Saunders, Absolem	42	DE	258
Annie	9	PA	274
Benjamin	72	PA	382
Casey	4	PA	274
Charlotte	28	DE	258
Dallas	2	PA	274
Elias	18	DE	293
Eliza J	21	DE	400
Elizabeth	14	DE	381
Elizabeth	27	DE	382
Elizabeth	56	DE	381
Ellen R	58	DE	382
Ellis	56	MD	381
George	5/12	DE	269
Griffith	60	DE	390
Henrietta	3	DE	11
James	15	DE	380
Joel	14	DE	380
John	2	DE	380
John	4	DE	269
Saunders, John	17	DE	381
John	19	DE	309
John	40	KY	274
John H	17	DE	382
Margaret	1/12	DE	11
Margaret	21	DE	375
Maria	24	DE	11
Maria	30	PA	274
Matilda	7	PA	274
Rebecca	20	DE	382
Richard	10/12	DE	274
Samuel	6	DE	298
Samuel	16	DE	381
Sarah	38	DE	380
Sarah A	20	DE	380
Stephen	44	DE	380
Vincent	25	DE	11
William	25	DE	382
William	25	DE	400
Wm	11	PA	274
Saurdon, C P	15	DE	165
L	14	DE	165
Savage, Laura S	64	VA	332
Savel, Anna P	12	MD	84
George A	7/12	DE	84
Isaac H	8	DE	84
James	43	MD	84
Margaret	38	MD	84
Savile, Jonathan	10	PA	62
Savill, Adaline	40	DE	159
Alexander	38	DE	159
Harriet	64	NJ	159
James H	41	DE	160
Saville, Diana	34	DE	272
John	37	DE	272
Saving, Barbara	13	DE	293
Jacob	11	DE	293
Joseph	18	DE	293
Joseph	43	PA	293
Mary E	9	DE	293
Samuel	20	DE	293
Sarah A	47	DE	293
Sarah J	14	DE	293
Savoy, Elener	42	DE	21
Hannah	11	DE	21
James	13	DE	21
Mary	9	DE	21
Michel	45	DE	21
Sawyer, Susan	70	MD	54
Saxon, Alfred J	21	DE	381
Ann	18	DE	217
Anna	39	NJ	134
Elizabeth	12	DE	217
Francis A	5	NJ	134
Joseph H	52	DE	381
Phebe	52	DE	381
Sarah W	20	DE	381
Saxton, Alfred	4	DE	300
Anna	26	DE	300
Isaac	32	DE	104
James	27	DE	300
William H	1	DE	300
William H	7	DE	102
William H	33	DE	134
Sayers, Ann	11	DE	6
Ann	41	IE	162
Anne	2	DE	162
Catherine	4	DE	6
Charles H	16	DE	162
Elizabeth	30	IE	6
Ellen	9	DE	6
Franklin	6	DE	162
George	4	DE	162
George	40	IE	162
Isabella	6	DE	6
Jane	11	DE	162
John	30	IE	6
Margaret	2	DE	6
Margaret	25	PA	308
Patrick	28	IE	290
William	28	IE	308
Scan, Margaret	20	DE	10
Scanlan, Alexander	14	PA	325
Cathrine	9	PA	325
Cathrine	46	PA	325
Charles	11	PA	325
Daniel	24	PA	325
James	49	PA	325
Jamma L	2	DE	325
Mary	18	PA	325
Samuel L	17	PA	325
Scanlin, Florence	29	PA	311
Hannah	23	MD	311
James W	1	DE	311
Scanlon, John (Rev)	33	IE	163
Scantlan, James	21	PA	101
Schnepp, Maria	22	GE	250
Schofield, Margaret	13	MD	143
Robert	2	DE	319
Scilion, Catherine	20	IE	166
Susan	22	IE	166
Scofield, Cerneul	25	PA	288
Emily	30	PA	288
Emma	21	GB	332
H R	30	PA	288
Henry	12	GB	320
James	23	GB	332
Jane	28	GB	320
John	4	DE	320
John	30	GB	320
Joseph	22	GB	320
Levina	9	DE	320
Margaret	13	DE	142
Mary	17	NJ	320
Samuel	12	DE	320
Sarah	47	IE	320
Sarah A	24	GB	320
Scot, Ann	35	PA	352
Joseph	1/12	DE	352
Richard	50	MD	352
Samuel	17	DE	369
Scotman, Mary	23	DE	215
Scott, Abigail	37	DE	385
Agnes	40	DE	38
Alice	19	MI	366
Ann	27	DE	308
Ann E	9	DE	242
Betsey	34	MA	53
Burtain	21	DE	324
Catharine	50	MD	242
Eliza	9	MD	334
Elizabeth	30	DE	232
Elizabeth	70	DE	242
Francis	3	DE	334
George	5	DE	334
Hanson	20	DE	242
Harriet	8	DE	308
Henry	12	PA	313
Isaac	2	DE	308
Isaac	30	DE	308
Isabella	9	MD	352
Jacob	41	MD	334
Jalinia	9/12	DE	20
James	30	PA	20
James	35	IE	352
Jane	13	MD	315
Jane	34	IE	352
Joel	--	DE	290
John	3	DE	20
John	20	DE	327
John	21	DE	323
Jno	--	DE	290
Joseph	53	GB	53
Laura	6	DE	20
Letitia	24	DE	323
Lydia	27	DE	20
Margaret	8	DE	385
Mary	7	DE	334
Mary	21	IE	167
Mary	73	DE	319
Mary E	12	DE	323
Mary J	1	DE	308
Rachel A	3	DE	385
Robert	4	DE	308

Name	Age	Place	No.
Scott, Robert	11	MD	334
Samuel	5	DE	385
Samuel	46	DE	385
Sarah	39	DE	90
Sarah A	22	DE	242
Sarah Jane	33	DE	352
Stephen	30	IE	352
Thomas	25	ST	50
Thomas	50	DE	242
Thomas L	13	DE	242
Timothy	65	DE	281
Virginia	6	DE	385
Walter	11	DE	368
William	3	DE	232
William	18	PA	273
William	21	IE	331
William	25	DE	242
Scotten, Elizabeth	6	DE	89
Scotton, Ann	16	DE	232
Anne	8	DE	234
Greenbury	12	DE	234
Greenbury	14	DE	237
Henry	15	DE	234
John	53	DE	232
Lydia	49	DE	232
Rachel	18	DE	232
Rebecca C	6/12	DE	234
Sarah J	26	DE	232
Sophia	30	DE	234
William	35	DE	234
William Jr	4	DE	234
Scout, Augustus	6	DE	124
Catharine	47	PA	269
Edwin	8	PA	266
Elizabeth	4	DE	124
Ellen	4	PA	269
George W	35	DE	124
Georgeanna	5	PA	266
James	2	DE	124
James	17	PA	269
Jerome	1	DE	252
Jesse	52	PA	269
Maria	30	DE	124
Mary A	8	PA	269
Mary M	18	DE	304
Rebecca	8	DE	124
Sarah	20	DE	267
Susan	31	PA	266
Thomas	14	PA	269
William H	15	DE	304
Wm	30	PA	266
Scrafton, Wilson	32	GB	270
Scranton, Edmond	10	GB	201
Edward	39	GB	201
Elizabeth	6	GB	201
Ellen	8	GB	201
Julia	3	DE	201
Mary M	39	GB	201
Sculford, George	24	NJ	134
Lewis C	1	DE	134
Mary J	30	DE	134
Scully, Biddy	36	IE	147
Catherine	7	DE	148
Edward	5	DE	147
Patric	40	IE	147
Sarah	9	DE	147
Scurr, Susan	16	MA	166
Scurry, Alice	25	MD	178
Sarah	40	MD	196
Seagraves, Martha	7	DE	253
Seak, Agnes	40	GB	39
Seal, Joshua	30	DE	20
Joshua T	46	DE	163
Lydia	52	PA	162
Mary	30	DE	20
Rachel	75	PA	163
Seals, Catharine	22	DE	227
Hester	21	DE	90
John	28	DE	227
Joseph F	4	DE	227
Maria E	1	DE	90
Martin	35	DE	90
Seals, Mary E	1	DE	227
Rebecca	3	DE	227
Seares, Elizabeth	8	DE	386
John	35	IE	386
Margaret	7	DE	386
Phebe A	8/12	DE	386
Robert	2	DE	386
Sarah	35	IE	386
Sarah J	3	DE	386
Thomas	15	IE	363
Searing, Catharine	15	DE	6
Emma	2	DE	6
George	20	DE	6
John	17	DE	6
John	46	PA	6
Mary J	13	DE	6
Sarah	5	DE	6
Sarah	44	DE	6
Sebley, William	17	DE	231
Sebo, John	50	DE	32
Mary	40	NC	153
Peter	73	FR	153
Rebecca	50	DE	32
Segars, Anne E	29	DE	187
David	27	DE	187
Elijah	4/12	DE	201
Elizabeth C	17	DE	218
James	8	DE	241
James Wesley	2	DE	186
John	25	DE	201
Joseph	3	DE	201
Joseph	13	DE	187
Margaret	22	DE	241
Margaret A	1	DE	201
Margaret R	12	DE	241
Martin	12	DE	187
Mary	19	DE	187
Mary A	2	DE	241
Mary A	10	DE	187
Matilda	30	MD	201
Rebecca	2	DE	201
Samuel	32	DE	187
Samuel D J A	2/12	DE	241
Samuel J	8	DE	187
Sarah J	7	DE	187
Seiney, Araminta	14	DE	253
Charlotte	7	DE	253
David	55	MD	253
Eliza	5/12	DE	268
Elizabeth	11	DE	268
Elizabeth	12	DE	253
Ella	2	DE	268
Emeline	10	DE	253
George	26	DE	253
James	4	DE	253
Jane	27	DE	251
Joshua	45	DE	268
Mary	4/12	DE	253
Mary	46	DE	253
Philis	30	DE	268
Sarah	6	DE	268
Sarah	18	DE	253
Selah, Amanda	9	PA	126
Charles	5	DE	126
Edwin	7	PA	126
Elizabeth	33	NJ	126
John	13	PA	126
Mary A	11	PA	126
Robert	47	PA	126
William	1	DE	126
Selas, Robert	19	DE	35
Selfridge, Rebecca	22	IE	319
Selinn, Rachel	17	DE	310
Selle, Rebecca	9	PA	362
Sellers, George	35	DE	28
Lavinia	40	DE	28
Matilda	41	DE	28
W R	57	DE	28
Semi, James	3	DE	322
Sempel, James	25	DE	191
Semple, Ann	40	DE	130
Daniel	50	PA	61
Semple, Helen	17	DE	130
Jane B	30	PA	61
Senie, David L	30	MD	321
John	5	DE	321
Sarah	22	DE	321
Thomas	7	DE	321
Senix, Eli	50	DE	159
Isaac	4/12	DE	371
Jennet	26	MD	371
Joseph	28	DE	371
T W	31	DE	371
Sentman, Jane	50	PA	308
Serby, Robert	55	DE	366
Sergent, Amelia	18	MD	20
Serkiner, Eleaner	1/12	DE	170
Eliza	35	DE	170
John W	33	MD	170
Mary Louisa	6	DE	170
Sertins, Lydia A	16	DE	373
Sevel, Phebe	36	DE	139
Sevil, David	44	DE	299
Edith	40	MD	299
Seward, Daniel	6	DE	36
Daniel	30	DE	195
Eliza	14	DE	195
John	11	DE	36
John	30	DE	36
Josiah	60	DE	174
Mary	28	DE	195
Mary	35	DE	36
Rebecca	2	DE	36
Thomas	22	DE	213
Sewel, Agnes	12	DE	56
Agness	15	DE	65
Benjamin	40	DE	65
Benjamin	55	MD	56
Catherine	70	GE	5
Edith	16	DE	56
Edith	17	DE	65
Henne	50	MD	56
Henrietta	38	DE	65
John	21	DE	56
Phebe	8	DE	56
Phebe	14	DE	65
Sarah	17	MD	56
Sarah	19	DE	65
Sewell, David	32	DE	345
Edward	24	DE	297
Henry	35	DE	284
James	56	MD	284
John	26	DE	216
Seymour, Anna	8	IE	173
Sha, Bridget	49	IE	105
Catherine	9	IE	105
John	50	IE	105
Mary	7	IE	105
Thomas	50	IE	51
Schakerford, Stephen	14	DE	171
William	22	DE	171
Shadd, Amelia	14	DE	101
Amelia	50	DE	100
Amelia	75	WI	100
Andrew	19	DE	101
Caroline	10	DE	101
Isaac	22	DE	101
Jeremiah	24	DE	100
Margaret	19	DE	101
Mary E	15	DE	101
Shades, Mary	62	DE	272
Shady, Catherine	27	IE	87
Mary A	9/12	DE	87
Peter	35	IE	87
Shaefer, Elijah	50	DE	202
Rebecca	50	DE	202
Shaes, Charles	3	IE	11
Charles	25	IE	11
Elizabeth	13	IE	90
Sarah	25	IE	11
Shafer, Alexander	5	DE	337
Caroline	39	DE	337
Charles	16	PA	89
Emily	16	DE	337

Name	Age	St	No
Shafer, John	11	DE	337
John	37	DE	337
Rachel	40	NY	122
William	15	DE	337
Zachariah	2	DE	337
Shaffer, Ann	5	DE	372
Shakespear, Benjamin	61	DE	380
Benjamin W	42	DE	355
Charles	12	DE	380
Elizabeth	8	DE	380
Mary	50	DE	380
Shakespeare, Alex	2	DE	364
Ann E	17	DE	356
Benjamin	2	DE	331
Benjamin A	24	DE	174
Benjamin W	43	DE	356
Caroline	26	DE	331
Catherine	35	DE	364
Edward	4	DE	331
Eliza Ann	8	DE	364
George	2	DE	356
James	9	DE	356
John	7	DE	356
John	35	DE	364
John	82	PA	356
Louis	5	DE	364
Margaret J	12	DE	356
Margaret Jane	12	DE	363
Mariah	36	PA	356
Mary	15	DE	356
Mary	39	MD	364
Rebecca	27	DE	377
Thomas	68	DE	364
William	4	DE	356
William	31	DE	331
Shamon, Solomon	30	DE	16
Shankley, Benjamin	23	DE	92
David M	2	DE	92
James A	4/12	DE	92
Mary J	23	DE	92
Rosanna	13	DE	342
Shannon, Abraham P	52	DE	374
Ann	18	IE	282
Ann W	53	DE	374
Barnard	45	IE	163
Bridget	70	IE	287
Elizabeth	20	IE	345
John	20	IE	356
Margaret B	21	DE	374
Mary	17	DE	374
Mary Ann	18	IE	345
Mary E	16	PA	391
Shaper, Charles	16	PA	90
Sharan, James	56	NJ	161
Sarah S	40	DE	161
Sharon, Catherine	17	IE	288
Sharp, Edwin	23	PA	320
Furdenan	35	PA	320
George W	3/12	DE	320
George W	19	DE	314
Henry	24	NJ	285
Joseph	3/12	DE	320
Joseph	45	DE	320
Martha	40	GB	400
Mary A	16	CN	272
Mary A	24	PA	320
Rebecca	26	PA	320
Ruth A	45	PA	320
Susan	15	PA	349
Thomas	35	GB	400
Wm W	2	PA	320
Sharpe, Ann	5/12	DE	104
Anna	9	PA	50
Anna	27	DE	28
Eli	17	DE	57
Eli	17	DE	104
Elizabeth	8	DE	104
Elizabeth	32	DE	104
Elizabeth J	70	PA	47
Emma	1	DE	19
George	13	DE	104
Henry	8	DE	104
Sharpe, Jesse	7	DE	19
Jesse	11	DE	104
Jesse	42	DE	104
Joseph	5	DE	104
Joseph	30	DE	17
Maria	31	PA	50
Martha	13	DE	120
Martha	40	GB	401
Mary	1	PA	28
Mary	2	DE	50
Mary	3	DE	19
Phebe	50	PA	17
Rachel	51	DE	168
Richard	42	DE	120
Sabilla	3	DE	104
Sarah	13	DE	18
Sarah	20	DE	17
Sarah	32	DE	18
Sarah	49	NJ	167
Thomas	38	DE	18
William	6	PA	50
William	28	PA	28
William H	33	PA	50
Sharpless, Amos	17	DE	383
Amos	61	DE	383
Ann	32	DE	359
Ann	50	DE	383
Anna	27	DE	383
Anna E	8	DE	358
Benjamin T	12	DE	358
Caleb	24	DE	382
Caleb	63	PA	358
Edward	14	DE	383
Elizabeth	43	PA	358
Emma	6	MD	359
Jehu	25	DE	382
Joel L	8/12	DE	383
Rebecca	22	PA	383
Samuel	21	DE	383
William	12	DE	383
Sharply, Eliza	35	DE	285
Elizabeth	70	DE	285
Esau	83	DE	295
Jacob	37	DE	285
Jane	40	DE	303
John	30	DE	295
John F	19	DE	303
Margaret	17	DE	303
Mary J	21	DE	295
Matilda	34	PA	285
Rebecca	10	DE	303
Stephen	15	DE	285
Susan	7/12	DE	295
Susan	35	DE	295
William	54	DE	303
William H	4	DE	295
Shaw, Aaron	53	NJ	306
Aaron W	13	NJ	306
Alice	17	PA	164
Andrew	13	DE	164
Ann	55	GB	44
Benjamin F	31	MD	243
Catharine	1	DE	225
Charles	3	DE	221
Charlotta A	9	DE	80
Clarissa	5	DE	80
Daniel J	53	MD	325
David	6	DE	80
David	56	IE	80
Eliza	17	DE	166
Eliza A	30	DE	166
Elizabeth	5	DE	268
Elizabeth	17	DE	80
Elizabeth	27	MD	44
Elizabeth	29	DE	243
Elizabeth	46	PA	80
Ellen	55	DE	44
Emeline	4/12	DE	243
Emeline	13	DE	80
Ezekiel	6	DE	268
Ezekiel	57	NJ	259
George T	2	DE	134
Shaw, Henry	22	GB	339
James	9	DE	226
James H	5	DE	243
John	31	NJ	268
John	56	GB	44
John P	3	DE	243
John T	12	CT	325
Joseph	32	GB	339
Martha	30	DE	268
Mary	1	DE	268
Mary	22	DE	44
Mary	44	MD	325
Mary	54	NJ	259
Mary E	10	MD	243
Mary J	23	DE	80
Mary R A	5	DE	226
Rebecca	23	PA	225
Ruth	35	GB	339
S D	13	PA	163
Samuel	30	DE	189
Sarah	15	DE	80
Sarah	25	DE	44
Sarah	51	NJ	306
Sarah A	13/12	DE	339
Sarah S	10	NJ	306
Stephen	6	DE	225
Stephen	52	DE	222
Temperance	20	DE	134
Thomas	2	DE	225
William	19	DE	80
William	27	GB	134
William	28	DE	225
Shayle, Rarance	25	GE	368
Shayne, John	60	IE	350
Shea, Thomas	50	IE	52
Shearer, Ann	35	DE	44
Ann	10/12	DE	44
Joseph	2	DE	44
Joseph	38	GE	44
Shed, Catherine	45	IE	71
Sheer, Jacob	20	DE	375
Shelden, Ann	80	GB	142
Mary	23	DE	316
Edward	34	PA	316
Shell, Samuel	30	DE	87
Shelton, John	13	PA	119
Shepard, Edward	35	NJ	378
Shepherd, Alonzo	16	PA	119
Clara	1	DE	119
Emma	3	IA	119
Hannah	40	DE	106
John	13	PA	119
John	40	PA	119
Josephine	5	PA	119
Letitia	40	DE	73
Marinda	29	PA	119
Mary	70	GB	294
Shepherdson, Anne E	19	PA	61
Hannah J	13	PA	61
Richard	41	GB	61
William H	3	DE	61
Sherdon, Auther M	22	DE	85
Margaret	29	IE	309
Sherene, Catharine	50	MD	342
Sheridan, Mary	20	IE	281
Sherky, Mary	58	DE	77
George W	23	PA	77
John B	26	DE	77
Sherman, John	30	NY	263
Sherry, Elizabeth	15	DE	342
Hannah	66	IE	22
Sherwood, James	30	DE	204
Ruth	25	DE	204
Shields, Bridget	11	IE	326
Bridget	20	IE	383
Charles	25	IE	308
Edward	24	IE	11
Elizabeth	9	IE	326
Hugh	30	IE	11
James	30	IE	383
Jane	3	DE	11
Mary A	3	DE	326

Name	Age	State	No.
Shields, Peter	7	DE	326
Rose	13	IE	326
Sarah	23	PA	11
Sarah	27	IE	11
Susan	52	PA	313
Susan	60	DE	15
Shige, Benjamin	30	GB	390
George	6	GB	390
Jane	27	GB	390
Samuel	1	DE	390
Shiner, Sarah B	13	NJ	165
Shinn, Benjamin F	36	NJ	234
Eliza	28	NJ	234
Sarah A	4	NJ	234
William	7	NJ	234
Shipley, Edward	29	DE	36
Elizabeth	40	DE	137
Elizabeth	45	DE	61
Elizabeth	67	DE	55
Emma	38	DE	137
Hannah	44	DE	137
Henry	48	DE	83
Hesper	53	DE	36
John	56	DE	137
Jonathan	14	DE	359
Maria	19	DE	338
Mary J	6	DE	8
Rebecca	12	DE	8
Rebecca	13	DE	352
Robert	8	DE	338
Sarah	42	DE	137
Sarah	80	DE	34
Susan	52	DE	312
Susanah	23	DE	36
Thomas	79	DE	34
William	17	DE	89
Wm	42	DE	338
Shipps, Andrew	3	DE	159
John	41	DE	159
Maria	23	DE	159
William H	8/12	DE	159
Shippy, Mary A	12	DE	214
Shirk, Elizabeth	16	PA	393
Shirley, James	69	MD	371
Shockley, David	55	DE	174
Edith	23	DE	172
Isaac	21	DE	196
James	22	DE	196
Levinia	25	DE	174
Mary J	3	DE	174
Sewell	35	DE	174
Shoebreck, Abrella	15	DE	121
Alicia	19	DE	121
Julia	44	DE	121
Richard	12	DE	121
Shoemaker, George	25	DE	81
Shoote, Asa	36	NJ	86
Short, Abraham C	3	DE	315
Abraham M	32	DE	315
Amanda M	14	DE	323
Anna	9	DE	293
Caroline	26	DE	376
Caroline A	2	DE	376
Clara	7	DE	293
Ella	7	DE	119
Ellen	5	DE	104
Ellen	40	DE	104
Emma B	12	DE	293
Hester A	32	DE	315
Jacob F	35	NY	119
James	67	DE	293
James A	22	DE	323
John	63	DE	293
Joseph	11	DE	323
Julia	2	DE	293
Julia C	3	DE	119
Lydia	14	DE	328
Lydia E	6	DE	315
Margaret J	1	DE	376
Margaretta	11	DE	293
Maria	5	DE	119
Maria A	2	DE	318
Short, Mary	50	DE	323
Mary E	4	DE	376
Mary E	8	DE	119
Nancy	64	DE	314
Rebecca	33	DE	318
Rebecca	47	DE	293
Sarah C	32	DE	119
William	6/12	DE	318
William	43	MD	318
William	50	DE	104
William H	29	DE	376
Williamina	10	DE	119
Shorter, George	19	PA	295
Shortlege, Hyram	39	PA	369
Joshua	2	PA	369
Lydia A	14	PA	369
Martha J	12	PA	369
Mary J	36	PA	369
Samuel	8	PA	369
Showwalter, Hannah	33	DE	129
Henry	9	DE	129
Jacob	32	PA	129
Mary	7	DE	129
Shrader, Abraham	59	GE	150
Ann	53	DE	150
Clara	16	DE	150
George	21	DE	150
Margaret A	11	DE	150
Mary	22	DE	150
Mrs	82	GE	150
Shrieves, James A	16	PA	102
Shubert, Isaac	57	PA	274
Sarah	6	MO	274
Sarah	55	PA	274
Susan	21	PA	274
Shull, Henry	13	DE	144
John J	36	NJ	144
Louisa	33	PA	144
William	8	DE	144
Shullcross, Anna	1/12	DE	206
Anna	29	PA	206
Jacob	5	DE	206
James	3	DE	206
Sarah F	34	PA	206
Shultz, Abraham	66	NY	307
Mary	67	DE	307
Shurden, John	18	DE	385
Shuster, Ann E	16	DE	135
Elizabeth	37	DE	255
Evelyn	11	DE	255
George	15	PA	269
Harriet	17	DE	135
James	2	DE	255
James	36	NJ	255
John L	4	DE	255
John L	64	DE	135
Joseph	6	DE	255
Lucy	20	DE	135
Mahala	45	DE	269
Mary	8	DE	255
Mary A	23	DE	135
Matilda	18	DE	135
Samuel	18	DE	269
Sarah	13	DE	255
Shute, Amanda	5	DE	279
Catharine	5/12	DE	279
Catharine	39	NJ	279
Elizabeth	6	DE	279
Emily	48	DE	188
John	15	DE	279
Rosella	12	DE	279
Sarah E	8	DE	279
William	14	DE	279
Sibley, Catherine	24	PA	128
Eldridge	29	MA	143
Josiah	27	PA	127
Siddons, Lardner	12	PA	348
Sides, Catherine	8	DE	122
Sikes, Caroline	38	DE	399
Isaac	38	DE	399
John T	3	DE	399
Mary S	4	DE	399
Silby, Amelia	66	MD	73
Luisa	8	MD	73
Perry	50	MD	73
Silcox, Amelia	8	DE	208
Anna	58	DE	212
Anna M	9	DE	208
Eliza	60	DE	208
Eliza J	4	DE	208
James	56	MD	208
James W	15	DE	208
John	3	DE	170
Lawrence	20	DE	212
Louisa	10	DE	208
Margaret A	17	DE	212
Rachel	29	DE	170
Sarah A	12	DE	208
Spencer	42	MD	170
William M	6	DE	208
Wilmina	5	DE	170
Siles, Ellen J	35	MD	340
Francis	18	MD	341
Mary A	16	MD	341
Orin	61	NC	340
Rebecca	60	MD	340
William	21	MD	340
Sill, Elizabeth	14	DE	16
Sillcox, Almira	7	DE	230
Ann E	4	DE	246
Ann G	48	PA	230
Charles	10/12	DE	246
Edward	11	DE	230
Edward	35	MD	230
Elias	40	DE	246
John	12	DE	230
Sarah	9	DE	246
Sarah	25	DE	246
Thomas	21	MD	230
William	5	DE	246
Sillitoe, Ann R	18	PA	314
Edward H	56	GB	314
Margaret	48	PA	314
William W	11	DE	314
Silver, Albert H	10	DE	291
Henry H	15	DE	291
Jacob	20	DE	374
Samuel	21	DE	291
Sarah	53	DE	291
Sarah E	16	DE	291
William	55	NJ	291
Wilson	54	NJ	297
Simmons, Amos	1	DE	53
Amos	33	GE	53
Angelina	23	PA	126
Ann	5	DE	335
Ann	8	DE	323
Ann	22	DE	326
Ann	34	DE	50
Ann	40	DE	28
Ann	52	DE	126
Ann E	2	DE	107
Anna	4	DE	53
Anna M	19	DE	153
Augustus	8	DE	53
Bandery	45	DE	28
Benjamin	15	DE	256
Benjamin	20	DE	186
Catharine	34	MD	325
Catharine A	1	DE	330
Catharine A	21	DE	297
Charles	4	DE	28
Charles	15	DE	53
Edward	7	DE	50
Edward T	18	DE	135
Edwards	34	DE	135
Eliza	3/12	DE	129
Elizabeth	14	DE	348
Elizabeth	30	DE	323
Elizabeth	35	GB	395
Ella	16	DE	34
Ellen	4	DE	173
Ellen	36	PA	173
Emeline	39	DE	53

Name	Age	State	No.
Simmons, Emily	2	DE	395
Emily	14	PA	50
Enos	6/12	DE	323
Ezekle E	22	DE	120
Frances	26	DE	72
Frederic	9	DE	50
Frisby	36	DE	325
George	7	DE	323
George	8	DE	326
George	12	DE	34
George	35	PA	330
George H P	28	DE	129
George L	3	DE	323
George W	6	DE	395
Hannah	22	DE	107
Hannah	23	DE	135
Harriet	35	GB	395
Harriet E	26	DE	323
Harry	7/12	DE	107
Harry	5	DE	355
Henry	11	DE	34
Henry	68	DE	235
Hetty	50	DE	235
Isaiah	3	DE	292
James	12	PA	50
James	14	DE	343
James	20	DE	56
James	38	PA	82
James	59	GB	395
Jane	65	MD	335
John	1	DE	222
John	4	DE	72
John	30	DE	135
John	32	DE	235
John	35	DE	222
John B	25	DE	126
John F	29	DE	297
John G	1	DE	395
Joseph H	1	DE	395
Josephine	3	DE	173
Joshua	14	DE	384
Joshua	47	DE	34
Julia S	2	DE	297
Leah J	5	DE	292
Leonas	9/12	DE	292
Lewis	13	DE	53
Louis	3	DE	219
Margaret	--	DE	290
Margaret	2/12	DE	50
Margaret	35	MD	330
Margaret J	19	DE	104
Margery	24	PA	129
Maria	1	DE	323
Maria	18	DE	56
Maria	40	DE	323
Maria	41	DE	292
Maria	45	DE	116
Martha	1	DE	72
Mary	2	DE	50
Mary	9	DE	323
Mary	10	DE	292
Mary	16	DE	53
Mary	35	DE	135
Mary	42	DE	34
Mary	50	DE	144
Mary	57	NJ	153
Mary A	5	DE	395
Mary A	6	DE	222
Mary A	7	DE	72
Mary A	35	GB	396
Mary E	8	DE	173
Mary E	25	DE	144
Mary J	4	DE	395
Mary J	5	DE	324
Minty	11	DE	322
Nathan	6	DE	173
Nathan	37	DE	173
Nicholas	7	DE	292
Perry	13	DE	295
Perry	40	DE	323
Rachel	12	DE	335
Rachel	28	DE	222
Simmons, Rachel	59	PA	135
Rachel A	23	DE	126
Rebecca J	4	PA	330
Richard	35	GB	395
Robert	--	DE	290
Robert	5	DE	222
Robert	19	DE	201
Samuel	8	DE	28
Samuel	10	DE	323
Samuel	35	GB	395
Samuel W	8	DE	158
Sarah	30	DE	144
Sarah	32	DE	135
Sarah	35	PA	82
Sarah E	7/12	DE	126
Sarah J	7	DE	224
Sarah J	8	DE	222
Shadrack	45	MD	295
Sophia	14	DE	34
Stephen	12	DE	292
Stephen	60	DE	323
Susan	28	DE	235
Thomas	45	DE	292
Thomas W	31	DE	323
Thompson	11	DE	153
William	4	DE	129
William	10	DE	135
William	24	DE	107
William	30	MD	72
William	35	PA	50
William	57	PA	153
William B	21	DE	135
Simon, David	24	IE	30
Simons, Charles H	30	PA	84
Ellen	24	PA	84
Emma E	8/12	DE	84
Joseph	16	PA	84
Josephine	2	PA	82
William	10	PA	82
Simper, Albert	3	DE	204
Hannah R	8	DE	204
Joshua	6	DE	204
Joshua	37	MD	204
Mary A	27	GB	204
Maryanetta	6/12	DE	204
Sarah A	10	DE	204
Simpers, Elizabeth	11	DE	384
Margaretta	6	DE	384
Martha	32	DE	384
Robert O	7	DE	384
Thomas	43	MD	384
Simpkins, Emma	24	IE	339
Mary	22	DE	262
William	21	DE	231
Simple, George	14	PA	294
Mary	18	DE	301
Simpler, Eliza	50	DE	315
Simpson, Alexander	13	DE	15
Alexander	30	PA	149
Alexander	37	IE	15
Alexander	40	ST	337
Allen	4	DE	28
Ann	37	DE	114
Ann J	20	DE	29
Anna	28	DE	285
Arthur	28	IE	193
Capt	40	DE	147
Caroline	18	DE	308
Caroline	41	NJ	149
Edith	66	PA	386
Eliza F	37	DE	318
Elizabeth	10	IE	28
Elizabeth	17	DE	94
Elizabeth	50	IE	29
Elizabeth	65	IE	162
Frances	18	DE	99
Frances	20	DE	158
George	2	DE	114
George C	30	DE	318
Henry	15	DE	15
Henry J	7	DE	114
Hester	18	IE	193
Simpson, Hester A	17	DE	277
Isaac	14	DE	262
James	7	DE	15
James	12	DE	372
James	14	IE	371
James	19	IE	23
James	20	DE	99
James	26	DE	285
James	50	IE	23
James	67	IE	162
Jane	2	DE	340
Jane	7	DE	340
Jane	35	GB	341
Jane	41	IE	372
John	9	DE	372
John	10	IE	363
John	10	IE	371
John	24	DE	22
John	35	PA	114
John	42	IE	372
Joseph	2	DE	15
Joseph	10	PA	340
Joseph	35	GB	341
Josephine	5/12	DE	285
Margaret	8	DE	162
Margaret	12	GB	340
Margaret	12	IE	371
Margaret	20	IE	23
Margaret	36	IE	15
Margaretta	10	DE	30
Mark	1	DE	372
Mary	13	DE	29
Mary L	6	DE	318
Moses	5	DE	340
Nathaniel	15	IE	23
Phillip	40	GE	50
Rebecca	16	DE	100
Robert D	6	DE	372
Robert N	4	DE	371
Sarah	5	DE	285
Sarah	15	DE	29
Sarah	17	IE	23
Sarah	28	DE	162
Sarah	34	IE	371
Sarah A	6	PA	149
Sarah A	20	GB	332
Sarah E	8	DE	318
Sophia	48	DE	182
Susanna	4	DE	285
Tempe	35	MD	147
Thomas	7	IE	371
Thomas	16	DE	288
Thomas	35	IE	371
William	2	DE	371
William	11	DE	15
William	16	IE	23
William	24	DE	100
William	62	DE	126
William	72	IE	29
William H	9	PA	149
William W	9	DE	114
Wilson	11/12	DE	277
Sims, James	3	DE	321
John	48	MD	148
John H	21	PA	148
Joshua L	16	PA	148
Margaret	48	PA	148
Margaret E	19	PA	148
Susannah E	17	PA	148
Sinex, Eli	73	DE	368
Mary	54	MD	159
Singer, Abraham	7/12	MD	59
David	3	MD	59
David	55	MD	59
Samuel	6	MD	59
Sarah E	9	MD	59
Singles, Ann	50	DE	399
Ann	65	DE	107
Benjamin	30	DE	399
Benjamin	55	PA	107
Edward	24	PA	108
Elizabeth	20	DE	399

Name	Age	Place	Page
Singles, George W	16	DE	399
John M	26	DE	399
Mahala	2	DE	399
Martha J	6	DE	399
Mary E	23	NJ	108
Mary L	2	DE	108
Rachel A	25	DE	399
Reuben G	3/12	DE	399
Thomas	23	DE	399
William H	4	DE	399
Singleton, Oswell	23	PA	357
Sinix, Ann	24	DE	381
Edmond R	2	DE	381
James S	1/12	DE	381
Nayamia	25	DE	381
Sinner, Ephraim	37	DE	311
Sister Ann	70	DE	112
Antonette	40	NY	164
Barrabas	35	IE	164
Bernard	55	MD	164
Constance	40	IE	164
Mary Eligins	21	IE	164
Mary Flora	45	IE	164
Remi	24	MD	164
Terrencia	40	PA	164
Victoria	42	IE	164
Sipple, Frank	14	DE	16
Thomas	29	DE	16
Perry	16	MD	381
Skaggs, Adaline	5	DE	223
Caroline	2	DE	223
Emaline	30	DE	223
Henry	7	DE	223
John	12	DE	223
John	39	DE	222
Thomas	36	DE	223
William	10	DE	223
William	36	DE	222
Skean, James	25	IE	80
Skeiss, Margaret	65	PA	275
Skelly, Angelina	21	DE	42
Deborah	52	DE	42
Sally	19	GA	42
Skinner, Frances	22	GB	162
George	42	GB	162
Sarah	46	GB	162
Slack, Ann	38	DE	56
Daniel	10	DE	334
Enos	64	NJ	338
Hester	60	DE	338
Jane	21	DE	56
Jane	89	PA	334
John	8	DE	334
Mary	14	DE	56
Mary	39	DE	56
Mary A	35	DE	334
Mary E	5	DE	334
Joseph	15	DE	334
Richard	12	DE	338
Richard T	15	DE	338
Richard T	16	DE	328
Samuel	2	DE	334
Sarah J	12	DE	334
William	46	DE	334
Slater, Eliza	35	PA	18
Emily	48	DE	189
John	8/12	DE	18
Mathew	35	GB	18
Sleating, Mahala	15	DE	328
Sleeper, Ann C	5	PA	154
Charles S	50	NJ	154
Elizabeth	70	PA	282
Elizabeth H	16	PA	154
James	72	NY	282
Joseph	30	PA	282
Mary E	10	PA	154
Phebe H	40	PA	154
Susan	32	PA	282
Sloan, Hannah	60	PA	334
Sarah	17	DE	271
Thomas	69	PA	334
Sluby, Mary	30	DE	73
Smallwood, Phoebe	14	DE	231
Sarah	59	MD	375
Washington	28	DE	233
Smally, Henry L	43	NJ	378
Isaac M	19	NJ	378
James H	21	NJ	378
John	12	NJ	378
Mary B	13	NJ	378
Tabitha B	45	NJ	378
William	17	NJ	378
Smith, Adam C	13	PA	384
Adeline	24	DE	313
Agness	23	IE	379
Albert	11	PA	269
Albert W	32	PA	50
Alexander	5/12	DE	167
Alexia	6	PA	50
Alfred	1	DE	354
Alfred	5	DE	273
Alfred	14	DE	275
Alice	7	DE	237
Allen	26	PA	61
Alpha	31	DE	67
Amanda	4/12	DE	304
Amanda A	12	DE	312
Amelia	26	PA	315
Amelia R	2	DE	190
Andrew	22	IE	97
Andrew	24	GE	142
Ann	3	DE	287
Ann	14	DE	12
Ann	39	DE	397
Ann	40	MD	255
Ann	48	MD	98
Ann	50	DE	11
Ann	58	DE	273
Ann	79	DE	149
Ann A	1/12	DE	379
Ann G	8	DE	305
Ann J	17	DE	273
Anna	1	DE	397
Anna E	3	DE	146
Anna E	2	DE	388
Anna E	17	DE	166
Anna E	19	DE	399
Annie C	10	DE	289
Asbury	18	DE	268
Atmore	1	DE	275
Atwood	1	DE	275
Avis	64	DE	219
Azariah F	33	DE	315
Benjamin	14	DE	337
Benjamin	33	DE	219
Benjamin H	15	GB	352
Benjamin R	1	DE	213
Bridget	19	IE	377
Burton	10/12	DE	275
C A	14	DE	21
C B F	36	DE	138
Caroline	10	DE	259
Caroline	24	DE	387
Caroline	25	DE	354
Catherine	8/12	DE	387
Catherine	9	DE	339
Catherine	25	IE	98
Catherine A	37	DE	331
Catherine E	22	DE	175
Cecelia	35	GB	339
Charles	10/12	DE	307
Charles	14	DE	337
Charles	18	DE	397
Charles	25	DE	212
Charles F	29	DE	175
Charles H	3	DE	315
Charles T	27	DE	369
Charles W	17	DE	4
Charlotte	3	DE	189
Charlotte	7	DE	130
Charlotte	11	DE	337
Charlotte	31	NJ	269
Cheney	12	PA	272
Christin	42	GE	303
Smith, Christopher C	16	DE	331
Clara	4	DE	388
Clara	5	DE	388
Clara	40	DE	268
Clara S	14	PA	12
Danial	25	PA	149
Daniel	21	IE	379
Daniel	70	DE	315
David	4/12	DE	146
David	3	DE	96
David	23	DE	279
David P	28	PA	189
Debra	18	PA	143
Dunham	30	DE	269
E E	36	NJ	137
Edmond	17	DE	273
Edmond L	6	DE	213
Edward	11	DE	303
Edward	30	IE	377
Edward A	4	DE	4
Edwin A	32	PA	189
Eleuthus D	40	IE	342
Eli	40	DE	377
Eli B	14	PA	272
Eli B	23	DE	273
Elihu	2	DE	179
Eliza	18	DE	10
Eliza	20	DE	178
Eliza J	9	DE	216
Eliza J	39	DE	4
Elizabeth	3	DE	303
Elizabeth	5	DE	387
Elizabeth	7	DE	389
Elizabeth	14	DE	309
Elizabeth	15	PA	127
Elizabeth	15	DE	348
Elizabeth	25	DE	388
Elizabeth	32	PA	50
Elizabeth	32	PA	287
Elizabeth	35	DE	369
Elizabeth	36	DE	377
Elizabeth	40	DE	292
Elizabeth	45	DE	66
Elizabeth	86	DE	161
Elizabeth A	11	DE	275
Elizabeth A	13	DE	377
Elizabeth A	16	DE	143
Elizabeth J	12	DE	272
Ellen	6	DE	289
Ellen	22	DE	73
Ellen	22	DE	304
Ellen	28	DE	300
Ellener	2	DE	47
Elmor	11	DE	369
Elwood	19	PA	273
Emeline	18	DE	46
Emeline	38	MD	287
Emma	3	DE	277
Emma	6	DE	369
Emma D	5	DE	304
Emma L	11	DE	273
Evelina	34	MD	146
Francis	4	DE	213
Franklin G	25	PA	189
Frederic	18	PA	163
Garret	44	NJ	273
George	6	DE	397
George	10	DE	303
George	13	DE	259
George	17	MD	28
George	20	DE	334
George	24	PA	399
George	30	DE	168
George	41	DE	264
George A	3/12	DE	283
George R	17	DE	321
George W	23	DE	278
Greensbury	45	MD	11
Hannah	8	DE	337
Hannah	9	DE	287
Hannah	13	DE	368
Hannah	29	DE	259

Name	Age	St	No	Name	Age	St	No	Name	Age	St	No
Smith, Hannah	43	DE	369	Smith, John	23	GB	86	Smith, Mary	5	DE	96
Hannah	60	PA	64	John	25	DE	320	Mary	8	DE	337
Hannah	60	DE	321	John	27	DE	375	Mary	10	DE	324
Hannah E	12	DE	138	John	34	NJ	213	Mary	12	DE	397
Harriet	1	DE	392	John	38	DE	308	Mary	13	DE	285
Harriet	26	PA	272	John	40	PA	127	Mary	14	DE	268
Harriet	28	NJ	213	John	40	GE	303	Mary	14	DE	272
Harriet	39	DE	264	John	43	IE	90	Mary	16	DE	161
Harry	8	NJ	89	John	46	MD	136	Mary	16	DE	291
Henry	7	DE	387	John	48	PA	287	Mary	22	PA	47
Henry	8	PA	127	John A	9	DE	4	Mary	25	IE	392
Henry	14	DE	91	John C	35	GB	3	Mary	27	PA	58
Henry	18	PA	251	John E	4	DE	369	Mary	29	DE	307
Henry	28	DE	313	John G	13	DE	339	Mary	36	DE	138
Henry	32	GB	287	John H	1	DE	273	Mary	37	PA	2
Henry	40	DE	67	John J	26	PA	389	Mary	45	DE	315
Henry Clay	4	DE	239	John L	21	DE	390	Mary	47	PA	389
Hester	1	DE	237	John M	6	DE	287	Mary	51	DE	273
Hester	34	DE	237	John N	25	PA	177	Mary	62	DE	113
Hetty	8	DE	289	John R	26	DE	175	Mary	63	DE	278
Horace	50	DE	268	John T	2	DE	387	Mary A	1	DE	308
Isaac	3	DE	275	John W	7/12	DE	279	Mary A	23	IE	100
Isaac	44	PA	272	John W	12	DE	237	Mary A	23	DE	297
Isaac	59	DE	273	John W	41	MD	4	Mary Ann	6	DE	387
Isabel	14	DE	237	Jno	47	DE	292	Mary C	34	DE	289
Isabella	48	GB	331	Jonathan C	17	DE	189	Mary E	4	PA	272
J Fleming	25	DE	161	Jonathan P	58	NJ	189	Mary E	4	DE	287
Jackson	25	DE	304	Joseph	10	DE	292	Mary E	15	PA	2
Jacob	5	DE	304	Joseph	21	DE	158	Mary E	16	DE	237
Jacob	26	DE	273	Joseph	30	PA	270	Mary E	18	DE	374
Jacob	35	DE	303	Joseph	45	DE	216	Mary E	28	PA	137
Jacob R	15	DE	389	Joseph	58	DE	313	Mary J	3	DE	269
James	4	DE	387	Joseph E	7	DE	275	Mary J	15	DE	305
James	7	DE	287	Joseph W	37	GB	321	Mary J	18	DE	276
James	7	DE	308	Josephine	1	DE	272	Mary J	31	DE	275
James	9	DE	91	Joshua	2/12	DE	50	Mary J	38	DE	149
James	14	DE	88	Joshua	18	DE	99	Mary P	1	DE	375
James	14	MD	146	Joshua	40	DE	206	Matilda	14	DE	279
James	14	DE	330	Joshua	47	DE	315	Moll	13	DE	219
James	15	DE	131	Julia A	18	DE	11	Molten	2	DE	283
James	15	DE	134	Julia A	26	DE	149	Nelson	6	PA	2
James	15	DE	268	Kate	9/12	DE	161	Nicholas	23	GE	50
James	17	PA	127	Lavinia	20	DE	375	Obadiah	27	MD	307
James	18	DE	324	Lavinia	30	DE	189	Oliver	50	DE	268
James	26	DE	46	Lenith	35	PA	305	Oscar	3	DE	137
James	26	GB	331	Leuticia	14	DE	69	P B	11	DE	339
James	30	DE	355	Leuvinia	11	DE	138	Patric	20	IE	88
James	33	DE	387	Levin	4	DE	397	Peter	1	DE	292
James	38	IE	339	Lewis	2	DE	138	Phebe	3/12	DE	287
James	40	DE	305	Lewis	18	DE	57	Phebe	5/12	DE	368
James	62	DE	113	Linten	8	PA	50	Priscilla	19	DE	64
James	79	DE	104	Louisa	13	DE	315	Prudence	20	DE	273
James A	2	DE	216	Louisa	23	DE	273	Purly P	2	DE	369
James A	2	DE	315	Luther	21	DE	186	Rachel	8	PA	2
James A	30	DE	388	Lydia	4	DE	283	Rachel	23	PA	273
James A B	42	DE	275	Lydia	5	PA	127	Rachel	28	PA	56
James F	41	DE	88	Lydia	19	DE	279	Rachel	34	PA	272
James H	36	MD	146	Lydia D	7	DE	239	Rachel A	3	DE	387
James P	13	DE	389	M A	4	DE	304	Rachel A	22	DE	175
James P	16	DE	275	M J	7	DE	304	Rebecca	2/12	DE	397
Jane	6	DE	307	Mahlon	8	DE	292	Rebecca	10	DE	275
Jane	9	DE	268	Malvina	4	DE	73	Rebecca	13	DE	254
Jane	18	MD	279	Margaret	6	DE	279	Rebecca	18	DE	304
Jane	27	MD	279	Margaret	7	DE	273	Rebecca	26	DE	239
Jane	45	IE	300	Margaret	22	DE	273	Rebecca	45	PA	304
Jane	45	DE	321	Margaret	24	IE	91	Richard	2/12	DE	315
Jane	83	PA	68	Margaret	55	DE	387	Richard	23	DE	123
Jane F	6	DE	320	Margaret A	4	PA	2	Richard	32	DE	179
Jane H	45	PA	274	Margaret C	14	DE	273	Richard	35	GB	96
Jane J	16	DE	377	Margaret T	19	DE	274	Robert	9	DE	360
Johanna	6	DE	216	Maria	6	DE	232	Robert	20	IE	88
John	1/12	DE	304	Maria	28	NJ	216	Robert	36	DE	325
John	7/12	DE	138	Maria	34	DE	96	Robert	42	PA	2
John	2	DE	73	Maria	53	DE	307	Robert H	5	DE	315
John	3	DE	308	Maria	60	DE	57	Robert J	9	PA	50
John	5	DE	273	Martha	16	DE	158	Robt	32	GB	331
John	9	DE	303	Martha	23	DE	161	Rosa	36	IE	98
John	10	DE	88	Martha	25	DE	283	Rosanna	17	MD	279
John	12	DE	313	Martha J	14	DE	308	Rosanna	48	NJ	189
John	13	DE	279	Martha M	26	DE	179	Rosel	22	DE	298
John	16	DE	255	Mary	2	DE	304	Sam	17	DE	397
John	23	GB	86	Mary	5	DE	96	Samuel	8	DE	313

Name	Age	St	Pg	Name	Age	St	Pg	Name	Age	St	Pg
Smith, Samuel	15	DE	304	Smith, William L	9	DE	305	Snyder, Sarah	12	DE	365
Samuel	16	DE	187	William P	21	DE	273	Thomas J	43	DE	301
Samuel	18	DE	393	William R	3	DE	189	William	28	GE	21
Samuel	21	DE	56	William T	28	MD	146	Sofus, Eliza	23	DE	335
Samuel	21	PA	282	William W	2	DE	320	Elizabeth	4	DE	335
Samuel	22	DE	85	Williamson	11	PA	21	Henry	6	DE	335
Samuel	50	DE	304	Windfield S	4	DE	389	Julia	1	DE	335
Samuel	56	DE	397	Smithers, Ann M	50	GB	360	Samuel	24	DE	335
Samuel P	11	DE	389	Charles H	19	PA	360	Sarah	3	DE	335
Sarah	2/12	DE	88	Edwin	13	PA	360	Soleby, Thomas	22	PA	282
Sarah	3	DE	303	Joseph	57	DE	170	Solom, Mary	83	SZ	145
Sarah	12	PA	50	Joyce	21	DE	54	Soloman, Danial	30	PA	91
Sarah	14	DE	273	Mary E	24	DE	170	Ella	2	DE	1
Sarah	14	DE	366	Nathaniel	63	DE	162	Ester	8	PA	91
Sarah	19	DE	167	Rachel E	54	DE	162	Ester	28	PA	91
Sarah	23	DE	175	Richard	14	PA	360	Jacob	32	PA	86
Sarah	26	PA	88	Smithson, John	35	DE	189	John J	27	DE	1
Sarah	28	DE	387	Martha J	48	DE	189	Margaret J	5	PA	91
Sarah	31	DE	304	Susan	21	PA	331	Mary	24	DE	1
Sarah	36	PA	275	Smitt, Charles H	30	PA	85	Rebecca J	4	DE	1
Sarah	47	DE	136	George	23	GE	85	Sarah	2	PA	91
Sarah	68	DE	99	Levinia	10	PA	62	Solomon, Edward	22	DE	31
Sarah A	17	DE	305	Margaret	50	GE	62	Sooy, Elma	48	NJ	299
Sarah A	17	DE	377	William	29	PA	85	Thomas	58	NJ	299
Sarah A	20	DE	2	Smyne, George W	2	DE	317	Soragin, Frances	23	IE	331
Sarah A	21	GB	130	Mary	28	DE	317	Sorden, John H	32	DE	49
Sarah A	30	DE	308	Rebecca A	3	DE	317	John T	1	DE	49
Sarah E	3	DE	274	Thomas	34	IE	317	Luvenia	24	PA	49
Sarah J	10	DE	348	Smyra, Sarah	85	PA	370	Sorrel, Hannah	25	PA	318
Sarah J	43	IE	91	Smyth, Amelia E	10	DE	146	John	23	DE	318
Sillinda	6	DE	305	Anna C	4/12	DE	59	Mary Ellen	3	DE	318
Solomon	7	DE	292	Anna E	67	DE	142	Rebecca	26	DE	318
Stephen	22	DE	253	Benjamin	2	DE	146	Samuel	20	DE	318
Stephen	22	DE	268	Clement B	22	DE	142	Thomas	26	PA	318
Susan	8	DE	308	David	5	DE	146	Thomas J	11	DE	319
Susan	25	DE	219	David	68	DE	142	Soulty, Robert	15	PA	163
Susan	29	MD	320	Emily B	27	DE	59	Southard, Amanda C	9	NJ	75
Susan	37	PA	127	Henry	40	DE	146	Augustus	3	DE	75
Tamer	30	DE	354	Hetty	27	DE	146	Eugene	5	DE	75
Tempy	30	DE	323	Lucy	27	DE	142	Letitia	18	NJ	75
Thomas	5	DE	146	Luke	3	DE	146	Samuel L	11	NJ	75
Thomas	6	DE	91	Mary A	25	DE	142	Sarah	39	NY	75
Thomas	6	DE	138	Mary B	2	DE	59	Stephen	16	NJ	75
Thomas	10	MD	163	William C	27	DE	59	Stephen	43	NY	75
Thomas	13	PA	127	William H	7	DE	146	Southwell, Elizabeth	39	MD	134
Thomas	38	GB	300	Sneath, Charles T	8	DE	319	Mary	14	DE	287
Thomas	40	PA	369	George R	13	PA	319	Thomas	10	DE	227
Thomas	42	GB	331	Lewis H	11	PA	319	Sowartz, Anne E	13	GB	283
Thomas C	71	DE	278	Rosanna A	40	PA	319	Christopher	38	GB	283
Thomas M K	40	PA	342	Samuel	15	DE	319	Mary T	14	GB	283
Thomas S	7	DE	315	Sarah J	6	DE	319	Sower, Allice	26	GB	368
Thomas T	8	DE	278	Thomas L	40	PA	319	George	7/12	DE	368
Wallace H	12	DE	216	Snicker, Ann	16	DE	329	George	30	GB	368
Walter	2	PA	50	Kennard	14	DE	315	Jesse	3	GB	368
Walter J	9/12	DE	4	Rebecca	20	DE	378	John	2	GB	368
Walter W	17	DE	321	Snider, Henry	10/12	DE	5	Sowerby, Caleb	33	MD	367
William	5/12	DE	179	Henry	36	GE	293	James T	8	PA	367
William	6	DE	303	Jane	37	GB	381	Mary J	4	DE	367
William	7	DE	96	Joseph	35	GB	381	Sharlott	31	PA	367
William	8	DE	244	Rebecca	20	DE	379	William	7	PA	367
William	8	DE	307	Snitcher, Isaac T	10	DE	380	Sowers, George W	6	DE	383
William	11	DE	91	John	55	NJ	380	Hannah	28	DE	383
William	12	DE	330	Mary	47	NJ	380	John	38	MD	383
William	15	DE	397	Richard	7	DE	380	Mary E	1	DE	383
William	16	DE	314	Samuel R	2	DE	380	William H	3	DE	383
William	25	PA	356	Snoral, Jane	45	PA	7	Spackman, Elizabeth	14	PA	332
William	26	DE	72	John	50	PA	7	Spakeman, Joanna	52	PA	305
William	26	DE	311	Snoval, Elizabeth	29	PA	26	John	50	PA	305
William	30	DE	228	Emily	6	PA	26	Mary G	24	DE	305
William	30	DE	239	James	33	PA	26	Sparagnay, Wilhel-			
William	30	MD	279	Jane	9	PA	26	mina	6	PA	371
William	30	PA	283	John	2	PA	26	Sparks, Alfred	1	DE	78
William	32	DE	73	Sarah	8	PA	26	Caroline	8	DE	144
William	40	MD	237	Snow, Julia A	34	MD	201	Christiana	37	DE	348
William	52	PA	389	Snowden, Rebecca	45	NJ	62	Dado	34	DE	95
William	56	DE	273	Snyder, Alice	16	PA	165	Eliza	28	MD	110
William	68	DE	175	Catherine	18	PA	165	George	25	NJ	30
William	70	DE	99	George	45	PA	136	George	30	DE	110
William C	5	DE	219	James	40	DE	360	George	37	MD	28
William H	13	DE	4	Jeremiah	25	GB	201	George	64	DE	110
William H	17	DE	389	Margaret	49	PA	301	Hannah	27	PA	144
William J	9	DE	237	Rebecca	13	PA	301	Hariot	37	MD	28

Sparks, John	5	DE	144	Spencer, Anna	29	DE	381	Springer, Elizabeth	23	DE	372
John	37	DE	144	Anne	70	DE	98	Elizabeth Jane	34	DE	358
John L	9	DE	95	Anthony	60	DE	73	Eveline	6/12	DE	348
Josiah	52	NJ	88	Catherine	14	DE	382	George	11	DE	348
Julia E	1	DE	348	Catherine J	5	DE	284	George	35	DE	348
Julia E	6	DE	110	Clara	9	PA	66	George M	5	DE	345
Kate	9/12	DE	144	Daniel	10	DE	382	Hannah S	12	DE	120
Laura D	30	MD	348	Elizabeth	13	PA	66	Harriet	65	IE	285
Margaret L	55	MD	199	Elizabeth	29	MD	304	Hester	38	DE	68
Mary	6/12	DE	78	Elizabeth	45	PA	66	Hester	41	DE	353
Mary	1	DE	95	Elizabeth	48	MD	284	Hester	45	DE	120
Mary	30	DE	110	Francis	7	DE	66	Hester A	8	DE	348
Mary A	3	DE	110	George W	10	PA	66	Isabel	30	DE	353
Mary J	18	PA	88	Henry	7	DE	382	James	12	DE	345
Rebecca	27	DE	97	Joel	15	DE	82	James	30	DE	358
Rebecca	28	DE	95	Joel	53	DE	82	James	44	DE	82
Rebecca	35	NJ	78	John	30	DE	202	James W	3	DE	348
Samuel L	21	MD	199	Joseph	77	DE	383	Jane	70	DE	375
Sarah	19	DC	30	Joseph Jr	27	DE	383	Jeremiah	47	DE	83
Susan	10/12	DE	110	Levi	56	DE	87	Jeremiah J	7	DE	82
William L	24	MD	199	Margaret	55	DE	82	Jesse	70	PA	376
Speakman, Agnes	3/12	DE	70	Mary	7	DE	284	John	6/12	DE	24
Clayton	3	DE	66	Mary	19	DE	46	John	30	DE	17
David F	5	DE	362	Mary	29	DE	128	John	35	DE	348
Edith	28	DE	66	Mary E	19	DE	383	John	43	DE	359
Eli T	1	DE	66	Nathaniel	17	DE	381	John	50	DE	82
Evan T	30	PA	66	Nehemiah	45	DE	382	John A	14	DE	68
George	20	DC	362	Nicholas	25	PA	66	John C	8	DE	120
Horacia	25	PA	115	Nicholas	48	PA	66	John S	2	DE	297
Isabella	24	DE	107	Peter	50	DE	284	Joseph	16	DE	68
James	25	DE	107	Rebecca	62	DE	73	Joseph	26	DE	18
John N	26	DC	362	Richard B	23	PA	128	Josephine	3	DE	120
Margaret	24	DE	70	Sarah	4	DE	66	Joshua	50	DE	375
Mary	25	DE	362	Sarah	10	DE	284	Levi	26	DE	24
Miller	55	PA	362	Sarah	45	DE	382	Lewis	2	DE	82
Rebecca	49	MD	362	William	17	DE	58	Lewis	12	DE	333
Sarah	14	DC	362	William	31	DE	49	Lewis	22	DE	129
William	3	DE	107	William H	1	DE	128	Lewis	46	DE	362
Spear, Andrew	14	DE	248	Spenser, Sarah	70	MD	38	Lewis H	7	DE	362
Eleanor	8	DE	248	Spicer, Edward W	4	DE	376	Lydia	35	DE	360
Elizabeth	7	DE	371	Emeline	5	DE	376	Margaret	--	DE	355
Elizabeth	12	DE	20	Outen	35	DE	376	Margaret	26	DE	355
Franklin	24	DE	371	Sarah A	33	DE	376	Margaret	62	DE	359
John C	43	DE	248	Spooner, Joseph	24	MA	59	Margaret	63	MD	104
John C Jr	12	DE	248	Spotswood, Anna R	4	DE	289	Margaret A	16	DE	362
Joseph	19	DE	20	Elizabeth W	14	VA	289	Margaretta H	14	DE	82
Margaret	3	DE	371	John B	42	VA	289	Martha	12	DE	360
Mary	15	DE	20	Lucy	1	DE	289	Mary	28	DE	360
Mary	32	MD	20	Maria L	16	VA	289	Mary	40	DE	362
Mary A	1	DE	371	Mary B	7	DE	289	Mary A	18	DE	82
Mary F	5	DE	248	Sarah	42	PA	289	Mary A	36	DE	359
Sarah F	2	DE	248	Susan B	12	VA	289	Mary Ann	21	DE	358
Sarah Jane	25	MD	371	Virginia	9	MD	289	Mary Ann	22	DE	364
Speare, John	47	IE	167	Sprigs, Mary	30	PA	304	Mary C	11	DE	68
Spece, Sarah A	8	DE	313	William	27	PA	304	Mary E	13	DE	362
Specie, Josephine	14	DE	296	Springbit, Alinda	5	DE	47	Mary E	14	DE	333
Speck, Sophia	19	GE	6	Daniel	12	DE	47	Mary E	24	DE	358
Spence, Ann	23	DE	273	Elizabeth	32	DE	47	Mary H	44	DE	82
Ann E	3	DE	137	John	14	DE	47	Mary Louisa	2	DE	353
Benjamin	25	DE	151	William	8	DE	47	Mary U	2	DE	345
Catherine	1	DE	137	Springer, Abel	18	DE	359	Peter	10	DE	333
Charles	66	DE	151	Adelia J	4	DE	362	Peter	25	DE	296
Danial	32	DE	153	Albert	8	DE	333	Peter	56	DE	333
Edgar	1	DE	332	Amanda	23	DE	355	Priscilla	18	DE	354
Eliza	36	IE	300	Amanda E	9/12	DE	362	Rachel	8/12	DE	375
Francis	14	DE	134	Ann Elizabeth	10	DE	345	Rachel	48	DE	362
James	10	IE	300	Anna M	5/12	DE	296	Rebecca	21	DE	18
James	24	DE	137	Anna M	24	DE	296	Rebecca	35	DE	348
James	40	DE	160	Arabella	30	DE	354	Rebecca	42	DE	345
Louisa	27	DE	292	Betsey	48	DE	130	Samuel	12	DE	82
Margaret	50	DE	134	Catherine	9	DE	359	Samuel	12	DE	358
Martha	22	DE	158	Catherine	16	DE	333	Samuel	15	DE	82
Martha	25	MD	332	Charles	24	DE	48	Samuel	41	DE	82
Matthew	8	IE	300	Charlotta	37	MD	82	Sarah	4	DE	24
Rachel	58	DE	151	Christopher	63	DE	167	Sarah	19	DE	129
Samuel	5	IE	300	Edmond G	5	DE	348	Sarah	35	DE	375
Sarah	16	IE	300	Edward L	18	DE	82	Sarah J	32	DE	348
Sarah E	21	DE	137	Eliza	20	DE	333	Sarah L	10	DE	82
Susanah H	29	NY	153	Eliza	45	DE	348	Stephen	28	DE	358
Walden	18	DE	134	Elizabeth	3	DE	68	Thomas	8	DE	345
William J	14	IE	300	Elizabeth	15	DE	359	Thomas	39	DE	348
Spencer, Angeline	23	DE	49	Elizabeth	47	PA	333	Thomas C	1	DE	358

Name	Age	State	Page
Springer, Victoria	18	?	167
William	3	DE	348
William	7	DE	68
William	22	DE	82
William	24	DE	167
William	44	DE	353
Sprole, Jacob	22	DE	110
Sprouls, Dorcas	20	PA	349
Sprout, Ann	36	MD	328
Jacob	40	MD	328
John	12	DE	328
Mary	8	DE	328
Mary	35	MD	328
Spruance, Horace	14	DE	401
Sprule, Hester	50	PA	2
Spry, Eliza A	31	DE	205
Catherine E	4	DE	205
Luff	32	DE	205
Mary J	7	DE	205
Rachel A	1	DE	205
Sarah A	8	DE	205
William H	10	DE	205
Spurway, Anna	22	GB	128
Joseph	29	GB	128
Squibb, Alfred	12	DE	298
Staart, Eliza	59	DE	287
Mary J	22	DE	287
Sarah	58	PA	287
Staat, Ann	36	DE	229
Elizabeth	21	DE	227
Emily S	5	DE	229
James H	14	DE	229
John	3	DE	229
Rebecca A	7	DE	229
Samuel	40	DE	229
Staats, Ann C	2	DE	216
Brack	12	DE	316
David	40	DE	245
David W	6	MD	247
David W	17	DE	216
Elijah M	23	DE	247
Eliza	23	DE	204
Henrietta	8	DE	216
Hezekiah	4	DE	204
Jacob	14	DE	216
James	35	DE	204
Jane	60	DE	233
John	15	DE	218
K A C P B	35	DE	216
Lavinia	14	DE	245
Margaret J	6	DE	216
Marietta	11	DE	216
Martha	13	DE	216
Mary	37	DE	216
Mary	50	DE	245
Mary	63	DE	247
Matthew	45	MD	204
Rebecca	20	MI	366
Rebecca	44	DE	245
Samuel	51	DE	245
Samuel J	14	DE	245
Sarah	37	DE	247
Sarah E	19	DE	216
Susan	9	DE	216
Susan B	48	DE	245
William	5	DE	245
Staatt, Elijah	21	DE	228
Stabury, Ephraim	18	DE	209
Stackhous, Caroline	20	NJ	360
Charles A	1	PA	360
Jacob	24	NJ	360
Stacy, William	15	PA	298
Stafford, Alexander	2	DE	295
Alexander	7	DE	250
Benjamin	22	DE	311
James	5	DE	295
James	35	DE	276
James	59	DE	313
Minte	41	DE	313
Phebe	5	DE	350
Robert	30	DE	295
Sarah	4	DE	295
Stafford, Sarah	20	DE	250
Sarah	27	DE	295
Susan	2/12	DE	295
Susan	28	DE	276
Wm	35	DE	249
Stagers, Abigal	5	DE	74
Adaline	35	DE	74
Ann	13	DE	20
Benjamin	36	DE	20
Charles W	3	DE	74
Edward	5	DE	20
Jorden	11	DE	74
Jorden	44	DE	74
Mary	32	NJ	20
Rebecca	8	DE	20
William	10	DE	20
Staid, Joseph	27	GE	48
Mary	25	GE	48
Stain, Eliza	52	IE	91
Elizabeth	20	NY	91
John	22	NY	91
Rosana	65	NE	91
Sarah	20	PA	91
Stalcup, Eliza J	28	DE	126
James	28	DE	126
John	24	DE	270
Maria C	4	DE	126
Mary L	6	DE	126
Taylor K	2	DE	126
Stamm, W	24	PA	165
Stamp, Milton	35	PA	32
Sarah	30	PA	32
Stanhope, Emma	5	DE	75
Hannah	40	DE	75
Henry	3	DE	75
Jacob	38	DE	75
John	12	DE	75
William	14	DE	75
Stanky, Sarah	2	DE	233
Stanley, William	15	MD	195
Stanly, Louisa	27	DE	233
Mary	20	DE	107
Susan	4	DE	233
Wesley	33	DE	233
Stansfield, Ann	8	GB	57
Hannah	11	GB	57
John	6	GB	57
Mary	13	GB	57
Samuel	46	GB	57
Sarah	1	DE	57
Sarah	35	GB	57
Stanton, Benjamin	60	DE	327
Elizabeth	9	DE	327
George W	28	DE	208
Isaac	26	DE	301
Joseph A	13	DE	327
Josiah	51	DE	327
Kitty	32	DE	145
Laura	11	DE	392
Lewis	19	DE	41
Margaret	16	DE	327
Margaret	19	DE	41
Maria	12	DE	327
Maria	53	DE	327
Mary	34	PA	167
Mary	46	MD	392
Mary A	2/12	DE	208
Mary A	15	DE	392
Rachel A	26	DE	208
Sarah	24	DE	301
Stapler, Hannah	60	DE	20
James	4	DE	58
Margaret A	10	DE	132
Mary	36	DE	132
Sarah	52	PA	58
Sarah	60	MD	317
Thomas	58	DE	58
William	10	DE	58
Staples, Ann R	11	MD	379
Elizabeth	56	DE	298
Freeman	13	MD	379
Fulton	17	MD	379
Staples, Henrietta	19	MD	379
James	1/12	DE	379
John	9	MD	379
Mary	24	DE	298
Sarah	44	MD	379
Stephen M	57	DE	298
Washington	15	MD	379
William	39	DE	379
William H	21	MD	379
Starke, Brack	12	DE	316
Starkey, Jane	52	MD	321
John	17	DE	4
John	20	MD	322
Newberry	17	DE	192
Newberry	90	DE	220
Newberry Jr	27	DE	220
Rany A	16	DE	220
Rebecca	27	DE	220
Rosanna	5	DE	322
Samuel	7	MD	322
Zachariah	53	MD	321
Starkler, Under	37	GE	125
Starling, Rosa	23	DE	286
Zeak	27	FE	309
Starr, Aaron	10	PA	39
Adaline	3	DE	39
Alonzo	5	DE	28
Amanda	9	DE	28
Ann E	24	DE	83
Anna	6	PA	39
Caless	78	DE	34
Catherine	26	MD	39
Charles	31	DE	364
Delia A	5	DE	124
Edward	8	DE	28
Edwin	25	DE	364
Elizabeth	35	DE	78
Elizabeth	67	MD	364
George	33	PA	364
Gilbert	42	DE	364
Hannah	36	PA	124
Harry	6	DE	78
Isaac	12	PA	124
Isaac	33	PA	39
Jacob	25	DE	83
Jacob	40	DE	124
Jacob O	9/12	DE	83
Jane	3	DE	78
Jane	40	DE	78
Jane	47	DE	63
John	50	DE	78
Joshua	40	DE	364
Joshua	80	PA	364
Lewis	40	DE	28
Lucy	14	PA	364
Margaret	32	PA	39
Mary	32	DE	78
Mary	33	DE	364
Mary M	15	DE	78
Morrison	9	DE	78
Moses	8	PA	39
Ruth	30	DE	28
Sarah	27	DE	364
Thomas	1	DE	78
Thomas	38	DE	78
William	11	DE	78
William	44	DE	364
Stasson, James	15	PA	331
Mary	40	IE	331
Mary J	10	DE	331
Matilda	4	DE	331
Susannah A	16	IE	331
Thomas	43	IE	331
Staten, Catherine	64	DE	328
Henry	21	DE	326
Henry	25	DE	328
Mary A	17	DE	328
Mary J	23	DE	328
Mary J	27	DE	329
John	51	DE	302
Susan	47	DE	302
Richard	14	DE	317

Name	Age	State	No.
Staats, Abraham	12	DE	141
Abraham	51	DE	141
Anne C	3	DE	215
David W	17	DE	215
George	9	DE	213
Henrietta	9	DE	215
Jacob	42	DE	215
Jacob Jr	15	DE	215
James R	27	DE	192
Margaret J	7	DE	215
Maria	40	DE	141
Martha	13	DE	215
Mary	1	DE	141
Mary	37	DE	215
Mary A	24	MD	193
Rachel	8	DE	141
Sarah	19	DE	215
Sarah E	14	DE	141
Susan E	11	DE	215
Thomas	4	DE	141
Thomas H	10	DE	193
William H	19	MD	193
Steal, Isaac V	2	PA	366
Margaretta	5	PA	366
Margaretta	28	PA	366
Milton	34	DE	355
Nathan	32	PA	366
William G	3	PA	366
Stean, Allice A	2	DE	107
Hannah	27	PA	107
James	25	NY	107
Mary E	4	DE	107
Stearn, Caroline	32	DE	17
Charles	32	DE	17
Suner	11	DE	364
Stedham, Catherine	72	DE	367
Edith	33	DE	365
Gilpin P	37	DE	365
Isaac	42	DE	300
James P	23	DE	365
Mary	60	DE	300
Mary A	9	DE	365
Rebecca M	21	DE	365
Sarah	20	DE	300
Sarah C	7	DE	365
Susan	26	DE	300
Susan	45	DE	370
Stedman, James	33	DE	371
Rosetta	34	DE	371
Steel, Adaline	16	DE	396
Elizabeth	20	PA	355
George W	7	DE	396
Hudson	11	DE	396
John	29	PA	355
John T	19	DE	396
Lucinda	14	DE	396
Margaret M	16	PA	355
Mary	47	DE	396
Milton	8	DE	355
Robert H	21	DE	396
Robt	57	PA	355
Silena	50	PA	355
Thomas	12	PA	355
Thomas	48	DE	396
Steele, Alfred	18	PA	27
Anna	67	DE	112
Catherine	23	CT	130
Dorsey	100	DE	167
Henry	40	DE	112
Isabella	15	IE	347
Jane	23	IE	154
Richard	23	DE	112
William	35	DE	150
Stemson, A E	41	NY	52
Anne M	10	NY	52
Danial M	6	NY	52
Earl L	14	NY	52
Margaret	50	NY	52
Samuel E	8	NY	52
Stephen, Ann Rebecca	11	DE	378
Foreman	13	DE	378
Fulton	17	DE	378
Stephen, Henrietta	19	DE	378
John	9	DE	378
Sarah	44	DE	378
Thomas	12	DE	378
Washington	15	DE	378
William	59	DE	378
William H	21	DE	378
Stephens, Albert	12	DE	331
Alexander	3	DE	344
Alexander	70	ST	344
Anna M	32	DE	371
Benjamin	40	MD	288
Caroline	18	PA	331
Christiana	1	DE	344
Christiana	65	ST	344
Elizabeth	7	DE	331
Harriet	26	PA	344
James	36	ST	344
John	2	DE	331
John B	35	DE	18
Mary	10	DE	331
Mary	46	PA	331
Rebecca	19	DE	97
Rebecca	60	IE	97
Samuel	20	DE	331
Thomas	16	DE	331
Thomas	49	PA	331
Stephenson, Ann	31	DE	124
Anna A	4	DE	124
Charles	44	GB	296
Danial	34	DE	124
Danial	55	MD	325
George	51	DE	303
Harriet	40	GB	296
Isaac	19	DE	10
Jacob	47	DE	303
Jane E	9	DE	124
Julia A	6	DE	124
Mary E	7/12	DE	124
Sarah A	11	PA	124
Susan	54	MD	325
Stepson, Anna	44	GB	309
Charlotte	15	GB	309
Emma	12	DE	309
John W	3	DE	309
Jonathan	34	GB	309
Joseph	6/12	DE	309
Margaret A	8	DE	309
Mary	18	GB	309
Melinda	6	DE	309
Sarah J	11	DE	309
Sterle, Clotilda	6	GE	310
Everhart	50	GE	310
Louisa	4	GE	310
Philomena	40	GE	310
Sterling, Allice	1	DE	300
Ashbury	9	DE	134
Ceasar	3	DE	379
Elizabeth	24	MD	300
Harriet E	15	DE	138
Henry	21	MD	267
Hugh	25	IE	302
James A	1	DE	301
Jane	50	DE	301
Jane A	25	IE	301
John H	11/12	DE	379
John Q	27	DE	301
Joseph W	12	DE	133
Mahala	15	DE	329
Martha	63	IE	302
Mary	3	DE	300
Michel	62	MD	133
Sarah	6/12	DE	300
Sarah	40	DE	54
Sarah	42	MD	133
Sarah J	23	DE	133
Theresa	25	DE	379
Thomas	22	DE	301
Thomas	28	DE	379
Thomas	67	IE	302
Thomas P	2	DE	301
Victor	4	DE	300
Sterling, Washington	27	DE	300
Wesley	17	DE	134
Stern, Ann	53	PA	361
Ann E	9	PA	361
George	50	PA	361
Ruel	2	DE	359
Sidney	14	PA	361
William T	18	PA	361
Sterne, Elwood	4	DE	358
John	22	PA	6
Lewis	41	DE	358
Mary A	32	DE	358
Sterrett, Alexander	5	DE	342
Ellen	27	IE	342
George	3	DE	342
James	7	DE	342
James	30	IE	342
Mary Jane	10	DE	342
Robert	1	DE	342
William	8	DE	342
Stetson, George	31	MA	58
Synthe	28	MA	58
William	15	MA	58
Steuart, Frances A	9	DE	290
Priscilla	35	PA	290
Stevens, Adaline	12	DE	169
Alfred	4/12	DE	201
Amanda	7	DE	201
Anna E	14	DE	201
Augustine	14	AL	165
Charlotte	35	DE	169
Daniel	14	DE	191
Daniel	39	NJ	201
David	41	NJ	173
Edward	5	DE	201
Elizabeth	25	DE	76
Emma	3	DE	201
Frances	19	NJ	169
George	25	DE	141
Hannah	33	NJ	173
Irwin	45	NY	169
Isaac	22	PA	8
Isaac	32	DE	76
James	19	IE	145
James H	15	DE	169
John	82	NJ	169
Lucinda	8	DE	169
Luisa	6	DE	76
Margaret	18	DE	8
Margaret	60	PA	8
Margaret E	9	DE	201
Mary	16	NJ	173
Mary J	16	DE	201
Sarah	17	NJ	169
Sarah	33	DE	201
Vashti	40	NJ	173
Stevenson, Abigail	7	DE	326
Alfred	5	DE	119
Almira H	22	PA	140
Ann	25	DE	138
Annie	12	DE	185
Anthony	23	DE	156
Caroline	32	DE	94
Daniel G	25	DE	178
David	15	DE	119
David	35	DE	94
Dianna	35	MD	326
Dorcas	3	PA	146
Eliza	20	DE	70
Eliza	30	PA	146
Elizabeth	25	DE	119
Elizabeth	26	PA	119
Emma	5	DE	326
Emma	17	DE	20
Henry	40	MD	146
Isaac	18	DE	273
Isaac	47	DE	82
Jacob	12	DE	70
Jacob	52	DE	70
James W	23	DE	140
John	12	DE	326

Name	Age	St	Pg
Stevenson, John	40	MD	326
John	59	ST	55
Kesiah	53	DE	70
Margaretta	20	DE	119
Martha	13	DE	119
Martha	79	DE	82
Martha J	7	DE	82
Mary	54	PA	119
Mary A	11	DE	82
Mary A	22	DE	119
Rebecca	24	DE	119
Richard	4	DE	295
Robert G	2	DE	94
Sarah A	30	DE	82
Sally	1	DE	326
Samuel	8	PA	146
Samuel A	2	DE	94
Sarah	60	MD	73
William	6	PA	146
William	15	DE	70
William	30	DE	119
William H	10	DE	326
Wm	26	DE	273
Steward, Andrew J	8	DE	374
Ann	38	IE	356
Anne J	10	DE	313
Catharine S	19	DE	313
Charles	12	DE	313
Charley	7	CN	366
Daniel B	15	DE	313
David	67	DE	374
David M	6/12	DE	374
Eliza	44	MD	339
Eliza A	9/12	DE	370
Elizabeth	8	IE	356
George W	4	DE	334
Hannah	27	MD	334
Hester	39	DE	374
Hester H	11	DE	374
James	32	DE	313
James	35	IE	356
James	44	DE	339
James	44	DE	374
James	86	DE	370
James H	14	DE	374
James T	10	MD	334
Jane	12	IE	336
John	1	IE	356
John	46	DE	339
Levic	12	DE	370
Lydia	19	DE	374
Margaret	3	DE	374
Martha	6	IE	356
Martha	21	MD	370
Martha A	5	DE	339
Mary	25	DE	313
Mary	30	DE	334
Mary E	7	DE	339
Mary J	19	IE	362
Mary J	21	DE	374
Rebecca B	48	PA	313
Robert	4	DE	366
Robert	31	DE	370
Samuel	35	DE	334
Sarah	1	DE	314
Sarah	26	CN	366
Seth	13	DE	334
Seth	29	DE	334
Susan	5	DE	313
Susan F	17	DE	374
Thomas	2	DE	366
Thomas	29	IE	366
Trudy	4	DE	334
William	14	DE	313
William B	2	DE	334
William W	6	DE	374
William W	49	DE	313
Stewart, A Crawford	3/12	DE	97
Agness	18	DE	70
Andrew	35	IB	395
Andrew	53	DE	2
Ann	22	IE	353

Name	Age	St	Pg
Stewart, Anne	15	DE	71
Anthony	50	IE	399
Caroline M	3/12	DE	103
Catherine	4	DE	71
Catherine	50	DE	155
Charles	16	PA	363
Charles	18	PA	62
Charles	23	IE	103
Charles	35	DE	70
Charles	70	DE	286
Charles C	2	DE	124
Charlotta	50	DE	90
Charlotte	30	NJ	249
Charlotte A	18	NJ	376
Clara C	15	DE	185
Clarissa	11/12	DE	21
Daniel	6	DE	15
Edward	38	MD	170
Edward W	7	DE	97
Elener F	2	DE	103
Eliza	50	DE	188
Eliza A	4	DE	311
Elizabeth	12	DE	71
Elizabeth	21	ST	331
Elizabeth	25	IE	341
Elizabeth	32	DE	70
Elizabeth	52	DE	310
Elizabeth	72	DE	120
Elizabeth	43	PA	311
Elizabeth A	8	DE	395
Elizabeth A	35	MD	124
Elizabeth F	5	DE	363
Esther	8	DE	395
George W	2	DE	143
Henry	40	DE	90
Homer	10	DE	189
Jackson	18	DE	189
James	37	IE	341
James	46	IE	346
James F	9	DE	97
James H	11	DE	118
James E	17	MD	176
James R	24	NJ	376
Jane E	3	DE	77
John	2	DE	143
John	5	DE	124
John	8	PA	62
John	8	DE	71
John	9	DE	363
John	19	DE	311
John	21	DE	271
John	30	DE	118
John	37	DE	15
John	39	IE	363
John S	44	DE	124
Joseph H	2	DE	311
Letitia	8	DE	15
Luisa	30	DE	35
Margaret	7/12	DE	311
Margaret	1	DE	71
Margaret	7	DE	363
Martha	40	IE	363
Martha J	7	DE	170
Mary	22	DE	8
Mary	32	DE	143
Mary	39	MD	15
Mary	62	ST	333
Mary A	11	DE	97
Mary A	16	DE	143
Mary A	30	DE	97
Mary E	2	DE	118
Mary E	4	DE	21
Mary J	14	DE	363
Matthew	13	DE	363
Peter	40	IE	395
Rachel	22	IE	103
Rachel	25	DE	311
Rachel A	25	DE	118
Rebecca	10	PA	62
Rebecca	11	DE	363
Rebecca	35	DE	395
Rebecca	40	PA	62

Name	Age	St	Pg
Stewart, Reuben	12	DE	143
Reuben	36	DE	143
Robert	21	DE	35
Saml	60	DE	266
Samuel A	5	DE	97
Samuel W	40	DE	97
Sarah	16	DE	62
Susan	30	PA	170
Thomas	14	DE	143
Thomas	20	MD	49
W H	44	DE	62
William	4	DE	62
William	16	DE	15
William	17	NJ	310
William	21	DE	299
William	23	IE	291
William	28	DE	311
William H	5	DE	170
Zackaraiah	1	DE	170
Stewartson, Margaret	17	PA	98
Stidham, A E	20	DE	28
Anna	30	DE	90
Anna M	20	DE	156
Anne C	4	DE	240
Arnold	20	DE	155
Daniel	17	DE	231
Elizabeth	35	DE	286
Elizabeth	48	DE	68
Elizabeth C	31	DE	240
Emmett F	5	DE	90
Franklin	7	DE	240
George	5	DE	91
George W	9/12	DE	90
Hannah	50	DE	24
Hannah	56	DE	284
Henry	66	MD	284
Isaac	52	DE	333
James	10	DE	240
John	7	DE	90
John L	11	DE	90
John S	35	DE	90
Joseph K	40	DE	90
Lewis	2	DE	90
Lewis W	33	DE	240
Margaret	50	DE	90
Martha	10	DE	90
Mary E	2	DE	240
Samuel	26	DE	167
Sarah	12	DE	90
Siney	37	DE	90
William H	7	DE	90
Stidman, Sabilla	35	DE	6
Stillborn, Henry	25	DE	10
Stillwell, Alfred	23	DE	391
Franklun	17	DE	374
Jacob	29	DE	374
James A	1	DE	399
John	28	DE	399
John	62	PA	374
Mary A	30	DE	399
Sarah	20	DE	374
Stilly, Mary A	5	DE	71
Priscilla	33	NJ	71
William	36	DE	71
Stilts, Godfrey	32	GE	131
Stimmell, Albert	20	PA	303
Frederic	68	PA	303
John	22	PA	303
Maria	53	DE	303
Sarah	18	PA	303
Stimson, Margaret	11	DE	355
William	32	DE	356
Stinson, James	45	PA	357
Margaret	11	PA	356
Stockdale, James	16	MD	164
Stockton, Mary	34	ST	108
Servilla	45	CT	108
Stoddard, Lucinda M	25	NH	13
Stokes, Abel	9	DE	111
Abel	49	PA	111
Alfred	7	DE	111
Caroline	3	DE	88

Name	Age	St	No.	Name	Age	St	No.	Name	Age	St	No.
Sullivan, John	27	DE	23	Sutton, William H	13	DE	310	Sweney, Thomas	10	IE	80
Mary	7	MD	23	Wm	14	DE	262	Edward H	40	IE	143
Noble	63	DE	297	Wm	38	MD	260	Swenye, Joseph	16	IE	45
Rachel	36	PA	304	Suzby, John	35	DE	270	Sweter, Elizabeth	36	DE	97
Robert	6	DE	297	Swallows, Susan	14	DE	252	Fanny	4	DE	97
Samuel W	9	MD	304	Swan, Ann	23	GB	373	Martha	8	DE	97
Sumers, George	4	DE	75	John	29	GB	373	William	44	DE	97
Margaretta	6	DE	75	Robert	18	GB	373	Swetman, Emma	12	DE	106
Mary	28	DE	75	William	3	GB	373	James C	51	NJ	106
Meley	1	DE	75	Swaney, Bernard	19	IE	79	Mary J	14	DE	106
Susan	3	DE	75	Edward	17	IE	79	Mary J	50	MD	106
Summer, Barbara	26	GE	157	James	26	IE	80	Swiggers, Hannah	3	PA	52
Charles	28	GE	157	John	22	IE	79	Jacob	40	GE	52
Summers, James	35	DE	297	John	52	IE	79	Julia	3/12	PA	52
William	10	DE	363	Mary	44	IE	79	Sarah	11	PA	52
Supley, Alfred J	7	PA	7	Swayne, Amanda M	5	DE	118	Sarah	36	PA	52
Amanda S	10	PA	7	Ann P	32	PA	150	Swigget, Isaac	50	DE	371
Elvira S	5	DE	7	Caleb T	56	PA	61	Mary	40	DE	371
Franklin	38	PA	7	Caroline	3	DE	350	Richard	1	DE	371
Hariot	3	DE	7	Charles	8	DE	350	Swiggitt, Isaac	11	DE	294
Hariot	40	NJ	7	Henry	32	PA	350	Swinborn, Anna M	1	DE	353
James T	3/12	DE	7	Hugh	19	IE	36	Swindell, Charles	23	PA	276
Wilber F	16	PA	7	Jesse	17	DE	135	Emma	11/12	DE	276
Suppil, James H	4	DE	123	Jesse	20	PA	118	Sarah	17	PA	276
John	36	DE	123	Mary	16	PA	118	Swinney, Mary Etta	19	DE	382
John W	2	DE	123	Mary K	63	GB	350	Swinson, Eliza	35	MD	268
Martha A	7	DE	123	Rebecca	44	PA	118	Switzgabe, Samuel	50	PA	357
Meletta	24	DE	123	Sarah	22	PA	118	Sykes, Ann	30	DE	228
Suret, Pender	12	CU	165	Sarah	25	PA	61	Cato	35	DE	228
Susman, Martin W	7	DE	37	Sarah	56	PA	61	Mary	10	DE	229
Sarah A	5	DE	37	William	13	PA	118	Hannah	35	DE	200
Susmin, Joanna	17	PA	15	William	45	PA	118	Hester	10	DE	192
Sussex, Jim	23	DE	192	Swazey, Samuel	9	DE	371	John	10	DE	228
Susuman, Adalade	24	PA	24	Sweatman, Ann	45	DE	223	Sylvester, Tempy A	13	DE	235
Madora	2	PA	24	Christopher D	6	DE	211				
Peter	35	PA	24	Clementine	6	DE	211	Tagart, Asena	57	PA	116
Sarah	4	PA	24	Clinton	11	DE	223	Calvin	35	PA	116
Susan	7	PA	24	Eliza	7	DE	223	Edward B	9	DE	116
Suthell, James	24	DE	239	Franklin	11	DE	221	Joel	5	DE	21
Sutherland, Roderic	30	WI	296	Hannah	23	MD	230	John	4	DE	21
Sutton, Adelia	3	PA	260	Herdeman	8	DE	211	John	20	DE	33
Albert	4	DE	261	Mary	18	DE	220	John	23	DE	87
Alexander	13	MD	330	Rachel	46	DE	221	John	36	PA	21
Alfred	5	DE	310	Rebecca	15	DE	223	Mary B	5	DE.	116
Amanda J	11	DE	310	Samuel	5	DE	223	Rachel	3	DE	21
Ana	6	RI	5	Simon	9	DE	223	Rosetta	25	PA	21
Ann	30	IE	5	Simon P	49	DE	221	Sarah	2	DE	21
Ann E	7	DE	310	Thomas	14	DE	223	Sarah	29	DE	116
Benjamin	19	MD	36	Thomas	16	DE	228	Taggart, Joseph	9	OH	303
Edward	17	DE	262	Thomas	17	DE	221	Joseph J	42	PA	303
Eliza	18	DE	262	William	18	DE	221	Mary A	2	DE	303
Emily J	1	PA	5	William	53	DE	223	Mary G	41	DE	303
Emma	8	DE	262	Sweeney, Barney	30	IE	325	Rebecca H	15	IL	303
Ephraim	32	NJ	310	Cathrine	24	IE	325	Talbot, Anabella	1	NJ	381
George M	18	MD	330	Daniel	28	IE	346	Charlotte	27	NJ	381
Hannah	14	MD	330	Ellen	10/12	DE	273	Forklow	38	MD	381
Henry	4	DE	262	Hugh	25	IE	345	Mary E	4	NJ	381
Hester E	3	DE	310	Hugh	28	IE	339	William	16	DE	368
Isabella	5	DE	311	James	2	DE	346	Talfrey, Sarah J	22	DE	229
Isaac	20	NJ	310	John	5/12	DE	325	John	4/12	DE	229
Isaac	59	NJ	310	Lucy	8	PA	273	William	28	DE	229
James	10	DE	311	Mariann W	65	IE	342	Tallarey, Phillip	66	DE	168
James N	50	DE	261	Mary	2	DE	339	Talley, Aaron	29	PA	274
John	3	RI	5	Mary	6	DE	346	Abner C	9/12	DE	282
John	3	DE	262	Mary	26	IE	346	Abner P	14	DE	275
John	36	IE	5	Mary A	5	PA	274	Amos S	16	DE	272
John	49	DE	262	Mary A	23	IE	339	Ann	78	DE	276
John	82	DE	260	Mary A	23	IE	339	Annavela W	6	DE	274
Joshua	9	MD	330	Sweeny, Ann	20	IE	300	Anna J	9/12	DE	272
Julia	1/12	DE	260	Catharine	44	IE	286	Anna L	15	DC	272
Julia A	20	DE	262	Charles	7	IE	286	Beulah	1	DE	280
Louisa	13	DE	262	Ellen	21	IE	286	Burton L	10	DE	282
Margaret	49	DE	262	James	5	IE	286	Caroline E	5	DE	272
Martha	33	NJ	262	John	12	IE	286	Caroline S	2/12	DE	280
Mary	4/12	DE	262	Michael	15	IE	286	Charity	23	DE	275
Ruth	54	NJ	310	Michael	45	IE	286	Charles	15	DE	282
Ruth A	17	NJ	310	Patrick	17	IE	286	Charles T	30	DE	273
Saml B	35	DE	262	Patrick	25	IE	368	Curtis	11	DE	275
Samuel	51	DE	219	William	30	DE	196	Curtis	21	DE	272
Sara	49	PA	330	Sweney, Bridget	40	IE	273	Curtis M	7	DE	282
Susan	26	DE	260	Catherine A	24	IE	80	Deborah	30	?	274
William	11	MD	330	Cornelius	45	IE	273	Edith	5	DE	282

Name	Age	State	Page	Name	Age	State	Page	Name	Age	State	Page
Taylor, Edmond	6	DE	398	Taylor, Martha	24	DE	357	Teas, Clara	4	DE	95
Edmond	19	DE	307	Martha J	16	MD	278	Ellen J	11	DE	95
Elbert	7	DE	199	Mary	28	MD	6	Salina	7	DE	95
Elias	36	DE	242	Mary	28	PA	41	Sarah	39	PA	95
Eliza	20	NY	134	Mary	34	DE	317	Joseph	40	DE	94
Elizabeth	14	MD	278	Mary	35	GB	58	Teddings, Saml	40	PA	264
Elizabeth	20	GB	66	Mary	44	PA	355	Teeney, Charles	8	DE	315
Elizabeth	23	DE	317	Mary	46	PA	35	Elizabeth	22	DE	315
Elizabeth	23	DE	355	Mary	46	DE	199	Joseph	22	DE	315
Elizabeth	61	DE	19	Mary	52	MD	304	Joseph	11/12	DE	315
Elizabeth	69	DE	276	Mary	55	IE	324	William H	4	DE	315
Elizabeth J	24	NJ	97	Mary	61	DE	307	Tempel, Samuel	30	DE	105
Ella	4	DE	317	Mary A	35	DE	211	Tempell, Ann	23	DE	41
Emenuel	5	MD	58	Mary A	36	PA	135	Temple, Clemence	14	DE	345
Emeline	20	DE	382	Mary E	4/12	DE	242	Hester	54	PA	345
Emma	1	DE	317	Mary E	5	MD	6	Howard	15	PA	345
Fanny	50	DE	137	Mary E	8	MD	278	Josephine	4	MD	123
Francis	16	IE	295	Mary E	18	MD	166	Mary	20	DE	345
Francis	45	MD	67	Mary J	10	DE	398	Mary A	18	DE	351
Franklin	23	DE	307	Mary J	19	MD	401	Samuel	60	PA	345
George	4	NJ	97	Mary R	22	DE	382	Sarah	22	DE	345
George	12	PA	297	Matilda B	8	DE	366	Sarah J	21	MD	123
George	20	PA	153	Newton J	1	DE	274	Simon	24	DE	123
George W	19/12	DE	366	Nicholas	11	DE	199	William	32	DE	345
Hannah	20	DE	221	Peter	29	NJ	97	Templeman, Anne	2	DE	209
Hannah	25	IE	296	Peter	60	VA	304	Clayton	5	DE	209
Hannah	28	DE	351	Phillis	2	DE	187	Ellen V	1/12	DE	209
Hannah	30	PA	153	Rachel A	27	PA	274	George	9	DE	209
Hannah	57	PA	274	Rebecca	7	DE	317	George C	40	MD	209
Harriet	24	PA	359	Rebecca	30	MD	30	Henry	27	DE	209
Henry	14	NJ	355	Richard	13	IE	294	Henry	74	MD	209
Hester	12	DE	222	Robert	1/12	DE	35	Mary	30	DE	209
Isaac	30	PA	30	Robert	2	PA	39	Mary E	14	MD	209
James	3/12	DE	296	Robert	2	DE	359	Mary E	33	DE	209
James	28	DE	316	Robert	22	DE	324	Richard H	12	DE	209
James	30	PA	286	Robert	30	IE	35	Sarah M	7	DE	209
James	31	GB	66	Robert	70	GB	137	Tench, Henry	20	DE	207
James	34	DE	26	Ruth	23	IE	292	Ternein, Catherine	32	IE	316
James	68	DE	366	Samuel	1	PA	359	Lawrence	30	IE	316
James C	23	DE	134	Samuel	30	DE	359	Terra, Henry	20	DE	207
James Jr	39	DE	366	Samuel	51	PA	355	Terrall, Eliza J	12	DE	397
James T	7	DE	366	Samuel	67	DE	307	George	58	PA	397
Jane L	14	DE	229	Sarah	3	DE	6	Lydia M	17	DE	397
Jeffrey	45	GB	330	Sarah	19	DE	216	Margaret	65	PA	397
Jennetta	2	DE	134	Sarah	24	PA	356	Terry, Adeline	2	DE	289
Jesse	29	DE	351	Sarah	28	DE	26	Benjamin	38	MD	175
Jobe	13	DE	354	Sarah	50	DE	210	Henry R	1	DE	175
John	5	DE	245	Sarah	50	MD	271	Howell	43	DE	289
John	6	DE	354	Sarah	52	GB	137	Margaret A	25	DE	175
John	18	PA	114	Sarah A	7	MD	278	Rebecca J	26	DE	289
John	21	PA	39	Sarah A	14	DE	354	Victor Alphion	8/12	DE	289
John	28	DE	357	Simon	20	DE	188	William H	4	DE	289
John	30	IE	297	Simon	49	MD	199	Terune, Alexander	30	DE	317
John	32	GB	137	Susan	28	DE	242	Thacker, John H	15	DE	401
John	34	DE	325	Susan	46	MD	278	Thatcher, Albert	37	DE	96
John H	4	MD	278	Venus	8/12	DE	221	Anna	36	DE	111
John M	4	DE	351	William	3	DE	221	Charles H	7	DE	96
John T	35	PA	39	William	3	DE	245	Emma	15	DE	96
John T Q	11/12	MD	398	William	14	DE	188	Huable	73	DE	139
John W	30	DE	366	William	14	PA	335	John	3	DE	96
Joseph	3	DE	398	William	22	PA	153	John	15	DE	111
Joseph	30	PA	398	William	25	DE	221	Joseph L	5	DE	96
Joseph K	19	PA	350	William	29	IE	296	Lydia	37	DE	96
Josiah	56	DE	229	William	35	DE	216	Malvina	13	DE	96
Julia	3	DE	317	William	74	GB	276	Mathew	9	DE	96
Juniper	42	MD	278	William J	1	PA	134	Sally A	32	DE	56
Levin	20	DE	260	William F	2	DE	366	Samuel A	38	PA	56
Luisa	11	DE	354	William W	33	MD	317	Wheeler	7	DE	111
Lydia	3	DE	216	Willia	6/12	DE	6	William	37	DE	111
Lydia	8	DE	354	Wm	13	PA	319	Thawley, Albert	4/12	DE	367
Lydia	18	NJ	355	Zachary	6/12	DE	343	Rachel A	22	PA	367
Lydia A	6	NJ	97	Tayton, James	34	GB	27	Thomas	27	MD	367
Lydia M	26	DE	366	Sarah	29	GB	27	Theiss, Margaret	65	DE	274
Margaret	3	DE	199	Tazewell, Elizabeth	15	MD	88	Thilon, Lucinda	20	DE	278
Margaret	21	PA	39	John	18	DE	23	Thomas, Adalade	27	DE	46
Margaret	27	DE	398	John	18	MD	88	Albert	3	DE	146
Margaret	40	IE	112	Robert	4	MD	88	Amanda	27	NJ	267
Margaret A	19	MD	278	Samuel	9	MD	88	Amanda J	13	DE	213
Margaretta	1	NJ	97	Sarah A	40	MD	88	Amos	35	DE	177
Martha	4/12	DE	307	William	12	MD	88	Ann	41	PA	139
Martha	2	DE	296	William	60	GB	88	Aquilla	2/12	DE	267
Martha	18	DE	307	Teapot, Benjamin	58	DE	315	Aquilla	33	DE	267

Name	Age	St	Pg	Name	Age	St	Pg	Name	Age	St	Pg
Thomas, Aquilla	65	MD	99	Thomas, Rebecca	27	DE	237	Thompson, Henry	13	PA	55
Betsey	28	MD	142	Renattes	79	MD	62	Henry	31	DE	69
Betsey	65	MD	113	Richard	44	DE	212	Henry	38	DE	151
Beula	28	DE	382	Robert	2	DE	159	Horace	21	PA	55
Caroline	1	DE	212	Robert	3	DE	215	Hugh	15	IE	190
Catharine J	2	DE	237	Robert	9	DE	283	Isaac	13	DE	297
Charles	1	DE	197	Robert	56	MD	113	Isaac	28	DE	303
Charles	49	PA	139	Samuel	17	DE	213	Isabella	13	IE	55
Charles F	7	DE	382	Samuel	21	DE	202	Jacob	9	DE	375
Charles L	4	DE	139	Samuel W	48	MD	63	Jacob	26	DE	247
Daniel	3	DE	316	Sarah	2	MD	63	Jacob	61	DE	340
Daniel H	28	MD	146	Sarah	4	DE	237	James	6	DE	300
David W	50	DE	212	Sarah	14	DE	139	James	8	DE	333
Edward	14	DE	46	Sarah	20	DE	234	James	17	DE	49
Edward	40	DE	212	Sarah	40	DE	262	James	30	IE	300
Elener	6/12	DE	237	Sarah E	6	DE	262	James	46	MD	110
Eliza	8	DE	46	Sarah E	29	MD	63	James	50	DE	246
Eliza	9	DE	212	Sarah J	4/12	DE	316	James	80	MD	327
Elizabeth	23	DE	46	Sarah J	1	DE	72	James H	4	DE	394
Elizabeth	28	DE	283	Susan	17	DE	309	Jane	8	DE	246
Ella J V	5/12	DE	21	Susan	23	DE	87	Jane	22	DE	361
Ellen	21	DE	110	Susan	28	MD	146	Jane	26	GB	71
Ellen W	50	DE	110	Susan	58	DE	212	Jane	40	MD	150
Ellener	59	MD	46	Thomas	30	DE	214	Jane	55	PA	40
Elmira	22	NJ	5	Westly	12	MD	316	Jane	63	PA	361
Emily	19	MD	158	William	1	DE	381	Jeremiah	70	DE	337
Emma L	9	DE	382	William	3	DE	316	Jethro	65	DE	246
Euphemia	16	PA	48	William	3	DE	319	Joel	25	DE	396
Evan	17	DE	139	William	4	DE	283	John	7	DE	321
Fanny	10	DE	105	William	6	DE	316	John	12	MD	77
Frances	1	DE	215	William	7	DE	159	John	17	PA	310
Frances	11	MD	316	William	11	MD	63	John	22	ST	110
Franklin	2	DE	397	William	29	MD	283	John	28	DE	247
George	2	DE	21	William	50	MD	316	John	45	PA	77
Hagar	40	DE	212	William	76	MD	46	John B	9	DE	217
Hannah	12	DE	137	William F	4	DE	212	Joseph	36	DE	217
Hannah	65	DE	216	William L G	5	DE	382	Josephine	11	DE	340
Henry	63	DE	385	William W	39	DE	382	Joshua	50	DE	293
Isaac	2	DE	267	Wm C	49	DE	262	Louisa	16	PA	55
Isaac	29	DE	21	Thompson, Alexander	1	DE	217	Lydia	3	PA	128
Isaac	70	DE	67	Alfred	6	DE	77	Lydia	23	DE	396
Isabella	54	MD	237	Alfred	30	MD	72	Margaret	22	DE	394
Israel	17	NJ	7	Allen	62	DE	69	Margaret	36	IE	85
James	3	DE	110	Amanda	1	DE	376	Margaret	39	DE	303
James	11	MD	63	Andrew	11	DE	375	Margaret E	18	MD	166
James	11	DE	382	Andrew	14	DE	352	Margaret J	3	DE	85
James	30	DE	212	Andrew J	11	MD	127	Maria	23	DE	150
John	1	DE	146	Ann	7	PA	127	Maria	47	DE	340
John	2	DE	1	Ann	9	MD	243	Mariah S	29	DE	69
John	4	DE	267	Ann	57	DE	128	Mart	28	DE	247
John	7	MD	63	Ann M	14	DE	332	Martha	3	DE	150
John	26	MD	110	Anna M	6	DE	375	Mary	17	PA	55
John	33	MD	265	Bula	47	PA	396	Mary	23	GB	71
John	50	DE	270	Catherine	6	DE	150	Mary	28	PA	40
John	57	DE	234	Catherine	9	DE	340	Mary	40	DE	246
John T	70	ME	90	Charles W	5	DE	361	Mary	56	DE	99
John W	34	MD	237	Charlotte	50	DE	337	Mary A	24	DE	61
Joseph	3	DE	159	Cyrus B	9	DE	361	Mary A	26	DE	143
Lucy	26	GB	265	Daniel	49	DE	396	Mary E	7	PA	284
Lydia	21	NJ	21	Dorcas	40	MD	327	Mary E	9	DE	150
Lydia	37	PA	212	Dorcas	60	MD	37	Mary E	17	MD	243
Margaret	57	DE	67	Edward	4/12	DE	150	Mary J	19	PA	99
Martha	30	MD	316	Edward	70	DE	155	Mr	54	DE	94
Martha A	11/12	DE	283	Eliza	20	IE	207	Priscilla	64	DE	299
Martha J	--	MD	186	Elizabeth	5	PA	128	Rachel	13	DE	340
Martha J	15	MD	112	Elizabeth	13	DE	375	Rebecca	24	DE	246
Martha J	15	MD	113	Elizabeth	36	DE	217	Rebecca	47	MD	77
Mary	2	DE	139	Elizabeth	46	DE	55	Rebecca A	1	DE	246
Mary	5	MD	63	Elizabeth	66	MD	393	Rebecca A	45	DE	246
Mary	12	DE	262	Ellen	38	PA	127	Rebecca B	36	PA	361
Mary	16	GB	127	Emily	19	PA	55	Richard	40	GB	368
Mary	18	DE	115	George	3	DE	217	Robert	2	DE	150
Mary	19	PA	301	George	15	MD	77	Robert	9	MD	128
Mary	25	DE	214	George	18	DE	375	Robert	25	MD	150
Mary	35	IE	282	George	28	DE	394	Robert	30	IE	85
Mary A	50	PA	90	George	35	DE	284	Robert	54	IE	99
Mary J	15	DE	212	George	38	DE	361	Robert J	6	DE	85
Narcisa	15	DE	141	Hamilton	4	DE	376	Robt	6	DE	217
Phebe A	45	DE	99	Hannah B	21	DE	142	Sally	4	DE	337
Rachel	14	MD	54	Hannah H	16	DE	396	Sarah	10	DE	246
Rachel W	7	DE	212	Hannah J	26	DE	361	Sarah	37	PA	375
Rebecca	25	DE	46	Helen	22	PA	55	Sarah A	26	PA	284

Name	Age	State	Page
Thompson, Sarah L	5	DE	247
Sarah M	18	DE	69
Seba	40	MD	72
Stephen	1	DE	85
Stephen	27	DE	299
Susanna	25	DE	341
T S	11	MD	164
Virginia	1	DE	44
William	9	DE	85
William	13	PA	127
William	39	DE	150
William	41	PA	127
William	50	IE	192
William	51	DE	128
William	53	DE	375
William	70	GE	86
Thomson, Alauisha P	10	DE	336
Amy	48	MD	369
Ann	43	PA	336
Ann M	14	DE	336
Anna	10	DE	389
Anna W	37	DE	389
Arvill	46	MA	358
Caroline	14	DE	389
Charles	2	DE	325
Charlotte	50	MD	259
Clara A	8	DE	336
Darcus	60	MD	327
Elizabeth	17	DE	375
Elizabeth	56	IE	331
Ella	8	DE	10
Ellen	30	DE	325
Emma	4	DE	389
George	5	DE	325
George	35	DE	325
Hetty	48	GB	353
J W (Dr)	48	VA	10
James	28	DE	201
James	70	MD	327
James M	17	DE	336
James W	12	DE	336
James W	14	DE	10
Jane	27	IE	336
John	12	GB	353
John	50	IE	336
John	55	GB	353
John A	20	DE	10
John P	19	DE	336
Joseph	8	DE	326
Josephine	12	DE	336
Josephine C	1	DE	389
Julia	18	DE	10
Lucy E	16	DE	10
Martha E	12	DE	389
Mary	4/12	DE	325
Mary E	8	DE	389
Nalbro	10	DE	10
Richard M	42	DE	357
Rosella M	21	PA	10
Saml	61	IE	336
Samuel	19	IE	379
Samuel E	40	MD	389
Sarah	22	PA	353
Sarah E	13	DE	336
Sarah P	12	DE	10
Sarah P	48	DE	10
William	22	GB	353
William A	23	DE	336
Victor S	17	DE	336
Thorn, Eliza P	3	DE	287
George	6	GB	287
George	29	GB	287
Mary	74	GB	287
Mary A	29	GB	287
Mary E	5	GB	287
Valentine	5/12	DE	287
William	64	GB	287
Thornton, Eliza	2	IE	315
Elizabeth	33	DE	233
James	32	IE	315
Margaretta	60	IE	315
Mary	20	IE	315
Thornton, Richard	21	IE	315
Thomas	48	DE	233
Thorp, Susan	35	DE	348
Tibbit, Elizabeth	9	DE	262
Tibbles, Ewing	22	PA	267
Tieg, James	22	IE	298
Tiely, Peter	42	IE	299
Tightcap, Henry	28	DE	225
Till, Apsom	13	DE	214
Henry	15	DE	309
Henry	43	DE	281
John	11	DE	286
Levi	25	DE	234
Philip	18	DE	233
Sarah	38	MD	112
Tillman, Ann	28	DE	241
Anna E	4	DE	368
Catharine	6	DE	241
Christopher J	3/12	DE	184
Chruse	72	MD	240
Eli	10	DE	184
Ellen	3	DE	241
Ellen	75	MD	240
George	2	DE	368
Henrietta	9	MD	258
Jacob	24	DE	368
Jane	50	MD	258
Jesse	40	MD	240
John	11	MD	258
John	35	DE	368
John	68	DE	212
Margaret	25	DE	368
Marian	1	DE	368
Mary	3	DE	365
Mary A	4	DE	368
Mary E	2	DE	368
Mary J	12	DE	184
Philip	25	DE	369
Rachel	30	DE	365
Richard	30	DE	365
Samuel	6/12	DE	241
Sarah	5	DE	241
Sarah	20	DE	368
Sarah	28	DE	368
Sarah	35	DE	184
Sewall	40	DE	184
Tillotson, Milly	80	MD	203
Tilman, Ann	28	DE	293
Catharine	8/12	DE	293
George	18	DE	99
George	22	DE	92
George	60	DE	202
Henrietta	1	DE	146
Jacob	18	DE	59
James	3/12	DE	92
Jim	22	DE	189
Joel	25	DE	189
John	23	DE	59
John	70	MD	59
Joshua	1	DE	26
Margaret	5/12	DE	59
Mary	25	DE	59
Mary A	4	DE	146
Matilda	26	MD	26
Rachel	21	DE	92
Rachel	29	MD	146
Rebecca	16	DE	59
Simon	29	DE	146
Thomas	14	DE	59
William	6	DE	26
William	21	DE	59
William	45	DE	26
Tilten, Elizabeth	17	NJ	78
Timmons, Eliza	24	MD	261
Georgianna	1	MD	261
John	3	MD	261
John	34	MD	261
Timpson, Charles	30	DE	357
Elizabeth	4	DE	357
George H	7	DE	357
Mary H	28	DE	357
Sarah Helen	8	DE	357
Timpson, Susanna	3	DE	357
Tindle, Danial	9	DE	153
Elener	11	DE	153
Eliza	48	PA	153
Mary	78	NJ	153
Robert	16	DE	153
Samuel	47	NJ	153
Sarah	18	DE	153
William	6	DE	153
Tingley, Hannah	43	DE	226
John W	8	DE	226
Joseph	20	DE	226
Martha	12	DE	226
Sarah A	15	DE	226
Stringer	23	DE	226
Stringer	56	DE	226
Tinney, Mary	62	PA	336
Tippet, Ann	25	DE	318
George	47	DE	318
George H	6	DE	318
Joshua E	3	DE	318
Mary F	6/12	DE	318
Samuel	11	DE	318
Sarah	13	DE	319
William	9	DE	319
Tippets, Daniel	22	DE	223
Elizabeth	50	DE	223
Rebecca	19	DE	223
Samuel	8	DE	223
Sarah E	2	DE	223
Tippett, Mary	27	DE	222
Tippin, Hannah	50	NJ	267
John	55	NJ	267
Titman, Anthony	32	GE	52
Titteny, Catherine	53	SZ	145
Titus, Catherine	17	NJ	111
David	13	NJ	111
Ellen J	34	NJ	111
Mary A	12	NJ	111
Sarah	10	NJ	111
Thomas	1	NJ	111
Thomas	40	NJ	111
Tobias, Hannah	11	DE	47
Hannah	50	DE	47
James	17	DE	369
Tobin, Hannah M	28	MD	383
James	--	GB	290
Margaret	1	MD	383
Rebecca	3	DE	383
Thomas	10	DE	383
William	35	NJ	383
Toby, Charles E	9	DE	177
Eliza J	29	DE	177
Franklin W	5	DE	177
John	30	DE	177
John W	1/12	DE	177
Mary L	3	DE	177
Tod, Clara	3	DE	79
Eli	6/12	DE	79
Eli	48	DE	79
Elmira	6	DE	79
Gideon F	16	DE	79
Lucinda	10	DE	79
Sally A	47	DE	79
William H	12	DE	79
Todd, Alfred	15	DE	86
Alfred	20	DE	154
Allen	30	GB	261
Amanda	9	DE	354
Ann	43	DE	63
Anna M	8	MD	377
Beulah	6	DE	298
Deborah P	28	PA	355
Eliza J	15	DE	375
Elizabeth	25	DE	299
Elizabeth J	12	DE	354
Esther	48	DE	375
Eunice	3	DE	354
Evelina	28	DE	154
Francis	4	DE	332
Frank	15	DE	63
George	20	DE	63

Name	Age	St	Pg	Name	Age	St	Pg	Name	Age	St	Pg
Todd, George A	4	DE	298	Topham, Sinthia	15	DE	321	Townsend, John	50	DE	77
Hannah	6	DE	332	Topin, George	4	DE	312	John F	2	DE	247
Hester	16	DE	357	Robert	36	DE	312	John J	3	DE	239
James	16	DE	276	Samuel	1	DE	312	John J	28	DE	169
James	17	PA	294	Sarah	6	DE	312	John S	38	DE	247
James	31	DE	299	Sarah	28	DE	312	Joseph	25	DE	77
John	36	DE	299	Susan	40	PA	363	Joseph F	25	DE	203
John	56	DE	375	Toppen, Amanda	26	DE	293	Joseph R	50	DE	112
John W	6/12	DE	298	Amanda	11	DE	254	Josephine	1	DE	77
Jonathan	33	GB	332	Ann	2	DE	291	Joshua	48	DE	246
Joseph	22	DE	63	George	5	DE	291	Margaret	12	DE	77
Joseph	45	DE	63	George	44	DE	254	Maria	59	DE	217
Joseph	50	DE	311	George B	7/12	DE	254	Marion F	1	DE	197
Josiah	70	MD	154	Jno	35	DE	291	Martha	7	DE	77
Levi	49	MD	377	Julia	36	NJ	254	Martha	28	DE	169
Lewis E	1	DE	299	Margaret	7	DE	254	Mary	9	DE	77
Martha L	13	DE	375	Mary	30	DE	291	Mary	10	DE	291
Mary	7	DE	332	Samuel	6	DE	291	Mary	59	DE	280
Mary	16	DE	82	Susan	12	DE	254	Mary A	6	DE	376
Mary	19	DE	154	Torbel, Anna	37	DE	371	Mary A	8	DE	241
Mary	26	DE	298	Anna E	18	DE	371	Mary A	24	DE	187
Mary	29	DE	332	Elizabeth	11	DE	371	Mary Anna	11	DE	305
Mary	70	IE	154	Franklin	6	DE	371	Mary G	56	DE	378
Mary A	34	PA	354	Peter	56	DE	371	Mary H	33	NJ	291
Mary Ann	41	MD	377	Rebecca	3	DE	371	Mary H	77	DE	112
Mary E	21	MD	377	William	17	DE	271	Rachel	41	DE	241
Petter	25	DE	32	Torbert, Catherine H	25	DE	112	Rachel	58	DE	172
Rachel M	15	MD	377	Hannah	26	DE	154	Rebecca	41	DE	305
Rebecca	63	PA	355	Tously, Jacob	50	DE	318	Rebecca V	1	DE	305
Robert	12	DE	63	Towel, Harry	25	GE	349	Richard	10	DE	241
Samuel	19	PA	294	Martha	23	IE	349	Saml	18	PA	365
Sarah	14	PA	346	Town, Annabella	6	DE	381	Samuel	14	DE	241
Tilly	49	IE	276	Annabella	30	DE	381	Samuel	37	DE	241
William	36	PA	354	Towns, Elijah	7/12	DE	181	Samuel	67	DE	172
William	39	DE	298	George W	16	MD	181	Samuel Jr	14	DE	241
William	60	IE	276	James R	42	DE	181	Sarah A	37	DE	239
Toland, Dennis	49	IE	306	James R Jr	2	DE	181	Sarah A	45	DE	172
Elizabeth A	63	MD	306	Mary	32	MD	181	Sarah C	5	DE	197
Margaret	19	DE	306	Mary R	12	DE	181	Sarah E	1	DE	203
Mary A	29	DE	306	Rebecca M	8	MD	186	Sarah J	7	DE	226
Tolbert, Anna M	22	DE	61	Townsend, Abigal	38	PA	321	Sarah J	16	DE	77
Hugh	27	DE	61	Alfred E	6	DE	305	Solomon	17	DE	305
William B	3	DE	61	Anamaria	19	MD	187	Solomon	44	DE	291
Tolson, Benjamin	6/12	DE	243	Ann	45	DE	77	Solomon H	13	DE	291
John	5	MD	243	Ann	54	DE	339	Stephen	73	DE	339
John V	32	MD	243	Ann	74	DE	226	Stephen G	22	DE	378
Samuel	7	MD	243	Ann E	20	DE	77	Sylvester	19	DE	305
Sarah A	26	MD	243	Anna M	31	MD	241	Sylvester	48	DE	321
Tomany, John	55	IE	286	Artemia	40	NJ	112	William	8	DE	291
Mary	8	DE	286	Catharine	1	DE	239	William H	7	DE	112
Mary	20	IE	286	Catharine	6	DE	143	William H	16	DE	241
Mary	65	IE	286	Charles M	2	DE	112	Zadock	15	DE	305
Tominy, Ann	19	IE	285	Charles W	23	DE	339	Zadock	42	DE	305
Barney	27	IE	285	Edmond L	16	DE	112	Towsand, Amos E	4	MD	327
Tompson, Anna	7	DE	347	Edward	30	DE	187	James L	2	MD	327
Emily	3	DE	347	Eliza	26	DE	143	John	9/12	DE	327
Hannah M	5	DE	347	Eliza	38	DE	291	Mary A	26	DE	327
Hellen A	4	PA	353	Eliza A	25	DE	203	Mary E	9/12	DE	327
Henry	1	DE	347	Elizabeth	24	MD	197	Silas	28	DE	327
John	32	PA	352	Elizabeth J	20	DE	112	Trainer, Agnis	3	DE	147
John	45	DE	347	Ellen	6	DE	77	Edward	13	PA	164
Lewis	33	DE	347	Eloisa J	13	DE	247	Henry	13	DE	55
Lydia	31	DE	347	Emaline	30	DE	239	Mary A	15	DE	130
Martha	26	PA	352	Enoch	22	DE	77	Philip	40	IE	147
Mary	2	DE	352	Esther	26	DE	187	Rosanah	44	IE	147
Mary P	8	DE	347	Franklin	6	DE	291	Thomas	11	DE	147
Sarah	37	PA	367	Franklin	13	DE	305	Trasinal, The Rev Mr	35	GB	145
William	15	NY	108	George L	9	DE	321	Travers, Edward	40	IE	168
William A	4	DE	352	George M	15	DE	112	Martha	28	MD	285
Tone, Agnes	40	ST	333	George R	21	DE	295	Thomas	15	DE	240
Frances	15	ST	333	George W	4	DE	197	Thomas	34	DE	187
Jenette	17	ST	333	George W	31	DE	197	Traverse, Aaron	55	MD	270
John	9	DE	333	Hannah	35	DE	172	Frances	2/12	DE	270
Michael	11	ST	333	Hannah E	10	DE	241	Rachel	4	DE	270
Toner, Ellen	28	IE	166	Harriet O	4/12	DE	169	Sarah	7	DE	270
Tony, Harry	18	DE	181	Henrietta	12	DE	241	Travise, Daniel	15	PA	296
Toodle, John	7	DE	205	Henry	3	DE	305	Daniel	50	IE	296
Mary	25	DE	205	Israel	35	DE	239	John	11	PA	296
Shadrack	30	DE	205	James	29	DE	143	Margaret	18	DE	296
Tool, James	40	IE	377	Janeth	36	DE	247	Margaret	50	IE	296
Toomer, Carrie F	17	VA	166	Job	57	DE	217	Trencher, John	12	PA	316
M J	19	VA	166	John	42	DE	241	Trevecca, Eliza	8	DE	160

Name	Age	State	Page
Trevecca, Henry	12	DE	160
John	40	DE	160
Mrs	35	DE	160
Susan	10	DE	160
Tribbit, Charles	30	DE	377
George H	5	DE	377
Jane	25	DE	377
Mary E C	10	DE	377
Tribble, Caroline	5	PA	142
Charles	9	PA	142
Charles	40	GE	142
Fredericia	34	GE	142
Henry	10/12	DE	142
Louisa	3	PA	142
Sophia	11	GE	142
William	13	GE	142
Tribet, Alexander	25	DE	296
Diana	4/12	DE	386
Diana	15	DE	386
Emeline	8	DE	386
Esther J	5	DE	386
Francis	38	DE	386
George W	7	DE	386
Mary	2/12	DE	386
Mary A	10	DE	386
Sabinia	31	DE	386
Susanna	3	DE	386
Tribit, Daniel	14	DE	338
Tribute, Andrew	24	DE	46
Anthony	55	DE	46
Mary	58	DE	46
Trift, Sarah	19	DE	217
Triggs, Elizabeth	38	GB	142
Richard	38	GB	142
Trimble, James	30	IE	329
Joseph	65	MD	356
Trinder, James	35	DE	380
Joseph	37	DE	380
Tripp, Sarah	75	DE	56
Trippet, John	18	DE	356
Troth, Eugene H	8	DE	374
Joseph Eugene	6	DE	374
Joseph N	38	NJ	374
Laura N	10	DE	374
Mary J	12	DE	332
Mary Josephine	12	DE	374
Laura A	10	DE	332
Narcissa J	37	MD	374
Truaty, Ramona	46	MD	67
Trueaxe, Benjamin	25	DE	232
Martha A	18	DE	232
Truet, Jemima	30	DE	396
Rebecca	2/12	DE	396
Truitt, Andrew	24	DE	141
Elizabeth	36	DE	160
Emma L	2	DE	107
Henry A	5	DE	107
Joseph L	8	DE	107
Martha A	17	DE	107
Martha M	15	NJ	166
Peter	56	DE	107
Sarah	34	DE	107
Thomas	30	DE	329
Truman, Jesse	68	DE	292
Henrietta	58	DE	292
Trush, Charles	19	DE	185
Truss, Anna L	5	DE	284
James	29	NJ	283
James W	3	DE	284
Margaret	27	NJ	283
Mary P	7	DE	283
Rosanna	28	NJ	288
Samuel P	27	NJ	288
Thomas L	5	DE	288
Trust, John	38	PA	357
Rebecca	32	PA	357
William	21	DE	381
Trusty, Ann	11	DE	284
Benjamin	25	DE	203
Catharine	16	DE	321
Charlotta	35	MD	154
Delia	17	MD	73
Trusty, Eliza	42	MD	73
Elizabeth	9	DE	73
Ellen	28	DE	73
Empson	12	MD	16
Empson	44	MD	16
Gasaway	24	PA	251
George	9	DE	323
George	21	MD	73
Isaac	8	MD	73
Isaac	35	DE	161
Isaac	40	MD	73
Jacob	30	DE	11
Jacob	40	DE	319
John	6/12	DE	321
Jonathan	6	DE	323
Joseph	5	DE	73
Joshua	18	DE	218
Joshua	60	DE	218
Kennard	20	DE	353
Levinia	1	DE	154
Margaret A	6	DE	154
Maria	6	DE	323
Mariah	40	DE	323
Mary	3/12	DE	323
Mary	15	MD	16
Matilda	65	DE	218
Ramond	16	MD	16
Rebecca	2	DE	323
Rebecca	8	MD	16
Samuel	22	DE	323
Sarah	15	DE	320
Sarah	15	DE	323
Sarah A	14	DE	218
Tabitha	13	DE	323
Warner	48	DE	323
William	13	DE	154
William	18	MD	16
Trute, Ann	62	DE	288
Truville, Mary	16	PA	394
Tucker, Abigal	4/12	DE	139
Amos	3	DE	139
Bridget	23	IE	265
Clement	65	DE	383
Delia	8	DE	92
Edward	9/12	DE	127
Hannah J	23	PA	346
Jacob	30	DE	92
Jerenine	4	DE	92
John	25	IE	265
Julia	9/12	DE	92
Julia	28	WI	92
Julia A	5	DE	139
Mary	25	IE	127
Patric	32	IE	127
Sarah A	34	DE	139
Thomas	30	PA	139
Ulis Antony	6	DE	92
Wm	22	PA	265
Tudor, Elizabeth	17	DE	365
Tullder, William	28	DE	363
Tumblers, John	22	DE	168
Tumlin, Amanda	6	DE	253
Frances	3	DE	253
John	36	DE	253
Martha	12	DE	253
Mary	8	DE	253
Sarah	11	DE	253
Sarah	33	DE	253
Tunnel, Charles	4	DE	59
Mary	28	DE	59
Sampson	30	DE	59
Turnbull, Adam	35	MA	300
George	33	DE	300
Mary	16	PA	393
Mary J	28	DE	300
William	37	GB	300
Turner, Ann	55	MD	368
Brooke T	56	GB	54
Byran	4	DE	24
Catharine	16	NJ	290
Catharine	54	DE	44
Catharine V	4	DE	116
Turner, Catharine V	4	DE	116
Charles	18	DE	366
Charlotta	27	GB	23
Danial	1	DE	93
Elizabeth	2	DE	366
Elizabeth	7	DE	300
Elizabeth	13	MD	239
Elizabeth	13	DE	286
Elizabeth	25	DE	383
Elizabeth	50	PA	54
Elizabeth	50	DE	280
Elizabeth L	6	DE	286
Emma	9	DE	116
George	2	DE	383
George	15	DE	110
George W	2	DE	286
George W	34	DE	275
Hannah	2	DE	313
Hannah	28	PA	24
Harriet E	27	DE	286
Henry	3	DE	251
Isaac	23	DE	255
Isaac	24	MD	313
Isaac	30	DE	383
John	7	DE	24
John D	46	DE	293
John M	53	VA	116
Joseph	25	PA	353
Joseph H	25	DE	350
Laura J	10	DE	286
Leonora	5	DE	287
Levi	14	DE	110
Lewis	1	DE	24
Louisa	25	DE	299
Lurana	11	DE	380
Margaret	2	DE	350
Margaret	44	DE	350
Margaretta	18	PA	110
Maria	25	DE	224
Mariah	20	DE	368
Martha J	17	DE	110
Mary	5/12	DE	384
Mary	12	DE	116
Mary	40	MD	280
Mary	43	PA	116
Mary	54	DE	350
Mary A	15	MD	197
Mary A	18	DE	285
Mary F	7	MD	224
Mary J	3/12	DE	280
Mary J	24	DE	366
Mary P	4	DE	286
Naomia	6	DE	24
Peter	39	DE	18
Priscilla J	20	PA	353
Rachel	38	DE	299
Rebecca	15	DE	286
Rebecca	18	DE	116
Rebecca	40	DE	286
Rebecca	54	DE	293
Robert	42	DE	299
Robert G	6	DE	116
Sarah	6/12	DE	366
Sarah	5	PA	44
Sarah	18	MD	280
Sarah	25	DE	313
Sarah	30	DE	350
Sarah	50	GB	23
Sarah A	20	DE	286
Sarah J	26	DE	93
Susan	20	NJ	280
Susan	37	PA	18
Susanna	11	DE	381
Susanna	20	MD	239
Thomas	25	GB	23
Thomas	25	GB	309
Thomas	31	DE	318
Thomas	43	DE	286
Tilghman	24	MD	280
Tilghman	26	DE	366
Tolbert	24	PA	110
Walter E	14	DE	293

Name	Age	St	No.
Turner, Washington	7	DE	299
Wesley	13	DE	166
Wesley	27	MD	24
William	10	DE	299
William	33	DE	93
Turpin, James	30	NJ	239
Tuthall, Biddy	15	IE	342
Catherine	18	IE	342
John	2	DE	342
Mary	35	IE	342
Michael	12	IE	342
Nancy	10	IE	342
Patrick	40	IE	342
Tweed, Alice	23	DE	385
Alice	25	DE	349
Alice	65	PA	349
Andrew	21	DE	349
Ann	32	DE	349
Elizabeth	5	DE	374
Emery	32	DE	353
Hester A	7	DE	374
Hester A	42	DE	374
Jeremiah	1	DE	353
John	11	DE	374
John	40	DE	23
John	59	DE	374
Mansel	27	DE	374
Mary	30	DE	349
Mr	50	DE	97
Rachel	34	DE	353
Robert	68	PA	349
William	7	DE	353
William	15	MD	353
William R	9	DE	374
Tweedy, Anna	25	MD	13
Caroline	23	MD	25
David	2	DE	134
David	60	DE	371
Elizabeth	7	DE	134
Ellen	50	DE	371
Emma	10	DE	134
Jacob	28	DE	25
Jacob	30	DE	13
Joshua	50	DE	374
Mary A	36	DE	134
Susan	41	DE	374
Washington	36	DE	134
Tybout, Elizabeth	27	PA	312
Georbe W	4	DE	312
George Z	34	PA	312
Lydia M	1	DE	312
Marion	7	DE	312
Tyler, Frederick	4	GB	256
James	26	GB	186
Martha	28	GB	256
Reuben	16	GB	186
Saml	28	GB	256
Thomas	25	GB	186
William H	12	PA	386
Tyndale, Elizabeth	23	DE	263
Tyson, Barstow	4/12	DE	22
Elijah	30	MD	22
Isaac	7	MD	22
Jacob	25	DE	171
Martha	26	DE	22
Martha	28	NJ	18
Mary	3	MD	22
Mary F	32	PA	351
Rebecca	26	DE	100
Rebecca	50	DE	397
Rebecca F	1	DE	351
Samuel	37	PA	351
Samuel T	9	DE	351
Sarah F	2	DE	351
William	7	PA	18
Uhler, Richard	32	PA	274
Underhill, John	19	PA	355
Underwood, Eliza	77	DE	349
(Unknown) Ann	20	IE	304
Capt	26	DE	85
Cesar	26	DE	94
(Unknown) Grace	50	MD	304
Harriet	16	DE	142
Rebecca	30	DE	98
Sophia	27	DE	142
Susan	20	IE	304
Unrugh, Louisa	2	PA	313
Matilda	27	DE	37
Washington	23	PA	37
William	24	PA	313
Updyke, Isaac	8	DE	373
Isaac	34	DE	373
John T	6	DE	373
Jonas	11	DE	373
Sarah	35	DE	373
William	13	DE	373
Urian, Harrison	8	PA	250
Howard	11	PA	250
Israel	38	PA	249
Louisa	18	DE	250
Mary	35	PA	250
Theodore	5	PA	250
Urmey, Charlotta	11	MD	69
Daniel	36	PA	69
George W	2	DE	69
Rebecca	32	DE	69
Uxington, Jane	52	GB	38
Vail, Alexander	12	DE	176
Alice J	5	DE	190
Angeline	4	DE	257
Anna L	10	DE	207
David C	18	DE	207
David C	19	DE	190
Elizabeth	32	DE	234
Elizabeth E	9	DE	176
Hannah	32	MD	257
Hannah	55	DE	207
Hannah L	21	DE	207
Harriet	11	MD	190
Harriet J	35	MD	190
James	45	DE	176
John	2	DE	257
John B	3	DE	190
John C	35	DE	190
John T	9	DE	234
Mary E	10	DE	214
Mary J	26	DE	176
Phebe	54	DE	384
Saml	4/12	DE	257
Samuel C	6	DE	190
Sarah J	6	DE	234
Thomas	8	DE	190
Thomas	38	DE	234
William S	6/12	DE	190
Wm	33	DE	257
Vair, Samuel	22	NJ	162
Valentine, Abraham	6	DE	321
Abraham	41	PA	321
Alexander	23	PA	285
Alfred	5	PA	139
Anna M	13	PA	346
Burton	8	DE	360
Eliza	10	PA	285
Elizabeth	10	DE	321
Elizabeth	12	PA	139
Elizabeth	32	DE	360
Ellen	12	DE	369
Ellenor	12	DE	321
Emma L	13	DE	124
Engle	7	PA	285
Ezra	64	PA	346
George	51	PA	285
Harriett	12	DE	299
Harrison	33	PA	366
Henry A	9	DE	360
James	3	PA	139
James	11	PA	285
John	21	PA	285
John	21	DE	360
Joseph	8	DE	321
Joshua S	38	PA	124
Levina	14	DE	360
Valentine, Lydia	2	PA	139
Mary	9	PA	139
Mary J	32	DE	321
Matilda	11	DE	321
Matilda	13	DE	360
Matilda	14	PA	139
Rachel A	33	DE	124
Robert	4	DE	321
Sarah	15	DE	360
Sarah	16	PA	285
Sarah	50	ST	285
Sarah A	11	DE	124
Thomas	17	PA	285
William	5	DE	360
William	16	PA	139
William	19	PA	285
William	35	DE	360
William H	1	DE	321
Valon, Daniel	11	DE	324
Vanartsdale, John	66	PA	360
Lina	52	DE	360
Vanburen, Martin	24	DE	312
Vance, Auther	1	PA	77
Auther B	30	PA	77
Bartholomew	5	PA	77
Elizabeth	32	DE	77
Grace	28	PA	77
James	30	PA	77
Mary	14	DE	321
Mary E	3	PA	77
Richard	22	DE	91
Serena	25	DE	91
Stephen	11	MD	304
Susan	8	DE	296
William	17	DE	321
William A	4/12	DE	91
Vandegrift, A Jack-son	35	DE	199
Abraham	16	DE	206
Abram	50	DE	202
Alfred	20	DE	206
Ann	31	DE	199
Caroline	2/12	DE	199
Christopher J	6	DE	188
Ellen	8	DE	188
Harrison	10	DE	206
Hester D	31	DE	188
Isaac H Jr	53	DE	206
Isaac W	18	DE	206
Jacob	50	DE	187
Jacob	60	DE	202
Jacob A	12	DE	206
James	13	DE	215
James M	35	DE	199
John	52	DE	257
John B	3	DE	199
J W	27	DE	209
Leonard G	1	DE	188
Leonard G	28	DE	211
Leonard G	37	DE	188
Leonard H	11	DE	280
Louis	65	DE	199
Martha	42	DE	206
Mary	28	DE	213
Mary A	25	MD	199
Mary A	34	DE	280
Nicholas	16	MD	193
Olivia	4	DE	199
Rebecca T	20	DE	202
Sarah	60	DE	202
Sarah R	19	DE	202
Susan E	6	DE	199
Vandergrift, Anna	3	DE	379
Anna J	33	DE	379
Charles	4	DE	152
Christopher	26	DE	185
Christopher	68	DE	185
Eliza R	5/12	DE	379
Elizabeth	10	PA	152
Elizabeth	24	DE	185
Elizabeth H	47	DE	181
Ellen	30	DE	185

Name	Age	St	Pg
Vandergrift, Frazier	17	DE	172
George	1	DE	395
George	31	DE	395
George W	6	DE	395
George W	7	DE	379
Hannah	28	DE	395
Joanna	66	DE	105
John M	40	PA	152
Josephine	9	DE	379
Leonard	29	DE	395
Leonard	52	DE	181
Louisa	18	PA	152
Martha A	5	DE	379
Mary	7	DE	152
Mary	38	PA	152
Mary E	9	DE	395
Mary P	19	DE	395
Matilda	11	DE	379
Miller	1	DE	152
Sarah	61	DE	379
Sarah E	5	DE	395
Sarah E	13	DE	379
Thomas	12	PA	152
Ward	44	DE	379
William	15	PA	152
William A	2	DE	395
Wilson	22	DE	172
Vandever, Alfred C	16	DE	3
Ann	51	DE	356
Catherine	26	DE	284
Chas M	5	DE	284
E M (Rev)	34	MA	159
Edwin G	6	MD	159
Eli	11	DE	356
Eliza M	34	CT	159
Elizabeth	12	DE	44
Elizabeth A	17	DE	256
Ellen	20	DE	279
Ellen	78	DE	62
Emma	7	DE	356
Henry	4	DE	3
Henry	4	DE	284
Isabella	30	DE	44
Jacob	56	DE	54
Jacob B	24	DE	281
John	47	DE	3
John B	28	DE	27
Lucinda	14	DE	3
Mary E	9	OH	159
Peter B	23	DE	284
Rachel A	17	PA	351
Rebecca	19	DE	281
Sarah	52	DE	72
Sarah A	44	DE	3
Sarah E	10	DE	3
Seferia A	20	DE	3
Thomas	60	DE	356
William	7	DE	207
William	14	DE	44
William L	25	DE	3
William M	30	DE	213
Vandiver, Amos C	4	PA	353
Hannah	23	PA	353
Jacob	1	PA	353
Thomas	26	DE	353
Vando, Ellen	23	IE	113
Vandyke, Amanda	2	DE	239
Ann S	48	MD	213
Baby boy	1/12	DE	243
Ephraim B	13	DE	243
George	3	DE	239
Jacob	32	DE	239
James M	16	MD	213
Jane	7	DE	243
Mary	25	DE	239
Mary	48	DE	243
Mary C	10	MD	213
Mary E	20	DE	243
Mary J	20	DE	243
Nicholas	40	DE	213
Sarah E	5	DE	239
Vandyke, William H	14	MD	213
William S	23	DE	243
Vaneman, John	2	DE	145
Joseph	24	DE	144
Levenia	3	DE	144
Mary	23	GB	144
Vanerbrace, Henry	2	DE	70
Laurence	30	DE	70
Mary	25	DE	70
Vanhekle, J	30	NY	17
Vanhicle, Charles	53	DE	270
John	34	GB	269
Joseph	6	DE	269
Margaret	1/12	DE	269
Margaret	45	DE	270
Mary	24	DE	270
Mary	28	GB	269
Mary	36	PA	261
Sarah	2	DE	269
William	12	DE	270
Vanhikle, Charles	1	DE	186
Emma	6	DE	186
Fredus P	31	DE	186
Isaac	3	DE	186
Latitia	--	DE	186
Rebecca	5	DE	186
Vanhorn, Catherine	8	DE	225
Ingeber	22	DE	183
Isaac	27	DE	225
Jacob	14	DE	225
Levi	2	DE	225
Rachel	49	DE	225
Thomas	30	DE	183
Vaniman, Charity	8	DE	43
Emeline	14	DE	43
James	5	DE	43
James	39	NJ	43
Robert	2	DC	43
Susan	32	MD	43
Vannissen, C	28	NJ	68
Mary E	29	NJ	68
Mary J	14	NJ	68
Vansant, Benjamin	40	DE	315
Eliza Jane	14	DE	363
George	75	DE	296
Hellen	10	DE	363
Isaac L	12	DE	363
James	6	DE	293
John	17	DE	329
John	45	DE	315
Joshua	20	MD	230
Margaret	4	DE	293
Maria	53	DE	329
Mary	37	PA	363
Mary Louisa	2	DE	363
Michel	9	DE	329
Rachel	19	DE	329
Robert	38	DE	315
Samuel	42	DE	363
Sarah	28	OH	293
Sarah	48	DE	296
Susannah	5	DE	363
Thomas	11	DE	329
William	7	DE	363
William	14	DE	329
William	30	DE	293
William	49	DE	329
Vantrump, Sabria	63	GE	167
Vanwinkle, Eliza	17	DE	220
Vanzant, Amanda	5/12	DE	375
Elizabeth	20	MD	177
Ellen	67	DE	375
Harriet	20	PA	375
Isaac	31	DE	375
John	35	DE	375
Vary, Deborah	30	DE	205
Hannah A	1	DE	205
James	6	DE	205
Richard	4	DE	205
Vaughn, Eliza L	71	DE	132
J. Frank	11	DE	28
Vaught, Rachel B	63	DE	51
Vaulk, Rebecca	6	IE	261
Veach, Ann	29	PA	339
Arabella	6/12	MD	340
Augusta	5	MD	340
Elizabeth J	19	DE	283
Ellen	60	DE	90
Emily	4	MD	340
Emily	30	MD	340
George	35	DE	339
James P	26	DE	283
Jane	47	DE	283
John	2	DE	339
John	63	DE	339
Joseph	32	DE	340
Martha	3	MD	340
Mary E	1	DE	339
Melvina	12	DE	283
Rachel	9	MD	340
Samuel	31	DE	288
Solomon	22	DE	135
Susanna	24	DE	283
W P	57	DE	283
William L	18	DE	283
William M	7	MD	340
Veal, Ann M	18	PA	288
George	51	GB	288
George W	15	PA	288
John	26	PA	288
Julia	5/12	PA	288
Julia	21	DE	288
Margaret J	48	PA	288
Melvina A	20	PA	288
William H	11	PA	288
Veast, John	30	GE	5
Veasy, Abraham	3	DE	22
Abraham	35	DE	22
Maria	33	DE	22
Rebecca	1	DE	22
Thomas	13	?	291
Veazy, Anna A	15	PA	311
Edward	51	MD	311
Edward T	17	PA	311
Eliza A	29	DE	376
Eliza F	11	PA	311
Elizabeth F	49	NY	311
George C	43	MD	311
George W	1	DE	376
Henry	39	DE	376
Henry E	26	DE	311
James L	7	DE	321
James L	35	MD	321
John	40	MD	192
John C G	19	PA	311
Joseph W	10	MD	312
Malinda	2	DE	376
Margaret H	23	DE	321
Maria E	24	DE	311
Mary A	4	DE	376
Mary E	20	PA	311
Norris	8	DE	376
Reed	6	DE	376
Sidney P	2	MD	312
Vecinty, Ab	52	NY	26
Albert M	1	DE	26
Ella	9	DE	26
Mary	34	DE	26
Phebe	7	DE	26
Vencir, Samuel	34	DE	371
Venn, Cornelius	23	GB	127
Hannah M	24	PA	127
James	67	IE	15
Veny, Calvin	8/12	DE	317
Emma	2	DE	317
John	27	DE	317
Sarah	27	DE	317
Verenia Procencia L	12	CU	164
Verga, Augustes	12	SZ	163
Vernon, Abner	24	PA	284
Abner	59	PA	284
Alfred	31	PA	94

Name	Age	St	No
Vernon, Alfred G	2/12	DE	94
Anna J	30	IE	91
Charles	9	DE	91
Colburn	20	PA	141
Eliza	16	PA	135
Eliza	42	PA	40
Elizabeth	3	DE	91
Emma S	4	PA	283
Esther	54	PA	284
George	16	PA	284
George W	30	PA	135
Hoopes	20	PA	141
Jane	50	PA	135
John	27	PA	283
John T	5	DE	91
Martha	25	PA	283
Mary	11/12	DE	91
Mary	21	DE	94
Mary	28	GB	284
Rebecca	30	DE	27
Rufus	50	PA	135
Samuel	24	PA	284
Thomas	40	IE	91
William	12	PA	284
Verria, Cortia	11	CU	165
Vible, Anne	27	DE	177
James	1	DE	177
Samuel	27	DE	177
Vickers, Elizabeth	19	DE	166
Vicks, Charles	64	DE	325
Elizabeth	25	DE	325
Isaac	40	DE	325
Mary	3	DE	325
Mary	62	DE	325
Victory, John	18	DE	86
View, Ann	14	DE	281
Charles	4	DE	170
Elizabeth	7	DE	200
Ezekiel	55	DE	235
Margaret	19	DE	171
Serey	89	DE	235
Viglin, Clara	10	VA	165
Marcellina	10	VA	165
Vincent, Conrad	2	MD	259
Daniel	49	DE	371
Elizabeth	30	MD	82
Elizabeth	39	DE	371
Francis	28	GB	139
Hanna J	6/12	DE	320
Harriet	23	PA	139
Henry	3	DE	141
Hetty	3/12	DE	259
Hetty	37	GE	259
James	23	DE	291
James	27	MD	320
John	2	MD	259
John	39	GE	259
Joseph	21	DE	296
Mary	9	PA	28
Mary	24	MD	82
Mary A	26	DE	320
Mary E	4/12	DE	141
Mary W	2	DE	139
Sarah E	23	DE	141
Truitt	26	DE	141
Vine, James	35	IE	322
Viney, Eliza	40	DE	333
Lott	37	DE	333
Moses	30	DE	227
Thomas	7	DE	333
Viniman, Mary	18	DE	44
Sarah	22	DE	44
Vining, Anna	4	DE	237
Ellen	7	DE	237
Emma	13	DE	287
Frances	12	DE	258
Frances A	8	DE	171
Harriett	9	DE	287
Hestalena	14	DE	286
James	1	DE	287
Jas S	37	DE	286
John	33	DE	258
Vining, John B	5	DE	287
John B	36	DE	287
Joseph A	33	DE	286
Louisa	2	DE	286
Margaret	7	DE	287
Margaret	32	DE	286
Maria	37	DE	286
Rebecca	2	DE	286
Rebecca	58	PA	283
Sarah	29	DE	258
Sarah M	33	DE	287
William H	20	DE	286
William H	39	DE	286
Vinson, Catharine	2	DE	329
Catharine	78	GE	329
Conrad	38	GE	329
George	6	GE	329
Jacob	9	GE	329
Jacob	27	GE	329
Jonny	12	GE	329
Mary	5	GE	329
Mary	14	GE	329
Mary	39	GE	329
Vinter, Benjamin	23	GB	323
Martha D	18/12	DE	323
Sarah	28	GB	323
Virtue, David	11	DE	149
Margaretta	14	DE	149
Mary E	16	DE	149
Rebecca	35	MD	149
Robert	52	DE	149
Samuel	8	DE	149
Voger, Henry	21	GE	142
Volla, Sarah	44	DE	104
Voshel, Anne	25	NJ	239
Francis A	6	MD	239
Gertrude	6	DE	205
James	32	DE	239
John C	32	DE	239
Mary E	2	DE	205
Sarah A	28	DE	205
Thomas	33	DE	205
William T	1	DE	205
Wadsley, Anna M	10	DE	309
Isabella M	18	DE	309
Joseph H	8	DE	309
Robert	16	DE	309
Robert	52	GB	309
Teresa	54	GE	309
Thomas	13	DE	309
Waggener, Ellen	40	DE	109
Wahn, John	10	DE	186
Wait, Francis D	55	MA	172
Sarah	63	PA	112
Waite, George W	50	NY	75
Joanna	47	NJ	75
Robert	18	NY	75
Sophia	19	PA	75
Walde, Harriet	20	NJ	85
Wales, Catherine	28	DE	30
John	19	DE	30
John	67	CT	30
Josephine	17	DE	30
Leonara E	26	DE	30
Matilda	22	DE	30
Waley, Rebecca	12	MD	207
Walker, Aaron	21	DE	354
Alexander	21	IE	328
Alexander	38	DE	388
Alice C	2	DE	232
Allice	14	PA	68
Andrew	70	DE	347
Ann	25	DE	86
Ann	27	DE	388
Ann	37	GB	328
Ann	50	DE	354
Ann A	3	DE	327
Ann C	12	DE	216
Ann W	33	DE	216
Anna	4	MD	237
Anna	5	DE	15
Walker, Anna	15	DE	162
Anna	24	MS	330
Anne C	7/12	DE	232
Benjamin	3	DE	68
Benjamin	9	DE	48
Benjamin	55	PA	68
Byher	6	DE	365
Caleb	33	PA	347
Caroline	9	DE	308
Catherine	1	DE	269
Catherine	29	DE	216
Catherine C	9	MD	237
Cecilia	9	DE	22
Collins D	10	DE	133
Cornelius	42	DE	269
David	19	DE	309
David	70	DE	261
Deborah	7	DE	352
Deborah A	13	DE	351
Dewitt C	16	DE	216
Dorcas	5	DE	327
Dorinda L	5	DE	328
Edith	35	PA	351
Edith	50	DE	347
Edwin	9	DE	388
Eliza	5	MO	48
Eliza	10	DE	269
Eliza	32	DE	269
Eliza J	22	PA	328
Elizabeth	19	DE	116
Elizabeth	24	PA	232
Elizabeth	24	DE	355
Elizabeth	40	PA	68
Elizabeth	40	DE	347
Elizabeth	64	DE	162
Elizabeth A	11	PA	328
Ellen	7	DE	15
Ellen	51	GB	68
Elmira	16	DE	352
Emily	20	DE	171
Emma	3	DE	354
Enos	4	DE	352
Enos	52	DE	353
Evans	12	DE	68
Ezekiel W	14	DE	68
Ezekle	47	PA	68
Fanny A	24	DE	162
Florence	1	DE	237
Frances M	1	DE	347
Francis	18	NJ	68
Franklin	3	DE	69
George	1	DE	234
George	22	MD	321
George	30	DE	327
George	48	GE	125
George H	7/12	DE	232
George W	9	DE	216
George W	13	DE	22
George W	13	DE	355
George W	24	DE	232
George W	40	IE	15
Hamath	17	DE	15
Hamatt	22	GB	68
Hannah	11	DE	15
Henry	11	DE	352
Henry	12	DE	269
Henry Clay	10	MD	237
Henry R	38	DE	216
Hellen	--	DE	347
Hester	35	MD	337
Hester	60	DE	347
Isaac	7	DE	269
Isaac	11	DE	337
Isaac	21	DE	86
Isaac	23	DE	22
Isaac	26	DE	232
Isaac P	41	DE	236
Isabella	48	GE	125
Jacob	35	DE	243
James	11	DE	68
James	38	DE	354
James	60	DE	26

Name	Age	St	Pg	Name	Age	St	Pg	Name	Age	St	Pg
Walker, Jane	5	DE	48	Walker, Rebecca	65	DE	355	Wallace, Anderson	35	DE	258
Jane	10	DE	81	Rhody A	13	DE	216	Andrew	5	DE	258
Jane	10	DE	119	Richard	13	DE	48	Clarissa	50	DE	41
Jane	63	DE	397	Richard	24	DE	322	David	3	DE	258
Jane	78	DE	48	Robert	7	DE	48	Dianna	54	MD	338
Jefferson	21	DE	391	Robert	13	DE	81	Edward	22	DE	300
Jefferson	22	DE	355	Robert	13	DE	324	Eliza	--	IE	290
Jerome	54	DE	355	Robert	35	DE	347	Elizabeth	22	DE	27
Joseph	37	PA	314	Robert H	17	VA	401	Elizabeth J	7	DE	137
Joseph	54	DE	215	Robt	30	GB	330	Henry	20	PA	359
Joseph H	15	DE	216	Rhyhu	6	PA	366	James	9	DE	253
John	10	DE	187	Sally	32	DE	48	James	40	DE	113
John	15	DE	48	Sam	25	SC	328	Joanah	7	DE	296
John	15	DE	59	Saml A	2	DE	328	John	25	DE	267
John	18	DE	15	Saml	12	DE	255	Julia	16	DE	113
John	27	DE	347	Samuel	1	DE	327	Lydia	21	DE	41
John	29	PA	48	Samuel	21	PA	401	Margaret	65	MD	127
John	30	DE	216	Samuel	28	GB	81	Nathan	66	DE	41
John	40	DE	48	Sarah	6	DE	216	Phoebe	16	DE	241
John	40	DE	167	Sarah	13	DE	352	Robert	45	PA	137
John	42	MD	119	Sarah	17	DE	354	Sarah	1	DE	258
John	49	DE	168	Sarah	25	DE	47	Sarah	7	DE	258
John	76	DE	347	Sarah	43	DE	22	Sarah	22	MD	250
John M	3/12	DE	119	Sarah	45	PA	352	Sarah	26	DE	258
John W	1/12	DE	216	Sarah	48	GB	81	Thomas	20	MD	325
Julia	14	DE	47	Sarah A	16	DE	119	William	20	MD	31
Julia	17	DE	22	Sarah A	26	DE	347	Wallas, Andrew	4	DE	388
July Ann	17	DE	361	Sarah E	12	DE	347	Belinda	21	DE	394
Laura	4	DE	388	Sophia	31	PA	48	David	3	DE	388
Leanora	25	NY	57	Susan	13	DE	119	Jane	9	DE	388
Levi	60	PA	354	Susan	18	PA	325	Sarah	29	DE	388
Louis A	29	DE	171	Susan	25	DE	243	Sarah E	1	DE	388
Louisa	18	DE	162	Susanah	15	DE	81	Walls, Benjamin	26	DE	184
Louisa J	7	DE	328	Thomas	2	DE	313	Mary A	1	DE	184
Lydia	66	PA	61	Thomas	17	IE	328	Mary A	24	DE	184
Lydia J	10	?	167	Thomas	21	DE	22	Walraven, Alfred	13	DE	154
Margaret	13	DE	269	Thomas	23	IE	326	Ann	42	DE	286
Margaret	40	IE	331	Thomas	26	DE	348	Anna	15	DE	154
Margarett	4	DE	326	Thomas	38	DE	48	Anna M	5	PA	56
Martha	18	DE	256	Thomas	52	DE	59	Eliza J	6	DE	286
Martha	38	IE	331	Thomas	70	DE	168	Elizabeth	12	DE	286
Martha M	26	PA	69	Thomas J	27	IE	328	Elizabeth	17	DE	154
Mary	15	DE	15	Unity	30	DE	162	Ella L	1	DE	56
Mary	23	IE	326	Washington	2/12	DE	69	Frederick	20	DE	287
Mary	26	DE	48	William	4	DE	48	Henrietta	27	GB	30
Mary	38	IE	347	William	14	DE	15	John	28	PA	56
Mary	40	SW	15	William	16	DE	22	Jonas	15	DE	286
Mary	46	DE	166	William	17	GB	81	Jonas	29	DE	30
Mary	48	PA	68	William	18	DE	322	Margaret	27	PA	56
Mary	48	?	168	William	19	DE	210	Mary	51	DE	287
Mary	57	PA	26	William	20	NY	68	Mary J	12	DE	180
Mary	71	DE	102	William	22	DE	347	Nicholas	30	DE	96
Mary A	3	DE	216	William	42	MD	337	Sarah	17	DE	30
Mary A	10	DE	348	William A	20	DE	389	Sarah J	6	DE	180
Mary A	16	DE	114	William H	2	DE	388	Thomas	18	DE	286
Mary A	18	DE	352	William H	14	DE	296	Thomas	51	DE	286
Mary A	32	PA	119	William H	19	MD	337	Walsh, James	--	DE	290
Mary A	35	?	167	William P S	4	DE	119	Sarah	66	DE	169
Mary A	45	DE	167	William W	16	DE	355	Walt, Mary	23	PA	132
Mary Ann	31	PA	347	Wilson W	23	DE	171	Samuel	21	PA	132
Mary E	4	DE	69	Wm	36	IE	328	Waltemberg, Ella	2	DE	112
Mary E	10	DE	354	Walkersen, Francis	2	DE	359	Francis	8	NY	112
Mary E	10	DE	354	Georgiana	8/12	DE	359	Francis	32	PA	112
Mary E	13	PA	328	Hannah J	7	DE	359	Harry	5	NY	112
Mary E	22	DE	327	James H	6	DE	359	Ida	3	NY	112
Mary E	25	DE	369	Robert	4	DE	359	Sarah	25	NY	112
Mary J	13	DE	337	Robert	79	DE	359	Walter, J Howard	3	DE	356
Mary S	6	DE	388	Robert Jr	31	DE	359	James	7	PA	288
Maryetta	22	DE	162	Sarah	28	DE	359	John S	30	PA	288
Moses M	41	PA	69	Sarah	40	DE	359	Lewis	36	PA	356
Newton B	21	DE	216	Walkin, Sarah	29	DE	38	Libe D	9	DE	356
Olivia A	36	MD	171	Wall, Andrew	18	IE	137	Lydia	4	DE	356
Phoebe	50	DE	213	Anna	12	IE	333	Martha	26	PA	288
Priscilla A	17	DE	314	Bridget	15	IE	333	Martha	36	PA	356
Rachel	7	DE	237	Ellen	11	IE	333	Mary	64	PA	361
Rachel	28	DE	354	Ellen	37	IE	333	Sarah J	22	DE	361
Rachel	34	PA	236	James	12	DE	231	William	54	DE	361
Rachel	50	MD	59	Jane	33	PA	34	Walters, Ann E	5	DE	309
Rebecca	3	VA	347	Joseph	34	GB	34	B Franklin	7	PA	117
Rebecca	4	DE	232	Mary	2	DE	34	Catherine	14	PA	117
Rebecca	16	DE	116	Miller	7	DE	34	Catherine	32	WL	138
Rebecca	22	PA	232	William	9	IE	333	David	5	DE	138

Name	Age	State	No.
Walters, Debby	38	PA	75
Debby A	7	PA	75
Edmond	1	PA	117
Elnor	25	DE	309
George S	1	DE	309
George W	5	PA	75
Hannah	35	PA	117
Henry	32	PA	309
J	20	AL	164
Jacob	36	PA	117
James	11	WL	138
James	25	PA	191
James M	2	PA	75
James W	3	DE	309
Jane	9	WL	138
John	17	DE	313
John H	10	PA	75
Joseph	10/12	DE	24
Leonard	40	PA	75
Mary J	9	PA	117
Naomi	25	PA	24
Richard G	14	DE	365
Samuel A	8	PA	117
Sarah	40	MD	35
Sarah A	20	MD	179
Sarah E	12	PA	75
Thomas	36	WL	138
Thomas	48	DE	24
William	14	DE	127
William	18	DE	39
William F	15	PA	75
William H	2	DE	138
Walton, Adrianna	9	PA	307
Andrew	25	DE	307
Anna	18	VA	166
E H	7	VA	166
Ephraim T	10	PA	307
Gibbons	20	PA	351
Hannah L	35	PA	306
Howard P	7	PA	307
Jacob	39	PA	306
Risey A	2	DE	307
Sidney	46	PA	60
William L	12	PA	307
Wantersalter, Geo	49	GE	35
Waples, Betty M	48	DE	186
Catherine	50	DE	95
Frank	3/12	DE	88
Gideon B	18	DE	401
Mira	40	DE	97
Peter	50	DE	33
S	16	DE	165
William	19	DE	97
Wolsey W	13	DE	97
Ward, Abraham	1	DE	65
Abraham	33	MD	65
Alfred	5	DE	45
Allen	64	PA	101
Amelia J	12	DE	290
Ann	20	DE	335
Ann	30	IE	166
Ann	46	DE	335
Arter D	18	VA	163
Caroline	5/12	DE	317
Caroline	14	DE	335
Catherine	25	IE	99
Catherine	55	PA	45
Danial	23	IE	80
Emeline	33	DE	284
Esther	32	NJ	314
George	50	MD	64
George W	11	DE	65
George W	37	MD	317
Hannah E	4	DE	386
Harriet	6	DE	65
Henry E	56	DE	334
James	2	DE	386
John M	2	DE	386
John A	2	DE	317
John S	9	DE	192
Joseph	41	NJ	314
Joseph C	24	DE	77
Ward, Lewis	8	DE	65
Lois	54	NC	101
Lydia S	4	DE	192
Margaret	27	DE	73
Martha	32	DE	385
Martha J	5	DE	284
Martina	4	DE	65
Mary	21	IE	287
Mary A	9	DE	284
Mary A	35	DE	192
Minte	53	MD	64
Minte	40	MD	65
Rachel	7	DE	335
Rhoda	33	DE	317
Sally A	30	DE	65
Samuel	2	DE	73
Samuel	19	DE	185
Samuel	30	MD	73
Sarah	4	DE	281
Sarah	16	IE	162
Steuard	35	DE	284
Thomas	9	DE	45
Thomas	40	GB	385
William	11	DE	284
William	11	DE	317
William	19	PA	24
William H	3	DE	73
Wardel, Alexander	23	DE	330
Margaret	22	DE	330
Ware, Albert	3	NJ	26
Amos	16/12	DE	328
Ann E	8	DE	328
Anna	9	NJ	264
Barbary	30	NJ	264
Catharine	10	DE	328
Dennis	12	DE	328
Emeline	6	NJ	264
James	8/12	DE	327
James	13/12	DE	327
James	5	DE	369
James	58	PA	327
James R	37	PA	369
Jane	16/12	DE	328
John	8	PA	369
Joseph	4	NJ	264
Joseph	6	DE	369
Joseph H	33	NJ	264
Margaret	30	DE	369
Mary	14	DE	328
Mary	20	IE	336
Mary	25	IE	338
Mary	29	IE	327
Mary A	3	DE	327
Rachel	40	PA	328
Rebecca	2/12	DE	264
Rebecca A	7	PA	327
Rebecca A	25	PA	327
Thomas	23	PA	327
Thomas J	18/12	DE	260
Victoria	6	DE	328
William	30	PA	327
William H	4	PA	327
Warfield, Joseph	73	DE	167
Waritel, Alexander	24	MD	381
Margaret	17	MD	381
Warley, Felix	14	SC	298
Warner, Charles	10	PA	232
Clintonia W	5	MD	319
David	12	DE	258
Elizabeth H	2	MD	319
Esther	71	DE	54
Gustavus N	10	MD	319
Hetty	27	DE	54
James H	38	PA	319
Jean	47	DE	54
John H	16	MD	319
Joseph T	50	DE	54
Maria	21	DE	290
Mary A	33	MD	319
Mary L	3/12	DE	319
Peter	55	PA	232
Peter J	16	PA	232
Warner, Peter Jr	16	PA	232
Rebecca	8	DE	365
Rebecca	45	NJ	232
Sarah	17	PA	232
Susannah	12	PA	232
Warren, Alfred DuP	2	DE	34
Amelia	47	NY	399
Angrine	25	NY	399
Anna M	4	DE	293
Benjamin	19	DE	326
Benson	4	DE	117
Charles	3	DE	293
Charles	25	DE	326
Charles	30	DE	389
Charles	35	DE	34
Charles H	56	DE	326
Eliza	26	DE	291
Elizabeth	58	DE	42
Ellen	10	DE	326
George	7	DE	300
George	15	NY	399
George	18	DE	218
George	40	DE	19
Hannah	26	PA	332
Hariett A	15	DE	326
Harry	4/12	DE	332
Harry	47	NY	399
Isabell	5	DE	326
James	45	MD	300
Jane	--	DE	177
John	12	DE	285
John	17	NY	399
John S	25	DE	320
Joseph	21	NY	399
Joshua	9	DE	19
Lewis S	10	DE	293
Margaret	6	DE	34
Martha	20	PA	304
Mary	14	DE	19
Mary	15	DE	326
Mary	30	DE	34
Mary	39	NJ	293
Mary A	46	DE	326
Mary E	4	DE	300
Mary F	2/12	DE	320
Matilda	5	DE	332
Matthew	35	MD	293
Nelson	12	NY	399
Obed	32	MD	291
Phillip	72	PA	152
Rebecca	35	DE	300
Rebecca J	10	DE	177
Robert	19	PA	175
Sarah	2	DE	332
Sarah	35	DE	19
Sarah J	22	DE	320
Theodore	27	NY	332
Thomas G	17	DE	326
Washington	9	DE	177
William	7	DE	177
William	10	DE	300
William H	10	NY	399
William W	6	DE	326
Warrington, Anne	11	DE	151
Ephraim	21	DE	386
James	2	DE	151
John C	9	DE	151
John W	43	DE	151
Mary A	40	MD	151
Mary E	6	DE	151
Sarah E	6	DE	151
Warrnel, Anna E	1	DE	356
Caroline S	7	DE	356
Elizabeth	31	DE	356
Nimrod	32	DE	356
Sarah M	5	DE	355
Warwick, Abraham W	8	DE	357
Amos B	48	NJ	257
Amos E	10	DE	357
Elizabeth A	21	DE	357
Esther J	19	IN	357

Warwick, Mary E	12	DE	357	Watson, Joseph G	5	DE	389	Way, Jacob	69	PA	361
Mary P	47	DE	357	Julia	14	PA	62	Jacob M	12	DE	362
Robert J	15	DE	357	Leander	1	DE	208	Jesse	20	PA	152
Washington, Ann	10	DE	319	Lewis L	8	DE	389	Joseph	48	DE	333
Ann E	49	DE	159	Mahala	45	DE	239	Lucretia	9	MD	356
Catherine A	59	PA	159	Margaret	5	DE	208	Martha	4	MD	356
Daniel B	1	DE	7	Margaret	5	IE	334	Mary	22	DE	381
Ester	28	PA	7	Margaret	11	IE	340	Mary E	1	DE	60
George	14	DE	328	Margaret	45	IE	340	Matilda	35	PA	362
George	16	DE	322	Margaret	49	PA	62	Matilda J	6	PA	362
Hariot	5	DE	21	Martha	2	DE	334	Malmoth H	14	MD	356
John H	53	PA	159	Mary	5	PA	12	Sarah	37	PA	356
Mary E	13	MD	7	Mary	15	PA	62	Thos H	28	PA	362
Sarah A	6	DE	7	Mary	22	DE	240	William R	27	PA	60
William	4	DE	7	Mary	33	DE	208	Wayne, John	16	NJ	374
William	35	PA	7	Mary A	17	IE	339	Wear, Alace	25	MD	61
Wasilewski, Alfred	35	PO	85	Mary A	18	DE	200	Ann	28	DE	19
Wason, Catherine	24	DE	161	Mary J	27	DE	389	Elizabeth	18	DE	19
Dorcas	42	DE	161	Mary L	2	MD	389	Frederic	35	GE	129
Julia	1	DE	161	Miles	13	DE	239	John W	28	MD	61
Wasson, Eliza J	25	DE	368	Mitchell	8	DE	239	Mary	13	DE	307
Waterman, Ann	70	DE	342	Mrs	34	PA	25	Mrs	33	GE	129
Waters, Alexander	23	MD	368	Rebecca	5	PA	67	Weare, Sarah	21	NJ	105
Catherine	4	DE	301	Richard	29	DE	239	William	1	DE	105
Daniel	18	DE	384	Robert	19	IE	148	Weaver, V	14	MD	165
Daniel	60	DE	384	Robt	45	IE	340	Webb, Adeline	11	DE	268
Jeremiah	16	DE	384	Rose	17	IE	340	Agnes J	3	PA	399
Lewis	13	DE	384	Ruth A	37	ND	397	Amanda M	9	DE	180
Nicholas	27	DE	387	Sarah	4/12	DE	239	Anna	15	DE	187
Rachel	58	DE	384	Silas B	9/12	PA	397	Anna J	7	PA	100
Watkins, Columbus	20	DE	172	Silas H	42	PA	397	Anna M	5	DE	180
Sarah	25	DE	168	Vilator	40	DE	41	Annette	4	DE	204
Wats, Cumirah	12	DE	334	William	9/12	DE	18	Arabella	14	DE	268
Watson, Abigal	40	PA	55	William	16	DE	189	Benjamin	10	DE	320
Absolem	7	PA	12	William	45	IE	18	David	10	DE	204
Absolem	30	DE	12	Wilson	8	DE	208	Edward J	13	DE	204
Adaline	35	DE	389	Wilson G	8	DE	208	Edwin F	13	DE	180
Alexander	14	DE	188	Wattles, Thomas	--	DE	178	Elisha	13	DE	180
Alfred	3	DE	239	Watts, Abby	1	DE	36	Ellen	11	DE	304
Alfred	30	PA	41	Alexander	14	GA	163	George	5	DE	187
Alexander	35	DE	208	Andrew	31	MD	264	George C	7	DE	180
Amanda	7	PA	397	Caroline	34	MD	300	Henry	4/12	DE	25
Ann	10	PA	12	Charles	7	DE	300	Henry H	8	DE	320
Ann	28	DE	12	Charlotta	30	GB	36	Hiram	9	DE	268
Ann	33	DE	193	Edward	22	IE	300	Isaac	15	DE	242
Ann	56	DE	245	Eliza	29	DE	364	Jacob	20	DE	247
Charlotta	8/12	DE	12	Elizabeth	16	DE	218	James	3	DE	187
Clark	34	IE	25	George	8	DE	300	James	23	DE	235
Darcus	28	MD	334	Hester A	28	DE	226	James	35	DE	268
David	13	DE	309	Jacob	35	GE	36	James	54	PA	10
Eben A	17	PA	397	James	45	MD	301	Jeremiah	27	MD	249
Edward L	10	DE	389	John	5	DE	264	John	3	DE	268
Elizabeth	24	PA	109	John	14	DE	364	Joseph	7	DE	187
Evan	12	DE	62	John	25	IE	336	Lydia	45	DE	10
F	17	MD	165	Joseph	15	DE	364	Lydia	47	DE	56
Fanny	37	IE	18	Lawrence	11	DE	364	Maria	34	IE	25
Frederic	41	GB	62	Lawrence	38	GE	364	Martha	17	MD	166
George	12	DE	239	Levi	13	DE	364	Mary	11	DE	10
George	19	MD	311	Mary	3	DE	264	Mary	26	PA	399
George	34	MD	334	Mary	4	PA	36	Mary	40	DE	187
George M	5	PA	397	Mary	8	DE	364	Mary A	9	DE	25
Hannah	20	IE	330	Mary	31	MD	264	Mary E	17	DE	204
Hannah A	14	PA	397	Susan A	5	DE	364	Mary F	4/12	DE	249
Harriet	7	DE	208	Tabitha	14	DE	226	Mary H	32	PA	100
Henry	68	DE	239	William	5	DE	300	Nemiah	45	DE	204
Henry A	4	DE	193	William	40	MD	226	Osmand B	11	DE	180
Isaac	4	PA	12	William N	10	DE	226	Rachel A	37	DE	180
Isabella	19	IE	340	Wattson, Allice	2	DE	267	Rachel A	47	DE	204
James	13	PA	18	Elizabeth	28	DE	267	Rachel P	35	PA	320
James	20	IE	340	Emery	30	DE	267	Rebecca	28	DE	249
James	22	DE	196	Henry	7/12	DE	267	Richard	40	IE	25
James W	38	PA	55	Joseph	25	DE	267	Richard H	10	PA	100
Jane	34	MD	121	Waugh, Rachel B	63	DE	52	Sarah	1	DE	268
Jane	82	DE	41	Way, Ann	65	DE	130	Sarah	31	DE	268
Jerry	3	PA	12	Caleb S	41	PA	362	Susan	23	DE	235
Jesse	25	PA	109	Chancey	42	PA	356	Thomas D	40	PA	100
Joel	12	PA	348	David	27	DE	381	Thomas F	26	GB	399
John	13	DE	299	David B	38	PA	294	Thomas J	5	PA	25
John	20	DE	193	Edwin	9	DE	362	William	1	DE	235
John	40	DE	172	Elizabeth	22	DE	60	William	18	DE	207
John H	10	PA	397	Elizabeth	28	DE	361	William	40	DE	187
Joseph B	5	PA	55	Hannah	12	MD	356	William A	20	DE	204

Name	Age	State	Page	Name	Age	State	Page	Name	Age	State	Page
Webb, William C	37	DE	181	Welch, George	18	DE	253	Weldon, Joseph H	17	DE	297
William H	11	DE	228	Honor	11	IE	333	Joseph H	45	DE	297
William P	4	DE	100	Jacob	30	IE	328	Levi	42	DE	298
Wm	5	DE	320	Jialala	28	IE	328	Lew Cass	2	DE	291
Wm	34	DE	320	John	12	IE	333	Lewis	34	DE	291
Webber, Charles	1	DE	208	John (Rev)	30	IE	325	Lydia A	14	DE	294
Charles	26	PA	208	Julia	34	IE	333	Mary	35	DE	305
Mary E	9	MD	208	Mary	15	IE	333	Mary	44	PA	293
Rachel	26	DE	208	Mary	40	IE	360	Mary A	21	DE	293
Weber, Anna	23	DE	322	Nancy	6	IE	333	Mary E	4	DE	293
Benjamin	64	PA	322	Patrick	9	IE	333	Phebe A	18	DE	292
Catherine	59	PA	322	Patrick	28	IE	345	Rebecca	12	DE	294
Edward	25	DE	322	Sarah	28	DE	326	Rebecca	20	DE	292
Eliza	24	DE	322	Thomas	27	IE	346	Rebecca	56	DE	305
Emily	20	DE	322	Thomas	36	IE	333	Sarah	20	DE	294
Weblents, Mary	5/12	DE	278	Welde, Charles	18	NJ	158	Sarah L	15	DE	292
Webley, Mary A	28	GB	386	Elizabeth	42	NJ	94	Wesley C	12	DE	292
Webster, Amanda	21	DE	297	Elizabeth	53	NJ	95	William	27	DE	293
Andrew W	20	DE	223	Emily J	8	DE	87	William A	4	DE	292
Ann E	10	DE	297	James	13	NJ	94	William A	15	DE	292
Anna M	10	DE	223	Joseph	19	NJ	95	William B	52	DE	292
Caroline	8	DE	297	Leonard	43	NJ	94	Wells, Abel	10	DE	238
Charles	3	DE	295	Lydia	23	NJ	158	Benjamin	24	PA	52
Clark	16	DE	278	Lydia	44	DE	87	Benjamin	32	PA	260
Clark	63	DE	278	Mary	21	NJ	95	Catharine	18	DE	238
Dickerson	12	DE	240	Morris	44	PA	87	Daniel	61	NJ	238
Eliza	25	DE	295	Morris M	7	DE	87	Francis	19	DE	238
Elizabeth	20	DE	240	Rebecca	9	NJ	94	George	45	DE	18
Elizabeth	21	DE	240	Rebecca	58	NJ	90	Hariot	23	PA	24
Ella	6	DE	297	Sarah	11	NJ	94	Harris	32	PA	24
Henry	46	DE	297	William	65	NJ	90	John	35	PA	24
Henry D	23	DE	223	William L	13	DE	87	John E	28	OH	62
Isaac	28	DE	278	Welden, Abner J	28	DE	127	Joshua	3	PA	24
Isaac S	3	DE	295	Jacob B	5	DE	244	Mahala	28	PA	24
James F	5	DE	223	John	3	DE	219	Mary	24	DE	260
Jane A	20	DE	278	Lydia	2	DE	127	Mary	42	PA	18
John	13	DE	297	Martha	1	DE	219	Rebecca	12	DE	238
John	27	DE	94	Martha J	11/12	DE	226	Rebecca	52	DE	238
John	42	DE	223	Mary A	22	DE	226	Samuel	18	IE	24
Jonathan	25	DE	239	Mary J	11	DE	220	Samuel	25	NJ	238
Martha	1/12	DE	240	Rayworth	31	DE	226	Sarah	17	PA	18
Martha	22	DE	278	Rebecca	23	NJ	127	Sarah E	60	DE	52
Mary	17	DE	297	Sarah	30	DE	219	Sophia	2	DE	24
Mary	33	DE	278	Sarah E	5	DE	219	Thomas	35	DE	260
Mary A	40	MD	223	Susan	25	DE	244	Walter	7	MD	260
Priscilla	41	DE	297	William	30	DE	219	Welsby, James	2	DE	73
Samuel	5	DE	295	William F	20	DE	220	Welser, Benj B	8	PA	280
Samuel A	2	DE	223	Weldon, Amy	32	PA	291	Benj B	37	PA	280
Sarah	15	DE	297	Ann	30	DE	293	Ebenezer	5	DE	280
Sarah J	7	DE	223	Anna R	12	DE	297	Eliza	58	DE	276
Susan E	15	DE	223	Anna W	17	DE	298	Elizabeth	33	MA	280
William	28	DE	240	Benton V	13	DE	220	Frances	3	DE	280
William H	1	DE	295	Beulah	35	DE	297	George W	14	PA	280
Weeks, Henry	30	MD	309	Beulah	45	NJ	294	Welsh, Ann	25	IE	13
Henry	52	DE	65	Catharine	1	DE	293	Anna	2	DE	13
Mary A	22	DE	307	Charles	20	DE	132	Brian	24	IE	334
Richard	1	DE	65	Charles E	1	DE	291	Charles	6	DE	173
Ruth	18	DE	65	Charles W	7	DE	132	Eli	30	DE	220
Sidney J	1	DE	307	Eliza	4	DE	294	George	2	DE	173
Weer, Elizabeth	28	DE	278	Eliza J	9	DE	297	Jacob	48	DE	80
Esther A	4	DE	278	Elizabeth	41	DE	298	Louisa	16	DE	247
Henry T	11	DE	278	Ella M	4	DE	132	Marcia E	1	DE	183
Isaac	52	DE	278	Ellen E	27	DE	132	Margaret	9	DE	173
Isaac D	22	PA	278	Elvira	21	DE	293	Margaret	23	DE	220
Mary	47	PA	278	Emily	8	DE	298	Margaretta	14	DE	79
Mary M	13	DE	278	George	9	DE	294	Martha	1	DE	220
Thomas C	16	PA	278	George	54	DE	295	Mary	4	GB	13
William C	18	PA	278	George E	20	DE	293	Mary A	46	DE	79
Weight, James	1	NY	313	George M	10	DE	298	Michel	24	IE	306
Weir, Catharine	8	DE	375	George W	15	DE	297	Nancy	41	DE	173
Catharine	48	DE	375	Hannah	22	DE	291	Rachel	7	DE	173
Margaret	6	DE	375	Hannah	33	DE	294	Richard T	13	DE	173
Robert	48	DE	375	Hannah R	16	DE	297	Rose	40	DE	173
Sarah	16	DE	375	Harriet	6	DE	291	William	3	DE	220
Uriah	18	DE	375	Henry H	9	DE	292	William	28	GB	13
William	11	DE	375	Isaac	1	DE	294	Wence, George	22	IE	190
Welch, Ann	20	IE	194	Isaac L	40	DE	293	Wenks, Archivald	46	MD	34
Benjamin	19	DE	380	Jacob	28	DE	294	Margaret	38	MD	34
Bridget	4	IE	333	Jacob S	36	IE	132	Martha	3	DE	34
Ellen	13	IE	333	James	16	IE	302	Rebecca	6	DE	34
Ellena	60	IE	326	Jane	26	DE	293	Were, Elener	60	DE	123
Francis	8	IE	333	John	61	DE	293	James	4	DE	145

Name	Age	St	Pg	Name	Age	St	Pg	Name	Age	St	Pg
Were, John	30	IE	145	Whitaco, Francis A	4	DE	287	White, Julia A	13	DE	290
Margaret J	2	DE	145	Sarah	6	DE	287	Lydia	22	DE	101
Sarah	22	IE	145	Whitacre, Ann H	34	DE	268	Lydia A	7	DE	91
Werney, Clement	35	DE	205	Clementine	37	DE	286	Margaret	11	DE	390
Wesley, Alfred	5	DE	241	Frances A	4	DE	286	Margaret	12	DE	353
James	9	DE	241	Elzena	8	DE	227	Margaret	23	IE	53
John	14	DE	247	Henry	35	DE	268	Margaret A	7/12	DE	156
Leonard	7	DE	241	Lydia	5	DE	227	Margaret A	6	DE	342
Levi	25	DE	121	Margaret	8	DE	191	Margaretta	6	DE	298
West, Ann	25	DE	247	Mary	28	DE	227	Maria	20	DE	210
Ann E	21	NY	296	Mary A	14	DE	227	Maria	23	DE	169
Benjamin M	8	DE	247	Sarah	1	DE	227	Maria	23	DE	257
Caroline	2	DE	247	Sarah	6	DE	286	Maria	26	DE	342
Cecelia	48	GB	319	Stewart	15	DE	309	Martha	16	DE	52
Charlotte	50	DE	247	William	6	DE	227	Mary	14	PA	113
David H	13	DE	247	William	30	DE	227	Mary	15	IE	49
Elizabeth	34	PA	354	Whitaker, George	21	PA	348	Mary	15	IE	72
Frances	32	DE	247	Whitbank, Henry	12	DE	327	Mary	21	IE	328
Isaac	25	DE	67	Whitbore, Alexander	18	DE	359	Mary	25	DE	322
J W D	6	NY	276	Whitcraft, Elizabeth	10	DE	243	Mary	27	DE	295
James	8	GB	319	Lydia	51	DE	243	Mary	35	IE	33
James	46	GB	319	Mary A	7	DE	243	Mary	38	DE	263
John	32	MD	354	William	16	DE	243	Mary A C	9	DE	353
John	77	MD	354	White, Adam	22	PA	58	Mary J	7	DE	311
John C	5	NY	296	Adam	68	DE	59	Perry	41	DE	342
Joseph	15	DE	247	Albertine	19	GE	133	Phebe	9	DE	298
Joseph	44	DE	247	Amanda	20	DE	160	Priscilla	2	DE	156
Joseph R	11	GB	319	Annavella	21	DE	295	Rachel	10	DE	49
Lavenia	11	DE	67	Ann E	25	DE	156	Rachel	25	DE	273
Lewis	25	DE	295	Anthony	22	DE	14	Rebecca	10	DE	59
Loretta	11	DE	247	Benjamin	22	DE	94	Robt	24	IE	328
Lydia	1	DE	354	Benjamin	28	GB	23	Robt	25	GB	275
Mary	6	DE	354	Benjamin	55	DE	169	Roselle	7	DE	72
Mary	10	DE	67	Biddy	30	IE	20	Sabastian	20	IE	20
Mary	24	DE	201	Catherine J	3	DE	342	Sally	46	DE	35
Patience	41	DE	67	Daniel	6/12	DE	342	Sally A	9	DE	91
Sarah	13	MD	10	Daniel	3	DE	59	Samuel	23	IE	210
Sarah A	16	DE	247	Daniel	26	DE	35	Samuel	39	DE	156
Sewall	17	DE	247	David	2	DE	59	Sarah	8	DE	35
Thomas	19	NY	203	Deborah A	40	PA	353	Sarah	26	DE	101
William	4	DE	354	Deborah S	14	DE	353	Sarah	30	DE	13
William M	3/12	DE	247	Edward	14	DE	225	Sarah	40	DE	91
Westbrook, Mary A	37	GB	287	Edward	18	IE	20	Sarah	50	DE	101
William T	12	GB	287	Edward	21	IE	72	Susan	22	IE	15
Westlake, Ann	68	GB	290	Eliza	19	MD	298	Thomas	17	DE	241
John	26	GB	290	Eliza	37	DE	387	Thomas	21	GB	311
Westley, John	9	NJ	269	Elizabeth	64	GB	295	Thomas	25	IE	294
Weston, James	20	PA	27	Frances C	4	DE	72	Thomas J	85	NY	113
Wetherald, Charles B	4	DE	307	Frederic	28	GE	133	Unice	18	IE	142
Emily B	27	DE	307	Frederic	32	GE	261	William	4	DE	176
Mary F	3	DE	307	George	3	DE	197	William	17	IE	72
William	31	GB	307	George	16	DE	311	William	18	GB	311
Wetsel, Gerana	10	DE	20	Hannah	14	DE	311	William	21	DE	205
Lewis	27	DE	20	Hannah A	7	DE	317	William	50	GB	311
Sarah	28	DE	20	Henry	11	DE	368	William	55	IE	72
Whaley, Jemima	8/12	PA	366	Henry	25	PA	94	Whitecraft, James	22	DE	335
Wham, Adam	77	PA	397	Henry	30	DE	295	Whitehall, Ann E	21	DE	107
Wheatley, Caroline	7	MD	328	Henry	55	DE	91	Nathan	36	DE	107
Catharine	48	MD	328	Henry B	72	VA	386	Whitehead, Ann H	34	GB	269
Elizabeth	13	MD	328	Henry Clay	5	DE	367	Henry	35	GB	269
Ezekiel	14	MD	328	Henry M	6	DE	311	Whitehill, Mary	17	PA	394
Martha	4	DE	328	Hester	40	DE	59	Whitelock, Elizabeth	24	DE	44
Millison A	1	DE	328	Isaac	4	DE	399	Hester	12	DE	44
Wheeler, Danial	60	DE	129	Isaac	6	DE	391	James	41	DE	44
Ella	4	DE	51	Isabella	45	GB	311	Whitely, Catharine	30	DE	161
Henry	3/12	DE	51	James	1	DE	288	Elizabeth	3	DE	161
Hester	23	DE	51	James	27	DE	199	Henry	1	DE	161
Isaac J	34	PA	51	James	40	DE	353	Mary	5	DE	161
Joshua	40	DE	246	James	69	IE	295	Nancy	27	NJ	161
Margaret	14	PA	392	Jane	14	PA	56	Ruther	21	DE	161
Margaret	52	DE	8	Jane	17	IE	328	William G	31	DE	161
Where, Rachel	30	DE	132	Jane	85	DE	52	Whiteman, Adaline	16	DE	375
Whibley, James	8	DE	376	Jane F	48	GB	72	Andrew Jackson	14	DE	363
James	37	GB	376	Janette	9/12	DE	169	Ann	44	NY	52
John	5	DE	376	Jennett	1	DE	322	Ann E	8	DE	359
John	48	GB	376	Jesse	25	DE	387	Anna	50	PA	363
Martin	19	NY	376	Joanna	22	IE	288	Benjamin	58	PA	374
Mary	27	GB	376	John	5	DE	197	Caroline	11	PA	357
Mary Ann	48	GB	376	John	22	NY	32	Catherine	1	DE	352
William	20	GB	330	John	23	GB	311	Charles	19	DE	362
Whirt, William	21	IE	384	Joseph	1	DE	399	Charles	23	DE	375
Whitaco, Clematine	37	DE	287	Josephine	2	DE	387	Christiana	23	DE	352

Name	Age	State	Page
Whiteman, Eliza	40	PA	357
Elizabeth	23	DE	362
Emma	2	DE	359
Emma	60	DE	367
Franklin	16	PA	357
Guilbert	17	DE	363
Hellen	19	DE	376
Henry	20	DE	362
Henry	60	PA	362
Henry M	37	DE	359
Israel	23	DE	362
Jacob	25	DE	362
Jacob	60	PA	376
Jacob	70	PA	362
Jane	69	PA	362
Jeremy	12	PA	357
John H	34	DE	359
Jonathan	46	NY	52
Josiah B	31	DE	362
Julia Ann	27	DE	362
Laura	5/12	DE	359
Lavenia	6	DE	359
Lemuel	27	DE	376
Luisanna	14	PA	357
Margaret	29	DE	359
Margaret J	11	DE	362
Margaret L	8/12	DE	376
Maria	58	NJ	375
Mary	62	PA	377
Mary Ann	5	DE	362
Matilda	30	PA	375
Samuel B	8	DE	351
Sarah	22	DE	363
Sarah	85	PA	95
Sarah S	3	DE	360
Susanna	20	DE	375
Thomas	40	PA	377
Washington	25	DE	352
William H	5	DE	376
Whitin, Lydia	38	PA	153
Ruben	40	NJ	153
Whitlock, Ellen	5	DE	176
Emily	15	DE	176
Eugene	7	DE	176
John	11	DE	176
John	40	MD	176
Rachel A	40	DE	176
Sewall	14	DE	176
Theodore	17	DE	176
Whitlocks, Abraham	2	DE	205
Ann	32	IE	205
Henry	41	GB	205
Joseph	5	PA	205
Julia	25	IE	205
Mary E	7	PA	205
Nathan	25	IE	205
Robert	3	PA	205
Whitman, Felix P	40	CT	299
Nancy W	24	PA	101
Whitmarsh, Nancy W	24	PA	102
Whitson, David	4	DE	300
George	8	DE	300
John	6	DE	300
Mary	34	IE	300
Thomas	11	IE	300
Thomas	35	IE	300
William	2	DE	300
Whittacre, Thomas	12	DE	204
Whittaker, Hannah	35	DE	170
Ismel	4	DE	170
James	9	DE	170
James	32	DE	170
William	2	DE	170
Whitten, Richard	83	PA	320
Whittington, Joseph	70	MD	159
Tabitha	60	MD	159
Mary	23	DE	333
Sam	29	GB	333
Whortenbury, John	55	MD	238
Wiatt, Sarah	47	DE	371
Thomas	20	DE	371
Wibley, Eliza	15	GB	393

Name	Age	State	Page
Wibley, Emeline	9	DE	364
Martin	19	DE	390
Zachariah	1	DE	364
Wickersham, Amanda W	13	DE	287
Amos H	44	PA	287
Caleb	28	PA	165
Eugene E	6	DE	287
Josephine L	11	DE	287
Llewellyn	4	DE	287
Mary	36	PA	123
Mary E	15	DE	287
Orlando L	9	DE	287
Sarah A	43	DE	287
Victoria L	11	DE	287
William F	8	DE	287
Wiggans, Emily W	2	DE	113
Matilda R	32	DE	113
Myra	4	DE	113
W B	30	NJ	113
Wiggelsworth, Edw F	2	DE	100
George W	8	DE	100
Hannah E	5	DE	100
John H	10	DE	100
Joseph A	5/12	DE	100
Josiah	56	GB	100
Margaret	37	GB	100
William	22	DE	100
Wiggins, Abraham	--	DE	227
Abraham	50	DE	227
Harriet	--	DE	227
Jacob	8	PA	354
Jacob	45	DE	170
Louisa	--	DE	227
Mary	15	DE	154
Mary	15	PA	166
Mary A	35	DE	355
Mrs	50	DE	154
Ruth	48	MD	170
Sarah A	--	DE	227
William	14	DE	180
William	14	DE	355
Wignkoop, Arelio	40	PA	162
Geradus	7	DE	162
S (Rev)	45	CT	162
Theodore	10	DE	162
Wilcox, Ann	45	GB	249
Anna	16	GB	183
Edward	16	PA	163
Robert	12	GB	249
William	12	GB	249
Wild, Augustus	15	PA	131
Augustus	40	GE	131
Catherine	1	PA	131
Charles	10	PA	131
Henry	6	PA	131
John	13	PA	131
Mary	4	PA	131
Mary	40	GE	131
William	16	PA	131
Wilde, Elizabeth	8	PA	41
Joseph	3	PA	41
Mark	18	GB	41
Mark	45	GB	41
Mary	15	NJ	298
Sarah	5	PA	41
Sarah	46	GB	41
Wilden, William	20	DE	361
Wilder, Benjamin F	28	PA	354
John	2	DE	354
Lydia	60	DE	20
Margaret A	23	DE	354
Mary E	1	DE	354
William	18	DE	169
Wilders, James	11	DE	222
Wilds, Jno	38	DE	288
John	31	DE	245
Wiley, Alden	16	DE	61
Ann	17	DE	318
Augustus	6	DE	321
Catharine	60	DE	337
David	40	DE	125
Elizabeth	20	DE	192

Name	Age	State	Page
Wiley, Hannah	24	DE	321
John	18	DE	61
John	26	DE	315
John	49	DE	321
Jonathan	32	DE	321
Josephine	5	DE	321
Letitia	47	PA	61
Margaret	7	DE	321
Mary	13	DE	125
Mary	16	NH	317
Mary	34	DE	321
Mary J	8/12	DE	321
Moses	8	AL	165
Rosanna	12	DE	321
Rosetta	3	DE	321
Sarah	50	DE	321
Stephen	49	DE	321
Susan	26	MD	125
William	7	DE	125
William	22	DE	61
Wilkins, Amanda	21	DE	209
Caroline	35	DE	175
Charles	6	DE	119
Charles L	10	DE	8
Edward	3	DE	119
Ellen	26	IE	31
Elmer	1	DE	390
Francis	1	DE	390
Garway	48	MD	209
George	45	DE	8
George H	7	DE	390
Hester	54	DE	209
James	30	PA	118
James H	7	PA	118
James H	18	DE	390
John A	28	DE	390
John C	17	MD	390
John R	47	DE	389
Joshua B	15	DE	389
Margaret	11	DE	389
Margaret	28	PA	118
Martha E	13	DE	390
Mary	25	IE	322
Mary E	3	DE	390
Mary E	39	MD	389
Monroe	10	PA	118
Rebecca	28	DE	390
Robert B	5	DE	390
Sarah	50	DE	8
Sarah J	17	DE	8
William	13	PA	119
Wm	24	PA	274
Wilkinson, Ann	10	DE	7
Ann	47	GB	286
Anne	43	DE	29
John	14	DE	7
Mary	35	GB	311
Mary	44	GB	286
Mary	84	GB	286
Mary J	12	DE	7
Mehitabel	2	DE	7
Rachel	65	DE	29
Rebecca	47	DE	29
Susan	35	DE	7
Thomas	15	DE	7
William	7	DE	7
William	40	GB	7
Willbank, Sarah A	11	DE	359
Willbanks, Jacob	19	DE	377
Joseph T	8	DE	377
Samuel	14	DE	373
Susanna	38	DE	377
Willet, Ann	2/12	PA	75
Mary	3	DE	4
Mary	20	DE	75
Stephen	2	DE	75
Willey, Absolam	47	DE	385
Anna E	15	PA	385
David	14	DE	339
Eliza	39	DE	385
Jane	1	DE	385
Scofield	18	PA	385

Name	Age	State	No.
Willey, Sinah	9	PA	385
Wilson	12	PA	385
William, James	14	DE	244
Sarah E	12	DE	376
Williams, Abraham	60	NJ	101
Alexander	3	DE	368
Alexander	16	DE	217
Alice	13	DE	308
Amanda	9/12	DE	194
Amy E	3/12	DE	383
Amy M	20	DE	383
Andrew	5	DE	176
Andrew	6	DE	324
Andrew	25	DE	323
Andrew	28	MD	194
Andrew J	17	NY	342
Andrew J	18	DE	176
Ann	20	DE	38
Ann	20	DE	247
Ann	25	IE	239
Ann	26	MD	23
Ann	60	DE	218
Ann	60	DE	236
Ann J	18	DE	210
Ann L	18	DE	284
Ann M	8	MD	340
Ann M	11	DE	323
Ann M	13	DE	394
Anna	49	IE	290
Anna E	21	PA	277
Anna M	30	DE	155
Anne	20	DE	248
Annie	19	DE	226
Benjamin	23	DE	325
Benjamin	24	DE	343
Betsey	18	DE	190
Caroline S	11	DE	330
Catharine	12	DE	219
Catharine	31	PA	260
Chamberlain	1/12	DE	335
Charles	5	DE	157
Charles	8	DE	228
Charles	10	DE	331
Charles	14	DE	339
Charles	15	DE	389
Charles	16	DE	294
Charles	20	PA	290
Charles	23	DE	217
Charles	28	DE	38
Charles H	7	DE	316
Charlesanna	13	DE	298
Charlotte	42	MD	263
Charlotte	65	MD	371
Chas	42	DE	285
Clara	5	DE	193
Clarence H	14	GA	319
Comfort	17	DE	302
Comfort	76	DE	192
Curtis J	1	DE	192
Daniel	8	DE	298
Darcas	56	DE	371
David	4	DE	148
David	16	DE	38
Diana	35	DE	380
Dinah	38	DE	67
Edward	16	DE	383
Edward	24	DE	98
Edward	48	DE	284
Edward	56	MD	325
Edwards	30	DE	98
Edwin P	1	DE	61
Elias	34	DE	368
Elijah	12	DE	217
Elijah	75	DE	217
Eliza	19	DE	27
Eliza	20	GB	342
Eliza	35	DE	217
Eliza J	11	DE	316
Elizabeth	10	MD	340
Elizabeth	16	DE	104
Elizabeth	28	DE	400
Elizabeth	29	PA	325
Williams, Elizabeth	29	PA	325
Elizabeth	52	DE	298
Elizabeth J	55	DE	101
Ella A	12	DE	342
Emeline	27	DE	316
Emily	19	DE	194
Emily	20	PA	292
Emma A	18	PA	124
Emma C	3	DE	193
Ester	3	DE	46
Esther	42	DE	230
Frances	35	DE	279
Francis T	17	GA	319
G H	7	PA	316
George	4	DE	338
George	4	DE	400
George	5	DE	285
George	49	DE	331
George W	6	DE	290
George W	30	DE	192
George W Jr	15	DE	192
Hannah	4	DE	155
Hannah	6	DE	194
Hannah	30	DE	46
Hannah	40	DE	38
Hanson	13	DE	339
Harriet	22	DE	35
Harriet	28	DE	396
Harriet	41	DE	98
Harriet J	2	DE	383
Harry	22	DE	383
Helen	5	PA	260
Henry	--	DE	290
Henry	13	DE	244
Henry	17	DE	294
Henry	17	DE	376
Henry	23	DE	247
Henry	40	GB	148
Henry J	35	MD	325
Hester A	10	DE	339
Horace	2	PA	260
Isaac	4	DE	387
Isaac	9	DE	316
Isaac	20	DE	308
Jacob	11	DE	316
Jacob	30	DE	338
Jacob	35	DE	316
James	1	DE	67
James	2	DE	400
James	3	DE	298
James	7	DE	23
James	16	DE	38
James	31	DE	67
James	35	DE	227
James	39	MD	340
James	43	MD	228
James	43	GB	321
James	45	DE	339
James	46	DE	98
James	50	DE	248
James	57	DE	192
James G	8	DE	339
James H	1	DE	324
James M Jr	4	DE	228
Jane	13	DE	41
Jane	13	PA	321
Jane	17	PA	346
Jane	20	DE	15
Jane	29	ST	148
Jane	42	DE	339
Jesse	17	DE	376
Joanah	23	DE	157
Joanna	7	DE	338
John	3/12	DE	67
John	10	PA	290
John	13	PA	383
John	14	DE	325
John	15	DE	321
John	18	DE	292
John	20	DE	400
John	30	GB	175
John	35	DE	260
Williams, John	35	DE	260
John C	5	DE	23
John T	5	DE	176
Jonathan	49	NJ	285
Joseph	6	DE	400
Joseph	21	DE	380
Joseph	26	DE	230
Joseph	30	DE	400
Joseph	66	DE	371
Joseph	74	DE	192
Joseph B	20	DE	382
Joseph Jr	36	DE	192
Josephine	2	DE	35
Josephine	2	DE	285
Judy	50	DE	217
Julia	9	DE	157
Julian	7	DE	285
Lady	47	DE	302
Laura	6/12	DE	176
Levi	30	MD	336
Levi	38	DE	178
Lewis	16	DE	384
Lewis B	6/12	DE	381
Louisa	3	DE	217
Louisa	18	MD	325
Louisa	28	DE	338
Lucretia A	8	WN	325
Lydia	34	DE	368
Margaret	7/12	DE	340
Margaret	1	DE	217
Margaret	4	DE	333
Margaret	13	DE	323
Margaret	15	PA	366
Margaret G	54	PA	124
Maria	3	DE	338
Maria	40	DE	248
Maria J	49	DE	284
Martha	7	PA	124
Martha A	14	MD	228
Mary	15	DE	289
Mary	24	DE	175
Mary	26	DE	38
Mary	31	MD	340
Mary	33	NJ	285
Mary	38	MD	285
Mary	40	IE	345
Mary	47	GB	321
Mary	60	DE	141
Mary	63	PA	129
Mary A	5	DE	316
Mary A	25	MD	84
Mary A	28	DE	98
Mary Ann	7	DE	197
Mary E	3	DE	339
Mary E	4	DE	316
Mary E	7	DE	228
Mary E	16	DE	247
Mary E	17	DE	218
Mary E	52	DE	342
Mary J	8	DE	204
Mary J	18	MD	340
Mary J	34	DE	323
Mary L	30	MD	228
Matthew	2/12	DE	256
Matthew	49	DE	286
Matthew W	29	NC	277
Minty	3	DE	226
Minty	35	DE	226
Nancy	19	MD	335
Nathaniel	5	MD	340
Nathaniel	25	DE	381
Nathaniel	27	PA	230
Nathaniel	30	DE	330
Oliver	26	DE	98
Oliver S	30	DE	110
Percival	2	DE	23
Perry	15	DE	203
Peter	--	DE	290
Peter	2	DE	387
Peter	18	DE	298
Peter	55	DE	298
Peter Jr	--	DE	290

Name	Age	St	No.
Williams, Phillis	58	DE	38
Rachel	5	DE	98
Rachel	15	PA	290
Rachel	16	PA	292
Rachel	20	DE	330
Rachel	25	DE	381
Rachel	30	DE	227
Rachel	46	DE	376
Rebecca	5	DE	298
Rebecca	25	DE	193
Rebecca	83	PA	279
Rebecca H	16	DE	284
Richard	40	DE	316
Richard	65	WL	129
Richard A	5	DE	339
Richard H	9	DE	342
Robt	4	DE	218
Sally A	2	DE	157
Sally A	33	DE	316
Samuel	7	DE	339
Samuel	17	DE	17
Samuel	30	PA	100
Samuel	30	PA	157
Samuel J	3	DE	383
Samuel T	7	DE	387
Sarah	2	DE	155
Sarah	2	DE	228
Sarah	22	DE	38
Sarah	50	DE	177
Sarah	62	DE	81
Sarah	76	MD	176
Sarah A	14	DE	386
Sarah A	19	DE	104
Sarah A	49	DE	377
Sarah E	2	DE	316
Sarah E	6	DE	350
Sarah E	15	PA	367
Sarah E	18	PA	4
Sarah J	19	DE	192
Sarah R	14	MD	340
Serena	29	DE	17
Sidney G	16	PA	124
Siney	54	DE	325
Spencer	3	DE	38
Spencer	14	DE	298
Spencer	25	DE	17
Spencer	28	DE	51
Susan	3	DE	98
Susan	30	DE	194
Theophilis	17	PA	290
Theophilis	60	PA	290
Thomas	1	DE	247
Thomas	11	DE	285
Thomas	35	DE	217
Thomas	53	GB	342
Timothy	35	DE	46
Warrington	4	PA	124
Wesley	14	MD	299
Wilhemina	18	DE	285
William	--	DE	290
William	2	DE	67
William	8	DE	324
William	11	DE	199
William	12	PA	290
William	30	DE	217
William	38	DE	376
William E	2	DE	325
William R	3	MD	340
Williamson, Ann	25	DE	133
Ann M	17	PA	128
Anna	13	DE	288
Anna	43	DE	30
David	4	MD	129
Eliza J	4	DE	133
Ellen	1	DE	133
George	56	DE	288
Harry	68	DE	288
Haslington A	28	MD	152
Henry	26	DE	133
Hester E	30	MD	152
John	21	DE	288
John	55	DE	128
Williamson, John F	15	PA	128
John F	32	MD	388
John M	2	DE	388
Laranna	80	DE	308
Lydia	35	MD	152
Margaret	2	DE	349
Margaret	18	DE	288
Margaret	32	DE	388
Margaret	33	DE	297
Maria	17	DE	149
Maria	53	PA	288
Mary	4/12	DE	133
Mary	14	MD	129
Mary	16	DE	288
Mary	50	PA	128
Mary A	30	MD	356
Mary J	25	DE	61
Mary J	30	DE	161
Matilda	24	IE	349
Rachel A	2	DE	297
Rebecca J	2	MD	356
Saml	35	IE	349
Samuel	28	PA	149
Sarah	21	MD	129
Sarah M	41	MD	129
Washington T	10	MD	129
William J	10	MD	388
William P	25	DE	61
Williard, Algernon C	11	PA	93
Benj T	6	DE	311
Charles A	9	DE.	311
Elizabeth J	8	PA	93
Emely	15	PA	93
Henry	8/12	DE	93
James A	4	DE	311
James H	29	PA	311
John A	6	PA	93
John A	46	PA	93
Letitia	1	DE	311
Lydia R	39	PA	93
Martin	13	PA	93
Mary	29	PA	311
Mary E	11	DE	311
Elizabeth J	12	PA	289
Willis, Ann	42	GB	322
Ann	62	NJ	377
Ann J	34	DE	153
Anne E	9	DE	321
Anthony	11	DE	300
Benjamin	9	DE	153
Benjamin	29	DE	267
Betsey	25	MD	154
Charles H	9/12	DE	322
Charlotta	49	GB	90
Dennis	2	DE	153
Elizabeth	11	ME	322
George S	16	ME	322
Hannah A	7	DE	153
James	17	DE	321
Jeremiah	6	DE	320
Jeremiah	55	DE	321
John	6	DE	322
John	12	DE	320
John	13	DE	153
Joseph	9	DE	322
Joseph	40	PA	90
Joseph	43	GB	322
Lara A	14	ME	322
Mary	21	DE	301
Mary E	3	DE	321
Miranda	15	DE	279
Sarah	25	PA	113
Stephen	74	NJ	377
Susan	39	DE	321
William	45	DE	153
William W	19	DE	311
Willits, Elizabeth W	24	DE	195
George Washington	14	DE	195
Horatio W	40	NJ	195
Merrit W	3	DE	195
Noah	18	DE	195
Sarah	12	DE	195
Willits, Thomas	30	DE	195
Waley	35	DE	195
Wills, James	60	DE	214
Martha	15	DE	214
Willson, James	22	PA	376
Willus, Lydia	38	DE	93
Wilmer, Ann	30	DE	159
Anne	30	DE	125
Henry	40	DE	125
James	20	PA	361
Malinda	31	PA	61
Sarah J	10	PA	61
William	31	MD	61
William B	8	PA	61
Wilmerson, Enoch	60	DE	255
Fanny	6	DE	255
Frances	30	DE	255
John	10	DE	255
Wilmot, Anna G	9	NJ	353
Catharine	2	DE	353
Christiana	35	PA	353
Lucy	4	DE	353
Rebecca	7	DE	353
Sarah G	12	NJ	353
William	45	GB	353
William W	15	NJ	353
Wilson, Abraham	36	DE	206
Adaline	1/12	DE	393
Adaline	16	DE	350
Agness	11	PA	370
Agness	52	IE	370
Alexander	21	MD	333
Alfred	1	DE	370
Allan J	13	DE	350
Amanda	3	DE	348
Amanda	4	DE	307
Amanda	10	DE	50
Amia	52	DE	12
Amos	1	DE	206
Andrew G	5	DE	120
Ann	2/12	DE	33
Ann	20	DE	33
Ann	32	PA	121
Ann	40	GB	50
Ann	41	MA	344
Ann	58	DE	385
Ann	59	DE	343
Ann E	1	MD	331
Ann M	2	DE	353
Ann M	4	PA	343
Anna	5	DE	65
Anna M	5	PA	121
Anna Maria	22	DE	98
Anne	12	DE	196
Anne	30	MD	59
Anne	42	DE	65
Anne E	9	DE	151
Ashbury	9	DE	338
Arma	7	DE	300
Beckey	36	DE	156
Belinda	11	DE	155
Benjamin	10	DE	38
Benjamin	27	MD	338
Benjamin	30	IE	389
Caleb	30	IE	334
Caroline	5	PA	343
Caroline	17	DE	45
Catharine	24	MD	331
Catharine	26	DE	212
Catharine	39	DE	303
Catharine	55	MD	308
Cecelia	3	DE	339
Chalmers	3	DE	120
Charles	3	DE	67
Charles	4	DE	157
Charles	12	MD	295
Charles	27	IE	370
Charles S	7	DE	307
Comfort A	7	DE	307
David	29	PA	355
David	38	DE	155
David	38	DE	392.

Name	Age	St	No	Name	Age	St	No	Name	Age	St	No
Wilson, David	46	DE	50	Wilson, James	21	DE	218	Wilson, Mary D	22	DE	352
David	50	DE	350	James	27	IE	339	Mary J	11	DE	350
David C	61	DE	98	James	44	DE	307	Mary J	39	DE	399
Edmond	14	DE	299	James	52	ST	295	Mary L	25	DE	392
Edward	9	DE	388	James	55	IE	370	Mary M	44	DE	287
Edward	30	PA	398	James A	12	DE	396	Mary R	16	DE	299
Edward	47	DE	179	James E	10	DE	200	Mary S	27	PA	343
Edwin	13	KY	13	James E	21	DE	229	Matilda	3/12	DE	121
Eli	51	DE	299	Jane	32	DE	98	Matilda	25	IE	199
Eliza	2	DE	33	Jane	48	DE	32	Milly A	34	PA	348
Eliza	14	DE	32	Jane	52	PA	350	Morris	30	DE	149
Eliza	23	PA	357	Janett	1	DE	339	Moses	35	DE	65
Eliza	28	DE	53	Jarrett	35	DE	157	Moses	40	DE	151
Eliza	60	IE	334	Jesse S	19	PA	355	Nathan	32	PA	122
Eliza J	1	DE	343	Jo Anna	44	DE	286	Lydia	38	DE	361
Eliza J	6	DE	156	John	3	DE	13	Peter	8	DE	47
Eliza R	45	NJ	350	John	5	DE	308	Peter	64	DE	47
Eliza Jane	10	DE	196	John	16	DE	250	Phebe	36	PA	346
Elizabeth	2	DE	348	John	25	DE	47	Phebe H	25	DE	350
Elizabeth	5	PA	123	John	26	DE	224	Phillip C	50	DE	361
Elizabeth	8	DE	370	John	31	PA	16	Pomphey L	8	DE	287
Elizabeth	10	DE	299	John	36	DE	173	Priscilla	17	DE	13
Elizabeth	13	DE	65	John	50	PA	393	Priscilla	18	DE	351
Elizabeth	17	DE	224	John C	24	DE	285	Purcy	23	DE	348
Elizabeth	18	PA	50	John G	6	PA	122	Rachel	12	DE	21
Elizabeth	18	DE	98	John T	9	DE	228	Rachel	18	DE	352
Elizabeth	18	DE	392	Joseph	7	DE	344	Rachel	39	DE	228
Elizabeth	22	DE	358	Joseph	58	GB	344	Rachel	45	PA	61
Elizabeth	25	DE	53	Joseph L	7	PA	13	Rachel	60	DE	285
Elizabeth	25	MD	398	Joseph M	28	PA	121	Rathnell	40	PA	388
Elizabeth	30	PA	61	Josiah	5	DE	157	Rebecca	36	DE	392
Elizabeth	50	DE	393	Julia	54	MD	47	Rebecca J	5	PA	16
Elizabeth	51	IE	12	Letitia	60	DE	99	Robert	29	DE	348
Elizabeth J	3	DE	121	Letitia J	4	MD	331	Robert M	14	PA	319
Ellen C	3	DE	349	Levi	9	DE	65	Robt	15	DE	215
Ellis	44	DE	299	Lewis	1	DE	399	Robt	31	DE	343
Elwood	4	DE	50	Lewis	25	DE	275	Rosanna	15	DE	65
Emeline	46	DE	329	Lorenso	8	PA	13	Ruth	11	PA	344
Ephragen	13	DE	348	Lucinda	11	DE	156	Ruth	50	DE	352
Francis	13	PA	374	Luisa	17	DE	2	Sabina	3	DE	156
Garrett	1	DE	67	Lydia A	7	DE	200	Samuel	4/12	DE	338
Garrett	1	DE	157	Lydia A	20	DE	351	Samuel	22	DE	215
Garrett	30	DE	67	Lydia P	22	DE	351	Samuel	29	DE	392
George	20	DE	254	Lydia R	13	DE	228	Samuel	62	PA	392
George	22	DE	293	Manlove	31	DE	231	Sarah	6	DE	132
George	23	MD	331	Margaret	3	DE	399	Sarah	13	PA	370
George	30	MD	350	Margaret	5	DE	389	Sarah	16	PA	344
George G	21	DE	133	Margaret	29	DE	389	Sarah	18	PA	61
George H	2	PA	123	Margaret	37	MD	396	Sarah	18	DE	311
George P	32	DE	399	Margaret	50	DE	392	Sarah	21	DE	276
Gordon	3	DE	393	Margaret A	21	DE	392	Sarah	26	PA	16
Hannah	10	DE	389	Margaret J	5	DE	348	Sarah	50	DE	53
Hannah	20	DE	350	Margaret J	21	DE	396	Sarah	50	DE	159
Hannah	25	MD	338	Maria	47	DE	307	Sarah A	19	DE	12
Hannah	30	DE	276	Maria M	10	DE	307	Sarah E	7	PA	343
Hannah	41	DE	348	Martha	9	DE	65	Sarah E	8	DE	157
Hannah	65	DE	272	Martha	15	DE	13	Sarah E	19	DE	285
Hannah A	9	DE	150	Martha	31	PA	349	Sarah E	49	DE	348
Hariot	40	MD	13	Martha	63	DE	183	Sarah J	3	DE	358
Harriet	1	DE	338	Martha A	26	MD	206	Sarah J	9	DE	348
Hellen E	13	DE	388	Martha E	2	DE	389	Sarah J	26	PA	339
Henry	1	DE	65	Martha M	35	DE	388	Sarah L	6/12	DE	200
Henry	14	DE	295	Mary	4	DE	287	Seker	23	PA	355
Henry	15	DE	65	Mary	6	DE	50	Sophia	6	DE	370
Henry	19	DE	193	Mary	6	DE	197	Sophia	28	DE	370
Henry	20	MD	331	Mary	8	DE	38	Stephen	23	DE	350
Henry	40	DE	65	Mary	17	DE	348	Susan	16	DE	132
Henry	60	DE	13	Mary	19	DE	54	Susan	32	DE	65
Henry A	19	DE	230	Mary	23	DE	173	Susan	38	DE	38
Horace	1	DE	53	Mary	25	DE	231	Susannah	16	DE	229
Hosea	39	DE	21	Mary	30	DE	200	Terence	73	DE	61
Isaac	5	DE	67	Mary	30	DE	348	Thomas	14	DE	12
Isaac	65	MD	308	Mary	32	DE	13	Thomas	18	DE	13
Isabella	25	DE	350	Mary	35	DE	21	Thomas	20	IE	284
J F (Dr)	32	DE	53	Mary	35	DE	42	Thomas	24	DE	224
Jacob	24	DE	308	Mary	38	PA	61	Thomas	27	DE	348
Jacob H	1	DE	16	Mary	38	IE	151	Thomas B	45	PA	389
James	4	DE	370	Mary A	19	DE	229	Vilet	29	DE	67
James	10	DE	67	Mary A	32	PA	122	Vilet	40	MD	157
James	10	DE	157	Mary Ann	18	PA	344	W W	35	PA	13
James	11	DE	338	Mary C	2	DE	355	William	1	DE	151
James	15	DE	307	Mary C	3	PA	303	William	4	DE	339

Name	Age	State	Page
Wilson, William	4	DE	355
William	13	DE	67
William	13	DE	338
William	16	DE	188
William	23	DE	276
William	24	IE	339
William	26	DE	119
William	27	DE	33
William	27	DE	285
William	34	DE	392
William	35	MD	38
William	37	PA	151
William	40	PA	61
William	40	DE	200
William	40	DE	228
William F	68	MA	183
William H	5/12	PA	123
William H	4	DE	200
William H	14	DE	157
William N	11	DE	228
William S	50	DE	352
William Sr	58	IE	339
William Z	5	DE	286
Wm H	17	PA	319
Zachary Taylor	2	DE	13
Wiltbank, Charles E	6	DE	275
Charles E	25	DE	278
Cornelius	19	DE	311
David	38	DE	275
Deborah A	30	PA	278
Eliza J	4	DE	275
Jesse	1	DE	275
John	26	DE	292
Jonathan O	60	DE	291
Lydia A	9	DE	275
Rebecca	33	DE	275
Wiltbanks, Elizabeth	11	DE	381
Esther	42	DE	381
John	62	DE	381
John	65	DE	383
Orson	3	DE	381
Samuel	6	DE	381
Samuel	46	DE	381
Thomas	8	DE	381
Wiltry, Edward	4	DE	351
James	10	PA	351
Martha	33	IE	351
William	31	IE	351
Win, Perry J B	14	PA	165
Wind, George	22	DE	190
Windle, Albert	8	PA	21
Allen	4	DE	31
Amelia	16	DE	69
Catherine	60	NJ	69
Frank	8	DE	112
Frank	10	DE	69
James	6	DE	31
Jonas	30	DE	177
Lewis	4/12	DE	21
Mary	3	DE	21
Mary J	25	DE	69
Rachel	27	DE	31
Rebecca	19	DE	177
Sarah	33	PA	21
Thomas	6	PA	21
William	39	PA	21
Windsor, Kennard	18	DE	305
Windward, Abner H	9	PA	349
Abner H	44	PA	349
Elizabeth E	2	PA	349
Elwood	5	PA	349
Julian	36	PA	349
Sarah A	12	PA	349
Wine, Michel	7	IE	147
Randolph	15	DE	3
Sarah	25	DE	203
Winemore, Ezra Ely	14	PA	319
Wingate, David	26	DE	21
Edward	50	MD	380
Ellis F	17	PA	380
Frances	21	MD	172
Frances	44	DE	172
Wingate, Hannah	20	DE	21
Henry	15	MD	205
Henry	28	DE	370
Jennie M	23	PA	380
Louisa	17	DE	349
Mahala	20	VA	371
Martha J	14	MD	172
Mary	44	MD	380
Mary	60	DE	216
Mary E	33	DE	172
Reuben	15	VA	399
Thompson C	21	PA	380
William	8/12	DE	21
William J	9	MD	172
Winne, David	32	DE	156
Winslow, Bridget	80	IE	33
Edward	2/12	DE	21
Elener	16	DE	33
Elizabeth	45	IE	33
Hannah	22	DE	21
Michel	26	DE	21
Victoria	2	DE	21
Winterhalter, Anna	15	DE	36
Elizabeth	21	DE	36
Ellen	12	DE	36
Hannah	10	DE	36
Magdaline	50	SZ	36
Wise, Ann E	13	DE	278
Charlotta	25	DE	31
Ephraim	2	DE	278
James	16	DE	278
James W	40	MD	278
John	26	MD	31
Joseph	75	DE	387
Louisa	10	DE	278
Mary	4	DE	278
Sarah	39	NJ	278
Sarah F	18	DE	278
Virginia	8	DE	278
Wishburgan, Doroella	22	GE	142
Wisnell, John	16	VA	293
Robert	14	DE	330
Wister, Frances A	6/12	DE	223
Louis	10	DE	223
Rebecca E	9	DE	223
Rhody A	19	DE	223
Witcraft, David	23	DE	361
Delia	19	PA	18
Rachel	21	DE	18
Witheson, Alexander	18	DE	358
Witman, Margaret	27	PA	265
Witmer, Henry	40	DE	154
Hetty A	4	DE	154
Jeffers	2	DE	154
Jesse	5	DE	154
Sarah	33	DE	154
Witsel, Adaline	20	DE	4
Dunetta	15	DE	4
Eliza	55	MA	4
Franklin	25	DE	4
George	18	DE	4
George	56	DE	4
Gerard	10	DE	19
Henry	2	DE	40
Henry	25	DE	40
Lewis	27	DE	19
Louisa	6/12	DE	40
Luvenia	21	DE	40
Sarah	28	DE	19
Wittinger, Rhoda	12	DE	116
Wolbert, James	24	DE	265
Wolf, Anna	20	DE	260
Benjamin B	14	DE	376
Daniel	42	DE	260
John	15	PA	260
John H	12	DE	376
Margaret A	16	DE	376
Mary	17	PA	260
Mary R	41	DE	376
Nathaniel	12	PA	260
Rebecca	42	DE	260
William D	22	MA	59
Wolf, William R	39	DE	375
Wm	19	PA	260
Wolfe, Daniel	29	DE	278
Eliza	63	DE	27
James	70	DE	27
Lydia	35	DE	27
Lydia	52	DE	278
Mary A	26	DE	278
Nathaniel	50	DE	278
William	21	DE	278
Wollason, Abraham	11	DE	370
Ann	50	PA	370
Anna	9	DE	370
Charles	40	NJ	370
Cyrus	13	DE	370
Cyrus C	13	DE	367
Isaac	5	DE	370
Rachel	40	NJ	370
Rebecca	14	DE	370
Thomas	15	MD	370
Wolleston, Adaline	3	DE	18
Adaline	39	DE	160
Ann	38	DE	58
Anna	12	DE	51
Anna W	25	DE	55
Caroline	11/12	DE	18
Catherine	80	DE	57
Emely C	10	PA	76
Henry A	12	PA	76
Hester	28	DE	18
Huther P	3	PA	76
James P	43	PA	76
Joseph P	51	PA	160
Joshua	33	DE	18
Margaret J	33	PA	76
Mary	4	DE	18
Mary A	14	PA	76
Samuel	60	DE	51
Susan	46	DE	55
Susanah	38	DE	51
Thomas	39	DE	58
Wolly, Mr	32	GB	143
Sarah	13	PA	34
Wolman, Anna	30	DE	18
David	31	PA	18
Wolsey, John	74	GB	336
Lydia	73	NJ	336
Wonderland, Alfred	15	NJ	386
Wonderlin, Andrew	33	NJ	359
Elizabeth	28	NJ	359
Hannah A	5	NJ	359
Hester	2/12	DE	359
Mary A	7	NJ	359
Wood, Alfred	5	DE	360
Ann	53	DE	158
Ann	56	DE	29
Anna	25	PA	152
Aquilla M	38	GB	287
Caroline E	2	DE	333
Catharine	14	ST	333
Clara E	7	DE	305
Eleanor	5	DE	273
Eliza	4	FR	288
Eliza	21	PA	337
Elizabeth	21	DE	76
Ellen	3	DE	370
George	1	DE	126
Hannah A	16	PA	165
Hiram	30	MD	389
Isaac	5	DE	333
James	3	DE	126
James	8	FR	288
James	22	IE	353
James A	4	DE	152
James F	13	PA	339
James H	11/12	DE	63
Jane	11	PA	360
Jane	12	ST	333
Jane	29	IE	63
Jane E	23	DE	389
Jane S	38	ST	333
John	24	PA	152

Name	Age	State	Page	Name	Age	State	Page	Name	Age	State	Page
Wood, John	26	PA	152	Woods, John	40	IE	334	Woollaston, Thomas	16	DE	382
John	34	GB	287	John M	52	DE	186	Thomas P	36	PA	300
John	56	DE	29	Joshua	26	DE	256	William	30	DE	171
John D	55	DE	153	Mary	16	DE	353	Woolson, Edward	12	DE	276
John M	10	FR	288	Rachael	22	DE	272	John A	14	PA	341
John M	46	PA	360	Rebecca	60	DE	188	John F	37	NJ	341
Joseph E	3/12	DE	389	Richard D	1	DE	360	Mary	37	PA	341
Leanora	10/12	DE	76	Rosanna O	5/12	DE	329	William	18	DE	276
Lewis H	3/12	DE	83	Roseland	21	DE	360	Wooten, Alfred P A	16	DE	401
Martha	18	DE	127	Samuel	34	IE	331	Words, John	73	DE	264
Mary J	21	DE	178	Sarah	28	DE	353	Rebecca	65	DE	264
Rebecca	1	DE	273	Sarah A	17	DE	210	Workman, Henry L	8	NY	369
Rodman R	26	PA	76	W Devere	24	PA	360	Levi	41	GB	369
Rosanah	3	DE	63	William	17	DE	362	Mary	38	GB	369
Samuel	13	DE	188	William	19	DE	283	Thomas	11	PA	369
Samuel	80	PA	29	William	44	PA	353	World, Alex	26	DE	258
Sarah A	2	PA	333	William H	6	DE	186	Worley, William	24	DE	72
Sarah A	30	MD	126	Woodward, Aaron	12	DE	364	Worrel, Alexander	31	DE	343
Sarah J	23	DE	83	Abner	22	DE	364	Rosetta	32	MD	343
Susanah H	1	DE	178	Abner H	9	DE	348	Samuel	10	DE	373
Thomas	1/12	DE	178	Abner H	49	DE	348	Worrell, Edward	47	DE	273
Thomas D	10	DE	309	Ann	40	PA	362	Elizabeth	17	DE	373
Thos	53	DE	284	Anna M	6	DE	364	Esther	17	DE	273
William	2	DE	76	Baby girl	1	DE	221	Jacob	21	DE	22
William	29	IE	63	Edward	4	DE	364	James	23	DE	373
William	30	DE	178	Elizabeth	16	DE	364	John	12	DE	373
William C	29	MD	126	Elizabeth	23	MD	365	Joseph	50	PA	373
William P	3/12	DE	370	Elizabeth	30	MD	221	Louisa	11	DE	273
Zelphia	45	PA	360	Elizabeth	43	DE	365	Louisa	35	DE	273
Woodan, Jno	21	OH	291	Elizabeth E	2	DE	348	Lucinda	19	DE	22
Woodard, Arthur	2	ME	15	Ellen	6	DE	362	Mary	25	DE	373
Danial	38	DE	133	Elwood	5	DE	348	Mary	30	DE	22
J	30	CT	15	Frederick	15	DE	364	Moses	45	DE	22
Jane	55	MD	98	George	10	DE	364	Rodney	3	DE	273
Kate	4	ME	15	George	22	DE	365	Sarah	51	PA	298
Mary	27	CT	15	Hannah	18	DE	364	Worrill, Emma	16	PA	383
Susanah	34	DE	133	Hannah	19	DE	20	Granville	13	DE	383
William	1	DE	133	James	10	DE	221	Hellen E	11	DE	383
William	65	MD	98	James	15	DE	368	Laura	1	DE	383
Woodbreeze, Jacob	55	DE	217	John	12	DE	243	Merriman	41	PA	383
Woodcath, Charles	20	DE	399	John	13	DE	365	Thomas	42	PA	383
Woodcock, Charles B	21	DE	132	John	14	DE	364	Worthington, Cather	70	PA	327
Emma	9	DE	132	John	45	PA	359	Harriet	32	PA	327
Henry A	4	DE	132	John W	12	DE	221	John	2	DE	333
Mary A	35	MD	132	Joseph	50	DE	364	Mary	28	DE	333
William	13	DE	132	Julian	36	DE	348	Rachel	24	DE	184
William	44	DE	132	Leonard	45	DE	365	Wrider, William	35	DE	366
Woodell, Acquilla	11	DE	48	Levin	2	DE	364	Wright, Abraham E	13	DE	330
Anna	9	DE	48	Margaret	11	DE	364	Alexander	32	IE	16
Eliza	14	DE	48	Margaret A	10	DE	362	Amanda	2	DE	329
Elizabeth	18	DE	48	Mary	40	DE	364	Ann	30	DE	236
John	16	DE	48	Mary Ann	3/12	DE	365	Ann	39	MD	329
Virginia	15	IE	114	Polk	4	DE	221	Ann	49	DE	87
Zebra	43	PA	48	Rebecca	15	DE	362	Ann E	16	DE	329
Woodland, Mary J	15	DE	358	Rebecca	42	PA	359	Ann J	6	DE	297
Woodroe, Catharine E	3	MD	380	Sarah	8	DE	364	Ann M	4	MD	325
Lydia	23	MD	380	Sarah	16	DE	365	Arnold	13	DE	396
Woodrough, Caleb S	6	DE	317	Sarah	60	PA	355	Caleb	9	DE	329
John L	1	DE	317	Sarah A	12	DE	348	Caleb	30	DE	251
Mary S	6	DE	317	Washington	46	PA	361	Caroline	21	DE	91
Rachel	12	MD	317	William	2	DE	365	Caroline F	6	DE	223
Rebecca	35	DE	317	William	19	DE	364	Catharine	7	DE	314
Sarah R	14	MD	317	William	60	PA	355	Catharine	10	DE	316
Simon M	10	MD	317	Wooliston, Amey	42	DE	380	Catharine	35	SE	340
Stephen	50	MD	317	Mary	73	DE	380	Catharine J	4	DE	223
Wm H	3	DE	317	Woollaston, Albert	7	DE	382	Charity A	32	DE	91
Woods, Ann	30	IE	329	Edward	12	DE	382	Charles	10	DE	87
B J	29	DE	272	George E	8	DE	382	Charles	14	MD	377
Clarissa	11	DE	186	Hannah E	10	DE	382	Charles	16	DE	203
David	10	DE	353	Joseph	42	DE	382	Charles J	16	DE	184
Eliza	30	IE	329	Josephine	1	DE	300	Clarra	7	DE	21
Eliza	35	IE	331	Louis P	14	DE	382	Cornelia	3	DE	256
Elizabeth V	15	DE	186	Mary	42	MD	382	Curtis R	28	DE	256
Gaines	6	DE	353	Mary A	27	DE	300	David	1	DE	223
George H	2	PA	329	Mary M	4/12	DE	300	David	7	DE	321
George P	13	DE	186	Sarah	11	PA	300	Delia	15	DE	284
Hannah	2	DE	353	Silvester	1	DE	382	Delilah	5	DE	240
Isaac	27	DE	252	Susan P	5	PA	300	Duffus	26	DE	63
Isaac	43	DE	210	Theodore	4	DE	382	Edmund R	7	DE	184
James	66	DE	359	Thomas	16	DE	382	Edward	3	DE	391
John	27	IE	346	Thomas P	36	PA	300	Edward Jr	1	DE	309
John	35	IE	329	William	30	DE	171	Eli	25	DE	41

Name	Age	State	No.
Wright, Elias	2	MD	325
Eliza A	9	DE	277
Elizabeth	14	DE	184
Elizabeth	19	DE	21
Elizabeth	28	DE	165
Elizabeth	40	DE	284
Elizabeth	44	DE	321
Elizabeth C	13	DE	284
Emma	3	DE	284
Emory	15	DE	299
Frances A	8	DE	230
Frank	24	DE	91
Franklin	1	DE	329
Franklin	34	PA	46
Frederick	13	DE	333
Garrison	15	DE	320
George	35	PA	286
George	40	DE	14
George W	12	DE	184
Grace	70	DE	378
Hannah	9	DE	91
Hannah	33	DE	220
Harriet	7	NJ	223
Harriet	57	DE	41
Harriet D	17	MD	332
Henrietta	1	DE	91
Henrietta	13	PA	316
Henry	12	DE	192
Henry Clay	5	DE	391
Hester	45	DE	91
Hester A	3/12	DE	313
Isaac	26	DE	91
Isaac	41	NJ	280
Isaac H	24	DE	87
Isabella	35	DE	233
Isiah	26	DE	214
Jacob B	1	DE	230
James	45	DE	316
Jane	10	DE	14
Jane	10	DE	245
John	3	DE	63
John	6	DE	316
John	8	DE	307
John	15	DE	87
John	27	DE	378
John	39	NY	223
John	54	DE	87
John	70	NJ	378
John F	14	NJ	223
John T	2	DE	329
John W	17	DE	222
Joseph	28	DE	284
Joseph	40	DE	256
Josephine	4/12	DE	256
Judith	67	NJ	378
Julia	9	DE	69
Louisa	1	DE	238
Louisa	9	DE	198
Louisa	11	DE	257
Louisa T	16	DE	332
Lydia M	23	NJ	184
Mahlon	19	NJ	184
Margaret	13	DE	41
Margaret	23	IE	284
Margaret A	22	DE	313
Margaret A	11	DE	233
Margaret R	11/12	PA	16
Maria	7	DE	287
Martha	1	DE	220
Martha	4	DE	256
Martha	20	MD	389
Mary	3/12	DE	63
Mary	3	DE	220
Mary	5	MD	334
Mary	7	DE	256
Mary	14	DE	322
Mary	18	MD	325
Mary	25	DE	251
Mary	27	DE	165
Mary A	20	PA	16
Mary A	29	DE	91
Mary Ann F	21	NJ	184
Wright, Mary E	3/12	DE	236
Mary E	5	DE	251
Mary E	7	DE	284
Mary E	14	PA	14
Mary E	39	NJ	223
Patience	37	DE	256
Peter	50	MD	321
Phebe	31	PA	46
Rachel	9	PA	38
Rachel	28	MD	316
Rachel	38	PA	391
Rachel A	9	DE	297
Rebecca	3	DE	251
Rebecca	8	DE	256
Rebecca	18	DE	87
Rebecca J	3	DE	236
Richard	15	DE	321
Richard	24	NJ	374
Richard	25	DE	21
Richard	38	NJ	391
Robert W	42	DE	233
Rosanna	45	DE	297
Sally A	10	DE	321
Samuel	9	NJ	223
Samuel	12	DE	122
Samuel	39	NJ	329
Samuel	41	MD	284
Samuel	49	DE	184
Samuel B	22	MD	389
Samuel N	9	DE	184
Samuel W	7	DE	329
Sarah	1	DE	251
Sarah	14	DE	256
Sarah	22	DE	63
Sarah	29	DE	230
Sarah	39	NJ	280
Sarah	44	NJ	184
Sarah	84	MD	278
Sarah J	9	DE	284
Siney	60	DE	91
Stephen	20	DE	203
Susan	30	DE	14
Susan	40	MD	101
Susan	42	DE	286
Thomas	4	DE	230
Thomas	13	DE	101
Thomas	15	DE	41
Thomas	15	MD	325
Thomas	27	DE	91
Thomas H	38	MD	230
Washington O	22	IE	319
Wilhelmina	24	MD	307
William	2	DE	63
William	13	DE	234
William	20	DE	209
William	21	DE	87
William	28	DE	91
William	28	DE	210
William	39	DE	220
William	45	PA	391
William C	14	DE	329
William J	1	DE	230
William T	14	DE	233
Wilmer	30	DE	236
Wyat, James	26	MD	371
James O	10/12	DE	371
Margaret	21	DE	371
Rebecca	23	DE	371
Robert	26	MD	371
William H	8/12	DE	371
William W	2	DE	371
Wyatt, Amanda	7	DE	325
Amelia	10	DE	292
Anna	4	DE	292
Catherine	13	DE	292
Catherine	59	DE	372
Eliza	18	DE	292
Eliza A	31	DE	325
Jane	7	DE	292
John G	33	DE	372
Latitia	25	DE	177
Mary	38	DE	292
Wyatt, Mary J	1	DE	325
Ott	40	DE	292
Peter	14	DE	291
Peter	14	DE	293
Rebecca	9	DE	292
Sarah	12	DE	325
Sarah A	27	DE	372
Sarah E	7	DE	372
Tilman	41	DE	325
Wayne	3	DE	325
Wilhelmina	9	DE	325
Wynkoop, Aurelia	40	DE	161
Geradis	7	DE	161
S (Rev)	45	DE	161
Theodore	10	DE	161
Wythes, Jane	28	PA	280
Joseph H	29	GB	280
Mary L	2/12	DE	280
Sarah J	2	PA	280
William	3	PA	280
Yarington, Hannah	50	DE	160
William	24	DE	160
William	60	CT	160
Yarnald, Jacob	40	DE	358
Mary	64	PA	358
Yarnall, Agness	58	PA	61
Yarnell, Jacob	16	PA	312
Samuel	21	PA	312
Sarah	19	PA	312
Yarnold, Ann	69	DE	365
Claten	5	DE	365
Elizabeth	37	DE	365
Ephraim	43	DE	365
Holton	15	DE	365
Jacob	3	DE	365
Jonathan	1	DE	365
Sarah	18	DE	365
Susan	9	DE	365
Yates, Francis	55	MD	284
Hudson Clifton	9	DE	194
Yearley, John	34	DE	181
John T	4	DE	181
Maria A	25	PA	181
Nathan B	3	DE	181
Samuel	10/12	DE	181
Yearly, Elizabeth	27	DE	14
Nathan	28	DE	14
Norroca	2	DE	14
Thomas	4	DE	14
Yearsley, James	20	DE	366
Margaret	58	DE	366
McCoy	15	DE	366
Nathan	58	DE	366
Samuel	23	DE	366
Yeates, Catherine L	20	PA	104
Charles	9	DE	45
Charles B	25	DE	104
Elizabeth A	49	DE	104
George	14	DE	45
Hannah	39	DE	45
James	2/12	DE	45
James	40	DE	45
John	5	DE	45
Sarah	16	DE	45
Yeatman, Alfred	12	DE	361
Benson	40	DE	361
George	14	DE	361
Hannah A	15	DE	361
James	4	DE	361
John	18	PA	361
Leuremma	36	DE	361
Mary	4	DE	361
Mary A	6	DE	361
Mary A	38	PA	361
Sarah	8	DE	361
Sarah E	10	DE	361
Thomas	49	DE	361
Yeats, Emma	3	DE	21
Emma	9	PA	17
John	7	PA	17
John	39	DE	17

Name	Age	State	No.
Yeats, Major	45	DE	21
Margaret	18	DE	17
Martha	12	PA	17
Mary	15	DE	17
Mary	35	DE	21
Mary	40	IE	17
Matilda	3	PA	17
Thomas	4	DE	21
Yellow, Eliza	24	DE	53
Yerden, Charles	12	DE	383
Elizabeth	10	DE	383
George W	7	DE	383
Sarah	14	DE	383
Yerrow, Mary	22	DE	9
Yoakes, Lewis	14	DE	351
Mary	65	PA	351
William H	11	DE	351
Yocum, John	40	PA	315
Mary	6	OH	315
Mary C	33	KY	315
Rebecca E	11	OH	315
Sarah A	3	OH	315
Wm C	1	OH	315
Yoker, Hannah	52	PA	348
Joseph	6	PA	348
Yokum, Mary A	36	DE	386
Richard	28	DE	386
William	3	DE	386
Young, Abigail	13	DE	231
Adelaide	8	DE	281
Agnes	56	NJ	336
Albert	2	DE	268
Amanda H	5	DE	358
Anna	1	DE	106
Anthony	18	DE	297
Anthony	19	DE	293
Arianna	2	DE	242
Barney	5	DE	298
Caroline	22	NJ	336
Catherine	17	IE	157
Catherine	31	DE	110
Catherine	83	DE	297
Cassius	5	DE	85
Corah R	8	DE	106
Daniel	21	DE	229
David	11	DE	374
David	12	PA	293
David	25	DE	286
David	53	DE	297
Dianna	47	DE	297
Drusilla	4	DE	387
Ellen	10	DE	106
Emma C	13	DE	106
Fanny	16	DE	185
George	6	DE	110
George	8	DE	268
George	11	DE	298
George	30	DE	268
Harriet	18	DE	147
Isaac	40	DE	72
Jacob	6	DE	298
James	3	DE	72
James	37	DE	242
Jane	9	MD	274
Jane	17	DE	174
Jane	18	IE	336
Jane	40	ST	185
Jannette M	14	DE	281
John	3	DE	298
John	29	DE	17
John	37	NY	77
Young, John B	10	DE	358
Joseph	9	IE	347
Josephine	4	DE	85
Julia	21	DE	85
Julia E	2	DE	85
Julia M	18	PA	142
Levi	40	DE	276
Lewis	32	DE	110
M Louisa	20	DE	332
Margaret	40	IE	347
Margaret	55	MD	195
Margaret J	1	DE	85
Martha	25	MD	268
Mary	18	DE	185
Mary	37	DE	46
Mary	45	DE	272
Mary	45	DE	341
Mary	78	PA	106
Mary A	16	MD	234
Mary J	21	DE	106
Melvina	19	DE	286
Minty	58	DE	72
Murray	13	DE	394
Nancy	48	DE	87
Nathaniel	54	DE	281
Rebecca Mc	10	DE	106
Richard	56	DE	341
Robert	7	DE	358
Robert	32	IE	347
Rufus P	32	PA	358
Sarah	8	DE	298
Sarah	19	MA	33
Sarah	49	DE	106
Sarah A	26	DE	242
Sarah A	32	DE	358
Sarah C	18	DE	106
Sarah E	5	DE	242
Sarah J	4/12	DE	358
Thomas	7	GB	384
Thomas	14	DE	174
Thomas	30	DE	380
Thomas	51	DE	106
Thomas E	6	DE	106
William	3	DE	110
William	25	IE	249
William	30	DE	85
William	40	DE	174
William	78	PA	308
Wm	4	DE	268
Wm	23	IE	261
Younger, Medford	11	MD	146
Sarah	14	DE	136
Sarah E	30	MD	146
Youngline, Jane E	7	NY	53
Zane, Basilda	28	PA	52
E R	25	PA	113
Hiram C	7	DE	332
Jonathan	33	PA	332
Mary A	33	MD	332
Zanes, David	40	NJ	96
Mrs	35	NJ	96
Philip	11	NJ	96
Zebbuth, Amos P	11	DE	347
Ann	60	DE	347
Anna	7	DE	347
Henrietta	8	DE	347
John	50	DE	347
Rebecca	18	DE	347
Zebley, Ann	39	DE	48
Ann	40	DE	304
Zebley, Anna C	8	DE	130
Benj	25	DE	293
Elizabeth	2	DE	128
Elizabeth	48	DE	108
Ella D	6	DE	130
Hannah	21	DE	128
Hannah	50	DE	293
Henry G B	3	DE	130
Jacob	60	DE	293
James	5	DE	304
James	17	DE	108
James	45	DE	304
John	8	DE	345
John	23	DE	128
John	35	DE	130
Lewis	14	DE	108
Magy	45	PA	279
Margarett	11	DE	304
Mary E	13	DE	130
Nann	13	DE	293
Outten	18	DE	319
Owen	18	DE	108
Owen	47	DE	108
Owen	64	DE	279
Sarah E	18	DE	293
Sarah J	30	DE	131
Thomas	26	DE	7
Zebly, Anthony	34	DE	5
Edward M	11	DE	307
Eliza	10	DE	5
Hannah	6	DE	285
Hannah	7	DE	307
Hannah	30	DE	285
Henry K J P	9	DE	307
Jacob	2	DE	5
James	3	DE	5
Jonathan	39	DE	306
Lewis	31	DE	285
Lewis A	3	DE	285
Margaret	40	DE	162
Martha H	34	DE	5
Mary	5/12	DE	307
Mary	6	DE	5
Mary	39	DE	306
Mary	81	DE	285
Mary L	1	DE	285
Rebecca J	5	DE	285
Samuel R	8	DE	285
Sarah	5	DE	307
Sarah E	10	DE	285
Sarah J	30	DE	130
Zeichler, Foltune	10/12	PA	162
George	28	GE	162
Unseden	28	GE	162
Zelby, Benjamin	18	NJ	165
Joseph S	14	NJ	165
Zigler, Ellen	45	MD	77
James	10	DE	77
John	50	GE	77
John M	5	DE	77
Zillias, John	30	DE	172
Zimmerman, Elener W	15	PA	129
Elizabeth	12	MD	144
Elizabeth H	19	PA	129
Henry W	13	PA	129
Percy S	21	PA	129
Rachel	52	PA	129
Susanah S	9	PA	129
Thomas B	30	PA	129
William	48	DE	129

Name	Age	State	Page
Abbot, Ann	56	DE	25
Eunice	5	DE	186
Mary A	12	DE	193
Richard	17	DE	60
Abbott, Amy	66	DE	42
Caroline	8	DE	28
Chloe	17	DE	84
David	60	DE	25
Edward J	18	DE	27
Eli	37	DE	69
Elizabeth	19	DE	28
Foster	5	DE	84
George	6	DE	69
George T	16	DE	28
Henry	4	DE	9
Isaac	13	DE	180
James	12	DE	69
John	48	DE	28
John	54	DE	69
John W	16	DE	69
Lydia L	16	DE	25
Margaret	21	DE	24
Mary	50	DE	84
Matilda	18	DE	28
Meroth	60	DE	84
Nancy	50	DE	85
Nehemiah	21	DE	24
Nicey A	13	DE	27
Phebe	37	DE	85
Sarah	52	DE	69
Susan C	13	DE	69
Unice	59	DE	28
William	10	DE	69
William H	18	DE	9
Abdale, Eliza	8	DE	13
Abdel, Bridget	13	DE	43
Lydia E	21	DE	52
Abdell, Elizabeth	16	DE	15
Elizabeth	40	DE	13
Lydia E	19	DE	13
Mary A	13	DE	13
Robert S	5	DE	13
Samuel E	3	DE	13
Sarah E	17	DE	13
Stephen	9	DE	13
Stephen	49	DE	13
William	15	DE	13
Abert, George	1	DE	54
Adams, Alfred	33	DE	233
Ann	23	DE	233
Ann L	17	DE	219
Bartholomew	28	DE	99
Catherine	17	DE	219
Catherine	40	DE	224
Catherine	50	MD	219
Charles	4	DE	99
Charles	13	DE	215
Charles H	16	DE	224
Charles M	32	DE	6
Charlotte L	29	DE	215
Clarissa	17	DE	109
Daniel	23	DE	219
Daniel	25	DE	208
Daniel	27	DE	149
Daniel A	14	DE	5
David	6/12	DE	223
Eda	65	DE	200
Edward	10	DE	221
Eleanor	23	DE	200
Eliza	3	DE	297
Eliza	65	DE	297
Eliza J	8	DE	223
Eliza R	43	DE	228
Elizabeth E	23	DE	6
Elizabeth H	16	DE	228
Elmer	3	DE	6
Eunica	60	DE	220
Garretson	4	DE	223
Garretson	56	DE	231
Garret	13	DE	223
George	7/12	DE	263
George	24	DE	211
Adams, George	25	DE	247
George H	21	DE	215
Henry	30	DE	247
Henry	38	DE	256
Hester Ann	8	DE	256
Hester C	9	DE	5
Isaac	17	DE	101
Isaac	25	DE	114
Isaac	38	DE	5
Isaac	40	DE	263
Jacob	13	DE	263
Jacob	19	DE	101
Jacob	25	DE	198
Jacob H	6	DE	242
James	10	DE	256
James B	12	DE	224
James E	15	DE	263
James M	18	DE	215
Jeremiah	37	DE	242
Jesse	11	DE	263
Jesse E	1	DE	233
John	7	DE	263
John	14	DE	109
John C	16	DE	223
John R	39	DE	223
John T	4	MD	211
Joseph T	18	DE	5
Josephine	10	DE	109
Kendal B	7	DE	273
Latitia	12	DE	99
Lavinia	34	DE	231
Leah	54	DE	149
Leah J	1	DE	150
Lovinia	5	DE	263
Manlove	43	DE	224
Margaret	3	DE	223
Margaret	12	DE	221
Margaret	13	DE	101
Margaret	22	DE	211
Margaret	38	DE	5
Margaret	47	DE	221
Maria E	13	DE	256
Martha	3	DE	256
Mary	1	DE	224
Mary	8	DE	101
Mary	19	DE	225
Mary	30	DE	297
Mary	32	DE	247
Mary	41	DE	221
Mary	75	DE	247
Mary A	11	DE	224
Mary A	33	DE	223
Mary C	20	DE	149
Mary E	1	DE	211
Mary E	8	DE	109
Mary E	13	DE	223
Mary E	23	DE	256
Mary J	35	DE	263
Mathew	65	DE	221
Matilda	2	DE	99
Nancy	12	DE	109
Nancy	34	DE	256
Nancy	35	DE	223
Nancy E	10	DE	223
Napoleon	10	DE	109
Nathan	36	DE	223
Nicholas W	52	DE	109
Rebecca	5	DE	256
Rebecca	6	DE	221
Rebecca	33	DE	220
Robert A	9	DE	224
Roger	25	DE	231
Roger	58	DE	219
Roger Jr	25	DE	219
Sallie W	6	DE	223
Sally	40	DE	101
Sally	40	DE	149
Sarah	8	DE	101
Sarah	16	DE	199
Sarah	19	DE	46
Sarah	20	DE	99
Sarah	35	DE	247
Adams, Sarah E	3	DE	233
Sarah J	29	DE	242
Shad	63	DE	133
Thomas	52	DE	256
Washington	21	DE	219
William	16	DE	219
William	19	DE	109
William	31	DE	219
William	43	DE	42
William	47	DE	247
William F	15	DE	256
Wm B	24	DE	211
Wm H	27	DE	200
Wm P	2	DE	223
Adkins, Arcada	65	DE	19
Catharine	--	DE	19
Charles H	15	DE	19
Elijah	21	DE	277
Harriet E	7	DE	19
Hetty	13	DE	19
Isaac	10	DE	114
Isaac	11	DE	19
Isaiah	55	MD	114
Jane	32	DE	114
Joseph (Capt)	37	DE	35
Lantay	1	DE	114
Louisa	1	DE	35
Ludovick	30	DE	20
Lydia	33	DE	19
Lydia E	10/12	DE	20
Martha	8	DE	35
Mary	47	DE	19
Mary J	9	DE	19
Miers B	21	DE	19
Peter	28	DE	19
Rhoda	17	DE	19
Rufus	32	DE	114
Sally	26	DE	35
Sarah A	28	DE	20
Sarah J	2	DE	20
Sarah Jane	10	DE	35
Thomas R	20	DE	19
William	7	DE	114
Wilson D	50	DE	19
Ake, Anda	50	MD	278
Hiram	10	DE	279
James	55	DE	118
John S	21	DE	279
Laura	13	DE	279
Mary	15	DE	279
Nancy	55	DE	117
Sarah	4	DE	279
Thomas	50	DE	120
Thomas D	52	MD	278
William	19	DE	279
William	55	DE	122
Allen, Ann	44	NJ	117
Ann M	32	DE	198
Betsey	40	DE	205
Burton	6	DE	165
Burton	21	DE	165
Caroline	13	DE	118
Caroline T	10	MD	211
Catherine	32	DE	53
Charles T	5	DE	118
David	17	NJ	118
Edward	14	DE	227
Eleanor	26	DE	165
Eliza A	30	DE	198
Elizabeth	16	DE	227
Elizabeth	22	DE	209
Elizabeth	45	DE	211
Elizabeth H	13	DE	205
Elizabeth J	14	MD	211
Enals	43	DC	198
Eunice	6	DE	97
Frank	2	DE	198
Hannah	35	DE	97
Hiram E	6	DE	204
Isaac W	6	DE	198
Isaac W	12	DE	210
J H A	13	DE	226

Name	Age	State	Page
Allen, Jacob	33	DE	204
James K P	5	MD	210
Jesse W	17	MD	211
John	7/12	DE	227
John	9	DE	165
John	22	DE	204
John H	23	DE	211
John J	19	NJ	118
John W	1	MD	210
John W	10	DE	198
Joseph	15	DE	198
Joseph B	19	DE	211
Joseph C	47	DE	211
Joseph D	47	NJ	117
Joshua	6	DE	213
Leah	60	DE	97
Leah	68	DE	165
Levin	41	DE	205
Levin J	1	DE	205
Lillie B	3	MD	211
Luzella	6	DE	206
Lydia J	3	DE	198
M W	37	DE	198
Margaret	5	DE	227
Margaret F	8	DE	198
Margaret P	9	DE	206
Margaret S	3	DE	205
Martha A	10	MD	210
Mary	30	DE	165
Mary	35	DE	210
Mary	36	DE	206
Mary C	8	MD	210
Mary E	13	DE	206
Mary R	6	MD	211
Mary T	10	DE	204
Nancy	12	DE	227
Nancy P	8	DE	205
Peter	5	DE	204
Pinkston J	3	DE	206
Rebecca	12	DE	205
Rebecca A	15	DE	206
Robert C	40	DE	206
Sallie	30	DE	228
Sallie A	11	MD	226
Sallie A	35	DE	204
Samuel	1	DE	204
Sarah C	12	DE	198
Selby H	9	DE	118
Solomon H	10	DE	205
Thomas A	3	MD	210
William	3	DE	227
William	6	DE	118
William	18	DE	210
William	36	DE	228
Wm	48	DE	210
Wm H	8	DE	206
Wm J	12	MD	211
Allis, Thomas H	6	DE	181
Anderson, Catherine	62	DE	49
Eliza J	7	MD	237
Elizabeth	17	DE	41
Elizabeth C	2	DE	135
Ellen	20	DE	41
Emeline	38	DE	236
Emilia E	12	DE	236
Emily	18	DE	41
Hetty	27	DE	135
James	15	DE	266
James	26	DE	162
James	31	DE	135
James	34	DE	42
James	51	DE	41
John	11	DE	135
John H	15	DE	236
Joseph	15	DE	222
Joshua W	8	DE	135
Margaret	16	IE	54
Martha	2	DE	236
Mary A	4	DE	135
Mary A E	14	DE	236
Nancy	78	DE	259
Nancy A	34	MD	222
Anderson, Sallie L	9	DE	237
Thomas H	5	DE	237
Venus	25	DE	2
William	45	DE	175
William J A	10	DE	236
Wm H	41	DE	236
Andre, Mary J	11	DE	136
Andrew, Agor	36	DE	212
Ann	25	DE	124
Benjamin B	20	DE	156
Benton	2	DE	144
Celia	36	DE	209
Charles H G	6	DE	212
David S	8	DE	212
Elizabeth	10	MD	209
Elizabeth	23	DE	144
Ellen	2	DE	124
Eunice	21	DE	233
Jacob	4	DE	212
James	15	DE	265
James	26	DE	161
James	28	DE	144
James M	6	MD	209
John	59	DE	156
John A	5	DE	144
Joshua	3	DE	144
Julia	13	DE	124
Levin A	33	DE	124
Martha	25	DE	156
Martha	64	DE	156
Mary	33	MD	209
Mary E	6/12	DE	212
Mary J	31	MD	212
Nancy	85	DE	239
Nancy C	2/12	DE	124
Peter A	4	DE	144
Saulsbury	39	DE	209
Sophia	62	DE	206
Tamsy	69	MD	209
William	1/12	DE	144
William	7	DE	137
William	10	DE	218
Andrews, Ager	36	DE	211
Charles H G	6	DE	211
David L	8	DE	211
Maria	13	DE	236
Maria	45	MD	236
Mary J	51	DE	211
Henry C	7	DE	236
Argo, Abigail	62	DE	72
Albert	8	DE	72
Andrew	14	DE	71
Andrew	27	DE	87
Eliza Ann	1	DE	87
Hester H	26	DE	71
John E	12	DE	31
Joseph	23	DE	71
Mary Ann	24	DE	87
Samuel T	7	DE	71
William B	1	DE	71
Armstrong, Charlott	35	MD	171
Arnold, Ann	55	DE	55
David S	13	DE	55
John	60	DE	55
Robert	15	DE	55
Arny, Joseph	17	DE	279
Atkins, Agnes	1/12	DE	165
Anna W	1	DE	33
Bevela	12	DE	165
Catharine S B	--	DE	33
Clara E	3	DE	33
Clayton	6	DE	165
David	7	DE	33
David H	7	DE	33
Eber	27	DE	155
Edward F	20	DE	179
Elijah	21	DE	168
Elijah	24	DE	155
Eliza	34	DE	155
Emily M	5	DE	33
George (Capt)	38	DE	33
George H	1/12	DE	169
Atkins, Isaac	42	DE	165
Isaac	54	DE	177
Isabel J	4	DE	155
James A	57	DE	179
James H	4	DE	169
Janet M	13	DE	185
Jason	5	DE	165
John	30	DE	28
Joshua	8	DE	165
Joshua B	7	DE	127
Kendal	19	DE	179
Letty	51	DE	179
Louisa	2	DE	155
Love	50	DE	168
Major M	26	DE	174
Margaret E	2	DE	169
Margaret H	1	DE	127
Mary	20	DE	168
Mary A	3	DE	127
Mary A	4	DE	181
Mary J	4	DE	33
Mary T	1	DE	174
Mitchell	60	DE	168
Nancy	27	DE	127
Noah	23	DE	168
Rufus M	2	DE	165
Samuel A P	20	DE	179
Samuel B	18	DE	145
Sarah	2	DE	165
Sarah	24	DE	169
Sarah	38	DE	165
Sarah A	1	DE	33
Sarah A	30	DE	33
Sarah E	9	DE	127
Serena	23	DE	174
Stanton	18	DE	168
Stephen	40	DE	185
Susan	19	DE	28
Theodore J	9	DE	33
Thomas	38	DE	127
Thomas J	31	DE	33
William	10	DE	165
William M	41	DE	169
Atkinson, Catherine	45	DE	221
Eliza A	18	DE	221
Erene	10	DE	221
Grove	59	DE	221
Harriet A	16	DE	221
James B	21	DE	221
John A	38	DE	221
Margaret A	8	DE	221
Martin L	6	DE	221
Austin, Benton	18	DE	91
Henry	30	DE	91
Isaac	60	DE	91
John W	5	DE	91
Rachael	33	DE	91
Sarah	66	DE	91
Sarah A	2	DE	91
William	7	DE	91
Aydelott, Caroline	7	DE	113
Clementine A	1	DE	113
David	29	DE	113
Jane	14	DE	113
John	22	DE	113
Love	19	DE	113
Margaret F	3	DE	113
Martha	33	DE	115
Mary	50	DE	113
Nathaniel H	19	DE	113
Stephen C	20	DE	112
Babe, Elizabeth E	23	DE	49,
James C	24	DE	49
James W	2	DE	49
Bacon, Amelia A	21	DE	239
Amy	18	DE	3
Ann	5	DE	25
Ann	18	DE	2
Daniel	18	DE	241
Dennis	20	DE	194
Edwin	22	DE	236

Name	Age	State	Page
Bacon, Edwin	22	DE	236
Eliza	20	DE	241
Eliza	20	MD	263
Eliza	25	DE	232
Elizabeth	13	DE	234
Elizabeth	25	DE	275
Elizabeth	29	DE	156
Gensy	31	DE	239
Harriet	15	DE	10
Harriet	16	DE	6
Henry	4	DE	262
Henry	6	DE	242
Henry	25	DE	241
Henry	69	DE	241
Isaac	80	DE	294
James	9	DE	294
James B	26	DE	232
Jane	17	DE	280
John	23	DE	239
John S	25	DE	236
Joseph	16	DE	241
Levin	14	DE	241
Lavinia	12	DE	241
Lydia A	9	DE	174
Margaret	2	DE	275
Maria	22	DE	290
Mary	2	DE	290
Mary	6	DE	241
Mary	25	DE	290
Mary	46	DE	241
Rhoda	67	DE	290
Samuel	76	DE	290
Samuel P	30	DE	263
Sarah P	5	DE	239
Sophia	79	DE	294
Thomas	21	DE	241
Bailey, Edward	16	DE	170
George R	1/12	DE	174
Hannah	65	DE	58
Hester	35	DE	50
Isaac	46	DE	244
John	13	DE	191
Joshua J	4	DE	174
Maria	40	DE	174
Nathaniel E	15	DE	145
Rhoda A	10	DE	174
Samuel	17	DE	188
William	23	DE	174
Zadock	17	DE	44
Baily, Benjamin	30	DE	155
Charles	13	DE	150
Eliza E	6	DE	244
Elizabeth	6	DE	245
Isaac J	8	DE	244
James	4	DE	245
James	17	DE	288
James R	19	DE	194
Jantha	10	DE	244
John L	45	DE	288
Jonah	32	DE	245
Jonathan	2	DE	245
Jonathan	61	DE	251
Joseph	18	DE	244
Levin	14	DE	244
Levinia	53	DE	288
Mahala	54	DE	251
Margaret	31	MD	245
Mary	50	DE	155
Mary E	12	DE	244
Sarah	19	DE	288
Baker, Absolem	14	DE	279
Albert	23	MD	162
Ann M	5	DE	201
Anna V	5	DE	33
Archibald	5	MD	278
Archibald	40	MD	278
Arena	11	DE	163
Asbury	15	MD	259
Bartem	22	DE	201
Bartrum	21	DE	217
Bayard	8	DE	279
Bisha	9	DE	163
Baker, Clarissa	23	DE	162
Daniel	44	DE	273
David	15	DE	279
David	23	DE	201
David D	4	DE	172
Drucilla	21	MD	163
Drucilla	22	MD	259
Elijah	2	DE	279
Elijah	45	MD	277
Eliza	6	DE	279
Eliza	40	DE	5
Eliza J	7	MD	281
Eliza M	16	DE	172
Elizabeth	21	DE	279
Elizabeth	27	DE	201
Elizabeth	35	DE	98
George	15	DE	273
George S	6/12	DE	33
Hetty J	4	DE	176
Jacob	9	DE	273
Jacob	26	DE	201
Jacob B	48	DE	274
James	13	MD	278
James	49	DE	172
Jane	16	DE	210
Jane	21	DE	233
Jesse	12	MD	259
John	1	DE	281
John	17	MD	277
John	23	MD	233
John A	7	DE	33
Jonathan	38	MD	162
Joseph	18	DE	279
Joshua G	54	DE	9
Kitty	35	MD	259
Lambert	5	MD	281
Lavinia	2	DE	233
Leah	13	DE	273
Luvenia	39	DE	281
Mahala	14	DE	162
Manlove	5	DE	273
Mariah	44	DE	273
Mary	14	DE	162
Mary	15	DE	278
Mary	19	DE	273
Mary	30	DE	162
Mary	34	DE	274
Mary F	3	DE	34
Milborn	13	MD	259
Minos	17	MD	281
Nancy	10	DE	162
Nancy	38	DE	172
Nancy	43	DE	279
Nancy	50	DE	28
Nancy	52	DE	274
Noble	7	MD	281
Peter E	8	DE	278
Priscilla	37	DE	176
Purnal	48	MD	259
Rachel	5	DE	162
Rosenia	1	DE	162
Salathiel	20	DE	278
Salathiel	43	DE	33
Sallie	56	DE	201
Samuel	41	MD	281
Sarah	4	DE	279
Sarah	5	DE	162
Sarah	31	MD	162
Sarah	45	MD	277
Sarah	50	MD	278
Sarah	53	DE	42
Sarah E	30	DE	9
Sarah H	29	DE	33
Seth W	13	DE	278
Simpson	8	DE	162
Smith	17	MD	260
Thomas	12	DE	273
Thomas	55	DE	274
Vilater A	10	DE	278
William	12	DE	162
William	17	DE	273
William H	1	DE	201
Baker, William S	15	DE	176
Ball, Anna	3	DE	36
Judy	66	DE	51
Baley, Mary E	24	DE	46
Sarah A	1	DE	46
Susan M	4	DE	46
William J	33	DE	46
Banem, Ann	35	DE	190
George A	8	DE	187
Henry	40	DE	190
John D	1	DE	190
William H	12	DE	190
Banks, Ann E	13	DE	143
Henry	32	DE	116
Jacob	39	DE	116
Jacob H	16	DE	136
James H	1	DE	116
John	26	DE	113
Joshua	1	DE	116
Lydia F	49	DE	143
Maria C	10	DE	143
Maria E	2	DE	116
Mary	1	DE	116
Mary	21	DE	117
Matilda	30	DE	116
Nancy	41	DE	115
Naomi	21	DE	113
Peter	56	DE	116
Rachel	3	DE	116
Samuel	25	DE	115
Sarah D	2	DE	116
Susan	28	DE	116
William P	1	DE	116
Banning, Alexander	5	MD	213
Ann	16	DE	96
Asbury	9	MD	213
Catherine	40	DE	209
Hetty	20	DE	205
Jacob G	2	MD	213
James	14	DE	96
James F	12	MD	213
Jeremiah	15	DE	96
Jesse	37	MD	213
John	2	DE	96
John M	6	MD	213
Kessiah	29	DE	209
Mary	4	DE	96
Priscilla	44	MD	213
Sally	6	DE	96
Sarah	36	DE	96
Thomas	11	DE	96
Thomas C	43	DE	96
Wm H	12	MD	213
Banson, Hannah E	6	DE	187
Barba, Joseph	23	FR	45
Barber, Mary J	16	DE	12
Barker, Aletha	37	DE	20
Anna E	8	DE	20
Anna L	2	DE	6
Burton C	4	DE	6
Eliza	54	DE	180
Eliza A	14	DE	180
Elizabeth	50	DE	171
Elizabeth	50	DE	176
Elizabeth L	26	DE	171
Elizabeth M	40	DE	191
George	6	DE	47
George	29	DE	192
Hannah	5	DE	47
Hannah	60	DE	47
Henry	1	DE	33
Henry L	3	DE	20
Henna	18	DE	38
James P	40	DE	4
John	12	DE	34
John	27	DE	32
John	45	DE	191
John D	7/12	DE	20
Joseph H	15	DE	171
Joseph R	4	DE	20
Joseph R	63	DE	180
Louisa	28	DE	13

Barker, Lydia	13	DE	39	Bayley, James R	19	DE	196	Bell, James	16	DE	271
Lydia C	10	DE	20	John	26	DE	88	Jeremiah	3	DE	272
Mary	5	DE	33	Phebe	50	DE	33	John H	82	DE	141
Mary	28	DE	59	William	1/12	DE	88	Josiah	18	DE	10
Mary C	6	DE	4	Baylis, Ann	21	DE	193	Julia	5	DE	271
Mary E	8/12	DE	59	Benjamin B	21	DE	178	Levin	4	DE	272
Mary E	7	DE	31	Cato	50	DE	187	Levin W	10	DE	272
Mary E	16	DE	184	Charlotte	34	DE	177	Louisa	22	DE	272
Mary L	30	DE	6	Clement	35	DE	177	Lovinia	3	DE	271
Mary N	45	DE	179	Elizabeth	7	DE	193	Lovinia	39	DE	271
Peter	76	DE	36	Emaline	28	DE	45	Maria	33	DE	137
Rachel A	25	DE	4	Hannah	13	DE	177	Mariah	40	DE	271
Robertson	35	DE	20	Henry	12	DE	177	Margaret	27	DE	271
Ruth	24	DE	33	James T	67	DE	178	Martha	17	DE	196
Sally	64	DE	13	John	8	DE	177	Mary	19	DE	63
Samuel	33	DE	62	John W	10	DE	193	Mary	35	DE	271
Sarah A	6	DE	20	Louisa	20	DE	193	Mary	40	DE	272
Shepard P H	5	DE	4	Mary	12	DE	193	Mary	60	MD	272
Thomas R	19	DE	180	Mary	58	DE	178	Mary E	12	DE	4
William	6	DE	33	Moses	4	DE	177	Milly	10	DE	55
William	30	DE	176	Moses	71	DE	193	Nancy	50	DE	63
William	30	DE	179	Nancy	65	DE	193	Nicholas	28	DE	272
William D	2	DE	4	Sarah	2	DE	177	Nicholas H	68	WN	272
Zadock	65	DE	171	Sarah A	25	DE	178	Peter	2	DE	63
Zadock T	22	DE	171	Solomon	16	DE	193	Peter	45	DE	137
Barlow, John	27	GB	124	Solomon	67	DE	193	Robert	4/12	DE	196
Barnard, Henry	14	DE	167	Bayliss, Hannah	17	DE	46	Robert	10	DE	271
Joseph S	53	NH	167	Bayman, Eliza	2	DE	17	Sarah	9	DE	272
Sarah S	42	DE	167	Henry C	6	DE	17	Thomas	74	DE	52
Barnes, Comfort	58	DE	117	Milley	35	DE	17	William	40	DE	271
Edward	27	DE	283	Zachariah	35	DE	17	Bennet, Betty P	4	DE	244
Barnet, George L	1	DE	115	Baynum, George W	35	DE	32	Brittania	59	DE	244
Luke	36	DE	115	Mary	18	DE	32	Henry R	10	DE	244
Mary W	35	DE	115	Mary	45	DE	32	John H	8	DE	244
Phebe	27	DE	152	Beach, Amelia A	21	DE	258	Levin M	50	DE	244
Sarah	63	MD	114	Arena	15	DE	257	Stephen J	16	MD	243
William	50	DE	114	Barney	23	DE	257	Stephen T	15	DE	243
Barr, David	30	DE	102	Charlotte	15	MD	254	Bennett, Aaron	33	DE	131
George	12	DE	102	Franky	13	DE	257	Abigail	45	DE	73
Hannah	60	DE	102	Hady	63	DE	257	Alfred	19	DE	74
Henry	21	DE	102	Isaac	10	MD	254	Ann M	8	DE	136
Hester	30	DE	102	Isaiah	24	DE	257	Arcada	45	DE	74
Hetty	8	DE	102	Jonathan	27	DE	241	Caleb	14	DE	85
John	17	DE	102	Jonathan	28	DE	257	Caroline	21	DE	81
Louis	17	DE	102	Kendal	21	DE	236	Catharine E	16	DE	74
Lovey	27	DE	102	Kendal	22	DE	257	Catharine R	5	DE	72
Lucy	28	DE	102	Levin	11	DE	257	Celia T	2	DE	72
Philip	4	DE	102	Nancy	24	DE	241	Charles D	28	DE	136
Robert	75	DE	102	Sarah	18	DE	257	David	28	DE	81
Robert P	30	DE	102	Sarah	52	DE	257	David H	5	DE	73
Barrett, Elizabeth	33	DE	31	Beacham, Nathaniel	29	DE	165	Edward	1	DE	81
Nathaniel	8	DE	31	Beadle, William	11	DE	186	Elias T	37	DE	72
Nathaniel	45	DE	31	Beal, Elizabeth	55	DE	142	Eliza	21	DE	85
Barrows, Emilia M	21	MD	232	John H	82	VA	142	Elizabeth	3	DE	72
Bartell, Henry C	5	DE	182	Beauchamp, Dinah	75	DE	74	Elizabeth	6	DE	77
Barten, Daniel	37	DE	28	Nancy	45	DE	196	Elizabeth	17	DE	74
Rachael	25	DE	28	Peter	75	DE	74	Elizabeth	20	DE	6
Bartlet, George J	1	DE	8	Rachael	35	DE	74	Elizabeth	20	DE	136
Nancy	44	DE	8	Beebe, George	18	DE	132	Elizabeth	28	DE	72
Bartlett, Ann W	13	DE	115	James	58	DE	132	Elizabeth	29	DE	72
Mary J	28	DE	208	Peggy	50	DE	132	Elizabeth	53	DE	31
Barton, Alice	1	DE	54	William	5	DE	132	Emeline S	17	DE	85
Alice	48	DE	54	Bell, Amanda	7	DE	272	George	11	DE	81
Burton	18	DE	163	Andrew	29	DE	207	George	30	DE	77
James	8	DE	163	Betsy	27	DE	63	George	72	DE	73
John	21	DE	163	Boze	46	DE	271	Grace	2/12	DE	131
Mary	24	DE	54	Charles	14	DE	271	Grace	16	DE	131
Isaac	45	DE	163	Charles	35	DE	271	Hester	4	DE	72
Nancy	6	DE	163	Clarisa	14	DE	272	Hester	4	DE	77
Nancy	40	DE	163	Easter	63	DE	272	Hetty	26	DE	131
Zena	13	DE	163	Easter	70	DE	272	Hetty A	23	DE	31
Barwick, Ann E	2	DE	226	Edward	24	DE	272	James	55	DE	136
Deborah	43	DE	224	Elizabeth	55	DE	141	James D	8	DE	72
Eliza M	4	DE	226	Elizabeth	67	DE	52	James E	1	DE	119
George W	5	DE	224	Elizabeth A	33	DE	271	Jehu	8	DE	135
Margaret E	8	DE	224	Emma	15	DE	272	Jehu	25	DE	136
Mary A	26	DE	226	George	12	DE	272	Jehu	84	VA	136
Nathan J	18	DE	224	Harriet	38	DE	271	Jerusha J	2	DE	119
James	28	DE	226	Henry	16	DE	57	John	21	DE	136
Bayers, Henry	10	DE	1	Henry H	7	DE	271	John	28	DE	119
Bayley, Elizabeth	27	DE	88	Jacob	20	DE	63	John	30	DE	129
Emond	21	DE	88	Jacob	60	DE	63	John	64	DE	74

Name	Age	St	Pg
Bennett, John S	23	DE	135
John T	63	DE	31
John W	10	DE	72
Joseph	28	DE	85
Joshua	2	DE	77
Joshua	20	DE	136
Leah Jane	17	DE	73
Levin H	21	DE	136
Lucy	28	DE	136
Major	49	DE	105
Mary	4	DE	135
Mary	8	DE	77
Mary	50	DE	73
Mary A	26	DE	73
Mary E	6	DE	72
Mary J	20	DE	119
Mary W	10	DE	72
Mercy D	42	DE	136
Miranda	6	DE	74
Nancy	5	DE	135
Nancy	31	DE	135
Nancy	67	DE	136
Nathaniel	8	DE	85
Nehemiah	20	DE	73
Nicholas	12	DE	105
Peter	2	DE	135
Priscilla E	1	DE	136
Purnel F	7	DE	73
Purnell	30	DE	73
Rhoda E	14	DE	136
Rhoda M	9	DE	135
Robert W	4	DE	136
Riley	31	DE	72
Sally	3	DE	77
Samuel D	31	DE	135
Sarah	25	DE	77
Sarah	25	DE	129
Sarah A	6	DE	119
Sarah J	1	DE	72
Slydia	4	DE	81
Stephen	5	DE	131
Stephen R	25	DE	31
Thomas A	11	DE	74
Trusten P M	9	DE	74
Virginia	2	DE	85
William	7	DE	105
William D W	7/12	DE	85
William H	8	DE	72
Benson, Ann	18	DE	21
Ann E	6	DE	40
Ann E	11	DE	285
Carline	16	DE	207
Charles H	12	DE	207
Elenor	17	DE	291
Elenor	18	DE	274
Eliza A	19	DE	207
Elizabeth	14	DE	207
Elizabeth	40	DE	41
Elizabeth	51	DE	207
Elizabeth	52	MD	236
George H	8	DE	207
Henry	61	DE	207
James A P	8	DE	41
Jansha	21	DE	207
John B	18	DE	261
John H	14	DE	41
Julia J	19	DE	263
Margaret	13	DE	41
Mary	16	DE	135
Mary A	15	DE	285
Milly A	17	DE	41
Nancy	40	DE	291
Nancy	48	DE	274
Sallie J	19	DE	262
Thomas	23	DE	291
Thomas	24	DE	274
William	54	DE	41
William S	11	DE	41
Benston, Halover C	17	DE	167
James H	8	DE	167
Margaret	42	DE	167
Margaret A	10	DE	167
Benston, Margaret A	10	DE	167
Peggy	50	DE	176
Benton, Catharine	25	DE	73
Cornelius	4	DE	31
Hannah	1	DE	31
Hannah E	12	DE	8
Henry	23	DE	73
Hester	9/12	DE	73
Heveloe	29	DE	31
James	6	DE	31
John	16	DE	31
John	31	DE	40
John	57	DE	9
Sarah J	25	DE	40
William A	3	DE	25
Betts, Ann	20	DE	84
Anna	50	DE	161
Anna E	9	DE	161
Benjamin B	12	DE	164
Charles	21	DE	161
David C	7	DE	122
Dennis	67	MD	201
Edward	11	DE	81
Eliza	6	DE	30
Eliza	41	DE	163
Elizabeth	22	DE	26
Elizabeth	45	DE	81
Elizabeth	53	DE	277
Emeline	34	DE	30
Emeline H	15	DE	163
Eunice W B	3	DE	164
Hannah W	15	DE	122
Harriet	9	DE	201
Hetty A	5	DE	122
Isaac	49	DE	81
Isaac J	27	DE	30
James	2	DE	81
James E	12	DE	161
James E	25	DE	26
James K	27	DE	84
Job	14	DE	282
John J	9	DE	122
John M	40	DE	122
Jonathan	18	DE	81
Joseph	6	DE	81
Joseph B	18	DE	161
Leah	54	DE	29
Louisa	13	DE	163
Manaen B	22	DE	163
Martha J	16	DE	161
Mary A	12	DE	122
Mary E	1	DE	30
Miers B	15	DE	161
Nancy	35	DE	122
Nancy E	8	DE	277
Nancy P	1	DE	122
Nathaniel	30	DE	277
Polly	63	DE	288
Rachel	20	DE	81
Rhoda	42	MD	201
Rhoda T	1	DE	201
Robert J	4	DE	30
Robert W	34	DE	30
Sally A	17	DE	163
Samuel	9	DE	161
Samuel	9	DE	164
Samuel	53	DE	163
Samuel	72	DE	161
Sarah	5	DE	30
Sarah A	18	DE	26
Sarah E	15	DE	81
Sarah J	20	DE	30
Silas J	11	DE	122
Sophia	21	DE	161
Stephen J	1	DE	30
Susan	7	DE	30
Walker	17	DE	81
William H	24	DE	277
Winget	24	DE	163
Winget	25	DE	166
Beverlin, Wm	28	IE	211
Beyman, Elizabeth	56	DE	36
Beyman, Elizabeth	56	DE	36
John	38	DE	36
Julia	36	DE	36
Seth T	13	DE	36
Beynum, Ann E	23	DE	33
Delthinia	11/12	DE	33
Ellen O	21	DE	20
Ellen O	49	DE	20
Elizabeth A	18	DE	20
Henry O	15	DE	20
Henry O	49	DE	20
James	28	DE	33
Biddle, George	2	DE	46
Isaiah	12	DE	77
Bignal, David	6	DE	192
Elizabeth	3	DE	192
Hetty	18	DE	16
John	9	DE	192
John	45	DE	192
Louisa	12	DE	192
Mary	42	DE	192
Susanna	15	DE	192
Bird, Hiram H	4	DE	263
Birtcher, James S	21	DE	180
John W	18	DE	180
Mary	43	DE	180
Robert	50	DE	180
Robert R	8	DE	180
Bishop, Ann C	7	DE	127
James	34	DE	127
James H	36	MD	131
Jane W	30	DE	131
John H	1	DE	131
Martha J	5	DE	127
Mary A	3	DE	131
Mary E	2	DE	127
Sarah H	31	DE	127
Bivins, James	40	DE	173
John	46	DE	158
Mary	30	DE	173
Priscilla	50	DE	158
Black, David	16	DE	82
David	47	DE	82
Ellis	9	DE	220
George F	22	DE	82
Henry	35	MD	220
James M	24	DE	82
Letitia	15	DE	220
Lucretia	12	DE	220
Nathaniel	17	DE	58
Rebecca	13	DE	220
Robert	8	DE	82
Robert	11	DE	58
Sarah	18	DE	82
Sarah	49	DE	82
Sophia A	15	DE	58
Wesly	14	DE	220
William E	14	DE	82
Wineford	6	DE	58
Blades, Charles	23	DE	243
Edward	31	DE	199
Ezekiel W	16	DE	115
James	14	DE	115
James	24	MD	244
James M	27	DE	199
Joshua	12	DE	30
Joshua H	19	DE	115
Leonard	7	DE	199
Mary	70	DE	199
Mary J	17	DE	115
Mary M	29	MD	199
Sarah	7	DE	199
Traphena	2	DE	199
William	37	DE	199
William J	1	DE	199
Blain, Ann E	12	DE	218
Elizabeth M	15	DE	218
Isaac	12	DE	126
James	6	DE	126
Blizzard, Alfred	10	DE	18
Alfred	10	DE	186
Ann E	9	DE	26

Name	Age	State	No.
Blizzard, Burton	21	DE	152
Catharine A	22	DE	186
Coard	5	DE	18
Coard E	5	DE	186
David	40	DE	5
David R	30	DE	192
Emily	17	DE	186
Emily	18	DE	18
George	25	DE	7
George A	2	DE	186
Gideon W	25	DE	186
Hannah	1	DE	186
Henry C	10	DE	26
James	17	DE	191
James	19	DE	187
James	19	DE	18
James E	24	DE	185
John T	19	DE	26
Joshua M	7	DE	26
Levin	45	DE	18
Levin	50	DE	186
Ludowick	22	DE	19
Lydia E	14	DE	192
Margaret A	19	DE	192
Martha J	18	DE	164
Mary	53	DE	142
Mary	60	DE	186
Mary A	22	DE	185
Mary J	23	DE	186
Milley	26	DE	6
Paynter F	52	DE	176
Peter	60	DE	142
Robert T	2	DE	192
Samuel	5	DE	18
Samuel	8	DE	186
Sarah	34	DE	26
Sarah	45	DE	18
Sarah	50	DE	186
Sarah A	20	DE	164
Sarah E	12	DE	36
Stephen	89	DE	186
Stephen E	14	DE	26
William B	58	DE	19
William H	5	DE	177
William J	1	DE	185
Blocksom, Adaline	4	DE	200
Amy	35	DE	200
Ann E	28	DE	11
Arthur	3	DE	200
Benjamin T	10	DE	11
David	25	DE	8
Dennis F	10/12	DE	200
Elizabeth	11	DE	200
Caroline	3	DE	11
Elizabeth	37	DE	11
Ellen	9	DE	200
Hannah E	7	DE	11
Hetty E	40	DE	11
Hetty Ann	17	DE	11
James	34	DE	11
Jesse	11	DE	11
Jesse	55	DE	11
John L	6	DE	12
John T	27	DE	207
Joseph	1/12	DE	11
Lydia A	9	DE	12
Lydia A	15	DE	17
Margaret	14	DE	28
Matilda	16	DE	11
Margaret A	2	DE	11
Priscilla	1	DE	12
Richard	4	DE	12
Richard	49	DE	11
Sarah E	16	DE	12
Sarah	12	DE	11
Shadrack	10	DE	200
Shadrack	54	DE	200
Robert	8	DE	11
Samuel	15	DE	11
Blocksum, Elizabeth E	9	DE	198
Leah	38	DE	198
Noah	39	DE	198
Blocksum, John E	11	DE	198
George W	12	DE	198
Noah	39	DE	198
Noah W	39	DE	198
Blossom, Benjamin M	7	DE	275
Emma	6/12	DE	275
James	14	DE	275
Leah	39	DE	275
Margaret	5	DE	275
Rachel	9	DE	275
Sarah	15	DE	275
Sarah H	18	DE	275
Spencer	47	DE	275
William	3	DE	275
Boice, Augustus	23	DE	203
Euphemia	27	DE	203
Bolton, Crecy	50	DE	97
David	5	DE	97
Eliza	7	DE	97
Margaret	11	DE	97
Smith	54	DE	97
William	19	DE	97
Boman, Eliza	11	DE	153
Samuel T	18	DE	189
Bonney, Samuel O	18	DE	92
William	10	DE	92
Bookfield, Isaac	17	DE	215
Bosten, Erenine	18	DE	223
James	2	DE	224
James	41	MD	223
Mary	38	DE	223
Mary A	6	DE	224
Sarah J	3	DE	224
Tilghman	2	DE	224
Bostin, Isaac	16	DE	224
Boston, Harriett	34	DE	198
Sallie S	11	DE	198
Bounds, Caroline	8	DE	157
Charles	7	DE	157
Charles	44	DE	157
Elizabeth	32	DE	179
George	5	DE	158
Hetty A	13	DE	157
Jacob	13	DE	179
James M	9	DE	179
Joseph	6	DE	179
Leah	43	DE	157
Leah A	26	DE	157
Mary E	1	DE	179
Plymouth	55	DE	179
Bowden, Ann	23	DE	161
Burton	18	DE	276
David	3	DE	276
James	25	MD	276
John	1	DE	276
John	21	DE	276
Kendal	24	DE	161
Leah	25	MD	276
Pellena F	2	DE	161
Sarah J	1	DE	161
Bowerscott, Geo W	30	DE	196
Bowery, Burton	6/12	NJ	40
Eliza	4	NJ	40
John	26	NJ	40
Sarah E	2	NJ	40
William	2	NJ	40
Bowman, Andrew	16	DE	255
Hetty	41	DE	258
Maria	10	DE	258
Samuel T	18	DE	188
Boyce, Ann	16	DE	282
Ann	24	DE	235
Ann	44	DE	295
Ann Eliza	8	DE	111
Ann M	20	DE	100
Charles	3	DE	245
Charles	3	DE	247
Comfort J	14	DE	237
Cyrus W	1	DE	291
Daniel	6	DE	245
Daniel	28	DE	247
David	6	DE	247
Boyce, David	43	DE	297
David	50	DE	290
David H	27	DE	291
Elisha	25	DE	235
Ellison	25	DE	100
Elison	55	DE	294
Eliza	42	DE	297
Elizabeth	18	DE	273
Elizabeth	19	NC	269
Elizabeth	21	DE	296
Fanny	56	DE	269
George	8	DE	297
George B	17	DE	294
George B	19	DE	294
George W	23	DE	269
George W	25	DE	273
Hannah	53	DE	290
Hetty	40	DE	290
Hiram	20	DE	290
James	6	DE	111
James	19	DE	293
James	43	DE	111
James N	87	DE	294
Jane	15	DE	295
John	5	DE	297
John	12	DE	294
John	19	DE	239
John	23	DE	269
John	26	DE	6
John	40	DE	297
John	52	DE	295
Jonathan	17	DE	294
Josea	17	DE	296
Joseph	61	DE	269
Joshua	21	DE	269
Julia	25	DE	291
Julia A	9	DE	269
Lavenia	29	DE	294
Margaret	27	DE	245
Margaret	27	DE	247
Martha	18	DE	296
Mary	2/12	DE	100
Mary	10	DE	297
Mary	30	DE	297
Mary	52	DE	297
Mary	56	DE	296
Miranda	10	DE	291
Nancy	12	DE	269
Noah	32	DE	297
Obed	10	DE	111
Peter	50	DE	297
Rebecca	20	DE	294
Robert	4	DE	291
Samuel	2	DE	245
Samuel	2	DE	247
Samuel	18	DE	239
Samuel	55	DE	290
Sarah	17	DE	239
Sarah R	37	DE	111
Thomas	9	DE	245
Thomas	9	DE	247
William	16	DE	293
Boyer, Samuel	31	DE	203
Bozman, Ann	25	DE	238
Columbia	7	DE	238
Edward	17	DE	227
Elizabeth	10	DE	227
Jensey	19	DE	214
John	40	DE	238
Louisa	16	DE	227
Mary	3	DE	238
Rebecca	52	DE	227
Revel	45	DE	227
Sarah	5/12	DE	238
William	13	DE	227
Bradley, Elijah	63	DE	93
Eliza	19	DE	83
George	15	DE	93
Melcha	65	DE	198
Susan	11	DE	93
Susan	50	DE	93
Talbot	8	DE	93

Name	Age	St	No.
Bradly, Aaron	15	DE	210
Allen R	22	DE	244
Anthony	4	DE	210
B H	25	DE	247
Caroline	37	DE	197
Charlotte	18	DE	229
Christopher	27	DE	244
Daniel	5	DE	197
David	16	DE	199
David H	2	DE	210
Delila	10	DE	252
Elizabeth	22	DE	244
Elizabeth	44	DE	252
Elizabeth	48	DE	244
Fordman	21	DE	252
Gatty	35	DE	206
George	5	DE	252
George	10	DE	203
Hannah	10	DE	210
Henry	19	DE	212
Hester	61	DE	245
Huffington	26	DE	245
Isaac	9	DE	211
Isaac	25	DE	197
Isaac W	12	MD	211
James	24	DE	243
James B	36	DE	244
James F	15	DE	245
James J	5	MD	245
James T	3/12	DE	206
Jesse A D	49	DE	244
John A B	18	DE	244
John D	5	MD	245
John W	4	DE	199
Joseph	19	DE	211
Joseph	28	DE	243
Joseph B	14	DE	244
Josephine	12	DE	244
Kezziah	50	DE	229
Lemuel	17	MD	245
Levinia	8	DE	210
Lucinda	24	DE	267
Lucinda A	35	MD	244
Major D	8	DE	245
Margaret	17	DE	210
Margaret	26	MD	243
Margaret E	17	DE	252
Maria J	7	DE	198
Mary	23	DE	247
Mary	71	DE	245
Mary A	23	DE	237
Mary E	13	MD	245
Mary J	13	DE	252
Peter	38	DE	210
Peter	40	DE	244
Phebe	24	DE	267
Phebe	42	MD	244
Phellan	51	DE	201
Philis W	8	DE	252
Rachel	38	MD	244
Rachel E	14	DE	244
Rebecca	3	MD	245
Richard	77	DE	244
Richard H	12	DE	244
Rosanna	12	DE	210
Sally	50	MD	245
Samuel	15	DE	252
Sarah	7	DE	203
Sarah	36	DE	210
Sarah	49	MD	244
Sarah A	19	DE	244
Sarah E	3	DE	199
Sarah E	18	DE	252
Sinah R	20	DE	244
Soverein	43	DE	252
Stephen T	22	DE	252
Susan	14	DE	223
Thomas	31	DE	243
Truman	39	DE	244
Wash J	19	MD	244
William	10/12	DE	267
William	24	DE	226
Bradly, Wm	7	DE	211
Brambley, Adam	28	MD	139
Isaac	11	DE	139
James	40	MD	139
John	12	DE	139
Joseph L	8	DE	139
Margaret	26	MD	139
Rebecca	80	MD	139
Sarah H	5	DE	139
Brasure, Amos	15	DE	142
Ann M	12	DE	127
Basheba	16	DE	112
Belitha	14	DE	154
Benton H	45	DE	127
Catherine	7	DE	142
Catherine	21	DE	127
Charlotte J	11	DE	168
Elijah	18	DE	127
Elijah	63	DE	94
Eliza D	12	DE	142
Elizabeth	12	DE	126
Elizabeth	13	DE	127
Elizabeth	34	DE	127
Elizabeth	39	DE	127
Emeline D	2	DE	112
Gardiner H	7	DE	168
George	15	DE	94
George	23	DE	154
Godfrey	53	MD	154
Hannah	22	DE	112
Henry J	24	DE	112
Hester A	16	DE	154
Hetty	12	DE	126
Hetty	34	DE	168
Jacob H	31	DE	126
James	32	DE	127
James	70	DE	126
James A	23	DE	127
James L	6	DE	127
John	4	DE	112
John	35	DE	168
John E	19	DE	127
John H	6/12	DE	168
Joseph	45	DE	154
Joseph B	17	DE	154
Joshua	9	DE	142
Joshua H	17	DE	171
Julia	11	DE	142
Lemuel	5	DE	142
Littleton	13	DE	142
Lovey	46	DE	154
Lydia	39	DE	142
Lydia A	9	DE	168
Margaret	6	DE	112
Margaret J	29	DE	126
Mary	11	DE	142
Mary	14	DE	127
Mary	15	DE	127
Mary C	4	DE	168
Mary Elizabeth	13	DE	112
Mary J	25	DE	112
Mitchel G	3	DE	127
Muriel P	1	DE	127
Perry	27	DE	154
Samuel S	1	DE	128
Sarah	46	DE	127
Sarah J	8	DE	127
Silas	4	DE	127
Sophia	70	DE	126
William J	51	DE	112
William T	20	DE	135
Brereton, Sarah	78	DE	38
Bretell, Eliza	10	DE	3
Mary	27	DE	7
Brewenton, Daniel	18	DE	47
Lidia	35	DE	64
Briley, Scarborah	24	MD	125
Brimer, Alexander	4	DE	162
Caleb	13	DE	162
Harriet	18	DE	162
Joseph	1	DE	163
Joshua	11	DE	162
Brimer, Joshua	11	DE	162
Mary	9	DE	162
Rachel	34	MD	162
Thomas	7	DE	162
Thomas	46	VA	162
Brinkley, Wm S	14	DE	292
Brinkloe, Caroline	2	DE	39
Catharine	13	DE	39
Charles	12	DE	55
Emeline	34	DE	55
John B	23	DE	3
Mariah	22	DE	39
Milley	55	DE	39
Peter	55	DE	39
Peter Wesley	4	DE	39
Robert	17	DE	39
Susan	20	DE	39
William	11	DE	39
William	15	DE	55
Brisington, Mathias	21	?	205
Brister, Zepa	26	DE	275
Britell, Mary	27	DE	6
Britenham, Kendal	26	MD	260
Mary	26	MD	260
Sabra	1	DE	260
Brittenham, Alfred	4	DE	54
Catharine	20	DE	28
Emma	2	DE	54
Hetty	10	DE	54
Hetty	36	DE	54
Joseph	17	DE	276
Joseph	47	DE	54
Moses	5	DE	28
Moses	26	DE	28
William	3	DE	28
Brittingham, Eliza A	2	DE	43
Elizabeth	48	DE	66
James	35	DE	43
John	45	DE	66
Levinia C	9/12	DE	67
Lidia H	19	DE	66
Mary	29	DE	43
Mary C	15	DE	66
Rachael	18	DE	67
Samuel H	23	DE	67
Thomas S	21	DE	181
Brookfield, Alexander	6	DE	230
Asbury	16	DE	206
Brister	60	DE	207
Charles W	1	DE	207
Eliza	7	DE	43
Elizabeth	28	DE	207
Elizabeth H	17	DE	207
Wm	14	DE	204
Zeppy	19	DE	197
Brown, Alberton	4	DE	223
Alsey	27	DE	240
Amanda M	6	DE	24
Amelia	21	DE	210
Andrew	18	DE	61
Ann	25	DE	218
Ann	25	DE	231
Ann	27	DE	223
Ann R	9	DE	223
Anthony	24	DE	100
Benjamin	60	DE	269
Betsy	45	DE	61
Catherine	35	DE	212
Charles	10/12	DE	218
Charles	6	DE	51
Charles H	4	DE	44
Charles M	3	DE	235
Chloe	35	DE	81
Comfort E	1	DE	44
Daniel	32	DE	240
Daniel	33	DE	218
Deborah	17	DE	205
Deborah	29	DE	235
Dennis	17	DE	205
Dinah	80	DE	225
Eliza	22	DE	216
Eliza	49	DE	210

Name			
Brown, Elizabeth	13	DE	81
Elizabeth	21	DE	204
Elizabeth J	6/12	DE	235
Eunica	32	DE	216
Frances	51	DE	197
Francis	12	DE	24
George	3	DE	240
George	14	DE	222
George	16	DE	217
George	17	GB	115
George	17	DE	269
George T	14	DE	24
George W	7	DE	196
Greensbury	62	DE	61
Greensbury L	10	DE	61
Hannah	26	DE	44
Harry	55	DE	294
Henry W	8	DE	210
Hester	28	DE	223
Hetty A	14	DE	131
Hugh	49	MD	210
Hugh C	16	DE	210
Humphreys	43	DE	24
Isaac	10	DE	81
Isaac	45	DE	81
James	2	DE	218
James	65	DE	215
James A	13	DE	210
James F	3/12	DE	207
Jesse	51	DE	210
John	15	GB	117
John	15	DE	131
John	16	DE	223
John	30	DE	223
John K	23	DE	204
John L	8	DE	44
Joseph	46	DE	204
Joshua	26	DE	217
Julia	1/12	DE	100
Ketty H	9	DE	136
Lavinia	25	DE	216
Leah	62	DE	269
Levin B	25	DE	210
Margaret	2	DE	224
Margaret	7	OH	223
Margaret	40	DE	201
Margaret C	26	DE	196
Margaret J	9	DE	24
Maria	39	DE	294
Maria	51	DE	210
Martha T	2	DE	61
Mary	6	DE	218
Mary	15	DE	210
Mary	25	DE	56
Mary	34	DE	131
Mary A	12	DE	223
Mary C	8	DE	235
Mary E	8/12	DE	240
Mary E	2	DE	51
Mary E	4	DE	196
Mary E	17	DE	24
Mary J	7	DE	131
Nathaniel H	10	DE	210
Nancy	71	DE	51
Rachel	5	DE	240
Rachel	18	DE	269
Rachel	38	DE	24
Rachel	45	DE	217
Rachel A	1	DE	235
Rebecca	19	DE	209
Robert L	25	DE	204
Robert W	9	DE	24
Sallie	38	DE	223
Samuel	17	DE	217
Sarah	23	DE	100
Sarah A	13	DE	210
Sarah E	2	DE	223
Sarah E	16	DE	210
Sarah H	45	DE	197
Sarah J	12	DE	217
Sarah W	18	DE	210
Shepherd	21	DE	210
Brown, Simon	29	DE	235
Sinah	73	DE	227
Sophia	25	DE	216
Soveren A	18	DE	210
Thomas	20	DE	209
Thomas	57	DE	217
Thomas H	18	DE	210
Thomas T	40	DE	223
Tilghman	26	DE	216
Urimina	1/12	DE	24
William	1	DE	223
William	28	DE	216
William	35	DE	44
William	35	DE	227
William P	31	DE	196
William Z	5	DE	44
Wm R	16	DE	217
Bruff, Ann M	4	PA	200
Elizabeth A	10	PA	200
John M	40	MD	200
Bruington, Sarah J	18	MD	201
Bruinton, Harriet	30	MD	260
Brumbly, Deany	48	DE	48
Wilson S	49	DE	48
Bryan, Burton	25	DE	281
Luvey	54	DE	281
Robert	21	DE	22
Sarah	50	DE	28
William	52	DE	281
Wolsy B	13	DE	281
Buchanan, Anna C	7	DE	73
Mary C	9	DE	73
Buck, Charles	64	DE	275
Elizabeth	52	DE	275
Emilia	80	DE	263
Kesiah	32	DE	214
Buckham, George	5	DE	230
Buley, Scarborah	24	MD	126
Bull, David	21	DE	113
Huldy J	14	DE	126
John	13	DE	113
John	45	DE	113
Josiah	45	DE	136
Lemuel	12	DE	131
Mannon	19	DE	113
Mary A	16	DE	113
Mary K	26	DE	113
Nancy	39	DE	136
William	1	DE	113
Bullett, Eunice J	25	DE	190
George R	3	DE	190
William	26	DE	190
Bunting, Anna	34	DE	132
Anna	35	DE	132
Arcada	15	DE	132
Catherine	7	DE	133
Charles	21	DE	132
Charlotte	3	DE	138
Charlotte	45	DE	132
Charlotte P	3	DE	133
Dolly	13	DE	138
Edward	15	DE	132
Eleanor	31	DE	132
Elijah	36	DE	132
Elizabeth	41	DE	132
Ephraim	13	DE	132
Gatty	7	DE	142
Gatty	20	DE	133
George	8	DE	138
George	9	DE	133
George	40	DE	132
Isaiah	18	DE	132
Jackson	1	DE	133
James	12	DE	133
John	2	DE	133
Joseph	11	DE	138
Julia A	2	DE	133
Lemuel	4	DE	133
Margaret	1	DE	138
Mary A	44	DE	133
Merril	46	DE	132
Milby	16	DE	132
Bunting, Milby	39	DE	138
Mitchell	17	DE	138
Neely	57	DE	133
Peter	7	DE	132
Prude	8	DE	133
Retty	41	DE	138
Samson	9	DE	133
Sarah	4	DE	138
William	11	DE	132
William	26	DE	133
Burbage, Ananias T	24	DE	117
Catharine B	24	DE	120
Elizabeth	22	DE	20
Henry S	59	DE	121
Henry W	25	DE	121
James	25	DE	134
John R	1	DE	117
Mary C	14	DE	120
Priscilla	25	DE	121
Sarah J	20	NJ	117
Silas H	3	DE	121
Thomas J	4	DE	21
Walter H	28	DE	120
Wethy	42	DE	120
William A	1/12	DE	21
Burr, David P	7	DE	46
Hudson	10	DE	46
Hudson	43	DE	46
Joseph A	18	DE	46
Martha H	43	DE	46
Sarah R	16	DE	46
William J	14	DE	46
Burrows, Amina	17	DE	66
Andrew	5	DE	226
Eli	26	DE	36
Eliza J	3	DE	18
Frances A	11	DE	18
George P	11	DE	66
Hetty	52	DE	20
James W	21	DE	66
Joseph	26	DE	20
Joseph A	3	DE	18
Louisa H	10	DE	20
Lydia	29	DE	18
Lydia	50	DE	66
Mahala	23	DE	36
Martha J	20	DE	66
Mary L	6	DE	18
Priscilla	10	DE	294
Sarah	8	DE	18
Sarah A	22	DE	54
Robert J	10	DE	66
Selby E	6/12	DE	18
Selby W	29	DE	18
William	24	DE	66
William	55	DE	66
Burton, Albertus	63	DE	46
Albian	76	DE	114
Alfred C	6	DE	169
Alfred S	7	DE	177
Alice	59	DE	49
Amarid	30	DE	172
Ann	15	DE	80
Ann	30	DE	61
Ann	75	DE	57
Anna	4	DE	193
Annlea	47	DE	183
Ann Eliza	24	DE	179
Arcada	59	DE	179
Benjamin	10	DE	56
Benjamin	40	DE	56
Benjamin	40	DE	173
Benjamin D	25	DE	173
Benjamin H	12	DE	190
Benjamin W T	1/12	DE	52
Caroline	4	DE	60
Caroline	6	DE	176
Caroline	8	DE	50
Catharine	8	DE	193
Catharine	25	DE	58
Catharine	25	DE	72
Catharine	28	DE	173

Name	Age		Page
Burton, Catharine	35	DE	56
Catharine	70	DE	177
Catharine C H	7	DE	51
Catharine E	5	DE	177
Cato	45	DE	193
Celia	2	DE	50
Celia	22	DE	56
Charles	4	DE	141
Charles	10	DE	176
Charles	50	DE	177
Charlotte	41	DE	188
Comfort	41	DE	56
Comfort	60	DE	58
Cornelius	4	DE	30
Cudgo	3	DE	189
Cudgo	64	DE	189
Cyrus	11	DE	193
Daniel	8	DE	193
Daniel	11	DE	173
Daniel	38	DE	80
David	2	DE	173
David	32	DE	170
David B	49	DE	56
David S	6	DE	183
Deborah	11	DE	45
Edward	5	DE	47
Edward	21	DE	186
Edward	25	DE	179
Edward A	9	DE	188
Edward S	9	DE	173
Edwin C	27	DE	177
Elhannon W	15	DE	45
Eli	20	DE	168
Elijah	25	DE	60
Elisha	17	DE	171
Eliza	1	DE	290
Eliza	2	DE	50
Eliza	17	DE	168
Elizabeth	15	DE	193
Elizabeth	17	DE	119
Elizabeth	27	DE	47
Elizabeth	34	DE	177
Elizabeth	35	DE	177
Elizabeth	41	DE	50
Elizabeth	60	DE	179
Elizabeth A	1	DE	171
Elizabeth L	35	DE	171
Elizabeth W	6	DE	51
Ellen	15	DE	168
Elmira	3	DE	56
Elsy	2	DE	60
Emeline	22	DE	193
Emily	21	DE	177
Emma Jane	3	DE	177
Eunice A	34	DE	179
Francis A	30	DE	177
Francis M	21	DE	10
Franklin E	3	DE	49
Frederick	4	DE	176
Gardiner H	11	DE	176
George	8	DE	74
George	9	DE	137
George	10	DE	193
George	14	DE	51
George	35	DE	61
George E	3	DE	191
George H	7	DE	173
George H	9	DE	181
George M	13	DE	156
George R	7	DE	194
Gideon M	19	DE	10
Gilbert	3	DE	172
Hannah	1	DE	30
Hannah	1	DE	176
Hannah	9	DE	6
Hannah	46	DE	137
Hannah	55	DE	51
Hannah A	6	DE	56
Hannah E	17	DE	186
Hannah P	45	DE	186
Hannah S	1	DE	191
Henry	23	DE	72
Burton, Henry	23	DE	72
Henry H	7	DE	190
Henry L	5	DE	171
Hester	7/12	DE	72
Hester E	9	DE	62
Hetty	4	DE	57
Hetty	32	DE	169
Hetty	40	DE	10
Hetty A	12	DE	192
Hetty H	19	DE	194
Heveloe	29	DE	30
Hiram R	8	DE	49
Isaac	30	DE	56
Isaac	85	DE	114
Isaac E	83	DE	171
Isaiah C S	20	DE	45
Jacob	25	DE	77
Jacob	50	DE	74
Jacob	51	DE	51
Jacob	56	DE	156
Jacob	80	DE	10
James	3	DE	77
James	6	DE	30
James	7	DE	184
James	10	DE	74
James	42	DE	193
James	70	DE	171
James A	37	DE	192
James D	2	DE	56
James S	2	DE	192
James T	40	DE	188
Jane	2	DE	56
Jane	28	DE	51
Job	8	DE	80
John	1	DE	77
John	3	DE	56
John	6	DE	137
John	10	DE	56
John	21	DE	119
John	23	DE	168
John	24	DE	179
John	45	DE	62
John	55	DE	119
John A	35	DE	177
John B	38	DE	184
John B	50	DE	183
John C	1	DE	56
John C	3	DE	177
John C	7	DE	62
John C	85	DE	190
John H	36	DE	176
John H	44	DE	194
John of J	60	DE	45
John P	26	DE	178
John R	37	DE	47
John R	45	DE	51
John S	21	DE	183
John W	50	DE	168
Joseph	8	DE	47
Joseph M	5	DE	177
Josephine M	14	DE	186
Joshua	40	DE	50
Joshua R	6	DE	50
Joshua S	42	DE	49
Judy	2	DE	51
Julia	20	DE	113
Laura J	7	DE	176
Leah A	1	DE	156
Lemuel	8	DE	56
Lemuel J	10	DE	50
Lemuel P	34	DE	191
Letty	50	DE	74
Lot	19	DE	51
Louisa	13	DE	47
Louisa A	11/12	DE	173
Louisa C	32	DE	176
Love	50	DE	168
Lydia	7	DE	77
Lydia	15	DE	74
Lydia	32	DE	176
Lydia	51	DE	177
Lydia A	3/12	DE	177
Burton, Lydia A	12	DE	50
Lydia E	36	DE	190
Lydia H	2	DE	190
Lydia H	17	DE	45
Lydia J	11	DE	193
Lydia R	5	DE	56
Maria	1	DE	61
Maria	8	DE	119
Maria	9	DE	144
Maria	58	DE	177
Maria S	24	DE	45
Martha	6	DE	72
Martha	17	DE	6
Martha A	12	DE	61
Margaret A	7	DE	178
Margaret A R	23	DE	6
Margaret W	6	DE	190
Mary	7	DE	171
Mary	10	DE	47
Mary	13	DE	80
Mary	25	DE	60
Mary	40	DE	62
Mary A	4	DE	62
Mary A	8	DE	61
Mary A	16	DE	190
Mary A	40	DE	192
Mary C	4	DE	50
Mary C	9	DE	177
Mary H	7	DE	186
Mary H	12	DE	179
Mary H	31	DE	177
Mary J	28	DE	178
Mary J	32	DE	51
Mary J	37	DE	191
Mary P	10	DE	194
Mary S	2	DE	52
Mary S	2	DE	177
Mary W	26	DE	190
Miers	8	DE	169
Milford	65	DE	58
Moses	12	DE	189
Naney	1	DE	119
Naney	60	DE	63
Naney M	22	DE	181
Nathaniel M	33	DE	181
Neecy	8	DE	170
Noah	55	DE	51
Patience	10	DE	80
Patience	36	DE	80
Patience	66	DE	189
Pemberton	2	DE	178
Peter R	5	DE	194
Peter R	28	DE	178
Peter W	31	DE	190
Phebe	44	DE	193
Phillis	60	DE	171
Polly	76	DE	194
Priscilla	20	DE	68
Rachel	19	DE	51
Rachel	25	DE	177
Reece	5	DE	61
Robert	4	DE	52
Robert	13	DE	119
Robert H	22	DE	179
Robert Hunter	5	DE	178
Rodney	1	DE	49
Rosanna	35	DE	193
Rosanna	93	DE	51
Rosey Ann	14	DE	60
Ruth	6	DE	60
Ruth H	7	DE	61
Ruth H	31	DE	49
Sallie A	19	DE	186
Sally	6	DE	172
Sally L	10	DE	49
Salmon R	30	DE	10
Sarah	6	DE	80
Sarah	6	DE	193
Sarah	8	DE	193
Sarah	12	DE	137
Sarah	18	DE	74
Sarah	28	DE	177

Name	Age	State	No.
Burton, Sarah	30	DE	57
Sarah	33	DE	184
Sarah	41	DE	15
Sarah	66	DE	46
Sarah	82	DE	193
Sarah A	1	DE	194
Sarah A	5	DE	190
Sarah A	17	DE	176
Sarah A	20	DE	173
Sarah A	27	DE	170
Sarah E	4	DE	56
Sarah E	4	DE	61
Sarah J	8	DE	156
Sarah J	38	DE	156
Sarah Jane	16	DE	10
Sarah P	37	DE	194
Sophia J	32	DE	178
Spencer	45	DE	137
Susan	9	DE	60
Susan	12	DE	74
Susan	25	DE	77
Susan	64	DE	172
Theodore	3	DE	176
Theodore H	14	DE	188
Thomas	14	DE	278
Thomas R	6	DE	278
Thomas W	45	DE	176
Virginia	1	DE	170
Walter	5	DE	49
Walter D	1	DE	178
Walter F	4	DE	169
William	4	DE	184
William	25	PA	45
William C	6	DE	156
William C	28	DE	179
William D	11	DE	119
William E	30	DE	170
William H	3	DE	56
William J	13	DE	56
William N	33	DE	177
William R	17	DE	183
William T	28	DE	177
Williard	1	DE	169
Woolsey	33	DE	169
Bury, Martha	25	DE	88
White	30	DE	88
Bustard, Charlotte W	35	DE	34
Butcher, Elizabeth	24	DE	9
Ellen	58	DE	9
Richard	29	DE	9
Butler, Ann	35	MD	220
Benjamin	12	DE	5
David A	7	DE	5
Elizabeth	49	DE	5
Ellen	15	DE	146
George	17	DE	146
Harriet	4	DE	5
James	21	DE	5
James	52	DE	5
Jemima	35	DE	9
Laban	30	MD	220
Margarett	15	DE	5
Mary	60	DE	146
Mary E P	5/12	DE	220
Mary J	17	DE	5
Nancy	30	DE	9
Sally A	19	DE	5
Samuel	60	DE	146
Sarah H	19	DE	146
Bynum, James H	5	DE	11
Cade, Andrew	14	DE	29
Ann B	28	DE	224
Asbury	13	DE	224
Elizabeth A	19	DE	224
John	33	DE	224
John B	3/12	DE	224
John H	2/12	DE	224
John H	15	DE	15
Leah	45	DE	29
Letty	20	DE	29
Nancy	56	DE	224
Cade, Sampson	50	DE	29
Samuel A	22	DE	121
Sarah	24	DE	211
Talbot	10	DE	29
Calaway, Bridget	35	DE	42
Calhoon, Charles H	1	DE	68
Comfort	15	DE	68
Elizabeth	10	DE	68
Elizabeth	40	DE	68
Joseph A	17	DE	68
Nancy	12	DE	68
Peter	49	DE	68
Rachael	6	DE	68
Sials	16	DE	283
Thomas	18	DE	57
Uphema	57	DE	283
William S	4	DE	68
Calhoun, Alexander	6/12	DE	297
Ann E	11	DE	116
Cedny	27	DE	297
David	29	DE	296
Eliza	24	DE	76
Ephraim	5/12	DE	116
Ephraim	38	MD	116
Ephraim P	6	DE	116
Francis Ann	23	DE	82
George C	5	DE	297
George W	4	DE	116
Hetty	24	DE	116
Hetty	29	DE	119
James A	8/12	DE	116
John	21	DE	282
John	33	DE	82
John	41	DE	116
John H	5	DE	119
John H	17	DE	116
Leonora F	3	DE	119
Lydia Ann	1/12	DE	82
Martha C	2	DE	119
Martha D	8	DE	116
Mary	2	DE	82
Mary A	2	DE	116
Nehemiah H	13	DE	116
Peter	30	DE	76
Sally	53	DE	76
Sarah	5	DE	76
Sarah	38	DE	117
Sarah E	4	DE	82
Silas	16	DE	282
Smiley	40	DE	119
Uphema	51	DE	282
William C	15	DE	116
Callars, Catherine	10	DE	2
Callaway, Alford	29	DE	294
Ann	57	DE	292
Arena A	3	DE	258
Benton W	28	DE	242
Bethena	12	DE	257
Charlotte	22	DE	241
Denis	14	DE	257
Eba	24	DE	269
Eben	60	DE	257
Eleanor	25	DE	242
Elihu	40	DE	257
Elijah	66	DE	269
Elisha	9	DE	273
Eliza	30	DE	295
Eliza H M	2	DE	242
Elizabeth	24	DE	269
Elizabeth	56	DE	273
Emeline	22	DE	258
Frances	6/12	DE	242
Frances	61	DE	242
George F	4	DE	295
Henry	28	DE	237
Hetty	45	DE	257
James	5	DE	257
James	21	DE	236
James	22	DE	273
Job M	25	DE	242
John	22	DE	258
John W	1	DE	295
Callaway, John W	33	DE	295
Jonas	3	DE	294
Joseph H	7	DE	295
Joseph S	22	DE	242
Josephus	12	DE	258
Kendal	81	DE	273
Levi	10	DE	258
Levin	1	DE	258
Levin	30	DE	233
Levin	64	DE	242
Levin S	6	DE	239
Malvina	2	DE	258
Mary	2	DE	269
Mary	12	DE	257
Mary	25	DE	233
Nancy	36	DE	247
Nancy A	10	DE	234
Nehemiah	61	DE	234
Nehemiah H	9	DE	234
Phebe	8	DE	239
Rebecca	25	DE	273
Sallie	41	DE	258
Sallie	52	DE	234
Samuel	1	DE	257
Samuel	28	DE	269
Samuel	30	DE	257
Sarah	7/12	DE	294
Sarah	4	DE	257
Sarah	24	DE	294
Sarah	30	DE	257
Washington	28	DE	258
William	4	DE	242
William	17	DE	292
William	20	DE	258
William	22	DE	269
William	24	DE	257
William F	6	DE	295
Wm S	10	DE	239
Calloway, George W	20	DE	218
Polly	68	DE	255
William	8	DE	256
Camel, Catharine	34	DE	73
Charlotte	20	DE	73
Elizabeth	24	DE	73
John	65	DE	73
Mary	35	DE	73
Mary	52	DE	73
Susan J	27	DE	73
Cameron, Asbury	23	MD	248
Burton	3	DE	248
Isaac	5	DE	248
Jane	19	MD	248
Julia A	9	DE	248
Lambert	11	MD	248
Leah	17	DE	248
Mary	43	MD	248
Nancy	15	MD	248
Noah	44	MD	248
Sarah	2	DE	248
William A	26	KY	164
Campbell, Ann M	8	DE	138
Benjamin	25	DE	140
Benton	2	DE	138
Burton	25	DE	288
Caroline	9	DE	138
Catharine	7	DE	138
Catharine	48	DE	132
Charles	4	DE	139
Christian	8	DE	139
Comfort	33	DE	288
Dolly	37	DE	132
Edward	3	DE	133
Eli	18	DE	133
Eli	52	DE	132
Eli	79	DE	133
Eliza	24	DE	132
Eliza	33	DE	72
Elizabeth	26	DE	139
Elizabeth	53	DE	132
Emily	9	DE	134
George	4	DE	138
George	14	DE	288

Name	No.	St	Pg
Campbell, George	23	DE	138
George W	1	DE	133
Henry	16	DE	133
Hester	59	DE	140
Isabella	14	DE	133
James	45	DE	133
Jane	20	DE	133
John	19	DE	140
Julia A	12	DE	138
Lambert	30	DE	138
Leander	5	DE	138
Lemuel	2	DE	138
Letty E	3	DE	138
Lydia	13	DE	141
Mary	4	DE	72
Mary	18	DE	132
Mary	24	DE	138
Mary	28	DE	138
Mary A	13	DE	133
Mary A E	9	DE	132
Morrell	60	DE	132
Reuben	62	DE	140
Robert	3	DE	72
Robert	35	DE	72
Sarah	22	DE	132
Sarah	40	DE	133
Sarah	41	DE	133
Sarah E	5	DE	138
Sarah J	8	DE	138
Simpson	28	DE	138
Willard	1	DE	138
William	4	DE	138
William	10	DE	288
William	15	DE	140
Wilson	29	DE	138
Wilson	3	DE	138
Cane, Samuel	12	DE	282
Cannon, Abraham	16	DE	204
Adaline	6/12	DE	205
Alexander	7	DE	200
Amanda	13	DE	259
Andrew	3	DE	270
Ann	6	DE	190
Ann	9	DE	275
Ann	13	DE	251
Ann	13	DE	270
Ann	33	DE	275
Ann	38	DE	241
Ann	40	DE	235
Ann	42	DE	290
Ann J	3	MD	213
Ann R	21	DE	200
Annis	41	DE	215
Anselem	17	DE	211
Antonietta	26	DE	207
Arcada	10	DE	204
Arcada	26	DE	207
Arthur	7	DE	286
Asbury	12	DE	214
Augusta	5	DE	219
Augustus	16	DE	207
Bartholomew M	4	MD	213
Bayard	3	DE	212
Benn	60	DE	209
Benton	51	DE	286
Boen	40	DE	190
Burton	23	DE	270
Byard	30	DE	42
Caroline	12	DE	217
Catherine	11	DE	296
Catherine	14	DE	210
Catherine	20	DE	222
Celia	32	DE	211
Cesar	19	DE	60
Charles	14	DE	207
Charles	18	DE	222
Charles R	5/12	DE	209
Charlotte	5	DE	2
Charlotte	6	DE	167
Charlotte	8	DE	222
Clary	34	DE	40
Cornelia	19	DE	285
Cannon, Cornelius	39	DE	209
Curtis	17	DE	203
Curtis	12	DE	222
Cyrus	43	DE	290
Cyrus W	20	DE	290
Daniel	2	DE	281
Daniel	54	DE	216
David	5	DE	270
David	6	DE	222
Drucilla M	19	DE	201
Ebinezer	37	DE	279
Eleanor	23	DE	167
Eleanor L	15	DE	210
Elijah	6	DE	279
Elijah	25	DE	199
Elijah	35	DE	40
Elisha W	16	DE	241
Eliza	13	DE	235
Eliza	24	DE	287
Eliza	49	MD	208
Eliza	52	DE	209
Eliza A	24	DE	208
Eliza J	17	DE	207
Eliza W	8	MD	213
Elizabeth	10	DE	280
Elizabeth	14	DE	240
Elizabeth	16	DE	275
Elizabeth	16	DE	224
Elizabeth	18	DE	211
Elizabeth	20	DE	206
Elizabeth	28	DE	219
Elizabeth	29	MD	216
Elizabeth	52	DE	224
Elizabeth	77	DE	287
Elizabeth A	12	DE	210
Elizabeth J	27	DE	280
Ellen	5	DE	224
Eveline	7/12	DE	206
Eveline	7	DE	204
Ephraim	11	DE	270
Esther	32	DE	286
Ezekiel	8	DE	229
Fatalus H	4	DE	280
Faustin P	52	DE	208
George	3	DE	286
George	13	MD	196
George	24	DE	270
George H	23	DE	285
George J	3/12	DE	224
George W	17	MD	213
George W	25	DE	241
Geo W	31	DE	201
Greensbury	35	DE	296
Harriet	1	DE	63
Harriet	17	DE	212
Harriet	20	DE	212
Harriet	58	DE	62
Harriett	8	DE	209
Harriett	60	DE	270
Henry H	32	DE	199
Henry P	3	DE	224
Hester	71	MD	210
Hester A	8	DE	199
Hester A	35	MD	213
Hetty	11	DE	270
Hetty	24	DE	63
Hetty W	36	DE	262
Hubert	22	DE	221
Huet	37	DE	228
Isaac	10	DE	241
Isaac	10	DE	279
Isaac	16	DE	270
Isaac	21	DE	286
Isaac	40	DE	240
Isaac	45	DE	209
Isaac	63	DE	279
Isaac B	6	DE	214
Isaac W	1	MD	216
Isabella	25	DE	200
Jacob	5	DE	209
Jacob	17	DE	204
Jacob W	17	DE	285
Cannon, James	6/12	DE	200
James	6	DE	240
James	9	DE	199
James	12	DE	207
James	18	DE	62
James	18	DE	224
James	21	DE	239
James A	7/12	DE	211
James B	56	DE	215
James D	40	DE	275
James H	27	DE	272
James M	15	MD	213
James M	30	MD	211
Jane	24	DE	215
Jeremiah	5	DE	204
Jeremiah	11	DE	250
Jeremiah	15	DE	195
Jerry	30	DE	212
John	7	DE	217
John	14	DE	285
John	33	MD	213
John A	3	DE	14
John A	19	DE	156
John C	5/12	DE	212
John E	9	DE	209
John H	2	DE	204
John H	27	DE	219
John T	41	DE	204
Johnson	29	DE	281
Joseph	3	DE	222
Joseph	3	DE	279
Joseph	9	DE	280
Joseph	47	DE	280
Joseph	59	DE	62
Joseph B	17	DE	285
Joseph B	53	DE	285
Joseph F	9	DE	210
Joseph H B	34	DE	280
Joseph K	30	DE	167
Joshua	22	DE	280
Joshua	44	DE	259
Josiah	3	DE	219
Josiah	12	DE	225
Julia	7	DE	225
Kesiah	29	DE	210
Killester	7	MD	213
Laury C	1	DE	286
Lavinia	45	DE	212
Letitia	21	DE	279
Levi	37	DE	204
Levi	60	DE	209
Levin	30	DE	60
Levin J	15	DE	200
Levinia E	2	DE	280
Levinia J	47	DE	280
Lillie N	10	DE	208
Louisa	13	DE	275
Louisa	13	DE	296
Lowder	41	DE	199
Lucy A	25	DE	286
Lurana	14	DE	270
Luther	11	DE	225
Lydia	25	DE	38
Lydia	35	DE	190
Lydia J	3	DE	190
Mahala	21	DE	270
Mahala	22	DE	212
Maranda	15	DE	157
Maranda	26	DE	281
Margaret	3	DE	275
Margaret	4	DE	235
Margaret	8	DE	279
Margaret	11	MD	213
Margaret	16	DE	229
Margaret	21	DE	270
Margaret	23	DE	233
Margaret	52	DE	240
Margaret A	35	DE	204
Margaret A B	36	DE	224
Margaret E	8	DE	209
Martha	12	DE	240
Martha	18	MD	225

Name	Ref
Cannon, Martha A	4 DE 208
Martha J	15 DE 210
Mary	7/12 DE 281
Mary	1 DE 216
Mary	9 DE 296
Mary	14 DE 275
Mary	15 MD 225
Mary	36 DE 208
Mary	36 DE 259
Mary	46 DE 286
Mary	48 DE 215
Mary	51 DE 200
Mary	67 DE 229
Mary	75 DE 272
Mary	76 DE 207
Mary A	12 DE 209
Mary A	22 DE 212
Mary B	55 DE 224
Mary C	8/12 DE 219
Mary E	1 DE 209
Mary E	7 DE 202
Mary E	10 DE 259
Mary H	2 DE 167
Mary J	2/12 DE 215
Mary J	6 DE 281
Mary J	19 DE 285
Mary M	33 DE 227
Mary P	8 DE 40
Mary T	11 DE 210
Matilda	12 DE 68
Minta	13 DE 190
Nancy	14 DE 283
Nancy	21 DE 275
Nancy	39 DE 201
Nancy	53 DE 210
Nancy	77 DE 199
Nancy R	9 DE 208
Nathaniel	5 DE 190
Nelson	38 DE 213
Nutter	50 DE 240
Penelopy	6 DE 283
Peter	47 DE 221
Peter R	41 DE 209
Petter	18 DE 270
Phillip W	28 DE 262
Plymouth	77 DE 212
Priscilla	26 DE 279
Priscilla	80 DE 233
Purnal	4 DE 206
Rachel	30 DE 209
Rachel	45 DE 229
Rebecca	15 DE 225
Rebecca	40 DE 11
Reece	34 DE 63
Regenia	2 DE 280
Richard W	8 DE 225
Robert	64 DE 285
Rose	26 DE 270
Rufus	10 DE 208
Sallie	14 DE 205
Sallie	42 DE 221
Sally T	5 DE 208
Sarah	5 DE 276
Sarah	19 DE 285
Sarah	22 DE 239
Sarah	22 DE 283
Sarah	24 DE 208
Sarah	28 DE 279
Sarah	48 DE 286
Sarah	50 DE 212
Sarah A	21 DE 272
Sarah A	37 MD 213
Sarah C	17 DE 199
Sarah E	1 DE 233
Sarah E	13 DE 40
Sarah E	16 DE 209
Sarah E	19 DE 261
Sarah H	20 DE 199
Sarah L	6 DE 210
Sarah M	22 DE 280
Sarah P	14 DE 224
Sena	12 DE 252
Cannon, Simon	5 DE 286
Simon	15 DE 190
Sina	13 DE 270
Stansbury	53 DE 225
Susan	50 DE 200
Tamsey C	14 DE 209
Theodore	25 DE 72
Thomas C	15 DE 68
Thomas L	28 DE 270
Thos J	34 DE 219
Trusten	5 DE 206
Trusten P	52 DE 207
Unis	1 DE 275
Washington	17 DE 241
Washington	20 DE 214
William	4 DE 240
William	11 DE 275
William	16 DE 222
William	23 MD 216
William	26 DE 293
William	35 DE 233
William	41 DE 224
William D	4 DE 167
William E	1 DE 40
William E	52 DE 280
William L	10 DE 224
William M	49 DE 208
William W	28 DE 272
Winey	40 DE 209
Wingate	14 DE 204
Wingate	23 DE 285
Wm	12 DE 285
Wm A	50 DE 212
Wm E	17 DE 210
Wm J	1 DE 208
Wm J	10 DE 209
Wm S	19 DE 210
Card, Levinia	8 DE 60
Cardiff, Elizabeth	50 DE 203
Carey, Abigail	56 DE 67
Albert	22 DE 22
Angeline	16 DE 67
Angeline W	22 DE 22
Ann	36 DE 118
Arthur C	5 DE 32
Bridget A	2 DE 20
Caroline S	11/12 DE 123
Catharine E	16 DE 20
Celia	34 DE 158
Charles H	6 DE 164
Charles W	2 DE 132
Clement	25 DE 88
Cornelius	27 DE 123
Cornelius J	25 DE 67
Daniel	1 DE 88
David	6 DE 88
David	8 DE 118
David	10 DE 39
David E	8 DE 58
David H	9/12 DE 22
Eli B	19 DE 67
Elijah	48 DE 163
Elijah	66 MD 139
Elisha	63 DE 24
Eliza A	12 DE 157
Eliza E	34 DE 128
Eliza J	32 DE 50
Elizabeth	20 DE 39
Elizabeth	31 DE 32
Elizabeth J	11 DE 50
Ellen	62 DE 128
Eunice	84 DE 164
George Ellen	1 DE 185
George M	18 DE 163
George S	2 DE 164
George W	26 DE 180
Hannah A	1 DE 180
Harriet H	6 DE 20
Henry	38 DE 24
Henry	39 DE 88
Henry W	19 DE 20
Hester	21 DE 22
Carey, Hester A	1 DE 24
Hester E	26 DE 139
Isaac	2 DE 129
Isaac	30 MD 132
James	20 DE 163
James	31 DE 32
James	37 DE 20
James A	4 DE 24
James A	4 DE 128
James A	6 DE 32
James A	33 DE 128
James B	5 DE 164
James M	16 DE 185
James T	11 DE 20
John	6 DE 118
John	17 DE 121
John	20 DE 185
John F	8 DE 39
John T	25 DE 164
Joseph	27 DE 185
Joseph H	17 DE 34
Joseph M	5 DE 39
Joseph S	27 DE 139
July Ann	34 DE 3
Lemuel	3 DE 118
Letty	57 DE 38
Letty J	14 DE 20
Louisa	9 DE 163
Louisa	39 DE 88
Louisa J	1 DE 128
Love	49 DE 163
Margaret	21 DE 185
Margaret	62 DE 121
Margaret	88 DE 185
Margaret H	5 DE 118
Mariah	27 DE 24
Martha	54 MD 139
Mary	16 DE 163
Mary	31 DE 129
Mary A	1 DE 22
Mary A	7 DE 129
Mary A	39 DE 20
Mary Ann	5 DE 88
Mary E	10/12 DE 20
Mary E	7 DE 20
Mary E	8 DE 128
Mary J	38 DE 88
Nancy	16 DE 164
Nancy	20 DE 121
Nancy	59 DE 159
Nancy W	2 DE 123
Nehemiah	62 DE 67
Patience	23 DE 180
Peter	20 DE 121
Peter	59 DE 121
Rachel	67 DE 171
Ralph P	5 DE 20
Reuben	8 DE 88
Robert F	14 DE 185
Robert H	39 DE 39
Sally	1 DE 88
Sarah	14 DE 163
Sarah	18 DE 115
Sarah	20 DE 123
Sarah	24 DE 132
Sarah A	9 DE 20
Sarah J	24 DE 164
Susan	34 DE 39
Susanna	6 DE 185
Susanna	47 DE 185
Sylvester	1 DE 118
Sylvester	38 DE 118
Theodore C	2 DE 39
Thomas	44 DE 50
Thomas	77 DE 42
Thomas D	31 DE 129
Thomas P	9 DE 185
William	22 DE 163
William A C	2 DE 50
William H	2 DE 24
William J	6 DE 128
William S	49 DE 164

Name	Age	State	Page
Carey, Woolsey	24	DE	115
Woolsey B	18	DE	185
Woolsey B	54	DE	185
Carl, Eliza	26	DE	45
Carlisle, Ann	35	DE	85
Ann	51	DE	108
Charles	5	DE	26
Eliza	16	DE	95
Eliza	17	DE	97
Elizabeth	33	DE	83
Emaline	18	DE	97
Emily	3	DE	97
George	2	DE	83
George	11	DE	97
Isaac	18	DE	95
Isaac	55	DE	95
James H	27	DE	87
Joel	60	DE	97
John	22	DE	224
John W	31	DE	97
Joseph	20	DE	97
Manlove	40	DE	85
Mary A	12	DE	19
Mary Ann	1	DE	97
Mary Ann	21	DE	97
Mary E	7	DE	87
Philis	50	DE	95
Rachael	14	DE	97
Rachael	26	DE	87
Robert	1	DE	87
Ruth	3	DE	87
Sallie	52	DE	97
Sally	19	DE	97
Samuel	14	DE	108
Sarah E	4	DE	97
Thomas	25	DE	83
William	2	DE	97
William	7	DE	85
William	15	DE	95
William	18	DE	108
William G	51	DE	108
William J	1/12	DE	83
William J	27	DE	98
Carmean, Benjamin	5	DE	264
Benjamin	35	DE	262
Cyrus	26	DE	264
Elias	10	DE	264
Elijah	4	DE	263
Elijah A	3	DE	262
Elizabeth	60	DE	264
Ephraim	19	DE	264
George W	24	DE	262
Jacob	9	DE	264
Jacob J	28	MD	263
Jane	22	DE	56
Jesse J	5	DE	262
Laura	8/12	DE	263
Mary	22	DE	263
Orasha	28	DE	259
Priscilla	2	DE	264
Priscilla	28	MD	262
Rachael	32	DE	264
Sally	40	DE	263
Thomas	23	DE	259
Umphra	2	DE	263
William	26	DE	263
Carpenter, Ann C	1	DE	79
Benjamin	5	DE	149
Benton	28	DE	77
Benson	35	DE	30
Charles	11	DE	100
Charlotte	27	DE	179
Comfort	14	DE	79
Daniel	9	DE	100
Edward	48	DE	38
Eleanor	23	DE	79
Eliza	1	DE	72
Eliza	24	DE	30
Elizabeth	20	DE	72
Elizabeth	41	DE	23
Elizabeth H	3	DE	173
Ellen	22	DE	100
Carpenter, Emily B	1	DE	38
George	6	DE	109
George	19	DE	79
George	40	DE	166
George Ann	1	DE	77
George T	1/12	DE	72
George T	32	DE	72
Gideon	10	DE	30
Hester	12	DE	77
Hannah	49	DE	109
Isaac	54	DE	79
Jacob	46	DE	109
James	11	DE	48
James	18	DE	109
James	28	DE	179
James	75	DE	47
James E	3	DE	179
Jane	25	DE	149
Jane S	40	DE	166
Jesse	23	DE	25
Jesse	23	DE	67
Job	33	DE	173
John	28	DE	72
John	30	DE	149
John W	10	DE	79
Joseph	22	DE	173
Julia A	22	DE	38
Lemuel	8	DE	5
Letty	5	DE	5
Letty	58	DE	100
Lovey	7/12	DE	100
Lovey	15	DE	109
Lydia	13	DE	38
Mahala	25	DE	77
Mahala	26	DE	173
Margaret	44	DE	48
Mary	3	DE	149
Mary	4	DE	77
Mary	8	DE	100
Mary	9	DE	31
Mary	71	DE	47
Mary A	12	DE	5
Mary A	28	DE	72
Mary E	11	DE	109
Mary J	8	DE	173
Mary S	23	DE	48
Miranda	8	DE	100
Nancy	2	DE	149
Nancy	6	DE	5
Nancy	20	DE	109
Nancy	20	DE	173
Nancy	32	DE	67
Noah	1	DE	179
Patience	50	DE	5
Peter	14	DE	173
Peter	22	DE	79
Rachel	11	DE	67
Rebecca	72	DE	13
Samuel	13	DE	38
Sarah	3	DE	5
Sarah	3	DE	72
Sarah	7	DE	149
Sarah	36	DE	66
Sarah A	14	DE	38
Sarah J	18	DE	67
Stephen	40	DE	5
Sylvester	18	DE	77
Thomas	14	DE	51
Thomas	46	DE	48
Thomas H	20	DE	48
William	3	DE	38
William	8	DE	109
William	15	DE	67
William	19	DE	72
William	31	DE	100
William	52	DE	67
Wingate	9	DE	5
Carroll, Ann	18	MD	216
Arthur	22	DE	209
Caroline	27	MD	224
Charles	16	DE	216
Eliza J	32	DE	228
Carrol, Elizabeth	4	DE	224
Elizabeth	20	MD	216
Isaac	29	DE	200
James	55	MD	216
Levin F	5/12	DE	228
Mary	28	DE	200
Melissa	13	DE	200
Priscilla	18	MD	216
Rebecca	47	MD	216
William	5/12	DE	224
William	13	DE	201
Wm H	12	DE	216
Wm S	33	DE	224
Carry, Ann E	3	DE	218
Elias	5	DE	218
Henry	10	DE	229
John	2/12	DE	218
John	23	DE	218
Rachel	27	DE	218
Robert	27	DE	218
Sarah	8	DE	218
Carsey, Charles	11	DE	58
Elizabeth	6	DE	62
Elizabeth	14	DE	58
Elizabeth	20	DE	46
James	50	DE	58
James	19	DE	62
Leah	16	DE	58
Martha	8	DE	58
Mary	3	DE	62
Mary	19	DE	47
Mary	42	DE	62
Miles	49	DE	62
Nancy	40	DE	58
Rachel	6	DE	58
Sarah	8	DE	62
Caruthers, Caleb B	2	DE	68
Catherine A	24	DE	68
Eliza A J	6/12	DE	68
Isaac	27	DE	68
Lydia R	4	DE	68
Patience B	55	DE	68
Patience J	16	DE	68
Cary, Ann	55	DE	228
Elijah J	2	DE	154
Elisha	34	DE	270
Eliza E	10	DE	270
Elizabeth	21	DE	153
Elizabeth	25	DE	228
Ephraim	45	DE	297
George	14	DE	221
Gideon R	20	DE	159
Harriet	30	DE	228
Jacob H	8	DE	270
James R	10	DE	11
Jane	33	DE	11
John	16	DE	215
Jonathan	38	MD	153
Leah	42	DE	297
Lemuel	40	DE	11
Letitia	26	DE	270
Margaret	5	DE	11
Margaret	16	DE	297
Mary	9	DE	297
Nehemiah	9	DE	221
George	14	DE	222
Sarah	4	DE	297
Sarah J	2	DE	153
Thomas B	23	DE	159
William	24	DE	148
Wooley	64	DE	159
Cashaw, John Neal	10	DE	207
Walter	20	DE	207
Cass, Lewis	2	DE	257
Caster, Planer	45	DE	245
Cathel, Elma E R	16	MD	237
Hester C	12	MD	237
Jonathan	56	MD	237
Lunitus	24	MD	237
Mary C	20	MD	237
Palmyra B	22	MD	237
Sallie T	53	MD	237

Name	Age	State	Page
Caulk, Ann M	24	MD	203
John D	39	MD	203
Sarah J	1	MD	203
William M	3	MD	203
Causy, Eunice	6	DE	220
Mary	9	DE	220
Cavender, John	60	DE	221
Cephas, James	20	DE	215
Ceruthy, Charlotte	26	DE	70
Elizabeth	23	DE	70
Jacob	18	DE	70
Philip	55	DE	70
Sally	54	DE	70
Thomas	21	DE	70
Chamberlin, Benjamin	8	DE	152
Charles	5	DE	150
Elizabeth	3	DE	150
Elizabeth	28	DE	152
George	10	DE	152
George	12	DE	152
George A	37	DE	150
John	62	DE	152
Lydia	36	DE	150
Mary A	6	DE	152
Nancy	57	DE	152
Sarah	3/12	DE	152
Sophia C	1	DE	152
William	36	DE	152
Chambers, George	40	GB	45
Hannah	10	DE	45
Lewis	12	DE	45
Mary A	13	DE	45
Peter	14	DE	45
Robert	1	DE	45
Ruth	39	DE	45
William	6	DE	45
Chandler, Ann	25	DE	277
Annanias	7	MD	133
Benjamin	20	DE	133
Catharine	48	DE	73
Eliza J	1	DE	76
Elizabeth	7	DE	76
Ellen	14	DE	137
Hiram	8/12	DE	277
James	38	DE	73
Jeremiah	7	DE	73
Mary	40	DE	76
Nancy	17	DE	143
Robert	6	DE	277
Thomas	4	DE	277
William	14	DE	73
William	29	DE	277
William	55	DE	76
Channel, Mary E	17	DE	116
Chapman, Benjamin	8	DE	296
Charles	17	DE	296
Handy	60	DE	296
Jane	40	DE	296
John	27	DE	292
Mary	3	DE	296
Susan	6	DE	296
Charick, James	50	MD	129
Sarah	63	DE	129
Charles, Henry	9	MD	139
Chase, Edward H	3	DE	6
Elizabeth	1/12	DE	28
George	5	DE	6
George B	26	DE	8
Jane	19	DE	28
James	1/12	DE	6
James	16	DE	241
James	51	DE	26
James F	32	DE	6
James R	25	DE	8
Isaac	23	DE	28
Lydia	7	DE	6
Margaret	45	DE	26
Mary	28	DE	6
Mary E	2	DE	8
Priscilla J	23	DE	8
Sarah	19	DE	9
Serena	50	DE	243
Chase, Susan	19	DE	26
William Thomas	6/12	DE	9
Cheesman, John	22	DE	223
Chipman, Ann E	4	DE	292
Eleanor	18	DE	268
James H	23	DE	268
John	22	DE	197
Joseph	18	DE	291
Margaret	21	DE	292
Mary	65	DE	197
Mary A	23	DE	268
Samuel	21	DE	268
Sarah A	11/12	DE	268
William	14	DE	291
Christopher, Armwell	14	DE	150
Benjamin	48	DE	150
Betsy	55	DE	195
Edward	40	DE	112
Elizabeth	16	MD	195
Hester	60	DE	151
Hetty E	2	DE	150
Isaac	16	DE	150
Isaac	69	DE	150
James	50	DE	195
Jane	39	DE	150
Kendal	15	MD	195
Mary	12	DE	265
Mary	36	DE	112
Sarah J	6	DE	150
Thomas	18	MD	195
William	21	MD	195
Clark, Ann	18	DE	60
Bevin	4/12	DE	178
Bridget A	18	DE	57
Daniel	19	DE	82
Edward M	7	DE	189
Eliza	50	DE	79
Ellen	25	DE	189
George	6	DE	79
George	14	DE	57
Gideon W	19	DE	115
Henry	4	DE	79
Hetty	15	DE	57
James	17	DE	245
James	18	DE	179
James	60	DE	117
James H	13	DE	140
Jesse	19	DE	79
John	1	DE	79
John	20	DE	57
Julia A	9	DE	245
Love	50	DE	117
Lydia	60	DE	178
Maria	41	DE	245
Maria E	7	DE	238
Mary A	15	DE	140
Mary A	20	DE	114
Mary Ann	22	DE	79
Mary B	2	DE	189
Mary C	20	DE	178
Minos	11	DE	57
Nancy	53	DE	82
Nathaniel	5	DE	245
Nathaniel	30	DE	114
Nathaniel	56	DE	57
Penelope A	10	DE	189
Robert	36	DE	189
Sarah E	12	DE	140
Sophia	24	DE	144
Sophia	60	DE	114
Tabitha	44	DE	140
Thomas	59	DE	79
Thomas H	3	DE	189
Unicy	7	DE	57
Unicy	50	DE	57
Washington	12	DE	245
William T	42	MD	140
Clarkson, Bayard	44	DE	227
Daniel	41	DE	227
Hannah	33	DE	227
James B	11	DE	196
James R	2	DE	227
Clarkson, Lewis E	9	DE	196
Robert	38	DE	196
Sarah A	32	DE	196
Clayton, John	1	DE	248
Thomas	14	DE	245
Clendaniel, Ahab	51	DE	89
Alfred	5	DE	28
Avery	23	DE	89
Benjamin	5	DE	76
Betsey	11	DE	89
Clement	55	DE	47
Caroline	2	DE	89
Cyrus	1	DE	65
Elias	38	DE	95
Eliza	15	DE	91
Elizabeth	6	DE	47
Elizabeth	22	DE	91
Elizabeth	28	DE	15
Elizabeth	59	DE	91
Emeline	3	DE	89
George	40	DE	76
George	79	DE	76
Harriet	43	DE	47
Hester A	30	DE	76
Hester M	38	DE	79
Isaac	7	DE	95
Isaac	21	DE	89
Isaac	63	DE	89
Jacob	14	DE	89
Jacob	75	DE	91
James	3	DE	65
James	11	DE	91
James	64	DE	76
Jemimah	10	DE	95
John	11	DE	76
John	23	DE	91
John	28	DE	89
John	28	DE	67
John A	11	DE	91
Joseph	10	DE	74
Joseph C	2	DE	15
Joshua	9	DE	89
Kendall B	11	DE	47
Luke	32	DE	28
Lydia A	32	DE	67
Lydia L	12	DE	47
Margaret	15	DE	89
Mary	22	DE	91
Mary	8	DE	79
Mary	18	DE	91
Mary	23	DE	95
Mary	30	DE	65
Mary A	20	DE	74
Matilda	10	DE	28
Nancy	14	DE	95
Nicey	10	DE	92
Pinkey	19	DE	91
Purnel	10	DE	79
Rachael	16	DE	89
Rachael	34	DE	40
Rachael	44	DE	90
Rhoda	8	DE	89
Sally	8	DE	76
Samuel	26	DE	95
Samuel S	10	DE	47
Sarah	53	DE	89
Spicer M D	12	DE	145
Thomas	12	DE	79
William	5	DE	15
William	14	DE	79
William	18	DE	90
William	30	DE	15
William	49	DE	79
William S	11/12	DE	47
Clifton, Ann	10	DE	57
Ann	20	DE	275
Asa	16	DE	87
Bemberton	2	DE	97
Betty	62	DE	31
Biddy	2	DE	87
Catharine	33	DE	96
Charlotte	26	DE	214

Name	Age	State	No.	Name	Age	State	No.	Name	Age	State	No.
Clifton, Curtis	9	DE	274	Codery, James	2	DE	256	Colborn, Elijah of J	40	DE	205
Eli	30	DE	275	John	1	DE	266	James H	5	DE	205
Eliza	2	DE	275	John	11	DE	256	Margaret J	3	DE	205
Eliza	50	DE	96	John	28	DE	259	Margaret L	41	DE	205
Eliza A	3	DE	90	Josiah	75	DE	259	Mary A	3	DE	205
Elizabeth	3	DE	274	Margaret	4	DE	266	William	24	DE	291
Elizabeth	18	DE	87	Nancy	22	DE	259	Wm L	2	DE	205
Elizabeth	24	DE	173	Nancy	27	DE	266	Colbourn, Arcada	1	DE	200
Elizabeth	38	DE	87	Patsy	40	DE	256	Cornelia	39	DE	200
Elizabeth	52	DE	49	Sarah	6	DE	266	Elizabeth	3	DE	199
Garrett	22	DE	87	Sarah	8	DE	259	Elizabeth	31	DE	199
George	6	DE	90	Solomon	14	DE	256	George R	1	DE	199
George	35	DE	214	Spencer M	41	DE	256	Georgianna	4	DE	200
Hannah	4	DE	96	William	17	DE	256	Jeremiah	30	DE	199
Hannah	15	DE	47	Codry, Aron	30	DE	280	John	3	DE	197
Hetty	16	DE	49	Eleanor	25	DE	280	John L	43	DE	196
James	12	DE	87	Elijah	15	DE	253	Joseph	9	DE	263
Jesse	34	DE	291	John	12	DE	256	Lavinia	28	DE	217
John	4	DE	87	Joseph	1	DE	280	Louisa E	9/12	DE	199
John	10	DE	90	Joseph	3	DE	256	Martha J	3	DE	199
John	50	DE	87	Margaret	30	DE	256	Mary	26	DE	263
Lovey	21	DE	219	Mary	7	DE	280	Mary A	7	DE	199
Maria	26	DE	87	Moulin	9	DE	280	Michael	39	DE	200
Mary	1	DE	214	Sarah	8/12	DE	256	Miranda	8	DE	200
Mary	8	DE	87	Rebecca	6	DE	280	Sarah L	7	DE	197
Mary	21	DE	220	William	8	DE	280	Sophia S	9	DE	217
Mary	28	DE	90	William	30	DE	256	Thomas J	32	DE	199
Mary	34	DE	291	Coffan, Betsy	35	DE	132	Thomas M	31	DE	216
Mary A	14	DE	274	David H	24	DE	188	William	30	DE	263
Nancy	8	DE	291	Elisha J	5	DE	155	Cole, Elizabeth	25	DE	257
Nancy	60	DE	275	Hannah	15	DE	132	Mary	28	DE	279
Nathan	66	DE	31	James B	27	DE	188	Priscilla	30	DE	279
Nathaniel	16	DE	218	John	8	DE	132	Washington	25	DE	257
Obediah	65	DE	275	John	40	DE	132	William	80	DE	279
Pemberton	14	DE	96	Margaret	14	DE	149	Coleman, Elizabeth	29	DE	55
Phoebe	25	DE	96	Mary	12	DE	132	Ellen	2	DE	54
Priscilla	45	DE	214	Mary	38	DE	155	George	6	DE	53
Rhoda A	8/12	DE	219	Mary	60	DE	188	Margaret	45	DE	53
Rhoda A	65	DE	214	Mary J	8	DE	155	Nancy	4	DE	53
Sarah	6	DE	274	Nehemiah	15	DE	177	Thomas	50	DE	53
Sarah	8	DE	90	Nehemiah	41	DE	155	Coles, Eliza	9	DE	205
Sarah E	3	DE	219	Peter M	1	DE	155	Eliza	42	DE	205
Sincey	52	DE	96	Ritty	6	DE	132	Hugh	15	DE	205
Susan T	2	DE	49	Robert	11	DE	149	Jeremiah	44	DE	205
William	2/12	DE	90	Samuel	19	DE	149	Levina	11	DE	205
William	10	DE	275	Sarah	10	DE	132	Samuel H	5	DE	205
William	12	DE	291	Sarah E	15	DE	155	William J	18	DE	205
William	23	DE	219	Thomas	63	DE	149	Colester, Peter	22	DE	31
William	31	DE	90	Thomas P	17	DE	149	Colhoun, Thomas	15	DE	30
William	35	DE	275	Coffin, Adaline J	10	DE	53	Collins, Aaron	70	DE	276
Zachariah	43	DE	274	Ann	37	DE	11	Adaline	3	DE	87
Clog, Eliza A	32	DE	129	David	6	DE	30	Adeline	28	DE	171
John	12	DE	135	David	6	DE	32	Alcy	60	DE	251
Clogg, David H	11	DE	143	David	31	DE	32	Alee	4	DE	130
Elizabeth	17	DE	143	David	35	DE	30	Alexander	5	DE	97
Hetty M	7	DE	143	Eliza	3	DE	30	Alfred B	12	DE	130
Coalscott, Harriet	15	DE	179	Eliza A	2	DE	32	Alfred T	21	DE	198
Coard, Eliza	30	DE	123	Elizabeth A	9	DE	21	Amelia	27	DE	265
Ellen	12	DE	118	Henrietta	1	DE	11	Andrew	23	DE	80
Henry	15	DE	122	Jane	25	DE	30	Angeline	4	DE	290
Henry	15	DE	123	Joseph	4	DE	21	Ann	13	DE	102
Jane	44	DE	121	Levin	11	DE	257	Ann	13	DE	116
Lavinia	9	DE	123	Margaret	50	DE	150	Ann	13	DE	276
Leah	60	DE	117	Mary A	2	DE	193	Ann	47	DE	180
Lydia	6	DE	123	Mary E	5	DE	11	Ann M	7	DE	140
Mary	50	DE	117	Mary E	7	DE	53	Annis	2	DE	222
Mary L	8	DE	121	Mary Hester	7/12	DE	21	Arabel	16	DE	290
Nancy	58	DE	117	Peggy	55	DE	74	Asbury	8	DE	252
Peter	55	DE	121	Robert	35	DE	21	Bartly M	30	DE	297
Phebe	13	DE	123	Robert	37	DE	11	Benjamin	9	DE	296
Sarah	11	DE	123	Samuel T	21	DE	12	Caroline	15	DE	161
Coats, Jency	54	DE	214	Sarah	2	DE	32	Caroline	15	DE	290
Mark A	19	DE	214	Sarah	10	DE	30	Catharine	1/12	DE	178
Wm J	13	DE	214	Sarah	35	DE	21	Catharine	4	DE	109
Wm N	54	DE	214	Sarah	35	DE	257	Catharine	29	DE	283
Cochran, Eliza	45	DE	242	Sarah A	4	DE	11	Catharine	35	DE	222
Codery, Benjamin	7	DE	256	Sarah J	28	DE	32	Celia	28	MD	219
Benjamin	31	DE	266	William F	8	DE	21	Charles	17	DE	202
Edward	9	DE	256	Colborn, Adalia	26	DE	204	Charles	17	DE	247
Elizabeth	72	DE	259	Amelia	1	DE	204	Charles	23	DE	109
James	2	DE	256	Catherine	14	DE	292	Charles	30	DE	251
John	1	DE	266	Edward	33	DE	204	Charles	47	DE	86

Collins, Charles H	7	DE	10	Collins, Henry	21	DE	252	Collins, Levin	25	DE 246
Charles W	13	DE	152	Henry	26	MD	248	Levin A	35	DE 248
Charlott	1	DE	97	Heston	55	DE	283	Levin B	17	DE 198
Cinthia	4	DE	97	Hetty	31	DE	246	Levina	14	DE 276
Clara B	33	DE	36	Hetty A	4	DE	171	Lovy	16	DE 290
Comfort	8	DE	248	Hiram	21	DE	248	Lurana	14	DE 259
Comfort	66	DE	248	Ida	2	DE	109	Lurany	4	DE 248
Comfort	70	DE	172	Isaac	8	DE	262	Luther W	52	DE 259
Cynthia	17	DE	98	Isaac	17	DE	242	Lydia	11	DE 98
Cyrus	1	DE	252	Isaac	23	DE	290	Lydia A	18	DE 211
Cyrus Q F	9	DE	147	Isaac	22	DE	246	Lydia J	19	DE 183
Cyrus W	16	DE	242	Isaac	54	DE	288	M Anthony	4	DE 210
David	33	DE	36	J P	32	DE	237	Mahala	5	DE 276
Dennis	20	DE	276	Jacob	14	DE	246	Margaret	5	DE 290
Doughty	55	MD	248	James	7	DE	87	Margaret	8	DE 268
Eben	22	DE	246	James	8	DE	283	Margaret	12	DE 198
Ebin	8	DE	277	James	23	DE	292	Margaret	27	DE 251
Eccleston	40	DE	198	James	62	DE	246	Margaret	56	DE 246
Edda	54	DE	288	James E	12	DE	248	Margaret C	11	DE 248
Edward	3	DE	198	James E	22	MD	213	Maria	7	DE 106
Eleanor J	6	DE	172	James H	3	DE	199	Maria	13	DE 98
Elena	52	MD	259	James H	8	DE	177	Maria A	11/12	DE 197
Elenor	26	DE	199	Jane	4	DE	102	Martha	2	DE 290
Eli	5	DE	283	Jane	7	DE	109	Martha	6	DE 106
Elias	8	DE	207	Jane	19	DE	200	Martha	14	DE 102
Elias	17	DE	276	Jane A	1	DE	10	Martha	18	DE 246
Elijah	2	DE	290	Jeffrey	20	DE	173	Martha	19	DE 197
Elijah	25	DE	197	Jeremiah	15	DE	259	Martha	23	DE 252
Elisha	22	DE	283	Jeremiah	23	DE	197	Martha J	12	DE 116
Elisha J	2	DE	183	Jeremiah	36	DE	198	Martha M	7	DE 248
Elizabeth	14	DE	262	Jerry	40	DE	97	Martin	20	DE 235
Elizabeth	15	DE	259	John	5/12	DE	211	Mary	10	DE 97
Elizabeth	20	DE	276	John	4	DE	170	Mary	12	DE 276
Elizabeth	21	DE	62	John	4	DE	206	Mary	12	DE 290
Elizabeth	25	DE	211	John	5	DE	259	Mary	13	DE 106
Elizabeth	27	DE	246	John	6	DE	248	Mary	20	DE 246
Elizabeth	28	DE	36	John	7	DE	283	Mary	21	DE 272
Elizabeth	31	DE	283	John	11	DE	276	Mary	21	DE 290
Elizabeth	32	DE	102	John	17	DE	109	Mary	24	DE 235
Elizabeth	32	DE	177	John	21	DE	202	Mary	25	MD 248
Elizabeth	33	DE	204	John	21	MD	248	Mary	27	DE 276
Elizabeth	50	DE	247	John	21	DE	283	Mary	39	DE 287
Elizabeth	54	MD	246	John	24	DE	199	Mary	40	DE 130
Elizabeth	70	DE	276	John	35	DE	10	Mary	49	DE 198
Elizabeth A	8	DE	191	John	36	DE	276	Mary A	3	DE 211
Elizabeth W	9	DE	116	John	38	DE	229	Mary A	5	DE 128
Ellen	8	DE	206	John	70	DE	78	Mary A	12	DE 137
Elzey	47	DE	276	John A D	16	DE	248	Mary A	16	DE 180
Emeline	25	DE	172	John B	6	DE	90	Mary A	33	DE 116
Emily S	3	DE	10	John B	64	DE	248	Mary Ann	28	DE 109
Emma H	13	DE	246	John G	27	DE	211	Mary E	2	DE 224
Ephraim	29	DE	287	John H	1	DE	36	Mary E	15	DE 198
Ephraim	50	DE	290	John M	8	DE	10	Mary F	9	DE 177
Eunice T	4	DE	177	John M	50	DE	180	Mary J	1	DE 248
Eunicey	52	DE	80	John W	21	DE	242	Mary J	6	DE 289
Euphemia J	19	DE	198	Jonathan	28	DE	62	Mary J	11	DE 152
Flora J	2	DE	36	Jonathan	32	DE	246	Mary J	14	MD 196
Gatty	18	DE	248	Joseph	6/12	DE	262	Melton	34	DE 199
George	10/12	DE	22	Joseph	1	DE	259	Minos	29	DE 290
George	15	DE	210	Joseph	19	DE	109	Moses	75	DE 251
George	16	DE	252	Joseph	25	MD	131	Nancy	15	DE 246
George	16	DE	288	Joseph A	40	DE	106	Nancy	18	DE 86
George	18	DE	264	Josephian	2	DE	211	Nancy	30	DE 106
George	30	DE	130	Josephus	4	DE	235	Nancy	30	DE 276
George	43	DE	247	Josiah	40	DE	290	Nancy	34	DE 290
George	45	DE	25	Josiah	47	DE	262	Nancy	38	DE 98
George W	29	DE	283	Josiah	80	MD	259	Nancy	47	DE 290
George W	37	DE	98	Julia	4	DE	290	Nancy	49	DE 152
Georgianna	4	DE	98	Kendle	23	DE	109	Nancy	52	DE 171
Grace	16	DE	130	Kendle T	23	DE	198	Nancy	78	DE 255
Handy	6	DE	252	Lamberson	17	DE	287	Noah	4	DE 276
Hannah	2	DE	106	Lazarus	16	DE	246	Noah	11	DE 209
Hannah	18	DE	265	Leah	12	DE	262	Noah	21	DE 246
Hannah	45	DE	106	Leah	12	DE	259	Noble	11	DE 290
Harmy	7	DE	290	Leah	45	DE	265	Omey	1	DE 290
Harriet	3	DE	90	Leah A	2	DE	209	Patience	17	DE 283
Harriet	34	DE	90	Leah J	14	DE	265	Patty	28	DE 109
Harriet A	5	DE	36	Lemuel	9	DE	288	Phebe	45	DE 86
Henrietta	10	DE	290	Letty	39	DE	10	Priscilla	1	DE 276
Henrietta	17	MD	213	Levi	54	DE	246	Rachel A	5	DE 10
Henry	9	DE	98	Levin	14	DE	252	Rachel A	5	DE 87
Henry	10	DE	252	Levin	25	DE	246	Rebecca	19	DE 170

Name	Age	St	Pg	Name	Age	St	Pg	Name	Age	St	Pg
Collins, Rebecca	28	DE	200	Commean, Eunice	5	DE	177	Connell, Charles	1	DE	39
Rhoda	45	DE	262	Hetty	10	DE	177	David H	23	DE	39
Rhoda	47	DE	259	John R	2	DE	177	Elizabeth	13	DE	31
Robert W	7	DE	36	Levin M	24	DE	157	Elizabeth	14	DE	14
Rose	18	DE	49	Luther	58	DE	157	Elizabeth	30	DE	110
Sallie	35	DE	224	Nancy	15	DE	177	Genet	11	DE	39
Sallie	50	DE	248	Nathaniel	38	DE	177	Hannah	13	DE	110
Sallie E	22	MD	248	Nelly	50	DE	157	Hetty D	46	DE	31
Sally	60	DE	78	Phenetta E	15	DE	157	Hetty J	15	DE	31
Samuel	17	DE	98	Sarah	8	DE	177	Joseph	47	DE	31
Samuel	25	DE	80	Sarah	35	DE	177	Lydia E	10	DE	31
Samuel C	40	DE	177	Thenetta	19	DE	157	Mary	15	DE	110
Samuel J	6	DE	211	Commian, Kendal	49	DE	150	Mary E	7	DE	31
Sandy	1	DE	251	Ritty	47	DE	150	Nancy	34	DE	30
Sarah	6	DE	276	Conaway, Andrew H	2	DE	17	Patience	22	DE	39
Sarah	13	DE	97	Ann	35	DE	197	William E	22	DE	31
Sarah	14	DE	166	Anna	4	DE	100	Connelly, Charles	21	DE	290
Sarah	15	DE	80	Arena	5	MD	213	David	25	DE	283
Sarah	19	DE	80	Charles H	9	DE	164	Elizabeth	19	DE	290
Sarah	19	DE	259	Charlotte	52	DE	283	Eliza	53	DE	290
Sarah	20	DE	297	Clayton	50	DE	147	Jacob	15	DE	290
Sarah	23	DE	251	Curtis	17	DE	97	Conner, Ann	42	DE	268
Sarah	25	DE	297	Danial	45	DE	197	David	30	DE	68
Sarah	43	DE	276	Daniel	10	DE	197	Frances E	16	DE	268
Sarah C	5	DE	116	Daniel	11	DE	212	John	8	DE	268
Sarah C	6	DE	183	Edward	4	DE	164	John	21	DE	4
Sarah C	10	DE	198	Elijah	5	DE	197	John	25	DE	268
Sarah E	2	DE	235	Eliza	3	DE	100	Joseph	9/12	DE	69
Sarah E	5	DE	177	Elizabeth	10	DE	147	Leah	12	DE	268
Sarah E	6	DE	287	Elizabeth	23	DE	212	Mahala	10	DE	34
Sarah E	7	DE	196	Elizabeth	35	DE	205	Martha	10	DE	268
Sarah E	14	DE	90	Elizabeth P	6/12	DE	17	Peter	45	DE	268
Sarah J	9	DE	36	George	28	DE	100	Sarah	26	DE	68
Sarah J C	4	DE	197	Henry	32	DE	97	Sarah E	3	DE	69
Sharp	13	DE	290	Henry C	7	DE	164	Spencer	14	DE	268
Solomon	6	DE	97	Hester	7	DE	212	Theodore	5	DE	268
Sovering	10	DE	196	James	1	DE	97	Theodore	35	DE	73
Stephen	31	MD	131	James C	15	DE	283	Connor, Catharine	60	DE	42
Stephen	74	DE	116	Jane	14	DE	197	George H	28	DE	49
Stephen A	2	DE	130	John	8	DE	101	George P	3	DE	49
Stephen P	7	DE	116	John	17	DE	283	Kate C	11/12	DE	49
Stephen S	22	DE	180	John	21	DE	147	Mary A	23	DE	49
Tamsey	25	DE	197	Lavenia	50	DE	205	Conovan, Elizabeth	9	DE	66
Theophilus	41	DE	109	Leah	24	DE	100	Conoway, Alfred	16	DE	105
Thom C	24	MD	213	Levin	14	DE	148	Amanda	2	DE	104
Thomas P	26	DE	183	Levin	17	DE	283	Ann	2	DE	103
Thos E	2	DE	199	Louisa	32	DE	164	Ann	37	DE	101
Washington	4	DE	251	Luisa	49	DE	147	Arthur	1	DE	10
William	3	DE	97	Lydia J	7	DE	17	Betsey	34	DE	101
William	5	DE	109	Mahala	2	DE	197	Brinkley	26	DE	98
William	7	DE	98	Margaret	22	DE	147	Celia	59	DE	109
William	8	DE	86	Margaret R	11	DE	164	Curtis	28	DE	103
William	10	DE	288	Maria	10	DE	283	Daniel	5	DE	103
William	13	DE	86	Martha L	3	DE	205	Dixon	36	DE	101
William	27	DE	98	Mary	1	DE	100	Elizabeth	12	DE	110
William	27	DE	171	Mary	14	DE	159	Elizabeth	22	DE	105
William	28	DE	235	Mary	14	DE	283	Elizabeth	26	DE	101
William E	9	DE	10	Mary	27	DE	6	Frances Ann	14	DE	110
William H	23	DE	266	Mary	55	DE	99	Hester	2	DE	101
William H	37	DE	36	Mary	55	DE	283	Isaac	1	DE	101
William T	5	DE	268	Mary A	33	DE	17	Isaac	14	DE	103
William V	4	DE	36	Mary E	16	DE	205	Isaac	18	DE	110
Wm T	50	DE	246	Morgan	7	DE	97	Isaac	23	DE	109
Wm W	5	DE	211	Nimia	19	DE	205	Isaac	60	DE	110
Winlock	39	DE	90	Noah	8/12	DE	212	Isaiah	1	DE	103
Zephora	20	DE	172	Noah	34	DE	164	Jackson	22	DE	103
Collison, Edward	6/12	DE	199	Purnal	13	DE	184	James	3	DE	104
Charles	5	DE	224	Sarah	8	DE	147	James	5	DE	101
John H	20	DE	229	Sarah	24	DE	97	James	6	DE	101
John M	35	MD	224	Sarah E	5	DE	295	James	12	DE	103
Mary A	17	DE	229	Selby	64	DE	283	James	14	DE	105
Rebecca	28	DE	229	Thomas	30	DE	10	James	54	DE	109
Sarah	41	DE	229	Thomas	33	DE	99	Jerry	8	DE	103
Stansbury	22	DE	229	William	14	DE	147	Jerry	55	DE	103
Twifort	41	DE	229	William	27	DE	164	Jesse	21	DE	110
William	29	DE	199	William A	36	DE	17	John	7	DE	101
Collister, Elizabeth	24	DE	201	William N	5	DE	17	John	9	DE	103
Henrietta A	28	DE	201	Wright	13	DE	147	John	10	DE	103
John M	65	DE	201	Wingate	12	DE	205	John	30	DE	98
Joseph W	10	DE	262	Connell, Alletta	13	DE	31	John R	29	DE	104
Mary A	58	DE	201	Asa	36	DE	30	Joseph	4	DE	101
Collum, Sinah	26	DE	197	Baptist S	30	DE	110	Joseph	25	DE	110

Name	Age	St	Pg	Name	Age	St	Pg	Name	Age	St	Pg
Conoway, Josiah	23	DE	105	Cooper, Edward	23	DE	240	Corday, Emily	7	DE	167
Julia	8	DE	109	Eleanor	32	DE	240	Joseph B	3	DE	167
Julia	9	DE	101	Elenor	41	DE	245	Josephine	9	DE	167
Levenia	29	DE	104	Elizabeth	25	DE	266	Kinsey A	34	DE	167
Levin	54	DE	105	George	31	DE	235	Louisa	1	DE	167
Levinia	10	DE	103	George W	12	DE	252	Margaret M	29	DE	167
Lewis	10	DE	110	Hamilton	24	MD	289	Stephen A	4	DE	167
Manlove	17	DE	103	Hannah	10	DE	266	Cordery, George E	11	DE	171
Mary	4/12	DE	103	Hannah	35	DE	38	John	32	DE	171
Mary	15	DE	103	Henry	2	DE	266	John R	14	DE	171
Mary	37	DE	103	Henry	13	DE	240	Lovey	32	DE	171
Mary Jane	18	DE	105	Henry	51	DE	239	Cordray, Perry W	14	MD	237
Matilda	45	DE	105	Hester	35	DE	239	Cordrey, Elisha	40	DE	233
Miles	11	DE	101	Hester	52	DE	224	Elisha	17	DE	233
Minus	3	DE	103	Hetty	49	DE	240	Cordry, B L	9	MD	248
Minus	38	DE	110	Isaac	10	MD	289	Elizabeth	22	DE	247
Nancy	48	DE	110	James	32	DE	36	Elizabeth	40	FR	248
Nathaniel	5	DE	101	James	47	DE	38	Joseph E	73	DE	248
Nathaniel	51	DE	101	Jane	21	DE	169	Spencer	75	DE	247
Noble	37	DE	101	Jane	25	DE	235	William	39	DE	247
Patience	65	DE	101	Jane	50	MD	266	Corney, Joseph	15	DE	21
Polly	40	DE	103	Joseph	12	DE	240	Lucey	40	DE	21
Purnel	22	DE	110	Keziah	3/12	DE	240	Lydia	4	DE	21
Rebecca	13	DE	104	Leah	63	ND	266	Nehemiah	13	DE	21
Richard	4	DE	101	Leonard	47	DE	224	Nehemiah	53	DE	21
Robert	2	DE	103	Levin J	11	DE	252	Rebecca	35	DE	21
Sally	58	DE	103	Lucy	5	DE	252	Cornish, Phillis	8	DE	108
Sarah	5	DE	105	Marana	5	DE	252	Richard	70	DE	108
Sarah	26	DE	98	Margaret	8	DE	252	Sarah	13	DE	108
Sarah	27	DE	103	Margaret	21	DE	239	Sarah	56	DE	108
Sarah	40	DE	103	Margaret	68	DE	245	Corsey, Eliza	44	DE	44
Wilford	10	DE	105	Mary	7/12	DE	252	Elizabeth	6	DE	63
Wilhelmina	7/12	DE	104	Mary	10	DE	240	James	19	DE	63
William	23	DE	101	Mary	12	DE	240	John	6	DE	44
William	28	DE	110	Mary	19	DE	38	John	60	DE	44
William	37	DE	101	Mary	32	DE	252	Lydia A	19	DE	44
Wm P	30	DE	205	Mary	47	MD	289	Martha	8	DE	44
Conwell, Ann A	18	DE	49	Mary	65	DE	59	Mary	3	DE	63
Ann C	34	DE	26	Mary A	8	DE	252	Mary	42	DE	63
Asa	36	DE	31	Mary A	36	MD	252	Mary J	18	DE	44
Comfort N	2	DE	31	Nancy	12	DE	235	Priscilla	16	DE	44
Cornelia	45	DE	49	Nancy	18	MD	289	Sarah	8	DE	63
Elizabeth	41	DE	54	Nancy	50	MD	263	Thomas	4	DE	44
Elizabeth R	8	DE	26	Noah	2	DE	252	William	1	DE	44
Emaline	9	DE	31	Noah	36	DE	252	William	24	DE	16
Hannah	6	DE	26	Peter	7	DE	240	Costen, Betsey	54	DE	44
Israel J	26	DE	49	Prudence	35	DE	240	Cottengim, Jacob	86	DE	173
Jacob	21	DE	54	Pusey J	20	DE	36	Cotter, Charles M	29	DE	214
Jacob	55	DE	49	Rhoda	1	DE	240	Cotting, Sarah	75	MD	124
Jacob A	16	DE	49	Rhoda	3	DE	266	Cottingham, Adaline	6	DE	197
James G M	7	DE	49	Rhoda	60	DE	235	Alfred	4	DE	197
John D C	12	DE	31	Robert	40	DE	240	Alfred	40	DE	197
John S	13	DE	49	Sampson	15	DE	266	Ann	44	DE	54
John M	2	DE	26	Sarah	17	DE	38	Ann E	7	DE	54
John T	35	DE	26	Shepperd	10	DE	238	Cassa	40	DE	101
Joseph	11	DE	54	Stephen T	1	DE	38	Charles	43	DE	101
Mary	15	DE	54	Susan	14	DE	38	Charles A	20	DE	197
Mary J	4	DE	26	Thomas	85	DE	240	Elizabeth	5	DE	102
Mary J	6	DE	26	William	4	DE	126	Harriet	27	DE	102
Nancy	34	DE	31	William	10	DE	18	Hester	2	DE	54
Nehemiah	5	DE	31	William	12	DE	294	Jacob	80	DE	172
Renck T	7	DE	31	William	21	DE	266	John	50	DE	114
Robert R	15	DE	31	William	38	DE	252	John	55	DE	197
Sarah E	4	DE	26	William	51	DE	240	John H	22	DE	197
Susan	25	DE	26	William J	6	DE	238	Joshua	22	DE	54
Thomas A	21	DE	49	Zephaniah	18	DE	266	Lavenia	38	DE	197
Thomas W	24	DE	54	Copse, Catherine	24	DE	5	Margaret	44	DE	197
William	3	DE	54	Joseph	28	DE	4	Robert	17	DE	54
William A	2	DE	26	Julia M	3	DE	5	Sarah	10	DE	102
William A	34	DE	26	Margaret	1	DE	5	Sarah E	10	DE	197
William A	45	DE	54	Corbin, Amanda	7	DE	212	Thomas E	14	DE	197
Cooper, Adaline	10	DE	240	Amelia	19	DE	212	Washington	16	DE	197
Alexandria	13	DE	266	Amos K	13	DE	212	William	13	DE	102
Amelia	8	DE	240	Mary A M	17	DE	212	William	50	DE	54
Amelia	70	MD	245	Matilda	48	DE	212	Cotts, Elizabeth	18	DE	98
Benjamin	11	DE	266	Sarah G	11	DE	212	John	25	DE	98
Benjamin	18	DE	266	Sarepta	21	DE	212	Coulborn, Amelia A	17	DE	202
Celia	5	DE	240	Stephen	11	DE	212	Elijah	49	DE	270
Charles W	55	DE	263	Twiford	47	DE	212	Isabel	12	DE	270
David R	10	DE	38	Wm A	15	DE	212	Jacob	6	DE	270
Edward	6	DE	266	Corcket, Margaret	38	DE	296	James Allen	4	DE	270
Edward	13	DE	18	William	11	DE	296	John Wesley	2	DE	271

Name	Age	State	No.	Name	Age	State	No.	Name	Age	State	No.
Coulborn, Marcellus	5	DE	202	Craig, Maria	23	DE	58	Culver, Amelia	41	DE	251
Margaret	38	MD	270	Samuel	24	DE	58	Arena	16	DE	255
Mary P	8	DE	270	Sarah A	3/12	DE	58	Augusta	21	MD	252
Michael	25	DE	197	William	27	DE	58	Benton	21	DE	255
Newton	23	DE	197	Cramfield, Burton	25	DE	289	Charles	2	DE	258
Priscilla	79	DE	272	Burton	51	DE	155	Charles	17	DE	251
Robert	10	DE	270	Comfort	23	DE	289	Charles	34	DE	258
Robert	77	DE	272	Edward	12	DE	155	Daniel	7	DE	256
Susan	43	DE	202	Eleanor	28	DE	173	Daniel	8	DE	255
Coulbourn, Isabel	12	DE	271	Eliza	19	DE	155	Daniel	45	DE	255
Lavenia	38	DE	197	Elizabeth	16	DE	155	Edward	10	DE	258
Mary	16	DE	197	Elizabeth	42	DE	155	Elias	12	DE	251
Coulbourne, Eliza	5	DE	242	George	14	DE	289	Elias	41	DE	252
Emeline	35	DE	242	Isaac	22	DE	155	Elijah	14	DE	258
Ezekiel	40	DE	242	Isaiah	30	DE	155	Elinor	22	MD	252
James	1	DE	242	Jacob	42	DE	173	Eliza	29	MD	246
John E	2	DE	242	James	4	DE	155	Eliza	38	MD	252
Coulter, Cornelius	69	DE	34	Love	25	DE	155	Garison	19	DE	256
Cornelius R	16	DE	34	Mary	2	DE	155	Gracy	13	DE	258
Daniel T	54	DE	77	Mary	26	DE	155	Greensbury	24	DE	255
Delilah	11	DE	77	Pemberton	10	DE	155	Handy	10	DE	252
Elijah	19	DE	77	Purnal	44	DE	155	Handy	14	DE	255
Eliza	52	DE	34	Sally	59	DE	155	Handy	22	DE	256
Elizabeth	12	DE	77	Sarah	14	DE	155	Handy	23	DE	255
Elizabeth	33	DE	17	William	10	DE	289	Henry P	41	DE	251
Elizabeth	45	DE	77	Craner, Eliza T	24	DE	212	Hester	60	DE	255
George	18	DE	77	Elizabeth	1	DE	212	Hetty E	10	DE	256
James	15	DE	77	Joshua	70	DE	212	Hiram	23	DE	264
James	30	DE	17	Joshua C	29	DE	212	Isaac	16	DE	251
Margaret W	18	DE	77	Craney, William W	23	IE	4	James	19	DE	258
Rhoda	20	DE	17	Crapper, Ann	26	DE	167	Jane	7	DE	251
Ruth M	53	DE	77	Eleanor	28	DE	167	John	22	DE	255
Sarah A	46	DE	34	Erasmus	19	DE	167	John J	28	DE	255
Thomas J	14	DE	77	Hannah	15	DE	167	Jonathan	8/12	DE	258
William J	8	DE	77	Joseph	49	MD	167	Joseph	5	DE	255
William V	52	DE	77	Martha	24	DE	167	Julia E	2	DE	251
Coverdale, Daniel	4	DE	107	Sarah	28	DE	125	Lavina G	13	DE	274
David	2	DE	47	Susan	7	DE	125	Lidia E	17	DE	255
David	45	DE	47	Thomas	3	DE	125	Lovy	28	DE	255
Elias	12	DE	34	Warner	16	DE	59	Lydia	4	DE	251
Elias	31	DE	41	William	9	DE	125	Lydia	7	DE	252
Elias	59	DE	33	William	36	VA	125	Mary	46	DE	255
Elizabeth	6	DE	47	Cray, Eliza	10	DE	209	Mary E	7	DE	258
Elizabeth	26	DE	72	Mahla	40	DE	198	Miranda Ann	8	DE	255
Elizabeth	36	DE	33	Crocket, Elenor	73	DE	296	Patience	18	DE	264
George A	4	DE	38	Jane	45	DE	256	Perry	15	DE	252
Jacob	30	DE	107	Jency	30	DE	296	Peter	50	DE	258
Jerry	28	DE	96	Leven	8	DE	296	Polly	58	DE	251
Joshua	1	DE	107	Robert	40	DE	257	Priscilla	15	MD	248
Levin J M	1	DE	38	Thomas	17	DE	282	Quilly	35	DE	258
Lydia	35	DE	47	Crockett, Charlotte	25	MD	234	Salathiel	13	DE	251
Margaret A	7	DE	34	Daniel	13	MD	238	Salathiel	13	DE	252
Mary	21	DE	96	John C	18	MD	238	Salathiel	48	DE	255
Mary	45	DE	41	Martha	9	MD	238	Sallie	8	DE	258
Mary	45	DE	72	Mary	49	MD	238	Sallie J	26	DE	269
Mary A	3	DE	72	Sallie A	19	MD	238	Sarah	14	DE	251
Mary L	4	DE	34	Sarah	21	DE	75	Tara	27	DE	255
Matilda	1	DE	96	Cropper, Sarah	21	DE	74	Umphra	18	MD	252
Mitchel	30	DE	6	Cubbage, John H	1	DE	213	William	12	DE	255
Mitchel	30	DE	38	Lenora	35	DE	213	Wilmoore	19	DE	251
Nancy	25	DE	38	Luther	7	DE	213	Wm	28	DE	246
Nathaniel	26	DE	72	Mary F	5	DE	213	Cummings, Susannah	70	DE	16
Priscilla	30	DE	107	Samuel	31	DE	213	Curry, Albert	32	DE	97
Stephen G	5/12	DE	47	Culber, Cornelius	21	DE	170	Alice	24	DE	85
Wesley	17	DE	34	Culberry, Angeline	34	DE	230	Elias	17	DE	97
Covington, Catherine	30	DE	292	Elizabeth	13	DE	230	Elizabeth	7	DE	12
Charles	10	MD	292	George	8	DE	230	Elizabeth	19	DE	225
Elizabeth	20	DE	243	Hester	11	DE	230	Ennals	30	DE	84
James	25	DE	243	Louisa	4	DE	230	James	13	DE	225
Wm	49	DE	292	William	6	DE	230	James	19	DE	97
Crague, Comfort C	12	DE	187	Wm M	41	DE	230	James	74	DE	225
Elizabeth M	9	DE	187	Cullen, Burton	25	DE	151	James B	33	DE	219
Hester	90	DE	177	Charles M	22	DE	1	Jeremiah	4/12	DE	85
James D	14	DE	187	Delane	22	DE	20	John	43	DE	225
John L	22	DE	181	Elisha D	48	DE	1	Joshua	8	DE	97
Lydia A	16	DE	181	Lydia W	25	DE	1	Julia	6	DE	85
Lydia A	17	DE	187	Margaret W	50	DE	1	Lot	5	DE	245
Lydia B	49	DE	187	Mary W	23	DE	1	Lucy A	3	DE	245
Robert	45	DE	187	Thomas	19	DE	142	Nancy	68	DE	97
Craig, Ellenor	18	DE	16	Culleny, Belinda	1	DE	222	Rebecca	24	DE	225
James L	15	DE	31	Sarah J	22	DE	222	Ruth A	2	DE	85
Lydia	45	DE	30	Culver, Amelia	10	DE	252	Sarah Ann	24	DE	97

Name	Age		Pg
Curry, Thomas	31	DE	219
William	38	DE	219
Dailey, Joshua	14	DE	29
Dalby, Simon B	75	DE	275
Dale, Ann	9	DE	79
Caroline	19	DE	136
Elizabeth	40	DE	79
James M	54	DE	136
Kittura	12	DE	136
Margaret	53	DE	136
Peter R	22	DE	136
Dalton, George	1	DE	90
Margaret	70	DE	298
Rachel	22	DE	90
Silas	25	DE	90
Daniel, Elias	30	DE	80
Elizabeth	47	DE	42
Emaline	28	DE	35
James	23	DE	80
James H	3	DE	80
Joshua	11	DE	85
Lavinia	25	DE	80
Mary	5	DE	80
Nehemiah	50	DE	80
Priscilla	50	DE	80
Riley H	62	DE	85
Sarah A	40	DE	85
Sippy	20	DE	80
Walter W	2	DE	85
William	6/12	DE	85
Daniels, James	24	DE	75
James A	14	DE	77
Joseph	10	DE	77
Letitia	40	DE	77
Mary	16	DE	77
Molton R	35	DE	77
Nancy	19	DE	77
William	14	DE	77
Darber, Clara	9	DE	196
Fanny	1	DE	196
Hester A	34	DE	196
James	45	DE	196
John E	13	DE	196
Darby, Alexander B	10	DE	72
Ephraim	52	DE	35
Ephraim J P	14	DE	35
James W	12	DE	35
Mary	47	DE	35
Mary J	19	DE	38
Miers	48	DE	38
Miers J	25	DE	35
Milly	44	DE	38
Nancy	41	DE	72
Miers	48	DE	38
Miers J	25	DE	35
Milly	44	DE	38
Nancy	41	DE	72
William J	21	DE	72
Dartus, Sarah	82	DE	282
Whitfield	45	DE	282
Dashields, Joseph H	10	DE	199
Nancy E	15	DE	232
Rebecca	37	DE	232
Rebecca A	7	DE	232
Windsor	61	DE	232
Wm W	25	DE	232
Davenport, Elizabeth	3	DE	47
Lydia	83	DE	47
Davidson, Ann	31	DE	72
Asariah	19	DE	150
Charles H	5	DE	155
Charlotte	25	DE	30
Charlotte	48	DE	137
Charlotte	56	DE	187
Cornelius	22	DE	35
Didani	28	DE	155
Eleanor	5	DE	137
Elijah	26	DE	155
Eliza A	24	DE	187
Eliza J	18	DE	27
Elizabeth	15	DE	27
Davidson, George B	5	DE	27
George L	6/12	DE	155
Henry E	4	DE	27
Hester	40	DE	27
Hester A	6	DE	27
Hester A	16	DE	154
Hetty	12	DE	137
Isaac	4	DE	154
Isaac	14	DE	86
Isaiah	59	DE	157
James	66	DE	187
James H	29	DE	61
James P	6	DE	188
Jane W	27	DE	150
John	6	DE	154
John	18	DE	137
John	20	DE	86
John	50	MD	137
John	52	DE	86
John H	6	DE	72
John H	13	DE	189
John M	22	DE	187
John R	11	DE	27
John W	17	DE	188
John W	33	DE	72
Joseph	14	DE	155
Joseph	36	DE	151
Joseph	45	DE	154
Josiah	15	DE	183
Lemuel	36	DE	145
Lemuel J	4	DE	72
Lydia E	6/12	DE	145
Margaret	19	DE	61
Martha	20	DE	137
Martha J	21	DE	188
Matilda A	17	DE	157
Mary	21	DE	151
Mary	47	DE	154
Mary A	17	DE	137
Mary E	10	DE	27
Mary E	21	DE	30
Mary T	20	DE	187
Nancy	62	DE	86
Nancy	64	MD	163
Nathaniel	24	DE	157
Noah	6	DE	154
Robert J	3	DE	145
Robert P	41	DE	27
Robert T	11	DE	72
Rufus R	4/12	DE	61
Samuel	25	DE	187
Samuel	50	DE	188
Samuel B	31	DE	150
Sarah C	2	DE	155
Sarah C	10	DE	188
Sarah E	7	DE	145
Susanna	3	DE	188
Thomas J	8	DE	27
William	20	DE	154
William C	12	DE	72
William H	7	DE	150
Davis, Alex	17	DE	227
Alfred J	19	DE	42
Amelia	16	DE	208
Ann	9	DE	82
Ann	25	DE	75
Ann	29	DE	32
Ann	50	DE	76
Ann E	1	DE	211
Ann E	24	DE	228
Ann Virginia	4	DE	1
Anna	3	DE	82
Anna C	12	DE	228
Anna J	21	DE	79
Augustus	28	DE	265
Brinkley	25	DE	24
Brinkley	75	DE	24
Caleb	7	DE	66
Caleb R	14	DE	71
Catharine	11	DE	76
Caroline	16	DE	24
Celia	27	DE	74
Davis, Charity	40	DE	82
Charles	25	DE	106
Charles W	11	DE	32
Charles W	13	MD	141
Comfort	63	DE	25
Daniel	21	DE	250
Daniel	55	DE	76
Edward	23	DE	77
Edward	30	MD	211
Eli	49	MD	141
Elijah	40	MD	288
Elisha	21	MD	141
Eliza	20	DE	76
Elizabeth	5	DE	75
Elizabeth	10	DE	71
Elizabeth	10	DE	106
Elizabeth	12	DE	69
Elizabeth	20	MD	212
Elizabeth	21	DE	211
Elizabeth	28	MD	141
Elizabeth	37	DE	246
Elizabeth	38	DE	125
Elizabeth	39	MD	208
Elizabeth	41	DE	52
Elizabeth	51	MD	142
Elizabeth C	2/12	DE	70
Elizabeth C	5	DE	145
Elizabeth P	30	DE	145
George	22	DE	76
George	25	DE	75
George	27	DE	74
George	51	DE	158
George M	13	DE	66
George M	43	DE	228
Henry	32	DE	75
Hester	29	DE	82
Hester	53	DE	79
Hester A	10	DE	69
Hester A	12	DE	24
Hester A	32	DE	69
Hester A	55	DE	24
Hester J	20	DE	77
Hetty	12	DE	125
Isaac H	30	MD	141
James	7	DE	125
James	8	DE	106
James	40	DE	125
James D	10	DE	56
James H	14	DE	33
James M	7	DE	77
Jane	26	DE	265
Jesse	21	MD	141
John	6	DE	106
John	6	DE	288
John	18	DE	76
John	19	MD	126
John	21	DE	266
John	47	DE	106
John E	9	MD	141
John J	36	DE	66
John M A	18	MD	208
John W	8	DE	66
John W	31	MD	1
Joseph E	6	DE	70
Joseph M	27	DE	71
Joshua	28	DE	24
Josiah	15	DE	182
Josiah	16	MD	126
Kiturah	46	DE	76
Levin T	11	MD	141
Lavinia E	24	DE	1
Lot W	27	DE	68
Lovey	25	DE	288
Lovey	37	DE	106
Lovinia	2	DE	265
Lydia	7	DE	75
Lydia	25	DE	266
Margaret	4	DE	228
Margaret	12	DE	246
Margaret A	9	DE	152
Mahala	31	DE	56
Maria	38	DE	66

Name	Age	St	Pg	Name	Age	St	Pg	Name	Age	St	Pg
Davis, Maria C	1	DE	66	Davis, William P	4	DE	71	Dazey, Joseph N	18	DE	125
Maria M	27	DE	71	William R	30	DE	22	Joshua	9	DE	117
Mark	5	DE	82	Wm A	38	MD	212	Leah	59	DE	122
Mark	16	DE	76	Daws, Joseph	15	DE	206	Louisa M	18	DE	121
Martha E	19	DE	142	Dawson, Anna C	6	DE	202	Margaret	15	DE	126
Mary	1	DE	69	Amy	32	DE	217	Mary	51	DE	117
Mary	5	DE	288	Bayard	51	DE	203	Mary J	15	DE	117
Mary	14	DE	76	Caroline	10	DE	217	Mary P	31	DE	121
Mary	20	MD	139	Charles	8	DE	217	Matilda	74	MD	121
Mary	22	DE	106	Charles W	12	DE	202	Nancy	52	DE	121
Mary	58	MD	126	Elizabeth J	16	DE	202	Nancy S	35	DE	121
Mary A	19	DE	77	Evie Ann	6	DE	217	Naomi	24	DE	122
Mary E	3	DE	75	George M	3	DE	202	Nathaniel P	58	DE	121
Mary E	17	MD	208	Hosea	40	DE	202	Neely	72	DE	122
Mary E	17	DE	246	James	11	DE	203	Prettyman M	51	DE	122
Mary H	5	DE	22	Jane	20	DE	203	Robert C A	12	DE	121
Mary J	2	DE	70	Josiah	39	MD	235	Rufus T	3	DE	121
Mary J	25	DE	70	Louisa A	8	DE	202	Sarah	18	DE	121
Mary J	25	DE	71	Luther	4	DE	203	Sarah	23	DE	117
Mary R	28	DE	68	Margaret	25	DE	213	Sarah A	5	DE	120
Mathew G	44	DE	208	Mary A	38	DE	202	Sophia	16	DE	117
Nancy	20	MD	217	Mary E	25	MD	235	Susan	33	DE	121
Nancy A	22	DE	157	Mary H	9	DE	222	Thomas	4	DE	115
Nancy C	8	DE	56	Mary H	14	DE	202	Thomas	29	DE	120
Nancy J	10	DE	24	Moses	42	DE	217	Thomas	39	DE	191
Nathan	34	DE	56	Prudence	63	DE	227	Thomas	54	DE	125
Nathaniel	4	DE	69	Rebecca	1	DE	213	Virginia E	21	PA	129
Nathaniel G	44	DE	69	Thomas	38	DE	222	Walter J	2	DE	121
Nehemiah	81	DE	68	Thomas H	4	MD	222	William	2	DE	116
Nehemiah H	1	DE	75	Thomas W	21	DE	244	William B	14	DE	117
Nehemiah H	4	DE	68	William S	3	MD	235	William J	27	DE	122
Nutter L	37	DE	82	William T	23	DE	259	Dazy, Jonathan C	21	DE	120
Paul	37	DE	52	Wm Hut	23	DE	203	Deal, Mary A	47	DE	209
Peggy	35	DE	137	Day, Asbury	20	DE	111	Dealen, Harriet	39	DE	123
Prudy	8	DE	125	Betty	64	DE	10	William W	38	MD	123
Purnel	15	DE	66	Elias A	22	DE	149	Dean, Charles H	8	DE	205
Rachel J P	4	DE	141	Eliza	10/12	DE	105	David	2	DE	48
Ritty	20	MD	126	Eliza A	15	DE	10	Elizabeth	12	DE	270
Robert	26	DE	76	Elizabeth	14	DE	111	Elizabeth	27	DE	30
Robert	26	DE	79	Henry H	13	DE	10	John W	29	DE	30
Robert A	5	DE	70	James	18	DE	111	John W	60	DE	56
Robert H	6	DE	71	James O	31	DE	105	Levin	33	DE	48
Robert M	30	DE	70	John	54	DE	111	Louisa	30	DE	48
Rowland J	3	DE	22	John H	9/12	DE	10	Mary	7	DE	48
Ruth E	2	DE	71	John W	4	DE	105	Mary E	5	DE	30
Sallie C	15	MD	208	Letitia	28	DE	105	Peter	1	DE	48
Samuel	11	MD	211	Leven D	36	DE	10	Sallie	70	MD	205
Samuel	12	DE	283	Lovey	54	DE	111	Sallie M	42	DE	236
Samuel C L	23	MD	141	Lydia J	3	DE	10	Sarah	60	DE	56
Sarah	3	DE	288	Mary	11	DE	111	William B	3	DE	30
Sarah	4	DE	106	Mary	32	DE	10	Delany, Abraham	10/12	DE	238
Sarah	6	DE	265	Mary E	7	DE	10	Ann	23	DE	240
Sarah	7	DE	69	Rowland B	11	DE	10	Clara	2	DE	240
Sarah	12	DE	106	Sarah	15	DE	149	Eleanor	10	DE	240
Sarah A	25	MD	141	William T	9	DE	10	John P	4	DE	240
Sarah C	1	MD	212	Dazey, Almira	5	DE	120	Keziah	32	DE	238
Sarah C	7	DE	70	Amos	21	DE	145	Minos	45	DE	238
Sarah E	1	DE	68	Ann	21	DE	144	Wm W	10/12	DE	240
Sarah E	7	DE	22	Caroline	6	DE	120	Wm W	37	DE	240
Sarah J	13	MD	212	Charles	5	DE	115	Demming, Barsheba	55	DE	46
Sarah R	36	MD	212	David	7	DE	115	Dennis, Ben	32	DE	242
Sina	53	DE	64	David	60	DE	117	Emila E	4	DE	241
Solomon	21	DE	24	Ebra	32	DE	129	Erasmus	6	MD	241
Solomon	75	DE	64	Edward P	29	DE	115	Mary	57	MD	278
Tabitha	25	DE	22	Eli R	24	DE	125	Mary J	26	DE	241
Thomas	2	DE	71	Elihu	8	DE	120	Denny, George	5	DE	151
Thomas	8	DE	76	Elizabeth	15	DE	125	Denton, Ann	18	DE	231
Thomas	14	DE	246	Elizabeth	20	DE	124	Deputy, Abigail	19	DE	71
Thomas	22	MD	139	Elizabeth S	1	DE	120	Andrew	23	DE	86
Thomas	65	DE	79	Ellen	17	DE	138	Ann E	1	DE	81
Thomas J	27	DE	71	Ellen B	28	DE	115	Ann E	20	DE	77
Unice	7/12	DE	77	Ellen C	20	DE	125	Benjamin	14	DE	77
William	5/12	DE	82	Hannah	55	DE	125	Betsy	70	DE	97
William	8/12	DE	22	Isaac A	3	DE	120	Comfort J	6	DE	82
William	4	DE	265	Isabella	8/12	DE	120	Daniel	57	DE	71
William	9	DE	241	James T	30	DE	144	David	6/12	DE	84
William	30	DE	258	James W	16	DE	125	David	17	DE	95
William	64	DE	32	Job R	1	DE	129	Eliza	7	DE	77
William F M	7	DE	214	John	11/12	DE	115	Eliza J	20	DE	82
William G	6	DE	141	John	16	DE	115	Elizabeth	7	DE	84
William H	13	DE	77	John	60	DE	125	Elizabeth	30	DE	82
William M J	3	MD	212	John G	4	DE	129	Elizabeth	70	DE	81

Name	Age	State	Page
Deputy, Gabriel	73	DE	97
George	13	DE	77
Henry	28	DE	91
Hester E	9	DE	82
James	14	DE	77
James	36	DE	82
James H	4	DE	82
Jesse	11	DE	77
Jesse	20	DE	90
Jesse	50	DE	77
John	20	DE	86
John	21	DE	89
John	23	DE	95
John H	3	DE	82
Jonathan	25	DE	89
Leah	25	DE	86
Lovey	60	DE	89
Mahala	26	DE	84
Martha	11	DE	81
Mary	6	DE	91
Mary	14	DE	77
Mary E	7/12	DE	77
Nancy	25	DE	81
Nancy	60	DE	40
Nathaniel	25	DE	84
Rachel	16	DE	86
Rachel Ann	11	DE	82
Robert J	4	DE	84
Samuel	2	DE	91
Sarah	7	DE	77
Sarah	14	DE	91
Sarah	56	DE	77
Sarah A	3	DE	84
Sarah E	1	DE	82
Sarah E	5	DE	81
Sarah R	19	DE	84
Sarah Ann	21	DE	91
Solomon	30	DE	81
Thomas H	24	DE	77
Vicey	50	DE	86
William	4	DE	78
William	4	DE	91
William	13	DE	95
Zachariah	62	DE	77
Derham, Elizabeth	33	DE	148
William	33	DE	148
Derickson, Alfred H	2	DE	174
Ann E	8/12	DE	8
Annanias D	2	DE	126
Annanias D	33	DE	126
Arthur	29	DE	114
Aurena	32	DE	124
Barbary A	30	DE	122
Benjamin	49	DE	128
Charles W	6	DE	120
Cornelia A	6	DE	122
Dagworthy	51	DE	194
Daniel	4	DE	193
David H	20	DE	129
Edward	8	DE	119
Elihu R	2	DE	130
Elisha	4	DE	120
Elizabeth	3	DE	120
Elizabeth	8	DE	144
Elizabeth	16	DE	128
Elizabeth	44	DE	122
Elizabeth C	3	DE	129
Elizabeth H	13	DE	144
Elizabeth T	26	DE	114
Esther C	6	DE	193
Gaddy Ann	26	DE	8
George	2	DE	119
George F	20	DE	194
George J	14	DE	129
George M Dallas	5	DE	8
George T	25	DE	130
Hannah	40	DE	193
Hannah	44	DE	128
Hester A	42	DE	237
Hetty	13	DE	144
Hetty A	12	DE	129
Hetty R	20	DE	174
Derickson, Hetty R	20	DE	174
Hetty J	11	DE	129
Irena	20	DE	130
Isaac C	7	DE	126
Isabella	13	DE	120
Isaiah V	12	DE	144
James	2	DE	122
James	11	DE	119
James	14	DE	144
James	29	DE	122
James	48	DE	129
James B	8	DE	117
James P	36	DE	117
James T	24	DE	120
Jane	32	DE	119
Jane	56	DE	114
Jehu B	6	DE	117
Jehu F	17	DE	145
Job	24	DE	117
Job H	2	DE	117
Job W H	31	DE	124
John	56	DE	144
John C	19	DE	120
John D	6	DE	144
John P	17	DE	144
John S	23	DE	174
John L	4	DE	129
John W	55	DE	150
Joseph	8	DE	120
Joseph B	10	DE	194
Joshua V	14	DE	144
Kitty	32	DE	144
Lemuel	45	DE	144
Lemuel H	32	DE	119
Levin	1	DE	120
Levin	23	DE	119
Levin H	40	DE	135
Lucy C A	3	DE	144
Margaret J	18	DE	114
Maria T	5	DE	129
Mary	53	MD	144
Mary A	8	DE	129
Mary A	8	DE	144
Mary A	16	DE	237
Mary A	24	DE	117
Mary A	26	DE	2
Mary E	24	DE	126
Mary J	22	DE	144
Mary M	4	DE	126
Matilda M	37	DE	136
Mitchell	51	DE	120
Nancy	16	DE	144
Nancy	38	DE	120
Nancy	39	DE	128
Nancy	58	DE	174
Nathaniel M	22	DE	128
Peter	1	DE	140
Priscilla	51	DE	140
Rhoda	1	DE	120
Rhoda	38	DE	120
Robert	2	DE	118
Robert	54	DE	114
Robert H	16	DE	114
Samuel D	6	DE	122
Samuel W	26	DE	8
Sarah	1/12	DE	119
Sarah	15	DE	144
Sarah	16	DE	129
Sarah	22	DE	120
Sarah	80	VA	136
Sarah A	4	DE	117
Sarah P	44	DE	129
Sophia	60	DE	119
Sophia J	4	DE	119
Stephen	10	DE	120
Stephen E	19	DE	144
Thomas	16	DE	120
Thomas	17	DE	143
Thomas	60	DE	119
W B	48	DE	237
William	15	DE	120
William	21	DE	144
Derickson, William	36	DE	144
William E	7	DE	8
William H	9	DE	144
Derrickson, Benjamin	12	DE	136
Emeline	6/12	DE	136
Hetty	37	DE	144
Hetty C	2	DE	136
John B	36	DE	136
Joseph	6	DE	136
Leah	55	DE	22
Levin H	8	DE	136
Lucy A	2	DE	136
Margaret J	4	DE	136
Mary	8	DE	136
Nathaniel	42	DE	144
Noah	15	DE	242
Peggy	47	DE	242
Peter M	16	DE	136
Priscilla	51	DE	195
Robert H	16	DE	115
Sarah	6	DE	136
Sarah	15	DE	136
Sarah	28	DE	136
Sarah H	15	DE	22
Thomas	17	DE	121
William	33	DE	22
Deshields, Elias	9	DE	263
Josephine	17	DE	268
Sarah J	7	DE	199
Thomas W	10	DE	187
Dickenson, Charles	2	DE	128
Elizabeth	30	DE	128
Ezekiel	8	DE	128
Ezekiel	40	DE	128
James	13	DE	128
Sarah E	5	DE	128
Wetha	10	DE	128
Dickerson, Alfred	3	DE	59
Allison	40	DE	90
Andrew	8	DE	59
Ann	4	DE	100
Catherine	4	DE	18
Catherine	15	DE	39
Charles	9	DE	100
Comfort	29	DE	59
Edward	6	DE	59
Elizabeth	29	DE	165
Elizabeth	58	DE	35
Elizabeth E	6	DE	18
Eunice	75	DE	4
George	42	DE	18
Georgianna	3	DE	90
Hannah J	2	DE	18
Harriet	28	DE	100
Hester	46	DE	62
Hester	48	DE	62
James	26	DE	165
James	35	DE	59
James H	13	DE	18
Jane	24	DE	192
John M	3	DE	164
Jonathan	35	DE	164
Julia Ann	12	DE	18
Julia J	6	DE	165
Luvinia	8	DE	18
Mary A	13	DE	165
Mary C	23	DE	90
Mary E	3	DE	165
Milla P	11	DE	164
Nancy	30	DE	165
Nathaniel	10	DE	18
Noah	39	DE	21
Patrick	21	DE	21
Peter	29	DE	192
Peter P	21	DE	35
Philip	25	DE	35
Rachel	34	DE	164
Richard S	24	DE	30
Russel	37	DE	100
Sarah	5	DE	100
Sarah	8	DE	165
Sarah	60	DE	11

Name	Age		Page	Name	Age		Page	Name	Age		Page
Dickerson, Sarah A	8	DE	166	Dingle, William	40	DE	150	Donovan, Alfred	21	DE	24
Sarah Jane	28	DE	63	Dobson, Henry	39	DE	43	Alfred B	3	DE	24
Stockely	28	DE	166	Dodd, Aaron	40	DE	20	Ann R	19	DE	40
Thomas	8/12	DE	103	Absolem	38	DE	36	Araminta	21	DE	40
William	8/12	DE	90	Ann	38	DE	59	Asbury	19	DE	23
William	7	DE	100	Asahel	43	DE	172	Avis	7	DE	23
William	35	DE	63	Athey	65	DE	20	Avis	29	DE	23
Dickinson, Ann	4	DE	105	Benjamin	4	DE	21	Barton	15	DE	23
Catherine J	13	DE	33	Charles	22	DE	31	Basheba	73	DE	23
Elisha	26	DE	105	Clayton	55	DE	31	Benjamin	25	DE	41
Eliza Beth	14	DE	86	Cornelius	48	DE	25	Bivens	7	DE	23
Elizabeth	20	DE	105	David	19	DE	31	Burton	29	DE	23
Jacob	20	DE	86	David	49	DE	16	Byard	23	DE	23
James	27	DE	14	Eliza J	2	DE	21	Charles	--	DE	23
Jonathan D	10	DE	28	Elizabeth	6	DE	20	Catharine	19	DE	23
Mary A	5	DE	14	Elizabeth	40	DE	21	Eli	60	DE	28
Mary E	1	DE	105	Elizabeth A	15	DE	59	Elizabeth	12	DE	41
Nancy	45	DE	14	Emily	6	DE	36	Foster	36	DE	27
Samuel James	3	DE	14	Emily	7	DE	36	George	7	DE	23
Sarah	26	DE	131	Frances	40	DE	188	George	8	DE	23
Sarah	59	DE	86	George	24	DE	31	George	22	DE	23
Sophia	33	DE	19	George T	12	DE	172	George D	4	DE	23
Dickison, Edmond	21	DE	19	Hannah	44	DE	60	George Henry	2	DE	23
George W	22	DE	19	Hannah C	7	DE	59	Henry	14	DE	29
James	21	MD	163	Hannah E	9	DE	37	Henry	20	DE	28
John H	3	DE	22	Hester	55	DE	189	Henry	30	DE	296
Jonathan	28	DE	22	Hester	78	DE	20	Hetty A	24	DE	23
Lusinia	18	DE	19	Hetty	25	DE	20	Job	73	DE	23
Nancy	40	DE	273	Hevon W	17	DE	196	John	3	DE	23
Nancy J	27	DE	22	Isaac	1	DE	20	John	35	DE	23
Dill, Alfrod	7	DE	288	James	8	DE	16	John of P	45	DE	41
Edward	5	DE	288	James	18	DE	25	Jonathan	26	DE	24
Edward	35	DE	288	James L	15	DE	59	Kendall	50	DE	23
Lavinia	31	DE	288	Jesse	15	DE	30	Leah	65	DE	23
Mary	1	DE	288	John	34	DE	20	Levin	3	DE	23
Sophia	3	DE	288	John	42	DE	21	Lipson	5	DE	23
Dingle, Angeline	11	DE	158	John H	10	DE	59	Maria	11	DE	41
Arnstaid	22	DE	167	Joseph H	39	DE	59	Mary	16	DE	29
Belfast	70	DE	168	Luther A	26	DE	37	Mary	27	DE	23
Bersheba	7	DE	158	Margaret	5	DE	59	Mary	37	DE	41
Caroline	7	DE	151	Martha	3	DE	37	Mary	70	DE	23
Catharine	15	DE	80	Mary	24	DE	20	Mary	80	DE	23
Charles	8	DE	142	Mary A	3/12	DE	172	Mary A	2	DE	23
David	10	DE	80	Mary A	2	DE	20	Mary E	11	DE	23
Eliza	10	DE	150	Mary A	36	DE	25	Mary J	4	DE	23
Elizabeth	40	DE	150	Mary E	12	DE	59	Mary J	6	DE	41
Emily H	12	DE	171	Mary H	45	DE	16	Mary P	1	DE	23
Erasmus	17	DE	112	Mary P	7	DE	16	Nancy	6	DE	23
George	11	DE	142	Matilda	32	DE	172	Nancy	26	DE	23
Henry	20	DE	167	Moses	25	DE	36	Nancy	36	DE	29
Isaac	11	DE	150	Nancy	55	DE	3	Nehemiah	53	DE	23
Isaac	13	DE	142	Peter	30	DE	20	Nicey	27	DE	27
Isaac	23	DE	167	Peter A	1	DE	20	Oliver	2	DE	23
Isaac	58	DE	142	Pettyjohn	30	DE	20	Peter	8	DE	41
Isabella	7	DE	158	Robert	29	DE	20	Peter	29	DE	23
Jacob	17	DE	142	Samuel J	13	DE	172	Peter S	30	DE	94
James	4	DE	151	Sarah	11	DE	36	Priscilla	9	DE	23
Jane	16	DE	150	Sarah	20	DE	36	Priscilla	18	DE	41
Jane	16	DE	156	Sarah E	5	DE	20	Priscilla	47	DE	23
Jane	50	DE	158	Sarah J	9	DE	188	Reuben	60	DE	23
Jane	95	DE	168	Seth	40	DE	188	Rhoda	1	DE	23
John	12	DE	112	Sophia A	25	DE	16	Riley	30	DE	23
John	15	DE	142	Unice	32	DE	30	Robert	15	DE	41
John	21	DE	158	Walter A	4	DE	172	Robert	33	DE	23
John	23	DE	173	William A	30	DE	60	Sally	23	DE	23
Julia	19	DE	153	William E	10	DE	172	Sally A	9	DE	23
Julia A	19	DE	112	William E W	3	DE	188	Sarah	1	DE	41
Julia A	20	DE	168	William G	3	DE	59	Sarah	10	DE	29
Leah	17	DE	153	Dodds, John W	5	DE	191	Sarah E	4	DE	23
Leah	65	DE	168	Dolby, Alhalanda	9	DE	103	Tabitha	2	DE	23
Love	14	DE	112	Benjamin	6	DE	281	Thomas	26	DE	40
Mary	5	DE	151	Hiram	2	DE	282	Westley	10	DE	23
Mary	40	DE	142	Isaac	26	DE	282	William	21	DE	23
Mary Ellen	4	DE	80	Jenny	7	DE	103	William	45	DE	23
Mary S	50	DE	112	John	35	DE	102	William T	6	DE	23
Nancy	45	DE	80	Mary	15	DE	282	Wingate	37	DE	29
Nathaniel	19	DE	142	Mary	35	DE	102	Zachariah	27	DE	23
Nathaniel	25	DE	158	Sallie	20	DE	103	Donohoe, James	9	DE	104
Rachel	45	DE	171	Sarah	3	DE	103	Jane	27	DE	104
Sarah J	8	DE	171	Sarah	25	DE	282	Nancy	8/12	DE	104
Thomas	12	DE	150	Donavan, Aerah	49	DE	23	Peter	29	DE	104
William	40	DE	150	Abraham	30	DE	28	Robert	3	DE	104

Name	Age	State	Page
Donovan, Avis	29	DE	23
Charity	11	DE	65
Denny	43	DE	43
Eliza	20	DE	93
Eliza J	11	DE	22
Elizabeth	8	DE	93
George Henry	2	DE	23
Gipson	38	DE	65
Hannah W	12	DE	43
Hetty	30	DE	65
James D	19	DE	22
James R	49	DE	22
John	15	DE	43
John	60	DE	43
John	7	DE	65
Joshua	9	DE	43
Leah	2	DE	93
Margaret	5	DE	65
Mary	19	DE	65
Mary J	28	DE	93
Nancy	5	DE	11
Nancy	41	DE	22
Peter	11/12	DE	93
Peter	71	DE	23
Peter S	30	DE	93
Rachel	13	DE	65
Reuben	4	DE	24
Riley	35	DE	23
Sarah	17	DE	65
Sarah E	16	DE	22
William	1	DE	65
William	14	DE	22
William	22	DE	43
Zachariah	15	DE	65
Dood, Amanda P B	8	DE	230
Clement	15	DE	230
Elizabeth	42	DE	230
Moses	47	DE	230
Wm H H	10	DE	230
Dorey, Ann T	25	DE	173
Benjamin H	60	MD	173
Benjamin R	18	DE	173
Edward	33	DE	129
George	10	DE	129
Jane	53	DE	129
Jesse	42	MD	170
John H	9	DE	173
Maria L	4	DE	129
Mary B	13	DE	173
Patience	43	DE	173
Sarah A	6	DE	129
William	12	MD	170
Dorman, Abraham H	15	DE	183
Ann E	8	DE	37
Catharine R	47	DE	183
David	48	DE	37
Ellenor	47	DE	37
Frances J	10	DE	183
Hetty	21	DE	34
John B	7	DE	16
Mary	12	DE	37
Mary C	12	DE	183
Nehemiah	23	DE	34
Nehemiah	44	DE	16
Peter W	17	DE	183
Samuel D	3	DE	37
Sarah A	7	DE	37
Thomas H	20	DE	38
William W	51	DE	183
Dorsey, John	1	DE	76
John	52	DE	76
Lovey J	22	DE	76
Doud, Ann S	29	MD	1
Dougherty, John	40	DE	202
Douglas, Henry C	20	MD	211
Douglass, George	6	DE	251
Henry	54	MD	251
Mary	35	MD	251
Mathias	15	DE	252
Sallie	14	DE	251
Downey, James	60	DE	160
Rachel	50	DE	160
Downing, Barrett	18	DE	22
Boze	76	DE	22
Ellenor	51	DE	22
Hiram T	17	DE	227
Irena E	11	DE	227
James	52	DE	227
James R	6	DE	227
John W	11	DE	205
Kizziah	55	DE	205
Margaret	67	DE	227
Margaret J	13	DE	227
Downs, Benjamin	6	DE	287
Caroline	36	MD	277
Catharine	22	MD	278
Clarisa	4	DE	278
Comfort	9	DE	287
George	3	DE	28
Isaac	9	DE	27
Isaac L	1	DE	162
Jacob	8	DE	287
James	20	MD	281
John	60	DE	218
John B	1	DE	218
Joshua	56	MD	281
Josiah	13	MD	277
Josiah M	35	MD	262
Julia A	8	MD	277
Lydia	32	DE	262
Margaret	5	DE	218
Mary	11	DE	287
Mary	56	MD	281
Mary J	26	DE	241
Merril	26	MD	162
Minos	17	MD	281
Nancy	9	MD	281
Noah	30	MD	278
Noah H	3	DE	162
Ritty	13	MD	281
Robert	2	DE	278
Sarah	25	MD	162
Sarah	49	DE	293
Stephen	2	DE	288
William	6	MD	277
William	48	MD	277
Wingate	21	MD	287
Wm J	3	DE	218
Dozey, Alfred	22	DE	53
Drain, Abraham	42	DE	193
Daniel	8	DE	193
Daniel	68	DE	150
Daniel S	16	DE	270
Elizabeth	12	DE	193
Elizabeth E	18	DE	150
Emeline	11	DE	64
George W	23	DE	270
Hannah	5	DE	193
Harriet	34	DE	193
Jacob	20	DE	64
James	17	DE	64
John	16	DE	193
Lovy	51	DE	270
Margaret	3	DE	193
Mary	50	DE	150
Robert	22	DE	64
Sallie	7	DE	193
Sally	55	DE	270
Shepherd	65	DE	270
Solomon	13	DE	193
Drane, Arminia	2	DE	45
Daniel	25	DE	45
Levinia	21	DE	45
Draper, Abigail R	5	DE	73
Alexander S	33	DE	73
Alfred	4	DE	29
Ann E	8	DE	70
Byard	15	DE	72
Catharine	22	DE	29
Edward	5	DE	74
Eliza	2	DE	64
Eliza	31	DE	70
Elizabeth	6	DE	70
Elizabeth	25	DE	70
Draper, Elizabeth E	35	DE	64
George	16	DE	70
George H	4	DE	70
Henry	18	DE	24
Henry C	12	DE	72
Henry R	33	DE	70
Henry W	22	DE	70
Hester	23	DE	72
Hester Ann	1	DE	29
James	14	DE	70
James	50	DE	34
James B	8	DE	73
John	9	DE	69
John	45	DE	30
John P	8	DE	113
Jonathan	40	DE	68
Joseph	2	DE	70
Joseph	6	DE	29
Joseph H	7	DE	70
Josephine	16	DE	56
Leah	60	DE	68
Lemuel	53	DE	72
Lydia	7	DE	70
Lydia L	9	DE	73
Mary	3	DE	70
Mary C	6	DE	70
Mary J	26	DE	70
Mary S	7	DE	73
Maud	35	DE	70
Miers	31	DE	70
Nancy	9	DE	31
Nehemiah D	6	DE	70
R	4	DE	70
Rachael	20	DE	85
Sarah	14	DE	72
Sarah	31	DE	73
Sarah E	27	DE	70
Sarah W	10	DE	70
Sina	50	DE	68
Thomas	5	DE	70
Thomas	18	DE	34
Thomas	35	DE	70
Thomas	75	DE	70
Wilhelmina	1	DE	70
William	7/12	DE	70
William	11	DE	24
William C	3	DE	73
Driggans, Julia	25	DE	45
Duffield, Edward	10	DE	49
Thomas	12	DE	49
Rody	45	DE	49
James	52	DE	49
Dutton, Elizabeth	19	DE	23
Elizabeth	22	DE	23
Ellenor	31	DE	22
Dugers, Letty	44	DE	183
Major	48	DE	183
Duhamel, Charles	30	DE	220
Levinia	30	DE	220
Mariam	6	DE	220
Duke, Arthur	24	DE	168
Charlotte	66	DE	168
Edward	14	DE	155
Henry	17	DE	155
Hiram	21	DE	168
James	40	DE	155
Jesse	20	DE	151
John H	6	DE	151
Littleton H	28	DE	151
Lurania A	8	DE	151
Mary C	1	DE	151
Nancy	34	DE	151
Nancy	40	DE	155
Parker	69	DE	168
Paynter	16	DE	155
William	40	DE	294
Dukes, Benjamin	5	DE	98
Emaline	3	DE	98
George	8	DE	98
George	41	DE	98
Isaac	6	DE	98
Jane	1/12	DE	98

Name	Age	State	Page
Dukes, John	4	DE	285
John	24	DE	153
Mary	2	DE	98
Mary	24	DE	153
Mary	30	DE	283
Mary	32	DE	98
Sarah A	11	DE	98
Samuel	35	DE	283
Thomas	9	DE	285
Virginia	4	DE	98
Walter C	2/12	DE	153
William	12	DE	98
Dulany, Levin W	24	DE	207
Martha	20	DE	207
Mary E	3	DE	207
Dulin, Benton	36	DE	248
Enoch	2	DE	247
Erasmus	4	DE	247
Leonel	8	DE	247
Olivia	12	DE	247
Patience	11	DE	247
Priscilla	36	DE	247
Duncan, Charles	9/12	DE	288
Levin	23	MD	288
Nancy	25	MD	288
Dunn, Ann M	15	DE	247
Asher	48	DE	223
David	10	DE	247
Eliza A	50	DE	223
James	7	DE	223
John H	13	DE	247
Mary	79	DE	205
William	4	DE	223
William	71	DE	247
Wm	24	DE	216
Dunning, Adeline V	19	DE	171
Barsheba	65	DE	47
Isaac J	21	DE	11
Jane	19	DE	2
James A	25	DE	171
Martha	57	DE	1
Martha T	2	DE	171
Valevia	4/12	DE	171
William	72	DE	1
Dunoho, Clement	6	DE	252
George	8	DE	252
Hiram	3	DE	252
James	27	DE	286
Jane	32	DE	252
Julia	1/12	DE	252
Maranda	23	DE	286
Margaret	22	DE	252
Minos	1	DE	252
Noah	10	DE	252
Sarah	2	DE	286
William	6	DE	286
Duran, Paul	21	FR	45
Dutton, Ann	16	DE	150
Ann	16	DE	149
Araminta	2	DE	199
Charity	16	DE	215
Comfort A	4	DE	22
Daniel	13	DE	215
Eliza	2	DE	215
Elizabeth	19	DE	22
Elizabeth	22	DE	22
Elizabeth	50	DE	22
Frances M	21	DE	11
George H	30	DE	22
Gideon W	19	DE	11
Isaac J	1	DE	23
Isaac T	28	DE	11
James	30	DE	22
James H	7/12	DE	207
James M	35	DE	199
James R	7	DE	43
Jane	42	DE	215
Jerry	10	DE	215
Jesse	31	DE	22
John	42	MD	215
John	51	DE	43
John Truitt	7	DE	22
Dutton, Josiah	49	DE	12
Levin P	24	DE	26
Lucy E	14	DE	22
Margaret	7	DE	215
Margaret	70	DE	297
Maria E	52	DE	22
Mary J	3	DE	22
Mary J	22	DE	22
Nancy	17	DE	26
Painter	8	DE	215
Peter L P	2	DE	22
Priscilla	24	DE	199
Sarah E	8	DE	22
Sarah Jane	16	DE	11
William	3	DE	215
William	30	DE	22
William A	5	DE	22
Dyer, Charles	27	DE	105
Eliza	3/12	DE	105
Elizabeth	24	DE	105
Dynes, Maria	16	DE	225
Dyre, Charlott	14	DE	94
Daniel	10	DE	94
Eleanor	33	DE	94
Hester	5	DE	94
Leonard	7	DE	94
Rebecca	3/12	DE	94
Sallie	2	DE	94
Thomas	61	DE	94
Eagin, Amelia	34	DE	213
Charlotte A	5	DE	213
Cornelia	27	MD	213
Elizabeth	19	DE	205
James	4/12	DE	213
Martha C	2/12	DE	205
Mary	68	DE	213
Mary Jane	26	DE	213
Sarah E	7	DE	213
Wm	23	DE	213
Wm H	3	DE	213
Easum, Henry	30	DE	263
Margaret	28	DE	263
Martha	7	DE	264
William	5	DE	264
Eddington, John H	17	DE	21
Mary J	1	DE	17
Sarah	24	DE	17
William	52	DE	17
Edwards, Eliza	6	DE	82
George	12	DE	82
Joseph	14	DE	82
Sarah Ann	1	DE	82
Stephen	55	VA	207
William H	9	DE	82
Eliot, John H	30	DE	147
Louisa H	23	DE	147
Lovenia	5	DE	148
Maranda	18	DE	148
Mary A	3	DE	148
Sarah E	8/12	DE	148
William J	2	DE	148
Winget	30	DE	148
Ellegood, Alexander	39	DE	230
Ann	13	DE	281
Ann	46	DE	282
Ann E	19	DE	282
Catherine	11	DE	40
Catherine	21	DE	282
Charles	13	DE	230
Elizabeth	18	DE	281
Elizabeth	38	DE	40
Elizabeth A	15	DE	230
Francis	37	DE	237
Georgianna	3/12	MD	203
John	15	DE	236
John	68	MD	234
John H	8	DE	56
John H	49	DE	40
John T	14	DE	230
Joseph	11	DE	230
Joseph	11	DE	239
Ellegood, Joshua	2	DE	56
Joshua A	6	DE	282
Julia A	32	DE	234
Julia Ann	16	DE	40
Lake	5	DE	56
Levin	2	MD	203
Levin	7	DE	230
Levinia	34	DE	56
Louisa	6	DE	40
Margaret	82	DE	281
Margaret L	10	DE	56
Martin W	9	DE	40
Mary	35	DE	230
Mary E	1	DE	40
Mary G	16	DE	282
Miranda	13	DE	40
Nancy	45	MD	203
Priscilla	7	DE	40
Rhoda A	5	DE	204
Robert	23	DE	282
Sarah	10	DE	230
Sarah	10	DE	282
Seth	7	DE	282
Shepherd	17	DE	282
Vinus	13	DE	282
William	13	DE	282
William	26	DE	170
William	40	DE	56
Ellensworth, David E	16	DE	216
Dennard	23	DE	216
Eliza	7	DE	77
Elizabeth	11	MD	237
Elizabeth	12	DE	85
Elizabeth	18	DE	86
Elizabeth	18	DE	90
Elizabeth	39	DE	35
George	39	DE	201
Harriet	10	DE	77
Henry	16	DE	34
James	17	DE	267
James E	9	DE	216
James P	6	DE	34
Jane	15	DE	27
John	13	DE	34
John	18	DE	216
Joseph	30	DE	85
Joshua J	37	DE	77
Levinia J	11	DE	120
Louisa	20	DE	216
Luke	30	DE	86
Luke	33	DE	90
Lydia	20	DE	67
Mary E	17	DE	262
Mary Ann	45	DE	77
Nancy	30	DE	86
Nancy	50	DE	90
Noble E	43	DE	34
Rachel A	7	DE	216
Rufus N	2	DE	34
Salathiel	13	DE	76
Sarah	49	DE	216
William	3	DE	77
William	7	DE	201
William W	11	DE	34
Wm S	12	DE	216
Ellingsworth, Andrew	43	DE	194
Benjamin	50	DE	160
Cornelius	5	DE	165
Cornelius	34	DE	165
Eliza C	7	DE	165
Eliza J	3	DE	160
James	25	DE	159
Louisa	8	DE	165
Love	23	DE	159
Lovey	54	DE	160
Margaret A	19	DE	160
Mary	1	DE	165
Mary	15	DE	160
Mary E	1	DE	160
Priscilla	30	DE	165
Robinson	20	DE	160
Samuel	19	DE	165

Ellingsworth, Sarah	8	DE	159	Elliott, Margaret	9	DE	265	Ellis, Elenora A	40	DE	253
Unicy	21	DE	160	Margaret	10	DE	229	Elijah	12	DE	196
William	11	DE	165	Margaret	11	DE	265	Eliza A	17	DE	253
Elliot, Aaron	17	DE	101	Margaret	18	DE	265	Elizabeth	4/12	DE	254
Amelia	15	DE	246	Margaret	50	DE	269	Elizabeth	64	DE	253
Elizabeth	15	DE	101	Margaret	57	DE	268	Emeline	20	DE	245
James A	3	MD	245	Margaret	55	DE	265	Fernetta	37	DE	255
Joseph	67	DE	101	Margaret A	1	DE	244	Ferry B	14	DE	255
Margaret A	1	DE	245	Mariah	16	DE	265	Frances	11	DE	256
Mary E	9/12	DE	101	Mary	13	DE	224	Francis	8	DE	254
Mary E	7	DE	245	Mary	17	DE	268	George	2	DE	266
Wm H	5	DE	245	Mary	20	DE	262	George R	10	DE	196
Elliott, Alfrod	8	DE	262	Mary	22	DE	261	George W	8	DE	254
Alfred	20	DE	268	Mary	24	DE	263	Geo W	30	DE	250
Andrew	32	DE	265	Mary	24	DE	267	Gillis	46	DE	195
Anthony	22	DE	268	Mary	27	DE	262	Gustavus	1	DE	253
Benjamin	13	DE	261	Mary	31	DE	265	Hetty P	26	DE	130
Benjamin	42	DE	265	Mary	37	MD	261	Isaac	20	DE	255
Bridgett	7	DE	265	Mary	40	DE	265	Isaiah	37	DE	130
Burton	2	DE	267	Mary	54	DE	261	James	9	DE	245
Burton	44	DE	261	Mary	55	DE	265	James	39	MD	255
Caroline	5	DE	242	Mary E	30	DE	244	James	44	DE	253
Charles	9	DE	259	Mary J	27	DE	244	James E	22	DE	257
Charlotte	28	DE	256	Matilda	8	DE	262	James S	6	DE	253
Elinor	6	DE	262	Nancy	14	DE	262	James W	11	DE	255
Elenor	11	DE	259	Nancy	19	DE	261	John	3	DE	266
Elias	40	DE	262	Nancy	30	DE	259	John	4	DE	245
Elijah	10	DE	265	Nancy	65	DE	265	John H	5	DE	130
Eliza	10	DE	261	Naoma	47	DE	261	Jonathan W	10	DE	253
Elizabeth	6	DE	246	Naomia	18	DE	261	Joseph	30	DE	252
Elizabeth	7	DE	261	Nathaniel J	26	DE	266	Joseph B	13	DE	254
Elizabeth	23	DE	261	Noah	64	MD	269	Joseph E	22	DE	245
Elizabeth	39	DE	262	Patty	31	DE	222	Joseph of W	40	DE	254
Elizabeth	60	DE	265	Paynter	16	DE	261	Josephine A	5	DE	254
Emeline	5	DE	261	Pernetta	6	DE	262	Josephus	4	DE	253
George	7	DE	259	Peter	11	DE	210	Julia A	30	DE	266
George	10	DE	263	Phillace	60	DE	233	Keasey A	28	DE	253
George W	10	DE	265	Rachel	13	DE	262	Laura A	1	DE	250
Henry W	35	DE	263	Robin	14	DE	261	Lavenia	42	MD	195
Hetty	33	DE	242	Rufus	14	DE	259	Lavenia E	5	DE	195
Hetty	43	DE	265	Sarah	10	DE	246	Leah	20	MD	250
Huet	75	DE	261	Sarah	14	DE	242	Littleton	50	DE	255
Jacob	4	DE	262	Sarah	58	DE	256	Mackinsa P	14	DE	255
Jacob	17	DE	242	Sarah C	9	DE	245	Maranda	2	DE	253
Jacob	19	DE	266	Sarah J	7	DE	235	Margaret E	14	DE	245
Jacob	29	DE	229	Sallie	20	DE	261	Martha	5	DE	255
Jacob	48	DE	268	Sally E	31	DE	223	Martha	14	DE	245
Jacob W	46	DE	261	Samuel	30	DE	256	Martin	12	DE	130
James	12	DE	263	Samuel B	35	DE	259	Mary	6	DE	250
James A	3	DE	244	Sarah	14	DE	265	Mary	7	DE	245
James T	7	DE	265	Sarah C	9	DE	244	Mary	37	DE	196
Jane	28	DE	229	Sarah E	3	DE	229	Mary	40	DE	256
Jeremiah	25	DE	268	Sarah J	6	DE	265	Mary	70	DE	130
John	2	DE	262	Selvy	50	DE	268	Mary A	8	DE	255
John	2	DE	263	Serach	64	DE	268	Mary A	16	DE	256
John	8	DE	262	Solomon H	34	DE	244	Mary F	4	DE	253
John	24	DE	237	Sophia	45	DE	242	Mary L A	2	DE	196
John	53	DE	242	Stockley	16	DE	259	Mathias	11	DE	245
John	60	DE	265	Stokely W	43	DE	261	Menelas	6	MD	253
Joseph	11	DE	262	Theodore	18/12	DE	265	Nancy	50	DE	255
Joseph	17	DE	259	Warren	4	DE	262	Noah	18	DE	245
Joshua	27	DE	267	William	1	DE	229	Phillian M	5	MD	196
Joshua S	31	DE	263	William	1	DE	263	Priscilla	13	DE	245
Josiah	3	DE	263	William	16	DE	265	Rachel	2	DE	253
Lavenia	27	DE	263	William	23	DE	266	Rachel	2	DE	255
Lavenia	43	DE	261	William	27	DE	261	Rebecca	4	DE	254
Levinia	8	DE	261	Wm H	5	DE	244	Rhoda	8	DE	266
Levinia	16	DE	261	Wm T	31	DE	235	Robert E	13	MD	195
Leah	12	DE	265	Wm W	24	DE	262	Samuel	1	DE	246
Leah	18	DE	262	Ellis, Amy	22	DE	15	Samuel	6	DE	78
Leonard	18	DE	267	Amy A	11	DE	254	Sarah	20	DE	256
Lewis	35	DE	265	Anna	68	DE	250	Sarah	48	DE	245
Lorenzo	12	DE	261	Archilla	3	DE	256	Sarah E	9	DE	255
Lurana	18	DE	266	Army	25	DE	235	Sarah E	15	MD	195
Lydia	1	DE	262	Cannon	18	DE	267	Sarah E	18	DE	253
Lydia	10	DE	225	Catesbury	6	DE	256	Sopheonea	7	MD	196
Machaiel	14	DE	265	Charlotte	14	DE	196	Stephen	5	DE	245
Mahala	17	DE	266	Charlotte	28	DE	250	Stephen	16	DE	235
Maria	2	DE	261	Charlotte E	10	DE	195	Stephen	32	DE	250
Maria	16	DE	242	David	1	DE	245	Stephen	46	DE	245
Margaret	5	DE	263	Eleanor	8	DE	236	Stephen E	12	DE	255
Margaret	8	DE	242	Eleanora A	40	DE	253	Susan A	35	DE	254

Name	Age	St	Pg	Name	Age	St	Pg	Name	Age	St	Pg
Ellis, Theodore	14	DE	253	Ennis, David R	13	DE	17	Evans, Catharine B	40	DE	119
Thomas	20	DE	255	Eliza A	10	DE	17	Catharine E	25	DE	122
Thomas	24	DE	266	Elizabeth	18	DE	150	Charles	5	DE	143
Thomas A	16	MD	195	Elizabeth	40	DE	80	Charles B	1	DE	122
William	37	DE	196	Elizabeth	49	DE	149	Charles D	15	PA	117
William R	12	DE	253	Elizabeth R	1	DE	149	Charles J	10	DE	54
William S	16	DE	254	Frederic	16	DE	79	Charles W	31	DE	120
Wm	15	DE	245	George B	11	DE	182	Charlotte	3	DE	290
Wm B	18	MD	195	George W	4/12	DE	18	Clarissa A	3	DE	143
Wm G W	8	IL	250	Henry	22	DE	80	Clement	42	DE	143
Elsey, Arnald A	50	DE	254	Henry W	2/12	DE	149	Cordelia	2	DE	119
Charles	13	DE	254	Hester	20	DE	80	Cordelia S	17	PA	117
Elizabeth	44	DE	254	James	19	DE	79	Cornelius F	8	DE	119
Lewis	6	DE	254	Jesse	45	DE	17	Cornelius W	6	DE	54
Sarah E	15	DE	254	John	3	DE	147	Curtis	3	DE	118
Elwell, Charles	3	DE	3	John	66	DE	8	Daniel	76	DE	135
Margaret	24	DE	3	John R	14	DE	149	David	27	DE	117
Philip	5	DE	3	John W	6	DE	182	David W	34	DE	119
Sarah	1	DE	3	Joseph J	42	DE	182	Eben	21	DE	117
Elzey, Alfred	34	DE	241	Joshua R	23	DE	182	Edgar L	8	DE	135
Levin	21	DE	238	Kitty	24	DE	147	Edward	22	DE	118
Mary	60	DE	241	Levinia	14	DE	80	Elijah	20	DE	123
Robert	64	DE	240	Louisa D	13	DE	9	Elisha	43	DE	119
Emerson, George	4	DE	291	Louisa E	22	DE	149	Elisha C D	12	DE	54
Rachel	2	DE	291	Margaret A	13	DE	9	Eliza	14	DE	38
Emily, C	5	DE	237	Margaret H	64	DE	16	Eliza	30	DE	117
Engard, Wm	26	PA	232	Martha A	16	DE	182	Eliza	48	DE	120
English, Brittana	4	DE	243	Martha A	23	DE	182	Elizabeth	6	DE	135
Charity	13	DE	243	Mary A	1	DE	147	Elizabeth	11	DE	213
Elisha	16	DE	288	Mellay M	16	DE	149	Elizabeth	14	DE	144
Elisha	57	DE	288	Nancy	46	DE	182	Elizabeth	18	DE	128
Harriet	40	DE	243	Sarah E	8	DE	17	Elizabeth	28	DE	119
James	23	DE	288	Sarah E	35	DE	17	Elizabeth	36	DE	144
John	9	DE	243	Stephen	34	DE	80	Elizabeth	77	DE	128
Joseph J	11	DE	288	Susan M	3	DE	18	Elizabeth D	31	DE	128
Levinia	50	DE	288	William B	21	DE	182	Elizabeth F	10	DE	53
Maria	5	DE	288	William B T	1	DE	182	Elizabeth L	10	DE	52
Nancy	75	DE	204	Eskards, Emelia C E	3	DE	196	Elizabeth M	30	DE	130
Sena	18	DE	243	Goldborough D	8	DE	196	Emma S	4	DE	54
Wm T	16	DE	243	Mary A	10	DE	196	Enoch R	18	DE	171
Engram, Alfred R	13	DE	179	Mary A	13	DE	196	Ezekiel	21	DE	120
Alla F	37	DE	164	Mary E	33	DE	196	Ezekiel	61	DE	120
Ann E	4	DE	165	Oakly T	43	DE	196	Ezekiel W	11	DE	124
Charles	50	DE	166	William S	3/12	DE	196	George	15	DE	39
Daniel	13	DE	158	Eskridge, Adaline	33	OH	207	Harriet	1/12	DE	144
Eliza	8	DE	164	Antoinetta	4	DE	206	Harriet	11	DE	52
Eliza	21	DE	166	Arcadia E	7	DE	206	Harriet J	12	DE	129
George	14	DE	166	Catherine	5	DE	207	Henrietta	6	DE	289
George T	16	DE	165	Catherine	33	DE	195	Henry	12	DE	38
Gincey	36	DE	164	David A	15	DE	195	Henry	24	DE	135
Henry	60	MD	171	Isabella L	2	DE	206	Henry	40	DE	143
Hetty A	24	DE	158	James	14	OH	207	Hester C	3	DE	121
Isaac	17	DE	166	James J	12	DE	273	Hetty	19	DE	118
James	20	DE	166	James L	9	MD	206	Hetty	38	DE	118
John	12	DE	166	Jeremiah	4	DE	274	Hetty J	33	DE	55
John	15	DE	158	Jeremiah	38	DE	273	Isaac	10	DE	118
Letty	35	DE	165	John	50	DE	207	Isaac	26	DE	117
Letty	19	DE	165	Jonathan	8	DE	273	Isaac	30	DE	120
Lydia	21	DE	158	Lorenzo D	6	DE	274	Isaac	48	DE	118
Margaret A	17	DE	170	Lydia	10	NJ	207	Isaac H	18	DE	123
Mary	7	DE	166	Margaret E	1	DE	206	Isaiah C	6	DE	130
Mary	28	DE	166	Margaret R	30	DE	206	Jacob	36	DE	130
Mary	41	DE	158	Mary	11	OH	207	Jacob	61	MD	289
Nathaniel	9	DE	171	Mary Ann	36	DE	273	James	10	DE	38
Nathaniel	44	DE	165	Samuel	36	DE	206	James	17	DE	76
Peter	50	DE	158	Uphany	6	DE	273	James	32	DE	289
Rachel	15	DE	165	William	5/12	DE	207	James	44	MD	137
Rhoda J	15	DE	170	William F	1	DE	195	James W	17	DE	124
Robert	1	DE	166	William F	12	DE	273	Jane C	7	DE	143
Sarah	7	DE	158	Evans, Aaron	3	DE	135	Jedediah D	11	DE	135
Sarah	9	DE	165	Abigail	60	DE	123	Jedediah D	45	DE	116
Sarah E	12	DE	170	Albert S	31	DE	121	Job	14	DE	120
Thomas	19	DE	165	Alfonso G	1	DE	117	John	1	DE	149
William	1	DE	166	Amanda	9	DE	117	John	4	MD	289
William	12	DE	171	Arcada	6	DE	128	John	16	DE	144
William C	13	DE	165	Archabald	38	DE	213	John	20	DE	118
Ennis, Adam	17	DE	149	Benjamin	42	DE	119	John	40	DE	130
Ann J	25	DE	16	Benjamin F	17	DE	119	John H	3	DE	137
Burton M	11	DE	149	Burton	8	DE	143	John J	16	DE	120
Caleb S	4	DE	16	Caroline	4	DE	119	John W	14	DE	136
Charity	7	DE	18	Catharine	6	DE	118	John W	15	DE	71
David P	29	DE	16	Catharine B	40	DE	119	Joshua	14	DE	118

Name			
Evans, Joshua T	4	DE	131
Lemuel	2	DE	119
Lemuel	9	DE	289
Lemuel	55	DE	117
Lemuel	63	DE	52
Lemuel H	9	DE	130
Louisa A J	6	DE	129
Love A	1	DE	120
Lucinda R	15	DE	119
Margaret	3	DE	144
Margaret	4	DE	117
Margaret	22	DE	119
Margaret	26	DE	119
Margaret D	6/12	DE	129
Martha	31	DE	135
Martin U B	14	DE	52
Mary	1	MD	289
Mary	5	DE	290
Mary	8	DE	144
Mary	8	DE	293
Mary	12	DE	119
Mary	21	DE	117
Mary	24	MD	137
Mary	25	DE	130
Mary	26	DE	119
Mary	58	DE	128
Mary	61	DE	119
Mary A	14	DE	119
Mary A	32	DE	143
Mary A	37	DE	213
Mary C	11/12	DE	54
Mary C	9	DE	121
Mary D	6/12	DE	129
Mary J	12	PA	117
Mary M	1	DE	144
Matilda	29	DE	289
Nancy	25	DE	290
Nancy	50	DE	52
Nancy	54	DE	121
Nancy	60	DE	116
Nancy C	3	DE	130
Nancy C	6	DE	121
Nancy J	10	DE	130
Naomi S	12	DE	135
Nathaniel M	5	DE	135
Nathaniel W	44	DE	135
Oliver	14	DE	124
Orland	6	DE	119
Rhoda	2	DE	122
Rhoda	46	DE	130
Rhoda L	3/12	DE	130
Rhoda M	21	DE	121
Rebecca A	1	DE	130
Samuel C	15	DE	123
Sarah	6	DE	144
Sarah	8	DE	290
Sarah	55	DE	123
Sarah A	2	DE	213
Sarah A	36	PA	117
Sarah E	16	DE	128
Sarah H	21	DE	120
Sarah R	6	DE	130
Sarah W	24	DE	130
Selby	30	DE	122
Selby	31	DE	122
Silas R J	3	DE	129
Silas W J	6	DE	119
Spencer	27	DE	290
Stephen H	26	DE	122
Stephen R	3	DE	119
Stephen R	41	DE	128
Stephen W	27	DE	119
Sylvester C	17	DE	119
Tabitha	9	DE	279
Thomas	4	DE	213
Thomas	52	DE	124
William	12	DE	144
William	52	DE	54
William	58	DE	123
William H	8	DE	54
William P	2	DE	121
William S	30	DE	119

Name			
Evans, William T	34	DE	130
Wm H H	9	DE	129
Zadock	72	DE	130
Zadock A	4	DE	130
Zadock J	8	DE	130
Ewing, Adolphus P	30	DE	2
Chloe	50	DE	2
Gustavus A	3	DE	2
Louisa M	27	DE	2
Mary Ann	1	DE	2
Ewings, Charles	5	DE	31
Eliza	7	DE	31
George	8	DE	31
Farmer, Caroline	2	DE	269
Charles	43	DE	269
Edwin	6	DE	269
John	11	DE	269
Martha	5	DE	269
Sarah	7	DE	269
Unicy	30	DE	269
Fassett, Elsey	40	DE	43
Fassitt, Elizabeth	24	DE	41
George	7	DE	41
Jacob	48	DE	41
Jacob E	3	DE	41
Mary E	8/12	DE	41
Peter F	18	DE	41
Sarah W	5	DE	41
William A	10	DE	41
Ferry, Amelia P	19	DE	116
Drucilla	4	DE	116
Edward P	25	NH	116
Mary V	1	DE	116
Fiddeman, Eliza	37	DE	91
Henry	11	DE	91
Henry B	42	DE	91
Mary	14	DE	91
Phillip	14	DE	91
Field, Joseph	40	DE	71
Joseph H	6	DE	72
Susan H	2	DE	72
Figgs, James H	25	DE	260
Jonathan	19	DE	260
Lucinda A	14	DE	260
Mary	52	DE	260
Fisher, A Ann	14	DE	13
Alexander R	24	DE	108
Cassandra	17	DE	108
Catharine	7	DE	106
Catharine	27	DE	108
Charles	5/12	DE	13
Charles	3	DE	190
Charles	12	DE	13
Comfort	22	DE	22
Daniel	26	DE	108
Eliza	28	DE	37
Elizabeth	6/12	DE	190
Elzey	12	DE	108
Emaline	18	DE	221
George	3	DE	22
George	5	DE	145
George	8	DE	190
George R	59	DE	77
Hetty A	20	DE	190
Hiram	18	DE	62
James	6	DE	106
James	20	DE	13
James	63	DE	106
James H	27	DE	297
James M	45	DE	189
John	22	DE	13
John H	32	DE	37
John T	1	DE	37
Joseph	17	DE	44
Joseph	23	DE	22
Joseph	50	DE	145
Joshua S	2	DE	145
Kitty	45	MD	128
Lorenzo	35	DE	96
Louisa	36	DE	97
Luther W	22	DE	108

Name			
Fisher, Luther W	22	DE	108
Lydia	23	DE	13
Mahala	30	DE	145
Manlove	26	DE	108
Manlove	55	DE	214
Margaret	5	DE	190
Margaret	16	DE	62
Martha J	17	DE	189
Mary	35	DE	214
Mary	54	DE	108
Mary H	7	DE	37
Myers	10	DE	3
Robert S	20	DE	62
Sally	40	DE	189
Samuel	3	DE	214
Samuel C	15	DE	108
Sarah	5/12	DE	22
Sarah	15	DE	106
Sarah	47	DE	106
Theodore	7	DE	108
Thomas	8	DE	62
Thomas C	3	DE	37
William	1	DE	214
William	13	DE	190
William D	11	DE	108
William H	5	DE	37
Fleetwood, Andrew	1	DE	104
Catherine	17	DE	104
Catherine	30	DE	100
Cyrus	7	DE	101
Cyrus	45	DE	100
Curtis	17	DE	101
Curtis	29	DE	230
Delphine	4	DE	100
Eliza	13	DE	104
Eliza	43	DE	105
Elizabeth	3	DE	101
Elizabeth	19	DE	104
Elizabeth	29	DE	230
Elizabeth	35	DE	100
Elizabeth	56	DE	100
Emaline	16	DE	104
George W	2	DE	104
James B	11	MD	207
James H	7	DE	230
Jane	30	DE	207
Jenny	2/12	DE	100
John	20	DE	10
John	29	DE	105
John	36	DE	100
Judith	63	DE	207
Judith L	1	DE	207
Julia Ann	6	DE	101
Juliann	6	DE	100
Margaret	8	DE	100
Mary	10	DE	100
Mary	26	DE	105
Mary E	4/12	DE	230
Mary E	27	DE	206
Nancy	10	DE	3
Philip	5	DE	104
Purnal T	31	DE	207
Ruth Ann	2	DE	100
Samuel	20	DE	104
Sarah	10	DE	101
Sarah	61	DE	101
Sarah H	5	DE	207
Tabitha	30	DE	104
William	14	DE	101
William	29	DE	206
William	41	DE	104
Wm J	2	DE	230
Fletcher, John T	24	MD	196
Marcellus W	13	MD	196
Flosset, William	36	MD	118
Flowers, Ann	55	MD	204
Charles	49	DE	204
Lucinda	15	DE	196
Amelia	10	DE	196
Mary E	21	DE	196
Matilda	26	DE	200
Owen	50	MD	196

Name	Age	ST	Pg
Flowers, Perry	26	DE	196
Rosina	4	DE	200
Sallie A	45	DE	196
Sarah E	1	DE	200
Wesley	32	DE	200
Floyd, Adam	34	DE	174
Eliza A	28	DE	174
John L	6	DE	174
Fooks, Ann J	50	DE	111
Ann M	14	DE	295
Benj F	20	DE	236
Benjamin	74	DE	236
Catherine	35	DE	282
Celia	44	DE	283
Charles B	20	DE	236
Cyrus Q	33	MD	147
Edward	13	DE	282
Elizabeth J	7	DE	236
Elizabeth W	36	DE	282
George	14	DE	250
Henry	17	DE	250
Henry P	14	DE	236
Hetty	22	DE	111
Isaac	8	DE	282
Isaac	48	DE	105
Isaac N	3/12	DE	111
John	1	DE	283
Jonathan B	33	MD	255
Lurana A	24	DE	255
Mary	34	DE	147
Mary E	2	DE	255
Matthew	3	DE	283
Nathan	40	DE	282
Priscilla	24	DE	282
Priscilla C	6	DE	147
Samuel	17	DE	282
Sarah	40	DE	236
Sarah	65	DE	282
Sarah A	2	DE	111
Thomas	28	DE	111
Thomas	70	DE	282
Foskey, Ann	3/12	DE	152
Asbury	9	MD	280
James	50	DE	280
Jannet	38	DE	152
Mary	2	DE	280
Mary	3	DE	152
Mary	65	DE	280
Nancy	5	DE	152
Sarah J	10	DE	152
William	42	DE	152
William H	8	DE	152
Wm	40	DE	289
Fosky, Abigale	30	DE	280
Celia	26	DE	290
Elizabeth	40	MD	260
James B	36	MD	260
Levenia	4	DE	90
Lovy	5	MD	260
Mary	8	MD	260
Matilda	5	DE	280
Nancy	7/12	DE	290
Nancy	40	DE	280
Noble	6	DE	290
Robert	3	MD	260
Winna	15	DE	266
Fossett, Joshua	60	DE	124
Solomon	40	DE	42
Taymer	61	DE	124
Fossitt, John	42	DE	35
Mary	5	DE	228
Mary A	10	DE	35
Peter C	1	DE	35
Sarah E	14	DE	35
Smith	12	DE	35
Foster, Abigail	46	DE	16
Ann	4	DE	16
Ann Maria	9	DE	11
Bainton	35	DE	147
Eliza	30	DE	147
Eliza	35	DE	10
James	56	DE	16
Foster, Lydia Jane	14	DE	16
Lucy	3	DE	16
Raimond	35	DE	10
Robert	10	DE	16
Sarah	1	DE	16
Thomas	15	DE	13
Woolsey	71	DE	57
Fountain, Abraham	56	DE	198
Andrew	11	DE	83
Catherine	7	DE	197
Edwin	11/12	DE	197
Elenor	4	DE	197
Elizabeth	31	DE	83
Elizabeth	45	DE	78
Flora	50	DE	198
Hetty	29	DE	197
James	1	DE	83
John	14	DE	83
Margaret	65	DE	83
Matthew D	48	DE	83
Solomon	13	DE	78
Trapheny	35	DE	78
William	16	DE	83
William H	25	DE	78
Z P	34	DE	197
Fowler, Ann	14	DE	188
Ann	60	DE	71
Benjamin	58	DE	18
Benton	41	DE	94
Eliza	31	DE	38
Ellen	27	DE	71
George	9	DE	39
George	20	DE	73
George H	16	DE	45
Harriet	36	DE	45
James	13	DE	94
Jeremiah	4	DE	71
Lewis P	2	DE	45
Lydia	3	DE	72
Lydia	12	DE	72
Lydia	45	DE	18
Mahala	35	DE	94
Mary	1	DE	38
Mary A	19	DE	94
Mary E	5	DE	72
Minty	5/12	DE	71
Robert	17	DE	25
Robert	34	DE	71
Samuel	4	DE	38
William	5	DE	38
William	34	DE	38
William M	45	DE	45
Frame, Alsey	52	DE	26
Clem T	12	DE	185
Elija J	2	DE	169
Elizabeth	18	DE	185
Elizabeth J	47	DE	185
Fanny	61	DE	169
Gatty	40	DE	177
George	16	DE	169
George W	17	DE	185
Hannah	40	DE	48
Henry	3	DE	190
Henry C	20	DE	185
Isabella	13	DE	169
Jane W	9	DE	185
John	10	DE	193
Mariah	18	DE	25
Mary A	18	DE	1
Mary V	25	DE	185
Matilda	15	DE	51
Paynter	23	DE	185
Peter	60	DE	169
Robert	6	DE	178
Robert	24	DE	203
Sarah J	6	DE	194
Simon	18	DE	177
Thalia H M	7	DE	185
Thomas J	15	DE	185
Frampton, Elisha	51	DE	212
John H	20	DE	212
Mary A	17	DE	212
Frampton, Sarah C	18	DE	212
Sarah R W	15	DE	212
Solomon	60	DE	212
Warren	22	DE	212
Frances, Caroline	19	DE	71
William	20	DE	71
Frank, Cato	18	DE	34
Franklin, Burton	55	DE	287
Clara	6	DE	287
George	1	DE	4
Thomas	25	DE	287
Fulcher, Erasmus W	20	DE	56
Hetty A	44	DE	56
Hetty E	7	DE	56
John	52	DE	56
John M	16	DE	56
Joseph F	10	DE	56
Martha A	12	DE	56
Mary W	22	DE	56
Furman, Abigail	19	DE	122
Amanda	9	DE	131
Ann M	13	DE	152
Arcada R	6	DE	122
Edwin P	13	DE	131
Elizabeth	27	DE	152
Gatty	36	DE	131
George	5	DE	131
Henry	18	DE	152
Hester	78	DE	122
Hetty J	15	DE	131
James	40	DE	122
James	47	DE	152
James A	10	DE	122
John	10	DE	152
John B	46	DE	131
John D	38	DE	124
John P	3	DE	122
Laura A	3	DE	131
Lemuel H	24	DE	122
Love A	4	DE	122
Lucinda	1	DE	131
Maria	24	DE	152
Martha	23	DE	152
Mary	60	DE	147
Mary C	9	DE	122
Mary E	36	DE	124
Mary F	30	DE	122
Mary J	15	DE	152
Mary P	5	DE	124
Phillip J	3	DE	124
Sarah A	1	DE	122
Sarah A	9	DE	124
William	20	DE	152
William E	20	DE	122
Furness, Agnes C	7	NY	121
Amanda P	2	DE	121
Charles	36	GB	121
Charles H	4	DE	121
Mary A	11	NY	121
Mary J	35	MA	121
Susan J	14	NY	121
William R	13	NY	121
Gadwin, Elizabeth	67	DE	85
Margaret	18	DE	85
Gaines, Charles W	17	DE	237
Harvey J	10	DE	237
John G	43	MD	237
Joseph H	13	DE	237
Lavinia	33	DE	237
Leah E	8	DE	237
Gally, F P	27	NY	197
Gam, Eliza	49	DE	292
George	57	DE	292
Isaac	18	DE	292
Levin	12	DE	292
Warren	16	PA	292
Gamm, Leah	23	DE	292
Gams, Chandler	24	DE	256
Esther	51	DE	256
Jane	25	DE	256
Leah	25	DE	234

Gams, Minty	8	DE	256	Gorden, Sina	72	DE	27	Gorman, George	17	DE	222
Garvie, Leah	23	DE	268	William	45	DE	56	Gosle, Ellenor	3	DE	38
Gatt, Elizabeth	35	MD	139	Gordon, Charles C	5	DE	49	Hetty A	26	DE	38
Gaul, Bentley	10	PA	113	David	31	DE	17	Letty	61	DE	38
Gib, Nelly G A	29	DE	50	Elizabeth S	38	DE	48	Samuel G	34	DE	38
Robert G A	13	DE	50	James	42	DE	48	Goslin, Ann M	11	DE	223
Gibbon, Eleanor	24	DE	151	Sarah H	8	DE	49	Catherine B	2	DE	223
John	28	DE	151	Gordy, Aaron	19	DE	267	Elizabeth	26	DE	107
Mary	21	DE.	151	Amilia	14	DE	267	Emma	17	DE	215
Meranda	13	DE	151	Ann	18/12	DE	275	George	6	DE	223
Samuel	61	DE	151	Aron N	28	DE	275	Hester	52	DE	215
Train	17	DE	151	Benjamin	5	DE	262	Hester L	14	DE	215
Gibbons, Eleanor	25	DE	174	Benjamin	12	DE	267	Isaac	58	DE	240
Elizabeth	12	DE	109	Benton H	35	DE	262	James B	4	DE	223
Frederick	18	DE	109	Chally	10	DE	267	James M	41	DE	223
Isaac	5	DE	109	Elizabeth	10	DE	294	Lovey	5	DE	107
John	1	DE	109	Elizabeth	32	DE	262	Nancy	30	MD	223
Louisa	30	DE	109	Elijah	4	DE	267	Sally	39	DE	265
Lucinda	5	DE	109	Eliza	2	DE	290	Waitman	45	DE	107
Mary	25	DE	109	Elizabeth	45	DE	267	Wm H	12	DE	223
Miles	11	DE	109	Emeline	3	DE	294	Gosly, Elijah	45	DE	244
Nancy	31	DE	109.	George	5	DE	275	Eliza T	1	DE	244
Olivia	16	DE	113	George L	4	DE	256	Martha	16	DE	244
Sarah	1	DE	109	Hetty	6	DE	262	Mary	25	MD	245
Sarah	65	DE	109	Jackson	27	DE	287	Sallie	34	DE	244
Gibs, Hester	87	DE	51	James	9	DE	290	Gothard, John	23	DE	20
Susan	18	DE	51	James	17	DE	235	Gotherd, Elisha	35	DE	15
Giffith, Ellen	3	DE	36	John	7	DE	275	James H	9	DE	15
Sally	25	DE	36	John	19	DE	287	Sally	30	DE	15
Giles, Ann E	13	DE	250	John	40	DE	235	Graham, Ann	40	DE	291
Edith	7	DE	250	John	52	DE	262	Benjamin	12	DE	291
Isaac	46	MD	250	John C	29	DE	256	Hester	6	DE	291
James S	14	DE	292	John H	29	DE	256	James	28	DE	268
Lucy	9	DE	250	Joseph	9	DE	267	James R	5	DE	268
Sallie	3	DE	250	Lavinia	7	DE	294	John	14	DE	291
Sarah E	34	DE	250	Louisa	8	DE	262	Kendal J	2	DE	268
Thomas	1	DE	250	Lurany	23	DE	275	Levin	2	DE	291
Gines, Bridget	60	DE	157	Margaret A	20	DE	235	Peter	4	DE	291
Ginley, James	14	DE	14	Maria	70	DE	235	Phillip	18	DE	291
Godfrey, Amos	21	MD	137	Mary	4	DE	294	Phillip	56	MD	291
Charlotte	3	DE	151	Mary	6	DE	262	Sarah	20	DE	297
Cornelius	19	DE	230	Mary	45	DE	262	Sarah	27	DE	268
Eliza J	2	DE	151	Mary E	3	DE	256	Uriah	16	DE	291
Elizabeth	26	DE	173	Mary M	38	DE	235	William	7	DE	268
Henry	50	DE	151	Matilda	23	MD	266	William	10	DE	291
George W	6	MD	128	Nancy	1	DE	287	Wm	25	MD	297
Isaac B	2	DE	173	Nancy	42	DE	276	Graves, Nancy	60	DE	29
Joseph C	4	DE	173	Nancy W	38	DE	238	Gray, Alfred	7	DE	112
Julia E	6	DE	173	Patience	15	DE	267	Amelia	41	MD	112
Levin D	39	MD	173	Peter	22	DE	290	Ann	12	DE	231
Levin J	6	DE	151	Priscilla	28	DE	294	Ann	30	DE	281
Martha	41	MD	128	Rebecca	21	DE	290	Annanias	12	DE	112
Mary	23	MD	128	Rhoda	26	DE	287	Annanias	42	MD	112
Mary E	35	DE	172	Sarah	2	DE	262	Ardelia	15	DE	252
Nathaniel D	24	DE	172	Sarah	12	DE	294	Benjamin	11	DE	143
Zippora	25	DE	151	Sarah	25	DE	256	Benjamin	47	MD	112
Godwin, Charles T	4	DE	135	Sarah E	33	MD	236	Biddy	9	DE	282
Charlotte	11	DE	183	Stephen	3	DE	262	Burton	5	DE	112
Comfort	39	DE	123	Stephen H	35	DE	294	Caroline	18	DE	281
David	13	DE	123	William	17	DE	267	Catharine	7	DE	225
David	47	DE	123	William	56	DE	267	Catharine	14	DE	112
Ebe W	1	DE	135	Gorley, Albina	2	DE	175	Ebe D	2	DE	143
Eliza J	17	DE	123	Benjamin	28	DE	145	Ebe D	49	MD	143
Elizabeth	16	DE	183	Catharine	34	DE	178	Eben	52	DE	281
George T	3	DE	135	Edward	12	DE	178	Ebinezar	17	DE	277
Jacob	13	DE	123	Elizabeth J	17	DE	178	Edward	7	DE	229
James W	18	DE	123	Frances	32	DE	179	Elija C	1	DE	112
John	33	DE	135	George H	9	DE	145	Eliza	10	DE	210
Maria	14	DE	123	George H	9	DE	175	Elizabeth	12	DE	277
Mary A	34	DE	135	Hector E	4	DE	179	Elizabeth	14	DE	229
Mary C	4	DE	123	John S	1	DE	179	Elizabeth	16	DE	137
Nancy T	5	DE	125	Louisa	5	DE	175	Elizabeth	25	DE	84
Naomi	47	DE	182	Louisa C	4	DE	177	Elizabeth	28	DE	76
Robert H	2	DE	123	Mary	5	DE	145	Elizabeth	46	DE	281
Sarah	6	DE	144	Mary A	6	DE	177	Elizabeth	50	DE	231
Tabitha	36	DE	125	Mary J	29	DE	175	Elizabeth A	13	DE	143
Thomas	22	DE	135	Peter C	40	DE	177	Emaline	2	DE	84
William H	36	DE	125	Salathel B	8	DE	178	Emeline H	26	DE	112
William J	2	DE	125	Samuel	2	DE	145	Fanny	4	DE	281
Gooden, Sarah	50	DE	52	Sarah J	2	DE	177	George	15	DE	231
Gorden, David	72	DE	27	William W	14	DE	177	George	19	DE	229
Sarah	75	DE	56	William W	37	DE	179	George L	16	DE	229

Name	Age	State	Page
Gray, Hannah	20	DE	125
Hester	9	DE	143
Hetty	10	DE	277
Hiram B	16	MD	139
Hooper	10	DE	231
Isaac	20	DE	281
James	5	DE	225
James	8	DE	252
James	40	DE	229
James B	20	DE	143
Jehu H	11	DE	143
Jesse	10	DE	112
John	12	DE	281
John	25	DE	133
John H	14	DE	143
Johnson	42	DE	143
Joshua	5	DE	64
Joshua	17	DE	112
Joshua	30	DE	225
Joshua	37	DE	76
Joshua	47	MD	277
Joshua	68	DE	76
Leah	7/12	DE	252
Levin C	13	DE	143
Levenia	28	DE	225
Louvinia	18	DE	277
Lydia	42	DE	143
Margaret	6	DE	281
Margaret	50	DE	76
Msrgaret	60	DE	84
Martha	16	DE	231
Mary	10	DE	289
Mary	19	DE	133
Mary	23	DE	229
Mary C	9	DE	144
Matilda	19	DE	142
Milby	17	DE	143
Mitchell	21	DE	143
Nancy	30	DE	252
Noah	6	DE	229
Peter	10	DE	231
Peter	22	DE	222
Rachel	14	DE	281
Samuel	5	DE	281
Samuel	9	DE	229
Samuel	18	DE	231
Sarah	2/12	DE	225
Sarah	13	DE	277
Sarah A	20	DE	277
Sarah E	14	DE	231
Sarah J	8	DE	21
Sena	13	NC	231
Susan A	20	DE	231
Thomas	15	DE	277
Thomas	22	MD	252
Thomas	46	MD	252
Thomas	55	DE	231
Thomas F	22	DE	252
Unicy	43	DE	143
William	10/12	DE	229
William	9	DE	112
William	18	DE	112
William	21	DE	281
William J	15	DE	143
William P	38	DE	84
Wm H	9/12	DE	229
Green, Allen	15	DE	262
Angelina	22	DE	166
Ann	24	DE	152
Arcada	13	DE	185
Benjamin	25	DE	185
Caroline	13	DE	295
Charles B	63	MD	262
Clarisa	40	DE	295
David	23	DE	166
Eliza	3	DE	296
Eliza H	11	DE	185
Eliza P	12	DE	176
Elizabeth	71	DE	262
Emila	22	DE	239
George	6/12	DE	296
George	19	DE	166
Green, George W	36	DE	176
Geo W	34	DE	296
Hetty	30	DE	176
Isabella	51	DE	169
Jacob	25	DE	197
James	25	DE	166
James H	13	DE	176
Jane	20	DE	197
Jannet B	15	DE	176
Jesse	46	DE	166
John	65	DE	185
John D	17	DE	176
John M	6	DE	176
Joseph	13	DE	166
Leah	16	DE	185
Lemuel	8	DE	11
Lesse	8	DE	166
Lewis	8/12	DE	197
Lydia	55	DE	185
Lydia B	30	DE	176
Maria	58	MD	239
Mariah	40	DE	6
Martha	2	DE	152
Mary	15	DE	176
Mary A	31	DE	239
Nancy K	47	DE	166
Paros	45	DE	295
Peter F	3	DE	176
Philip	20	DE	176
Philip	51	DE	176
Samuel	8	DE	10
Sarah A	6	DE	167
Sarah E	8	DE	176
Sarah E	26	DE	239
Sophia	25	DE	296
Stephen	60	DE	239
Thomas	40	DE	296
William	4	DE	176
William	10	DE	262
William B	20	DE	185
William G	7	DE	10
Greenly, Celia	6	DE	37
Clarissa A	3/12	DE	37
David	50	DE	11
Elizabeth	18	DE	11
Elizabeth	58	DE	11
George	36	DE	37
John	32	DE	18
Louisa	27	DE	18
Mary	50	DE	69
Mary A	3	DE	18
Newel	7	DE	245
Robert	25	DE	11
Mary E	8	DE	37
Sarah	35	DE	37
Sarah A	2	DE	37
Sarah C	1	DE	18
Thomas	27	DE	11
Grey, Elizabeth E	18	DE	21
Joseph	49	DE	21
Sarah	56	DE	21
Gridy, Isaac P	28	DE	225
Griffeth, Mary	52	DE	41
Griffin, Charlotte	11	DE	276
Mary J	9	DE	177
Griffith, Albert	5	DE	96
Angeline	7	DE	226
Ann	1	DE	96
Ann E	19	DE	108
Ann R	9	DE	108
Caleb	10	DE	96
Catharine	5	DE	108
Catharine	27	DE	97
Cyrus	37	DE	225
Ellen	3	DE	35
Eliza	7	DE	108
Elizabeth	38	DE	108
George	5	DE	97
Humphreys	18	DE	108
James	14	DE	96
James	23	DE	97
James W	31	PA	229
Griffith, Jeremiah	16	DE	108
John	3	DE	225
John	4	DE	270
John	13	DE	96
John W	1	DE	108
John W	2	DE	92
Joshua	8	DE	96
Joshua	38	DE	96
Lovey	3	DE	97
Major	30	MD	270
Margaret L	6	DE	108
Maria	8	DE	108
Mary	22	DE	270
Mary	48	DE	108
Mary	53	DE	40
Mary A	11	DE	108
Mary E	7	DE	97
Mary E	14	DE	108
Mary E	17	DE	92
Maria	32	DE	96
Nancy	40	DE	218
Okerd	8	DE	126
Rhoda A	3	DE	199
Sally	35	DE	35
Samuel	21	DE	108
Sarah A	19	DE	225
Sarah A	21	DE	108
Sarah C	2	DE	229
Sarah J	13	DE	108
Turner	44	DE	108
William	2	DE	97
William	2	DE	270
William	11	DE	108
William C	49	DE	108
William H	17	DE	108
Zachariah	34	DE	97
Grimmer, Sarah	23	DE	150
Grinmon, William	13	DE	174
Groves, Elie A	17	DE	74
George	40	DE	96
Jeremiah	14	DE	74
Jeremiah	38	DE	74
Joseph	3	DE	74
Joseph	24	DE	72
Joseph	25	DE	31
Mary	25	DE	96
Mary	38	DE	74
Mary A	1	DE	74
Molton W	2	DE	74
Nehemiah H	38	DE	68
Solomon	9	DE	74
Gum, Ann	24	DE	151
Charles	10	DE	152
Francis M	2	DE	152
Lovenia C	9/12	DE	152
Manaen	42	DE	152
Martha	2	DE	151
Martha A	9	DE	152
Mary E	6	DE	152
Sarah	38	DE	152
Sarah J	4	DE	152
William A	8	DE	152
Gunn, Eliza	44	DE	292
George	57	DE	292
Isaac	18	DE	292
Levin	12	DE	292
Warren	16	DE	292
Gurley, Letitia	19	DE	53
Hadden, Albert	15	MD	279
Elizabeth	7	DE	279
Joseph	5	DE	279
Lemuel	19	MD	279
Nancy	44	DE	279
Thomas	3	DE	279
Haines, Allen	45	NJ	196
Lavenia	25	DE	196
Hale, Taymer	66	DE	137
Hall, Alfred H	28	DE	118
Alice	30	DE	118
Amanda D	6	DE	235
Andrew T	15	DE	119

Name	Age			Name	Age			Name	Age		
Hall, Angeline	18	DE	264	Hall, John H	11	DE	234	Hall, William T	28	DE	201
Ann	15	DE	127	John H	25	DE	235	William W	39	DE	263
Ann E	9	DE	38	John M	5	DE	291	Wm K	39	DE	234
Ann E	13	DE	119	Joseph	20	DE	55	Wm S	31	DE	234
Anna	6	DE	35	Joseph	21	DE	117	Wm T	8	DE	234
Burton M	32	DE	172	Joshua	11	DE	122	Zadock	78	DE	118
Caroline	26	DE	36	Julia	4	DE	122	Halloway, Aaron	25	MD	127
Catharine	29	DE	110	Kendal S J	3	DE	120	Annanias	25	DE	137
Catharine	40	DE	119	Laura	5	DE	35	Charlotte	22	DE	137
Charles	2	DE	127	Laura C	3	DE	235	David	26	DE	127
Charles	8	DE	122	Leah	60	DE	121	Ellen C	7	DE	132
Charles	28	DE	127	Lemuel A	3/12	DE	123	Henry W	21	DE	153
Charles	46	DE	127	Lemuel A	74	DE	123	Jacob	22	MD	139
Charles M	9	DE	123	Lemuel C Jr	29	MD	123	Jane	25	DE	137
Charlotte	9	DE	53	Levi	31	DE	110	John C	4	DE	137
Cornelius J	13	DE	117	Margaret	29	DE	294	Joshua	30	MD	132
Daniel	62	DE	123	Maria C	1	DE	119	Josiah	26	DE	53
David	19	DE	55	Maria E	14	DE	234	Margaret	20	DE	127
David	60	DE	119	Mariah	14	DE	263	Martha	16	DE	122
David M	3	DE	53	Martha	1	DE	263	Peter W	31	DE	137
Derenda	75	DE	57	Martha	31	DE	53	Sarah E	2	DE	53
Dinnah	48	DE	295	Martha E	5	DE	234	William T	30	DE	137
Edward	9	DE	110	Mary	4	DE	263	Hallum, Arcada	59	DE	57
Edward	19	DE	15	Mary	14	DE	55	Lydia B	12	DE	57
Edwin M	20	DE	118	Mary	25	DE	49	Thomas	64	DE	57
Elijah	3	DE	264	Mary	75	DE	118	William T	12	DE	57
Elijah J	2	DE	234	Mary A	9	DE	53	Ham, Ann E	12	DE	217
Eliza	17	DE	55	Mary A	19	DE	172	Elizabeth M	15	DE	217
Eliza	26	DE	35	Mary A	52	DE	120	Hamilton, Jacob	1	DE	226
Eliza	46	DE	117	Mary C	40	MD	125	James	5	DE	267
Elizabeth	21	DE	119	Mary E	22	DE	295	John	60	DE	99
Elizabeth	25	DE	295	Mary H	3	DE	117	John C	31	DE	226
Elizabeth	34	DE	234	Mary J	7	DE	234	Joseph	6	DE	288
Elizabeth	34	DE	263	Miles S	24	DE	298	Leah	60	DE	99
Elizabeth	50	DE	119	Nancy	6	DE	264	Maranda	23	DE	159
Elizabeth F	3	DE	123	Nancy	34	DE	119	Purnal	50	DE	159
Ferdinand S	11/12	DE	115	Nancy	38	DE	127	Sarah E	3	DE	226
Flory	51	DE	119	Nancy	60	DE	234	Sarah T	25	DE	226
George	2/12	DE	110	Nancy	64	DE	264	Susan A	5	DE	226
George	7	DE	235	Nathaniel	22	DE	57	Hammond, Amelia	75	DE	2
George	56	DE	31	Phillip	7	DE	264	Charles H	9	DE	6
George A	12	DE	38	Phillip W	6	DE	234	Charlotte	8	DE	13
George H	27	DE	49	Phillip W	25	DE	123	Elizabeth	34	DE	6
Greensbury	53	DE	291	Polly	65	DE	298	George	16	DE	5
Hannah	28	DE	291	Priscilla	17	DE	117	James A	7/12	DE	6
Hannah	32	DE	122	Rebecca	10	DE	55	John	5	DE	6
Hannah	55	DE	127	Rhoda	23	DE	127	Louder	39	DE	6
Henry	7	DE	55	Richard M	42	DE	38	Martha	35	DE	6
Henry	17	DE	55	Sallie	30	DE	234	Mary	11	DE	6
Henry F	6	DE	119	Sallie A	16	DE	234	Mary E	3	DE	6
Henry F	58	DE	55	Samuel	19	DE	119	Matiah	35	DE	6
Hester	19	DE	131	Sarah	1	DE	264	Milly A	11	DE	6
Hester	53	DE	55	Sarah	16	DE	263	Nathaniel	17	DE	36
Hetty	18	DE	59	Sarah	24	DE	119	Purnell	13	DE	6
Hetty	18	DE	127	Sarah	30	DE	264	William	42	DE	6
Hetty	39	DE	117	Sarah	44	MD	123	Hancock, Albert	21	MD	137
Houston	35	DE	35	Sarah	46	DE	31	Ann	20	DE	22
Isaac	1	DE	122	Sarah A	29	DE	31	Edward	3/12	DE	173
Isaac	21	DE	127	Sarah C	18	DE	119	Frederick T	2	DE	188
Isaac	45	DE	122	Sarah D	28	DE	119	George	10	DE	173
Isabella	17	DE	118	Sarah E	1	DE	234	Henry	55	DE	173
Isaiah W	5	DE	119	Sarah E	8	DE	150	Hetty	20	DE	173
Jacob W	43	DE	53	Sarah E	19	DE	37	Hetty Amea	22	DE	62
James	25	DE	36	Sarah G	58	DE	120	Isaac	23	DE	22
James F	1	DE	123	Sarah J	7	DE	36	Jacob	22	DE	173
James K	8	DE	263	Sarah J	15	DE	119	James	17	DE	173
James K	9	DE	234	Shadarick M	30	DE	264	James B	43	DE	188
Jane	6	DE	122	Simon W	29	DE	294	John	7	DE	173
Jane	22	DE	123	Taymer	3	DE	124	Martha J	4	DE	188
Jane	22	DE	31	Thomas	14	DE	123	Mary	50	DE	18
Jane	25	DE	235	Turpin	21	DE	298	Mary A	34	DE	188
Jane E	4	DE	234	Turpin	35	DE	233	Mary J	18	DE	18
Jasper	35	DE	234	William	2	DE	35	Milla A	11	DE	173
Jincy	38	DE	38	William	8	DE	264	Rebecca	30	DE	173
John	2	DE	110	William	12	DE	122	Sarah	1	DE	22
John	4	DE	294	William	68	DE	298	William	18	DE	173
John	10	DE	263	William C	28	DE	118	William	20	DE	152
John	20	DE	59	William D	8	DE	119	William	46	DE	18
John C	11	DE	119	William E	12	DE	31	Hand, Emaline	35	DE	25
John C	16	DE	31	William H	4	DE	110	Mary	4	DE	38
John C	40	DE	123	William R	40	DE	119	Handy, Angeline	14	DE	64
John E	21	DE	38	William S	57	DE	117	Cassandare	18	DE	64

Name	Age	St	No	Name	Age	St	No	Name	Age	St	No
Handy, Emmarella	37	DE	64	Harmon, Elizabeth	17	DE	188	Harris, Eliza J	6	DE	141
Francis	60	DE	218	Elizabeth	31	DE	149	Eliza M	15	DE	1
Grace	48	DE	218	Elizabeth A	16	DE	150	Elizabeth	5	DE	195
John	21	DE	205	Ellen	19	DE	167	Elizabeth	17	DE	192
John	22	DE	209	Eunice J	12	DE	167	Elizabeth	35	DE	195
Judah A	3	DE	218	Garretson	44	DE	178	Erasmus W	9	DE	14
Samuel	16	DE	49	Harriet	32	DE	184	George	10	DE	141
Samuel	40	DE	64	Henry	15	DE	158	George	40	DE	3
Hanson, Elizabeth	34	DE	42	Hetty	20	DE	38	Hannah	25	DE	53
Louisa	14	DE	184	Hetty	50	DE	40	Harriet	8	DE	192
Mary	45	DE	42	Israel	6	DE	56	Henry	10	DE	192
Hanzor, Ann	42	DE	180	James	21	DE	128	Henry	60	DE	145
Eleanor	4	DE	184	James B	11	DE	184	Hetty	50	DE	192
Eli	39	DE	184	Jehu	20	DE	128	Hetty A	16	DE	1
Hester	75	DE	184	John	17	DE	128	James	1	DE	192
Jacob	56	DE	184	John	25	DE	38	James A	9	DE	195
James	4	DE	180	John R	41	DE	187	Jeremiah	54	DE	192
Jeremiah	47	DE	184	John W	1	DE	187	John W	7	DE	195
John	15	DE	184	John W	15	DE	167	Joseph	39	MD	141
John	63	DE	180	John W	16	DE	92	Joshua P	1	DE	141
Josephine	7	DE	184	Josephine	4	DE	187	Kitty	12	DE	104
Milkey	60	DE	184	Julia A	29	DE	56	Levica	4	DE	141
Nancy	54	DE	184	Leah	50	DE	149	Levin J	3	DE	141
Nancy	66	DE	180	Louisa C	4	DE	187	Levin J	8	MD	202
Robert	9	DE	180	Love	29	DE	149	Lewis	11	DE	192
Shepherd	49	DE	180	Lovenia	42	DE	178	Mahala A	11	MD	141
Thomas A	11	DE	180	Lovinia	38	DE	187	Manuel	10	DE	104
Harding, Elizabeth	30	DE	111	Lydia	35	DE	189	Margaret	11	DE	195
Julia	12	DE	111	Lydia F	7	DE	187	Margaret	50	DE	195
Thomas	45	DE	111	Lydia J	3	DE	189	Margaret J	1	DE	202
Hare, Elizabeth	18	DE	241	Margaret	7	DE	56	Martha	28	DE	209
Hargis, James	49	DE	222	Margaret	27	DE	149	Martha J	36	DE	14
James H	3	MD	222	Martha	27	DE	183	Mary H	2	DE	195
Levi	1	MD	222	Mary	13	DE	128	Mary R	39	DE	1
Sarah E	28	VA	222	Mary	22	DE	39	Mary S	38	DE	3
Hargus, Comfort	25	DE	48	Mary	35	DE	49	Nathaniel P	49	DE	1
Cuff	70	DE	55	Mary	40	DE	173	Patience	6	DE	192
Diannah	55	DE	55	Mary A	25	DE	50	Rhoda	33	DE	141
Hannah	4	DE	63	Mary J	9	DE	187	Robert	31	DE	53
Hetty A F	10/12	DE	63	Minta	13	DE	189	Rosa	52	DE	104
Jeremiah	10	DE	60	Mitchell	15	DE	187	Sarah	6	DE	192
John	17	DE	2	Morris	24	DE	62	Sarah E	26	DE	202
Margaret	11	DE	63	Nathan	17	DE	167	Somerset	64	DE	104
Maria	2	DE	63	Nathaniel	5	DE	189	William	16	DE	192
Matilda	5	DE	63	Nehemiah	1	DE	184	William	51	DE	14
Matilda	40	DE	63	Nehemiah	6	DE	184	William J	33	MD	202
Robert	12	DE	60	Peggy	60	DE	92	Wm	35	DE	195
Robert	65	DE	63	Rachel	83	DE	167	Wm J	5	DE	202
Harlen, David	22	OH	237	Robert	11	DE	178	Harrison, William	17	MD	190
Harman, Absalom	4	DE	63	Sarah	4	DE	183	Hart, Ann R	17	DE	190
George	14	DE	293	Sarah	14	DE	56	Arthur J	7	DE	190
Hannah	23	DE	63	Sarah	21	DE	184	David S	10	DE	188
Henry	8	DE	293	Sarah A	9	DE	187	Elizabeth A	11	DE	191
John	2	DE	63	Sarah J	9	DE	173	Hetty A	16	DE	180
Jonathan	45	DE	293	Simon	15	DE	189	Isaac A	43	DE	188
Joseph	18	DE	262	Sophia J	7	DE	187	Isaac T	12	DE	179
Josiah	18	DE	293	Theodore	11	DE	187	John E	6	DE	188
Judy	70	DE	62	Thomas	3	DE	184	Joseph A	10	DE	190
Lavinia	45	DE	293	Turner	25	DE	150	Lydia A	5	DE	190
Matthias	22	DE	78	Vashti	24	DE	92	Margaret R	3	DE	190
Nancy	16	DE	293	Whittleton	10	DE	178	Mary A	34	DE	190
Painter	25	DE	63	William	15	DE	187	Mary E	8	DE	34
Robert	1/12	DE	63	William	38	DE	187	Mary H	8	DE	188
Sally	20	DE	78	William Jr	60	DE	92	Peter R	16	DE	188
Zachariah	8	DE	293	Woolsey	10	DE	56	Rhoda W	35	DE	188
Zachariah	12	DE	293	Woolsey	30	DE	56	Samuel	23	DE	192
Zachariah	70	DE	62	Zadock	52	DE	173	Susanna	42	DE	179
Harmon, Adonijah	34	DE	184	Harper, Catharine	14	DE	83	Thomas	37	DE	190
Ann	6	DE	189	Hetty	8	DE	83	William A	13	DE	188
Ann	14	DE	150	Jane	18	MD	225	Harvey, Jacob	20	DE	166
Ann M	8	DE	128	John	2	DE	83	Jacob	24	DE	165
Ann M	8	DE	184	Joseph	11	DE	83	Hasting, Archellia	41	DE	232
Benjamin	60	DE	40	Mary Jane	33	DE	83	Dewitt	21	DE	216
Betsey	60	DE	150	Sarah	18	DE	172	Eli	76	DE	249
Boen	40	DE	189	Thomas R	20	DE	4	Eliza	42	DE	232
Burton	22	DE	167	Trusten	8	DE	83	Frances	52	MD	217
Charles S	2	DE	173	Harris, Alburton	10	DE	209	Harris P	7	DE	217
Coard	21	DE	184	Altha V	8	DE	209	John H	4	DE	232
Delila	44	DE	128	Ann	35	DE	1	Joseph	6	DE	232
Eleanor	41	DE	187	Catherine F	2	DE	2	Joseph	11	DE	216
Eliza	33	DE	167	Edward P	13	DE	1	Justin	1	DE	232
Eliza A	22	DE	184	Eleanor A	16	DE	1	Peter E	10	DE	232

Hasting, Priscilla	12	DE	232	Hastings, Jane	16	DE	259	Hastings, Samuel	45	DE	296
Sallie S	14	DE	232	John	26	DE	257	Samuel B	8	DE	258
Wm N	18	DE	232	John E	4	DE	249	Sarah	1	DE	255
Hastings, Alexandra	32	DE	170	John H	22	DE	283	Sarah	4	MD	254
Anna	1	DE	257	John M	35	DE	247	Sarah	7	DE	257
Anna	14	MD	254	John T	7	DE	254	Sarah	7	DE	263
Anthony G	31	PA	170	John W	12	MD	250	Sarah	8	DE	296
Asbury	27	DE	293	Jonathan	22	DE	249	Sarah	12	DE	245
Beacham	26	MD	254	Joseph	9	DE	278	Sarah	15	DE	278
Benjamin	15	DE	283	Joseph	12	DE	263	Sarah	21	DE	292
Benjamin	42	DE	257	Joshua	2	DE	247	Sarah	35	DE	296
Benjamin B	17	MD	241	Joshua	4	DE	250	Sarah	40	DE	265
Caroline	7	DE	255	Joshua	13	DE	281	Sarah	53	DE	286
Catharine	31	DE	154	Joshua	38	DE	263	Sarah	71	DE	259
Celia	25	MD	254	Joshua J	7	DE	154	Sarah E	5	DE	3
Charles R	3	DE	170	Julia A	11	DE	249	Sarah E	12	DE	253
Charlotte	2	DE	3	Julia A	18	DE	255	Seth	12	DE	257
Clement	50	DE	278	Julia A	25	DE	293	Sina	60	DE	256
Colwell	21	DE	265	Julian	6	DE	256	Solomon	15	DE	296
Cornelia	3	DE	247	Kendal	15	DE	227	Stayton	7	DE	241
Cyrus	10	DE	259	Lavenia	3	DE	263	Susan E	10	DE	170
Daniel	30	DE	255	Lavenia	11	DE	256	Thomas	30	MD	254
Daniel	40	DE	259	Lavinia	12	MD	254	William	5	DE	241
David	12	DE	247	Leah	13	DE	256	William	6	DE	263
Eben	24	MD	254	Leonard	62	DE	265	William	8	DE	296
Edward	5	DE	258	Levin	4	DE	255	William	11	DE	265
Edward T	1	DE	170	Levin	18	DE	259	William	12	DE	259
Elam	19	DE	256	Lidia A	18	DE	257	William	13	DE	278
Elenor	15	DE	255	Lovey	28	DE	256	William	17	DE	256
Elenor	25	DE	296	Luther	29	DE	3	William	45	DE	245
Elenor	30	DE	263	Luther W	24	DE	246	William B	5	MD	254
Eli	11	DE	255	Lydia	17	MD	254	William D	4	DE	170
Elihu	10	MD	254	Mahala	70	DE	255	William H	33	DE	154
Elihu	23	DE	257	Margaret	7	DE	247	William L	8	DE	154
Elihu	24	DE	249	Margaret	22	DE	247	William W	15	DE	254
Elihu	60	DE	256	Margaret	46	DE	278	Winder	31	DE	256
Elijah	2	DE	256	Maria	12	DE	248	Winder	38	DE	255
Elijah	11	DE	255	Maria	34	DE	249	Wm C	30	DE	234
Eliza E	8	MD	247	Maria J	6	DE	154	Zedekiah P	23	DE	286
Elizabeth	2	MD	254	Mariah	10	DE	263	Hasty, Eliza	40	DE	249
Elizabeth	5	DE	255	Martha	1	DE	259	Hatfield, Caroline E	7	DE	3
Elizabeth	11	DE	250	Martha	2	DE	255	Elijah	64	DE	149
Elizabeth	11	DE	296	Martha	3	DE	247	Eliza	22	DE	97
Elizabeth	20	DE	255	Martha	5	MD	255	Elizabeth	16	DE	231
Elizabeth	26	DE	3	Martha	6	DE	253	Elizabeth	83	DE	101
Elizabeth	30	DE	255	Martha	26	MD	255	Emma	18	DE	231
Elizabeth	33	MD	247	Mary	1	DE	278	George W	4	DE	3
Elizabeth	64	DE	159	Mary	4	DE	255	Harrison	10	DE	97
Elizabeth A P	31	DE	170	Mary	9	DE	255	Hester	18	DE	231
Ellen	4	DE	131	Mary	18	DE	265	Jane T	29	DE	3
Elzey	26	MD	257	Mary	19	DE	246	Joseph	24	DE	97
Esther	40	MD	254	Mary	47	DE	246	Leonard	24	DE	231
Ezekiel	3	DE	257	Mary	55	DE	265	Mary	1	DE	97
Fillis	23	DE	257	Mary A	8	DE	170	Mary	59	DE	230
Frederick	1	DE	257	Mary E	6/12	DE	170	Nelly	46	DE	149
Frederick	30	DE	258	Mary E	4	DE	259	Sallie	64	DE	101
Gatty	15	DE	267	Mary E	12	MD	254	Theodore W	10/12	DE	3
Geo W	1	DE	296	Mary H	10	DE	154	Thomas	30	DE	3
Gracy	22	DE	258	Matilda	1	DE	263	Willard H	30	DE	231
Gracy	35	DE	259	Matilda	15	DE	253	William P	11	DE	27
Hamel	21	DE	249	Matilda	27	DE	254	Hatwell, J S	44	GB	237
Henry	6	DE	131	Miranda	3	DE	255	Hayden, Major	29	DE	87
Henry	31	DE	259	Moses	50	MD	254	Sarah	25	DE	87
Henry A	6	DE	170	Nancy	8	DE	259	Hayman, Elinor	25	MD	217
Hester	13	DE	253	Nancy	9	DE	245	Martha J	5	MD	217
Hester	28	DE	257	Nelly	4	DE	245	Martin	47	MD	217
Hetty	5	MD	254	Nutter	30	DE	241	James	21	MD	217
Hezekiah	23	DE	263	Patience	6	DE	257	Julia	8	MD	217
Hezekiah	51	MD	253	Patience	8	MD	254	Hays, Catharine	24	DE	87
Irena	5	DE	256	Perry	43	DE	249	Henry	12	DE	87
Isaac	23	DE	265	Philip	1	DE	296	James	20	DE	63
Isaac	29	DE	247	Priscilla	1	DE	241	John	14	DE	72
Isaac W	8	DE	253	Priscilla	28	DE	241	John	26	DE	87
Jackson	3	DE	241	Rachel	20	DE	245	John	51	DE	87
Jacob	3	DE	256	Rachel	35	DE	254	John P	1	DE	87
Jacob	7	MD	258	Rhoda	5	DE	278	Mary	36	DE	87
Jacob F	8	DE	170	Richard T	34	PA	170	Mary	62	DE	87
James	1	DE	246	Robert W	2	DE	154	Nancy	43	DE	213
James	3	MD	254	Sallie	35	DE	253	Sarah E	3	DE	87
James	10	DE	296	Sallie A	19	DE	249	Susan	28	DE	87
James	34	DE	249	Sally	60	DE	249	Thomas	49	DE	87
James W	2	DE	253	Samuel	5	DE	296	Hazle, John C	29	DE	13

Name	Age	St	No	Name	Age	St	No	Name	Age	St	No
Hazle, Kensey S	11	DE	13	Hazzard, Mary E	4	DE	36	Hearn, Charlotte	15	DE	274
Robert W	12	DE	13	Mary E	6	DE	39	Charlotte	16	DE	254
Sally	40	DE	13	Mary F	11	DE	201	Charlotte	22	DE	236
William	35	DE	13	Mary P	27	DE	39	Clement	30	DE	280
William H	8	DE	13	Matilda	6	DE	73	Daniel	6	DE	253
Hazzard, Abraham	55	DE	40	Melvin	62	DE	42	Daniel	37	MD	238
Abram	8	DE	40	Milly	30	DE	68	David	13	DE	274
Adaline L	1/12	DE	199	Milly	56	DE	73	Dolly	35	DE	275
Ann	43	DE	192	Milly	65	DE	66	Drucilla	9	DE	260
Ann	59	DE	197	Minus	25	DE	68	Ebenezer	5	DE	273
Ann C	30	DE	194	Monroe	5	DE	29	Ebenezer	17	DE	260
Anna H	4	DE	199	Moses	50	DE	73	Edward	4	DE	280
Annis	3	DE	31	Nancy	14	DE	151	Edward	5	DE	260
Anthony	7	DE	29	Nancy	35	DE	73	Eleanor	35	DE	253
Arthur	38	DE	194	Nancy	53	DE	42	Elena	35	DE	255
Catharine	12	DE	73	Nancy	63	DE	192	Elenor	30	DE	258
Catharine	30	DE	85	Owens	3	DE	32	Elijah	3	DE	273
Charlotte	6	DE	73	Patience	25	DE	68	Elijah	5	DE	273
Charlotte	22	DE	34	Patience	67	DE	194	Elijah	7	DE	254
Daffy	18	DE	29	Patience E	9	DE	70	Elijah	8	DE	253
Daniel	60	DE	174	Phebe	9	DE	29	Elijah	30	DE	237
Daniel J	15	DE	192	Philis	53	DE	42	Elisa	40	DE	257
David	2	DE	72	Phoebe Ann	5/12	DE	68	Elivia	9	DE	267
David	9	DE	85	Return	49	DE	36	Eliza J	23	DE	262
David	12	DE	73	Rhodes	43	DE	199	Eliza J	34	DE	238
David	17	DE	192	Richard	33	DE	194	Elizabeth	5	DE	261
David	19	DE	29	Robert	16	DE	40	Elizabeth	9	DE	198
David	69	DE	31	Robert	28	DE	194	Elizabeth	10	DE	236
David F	9	DE	36	Robert C	18	DE	192	Elizabeth	17	DE	261
Derick B	1	DE	169	Salie	70	DE	72	Elizabeth	18	DE	253
Edward B	7	DE	169	Sallie W	7	DE	201	Elizabeth	22	DE	254
Eliza	25	DE	31	Sally	50	DE	199	Elizabeth	38	DE	258
Eliza J	1	DE	73	Samuel	10	DE	29	Eunice	7	DE	234
Elizabeth	18	DE	73	Samuel	28	DE	57	Eunicy	10	DE	261
Elizabeth	25	DE	194	Samuel	37	DE	29	Eurila	9	DE	234
Elizabeth	32	DE	194	Samuel J	21	DE	199	Frances	5	DE	255
Elizabeth	33	DE	36	Sarah	35	DE	85	Frances	8	DE	236
Elizabeth	67	DE	31	Sarah J	6	DE	66	Frances	37	DE	236
Ellen	7	DE	36	Sina	55	DE	174	Frances	75	DE	258
Elsey	4	DE	29	Solomon	8	DE	73	Franky	2	DE	273
Emaline	7	DE	10	Susan	20	DE	36	George	24	DE	280
Emaline	28	DE	193	Sylvester	22	DE	36	George H	15	DE	259
Emma S	3	DE	201	Thomas	15	DE	15	George W	15	DE	236
Exenine J	31	DE	201	Thomas	42	DE	194	George W	30	DE	262
Francis	13	DE	198	Thomas R	17	DE	199	George W C	26	DE	260
Francis	80	DE	199	Wain	15	DE	29	Harriet	42	DE	259
Francis M	17	DE	191	Wilber F	9	DE	201	Harriet E	2	DE	238
Genet	25	DE	66	William	12	DE	85	Harriet H	22	DE	260
George	2	DE	31	William	13	DE	49	Henry C	7	DE	238
Georgianna	14	DE	201	William	14	DE	40	Hiram	19	DE	265
Gertrude	1	DE	85	William	40	DE	201	Howard	33	MD	241
Hanley E	10	DE	36	William A	10	DE	194	Isaac	3	DE	258
Hannah	11	DE	31	William A	37	DE	39	Isaac	5	DE	254
Hannah	33	DE	29	William C	46	DE	192	Isaac	8	DE	236
Harriet A	20	DE	192	William H	10	DE	199	Isaac	15	DE	280
Harris	6	DE	85	William L	1	DE	73	Isaac	17	DE	259
Hester	8	DE	29	William R	4	DE	169	Isaac	32	DE	237
Hetty	16	DE	85	William W	5	DE	193	Isaac R	31	DE	243
Jacob	60	DE	66	Hearn, Alfred W	8	DE	236	Isaac S	18	DE	264
James	12	DE	69	Amanda	12	DE	254	Isaac T	10	DE	270
James D	10	DE	169	Amanda	24	MD	260	Isaac of S	35	DE	255
James L	19	DE	199	Amanuel B	43	MD	280	Jacob	8	DE	264
Jerry	13	DE	29	Amelia	37	DE	238	Jacob	25	DE	237
John	17	DE	29	Amelia E	4	DE	238	Jacob	50	DE	264
John	18	DE	40	Andrew	20	MD	248	Jacob K	8	DE	264
John	36	DE	194	Ann	4	DE	257	James	9	DE	280
John A	26	DE	81	Ann E	9	DE	238	James	12	DE	260
John A	36	DE	85	Ann M	31	DE	260	James	24	MD	254
John C	29	DE	34	Arzel	46	DE	273	Jane	22	DE	238
John C	34	DE	169	Benjamin	1	DE	235	Jane	50	MD	243
John E	24	DE	193	Benjamin	14	DE	261	Jane S	22	DE	277
Leah	54	DE	40	Benjamin	30	DE	273	Joanna	60	DE	265
Letitia	1	DE	36	Benjamin	49	DE	280	John	1	DE	258
Lovey	65	DE	73	Benjamin	60	DE	265	John	7	DE	280
Lucinda M	51	MD	199	Benton	10	MD	254	John	12	DE	261
Margaret A	4	DE	39	Burton R	40	DE	253	John C	7	DE	236
Mary	3	DE	29	Caroline	8	DE	254	John H	16	DE	260
Mary	18	DE	73	Caroline	26	DE	236	Jonathan	21	DE	262
Mary	29	DE	169	Catharine	23	DE	280	Jonathan	40	DE	267
Mary	30	DE	57	Catharine	30	DE	273	Jonathan A	15	DE	255
Mary A	8	DE	27	Charles A	1	DE	235	Jonathan A	38	DE	236
Mary E	1/12	DE	36	Charlotte	10	DE	264	Jonathan of J	51	DE	236

Name	Age	State	No.
Hearn, Joseph	10	DE	254
Joseph	12	DE	280
Joseph	15	DE	258
Joseph	33	DE	264
Joseph	50	DE	262
Joseph E	24	DE	262
Joseph J	29	DE	260
Joseph W	1	DE	237
Julia	5	DE	277
Julia	13	DE	254
Julia	21	DE	264
Julia J	11	DE	267
Kendal B	50	DE	241
Kendal B of T	41	DE	258
Kesiah	51	DE	261
Lavina	45	DE	254
Lavinia E	6	DE	237
Leah	31	DE	42
Levi	24	DE	236
Levin	21	DE	273
Levin	46	DE	261
Louder	34	DE	277
Louisa	11	DE	234
Louisa	14	DE	261
Lovena	21	DE	236
Lovenia	20	DE	264
Lovenia	31	DE	264
Lovina	9	DE	260
Lovy	16	DE	264
Luthey	13	DE	255
Marcelus	11	DE	253
Margaret	9	DE	264
Margaret	20	DE	233
Margaret	23	MD	261
Margaret	40	DE	274
Maria	30	DE	236
Maria J	11	DE	238
Mariah	10	DE	264
Marlin L	42	DE	235
Martha	1	DE	260
Martha	10	DE	253
Martha A	2/12	DE	236
Martha F	4	DE	238
Martin	3	DE	234
Martin	16	DE	253
Mary	2	DE	258
Mary	2	DE	264
Mary	5	DE	234
Mary	11	DE	274
Mary	12	DE	261
Mary	12	DE	280
Mary	16	DE	254
Mary	20	DE	261
Mary	29	DE	273
Mary	50	DE	236
Mary E	5	DE	271
Mary E	7	DE	277
Mary E	9	DE	253
Mary E	10	DE	243
Mary E F	2	DE	236
Matilda	11	DE	255
Minos	18	MD	254
Mitchael	22	DE	241
N	62	DE	238
Nancy	35	DE	267
Nandra	5	DE	267
Noah	49	MD	261
Patrick H	14	DE	236
Patty	41	DE	260
Phebe	43	DE	280
Phillip	13	DE	259
Polly	70	DE	254
Rachel	2	DE	253
Rachel	45	DE	241
Rebecca P	13	DE	260
Sallie	30	DE	237
Sallie A	5	DE	237
Sallie A	10	DE	258
Samuel	8	DE	258
Samuel S	6	DE	237
Sarah	1	DE	273
Sarah	6	DE	258
Hearn, Sarah	7	DE	255
Sarah	11	DE	260
Sarah	12	DE	239
Sarah	15	DE	265
Sarah	36	DE	234
Sarah	40	DE	261
Sarah	71	DE	280
Sarah A	22	DE	241
Sarah C	14	DE	238
Sarah E	15	DE	234
Simons	60	DE	277
Spencer	60	DE	258
Stephen B	6	DE	236
Thomas	4	DE	253
Thomas	4	DE	264
Thomas	14	DE	258
Thomas	17	DE	265
Thomas	40	DE	280
Thomas N	28	DE	262
Thomas W	19	DE	254
Tilghman	30	DE	275
William	2	DE	280
William	7	DE	264
William	8	DE	272
William	9	DE	255
William	11	DE	270
William	12	DE	264
William	13	DE	267
William	14	DE	253
William	16	DE	261
William	17	DE	258
William	50	DE	254
William H	33	DE	270
William of S	33	DE	258
William S	4	DE	236
Winder C	8	DE	255
Windon	32	DE	237
Wm J	8	DE	237
Wm R	21	DE	241
Zephora	30	DE	270
Hearl, Nelly	45	DE	140
Heathers, Hester J	40	DE	29
Horatio	42	DE	29
John M	1	DE	29
Martha J	11	DE	29
Samuel K	5	DE	29
William B	8	DE	29
Heaveloe, Buster	15	DE	60
Chloe	60	DE	65
Edwin	7	DE	60
Elizabeth	12	DE	43
Erasmus	2	DE	43
George	14	DE	43
Harriet E	1	DE	43
Henry H	4	DE	60
Isaac	4	DE	43
James	10	DE	43
John	16	DE	43
John	40	DE	60
Lydia	55	DE	65
Mary	36	DE	43
Mary J	17	DE	50
Moses	11	DE	60
Moses	40	DE	43
Nero	60	DE	65
Roseanna	40	DE	60
Ruth	20	DE	65
Sally	8	DE	43
Sarah	9	DE	60
Sarah	80	DE	65
Stafford	18	DE	60
Stewart	19	DE	60
Hebaloe, Asbury	6	DE	27
Bernard	20	DE	27
Greensbury	15	DE	27
Margaret J	9	DE	27
Thereby	44	DE	27
William	19	DE	27
Hebeloe, Alfred	24	DE	28
Bennett	44	DE	27
James	12	DE	28
John	51	DE	28
Hebeloe, John W	11	DE	28
Mary	48	DE	28
Sarah	17	DE	28
Heidran, John	12	DE	71
Helm, Hillard	25	DE	150
Jannet K	42	DE	114
John	2	DE	150
Martha	16	DE	114
Mary	2/12	DE	150
Peleg W	49	DE	114
Peter N B	37	DE	150
Rhoda A	4	DE	150
Thomas	6	DE	150
William	14	DE	114
Hemmons, Hester A	14	DE	203
Margaret J	2	DE	203
Martha C	10	DE	203
Ruth	30	DE	203
Sarah E	12	DE	203
Thomas	41	DE	203
Henderson, Benjamin	38	DE	173
Catharine A	7	DE	173
Edward N	11	DE	173
Elizabeth	33	DE	173
Elizabeth M	2	DE	173
Isaac	12	DE	10
Isaac	31	DE	249
Mary	45	DE	84
Mary E	13	DE	84
Phillis	30	DE	247
Rhoda	57	DE	249
William	18	DE	84
Wm	40	DE	247
Hendle, Ann	23	DE	107
Caleb	10	DE	107
Elizabeth	19	DE	107
Jacob	76	DE	107
John B	26	DE	107
Jonas	28	DE	107
Nancy	51	DE	107
Henry, Albert	12	DE	31
Charles	18	DE	50
Columbus W	34	DE	249
Edward	7	DE	234
Garison	9	DE	3
George	3/12	DE	234
George	6/12	DE	249
George	30	DE	234
Isaac	35	DE	253
Jane	34	DE	249
John	2	DE	263
John	7	DE	249
John S	28	DE	252
Margaret	5	DE	249
Martha	7	DE	252
Mary	5	DE	252
Mary E	2	DE	234
Patrick	4	DE	252
Sallie E	18	DE	253
Sarah	29	DE	252
Sarah	30	DE	234
Thomas	2	DE	249
William	2	DE	252
William	9	DE	249
Hepran, David	50	DE	57
Elizabeth	37	DE	57
Henry	13	DE	57
John	8	DE	57
William	3	DE	57
Herman, Abby	66	DE	117
Morris	24	DE	63
Heveloe, Cornelius	16	DE	78
Edward	3	DE	78
James	33	DE	29
Jane H	10	DE	74
Mary	35	DE	78
Nehemiah	35	DE	74
Peter	7	DE	74
Purnel	12	DE	74
Sarah	25	DE	74
William	14	DE	78
Hevilo, Cornelius	23	DE	24

Name	Age	State	Page	Name	Age	State	Page	Name	Age	State	Page
Hevilo, Matilda	20	DE	24	Hickman, Lucinda	4	DE	130	Hignut, Margaret A	22	DE	220
Sarah	79	DE	24	Lydia	38	DE	51	Mary E	4	DE	221
Hewes, Hetty A	4	DE	117	Mannan	34	DE	293	Mary E	14	DE	220
Hickman, Adalaide	6	DE	112	Maria	13	DE	130	Matilda	11	DE	220
Albertine	6	DE	51	Martha	10	DE	51	Nancy	68	MD	220
Alfred	1	DE	50	Martha	18	DE	154	Sarah A	16	DE	220
Amanda	37	DE	138	Martha E	11	DE	71	Sarah E	8	DE	221
Ann E	5	DE	4	Mary	9	DE	112	Sophia A M	9	DE	220
Annanias	19	DE	143	Mary	12	DE	130	Hill, Benjamin	3	DE	257
Annanias	85	DE	143	Mary	21	DE	134	Caroline	17	DE	105
Bridget	46	DE	141	Mary	22	DE	134	Charles A	17	DE	237
Burton	5	DE	153	Mary	25	DE	75	Clement	40	DE	113
Caleb	9	DE	130	Mary	26	DE	168	Columbus W	7	DE	257
Caleb J	7	DE	71	Mary	41	DE	112	Cornelia A	30	DE	188
Caleb	10	DE	135	Mary	52	DE	47	David	8	DE	105
Catharine	14	DE	112	Mary A	5	DE	138	Diannah	40	DE	188
Charles	1	DE	138	Mary C	4	DE	5	Edward	12	DE	105
Charles	20	DE	112	Mary E	11	DE	141	Elija	37	MD	237
Charles C	17	DE	47	Mary J	1	DE	71	Elijah	11	DE	141
Charles H	6	DE	143	Mary S	17	DE	51	Eliza	18/12	DE	296
Clara A	1	DE	141	Matilda	35	DE	130	Eliza	9	DE	237
Deborah	2	DE	153	Matilda A	2	DE	134	Eliza	24	DE	296
Edward	4	DE	133	Nancy	17	DE	112	Elizabeth	16	DE	123
Edward H	28	DE	50	Nancy	40	DE	72	Elizabeth	20	DE	97
Eleanor	6	DE	135	Nancy	50	DE	137	Elizabeth	40	DE	171
Eleanor	20	DE	138	Napoleon	11	DE	47	Elizabeth	48	DE	122
Eleanor	21	DE	143	Nathaniel	14	DE	134	Elizabeth	60	MD	128
Eliza	21	DE	47	Nathaniel D	40	DE	51	Elizabeth	61	DE	89
Elizabeth	18	DE	138	Nevet B	11	DE	142	Elizabeth	66	DE	188
Elizabeth	19	DE	139	Patty	19	DE	132	George	1	DE	80
Elizabeth	54	DE	142	Pemberton	3	DE	134	George W	15	DE	250
Elizabeth	64	DE	137	Prudence	63	DE	134	Hannah	30	DE	113
Elizabeth J	9	DE	142	Rachel	28	DE	293	Henry	1	DE	171
Elmira E	2	DE	143	Rachel A	1	DE	71	Henry	15	DE	215
Emily	13	DE	47	Rebecca J	7	DE	4	Henry B	36	DE	171
George	7	DE	138	Richard	9	DE	153	Henry E	40	MD	122
George	30	DE	75	Richard	17	DE	130	Hetty	17	DE	39
George	30	DE	4	Richard	48	DE	130	James	12	DE	123
George	71	DE	47	Rufus W	1	DE	4	James H	6	DE	105
George E	12	DE	143	Sarah	1	DE	142	James P	9	DE	128
Hannah E	4	DE	4	Sarah	7	DE	130	James W	14	DE	237
Harbeson	5	DE	112	Sarah	8	DE	293	Jane	16	DE	59
Henry	8	DE	134	Sarah	12	DE	153	Jincy	40	DE	105
Henry	11	DE	112	Sarah	15	DE	75	John	18	DE	219
Henry	49	DE	112	Sarah	30	DE	161	John	40	MD	250
Hetty	9	DE	138	Sarah	82	DE	143	John A	18	DE	141
Hetty	9	DE	142	Sarah A	4/12	DE	4	John C	7/12	DE	257
Hetty	30	DE	4	Sarah A	28	DE	71	John W	24	DE	126
Isaiah	20	DE	134	Sarah A	60	DE	167	Jonathan	10	DE	105
Jacob	37	DE	141	Selby	8	DE	130	Joseph	8	DE	257
James	63	DE	134	Selby	9	DE	141	Joshua	2	DE	80
James A	31	DE	122	Selby J	50	DE	134	Joshua	18	MD	143
Jane	6	DE	134	Sophia	10	DE	130	Joshua	22	DE	250
Jane	21	DE	143	Sophia	31	DE	122	Josiah	23	DE	250
Jane	24	MD	141	Sophia	60	DE	134	Kensy J	30	DE	296
Jane	28	DE	4	Susan L	20	DE	50	Lavinia	10	DE	250
Jehosabeth	19	DE	161	Virginia	3	DE	130	Lemuel	40	DE	167
Jeptha	45	DE	138	William	3/12	DE	130	Manaan	48	DE	105
John	3	DE	153	William	7	DE	141	Manlove	14	DE	105
John	5	DE	141	William	8	DE	142	Margaret A	18	DE	170
John	22	DE	153	William	10	DE	75	Margaret E	8	DE	171
John	24	DE	143	William	22	DE	153	Maria	41	DE	167
John	25	DE	143	William	43	DE	141	Martha A	6	DE	250
John	58	DE	142	William	52	DE	153	Mary	10	DE	296
John	60	DE	226	William B	8	DE	143	Mary	18	MD	128
John	70	DE	137	William B	42	DE	134	Mary	48	DE	237
John B	10	DE	143	William P	3	DE	122	Mary	75	DE	117
John H	2	DE	4	William R	50	DE	71	Mary E	6	DE	171
John S	12	DE	51	Hicolls, Mary	7	DE	218	Mathew M	11	DE	237
John W	22	DE	161	Higman, Catherine	5	DE	214	Miranda	8	DE	296
Jonathan	64	DE	161	James E	3/12	DE	214	Nancy	13	DE	257
Joseph	40	DE	4	John	29	DE	214	Nancy	50	DE	97
Julia	22	DE	134	John W	30	DE	214	Nancy	62	DE	113
Leah	24	DE	161	Mary E	27	DE	214	Naomia	35	DE	127
Letitia	15	DE	51	Rachel	2	DE	214	Napoleon	2	DE	105
Levin J	1	DE	161	Hignut, Andrew C	16	DE	220	Niven	18	DE	171
Lewis	19	DE	47	Elenor	16	MD	221	Peter	13	DE	77
Littleton	25	DE	134	Elija M	20	DE	220	Rachael	30	DE	257
Louisa	39	DE	134	Elijah	60	MD	220	Rachael	40	DE	45
Love	30	DE	153	George W	11	DE	221	Rachel	20	DE	250
Love	41	MD	141	Isabel	17	DE	220	Rebecca	5	DE	97
Lucinda	4	DE	130	John H	20	DE	220	Rosanna	25	DE	80

Name	Age	St	No
Hill, Samuel	83	DE	113
Sarah	4	DE	81
Sarah	4	DE	105
Sarah	6	DE	296
Sarah	40	DE	250
Stephen	18	DE	89
Susan	4	DE	97
Thomas	10	DE	257
William	1	DE	97
William	6	DE	80
William	12	DE	257
William	13	DE	296
William	20	MD	123
William	38	DE	80
William	44	MD	257
William T	27	MD	202
Zadock	78	DE	117
Hillman, Arcada	58	DE	58
Clara	20	DE	84
Elizabeth C	11	DE	84
Ezekiel	2	DE	84
Hester A	6	DE	84
Letitia	18	DE	84
Lydia B	12	DE	58
Mary E	15	DE	84
Rachael	27	DE	84
Sarah E	2	DE	84
Thomas	16	DE	84
Thomas	40	DE	84
Thomas	64	DE	58
William T	12	DE	58
Hindebagh, Jacob	60	DE	42
Sarah	29	DE	42
Hines, Ann	35	DE	197
Charles K	24	DE	198
Eliza A	6	DE	197
Emma J	20	DE	198
Hester	18	DE	198
Levinia	55	DE	198
Martha B	7	DE	197
Sallie R	4	DE	197
Thomas	2	DE	197
Thomas	16	DE	198
Thomas	58	DE	198
William	38	DE	197
Hinley, Eliza	32	DE	101
James	32	DE	101
John	7/12	DE	101
Mary	6	DE	101
Sallie	15	DE	101
Theophilus	8	DE	101
William	2	DE	101
Hitch, Albert	5	DE	248
Arcadia	12	DE	225
Arthur	3	DE	248
Benjamin	35	DE	248
Clement	7	DE	218
Clement	48	MD	225
Daniel	5	DE	218
David	5	DE	225
David	8	DE	226
Elgate	13	DE	218
Elijah	43	DE	248
Elizabeth H	35	DE	233
Elma	11	DE	218
Euphema	34	DE	248
George	7	DE	248
George	9	DE	293
Henry	39	MD	218
Hester A	3	DE	233
Isaac J	10	DE	233
James	27	DE	232
James E	8	DE	218
Jane	27	MD	232
John H	18	DE	226
Josephus	11	DE	248
Joshua	52	DE	257
Laura	9	DE	248
Leah A	45	DE	248
Levin	5	DE	293
Levin	23	DE	232
Levin E	35	DE	233
Hitch, Levinia L	15	DE	233
Maria	16	DE	248
Martha	6/12	DE	248
Margaret	39	DE	218
Mary	1	DE	232
Mary	2	DE	293
Mary	19	DE	248
Mary	25	DE	232
Mary E	9	DE	218
Miranda	33	DE	293
Nancy	40	DE	257
Sarah	15	DE	293
Sena	48	DE	225
Sovereign H	2	DE	218
Thomas	10/12	DE	293
William	11	DE	293
William	49	DE	293
William T	6	DE	233
William W	26	DE	225
Hitchens, Alexander	26	DE	142
Amanda	14	DE	52
Caroline	13	DE	233
Caroline	16	DE	267
Catharine	16	DE	52
Charles J	28	DE	263
Comfort	23	DE	52
Cotsman	28	DE	250
Cyrus	18	DE	283
Daniel	15	DE	291
Edmond	6	DE	249
Edmond	25	DE	295
Edmond	59	DE	294
Edward	26	DE	52
Elenor	19	DE	285
Elenor	23	DE	263
Elihu	37	DE	261
Elijah	3	DE	288
Elijah	6	DE	160
Elijah	37	DE	233
Elijah	38	DE	264
Eliza J	4	DE	263
Eliza J	22	DE	241
Elizabeth	7	DE	281
Elizabeth	14	DE	156
Elizabeth	20	DE	282
Elizabeth	35	DE	283
Elizabeth	42	DE	263
Elizabeth	76	DE	264
Elizabeth A	29	DE	52
Elizabeth J	22	DE	242
Ellen	14	DE	60
Ellen	18	DE	52
Emaline	18	DE	37
Georgianna	3	DE	264
Georgianna	7	DE	233
Gideon B	31	DE	283
Giles	26	DE	285
Hannah	25	DE	52
Henrietta	50	DE	285
Henry	11	DE	285
Holland D	11	DE	264
Hudson	12	DE	285
Isaac	21	DE	146
Isaac	68	DE	250
Jacob	10	DE	112
James	6	DE	292
James	38	DE	112
James	39	DE	288
James	41	DE	257
Jane	2	DE	28
Jane	34	DE	288
Jas H	27	DE	296
Jeremiah	40	DE	242
John	3	DE	286
John	7	DE	237
John	7	DE	263
John	10	DE	288
John	23	DE	294
John	25	DE	294
John	30	DE	292
John H	5	DE	112
John H	19	DE	285
Hitchens, John M	6	DE	242
Joseph	13	DE	112
Josephine	11	DE	52
Joshua	4	DE	263
Lavinia	2	DE	261
Lavinia	19	DE	1
Lavinia	31	DE	261
Lavinide A	11	DE	233
Levin	7	DE	261
Levinia	4	DE	293
Lou	23	DE	112
Louisa	4	DE	264
Louisa	9	DE	233
Louisa	9	DE	294
Louiza	3	DE	295
Louvenia	9	DE	264
Lovey	15	MD	248
Margaret	28	DE	250
Martha	5	DE	242
Martha	31	DE	295
Martha	35	DE	28
Martha A	17	DE	263
Mary	2	DE	52
Mary	4	DE	261
Mary	5	DE	242
Mary	22	DE	250
Mary	28	DE	264
Mary	30	DE	233
Mary	30	DE	286
Mary	40	DE	242
Mary	50	MD	285
Mary E	6/12	DE	250
Mary J	20	DE	52
Miller	20	DE	285
Miller E R	9/12	DE	234
Millis	7/12	DE	285
Milton E	8/12	DE	264
Nancy	35	DE	267
Nancy	45	DE	250
Nancy	49	DE	52
Nathaniel	29	DE	285
Nelly	40	DE	250
Noah	22	DE	285
Norman	12	DE	283
Nutter	2	DE	263
Patty	69	DE	259
Peter	28	DE	286
Pollard E	12	DE	234
Polly	22	DE	249
Priscilla	18/12	DE	286
Priscilla	25	DE	283
Priscilla	60	DE	294
Robert	25	DE	249
Samuel	8	DE	288
Samuel	16	DE	234
Samuel	18	DE	264
Samuel F	73	DE	292
Samuel J	18	DE	242
Sarah	2	DE	295
Sarah	6	DE	159
Sarah	8	DE	264
Sarah	9	DE	263
Sarah	13	DE	267
Sarah	15	DE	261
Sarah	22	DE	285
Sarah E	10	DE	234
Selby	9	DE	52
Selby	60	DE	52
Smith	52	DE	285
Severin	65	DE	294
Unicy	58	DE	294
Virginia	13	DE	264
William	4	DE	288
William	5	DE	285
William	9	DE	261
William	37	DE	52
Wm	18	DE	221
Wm	18	DE	296
Wm E	12	DE	242
Hitchings, Alfred	43	DE	165
Caroline	13	DE	165
Dolby	50	DE	160

Name	Age	St	Pg
Hitchings, Edward	1	DE	148
Eli	30	DE	151
Eliza A	1	DE	151
Emeline	11	DE	165
George	19	DE	165
George	23	DE	160
Hester A	20	DE	160
Isaac	24	DE	160
Manlift	11	DE	160
Maranda	25	DE	148
Margaret	50	DE	160
Mary	20	DE	151
Mary E	4	DE	165
Merrick	40	DE	151
Mitchell	17	DE	160
Philip	16	DE	165
Samuel	22	DE	160
Susan	44	DE	165
Martin	43	DE	109
William	24	DE	169
Hite, Anna	3	DE	84
James	1	DE	84
Joseph	33	DE	84
Mary	30	DE	84
Mary Ann	23	DE	85
Nancy J	18	DE	84
Samuel	5	DE	84
William	20	DE	85
Hobbs, Benton	11	DE	220
Benton	41	DE	220
Bethany	7	DE	78
Catherine	50	DE	220
Charles W	11/12	DE	220
Eleanor	26	DE	219
Elisha	15	DE	220
Enoch	42	DE	220
Frances	6	DE	220
Georgetta	7	DE	220
Henry	15	DE	220
Henry C	5	DE	220
John	33	DE	73
John R	8	DE	73
Josephine	3	DE	220
Levinia	9	DE	78
Levinia	35	DE	78
Margaret Jane	4	DE	78
Mary	5/12	DE	73
Mary	36	DE	207
Mary E	9	DE	220
Mary E	2	DE	219
Mary E	31	MD	220
Mathias	4	DE	73
Nancy	17	DE	220
Nancy	70	MD	220
Nehemiah	1	DE	78
Priscilla	32	DE	73
Rachael	13	DE	78
Sarah	15	DE	78
Saulsbury	32	MD	219
Sena	8	DE	220
Sylvester	38	DE	78
William F	1	DE	220
Holland, Albert	4	DE	15
Albert	42	DE	52
Alfred	16	DE	59
Almira	14	DE	12
Alsey	29	DE	194
Amanda	2	DE	73
Andrew	29	DE	17
Andrew B	4	DE	13
Andrew J	1	DE	17
Ann	45	DE	74
Ann E	8	DE	13
Ann M	7	DE	70
Arcada	18	DE	16
Celia	24	DE	13
Charles	18	DE	59
Charles F	9	DE	12
Comfort	13	DE	58
Comfort	70	DE	63
Comfort J	8	DE	70
Cornelius	44	DE	59
Holland, Cotta	47	DE	13
Cyrus	2	DE	14
Cyrus	59	DE	13
Daffy A	21	DE	39
Daniel	57	DE	58
David	15	DE	59
David	25	DE	39
David H	8	DE	75
David H	20	DE	73
Ebe	49	DE	14
Edward H	31	MD	139
Eleanor	42	DE	59
Eli	21	DE	13
Elijah	46	DE	59
Elisha	45	DE	12
Eliza	16	DE	12
Eliza A	4	DE	140
Eliza A	18	DE	13
Eliza J	22	DE	39
Elizabeth	26	DE	33
Elizabeth	28	MD	132
Elizabeth	50	DE	14
Elizabeth	55	DE	16
Elizabeth J	23	DE	16
Elizabeth M	27	DE	17
Ellenor	10	DE	13
Frances	40	DE	58
George	12	DE	59
George	13	DE	27
Hannah	17	DE	14
Hannah	18	DE	13
Hetty	11	DE	59
Hetty	19	DE	14
Hetty E	18	DE	57
Hester A	28	DE	17
Jacob	15	DE	15
Jacob	27	DE	14
James	23	DE	13
James	25	DE	15
James C	7	DE	66
James H	5	DE	13
Jeremiah	16	DE	13
Jeremiah	50	DE	75
John	8	DE	14
John	9	DE	66
John	13	DE	15
John	14	DE	58
John	24	DE	221
John	26	DE	72
John	33	DE	74
John O	34	DE	70
Joseph	7	DE	59
Joseph	14	DE	14
Joseph C	7	DE	17
Joshua	11	DE	58
Louisa	38	DE	12
Lucy A	7	DE	58
Lydia	15	DE	69
Lydia A	8	DE	17
Martha	6	DE	75
Mary	13	DE	13
Mary	13	DE	17
Mary	42	DE	59
Mary	50	DE	52
Mary A	2	DE	33
Mary A	20	DE	136
Mary E	19	DE	73
Mary J	6	DE	74
Mary S	13	DE	12
Milly	45	DE	75
Moses	8	DE	75
Nancy	31	MD	139
Noah	25	DE	31
Noah	26	DE	33
Patience E	11/12	DE	59
Richard	23	DE	221
Richard	47	DE	16
Robert C	5	DE	12
Sarah	22	DE	72
Sarah E	4	DE	33
Sarah H	3	DE	75
Sarah P	7	DE	12
Holland, Silas	13	DE	68
Susan	18	DE	75
Tabitha	13	DE	14
William	3	DE	140
William	11	DE	14
William S	20	DE	12
William T	4	DE	17
William Wesley	5	DE	39
Hollaway, Abel	29	DE	127
Ezekiel W	4	DE	127
James	9	DE	127
John G	3	DE	132
Kitty	30	DE	127
Mary	28	DE	132
Mary C	7	DE	127
Sarah M	1	DE	132
Thomas J	5	DE	132
Hollis, George	20	DE	220
Malba	16	DE	220
Hollock, Louisa	20	DE	170
Holloway, Aaron	62	MD	139
Annanias W	25	DE	136
Armwell L	2	DE	136
Charles	7/12	DE	53
Charlotte	4	MD	125
Charlotte	22	DE	136
Ebe	30	DE	142
Elisha	24	DE	142
Eliza S	26	DE	53
Elizabeth	26	DE	142
Fanny	50	MD	139
George B	58	MD	142
Hannah	22	DE	142
Hannah	56	MD	142
Henry	11	MD	125
Henry M	21	DE	154
Jacob	20	MD	140
James	5	MD	125
James	23	OH	125
James	25	DE	136
Jane	25	DE	136
Jedilah	35	DE	142
John E	4	DE	136
Joseph	22	MD	132
Julia	8	MD	125
Kenard	2	MD	125
Lana A	1	DE	142
Levin J	5	DE	136
Rachel	33	MD	125
Sarah	21	DE	132
Sarah	50	MD	139
Sarah	50	MD	140
Tabitha	21	DE	142
Thomas	16	DE	142
Thomas	20	MD	139
Thomas	22	DE	142
William T	30	MD	136
Holsten, Elisha	22	DE	25
James	35	DE	25
James A	9	DE	25
Jenny	35	DE	25
John	50	DE	25
Lemuel D	6	DE	25
Mary	3	DE	25
Nancy	45	DE	25
Sarah E	3	DE	25
William	30	DE	25
William H	1	DE	25
Holstein, Eliza	40	DE	91
James A	3	DE	84
Joseph	14	DE	91
Polina	28	DE	84
Sarah	2	DE	84
Thomas	42	DE	84
Holston, Ann	58	MD	128
Levin	31	MD	128
Robert	18	DE	128
Sarah	31	DE	128
Holt, Alfred	9	DE	274
Caroline	26	DE	272
Cyrus	2	DE	122
Daniel	31	DE	272
Elizabeth M	23	DE	122

Name	Age	St	Pg	Name	Age	St	Pg	Name	Age	St	Pg
Holt, George	4	DE	272	Hopkins, Elizabeth	6/12	DE	57	Hopkins, Robert	45	MD	270
Henry	5/12	DE	122	Elizabeth	16	DE	164	Samuel	7	DE	57
Hester A	20	DE	272	Elizabeth	19	DE	201	Samuel	26	DE	174
Isaac	7	DE	274	Elizabeth	21	DE	174	Sarah	12	DE	269
James F	36	DE	122	Elizabeth	22	DE	271	Sarah	14	DE	41
John W	2	DE	198	Elizabeth	45	DE	270	Sarah	14	DE	89
Maranda	2	DE	122	Emeline	29	DE	269	Sarah	17	DE	164
Martha	28	DE	272	George	6	DE	165	Sarah	26	DE	60
Mary	3	DE	272	George	19	DE	41	Sarah	31	DE	113
Mary	33	DE	198	George E	2	DE	60	Sarah	44	DE	41
Metchel	27	DE	272	George H	6/12	DE	186	Sarah A	13	DE	282
Miles S	24	DE	297	Hazlett	32	DE	89	Sarah E	4	DE	174
Missouri A	7	DE	272	Henry	10	DE	164	Sarah L C	19	DE	159
Polly	65	DE	297	Henry L	31	DE	201	Solomon	4	DE	41
Rebecca	7/12	DE	272	Hester	12	DE	41	Sophia Ann	4	DE	63
Samuel	25	DE	272	Hester A	15	DE	38	Thomas	4	DE	60
Turpin	21	DE	297	Jacob	59	DE	164	Washington	21	DE	270
William	6/12	DE	272	James	23	DE	159	William	11/12	DE	270
William	68	DE	297	James	29	DE	165	William	6	DE	41
William W	30	DE	198	James	53	DE	271	William	25	DE	180
Hood, Amy	21	DE	12	James A	16	DE	16	William	49	DE	41
David	37	DE	42	James H	10	DE	171	William A	2	DE	113
Eliza B	17	DE	173	James H	15	DE	43	William E	2	DE	63
Alfred B	5	DE	16	James W	12	DE	113	William H	1	DE	152
Alvin	14	DE	32	Jane	5	DE	37	William S	10	DE	57
Charles	10	DE	292	Jane	21	DE	201	Winiford	53	DE	16
George	9	DE	61	Jane C	2	DE	174	Wm C	39	DE	269
Eliza B	17	DE	172	Jaruscy	45	DE	271	Horn, Thomas	16	DE	224
Hannah	64	DE	61	Jehu B	10	DE	113	Horsey, Amanda	10	DE	198
Harriet	9	DE	158	John	3	DE	165	Ann	55	DE	266
Harriet	24	DE	149	John	19	DE	164	Biddy	34	DE	266
Henrietta	33	DE	292	John	21	DE	159	Catherine	66	DE	266
Henry	25	DE	12	John	23	DE	270	Charles	13	DE	266
Henry C	35	DE	176	John D	10	DE	113	Charles H G	2	DE	211
Hester A	28	DE	16	John D	36	DE	113	Edward	6	DE	198
Isaac	12	DE	158	Jos C	30	DE	195	Elijah	20	DE	211
Isaac	16	DE	292	Joseph	1	DE	89	Eliza	30	DE	198
Isaac	59	DE	292	Joseph H	4	DE	180	Elizabeth	13	DE	292
James	38	DE	16	Joshua	23	DE	293	Fanny G	3	DE	198
James H	7	DE	176	Josiah	24	DE	58	George H	3	DE	211
John	21	DE	37	Julia A	8	DE	269	Jacob B	11	DE	214
John	25	DE	31	Julia A	35	DE	195	James	40	DE	266
John	28	DE	61	Levi G	22	DE	159	Jane	6	DE	266
John R	5	DE	176	Levin	31	DE	60	John C	16	DE	198
Joseph	4	DE	147	Levin	72	DE	159	Josephine	13	OH	214
Lydia	3	DE	12	Levin S	31	DE	152	Maranda	10	DE	266
Margaret	34	DE	176	Levin S	37	DE	57	Mariah	14	DE	266
Margaret R	10	DE	176	Louisa	5	DE	89	Mary	7	DE	198
Martha	6	DE	16	Louvena	26	DE	159	Matilda	1	DE	266
Mary A	6	DE	147	Mahala	15	DE	41	Nathaniel	16	DE	214
Mary C	2	DE	176	Margaret	6	DE	269	Revel	37	DE	214
Mary Susan	1	DE	12	Margaret	35	DE	57	Samuel S	11	DE	293
Samuel	35	DE	149	Margaret P	3	DE	180	Sarah	8	DE	266
Hooper, Amelia	15	DE	241	Martha	3	DE	164	Smith	2	DE	266
Annis	60	DE	201	Martha	19	DE	152	Thomas J	6	DE	211
Araminta	75	DE	211	Mary	1	DE	165	William	9/12	DE	198
Bethany	7	DE	201	Mary	4	DE	269	William	9	DE	293
Charles H	15	DE	211	Mary	6	DE	89	Horsy, Andrew J	22	DE	241
Charlotte	65	DE	210	Mary	25	DE	16	Arcadia	23	DE	211
Draper	60	DE	201	Mary	25	DE	270	Eliza	48	DE	241
Eliza	47	DE	210	Mary	26	DE	171	Elizabeth	34	DE	214
H D	25	DE	197	Mary	34	DE	89	Ellen W	26	MD	234
Harriet	20	DE	202	Mary A	1	DE	180	Emeline	35	DE	241
John W	7	DE	201	Mary A	5	DE	57	George W	25	MD	234
Rhoda	1	DE	202	Mary A	30	DE	63	Goodwin	74	DE	208
Hopkins, Adaline	8	DE	89	Mary A E	2	DE	195	Harriet E	8	DE	211
Alexander	23	DE	270	Mary C	2	DE	41	Jacob R	11	OH	215
Alfred	22	DE	156	Mary E	9	DE	282	James	9	DE	212
Ann E	3	DE	159	Mitchel	7/12	DE	89	James H	11	DE	214
Ann M	4	DE	113	Nancy M	23	DE	180	Jesse	50	DE	215
Arpy	22	DE	58	Nathaniel	3	DE	164	Lenah	43	DE	215
Charity	24	DE	186	Nehemiah	15	DE	270	Lewis	11	DE	215
Charlotte E	9	DE	195	Noah	7	DE	41	Martha J	5	DE	234
Cornelia A	4	DE	195	Peter	14	DE	15	Mary E	2	DE	214
David	1	DE	61	Peter	46	DE	16	Nathan	33	DE	228
David	16	DE	159	Peter B	8	DE	114	Nathaniel	16	DE	215
David	17	DE	202	Philip	26	DE	172	Nathaniel	23	DE	241
David	32	DE	63	Priscilla	18	DE	236	Nathaniel	47	DE	211
Elias	4/12	DE	41	Prudence J	1	DE	63	Nathaniel	57	DE	241
Eliza	17	DE	270	Rebecca H	6	DE	195	Samuel	11	DE	292
Eliza	21	DE	165	Robert	2	DE	57	Samuel H	26	DE	241
Eliza	51	DE	159	Robert	20	DE	16	Samuel H	27	MD	234

Name	Age	State	No.	Name	Age	State	No.	Name	Age	State	No.
Horsy, Sarah	43	DE	216	Houston, Priscilla	40	DE	91	Hudson, Ann M	14	DE	90
Sarah	53	DE	208	Reuben	7	DE	91	Ann W	22	DE	144
Sarah P	7	DE	215	Robert	4	DE	91	Anna	6	DB	127
Sylva A	2	DE	228	Robert A	46	DE	1	Annanias	2	DB	123
Thomas	5	DE	214	Robert B	47	DE	155	Arlinda	12	DB	123
Thomas C	2	MD	234	Robert J	8	DE	156	Armwell	13	DE	138
William	9	DE	292	Sallie P	17	DE	60	Barsheba	36	DE	90
William H	29	DE	198	Samuel	6	DE	158	Benjamin	9	DE	78
Winny	30	DE	228	Sarah	6	DE	91	Benjamin	26	DE	237
Wm F	11/12	DE	215	Sarah	11	DE	3	Benjamin	31	DE	144
Hosea, Anna	13	DE	264	Sarah	20	DE	49	Benjamin	42	DE	130
Arnold	7	DE	264	Sarah	22	DE	235	Benton C	22	DE	143
Benjamin	12	DE	264	Sarah	25	DE	46	Bolitha	24	DE	126
Charlotte	17	DE	264	Sarah	35	DE	91	Caroline	21	DE	151
George	30	DE	264	Sarah	35	DE	172	Catharine	7	DE	61
James W	26	DE	232	Sarah A	24	DE	172	Catharine	8	DE	141
John	18	DE	264	Sarah J	3	DE	91	Catharine	10	DE	140
John	57	DE	264	Sheppard P	41	DE	60	Catharine	60	DE	138
Lovina	10	DE	264	Theodore	8	DE	175	Catharine A	14	DE	121
Margaret	11	DE	264	Thomas	9	DE	202	Charles	12	DE	141
Mary	8	DE	264	Wilber	4	DE	3	Charles	17	DE	73
Nancy	45	DE	264	William	21	DE	202	Charlotte	11	DE	137
Perry	20	DE	264	William A	5/12	DE	156	Charlotte V	5	DE	140
Risdon	8	DE	264	William F	3	DE	44	Clarissa P	11	DE	121
William	5	DE	264	Zilla	33	DE	202	Clayton W	47	DE	168
Hoskins, James W	32	NC	232	Hove, Harriet	9	DE	159	Clement	49	DE	90
Sarah	45	DE	85	Howard, Benjamin A	30	DE	112	Comfort	40	DE	156
Thomas	19	DE	85	Charles	5	DE	117	Comfort	68	DE	121
Houston, Alexander	50	DE	172	Clara	1	DE	112	Comfort L	18	DE	143
Amelia	16	DE	202	Daniel T	1	DE	172	Cornelius	35	DE	80
Ann	11	DE	91	Eleanor	3	DE	253	Cyrus	6	DE	63
Benjamin	19	DE	91	Eleanor	28	DE	253	Daly	52	DE	127
Borah C	3	DE	272	Elijah	14	DE	117	Daniel	10/12	DE	80
Catherine	70	DE	5	Elijah	47	DE	117	Daniel	73	DE	283
Caroline	7	DE	91	Elizabeth	9	MD	253	David	1	DE	61
Celia G	29	DE	91	Elizabeth	20	MD	128	David	6	DE	130
Charles	12	DE	156	Elizabeth	34	DE	143	David	19	DE	118
Charles B	4	DE	156	Elizabeth K	63	DE	122	David	24	DE	38
Clement	73	DE	91	Francis A	25	DE	126	David	25	DE	143
Clement Jr	30	DE	91	George	7	DE	117	David	45	DE	141
Curtis	38	DE	91	Geo W	14	DE	200	David	90	DE	130
Edward W	7	DE	171	Geo W	32	DE	112	David H	12	MD	163
Edward W	12	DE	156	Isaiah	2	DE	117	David J	6/12	DE	189
Elijah	24	DE	46	James	34	MD	253	Dingle	40	DE	168
Eliza	10	DE	202	Jane R	61	DE	47	Eben	25	DE	139
Elizabeth	32	MD	171	Jesse	19	DE	199	Edward	12	DE	112
Elizabeth	67	DE	5	John	1	DE	117	Elijah	16	DE	138
George H	4/12	DE	202	John	25	DE	128	Elijah	20	MD	163
Hannah	26	DE	52	John W	11	DE	199	Elisha	17	DE	139
Henry	21	DE	147	Joshua R	10	DE	112	Eliza	4	DE	91
Henry A	3	DE	156	Julia A	42	DE	199	Eliza	30	DE	61
Hetty	25	DE	170	Leah	22	DE	112	Eliza A	21	DE	141
Isaac	39	DE	91	Margaret	20	DE	47	Eliza J	12	DE	61
Isaac H	16	DE	156	Mary	11	MD	253	Eliza J	12	DE	139
Isaac H	51	DE	156	Mary	67	DE	200	Elizabeth	3	DE	140
Jacob	8	DE	158	Mary P	9/12	DE	114	Elizabeth	6	DE	44
Jacob	60	DE	158	Nancy	44	DE	112	Elizabeth	8	DE	80
James	66	DE	91	Rachel	7	MD	253	Elizabeth	12	DE	130
James A	42	DE	171	Rhoda	65	DE	112	Elizabeth	12	DE	141
James H	7	DE	202	Robert	50	DE	112	Elizabeth	15	DE	138
Jane	32	DE	91	Sarah	20	DE	47	Elizabeth	19	DE	139
John	55	DE	202	Sarah	36	DE	117	Elizabeth	23	DE	189
John M	18	DE	156	Sarah E	17	DE	126	Elizabeth	25	DE	137
John W	14	DE	202	Thomas	71	DE	47	Elizabeth	29	DE	65
Jonas W	35	DE	5	William	6	MD	253	Elizabeth	30	DE	168
Joseph M	15	DE	60	William	8	DE	117	Elizabeth	42	DE	141
Julia A	5	DE	202	William	45	DE	143	Elizabeth	43	DE	127
Louisa	2	DE	202	Howell, Sarah	84	DE	140	Elizabeth	52	DE	140
Lydia B	41	DE	156	Hubbard, Amelia	80	DE	212	Elizabeth	53	DE	43
Margaret	22	DE	202	Cassa	23	MD	208	Elizabeth A	7	DE	153
Margaret A	38	DE	5	John	2	MD	208	Elizabeth A	18	DE	140
Margaret E	11/12	DE	171	Joseph J	14	DE	291	Elizabeth J	14	DE	12
Maria	6	DE	91	Maranda	11	DE	218	Elizabeth P	13	DE	127
Maria	12	DE	236	Hudson, Aaron	3	DE	130	Ellen	23	DE	138
Maria C	1	DE	91	Alexander	10	DE	82	Ellen	40	DE	82
Martin	18	DE	202	Alexha	49	DE	131	Emeline	8	DE	127
Mary	57	DE	158	Alfred	2	DE	44	Emiry	18	DE	82
Mary R	4	DE	44	Alfred	25	DE	139	Ezekiel P	20	DE	128
Matilda	8	DE	172	Amanda	18	DE	138	Ezekiel W	2	DE	120
Nancy	67	DE	91	Angeline	1	DE	151	Francis	1	DE	78
Nancy	70	DE	199	Ann	2	DE	60	Gatty	48	DE	137
Phillis	11/12	DE	172	Ann	13	DE	137	George	11	DE	112

Hudson, George	15 DE 283	Hudson, Joshua	54 MD 163	Hudson, Nancy E	2 DE 134
George	17 DE 137	Joshua R	10 DE 113	Nathaniel	20 DE 139
George	18 DE 139	Joshua W	4 MD 163	Neal	20 DE 140
George T	16 DE 130	Julian Ann	23 DE 78	Nehemiah	16 DE 82
Godfrey	5 DE 169	Lavenia	62 DE 296	Noah	24 DE 140
Hannah	8 DE 112	Leah	50 DE 283	Parker W	20 DE 78
Hannah	38 DE 112	Lemuel	11 DE 169	Peter	2 DE 134
Harriet	20 DE 166	Lemuel	13 DE 140	Peter	15 DE 61
Harriet	22 DE 283	Lemuel	35 DE 153	Peter	20 DE 78
Harriet	30 DE 140	Lemuel	53 DE 140	Peter	30 DE 60
Henrietta	21 DE 134	Lemuel D	35 DE 120	Peter	30 DE 77
Henry	13 DE 76	Lemuel P	1 DE 140	Peter R	16 DE 140
Henry	30 DE 296	Letty	16 DE 140	Polly	40 DE 130
Henry	33 DE 36	Letty	18 DE 136	Polly	50 DE 139
Henry	41 DE 121	Letty	44 DE 138	Prudence	20 DE 139
Henry B	7/12 DE 139	Levin	2 DE 112	Prudy	22 DE 137
Henry C	12 DE 13	Levin	19 DE 141	Purnel P	1 DE 141
Henry G	11 DE 123	Levin	21 DE 155	Rachael	3 DE 63
Hester J	8 DE 130	Levin	46 MD 112	Rachael	36 MD 128
Hetty	4 DE 63	Levin	49 DE 140	Rachael	51 DE 78
Hetty	18 DE 168	Liben	9 DE 138	Rebecca	27 DE 44
Hetty	49 DE 138	Louisa J	3 DE 141	Retty	25 DE 138
Hetty C	25 DE 120	Lovey	7 DE 169	Reuben	32 DE 78
Hetty J	1 DE 121	Lovey	49 DE 139	Ritty	14 DE 139
Houston	1 DE 91	Luinham	7 DE 140	Robert	10 DE 123
Isaac	6 DE 137	Lydia	12 DE 140	Robert	11 DE 139
Isaac	40 DE 82	Lydia	21 DE 118	Robert	19 DE 69
Isaac	49 DE 137	Lydia	45 DE 76	Robert	26 DE 138
Isabella	3 DE 127	Manaan	23 DE 133	Rufus	30 DE 151
Isaiah	6 DE 141	Manaan	21 DE 138	Ruth	50 DE 63
Isaiah	14 DE 139	Margaret	7 MD 163	Thomas	5 DE 62
Isaiah	49 DE 139	Margaret	8 DE 163	Thomas R	27 DE 189
Jacob	12 DE 63	Margaret	31 DE 153	Thomas W	22 DE 36
Jacob H	11 DE 130	Margaret J	2 DE 153	Sally	20 DE 138
James	1 DE 60	Margaret E	2 DE 36	Sally Ann	13 DE 82
James	6 DE 80	Maria	24 DE 143	Samson	55 DE 63
James	9 DE 139	Maria	35 DE 80	Samuel	13 DE 169
James	14 DE 59	Martha	10 DE 63	Samuel	50 DE 36
James	17 DE 118	Martha	70 DE 154	Samuel D	14 DE 36
James	17 DE 141	Mary	2 DE 82	Samuel M	45 DE 127
James	18 DE 5	Mary	6 DE 112	Samuel W	10 DE 127
James	49 DE 91	Mary	9 DE 139	Sarah	8/12 DE 112
James H	1 DE 120	Mary	11 DE 90	Sarah	2 DE 78
James H	4 DE 151	Mary	11 DE 140	Sarah	6 DE 91
James H	12 DE 78	Mary	14 DE 283	Sarah	9 DE 137
James L	14 DE 140	Mary	16 DE 168	Sarah	14 DE 118
Jane	5 DE 138	Mary	20 DE 70	Sarah	20 DE 138
Jane	25 DE 60	Mary	24 DE 128	Sarah	21 DE 135
Jane A	16 DE 140	Mary	30 DE 123	Sarah	50 DE 283
Jenny	69 DE 82	Mary	40 DE 78	Sarah	82 DE 83
Jeremiah	17 DE 130	Mary	40 DE 130	Sarah A	28 DE 83
Jeremiah	40 DE 130	Mary	40 DE 140	Sarah C	2/12 DE 144
Jeremiah B	35 DE 128	Mary	54 DE 36	Sarah F	5 DE 153
John	2 DE 151	Mary	77 DE 141	Sarah H	6 DE 41
John	4 DE 123	Mary A	10/12 DE 237	Sarah W	13 DE 121
John	5 DE 128	Mary A	8 DE 120	Sarah W J	40 DE 121
John	11 MD 163	Mary A	16 MD 163	Selah C	15 DE 127
John	14 DE 112	Mary Ann	24 DE 36	Seth	65 DE 139
John	19 DE 128	Mary C	5 DE 128	Shady	26 DE 154
John	19 DE 139	Mary C	11 DE 45	Simpson	14 DE 141
John	24 DE 73	Mary E	2 DE 144	Sip	18 DE 80
John	40 DE 82	Mary H	2 DE 130	Sophia	60 DE 128
John	45 DE 76	Mary H	2 DE 189	Stephen	7 DE 138
John	45 DE 118	Mary H	2 DE 130	Susan	25 DE 41
John	50 DE 61	Mary H	3 DE 130	Susannah	25 DE 237
John B	5 DE 41	Mary H	16 DE 127	Thomas	5 DE 61
John G	3 DE 121	Mary H	42 MD 163	Walter	31 DE 41
John H	3 DE 144	Mary J	6 DE 123	William	7 DE 33
John H	11 DE 138	Matilda	4 DE 82	William	8 DE 123
John H	20 DE 127	Matilda	22 DE 139	William	18 DE 138
John MC	3 DE 169	Micala	9 DE 141	William	20 DE 130
John N	4 DE 120	Milford	7 DE 63	William H	8 DE 90
John P	40 DE 156	Michaela	18 DE 137	William H	9 DE 121
John W	11 DE 78	Nancy	5 DE 130	William H	35 DE 123
John W	42 DE 83	Nancy	13 DE 140	William H W	24 DE 135
Joseph	8 DE 44	Nancy	14 DE 130	William J	4 DE 127
Joseph	8 DE 91	Nancy	21 DE 138	William L	24 DE 134
Joseph A	26 DE 83	Nancy	26 DE 128	William M	1 DE 143
Joseph D	14 MD 163	Nancy	46 DE 168	Williamina C	1 DE 135
Joseph J	9 DE 130	Nancy	60 DE 136	Wm	4 DE 283
Joshua	19 DE 4	Nancy C	17 MD 163	Woolsey	43 DE 44
Joshua	40 DE 138	Nancy E	2 DE 128	Huffington, Amelia	12 DE 239

Huffington, Charles	6	DE	240	Hurst, Chester	19	DE	98	Isaacs, John	49 DE 101
Clarinda	13	DE	198	Ellen	13	DE	98	Joseph	11 DE 101
Deborah	14	DE	239	John T	41	DE	98	Joseph	41 DE 106
Eliza D	6	DE	110	Joseph	3	DE	98	Julia	6 DE 111
Harriet	25	DE	110	Mary	11	DE	98	Levin	28 DE 101
James	8	DE	240	Mary	16	DE	98	Levinia	12 DE 101
James	40	DE	110	Mary	45	DE	98	Louis	8 DE 101
James	40	DE	240	Samuel	21	DE	98	Lovey	28 DE 111
Jane	19	DE	239	William	1	DE	98	Margaret	1 DE 111
John	19	DE	110	Hust, Nancy	37	DE	42	Margaret	12 DE 106
John	45	DE	239	Nancy	41	DE	42	Margaret	26 DE 106
John	82	VA	201	Huston, Caroline	20	DE	91	Martha	6 DE 106
John M	4	DE	110	Elisha	28	DE	272	Mary	1 DE 101
Luraney J	1	DE	240	James	26	DE	91	Mary	4 DE 111
Mahala	4	DE	240	Jane	11	DE	91	Mary Ann	32 DE 101
Mary	2	DE	110	John	16	DE	91	Minus	10 DE 111
Mary	10	DE	239	Joseph	23	DE	205	Minus	38 DE 111
Mary	30	DE	240	Mary	40	DE	79	Noah	34 DE 101
Mary Ann	30	DE	110	Robert	13	DE	204	Owen	3 DE 101
Mary L	1	DE	110	Vardin R	5	DE	272	Owen	69 DE 101
Rachel	68	DE	201	Zephora	25	DE	272	Sarah	2 DE 106
Rebecca	2	DE	240	Hutchins, James	17	DE	231	Sarah	3 DE 111
Robert	15	DE	297	Hutson, Elizabeth	32	DE	170	Isham, Margaret	28 MD 126
Samuel	5	DE	240	James A	42	DE	170		
Sarah Ann	10	DE	110					Jack, Alsey	15 DE 40
Susan	42	DE	239	Ingram, Ann L	7/12	DE	75	Cornelius	60 DE 47
Susan A	8	DE	239	Anthony	28	DE	75	Eli	19 DE 70
William	20	DE	239	Elizabeth	40	DE	75	Eliza	40 DE 30
William L	8	DE	110	Elizabeth J	11	DE	71	Elizabeth J	4 DE 44
Hughes, Ann	48	DE	237	James S	5	DE	75	Francis	12 DE 30
Hester	34	DE	198	John	33	DE	75	Israel	38 DE 44
Hester A	27	DE	225	John B	2	DE	75	Jacob	70 DE 40
Hetty A	8	DE	115	Leah J	16	DE	71	John	10 DE 62
James	18	DE	115	Mary	51	DE	80	John	34 DE 30
John	17	DE	115	Mary Elizabeth	18	DE	80	Mary J	26 DE 44
John	40	MD	115	Matilda	8	DE	80	Nancy	2 DE 62
Luraney	50	DE	237	Nathaniel	40	DE	71	Samuel	22 DE 42
Maria E	11	DE	237	Nathaniel M	2	DE	71	Sip	17 DE 69
Mary	11	DE	115	Nathaniel T	3	DE	75	Ugenia	1 DE 44
Mary E	14	DE	235	Nehemiah R	8	DE	75	William	20 DE 66
Matilda J	20	DE	237	Robert	52	DE	80	Jackson, Ann	28 DE 35
Nancy	23	DE	115	Sarah A	27	DE	75	Ann	66 DE 33
Peter	13	DE	115	Sarah E	--	DE	75	Ebenezer	29 MD 205
William J	6/12	DE	115	Sarah F	7	DE	71	Eliza	30 DE 246
Humphris, Wm	18	MD	232	Smart	35	DE	71	Elizabeth	14 DE 39
Hunt, Wm G	17	DE	213	Thomas	12	DE	80	Elizabeth	33 DE 216
Hunter, Eliza A	22	DE	189	Thomas R	13	DE	71	Hester	32 DE 205
Eliza J	7/12	DE	13	William	14	DE	80	Hetty	10 DE 39
Emily	20	DE	189	Insley, Allice V	10/12	DE	205	Isaac	40 DE 39
Jane	48	DE	189	Amelia	8	DE	205	James H	30 MD 246
Joseph	25	DE	189	Cyrus	14	DE	275	James M	4 DE 216
Sarah	16	DE	189	Elijah	9	DE	205	John	4 DE 246
Hurdel, Ann E	5	DE	187	Eliza	5	DE	205	John H	3 MD 205
Comfort	30	DE	187	Eliza	29	MD	205	Julius	54 DE 33
Eleanor	23	DE	182	Jacob	37	MD	205	Louisa	21 DE 39
Hannah	21	DE	178	James M	32	DE	90	Margaret A	5 MD 205
Isabella N	2	DE	187	Martha	3	DE	205	Martha A	4 DE 216
Jacob F	24	DE	178	Mary	14	DE	205	Mary E	10 DE 216
John A	4/12	DE	182	Rachel W	75	DE	205	Peter	19 DE 9
Joseph C	30	DE	182	Sarah	13	DE	90	Peter	28 DE 33
William M	28	DE	187	Sarah	31	DE	90	Peter	58 DE 33
William T	1/12	DE	187	William	12	DE	205	Phebe	60 MD 200
Hurley, Adaline	25	DE	101	Insly, Angeline	11	DE	234	Robert B	7 DE 216
Ann E	20	DE	209	Mary	25	DE	234	Wesley	38 DE 216
Clement	45	DE	76	Irons, Absolem	59	DE	167	Wm C	1 DE 205
Elizabeth	56	DE	76	Andrew B	7	DE	151	Wm W	2 DE 216
Sarah	10	DE	101	Charles C	40	DE	151	Jacobs, Alexander	10 DE 57
Sarah	53	DE	101	David L	3	DE	151	Alice	56 DE 113
Wesley	12	DE	101	Hetty J	35	DE	151	Andrew	20 DE 224
Wingate	1	DE	101	Jane	52	DE	167	Ann	52 DE 79
Hurly, Benton W	23	DE	209	Joshua H	18	DE	170	Annis	35 DE 211
John H	8/12	DE	71	Major	21	DE	167	Aron	25 DE 210
Joshua C	27	DE	71	Mary A	40	DE	170	Bell J	10 DE 211
Mary E	2	DE	71	Sallie A	12	DE	170	Cedney	40 DE 225
Mary W	20	DE	209	Zepporah	82	DE	114	Charles	21 DE 205
Sarah A	23	DE	71	Isaacs, Betsy	50	DE	101	Curtis M	24 DE 212
Hurst, Alexine	17	DE	98	Elizabeth	19	DE	111	Eben	62 DE 113
Angeline	9	DE	98	George Ellen	10/12	DE	106	Edward	16 DE 211
Ann	36	DE	98	Hester	5	DE	101	Eleanor	27 DE 213
Ann	13	DE	98	Hiram	8	DE	111	Eliza	29 DE 10
Benjamin	16	DE	98	John	6	DE	101	Eliza E	8 DE 79
Caroline	8	DE	98	John	24	DE	111	Elizabeth	10/12 DE 52

Name			
Jacobs, Elizabeth	22	DE	227
Emeline	4	DE	58
George	8	DE	7
George	25	DE	63
George C	1	DE	227
George W	12	DE	209
Georgianna	2	DE	7
Hannah	62	DE	137
Harriet A J	9	DE	7
Henrietta	50	DE	212
Henrietta W	6	DE	213
Henry C	9	DE	213
Hester	18	DE	49
Isaac	14	DE	106
James	6	DE	7
James	21	DE	208
James	72	DE	137
Jane	16	DE	63
Jane	65	DE	153
Jane T	4	DE	106
John	59	DE	58
John	60	DE	137
John M	19	DE	137
John T	3	DE	222
John W	36	DE	196
Julia Ann	45	DE	106
Levin	66	DE	153
Levinia R	5	DE	213
Loseby	31	DE	222
Lucy	17	DE	57
Lurany	41	DE	217
Luther F	17	DE	212
Lydia	50	DE	58
Mahala J	20	DE	210
Manuel	14	DE	63
Manuel	45	DE	63
Margaret	6	DE	58
Maria	14	DE	207
Maria	20	DE	63
Mary	4	DE	63
Mary	6	DE	210
Mary	26	DE	7
Mary	31	DE	168
Mary	35	DE	52
Mary E	2	MD	213
Mary E	20	DE	93
Minus	28	DE	7
Nancy	4	DE	10
Nathaniel	46	DE	106
Nicey	59	DE	93
Noah J	14	DE	10
Rachael Ann	12	DE	79
Rhoda A	30	DE	7
Rhosalin	14	DE	212
Robert	30	DE	7
Rosanna	3/12	DE	7
Rufus K	21	DE	212
Sanballet	1	DE	222
Sarah	16	DE	224
Sarah C	13	DE	211
Sarah J	11	DE	153
Sinah A	25	DE	222
Stansbury	1	DE	7
Stansbury	59	DE	213
Starling	22	DE	10
Stephen	1	DE	211
Thomas	61	DE	211
Thomas H B	8	DE	211
Timothy	43	DE	10
William	51	DE	79
Wm A	29	DE	227
Wm K	33	DE	213
Jailot, James	85	DE	277
Jalt, Archabald	14	DE	153
John	63	MD	153
John W	19	DE	153
Lanta E	17	DE	153
Obediah	21	DE	153
Rhoda	52	DE	153
James, Ahasmerus	22	DE	101
Ahasmerus	33	DE	104
Ann	6	DE	104
James, Ann	6	DE	104
Ann G	28	DE	208
Ann H	21	DE	266
Betsy	24	DE	105
Betsy	62	DE	182
Branson	23	DE	283
Charles	8	DE	104
Charles W	5	DE	2
Colwell	10	DE	283
Colwell	44	DE	283
Cornelius C	14	DE	297
Edward	78	DE	239
Eleanor H	39	DE	2
Elenor	31	DE	249
Elias	9	DE	28
Elias	39	DE	2
Eliza J	18	DE	283
Elizabeth	5	DE	119
Elizabeth	7	DE	28
Elizabeth	12	DE	293
Elizabeth	25	DE	104
Elizabeth	51	DE	266
Elizabeth	60	DE	121
Emaline	31	DE	28
Ezekiel	29	DE	104
George	5	DE	283
George W	35	DE	293
Henry	13	DE	28
Henry	15	DE	283
Henry A	24	DE	266
Isaac	3/12	DE	101
Isaac	1	DE	142
Isaac	18	DE	283
Isaac W	32	DE	119
Jacob	3	DE	104
John	2	DE	104
John	32	DE	121
John	45	DE	28
John E	8	DE	283
John S	30	DE	208
Joseph H	4	DE	208
Joshua	3	DE	119
Joshua	5	DE	283
Joshua	32	DE	101
Joshua	38	DE	283
Julia Ann	32	DE	104
Julia F	12	DE	297
Leah	19	DE	283
Leah	22	DE	293
Leah A	15	DE	283
Levin	2	DE	28
Margaret A	11	DE	2
Maria	3	DE	293
Martha	17	DE	283
Martha T	7	DE	2
Mary	5	DE	104
Mary	12	DE	73
Mary	19	DE	284
Mary	21	DE	101
Mary	60	DE	249
Mary A	5	DE	104
Mary A	34	DE	239
Mary A	35	DE	297
Mary E	13	DE	2
Mary E	13	DE	283
Mary E	27	DE	283
Mary J	42	DE	283
Mary K	31	DE	119
Minos F	16	DE	266
Nancy R	9	DE	119
Noah	7	DE	283
Noah H	10	DE	283
Phebe	28	DE	249
Philip	2	DE	105
Philip	20	DE	122
Robert	10/12	DE	283
Robert L	40	DE	283
Rubin	9	DE	283
Sallie	70	DE	269
Samuel	2	DE	208
Sarah	10	DE	104
Sarah	24	DE	232
James, Sarah E	9	DE	2
Sarah E	14	DE	266
Tempy	18	DE	283
Tharp	7	DE	271
Thomas	20	DE	283
William	13	DE	24
William D	7	DE	119
William E	2	DE	2
Winget	40	DE	158
Wm	26	DE	239
Wm H	10	DE	297
Jarman, Ann	13	DE	292
Benjamin N	7	DE	257
Burton H	7	DE	266
Drucilla	19	DE	278
Eby	55	DE	259
Elenor	70	DE	266
Emeline	14	DE	278
Esther	76	DE	290
Henry	37	DE	277
Isaac	24	DE	278
Isaac	54	DE	292
Isaac T	58	MD	278
Jacob	6	DE	266
James	6	DE	292
James	17	DE	278
James R	41	DE	256
James S	15	DE	257
Jane	1	DE	293
Job	23	DE	259
John	56	DE	259
John W	37	DE	292
Lambert L	18	DE	256
Lavinia	9	DE	292
Louisa	8	DE	266
Lovy	7	DE	266
Lovy	50	DE	256
Mariah	44	DE	266
Mary	5	DE	292
Mary	45	DE	266
Mary E	20	DE	256
Mary J	6	DE	259
Nancy	13	DE	277
Nancy	47	DE	266
Phillip	4	DE	292
Rachael	53	DE	278
Sarah	7	DE	292
Sarah	15	DE	266
Sarah	36	DE	292
Sarah E	8	DE	295
William	8	DE	266
William	15	DE	259
William H	30	DE	266
William of L	47	DE	266
Jarmon, Hannah	4	DE	266
Theodore	2	DE	266
Jarvis, Ann M	14	MD	119
Ann M	15	DE	119
James W	2	DE	119
Martha E	4	DE	119
Martha H	28	DE	119
Jeffers, Ann E	6	DE	46
Eliza	31	DE	46
Frances	10/12	DE	46
Hannah	5	DE	46
Hannah	9	DE	33
Jacob	21	DE	33
John	23	DE	46
Jonathan	49	DE	46
Mary C	23	DE	34
Mary E	14	DE	33
Mary E	20	DE	46
Peter	21	DE	34
Sarah	54	DE	34
William	34	DE	34
Jefferson, Ann	11	DE	105
Ann W	38	DE	105
Anna	16	DE	66
Anna	8	DE	110
Asa	28	DE	6
Clarissa A	14	DE	145
Clementine W	4	DE	145

Name	Age	St	No.	Name	Age	St	No.	Name	Age	St	No.
Jefferson, Cyrus	39	DE	109	Jester, Elias H	8	DE	219	Johnson, Charlotte	23	DE	168
Diana	1	DE	75	Eliza	16	DE	23	Clarissa	30	DE	191
Eliza A	20	DE	66	Eliza	27	DE	219	Comfort	6	DE	181
Elizabeth	10	DE	110	Elizabeth	13	DE	86	Comfort	43	DE	29
Elizabeth	15	DE	105	George	4	DE	20	Comfort C	5	DE	29
Elizabeth	18	DE	49	George W	2	DE	18	Curtis J	12	DE	86
Elizabeth	20	DE	7	Hudson	22	DE	219	Cyntha	10	DE	88
Elizabeth	30	DE	110	Isaac	14	DE	22	David	32	DE	25
Elizabeth	59	DE	105	Isaac	38	DE	219	David	33	DE	86
Elizabeth	72	DE	34	James	21	DE	86	David C	9	DE	115
Gilley	10	DE	109	John H	2	DE	219	David H	19	DE	173
Hannah	14	DE	109	Lydia	11	DE	219	David J	2	DE	179
Henry	21	DE	73	Mary	45	DE	86	David M	8	DE	148
Hester J	6	DE	75	Mary A	15	DE	228	Deputy	28	DE	81
James	8	DE	105	Mary A	16	DE	219	Dinah	60	DE	88
James	9	DE	75	Mary C	1	DE	219	Edward	7	DE	83
James R P	3	DE	67	Miranda	18	DE	219	Edward	8	DE	97
James V	11	DE	146	Nancy	46	DE	25	Edward C	11	DE	189
Jeremiah	37	DE	75	Pollard	23	DE	219	Eleanor A	16	DE	148
John	16	DE	109	Rachael	19	DE	91	Elisha	60	DE	87
John S	7	DE	145	Rhoda	10	DE	219	Eliza	14	DE	163
John W	35	DE	110	Ruth	24	DE	90	Eliza	35	DE	180
Joshua E	14	DE	145	Samuel	10	DE	86	Eliza	40	DE	281
Julia J	13	DE	145	Samuel	13	DE	219	Eliza	50	DE	87
Kitty	25	DE	145	Sarah A	3	DE	25	Eliza E	2	DE	181
Levin	9	DE	105	Sarah A	31	DE	18	Eliza E	10	DE	33
Lydia A	38	DE	66	Solomon	26	DE	91	Eliza J	2	DE	83
Margaret A	3	DE	145	Sylvester	17	DE	86	Eliza M	6	DE	25
Mary A	5	DE	145	Thomas	29	DE	18	Elizabet	22	DE	32
Mary A	11	DE	75	Thomas	26	DE	20	Elizabeth	7	DE	260
Mary E	14	DE	33	Washington	28	DE	90	Elizabeth	8	DE	176
Mary E	17	DE	109	William	12	DE	86	Elizabeth	10	DE	191
Mary H	14	DE	179	Jiles, Elizabeth	8	DE	295	Elizabeth	11	DE	179
Mary H	30	DE	145	Isaac	12	DE	295	Elizabeth	15	DE	20
Mary L	26	VA	120	Jacob	5	DE	295	Elizabeth	20	DE	21
Nancy	53	DE	179	John	14	DE	295	Elizabeth	21	DE	88
Paynter	50	DE	179	Mary	36	DE	295	Elizabeth	23	DE	153
Rebecca	4	DE	75	William	41	DE	295	Elizabeth	24	DE	186
Rebecca	50	DE	145	Jines, Louisa	2	DE	151	Elizabeth	25	DE	15
Rebecca	75	DE	75	Love	25	DE	151	Elizabeth	25	DE	32
Richard M	4	DE	120	Robert	27	DE	151	Elizabeth	26	DE	193
Robert	7	DE	109	Thomas	4	DE	151	Elizabeth	32	DE	179
Robert B	20	DE	145	Johnson, Abraham	21	DE	189	Elizabeth	41	DE	87
Robert J	53	DE	145	Abraham	24	DE	186	Elizabeth	48	DE	182
Robert W	40	DE	145	Albert J	21	DE	21	Elizabeth	53	DE	186
Sabrey	5	DE	109	Alexander	5	DE	87	Elizabeth	60	DE	97
Samuel	1	DE	110	Alexander	30	DE	13	Elizabeth A	10	DE	29
Samuel B	17	DE	76	Alexander	50	DE	87	Elizabeth A	23	DE	116
Sarah	54	DE	33	Alexandra	18	DE	19	Ellen	25	DE	13
Sarah E	1	DE	145	Alfred	3	DE	193	Ellen	64	DE	191
Sarah J	9	DE	109	Ann	15	DE	181	Ellen L	13	DE	182
Susan	36	DE	75	Ann	35	DE	189	Elmer V	19	DE	33
Thomas	6	DE	110	Ann E	30	DE	112	Emily C	5	DE	189
Thomas	9	DE	67	Ann J	45	DE	179	Eunice A	34	DE	178
Thomas H	10	DE	145	Ann S	20	DE	182	Frances	14	DE	189
Thomas P	45	DE	66	Annanias	21	DE	163	George	7	DE	280
Virginia F	6	DE	66	Annanias D	62	DE	149	George	10	DE	163
Walter E	42	DE	120	Arrana	7	DE	189	George E	6/12	DE	180
William	10	DE	105	Arthur H	3	DE	189	George M	4	DE	186
William	11	DE	110	Asa	35	DE	145	George P	10	DE	112
William	12	DE	109	Asa G	32	DE	147	Geroge P	27	DE	136
William	34	DE	33	Asa S	19	DE	182	George P	70	DE	115
William	40	DE	105	Asahel	43	DE	182	George W	1	DE	188
William	45	DE	145	Asbury	5	DE	147	George W	4	DE	112
William J	2	DE	7	Auther R	56	DE	260	George W	4	DE	178
William P	21	DE	66	Benjamin	8	DE	87	George W	8	DE	149
Zippora	30	DE	145	Benjamin	17	DE	149	George W	13	DE	83
Jenkins, Eleanor C	13	DE	215	Benjamin	56	DE	163	George W	40	DE	83
J J	31	DE	202	Benjamin B	23	DE	173	Grace	9	DE	179
Lizzie	1	DE	202	Bennett	38	DE	29	Hannah	10	DE	189
Maria	27	DE	202	Benton H	37	DE	115	Hannah P	20	DE	116
Mary Ann	5	DE	202	Brinkloe	63	DE	173	Harriet	16	DE	175
Jepson, Margaret	58	DE	54	Brook A	24	DE	45	Harriet	53	DE	163
Samuel	65	DE	54	Burton	51	DE	180	Henrietta	28	DE	29
Jester, Ally	50	DE	219	Burton	67	DE	188	Henry	11	DE	260
Ann	27	DE	20	Catherine	5	DE	13	Henry	19	DE	233
Benjamin	11	DE	18	Catherine A	25	DE	173	Henry C	19	DE	163
Benjamin C	23	DE	91	Charles H	3	DE	180	Henry D	23	DE	184
Daniel	20	DE	17	Charles H	27	DE	97	Henry M	32	DE	173
Deborah	25	DE	219	Charles R	6	DE	186	Henry R	22	DE	182
Elias	18	DE	22	Charles T	7	DE	148	Henry R	27	DE	112
Elias H	8	DE	219	Charlotte F	10/12	DE	189	Henry W	15	DE	29

Name	Age	DE	Pg	Name	Age	DE	Pg	Name	Age	DE	Pg
Johnson, Henry W	40	DE	29	Johnson, Margaret	12	DE	184	Johnson, Return	1/12	DE	32
Hester	50	DE	14	Margaret	22	DE	89	Return	3/12	DE	32
Hetty	24	DE	112	Margaret A	5	DE	167	Return	3/12	DE	193
Hetty A	1	DE	25	Margaret A	16	DE	33	Rhoda A	26	DE	115
Hetty A	8	DE	189	Maria	3	DE	115	Rhoda A	30	DE	89
Hetty A	28	DE	147	Maria	11	DE	83	Rhoda M	23	DE	188
Hetty H	10	DE	149	Maria W	14	DE	116	Richard	18	DE	159
Hetty H	36	DE	148	Martha	10	DE	97	Richard A	60	DE	186
Hiram	26	DE	145	Martin F	32	DE	174	Richard M	4	DE	88
Isaac	23	DE	97	Mary	11	DE	183	Robert	6	DE	179
Isaac	25	DE	14	Mary	23	DE	97	Robert	11	DE	116
Isaac	57	DE	116	Mary	24	DE	166	Robert	18	DE	163
Isaiah	2	DE	32	Mary	27	DE	81	Robert	18	DE	188
Isaiah	4	DE	193	Mary	42	DE	97	Robert	62	DE	193
Jack	23	DE	87	Mary	44	DE	183	Robert B	14	DE	189
Jacob	4	MD	209	Mary	55	DE	149	Robert L	33	DE	167
James	8	DE	83	Mary	62	DE	193	Robert M	36	DE	148
James	16	DE	163	Mary	66	DE	115	Rosa	40	DE	116
James	26	DE	97	Mary A	4/12	DE	148	Rufus W	6	DE	189
James	30	DE	183	Mary A	13	DE	179	Sally	35	DE	87
James	76	DE	97	Mary A	21	DE	182	Samuel	18	DE	74
James A	4	DE	21	Mary E	1	DE	36	Samuel B	12	DE	186
James A	25	DE	21	Mary E	1	DE	178	Samuel R P	1	DE	29
James G	19	DE	180	Mary E	1	DE	183	Samuel W	41	DE	181
James H	1	DE	29	Mary E	4	DE	25	Sarah	6	DE	179
James M	11	DE	182	Mary E	4	DE	167	Sarah	24	DE	189
Jane	9	DE	181	Mary E	12	DE	149	Sarah	25	DE	36
Jane	33	DE	112	Mary E	13	DE	189	Sarah	47	DE	17
Jane	33	DE	186	Mary E	20	DE	97	Sarah	47	DE	150
Jane M	40	DE	83	Mary E	20	DE	192	Sarah	90	DE	285
John	1	DE	97	Mary H	1/12	DE	147	Sarah A	6/12	DE	167
John	2	DE	87	Mary J	27	DE	33	Sarah Ann	13	DE	87
John	4	DE	191	Mary J	29	DE	25	Sarah E	1	DE	186
John	22	DE	166	Mary M	10	DE	187	Sarah E	3	DE	182
John	24	DE	97	Mary N	9	DE	182	Sarah E	6	DE	33
John	24	DE	145	Mary S	8	DE	29	Sarah E	9	DE	88
John	28	DE	81	Maryana	15	DE	14	Sarah E	12	DE	182
John A	20	DE	116	Matilda	9	DE	179	Sarah J	1	DE	164
John B	7	DE	180	Miles	16	DE	163	Sarah J	14	DE	148
John D	6	DE	147	Minos	30	DE	148	Sarah M	17	DE	173
John D	28	DE	188	Minus	31	DE	17	Sarah P	5	DE	150
John E	3	DE	189	Miranda	18	DE	20	Sarbra	7	DE	275
John H	2	DE	13	Mitchell	65	DE	191	Sopha A	18	DE	182
John H	4	DE	81	Nancy	16	DE	130	Sophia	14	DE	179
John H	8	DE	191	Nancy	20	DE	174	Sophia	21	DE	163
John L	31	DE	36	Nancy	23	DE	174	Sophia	28	DE	186
John W	1	DE	21	Nancy	47	DE	186	Susan	23	DE	136
John W	1	DE	149	Nancy	50	DE	182	Susan	60	DE	275
John W	7	DE	148	Nancy	58	DE	116	Susan E	2	DE	25
Joseph	22	DE	174	Nancy	69	DE	87	Sylvester	5	DE	180
Joseph C	30	DE	148	Nancy A	26	DE	145	Tabitha	22	DE	182
Josephine	6/12	DE	97	Naomi J	5	DE	179	Theodore	21	DE	87
Josephus	16	DE	182	Nathan	22	DE	97	Thomas	18	DE	163
Joshua	10	DE	127	Nathaniel	45	DE	33	Thomas	26	DE	174
Joshua	33	DE	87	Nathaniel B	7	DE	33	Tilman S	29	DE	163
Joshua S	7	DE	148	Nathaniel H	37	DE	88	Umphries B	18	DE	188
Joshua B	6/12	DE	115	Nathaniel M	34	DE	186	Whittleton	38	DE	189
Joshua H	2	DE	112	Neely	38	DE	189	William	3	MD	260
Josiah	1/12	DE	174	Nepthem	3	DE	149	William	4	DE	136
Kitty A	12	DE	115	Noah	20	DE	182	William	5	DE	148
Kitty A	15	DE	182	Noble	45	DE	179	William	7	DE	150
Leah	50	DE	176	Patience	22	DE	188	William	13	DE	180
Lemuel	47	DE	189	Paynter	8	DE	163	William	14	DE	97
Lenard	10	DE	188	Paynter	27	DE	19	William	30	DE	14
Levenia W	3	DE	147	Paynter	47	DE	163	William	30	DE	178
Levi	13	DE	163	Perry P	23	DE	173	William	45	DE	1
Louisa	7	DE	88	Peter	36	DE	112	William A	1	DE	182
Louisa	13	DE	180	Peter	60	DE	97	William A	4	DE	36
Louisa A	15	DE	188	Peter	66	DE	116	William B	25	DE	186
Love R	19	DE	182	Peter P	25	DE	15	William D	4	DE	181
Lovenia	3	DE	148	Purnal	21	DE	163	William E	2	DE	167
Lovenia	6	DE	149	Purnal	75	DE	183	William E	12	DE	182
Lovenia	61	DE	149	Purnal R	16	DE	182	William K	15	DE	83
Lovey	30	DE	148	Rachel	18	DE	183	William M	34	DE	182
Lovey J	22	DE	149	Rachel	20	DE	168	William M	53	DE	182
Lydia	37	DE	181	Rachel	40	DE	163	William P	2	DE	153
Lydia F	19	DE	193	Rachel	50	DE	89	William S	17	DE	149
Manlove	42	DE	87	Rachel C	17	DE	116	William T	1	DE	88
Maomy	21	DE	21	Rachel E	2	DE	174	Winget	3	DE	148
Maranda	22	DE	174	Rebecca	12	DE	81	Winget	70	DE	166
Margaret	2/12	DE	19	Rebecca	28	DE	148	Winget of A	32	DE	153
Margaret	11	DE	87	Rebecca	43	DE	87	Zadock H	1	DE	153

Name	Age	St	No	Name	Age	St	No	Name	Age	St	No
Joice, Sallie A	10	DE	199	Jones, James	49	DE	70	Jones, Thomas	5	DE	261
Jones, Agnes	19	DE	25	James D	5	DE	148	Thomas	14	DE	111
Alexander	28	DE	223	James H	2	DE	217	Thomas A	48	DE	111
Alfred	21	DE	26	Jeremiah	31	DE	276	Thomas R	45	DE	125
Amanda	2/12	DE	147	Jeremiah	75	DE	279	Unicy	35	DE	280
Amy	7	DE	25	Jessisi	35	DE	78	Waitman	53	DE	225
Ann	48	DE	225	John	14	DE	78	William	7	DE	78
Ann C	11	DE	157	John	16	DE	111	William	8	DE	111
Ann L	1	DE	217	John	18	DE	69	William	14	DE	157
Ann R	24	DE	86	John	35	DE	290	William	49	DE	147
Annanias	24	MD	163	John	38	DE	221	William	52	DE	157
Augustus	45	DE	210	John	54	DE	164	William F	24	DE	1
Bayard	37	DE	196	John B	15	DE	210	William P	20	DE	164
Benjamin	3	DE	70	John H	4	DE	25	Wm	35	DE	221
Benjamin B	22	DE	172	John M	11	DE	164	Wm H	2	DE	223
Burten	2	DE	147	John P	26	DE	157	Wm Jr	34	MD	203
Burton	52	DE	146	John W	4/12	DE	196	Wm R	4	DE	210
Caleb W	6	DE	210	Jonah	70	DE	290	Zachariah E	17	DE	147
Caroline	7	DE	32	Joseph R	3	DE	289	Jonson, Jacob	4	MD	209
Caroline	18	DE	242	Joshua	4	DE	143	Jorden, John	25	DE	107
Caroline	31	MD	203	Julia A	2	DE	147	Phebe	23	DE	107
Catherine	44	DE	4	Kinsey	18	DE	69	Joseph, Abigail	33	DE	12
Charles H	2	DE	221	Leah	12	DE	146	Adelphine H	8	DE	192
Charles R	4	DE	164	Laura	5/12	MD	203	Adolphus E	2	DE	20
Charlotte	21	DE	289	Lavenia	5	DE	290	Alfred	4	DE	187
Clement	28	DE	217	Levin J	13	DE	143	Alfred	17	DE	41
Comfort	67	DE	289	Lovy	17	DE	289	Alfred D	10	DE	192
Comfort J	46	DE	164	Lovy	52	MD	289	Almira C	1	DE	181
Cyrus	22	DE	157	Lurany	23	DE	217	Ann E	9	DE	188
Daniel	10	DE	111	Lurena	23	DE	146	Ann E	13	DE	181
David	30	DE	86	Luther	30	DE	201	Benjamin	37	DE	156
Deborah	31	DE	221	Luvena	39	DE	146	Betsy M	13	DE	58
Ebe	8	DE	143	Luvina	7	DE	147	Boze B	6	DE	23
Ebe	32	MD	143	Lydia	10	DE	143	Catharine	10	DE	18
Edward	6	DE	157	Lydia A	14	DE	148	Catharine	10	DE	41
Edward	24	DE	219	Mahala	55	DE	210	Catharine	11	DE	64
Elias	6/12	DE	221	Martha	12	DE	157	Caroline	32	DE	156
Eliza	1	DE	289	Martha	40	DE	125	Cassandria W	10	DE	181
Eliza	16	DE	147	Mary	7	DE	111	Dagworthy D	11	DE	188
Eliza	26	DE	25	Mary	7	DE	144	Daniel F	5	DE	57
Eliza	48	DE	1	Mary	10	DE	147	David H	20	DE	184
Eliza A	5	DE	69	Mary	25	DE	260	Edward	30	DE	188
Elizabeth	5	DE	221	Mary	40	DE	210	Eli T	50	DE	64
Elizabeth	12	DE	111	Mary A	4/12	DE	223	Elias	1	DE	181
Elizabeth	33	DE	221	Mary A	41	DE	279	Elihu	14	DE	187
Elizabeth	35	MD	289	Mary E	1	DE	86	Elisha	47	DE	187
Elizabeth	39	DE	69	Mary J	5	DE	78	Elisha J	1	DE	184
Elizabeth	48	DE	226	Mary J	16	DE	148	Eliza A	15	DE	18
Elizabeth D	1/12	DE	157	Mary J	18	DE	219	Elizabeth	9	DE	181
Elizabeth J	28	DE	1	Mary M	12	DE	210	Elizabeth	16	DE	187
Ellen	23	DE	223	Nancy	7	DE	143	Elizabeth	20	DE	149
Emeline	16	DE	157	Nancy	10	DE	290	Elizabeth	24	DE	190
Emily A	20	DE	172	Nancy	30	DE	111	Elizabeth	33	DE	20
Emily S	21	DE	157	Naomy	35	DE	82	Elizabeth	38	DE	23
Erasmus	20	DE	69	Nathan A	10	DE	210	Elizabeth	39	DE	18
Ezekiel	7	DE	111	Nathaniel	26	DE	242	Elizabeth	39	DE	41
Ezekiel	35	DE	111	Philis	18	DE	157	Elizabeth	44	DE	182
Garison	8	DE	1	Phillip C	15	DE	1	Elizabeth	57	DE	182
George	8	MD	203	Phillip C	47	DE	1	Elizabeth A	5	DE	186
George	25	DE	25	Prudence	20	DE	4	Elizabeth A	11	DE	181
George A	16	DE	164	Purnal	50	DE	242	Elizabeth A	18	DE	41
George W	25	DE	289	Purnel	9	DE	41	Elizabeth B	35	DE	188
Gibson	49	DE	78	Rebecca	18	DE	290	Elizabeth R	61	DE	188
Gillis	55	MD	279	Rebecca	52	DE	157	Elizabeth W	3	DE	14
Hannah	5	DE	289	Richard	23	NJ	232	Ellen	21	DE	163
Harriet	30	DE	253	Robert	9	DE	69	Emeline	6	DE	187
Henry	3	DE	111	Rhoda	5	DE	111	Emeline	40	DE	187
Henry	12	DE	69	Sallie	36	DE	196	Emily	13	DE	41
Henry	20	DE	225	Sally	55	DE	25	Emily	13	DE	18
Henry	26	DE	25	Samuel P	8	DE	210	Ephraim C	63	DE	14
Hester A	20	DE	1	Sarah	1	DE	69	Eunice	72	DE	186
Isaac	14	DE	26	Sarah	5	DE	111	Frances	54	DE	182
Isaac	25	DE	290	Sarah	10	DE	78	Gardener W	8/12	DE	176
Isaac	74	MD	226	Sarah	31	DE	111	Gardener W	7	DE	20
Isabella	11	MD	203	Sarah	46	DE	279	George	18	DE	30
Jacob	6	DE	289	Sarah A	2	DE	86	George M	43	DE	181
Jacob	12	DE	143	Sarah A C	14	DE	210	George W	22	DE	188
Jacob	25	DE	280	Serenia	9	DE	111	Gideon H	24	DE	8
Jacob	65	DE	289	Solomon	12	DE	111	Hannah	23	DE	187
James	1	DE	78	Susan E	5	DE	25	Hannah	60	DE	187
James	22	DE	30	Thomas	4	DE	196	Hannah T	3	DE	181
James	45	DE	148	Thomas	5	DE	261	Harriet	14	DE	187

Name	Age	St	No.
Joseph, Henry C	18	DE	182
Henry D	36	DE	187
Hezekiah	28	DE	192
Hester	8	DE	186
Hester J	4	DE	62
Hetty R	17	DE	181
Isaac B	2	DE	156
Isabella	11	DE	181
James	6	DE	182
James B	34	DE	37
James H	7	DE	188
Jane	6	DE	18
Jane	6	DE	41
Jane	21	DE	62
Jesse E	11	DE	58
Jesse P	35	DE	176
John	8	DE	156
John C	4	DE	14
John H L	14	DE	181
John M	5	DE	181
John P	34	DE	186
John W	33	DE	12
Jonathan	20	DE	22
Jonathan	48	DE	181
Josephine	2	DE	57
Joshua B	3	DE	192
Julia A	31	DE	182
Leah Jane	7	DE	14
Lemuel	39	DE	58
Letty	61	DE	192
Levin	16	DE	182
Louisa B	13	DE	193
Louisa C	6	DE	181
Lydia	37	DE	58
Lydia J	21	DE	145
Margaret	15	DE	23
Margaret A	4	DE	182
Marian	11	DE	37
Mary	23	DE	192
Mary	33	DE	62
Mary	36	DE	181
Mary	47	DE	182
Mary	51	DE	64
Mary	52	DE	8
Mary A	6	DE	156
Mary A	14	DE	8
Mary B	34	DE	19
Miranda	8	DE	18
Miranda	8	DE	41
Miranda A	5	DE	20
Nathan H	5	DE	192
Nathan H	35	DE	192
Nehemiah	22	DE	187
Noah	51	DE	182
Pauline	9	DE	20
Paynter	50	DE	19
Paynter A	3	DE	23
Peter P	8	DE	182
Pinkey	12	DE	37
Rachel	19	DE	176
Rebecca	26	DE	192
Rebecca	31	DE	156
Rhoda	19	DE	64
Rhoda A	4	DE	37
Robert	16	DE	181
Robert	42	DE	23
Rufus	3	DE	181
S White	33	DE	57
Samuel	60	DE	149
Samuel	64	DE	192
Sarah	1	DE	163
Sarah	9	DE	187
Sarah	20	DE	184
Sarah	34	DE	37
Sarah C	7	DE	58
Sarah E	6/12	DE	23
Sarah J	7	DE	181
Sarah M	28	DE	192
Sarah W	24	DE	186
Sarah W	25	DE	57
Sarah W	30	DE	192
Sylvester	30	DE	192
Tatum P	24	DE	19
Joseph, Theodore	16	DE	64
Theodore P	2	DE	37
Thomas	11	DE	187
Thomas	17	DE	187
Thomas A	17	DE	18
Thomas H	12	DE	192
Thomas H	60	DE	187
Thomas J	3	DE	181
Thomas T	33	DE	20
Velinda	10	DE	23
William	5	DE	188
William	26	DE	55
William	65	DE	188
William C	10	DE	156
William C	31	DE	181
William E	39	DE	18
William E	39	DE	41
William J	9/12	DE	18
William W	49	DE	190
William S	9/12	DE	41
Zachariah	28	DE	64
Zachariah S	28	DE	62
Jourdon, Alfred	38	DE	84
Clement	2	DE	84
Clementine	24	DE	84
Joy, Alfred D	21	WN	20
Justice, Charlotte	7	DE	122
Elizabeth	70	DE	42
John H	5	DE	122
Martha	46	DE	42
Justis, Ann	18	DE	164
Benjamin	5	DE	125
Elijah	46	DE	164
Elizabeth	36	DE	125
Hetty	2	DE	125
Isaac	14	DE	125
James	44	VA	125
John	9	DE	125
John	14	DE	295
Rachel	30	DE	129
Rachel	30	DE	136
Sarah	11	DE	153
Sarah	13	DE	125
Sarah	40	DE	164
Thomas	11	DE	125
William	16	DE	125
Kane, Daniel	45	GE	237
Eliza	6	DE	69
Elizabeth	4	DE	237
James	39	DE	69
James M	2	DE	69
Mary	37	DE	69
Mary	50	DE	237
Mary E	12	DE	69
Solomon	9	DE	69
Karsey, James	50	DE	59
Kelley, Peter	21	MD	164
Kender, Ann E	21	DE	211
Caleb D	24	DE	211
Mary F	9/12	DE	211
Keniken, Clayton	28	DE	249
John	30	DE	249
Mary	23	DE	249
Kenneken, Ann	41	DE	296
Wm	51	DE	296
Kennekin, Elenor	35	DE	250
George	5	DE	250
Harriet	8	DE	250
Leah	6	DE	250
Mary	11	DE	250
Mary	27	DE	247
Perry	36	DE	246
Stephen	55	DE	250
Waitman	14	DE	250
Kennikin, Elizabeth	52	DE	243
Getty	15	DE	243
Margaret E	20	DE	243
Mathew	67	DE	243
Priscilla	26	DE	243
Thomas	44	DE	243
Wm B	46	DE	243
Kenny, Amelia	8	DE	257
Ann E	10	DE	238
Ann G	17	DE	290
Elenor	22	DE	257
Elijah	8	DE	257
Elijah C	27	DE	249
George	21	DE	249
Harriet	35	DE	249
Jacob B	38	DE	238
James	17	DE	257
James E	15	DE	249
Jesse	5	DE	249
John	17	DE	236
John	19	DE	249
Joshua	7	DE	249
Joshua	58	DE	249
Julia A	22	DE	249
Marry	11	DE	257
Mary	40	DE	257
Mary E	1	DE	238
Oliver J	8	DE	249
Sallie	27	DE	249
Samuel	29	DE	249
Sarah	2	DE	249
Sarah	24	DE	238
Sarah	55	DE	249
Waitman	33	DE	249
William	13	DE	257
William J	11	DE	257
Kery, George C	8	DE	59
Killey, Peter	21	DE	163
Killum, John	60	DE	170
Martha	40	DE	170
Kimmey, Aaron	37	DE	19
Ann K	29	DE	19
Caroline W	5	DE	19
Jacob S	4	DE	19
James D	7	DE	37
James P	10	DE	19
John H	8	DE	19
John M	10	DE	19
Laura	5	DE	19
Mary Ann	2	DE	19
Mary J	12	DE	19
Priscilla	6	DE	19
Purnel P	37	DE	19
Sarah	31	DE	19
Kimmy, Aaron	75	DE	92
Alexander	35	DE	61
Alfred	12	DE	212
Elizabeth	31	DE	61
Elsey	8	DE	92
George W	7	MD	220
John	4	DE	61
Lovey	60	DE	92
Mary E	1	DE	61
Oliver	41	DE	213
Kinder, Alace	38	DE	208
Caroline	8	DE	211
Caroline A	2/12	DE	208
Castilia	12	DE	211
Castitia	45	MD	214
Charlotte	16	DE	214
Daniel B	33	DE	208
David B	2	DE	214
David S	16	DE	208
Edmond C	3	DE	208
Eliza A	14	DE	211
Eliza A	18	DE	208
Eliza A	48	DE	211
Elizabeth R	9	DE	214
Henry C	5	DE	208
Isaac	77	DE	208
Isaac L	17	DE	214
Isaac N	2	DE	208
Jacob	41	DE	214
Jacob O	12	DE	208
John	47	DE	214
John L	12	DE	214
Lewis	14	DE	214
Lovy A	8	DE	208
Martha	16	DE	211

Name	Age	State	No.	Name	Age	State	No.	Name	Age	State	No.
Kinder, Mary	37	DE	214	King, Matthew	4	DE	281	Knowles, Emeline	9	DE	243
Mary A C	7	DE	211	Nancy	17	DE	280	Emma	5	DE	268
Mary E	19	DE	208	Nancy	60	DE	202	Ephraim	27	DE	244
Mary E	25	DE	208	Nathaniel	32	DE	281	Esther	91	DE	249
Mary M	18	DE	214	Noble	27	DE	277	George	6/12	DE	100
Owen	44	DE	208	Noble	28	DE	281	George	3	DE	247
Rhoda	71	DE	208	Priscilla	9	DE	32	George	22	DE	268
Rhoda A	22	DE	211	Rachel	9	DE	281	Gideon W	23	MD	244
Rhoda J	14	DE	208	Rhoda	43	MD	237	Hester	2	DE	243
Samuel	14	DE	214	Robert	7	DE	32	Hester	53	DE	242
Sarah C	14	DE	214	Rodney	5/12	DE	55	Isaac	23	DE	275
Sina W	3	DE	208	Ruth	15	DE	277	Jacob	1	DE	275
Sinah W	16	DE	211	Sarah	18	DE	280	James	28	DE	274
Stephen W	7	DE	214	Sarah	26	DE	267	James W	17	DE	244
Tilghman D	29	DE	214	Sarah	32	DE	15	Jane	28	DE	100
Warren	49	DE	211	Sarah	63	DE	14	Jane	38	DE	100
Wesley S	5	DE	214	Sarah A	4	MD	237	John	8	DE	100
King, Ann	40	DE	202	Sethy	60	DE	277	John	17	DE	100
Anna	50	DE	199	Sully	67	MD	289	John	47	DE	243
Benjamin	11	DE	277	Susan	30	DE	202	Joseph	1	DE	247
Benjamin J	11	MD	289	Susan E	19	DE	14	Joseph	3	DE	275
Byard	16	DE	24	Thomas H	14	DE	15	Josephine	9	DE	244
Byard	16	DE	32	William	6	DE	277	Julia	9	DE	100
Catherine J	29	DE	44	William	21	DE	202	Julia A	24	DE	244
Cornelius	19	DE	15	William C	33	DE	267	Letty	9	DE	100
David	50	DE	202	William H	13	DE	15	Louisa	6	DE	100
David C	11	DE	202	Wm S	21	DE	234	Lurany	24	DE	275
David H	33	DE	43	Wingate	12	DE	32	Maria	8	DE	268
Dennis	12	DE	15	Zephora	4	DE	273	Martha	19	DE	268
Eliza A	17	DE	121	Kinnekin, Sallie	17	DE	249	Mary	18	DE	100
Elizabeth	5	DE	32	Kinney, Ann	35	DE	3	Mary	20	DE	273
Elizabeth	14	DE	202	Catherine	39	DE	198	Mary	41	DE	244
Elizabeth	15	DE	283	Jacob	31	DE	3	Mary	48	DE	100
Elizabeth	18	DE	237	Mary	60	DE	3	Mary A	10	DE	291
Elizabeth	25	DE	281	Kinny, Eleanor	49	DE	242	Mary A	18	DE	239
Elizabeth	50	DE	277	George	21	DE	248	Mary A	24	DE	268
Elizabeth	50	MD	289	James E	15	DE	249	Mary J	4	DE	244
Ellen	20	DE	202	John	17	DE	235	Mary J	24	DE	244
Ellenor	25	DE	32	John	19	DE	249	Mary P	19	MD	244
Emeline	21	DE	225	Julia A	22	DE	249	Mentin	4	DE	100
Eunice	7	DE	202	Leah	50	DE	234	Nancy	40	DE	244
Francis	33	MD	237	Samuel	49	DE	242	Rebecca	18	DE	246
George	3	DE	15	Kirk, Sarah E	22	DE	77	Rebecca A	18	DE	242
George	5	DE	267	Kirkman, Charles H	3	DE	235	Richard	9	DE	247
George E	28	DE	241	James A	16	DE	235	Richard	17	DE	243
George H	17	DE	14	John M	8	DE	235	Robert	21	DE	100
Hannah	12	DE	15	Phanny E	10	DE	235	Robert E	21	DE	242
Henry	7	DE	62	Kirkpatrick, Edward	22	DE	167	Samuel	6	DE	244
Henry	54	DE	62	Hamilton	37	DE	167	Samuel	26	DE	101
Hessy	6/12	DE	32	Isabella	10	DE	167	Sanpta	5	DE	243
Hetty	3	DE	267	John	7	DE	167	Sarah	7	DE	100
Hugh	65	DE	15	Maria	48	DE	167	Sarah	13	DE	268
Isaac	19	DE	62	Knocks, Benjamin E	13	DE	217	Sarah	46	DE	268
Isaac	55	DE	62	James R	15	DE	217	Thomas	15	DE	244
James	37	DE	15	Jonathan	22	DE	217	Thomas	18	DE	273
James	52	DE	277	Martha J	3	DE	217	William	3	DE	244
James C	20	DE	14	Mary L	2	DE	217	William	14	DE	273
James H	6	DE	273	Rhoda K	10	DE	217	William	25	DE	100
John	3	DE	277	Samuel	46	DE	217	William J	2	DE	244
John	4	DE	32	Samuel F	8	DE	217	Wilson	51	DE	268
John	19	DE	62	Sarah	45	DE	217	Wm	27	DE	247
John	19	DE	202	Sarah A	17	DE	217	Wm	65	DE	244
John	46	DE	32	Wm H	16	DE	217	Wm S	14	DE	242
John C	10	DE	249	Knowles, Amelia	46	DE	243	Knowls, Frederic	13	DE	110
Joseph S	3	DE	15	Ann J	21	DE	274	Jacob	33	DE	110
Joshua	8	DE	289	Arcada	38	DE	244	John	3	DE	110
Joshua	9	DE	277	Asena	72	DE	247	Louisa	1	DE	110
Lucy	13	PA	235	Cannon	49	DE	244	Nancy	33	DE	110
Lurena	17	DE	277	Caroline	6	DE	100	Rachel	9	DE	110
Maranda	20	DE	281	Catherine	16	DE	273	Theodore	5	DE	110
Margaret	13	DE	32	Charlotte	17	DE	242	Knox, Aurena	2	DE	123
Maria	7	DE	267	Daniel	12	DE	100	Eleanor	45	DE	123
Mary	7/12	DE	267	Daniel	51	DE	100	George W	19	DE	123
Mary	14	DE	32	David	31	DE	243	James	44	DE	123
Mary	24	DE	277	Eleanor	11	DE	243	James H	14	DE	123
Mary	25	DE	289	Elijah	12	DE	244	Sarah E	10	DE	123
Mary	35	DE	222	Eliza	3	DE	274	William	6	DE	123
Mary	50	DE	15	Eliza	15	DE	100	Kolhoun, Elizabeth	25	DE	26
Mary A	14	DE	202	Eliza	50	DE	273	Caroline	20	DE	26
Mary E	4	DE	15	Elizabeth	2	DE	100	George	14	DE	26
Mary J	7	DE	61	Elizabeth	28	MD	247	George	44	DE	26
Mary L	35	DE	273	Emeline	2	DE	243	Gideon	16	DE	26

Name	Age	St	Pg
Kolhoun, James	9	DE	26
Jonathan	68	DE	26
Leah	35	DE	26
Nancy	76	DE	26
Thomas	17	DE	26
Kollock, Alfred	10	DE	2
Amanda	11	DE	7
Ann W	16	DE	156
Benjamin	55	DE	59
Cyrus	9	DE	7
David J	7	DE	59
Dianna C	73	DE	51
Edward	7	DE	2
Elizabeth M	5	DE	59
Elizabeth R	14	DE	156
George	74	DE	4
Hannah	23	DE	3
Hetty	24	DE	3
Isaac	33	DE	7
Jacob M	37	DE	2
James F	33	DE	8
James P W	60	DE	6
John	65	DE	3
Joseph	45	DE	156
Joseph A	2	DE	156
Margaret	6	DE	2
Martha F	32	DE	6
Mary	5	DE	2
Mary	35	DE	7
Mary	38	DE	4
Mary	44	DE	59
Mary	55	DE	3
Mary C	10	DE	156
Mary E	40	DE	2
Mary J	1	DE	7
Mary J	20	DE	59
Patience	60	DE	4
Robert	16	DE	7
Robert H	18	DE	156
Sarah	42	DE	156
Sarah E	7	DE	7
Thomas	4	DE	7
William D	10	DE	59
William J	6	DE	128
William S	12	DE	156
Korsine, Christian	40	GE	226
Lack, Nancy	47	DE	58
Lacey, Elizabeth	52	DE	189
Hutcher	56	DE	189
John	26	DE	182
John S	26	DE	165
Mary A	30	DE	189
Robert	57	DE	165
Lacy, John C	23	DE	13
Maranda E	16	DE	13
Mary	57	DE	13
Priscilla L	28	DE	34
Robert	34	DE	34
William A	9/12	DE	34
Zadock B	59	DE	13
Ladd, William	14	DE	68
Lafet, Elizabeth	5	MD	281
Julia A	6	DE	281
William	1	MD	281
William	30	MD	281
Lafetre, Joseph	33	DE	55
Laman, Catherine	17	DE	48
Lamb, Sarah	22	DE	145
Lamden, John	18	DE	246
Joshua	40	DE	246
Mary	15	DE	246
Sarah	40	DE	246
Wm	16	DE	246
Lamdin, Robert	28	DE	109
Lane, Isaac	22	DE	30
Leah M	9	DE	228
Langrell, Daniel F	9	DE	195
Elizabeth	39	DE	221
John	40	DE	195
Mary J	35	DE	195
Sarah M	7	DE	195
Langrell, Sarah M	7	DE	195
Lank, Ann	38	DE	272
Cannon	40	DE	266
Catharine	7	DE	272
Elizabeth	15	DE	272
Hannah J	16	DE	57
James	26	DE	57
James A	1/12	DE	38
John	30	DE	38
John E	1	DE	57
Joseph E	2	DE	38
Letty E	22	DE	38
Levin	10	DE	272
Levin	60	DE	272
Margaret	13	DE	272
Maria	22	DE	235
Mariah	24	DE	57
Megruda B	3	DE	235
Mitchel	56	DE	57
Robert	4	DE	272
Sophia	50	DE	57
Thomas	30	DE	235
Uris E	24	DE	272
William H	4	DE	38
William L	19	DE	57
Lankford, Ann	43	DE	205
Elizabeth	16	DE	206
John H	17	DE	205
John W	32	MD	221
Leah J	11	DE	205
Littleton	50	MD	204
Martin V B	10	DE	205
Mary A	31	MD	221
Mary E	10	MD	221
Nancy H	4	DE	205
Noah	14	DE	205
Rebecca E	9	MD	221
Sallie H	8	DE	205
Sarah A	5/12	DE	221
Wm W	6	MD	221
Lark, Hannah J	10	DE	12
James M	16	DE	12
Leven J	17	DE	12
Mary	43	DE	12
Mary	50	DE	12
Mary E	14	DE	12
Moses	20	DE	30
Nancy J	17	DE	12
Ruthy A	12	DE	12
William	42	DE	12
William D	21	DE	15
Larnier, Ann	30	DE	269
George	8/12	DE	269
Margaret	7	DE	269
Mary	5	DE	269
Thomas	4	DE	269
Thomas	34	MD	269
Lavender, Catherine	23	DE	44
Charles	7	DE	44
John D	3	DE	44
John Jr	33	DE	44
Oscar	1	DE	44
Law, Ann A	20	DE	118
Charles R	8	DE	118
Ezekiel P	14	DE	118
George E	4	DE	118
Harriet B	4	DE	118
James	48	DE	118
James H L	18	DE	118
Levin W	9	DE	118
Mary E W	11	DE	118
William L	19	DE	118
Lawder, Elizabeth	24	DE	239
Lawler, Elizabeth	19	DE	151
Lawles, Ann E	5	DE	172
Hetty	40	DE	172
John C	2	DE	172
Joseph S	8	DE	172
Nathaniel	35	DE	172
Sarah E	11	DE	172
Lawless, Eliza J	9	DE	227
James	42	DE	227
Lawless, Jane	32	DE	227
John	19	DE	8
Julia A	11	DE	227
Mary	20	DE	8
Robert	14	DE	8
Lawrence, Alexandria	36	DE	168
Ann T	14	DE	137
Hannah	16	DE	168
Hannah	59	DE	168
Lydia L	21	DE	168
Laws, Alexander	19	DE	296
Ann	3	DE	229
Ann	45	DE	297
Anthony	60	DE	297
Augustus	14	DE	296
Augustus	58	DE	296
Beth	70	DE	225
Charlotte	23	DE	297
Charlotte	64	DE	215
Cornelius	17	DE	297
Cyrus	9	DE	297
Cyrus	19	DE	296
Dennis	21	DE	297
Edward	24	DE	282
Eliza	11	DE	297
Flora	56	DE	225
Hannah	30	DE	1
Harriet L	23	DE	234
Jannet	4	DE	114
Joanna	7	DE	297
John	32	DE	234
John R	3	MD	234
Leah	19	DE	209
Margaret	12	DE	296
Mary	23	DE	282
Mary	24	DE	201
Mary A	20	DE	296
Mary E	6	DE	234
Nathan	13	DE	297
Robert	21	DE	296
Sallie	74	DE	215
Samuel	68	DE	215
Willie	7/12	DE	234
Lawson, Arcada	30	DE	184
Charlotte	20	DE	15
Daniel	5	DE	184
David A	9	DE	165
David T	2	DE	184
George	11	DE	184
Hamilton	21	DE	193
Henry	50	DE	165
Henry H	21	DE	165
Henry J	20	DE	184
Hester J	3	DE	165
Hetty A	5	DE	190
James L	34	DE	190
Jehu	9	DE	190
John	5	DE	184
John	7	DE	184
John M	17	DE	165
Lydia H	2	DE	190
Maria	14	DE	184
Martha	18	DE	182
Martha A	17	DE	193
Mary	48	DE	193
Mary A	15	DE	184
Mary E	10	DE	165
Mary J	31	DE	190
Nathaniel	19	DE	193
Robert	9	DE	184
Robert	23	DE	193
Robert	45	DE	184
Sarah	45	DE	165
Selby	17	DE	184
Thomas	14	DE	57
Thomas A	15	DE	165
William	7	DE	165
Zadock J	12	DE	190
Layton, Alfred L	2	DE	211
Alsey	66	DE	85
Benton	70	DE	108
Burton	23	DE	160

Name	Age		No.	Name	Age		No.	Name	Age		No.
Layton, Burton	54	DE	218	Layton, William	24	DE	130	Lekate, James	2	DE	291
Caleb	11	LE	134	Leach, Amelia	31	MD	206	Jeremiah	37	DE	289
Caleb	17	DE	209	Elizabeth	8	MD	206	Nancy	28	DE	289
Caleb R	24	DE	1	John H	4	DE	206	Peter	30	DE	291
Caleb S	52	DE	1	Lillie C	1	DE	206	Sabra	4	DE	289
Charles	52	DE	79	Margaret A	9	DE	206	Samuel	2	DE	289
Charlotte E	20	DE	224	Perry T	33	MD	206	Sarah	8	DE	289
Clement	60	DE	85	Lecate, Benjamin	24	DE	233	Sovereign	3	DE	289
Daniel John	16	DE	1	Betsy	58	DE	233	Lekite, Cyrus H	2	DE	146
Ebe	44	DE	133	Brittiana	30	MD	206	Mary E	4	DE	146
Elbert	15	DE	229	Charles M	6	DE	206	Samuel	33	DE	146
Eli T	13	DE	160	Euphama	44	DE	267	Sarah	21	DE	146
Eli W	10	DE	125	George W	2	DE	206	Sarah J	5/12	DE	146
Elisha	4	DE	133	Hetty	5	DE	288	Lekites, Charles	24	DE	164
Elizabeth	53	DE	160	Levin	66	DE	233	Isaac	22	DE	124
Elizabeth A	18	DE	152	Mary A	18	DE	233	Jane	26	DE	164
Elizabeth E	2	DE	218	Polly	55	DE	232	Lemuel	25	DE	124
Garret S	24	DE	224	Sallie A	24	DE	233	Mary A	4	DE	124
Hanna	2	DE	133	Samuel W	1	DE	288	Nancy	61	DE	124
Hester	16	DE	133	Sarah A	5	DE	233	Lemmer, John	32	DE	213
Hester	18	DE	111	Thomas	10	DE	233	Sarah A	24	DE	213
Hester	21	DE	85	Thomas	55	DE	267	Lennon, Ann	21	DE	102
Hester A	17	DE	160	Wilbank	8	DE	267	Charles	6	DE	102
Hester Ann	19	DE	1	William	50	DE	232	Daniel	12	DE	102
Hulby	41	DE	133	Wm W W	5	DE	206	Daniel	35	DE	102
Isabella	15	DE	133	Lecats, Levin	25	DE	205	Elias	10	DE	102
James B	28	DE	211	Lecatt, Amanda	15	DE	2	Jane	5	DE	102
James M	24	DE	160	Ann	24	DE	259	Louisa	9	DE	102
Jane C	2	DE	157	Burton	8	DE	256	Lepo, Margaret	32	DE	55
Jannet	35	DE	133	Caroline	7	DE	258	Samuel	32	DE	55
Jerome	20	DE	209	Charlotte	23	DE	258	Lewis, Angeline	9	DE	269
Jesse	28	DE	209	Ebin	80	DE	258	Ann	5	DE	55
John	10	DE	130	Ebinezer	5	DE	258	Benjamin	12	DE	269
John	16	DE	85	Elijah	45	DE	255	Casias A	4	DE	162
John	25	DE	111	Elisha	24	DE	258	Catharine	10	DE	162
John W	58	DE	108	Garrison	14	DE	258	Charles	19	DE	269
Joseph	14	DE	133	George	1	DE	264	Charles R	6	DE	153
Joseph	24	DE	210	Hetty	50	DE	255	Charlotte	28	DE	153
Joseph B	30	DE	170	James	24	DE	258	Clarissa	9	DE	162
Joshua S	7	DE	125	Job	30	DE	24	David	16	DE	269
Lavinia Jane	11	DE	1	John W	1	DE	24	Diannah	30	DE	186
Levinia	50	DE	79	John W	25	DE	258	Edward	10	DE	63
Lovey	40	DE	130	Joseph	8	DE	258	Eliza	1	DE	55
Maranda M	9	DE	160	Leonard	21	DE	258	Eliza	7	DE	162
Margaret A	2	DE	157	Levin	3	DE	258	Eliza J	1/12	DE	44
Margaret L B	11	DE	1	Lovy	28	DE	258	Elizabeth	25	DE	54
Mark	4	DE	10	Luther	21	DE	258	Elizabeth	26	DE	162
Mary	17	DE	130	Margaret	49	DE	258	Emeline	5	DE	153
Mary	22	DE	125	Mary	50	DE	258	Emma	14	MD	269
Mary A	10	DE	133	Mary A	6/12	DE	258	George	2	DE	269
Mary A	21	DE	170	Matilda	28	DE	264	George	39	DE	162
Mary E	18	DE	125	Milly	25	DE	24	George	55	DE	186
Mary P	8/12	DE	170	Minos	13	DE	258	Hannah	35	DE	55
Matilda	12	DE	133	Perry	16	DE	258	Henry E	9	MD	269
Mills H	45	DE	125	Soveren	24	DE	264	Hetty	16	DE	47
Mitchel	11	DE	224	Thomas	12	DE	258	Hetty	35	DE	55
Nancy	8	DE	134	Thomas C	24	DE	256	Hiley	26	DE	162
Nancy	12	MD	125	Tirsy	27	DE	258	Isaac	11	DE	162
Nancy	33	MD	125	William	3	DE	258	Isaac	40	DE	55
Parnal	21	DE	209	William	50	DE	258	Jacob	1	DE	162
Pemberton	5	DE	134	Winder	19	DE	258	Jacob	14	DE	55
Penelope R	14	DE	1	Winder	30	DE	258	Jacob	45	DE	55
Penelope R	50	DE	1	Wingate	50	DE	258	James	12	DE	55
Rebecca	57	DE	218	Lecompt, Deborah	3	DE	220	James H	6	DE	44
Robert	40	DE	133	Elijah W	16	DE	220	Jesse	35	DE	44
Sally Ann	23	DE	85	Eliza A	5	DE	220	John	1	DE	162
Samuel	21	DE	111	George	42	DE	220	John H	8	DE	63
Samuel	25	DE	85	John	7	DE	220	John W	6	DE	162
Samuel H	26	DE	152	Sarah	11	DE	220	John W	18	DE	223
Sarah	65	DE	209	Sophia	38	DE	220	Joseph	31	DE	153
Sarah	71	DE	209	Ledman, Sarah	48	DE	211	Joseph	55	DE	240
Sarah E	1	DE	152	Wm	17	DE	211	Julia	18	DE	162
Sarah E	7	DE	160	Lekat, Lovy	66	DE	288	Julia C	1	DE	162
Sarah E	22	DE	211	Mahala	25	DE	288	Kendle M	79	MD	269
Sarah E	22	DE	209	Lekate, Ann	4	DE	289	Leah	18	DE	269
Shady	16	DE	133	Daniel	35	DE	289	Leah	25	DE	162
Tabitha	6	DE	133	David	6	DE	291	Lucy	12	DE	278
Tilghman	36	DE	222	Eleanor	29	DE	293	Lurany	46	MD	269
Tilman	30	DE	111	Elijah	55	DE	293	Lydia	17	DE	55
Warner S	14	DE	160	Hannah	58	DE	293	Margaret	16	MD	269
William	8	DE	133	Hetty	6	DE	289	Margaret	40	DE	162
William	16	DE	229	Hetty	27	DE	291	Martha J	17	DE	224

Name	Age	State	Page
Lewis, Mary	16	DE	52
Mary		DE	162
Mary A	28	DE	44
Mary E	8	DE	162
Mesack	69	MD	269
Nancy	36	DE	162
Nathaniel	30	DE	232
Perry	32	DE	162
Peter	5/12	DE	55
Peter	14	DE	269
Peter	28	DE	54
Peter	65	DE	51
Phillip M	3	MD	269
Rachael	11	DE	55
Rachael	13	DE	54
Rachael	76	WN	269
Rachel	18	DE	290
Sarah	2	DE	153
Sarah	8	DE	162
Sarah	11	DE	54
Sarah E	2	DE	44
Simon	6	DE	55
Stephen	14	DE	162
Stephen	16	DE	55
Stephen	84	DE	161
Thomas	12	DE	162
Thomas	13	DE	162
Thomas	48	DE	162
William	5	DE	162
William	22	DE	269
Wm H	11	MD	269
Wright	18	MD	208
Zipora	34	DE	162
Lidnum, Henry	24	DE	214
Mary	56	DE	214
Noah	28	DE	214
Likey, Thomas H	10	DE	11
Limmes, John	33	DE	212
Sarah A	24	DE	212
Linch, Alexander	7	DE	223
Ann	25	DE	226
Ann	45	DE	223
David	35	DE	226
Elizabeth	16	DE	28
John H	3	DE	226
Margaret E	10	DE	223
Maria	15	DE	223
Mary A	4	DE	226
Rhoda	5	DE	223
Sarah	66	DE	267
Sarah A	16	DE	223
William	9	DE	223
William	45	DE	223
Lindell, Lydia	24	DE	30
Roby	28	DE	30
Lindle, Nancy	37	DE	15
Tamer	66	DE	33
Thomas	23	DE	24
Lindsay, Letty	16	DE	141
Lines, Ann	1	DE	99
Charlott	21	DE	106
David J	28	DE	99
Elizabeth	50	DE	292
Elizabeth	60	DE	106
George	3	DE	99
Henry	10	DE	24
Hester	10	DE	271
James	1	DE	106
Rebecca	22	DE	99
Richard	53	DE	106
Sally	2	PA	99
William	25	DE	106
William	43	DE	292
Wm	50	DE	292
Lingo, Alfred B	17	DE	183
Alfred P	9	DE	184
Andrew M	7	DE	184
Angeline	36	DE	183
Ann A	3	DE	180
Benjamin G	40	DE	183
Catharine	3	DE	183
Catharine	31	DE	177
Lingo, Charles H	3	DE	177
Clara	8	DE	158
Comfort	8	DE	191
Comfort E	9	DE	191
Cyrus	32	DE	184
Daniel	40	DE	177
David B	27	DE	151
Deborah C	23	DE	183
Edward	11	DE	158
Edward	12	DE	184
Eli	18	DE	12
Eli J S	5	DE	159
Elisha	66	DE	183
Eliza	14	DE	268
Eliza A	2	DE	184
Eliza A	9	DE	177
Eliza A	26	DE	180
Elizabeth	10	DE	268
Elizabeth	40	DE	183
Elizabeth	41	DE	268
Elizabeth E	3	DE	191
Erasmus M	12	DE	191
Francis A B	1	DE	178
Gardiner M	1	DE	151
George T	14	DE	183
Hammon	35	DE	191
Harriet	57	DE	183
Harriet P	2/12	DE	183
Henry	70	DE	184
Henry L	19	DE	184
Hetty J	15	DE	183
Hetty R	16	DE	183
Isabella	13	DE	183
Isabella	15	DE	151
Jane	40	DE	158
Jesse	67	DE	183
John	51	DE	191
John C	21	DE	191
John H	7	DE	177
John H	10	DE	191
Joseph B	11	DE	177
Joseph H	8	DE	191
Lemuel	24	DE	151
Lemuel B	35	DE	178
Letty A	19	DE	151
Levin	14	DE	158
Lewis	4	DE	184
Lewis J	6	DE	191
Louisa	9	DE	183
Louisa C	20	DE	183
Margaret J A	5	DE	178
Martha C	22	DE	178
Mary	39	DE	191
Mary A	5	DE	159
Mary C	11	DE	191
Mary W	29	DE	191
Matilda A	3/12	DE	191
Miers B	22	DE	183
Minos	16	DE	268
Nancy	30	DE	159
Paynter E	27	DE	183
Salathe E	2	DE	191
Sallie	38	DE	204
Samuel H	4/12	DE	180
Samuel W	24	DE	184
Sarah A	18	DE	183
Unicy A	3	DE	159
William	2	DE	268
William	17	DE	183
William	24	DE	183
William H	12	DE	191
William H	35	DE	178
William J	36	DE	180
William W	36	DE	159
Wilson	41	DE	268
Little, Cornelia	71	DE	62
Henry	65	DE	211
Littleton, Charlotte	2	DE	229
Daniel	26	DE	270
D S	38	DE	229
Edward H	13	DE	163
Elizabeth	49	MD	163
Littleton, Love J	6	DE	163
Mary	30	DE	229
Mary B	8	DE	229
Nancy L	3	DE	229
Samuel	54	MD	163
Sarah W	15	DE	163
Sharp M	8	DE	163
William M	1	DE	163
Livingston, Fanny E	11	DE	84
John	9	DE	84
Nathan	3	DE	84
Sarah Ann	33	DE	84
Thomas	34	DE	84
Thomas E	2/12	DE	84
William H	5	DE	84
Lloyd, Ann E	19	DE	205
Catharine	43	DE	195
Charles W	5	DE	205
Cyrus	11	DE	195
Eleanor	14	DE	205
Elizabeth	6/12	DE	200
Ezekiel	15	DE	197
George	17	DE	195
James	24	DE	195
John L	8	DE	205
Lavenia	21	DE	195
Maria	11	DE	205
Nancy	51	DE	296
Sallie A	17	DE	199
Samuel	13	DE	195
Sylvester	6	DE	195
William J	20	DE	195
Lockam, Elizabeth	14	DE	38
Hetty	10	DE	38
Isaac	40	DE	38
Louisa	21	DE	38
Lockrider, Isaac	15	DE	182
James	16	DE	185
James	17	DE	182
Mary A	8	DE	182
Nancy	46	DE	182
Sarah E	11	DE	182
Thomas B	4	DE	182
William H	16	DE	182
Lockwood, Adeline	8	DE	172
Amy	1	DE	150
Angeline	1	DE	150
Benjamin	10	DE	140
Burton W	37	DE	150
Caleb	65	DE	128
Caroline	33	DE	172
Charles H	11	DE	152
Eli	70	DE	131
Eliza	21	DE	4
Eliza A	19	DE	178
Elizabeth	60	DE	150
Eunice W	37	DE	178
George	2	DE	168
George	16	DE	152
Hamilton W	7	DE	178
Hannah	2	DE	152
Henry	11	DE	152
Henry	45	DE	152
Hetty	14	DE	152
Isaac	15	DE	128
Isaac J	9	DE	172
Isaiah	50	DE	140
James	45	DE	140
James	49	DE	152
Jane	1	DE	45
Jannet	18	DE	152
Jannet	19	DE	153
John	7	DE	152
John	11	DE	172
John	20	DE	140
John	22	DE	128
John	44	DE	172
Letty	19	DE	140
Levin	20	DE	177
Levin	40	DE	178
Levin J	9	DE	178
Louisa	21	DE	150

Name	Age	State	No.	Name	Age	State	No.	Name	Age	State	No.
Lockwood, Love	28	DE	168	Lofland, Martha	10/12	DE	76	Long, George R	42	DE	153
Luthina	3	DE	150	Martha	26	DE	76	Hannah	32	MD	141
Margaret A	14	DE	152	Mary	4	DE	142	Henry	33	DE	47
Mary	5	DE	152	Mary	9	DE	131	Henry A	24	DE	137
Mary	8	DE	140	Mary	13	DE	74	Hester	36	DE	139
Mary E	1/12	DE	4	Mary	14	DE	229	Hetty	7	DE	161
Mary M	31	DE	150	Mary	40	DE	95	Hetty	25	DE	161
Matilda	5	DE	178	Mary	46	DE	107	Hetty J	19	DE	124
Milkey T	8/12	DE	178	Mary	49	DE	80	Hetty R	4	DE	194
Nancy	4	DE	178	Mary A	18	DE	30	Isaac	6	DE	168
Noah	63	DE	150	Mary C	4	DE	76	Isaiah	37	DE	141
Peter	35	DE	168	Mary E	2	DE	80	Jane	15	DE	167
Peter B	17	DE	178	Mary E	11	DE	88	Jane	21	DE	138
Rachel	40	DE	152	Mary W	6	DE	67	Jane	41	DE	153
Rebecca	11	DE	178	Nancy	44	DE	30	Jannet	6	DE	124
Robert M	2	DE	178	Nancy	84	DE	42	Jeremiah	25	DE	224
Samuel	28	DE	4	Nancy R	59	DE	32	Jesse L	29	DE	236
Sarah	9	DE	152	Parker	40	DE	88	John	3	DE	138
Sarah	13	DE	178	Peter F	1	DE	67	John D	10	DE	194
Sarah	40	DE	152	Robert	5	DE	229	John H	40	DE	136
Selah A	7	DE	172	Samuel	8	DE	67	John T	22	DE	153
Susan	10	DE	63	Sarah	13	DE	74	John T	24	DE	139
Tabitha	55	DE	128	Sarah	19	DE	107	Joseph	2	DE	168
Lodge, Benjamin B	4	NJ	57	Sarah	20	DE	95	Joseph	70	DE	139
Frances A	9	NJ	57	Sarah Ann	5	DE	80	Joseph T	6	DE	132
George W	8	NJ	57	Sarah Ann	19	DE	88	Joshua P	28	DE	139
John K L	11	NJ	57	Sarah P	13	DE	229	Lemuel	6	DE	138
Martin W	6	NJ	57	Solomon	39	DE	30	Levin C	1	DE	141
Mary	14	NJ	57	Sophia	43	DE	131	Lorenzo	12	DE	140
Mary J	14	NJ	57	Stephen H	6	DE	76	Lovey J	6	DE	141
Samuel D	2	DE	57	Susan	9	DE	80	Lydia	1	DE	161
Samuel J	40	NJ	57	Tristram P	5	DE	67	Lydia	33	DE	140
William G	13	NJ	57	Vina	1	DE	74	Mahala	34	DE	167
Loffland, David	12	DE	31	William	11	DE	131	Mahala	66	DE	139
David	44	DE	31	William	15	DE	30	Mansen	21	DE	161
Elias	4	DE	31	William	18	DE	229	Margaret	22	MD	137
Ruth A	15	DE	31	William	49	DE	80	Margaret A	12	DE	167
Samuel M	14	DE	31	William A	5	DE	88	Margaret W	28	DE	47
Sarah A	40	DE	31	Wingate	15	DE	30	Maria C	3	DE	140
Sarah C	6	DE	31	Logan, Isabel	3	DE	37	Maria W	17	DE	124
Susan	1	DE	31	Logwood, George	4	DE	61	Mary	4	DE	161
Lofland, Alexander	10	DE	229	Perry	5	DE	61	Mary	12	DE	167
Alfred	3	DE	67	Lokey, Thomas H	10	DE	12	Mary A	9	DE	138
Ann	16	DE	107	Loky, John	57	DE	289	Mary A	11	DE	141
Ann	17	DE	95	Joseph	49	DE	42	Mary A	23	DE	152
Ann	34	DE	67	Lavinia	8/12	DE	289	Mary C	3	DE	162
Celia	33	DE	76	Leah	7	DE	289	Mary C	4	DE	139
Clement C	45	DE	131	Mary	6	DE	289	Mary J	24	DE	136
David	33	DE	107	Sarah	25	DE	289	Mary J	27	DE	236
David	41	DE	74	Loman, Catherine	17	DE	49	Nancy	8	DE	124
Edward	10	DE	95	Long, Amanda	6	DE	140	Nancy	38	DE	161
Elias	10	DE	107	Ann	27	DE	194	Nancy	49	DE	124
Elias	45	DE	95	Benjamin	46	DE	138	Nathaniel	8	DE	167
Elias	47	DE	107	Caleb	45	DE	167	Nathaniel	15	DE	138
Eliza	18	DE	229	Charles	3/12	DE	47	Patience A	6	DE	194
Eliza	40	DE	74	Charles	35	DE	115	Rachel	11	DE	161
Eliza J	9	DE	76	Charles H	12	DE	138	Rebecca	75	DE	140
Elizabeth	42	DE	88	Charles H	17	DE	167	Richard	7	DE	161
Elizabeth C	19	DE	33	Clara J	1	DE	137	Robert	1	DE	139
Erasmus	16	DE	32	Clarissa	9	DE	161	Robert	29	DE	152
Francis A	8	DE	76	Clarissa A	7	DE	141	Robert	39	DE	194
George	10	DE	74	Daniel J A	4	DE	141	Ruth	2	DE	139
George	11	DE	229	David	41	DE	161	Samuel	13	DE	167
Grace	4	DE	74	Eben	2	DE	139	Sarah	1	DE	167
Hetty J	15	DE	67	Eben	9	DE	140	Sarah	11	DE	140
Hiram	7	DE	229	Ebenezer	7	DE	236	Sarah A	5	DE	138
James	12	DE	67	Elisha	1	DE	134	Sarah J	19	DE	137
James P	8	DE	88	Elisha	40	DE	140	Sarah W	2	DE	136
Jesse	29	DE	76	Eliza	29	DE	139	Seth	26	DE	138
John	7	DE	95	Eliza J	2	DE	138	Sophia	68	MD	140
John	8	DE	107	Elizabeth	16	DE	161	Stephen	18	DE	138
John	9	DE	131	Elizabeth	28	DE	139	Susanna	22	DE	139
John	34	DE	76	Elizabeth	29	DE	115	Sydinham	30	DE	137
John W	16	DE	88	Elizabeth	48	DE	138	Sylvester B	3	DE	139
Joseph	5	DE	131	Elizabeth	55	DE	137	William	6/12	DE	194
Joshua	10	DE	67	Elizabeth D	2	DE	136	William	10	DE	141
Joshua	40	DE	67	Elizabeth M	8	DE	194	William	33	DE	161
Levin	18	DE	31	Emma B	2	DE	47	William	51	DE	124
Littleton M	30	DE	67	George	1	DE	236	William J	3	DE	152
Luke L	5	DE	67	George	7	DE	167	Zeno	14	DE	140
Manuel	8	DE	74	George	20	DE	140	Zeno	73	DE	140
Margaret	38	DE	67	George	22	DE	138	Longo, Elizabeth	37	DE	184

Name	Age	St	Pg	Name	Age	St	Pg	Name	Age	St	Pg
Lookwood, Eliza	21	DE	5	Loyd, Esther	48	MD	250	Lynch, Gilbert	48	DE	135
Lord, David	18	DE	222	Frances	16	DE	275	Greensbury	35	DE	8
Henry	9	MD	222	Francis	22	DE	271	Hannah	40	DE	176
Henry	42	MD	222	George W	9	MD	250	Hester	7	DE	130
Luther	8	DE	222	Jacob W	10	DE	272	Hester A	1	DE	143
Richard	7	DE	222	James	4	DE	272	Hester C	1	DE	67
Nancy	43	DE	222	Jane	20	DE	271	Hetty	9	DE	131
Sarah	6	DE	222	Jane	21	DE	269	Hetty	9	DE	135
Lotman, James	55	DE	90	John	2	DE	272	Hetty	37	DE	266
John	22	DE	90	John	48	DE	272	Hetty A	4	DE	143
Peggy	55	DE	90	John W	3	MD	250	Hetty C	15	DE	128
Louder, Elizabeth	35	DE	240	Levi	17	MD	250	Isaiah	31	DE	135
Jacob	59	DE	240	Louisa J	12	DE	272	Jacob	11	DE	130
John H	3/12	DE	240	Maria	23	MD	250	Jacob	13	DE	142
Matilda	4	DE	240	Mary	14	DE	271	James	1	DE	94
Stephen	11	DE	240	Sarah	55	DE	271	James	14	DE	266
Low, Andrew	23	DE	287	William	6	DE	272	James	19	DE	129
Edward	9	DE	258	William	10	DE	275	James	36	MD	128
Eliza	16	DE	278	William	16	DE	271	James	42	DE	142
Elizabeth	24	DE	287	William	51	MD	250	James W	24	DE	186
Elizabeth	40	DE	266	William B	5	MD	250	Jane	6	DE	131
Ephraim	14	DE	278	Willis	55	DE	271	Jane	25	DE	143
Francis	12	DE	267	Zepha	18	DE	271	Jane W	20	MD	130
Hetty	4	DE	258	Lucas, Edwin M	27	MD	224	Jannet	30	DE	135
Hetty	17	MD	254	Luff, Jane	17	DE	46	John	4	DE	135
Isaac	16	DE	266	Lugey, Catharine D	21	DE	71	John	6	DE	266
James	17	DE	258	Thomas	21	DE	71	John	11	DE	135
James	48	DE	287	Lunch, Caleb	17	DE	130	John	14	DE	131
John E	42	DE	258	Lundon, Joseph	45	DE	84	John	31	DE	176
Keziah	30	DE	258	Lynch, Aaron	29	DE	135	John	47	DE	266
Lavinia	13	DE	258	Abrena	3	DE	131	John	77	DE	130
Levin	16	DE	263	Absalom	25	DE	67	John D	31	DE	143
Lovy	5	DE	258	Adzer	1	DE	266	John E	8	DE	8
Lurana	41	DE	278	Alfred	4	DE	131	John L	20	DE	164
Mahala	12	DE	278	Alfred	26	DE	130	John W	36	DE	128
Mary A	9	MD	254	Alward M	23	DE	134	Joseph	6	DE	131
Mary A	11	DE	204	Amanda	7	DE	266	Joseph	27	DE	143
Mary A	19	DE	287	Ann	28	DE	93	Joseph B	9	DE	135
Minos	18	DE	278	Belinda	7	DE	135	Joshua	5	DE	142
Nancy	17	DE	278	Caleb	17	DE	142	Joshua	9	DE	93
Patience B	15	MD	254	Caleb M	4	DE	143	Joshua	26	DE	90
Rachel	44	DE	287	Cassy	9	DE	68	Joshua T	4	DE	114
Ruth	6	MD	254	Catharine M	18	DE	135	Joshua T	40	DE	131
Samuel	14	DE	208	Charles C	2/12	DE	8	Juliann	13	DE	266
Samuel	44	DE	266	Charlotte	12	DE	131	Lambert A	1	DE	131
Sarah	5	DE	278	Comfort	40	DE	135	Lemuel	8	DE	129
Sarah	20	DE	263	Comfort A	9	DE	50	Lemuel	41	DE	130
Thomas	44	DE	278	David	7	DE	94	Leonora	4	DE	130
William	12	MD	254	David	7	DE	142	Levi	25	DE	143
Wingate	6	DE	278	David	19	DE	67	Levin	9	DE	130
Lowe, Charlotte	17	DE	242	David R	5	DE	8	Margaret	12	DE	129
Cyrus	1	DE	296	Edward	6	DE	129	Maria	8	DE	131
Cyrus	21	DE	232	Edward D	36	DE	136	Maria	6	DE	67
Ebenezer	18	DE	254	Edward J	7	DE	136	Martha	21	DE	135
George	14	DE	242	Eleanor	13	DE	130	Mary	10	DE	131
George	23	3	201	Elias	8	DE	131	Mary	22	DE	49
James	13	DE	287	Elijah	2	DE	131	Mary A	16	DE	130
James	16	DE	242	Elijah	44	DE	129	Mary A	22	DE	134
James	19	DE	287	Eliza	4	DE	266	Mary A	24	DE	176
James	23	DE	254	Elisha	40	DE	191	Mary A	43	DE	114
James	45	DE	242	Elisha M	2	DE	8	Mary C	2	DE	143
John	10	DE	242	Eliza J	2	DE	135	Mary E	3/12	DE	176
Letty	19	DE	237	Elizabeth	3	DE	129	Mary E	16	DE	266
Mahala	32	DE	242	Elizabeth	14	DE	136	Mary E	26	DE	8
Margaret	3	DE	296	Elizabeth	15	DE	67	Mary J	10	DE	135
Marvel	6	DE	242	Elizabeth	15	DE	130	Mary J	13	DE	67
Matilda	10	DE	287	Elizabeth	19	DE	142	Mary W	42	DE	134
Miranda	17	DE	287	Elizabeth	20	DE	67	Matilda	9	DE	142
Nancy	8	DE	242	Elizabeth	20	DE	135	Matilda A	2	DE	167
Patience	7	DE	287	Elizabeth	21	DE	143	Minus	40	DE	67
Peggy	54	DE	254	Elizabeth	37	DE	129	Nancy	15	DE	129
Rachel	8	DE	287	Elizabeth	43	DE	142	Nancy	15	DE	142
Samuel	9	DE	287	Elizabeth	57	DE	135	Nancy	18	DE	135
Sarah	3	DE	242	Elizabeth	59	DE	82	Nancy	32	DE	136
Sarah	7	DE	296	Emily S	3/12	DE	50	Nancy	65	DE	131
Sena	50	DE	254	Ezekiel	33	DE	131	Nancy T	15	DE	135
Silas	12	DE	254	Ezekiel W	13	DE	135	Narissa	36	MD	131
William	64	DE	253	Gatty	12	DE	132	Peter	15	DE	176
Loyd, Alexander	11	MD	250	George	10	DE	128	Prudence	6	DE	128
Atiles	24	DE	271	George	11	DE	162	Prudence	34	DE	128
Bethany	27	DE	272	Gideon W	17	DE	114	Rachel	17	DE	67
Charles	11	DE	271	Gilbert	1	DE	129	Rachel A	9	DE	143

Name	Age	St	Pg	Name	Age	St	Pg	Name	Age	St	Pg
Lynch, Rebecca	41	DE	114	Macklin, John	49	DE	21	Manship, Charles	38	DE	35
Rebecca J	9	DE	114	Jonathan	16	DE	94	Charlott	11	DE	35
Reuben	6	DE	131	Louisa	22	DE	91	Jane E	17	DE	35
Reuben	41	DE	131	Margaret	6/12	DE	96	Martha J T	5	DE	35
Rhoda E	6	DE	143	Margaret J	10	DE	94	Sarah E	7	DE	35
Ritty	18	DE	135	Mary	14	DE	94	William C	15	DE	35
Robert	6	DE	176	Mary	17	DE	259	Marene, Elizabeth	46	DE	247
Robert	32	DE	93	Mary	20	DE	94	Griffeth	56	DE	247
Robert	35	DE	49	Mary	25	DE	96	Jacob R	24	DE	247
Sally A	12	DE	94	Mary	54	DE	233	Marey, Celia	34	DE	159
Samuel	1	DE	131	Mary A	40	DE	24	Marker, Cyrus	2	DE	95
Samuel	5	DE	266	Mary M	8	DE	94	Cyrus	35	DE	95
Sarah	3	DE	136	Nancy	15	DE	259	James	5	DE	95
Sarah	3	DE	142	Nancy	17	DE	233	Margaret	35	DE	95
Sarah	9	DE	266	Nehemiah	3	DE	94	Mary	16	DE	95
Sarah	10	DE	129	Obediah	62	DE	95	Nancy	7	DE	95
Sarah	13	DE	131	Rachel	13	DE	21	Sarah	48	DE	42
Sarah	16	DE	67	Sallie	55	DE	95	Marriner, Catharine	85	DE	165
Sarah	31	DE	131	Sally	52	DE	259	Edward J	11	DE	166
Sarah	36	DE	130	Sarah	4	DE	96	Eliza A	6	DE	188
Sarah	40	DE	67	Sarah	51	DE	21	Elizabeth P	2	DE	66
Sarah	60	DE	191	Sarah	55	DE	233	George E	4	DE	188
Sarah A	4	DE	8	Sarah A	25	DE	21	Hetty	44	DE	188
Sarah A	11	DE	67	Tilghman	28	DE	21	Hetty J	1	DE	188
Sarah A	21	DE	143	Virden	28	DE	21	John	13	DE	164
Sarah E	6	DE	50	William	7	DE	91	Joseph	32	DE	66
Sarah E	7	DE	135	William	18	DE	94	Mary W	16	DE	188
Tabitha	88	VA	136	Mackson, Wm C	1	DE	206	Robert	63	DE	188
Thomas Henry	3	DE	50	Madison, Catharine	21	DE	68	Robert K	14	DE	188
William	1	DE	143	George H	5	DE	68	Sarah E	24	DE	66
William	7	DE	176	James	29	DE	68	Thomas	36	DE	180
William	11	DE	142	Mary C	3	DE	68	Marsh, Andrew	17	DE	60
William	12	DE	266	Nelly	1	DE	68	Ann	14	DE	59
William	38	DE	176	Magee, Arcada	29	MD	141	Ann M	3	DE	240
William E	7	DE	8	Biddy	8	DE	289	Charles	17	DE	56
William H	1	DE	130	Charles H	12	MD	141	Cyrus	5	DE	240
William J	5	DE	128	George W	2	DE	289	David	4	DE	285
Lyons, Daniel	22	IE	45	Henalotta C	4	MD	141	Elizabeth	25	DE	240
Hannah	42	DE	6	Hetty	6	DE	289	Elizabeth	26	DE	239
Joseph B	14	DE	6	Hetty E	8	DE	266	Elizabeth W	1	DE	61
Laban L	44	DE	6	John	39	MD	141	Emily B	12	DE	43
Rodney E	13	DE	6	Joshua	4	DE	289	Erasmus D	41	DE	43
Silas	15	DE	6	Julia	10	DE	289	Erasmus W	3	DE	43
				Julia B	25	DE	266	Henry	24	DE	285
Macallum, Caroline J	22	MA	127	Julia T	14	MD	141	Hetty	25	DE	61
John	50	CT	126	Levin H	6	MD	141	Hugh C	17	DE	43
John R	11	MA	127	Nasha	60	MD	127	James	60	DE	56
Leonard M	20	MA	127	Sarah	25	DE	289	James P W	26	DE	193
Maria	50	CT	127	Thomas B	2	MD	141	Jane	61	DE	59
Macklin, Alfred	7/12	DE	91	William	16	MD	141	John A	23	DE	193
Alfred	25	DE	21	Mahoney, Elizabeth	21	DE	198	John C	11	DE	60
Ann	2	DE	91	Mary	22	DE	198	Joseph W	10	DE	43
Ann	17	DE	21	Makin, Cyrus	13	DE	96	Leah	2	DE	285
Ann	38	DE	94	Maloney, William	42	DE	223	Lemuel	30	DE	61
Ann E	1	DE	94	Manford, Catharine	80	DE	126	Levin	8	DE	240
Ann Eliza	3	DE	90	Manlove, Asa	42	DE	58	Lydia	56	DE	60
Barkley	19	DE	21	Catharine	25	DE	72	Lydia A	39	DE	193
Caroline	15	DE	24	Cotter A	15	DE	72	Margaret R	27	DE	60
Charles	6	DE	96	David	14	DE	41	Maria	4	DE	239
Charles	14	DE	94	Elias	10	DE	72	Marshal	30	DE	240
Charles	48	DE	94	Genet E	6	DE	44	Mary	4	DE	60
Curtis	2	DE	96	Grace A	14	DE	73	Mary	60	DE	56
Curtis	63	DE	86	Hannah	23	DE	58	Mary A	24	DE	60
Daniel	11	DE	96	Hester A	4	DE	73	Mary E	14	DE	43
Eleanor	60	DE	86	Isabel	8	DE	72	Mary E	22	DE	193
Eli	20	DE	94	James H	9	DE	73	Mathew	30	DE	60
Elizabeth	2/12	DE	90	James M	16	DE	58	Matilda	6	DE	239
Elizabeth	13	DE	259	John W	1	DE	72	Peter	34	DE	61
Elizabeth	16	DE	233	Lydia	3	DE	73	Peter	48	DE	59
Elizabeth	27	DE	21	Mary E	34	DE	44	Sarah	22	DE	61
George	5	DE	94	Morris	60	DE	73	Sidney A	15	DE	60
George	32	DE	96	Nehemiah	6	DE	72	Susan	43	DE	43
George H	12	DE	86	Peter	7	DE	15	Theodore	38	DE	239
Henry	25	DE	92	Peter	40	DE	44	Theodore W	6	DE	43
Henry	26	DE	90	Philip	43	DE	72	Thomas	19	DE	56
Jessisi	24	DE	90	Robert H	1	DE	73	Thomas C	28	DE	60
Jessisi	23	DE	91	Sally	25	DE	73	Thomas P	8	DE	43
Job	2	DE	233	Samuel	16	DE	59	William J	3	DE	61
Job	53	DE	259	Williim J	13	DE	25	Marshal, Caroline	26	MD	250
John	12	DE	95	William R	4	DE	44	James H	31	MD	250
John	22	DE	91	Manship, Alfred H	13	DE	35	Mary E	4	MD	250
John	43	DE	24	Araminty	38	DE	35	William	6	MD	250

Name	Age	State	Page
Marshall, Aaron	1	DE	46
Aaron	59	DE	31
Aaron M	16	DE	31
Ann E	25	DE	120
Catharine	14	DE	45
Catharine	70	DE	48
Charles	24	DE	45
David	11	DE	49
David J	37	DE	45
Eliza	43	DE	49
Eliza A	35	DE	45
Elizabeth	7	DE	49
Elizabeth	44	DE	54
Ellen M	21	DE	49
Francis	5/12	DE	45
Hannah	13	DE	31
Henrietta E	19	DE	45
Henry	20	DE	31
Hetty	44	DE	45
Jacob	50	DE	46
Jacob A	11	DE	46
Jacob A	36	DE	48
James	17	DE	49
Jane	48	DE	31
Jane E	18	DE	31
John	5	DE	45
John	8	DE	46
John	12	DE	54
John	19	DE	49
John	46	DE	49
John	46	DE	54
Lydia	18	DE	45
Margaret	22	DE	55
Mary	34	DE	46
Mary A	17	DE	69
Mira	4	DE	54
Sally	8	DE	45
Samuel	11	DE	31
Samuel D	4	DE	46
Sarah	20	DE	69
Thomas	2	DE	45
Thomas	8	DE	31
William	14	DE	49
William M	11	DE	45
William M	44	DE	45
Martch, James H	9	MD	199
Martin, Alice	60	DE	43
Ann E	4	DE	4
Anna	5	DE	35
Catharine	2	DE	59
Catharine	29	DE	4
Catharine	40	DE	59
Ebe	14	DE	19
Eleanor	22	DE	240
Elizabeth	40	DE	43
Elizabeth	45	DE	35
Ellen	38	DE	30
Emeline	32	DE	166
Emily	26	DE	43
Erasmus	13	DE	59
Hannah	1	DE	43
James	2/12	DE	181
James	50	DE	30
James	50	DE	43
James H	2	DE	198
James M	9	DE	4
James M	15	DE	43
John	6	DE	59
John	19	DE	43
John	40	DE	166
John D	26	DE	181
John W	7	DE	4
Lorenzo D	41	DE	59
Lydia	11	DE	59
Lydia	16	DE	35
Lydia A C	10	DE	43
Margaret	30	DE	43
Mary	16	DE	181
Mary	18	DE	35
Mary	38	DE	43
Mary	50	DE	19
Mary E	12	DE	166
Martin, Mary H	13	DE	19
Nancy T	6	DE	19
Peter	34	DE	4
Robert H	13	DE	43
Ruth E	4	DE	43
Samuel	10	DE	35
Samuel	45	DE	35
Sarah E	4	DE	166
Sarah E	16	DE	30
Sarah J	4	DE	59
Stephen P	15	DE	30
Susan	11	DE	60
William	52	DE	19
William C	5	DE	43
William H	11	DE	4
William P	20	DE	70
William S	12	DE	19
Marvel, Aaron	13	DE	176
Aaron	58	DE	25
Aaron B	1/12	DE	149
Aaron B	44	DE	149
Abraham H	62	DE	3
Alfred B	8	DE	170
Alfred H	14	DE	188
Alfred S	4	DE	200
Alfred W	6	DE	150
Ann E	34	DE	3
Atha A	3	DE	201
Catherine H	34	DE	200
Cinty	26	DE	25
Dagworthy	19	DE	25
David	1	DE	9
David	22	DE	25
David	52	DE	170
Edward	18	DE	156
Elias R	6	DE	174
Eliza	22	DE	95
Eliza	25	DE	55
Eliza	32	DE	173
Eliza C	30	DE	188
Eliza E	1	DE	188
Elizabeth	3	DE	164
Elizabeth	30	DE	174
Elizabeth	46	DE	170
Elizabeth	48	DE	176
George	1	DE	55
George	3	DE	149
George P	52	DE	176
George W	6	DE	175
Harriet	10	DE	104
Hetty	7	DE	174
Hetty E	2	DE	9
Hiram	15	DE	25
Hiram N	5	DE	164
Jackson	18	DE	148
James	6	DE	257
James	10	DE	174
James	19	DE	257
James D	10	DE	201
James E	17	DE	200
James H	8	DE	3
James H	10	DE	173
James W	30	DE	260
Jane	16	DE	145
Job	45	DE	174
John	10	DE	100
John	18	DE	100
John	47	DE	150
John H	6	DE	201
John P	1	DE	150
John T	6/12	DE	53
John W	1	DE	200
Joseph	8	DE	257
Joseph	43	DE	150
Joseph H	25	DE	25
Joseph J	2	MD	260
Joseph R	19	DE	150
Josiah	28	DE	104
Josiah	70	DE	100
Joshua	26	DE	239
Joshua B	4	DE	9
Julia A	34	DE	149
Marvel, Julian	20	MD	260
Lemuel	28	DE	3
Letty A	3	DE	150
Letty A	24	DE	180
Levina	77	DE	149
Lorenzo	6/12	DE	257
Louisa	18	DE	70
Louvenia	3/12	DE	149
Lovey	18	DE	104
Lovey	63	DE	100
Manaan B	42	DE	188
Margaret	69	DE	200
Margaret P	2	DE	188
Maria	57	DE	25
Martha	23	DE	257
Martha J	10	DE	150
Mary	25	DE	156
Mary	33	DE	200
Mary	61	DE	156
Mary E	4	DE	188
Mary E	12	DE	150
Mary J	6	DE	200
Miller A	5	DE	149
Nancy A	40	DE	178
Nancy C	22	DE	9
Nathaniel	15	DE	174
Nathaniel H	2	DE	180
Nuter	40	DE	149
Parker	15	DE	100
Perry P	35	DE	201
Peter	2	DE	149
Peter	53	DE	156
Peter P	22	DE	164
Philip	71	DE	174
Philip Jr	33	DE	174
Priscilla	24	DE	164
Priscilla A	30	DE	3
Purnell	16	DE	100
Rachel	81	DE	9
Roda	25	DE	52
Samuel	2	DE	104
Sarah	1	DE	260
Sarah	2	DE	257
Sarah	11	DE	174
Sarah	14	DE	149
Sarah	30	DE	257
Sarah	72	DE	149
Sarah A	6	DE	188
Sarah A	25	DE	239
Sarah A	35	DE	150
Sarah A	59	DE	257
Sarah M	20	DE	150
Susan	1	DE	150
Theodore W	36	DE	180
Thomas	13	DE	188
Thomas E	16	DE	25
Thomas R	32	DE	9
Unicy	27	DE	150
Warner	25	DE	45
Warren	10	DE	104
Wesley	7	DE	182
William	2	DE	267
William	4	DE	257
William	8	DE	100
William	21	DE	265
William	33	DE	70
William E	37	DE	201
William S	5	DE	3
William T	12	DE	173
William P	35	DE	257
Wm T	9	DE	200
Zipporah A	3	DE	3
Marvell, James	31	DE	267
Lydia	22	DE	293
Mary	20	DE	267
Tharp	4	DE	269
Wm	18	DE	297
Marvil, Benton H	24	DE	8
Clara M	14	DE	8
Edward	60	DE	8
Louisa E	13	DE	8
Mary	18	DE	8

Name	Age	State	No.
Marvil, Mary A	18	DE	8
Mary E	14	DE	8
Marvill, Joshua	26	DE	240
Levin J	17	DE	238
Sarah A	25	DE	240
Wm	35	NH	246
Marvin, Anna	12	DE	227
Elizabeth	24	DE	227
Garretson	25	DE	227
William	18	DE	296
Masley, Ann	24	DE	50
Cornelius	28	DE	50
George	1	DE	50
William	4	DE	50
Mason, Hannah	28	DE	79
James	7	DE	79
John	9	DE	79
Joseph	10	DE	79
Joseph	35	DE	79
Lydia	60	DE	79
Mary	5	DE	79
Nicey	30	DE	37
Robert	23	DE	37
Susan	20	DE	80
Massa, Caroline	10/12	DE	271
Elijah	28	MD	278
Eliza	8	DE	271
James	21	DE	238
Leonard	4	DE	271
Lorenzo	6	DE	271
Luisa	20	DE	278
Margaret	37	DE	271
Martin	34	DE	271
Nancy	33	DE	271
Turpin	13	DE	205
William	10	DE	271
Zachariah	45	DE	271
Masser, George	21	DE	283
Margaret	45	DE	293
Sarah	16	DE	293
Massey, Alexander	46	DE	60
Andrew	60	DE	38
Arzelia	3	DE	273
Asbury B	4	DE	43
Charity J	3	DE	60
Easter	33	DE	273
Eli	9	DE	95
Eli	45	DE	272
Eliza	5	DE	272
Eliza	9	DE	273
Eliza A	12	DE	176
Elizabeth	15	DE	192
Eunice	26	DE	192
Frances	10	DE	272
George	6	DE	38
Hannah	6	DE	192
Henry	2	DE	192
Hetty	36	DE	43
Jarvis	43	DE	95
John A	1	DE	60
John S	23	DE	192
Joshua	12	DE	43
Kesiah	16	DE	95
Lavinia	46	DE	95
Lovy	13	DE	273
Mary P	4	DE	192
Matilda	1	DE	95
Matthias	11	DE	273
Nancy	6	DE	273
Nancy	72	DE	274
Nathan	19	DE	272
Peter	8	DE	43
Phebe	55	DE	38
Priscilla	38	DE	272
Rachael	10	DE	95
Rachael	16	DE	273
Sarah C	5	DE	60
Sarah J	23	DE	60
Shepherd	18	DE	273
Tabitha	49	DE	192
William	12	DE	95
William	34	DE	43
Massey, William	48	DE	273
Williard	8	DE	272
Massy, Hester	9	DE	268
Hetty	14	DE	38
Mary	44	DE	268
William	17	DE	268
Mastin, Elizabeth	41	DE	204
H H	41	DE	204
Joseph J	10	DE	204
Lenora L	6	DE	204
Levinia E	8	DE	204
Luraney C	12	DE	204
Mary J	13	DE	204
Sarah A	15	DE	204
Maston, Elisa	33	DE	273
James	36	DE	273
Julian	9	DE	273
Margaret	13	DE	273
Martha	5	DE	273
Sarah	7	DE	273
Uphany	3	DE	273
Mathews, Amelia A	14	DE	293
Casandra	18	DE	295
Catharine	25	DE	290
Cynthia	18	DE	293
David	22	DE	146
Eleanor	45	DE	293
Elisha	11	DE	294
Elizabeth	20	DE	295
Elizabeth	22	DE	286
Elizabeth	29	DE	290
Euphama	20	DE	293
George	10	DE	290
George	21	DE	242
Henry C	15	DE	294
Hetty	40	DE	286
Hetty G	19	DE	294
Hezekiah	13	DE	294
Hezekiah	53	DE	294
Isaac	2	DE	290
James	45	DE	262
Janet	13	DE	262
John	10	DE	148
John	58	DE	295
John H	22	DE	295
John J	24	DE	290
Leah	57	DE	295
Levin	16	DE	148
Levinia	9	DE	262
Levinia	26	DE	263
Luraney E	9	DE	293
Margaret	4	DE	262
Margaret	11	DE	290
Maria	15	DE	262
Mary	3	DE	286
Mary	12	DE	236
Mary	12	DE	262
Mary	56	DE	148
Mary M	17	DE	294
Matilda	14	DE	295
Nancy	60	DE	293
Nancy M	27	DE	293
Nutter J	55	DE	290
Phillip C	16	DE	295
Phillip W	51	DE	293
Sallie	35	DE	262
Sampson	58	DE	148
Samuel	40	DE	286
Sarah	9/12	DE	286
Sarah	13	DE	263
Stansbury E	16	DE	293
Tolbert	28	DE	147
Wingate	25	DE	286
Wingate	61	DE	293
Maul, Ann	50	DE	51
Carter A	12	DE	64
Hannah	25	DE	51
Minty	76	DE	42
Maull, Alsey	55	DE	55
Ann	30	DE	63
Ann	40	DE	171
Ann	60	DE	45
Maull, Arange	38	DE	63
Catharine	33	DE	49
Charles	8	DE	49
Charles	16	DE	51
Cotter A	12	DE	63
Cyrus	70	DE	1
David	7	DE	51
Edward	7	DE	49
Edward	15	DE	51
Edward	35	DE	49
Eliza A	16	DE	171
Emily	11	DE	51
Emily	33	DE	51
Emma	1	DE	51
Fanny	1/12	DE	49
Frances A	31	DE	12
Franklin	6	DE	49
George	36	DE	49
George W	43	DE	3
Hannah	13	DE	51
Hannah	29	DE	49
Hannah	50	DE	51
Hannah R	28	DE	52
Harriet	3	DE	64
Harriet	47	DE	1
Harry	53	DE	51
Harry	55	DE	45
Henry	1	DE	49
Henry	14	DE	64
Henry	15	DE	55
Henry	38	DE	52
Henry C	20	DE	170
Henry G	6	DE	12
Henry Sr	66	DE	52
Hetty	3	DE	49
Hetty	13	DE	43
James	7	DE	64
James	79	DE	1
James E	8	DE	12
James H	15	DE	3
James R	53	DE	51
Jane	18	DE	34
John	9	DE	45
John	78	DE	51
July A	46	DE	3
Lemuel	46	DE	171
Louisa	21	DE	52
Mary	5	DE	49
Mary	10	DE	51
Mary	26	DE	52
Mary	62	DE	52
Mary	64	DE	52
Mary	77	DE	51
Mary E	6	DE	49
Mary J	18	DE	51
Purnel	32	DE	12
Rosanna	5	DE	64
Sally	18	DE	51
Sally	18	DE	52
Sally	58	DE	34
Samuel	16	DE	51
Thomas	9	DE	63
Thomas	38	DE	51
William	2	DE	64
William	3	DE	51
William T	41	DE	51
Maxfield, Emaline	38	DE	9
Harriet	1/12	DE	9
William E	6	DE	9
Maxwell, John	26	DE	149
May, Walter R	7	DE	2
Mayfield, William	65	DE	68
McBride, Celia	6	DE	85
John	54	DE	85
John H	8	DE	85
Robert W	16	DE	85
Sarah	12	DE	85
Sarah	47	DE	85
McCabe, Amos	24	DE	133
Ann	20	DE	134
Ann	27	DE	125
Arthur	11	DE	137

Name	Age	ST	Pg
McCabe, Asher	5	DE	154
Barton T	26	DE	138
Caleb	14	DE	133
Charles	1	DE	133
Charles W	2	DE	154
Charlotte	11	DE	137
Edward	26	DE	138
Edward	60	DE	153
Eli	19	DE	134
Elijah	16	DE	133
Elisha	24	DE	133
Eliza	50	DE	133
Elizabeth	16	DE	133
Elizabeth	18	DE	153
Elizabeth	57	MD	133
Elizabeth J	11	DE	134
Garretson	3	DE	133
Garretson	30	DE	134
Garretson	61	DE	133
George	14	DE	137
Handy	2	DE	134
Henrietta	24	DE	154
Henry	18	DE	137
Hester	10	DE	137
Hetty	26	DE	137
Isaac	47	DE	137
Isaac C	30	DE	154
Jane	20	DE	139
John	22	DE	133
John	27	DE	133
Joseph	22	DE	134
Joseph	54	DE	134
Josiah	25	DE	153
Levin	21	DE	134
Levin J	1	DE	134
Lucinda	3	DE	134
Margaret D	25	DE	137
Mary	3	DE	137
Mary	23	DE	133
Nancy	14	DE	14
Nancy	54	DE	14
Patience	14	DE	13
Sarah	6	DE	137
Sarah	24	DE	134
Sarah	50	DE	153
Sebo	1	DE	137
William	19	DE	133
William	30	DE	134
McCalsey, Daniel	23	DE	111
John W	25	DE	111
Joshua	65	DE	111
Mary J	12	DE	111
Priscilla	60	DE	111
McCauley, Alfred H	1	DE	10
Edmond P	4	DE	10
Edward	14	DE	99
Edward	28	DE	10
Eliza	38	DE	100
Elizabeth	6	DE	99
Elizabeth	8	DE	10
Elizabeth	39	DE	99
George	12	DE	86
Hester	5	DE	79
John H	12	DE	99
Joseph P	7	DE	10
Josiah	4	DE	100
Letitia	7	DE	79
Margaret J	16	DE	99
Mary	11	DE	79
Mary C	10	DE	99
Nancy	26	DE	10
Nancy	37	DE	79
Peter	34	DE	100
Priscilla	4	DE	100
Robert	9	DE	79
Robert	38	DE	99
Robert	61	DE	79
Sarah	44	DE	42
Trusten P	1	DE	79
William	18	DE	79
McCaulley, Dorcas	12	DE	86
Eliza J	10	DE	86
McCaulley, Elizabeth	45	DE	86
John	6	DE	86
Trust	4	DE	86
Trust P	50	DE	86
McColley, James	40	DE	31
Mahala	2	DE	31
Mary E	7	DE	31
Priscilla	25	DE	31
Purnel	3	DE	31
Rhoda A	5	DE	31
McCollister, Joseph	15	DE	281
McCormick, Eliz A	19	DE	136
Ellen	28	DE	136
Nancy	16	DE	136
Nancy	49	DE	136
Robert	11	DE	136
Sarah J	2	DE	136
Thomas	13	DE	136
Thomas	56	DE	136
William	22	DE	136
McCorna, Patrick	24	IE	45
McCraiken, Ann	64	DE	53
Harvey H	59	DE	53
Samuel	22	DE	53
McCray, Alfred	3	DE	178
Charlotte	17	DE	112
Edward	29	DE	178
Elizabeth	21	DE	153
Harriet	35	DE	169
James	2	DE	169
John	8	DE	169
John	13	DE	169
Joseph	40	DE	169
Lemuel	11	DE	169
Louisa	19	DE	169
Lydia	25	DE	178
Margaret	14	DE	151
Mary	9	DE	169
Mary	17	DE	169
Matilda	4	DE	169
Peter	36	DE	169
Peter	56	DE	8
Sarah	5	DE	169
Sophia	37	DE	169
William	8/12	DE	178
McCullins, Edward	1	DE	135
McDowel, Benjamin	10	DE	285
Elizabeth	24	DE	285
Ephraim	57	MD	245
Joshua	19	DE	283
Joshua	19	DE	285
Julia	15	DE	285
Nancy W	48	DE	285
Sarah J	3	DE	285
Zachariah	7	DE	285
McDowell, Clara	20	DE	166
Eli	24	DE	172
Elijah	50	DE	173
John S	5	DE	173
Julia	25	DE	178
Mary	10	DE	173
Mary	28	DE	68
Mary A	4/12	DE	68
Mary A	19	DE	173
Rebecca	2	DE	68
Sarah E	4	DE	68
Sarah G	8	DE	173
Susanna	15	DE	172
William	28	DE	68
McFadden	25	MD	6
Sarah	18	MD	6
McFarland, Andrew	13	DE	50
McFerran, Joseph A	23	DE	34
Margaret	58	DE	34
McGee, Alace E	2	DE	166
Ann E	1	DE	182
Anna H	5	DE	35
Arthur	25	DE	130
Bridget	29	DE	14
Charles B	5	DE	143
Eliza Emily	2	DE	14
Eliza J	12	DE	166
McGee, Elizabeth	17	DE	30
Elizabeth	42	DE	166
Elizabeth	70	DE	182
Elizabeth	72	MD	117
Ellen	63	DE	162
George	27	DE	37
George	46	DE	166
Henry	17	DE	182
Hetty	14	DE	166
Isaac	18	DE	185
James	20	DE	61
James	74	DE	42
Jane M	33	DE	187
John	25	DE	115
John	70	DE	182
John H	9	DE	166
John R	3	DE	187
John W	37	DE	188
Letty H	10	DE	188
Levin J	25	DE	182
Lydia	5	DE	35
Lydia	32	DE	187
Martha J	29	DE	143
Mary	21	DE	182
Mary A	2	DE	115
Mary A	22	DE	182
Mary C	19	DE	187
Mary E	5/12	DE	187
Mary E	12	DE	187
Mary J	20	DE	115
Mary Jane	5	DE	184
Moses	31	DE	187
Moses	61	DE	185
Noah	33	DE	35
Patience	34	DE	35
Peter	32	DE	14
Rhoda	23	DE	182
Sarah	60	DE	185
Sarah E	7	DE	14
Theodore M	6	DE	166
Thomas	63	DE	182
Thomas J	8	DE	188
Thomas P	35	DE	187
William	15	DE	194
William	61	DE	37
William C	4	DE	188
William G	2/12	DE	14
William H	1/12	DE	115
William H	2	DE	187
William T	23	DE	182
McIlvain, Alfred	24	DE	184
Benjamin	31	DE	72
Benjamin	56	DE	47
Benjamin P	9	DE	182
Cesar	85	DE	51
Clara	55	DE	35
David	45	DE	55
Elizabeth C	7	DE	36
Elizabeth M	45	DE	184
Emily	22	DE	55
Frances A	6	DE	14
Handy	36	DE	187
Harriet	40	DE	187
Harriet A	4/12	DE	187
Harriet J	20	DE	184
Henry S	18	DE	47
James	5/12	DE	72
James F	13	DE	47
Jane	70	DE	55
John	2	DE	72
Laura	1	DE	184
Lewis M	10	DE	184
Margaret	25	DE	72
Mary	60	DE	2
Mary E	7	DE	72
Mary Ruth	14	DE	14
Richard	4	DE	60
Robert	4	DE	72
Robert	25	DE	2
Sarah	55	DE	47
Wrixon	2	DE	184
McKim, Arthur	5	DE	3

Name	Age	State	Page
McKim, John L	14	DE	3
John M	37	PA	3
Mary	3	DE	3
R Heber	12	PA	3
Susan A	37	IE	3
McNeal, Ephraim W	33	MD	141
Margaret	2	DE	142
Mary L	22	DE	141
Rebecca C	27	MD	139
Woolsey T	36	MD	139
McNelly, Benjamin	13	DE	200
James	10	DE	200
Jeremiah	54	MD	200
John D	20	DE	200
Mary A	22	DE	200
William S	25	DE	200
McNeely, Agnes	8	DE	200
Sophoma S	4	DE	200
Mears, Fanny	63	DE	84
Mary A	31	DE	84
Sallie	23	MD	217
Meers, Burton	25	DE	148
Charles P	2	DE	148
Edward B	9	DE	159
Eliza J	12	DE	159
Hannah	23	DE	148
Hannah A	6	DE	158
John T	11	DE	158
Louisa	15	DE	158
Lovenia	14	DE	158
Mary A	34	DE	158
Mary J	3	DE	148
Mary W	2	DE	158
Richard B	9	DE	158
Robinson	45	DE	158
Sarah A	25	DE	148
Melson, Abraham	70	DE	285
Ann M	13	DE	285
Benjamin	4	DE	285
Benjamin	43	DE	285
Benjamin H	15	DE	286
Daniel	9	DE	279
David	8	DE	285
Eleanor	22	DE	285
Eli	1	DE	285
Eliza	22	DE	150
Elizabeth	28	DE	285
Elizabeth	30	DE	16
George	2	DE	260
George	6	DE	285
Hannah	8	DE	16
Isaac	7	DE	285
James	27	MD	278
Jane	15	DE	285
Jane	17	DE	285
Jane	21	DE	285
John	4	DE	285
John	5	DE	285
John	10	DE	294
John	15	DE	285
John	26	DE	117
John	63	DE	285
Joseph	14	DE	150
Josiah H	38	DE	294
Levin	30	DE	285
Mahala	30	MD	260
Major	90	DE	42
Mary	55	DE	285
Mary A	11	DE	285
Mary A	39	DE	285
Nancy	26	DE	157
Nathaniel	28	DE	285
Phillip	6	DE	285
Rhoda C	15	DE	285
Rhodes	40	DE	16
Samuel R P	1	DE	16
Sarah	1	DE	285
Sarah	19	DE	285
Sarah	29	DE	285
Sarah	38	DE	294
Sarah E	16	DE	285
Stephen	26	DE	157
Melson, Thomas	20	MD	162
Walter	24	DE	285
William	2	DE	285
William	27	MD	260
Wm	34	DE	285
Melvin, Elizabeth	83	DE	126
Gatty T	45	MD	131
Hannah	28	DE	115
John	39	MD	126
Peggy P	29	MD	126
Merril, William	21	DE	264
Merriner, Eliz P	2	DE	67
Joseph W	32	DE	67
Sarah E	24	DE	67
Messick, Albert	8	DE	108
Albert	15	DE	103
Alfred	30	DE	215
Amelia	30	DE	99
Ann	4	DE	215
Ann	30	DE	282
Anna	4	DE	99
Anne	15	DE	66
Avis	9	DE	27
Benton	7	DE	99
Benton	8	DE	165
Biddy	14	DE	295
Burton J	4	DE	167
Caroline	3	DE	282
Catherine C	7	DE	66
Charles	13	DE	295
Charles H R	6	DE	238
Charles R	7	DE	166
Clayton	9	DE	282
Covington	45	DE	108
Daniel	17	DE	286
Daniel	19	DE	152
David	30	DE	148
David C	16	DE	165
Edward	5	DE	296
Edward R	16	DE	48
Eleanor	66	DE	164
Eli	40	DE	219
Elias J	17	DE	12
Elisha	56	DE	5
Eliza	33	DE	33
Eliza	49	DE	197
Eliza E	1	DE	33
Eliza J	1	DE	12
Eliza J	18	DE	295
Elizabeth	4	DE	282
Elizabeth	16	DE	282
Elizabeth	22	DE	83
Elizabeth	25	DE	167
Elizabeth	27	DE	27
Elizabeth	30	DE	165
Elizabeth	36	DE	297
Elizabeth	43	DE	282
Elizabeth	54	DE	28
Elizabeth	57	DE	295
Elizabeth	80	DE	27
Elizabeth A	9	DE	28
Eveline	6	DE	165
Emilia L	9	DE	238
Eunice	10	DE	297
George	15	DE	103
George	15	DE	108
George	24	DE	27
George A	9	DE	167
George M	5	DE	4
George R	5	DE	27
George R	14	DE	48
George T	9	DE	158
George T	19	DE	12
Henry	15	DE	216
Henry	39	DE	283
Henry	43	DE	215
Henry H	4	DE	27
Hester	10	DE	99
Hetty	4	DE	27
Huldy	27	DE	283
Isaac	2	DE	283
Jacob	12	DE	197
Messick, Jacob	15	DE	286
Jacob	18	DE	295
Jacob	27	DE	259
James	7	DE	282
James M	7	DE	158
James W	30	DE	295
Jane	7	DE	99
Jane	18	DE	69
Jane	40	DE	295
Janly	3	DE	216
Job	45	DE	282
John	1	DE	296
John	33	DE	18
John	43	DE	99
John	48	DE	282
John H	12	DE	12
John H	35	DE	166
John W	7	DE	4
John W	14	DE	282
Joseph	19	DE	156
Joseph	20	DE	166
Joseph H	5	DE	33
Joseph M	35	DE	33
Juel	10	DE	282
Julia	14	DE	282
Julia A	16	DE	297
Julia A	20	DE	295
Julian	15	DE	197
Kensy	9	DE	295
Lavenia	20	DE	286
Levi	30	DE	27
Levi	40	DE	165
Lovey	56	DE	5
Lydia	13	DE	282
Lydia	38	DE	282
Lydia A	10	DE	48
Mahala	17	DE	108
Margaret	9	DE	235
Margaret	24	DE	5
Margaret	25	DE	148
Margaret A	14	DE	12
Martha	27	DE	215
Mary	5/12	DE	99
Mary	1	DE	282
Mary	15	DE	215
Mary	26	DE	286
Mary	32	DE	238
Mary	65	DE	12
Mary A	40	DE	12
Mary E	16	DE	166
Mary E	19	DE	66
Mary J	3	DE	158
Mary J	7	DE	215
Matilda	45	DE	158
Miles	5	DE	286
Miles	34	DE	238
Miles E	7	DE	103
Miles of J	35	DE	103
Minos	42	DE	166
Minos	45	DE	12
Minus	40	DE	28
Mitchell	45	DE	158
Nancy A	2	DE	166
Nathan	12	DE	99
Nathan	27	DE	5
Nathan	32	DE	282
Nathan	66	DE	282
Nathaniel	21	DE	295
Nehemiah	16	DE	66
Nehemiah	21	DE	108
Nehemiah	47	DE	66
Nehemiah	49	DE	295
Nehemiah J	17	DE	9
Nelly	48	DE	166
Patience	37	DE	66
Patty	20	DE	282
Phebe	22	DE	286
Phillip	5	DE	282
Prettyman	9	DE	215
Purnel	8	DE	297
Rachel	11	DE	108
Ritty	47	DE	99

Name	Age	State	No.	Name	Age	State	No.	Name	Age	State	No.
Messick, Robert	11	DE	282	Milby, George	8	DE	193	Miller, Matilda	9	DE	60
Robert	13	DE	215	Hester A	39	DE	62	Milley	31	DE	45
Robert H	13	DE	165	Hestera	21	DE	32	Nancy	52	DE	60
Ruth	45	DE	48	Hetty	31	DE	75	Nehemiah	14	DE	187
Sallie	39	DE	215	Hetty	61	DE	16	Parris	65	DE	113
Sally	36	DE	4	Jackson B	18	DE	172	Rebecca	60	DE	32
Sally A	3	DE	28	James H	5	DE	66	Risdon	40	DE	240
Samuel	7	DE	286	Joseph	33	DE	60	Roland	8	DE	183
Samuel	7	DE	295	Lydia	24	DE	172	Rosanna	8	DE	240
Samuel	13	DE	215	Mary	30	DE	3	Sarah	20	DE	30
Sara	28	DE	27	Mary	31	DE	14	Sarah	41	DE	183
Sarah	5	DE	295	Mary A	12	DE	62	Timothy	4	DE	240
Sarah	5	DE	297	Mary H	6/12	DE	32	William	8	DE	257
Sarah	14	DE	295	Mary H	7/12	DE	76	Milligan, Ann M	3	DE	206
Sarah	16	DE	295	Nancy	35	DE	66	Mary E	11	DE	206
Sarah	26	DE	164	Nathaniel	41	DE	14	Millis, Alley	3	DE	56
Sarah	27	DE	166	Peter	25	DE	172	David T	45	DE	56
Sarah	45	DE	18	Peter	50	DE	66	Harriet	9	DE	56
Sarah	48	DE	295	Rhoda	68	DE	3	John H	12	DE	56
Sarah	72	DE	282	Rhoda R	17	DE	66	Lacey	35	DE	56
Sarah A	14	DE	158	Rowland P	6/12	DE	14	Mills, Charles	39	DE	61
Sarah E	1	DE	27	Sarah	30	DE	236	David	1	DE	78
Sarah E	7	DE	33	William	19	DE	66	David	5	DE	61
Sarah E	33	DE	103	William	38	DE	32	Drucilla	28	MD	248
Selby	40	DE	297	William	68	DE	16	Eliza A	27	DE	252
Seth	45	DE	48	William C	37	DE	75	Elizabeth	15	DE	61
Sina	47	DE	108	Zadock	49	DE	62	Elizabeth	18	DE	254
Stanley	27	DE	99	Miller, Alcey	30	DE	256	Elizabeth	23	DE	78
Stansbury	25	DE	197	Almon	4	DE	240	Elizabeth	45	MD	254
Susan	2	DE	148	Alsey	13	DE	60	Elizabeth J	19	DE	254
Susan	17	DE	103	Amos	9	DE	124	George W	6/12	DE	61
Susan	60	DE	148	Ann	20	DE	52	Hudson L	48	MD	254
Susan E	12	DE	158	Ann E	1	DE	45	James	24	MD	254
Tansy	9	DE	215	Asa	4	DE	257	James E	4	DE	61
Theodore	12	DE	295	Benjamin	8	DE	124	John	38	DE	248
Theophilus	11	DE	238	Charles	11	DE	208	John Clayton	1	DE	249
Unice	3/12	DE	28	Colman	44	DE	256	Lucrisa	13	DE	248
Virginia	8/12	DE	166	David	2	DE	60	Maria	30	DE	61
William	1	DE	282	David	9	DE	240	Martin M	25	MD	254
William	21	DE	103	David	21	DE	185	Mary A	12	DE	61
William	25	DE	83	David	30	DE	58	Miles	24	DE	78
William	35	DE	283	David	31	DE	16	Olivia	1	DE	254
William	55	DE	27	Edward	11	DE	60	Patty E	5	DE	248
William C B	3	DE	33	Elizabeth H	11	DE	127	Rachel	20	DE	254
William E	2	DE	167	Ellen	18	DE	183	Rufus	1	DE	254
William J	7	DE	12	Esther	31	DE	48	Sarah	9	DE	61
William R	3	DE	103	George T	11	DE	256	Sarah	19	MD	254
Wilson	48	DE	295	George W	20	DE	6	Susan J	4	DE	248
Winget H	5	DE	158	Hannah	50	GE	32	Milman, Ann C	17	DE	76
Metcalf, Alfred	1	DE	52	Hannah	58	DE	113	David	20	DE	79
Andrew	12	DE	52	Hannah J	1	DE	58	Edward	17	DE	79
Eliza	4	DE	52	Henry	26	DE	275	Elizabeth	13	DE	76
Eliza	4	DE	62	Henry	30	DE	240	Elizabeth	28	DE	90
Hetty	40	DE	52	Hester A	22	DE	58	George W	10	DE	66
John	9	DE	52	Hetty	9	DE	62	Harriet	17	DE	75
John	40	DE	52	Hetty R	7	DE	124	Hester	45	DE	79
Joseph	4	DE	52	Isaac	10	DE	183	James	3	DE	90
Stephen	40	DE	52	Isaac	20	DE	59	Jeremiah	16	DE	29
Thomas	14	DE	52	Isaac	40	DE	183	Jesse	30	DE	90
Michal, Lydia	20	DE	2	Jacob	20	GE	32	John R	25	DE	75
Midcass, Alsey	28	DE	44	James	27	DE	45	Jonathan	8	DE	66
Charlotte	5	DE	191	James	50	DE	60	Jonathan	11	DE	76
Elizabeth	9	DE	191	James H	11	DE	240	Jonathan	13	DE	111
Jacob	45	DE	191	Jane	15	DE	60	Jonathan	16	DE	79
Jane	20	DE	71	Jane	44	DE	124	Jonathan	23	DE	66
Milla	30	DE	191	Jenkins	44	MD	124	Jonathan	68	DE	75
Richard	19	DE	73	John	7	DE	32	Joseph	24	DE	75
Woodey	6	DE	187	John	56	GE	32	Michael	18	DE	76
Middleton, Elizabeth	22	DE	40	Levinia A	6	DE	240	Michael	41	DE	79
Miflin, Comfort	70	DE	4	Louisa	12	GE	32	Martha	27	DE	66
Emeline J	4/12	DE	4	Lydia P	12	DE	124	Mary	17	DE	90
Mary	25	DE	4	Major	25	DE	43	Nicy T	4	DE	66
Moses	25	DE	4	Maria	6	DE	63	Sally	60	DE	75
Rachel R	3	DE	4	Maria P	3	DE	124	Sarah	1	DE	90
Tamsey D	5	DE	4	Margaret	8/12	DE	48	Susan	6	DE	90
Milbey, Arthur	2	DE	55	Margaret	14	GE	32	William H	6	DE	66
Cato	10	DE	55	Martha A	6/12	DE	240	Milvy, Mary	10/12	DE	62
Edward	29	DE	55	Mary	15	DE	52	Minor, Fithin	56	VT	199
Eliza	17	DE	55	Mary	18	DE	32	Martha J	25	DE	199
Milby, Anna	2	DE	236	Mary	32	DE	240	Minos, Beacham	7	DE	224
Arthur	40	DE	236	Mary	77	DE	63	Minus, Catharine	8	DE	52
Eliza	16	DE	34	Mary A	6	DE	257	Mitcheal, Hester	70	DE	50

Name	Age	State	Page	Name	Age	State	Page	Name	Age	State	Page
Mitcheal, Pompey	71	DE	50	Mitchel, Stephen	35	DE	5	Moore, Charles N	51	DE	251
Mitchel, Amos	1	DE	277	Stephen	50	MD	277	Charlotte	2	DE	217
Ann	29	DE	96	Tamer	49	DE	225	Charlotte	23	DE	195
Ann	40	DE	292	Thomas	8/12	DE	8	Clarisa	22	DE	271
Archibald	5	DE	279	Thomas	12	DE	276	Clayton	7	DE	270
Benjamin	2	DE	278	Thomas	40	DE	276	Colwell	32	DE	238
Benjamin	11	DE	278	Unica	8	DE	278	Colwellsbury	10	DE	247
Betty	25	DE	5	Vilator A	10	DE	279	Curtis	6	DE	247
Burton	33	DE	278	William	16	MD	278	David	9	DE	271
Charlotte	5	DE	278	Wingate	11	DE	278	David	17	MD	244
Charlotte	10	DE	276	Zephora	4	DE	276	David	28	DE	204
Cinthy	21	DE	49	Zepy	26	DE	278	David	67	DE	137
Edward	8	DE	276	Mitchell, Alfred	2	DE	169	David W	20	DE	268
Elijah	2	DE	276	Catherine	16	DE	3	Derick	9	DE	172
Elijah	65	DE	278	Charles	1/12	DE	161	Drucilla	30	DE	271
Elisha	22	DE	276	Charles F	1	DE	162	Eccleston	56	DE	274
Eliza	16	DE	278	Daniel	24	DE	276	Edward D	28	DE	137
Eliza	34	MD	278	Daniel	60	DE	169	Edward W	27	DE	234
Elizabeth	4	DE	5	David H	1	DE	169	Eleanor	74	MD	202
Elizabeth	12	MD	276	Edward J	5	DE	162	Elenor	15	DE	296
Elizabeth	33	DE	278	Eliza J	7	DE	5	Elenor	40	DE	296
Emelia	35	MD	276	Elizabeth	26	DE	162	Elenor	49	DE	274
Fanny	22	MD	277	Eunice	30	DE	1	Elias	2	DE	155
Gatty	3	DE	277	Hannah	23	DE	169	Elijah	83	?	213
George	47	MD	278	Harriet	10	DE	165	Eliza	45	DE	232
Hanabel	60	DE	225	Henry B	7	DE	162	Eliza A	2	DE	114
Harriet	21	MD	279	Hetty	16	DE	169	Eliza E	22	DE	239
Hester	6	DE	276	Jacob	40	DE	170	Eliza E	28	DE	271
Hetty	8	DE	278	John	25	DE	225	Elizabeth	16	DE	207
Hetty	9	DE	277	Lydia	4	DE	169	Elizabeth	25	DE	238
Hetty	23	DE	278	Lydia	17	DE	169	Elizabeth	41	DE	218
Hiram	5	DE	278	Mahala A	4	DE	162	Elizabeth A	2	DE	172
Huldy	50	MD	277	Margaret	16	DE	276	Elizabeth A	12	DE	204
Isaac	4	DE	276	Maria	21	DE	161	Emeline	13	DE	151
Isaac	28	DE	277	Mary	1/12	DE	1	Emeline	20	DE	274
Isaac B	48	DE	277	Mary	3	DE	169	Emeline	33	DE	172
Isaac J	40	MD	276	Mary J	10	DE	170	Ephraim	34	DE	217
James	8	DE	277	Nancy	21	DE	169	Esther	83	DE	271
James R	21	DE	96	Nancy	32	DE	170	Ezekiel	4	DE	247
Jesse	13	DE	170	Nathan	17	MD	123	George	8/12	DE	270
John	3	DE	8	Patience	6	DE	117	George	3	DE	250
John	7	DE	278	Patience	61	DE	169	George	7	MD	217
John	9	DE	276	Rhoda	2	DE	169	George	22	DE	156
John	12	DE	277	Rufus	15	DE	161	George	25	DE	274
John	22	DE	278	Ruth Ann	2	DE	1	George	75	DE	64
John	25	DE	224	Samuel	31	DE	161	George W	28	DE	239
Joseph	19	DE	96	Sarah	8	DE	155	Georgianna	1	DE	201
Joseph	35	DE	8	Wesley	32	DE	161	Harriet G	7	DE	64
Julia A	24	DE	276	William	2	DE	169	Henry	18	DE	156
Julian	20	DE	276	Zippora	14	DE	169	Henry	23	DE	270
Leah	3	DE	278	Mitchelmore, Mary	65	DE	56	Henry	25	DE	289
Lemuel	27	DE	276	Moger, Hetty	8	DE	267	Henry S	18	DE	273
Louder	2	DE	278	John	35	DE	267	Hester	7	DE	137
Levina	1	DE	277	John W	5	DE	267	Hester A	13	MD	244
Lovenia	2	DE	277	Julia A	21	DE	267	Hetty	8	DE	247
Lovenia	14	DE	278	Julia A	25	DE	267	Hetty	25	DE	114
Margaret	4	DE	278	Martha	2	DE	267	Hetty	59	DE	154
Margaret	20	MD	276	Mary J	5	DE	267	Hetty A	30	DE	137
Mary	3	DE	278	William	1	DE	267	Isaac	1	DE	247
Mary	15	DE	279	Monroe, Mary	6	DE	61	Isaac	30	DE	172
Mary	19	DE	277	Mooney, John	60	DE	283	Isaac	33	DE	271
Mary	30	DE	294	Julia A	15	DE	283	Jacob	2	DE	232
Minos	1	DE	276	Sarah	12	DE	283	Jacob	21	DE	233
Nancy	8	DE	277	Moore, Albert W	2	DE	238	James	5/12	DE	251
Nancy	28	DE	8	Alexander	23	MD	201	James	24	DE	270
Nancy	36	DE	278	Ally	24	DE	202	James	25	DE	172
Peter	8	DE	279	Amelia	30	DE	250	James	48	DE	156
Phebe	9	DE	278	Andrew	9	DE	234	James A	8	DE	232
Pompey	9	DE	7	Ann	3	DE	270	James of J	70	DE	155
Pompey	12	DE	5	Ann	10	DE	250	Jane	13	DE	83
Rebecca	35	DE	276	Ann	18	DE	254	Jannas	12	DE	251
Richard	23	DE	279	Ann	50	DE	295	John	3	DE	217
Robert	25	MD	278	Ann A	22	DE	204	John	4	DE	250
Rufus	34	DE	278	Ann E	9	DE	217	John	14	DE	250
Salathiel	20	MD	279	Ann E	9	DE	295	John	27	?	213
Sarah	1	DE	278	Bayard	36	DE	271	John	49	DE	234
Sarah	5	DE	277	Benjamin	11	DE	251	John	50	DE	172
Sarah	6	DE	276	Benjamin J	10	DE	234	John D	5	DE	244
Sarah	10	DE	278	Catharine	3	DE	247	John E	1	DE	137
Sarah	50	MD	279	Celia A	2	DE	213	John J	8	DE	204
Sarah	62	DE	278	Charles H	6	DE	271	John M	40	DE	155
Seth W	13	DE	279	Charles H	25	DE	241	John of J	21	DE	168

Name	Age	St	No
Moore, John P	20	DE	137
John P	37	DE	114
John R	33	DE	2
John T	31	DE	234
Jonah A	33	DE	236
Jonathan	42	DE	270
Joseph	36	DE	271
Joseph H	7	DE	155
Josiah A	33	DE	235
Joshua	68	DE	203
Joshua H	22	DE	172
Julia A	12	MD	244
Julia J	8	DE	232
Julia J	17	DE	274
Julian	14	DE	274
Kendal	24	DE	202
Leah	35	DE	242
Leah J	2	DE	271
Leonor	14	DE	151
Levenia	60	DE	64
Levin	15	MD	218
Levin	18	DE	274
Lewis	30	DE	198
Louisa	9	DE	213
Louisa	14	DE	152
Louisa	15	DE	270
Louisa	16	DE	234
Louisa	25	DE	39
Louisa	38	DE	159
Louther T	47	DE	232
Lovey	26	DE	142
Lucinda C	5	DE	137
Lurana	15	DE	273
Luther	12	DE	274
Luther T	1	DE	39
Margaret	4	MD	213
Margaret	21	DE	269
Margaret	27	DE	273
Margaret A	3	DE	154
Maria	24	DE	154
Maria	26	DE	168
Mariah	10	DE	270
Mariah T	19	DE	273
Martha	16	DE	251
Martha	33	DE	271
Martha J	12	DE	234
Mary	16	DE	215
Mary	16	DE	274
Mary	21	DE	270
Mary	25	DE	154
Mary	26	DE	272
Mary	39	DE	244
Mary A	30	DE	154
Mary A	30	DE	159
Mary C	30	DE	235
Mary E	4	DE	238
Mary E	17	DE	251
Mary E	18	MD	244
Mary M	15	DE	254
Mary S	6/12	DE	202
Matilda	18/12	DE	269
Matilda	26	DE	218
Matilda C	11	DE	232
Milcha	65	MD	238
Miles	24	DE	195
Minos	5/12	DE	250
Missouri	3	DE	202
Myers	25	DE	142
Nancy	5	DE	272
Nancy	27	DE	155
Nancy	46	DE	270
Nancy	55	DE	156
Nancy	60	DE	151
Nancy	65	DE	155
Nancy M	48	DE	172
Nicy	38	DE	270
Peggy	65	MD	213
Peter	28	DE	114
Polly	42	DE	251
Priscilla	49	DE	234
Rachael	23	DE	274
Rachel	22	DE	154
Moore, Rachel A	1	DE	196
Rachel M	40	DE	155
Rebecca	3	DE	244
Robert	70	DE	251
Robert	83	DE	159
Sallie	73	DE	243
Sallie A	27	DE	234
Samuel	1	DE	114
Sarah	7	DE	270
Sarah	17	DE	200
Sarah	17	DE	296
Sarah	25	DE	213
Sarah	65	DE	137
Sarah A	10	DE	218
Sarah A	22	DE	250
Sarah J	2	DE	204
Sarah J	18	DE	137
Shepherd P	28	DE	155
Stephen	16	DE	247
Stephen	30	DE	168
Thomas	12	MD	213
Thomas A	26	DE	39
Thomas A	38	DE	159
Thomas H	31	DE	137
Thomas L	58	DE	270
Thomas W	4	DE	254
Turpin	13	DE	270
Washington	5	DE	155
Whitfield	42	DE	247
William	2	DE	64
William	9	DE	251
William	22	DE	274
William	23	DE	269
William	25	DE	154
William	60	DE	152
William B	3	DE	155
William J	13	DE	274
Wilson	18	DE	270
Wm G	23	DE	273
Wm S	24	DE	201
Wm W	14	MD	217
Woolsey	2	DE	155
Morewood, George	11	DE	59
Morgan, Almira	13	DE	198
Amelia H	39	DE	205
Andrew	25	DE	96
Ann	20	DE	111
Ann Eliza	5	DE	272
Anna	60	DE	230
Benjamin	25	DE	111
Benjamin	70	DE	111
Caroline	3	DE	272
Charles	3/12	DE	205
Charles	11	DE	109
Cyrus	15	DE	109
Elijah	45	DE	272
Elijah A	29	DE	272
Eliza C	10	DE	205
Elizabeth	8	DE	109
Elizabeth	14	DE	205
Elizabeth	23	DE	199
Elizabeth	58	DE	273
Emma	5	DE	282
George	35	DE	111
George D	45	DE	111
George W	2	DE	273
Hannah	8	DE	110
Henry H	9	DE	282
Hester	12	DE	110
Hester	17	DE	273
Hester	24	DE	96
Jacob	14	DE	109
Jacob	22	DE	272
Jacob	25	DE	110
Jacob	60	DE	274
Jacob T	1	DE	205
James	4	DE	110
James	7	DE	111
James	25	DE	274
James	31	DE	230
James W	24	DE	110
Jane	17	DE	110
Morgan, Jane	18	DE	111
Jane	23	DE	234
Jehu	5	DE	111
Jincy	55	DE	109
John	1	DE	96
John	10	DE	111
John	15	DE	272
John	17	DE	275
John	20	DE	204
John	37	DE	109
Joseph A	9	DE	205
Joshua	3/12	DE	110
Josiah	25	DE	234
Jullena W	6	DE	205
Lorenzo	18	DE	275
Lorenzo	30	DE	111
Lorenzo	45	DE	112
Margaret	5	DE	272
Martha	11	DE	110
Martha A	4	DE	205
Mary	23	DE	272
Mary	40	DE	111
Mary	65	DE	111
Mary Ann	34	DE	110
Mary J	3	DE	109
Michel J	6	DE	282
Penkston	50	DE	198
Peter	18	DE	109
Rachael	3	DE	96
Rebecca	24	DE	109
Rebecca C	12	DE	205
Robert	14	DE	110
Samuel	13	DE	110
Samuel	30	DE	109
Sarah	8	DE	272
Sarah	40	DE	111
Sarah	45	DE	272
Sarah E	22	DE	282
Stephen	21	DE	275
Stephen	40	DE	110
Suketty	28	DE	231
Unice	3	DE	110
Unis	8	DE	282
Wesley	59	DE	273
William	16	DE	110
William	23	DE	274
William W	7	DE	205
Wm W	34	DE	282
Wm W	70	DE	98
Zelly	60	DE	274
Zephora	12	DE	272
Morris, Alfred	21	DE	31
Amanda	7	DE	145
Andrew	15	DE	265
Ann	27	DE	265
Ann	39	DE	28
Ann M	21	DE	216
Ann R	8	DE	226
Anniah	12	DE	132
Anthalina	23	DE	174
Augusta	2	DE	271
Bayard	2	DE	132
Benjamin	17	DE	174
Benjamin B	16	DE	19
Bevins	24	DE	31
Bevins	26	DE	37
Burton	20	DE	175
Burton	22	DE	271
Caleb L	21	DE	145
Celia A	13	DE	107
Charity A	13	DE	206
Charles	7	DE	229
Charles H	6	DE	107
Charles J	12	DE	221
Charlotte E	3	DE	31
Columbus	2	DE	203
Curtis	17	DE	226
Curtis	18	DE	212
David	21	DE	248
David	31	MD	218
David M	8	DE	175
Deborah	15	DE	220

Name	Age	St	Pg	Name	Age	St	Pg	Name	Age	St	Pg
Morris, Derick B	19	DE	171	Morris, John H	4	DE	132	Morris, Polleno T	3	DE	179
Drucilla	28	DE	266	John H	7	DE	203	Purnal	5	DE	265
Edward	4	DE	57	John J	7	DE	31	Rachael	20	DE	107
Edward	7	DE	32	John J	59	DE	31	Rachel	39	DE	132
Edward	47	DE	226	John P	5	DE	265	Rachel W	40	DE	154
Edward P	30	DE	83	John R	23	DE	233	Rebecca	6	DE	32
Eleanor	50	DE	226	John W	40	DE	54	Rebecca	7	DE	32
Elenor	6	DE	295	Jonathan	20	DE	36	Richard	5	DE	62
Elinor	85	DE	231	Jonathan C	7	DE	226	Robert	12	DE	31
Elisha	18	DE	203	Joseph	1	DE	32	Robert	12	DE	193
Eliza J	11	DE	132	Joseph	12	DE	134	Robert	15	DE	32
Eliza J	19	DE	227	Joseph	35	DE	170	Robert	16	DE	217
Elizabeth	1	DE	104	Joseph	47	GE	62	Robert	61	DE	174
Elizabeth	8	DE	227	Joseph	75	DE	134	Robert R	11	DE	31
Elizabeth	9	DE	229	Joseph B	2	DE	175	Rosanna	25	DE	265
Elizabeth	12	DE	174	Joseph B	52	DE	145	Sally H	30	DE	174
Elizabeth	14	DE	220	Joseph H	7	DE	154	Sarah	5	DE	107
Elizabeth	18	DE	175	Josephus	8	DE	247	Sarah	12	DE	265
Elizabeth	35	DE	170	Joshua	9	DE	226	Sarah	29	DE	62
Elizabeth	44	DE	231	Joshua C	22	DE	171	Sarah	55	DE	221
Elizabeth	46	DE	145	Joshua S	18	DE	145	Sarah A	10	DE	219
Elizabeth	48	DE	14	Joshua W	7	DE	19	Sarah A	14	DE	132
Elizabeth	48	DE	166	Julia	2	DE	174	Sarah B	19	DE	54
Elizabeth	60	DE	175	Leah A	13	DE	135	Sarah E	3	DE	226
Elizabeth A	16	DE	31	Lemuel	4	DE	134	Sarah E	5	DE	179
Elizabeth B	17	DE	54	Letitia	40	DE	31	Sarah E	6	DE	37
Elizabeth C	9	DE	132	Letitia	46	DE	32	Sarah E	14	DE	31
Elizabeth J	39	MD	235	Letty A	7	DE	170	Sarah J	11	DE	135
Ellen	15	DE	19	Levi	62	DE	39	Sarah J	19	DE	221
Ellen	32	DE	83	Levin	45	DE	134	Sarah J	22	DE	145
Ellen	40	DE	226	Levin	28	DE	265	Sarah J	23	MD	233
Ellenor	30	DE	37	Levinia	30	DE	104	Silas	40	DE	203
Emeline	14	DE	265	Lorenzo D	40	DE	206	Stephen	11	DE	193
Emma	15	DE	271	Lovenia	17	DE	265	Stephen	23	DE	221
Eunice	6	DE	226	Lovey	38	DE	19	Stephen	80	DE	175
Francis	10	DE	31	Lydia B	23	DE	174	Stephen C	33	DE	175
Francis	13	DE	32	Mahala J	11	DE	220	Stephen W	22	DE	124
George	7	DE	83	Margaret	32	DE	54	Tabitha	75	DE	134
George	21	DE	83	Margaret	35	MD	247	Temperance	9	DE	148
George	34	DE	265	Margaret J	13	DE	145	Thomas	3/12	DE	39
George H	6	DE	175	Maria	5/12	DE	226	Thomas	17	DE	31
George S	10	DE	19	Martha	7	DE	292	Thomas	18	DE	32
George T	25	DE	135	Martha A	16	DE	123	Thomas	45	DE	31
Hannah	5	DE	174	Martha E	24	DE	275	Thomas	48	DE	32
Hannah	66	DE	265	Mary	1	DE	266	Thomas C	6	DE	54
Harriet	19	DE	258	Mary	2	DE	135	Thomas E	15	DE	226
Henrietta	12	DE	220	Mary	10	DE	265	Thos	35	DE	247
Henrietta	37	MD	220	Mary	24	DE	107	Truston R	28	DE	174
Henry	12	DE	39	Mary	30	DE	218	Washington	5	DE	154
Henry	19	DE	265	Mary	31	DE	175	William	2	DE	226
Hester A	4	DE	218	Mary	32	DE	206	William	3	DE	132
Hetty	30	DE	39	Mary	34	DE	134	William	6	DE	104
Heveloe	45	DE	28	Mary	50	DE	135	William	8	DE	265
Hezekiah	31	DE	226	Mary A	10	DE	166	William	10	DE	178
Hiram	17	DE	174	Mary A	20	DE	172	William	18	DE	14
Isaac	9	DE	134	Mary A	27	DE	179	William	31	DE	265
Isaac	10	DE	247	Mary A	37	DE	206	William	32	DE	104
Isaac H	11	DE	206	Mary C	30	DE	228	William	33	DE	69
Isabella	13	DE	203	Mary E	5	DE	132	William	54	DE	54
Jackson	7	DE	134	Mary E	6	DE	237	William	58	DE	175
James	10/12	DE	233	Mary E	9	DE	226	William C	5/12	DE	19
James	6	DE	247	Mary E	33	DE	203	William C	25	DE	124
James	8	DE	61	Mary E	42	DE	227	William L	17	DE	166
James	11	DE	14	Mary J	22	DE	271	William L	32	DE	179
James	21	DE	107	Matilda	46	DE	219	William W	12	DE	226
James	23	DE	266	Milly	96	DE	42	Wingate	47	DE	19
James	25	DE	171	Minty	34	DE	265	Wm	39	DE	235
James G	5	DE	206	Mitchell	38	DE	132	Wm E	8	MD	235
James R	9	DE	32	Nancy	22	DE	17	Wm F	12	DE	206
James R	19	DE	226	Nancy	30	DE	14	Woolsey	2	DE	154
James of J	70	DE	154	Nancy	48	DE	31	Zipora L	58	DE	174
Jane	36	MD	265	Nancy	58	DE	270	Morten, David A	16	DE	199
Jane	61	DE	36	Nancy	65	DE	154	Edward L	13	DE	199
Jeremiah	12	DE	265	Nancy U	48	DE	171	Emma	26	PA	199
Jeremiah	32	DE	228	Nathaniel	83	DE	44	Hugh	51	DE	199
Job P	6	DE	170	Nathaniel M	20	DE	145	Hugh Jr	20	DE	199
John	15	DE	62	Patience	19	DE	174	Ida	2	PA	199
John	22	DE	227	Peter	2	DE	265	John E	16	DE	199
John	29	DE	107	Peter	30	DE	219	Luther	25	DE	199
John	41	DE	265	Peter	39	DE	206	Mary A	4	PA	199
John	52	DE	179	Peter T	1	DE	206	Samuel J K	18	DE	199
John E	6/12	DE	218	Phillip J	4	DE	226	Sophia	52	DE	199

Name	Age	St	Pg	Name	Age	St	Pg	Name	Age	St	Pg
Morton, William P	20	DE	71	Murray, Clarissa	5	DE	140	Musser, Julia	7	DE	139
Moseley, Ann	12	DE	27	David	7	DE	140	Lot	43	DE	139
Caleb	35	DE	27	David	15	DE	134	Nancy	37	MD	139
Catherine	16	DE	27	David	60	DE	142	Ritty	5	DE	139
Catherine	52	DE	27	Elinor J	41	DE	134	Sarah	12	DE	139
Cornelius	8	DE	27	Elijah	38	MD	137	Vilator	14	DE	139
Elzey	49	DE	27	Elisha	21	DE	142	Mustard, Ann P	5	DE	37
Grace	45	DE	27	Eliza	30	DE	140	Caroline	32	DE	33
Israel	12	DE	27	Elizabeth	50	DE	140	Cornelius	46	DE	51
James	3	DE	27	Elizabeth M	1	DE	134	David A	3	DE	33
John	6	DE	27	Emeline	12	DE	139	David H	34	DE	33
Louthey	7	DE	27	Emma J	9	DE	134	David S	14	DE	51
Maria	8	DE	27	George	37	DE	140	Eliza A	36	DE	37
Nehemiah	17	DE	39	Henrietta	10	DE	134	George H	26	DE	37
Peter	12	DE	61	Henry	1	DE	134	James S	1	DE	37
Phillis	28	DE	27	Henry B	19	DE	123	John B	41	DE	37
Robert B	4/12	DE	192	Isabel	17	DE	142	John H	15	DE	37
Ruth	6	DE	27	Isaiah	13	DE	141	Margaret C	5	DE	33
Susan	85	DE	27	Jane	8	DE	139	Mary E	7	DE	37
William	45	DE	27	Jeannet	18	DE	140	Milford	50	DE	190
Mosley, Albert	32	DE	192	Jonathan	9	DE	134	Robert W	11	DE	51
Ann M	35	DE	22	Joseph	21	DE	139	Myeshon, Jackson	21	DE	134
Cornelius	28	DE	51	Joshua S	2	DE	123	Nailer, David	17	DE	30
Dunning	19	DE	173	Julia	11	DE	141	Mary J	15	DE	30
Elisha	18	DE	21	Laban H	35	DE	134	Sarah A R	20	DE	30
Eliza	3	DE	21	Lambert	12	DE	134	William B	18	DE	30
Ellen	8	DE	167	Leanore	1/12	DE	140	Naul, David W	19	DE	3
George	25	DE	25	Levin	19	DE	140	Naull, James	8	DE	51
Henry	11	DE	21	Levin W	4	DE	138	Naylor, Mary J	16	DE	72
John	12	DE	21	Lovenia	19	DE	140	Neadam, Ann	28	DE	98
John	35	DE	21	Luvena	7	DE	134	William	30	DE	98
Mary E	6	DE	155	Margaret	3	DE	138	Neal, Ann D	48	DE	203
Sarah	16	DE	21	Margaret A	1	DE	142	Annis	52	DE	221
Sarah	43	DE	156	Maria	41	DE	134	Anthony	28	DE	273
Sarah A	26	DE	192	Martha	17	DE	134	Arthur	27	DE	209
Mumford, Caroline	27	DE	168	Martha	91	DE	133	Catharine	60	DE	209
Caroline	28	DE	153	Mary	15	DE	142	Charles W	1	DE	209
Catharine	74	DE	131	Mary	40	DE	134	Eli	10	DE	213
Charles	7	DE	140	Mary A	7	DE	138	Eliza	18	DE	296
Eleanor	32	DE	158	Mary E	4	DE	134	Elizabeth	1/12	DE	213
Henry	4	DE	153	Mary J	4	DE	141	Elizabeth	17	DE	209
Henry	4	DE	168	Milburn	59	DE	140	Elizabeth	25	DE	285
Hetty	39	DE	169	Minos	3	DE	140	Elizabeth	50	DE	209
Isaac	3/12	DE	170	Nancy	51	DE	140	Elizabeth A	17	DE	209
Isaac J	48	DE	169	Nathan J	25	DE	141	Harriet	11	DE	221
Isaiah	8	DE	168	Nehemiah R	3/12	DE	123	Hetty	40	DE	213
James	18	DE	168	Nelly	16	DE	140	Jacob	2	DE	207
James	19	DE	153	Peter	24	DE	140	Jacob R	28	DE	204
Jesse	2	DE	153	Rachel	26	DE	123	James	6/12	DE	218
Jesse	2	DE	168	Rachel	60	DE	142	John	12	DE	208
John	1/12	DE	153	Rebecca	45	DE	140	Joseph	1	DE	207
John	6	DE	170	Reuben	3	DE	134	Joseph	45	DE	209
John	26	DE	168	Richard	22	DE	140	Joseph	65	DE	209
John	34	DE	153	Ritty	28	DE	142	Josiah	13	DE	281
John W M	10	DE	131	Robert	15	DE	139	Josiah	35	DE	218
Josiah L	35	MD	131	Robert	35	DE	139	Levi	42	DE	218
Littleton N	12	DE	131	Rufus	27	MD	142	Louisa C W	19	DE	1
Margaret	29	DE	158	Sarach A	9	DE	140	Lucy	77	?	213
Mary	35	MD	131	Sarah	10	DE	139	Margaret	7	DE	281
Mary J	19	DE	140	Sarah	20	DE	142	Margaret	25	DE	273
Nisa	11	DE	170	Sarah	24	MD	137	Margaret	22	DE	218
Robert	43	DE	158	Sarah E	5	DE	134	Margaret	37	DE	281
Ruth C	1	DE	131	Sarah J	5	DE	134	Martha A L	14	DE	203
Samuel	9	DE	170	Sarah J	15	DE	140	Mary	2	DE	282
Samuel	52	DE	158	Sasha	55	DE	140	Mary	8	DE	214
Sarah	40	DE	5	Stephen W	31	DE	134	Mary A	47	DE	208
Sarah A	13	DE	140	Thomas	10	DE	140	Miranda	7	DE	285
Sarah A	13	DE	170	Thomas H	4	DE	142	Moses	13	DE	296
Thomas E	4	DE	131	William	11	DE	140	Nancy	44	DE	209
William	16	DE	170	William	15	DE	134	Nelson	9	DE	215
Murray, Albert J	4	DE	134	Musgrove, Ann Eliza	6	DE	82	Phebe	52	DE	296
Ann	27	DE	142	George	1	DE	82	Phillip	30	DE	285
Ann M	10	DE	134	James	8	DE	82	Polly	6	DE	285
Ann M	10	DE	142	Mary	5	DE	82	Pompey	62	DE	296
Anna	52	DE	142	Rosella	13	DE	82	Robert	5	DE	281
Benjamin J	14	DE	134	Sarah Ann	37	DE	82	Robert	19	DE	213
Caleb	28	DE	123	William	23	DE	82	Sarah	9	DE	281
Caleb W	53	DE	142	William Jr	46	DE	82	Sarah	17	DE	213
Catharine	8	DE	141	Musser, Absalom	9	DE	139	Sarah A	24	DE	209
Catharine	12	DE	134	Asher	5	DE	139	Solomon	9	DE	285
Charles L	8	DE	134	Caroline	2	DE	139	Thomas	39	DE	281
Charlotte	1	DE	138	John P	16	DE	139				

Name	Age	State	Page
Neal, Thomas	85	DE	213
Weldon W	25	DE	1
William	21	DE	203
William H H	11	DE	203
William Jr	23	DE	209
Wm C	11	DE	215
Wm Sr	59	DE	208
Neall, Jane	14	DE	269
Newbold, Absolem	45	DE	48
Hannah	50	DE	48
Newcomb, Cornelia	55	DE	53
Henry	15	DE	53
Sarah G	18	DE	53
Wesley	22	DE	53
William	68	DE	53
Newdam, Ann	3	DE	98
Newton, Benjamin	62	DE	158
Elizabeth	62	MD	158
Nicholls, Albert	25	DE	206
Ann	12	DE	218
Cassa	25	DE	206
Eccleston	50	DE	227
Elizabeth	19	DE	245
Hester	25	DE	224
John	22	DE	224
Joseph	60	DE	206
Kitty	45	MD	203
Levin	5	MD	203
Sallie	13	DE	219
Sallie	60	DE	245
Woolston	50	DE	226
Nichold, Lydia	19	DE	60
Nichols, Catharine	7	DE	109
Charles	26	DE	114
Edward D	22	DE	114
Hester Ann	27	DE	109
James H	3/12	DE	109
Mary J	28	DE	114
Nancy	53	DE	114
Nehemiah R	1	DE	109
Parker	60	DE	114
Robert M	31	DE	114
Sarah A	20	DE	114
Thomas	28	DE	109
William T	14	DE	114
Nicholson, Amelia	26	DE	234
Augusta J	2	DE	234
Harlen	3	DE	234
James W	27	MD	237
Martha A	22	MD	237
Mary L	3/12	MD	237
Wm H	31	DE	234
Nicolls, Abraham	60	MD	218
George	20	DE	218
Harriet	5	DE	218
Harriet	60	DE	218
Harrison	9	DE	218
John	12	DE	218
Jonathan	20	DE	248
Noah	4	DE	218
Sallie	13	DE	218
William	18	DE	218
Norbert, Theodore P	18	DE	181
Noble, Charles	51	DE	212
Charlotte W	11	MD	208
Clementine	2	DE	208
Elizabeth	52	MD	221
Harriet	37	MD	208
Harriet W	4	DE	208
Jonathan T	25	MD	212
Joseph W	16	MD	208
Mahala	52	MD	212
Martha V	9	DE	208
Mary E	12	DE	221
Phillip	25	DE	221
Rebecca A	15	DE	221
Rhoda E	7	DE	208
Solomon T	40	MD	208
William	17	DE	221
Norman, Benjamin	10	DE	47
Celia	10	DE	47
Clementine	10	DE	46
Norman, John	5	DE	47
Mariam	72	DE	46
Mary	19	DE	46
Mary	34	DE	47
Miller R	42	DE	46
Molten	7	DE	46
Purnal	2	DE	47
Purnal	35	DE	47
Rody	3	DE	46
Ruth	2/12	DE	46
Sarah	38	DE	46
Thomas	76	DE	47
William	7	DE	47
William	13	DE	46
Northerman, J W	19	MD	203
Norwood, Ann	4	DE	174
Charles	30	DE	32
Charity	45	DE	173
Eli	48	DE	173
Elizabeth	9	DE	184
John R	3/12	DE	187
Sally A	31	DE	187
Stephen	33	DE	187
William E	3	DE	187
Woolsey B	2	DE	187
Nutter, Ann	18	DE	195
Ann M	3	DE	223
Benjamin B	3	DE	202
Betsy A	21	MD	250
Caleb W	9	DE	223
Eliza A	35	DE	223
Charles J	16	DE	223
Clement	11	DE	223
David	30	DE	245
David J	7/12	DE	223
Eben	8	DE	245
Edna A	18	DE	212
Ephraim	35	DE	202
Henry	16	DE	203
Henry	48	DE	271
Hetty	11	DE	107
Hetty	45	DE	107
James	22	DE	271
James	45	DE	223
Jane	1	DE	251
Jane	26	DE	245
John N	15	DE	223
Julia	40	MD	250
Mary	10	MD	250
Moses	5	DE	223
Moses A P	11/12	DE	202
Nut	60	DE	271
Risden	70	DE	42
Sarah	1	DE	212
Sarah	6	DE	251
Wm H	13	DE	223
Zebeda	48	DE	107
Oakey, Elizabeth	18	DE	124
Griffith	51	DE	124
Leah	1	DE	124
Mary J	3	DE	124
Neely	46	DE	124
Robert	27	DE	124
Vina	46	DE	124
O'Beyman, Elizabeth	18	DE	21
Ellen	21	DE	21
Ellen	49	DE	21
George W	5	DE	21
Harriet	7	DE	21
Henry	15	DE	21
Henry	48	DE	21
Obier, Adaline	10	DE	207
Augustus	6	DE	207
Celia	39	MD	207
Celia A	13	DE	207
Eliza E	8	DE	207
Emelia	2	DE	207
George	5	DE	217
Isaac	49	DE	207
Isaac C	11	DE	207
Isaac J	7/12	DE	210
Obier, Isaac J	7/12	DE	210
Jacob P	14	DE	207
Jesse	8	DE	207
Joshua	43	DE	208
Martha J	6/12	DE	207
Mary C	16	DE	207
Mary J	46	DE	207
Sarah E	4	DE	207
O'Day, John L	12	DE	196
Martha A	2	DE	196
Mary C	6	DE	196
Nancy R	32	DE	196
Sarah E	10	DE	196
William	34	DE	196
William S	8	DE	196
Okey, Griffith	8	DE	127
Martha	18	DE	191
Samuel	65	DE	63
William	30	DE	191
Oliphan, Ann	8	DE	267
Cassanda	40	DE	267
Elizabeth	70	DE	263
James	12	DE	267
Rebecca	16	DE	267
Thomas	20	DE	263
William	42	DE	267
Oliphant, Charlotte	56	DE	288
David	5	DE	241
Elijah	22	DE	288
Mary	19	MD	288
Olivant, David	55	DE	280
Keturah	55	DE	280
Oliver, Ann C	7	DE	34
Charity	6	DE	37
David	60	DE	38
Elijah W	31	DE	258
Eliza	48	DE	34
George H	51	DE	34
Hetty	55	DE	38
Isaac	8	DE	258
Isaac J	8/12	DE	209
James W	8/12	DE	22
Jasper	1	DE	258
Jeremiah	2	DE	37
John W	28	DE	22
Joseph	4	DE	37
Joseph	40	DE	37
Julia A	32	DE	258
Martha	7	DE	38
Martha A	8	DE	37
Mary	21	DE	22
Mary J	36	DE	171
Nutter	4	DE	258
Priscilla	55	DE	53
Samuel W	16	DE	5
Sarah E	10	DE	37
Sarah J	5	DE	171
Susan E	13	DE	37
Theophilus	19	DE	258
Thomas	37	DE	171
William	5	DE	258
William	14	DE	179
O'Neal, Abigail	49	MD	291
Alexander	42	DE	195
Andrew	22	DE	228
Angelina	11	DE	238
Ann	39	DE	297
Catherine	2	DE	297
Christiana	22	DE	292
Daniel	2	DE	295
David	35	DE	295
Eliza	17	DE	295
Elizabeth	12	DE	228
Elizabeth	45	DE	292
George	7	DE	295
George S	12	DE	195
Hamilton	40	DE	238
Henry	5	DE	295
John	17	DE	297
John H	14	DE	195
Jonah	4	DE	291
Jos T	9	DE	292

Name	Age	State	Page
O'Neal, Josephus	11	DE	295
Josiah	66	DE	291
Lavenia	9	DE	295
Lurany	30	DE	238
Maria	1	DE	291
Martha	10	DE	297
Mary	25	DE	291
Mary	30	DE	295
Rachel	33	DE	195
Robert	7	DE	297
Samuel	24	DE	292
Sarah	3	DE	291
Sarah A	8/12	DE	292
Sarah M	5	DE	196
Susan H	9	DE	195
Thomas	13	DE	295
Wm	25	DE	291
Wm	42	DE	297
Oney, Charlotte	14	DE	222
David	12	DE	38
David	45	DE	38
Elizabeth	40	DE	38
Greensbury	12	DE	239
Horatio	70	DE	280
John	52	DE	281
Joseph	17	DE	280
Martha J	24	DE	241
Nancy	13	DE	281
Rebecca	20	DE	285
Sarah	11	DE	179
Sarah A	4	DE	241
Tempy	19	DE	42
Oram, George	3	DE	158
James	7	DE	158
Orr, Anthony	9	DE	44
Elizabeth	47	DE	44
William	24	DE	44
Osburn, Anna M	14	DE	230
Caroline A	10	DE	230
Catherine A	17	DE	230
Joseph	50	DE	230
Joseph T	6	DE	230
Mary A	35	DE	230
Susan A	31	DE	230
Otwell, Biard	47	DE	160
Clarisa	23	DE	287
Eliza	38	DE	160
Eliza J	6	DE	160
Eunice A	10	DE	160
Jane	64	DE	160
John C	40	DE	160
John T	63	DE	160
Joseph C	18	DE	160
Julia J	10	DE	171
Lavinia	2	DE	221
Lavinia	34	DE	287
Letitia	55	DE	221
Lucinda	17	DE	214
Mary	13	DE	287
Mary	16	DE	160
Mary	73	DE	160
Mary J	3	DE	160
Obadiah J	15	DE	160
Otha A	8	DE	160
Rufus A	6	DE	160
Samuel S	12	DE	160
Sarah	15	DE	287
Sarah	25	DE	221
Sarah A	34	DE	160
Sarah E	9	DE	160
Selby	36	DE	171
Susan	34	DE	171
Watson T	13	DE	160
Wesley	31	DE	221
William	38	DE	287
William T	14	DE	160
William W	11	DE	160
Ousterbridge, Ann	9	DE	188
Outen, Ezekiel	13	DE	110
George	1/12	DE	110
James	41	DE	110
John	11	DE	110
Outen, Margaret A	18	DE	110
Martha	4	DE	110
Mary	7	DE	110
Mary	41	DE	110
Nicholas A	12	DE	110
Sophia	16	DE	110
Outin, Elizabeth	40	DE	82
John	15	DE	82
Joshua	23	DE	82
Leah Elizabeth	13	DE	82
Lewis	52	DE	82
Margaret Ann	1	DE	82
Outten, Andrew	32	DE	197
Caroline	11/12	DE	197
Catharine	24	DE	202
George Ann	3	DE	197
James	17	DE	202
John R	25	DE	202
Joseph W	15	DE	202
Levina	3	DE	264
Louisa A	2	DE	203
Lucinda	47	DE	202
Margaret	21	DE	203
Mary	20	DE	275
Mary	23	DE	197
Patty	21	DE	264
Sarah J	9/12	DE	203
William	30	DE	264
William H	50	DE	202
Wm H	4	DE	197
Owens, Aaron	60	DE	243
Aaron S	25	DE	243
Alexine	12	DE	107
Ann L	18	DE	243
Anna	27	DE	106
Aron	4	DE	245
Biddy E	25	DE	245
Charles	5/12	DE	88
Charlotte	5	DE	88
Clayton	34	DE	245
David	9	DE	107
David	12	DE	88
Elijah M	31	DE	270
Elizabeth	37	DE	111
Elizabeth	57	DE	240
George	3	DE	245
George	50	DE	88
Hamilton	4	DE	243
Hiram	22	DE	243
Isaac	22	DE	107
Isaac W	16	DE	243
James	1	DE	106
James	20	DE	111
James H	30	DE	274
Jane	70	DE	270
John	11	DE	106
John	25	DE	111
John	25	DE	197
Jonathan	34	DE	106
Josiah	51	DE	243
Lydia Ann	8	DE	88
Margaret	2	DE	274
Margaret	6	DE	106
Margaret	20	DE	107
Mary	32	DE	274
Mary	44	DE	88
Rachael	47	DE	111
Sarah	2	DE	245
Sarah	3	DE	274
Thomas	77	DE	270
Uriah	27	DE	243
Paine, Charles	12	MD	212
Painter, George	6	DE	16
James	10	DE	16
Jane	36	DE	60
Mary	63	DE	60
Mary A	6	DE	60
Sarah	5	DE	60
Thomas	2	DE	60
Thomas	35	DE	60
Palmer, Alissa	30	DE	20
Palmer, Ann	18	DE	111
Ann B	29	DE	192
Catharine	8	DE	174
Comfort	81	DE	19
David	16	DE	2
David	16	DE	111
Edward	12	DE	174
Egda	47	DE	174
Elia	36	DE	186
Elizabeth	10	DE	51
Elizabeth	12	DE	21
Elizabeth	29	DE	16
Elizabeth	50	DE	17
Elizabeth J	14	DE	28
Ellice	4	DE	260
Emily	5	DE	16
Frances	4	DE	16
Garretson	4	DE	21
George W	6	DE	28
Greensbury	10	DE	28
Henry R	23	DE	192
Hetty	44	DE	44
Hetty A	7	DE	186
Hetty J	14	DE	192
Hetty J W	12	DE	51
Jackson	43	DE	28
James	8	DE	16
James	10	DE	111
John	15	DE	20
John	56	DE	51
John C	15	DE	189
John S	5	DE	186
John W	28	DE	196
Joseph	12	DE	260
Joseph	50	DE	260
Joseph M	4	DE	186
Julia	25	DE	110
Lemuel	4	DE	191
Letty M	10	DE	174
Luther	6	DE	260
Lydia B	1	DE	189
Maria	13	DE	20
Martha	16	DE	260
Martha U	13	DE	28
Mary	34	DE	189
Mary A	24	DE	191
Mary E	36	DE	186
Mary J	3	DE	189
Matilda	45	DE	260
Nancy	60	DE	190
Nancy J	18	DE	17
Patience	17	DE	180
Patience A	14	DE	174
Robert E	1	DE	180
Sabrey	50	DE	110
Sabrey	50	DE	111
Sally A	8	DE	22
Sampson	4	DE	22
Samuel	28	DE	192
Sarah	44	DE	28
Sarah	45	DE	31
Sarah A	2	DE	191
Sarah E	6	DE	21
Stephen	15	DE	34
Sylvester W	30	DE	20
Tabitha	20	DE	192
Tabitha	56	DE	51
Thomas	36	DE	189
William	25	DE	190
William	27	DE	16
William	50	DE	189
William B	54	DE	17
William W	4	DE	20
William W	7	DE	189
Woolsey B	6	DE	174
Woolsey H	52	DE	174
Panard, Daniel	50	DE	133
Jane	40	DE	133
John	4	DE	133
Pane, Lorenzo D	40	DE	34
Mary	36	DE	34
Parcast, William J	12	DE	157

Name	Age	ST	Pg	Name	Age	ST	Pg	Name	Age	ST	Pg
Parden, Eleanor	24	DE	239	Parker, Peter	16	DE	162	Parsons, Mary A	32	DE	192
Pardo, Angelia	4	DE	97	Peter	56	DE	21	Mary E	11	DE	184
Charlott	26	DE	97	Peter C	40	DE	35	Matilda	9	DE	279
John	7	DE	97	Priscilla	19	DE	226	Matilda	11	DE	279
John	32	DE	97	Prudence A	7	DE	162	Nancy	17	DE	280
Pardue, Hester A	2	DE	241	Robert A	14	DE	35	Noah	23	DE	279
James M	1	DE	241	Samuel	30	DE	162	Noah	24	DE	279
Mary	25	DE	241	Sarah	21	DE	260	Phebe	16	DE	279
Thomas	28	DE	241	Sarah C	2/12	DE	21	Phillip E	4	DE	260
Parkeal, Ann R	13	DE	39	Sarah E	1	DE	9	Priscilla	18	DE	279
Priscilla A	29	DE	39	Sina	39	DE	50	Robert Burton	3	DE	61
Samuel	39	DE	39	Theodore	7	DE	50	Susan	25	MD	280
Sarah E	11	DE	39	Theodore	22	DE	240	Theodore	5	DE	279
Wilhamina	2/12	DE	39	Theodore W	25	DE	35	William	28	DE	279
Parker, Adelaide W	4	DE	6	Thomas	28	DE	277	William	36	MD	279
Albert	6	DE	162	Thomas	65	DE	58	William B	56	MD	279
Alexine	6/12	DE	35	Thomas	67	GB	162	William P	17	DE	61
Baker	53	DE	9	Truitt	5	DE	9	William W	27	MD	280
Benjamin	2	DE	260	Warren	40	MD	138	Passwater, Alexander	23	DE	94
Betty	12	DE	162	William	6/12	DE	260	Betsy	40	DE	103
Burton	14	DE	9	William	5	DE	9	Eliza	12	DE	94
Caroline	24	DE	34	William	18	DE	240	Elizabeth	30	DE	94
Catherine	35	DE	139	William	30	DE	240	James	1	DE	103
Charlotte	27	DE	21	Wm	27	DE	210	Jesse	21	DE	103
Clara	10/12	DE	35	Parkhurst, Ann	33	DE	107	Jesse	50	DE	94
Deborah	25	DE	35	Daniel H	8	VA	107	Jesse J	2	DE	226
E L D	25	GA	232	Ellen O	10	VA	107	John	8	DE	103
Elijah	21	DE	218	Virginia	14	VA	107	John	25	DE	94
Elijah M	31	MD	260	William C	37	MA	107	John	47	DE	103
Elisha	35	DE	162	William J	12	VA	107	Kinsey	21	DE	103
Eliza	2	DE	10	Parks, Matilda	30	DE	79	Levi	13	DE	103
Eliza	25	DE	162	William	38	DE	79	Levinia	2	DE	103
Eliza	31	DE	35	Parmer, Araminta A	5	DE	245	Manlove	19	DE	103
Elizabeth	17	DE	240	Henry	7	DE	276	Margaret	5	DE	103
Elizabeth	17	DE	240	Isaac	4	DE	276	Marvel	22	DE	103
Elizabeth	24	DE	277	Isaac	35	DE	276	Nancy	20	DE	103
Elizabeth	66	DE	162	James	40	DE	245	Nancy	45	DE	94
Elizabeth	73	DE	13	John	13	MD	276	Polly	21	DE	103
Emaline	25	DE	9	Joseph H	6/12	DE	276	Richard	22	DE	94
Fanny	3	MD	226	Joshua H	6/12	DE	276	Robert	16	DE	103
Frederic J	2	DE	35	Maria	18	DE	290	Sally	10	DE	103
Gardner A B	2	DE	6	Martha	10	MD	276	Thomas	15	DE	94
Gatty	2	DE	277	Mary	3	DE	245	William	1	DE	103
George	4	DE	21	Mary	8	MD	276	Passwaters, Eliza A	22	DE	226
George	9	DE	162	Mary A	25	DE	245	James E	6	DE	226
George	40	DE	162	Priscilla	25	DE	276	John	13	DE	226
Hannah C	19	DE	34	Rhoda	38	DE	245	Nancy	41	DE	226
Hannah M	33	PA	6	Sallie	1	DE	245	Rebecca J	3	DE	226
Harriet	2	DE	21	Sallie	57	DE	245	Sarah E	12	DE	226
Henry	13	DE	9	Seth	5	DE	276	William	38	DE	226
Henry	21	DE	193	William	12	MD	276	William A	2	DE	226
Hetty A	9	DE	50	Parreh, Eliza	35	DE	66	Wingate	28	DE	226
Hetty B	43	DE	35	Parson, John	25	DE	261	Paswaters, Boaze	36	DE	68
Isaac	50	DE	240	Margaret L	22	DE	261	Boaze D	4	DE	68
James	7	DE	162	Parsons, Amanda E	14	DE	61	Charlotte	37	DE	89
James A	38	DE	6	Clementine S	6	DE	192	James H	9	DE	68
John	8	DE	9	Ebenezer	9	DE	279	James H	9	DE	89
John	10	DE	162	Elijah J	32	DE	277	Mary E	2	DE	68
John	13	DE	174	Elizabeth	36	DE	279	Nancy	39	DE	68
John	39	DE	50	Elizabeth C	1	DE	61	Samuel	5	DE	89
John E	25	DE	1	Hannah	50	DE	280	Sarah E	6	DE	68
Joseph	20	DE	162	Henry	14	DE	279	Sylvester	34	DE	89
Joseph H	1	DE	210	James	25	MD	280	William B	13	DE	68
Julia A	27	DE	210	James F	9/12	DE	260	Patton, Rebecca J	20	DE	216
Julian	4	DE	277	John	6/12	DE	280	Thomas	31	DE	216
Levin	11	DE	240	John	10	DE	280	Paynter, Ann	44	DE	58
Luther	9	DE	240	John	25	DE	260	Ann	56	DE	57
Mahala	34	DE	9	John	40	DE	61	Anna	14	DE	53
Margaret E	11	DE	35	John	48	MD	280	Caleb R	18	DE	15
Margaret J	7	MD	210	John E	9	DE	179	Daniel	70	DE	57
Marian W	7	DE	6	Levinia	38	DE	61	David	3	DE	50
Martha	14	DE	162	Louder	7	DE	279	David	10	DE	15
Mary	3	DE	162	Louisa H	7	DE	61	David E	16	DE	178
Mary	8	DE	277	Lovenia	3	DE	279	David R	10	DE	15
Mary	30	DE	162	Lucinda	2	DE	260	Eliza A	37	DE	48
Mary	55	DE	38	Lucinda	17	DE	279	Elizabeth	45	DE	58
Mary A	9	DE	9	Margaret H	1	DE	192	Elizabeth	76	DE	64
Mary A	50	DE	34	Margaret L	22	DE	260	Emma R	7	DE	15
Mary E	5	DE	6	Mary	8/12	DE	279	George	8	DE	61
Mary E	7	DE	35	Mary	1	DE	279	George	21	DE	57
Mary E	24	DE	240	Mary	53	MD	279	Hannah	14	DE	176
Nancy	6	DE	277	Mary A	12	DE	61	Henry	13	DE	179

Name	Age	State	No.
Paynter, Hetty	58	DE	52
Hetty	66	DE	48
Hetty A	14	DE	48
James	8	DE	50
James	17	DE	58
Jane	30	DE	48
John	80	DE	58
Joseph H	7	DE	48
John H	12	DE	15
John R	6	DE	48
Lemuel D	20	DE	181
Margaret	17	DE	13
Margaret	75	DE	62
Mary	10	DE	57
Mary	12	DE	58
Mary	18	DE	61
Moses	11	DE	58
Nancy	16	DE	62
Nathaniel	45	DE	87
Rece	55	DE	57
Richard	16	DE	61
Richard	39	DE	48
Richard	45	DE	61
Richard S	1	DE	48
Ruth	20	DE	13
Sally A	38	DE	15
Sallie F	4	DE	48
Samuel	12	DE	13
Samuel	12	DE	53
Samuel	18	DE	59
Samuel	55	DE	13
Samuel E	11	DE	48
Samuel E	45	DE	48
Samuel E	49	DE	15
Samuel S	16	DE	15
Sarah	25	DE	50
Sarah J	20	DE	34
Sirman	2	DE	57
Solomon	9	DE	13
Solomon	36	DE	34
Thomas	34	DE	50
Walter J	3	DE	192
William	16	DE	193
Pence, John	17	MD	202
Penn, Arpy	1	DE	65
Arpy	36	DE	65
John W	4	DE	65
Joshua	1	DE	65
Joshua L	45	DE	65
Pennawell, Catharine	16	DE	9
Charles	25	DE	9
Elmira	48	DE	9
George	27	DE	9
John	18	DE	9
Pennewell, Amelia	60	DE	239
Ann E	19	DE	226
Caroline	20	DE	296
Charles	25	DE	171
David	10/12	DE	226
Lemuel	21	DE	281
Lydia	27	DE	226
Mary	55	MD	281
Nancy	60	MD	226
Samson	23	DE	226
Sarah	18	DE	283
Silas J	24	DE	281
Pensey, Edward	8	DE	279
Ephraim W	38	DE	279
Ionna	10	DE	279
Kingsbury	11	DE	279
Nancy	30	DE	279
Penter, Charles H	3	DE	195
George R	7	DE	195
Hester	32	DE	195
Lurany	2/12	DE	195
Margaret O	9	DE	195
Mary L	10	DE	195
Socrates R	5	DE	195
William D	38	DE	195
Pentor, Ann	18	DE	230
Elizabeth	70	DE	273
Henrietta S	9	DE	195

Name	Age	State	No.
Pentor, James	78	DE	273
James E	5	DE	195
John D	11	DE	195
Lorenzo T	2	DE	195
Margaret A	13	DE	195
Mary	44	DE	273
Sallie	39	DE	195
Samuel C	15	DE	195
Susan	49	DE	273
William L	2/12	DE	195
Wm of S	37	DE	195
Pepper, Alfred	6	DE	7
Arthur	7	DE	9
Asbury	36	DE	9
Asbury W	7	DE	9
Caroline	7	DE	7
Catharine	28	DE	19
Catharine	30	DE	9
Charles	1	DE	7
Charles M	8	DE	19
Charles T	10	DE	9
Chloe A	9	DE	9
David	45	DE	9
David M	11	DE	9
David T	3	DE	149
Edward	32	DE	7
Edward W	6	DE	145
Eli	1	DE	9
Eli	82	DE	145
Eliza J	9/12	DE	8
Eliza W	4	DE	9
Elizabeth E	19	DE	8
George	10	DE	7
George H	4	DE	145
Greensbury	33	DE	8
Hannah	4	DE	7
Harriet A	15	DE	9
Henry	34	DE	149
Henry E	5	DE	28
Henry N	30	DE	28
Henry R	31	DE	293
Hetty	35	DE	145
Hetty J	9	DE	145
Isaac D	6/12	DE	7
Joshua S	11	DE	145
Joshua W	42	DE	145
Julia	36	DE	293
Lavinia	29	DE	7
Levin	24	DE	149
Levin A	1	DE	149
Levinia	3	DE	8
Luther M R	6	DE	9
Lydia E	5	DE	9
Margaret	33	DE	7
Martin M	8	DE	7
Mary A	7	DE	8
Mary A	8	DE	28
Mary A	16	DE	145
Mary E	13	DE	7
Mary E	13	DE	9
Nancy E	8	DE	7
Naomi	38	DE	9
Peter	29	DE	7
Rachel	33	DE	7
Rachel A	4	DE	10
Rhoda W	3	DE	7
Robert	28	DE	19
Robert G	1	DE	19
Sarah	25	DE	149
Sarah E	4	DE	7
Sarah E	5	DE	8
Thomas	29	DE	7
Walter W R	2	DE	10
William E	2	DE	7
Percy, George	25	DE	149
Perkins, Brinkley	28	DE	100
Eliza	30	DE	229
Elizabeth	10	DE	229
Holland	29	DE	100
Jane	12	DE	229
Jerry	6	DE	100
John W	1	DE	229

Name	Age	State	No.
Perkins, Joseph	8	PA	292
Lovey	2	DE	100
Lovey	4	DE	100
Mary	1	DE	100
Mary	2	DE	229
Mary	35	DE	229
Nancy	16	DE	229
Sarah	10	PA	292
Vincent	59	DE	229
Warren	23	DE	229
Wesly	30	DE	229
William	4	DE	229
Pernal, John	12	DE	292
Perry, Charles	9	DE	185
Daniel	12	DE	44
David C	17	DE	14
Elizabeth E	5	DE	14
George	25	DE	148
Hannah	60	DE	29
Hetty E	4	DE	189
Jane E	34	DE	189
John M	38	DE	189
Lydia A	43	DE	14
Margaret A	13	DE	14
Sallie A	1	DE	189
Samuel M	10	DE	14
Thomas J	22	DE	14
William	6	DE	189
Peters, Albert	55	DE	54
James	10	DE	43
James	29	DE	54
Mary	49	DE	54
Petty, Phebe	70	DE	254
Pettyjohn, Abel J	13	DE	11
Adelaid	3	DE	5
Ann	49	DE	21
Benjamin T	5	DE	182
Catharine	40	DE	18
Charles	5	DE	99
Charles	7	DE	26
Clement	45	DE	73
Ebenezer	11	DE	40
Elijah	4	DE	41
Eliza J	3	DE	41
Elizabeth	25	DE	53
Elizabeth	30	DE	41
Esther	6	DE	9
Frances A	14	DE	73
George	34	DE	99
George W	2	DE	19
George W	22	DE	19
Hannah	5	DE	5
Heveloe	1	DE	41
Isaac	17	DE	41
Isabella	16	DE	18
Israel	12	DE	73
Jacob	7	DE	40
James	2	DE	40
James	5	DE	40
James	7	DE	99
James	38	DE	40
James	40	DE	88
James	54	DE	5
James E	3/12	DE	22
Jane	35	DE	73
John	11	DE	40
John	15	DE	5
John W	11	DE	88
Joseph	9	DE	88
Joseph	11	DE	73
Julia	22	DE	34
Julia A	13	DE	40
Levin	45	DE	40
Louisa	13	DE	88
Lydia	6	DE	73
Margaret	12	DE	41
Martha	30	DE	99
Mary	1	DE	73
Mary	25	DE	10
Mary	32	DE	9
Mary A	24	DE	19
Mary Ann	9	DE	40

Name	Age	State	No.	Name	Age	State	No.	Name	Age	State	No.
Pettyjohn, Mary E	23	DE	182	Phillips, Eliza	34	DE	160	Phillips, Kendal J	38	DE	201
Matthew	18	DE	24	Eliza	38	DE	253	Leah	7	DE	164
Minty	40	DE	23	Eliza C	10	DE	204	Leah	13	DE	251
Molly	24	DE	22	Elizabeth	6	DE	159	Leah E	6	DE	253
Moses	31	DE	9	Elizabeth	7	DE	280	Lemuel H	3	DE	169
Nancy	65	DE	9	Elizabeth	12	DE	251	Lemuel W	39	DE	200
Phebe	2	DE	73	Elizabeth	14	DE	42	Levin	2/12	DE	159
Phillis	35	DE	40	Elizabeth	14	DE	204	Levin	4	DE	242
Phoebe	43	DE	88	Elizabeth	14	DE	274	Levin	73	DE	216
Pinkey	39	DE	40	Elizabeth	27	DE	246	Levin L	19	DE	216
Rhoda	6	DE	40	Elizabeth	30	DE	159	Lorenzo	4	DE	250
Richard	55	DE	18	Elizabeth	42	DE	251	Louisa	11	DE	164
Sarah	2	DE	53	Elizabeth	42	DE	253	Louisa	40	DE	159
Sarah J	7	DE	182	Elizabeth	52	DE	164	Lovenia E	16	DE	160
Sarah J	9	DE	88	Elizabeth E	13	DE	216	Luther W	1	DE	200
Sophia	8	DE	99	Elizabeth J	26	DE	164	Maranda	1	DE	251
Stephen	30	DE	53	Elizabeth S	22	DE	164	Marcelus	15	DE	252
Susan J	4	DE	19	Emeline	6/12	DE	250	Margaret	3	DE	251
Thomas	8	DE	40	Emeline	10	DE	159	Margaret	4	DE	247
Truitt	29	DE	182	Emeline	22	DE	242	Margaret	11	DE	252
William	1	DE	182	Emily	9	DE	164	Margaret	44	MD	216
William	27	DE	19	Eunice	63	DE	160	Margaret C	17	DE	216
William	50	DE	41	Eunice R	46	DE	164	Margaret H	19	DE	159
William E	4	DE	40	Frederic	7	DE	246	Margaret J	8/12	DE	200
Wrixam	40	DE	41	Gardiner	17	DE	164	Maria	9	DE	243
Zachara	2	DE	41	George	13	DE	247	Maria	31	MD	252
Zachariah	25	DE	22	George	14	DE	245	Martha	5	DE	253
Phenix, Emily	24	DE	58	George	16	DE	280	Martha A	4	DE	204
Gideon	15	DE	58	George	46	DE	253	Martha A	14	DE	251
Gideon	62	DE	57	George H	28	DE	291	Mary	2	DE	252
James	30	DE	57	George W	1	DE	253	Mary	4	DE	164
Mamex	55	DE	57	Goldbrook	28	MD	243	Mary	6	DE	251
Mary	26	DE	57	Greensbury T	14	DE	160	Mary	6	DE	253
Philips, Edward C	16	DE	53	Hamilton S	11	DE	159	Mary	9	DE	159
James	29	DE	13	Henry	18	DE	274	Mary	9	DE	252
Sarah	29	DE	13	Henry L	3	DE	201	Mary	16	DE	274
Phillip, Arthur B	9	DE	149	Hester	10	DE	273	Mary	18	DE	280
Mary	36	DE	149	Hester A	2	DE	242	Mary	22	DE	251
Sarah E	1	DE	149	Hetty A	4	DE	169	Mary	24	DE	159
Phillips, Albert	8	DE	245	Hiram	23	DE	251	Mary	47	DE	274
Alcy	11	DE	251	Ignius	37	DE	205	Mary	50	MD	281
Ally F	1	DE	201	Isaac	3/12	DE	143	Mary A	25	DE	160
Amelia	16	DE	291	Isaac	2	DE	251	Mary A	30	DE	200
Amelia	53	MD	291	Isaac	7	DE	20	Mary Ann	16	MD	279
Amelia H	39	DE	204	Isaac G	33	DE	242	Mary C	10	DE	253
Ann	12	DE	280	Isaac T	1	DE	251	Mary C	21	DE	251
Ann	36	DE	246	Jacob	26	DE	159	Mary E	10	DE	251
Anna	4	DE	253	Jacob	67	DE	164	Mary E	18	DE	247
Arcada W	26	MD	243	Jacob T	1	DE	204	Mary E	20	DE	23
Augustus	9	DE	246	James	3	DE	251	Mary E	35	DE	251
Azarius	22	DE	251	James	11	DE	280	Mary J	1	DE	246
Benjamin	32	DE	169	James	16	DE	247	Mary J	9	DE	243
Blaney	58	DE	149	James A	14	DE	204	Mary J	14	DE	170
Burton	47	DE	160	James A	26	DE	252	Mary P	20	DE	143
Cadmus S	8	DE	253	James H	18	DE	246	Matilda	28	DE	273
Celia	12	DE	274	James J B	12	DE	216	Milla A	8	DE	159
Celia	61	DE	249	James W	23	DE	197	Nancy	24	DE	159
Charles	3/12	DE	204	James W F	16	DE	253	Nancy	63	DE	242
Charles	4	DE	159	Jesse H B	3	DE	216	Nancy A	20	DE	291
Charles	45	DE	159	John	1	DE	246	Nancy H	16	DE	159
Cyrus S	37	DE	204	John	2	DE	280	Nancy J	4	DE	13
Daniel	43	DE	252	John	8	DE	164	Naomi	56	DE	159
Daniel	50	DE	274	John	20	DE	159	Nathaniel	19	DE	164
David	67	MD	281	John	28	DE	173	Nathaniel	47	DE	164
Darius M	33	DE	250	John B	23	DE	160	Noah J W	3	DE	243
Dennis	9/12	DE	273	John C	2	DE	169	Parker	5	DE	280
Dennis	39	DE	273	John M	50	DE	245	Patty A	29	DE	243
Drusilla	7	DE	247	John N	48	DE	280	Priscilla	13	DE	159
Drusilla	8	DE	273	John S	14	DE	251	Priscilla	30	DE	160
Edward	14	DE	280	John T	4	DE	239	Priscilla	46	DE	159
Egentine	6	DE	238	John T	14	DE	252	Purnal	14	DE	159
Eleanor	23	DE	250	Joseph	4	DE	273	Rachel	7	DE	251
Eleanor	39	DE	247	Joseph	20	PA	211	Rachel A	12	DE	253
Eleanor	46	MD	252	Joseph	48	DE	251	Rebecca C	12	DE	204
Elihu G	36	DE	160	Joseph	60	DE	159	Rebecca R	3/12	DE	160
Elijah	27	DE	243	Joseph A	9	DE	204	Rhoda	2	DE	159
Elijah M	26	DE	159	Joseph H	14	DE	159	Robert	10	MD	224
Elinor	12	DE	252	Joseph J W	4	DE	243	Robert	12	DE	159
Elinor	36	DE	200	Joshua	16	DE	164	Roger	34	DE	252
Eliza	7	DE	274	Joshua	50	DE	164	Rufus	17	DE	252
Eliza	20	DE	159	Josiah	19	DE	23	Sallie A	1	DE	239
Eliza	31	DE	169	Julius W	6	DE	204	Sallie A	18	DE	243

Name				Name				Name			
Phillips, Sallie P	10	DE	265	Piper, Unice L	26	DE	24	Polk, Robert	14	DE	108
Samuel	10	DE	274	William	31	DE	159	Robert	44	DE	229
Samuel	50	DE	252	William H	21	DE	2	Sarah	2	DE	217
Samuel J	20	DE	252	Pippen, Elizabeth	16	DE	253	Sarah	5	DE	292
Sarah	3	DE	159	Isaac	18	DE	253	Sarah	52	DE	36
Sarah	9	DE	251	Isaac	52	DE	253	Sarah A	29	DE	216
Sarah	9	DE	280	John	4	DE	253	Sarah A	35	DE	229
Sarah	10	DE	247	Prudence	42	DE	253	Sarah P	14	DE	229
Sarah	11	DE	164	Sallie	8	DE	253	Simon	17	DE	235
Sarah	28	DE	238	Plumer, Hudson	18	DE	282	Suthy A	42	DE	232
Sarah	37	DE	201	Plummer, Ann	35	DE	93	Tabitha	30	MD	196
Sarah	42	DE	280	Charlott	18	DE	87	Thomas	3	DE	214
Sarah E	8	DE	243	Elizabeth	25	DE	174	Trusten	10	DE	216
Sarah E	10	DE	160	Ellen	3	DE	28	William	5	DE	7
Sarah J	6	DE	169	George	1	DE	28	William	10	DE	292
Spencer	76	DE	160	George	10	DE	87	William	28	DE	196
Spencer A	13	DE	164	Jane	19	DE	87	Wm	16	DE	220
Tabitha	12	DE	252	James	44	DE	93	Wm	35	DE	292
Theodore	7/12	DE	13	Jincy	4	DE	87	Wm C	35	DE	216
Theodore	34	DE	243	John	7	DE	87	Ponder, James	29	DE	33
Thomas	1	DE	247	John	65	DE	87	John	58	DE	33
Thomas	15	DE	251	John W	6/12	DE	174	Lydia	30	DE	34
Thomas	49	DE	247	Mary C	2	DE	174	Melissa	10	DE	34
Thomas	66	DE	159	Nicy	31	DE	28	William	33	DE	34
Thomas J	41	DE	246	Patience	63	DE	87	Pool, Alfred P	16	DE	113
Thomas S	22	DE	159	Robert	26	DE	174	Ann	30	DE	48
Thomas W	8	DE	243	Sarah	11	DE	93	Benjamin R	28	DE	114
Uphany	6	DE	273	Silas	21	DE	87	Charles H	3	DE	48
William	9/12	DE	253	Wallis	20	DE	149	Elizabeth	20	DE	184
William	3	MD	273	William	9	DE	28	Erasmus M	19	DE	113
William	4	DE	246	Poasley, Gatty	29	DE	124	George B	11	DE	48
William	6	DE	250	Polite, Herman	45	DE	58	George J	1	DE	114
William	7	DE	274	Leah C	41	DE	58	Gilbert W	26	DE	112
William A R	38	DE	253	Mary J	19	DE	58	Henry W	21	DE	113
William S	24	DE	164	Polk, Abby	59	DE	98	Hester W	56	DE	184
William W	7	DE	204	Abraham	1	DE	218	John T	38	DE	48
William W	22	DE	291	Abraham	65	DE	218	John W	9	DE	113
Wm	15	DE	291	Alfred	3	DE	98	John W	24	DE	184
Wm R	25	DE	216	Amelia	45	DE	235	Joshua R	14	DE	113
Wm S	30	DE	246	Ann	28	DE	217	Ketturah	42	DE	112
Phippin, Isabel	23	DE	237	Caroline	8	DE	216	Ketturah J	2	DE	113
Pierce, Arcada	22	DE	80	Coloran	4	DE	217	Mary R	25	DE	114
Comfort J	27	DE	80	Daniel	4	DE	108	Perry	58	DE	112
Henry	25	DE	78	David	14	DE	227	Rebecca A	11	DE	113
Hester	23	DE	78	Eliza	33	DE	292	Robert W	6	DE	113
Jane	40	DE	54	Elizabeth	9	DE	36	Sarah	77	DE	188
John	6	DE	80	Elizabeth C	2	DE	216	Poole, Charlotte	15	DE	165
John	11	DE	54	Ellen	1	DE	216	Porter, Maria L	19	DE	84
Mark	3	DE	78	Emila	1	DE	229	Sally P	54	DE	84
Sarah Catherine	4	DE	80	Emma	3	DE	237	William	54	DE	84
Thomas	1	DE	78	Fardric	30	DE	217	Postles, David	21	DE	72
William	3	DE	80	George	28	DE	108	John	2	DE	72
William	33	DE	80	George	44	DE	235	Mary	65	DE	72
Pills, Arnold	50	DE	261	George W	7	DE	196	Sarah A	19	DE	72
Nancy	1	DE	261	George W	20	DE	208	Potter, Benjamin	16	DE	79
Sarah	22	DE	261	Hannah	60	DE	218	Caroline	14	DE	79
Piper, Benjamin	10	DE	146	Henry	3	DE	235	Celia	40	DE	79
Benjamin B	5	DE	143	Hetty	6	DE	292	Deborah	2	DE	79
Comfort	39	DE	159	Isaac	14	DE	253	Eliza	48	DE	88
Eliza	19	DE	4	Isaac	30	DE	196	James	15	DE	88
Elizabeth	18	DE	1	Isaac	30	DE	199	James	50	DE	87
Flora	55	DE	136	Isaac J	8	DE	196	Mary	20	DE	88
George H	5	DE	159	James K	10	DE	55	Mary Ann	18	DE	80
Hannah	71	DE	159	James of John	40	DE	87	Mary J	9	DE	88
Henry	22	DE	66	Jas R	15	DE	227	Potts, Bayard	17	DE	197
James H	11/12	DE	4	Jesse	76	DE	228	Powell, Isaac	6	DE	127
John	45	DE	24	Job	79	DE	266	Pratt, Fredric	9	DE	226
John O	18	DE	2	John	16	DE	36	Henry	35	DE	226
Josiah M	11	DE	10	John	17	DE	108	Janette	31	DE	226
Kasy	22	DE	67	John L	8	DE	229	Sarah	7	DE	226
Kitten	28	DE	143	John W	11	DE	87	Prettyman, Aaron B	8	DE	146
Love A	1	DE	143	Joseph	9	DE	87	Abigail	4	DE	17
Maranda	16	DE	159	Leah	14	DE	292	Ada C	7	DE	45
Mary E	3	DE	143	Louisa	13	DE	87	Adda	6	DE	211
Mary E	9	DE	24	Lovey A	12	DE	229	Alfred B	11	DE	184
Mitchel	17	DE	65	Martha	7	DE	235	Amanda C	4	DE	38
Nancy	43	DE	24	Mary	30	DE	237	Amy	23	DE	17
Nancy M	12	DE	146	Mary A	3	DE	229	Angeline	5	DE	55
Prince	34	DE	159	Mary E	5	DE	217	Ann	9	DE	55
Robert	28	DE	143	Mary E	10	DE	218	Ann	30	DE	191
Sarah	8	DE	159	Nancy	34	DE	225	Asbury	3	DE	9
Sarah T	39	DE	2	Phoebe	43	DE	87	Asbury W	42	DE	45

Name	Age	State	Page
Prettyman, Bagwell B	23	DE	161
Burton	65	DE	145
Burton C	26	DE	187
Catharine	8	DE	47
Charles H	9	DE	188
Charles K	12	DE	56
Charles P	7	DE	201
Charlotte	17	DE	179
Clarissa	1	DE	201
Clarissa	3	DE	187
Comfort	62	DE	181
Cornelius	6	DE	199
Cornelius	6	DE	199
Cornelius	27	DE	146
Cornelius P	4	DE	9
Curtis	26	DE	9
Daniel A	22	DE	1
David H	12	DE	201
David M	3	DE	45
David M	35	DE	187
E P	34	DE	201
Edward	10	DE	201
Edward H	14	DE	56
Elisha	58	DE	36
Eliza	52	DE	47
Eliza	40	DE	19
Eliza A	26	DE	187
Eliza A	41	DE	199
Elizabeth	17	DE	93
Elizabeth	22	DE	63
Elizabeth	33	DE	9
Elizabeth	35	DE	229
Elizabeth	41	DE	54
Elizabeth	45	DE	64
Elizabeth	83	DE	9
Elizabeth	92	DE	181
Elizabeth A	18	DE	14
Elizabeth B	40	DE	45
Ellen F	29	DE	184
Emeline	15	DE	145
Francis	15	DE	45
Genet	31	DE	55
George	10	DE	17
George C	8/12	DE	187
George H	7	DE	150
George W	1	DE	38
Georgianna E	9	DE	56
Gideon	23	DE	44
Hester	5	DE	211
Hester	12	DE	75
Hester A	5	DE	45
Hetty	50	DE	36
Hetty A	36	DE	14
Hughett	12	DE	229
Isaac	33	DE	17
Jacob	12	DE	54
Jacob	35	DE	102
Jacob W	45	DE	199
James	8	DE	36
James	15	DE	225
James	27	DE	44
James	40	DE	150
James	64	DE	191
James E	9	DE	199
James H	49	DE	229
Jane	52	DE	160
Joe	50	DE	56
John	32	DE	9
John	37	DE	184
John	45	DE	64
John C	4	DE	146
John C	41	DE	222
John H	28	DE	191
John W	11	DE	160
Joseph H	10	DE	146
Joseph R	15	DE	179
Josephus A	23	DE	146
Joshua	25	DE	55
Joshua S	1	DE	17
Josiah	22	DE	93
Lemuel	40	DE	36
Lemuel A	5	DE	36
Prettyman, Levin	10	DE	222
Lidia H	19	DE	64
Liston H	9	DE	150
Louis	19	DE	56
Louisa W	21	DE	164
Lovenia	18	DE	145
Lovenia A	19	DE	161
Lovey	62	DE	63
Lovey E	14	DE	36
Lucy	43	DE	9
Lydia A	2	DE	187
Lydia A	52	DE	189
Lydia E	22	DE	191
Lydia G	10	DE	54
Lydia H	13	DE	187
Lydia M	3	DE	14
Margaret E	1	DE	187
Margaret E	2	DE	17
Margaret J	14	DE	14
Margaret J	21	DE	38
Martha B	15	DE	199
Mary	7	DE	222
Mary	23	DE	9
Mary	23	DE	188
Mary	29	DE	191
Mary	32	DE	187
Mary	33	DE	17
Mary	40	DE	37
Mary	45	DE	9
Mary	48	DE	222
Mary	52	DE	44
Mary	60	DE	191
Mary	70	DE	62
Mary A	4	DE	201
Mary A	7	DE	229
Mary A	16	DE	75
Mary Ann	23	DE	1
Mary C	15	DE	64
Mary C	18	DE	44
Mary E	3	DE	9
Mary E	12	DE	45
Mary H	8	DE	54
Mary J	11	DE	164
Mary J	13	DE	160
Mary J	23	DE	146
Mary V	9/12	DE	56
Milla	38	DE	164
Nancy	28	DE	146
Nancy	50	DE	17
Nancy	57	DE	184
Nancy S	2/12	DE	9
Nathan	17	DE	20
Nehemiah	10	DE	75
Nehemiah	62	DE	75
Olivianna	2	DE	187
Patience	55	DE	181
Percy	26	DE	68
Peter	10	DE	36
Peter	13	DE	10
R D	39	DE	201
Rachel	9	DE	293
Rachel	20	DE	68
Rachel	48	DE	75
Rachel	66	DE	145
Rebecca	14	DE	36
Robert	35	DE	146
Robert	35	DE	191
Robert	62	DE	191
Robert of W	57	DE	159
Sallie E	18	DE	45
Samuel	40	DE	37
Samuel T	1	DE	150
Sarah	7	DE	17
Sarah	12	DE	55
Sarah	25	DE	102
Sarah	46	DE	159
Sarah	48	DE	56
Sarah	53	DE	17
Sarah A	8	DE	9
Sarah A	31	DE	201
Sarah E	3	DE	146
Sarah E	15	DE	189
Prettyman, Sarah H	4	DE	15
Scarborough	36	DE	150
Stephen S	64	DE	17
Thomas	46	DE	9
Thomas E	9	DE	45
Thomas P	6	DE	150
Unice	3	DE	17
Winget	38	DE	164
William	28	DE	17
William	57	DE	189
William C	7	DE	14
William C	35	DE	38
William D	7	DE	160
William E	6	DE	10
William H	1/12	DE	17
William H	5	DE	187
William M	2	DE	68
William T	2	DE	184
William T	11	DE	179
William W	17	DE	189
Price, Mary	14	DE	49
Pride, Eliza J	10	DE	59
Elizabeth	16	DE	181
Elizabeth	40	DE	292
George	30	DE	16
George R	12	DE	181
Greensbury	50	DE	101
Harriet G	23	DE	1
James H	14	DE	181
James M	20	DE	59
Job	35	DE	2
John	26	DE	16
John	30	DE	14
John C	3	DE	59
John T	2	DE	181
Margaret H	6	DE	181
Martha S	5	DE	59
Mary	28	DE	41
Mary E	18	DE	58
Mary J	8	DE	181
Minty	24	DE	58
Nancy	12	DE	59
Nancy	60	DE	16
Nelly	35	DE	181
Rachel	65	DE	2
Robert D	10	DE	181
Ruth V	5/12	DE	59
Sarah	36	DE	101
Sarah M	20	DE	58
Selby	18	DE	35
Winget	40	DE	181
Zachariah	39	DE	58
Prince, Eliza A	--	DE	173
Pritchet, Daniel	17	DE	215
James	45	DE	252
Maria	30	DE	252
Mary C	3	DE	252
Theophilus C	2	DE	252
Proctor, Cornelia	31	DE	198
Elisha	30	DE	198
Elizabeth	9	DE	198
Pullet, Eliza	4	DE	164
Hetty J	1	DE	164
Mary	29	DE	164
Woolsey P	34	DE	164
Purnal, Adam	35	MD	260
Benjamin	10	DE	233
Caleb	1	DE	233
Denny	1	DE	260
Hetty	8	DE	233
Isaac	9	DE	233
Jane	45	DE	233
John	70	DE	233
Joseph	6	DE	233
Lemuel	30	MD	233
Mahala	2	DE	233
Mariah	7	DE	260
Mary	30	DE	234
Nancy	40	DE	234
Sarah	35	DE	260
Thomas	12	DE	65
Purnall, David C	16	DE	65

Name	Age	State	Page
Purnall, Mary	12	DE	65
Reuben	10	DE	65
William	14	DE	65
Purnel, Hannah	70	DE	37
Peter	16	DE	37
Purnell, Ann E	16	DE	7
Ann M	12	DE	37
Charles T	11	DE	7
David	9	DE	37
David S	13	DE	7
Eliza	27	DE	37
Jacob	7	DE	37
James T	45	MD	7
Lot	50	DE	37
Lydia H	2	DE	37
Mary R	41	DE	7
Mary S	3	DE	7
Sarah J H	7	DE	7
Pursey, Anna	25	DE	280
Rhoda	45	DE	280
Thomas	14	DE	280
Pusey, Anderson	35	DE	241
Angeline	7	DE	47
Benjamin S	7/12	DE	238
Cyrus	13	DE	294
E T	31	DE	238
Edward	8	DE	280
Eleanor	40	DE	293
Eleanor	57	DE	294
Eliza	17	DE	294
Eliza	39	DE	293
Eliza	44	DE	275
Eliza J	4	DE	241
Elizabeth A	26	DE	292
Emeline	24	DE	197
Ephraim H	38	DE	280
Gatty	8	DE	294
George	4	DE	294
George W	8	DE	241
Harry	25	DE	268
Henry	6	DE	197
Isaac	10	DE	294
Jacob	6	DE	294
James	49	DE	293
James E	9	DE	9
John	7	DE	293
John	10	DE	294
John	45	DE	275
John S	3	DE	241
John S	22	DE	171
Julia A	15	DE	294
Kingsbury	11	DE	280
Lavinia	4	DE	294
Lavinia P	1	DE	241
Louisa	10	DE	280
Margaret J	23	MD	238
Mary	5	DE	268
Mary	16	DE	294
Mary	38	DE	293
Mary A	22	DE	173
Nancy	18	DE	293
Nancy	30	DE	280
Nancy	33	DE	241
Nathaniel	12	DE	294
Puab	34	DE	197
Samuel	6	DE	294
Sarah	19	DE	293
Sarah E	3	DE	238
Sarah E	6	DE	241
Thomas	38	DE	268
Thomas J	1	DE	197
Wm H	18	DE	294
Pusy, Alexander	7	DE	286
Ann	24	DE	286
Eliza	26	DE	286
George	29	DE	287
George M	23	DE	286
James	18	MD	281
John J	35	DE	286
Louisa	4	DE	286
Martha	1	DE	286
Quillen, Ebe	14	DE	120
Elizabeth	48	DE	274
Ellen J	12	DE	120
Hetty A	36	DE	118
Hetty J	8	DE	144
John	25	DE	271
Joseph H	5	DE	118
Josiah	25	DE	274
Lacy C	1	DE	118
Lucy	44	DE	120
Mahala E	5	DE	118
Mariah	20	DE	271
Mary A	12	DE	118
Nathaniel	14	DE	120
Oakley	18	DE	274
Peter	40	DE	120
Robert	17	DE	120
Robert	40	DE	118
Sarah M	8	DE	118
William	12	DE	120
Ragly, Sally	12	DE	48
Ralph, Betsy	65	DE	241
Caroline	18	DE	249
Charles J	13	MD	253
David	6	DE	251
James	20	DE	242
Machelan	40	DE	257
Mary	62	DE	241
Nancy	41	DE	254
Nancy	72	DE	241
Phillis	1	DE	251
Phillis	70	DE	257
Polly	40	DE	249
Samuel	18	DE	251
Sarah A	3	DE	251
Sarah S	38	DE	251
Thomas	45	DE	254
Thomas Sr	79	DE	254
Thomas T	27	DE	257
William	20	DE	254
Wm	77	DE	254
Ratcliff, Alexzine	20	DE	82
Elizabeth	20	DE	88
Elizabeth	47	DE	107
Frances Ann	4	DE	88
James	20	DE	88
James H	21	DE	107
Jane	6	DE	107
John	49	DE	88
John W	9	DE	88
Nancy	44	DE	88
Nutter	21	DE	88
Nutter	48	DE	107
Rachael	15	DE	107
Rachael Ann	18	DE	88
Reuben	1	DE	88
Samuel	7	DE	88
William	18	DE	107
William W	24	DE	82
Ratliff, George	33	DE	7
Louisa	28	DE	7
Rawlins, Charles A	26	DE	107
David	7/12	DE	107
Henry	8	DE	105
James	28	DE	105
Judy	63	DE	106
Lot	63	DE	105
Philip	17	DE	105
Sabrey	20	DE	107
Thomas	8	DE	106
Thomas	19	DE	107
Thomas	24	DE	106
Record, Elizabeth	15	DE	48
Robert W	29	DE	42
Records, Alexander	23	DE	247
Anslem	25	DE	225
Baxter	22	DE	247
Bayla	22	DE	245
Benjamin	17	DE	225
Benjamin	28	DE	61
Catherine	12	DE	224
Records, Charles	8/12	DE	242
David H	5	DE	248
Edward W	2	DE	248
Elizabeth	10	DE	227
Elizabeth	13	DE	224
Elizabeth	19	DE	223
Elizabeth	28	DE	247
Elizabeth	43	DE	248
Ella	12	DE	230
Henry C	11	DE	248
Hester	7	DE	245
Hester	7	DE	247
Isaac	25	DE	247
James	24	DE	280
John R	22	DE	223
John T	19	DE	216
Jonathan T	9	DE	248
Joseph	13	DE	248
Joseph	25	DE	223
Joshua	25	DE	245
Joshua	23	DE	247
Mary	3	DE	286
Mary	24	DE	280
Mary A	19	DE	223
Mary D	17	DE	248
Mary E	13	DE	250
Phebe	25	DE	242
Samuel H	7	DE	248
Sarah	3	DE	280
Sarah	25	DE	250
Sarah E	1	DE	223
Temperance	53	DE	61
Thomas	9	DE	286
Thomas S	15	DE	248
Thomas W	43	DE	248
Unicy J	32	DE	286
Wesley	16	DE	215
William	6	DE	286
Wm	25	DE	250
Wm D	36	DE	286
Redden, Alcy	75	DE	291
Amelia	51	DE	240
Benjamin	33	DE	291
Cassa	20	DE	291
Emaline	21	DE	24
Harriet	30	DE	249
James	72	DE	24
John	28	DE	226
John H	24	DE	240
Joseph W	15	DE	3
Leven	22	DE	240
Margarett	46	DE	2
Mary	72	DE	24
Nancy J	2	DE	291
Nehemiah	45	DE	232
Samuel	19	DE	3
Samuel E	37	DE	42
Sarah	6/12	DE	249
Stephen	9	DE	291
Thomas	6	DE	212
Thomas	12	DE	3
Thomas	55	DE	240
Washington	30	DE	228
William H	18	DE	2
William O	43	DE	2
Wm T	3	DE	291
Reddick, Eliza	25	DE	167
John W	26	DE	167
Sarah E	2	DE	167
Reddin, Alfred	5	DE	3
Reed, Abraham	24	DE	26
Alexander	18	DE	41
Alfred	12	DE	41
Amelia	57	MD	216
Andrew J	6	DE	195
Ann	8	MD	227
Benjamin	42	DE	29
Cecily C	22	DE	41
Daniel	47	DE	220
Donovan	57	DE	26
Elenor	19	MD	220
Eliza	10	DE	66

Name	Age	St	Pg
Roach, Hester A	16	DE	208
Hester A	26	DE	201
Hetty	1	DE	27
Isabella	30	DE	200
Isabella	51	DE	201
James	10	DE	69
James	41	DE	66
James B	25	DE	23
James C	30	DE	25
Jane	19	DE	201
Jeremiah	21	DE	206
John	9	DE	53
John	13	DE	27
John	24	DE	69
John	25	DE	208
John	32	DE	63
Letitia	22	DE	63
Louisa	5	DE	212
Louisa	25	DE	25
Louisa	49	DE	157
Louisa Ann	2/12	DE	63
Margaret	22	DE	53
Maria J	1	DE	200
Mary	3	DE	69
Mary	10	DE	36
Mary A	5	DE	27
Mary A	14	DE	23
Mary E	2	DE	208
Mary H	4	DE	70
Mary J	10/12	DE	69
Mary J	10/12	DE	70
Nancy	24	DE	9
Nancy	52	DE	28
Rachel A	28	DE	70
Richard	78	DE	66
Robert	12	DE	53
Robert	14	DE	55
Robert	20	DE	73
Sarah	5	DE	149
Sarah	44	DE	53
Sarah J	3	DE	23
Sarah J	7	DE	27
Sarah M	35	DE	23
Stephen	40	DE	200
Susan	4	DE	27
Susan	29	DE	27
Theodore	2	DE	69
Thomas	18	DE	70
Thomas	50	DE	69
Thomas J	1	DE	70
Turpin	18	DE	206
William	9	DE	25
William	16	DE	53
William	16	DE	69
William	41	DE	26
William	51	DE	28
William C	9	DE	149
William E	8/12	DE	208
Wittington	45	DE	53
Robbins, Alice A	8	DE	26
Ann	74	DE	15
David	22	DE	24
David	35	DE	26
David	76	DE	15
David H	22	DE	15
Eliza	20	DE	15
Elizabeth	28	DE	24
Elizabeth	45	DE	15
Emaline	14	DE	24
Hannah	22	DE	15
James C	42	DE	15
James M	6	DE	26
Jane	24	DE	24
Jane B	38	DE	25
Jane C	3	DE	25
John	4	DE	26
John	69	DE	15
John P	30	DE	15
Jonah	2	DE	26
Joseph	19	DE	24
Joseph	65	DE	24
Lydia	33	DE	26
Robbins, Lydia B	59	DE	15
Lydia L	8	DE	25
Mary	55	DE	24
Mary C	2/12	DE	15
Mary J	26	DE	15
Sally A	2	DE	15
Sarah	32	DE	29
Sarah A	9	DE	15
Sarah H	11	DE	25
William	17	DE	24
William	33	DE	29
Robert, Charlotte	18	DE	256
Roberts, Geo M	24	MA	225
Hetty A	41	DE	142
James S	18	DE	142
John H	21	DE	143
Mary E	14	DE	143
William	50	DE	142
Robertson, William	31	DE	62
Robinson, Abraham	30	DE	171
Alexander	8	DE	225
Alfred	2	DE	27
Alfred	29	DE	171
Alfred P	8	PA	5
Alfred P	32	DE	5
Allen	9/12	DE	20
Amaretta	50	DE	53
Amelia	41	DE	27
Ann	4/12	DE	20
Ann C	8	DE	180
Ann E	6	DE	197
Anslem	40	DE	225
Anslum	5	DE	225
Benjamin	50	DE	51
Benjamin M	17	DE	194
Burton	18	DE	170
Caroline	21	DE	179
Cassandra M	12	DE	180
Cato	76	DE	42
Cedny	42	DE	225
Cesar	74	DE	194
Charity	14	DE	199
Charles	2	DE	165
Clara C	30	DE	5
David H	3	DE	192
Edward	1	DE	171
Eliza	28	DE	171
Eliza A	28	DE	197
Eliza A	29	DE	218
Elizabeth	2	DE	30
Elizabeth	10	DE	48
Elizabeth	19	DE	176
Emily	34	DE	48
Emma J	8/12	DE	48
Ennals	23	DE	56
George	7	DE	27
George	8	DE	125
George	10	DE	205
George	30	DE	193
George	53	DE	168
George J	12	DE	5
George W	9	DE	194
Hannah	40	DE	117
Harriet Ann	45	DE	51
Henrietta	2	DE	197
Henry	3	DE	171
Henry	28	DE	192
Henry	40	DE	74
Henry	50	DE	72
Hetty	30	DE	194
Hetty	61	DE	176
James	8	DE	48
James	13	DE	129
James	14	DE	117
James H	5/12	DE	218
James H B	1	DE	192
Jesse W	30	MD	197
John	11/12	DE	30
John	14	DE	27
John	57	DE	180
John T	5	DE	192
Joseph	4	DE	225
Robinson, Joseph	8	DE	117
Joseph	10	DE	19
Joshua	17	DE	168
Joshua	22	DE	117
Joshua B	9	DE	29
Joshua C	4/12	DE	191
Julia	30	DE	42
Kate A	8	DE	51
Ketty	15	DE	117
Louisa	19	DE	224
Louisa C	8	DE	179
Love	19	DE	117
Lovey	26	DE	225
Lucony	20	DE	3
Louisa	20	DE	218
Louisa	20	DE	29
Luisa	55	DE	53
Major	11	DE	27
Margaret	8	DE	172
Margaret A	6/12	DE	225
Margaret J	4	DE	218
Martha A	9	DE	27
Mary	6/12	DE	29
Mary A	5	DE	48
Mary C	10	DE	191
Mary C	1	DE	225
Mary E	25	DE	171
Mary E	13	DE	229
Mary P	41	DE	191
Mary S	50	DE	168
Milla	30	DE	225
Mitchel	38	DE	171
Moses	67	DE	3
Moses	4	DE	117
Nancy	27	DE	171
Nancy	5	DE	172
Nathaniel	15	DE	168
Nathaniel	62	DE	168
Nathaniel	4	DE	29
Nehemiah	70	DE	29
Paris	35	DE	194
Parker	11	DE	168
Peter	4	DE	194
Peter P	35	DE	209
Phillip	47	DE	3
Rachel	54	DE	168
Rachel	5	DE	218
Rebecca J	6	DE	30
Reuben T	38	DE	48
Robert	5	DE	225
Sarah A	28	DE	192
Sarah A	53	DE	179
Sarah R	2	DE	194
Solomon L	5	DE	171
Thomas	10	DE	5
Thomas	24	DE	193
Thomas	57	DE	27
Thomas	58	DE	179
Thomas	8	DE	191
Thomas B	5	DE	27
Thomas C	9	MD	197
Wilhamina	3	DE	30
William	7	DE	225
William	7	DE	176
William H	21	DE	194
William S	40	MD	197
William T	28	DE	218
Wm	85	DE	59
Rodes, Casar	71	DE	59
Caty	50	DE	59
Eliza	62	DE	59
John	8	DE	59
Matilda	5	DE	16
Rogers, Hetty	12	DE	16
Hetty	32	DE	16
Isaac	10	DE	16
John	6	DE	54
John P	40	DE	54
Lambert	12	DE	54
Mary J	27	DE	16
Sarah	8	DE	2
Rodney, Caleb	30	DE	286
Caroline			

Name	Age	St	Pg	Name	Age	St	Pg	Name	Age	St	Pg
Rodney, Daniel	52	DE	286	Rogers, Isaac B	1	DE	222	Rollin, Priscilla E	19	MD	206
David H	9/12	DE	1	Isaac H	18	DE	112	Rolstin, Jeremiah	60	MD	200
Edward L	12	DE	1	Jacob	10	DE	127	Roop, Dorothy	31	GE	35
Eliza L	13	DE	1	Jacob	40	DE	127	Henry	4	DE	35
George	52	DE	285	Jacob	45	DE	3	John M	36	GE	35
George W	10	DE	50	James E	13	DE	146	Lydia	4/12	DE	35
Hannah H	12	DE	50	Jane	25	DE	222	Mary	6	NY	35
Hetty	18	DE	10	Joel H	12	DE	146	Rose, Celia	2	DE	216
Jane	11	DE	286	John	21	DE	146	Celia	50	DE	111
Jane	18	DE	285	John	22	DE	125	Elizabeth	30	DE	216
Jane	40	DE	286	John	77	DE	146	Margaret	8	DE	216
Jessica	6	DE	1	John L	15	DE	141	Mary A	6	DE	216
John	24	DE	286	John P	6	DE	55	James B	4	DE	216
John	41	DE	60	John T	8	DE	146	John W	28	DE	216
John D	37	DE	1	John W	4	DE	147	Henry W	14	DE	204
John W	5	DE	286	John W	34	DE	147	Hester A	23	DE	217
Julia A	2	DE	285	Joshua	9	DE	128	Wm	31	DE	217
Keturah	46	DE	285	Joshua	33	DE	128	Ross, Caleb	9	DE	210
Keturah B	10	DE	1	Julia A B	19	DE	126	Caleb	26	DE	28
Margaretta A	5	DE	50	Laban O	62	DE	126	Caroline	6	DE	207
Mary	20	DE	286	Lafayetta	16	DE	2	Catherine	10	DE	213
Mary Ann	2	DE	295	Lambert	46	DE	55	Charles A	4	DE	208
Mary B	35	DE	50	Leah E	15	DE	146	Charles H	3	DE	213
Mary O	38	DE	1	Letty	44	DE	146	Clement	37	DE	208
Mary R	4	DE	1	Letty A	5	DE	146	Edgar E	5/12	DE	210
Mary R	8	DE	50	Lovenia E	2	DE	149	Elizabeth	26	DE	77
Nancy	39	DE	295	Lovenia E	46	DE	146	Elizabeth	28	DE	210
Nicholas R	38	DE	49	Loveny E	6/12	DE	146	Ellen	24	DE	53
Penelope H	43	DE	50	Margaret	17	DE	146	Emma	4	DE	207
Rebecca	69	DE	50	Margaret J	16	DE	146	Eunice	30	DE	207
Robert M	33	DE	286	Maria	38	DE	146	George H	6	DE	210
Sarah	15	DE	286	Martha J	13	DE	141	James J	4	DE	210
Sarah	17	DE	159	Mary	2	DE	128	Leonard	10	DE	208
Sarah	21	DE	285	Mary	8	DE	128	Leonard S	8	MD	208
Sarah F	82	DE	49	Mary	22	DE	147	Letitia	7	DE	210
Susan	6	DE	52	Mary A	17	DE	141	Lydia	18	DE	208
Susan P	3	DE	50	Mary D	42	DE	222	Maria	37	DE	208
Thomas O	7	DE	286	Mary J	12	DE	55	Martha	2	DE	275
Wm H	9	DE	286	Mary J	23	DE	146	Martha	17	DE	213
Roe, Elizabeth	37	DE	42	Mary P	12	DE	1	Mary	35	DE	213
Thomas R	2	DE	42	Mary S	9	DE	2	Mary E	1	DE	213
Rogers, Adelaide	4	DE	222	Mary W	22	DE	126	Matilda	43	DE	212
Adeline	23	DE	2	Matilda A	10	DE	146	Polly	67	DE	200
Alma C	11	DE	141	Milly A	13	DE	1	Rachael	4	DE	77
Annanias	1	DE	141	Minus	21	DE	146	Rachel	40	DE	275
Annanias	26	DE	126	Nancy	19	DE	128	Rebecca	75	DE	42
Asa W	1	DE	146	Nancy	31	DE	146	Robert W	3	DE	53
Bethana	31	DE	141	Nancy	20	DE	146	Sallie	71	DE	200
Caleb	21	DE	125	Nancy T W	15	DE	126	Samuel	40	DE	53
Clarissa A	6/12	DE	141	Nathaniel	13	DE	146	Samuel R	17	DE	53
Clarissa M	12	DE	126	Patience C	9	DE	146	Sarah	41	DE	42
Clarissa T	3	DE	1	Penelope W	6	DE	146	Sylva J	8	DE	208
Comfort	45	DE	124	Peter	1	DE	127	Theodore	2	DE	208
Comfort A	3	DE	127	Philip	50	DE	146	Thomas	52	DE	77
Curtis	7	DE	146	Robert	21	DE	5	Thomas G	8	DE	213
Curtis A	38	DE	146	Robert B	2	DE	146	William E	5	DE	213
Daniel	18	DE	146	Sarah	11	DE	3	Willie M	2	DE	210
Daniel	51	DE	146	Sarah	11	DE	146	Wm	43	DE	213
Eleanor	8	DE	146	Sarah	12	DE	125	Wm H	37	DE	210
Eliza	32	DE	1	Sarah	45	DE	2	Roten, Marianna	20	DE	95
Eliza C	11	DE	1	Sarah	46	DE	146	Robert	25	DE	95
Elizabeth	6	DE	127	Sarah A	2/12	DE	149	Thomas	27	DE	42
Elizabeth	25	DE	146	Sarah A	11	DE	146	Rowelton, Gustavus	17	DE	46
Elizabeth T	20	DE	112	Sarah C	21	DE	149	Rowland, Adeline M	37	DE	46
Emeline	4	DE	146	Sarah E	7	DE	1	Catherine	44	DE	47
Gatty	18	DE	125	Solomon	23	DE	133	David	8	DE	47
George	7	DE	2	Stephen	26	DE	146	David J	45	DE	47
George	19	DE	146	Thomas H	7	DE	146	Jacob A	30	DE	50
George	50	DE	146	Thomas T	41	MD	141	James	61	DE	50
George H	5	DE	146	Walter	1	DE	2	John S	5	DE	47
George P	10	DE	128	Walter G	9	DE	146	Joseph	15	DE	46
George W	19	DE	146	William	2	DE	141	Letty	34	DE	42
Greensbury	33	DE	1	William	6	DE	128	Louisa	7	DE	46
Greensbury A	8	DE	1	William	27	MD	141	Margaret	16	DE	46
Hannah	33	DE	127	William	53	DE	2	Mary A	13	DE	46
Hannah	41	MD	141	William A	2/12	DE	1	Mary A	15	DE	46
Harrison	14	DE	146	William F	3	DE	222	Sarah R	56	DE	50
Henrietta	28	DE	128	Winget	28	DE	149	Sarah S	35	DE	50
Henry	6	DE	144	Wm E	36	DE	222	Susan	28	DE	50
Hetty M	6	DE	141	Zippora	67	DE	146	Theodotia	11	DE	46
Isaac	4	DE	128	Rollin, Elizabeth	3/12	DE	206	Thomas	57	DE	46
Isaac	10	DE	125	John	25	DE	206	Rowlins, John	31	DE	230

Name	Age	St	No	Name	Age	St	No	Name	Age	St	No
Rowlins, Leah	29	DE	230	Rust, Amy	36	DE	29	Salmons, Eliza	4	DE	81
Margaret V	3	DE	230	Ann	25	DE	226	Eliza	35	DE	10
William	33	DE	230	Ann E	31	NY	234	Eliza	40	DE	99
Wm W	1	DE	230	Arcada	44	DE	185	Eliza	52	DE	182
Runnels, Alsey	14	DE	25	Caleb F	30	DE	234	Elizabeth	8	DE	11
Hetty	7	DE	25	Charles D	7	DE	223	Elizabeth	11	DE	10
James	16	DE	29	Charles H	17	DE	185	Elizabeth	27	DE	39
Mary A	10	DE	25	Charles N	8	DE	234	Francis J	2	DE	10
Russam, Eliza	40	DE	209	David L	11	DE	26	George	11	DE	177
Russel, Alfred	3	DE	52	Edward	22	DE	124	George D	12	DE	182
Alfred	24	DE	29	Elza	11	DE	223	Hetty	18	DE	29
Anna	7	DE	51	Eliza	18	DE	29	Hetty A	18	DE	36
Anna	26	DE	70	Eliza	37	DE	223	Isaac	35	DE	39
Betsy	3	DE	50	Eliza A	12	DE	29	James	23	DE	104
Catharine	19	DE	93	Eliza J	3	DE	185	James	33	DE	11
David	15	DE	29	Elizabeth T	15	DE	20	Jane	19	DE	106
Edward	20	DE	51	Ephraim	49	DE	124	Jane	35	DE	10
Edwin	19	DE	93	George	24	DE	124	Jane A	6	DE	81
Elias	37	DE	70	George A	5	DE	29	John	2	DE	174
Eliza	5	DE	94	George T	20	DE	20	John	8	DE	106
Ellen	30	DE	51	Harriet	50	DE	20	John	13	DE	177
Hester H	13	DE	52	James	21	DE	124	John	16	DE	10
Hetty	4	DE	3	James	34	DE	185	John	26	DE	85
James	10	DE	93	John	12	DE	223	John	50	KY	171
James	16	DE	83	John	28	DE	124	John P	36	DE	177
James R	5	DE	50	John B	24	DE	136	John S	50	DE	182
James R	37	DE	50	Julia A	1	DE	185	Johnson	13	DE	106
John	42	DE	94	Louisa	5	DE	185	Joseph	10	DE	106
John	50	DE	23	Luther D	6	DE	234	Josephine	4	DE	45
Joseph	58	DE	93	Lydia	27	DE	221	Letty	3/12	DE	177
Joshua	5/12	DE	70	Maria	48	DE	16	Lovey	6	DE	10
Louisa	36	DE	94	Maria E	7	DE	16	Lovey	40	DE	106
Lydia	8	DE	50	Margaret J	2	DE	185	Lovey	42	DE	30
Martha	10	DE	50	Mary	52	DE	37	Mary	30	DE	81
Martin	4	DE	93	Mary A	3	DE	224	Mary A	6	DE	36
Mary	24	DE	93	Mary A	7	DE	221	Mary A	6	DE	39
Mary	51	DE	16	Mary A	49	DE	124	Mary A	12	DE	10
Mary	58	DE	52	Mary C	14	DE	185	Mary Ann	25	DE	85
Mary	68	DE	29	Mary H	10	DE	185	Mary Ann	25	DE	104
Mary A	36	DE	50	Mary J	17	DE	20	Mary Jane	2	DE	104
Mary H	1	DE	50	Peter	46	DE	20	Matilda	1	DE	104
Mary J	21	DE	3	Peter A	21	DE	188	Miers	4	DE	39
Mary P	17	DE	51	Peter W	13	DE	20	Milly Ann	10	DE	11
Nancy	17	MD	209	Sarah	40	DE	223	Nancy	35	DE	177
Nancy	54	DE	54	Sarah E	21	DE	188	Patience D	25	DE	11
Rebecca	20	DE	94	Sarah H	37	DE	185	Robert	13	DE	36
Robert	69	DE	29	Sarah K	26	DE	185	Robert W	14	DE	177
Robert R	37	DE	52	Sylvester H	38	DE	29	Roland	23	DE	104
Sabrey	9	DE	94	Thomas	44	DE	185	Sarah	18	DE	45
Sallie	45	MD	219	Thomas B	13	DE	185	Sarah	54	DE	41
Samuel	5	DE	52	William B	42	DE	185	Sarah A	10	DE	182
Samuel	35	DE	29	William C	3	DE	234	Sarah C	1	DE	10
Sarah	4	DE	15	William H H	9	DE	185	Sarah S	9	DE	39
Sarah	14	DE	93	William T	6/12	DE	188	Short	9	DE	10
Theodore	8	DE	94	William T	9	DE	16	Theodore	4	DE	177
Thomas	19	DE	46	Woodman S	31	DE	37	Theophilus	4	DE	10
Warren	11	DE	23	Ryan, Ann	20	DE	108	Theophilus	42	DE	10
William	12	DE	50	David	22	DE	108	Thomas	76	DE	177
William	16	DE	94	Elisha E	29	MD	129	William	6	DE	106
William	22	DE	29	Elizabeth	14	DE	108	William	57	DE	36
William	73	DE	51	Elizabeth	40	DE	107	Wingate	40	DE	30
William N	20	DE	8	Elizabeth T	23	DE	129	Sammins, Benjamin W	7	DE	81
William P	40	DE	3	George	29	DE	97	Caleb W	23	DE	81
Russell, Adaline	16	DE	202	James	2	DE	97	Emeline	10	DE	81
Charles	5	DE	6	James	19	DE	108	George	14	DE	81
David	30	DE	15	Maria	20	DE	107	Mary E	19	DE	81
Edward	3	DE	6	Mary Ann	13	DE	97	Sarah	48	DE	81
Eliza	25	DE	15	Priscilla	23	DE	97	Sarah Ann	11	DE	81
George	4	DE	6	Ritty	40	DE	108	William	52	DE	81
Isaac	41	DE	6	Sarah A T	1	DE	129	William H	24	DE	81
James	11	DE	6	Thomas	17	DE	108	Sammons, Caleb	13	DE	55
Nancy	44	DE	6	Thomas	22	DE	45	Caleb	16	DE	47
Sally A	17	DE	6	William	2	DE	107	James	26	DE	54
Sarah A D	38	DE	202	William B	50	DE	108	Leah J	29	DE	54
Thomas	14	DE	202	William Jr	30	DE	107	Samon, Mary H	7	DE	185
William	14	DE	6	Salmons, Anna	18	DE	99	Samons, George C	5	DE	89
William	77	DE	3	Bolitha	46	DE	106	Julianna	5/12	DE	89
Russum, Ann	50	DE	218	Catharine	51	DE	36	Minus L	30	DE	89
Mitchel	40	DE	218	David	1	DE	99	Sarah Ann	30	DE	89
Rust, Absolem	7	DE	185	David R S	6	DE	11	Sarah C	2	DE	89
Absolem	41	DE	16	Edward	15	DE	106	Samson, Charles H	2	DE	154
Alexander	5	DE	185					Elizabeth	16	DE	225

Name	Age	State	No.	Name	Age	State	No.	Name	Age	State	No.
Samson, Ellen S	5	DE	225	Scott, Eleanor	43	DE	146	Serman, Isaac W	25	DE	232
Henry P	3	DE	225	Eliza	20	DE	145	James E	4	DE	236
James	31	DE	154	Eliza	20	DE	146	Lucinda	33	DE	236
Jannet	33	DE	154	Eliza E	20	DE	71	Hannah	50	DE	53
Luvisa J	3	DE	154	Elizabeth	7	DE	219	Shanklin, Celia A	11	DE	33
Margaret A B	36	DE	225	Elizabeth	7	DE	224	Eliza	35	DE	33
Mary B	55	DE	225	Elizabeth	27	DE	221	Joseph	38	DE	33
Phillip L	3/12	DE	225	Elizabeth	50	DE	127	July Ann	19	DE	3
Sarah P	14	DE	225	Eunice	67	DE	224	Mary	77	DE	49
William	41	DE	225	Evan	76	DE	224	Matilda	1	DE	33
William L	10	DE	225	Francis	14	DE	271	Robert	21	DE	3
Sanders, Charles C	45	DE	236	George	7	DE	113	Robert H	4	DE	33
Elizabeth	45	DE	239	George	12	DE	275	Sarah E	6	DE	33
Margaret	10	DE	239	George	39	DE	146	Shannon, John H	60	DE	227
Sallie A	52	DE	236	George W	1	DE	160	Mary	21	DE	250
Sarah A	22	DE	236	James	5	DE	113	Sharp, Abram	14	DE	95
Simon	45	DE	239	James	14	DE	275	Ada	46	DE	22
Thomas B	16	DE	236	James	49	DE	275	Ada J	8	DE	22
Sandhover, William	28	GE	200	James H	26	DE	71	Alexander	8	DE	107
Satefield, Archibald	51	DE	222	James M	6	DE	146	Andis	45	DE	159
Charlotte	10/12	DE	222	John	17	DE	224	Ann	70	DE	93
Charlotte S	58	DE	222	John	18	DE	226	Ann M	11	DE	78
John	10	DE	222	John	26	DE	198	Anna	69	DE	92
Mary C	7	DE	222	John V	41	DE	113	Asbury	14	DE	92
Matilda	12	DE	222	John W	14	DE	224	Beniah	38	DE	78
Sarah	9	DE	222	Levi	8	DE	275	Benton	30	DE	93
William	5	DE	222	Louisa	15	DE	145	Byard	45	DE	95
Saterfield, Mary	12	DE	75	Manain	4	DE	113	Caleb	9	DE	95
Mary	37	DE	61	Mary	35	DE	113	Celia	35	DE	226
Sathberry, Anna	45	DE	121	Mary	41	DE	160	Clandberry	51	DE	92
Edward	6	DE	121	Mary	46	DE	271	Clement	32	DE	95
Henry	50	DE	121	Mary J	14	DE	113	Clement	72	DE	95
Kitty A	14	DE	121	Matilda	23	DE	198	David	6	DE	90
Martha	45	DE	121	Mitchel	23	DE	275	David	9	DE	72
Martha P	11	DE	121	Mitchel	46	DE	160	Eli	17	DE	95
Peter T	2	DE	121	Nathaniel	19	DE	87	Eliza	10	DE	92
Satterfield, Harriet	21	DE	98	Noah	25	DE	221	Eliza	42	DE	92
James	26	DE	98	Purnell	23	DE	33	Elizabeth	14	DE	95
John	12	DE	98	Robert E	2/12	DE	71	Elizabeth	33	DE	90
Mary Ann	24	DE	98	Sally	8	DE	271	Elizabeth	40	DE	95
William	16	DE	98	Sarah	18	DE	275	Emily	44	DE	12
William	20	DE	98	Sarah	33	DE	224	Frances Ann	7	DE	94
Saulsbury, Anna S	25	DE	8	Sarah	47	DE	275	George	17	DE	107
Williard	30	DE	8	Thomas	16	DE	137	Henry	14	DE	12
Saunders, Andrew	10	DE	104	Thomas	16	DE	275	Henry	43	DE	22
Amy	48	DE	104	Thomas	17	DE	113	Hester	45	DE	107
Catharine	23	DE	45	Thomas J	3	DE	71	Hetty	49	DE	181
Charles	7	DE	45	Walter	17	DE	41	Isaac	13	DE	27
Cornelius	21	DE	239	William	21	DE	33	Jacob	5	DE	27
Elizabeth A	3	DE	238	William	21	DE	275	James	55	DE	181
Harriet E	23	DE	238	William	47	DE	271	James S	35	DE	94
Henry L	1	DE	238	Zachariah	56	DE	33	Jane	16	DE	249
John	25	DE	238	Schribner, Ann	70	DE	83	Jane	25	DE	21
John	74	DE	54	Elizabeth	18	DE	83	Jesse	10	DE	90
John D	3	DE	45	Elizabeth	34	DE	83	Jesse	19	DE	92
John Jr	33	DE	45	John W	41	DE	83	Job	4	DE	90
Lucinty	16	DE	104	William A	32	DE	83	Job	14	DE	90
Milford	51	DE	104	Sedgwick, Charlotte	42	DE	225	Job	39	DE	40
Oscar	1	DE	45	Daniel	11	DE	225	Job	66	DE	92
Thomas	7	DE	104	George	6	DE	225	Job	68	DE	93
Savage, Elisha	56	MD	262	John	14	DE	225	John	4	DE	21
Elizabeth	8	DE	262	John	55	DE	225	John	12	DE	93
Harrison	10	DE	262	Joseph	21	DE	225	John	50	DE	27
Isaac	5	DE	262	William	2	DE	225	John P	3	DE	27
Jane	13	DE	262	Willis	9	DE	225	John W	14	DE	90
Lovey	3	DE	262	Seaborn, Edwin	5	DE	233	Jonathan	20	DE	21
Mary	13	DE	262	Selby, Daly	22	DE	133	Jonathan J T	10	DE	22
Mary J	14	DE	50	Elijah	10	DE	66	Joseph	30	DE	95
Nelly	46	DE	262	Isaac	21	MD	196	Joshua	35	DE	107
Schillinger, John	7	DE	50	Jane	3/12	DE	133	Josiah	15	DE	22
Stratton B	4	DE	50	Jane C	10	DE	133	Kinsey J	5	DE	22
Susan	36	DE	50	Josiah	28	MD	133	Leah	25	DE	95
Susan H	1	DE	50	Margaret	7	DE	133	Margaret	40	DE	92
Thomas E	16	DE	50	Nathaniel	22	MD	128	Mariah	42	DE	21
William	11	DE	50	Samson	58	MD	133	Mary	11	DE	90
William	40	DE	50	Sarah	45	DE	133	Mary	16	DE	95
Schock, Charles	36	GE	226	Sarah C	12	DE	133	Mary	30	DE	93
Scott, Ann M	14	DE	127	Sarah E	20	DE	196	Mary	39	DE	22
Curtis	1	DE	221	Sarah M	5	DE	133	Mary	46	DE	3
Curtis	35	DE	224	Williard S	2	DE	133	Mary	79	DE	22
Curtis W	9	DE	113	William C	3	DE	133	Mary Ann	9	DE	92
Ebby	22	DE	275	Serman, Caleb	12	DE	233	Mary E	6	DE	27

Name	Age	State	No.	Name	Age	State	No.	Name	Age	State	No.
Sharp, Mary J	5	DE	92	Shockley, Cyrus	48	DE	78	Short, Ann	50	DE	102
Matilda	40	DE	95	David H	4	DE	5	Anna	27	DE	147
Molly	3	DE	21	David W	21	DE	67	Arpha	35	DE	147
Nancy	3	DE	90	Edward	5	DE	5	Arpha A	5	DE	147
Nancy	79	DE	92	Edward C	7	DE	163	Asbury	14	DE	146
Nathaniel	15	DE	12	Elias	10/12	DE	26	Caldwell	8	DE	148
Nehemiah	8	DE	90	Elias	27	DE	67	Caleb	14	DE	151
Nehemiah	36	DE	90	Elias	56	DE	76	Caroline	10	DE	148
Noah	18	DE	107	Elijah	16	DE	163	Castilia J	1	DE	215
Patience	8	DE	92	Eliza E	5	DE	261	Catherine	3/12	DE	26
Priscilla	5/12	DE	27	Elizabeth	5	DE	83	Catherine	10	DE	102
Priscilla	6	DE	94	Elizabeth	7	DE	74	Catherine W	22	DE	148
Priscilla	35	DE	27	Elizabeth	8	DE	28	Charles	6	DE	154
Purnel	48	DE	92	Frances Ann	10	DE	82	Comfort	47	DE	174
Rachel	10	MD	212	George	18	DE	70	Daniel	26	DE	102
Rhoda D	30	DE	78	George	18	DE	76	Daniel	60	DE	102
Roland	3/12	DE	78	Hannah A	21	DE	68	Daniel E	31	DE	215
Rosina	6	DE	95	Henry	30	DE	86	Edward	36	DE	147
Sallie	6	DE	95	Henry	31	DE	89	Edward	42	DE	30
Samuel	4	DE	94	Hesekiah W	16	DE	163	Elena	23	DE	279
Sarah	18	DE	95	Hester J	4	DE	70	Elena A	17	DE	147
Sarah	41	DE	94	James	35	DE	74	Eli	6	DE	147
Silas	6	DE	92	Jeremiah	2	DE	26	Elias T	25	DE	169
Theophilus	2	DE	93	John	14	DE	67	Eliza	7/12	DE	102
Thomas	19	DE	95	John	38	DE	5	Eliza	10	DE	29
Thomas	22	DE	95	John M	17	DE	70	Eliza	16	DE	289
William	2	DE	90	Jonathan	8	DE	5	Eliza A	16	DE	4
William	4	DE	78	Joseph H	5	DE	26	Elizabeth	2	DE	147
William	10	DE	90	Kendle B	12	DE	76	Elizabeth	6	DE	102
William	13	DE	31	Lemuel	12	DE	76	Elizabeth	9	DE	159
William	14	DE	95	Lemuel	35	DE	82	Elizabeth	18	DE	49
William	15	DE	107	Lemuel	56	DE	76	Elizabeth	29	DE	102
William	38	DE	95	Letty J	33	DE	26	Elizabeth	36	DE	151
William E	12	DE	22	Levenia	21	DE	216	Elizabeth	62	MD	7
Shaster, John	8	DE	51	Lydia J	17	DE	67	Elizabeth	74	DE	157
Shatt, James	11	DE	291	Martha	9	DE	164	Elizabeth R	1	DE	159
Shepherd, Charlotte	24	DE	214	Mary	16	DE	78	Emeline	3	DE	281
Edith	17	DE	67	Mary	25	DE	86	Emeline	15	DE	51
James	22	DE	67	Mary	26	DE	89	Esther	20	DE	7
John	25	DE	214	Mary E	5	DE	67	Esther	70	DE	148
Joseph	22	DE	68	Matilda	13	DE	67	Francis	2	DE	102
Mary	40	DE	67	Mealy	9	DE	26	Francis	84	DE	159
Mary A	25	DE	67	Nancy	53	DE	67	Francis W	5	DE	168
Sarah	21	DE	177	Peter D	45	MD	163	George	4	DE	105
William	56	DE	67	Philis	65	DE	78	George	7	DE	154
Sherdon, Eleanor	51	DE	166	Purnel	26	DE	85	George Ann	4	DE	148
John	36	DE	166	Robert H	2	DE	70	George W	7	DE	148
Philip	11	DE	166	Robert H	3	DE	74	Gilley G	63	DE	102
Sherman, George	37	DE	17	Robinson	28	DE	68	Gilly	30	DE	102
George W	1	DE	17	Rhoda A	7	DE	67	Gilly M	24	DE	102
John	11	DE	286	Samuel	6/12	DE	74	Hannah	1	DE	146
John	25	DE	17	Sarah	15	DE	70	Hannah	8	DE	276
Mary	68	DE	17	Sarah	24	DE	71	Hannah	13	DE	159
Mary E	8	DE	17	Sarah	46	MD	163	Hannah	74	DE	160
Sarah	37	DE	17	Sarah E	1	DE	68	Hannah A	10/12	DE	9
Thomas S	4	DE	17	Shelly	12	DE	163	Henry	5	DE	276
Sherwood, Deborah	51	DE	229	Stephen	2	DE	67	Henry	9	DE	81
Shields, Bartly	11	DE	269	Susan	4	DE	74	Henry	12	DE	154
David	50	DE	269	Susan	32	DE	82	Henry	12	DE	159
George	8	DE	269	Susan	65	DE	5	Henry C	3	DE	168
Laura	3	DE	269	Susan C	10	DE	5	Hester A	5	MD	215
Louisa	5	DE	269	Thomas	20	DE	70	Hester A	8	DE	147
Mary	40	DE	269	Thomas L	20	DE	163	Hester A	13	DE	169
Shiffield, Patrick	23	IE	230	William P	19	DE	216	Hester A	15	DE	148
Shiles, Hester	49	DE	203	William V	33	DE	67	Hetty	15	DE	295
Shiply, Celia	17	MD	201	Wilson	23	DE	67	Hiram S	25	DE	148
J P H	28	MD	201	Wilson	60	DE	67	Hurman	12	DE	152
William J	1	DE	201	Shockly, Clement	55	DE	223	Isaac	11	DE	293
Shock, Alcia D	4/12	DE	226	Dinah	55	DE	223	Isaac	14	DE	107
Emila P	3	MD	226	Levinia	21	DE	217	Isaac	25	DE	289
Sarah	40	DE	226	Short, Agnes	5	DE	102	Isaac	42	DE	285
Shockley, Alfred T	1	DE	6	Alfred	33	DE	81	Isaac W	27	DE	147
Ann	3	DE	68	Alicy	8	DE	289	James	2	DE	148
Ann	30	DE	74	Allen	34	DE	4	James	5	DE	103
Ann E	19	DE	67	Alta	75	DE	163	James	10	DE	148
Barsheba	1	DE	82	Amanda J	16	DE	169	James	13	DE	174
Catharine	28	DE	67	Amy	37	DE	4	James	23	DE	295
Catharine	51	DE	70	Ann	9	DE	102	James	25	DE	102
Charity	51	DE	76	Ann	24	DE	102	James	40	DE	170
Charles	35	DE	26	Ann	29	DE	168	James C	18	DE	169
Charles W	5	DE	68	Ann	30	DE	266	James E	2	DE	42
Charlotte	32	DE	5	Ann	36	DE	147	James E	4	DE	147

Name	Age		No.	Name	Age		No.	Name	Age		No.
Short, James T	14	DE	107	Short, Nathaniel	46	DE	107	Short, Winget	10	DE	147
Jane	28	DE	147	Nathaniel W	3	DE	4	Winget	60	DE	154
Jane	51	DE	155	Neomy	21	DE	295	Woolsey	24	DE	154
Jerry	30	DE	237	Nutter	40	DE	29	Zippora	7	DE	147
John	3	DE	81	Obadiah W	20	DE	169	Showell, David	25	DE	189
John	3	DE	102	Painter A	13	DE	9	Mary	60	DE	115
John	9	DE	147	Patience	38	DE	285	Sarah	27	DE	189
John	11	DE	105	Peter	34	DE	147	Sarah H	8/12	DE	189
John	18	DE	148	Peter R	2	DE	147	Siley, George	30	MD	260
John	32	DE	102	Phebe	25	DE	29	Margaret	25	DE	260
John	40	DE	281	Philip	3	DE	174	Simmons, Julia	10	DE	55
John	48	DE	36	Philip	9	DE	147	Mary	40	DE	55
John B	27	DE	279	Philip	6	DE	168	Simpler, Alfred	9	DE	58
John C	21	DE	102	Philip	32	DE	159	Amanda A	10	DE	88
John E	15	DE	30	Philip	42	DE	168	Amos	40	DE	194
John H	5	DE	147	Philip	55	DE	169	Andrew E W	3	DE	26
John H	5	DE	151	Philip R	9	DE	170	Andrew J	21	DE	185
John H	25	DE	295	Philip of J	62	DE	295	Arcada	57	DE	185
John M	30	DE	148	Philip of N	23	DE	295	Arrena M	17	DE	185
John R	9	DE	169	Priscilla	27	DE	102	Barbary	1	DE	53
John S	1	DE	154	Purnal	60	DE	147	Benjamin	14	DE	146
John S	2	DE	148	Purnel	39	DE	102	Burton	31	DE	53
John S	28	DE	105	Purnel	43	DE	9	Caleb M	1/12	DE	20
John T	2	DE	158	Rachel	10	DE	168	Charles H	4	DE	58
Joseph	27	DE	277	Rachel	40	DE	174	Clara S	10/12	DE	26
Juel M	12	DE	147	Rachel	61	DE	172	Clowy	4	DE	53
Julia	2	DE	105	Rebecca	21	DE	26	Coard	42	DE	116
Julia A	23	DE	169	Robert	5	DE	174	David	6	DE	53
Julia Ann	45	DE	107	Ruben	5	DE	168	David	16	DE	50
Julia J	10	DE	4	Saborah	25	DE	148	David	20	DE	176
Lavenia	48	DE	295	Sally	22	DE	102	David	30	DE	88
Leah	6/12	DE	279	Samson	6	DE	174	David	44	DE	53
Leah A	1	DE	147	Samuel	3/12	DE	102	David	71	DE	50
Leonard	11	DE	147	Samuel	7	DE	102	David H	30	DE	185
Letty	20	DE	281	Samuel	17	DE	204	David M	4	DE	185
Letty A	23	DE	154	Samuel	28	DE	102	David R	12	DE	50
Levi	51	DE	159	Sarah	6/12	DE	295	Eli	22	DE	54
Levi	69	DE	277	Sarah	8/12	DE	105	Elias T	8	DE	123
Louisa	16	DE	150	Sarah	3	DE	266	Eliza	24	DE	26
Lucinda	6/12	DE	102	Sarah	3	DE	279	Eliza	38	DE	53
Lurana	17	DE	151	Sarah	9	DE	295	Eliza A	14	DE	185
Lurany	60	DE	148	Sarah	10	DE	146	Eliza J	11	DE	16
Luther	30	DE	30	Sarah	13	DE	102	Eliza J	24	DE	20
Luthy	50	DE	174	Sarah	22	DE	159	Elizabeth	9	DE	116
Lydia A	20	DE	46	Sarah	23	DE	289	Elizabeth	20	DE	185
Manaen	36	DE	148	Sarah	40	DE	168	Elizabeth	26	DE	13
Maranda	35	DE	161	Sarah	51	DE	159	Elizabeth	40	DE	185
Margaret	22	DE	148	Sarah	56	DE	295	Elizabeth A	3	DE	176
Margaret	31	DE	81	Sarah A	16	DE	147	Elizabeth N	28	DE	123
Margaret J	1	DE	168	Sarah A	19	DE	168	Emaline	35	DE	26
Maria	6	DE	102	Sarah J	15	DE	174	Emily	27	DE	53
Maria	9	DE	154	Selby H	1	DE	168	Emma C	5	DE	26
Maria	21	DE	102	Shadrach	1	DE	281	Fletcher L	9	DE	194
Maria	21	DE	296	Shadrach	18	DE	289	George	7	DE	88
Maria	34	DE	102	Solomon	61	DE	295	George	25	DE	85
Maria H	7/12	DE	147	Stanley	1	DE	154	George W F	1	DE	185
Martha	18	DE	295	Stansbury	24	DE	155	Gideon J	31	DE	192
Mary	5	DE	81	Stephen E	14	DE	169	Hannah B	3	DE	186
Mary	12	DE	174	Susanna	16	DE	179	Henry	22	DE	149
Mary	13	DE	168	Thomas	8	DE	174	Henry D	8	DE	178
Mary	20	DE	279	Thomas	19	DE	189	Hetty	23	DE	34
Mary	47	DE	154	Thomas W	1/12	DE	147	Isaac	26	DE	13
Mary	52	DE	169	Thomas W	31	DE	147	James	65	DE	185
Mary	60	DE	116	Thos	27	DE	296	James B	27	DE	185
Mary A	2	DE	26	Torbert	5	DE	175	James H	2	DE	185
Mary E	3	DE	215	Truman	12	DE	151	James M	22	DE	178
Mary E	6	DE	4	Uriah	32	DE	289	Jane R	30	DE	192
Mary J	7	DE	147	Vestates	2	DE	168	John C	17	DE	26
Mary P	9	DE	9	Vina	14	DE	147	John H	3	DE	194
Matilda	37	DE	215	William	7	DE	81	John H	9	DE	185
Miller	9	DE	159	William	16	DE	146	John of J	25	DE	20
Minos	22	DE	289	William	16	DE	148	Joseph	18	DE	15
Minus	6	DE	29	William	17	DE	168	Joshua	16	DE	88
Moses	54	DE	155	William	19	DE	159	Josiah	35	DE	186
Nancy	1	DE	289	William	29	DE	26	Leah E	6	DE	16
Nancy	25	DE	277	William	41	DE	266	Leah H	22	DE	176
Nancy	28	DE	105	William A	32	DE	168	Leah J	8	DE	186
Nancy	40	DE	148	William H	4	DE	168	Lovey	23	DE	185
Nancy	42	DE	289	William H	14	DE	9	Lydia	7/12	DE	26
Nancy	43	DE	1	William J	5	DE	148	Lydia	40	DE	20
Nancy	46	DE	9	William S	44	DE	7	Lydia H	7	DE	185
Nancy	47	DE	146	William T	5	DE	267	Lurena	52	DE	185

Name	Age	State	No.	Name	Age	State	No.	Name	Age	State	No.
Simpler, Manaen S	25	DE	185	Smallwood, Eliza	17	MD	126	Smith, Hetty	70	DE	238
Margaret	11	DE	53	Elizabeth	38	DE	129	Isaac	6	DE	99
Martha	27	MD	116	Gatty	47	MD	126	Isaac	27	DE	287
Martha	35	DE	16	James	24	MD	126	Israel	6	DE	103
Mary	19	DE	54	Littleton	11	DE	126	Jacob	3	DE	103
Mary	42	DE	178	Rhoda	22	MD	126	Jacob	5	DE	80
Mary A	43	DE	194	Samson	8	DE	126	Jacob	8	DE	198
Mary A	3	DE	185	Samson	57	MD	126	Jacob	35	DE	200
Mary A	7	DE	58	Sarah	19	MD	126	Jacob	49	DE	103
Mary D	6	DE	26	Smart, Alexander	23	DE	18	Jacob E	8	DE	230
Mary E	2	DE	13	Elizabeth	51	DE	24	James	3	DE	103
Mary J	14	DE	176	Smith, Alfred	40	DE	201	James	7	DE	105
Mary P	10	DE	186	Ally	50	DE	231	James	8	DE	103
Matilda A	3/12	DE	16	Amelia	6	DE	201	James	11	DE	198
Matilda A	9	DE	53	Amelia	6	DE	287	James	23	DE	287
Peter	26	DE	20	Andrew	28	DE	230	James H	14	DE	197
Peter R	55	DE	185	Angeline G M D	6	DE	195	James H	3	MD	203
Roland P	4	DE	194	Ann	26	DE	103	James H	4	DE	296
Sally	32	DE	33	Ann	32	MD	203	James T	3	DE	55
Sally E	12	DE	26	Ann	42	DE	91	James T	6	DE	230
Samuel M	23	DE	26	Ann M	11	DE	99	Jane	26	DE	205
Sarah	7	DE	16	Anna J	38	DE	195	Jane	30	DE	229
Sarah	27	DE	185	Arpy	4	DE	99	Jesse	9	DE	106
Sarah	33	DE	186	Asa	11	DE	107	Joanna	7	DE	103
Sarah C	6	DE	186	Benjamin	26	DE	264	Job	11	DE	89
Sarah J	18	DE	178	Benjamin	49	DE	166	John	2/12	DE	103
Susana	52	DE	186	Benjamin	55	DE	76	John	2	DE	264
Susana E	3	DE	192	Brittania	31	DE	104	John	4	DE	215
Theodore T	15	DE	194	Chalton	7	DE	99	John	6	DE	217
Thomas O	4/12	DE	185	Chalton	13	DE	107	John	7	DE	91
Thomas S	42	DE	123	Chalton	44	DE	99	John	8	DE	264
William	24	DE	58	Charles	64	DE	200	John	17	DE	103
William	48	DE	176	Charles J	42	MD	203	John	19	DE	287
William E	17	DE	16	Charlotte	28	DE	230	John	30	DE	228
William G	17	DE	194	Daniel	17	DE	231	John	37	DE	103
William H	40	DE	16	Daniel	28	DE	264	John	70	DE	59
Simpson, Ann	50	DE	221	David	1	DE	105	John A	4	DE	218
Benjamin	54	DE	221	David	6	DE	103	John A	7	DE	59
Henrietta	25	DE	227	David	6	DE	106	John B	36	DE	200
James	24	DE	221	David	42	DE	218	John H	13	DE	207
John	33	DE	215	David	50	DE	42	John S	38	DE	296
Mahala	66	DE	227	David	53	DE	80	Joseph	7	DE	296
Margaret	25	DE	215	David E	1	DE	217	Joseph	22	DE	287
Rebecca	20	DE	221	David R	8	DE	51	Joseph	67	DE	236
Sarah	23	DE	215	David R	30	DE	105	Joseph A	11/12	DE	203
Sarah	32	DE	227	David R	32	DE	91	Joseph A	27	DE	287
William	14	DE	221	Eben	12	DE	290	Josephus	1	DE	103
Wm B	31	DE	227	Edward B	13	DE	2	Josiah S	42	DE	107
Wm M	64	DE	227	Eli	25	DE	103	Judy	40	DE	7
Sipple, Anna E	11/12	DE	2	Eliza	1	DE	201	Julia A	31	DE	200
Caleb B	41	DE	2	Eliza	11	DE	218	Julius	37	DE	229
Edgar R	4	DE	2	Eliza	57	DE	231	Kendal	27	DE	104
George Ellen	8	DE	2	Eliza J	9	DE	287	Kitty	29	DE	106
Henrietta	28	DE	239	Elizabeth	6/12	DE	287	Lawrenson	25	DE	231
Hester	40	DE	92	Elizabeth	9	DE	79	Leah	35	DE	215
James	1	DE	239	Elizabeth	16	DE	215	Lemuel	21	DE	99
James	60	DE	92	Elizabeth	16	DE	228	Lemuel	54	DE	99
James W	10	DE	2	Elizabeth	25	DE	79	Levi	65	DE	103
John M	12	DE	2	Elizabeth	26	DE	218	Levin	9	DE	275
John T	4	DE	239	Elizabeth	30	DE	264	Levin	12	DE	103
Julia	15	DE	230	Elizabeth	68	DE	264	Littleton	25	DE	103
Julia J	5	DE	239	Elizabeth H	14	DE	181	Lovenia	25	DE	264
Maria	50	DE	236	Elizabeth K	1	DE	236	Lovey	18	DE	105
Martha	15	DE	236	Elizabeth M	43	DE	181	Luraney	38	DE	201
Mary A	27	DE	2	Ezekiel	45	DE	106	Lydia	27	NJ	236
Mary A	28	DE	2	Garrett	1	DE	91	Mahala	50	DE	210
Nancy	5	DE	92	Gatty E	22	DE	281	Major	12	DE	195
Robert	32	DE	277	George	1	DE	104	Major	19	DE	197
Robert	56	DE	236	George	1	DE	225	Major	40	DE	215
Rosanna	6	DE	2	George	2	DE	264	Margaret	3	DE	107
Sarah E	7	DE	92	George	5	DE	91	Margaret	7	DE	106
Thomas B	35	DE	2	George	7	DE	99	Margaret	14	DE	99
William	2	DE	92	George	14	DE	104	Margaret	27	MD	225
Wm	31	DE	239	George	80	DE	238	Margaret	35	DE	107
Skidmore, Henry	33	DE	37	George E H	3/12	DE	236	Margaret A	4/12	DE	216
Mary	11/12	DE	37	Gray	7	DE	107	Margaret A	12	DE	181
Sarah	34	DE	37	Hannah	12	DE	99	Marshal	33	DE	264
Smallen, Elijah	4	DE	226	Henrietta	5	MD	203	Martha	12	DE	215
Elinor	30	DE	226	Henry	23	DE	225	Martha A	8	DE	195
Elizabeth	2	DE	226	Henry H	35	DE	106	Martin	13	MD	203
Joseph	19	DE	226	Hester	1	DE	103	Marvel	17	DE	99
Whittington	51	MD	226	Hester	3	DE	7	Mary	7/12	DE	107

Name	Age	St	Page
Smith, Mary	4	DE	105
Mary	10	DE	229
Mary	11	DE	103
Mary	18	DE	46
Mary	18	DE	103
Mary	25	DE	55
Mary	30	DE	9
Mary	30	DE	106
Mary	37	DE	89
Mary	37	DE	103
Mary	48	DE	197
Mary	76	DE	41
Mary A	9	DE	218
Mary Ann	14	DE	99
Mary Ann	35	DE	99
Mary E	1	DE	99
Mary E	6	DE	89
Mary E	35	DE	2
Mary J H	2	DE	230
Mary W	9	DE	181
Mathew	29	DE	55
Milly	5	DE	103
Milly	43	DE	103
Minos	16	DE	290
Miranda	5	DE	104
Mitchel	28	DE	9
Nancy	35	DE	217
Nancy	43	DE	290
Nancy	59	MD	199
Nancy	63	DE	200
Peter	2	DE	80
Peter	40	DE	80
Phillip N	11	DE	2
Polly	2	DE	106
Prittyman	21	DE	99
Purnel	4	DE	103
Rachel	60	DE	7
Rachel	62	DE	89
Rebecca	62	DE	104
Rebecca J	12	DE	59
Reginia	9	DE	91
Reuben	45	DE	7
Rhoda A	33	DE	296
Robert	14	DE	99
Robert	49	DE	99
Robert M	8	DE	76
Robert M	59	DE	287
Rufus	13	DE	103
Ruth	50	DE	59
Sallie	14	DE	215
Sally	18	DE	103
Sallie Ann	34	DE	99
Sampson	25	DE	281
Samuel	10	DE	166
Samuel	12	DE	104
Samuel	17	DE	104
Samuel	24	DE	79
Sarah	5	DE	201
Sarah	5	DE	264
Sarah	30	DE	80
Sarah	33	MD	264
Sarah	48	DE	166
Sarah	48	DE	287
Sarah A	7	DE	89
Sarah A	19	DE	147
Sarah E	15	DE	2
Silas	50	DE	181
Silas J	6	DE	181
Susan	13	DE	287
Susan A	4	DE	89
Susanna J	2	DE	181
Tabitha	33	DE	104
Theophilus	1	DE	9
Walter	9	MD	203
Wesly	53	DE	231
William	8/12	DE	79
William	2	DE	89
William	3	DE	103
William	9	DE	105
William	13	DE	215
William	16	DE	99
William	19	DE	99
Smith, William	21	DE	83
William	21	DE	89
William	32	DE	264
William	38	DE	89
William	45	DE	104
William E	2	DE	225
William F	15	DE	34
William H	12	DE	230
William H	16	DE	197
William H	55	DE	197
Wm H	2	DE	218
Smithers, Caroline E	1	DE	32
Mary J	20	DE	32
William A	24	DE	32
Sorden, Almira	7	DE	211
David	50	DE	14
Edward	21	DE	215
Elizabeth	2	DE	227
Frances	50	DE	14
George	20	DE	218
Henry	28	DE	230
Jane	17	DE	220
John	42	DE	225
Joshua	2	DE	229
Julia	75	DE	227
Lewis C	2	DE	217
Margaret	3/12	DE	220
Martha J	3	DE	230
Nancy	26	DE	230
Rebecca A	1	DE	230
Rhoda	4	DE	217
Sinah	39	DE	225
Sourden, Leah	9	DE	24
Samuel A	9	DE	24
Spanish, Eliza	3	DE	108
Elizabeth	4	DE	108
John	1	DE	108
John	38	DE	108
Letitia	5	DE	108
Sarah	29	DE	108
William	6	DE	108
Spaulding, Catherine	33	DE	7
George M	5	DE	7
Joseph T	1	DE	7
Joseph W	54	DE	7
Spear, George W	3	DE	204
James P	17	DE	204
John H	36	DE	204
Louisa A	9	DE	204
Lovy H	1	DE	204
Maria J	11	DE	204
Sarah C	5	DE	204
Sarah E	35	DE	204
Wm T	7	DE	204
Speer, Charles	13	DE	248
Curtis	56	DE	291
David	1	DE	248
Dolly	35	DE	274
Edward	12	DE	291
John	8	DE	291
Lovey	6	DE	291
Mahala	10	DE	291
Mary Ann	18	DE	248
Sarah	4	DE	291
Sarah	34	DE	291
Tilghman	1	DE	291
Tilghman	30	DE	274
Tilghman	74	DE	274
Spence, Elizabeth	9	DE	228
Henry	11	DE	228
Margaret	7	DE	228
Mary A	32	DE	228
Mary E	23	DE	203
William	18	DE	203
Spencer, Benjamin	12	DE	243
Celia	33	DE	245
Charles	7	DE	78
Donovan	66	DE	78
Edward	3	DE	286
Elizabeth	30	DE	243
Elizabeth	66	DE	224
Elizabeth E	6	DE	243
Spencer, George H	8	DE	243
Henry	25	DE	78
Henry	35	MD	245
James	42	DE	245
John	5	DE	245
Joshua	30	DE	83
Keziah	14	DE	243
Levi	2	DE	246
Levin	58	DE	210
Levin J	4	DE	243
Maria	17	DE	245
Maria	24	DE	78
Martha	13	DE	83
Mary	35	DE	85
Mary Ann	8	DE	78
Mary J	7	DE	246
Matilda	23	DE	83
Nehemiah	48	NY	177
Samuel	40	DE	243
Samuel J	11	DE	243
Sarah	8	DE	245
Sarah	35	DE	246
Sarah E	12	DE	246
Sarah E	14	DE	78
William	27	DE	42
Wm R	2	DE	243
Spicer, Agnes	22	DE	101
Alfred	11	DE	109
Amia M	4	DE	209
Charles	5	DE	105
Curtis A	6	DE	174
Elija	54	DE	148
Elijah J	10	DE	209
Eliza	34	DE	105
Elizabeth	20	DE	105
Elizabeth	60	DE	106
Ellen F	13	DE	174
Ezekiel	7	DE	105
George G	6	DE	209
George W	3	DE	205
Hester	20	DE	226
Hiram J	10	DE	148
James	20	DE	36
James	25	DE	106
James	38	DE	105
James E	14	DE	109
James P	17	DE	205
Johanan D	22	DE	148
John	3	DE	105
John H	27	DE	101
John H	36	DE	204
John M	23	DE	36
Joseph	1	DE	105
Julia A T	9	DE	145
Kitty A	36	DE	145
Lavinia	45	DE	219
Louisa A	9	DE	205
Lovy H	1	DE	205
Lydia F	1	MD	209
Margaret	3	DE	101
Margaret A	1	DE	145
Maria J	11	DE	205
Mary	30	DE	174
Mary A	21	DE	21
Mary E	7	DE	145
Mary E	9	DE	109
Nancy	11	DE	105
Neely	50	DE	148
Noah	20	DE	148
Rachel A	10	DE	174
Rhoda J	16	DE	145
Robert	1	DE	102
Robert B	15	DE	174
Sally Ann	23	DE	101
Sarah	9	DE	105
Sarah	23	DE	105
Sarah C	5	DE	205
Sarah E	13	DE	174
Sarah E	31	DE	109
Sarah E	35	DE	205
Sarah W	11	DE	145
Sina	36	DE	209

Name	Age	St	No
Spicer, Theodore	18	DE	21
Theodore A	5/12	DE	21
Theophilus	5	DE	109
William	28	DE	105
William	30	DE	101
William	36	DE	174
William A	12	DE	106
William E	7	DE	109
William E	9	DE	174
William E	30	DE	36
William J	12	DE	148
William J	21	DE	21
William W	40	DE	209
Wm T	7	DE	205
Zipporah M	15	DE	145
Staat, Wm G	12	DE	214
Stafford, Martha J	20	DE	42
Mary N	63	DE	213
Wm H	24	DE	213
Stapleford, John H	18	DE	41
Starr, Hester	69	DE	29
Stayton, Amos	56	DE	92
Amos J	4	DE	224
Ann	42	DE	96
Charles	4	DE	96
Edwin	14	DE	89
Eli	12	DE	92
Eliza	25	DE	96
Elizabeth	50	DE	89
Eunice	12	DE	92
George W	18	DE	224
Isabel	14	DE	92
Jackson	17	DE	89
James	75	DE	89
Lewis	6/12	DE	96
Lewis P	30	DE	96
Louisa	11	DE	96
Margaret	5	DE	96
Mary J	28	DE	224
Nancy	46	DE	92
Nehemiah N	29	DE	224
Rebecca	1	DE	224
Thomas	2	DE	96
Thomas	9	DE	96
Thomas	42	DE	96
William	16	DE	92
William	48	DE	92
Wm M	3	DE	224
Steel, Amey	27	DE	79
Charles J	12	DE	122
Daniel	30	DE	157
David	6	DE	157
Eliza	1	DE	7
Eliza	40	DE	177
Ellen	6	DE	179
Fanny	33	DE	178
Hannah	28	DE	157
Hannah	37	DE	114
Hetty	19	DE	58
Hetty A	3	DE	116
Hetty E	11	DE	122
Isaac	8	DE	115
Isaac	43	DE	178
Ishmael	22	DE	7
Jacob	2	DE	178
James	14	DE	122
James	17	DE	178
James	46	DE	7
James M	8	DE	7
Jane	5	DE	122
John	21	DE	122
John	45	DE	122
John B	4	DE	157
John C	6	DE	7
John K	3	DE	122
John M	27	DE	79
John W	38	DE	177
Joshua	28	DE	178
Joshua	34	DE	116
Julia Ann	7	DE	7
Louvenia	26	DE	178
Lydia A	7	DE	122

Name	Age	St	No
Steel, Mary	18	DE	115
Mary	24	DE	116
Mary	43	DE	122
Mary A	12	DE	177
Mary C	1	DE	116
Mary E	16	DE	122
Mary J	18	DE	178
Mary R	5	DE	122
Myers B	21	DE	122
Nancy	51	DE	122
Nathaniel	2	DE	157
Nathaniel M	48	DE	114
Penelope	35	DE	7
Peter	8	DE	122
Peter W	11	DE	8
Presgrove	70	DE	22
Purnal	28	DE	230
Sarah	17	DE	7
Sarah	19	DE	122
Sarah A	7/12	DE	178
Sarah A	14	DE	115
Sina	69	DE	78
Thomas N	18	DE	122
Thomas R	17	DE	122
Thomas W	50	MD	122
William	4	DE	7
William	11	DE	122
William	21	DE	115
Steen, Curtis	77	DE	148
Curtis H	8	DE	157
Eliza A	11	DE	157
Elizabeth	40	DE	157
Ellen	48	DE	160
Ephraim	43	DE	160
George	3	DE	157
Ginsey	24	DE	119
James	3	DE	148
James	6	DE	157
James	24	DE	148
Julia	16	DE	160
Julia	22	DE	166
Levin	1	DE	166
Louisa	19	DE	160
Lovenia	64	DE	148
Lovenia J	4	DE	166
Naomi	22	DE	148
Peter	3	DE	119
Peter	16	DE	157
Thomas	40	DE	166
William	2	DE	148
William	17	DE	157
Stephens, Ann	17	DE	155
Charles	27	DE	155
Daniel	16	DE	226
Darius M	33	DE	249
Ebby	13	DE	226
Eleanor	23	DE	249
Emeline	6/12	DE	249
Frances	11	DE	226
Frederick	7/12	DE	24
George	6/12	DE	155
Henry	22	DE	157
Hester	20	DE	155
Hester J	12	DE	155
James	3	DE	249
Jane	22	DE	157
John	23	DE	24
Joseph	6	DE	155
Joshua	16	DE	155
Lorenzo	4	DE	249
Lydia	8	DE	155
Margaret A	2	DE	155
Martha C	2/12	DE	157
Mary A	19	DE	24
Nice	62	DE	156
Richard	25	MD	249
Robert	10	DE	155
Ruben	14	DE	155
Ruben	65	DE	155
Ruth	43	DE	155
Sarah	5	MD	249
Sarah	23	DE	226

Name	Age	St	No
Stephens, Solomon	28	DE	226
Susan	25	DE	249
William	51	DE	155
William	6	DE	249
William J	2	DE	226
Stephenson, Angelica	5	DE	191
Caroline R	4	DE	191
Eliza	25	DE	191
Erasmus E	3/12	DE	12
George A	3	DE	12
Jesse B	32	DE	191
Joseph R	3	DE	14
Kendal R	12	DE	191
Lemuel W	32	DE	12
Lena	23	DE	191
Letty J	1	DE	191
Lovenia W	24	DE	191
Lydia A	16	DE	191
Mary	50	DE	191
Mary A	27	DE	14
Nancy J	8	DE	191
Peter R	23	DE	67
Rhoda A	29	DE	191
Robert A	32	DE	14
Robert C	1	DE	14
Robert D	2	DE	191
Robert D	38	DE	191
Sarah	35	DE	12
Sarah E	10	DE	192
Sarah P	1	DE	192
Sophia	70	DE	14
Susan	21	DE	67
Wesley W	28	DE	191
William C	12	DE	34
William N	20	DE	191
William T	3	DE	191
Stevens, Joseph	1	DE	140
Nancy	54	DE	140
Sarah	20	DE	140
Thomas	25	DE	140
Stewart, Clara	1	DE	109
David	3	DE	228
Harriet M	12	DE	209
Henry	26	DE	88
James	3	DE	88
James D	28	DE	109
James J	30	DE	87
Jane E	6	DE	207
John	33	DE	297
John S	2	DE	228
Julia Ann	20	DE	109
Mahala	3	DE	297
Mahala	60	DE	297
Mary	30	DE	297
Mary	38	DE	296
Mary A	22	DE	228
Peter	7	DE	294
Robert	19	DE	87
Sarah	32	DE	88
W	29	DE	229
William	6	DE	88
William	10	DE	297
Wm N	7/12	DE	228
Wm W	29	DE	228
Stockley, Alfred	21	DE	61
Ann	29	DE	59
Anna	6/12	DE	61
Betsy	10	DE	61
Burton	54	DE	61
Charles C	31	DE	170
Comfort	40	DE	59
Eliza	42	DE	57
Eliza A	1	DE	59
Ellen	59	DE	61
Emeline B	7	DE	57
Eunice	64	DE	186
George	17	DE	52
George	40	DE	43
George E	17	DE	62
George M D	5	DE	57
Hannah	13	DE	61
Hannah	63	DE	55

Stockley, Henry	2	DE	59	Stuart, Reuben A	11	DE	84	Swain, Anderson	10	DE	102
Henry	29	DE	59	Robert	11	DE	26	Ann	9/12	DE	102
Henry L	4	DE	61	Samuel	18	DE	53	Benjamin	33	DE	293
Hetty	11	DE	47	Sarah	1	DE	109	Cenah W	4	DE	215
James	13	DE	57	Sarah	5	DE	109	Cornelius P	9	DE	215
John	5	DE	59	Sarah	8	DE	230	Eliza	42	DE	217
John	10	DE	57	Sarah	24	DE	297	Elizabeth	27	DE	104
Lemuel	24	DE	57	Sarah P	6	DE	19	Eunice	33	DE	102
Mary	3	DE	59	William	4	DE	230	George	23	DE	102
Moses	11	DE	61	William	14	DE	233	George A	11	DE	217
Moses	77	DE	186	Sudler, Elizabeth	24	DE	153	Gilley	14	DE	102
Sally	60	DE	63	James T	19	DE	222	Hannah	17	DE	102
Sally Jr	18	DE	63	John E	17	DE	222	Hudson D	25	DE	225
Sarah A	14	DE	62	John R (Dr)	53	DE	222	James	3/12	DE	102
Sarah A	23	DE	61	Joseph B	25	DE	153	James	35	DE	104
Sarah B	23	DE	61	Laura	3	DE	222	James	45	DE	217
Thomas	51	DE	57	Mary C	63	DE	222	James	69	DE	55
William	16	DE	57	Sarah A	31	DE	222	James S	1	DE	104
William B	2	DE	61	Sarah B	8	DE	222	John	3	DE	102
William R	9	DE	179	William F	10	DE	222	John	20	DE	99
Woodman	30	DE	61	Sulivan, Angeline	13	DE	219	John	25	DE	102
Stokeley, Benjamin	40	DE	201	Charlotte	7	DE	261	John	74	DE	99
Eliza F	40	DE	201	Charlotte	63	DE	261	John B	27	DE	99
Martha	30	DE	200	Charlotte J	7	DE	233	Julia A	3	DE	217
Mary	64	DE	200	Edmon	5	DE	261	Leah J	16	DE	215
Oney	65	DE	288	Edward B	5	DE	234	Levinia	20	DE	102
Sarah	9	DE	282	Eleanor	31	DE	261	Levinia E	3	DE	99
Street, Alfred	20	DE	170	Elizabeth	40	DE	261	Lucy Ann	3	DE	104
Catharine	4	DE	176	Henry M	4	DE	219	Margaret Jane	5	DE	104
David	28	DE	176	James	40	MD	219	Martha	29	DE	99
Frances	4	DE	176	James R	35	DE	264	Mary	30	DE	293
Hannah	30	DE	176	John	25	DE	267	Mary	41	DE	215
Isaac	2	DE	176	Joseph	11	DE	219	Mary Ann	22	DE	99
Jane	20	DE	177	Joseph	11	DE	261	Mary P	1	DE	225
Jeremiah	97	DE	177	Joseph	14	DE	261	Mary P	13	DE	100
John	5	DE	176	Joseph T	11	DE	233	Matilda	15	DE	102
Mary	2/12	DE	176	Levin	41	DE	261	Polly	56	DE	99
Nancy	50	DE	177	Levinia	3	DE	261	Priscilla	24	DE	99
Patience	23	DE	177	Levinia E	5	DE	233	Robert D	16	DE	217
Priscilla	70	DE	183	Margaret	2	DE	261	Sarah	21	DE	102
Theophilus	25	DE	176	Margaret C	3	DE	233	Sarah A	27	DE	225
Winget	68	DE	177	Mary E	16	DE	219	Spencer	16	DE	102
Stuart, Angeline	9	DE	84	Sallie	32	DE	233	Theophilus	11	DE	102
Ann	45	DE	230	Sarah	9	DE	261	Thomas B	9	DE	217
Ann E	12	DE	233	Sarah	32	DE	261	Trusten	11	DE	215
Caleb R	40	DE	233	Sarah	40	DE	219	Uriah J	5	DE	217
Carolin G	28	DE	230	Sarah A	9	DE	219	Walter	29	DE	102
Charles	14	DE	5	Sarah E	9	DE	233	William	20	DE	102
Charles	63	DE	5	Thomas	35	DE	261	William	45	DE	215
David	40	DE	19	Thomas	67	DE	261	William	70	DE	102
David A	9	DE	19	Thomas W	34	DE	233	Zepporah	21	DE	102
Ebe J	3	DE	19	William	31	DE	8	Swats, David	28	GE	237
Emma J	1	DE	19	Summers, Cato	53	DE	53	Sweeney, Charles	6	DE	45
George W	32	DE	109	Charlotte	45	DE	53	Edward	12	DE	45
Georgianna	6	DE	84	Diana	12	DE	51	Elizabeth	8	DE	45
Greensbury	11	DE	19	Mariah	8/12	DE	51	John	14	DE	45
Hester	40	DE	19	Mary	27	DE	51	John	50	DE	45
Hetty	10	DE	233	Thomas	4	DE	51	Mary	17	DE	45
Isaac	35	DE	84	Surman, Burton H	7	DE	265	Swiggett, Ashland	6	DE	2
James	38	DE	230	Elenor	70	DE	265	Sarah	25	DE	199
Jane	16	DE	293	Hannah	4	DE	265	William	8	DE	2
John M	14	DE	19	Jacob	6	DE	265	William H	37	DE	1
John W	8	DE	213	Louisa	8	DE	265				
Joseph	8	DE	233	Lovey	7	DE	265	Talbert, Alfred T	17	DE	6
Joseph	17	DE	230	Mariah	44	DE	265	Arthur H	13	DE	6
Joseph	52	DE	297	Mary	45	DE	265	Catherine A	43	DE	6
Joseph B	25	DE	154	Nancy	47	DE	265	Edward	6	DE	6
Julia	4	DE	230	Sarah	15	DE	265	Jonathan R	1	DE	6
Levinia	24	DE	109	Theodore	2	DE	265	Jonathan R	48	DE	6
Lizzie	1	DE	230	William	8	DE	265	John T	12	DE	167
Louisa	17	DE	19	William H	38	DE	265	Martha J	10	DE	6
Martha	29	DE	233	William of L	47	DE	265	Mary Anna	15	DE	6
Martha A	14	DE	230	Sutherlan, John W	10	MD	214	William E	18	DE	6
Mary	6	DE	233	Sutherland, Ann M	35	MD	220	Talbot, Coard B	10	DE	5
Mary	11	DE	230	Arthur T	3/12	DE	220	Hester	40	DE	62
Mary	30	DE	84	Henrietta	7	DE	220	Nancy	48	DE	102
Mary E	2	DE	84	James	40	MD	220	Warren	25	DE	102
Mary E	4	DE	109	John W	9	DE	220	Tarr, Betsey	62	DE	181
Mitchael	10	DE	230	John W	10	DE	213	Tatman, Ann	55	DE	81
Nancy	50	DE	5	Mary E	4	DE	220	Charles	3	DE	96
Nancy	61	DE	19	Swain, Abby	45	DE	102	Collins	18	DE	81
Penelope	16	DE	233	Alfred	13	DE	102	James	55	DE	91

Name	Age	St	No.
Tatman, Jane	14	DE	96
Jerry	7	DE	81
John	22	DE	91
John	25	DE	81
Margaret	4	DE	81
Mary Ellen	14	DE	81
Mitchel	56	DE	81
Peggy	55	DE	91
Purnel	52	DE	96
Sarah	32	DE	96
William	47	DE	7
Taylor, Abraham	28	DE	237
Ann L	5	DE	152
Charles	21	DE	135
Clarissa A	3	DE	125
Cornelia E	6/12	DE	257
David J	5	DE	120
Edward	26	DE	296
Elias	22	DE	124
Elias	31	DE	237
Elias	61	DE	292
Eliza A	1	DE	120
Elizabeth	1	DE	121
Elizabeth	15	DE	228
Elizabeth	26	DE	257
Elizabeth	32	DE	219
Elizabeth	45	DE	272
Elizabeth	49	DE	292
Emeline	3	DE	121
George T	33	DE	125
Harriet	30	DE	219
Hester	55	DE	219
Hester A	9	DE	219
Hester J	16	DE	125
Hester J	16	DE	135
Hugh	14	DE	76
Isaac E	3	DE	120
Isabella	10	DE	150
James	10	FR	296
James	30	DE	126
Jane	23	DE	76
John	13	DE	272
John	26	DE	121
John	32	DE	126
John	32	DE	292
John	68	DE	292
John M	32	DE	123
Joseph	3	DE	152
Joseph	16	DE	272
Lavenia	22	DE	296
Lovey	4	DE	76
Lovey A	27	DE	120
Lovey C	11	DE	152
Lucy A	2	DE	123
Lydia	20	DE	135
Maria	33	DE	152
Mary	26	DE	126
Mary	70	MD	281
Mary A	6	DE	121
Mary A	21	DE	123
Mary C	8	DE	120
Nancy C	2	DE	125
Nancy W	40	DE	136
Parson	25	DE	277
Patience	36	DE	275
Peggy	40	DE	150
Peggy	61	MD	126
Priscilla	2	DE	150
Priscilla	11	DE	154
Priscilla	12	DE	151
Rachel M	23	DE	125
Reuben	5	DE	76
Sarah	2	DE	76
Sarah	4	DE	275
Sarah	11	DE	219
Sarah	26	DE	272
Sarah	56	DE	292
Sarah A	22	DE	121
Sarah P	7	DE	152
Sarah W	5	DE	125
Solomon	19	DE	272
Stephen	10	DE	219
Taylor, Stephen	16	DE	136
Thomas	31	DE	125
William	18	DE	292
William	28	DE	76
William	38	DE	152
William	46	DE	275
William R	32	MD	120
Teague, John	39	DE	101
Martha	1	DE	101
Mary	30	DE	101
Sarah	3	DE	101
Templer, Caleb M	11/12	DE	21
Eliza J	24	DE	21
Peter	26	DE	21
Tendel, Benton	35	DE	105
Eliza	49	DE	104
Elizabeth	10	DE	104
Elizabeth	25	DE	105
George	14	DE	105
Hannah	11	DE	104
Harrison	9	DE	104
Isaac	12	DE	105
James	4	DE	105
John	18	DE	105
John	25	DE	104
John	62	DE	104
Jonathan	9	DE	105
Joseph	16	DE	204
Mahala	18	DE	104
Margaret	30	DE	104
Mary Ann	1	DE	105
Matilda	32	DE	105
Miles	60	DE	105
Miles Jr	34	DE	104
Nancy	52	DE	105
Onatalina	2	DE	104
Peter	7	DE	105
Sarah	6	DE	104
Sarah	14	DE	104
Theophilus	6	DE	105
Thomas	15	DE	105
Vashti	36	DE	105
William	8	DE	104
Tennant, Bangor	63	DE	228
John	20	DE	222
John H	10	DE	224
John H	11	DE	228
Sarah	30	DE	228
Sophia	8	DE	228
Terman, Ann	21	DE	103
Charles	6	DE	103
Daniel	12	DE	103
Daniel	35	DE	103
Elias	10	DE	103
Jane	5	DE	103
Louisa	9	DE	103
Terry, Elizabeth	50	DE	39
John H	21	DE	39
Mary L	15	DE	39
Tharp, Celia	65	DE	227
Elisha D	43	DE	90
Elizabeth	33	DE	89
Elizabeth	43	DE	90
George	20	DE	90
James	35	DE	220
Jesse	10	DE	89
Job	4	DE	89
John W	14	DE	89
Nehemiah	8	DE	89
Nehemiah	36	DE	89
Sophia	14	DE	90
William	9	DE	90
Thom, Adam	14	DE	78
Thomas, Ann	62	DE	113
Catherine H	8	DE	157
Elizabeth	18	DE	142
James	18	DE	44
James	31	DE	113
Jane	21	DE	134
Jane	21	DE	134
Joseph H	2	DE	157
Littleton	14	DE	134
Thomas, Littleton	14	DE	134
Margaret	4	DE	134
Mary	10	DE	157
Nathaniel H	44	DE	157
Rachel B	20	DE	113
Rebecca	24	DE	134
Rhoda C	6	DE	157
Ritty	56	DE	134
Sarah E	30	DE	157
Thompson, Albert J	2	DE	59
Amaril	40	DE	190
Amelia	28	DE	271
Ann E	2/12	DE	59
Arbetty	4	DE	271
Arena	7	DE	267
Augustus	7	DE	270
Augustus	35	DE	270
Benjamin	8	DE	129
Catherine	3	DE	61
Catherine	31	DE	235
Cornelia	6	DE	129
Eleanor	21	DE	155
Eleanor	26	DE	270
Elizabeth	5	DE	160
Elizabeth	8	DE	59
Elizabeth	9	DE	1
Elizabeth	14	DE	129
Elizabeth	26	DE	156
Elizabeth B	16	PA	119
Estella E	5	DE	235
George	8	DE	271
George	19	DE	59
George E	1	DE	235
George H	6/12	DE	51
Haister	26	DE	155
Hannah	38	DE	129
Harriet	3	DE	190
Henry	22	DE	51
Henry	23	DE	84
Henry	34	DE	271
Hetty	26	DE	61
Isaac	6	DE	271
Isaac J	23	DE	155
James	2	DE	271
James	3	DE	267
James	22	DE	235
James B	6/12	DE	190
James T	6	DE	59
Jane	80	DE	62
Jane C	4	DE	59
Jeremiah	3	DE	156
John	9	DE	270
John	15	DE	177
John	29	SW	59
John C	11	DE	59
Joshua	8	DE	156
Josiah	16	DE	241
Josiah	40	DE	129
Julia A	11	DE	267
Lydia	3/12	DE	61
Major	3	DE	129
Margaret	5	DE	270
Margaret	8	DE	50
Margaret	18	DE	84
Maria	22	DE	235
Mary	5	DE	190
Mary	10	DE	129
Mary	62	DE	42
Mary A	8	DE	61
Mary A	26	DE	235
Mary Ann	30	DE	85
Mary E	6	DE	166
Melisa	50	DE	155
Nancy	38	DE	267
Nancy	60	DE	266
Nathaniel	25	DE	85
Nathaniel	28	MD	235
Orange	12	DE	191
Rachel E	28	DE	287
Rhodes	39	DE	61
Robert	6	DE	156
Samuel	17	DE	241

Name	Age	St	No.	Name	Age	St	No.	Name	Age	St	No.
Thompson, Sarah	4	DE	85	Timmons, Isaac W	14	MD	154	Tingle, Elizabeth	17	DE	158
Sarah	18	DE	51	James	16	DE	132	Elizabeth	24	MD	139
Sarah	38	DE	59	James C	3	DE	157	Elizabeth	86	DE	167
Sina Jane	12	DE	61	James M	20	MD	154	Elizabeth R	48	DE	125
Solomon	45	DE	190	James W	35	MD	142	Fanny	10	DE	158
Susan	10	DE	61	Jancy	17	DE	132	George	13	DE	156
Thomas	72	DE	246	Jane	17	DE	50	Haiselet	6	DE	170
Wally	1	DE	156	Jane	17	DE	157	Harriet E	1	DE	137
Wally	28	DE	156	John	22	dE	157	Henry	6	DE	50
William	11	DE	129	Josiah	14	DE	132	Henry	8	DE	178
William	11	DE	270	Leonia	41	DE	132	Henry	14	DE	167
William C	2	DE	85	Levi	76	DE	289	Henry	19	DE	151
William E	1	DE	235	Levi D	22	DE	289	Hetty	4	DE	170
William T	12	DE	59	Lovey	20	DE	142	Hetty	6	DE	132
Wm	32	DE	235	Martha	9	DE	132	Hetty A	7	DE	137
Thorn, Adam	14	DE	77	Mary	19	DE	157	Isaac W	14	DE	125
Elijah	10	DE	212	Mary	45	DE	289	Jacob	8	DE	156
Thoroughgood, Ann	12	DE	166	Nancy	60	DE	289	Jacob	40	DE	158
Ann E	1	DE	180	Noble	25	DE	289	Jacob	79	DE	156
Avaline	6	DE	190	Purnetta	27	DE	289	James	30	DE	172
Catherine W	3/12	DE	191	Rebecca A	6	MD	154	James	38	DE	125
Daniel	42	DE	55	Sarah	11/12	DE	289	James Henry	3	DE	172
Eleanor	2	DE	190	Sarah	4	DE	132	John	8	DE	158
Eliza	32	DE	180	Sarah	7	DE	290	John	31	DE	143
Eliza A	3	DE	170	Sarah	23	DE	151	John	34	DE	170
Elizabeth	27	DE	55	Sarah	23	DE	157	John M	22	DE	167
George	8	DE	189	Sarah	29	DE	289	John S	1	DE	143
George M	18	DE	83	William	13	DE	157	Josephine	5	DE	167
Henry	11	DE	171	William	13	DE	175	Julia	43	DE	167
James P	7	DE	179	Tindal, Alfred	7	DE	110	Julia A	11	DE	167
Jane	30	DE	190	Benton	35	DE	104	Kitty	45	DE	161
John B	25	DE	180	Comfort	15	DE	110	Leah	65	DE	169
John D	3	DE	55	Eliza	49	DE	103	Louisa	15	DE	158
John E	9	DE	179	Elizabeth	10	DE	103	Levin D	19	DE	125
John E	11	DE	166	George	14	DE	104	Levinia C	3	DE	137
Lewis	18	DE	177	Hannah	11	DE	103	Lydia	20	DE	136
Lydia	23	DE	170	Harrison	9	DE	103	Manaen	18	DE	153
Mary	4	DE	170	Henry	16	DE	110	Maria	6	DE	156
Nathaniel	35	DE	170	Isaac	12	DE	104	Martha	8	DE	170
Peter	21	DE	177	James	4	DE	104	Mary	11	DE	156
Robert	4	DE	193	John	62	DE	103	Mary	19	DE	158
Robert L	9	DE	167	John	65	DE	109	Mary	35	DE	137
Sarah	15	DE	177	Jonathan	9	DE	104	Mary	36	MD	132
Sarah	30	DE	179	Mary Ann	1	DE	104	Mary	40	DE	50
Sarah A	15	DE	166	Peter	7	DE	104	Mary J	12	DE	161
Simeon W	19	DE	179	Sarah	14	DE	103	Mary J	19	DE	143
William	13	DE	166	Sarah	17	DE	109	Matthias	14	DE	162
William M	35	DE	179	Tindle, Barsheba	24	DE	82	Phillis	40	DE	158
William M	38	DE	166	David R	1	DE	71	Polena	13	DE	158
William N	1	DE	170	David R	25	DE	71	Robert	15	DE	156
William N	2	DE	179	James	30	DE	82	Sarah	40	DE	156
Tier, Eliza	40	DE	188	Joanna	4/12	DE	71	Sarah	60	MD	135
Eliza	41	DE	158	John	11	DE	60	Sarah J	5	DE	137
Tilney, Aletha M C	16	DE	39	John	12	DE	95	Solomon	24	MD	139
Hannah	46	DE	39	Joseph	25	DE	95	Susan	14	DE	121
John	42	DE	39	Joshua	17	DE	95	William	1	DE	139
John S	14	DE	171	Mary	3	DE	82	William	3	DE	132
Mary A	3	DE	171	Mary	16	DE	95	William	24	DE	167
Mary S	29	DE	171	Mary E	3	DE	71	William	45	DE	161
Robert H	12	DE	39	Nancy	24	DE	95	Tinker, Achsah M	7/12	DE	62
Robert M	38	DE	171	Sarah A	32	DE	71	Anna	6	NJ	62
Robert P	7	DE	171	Sarah E	8	DE	71	Dudley B	38	NJ	62
William E	5	DE	171	Tingle, Albert	17	DE	161	Eliza A	32	NJ	62
Timmons, Aaron W	9	MD	154	Alfred	35	DE	137	Emma H H	8	NJ	62
Anda	48	MD	154	Amy	75	DE	46	Sally L	11	NJ	62
Angeline	2/12	DE	132	Ann	15	DE	156	Tire, Eben	18	DE	294
Bersheba	10	DE	157	Ann	21	DE	158	James	15	DE	294
Catherine	2	DE	132	Ann M	12	DE	132	Jane	22	DE	276
Cyrus	6	DE	132	Annanias	11	DE	134	John	7/12	DE	276
Daniel	49	DE	157	Annanias R	53	DE	125	Mary	2	DE	276
Elizabeth	34	DE	289	Angelia	1	DE	161	Matilda	45	DE	294
Esther	85	MD	139	Belfast	70	DE	169	Minos	25	MD	276
Eunice	30	DE	289	Benjamin	47	DE	132	Peter	22	MD	276
Fanny	50	MD	139	Brister	44	DE	50	Todd, A G	43	DE	227
Fanny C	17	MD	154	Caroline	14	DE	158	Alfred H	5	DE	219
George	5	DE	157	Caroline	22	DE	170	Ann	43	DE	221
Handy	45	DE	132	Charles	10	DE	50	Benjamin	8	DE	275
Hannah	3	DE	157	Charles C	12	DE	125	Charles J	9	DE	227
Hannah	42	DE	157	David B	8	DE	161	Charles W	16	DE	25
Henry	7	DE	157	Edward	17	DE	167	Charlotta E	3	DE	227
Henry	12	DE	132	Elizabeth	9	DE	170	Charlotte	25	DE	216
Isaac	40	MD	154	Elizabeth	12	DE	167	David T	12	DE	216

Name	Age	State	No.
Todd, Eleanor	23	DE	227
Elizabeth A	11	DE	227
Ennals	8	DE	216
George	8	DE	231
George M	1	DE	227
Henry	18	DE	227
Henry	36	DE	219
Jacob C	11	DE	216
James R	13	DE	219
John	5	DE	216
John A	4	DE	227
John H	18	DE	221
John W	8	DE	219
Levin	49	DE	221
Louisa	16	DE	221
Luther	1	DE	216
Mary E	16	DE	227
Mary P	4	DE	216
Priscilla	28	DE	219
Sarah D	6	DE	216
Sarah E	5	DE	219
Sarah E	22	DE	221
Wm	34	DE	217
Wm A	2	DE	219
Wm H	10	DE	216
Wm M	14	DE	227
Tompson, Rachel E	28	DE	288
Toomey, Alexzina	4	DE	151
Angeline	6	DE	151
Ann	28	DE	151
Edward	2	DE	154
Eliza	3	DE	190
Elizabeth A	1/12	DE	154
Hannah	13	DE	113
Jane	35	DE	190
Levi	21	DE	113
Louvenia J	3	DE	154
Margaret	16	DE	113
Martha	25	DE	154
Matilda B	22	DE	113
Neely	61	DE	113
Nehemiah	1	DE	190
Nehemiah	45	DE	190
Sarah C	10	DE	190
Thomas	9	DE	151
Thomas R	28	DE	154
William	4	DE	154
William B	76	DE	113
William T	33	DE	151
Torbert, Adeline	14	DE	285
Anne E	5	DE	5
Calesbury	4	DE	285
Catherine B	12	DE	188
Eli	45	DE	4
Elizabeth	29	DE	285
Elizabeth	33	DE	294
Elizabeth	76	DE	4
George	5	DE	285
George	30	DE	5
Hamilton	31	DE	285
Hannah E	4	DE	5
James	9	DE	285
Jane	28	DE	5
John P	59	DE	294
John T	13	DE	285
Jonathan	8	DE	192
Levenia	7	DE	294
Martha	6/12	DE	294
Mary	12	DE	294
Mary A	37	DE	285
Mary M	4	DE	192
Nancy	61	DE	294
Penelopy	3	DE	294
Robert	19	DE	294
Rufus W	1	DE	5
Sarah	5	DE	294
Sarah	20	DE	294
Tabitha	11	DE	4
Tabitha	52	DE	4
Walter	25	DE	294
Watson	34	DE	294
William	11	DE	285
Torbert, William A	14	DE	5
William H	11	DE	3
Wm	8	DE	294
Towers, Andrew J	6	DE	6
Elizabeth	20	DE	208
James	13	DE	214
Nancy	16	DE	208
Rhoda	47	MD	6
Townsend, Alexander	12	DE	291
Ann C	42	DE	114
Catherine A	26	DE	128
Charles	8	DE	113
Charles W	5	DE	114
Ebe	29	DE	115
Eben	21	DE	117
Eben	80	DE	240
Edward	36	DE	113
Elias J	26	DE	77
Elizabeth	46	DE	116
Elizabeth	55	DE	3
Elizabeth A	21	DE	115
Joshua C	31	DE	115
George	11	DE	79
George H	4	DE	73
Grace	25	DE	113
Hannah	66	DE	128
Henry L	6	DE	114
Hester	20	DE	79
Hetty	63	DE	117
Hetty A	11	DE	117
Isaac	14	DE	116
Isabella	74	DE	117
James	5	DE	116
James	41	MD	116
James H	6	DE	116
James K	24	DE	115
Jane C	7	DE	114
John	35	SW	73
John	36	DE	74
John	67	DE	117
John C	1	DE	115
John S	4	DE	115
Lake	20	DE	115
Leah	3	DE	74
Lemuel	18	DE	79
Major	58	DE	115
Maria C	3	DE	116
Martha A	3	DE	114
Martha E	10	DE	116
Martha R	33	DE	117
Mary	4	DE	113
Mary	24	DE	73
Mary	25	DE	74
Mary	50	DE	79
Mary	61	DE	74
Mary A	1	DE	74
Mary A	13	DE	114
Mary A	19	DE	116
Mary E	10	DE	3
Mary E	18	DE	77
Mary J	8	DE	117
Mary J	60	DE	113
Moses	70	DE	240
Noah	78	DE	71
Noah	53	DE	79
Peter	36	DE	117
Peter	58	DE	291
Prince	55	DE	3
Purnel	62	DE	74
Rachel	50	DE	291
Rachel	65	DE	240
Sabra	76	DE	266
Sarah	3	DE	113
Sarah	11	DE	79
Sarah	26	MD	115
Sarah	56	DE	115
Sarah C	6	DE	117
Stephen H	9	DE	114
Thomas	20	DE	79
Wash	7	DE	74
William	14	DE	79
Zadock	66	MD	128
Townsend, Zadock P	8	DE	117
Zadock P	11	DE	114
Tracey, Catherine	3	DE	116
Edward	6	DE	113
Elizabeth	10	DE	113
Hannah L J	15	DE	126
Hetty	16	DE	115
Hetty	16	DE	115
James	2	DE	113
James T	12	DE	126
John	8	DE	113
John	11	DE	116
John H	21	DE	126
John W	38	MD	116
Mary A	34	DE	116
Nancy	40	DE	126
Rebecca H	7	DE	116
Robert	20	DE	113
Sally	37	DE	113
Tracy, Hannah	20	DE	126
William	8	DE	113
Trader, Caroline	1	DE	202
George	6	DE	202
Lucinda	18	DE	236
Margaret	24	DE	202
Traider, Elizabeth	40	DE	286
Levinia	10	DE	286
Margaret	18	DE	286
Mary	13	DE	286
Robert	50	DE	286
William	19	DE	286
Trail, Durwood W	30	MD	248
Trehearn, Arthur	2	MD	6
Arthur M	47	MD	5
Cyrus	5	MD	6
Jackson	10	MD	5
Sarah	37	MD	5
Thompson	6	MD	6
Treuit, Joshua	46	DE	87
Truit, Angeline	6	DE	83
David	12	DE	86
Elizabeth	3	DE	84
Garrett W	17	DE	83
John	14	DE	86
John C	41	DE	83
John W	14	DE	83
John W	15	DE	24
Joshua	46	DE	86
Lydia	80	DE	72
Margaret	8	DE	84
Marmy	4	DE	83
Mary	8/12	DE	86
Mary	3	DE	86
Mary	40	DE	86
Mary M	6	DE	84
Sarah	6	DE	86
Sarah	38	DE	83
Sarah	39	DE	86
Sarah A	27	DE	83
Sarah C	9	DE	83
Thomas H	30	DE	83
William	17	DE	86
Truitt, Alexander	34	DE	91
Alfred W	5	DE	85
Andrew C	7	DE	152
Andrew C	16	DE	144
Andrew V	42	DE	91
Ann	1	DE	91
Ann	3	DE	94
Ann	9	DE	279
Ann	18	DE	287
Ann M	16	DE	293
Air	12	DE	153
Asbury	25	DE	279
Avis	3	DE	24
B R	22	DE	288
Beniah W	17	DE	85
Benjamin	9	DE	89
Benjamin	21	DE	279
Benjamin	55	DE	153
Burton B	36	DE	287
Caleb	11	DE	294

Name	Age		Page
Truitt, Catherine	39	DE	85
Collins	21	DE	127
Cyrus	13	DE	293
Daddany	25	DE	153
David	16	DE	91
David	18	DE	153
David R	40	DE	68
David S	15	DE	85
Eleanor	84	DE	287
Elijah	5	DE	287
Elijah S H	3	DE	144
Elisha	6	DE	287
Eliza	2/12	DE	89
Eliza	7	DE	94
Eliza	39	DE	91
Eliza	40	DE	68
Eliza H	22	DE	161
Eliza Jane	7	DE	24
Elizabeth	14	DE	91
Elizabeth	26	DE	166
Elizabeth	28	DE	278
Elizabeth	30	DE	279
Elizabeth	35	DE	286
Elizabeth	58	DE	286
Elizabeth	66	DE	286
Elizabeth A	12	DE	144
Elizabeth C	47	DE	144
Elizabeth E	1	DE	287
Elsey	60	DE	24
Elsey	52	DE	94
Emory J	7	DE	127
George	6/12	DE	287
George	4	DE	278
George	5	DE	153
George	7	DE	287
George	8	DE	94
George	9	DE	24
George	16	DE	279
George R	18	DE	112
Granbury	30	DE	287
Greensbury	21	DE	293
Hamilton B	26	DE	161
Henry	10	DE	287
Henry B	32	DE	286
Henry C	17	DE	161
Henry S	10	DE	85
Hester M	15	DE	70
Hetty	53	DE	288
Hiram G	10	DE	144
James	5	DE	287
James	8	DE	91
James	15	DE	127
James	18	DE	91
James	20	DE	287
James	53	DE	286
James	59	DE	161
James E	5	DE	127
Jane R	20	DE	112
John	5	DE	68
John	5	dE	91
John	13	DE	24
John	68	DE	287
John A	8	DE	85
John L	7	DE	287
John S	44	DE	85
Joseph	9	DE	287
Joseph M	23	DE	287
Joseph S	23	DE	287
Joshua	16	DE	89
Josiah	6	DE	285
Leah	6	DE	294
Leah	55	DE	294
Levin	15	DE	294
Levinia	2	DE	287
Levinia	10	DE	293
Levinia	26	DE	287
Louisa	18	DE	277
Lovenia	18	DE	161
Lurany	25	DE	287
Mahala	34	DE	91
Mahala	44	MD	293
Martha H	6/12	DE	287
Truitt, Martha H	44	DE	112
Mary	8	DE	287
Mary	9	DE	294
Mary	13	DE	34
Mary	15	DE	24
Mary	20	DE	127
Mary	20	DE	153
Mary	25	DE	112
Mary	43	DE	286
Mary	66	DE	77
Mary A	9	DE	287
Mary E	12	DE	85
Mary R	40	DE	285
Mathew	36	DE	278
Mesach	74	MD	278
Miles D	25	DE	161
Nancy	17	DE	94
Nehemiah	14	DE	89
Nehemiah	50	DE	89
Noah	22	DE	287
Oney	22	DE	295
Pemberton	1	DE	91
Peter	53	DE	288
Peter	60	DE	294
Phillip	51	DE	263
Rachael	20	DE	89
Rebecca	18	DE	288
Renney J	21	DE	161
Rhoda A	70	DE	71
Robert	5	DE	24
Robert	5	DE	94
Rucilla	22	DE	153
Sallie A	25	DE	94
Sally	35	DE	24
Sally A	11	DE	24
Sally A	18	DE	89
Sally A	50	DE	89
Samuel	12	DE	89
Samuel	24	DE	279
Sarah	10	DE	91
Sarah	12	DE	287
Sarah	13	DE	294
Sarah	16	MD	127
Sarah	17	DE	263
Sarah	28	DE	287
Sarah	38	DE	153
Sarah	45	DE	287
Sarah	50	DE	153
Sarah A	9	DE	153
Sarah E	13	DE	161
Sarah J	9	DE	144
Sarah P	40	DE	286
Solomon	17	DE	75
Thomas	45	DE	290
Thursey	39	MD	263
William	1	DE	24
William	1	DE	94
William	3	DE	287
William	6	DE	278
William	18	DE	287
William	49	DE	293
William A	3	DE	91
William A	28	DE	277
William B	2	DE	85
William J B	13	DE	144
William M	19	DE	293
William R	50	DE	144
William W	4	DE	152
Trumans, Levi	76	MD	288
Levi D	22	DE	288
Sarah	29	DE	288
Trust, Denard W	30	MD	247
Trusty, Asbury	20	DE	202
Eliza A	5	DE	202
Hester A	12	DE	202
John	40	DE	202
Julia A	1	DE	202
Margaret A	11	DE	202
Sarah	31	DE	202
Wm A	3	DE	202
Truxton, Elizabeth	26	DE	48
Elizabeth	77	DE	46
Truxton, Sarah A	25	DE	46
Thomas	48	DE	46
Thomas J	2	DE	46
William H H	13	DE	46
Tubbs, Burton R	63	DE	135
David	16	DE	298
Edward H	12	DE	135
John	23	DE	297
Mary	21	DE	297
Mitchel	7	DE	297
Moses	57	DE	297
Priscilla	47	DE	297
Sarah	15	DE	297
Sarah	63	DE	135
Tabitha	10	DE	297
William	12	DE	297
Tucker, Andrew	9	DE	88
Benjamin	16	DE	89
Elizabeth	75	DE	42
Jesse	33	DE	88
John	29	DE	89
John T	5	DE	89
Nancy	37	DE	89
Nancy	42	DE	88
Tule, Milly	80	DE	41
Tull, Andrew	32	DE	203
Ann M	23	MD	202
Catherine	20	MD	196
Eleanor	16	DE	203
Eliza A	7	MD	204
Elizabeth	22	DE	204
Elizabeth C	1	DE	196
Emaline	28	DE	203
George H	1	MD	203
Hannah	67	DE	203
John	25	?	196
John	25	DE	203
John H	5	MD	203
John W	10	DE	204
Peter	33	DE	204
Rachel	22	DE	196
Rachel	64	DE	238
Rebecca	35	DE	203
Robert	27	DE	203
Robert T	5	DE	204
Rose A	39	DE	204
Samuel	35	DE	204
Sarah J	8	DE	203
William	31	DE	203
Wm C	12	DE	204
Tunnell, Albert	10	DE	55
Amanda	12	DE	7
Ann E	25	DE	120
Ann M	16	DE	115
Anna	3	DE	55
Arcada	48	DE	251
Benjamin E	6	DE	120
Bertha M	13	DE	115
Charles	7	DE	115
Charles	46	DE	7
Charles P	7	DE	7
Ebe W	5	DE	115
Edward	16	DE	232
Edward S	27	DE	120
Edwin A	5	DE	7
Eliza A	15	DE	120
Eliza R	1	DE	7
Elizabeth	19	DE	115
Elizabeth	36	DE	55
Emila	25	DE	232
Flora	30	DE	136
George	1	DE	136
George	8	DE	116
George	18	DE	232
George	40	DE	55
George T	6	DE	7
George W	3	DE	120
Hannah	5	DE	52
Hannah	5	DE	115
Hannah	5	DE	151
Hannah E	15	DE	7
Henry	46	DE	120

Name	Age	St	No.	Name	Age	St	No.	Name	Age	St	No.
Tunnell, Henry C	19	DE	120	Turner, William	32	DE	214	Vaughn, Eliza A	18	DE	12
Henry M	17	DE	115	William	42	DE	118	Elizabeth	21	DE	10
Hetty	46	DE	6	William E	14	DE	11	Frances	5	DE	12
Isaac	6	DE	116	Turpin, Angeletta	24	DE	239	Hannah	52	DE	10
Isaac	18	DE	7	Asa	27	DE	259	Hannah Caroline	9	DE	10
Isaac	40	DE	151	Benjamin	1	DE	259	James	28	DE	295
Isaac	82	DE	6	Elenor	30	DE	259	Jane	34	DE	45
Isaac E	11	DE	115	Elinor C	13	DE	216	Jane	50	DE	10
James A	11	DE	120	Gatty	50	DE	259	John N	7	DE	10
James H	21	DE	115	James E	25	DE	239	Joseph	33	DE	292
James M	55	DE	115	Jane	18	DE	201	Joseph	35	DE	37
Jane	10	DE	7	Josephus	4	DE	259	Joseph	58	DE	292
Jane A	12	DE	55	Lucinda	3	DE	206	Joseph B	52	DE	10
John	15	DE	115	Luther	3	DE	259	Juliann	7	DE	10
John	59	DE	120	Margaret	21	DE	206	Levin D	24	DE	10
John V	22	DE	120	William	28	DE	201	Margaret	6	DE	12
Joseph C	3	DE	120	Wm	3/12	DE	206	Margaret	38	GB	54
Maria	2	DE	116	Tusley, Rachel W	75	DE	204	Mary	2/12	DE	10
Maria	30	DE	115	Twiford, Catherine	46	DE	208	Mary	12	PA	45
Martha A	10	DE	115	Charles A	8	DE	208	Mary	38	DE	51
Mary	6/12	DE	151	Charlotte	12	DE	212	Mary L	13	DE	12
Mary	5	DE	55	Cordelia	35	DE	221	Matilda	31	DE	292
Mary	19	DE	232	John H	48	DE	208	Nancy D	11	DE	10
Mary E	40	DE	120	John T	25	DE	208	Nathan	15	DE	210
Nathaniel	52	DE	115	Martha T J	11	DE	208	Nathaniel	58	DE	10
Nathaniel W	11	DE	120	Sinah	40	DE	221	Pinkey	21	DE	10
Sallie A	9/12	DE	7	Wm	72	?	221	Richard	1	PA	45
Samson	90	DE	169	Twilly, Charlotte	26	DE	249	Richard	50	GB	54
Sarah	21	DE	55	Emeline	17	DE	249	Robert	9	DE	12
Sarah	35	DE	7	George C	8	DE	244	Samuel	28	DE	11
Sarah	80	DE	169	James	46	DE	249	Sarah	28	PA	45
Sarah C	49	DE	120	James E	6	DE	249	Sarah A	22	DE	295
Scarborough	9	DE	115	John R	5	DE	244	Sarah D	31	DE	292
Stephen H	14	DE	120	Joseph P	17	DE	249	William	16	DE	12
Susan	30	DE	151	Julia A	10	DE	249	William	31	GB	45
Thomas W	8	DE	115	Levin	35	DE	249	William D	17	DE	10
Unice	35	DE	7	Manuel	12	DE	244	Veasey, Jonah	31	DE	20
Wilbur F	10	DE	7	Maria	12	DE	249	Julia Ann	27	DE	20
William	8	DE	116	Mary	47	DE	249	Lydia Ann	7	DE	20
Wm	51	DE	232	Mary J	10	DE	249	Margaret C	4	DE	20
Tunnons, Ezekiel	37	DE	289	Mary P	17	DE	244	Nathaniel T	1	DE	20
Lavenia	29	DE	289	Nancy	35	DE	244	William	9	DE	20
Turner, Alsey	60	DE	228	Robert	15	DE	249	William H	8	DE	42
Catherine	8	DE	118	Robert	46	DE	244	Venables, Ann	1	DE	246
Elias P	1	DE	214	Robert	80	DE	249	Catherine	42	DE	246
Eliza	23	DE	5	Sallie E	10	DE	244	Margaret	8	DE	246
Elizabeth	12	DE	11	Samuel	2	DE	249	Mary	6	DE	246
Elizabeth	41	DE	118	Sarah	4	DE	249	Robert	4	DE	246
Elizabeth	47	DE	115	Thomas J	15	DE	244	Robert J	48	DE	246
Elizabeth	70	DE	128	Tyre, Burton	4	DE	124	Sarah	11	DE	246
Elizabeth A	12	DE	214	Burton	40	DE	124	Vent, Abel	66	DE	35
Henry	9	DE	115	George	20	DE	124	Adeline H	7	DE	34
Isaac	13	DE	118	Hannah	2	DE	124	Charles	1	DE	34
Israel	10	DE	11	Jacob	14	DE	124	Cornelius	35	DE	34
Israel	33	DE	11	James	17	DE	124	David	25	DE	35
James	50	MD	115	Mitchell	19	DE	124	Eleanor	53	DE	3
John	16	DE	118	Nancy	40	DE	124	Elizabeth	11	DE	3
John M	2/12	DE	214	Vane, Ann E	21	DE	70	Elizabeth	22	DE	17
John W	7	DE	66	Bartholomew	17	MD	220	Elizabeth S	31	DE	48
Jonathan	23	MD	8	Catherine	23	DE	70	Ellen	45	DE	34
Jonathan W	16	DE	120	Caroline	15	DE	70	Ellen B	17	DE	34
Joshua J	17	DE	130	Flora	55	DE	70	Emily B	15	DE	38
Lazarus	4/12	DE	66	Henry	55	DE	70	Jackson	21	DE	34
Lazarus	57	DE	292	Mary J	25	DE	70	James M	41	DE	11
Luther E	4	DE	214	Sarah A	17	DE	70	Jany J	2	DE	35
Lydia T	49	DE	43	Sarah E	3	DE	70	Joannah	5	DE	34
Margaret C	7	DE	115	William	13	DE	70	John	76	DE	34
Martha	8	DE	214	Vankirk, Frances E	3	DE	80	Joseph	55	DE	3
Martha	53	DE	292	Joshua	7	DE	80	Margaret	30	DE	34
Mary	33	DE	11	Joshua B	8	DE	80	Maria S	14	DE	35
Mary	34	DE	214	Lemuel	16	DE	80	Mary	24	DE	35
Mary C	2	DE	118	Mary	2	DE	80	Mary H	12	DE	34
Mary C	8	DE	222	Mary Catherine	5	DE	80	Mary M	36	DE	11
Mary E	10	DE	4	Penelope	34	DE	80	Nancy	54	DE	35
Mary P	16	DE	43	William	41	DE	80	Sarah E	19	DE	3
Mary R	66	DE	49	Vaughn, Angeline	24	DE	295	Susan T	19	DE	35
Paynter S	50	DE	43	Arcada G	18	DE	10	William S	23	DE	17
Rebecca A	20	MD	8	Charles	47	DE	12	William W	10	DE	34
Sarah M	6	DE	214	Charles R	22	DE	10	Venter, Martha	6	DE	73
Thomas	8	DE	11	Clara	2	PA	45	Vesey, Arcada D	28	DE	17
Thomas W B	18	DE	43	Edward M	22	DE	12	Arcada R	5	DE	17
William	6/12	DE	214					Edward J	3	DE	17

Name	Age	ST	Pg
Vesey, John R	14	DE	180
Mary A	1	DE	17
Nathaniel T	23	DE	189
Sarah	45	DE	194
Susanna B	19	DE	189
William W	30	DE	17
Vessels, Charlotte	44	DE	191
Jemmenica	44	DE	200
John	25	DE	200
Miers B	23	DE	191
William F	49	DE	191
Vickars, Alexine	17	DE	63
Vickers, Alfred T	3	DE	172
Benton	32	DE	133
Cassandra A	10	DE	180
Catharine J	1	DE	179
Edward W	7	DE	172
Elizabeth	48	DE	63
Elizabeth S	40	DE	158
Elizabeth W	17	DE	208
Fanny	23	DE	172
Isaac B	4	DE	158
Isaac O	41	DE	158
John B	29	DE	179
John H	6/12	DE	156
Joseph	5	DE	172
Joseph	9	DE	63
Joseph	70	DE	158
Margaret	24	DE	156
Mary B	6	DE	158
Mary E	21	DE	179
Nancy	49	DE	168
Nancy	50	DE	153
Nathaniel	30	DE	172
Obadiah A	18	DE	158
Rachel	52	DE	158
Rebecca	61	DE	133
Samuel	18	DE	63
Samuel G	50	DE	63
Sarah A	7	DE	172
Sarah Elizabeth	2	DE	63
Washington	8	DE	197
William	14	DE	156
William J	12	DE	158
William N	15	DE	179
Vickery, Harriet A	4	DE	134
Hetty	24	DE	114
Julia A	27	DE	133
Lemuel	32	MD	114
Martha P	7	DE	114
Sarah E	4	DE	114
Vicky, Sarah	69	DE	276
Victor, Henry	16	DE	212
John W	17	DE	214
Vincent, Betsey	33	DE	216
Charles	1	DE	216
Collins	10	DE	216
Comfort	34	DE	239
Emeline	34	DE	239
George	24	DE	96
George	52	DE	241
Harriet	9	DE	110
Hetty	2	DE	96
James	7	DE	216
James	35	DE	216
James K B	3	DE	239
Jane	20	DE	200
Jemima	6	DE	239
Jemima	70	DE	239
John	13	DE	241
Joseph	3	DE	110
Juliann	10	DE	110
Levin	60	DE	96
Margaret	6	DE	216
Margaret	26	DE	294
Margaret	33	DE	110
Maria J	2	DE	239
Mary	18	MD	241
Mary A	18	DE	239
Mary E	15	DE	110
Mary H	12	DE	152
Menego	30	DE	293
Vincent, Nelly	49	DE	96
Noah	30	DE	100
Peter	9	DE	216
Priscilla	20	DE	100
Priscilla	65	MD	241
Ridgeway	39	DE	239
Ruth	5	DE	96
Solomon	44	DE	110
Theodore C	12	DE	110
Warren	21	DE	110
William	4	DE	294
William T	6	DE	111
Wm S	3	DE	217
Vinson, Amelia	3	MD	260
Caroline T	7	DE	282
Elias G	2	DE	37
Eliza	30	DE	37
Elizabeth	18	DE	260
George	6	MD	260
George	22	DE	252
George H	24	DE	281
Gideon	9	DE	282
Hetty J	13	DE	37
Isaac	23	DE	263
Isabel	10	DE	260
James	13	MD	260
Job	10	DE	252
Joseph	1	DE	282
Joseph W	31	MD	281
Kesiah	6	DE	282
Leah	32	DE	282
Levi	13	DE	252
Levin	36	DE	282
Louisa	21	DE	263
Lucinda	40	DE	252
Mahala	7	DE	37
Margaret	26	DE	293
Margaret	46	DE	260
Martha A	12	DE	252
Mary	1	DE	283
Mary	4	DE	282
Nancy	3	DE	282
Nancy	27	DE	282
Noah	9	DE	282
Noah	10	DE	282
Patty	1	DE	282
Perry	22	DE	252
Priscillia	31	DE	267
Sarah J	20	MD	281
Stephen	38	DE	37
Thomas	5	DE	282
William	4	DE	293
William	17	DE	251
William	22	DE	260
William	22	DE	264
Virden, Anna	3	DE	46
Benjamin	29	DE	17
Elizabeth	30	DE	46
Ellen	49	DE	17
Ellen M	16	DE	17
Henry	7	DE	46
Henry	32	DE	46
James H	18	DE	17
John	1	DE	46
Joseph B	24	DE	17
Margaret	9	DE	46
Mary	5	DE	46
Sarah A	20	DE	17
Sarah M	12	DE	17
Thomas	12	DE	46
Voss, Mary	20	DE	223
Nehemiah	10	DE	86
Nehemiah	37	DE	86
Obediah	23	DE	25
Rachel	22	DE	86
Sally	54	DE	86
William	31	DE	86
William	63	DE	86
Vyland, Andrew	68	MD	220
Jason	33	MD	220
Louisa	4	DE	220
Nancy	60	MD	220
Vyland, Sarah	50	DE	220
William	22	MD	220
Wadkins, Ann J	13	DE	218
David S	15	DE	218
Henrietta	10	DE	218
Joseph D	3	DE	218
Mary E	6	DE	218
Thomas	49	DE	218
Wadman, Cassandra	29	MD	224
Harriet	42	DE	224
Luther C	50	MD	224
Waggamon, Elizabeth	22	DE	10
Martha A	5	DE	10
Mary Ann	47	DE	10
Mary H	9	DE	10
Wainwright, Amelia	29	DE	238
Angeline	8	DE	180
Arcada	3	DE	238
Charles	50	DE	203
Hetty	3	DE	289
Isaac H	6	DE	238
James	29	DE	238
James J	22	DE	205
James L	52	DE	291
Jane	7	DE	238
John	4	DE	205
John	50	DE	289
John M	55	DE	205
Joseph	5	DE	289
Joseph	12	DE	205
Laura E	1	DE	238
Lovy	1	DE	289
Lovy	50	DE	289
Mahala	51	DE	291
Mary	7	DE	289
Nancy	60	DE	205
Nelly	50	DE	203
Richard	15	DE	206
Sallie A	12	DE	203
Sarah	5	DE	290
Silas C	26	DE	205
William	8	DE	205
Wm H	15	DE	203
Wales, Charles H	9/12	DE	9
Charlotte	36	DE	18
Eliza	23	DE	9
George	26	DE	9
Jesse	10/12	DE	12
Mary	29	DE	12
Mary P	7	DE	12
Nancy	4	DE	12
Samuel	6	DE	11
Samuel	34	DE	11
Thomas	17	DE	11
Waley, Elizabeth	40	DE	237
Isaac J	22	DE	237
James	18	DE	237
Letitia	19	DE	237
Walker, Catharine	19	DE	44
Catherine	6	DE	53
Charles L	1	DE	129
Comfort	14	DE	52
Daniel G	36	DE	129
David	8	DE	53
David	64	DE	52
Elizabeth	4	DE	274
Elizabeth	4	DE	274
Ellen	43	DE	11
George	23	DE	44
Harriet	30	DE	28
Hetty	10	DE	53
James	38	VA	274
Jane C	9	DE	129
John	16	DE	185
John	31	DE	52
Joseph	37	DE	52
Lambert	14	DE	53
Leah	35	DE	52
Martha	29	DE	129
Mary	5	DE	127
Mary	53	DE	60

Name	Age	State	Page
Walker, Mary A	4	DE	129
Nancy	2	DE	28
Rhoda E	3/12	DE	28
Sarah	2	DE	274
Sarah	30	DE	11
Stephen J	6	DE	129
Thomas	39	DE	11
Thomas	40	DE	60
Thomas	84	DE	11
Unicy	35	DE	274
William	4	DE	53
William	10	DE	112
William	35	DE	28
Wall, Absolem	21	DE	159
Eleanor	31	DE	165
Eli	22	DE	159
George S	4	DE	165
James	30	DE	165
James	52	DE	159
James E	12	DE	165
Mary J	8	DE	165
Nancy C	2	DE	165
Samuel T	10	DE	165
Sarah	52	DE	159
William H	6	DE	165
Wallace, Amelia	8	DE	291
Bell J	9	DE	207
Dolly	6	DE	291
Elizabeth	29	DE	198
Elizabeth	29	DE	291
Henry	41	MD	207
Isabella	16	DE	198
Jacob W	22	DE	198
John	2	DE	66
John H	24	DE	198
John W	36	DE	291
Lemilia	60	MD	207
Lewis E	10	DE	198
Levin	5	DE	291
Margaret	50	MD	198
Mary	4	DE	291
Sarah A	31	DE	198
Wm S	7	DE	291
Waller, Ann	30	DE	235
Ann	52	DE	290
Ann	52	DE	291
Benjamin	35	DE	250
Benjamin F	23	DB	253
Caroline	22	MD	253
Catharine	12	DE	230
Ebenezer	33	DE	250
Eby A	4	DE	242
Eleanor	7	DE	250
Frances	33	DE	234
George	2	DE	292
Hamilton	35	DE	253
Isma	30	DE	235
James	14	DE	250
James L	4	DE	235
James L	42	DE	235
Jane	45	MD	253
John T	9	DE	250
Jonathan	6/12	DE	242
Jonathan	7	DE	253
Jonathan	35	DE	242
Joseph	3	DE	253
Julia	50	MD	232
Julia A	16	MD	232
Julia A	21	DE	253
Lavinia	7	MD	234
Leah	7	DE	254
Mansel	5	DE	250
Maria	73	DE	254
Mary	65	DE	253
Mary A	25	DE	292
Mary E	23	MD	253
Nelson	50	DE	232
Peter	9	MD	253
Peter	21	DE	195
Phany K	33	DE	235
Phillace E	8	DE	242
Polly E	19	MD	253
Waller, Priscilla	40	DE	250
Rachel	34	DE	242
Rachel	35	DE	250
Rachel	68	MD	253
Rachel E	2	DE	242
Richard	3	DE	250
Sarah	9	MD	234
Sarah	16	DE	258
Sarah E	7	DE	243
Sarah J	6	DE	242
Stansbury J	29	DE	292
Stephen	18	DE	269
Thomas W	10	DE	242
William	16	DE	250
William T	14	MD	232
Wm	8	DE	288
Walls, Absolem	31	DE	158
Alace C	13	DE	190
Alfred	17	DE	93
Ann	27	DE	4
Ann M	54	DE	182
Asa	20	DE	96
Asa	30	DE	43
Cash	10	DE	43
Catharine	38	DE	34
Catherine	6	DE	34
Catherine	44	DE	43
Celia	9	DE	81
Charles E	11	DE	34
Charles H	7/12	DE	8
Charlotte	12	DE	181
Charlotte	36	DE	17
Charlotte	45	DE	184
Clarissa	22	DE	94
Edward	35	DE	57
Edward R	15	DE	186
Eli	22	DE	158
Eli	47	DE	190
Eliza	4	DE	93
Eliza	15	DE	181
Eliza	23	DE	8
Eliza	43	DE	93
Eliza	45	DE	69
Eliza A	18	DE	184
Eliza A	20	DE	184
Eliza T	3	DE	186
Elizabeth	19	DE	34
Elizabeth	46	DE	180
Elizabeth E	14	DE	186
Elizabeth M	13	DE	188
Emily W	16	DE	184
Ennals	13	DE	81
Eunice J	30	DE	186
Gideon	10	DE	186
Gideon	42	DE	186
Gilley	20	DE	186
Hannah	3/12	DE	96
Hannah	24	DE	67
Hannah	41	DE	57
Hannah M	5	DE	186
Harriet	45	DE	186
Harriet J	16	DE	186
Henry	15	DE	181
Hester	6	DE	181
Hester E	15	DE	190
Hetty	25	DE	93
Hetty A	20	DE	43
Isabella	44	DE	184
James	13	DE	93
James	52	DE	158
James H	22	DE	190
James P	53	DE	182
Jesse	10/12	DE	11
Jessissi E	19	DE	81
John	22	DE	69
John	50	DE	186
John C	10	DE	186
John E	18	DE	186
John W	21	DE	190
Jonathan W	14	DE	184
Josiah D	8	DE	190
Lafaette	17	DE	186
Walls, Laura J	9	DE	186
Lemuel R	7	DE	186
Lemuel M	29	DE	183
Lemuel W	13	DE	145
Letty E	8	DE	186
Margaret	45	DE	186
Margaret A	22	DE	183
Mary	29	DE	11
Mary E	12	DE	186
Mary J	16	DE	186
Mary P	7	DE	11
Matilda	42	DE	183
Nancy	4	DE	11
Nancy	51	DE	181
Nehemiah	71	DE	186
Nehemiah R	15	DE	34
Nehemiah W	39	DE	34
Patience	35	DE	43
Peter	2	DE	96
Peter	48	DE	182
Peter S	10	DE	190
Prettyman	3	DE	181
Priscilla	15	DE	69
Purnal	25	DE	67
Rachel A	10/12	DE	43
Renatus	33	DE	186
Rhoda A C	11	DE	186
Robert	61	DE	183
Robert J	11	DE	68
Samuel	11	DE	180
Sarah	19	DE	181
Sarah	52	DE	158
Sidney	17	DE	96
Simon D	20	DE	190
Stephen A	26	DE	186
Susan	6	DE	57
Thomas	52	DE	43
Thomas	77	DE	11
Thomas P	27	DE	4
Thomas P	63	DE	181
William	1	DE	67
William	22	DE	93
William	48	DE	184
William	83	DE	93
William H	8	DE	69
William T	49	DE	69
William Z	23	DE	81
Winfield S	1	DE	186
Walston, Catharine	30	DE	274
Charles M	19	MD	249
David	10	DE	271
Elenor	56	DE	271
George	45	DE	249
James	36	DE	271
John C	15	DE	249
Julia A	40	MD	249
Lambird E	10	DE	249
Levin	40	DE	271
Louisa	7	DE	249
Mary J	2	DE	249
Nancy	30	DE	271
Thomas	6	DE	249
William	60	DE	271
Walter, Alsey	20	DE	114
Caprel	50	DE	114
Cato	60	DE	116
Ebe	30	DE	116
Elizabeth	6	DE	286
Hager	17	DE	285
Henry	12	DE	285
James	25	DE	114
Jonathan	19	DE	204
Lemuel	34	DE	169
Lydia A	2	DE	114
Maria E	6	DE	116
Martha A	2	DE	116
Mary	29	DE	116
Reuben	35	DE	116
Sarah	42	DE	114
Wandom, Ann	20	DE	138
George	26	MD	138
James	20	DE	137

Name	Age	State	Page
Waples, Adeline	33	DE	8
Alfred	6	DE	180
Amos T	16	DE	152
Angeline	6	DE	70
Angeline	19	DE	152
Ann	30	DE	52
Ann	45	DE	44
Anna	44	DE	152
Barsheba A	26	DE	1
Benjamin	10/12	DE	66
Benjamin F	30	DE	66
Benjamin O	25	DE	62
Betsey	33	DE	48
Bill	20	DE	47
Burton M	10	DE	180
Catherine	10	DE	153
Catherine A	9	DE	179
Celiah	54	DE	173
Cornelia A	8	DE	70
Cornelius	4	DE	60
Cornelius	19	DE	180
Cornelius	63	DE	180
David	40	DE	44
David M	8	DE	181
Edgar C	11	DE	1
Eliza	10	DE	169
Elizabeth	16	DE	45
Elizabeth	23	DE	62
Elzey	19	DE	52
George	14	DE	169
George	28	DE	58
George B	11	DE	152
Gideon B	17	DE	34
Grace A	38	DE	152
Hannah	7	DE	14
Henry	7	DE	46
Henry	16	DE	27
Isaac	73	DE	179
James E	13	DE	180
Jane	36	DE	173
Jane	49	DE	180
John	36	DE	70
John B	9	DE	1
John B	46	DE	1
John M	9	DE	37
John T	7	DE	157
John V	32	DE	112
Joseph	15	DE	152
Joseph B	3	DE	66
Joseph H	18	DE	180
Lemuel W	27	DE	184
Letty	7	DE	152
Levinia E	3	DE	70
Louisa B	6	DE	44
Lydia	61	DE	157
Manuel	20	DE	43
Margaret A	22	DE	184
Margarey	6	DE	60
Maria	17	DE	152
Mary	17	DE	152
Mary A	10	DE	44
Mary A	34	DE	157
Mary A	43	DE	179
Mary C	13	DE	173
Mary C	18	DE	184
Mary E	6/12	DE	179
Mary J	25	DE	58
Mary J	32	DE	37
Martha J	13	DE	152
Matilda	42	DE	84
Michael C	4	DE	44
Moses	41	DE	37
Moses	58	DE	121
Peter	1/12	DE	169
Peter	54	DE	179
Peter	68	DE	61
Peter C	6	DE	152
Peter R	38	DE	112
Polly C	27	DE	179
Rachael	58	DE	8
Rachel J	20	DE	184
Rhoda	36	DE	169
Waples, Robert	41	DE	169
Robert	61	DE	184
Robert C	1	DE	62
Robt M	10	DE	70
Ruth J	3	DE	179
Sally T	5	DE	157
Sarah	16	DE	171
Sarah	35	DE	60
Sarah	43	DE	34
Sarah	70	DE	33
Sarah A	5	DE	169
Sarah E	15	DE	34
Sarah L	8	DE	152
Serina	35	DE	70
Sina	60	DE	121
Solomon	20	DE	177
Sophia	9	DE	157
Stephen H	21	DE	49
Susan R	27	DE	66
Thomas	51	DE	152
Thomas	54	DE	173
Thomas	68	DE	157
William D	11	DE	157
William E	37	DE	179
Zadock A	8	DE	117
Ward, Ann	48	DE	256
Benjamin	11	DE	262
Benjamin	41	DE	262
Burton	6	MD	261
Catherine	48	DE	261
Cyrus	3	DE	262
Cyrus	29	DE	295
Daniel	51	DE	76
Edward	2	DE	76
Elijah	4	MD	261
Elizabeth	3	DE	261
Elizabeth	6	DE	259
George	4	DE	259
Gillis	21	DE	262
Harriet A	4	DE	229
Jacob	17	DE	234
James	28	DE	282
James	51	DE	261
James	70	DE	76
James W	5	DE	229
John	15	DE	262
John	33	DE	228
John II	18	DE	261
Joseph	3	DE	262
Joseph	12	DE	259
Joseph	16	DE	234
Joseph	29	DE	76
Lavinia	6	DE	262
Lavinia	13	DE	256
Leah	12	MD	261
Leonard	35	DE	261
Levinia	39	DE	261
Lovy	17	DE	261
Margaret	7	DE	76
Margaret	32	DE	228
Mary	1	DE	262
Mary	25	DE	261
Mary	27	DE	76
Mary	27	DE	229
Mary J	8	DE	259
Mary L	9/12	DE	228
Mary P	3	DE	229
Nancy E	19	DE	262
Priscilla A	35	DE	259
Samuel	3	MD	261
Samuel	45	DE	259
Sarah	41	DE	261
Sarah	50	DE	262
Sarah A	4	DE	228
Thomas	2	DE	259
Umphres	10	DE	259
William	6	DE	76
William	8	DE	261
William	9	DE	262
William	29	DE	229
William J	8	DE	261
Wm J	3/12	DE	229
Ward, Wm J	3/12	DE	229
Ware, Charles	9	DE	49
Francis A	12	DE	49
Hetty	35	DE	49
Thomas W	37	DE	49
William	11	DE	49
Warfield, Jane	27	MD	201
John W	8	MD	201
Jos H	6	MD	201
Jos N	32	MD	201
Samuel J	3	MD	201
Sarah A	8/12	DE	201
Waring, William A	2	DE	184
Warington, John	4	DE	285
Levinia	6	DE	285
Martha	8	DE	285
Sarah	27	DE	285
William	1	DE	285
William J	35	DE	285
Warren, Adeline	14	DE	66
Alexander	19	DE	28
Ann C	6	DE	82
Ann E	2	DE	68
Ann N	6	DE	39
Arpy	58	DE	66
Beniah	9/12	DE	75
Braz	26	DE	67
Charles	10	DE	211
David	30	DE	75
David	31	DE	94
David O	2	DE	66
Ebenezer P	32	DE	36
Edward	21	DE	8
Eliza	12	DE	65
Eliza	39	DE	67
Eliza A	12	DE	66
Eliza A	12	DE	67
Elizabeth	12	DE	85
Elizabeth	26	DE	66
Elizabeth A	13	DE	28
Elizabeth E	14	DE	145
Ellen	22	DE	75
Emeline L	20	DE	145
Francis A	6/12	DE	86
George	13	DE	5
George H	23	DE	39
Grabiel	18	DE	28
Grace	65	DE	67
Henry C	8	DE	67
Hester	23	DE	94
Isaac	6	DE	85
Isaac K	5	DE	66
Isaac T	23	DE	66
Jacob S	18	DE	145
James	15	DE	67
James	24	DE	86
James H	4	DE	66
Jenkins W	49	DE	5
Jeremiah	40	DE	85
John	35	DE	67
John of B	38	DE	66
John R	40	DE	28
John P	6	DE	28
John S	2	DE	165
John W	18	DE	8
Joseph	17	DE	8
Joshua	6/12	DE	94
Julia Ann	13	DE	82
Kendle	12	DE	94
Lavenia E	3	DE	36
Lovey	14	DE	94
Major Sr	82	DE	8
Margaret	33	DE	36
Maria	6	DE	67
Mary	7/12	DE	85
Mary	44	DE	67
Mary D	6	DE	36
Mary E	11	DE	67
Mary J	27	DE	229
Mary J	28	DE	165
Mary O	11	DE	2
Mary R	2	DE	229

Name	Age	St	No.	Name	Age	St	No.	Name	Age	St	No.
Warren, Mary R	46	DE	39	Warrington, Eliza J	5	DE	189	Warrington, WilliamH	15	DE	183
Milly	40	DE	85	Eliza J	6	DE	183	William R	3	DE	161
Mitchel	42	DE	83	Elizabeth	15	DE	48	Zena	71	MD	132
Nancy	1	DE	94	Elizabeth	20	DE	183	Warters, Job	5	DE	272
Nancy	20	DE	67	Elizabeth	24	DE	184	Robert	13	DE	272
Nancy	25	DE	29	Elizabeth	44	DE	189	Sarah	95	DE	272
Nancy	35	DE	94	Elizabeth M	36	DE	183	Washington, Philip	6	DE	72
Nancy	55	DE	75	Emma P	5/12	DE	16	Wasley, Elizabeth	58	DE	52
Nancy	58	DE	36	George C	2/12	DE	181	Hannah B	37	DE	52
Nancy	86	DE	66	George C	7	DE	160	Harry W P	13	DE	52
Penelope	29	DE	175	George H	1	DE	236	John D	10	DE	52
Rachel	2	DE	86	George W	3	DE	132	Watsin, Mary E	23	DE	80
Rachel	30	DE	67	Hannah E	12	DE	183	Watson, Absolem	27	DE	37
Richard	27	DE	145	Harriet P	21	DE	36	Ann	4	DE	155
Robert	3	DE	82	Henrietta	30	DE	11	Ann	29	DE	71
Robert	7	DE	94	Hetty	2	DE	34	Ann	31	DE	80
Robert	15	DE	8	Hetty	14	DE	183	Ann	45	DE	173
Robert	20	DE	28	Hetty	25	DE	289	Ann E	1	DE	73
Robert	50	DE	82	Hetty	29	DE	236	Arabel	4/12	DE	83
Robert	56	DE	145	Hetty A	11	DE	161	Arabel	5/12	DE	82
Robert R	22	DE	145	Hetty R	17	DE	183	Beniah	4	DE	73
Rufus M	19	DE	5	Isaac	21	DE	288	Beniah	7	DE	85
Ruth	1	DE	82	James	10	DE	48	Biddy	15	DE	81
Samuel	3	DE	94	James D	30	DE	184	Burton	36	DE	71
Samuel	16	DE	66	James F	46	DE	183	Caroline	33	DE	55
Samuel	38	DE	165	James H	1	DE	184	Charity	7	DE	81
Samuel	62	DE	94	Jane A	33	DE	13	Charles	35	DE	76
Samuel H	7	DE	28	Jane A	38	DE	181	Cornelius	39	DE	74
Sarah	16	DE	259	John	19	DE	288	Curtis S	40	DE	85
Sarah A	19	DE	67	John	22	DE	160	Daniel	18	DE	79
Sarah Ann	14	DE	85	John	33	DE	16	Daniel	18	DE	150
Sarah Ann	35	DE	82	John H	5	DE	160	David	75	DE	76
Sarah E	8	DE	165	John M	3	DE	185	David S	25	DE	76
Sarah M	17	DE	39	John T	6	DE	183	Deborah	28	DE	74
Sina	8	DE	85	Joseph	61	DE	145	Dinah	40	DE	222
Sina	23	DE	86	Josephine	1	DE	183	Edward	7	DE	155
Sina	25	DE	67	Josephine	8	DE	161	Edward	35	DE	55
Sina	40	DE	28	Josiah J	10	DE	132	Eleanor	36	DE	153
Sophia	8	DE	86	Kendal J	14	DE	183	Elias	2	DE	80
Spicer	29	DE	68	Laura A	3	DE	181	Elias	14	DE	68
Stephen	28	DE	86	Levin	24	DE	236	Elisha	36	DE	155
Stephen Jr	28	DE	66	Luvinia	2	DE	16	Eliza	10	DE	151
Susan	21	DE	68	Margaretta	33	DE	16	Eliza	19	DE	154
Susan E	4/12	DE	68	Margaretta	4	DE	16	Eliza A	13	DE	76
Unice	78	DE	17	Maria	29	DE	161	Eliza Jane	24	DE	81
Wesley F	16	DE	5	Mary	18	DE	236	Elizabeth	7	DE	57
William	17	DE	67	Mary A	2	DE	183	Elizabeth	30	DE	82
William	20	DE	39	Mary B	23	DE	145	Elizabeth	33	DE	83
William	20	DE	94	Mary E	7	DE	189	Elizabeth	64	DE	83
William	44	DE	67	Mary U	6	DE	16	Elizabeth B	7	DE	73
William	48	DE	39	Nancy	20	DE	5	Ellen	16	DE	81
William S	3	DE	68	Nancy	60	DE	288	Eunice	9/12	DE	228
William W	3	DE	28	Nathaniel R	33	DE	181	Eunice	10	DE	222
Warrick, Mary R	50	DE	43	Peter	17	DE	189	George	5	DE	68
Samuel	48	DE	43	Peter	46	DE	45	George	6	DE	85
Warring, James E	3	DE	184	Priscy E	13	DE	132	Handy	9	DE	255
Rhoda A	24	DE	184	Purnel S	6	DE	46	George	11	DE	155
William T	23	DE	184	Rebecca E	38	DE	48	George B	33	DE	74
Warrington, Alfred C	16	DE	13	Renatus	25	DE	160	George B	38	DE	83
Alfred M	7	DE	160	Richard W	15	DE	132	George M	15	DE	147
Ann	8	DE	148	Robert	30	DE	11	George W	3	DE	55
Ann	52	DE	160	Robert	56	DE	183	George W	31	DE	228
Arcada	30	DE	158	Rowland P	2	DE	13	Handy	40	DE	155
Arena C	2	DE	132	Ruth A	13	DE	46	Henry	14	DE	112
Bagwell	1	DE	160	Sally	25	DE	288	Henry	16	DE	168
Bailey A	4	DE	48	Samuel	34	DE	160	Henry	19	DE	83
Benjamin	26	DE	149	Samuel P	1	DE	160	Henry	26	DE	83
Benjamin B	6	DE	236	Sarah A	7	DE	13	Henry	35	DE	151
Benjamin S	35	DE	189	Sarah E	2	DE	236	Hetty	11	DE	169
Bill	17	DE	17	Sarah L	6	DE	161	Hetty	40	DE	75
Caroline	27	DE	160	Silas	21	DE	183	Hetty	62	DE	170
Catharine	32	MD	132	Silas M	12	DE	189	Isaac	3	DE	228
Charles R	13	DE	13	Silas M	45	DE	189	Isaac	40	DE	153
Coard	39	DE	13	Stephen	23	DE	145	Isaac H	4	DE	154
Comfort	46	DE	183	Susan	8	DE	3	Isabella	6	DE	173
Cornelius B	33	DE	183	Susan B	45	DE	46	Isabella	14	DE	81
David M	18	DE	10	Susannah E	8	DE	16	James	4	DE	85
David P	14	DE	189	Thomas	31	DE	161	James	11	DE	156
E H	36	DE	236	William	3/12	DE	236	James	43	DE	155
Edward D	31	DE	236	William	5	DE	13	James J	19	DE	76
Eleanor	23	DE	149	William	60	DE	288	Jane	4/12	DE	79
Elijah	38	MD	132	William B	40	DE	48	Jeremiah	18	DE	74

Name	Age		Pg
Watson, John	2	DE	228
John	12	DE	155
John	14	DE	150
John	19	DE	71
John	27	DE	85
John	27	DE	158
John	40	DE	129
John B	2	DE	129
John M	3	DE	137
John T	7	DE	158
Jonathan	9	DE	9
Joseph	1	DE	85
Joseph	6	DE	228
Joseph	10	DE	191
Joseph	18	DE	81
Joseph	44	DE	228
Joseph	55	DE	81
Josephine	8	DE	228
Kensey A	6	DE	188
Kitty C	16	DE	155
Lemuel	4/12	DE	173
Louisa	13	DE	71
Lydia	27	DE	158
Lydia	27	DE	173
Luvinia C	7	DE	154
Margaret	60	DE	85
Margianna	25	DE	81
Maria	33	DE	76
Mariah	24	DE	85
Martha A	1	DE	37
Martha J	12	DE	154
Mary	25	DE	158
Mary	40	DE	129
Mary	44	DE	79
Mary	45	DE	81
Mary	66	DE	228
Mary	70	DE	156
Mary A	3	DE	151
Mary A	7	DE	173
Mary Ann	10/12	DE	80
Mary C	11	DE	154
Mary E	4	DE	183
Mary E	23	DE	79
Mary J	6	DE	160
Mary J	7	DE	76
Mary J	24	DE	228
Mary J	28	DE	228
Matilda	38	DE	155
Milton	18	DE	69
Minos	10	DE	150
Mitchell	8	DE	179
Myranda	7	DE	62
Nancy	11	DE	155
Nancy	17	DE	80
Nancy	29	DE	73
Nancy	37	DE	155
Nathaniel	30	DE	173
Nicholas	13	DE	155
Nutter C	12	DE	74
Paynter	40	DE	112
Peter R	5	DE	137
Priscilla	14	DE	83
Priscilla	74	DE	55
Priscilla Ann	15	DE	82
Purnal	6	DE	155
Pusey	8	DE	222
Rachel	6	DE	155
Rachel	15	DE	153
Rachel A	7	DE	185
Ritty A	9	DE	154
Robert	5	DE	158
Robert	13	DE	82
Robert H	13	DE	84
Robert T	8	DE	85
Rowland	15	DE	13
Sallie	6	DE	228
Sarah	2	DE	158
Sarah	20	DE	85
Sarah	40	DE	151
Sarah A	14	DE	154
Sarah C	13	DE	75
Sarah C	38	DE	85
Watson, Sarah E	10	DE	74
Sarah E	10	DE	80
Sarah E	22	DE	83
Sarah J	6	DE	151
Smith	40	DE	75
Sophia	72	DE	34
Susan	5	DE	74
Susan	9	DE	37
Susan	25	DE	37
Susan E	6	DE	75
Thomas	21	DE	79
Thomas	39	DE	83
Thomas	43	DE	82
William	9	DE	155
William	14	DE	155
William	24	DE	79
William	46	DE	80
William B	4	DE	71
William B	32	DE	73
William E	6	DE	55
William H	7	DE	80
William J	3	DE	222
Watts, Lemuel	32	DE	168
Rosannah	1	DE	56
Weans, Ezekiel W	11	DE	125
Webb, Ann	3	DE	96
Ann	5	DE	96
Betsy	14	DE	95
Catherine	10	DE	78
Charles	13	DE	81
Charles	46	DE	81
Eliza	14	DE	78
Eliza	25	DE	95
Eliza	39	DE	238
Eliza A	8	DE	160
Eliza A	8	DE	167
Eliza J	14	DE	78
Elizabeth	19	DE	86
Emeline	10	DE	160
Emery	19	DE	78
Eunice	25	DE	96
George	13	DE	95
George	15	DE	78
Isaac C	30	DE	95
Jacob	55	DE	78
Jacob	55	DE	89
Jesse	38	DE	78
Jessisi	50	DE	78
James	25	DE	78
James	27	DE	96
James J	40	DE	166
James R	4	DE	166
James R	6	DE	160
Jane	7	DE	95
Jane	20	DE	78
John	1	DE	95
John	2	DE	78
John	23	DE	86
Jonas	45	DE	160
Joshua	30	DE	96
Louisa J	6	DE	81
Lovey	4/12	DE	96
Mary	3	DE	96
Mary	5	DE	95
Mary	17	DE	166
Mary	48	DE	77
Mary A	24	DE	96
Mary E	3	DE	81
Mary Jane	26	DE	81
Mason	31	DE	81
Nancy	53	DE	89
Nancy	55	DE	81
Nancy	56	DE	81
Priscilla	40	DE	166
Priscilla	44	DE	160
Rachael	11	DE	81
Rachael	17	DE	81
Robert	21	DE	81
Sally	23	DE	81
Sarah	7	DE	78
Sarah Ann	4	DE	81
Thomas	18	DE	78
Webb, William	4/12	DE	86
William	18	DE	81
William	39	DE	86
Welba, Sena A	22	DE	230
Welbrun, Catharine	14	DE	124
Ellen	11	DE	124
George	40	DE	124
Hannah	10	DE	124
Mary	35	DE	124
Nancy	8	DE	124
Robinson	1	DE	124
Semra	3	DE	124
William	16	DE	124
Welby, Cannon	31	DE	229
Eliza	28	DE	22
Elizabeth	8	DE	286
Francis	38	DE	22
George	12	DE	227
Henry E	24	DE	22
Hester A	8	DE	202
Hester A	25	DE	222
John	13	DE	286
Joseph	28	DE	232
Joseph N	5	DE	222
Levin W	33	DE	227
Louisa	20	DE	22
Loxly	31	DE	222
Lucinda	6	DE	22
Margaret	23	DE	229
Maria	28	DE	227
Martha	11	DE	286
Mary A	1	DE	227
Nancy	21	DE	227
Nathaniel	40	DE	220
Philip	63	DE	21
Sarah A	22	DE	229
Sarah J	4	DE	227
Susan	35	DE	220
Unice	54	DE	21
William D	12	DE	220
Wm E	7	DE	227
Welch, Ana E	23	DE	106
Clara E	7	DE	35
Elizabeth	50	DE	71
Emily J	5	DE	66
Frances	13	DE	65
George	9	DE	71
George F	5	DE	35
George M	16	DE	65
Herbert A	1	DE	35
James	16	DE	106
James	27	DE	106
John B	3	DE	66
Joseph O	28	DE	225
Luther H	48	DE	65
Margaret	7	DE	66
Martin	16	IE	52
Mary	11	DE	66
Mary	38	DE	65
Mary A	10	DE	35
Mary P	32	DE	35
Nathaniel	16	DE	68
Nehemiah D	41	DE	35
Sarah	14	DE	65
Thadeus P	3	DE	35
Thomas	12	IE	52
Weldon, Ellen	4	DE	18
George	2	DE	18
Frances	18	DE	18
Jane	20	DE	137
Jane	24	DE	131
Joseph of E	25	DE	18
Welham, Alfred	56	DE	199
Elizabeth A	26	DE	199
Well, Charles T	22	DE	193
George M	20	DE	193
John M	45	DE	193
Margaret	46	DE	193
Mary	18	DE	193
Sarah E	12	DE	193
Weller, Clarisa	19	DE	256
Welles, Hiram	8	DE	89

Name	Age	State	Page	Name	Age	State	Page	Name	Age	State	Page
Welles, Julianna	30	DE	89	West, Elizabeth	31	DE	54	West, Mary	4	DE	286
Mary E	8	DE	89	Elizabeth	37	DE	161	Mary	6	DE	115
Solomon	30	DE	89	Elizabeth	60	DE	147	Mary	6	DE	281
Wellin, Catherine	30	DE	200	Ellen	56	DE	161	Mary	16	DE	54
Isaac	34	DE	200	Emily	19	DE	53	Mary	16	DE	288
Wells, Daniel J	15	DE	260	Ephraim	19	DE	164	Mary	22	DE	163
Edward	7/12	DE	276	Ephraim	34	DE	288	Mary	30	DE	49
Elizabeth	2	DE	153	Esther	7	DE	285	Mary	34	DE	11
Emeline	27	DE	276	Ezekiel L	16	DE	123	Mary	45	DE	285
Ephrain	30	MD	276	George	6	DE	11	Mary	56	DE	158
Freeborn G	45	DE	260	George	11	DE	289	Mary	60	DE	262
Garritson	1	DE	162	George	35	MD	115	Mary A	19	DE	52
James	1	DE	276	George H	18	DE	123	Mary A	30	DE	19
Jane	31	DE	153	George T	19	DE	277	Mary A	42	DE	54
Jesse T	18	DE	260	Grace	2	DE	116	Mary D	7	DE	47
John	12	MD	162	Greensbury E	1/12	DE	180	Mary H	14	DE	123
John	16	DE	287	Handy	26	DE	147	Mary J	18	DE	161
Joseph	21	DE	287	Hannah R	25	DE	32	Mary J E	17	DE	163
Joseph	25	DE	287	Hetty	25	DE	168	Middy	36	DE	281
Kendal	3	DE	153	Hetty	34	DE	289	Milby	51	DE	161
Lurany	30	DE	287	Hetty A	9	DE	113	Nancy	2	DE	277
Mary	22	DE	287	Hellen	29	DE	150	Nancy	5	DE	147
Penn	24	DE	287	Isaac	5	DE	288	Nancy	15	DE	288
Pirnetta	25	DE	162	Isaac	7	DE	289	Nancy	19	DE	114
Sabra	46	MD	260	Isaac	60	DE	286	Nancy	32	DE	288
Sarah	17	DE	161	Isaac C	7	DE	123	Nancy	38	DE	114
Sarah	56	DE	161	Isaac C	45	DE	123	Nancy	38	DE	123
Thomas	35	DE	153	Jacob	14	DE	54	Nancy	65	DE	114
Thomas Jr	61	DE	161	Jacob	56	DE	54	Nancy A	22	DE	161
William	28	DE	277	Jacob J	7	DE	161	Nancy W	22	DE	163
William H	30	MD	162	Jacob J	22	DE	180	Naomi	18	DE	259
West, Abel	30	DE	288	James	3	DE	290	Painter	8	DE	288
Adaline	7	DE	90	James	72	DE	233	Patience F	15	DE	90
Albert	25	DE	286	James A of B	6	DE	158	Paynter G	14	DE	161
Alcy	23	DE	286	James D	10	DE	123	Peter W	2	DE	114
Alcy	60	DE	286	James F	10/12	DE	6	Phillip	13	DE	288
Alice	62	DE	56	Jane	5	DE	235	Phillip	22	DE	259
Amanda	12	DE	6	Jane	27	DE	286	Phillip	22	DE	280
Amelia	17	DE	288	Jane	33	DE	115	Phillip	31	DE	113
Amy Jane	18	DE	280	Jane	37	DE	114	Phillip	31	DE	150
Andrew	36	DE	288	Jannet	37	DE	114	Phillip A	63	DE	180
Ann	20	DE	180	Jehu	74	DE	161	Priscilla	6	DE	289
Bailey	42	DE	54	John	2	DE	6	Priscilla N	8	DE	288
Bartimus	17	DE	28	John	11	DE	53	Rachel	2	DE	168
Bayard	8/12	DE	286	John	29	DE	32	Rachel R	17	DE	114
Benjamin	7	DE	53	John	37	DE	290	Rebecca	12	DE	49
Benjamin M	1	DE	161	John	41	DE	6	Rebecca W	7	DE	114
Burton	13	DE	289	John	75	DE	163	Reuben	7	DE	115
Burton	52	DE	288	John M	1	DE	151	Reuben	37	DE	114
Catherine	14	DE	53	John P	26	DE	277	Ritty A	21	DE	114
Catherine R	4	DE	54	Joseph	7/12	DE	288	Robert	4	DE	11
Charles	3	DE	285	Joseph	1	DE	163	Robert	34	DE	11
Charles H	19	DE	114	Joseph	8	DE	90	Robert	38	DE	47
Charles P	11	DE	11	Joseph	15	DE	158	Ruth	48	DE	52
Charlotte	25	DE	286	Joshua	19	DE	288	Ruth	3	DE	53
Charlotte	40	DE	113	Joshua C	4	DE	114	Samuel	12	DE	54
Citturah	6	DE	54	Joshua C	62	DE	114	Samuel	21	DE	115
Clarissa	49	DE	54	Lambert	26	DE	169	Samuel	51	DE	53
Clementine	31	DE	47	Leah	6/12	DE	90	Sarah	2	DE	147
Clementine S	49	DE	49	Leah	5	DE	289	Sarah	3	DE	281
Cornelius	25	DE	288	Lemuel	26	DE	168	Sarah	6	DE	286
Curtis S	3	DE	52	Lemuel	59	DE	113	Sarah	9	DE	115
Daniel	7	DE	147	Lewis	14	DE	171	Sarah	10	DE	288
David R	10	DE	54	Lewis	60	DE	47	Sarah	15	DE	180
Davis	25	DE	290	Louisa	12	DE	161	Sarah	18	DE	288
Deborah A	23	DE	53	Louisa	16	DE	23	Sarah	21	DE	277
Edward	22	DE	53	Louisa H	2/12	DE	47	Sarah	22	DE	151
Eleanor	25	DE	147	Louisa M	12	DE	163	Sarah C	13	DE	114
Eleanor	54	DE	163	Lovenia	8/12	DE	290	Sarah C	13	DE	194
Elenor	30	DE	8	Lozeny	18	DE	90	Sarah E	8	DE	11
Elenor	37	DE	286	Lucinda	16	DE	24	Sarah E	17	DE	129
Eli P	29	DE	161	Luke	4	DE	116	Spencer	29	DE	147
Eli P	29	DE	163	Mahala	28	DE	290	Stockley	22	DE	10
Elisha J	30	VA	129	Margaret	5	DE	290	Stockley C	10	DE	161
Eliza	18	DE	53	Margaret	26	DE	147	Thomas	24	DE	151
Eliza	36	DE	6	Margaret	28	DE	233	Thomas of R	64	DE	158
Elizabeth	1	DE	114	Margaret C	8	DE	47	Thomas P	13	DE	180
Elizabeth	1	DE	147	Margaret J	4	DE	7	Thomas W	3	DE	163
Elizabeth	8	DE	54	Maria	5	DE	285	Unicy	14	DE	279
Elizabeth	13	DE	147	Martha	4	DE	168	William	6	DE	290
Elizabeth	14	DE	147	Martha	14	DE	52	William	9	DE	53
Elizabeth	21	DE	164	Martha A	5	DE	114	William	15	DE	285

West, William	21 DE 164	Wheatly, William	19 DE 269
William	45 DE 52	William	56 MD 269
William A	18 DE 54	Wheeler, Elias R	9 DE 150
William H	14 DE 6	James	23 DE 86
William Russell	9 DE 11	Mary E	12 DE 188
William T	25 DE 113	Rhoda Ann	22 DE 86
Wilmo	25 DE 163	William	24 DE 86
Wingate	28 DE 281	White, Alice	43 DE 14
Wetherby, Lazarus	5 DE 245	Alice A	27 DE 53
Leah A	14 DE 245	Adaline	8/12 DE 15
Mary	8 DE 245	Alfred	10 DE 15
Mary	48 MD 245	Alfred	21 DE 16
Moses	11 DE 245	Andrew R	12 DE 16
Whaite, Elizabeth	W2/12 DE 59	Ann	7 DE 45
Whales, Elias G	9 DE 149	Ann	45 DE 15
Whaley, Elizabeth	16 DE 293	Ann E H	6 DE 73
Isaac	22 DE 263	Anna	3 DE 39
Letty	20 DE 263	Ansley M	2 DE 83
Purnal	6 DE 277	Arena	2 DE 255
William	1 DE 9	Benjamin D	37 DE 15
William	21 DE 234	Betsy	19 DE 54
Wharton, Amanda D	5 DE 170	Catherine	8 DE 16
Amy	22 DE 92	Charity A	9 DE 56
Anna	23 DE 92	Charlotte	6 DE 39
Charles H	9/12 DE 235	Charlotte E	7 DE 33
Dean	23 DE 150	Comfort	80 DE 15
Edward T	10 DE 170	Daniel	11 DE 58
Eliza	16 DE 118	Daniel	60 DE 56
Elizabeth	32 DE 170	David	9 DE 62
Elizabeth	43 DE 117	David	23 DE 56
Elizabeth	60 DE 296	David H	5 DE 58
Hetty	7 DE 118	Edward	3/12 DE 39
Isaac R	38 DE 121	Edward J	4/12 DE 33
James	11 DE 118	Edward W	2/12 DE 58
James H	8 DE 170	Eliza W	24 DE 15
James H	29 DE 92	Elizabeth	3 DE 44
Jane	18 DE 118	Elizabeth	18 MD 241
John	19 DE 118	Elizabeth	32 DE 203
John	28 DE 173	Elizabeth	38 DE 255
John B	10 DE 120	Elizabeth	45 DE 44
John W	20 DE 156	Elizabeth	60 DE 153
Joseph	27 DE 235	Elizabeth A	26 DE 34
Joshua	35 DE 170	Ellen R	8 DE 83
Julia A	45 DE 121	George	3 DE 43
Love H	35 DE 151	George E	2 DE 225
Lurany	21 DE 235	George W	11 DE 83
Margaret	46 DE 118	George W	39 DE 83
Maria	18 DE 118	Geo P	38 DE 225
Martin	33 DE 121	Hannah	2 DE 58
Mary	2 DE 117	Hannah	45 DE 56
Mary	35 DE 72	Hannah W	22 DE 53
Mary A	8 DE 121	Hannah W	53 DE 53
Mary E	3 DE 92	Harriet	30 DE 43
Mary H	7 DE 170	Henry	15 DE 62
Nathaniel	40 DE 151	Henry	75 DE 43
Philip H	9 DE 122	Henry J	20 DE 15
Philip W	38 DE 122	Hetty	37 DE 15
Rhoda C	7 DE 151	Hetty J	3 DE 15
Sarah	36 DE 122	Hiram	9 DE 228
Sarah E	5/12 DE 170	Hiram	11 DE 218
Sarah E	4 DE 121	Isaac	42 DE 32
Sarah J	3 DE 151	Jacob	10 DE 58
Smart	50 DE 72	Jacob	39 DE 33
Stephen	7 DE 123	Jacob M	38 DE 39
Stephen	9 DE 118	James	42 DE 37
Walter J	2 DE 122	James	45 DE 14
William	13 DE 118	Jane	17 DE 255
William	41 DE 118	Jesse	56 DE 16
William H	10 DE 151	John	4 DE 255
William H	36 DE 117	John	13 DE 52
Wheatly, Andrew	2 DE 270	John	31 DE 15
Eleanor	51 DE 269	John	34 DE 58
Elizabeth	26 DE 269	John H	4/12 DE 43
James B	14 DE 269	Jonas	22 DE 15
Jeremiah	1 DE 230	Joseph	8 DE 63
Maranda H	16 DE 269	Joseph G	22 MD 263
Martha	8 DE 270	Joseph J	25 MD 260
Nancy	23 DE 270	Lavenia	22 MD 263
Seth B	17 MD 220	Lavenia	22 MD 261
Stansbury J	9 DE 270	Leonard W	11 DE 225
Turpin M	11 DE 269	Louisa	6 DE 56
Uphena	8 DE 270	Lucy P	4 DE 225

White, Luvenia A	13 DE 35		
Lydia	12 DE 56		
Lydia A	19 DE 152		
Lydia J	10 DE 16		
Margaret	6 DE 15		
Margaret	34 DE 56		
Margaret	80 DE 14		
Mariah	30 DE 37		
Mary	12 DE 255		
Mary	45 DE 32		
Mary A	10 DE 16		
Mary A	13 DE 16		
Mary C	1 DE 56		
Mary E	8 DE 15		
Mernerva A	7 VA 203		
Nancy	9 MD 6		
Nancy	52 DE 16		
Orange	36 DE 56		
Peter	39 MD 255		
Purnal	33 MD 203		
Robert	6 DE 44		
Robert	17 DE 56		
Robert	59 DE 15		
Robert C	22 DE 34		
Robert M	24 DE 152		
Rosena S	4 ? 203		
Sally	46 DE 44		
Samuel	20 DE 56		
Samuel	20 DE 62		
Samuel C	9 MD 203		
Sarah	1 DE 123		
Sarah	14 DE 255		
Sarah	15 DE 56		
Sarah	25 DE 58		
Sarah	32 DE 33		
Sarah	32 DE 39		
Sarah A	2 DE 33		
Sarah A	13 DE 62		
Sarah C	14 DE 83		
Sarah T	12 DE 44		
Sarah W	37 DE 83		
Sheppard	9 DE 44		
Sophia E	35 DE 225		
Theodore W	10 MD 203		
Twilly E	8 DE 255		
Wallace	10 DE 15		
William	6 DE 58		
William	10 DE 33		
William	10 DE 39		
William	55 DE 44		
William H	10 DE 44		
William W	34 DE 15		
Wm H	25 MD 232		
Winder	6 DE 255		
Wrixam W	27 DE 53		
Wiggin, Nancy	19 DE 125		
Wilbey, Gideon	21 DE 42		
Wilburn, Ellen	10 DE 125		
Nancy	8 DE 125		
Robinson	1 DE 125		
Serena	3 DE 125		
Wilby, Abner	34 DE 39		
Adaline D	11 DE 220		
Albert	12 DE 228		
Alexander	7 DE 223		
Ann M	8 DE 228		
Burton S	9 DE 230		
Edward	5 DE 222		
Edward	40 DE 230		
Eliza	28 DE 21		
Elizabeth	24 DE 39		
Elizabeth	38 DE 228		
Frances	38 DE 21		
Garrett L	18 DE 230		
Henry E	24 DE 20		
Hetty	21 DE 76		
Hiram	3 DE 222		
James	13 DE 222		
James A	6 DE 39		
John	6 DE 222		
John	43 DE 111		
John E	11 DE 223		

Name	Age	State	Page
Wilby, Joseph F	1	DE	223
Josephine	7	DE	230
Joshua C	13	DE	230
Julia A	27	DE	35
Louisa	20	DE	21
Louisa K	10/12	DE	230
Lucinda	6	DE	21
Martha	7/12	DE	39
Mary J	12	DE	228
Mary H	7/12	DE	76
Nancy	21	DE	292
Nehemiah	40	DE	223
Philip H	4	DE	39
Philip J	3	DE	228
Rebecca A	15	DE	230
Sarah	16	DE	228
Sarah	38	DE	222
Sarah E	10/12	DE	222
Solomon	42	DE	228
Susan	35	DE	223
William H	12	DE	223
Wilcots, Mary	22	DE	70
Mary F	38	DE	71
Purnal	23	DE	70
Wilcox, Catherine	7	DE	73
Joseph	25	DE	70
Wilcuts, _____	10	DE	71
Elizabeth	29	DE	70
Hester	8	DE	70
John	36	DE	70
John H	12	DE	70
Mary	6	DE	70
Mary A	24	DE	70
Purnel A	1	DE	70
Robert H	9	DE	70
William J	14	DE	70
Wilkenson, Margaret	40	MD	140
Wilkins, Angeline	26	DE	28
Charlotte S	1	DE	11
Eli W	4	DE	11
Eliza J	1	DE	68
George	11	DE	68
James	36	DE	68
James B	7	DE	11
John	32	DE	28
John A	4	DE	28
Letty	34	DE	68
Letty A	7	DE	68
Mary E	14	DE	68
Nelly P	2	DE	28
Rebecca	3	DE	11
Rowland	3/12	DE	28
Sarah A	9	DE	68
Sarah A	21	DE	11
Thomas J	4	DE	68
William	26	DE	280
William	33	DE	11
Wilkinson, Angelina	12	DE	88
Caroline	4	DE	88
David	1	DE	88
James	76	DE	88
John	35	DE	88
Levin	65	DE	88
Mary	8	DE	20
Permelia	46	DE	88
Sally	35	DE	88
Samuel	10	DE	88
Sarah	6	DE	88
Thomas	5	DE	88
William	13	DE	88
Willen, Charles	11	DE	209
Charles	25	DE	99
Charles	45	DE	209
Eliza A	30	DE	209
Elizabeth	4	DE	209
George	20	DE	99
Isaac	8	DE	99
Isaac	68	DE	99
James	8	DE	209
John	11/12	DE	100
Joseph	3/12	DE	209
Leah	19	DE	99
Willen, Mary	15	DE	99
Mary	15	DE	209
Mary	26	DE	99
Mary C	47	DE	99
Mary E	15	DE	205
Samuel	27	DE	99
Thomas	12	DE	99
Thomas	59	DE	99
William	2	DE	100
William	4	DE	209
William	18	DE	205
Willeson, Matthias	11	DE	139
Willey, Ann	7	DE	98
Ann	36	DE	98
Ann	41	DE	106
Anna	31	DE	108
Anna	36	DE	98
Burton A	12	DE	156
Caroline	2	DE	98
Catherine	28	DE	108
Charles C	6	DE	156
Cohen P	4	DE	55
Cyrus	10	DE	108
Daniel	13	DE	98
Daniel	24	DE	99
Ebenezar	1	DE	98
Eleanor	22	DE	156
Eli	35	DE	47
Eliza	8	DE	98
Eliza	12	DE	106
Eliza Ann	17	DE	98
Ezekiel	6	DE	108
Ezekiel	20	DE	98
Foster	17	DE	108
George	5	DE	38
George	10	DE	98
George	10	DE	99
George	18	DE	15
George R	55	DE	38
Gideon	21	DE	41
Greensbury	30	DE	15
Hester	35	DE	98
Isaac	1	DE	107
James	11	DE	94
James	11	DE	98
James	14	DE	51
James	16	DE	106
James	26	DE	291
Jeremiah	38	DE	94
John	5	DE	94
John	16	DE	291
John C	5	DE	55
Joseph	7	DE	98
Joseph	12	DE	95
Joshua	55	DE	55
Kendal	5	DE	291
Kesiah	49	DE	55
Lemuel A	7	DE	34
Levenia	24	DE	164
Louder	6	DE	108
Lovey	3	DE	98
Lucinty	14	DE	47
Margaret	9/12	DE	107
Margaret	6	DE	95
Margaret	16	DE	94
Margaret	34	DE	94
Margaret A	1	DE	156
Mary	4	DE	107
Mary	6	DE	98
Mary	34	DE	94
Mary	35	DE	38
Mary A	24	DE	99
Mary Ann	8	DE	108
Mary C	4	DE	98
Mary E	15	DE	38
Mary E	17	DE	98
Minus	41	DE	108
Mitchel	11	DE	108
Moses R	5/12	DE	55
Nancy	27	DE	164
Nancy	28	DE	108
Nancy	39	DE	156
Willey, Nancy	59	DE	108
Nancy P	1	DE	108
Nathaniel	36	DE	98
Peter	14	DE	98
Rachel	15	DE	98
Rebecca	40	DE	291
Richard	7	DE	106
Robert	3	DE	98
Robert	26	DE	107
Robert	38	DE	94
Robert J	45	DE	98
Sallie	2	DE	94
Samuel	7	DE	291
Samuel	11	DE	46
Samuel	15	DE	106
Samuel J	41	DE	106
Sarah	15	DE	291
Sarah	30	DE	108
Sarah E	6	DE	98
Sheppard	12	DE	98
Simeon	24	DE	99
Solomon	36	DE	156
Theodore	31	DE	99
Tilman	22	DE	108
Vashti	20	DE	108
Whitman	3	DE	108
Whitman	57	DE	108
William	8	DE	94
William	20	DE	291
William	21	DE	98
William	38	DE	107
William	45	DE	98
William H	9	DE	156
William J	29	DE	164
Willger, Emma	1	DE	136
Jacob A	45	DE	136
James	10	DE	136
John	16	DE	136
Joshua T	18	DE	136
Maria	41	DE	136
Matilda	13	DE	136
Robert	4	DE	136
Thomas	11	DE	136
William	6	DE	136
Willgos, Clarissa A	20	DE	125
Ephraim H	22	DE	125
Joshua J T	1	DE	125
Williams, Alepha	71	DE	266
Alfred	22	DE	136
Amelia C	19	DE	172
Ann	4	DE	90
Ann	18	DE	88
Ann	18	DE	106
Ann	26	DE	124
Ann	68	DE	202
Ann	70	DE	3
Ann E	34	DE	90
Ann M	6	DE	126
Arcada	19	DE	125
Ark	16	DE	106
Benjamin	10	DE	292
Benjamin	21	DE	88
Betsey	38	DE	87
Bill	8	DE	90
Catherine	8	DE	90
Charles	16	DE	137
Charles G	9/12	DE	206
Charles M	8	DE	212
Confort	31	DE	121
Daniel	2	DE	124
Daniel	20	DE	196
David	2	DE	95
David	6	DE	206
David	15	DE	272
David	30	DE	95
David	45	DE	272
David A	21	DE	205
Ebe T	2/12	DE	126
Ebenezer F	28	DE	126
Edward	17	DE	215
Edward	21	DE	125
Eleanor J	20	DE	127

Name	Age	St	Pg	Name	Age	St	Pg	Name	Age	St	Pg
Williams, Elenor	33	DE	266	Williams, Lemuel S	24	DE	126	Williams, Townsend	41	DE	106
Eliann	30	DE	95	Levinia	39	DE	199	Waitman	20	DE	79
Elihu	29	DE	273	Lilly T	45	DE	272	Whittington	10	DE	88
Elijah	4	DE	125	Lorenzo B	4	DE	207	Whittington	26	DE	206
Elijah	61	DE	242	Louisa	3	DE	266	Whittington M	6	DE	88
Eliza	8/12	DE	266	Louisa H	8	DE	126	William	6	DE	88
Eliza	22	DE	87	Lovey	25	DE	273	William	14	DE	50
Eliza A	25	DE	212	Luther	40	DE	266	William	19	DE	124
Eliza J	9/12	DE	170	Lydia	8	DE	142	William	28	DE	80
Eliza J	20	DE	242	Lydia	9	DE	212	William	32	DE	84
Elizabeth	13	DE	266	Lydia	11	DE	90	William H	14	DE	172
Elizabeth	16	DE	125	Margaret	11	DE	154	William L W	18	DE	126
Elizabeth	19	DE	154	Margaret	24	DE	268	Wm	21	DE	285
Elizabeth	24	DE	206	Margaret	30	DE	271	Wm	35	DE	212
Elizabeth	30	DE	212	Margaret	34	DE	228	Wm H	6	MD	212
Elizabeth	38	NJ	117	Margaret A	26	MD	206	Wilson	41	DE	39
Elizabeth	45	DE	154	Margaret E	17	DE	126	Zadock	12	DE	84
Elizabeth A	10	DE	25	Maria	11	DE	227	Willian, Thomas	25	DE	209
Elizabeth D	22	DE	172	Maria	36	DE	207	Willie, Jeremiah	38	DE	95
Elizabeth H	28	DE	126	Maria J	20	DE	84	Willin, Mary E	15	MD	206
Elizabeth T	20	DE	207	Mark A	26	DE	200	Wm	18	MD	206
Ellen E	3	DE	126	Martha	7	DE	266	Willis, Amelia	52	DE	94
Emeline	26	DE	126	Martha	12	DE	88	Fisher	62	DE	94
Ezekiel C	25	DE	127	Martha	17	DE	192	Frances	16	DE	94
George	10	DE	207	Martha E	4	DE	121	Frances	45	MD	219
George A	7	DE	84	Martha F	4	DE	206	Jefery	48	DE	94
George S	6	DE	207	Martha T	10	DE	84	Jenny	50	DE	94
George S	33	DE	126	Mary	2	DE	269	John	9	DE	94
George W	6	DE	263	Mary	3	DE	271	John	21	DE	94
George W	35	DE	225	Mary	15	DE	225	Nancy	77	DE	291
Gillis	17	DE	100	Mary	22	DE	142	Peggy	30	DE	94
Hannebel	59	MD	126	Mary	29	DE	242	Sarah	12	DE	94
Harriet	38	DE	25	Mary	33	DE	273	Willisams, David	2	DE	96
Harriet	43	DE	26	Mary	39	DE	198	Willy, Isaac R	28	DE	224
Henry	20	DE	131	Mary	47	DE	125	James	14	DE	52
Henry	40	DE	268	Mary C	6	DE	206	Wilson, Alexander	14	DE	234
Henry	40	DE	271	Mary E	4	DE	126	Almira	4	DE	213
Henry J	26	DE	84	Mary E	4	DE	206	Ann	37	DE	182
Hester	12	DE	272	Mary E	5	DE	100	Ann	45	DE	225
Hester	24	DE	80	Mary E	5	DE	142	Ann	67	DE	226
Hester	77	DE	131	Mary E	16	DE	88	Ann J	12	DE	263
Hester J	3	DE	142	Mary E	44	DE	172	Ann M	24	DE	240
Hester L	1	DE	212	Mary J	14	DE	127	Anna	60	DE	3
Hetty	44	DE	100	Mary M	2/12	DE	126	Anna	68	DE	8
Hetty	45	DE	238	Mathias	65	DE	241	Arena R	7	DE	181
Hetty C	6	DE	126	Morgan	24	DE	228	Asa Jr	25	DE	23
Hiram	9	DE	106	Nancy	17	DE	87	Asa Sr	60	DE	23
Isaac	6	DE	124	Nancy	45	DE	88	Asa T	1	DE	12
Isaac	11	DE	100	Nancy	51	DE	237	Barclay	50	DE	43
Isaac	19	DE	272	Nancy	64	DE	118	Benjamin	14	DE	66
Isaac	50	DE	136	Nancy C	2	DE	206	Benjamin F	1	DE	190
Isaac	63	DE	238	Nancy J	17	DE	126	Catherine	8	DE	242
Isaac H	13	DE	238	Nancy M	7	DE	206	Catherine	20	DE	190
Isaac W	10	DE	207	Nathan	68	DE	131	Charles	32	PA	46
James	2/12	DE	212	Nelly	55	DE	136	Celia	36	DE	247
James	9	DE	266	Newton	35	DE	206	Charity	45	DE	243
James	12	DE	100	Peter	15	DE	90	Charity	60	DE	39
James	25	DE	142	Peter	20	DE	90	Charles W	15	DE	176
James H	10/12	DE	273	Phebe A	13	DE	154	Coard	12	DE	190
James L	30	DE	126	Planer	55	DE	207	Comfort	13	DE	22
Jane	21	DE	200	Polly	55	MD	242	Comfort	31	DE	4
Jesse	30	MD	212	Prudence A M	20	DE	126	Curtis	5	DE	23
John	1	DE	95	Rachael	24	DE	88	Cyrus M	3	DE	46
John	2	DE	100	Samuel	18	DE	90	Daniel B	28	DE	190
John	7	DE	124	Samuel	19	DE	87	Daniel F	44	DE	243
John	10	DE	90	Samuel	31	DE	142	David	8	DE	228
John	12	DE	106	Sarah	13	DE	90	Donovan William	6	DE	12
John	14	DE	125	Sarah	15	DE	87	Ebenezer	17	DE	12
John	19	DE	273	Sarah A	24	DE	142	Edward J	23	DE	190
John	30	DE	112	Sarah Ann	20	DE	88	Edward R	11	DE	8
John	30	MD	206	Sarah C	9	DE	126	Eli G	30	DE	58
John	43	DE	90	Sarah E	3	DE	80	Eli W	19	DE	12
John H	1	DE	142	Sarah E	5	DE	212	Elias R	8	DE	181
John H	27	DE	199	Sarah E	24	DE	126	Eliza J	8	DE	12
John T	8	DE	25	Sarah H	11	DE	126	Eliza J	9	DE	69
John W	5	DE	126	Smith	80	DE	273	Elivia A	6	DE	227
John W	15	DE	88	Sophia	22	DE	126	Eliza	24	DE	3
John W	58	DE	126	Stephen	48	DE	88	Eliza	30	DE	24
Joseph A	8	DE	207	Thomas	10	DE	173	Elizabeth	4	DE	246
Joshua	45	DE	154	Thomas	46	DE	100	Elizabeth	20	DE	185
Joshua T	2	DE	126	Thomas	50	GB	172	Elizabeth	25	DE	97
Lemuel	23	DE	121	Thomas J	12	DE	125	Elizabeth	28	DE	76

Name	Age	State	Page
Wilson, Elizabeth	31	DE	15
Elizabeth	32	DE	19
Elizabeth	32	DE	8
Elizabeth	38	DE	228
Elizabeth	40	DE	238
Elizabeth	50	DE	190
Elizabeth	60	DE	16
Elizabeth	69	DE	8
Elizabeth	73	DE	219
Elizabeth A	4	DE	12
Elizabeth C	29	DE	22
Elizabeth E	12	DE	176
Elizabeth H	4	DE	13
Ellena	19	DE	23
Elenor	19	DE	23
Elsey	3	DE	18
Elton	4	DE	19
Elzey	56	DE	18
Eunicy	46	DE	256
Fanny E	10	DE	227
Frances	18	DE	19
Gaysworthy D	6	DE	4
Geo	37	DE	246
George	3	DE	19
George	4	DE	246
George	16	DE	18
George	25	DE	66
George F	15	DE	182
George F	20	DE	176
George M	9	DE	190
George W	5	DE	4
Hannah	8	DE	15
Henry	3	MD	281
Henry	35	DE	1
Henry	35	DE	19
Hetty E	8	DE	18
Hetty J	7	DE	38
Hetty W	20	DE	190
Hiram	14	DE	246
Hiram	20	DE	43
Hosea	40	DE	84
Jacob	45	DE	176
Jacob	50	DE	13
James	1	DE	13
James	4	DE	43
James	10	DE	233
James	28	DE	26
James	30	DE	76
James A	11	DE	22
James T	2	DE	62
James P	30	DE	8
Jane	20	DE	16
Janie	28	DE	26
Jarviss W L	1	DE	8
Jeremiah	16	DE	226
Jesse W	3	DE	190
John	10/12	DE	283
John	7	DE	19
John	15	DE	282
John	21	DE	43
John	25	DE	38
John	32	DE	8
John	39	DE	226
John A B	1	DE	38
John C	1	DE	62
John of A	39	DE	18
John Sr	69	DE	8
Jonathan	14	DE	78
Jonathan J	39	DE	182
Joseph	47	DE	12
Joseph of E	25	DE	19
Kendal B	3	DE	181
Kenasy A	6	DE	187
Leah H	29	DE	190
Leah W	28	DE	12
Letitia	33	DE	62
Letitia A	1	DE	13
Levi	17	DE	190
Levicey W	7	DE	8
Louisa	19	DE	43
Louis	23	DE	97
Lydia	32	DE	69
Wilson, Lydia A	7	DE	69
Lydia C	50	DE	190
Lydia H	6	DE	18
Mahala	4	DE	12
Major E	13	DE	12
Major H	12	DE	190
Major Jr	35	DE	8
Maomy	15	DE	22
Marcus E	4	DE	227
Margaret	1	DE	228
Margaret	8	DE	8
Margaret	26	DE	62
Margaret	37	DE	12
Margaret	48	DE	22
Margaret E	6	DE	190
Margaret E	10	DE	13
Margaret M	25	DE	58
Margaret R	5	DE	8
Margaret R	5	DE	18
Martha A	7	DE	180
Mary	11	DE	39
Mary	28	DE	8
Mary	30	DE	246
Mary	35	DE	84
Mary	40	DE	32
Mary	60	DE	18
Mary A	11	DE	62
Mary A	14	DE	62
Mary A	15	DE	12
Mary A	30	DE	13
Mary C	9	DE	4
Mary C	10	DE	190
Mary C	3	DE	228
Mary E	10	DE	18
Mary E	14	DE	80
Mathew D	24	MD	252
Matilda	29	DE	46
Matthew	40	IE	19
Minus C	32	DE	4
Nancy	11	DE	145
Nancy	26	DE	190
Nancy	45	DE	13
Nancy	64	DE	181
Naomi	20	DE	18
Naomi	48	DE	18
Naomi P	2	DE	176
Nathaniel H	11	DE	181
Patience	2	DE	18
Peter	17	DE	18
Peter L	9	DE	12
Rachael	14	DE	84
Rachel A	6	DE	176
Rachel Jane	13	DE	18
Reuben	4/12	DE	58
Reuben	60	DE	16
Reuben P	34	DE	12
Rhoda	31	DE	23
Rhoda	35	DE	283
Rhoda	43	DE	15
Richard	75	DE	19
Riley C	5	DE	69
Robert	25	DE	97
Robert E	1	DE	190
Robert George	2	DE	19
Robert R	2	DE	66
Ruth	55	DE	23
Ruth E	1	DE	69
Ruthy	26	DE	12
Samuel	29	DE	46
Samuel B	6	DE	190
Samuel P	9	DE	32
Samuel R P	1	DE	15
Sarah	5	DE	283
Sarah	6	DE	39
Sarah	8	DE	246
Sarah	16	DE	78
Sarah	32	DE	38
Sarah	37	DE	185
Sarah A	9	DE	18
Sarah A	14	DE	16
Sarah A	18	DE	190
Sarah A	29	DE	38
Wilson, Sarah E	1	DE	12
Sarah E	11	DE	43
Sarah J	5	DE	66
Sarah J	15	DE	32
Sarah J	22	DE	66
Sena	18	DE	252
Stephen	12	DE	246
Sophia	5	DE	243
Susanna	43	DE	176
Susanna T	14	DE	190
Tabitha E	2	DE	190
Theodore J	17	DE	22
Theodore J	42	DE	227
Thomas	9	DE	20
Thomas	15	DE	18
Thomas	16	DE	224
Thomas	23	DE	13
Thomas	25	DE	12
Thomas	25	DE	16
Thomas	25	DE	18
Thomas	36	DE	15
Thomas	56	DE	62
Thomas	78	DE	40
Thomas D	14	DE	43
Thomas E	3	DE	8
Thomas R	32	DE	69
Warrington O	45	DE	190
William	1	DE	181
William	21	DE	36
William	41	DE	38
William	50	DE	18
William J	50	DE	190
William M	1	DE	19
Wm B	56	DE	227
Zachariah P	50	DE	22
Wiltbank, Alfred T	21	DE	49
Ann	6	DE	51
Anna	1	DE	48
Brister	37	DE	50
Charles	8	DE	48
Charles William	6/12	DE	63
Comfort	35	DE	51
Cornelius	38	DE	48
Daffy	80	DE	29
David	4	DE	63
David	61	DE	25
David A	9	DE	25
Diana	34	DE	63
Eliza P	51	DE	49
Elizabeth	5	DE	48
Elizabeth	21	DE	25
George	7	DE	48
George	13	DE	48
George L	3	DE	63
Harriet	12	DE	63
Hester	36	DE	63
Hetty	29	DE	48
Hetty	30	DE	48
James	12	DE	50
James	18	DE	29
Jane	4	DE	48
Jeremiah	5	DE	58
Jerry	35	DE	58
John Cornelius	10	DE	48
John H	25	DE	25
Louisa	6	DE	63
Margaret E	18	DE	25
Mary	8	DE	58
Mary C	3	DE	63
Mary C	16	DE	25
Pompey	57	DE	63
Rachael	30	DE	58
Robert	11	DE	48
Ruth	30	DE	50
Sarah	14	DE	49
Sarah	52	DE	25
Thomas	3	DE	48
Thomas	42	DE	25
Weymouth	77	DE	29
William	10	DE	58
Windham, John	18	DE	297
Windser, Harriet	16	DE	2

Windsor, Ann 29 DE 4
C C 47 DE 239
Charles H R 3 DE 4
Elizabeth 11 DE 218
Elizabeth 11 DE 230
Elizabeth 48 DE 230
Emeline 17 DE 256
George 14 DE 230
George 25 DE 281
Gibson 27 DE 268
Hugh R 1 DE 239
James H 21 DE 256
Jane 20 DE 268
Joanna 18 DE 239
John 22 DE 230
John 49 DE 292
John 68 DE 6
John 73 MD 198
John C 3 DE 279
John McFee 4/12 DE 4
John P 8 DE 239
Joseph 14 DE 256
Joseph 21 DE 292
Joseph B 17 DE 239
Julia A 10 DE 4
Margaret 2 DE 268
Maria J 20 DE 239
Martha 10 DE 295
Mary 30 DE 232
Mary A 3 DE 256
Mary A 44 DE 239
Nancy (wid) 44 DE 256
Philip 32 DE 4
Samuel 13 DE 292
Sarah 16 DE 292
Thomas B 2 DE 279
Thos A 23 DE 232
William John 18 DE 256
Wine, John M 40 DE 178
Mary 39 DE 178
Wines, Mary E 17 DE 24
Wingate, Cannon 26 DE 287
Cannon 39 DE 290
Caroline 19 DE 280
Comfort 38 DE 4
Drucilla C 24 DE 228
Eliza 23 DE 290
Elizabeth 18 DE 242
Eveline E 8/12 DE 228
George 3 DE 280
Hannah 4 DE 4
Hezekiah 5 DE 290
Hezekiah 74 DE 217
Isaac C 20 DE 233
Isaac N C 21 DE 217
Isabel H 1 DE 4
John 13 DE 233
John 21 DE 42
John B 27 DE 228
Josephine 3 DE 4
Julia A 12 DE 275
Kendle B 32 DE 4
Laura A 2 DE 228
Levin 14 DE 208
Lurany 6 DE 280
Lydia C 6 DE 4
Margaret A 8 DE 4
Mary 15 DE 280
Mary C 9 DE 4
Mathew C 18 DE 233
Mathew G 43 DE 233
Nancy 43 DE 233
Nancy 62 DE 171
Nancy 62 DE 217
Phillip 3 DE 290
Phillip 9 DE 280
Phillip 40 DE 280
Phillip G 17 DE 233
Rachel 40 DE 280
Sarah 13 DE 238
Sarah E 10 DE 4
Thomas H 1 DE 228

Winget, Ann M 9 DE 156
Burton J 39 DE 156
Catharine M 1/12 DE 156
Charles T 9 DE 183
David M 23 DE 183
Elizabeth M 20 DE 156
Emeline 12 DE 179
James M 21 DE 183
Job 26 DE 156
John M 25 DE 183
Lucinda J 11 DE 156
Mary 50 DE 183
Mary A 12 DE 183
Nancy 63 DE 156
Thomas R 16 DE 183
Winn, James 12 DE 228
Joseph 46 DE 228
Leah 30 DE 228
Margaret A 4 DE 228
Theodore 9 DE 228
Winright, Angeline 8 DE 180
Sarah E 13 DE 180
Wise, Ann 25 DE 81
Charles 30 DE 81
Wolf, Aby 41 DE 63
Mary E 5/12 DE 236
Wolfe, Abigail 55 DE 57
Ann 46 DE 39
Anna 10 DE 48
Charlotte F 18 DE 39
Daniel 23 DE 47
David C 16 DE 39
David R 42 DE 236
Edward T 9 DE 236
Eliza B 23 DE 39
Elizabeth 40 DE 48
Elizabeth S 4 DE 49
Ellen 42 DE 236
Erasmus W 5 DE 236
George S 12 DE 48
George W 14 DE 236
Hannah 21 DE 47
Hannah 27 DE 60
Henry 12 DE 48
Henry 40 DE 48
Henry A 1 DE 48
James A 24 DE 5
Jane 8 DE 48
Jane 30 DE 60
Jerry 60 DE 48
Joanna R 11 DE 47
John 18 DE 48
Kesa P 21 DE 53
Luisa 47 DE 5
Lydia 43 DE 47
Margaret M 16 DE 5
Mary B 9 DE 48
Nathaniel 2 DE 48
Priscilla 16 DE 57
Reed 48 DE 48
Reese U 15 DE 47
Russell 15 DE 47
Wesley 47 DE 5
William 4 DE 48
William P 22 DE 5
William W 14 DE 58
William W 51 DE 39
Wolford, George 15 DE 8
Wood, Harriet 24 DE 148
Samuel 36 DE 148
Woodard, Caroline 19 DE 84
James 23 DE 84
John 1 DE 84
John 26 DE 84
Thomas 10 DE 84
Woodland, Elisha 38 DE 239
Elizabeth 31 DE 239
Hiram 10 DE 239
Mariah 39 DE 238
Mary E 6 DE 238
Matilda 11 DE 239
Nancy J 14 DE 207

Woodland, Noah J 10 DE 238
Sarah 4 DE 239
Sarah J 5 DE 239
Tempa 58 DE 239
Wm M 1 DE 239
Woolford, Andrew 3 DE 251
Bartholomew 40 DE 243
Bridget 46 DE 251
Caroline 74 DE 243
Charles 6 DE 180
Diannah 44 DE 180
Edward 1 DE 243
Emilia 3 DE 251
Esther 21 DE 251
George 6 DE 251
George 13 DE 180
Hannah 12 DE 180
Henrietta 9 DE 180
Henry 5 DE 251
Jane 7 DE 243
James D 27 MD 250
John 5 DE 243
John 8 DE 180
John 42 DE 180
Leah 25 DE 251
Levin 5 DE 243
Levin 19 DE 251
Louisa 20 DE 238
Maria 22 MD 238
Maria 23 DE 251
Martha 4 DE 243
Mary 2 MD 250
Matilda A 16 DE 180
Priscilla 22 MD 250
Rebecca 9 DE 243
Samuel 3 DE 243
Samuel 17 DE 180
Sarah 7/12 DE 251
Sarah 26 DE 243
Thomas 22 DE 238
Thomas 72 DE 243
William 21 DE 180
Wm J 10 DE 243
Wooten, Upshird 59 DE 121
Wootten, Albert P R 15 DE 2
Amelia 70 DE 267
Amelia A 7 DE 237
Arena 40 DE 275
Edward 43 DE 2
Eleanor 27 DE 263
Eleanor M 16 DE 237
Elijah 26 DE 263
Elizabeth 41 MD 237
George W 10 DE 237
George W 44 MD 237
Gideon W 39 DE 275
Henrietta 35 DE 268
John 23 DE 267
Lavenia 53 DE 2
Martha 3 DE 267
Mary 18 DE 293
Mary J 14 DE 237
Mary R 42 DE 2
Peter 45 DE 267
Polly 14 DE 275
Sarah 7 DE 267
Sarah 13 DE 275
Sarah 23 DE 267
Sarah 50 DE 263
Sarah 60 DE 150
William 30 DE 2
Wm A 10 DE 268
Wootton, Isaac 19 DE 241
Isaac 70 DE 242
Jacob 47 DE 241
Louisa E 6 DE 241
Maria 3 DE 242
Maria 40 DE 241
Mary 68 DE 242
Mary E 17 DE 241
Nathaniel 26 DE 242
Nutter G 35 DE 241

Name	Age	St	Pg	Name	Age	St	Pg	Name	Age	St	Pg
Wootton, Sarah J	25	DE	241	Wright, Ann	5	DE	274	Wright, Nelly	56	DE	209
Warren	5	DE	241	Ann	31	DE	62	Nicholas	29	DE	100
Worden, Edward	8	DE	256	Ann	50	DE	285	Patience	8/12	DE	44
George	15	DE	256	Ann J	12	MD	207	Peter	30	DE	62
Isaac	13	DE	256	Ann M	2	DE	60	Philip	25	DE	193
John G	17	DE	256	Cannon	26	DE	286	Return	4/12	DE	193
Lurana	23	DE	256	Cassandra	45	DE	173	Rhoda A	14	DE	214
Mahala	43	DE	256	Catherine	33	MD	217	Sallie	12	MD	245
Mary	20	DE	256	Charles	1	DE	215	Sallie C	12	DE	173
Nancy	22	DE	256	Charles	40	DE	245	Sallie C	13	DE	8
Sylvester	45	DE	256	Charles	51	DE	215	Samuel S	34	DE	13
William	10	DE	256	Curtis W	10	DE	173	Sarah	10	DE	44
Workman, Ann m	9	DE	24	David	4	DE	44	Sarah E	3	DE	172
Charles	3	DE	248	Elisha	22	DE	193	Sarah E	3	DE	209
Ebenezer E	7	DE	21	Eliza A	12	DE	172	Sena	39	DE	214
Edward	4	DE	285	Eliza A	30	DE	215	Sophia W	6	DE	215
Edward	11	DE	292	Elizabeth	5	DE	62	Thomas	22	DE	204
Eliza	5	DE	260	Elizabeth	11	DE	217	Walter	14	DE	44
Eliza	5	DE	278	Elizabeth	16	DE	286	Warren	40	DE	60
Eliza	1	DE	285	Elizabeth	35	DE	60	Warren	47	DE	44
Elizabeth	5	DE	24	Elizabeth	46	DE	172	Wesley B	14	DE	1
Elizabeth	11	DE	260	Elizabeth	66	DE	209	William	2	DE	274
Elizabeth	18	DE	288	Elizabeth W	4	DE	214	William	7	DE	275
Elizabeth	40	DE	292	Ellen	21	MD	203	William	15	MD	216
Elizabeth	43	DE	285	Emeline	3	DE	275	William	16	DE	217
Elizabeth A	9	DE	21	Emma	7	DE	173	William	18	DE	32
Garrison	2	DE	260	Fortnell	79	DE	13	Wm	16	DE	205
Henry	22	DE	196	Frederick	19	DE	178	Wm W	26	MD	203
Isaac	6	DE	285	Gardiner H	43	PA	173	York, Alfred	11	DE	22
Jacob	7	DE	24	George	5	DE	275	Alley	56	MD	272
James	23	DE	285	Hannah	22	DE	193	Charles	3	DE	196
James H	2	DE	21	Harrison	7	DE	172	Eliza	45	DE	22
Jane	17	DE	285	Henry	54	DE	222	Esther	40	DE	196
Jesse	29	DE	1	Hetty	6	DE	44	Isaac	11/12	DE	196
John	2	DE	260	Holland	28	DE	274	Jeremiah	15	DE	33
John	4	DE	293	Hugh M	4	DE	215	John	12	DE	196
John	12	DE	248	Isaac R	20	DE	214	Lazarus	16	DE	3
John	30	DE	21	Jacob	39	DE	62	Lazarus	61	DE	22
John	44	DE	260	Jacob	50	DE	172	Margaret J	14	DE	280
John	44	DE	292	James	1	DE	62	Nathan	56	DE	272
John W	5	DE	21	James	14	DE	267	Matilda	6	DE	22
Joshua	42	DE	278	James	51	MD	207	Obed	45	DE	196
Julia	8	DE	285	Jane	22	DE	56	Samuel	9	DE	195
Julia	10	DE	248	Jeremiah	26	MD	274	Sarah	5	DE	196
Julia	10	DE	248	John	20	DE	285	Young, Abigail	16	DE	71
Leah	2	DE	248	John	44	DE	275	Abner A	2	DE	75
Levin	15	DE	285	John S	8	DE	215	Alexander	5	DE	28
Levin	50	DE	285	John T	18	DE	217	Alexander	29	DE	27
Lurany	8	DE	248	Joseph	19	DE	44	Ann	8	DE	32
Mahala	2	DE	256	Joseph J H	2	MD	203	Anna	5	DE	75
Mahala	9	DE	248	Julia A	44	DE	275	Catherine E	15	DE	74
Maomy	40	DE	24	Keturah	13	DE	285	Charles	44	DE	74
Mariah	10/12	DE	278	Laura M	10	DE	215	Clement	16	DE	74
Mary	7	DE	278	Leah	49	DE	245	Daniel	72	DE	75
Mary	31	DE	248	Letitia	25	DE	228	David	13	DE	32
Mary A	15	DE	248	Letty	5	DE	172	David E	7	DE	75
Miranda	7	DE	248	Letty	30	DE	62	Diana	70	DE	75
Philip	44	DE	24	Levin	9	DE	44	Dinah M	22	DE	74
Purnel	22	DE	288	Lewis N	46	MD	214	Edward	21	DE	26
Robert	11	DE	24	Louisa	12	DE	44	Edward	21	DE	71
Sally	27	DE	21	Lucinda	6	DE	217	Eliza J	4	DE	35
Sarah	6	DE	248	Lydia C	2	DE	194	Elizabeth	18	DE	31
Sarah	7	DE	293	Margaret	5	DE	60	Francis	12	DE	87
Sarah	9	MD	260	Margaret	69	DE	13	Henry	6	DE	32
Sarah	11	DE	285	Margaret A	29	DE	209	Hester	4	DE	75
Sarah	33	MD	278	Margaret E	2	DE	243	James	10	DE	32
Sarah	34	DE	260	Margaret J	1	DE	209	James	13	DE	87
Sarah A	14	DE	248	Maria	42	DE	44	James H	7	DE	28
Sophia	1	DE	288	Maria E	5	DE	209	Jane	57	DE	42
Talbot	3	DE	24	Martha	7	DE	274	Jeremiah	2	DE	28
Thomas	13	DE	285	Martha	26	DE	100	John	17	DE	74
Thomas	40	DE	292	Mary	3	DE	62	Joseph	6	DE	87
Wolsey B	14	DE	260	Mary	7	DE	60	Joseph	43	DE	75
Wesley	1	DE	24	Mary	13	MD	216	Lydia	17	DE	71
William	8	DE	278	Mary	14	DE	217	Lydia C	1	DE	35
William	12	DE	292	Mary	25	DE	243	Maria	40	DE	35
William	15	DE	248	Mary	25	DE	243	Mary	50	DE	74
William	24	DE	260	Mary C	10	DE	172	Mary A	30	DE	74
Winny A	19	DE	260	Mary E	10/12	DE	214	Mary A	34	DE	32
Wm	35	DE	248	Milky	70	DE	250	Mary E	3	DE	87
Wright, Abram	60	DE	31	Morris	21	DE	44	Mary E	9	DE	74
Alford	30	DE	209	Sally	56	DE	209				

Young, Mercy	35 DE 75	Young, Rebecca	20 DE 75	Young, Solomon	24 DE 75
Milton H	13 DE 74	Rouse	37 DE 32	Susan	14 DE 74
Moses	15 DE 75	Sarah	20 DE 27	Susannah	30 DE 87
Nathaniel	10 DE 87	Sarah E	4 DE 28	Timothy P	35 DE 87
Philip	50 DE 35	Sarah E	7 DE 87	William C	12 DE 74
Philis	50 DE 71	Sarah E	11 DE 75	William H	5 DE 75
Rachel D	5 DE 74	Solomon	21 DE 71		

ERRATA
KENT COUNTY

Gilbreath, Emmet	2 DE 161	Hammeton, Isaac	16 DE 110

NEW CASTLE COUNTY

Bartle, Emma	8 DE 41	Matthews, Charles	40 MD 335	McKerson, Elizabeth	17 DE 288
Eccoff, William	3 DE 361	McCambridge, Bernard	26 IE 163	Pierce, John T	39 DE 276
Edwards, George	4/12 DE 260	McCracken, John	17 DE 304	Sluby, Michel	26 PA 73
Harris, Emeline	6 DE 46	McIntire, Ann	25 IE 163	Sweney, Joseph	15 IE 80
Hinson, Mary J	2 DE 73	McKerson, Ann H	46 DE 288	Taylor, Martha	23 DE 191
Lindsey, Anne	4 DE 29	Edward	22 DE 288		

SUSSEX COUNTY

Connell, Comfort N	2 DE 30	Davidson, Eliza C	5 DE 146	Gorley, Zilla	23 DE 145
Emaline B	9 DE 30	Elizabeth P	30 DE 146	Timmons, Isaac W	14 MD 154
John D C	12 DE 30	Ellen	45 DE 188	Tingle, Elizabeth	17 DE 158
Nehemiah J	5 DE 30	George	23 DE 154	Truxton, Louisa	10 DE 46
Robert R	15 DE 30	Elliott, Margaret	9 DE 256	Margaret W	25 DE 46
Rouse Y	7 DE 30